ADVANCED FINANCIAL ACCOUNTING

FOURTH EDITION

Clarence Byrd
Athabasca University

Ida Chen
Clarence Byrd Inc.

Prentice
Hall

Toronto

National Library of Canada Cataloguing in Publication Data

Byrd, Clarence E.
    Advanced financial accounting/Clarence Byrd, Ida Chen.

Accompanied by: Solutions manual.
Once every 2 to 3 years.
[1st ed.]-
ISSN 1487-590X
ISBN 0-13-089611-X (4th ed.)

1. Accounting.   I. Chen, Ida.   II. Title.

HF5635.B95   657.048   C99-301669-3

Vice President, Editorial Director: Michael J. Young
Senior Acquisitions Editor: Samantha Scully
Marketing Manager: Cas Shields
Associate Editor: Pamela Voves
Production Editor: Marisa D'Andrea
Production Coordinator: Andrea Falkenberg
Art Director: Mary Opper
Cover Design: Anthony Leung
Cover Image: Corel Photo Library/Marble Textures

1 2 3 4 5   07 06 05 04 03

Printed and bound in Canada.

Preface

What Is "Advanced" Financial Accounting?

Most Canadian universities and colleges offer either one or two courses in "advanced" financial accounting. Depending on the organization and the province in which it operates, all of Canada's professional accounting organizations require their students to complete one or both of such courses. Clearly there is a need for a text that deals with this subject.

Unfortunately, there is no general agreement as to the content that should be included in such a text. This was confirmed by a survey conducted by Pearson Education Canada, the publisher of this book. While there was general agreement that business combinations and the preparation of consolidated financial statements, as well as the translation of foreign currency transactions and foreign currency financial statements should be included, there was little agreement as to the other subjects that should be included under the general designation of "advanced" financial accounting.

In our view, any distinction between "advanced" and "intermediate" subjects in financial accounting is fairly arbitrary. We are devoting considerable effort to the idea that, subsequent to some type of introductory exposure to basic accounting skills, accounting should be taught on a subject by subject basis. Rather than relegating a subject such as long term investments to an intermediate accounting course because it is on the asset side of the balance sheet, we believe that it should be taught in a comprehensive and integrative manner. This requires recognition that some of the accounting procedures related to this subject cannot be dealt with in the absence of knowledge of consolidation procedures, the income tax law related to the cost and equity methods, and the possibility that such investments involve a business combination transaction.

As this approach is not currently used in university and college courses or professional accounting programs, we have produced this new edition of our version of what constitutes advanced financial accounting in Canada. The first ten Chapters cover the mandatory subjects of long term investments, business combinations, preparation of consolidated financial statements, and the translation of foreign currency transactions and foreign currency financial statements. The remaining Chapters, along with the justification for their inclusion, are as follows:

> **Chapters 11 And 12 - Income Taxes** Chapter 11 provides comprehensive treatment of the basic issues involved in accounting for income taxes. It presents the material at an advanced level and assumes, unlike the coverage of this subject in intermediate accounting texts, that the student has a good understanding of both personal and corporate taxation. Chapter 12 extends this coverage to some additional but less basic issues, including the tax aspects of business combination transactions and refundable taxes.

Chapter 13 - Partnerships This Chapter covers accounting for partnerships. While this subject is given some coverage in introductory courses, it is not generally covered in intermediate texts. It is an important subject in terms of professional practice and, as a consequence, we believe that it should be covered here.

Chapter 14 - Not-For-Profit Organizations The subject here is not-for-profit accounting. After business combinations and foreign currency translation, this is the most commonly covered subject in advanced financial accounting courses. While we recognize the great diversity in practices that exist in this important area, our focus is on the Sections of the *CICA Handbook* that provide detailed guidance on issues that are unique to not-for-profit organizations. Detailed coverage is given to the materials in *Handbook* Sections 4400 through 4460.

Chapter 15 - Financial Instruments This is a completely new Chapter in this edition of the text, prepared by Professor Teresa Anderson of the University Of Ottawa. While some parts of this subject are dealt with in various chapters of intermediate texts, this presentation integrates the material into a single Chapter. Coverage includes the current Section 3860, "Financial Instruments - Presentation And Disclosure", as well as proposed additions to the *CICA Handbook*.

Chapter 16 - Segment And Interim Reporting This Chapter deals with the subject of segment disclosures and interim financial reporting. While we do not view this material as being particularly "advanced" in nature, it is not covered in intermediate texts and is of considerable significance.

There are many other candidates for coverage under the banner of "advanced" financial accounting. It is our personal belief that both accounting for leases and accounting for pensions are subjects of sufficient complexity to warrant coverage here. In addition, subjects such as related party transactions and impaired loans involve very complex issues that would be difficult to deal with at the intermediate level. However, we believe that this book contains a relevant group of materials that can provide the basis for either a one semester or a two semester course in advanced financial accounting.

If you have alternative views on the appropriateness of the subjects we have chosen, we would very much like to hear from you.

Using This Book

The Accompanying CD-ROM
A unique feature of this text is the availability of additional materials on the CD-ROM that accompanies this text. It contains two major publications from the Virtual Professional Library of the Canadian Institute Of Chartered Accountants (CICA). These are:

Guide To Canadian Financial Reporting This is our comprehensive guide to the content of the *CICA Handbook* in particular, and Canadian financial reporting in general. It contains a detailed Chapter for each accounting *Handbook* Section, including materials on text subjects that we felt were too detailed for the general reader (e.g., summaries of EIC Abstracts on such subjects as foreign currency translation). This material can also be of use in situations where an instructor wishes to cover subjects that are not included in the text.

Financial Reporting In Canada - 2001 Edition This widely used publication is published each year (Heather Chapman is our co-author on this publication) and contains a survey of the accounting practices of 200 publicly traded companies. In addition to the statistics resulting from the survey, the publication contains examples from annual reports which illustrate the application of each *CICA Handbook* Section on accounting. This widely used publication is a unique resource for reviewing the manner in which Canadian companies actually apply accounting standards.

In addition to these publications, the CD-ROM also contains Chapter 8 of the text. Chapter 8 covers advanced topics in preparing consolidated financial statements. As our text serves as a comprehensive reference for Canadian consolidation procedures, we did not want to eliminate this material. However, we found that most instructors do not cover these topics in university or college courses. Given this situation, our compromise solution was to remove the material from the already lengthy paper version of the text and include it as an electronic .pdf file on the accompanying CD-ROM.

Official Pronouncements

The content of the text is current to *CICA Handbook* Revision No. 14 (March, 2002).

This text contains a large number of quotations from the *Handbook* of the Canadian Institute Of Chartered Accountants. In the *Handbook*, the paragraphs that represent official pronouncements are italicized. We will observe this convention in the quotations presented in our material.

In previous editions of the text, we have included summaries of relevant EIC Abstracts, either in the body of the text, or in an Appendix to the relevant Chapter. While the text still contains references to some of the more important of these Abstracts, we have removed all of the summaries. However, these summaries are still available as part of the *Guide To Canadian Financial Reporting* which is included on the CD-ROM that accompanies the text. There is a reference at the end of chapters with related EIC Abstracts that provides a list of the relevant Abstracts summarized in the *Guide*.

Problem Material

The text contains three types of problem materials. They can be described as follows:

Exercises   These are very directed problems that are included at appropriate points in the text material. They are designed to test your understanding of the material which you have just read and will be of maximum benefit if they are attempted as you work through the text material. These Exercises are included in Chapters 2 through 11, with the solutions provided in an Appendix that follows Chapter 16.

Self Study Problems   These are less directed problems which may deal with more than one issue. They are located at the end of the relevant Chapter, with solutions provided in the Appendix that follows Chapter 16. There are no Self Study Problems for Chapters 12, 14, or 16.

Assignment Problems   These problems are included at the end of each Chapter. Solutions to these problems are only available to instructors through a Solutions Manual that is provided to instructors.

Other Matters

Acknowledgments

The materials in this text have been developed over the course of many years. During this period they have been used by thousands of Canadian accounting students. Many of these students, as well as their instructors, have contributed to the development process by making suggestions for improvements and by helping us find the errors and omissions that are integral to such a process. We would like to thank all of these people for their assistance in improving these materials as well as for their patience in dealing with any problems found in earlier editions.

Through the efforts of Pearson Education Canada, a number of people have reviewed the previous edition of this text and provided us with their comments. They are:

- Loretta Amerongen, University of Alberta
- Betty Bracken, Niagara College
- Pauline Downer, Memorial University of Newfoundland
- Maureen Fizzell, Simon Fraser University
- Donald Lockwood, University of British Columbia
- Neville Ralph, Mount Allison University
- Deirdre Taylor, Ryerson Polytechnic University

It is invaluable to us to have feedback from users of this book. We appreciate their assistance in helping us improve the text.

We would especially like to acknowledge the work of Professor Teresa Anderson of the University Of Ottawa. Professor Anderson was the author of both the text and the problem material that constitutes Chapter 15 of this text, "Financial Instruments".

We are very much aware that this book would not be possible without the efforts of the staff at Pearson Education Canada. Pamela Voves provided constant assistance with all of our needs in the development and completion of this book. We look forward to working with Ms. Voves on the new edition of our *Canadian Tax Principles* which will be available for the fall of 2002.

Also of great importance to us is our long standing relationship with Pearson Education Canada's acquisitions editor, Samantha Scully. We are notoriously difficult to work with. Fortunately, with Ms. Scully's assistance, we have been able to satisfy our need for editorial independence within the context of publishing books under the banner of one of Canada's largest publishing organizations.

Related Web Sites

The web site for all texts written by Byrd and Chen and published by Pearson Education Canada is as follows:

www.pearsoned.ca/byrdchen

Other web sites that provide useful resources related to accounting standards are as follows:

Canadian Institute of Chartered Accountants   http://www.cica.ca

International Accounting Standards Board   http://www.iasc.org.uk

Financial Accounting Standards Board (US)   http://www.fasb.org

American Institute of Certified Public Accountants   http://www.aicpa.org

SEDAR   http://www.sedar.com/

This last reference is an acronym for "System For Electronic Document Analysis And Retrieval". It is of particular importance in that it contains all of the documents, including annual reports, that are filed with the provincial securities commissions that regulate securities trading in Canada.

A Final Word

As always, we have made every attempt to provide you with material that is free of errors and omissions. However, we are aware that such attempts are never completely successful. We apologize for any inconvenience that these errors and/or omissions may cause for you. Please advise us of any errors or other problems that you encounter.

We hope that you find this publication useful and welcome any suggestions for additions or improvements. These can be sent to us at:

Clarence Byrd Inc.
139 Musie Loop Road
Chelsea, Quebec   J9B 1Y6

e-mail address: byrddawg@passport.ca

Clarence Byrd	Athabasca University
Ida Chen	Clarence Byrd Inc.
Teresa Anderson	University of Ottawa (Chapter 15)

June, 2002

Table of Contents

Chapter 3
Business Combinations

Chapter 4
Consolidated Balance Sheet At Acquisition

Chapter 5

Consolidation Subsequent To Acquisition (No Unrealized Intercompany Profits)

Chapter 6

Consolidation Subsequent To Acquisition (Including Unrealized Intercompany Profits)

Chapter 10
Translation Of Foreign Currency Financial Statements

Chapter 11
Accounting For Income Taxes: Basic Issues and Procedures

Chapter 14
Accounting For Not-For-Profit Organizations

Chapter 14, continued

Chapter 15
Financial Instruments

Chapter 16
Part One:
Segment Disclosures

Part Two:
Interim Financial Statements

Chapter 16, continued

Appendix
Solutions to Exercises and Self-Study Problems

Chapter 1

Business Combinations and Long-Term Investments: Introduction and Overview

Introduction

1-1.   The first eight Chapters of this text deal with a group of related subjects which typically constitute the core material of most advanced financial accounting courses. These related subjects are:

- long-term investments
- business combinations
- consolidated financial statements

1-2.   When a long-term investment is made, the result may or may not be a business combination. Correspondingly, some business combination transactions result in an ongoing long-term investment situation. However, other business combination transactions may result in a single legal entity with no continuing intercorporate holding of securities. In those business combinations where there is a continuing long-term investment relationship, the preparation of consolidated financial statements will be required.

1-3.   Given this situation, the purpose of this Chapter is to provide a description of each of the individual subject areas listed, along with a general explanation of how the subjects relate. While the content of this Chapter is non-technical in nature, a familiarity with the individual subjects, as well as with the basic relationships between them is essential to an understanding of the more technical material which follows in Chapters 2 through 8.

Definitions And Classification

Long-Term Investments

Long-Term Vs. Temporary

1-4. The *CICA Handbook* contains Recommendations for both temporary investments (Section 3010) and long-term investments (Sections 3050 and 3055). While an investment in a security that matures in less than one year — for example, a Government of Canada 90 day Treasury Bill, is clearly temporary — the classification of other securities can be less obvious.

Such other securities would include both debt securities with various maturity dates, as well as equity securities which generally have no maturity date.

1-5.   In general, the classification of these other securities is dependent on the intent of management. As an example of this, consider a company which acquires 1,000 shares of another publicly traded company. If the investment simply reflects a temporary excess of cash and management intends to dispose of the shares in the next six months, the shares would be classified as a temporary investment. Alternatively, if management has acquired the shares as part of a long-term strategy of investing in a particular industry segment, the investment would be accounted for as a long-term investment.

Separate Legal Entities

1-6.   A corporation can invest in another corporation either by acquiring assets or, alternatively, by acquiring securities. When the asset approach is used, the assets are recorded on the books of the acquiring company and accounted for as per the other assets of the corporation. While an investment has been made, there would be no separate disclosure of a long-term investment balance.

1-7.   Alternatively, when debt or equity securities are acquired, there is a continuing investment relationship between two separate and distinct legal entities. This is depicted in Figure 1-1.

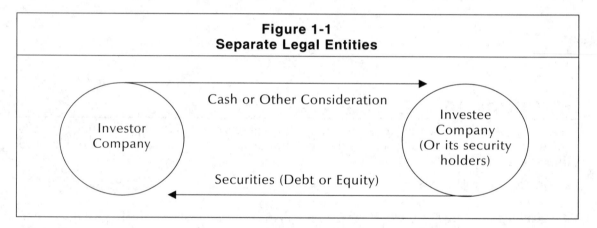

Figure 1-1
Separate Legal Entities

Cash or Other Consideration

Investor Company

Investee Company (Or its security holders)

Securities (Debt or Equity)

1-8.   As can be seen in Figure 1-1, the enterprise that has paid the consideration and acquired the securities will be referred to as the investor company. This enterprise can either acquire the other company's securities directly from the other company or, alternatively, the securities can be acquired in secondary markets from other investors. Regardless of the route chosen, the company whose securities are held will be referred to as the investee company.

1-9.   As noted in Figure 1-1, the investor company can acquire either debt or equity securities of the investee company. However, most of our Chapter 2 discussion of long-term investments will focus on the acquisition and holding of equity securities. This focus reflects the fact that there are few accounting problems associated with long-term holdings of debt securities.

1-10.   In the preceding paragraphs, we have referred to the investor "company" and the investee "company". There are, of course, many situations in which the investor, the investee, or both may be unincorporated business entities. In those cases where such business entities must apply generally accepted accounting principles (GAAP), the *CICA Handbook* Recommendations are clearly applicable. However, in order to avoid the additional complications associated with other forms of business organizations, we will generally focus on long-term investment situations in which both the investor and the investee are incorporated businesses.

Classification

1-11.   There are a variety of ways in which we could classify long-term investments in equity securities. From the point of view of determining the appropriate accounting treatment, the most widely used classification system is based on the degree to which the investor corporation can influence or control the operating, financing, and investing decisions of the investee corporation.

1-12.   In actual fact, the degree of influence or control available to an investor is a continuous variable which is not subject to completely defensible divisions. However, standard setters in Canada and other countries have found it useful to identify four categories of long-term investment relationships. These categories can be described as follows:

* Situations in which the investor has no influence or control over the investee .

* Situations in which the investor has significant influence, but not control, over the investee.

* Situations in which the investor has control over the company.

* Situations in which the investor company shares control of the investee with another investor.

1-13.   In those situations where the investor has no significant degree of control over the investee (a portfolio investment), there is little that would distinguish a long-term investment from any of the other non-current assets included in the investor's Balance Sheet. Reflecting this fact, the holding of the investee's securities is treated in a manner analogous to the treatment of most other assets. This method is known as the cost method of accounting for long-term investments and is explained in detail in Chapter 2.

1-14.   Between investment situations involving no control and those involving control, there are situations in which the investor is able to exercise a significant amount of influence over the affairs of the investee. When this is the case, the accounting will be modified to reflect this ability to significantly influence the investee. The accounting method that results from these modifications is referred to as the equity method of accounting for long-term investments. Implementation of the equity method requires the same adjustments that are used in the preparation of consolidated financial statements. This means that, while we can introduce the equity method in our general coverage of long-term investments in Chapter 2, we will have to return to this subject in Chapter 6 after completing our coverage of the preparation of consolidated financial statements.

1-15.   A third category of long-term investments involves situations in which the investor is able to exercise control over the operating, financing, and investing activities of the investee (subsidiary). In this situation, the investor is generally in a position to operate the two separate legal entities as a single economic entity. Given the presence of the entity assumption — an accounting assumption which requires the accountant to focus on the economic entity — it is necessary to prepare financial statements which reflect the presence of this single economic entity. These statements, which ignore the separate legal existence of the investor company and investee company, are referred to as consolidated financial statements. Chapters 4 through 8 deal with the complex procedures associated with the preparation of such statements.

1-16.   The final long-term investment category reflects the fact that today's business practices involve a growing number of situations in which two or more corporations organize a separate entity to undertake some form of business activity. Such entities, commonly referred to as joint ventures, are usually organized in a manner such that control is shared by the various investor companies. Under current accounting Recommendations, such investments must be accounted for using proportionate consolidation. As is the case with regular consolidation procedures, proportionate consolidation accounts for the investor and investee as a single economic unit. However, the resulting statements include only a proportionate share of the assets, liabilities, expenses, and revenues of the investee company. While there is a limited discussion of joint ventures in Chapter 2, they are covered in detail in Chapter 8.

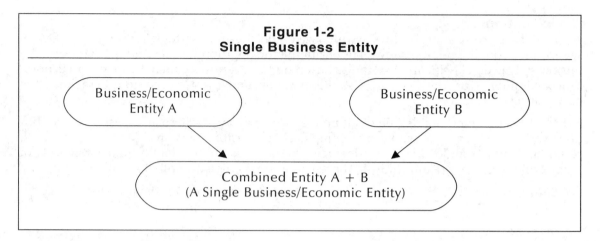

Figure 1-2
Single Business Entity

Business/Economic Entity A

Business/Economic Entity B

Combined Entity A + B
(A Single Business/Economic Entity)

Business Combinations
Defined

1-17.   The term business combination is defined in Section 1581 of the *CICA Handbook* as follows:

> **Paragraph 1581.06(a)**   A business combination occurs when an enterprise acquires net assets that constitute a business, or acquires equity interests of one or more other enterprises and obtains control over that enterprise or enterprises.

1-18.   This definition is illustrated graphically in Figure 1-2. In examining this Figure, it is important to understand that there is a difference between the legal and the accounting meanings of the term, business combination. In some situations, the economic unification of two businesses will be accompanied by an actual legal amalgamation of their assets. For example, if Entity A pays cash to acquire all of the assets of Entity B, the combined assets of the two entities will wind up on the books of a single legal entity. A similar result would occur if the assets of both Entity A and Entity B were transferred to a new entity established for this purpose. In such situations, the economic and legal entities coincide, and this serves to clearly establish the appropriate accounting entity.

1-19.   However, as is indicated in the definition of the term, a business combination may be accomplished through one business entity gaining control over the other through an acquisition of shares. For example, Entity A might acquire 100 percent of the outstanding voting shares of Entity B. In this case, the combining enterprises, Entity A and Entity B, retain their separate identities and, from a legal point of view, no business combination has taken place. In substance, however, this situation is no different from the one described in the preceding paragraph. The assets of both Companies are now under common control and, from an economic point of view, a business combination has occurred. As noted previously, the entity assumption requires that accountants focus on economic substance rather than legal form. This means that the accounting procedures will focus on the fact that there has been an economic amalgamation which has resulted in a single economic entity. The resulting financial statements, which ignore the separate legal existence of the two Companies, are referred to as consolidated financial statements.

Classification

1-20.   Prior to 2001, Canadian accounting standards identified two different types of business combination transactions. These standards took the position that, in the great majority of business combination transactions, one of the combining companies will emerge as the dominant or controlling organization. This type of situation is distinguished by the fact that this dominant company can be identified as the acquiring company. In such cases, the business combination transaction could be viewed in much the same manner as any other purchase of assets. This view was reflected in the requirement that the purchase method of accounting be used when one of the acquiring companies could be identified as the acquirer.

1-21.   While indicating the belief that, in the great majority of business combination transactions an acquirer could be identified, the Accounting Standards Board also provided for a different scenario. The Board indicated that, in some rare situations, companies could combine without any one of the predecessor companies obtaining control. This could happen if the combination involved companies of relatively equal size and value or, alternatively, if more than two enterprises were involved in the combination. When such situations occurred, it was felt that it would not be possible to identify an acquirer. The recommended accounting procedure for this type of business combination was the pooling of interests method.

1-22.   The pooling of interests method was based on the position that, because an acquirer could not be identified, there was no acquisition of assets and no need for a new basis of accounting for the assets of either company. This meant that increases in the fair value of assets and goodwill of the combining companies was ignored. As these additions to the assets were not recorded, they did not have to be amortized, resulting in both higher income levels and higher rates of return on the lower asset values.

1-23.   In July, 2001, a new *CICA Handbook* Section 1581, "Business Combinations", was introduced to replace the now superseded Section 1580 which dealt with the same subject. In Section 1581, the Accounting Standards Board takes the position that an acquirer can be identified in all business combination transactions. Based on this view, the purchase method is now required for all Canadian business combination transactions. With this decision, the Board has eliminated the pooling of interests method from Canadian GAAP.

1-24.   There is some question as to whether this was an appropriate conclusion. Using the now superseded Section 1580, accountants were able to conclude that there were some situations in which no acquirer could be identified. While this was not a common occurrence, there was a fairly clear indication that such situations did exist. As discussed in the following section, the fact that the Accounting Standards Board decided not to recognize such situations is probably a reflection of their desire to harmonize Canadian accounting standards with those of the U.S.

Harmonization Of Standards In Canada And The U.S.

1-25.   Prior to the issuance of Section 1581, the application of Canadian standards resulted in almost all business combination transactions being accounted for by the purchase method as an acquirer could almost always be identified. This was not the case in the U.S. Under their Accounting Principles Board Opinion No. 18, pooling of interests accounting could be used in most business combination transactions where the consideration used was shares. As a consequence, pooling of interest accounting was very widely used in the U.S.

1-26.   This situation was heavily criticized by both users and the U.S. Securities and Exchange Commission (SEC), resulting in a situation that clearly required change. After lengthy deliberations, the Financial Accounting Standards Board (FASB) concluded that the best solution was complete elimination of the pooling of interests method. In June, 2001, the FASB issued Statement of Financial Accounting Standards No. 141, *Business Combinations*, which effectively eliminates the use of pooling of interests accounting in the U.S. by requiring that all business combination transactions be accounted for by the purchase method.

1-27.   It is likely that Canada's decision to take the same approach reflects the expressed goal of the Accounting Standards Board to harmonize Canadian GAAP with that of the U.S. In this context, it is interesting to note that International Accounting Standard No. 22, *Business Combinations*, continues to provide for the use of pooling of interests accounting. While at one point in time it appeared that the major focus of the Accounting Standards Board was on harmonizing Canadian standards with those put forward by the International Accounting Standards Board, the emphasis seems to have shifted towards giving priority to harmonizing Canadian standards with those of the U.S.

1-28.   Chapter 3 contains a much more detailed discussion of the choice of accounting methods for business combination transactions.

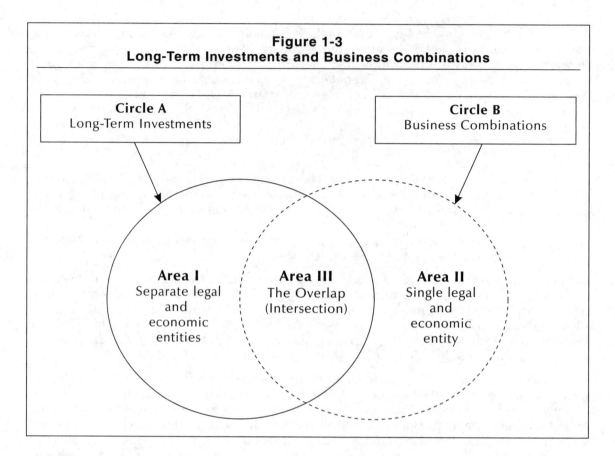

Figure 1-3
Long-Term Investments and Business Combinations

Circle A
Long-Term Investments

Circle B
Business Combinations

Area I
Separate legal
and
economic
entities

Area III
The Overlap
(Intersection)

Area II
Single legal
and
economic
entity

The Overlap

1-29.   In reading the preceding material it may have occurred to you that certain situations can involve both a business combination transaction as well as an ongoing long-term investment relationship. From the point of view of long-term investments, this involves a situation in which the investor and investee entities are treated as a single accounting entity. The same situation, described from the point of view of business combinations, could be described as a business combination in which the companies retain their separate legal identities. This is shown graphically in Figure 1-3.

1-30.   As can be seen in Figure 1-3, if Circle A represents the subject matter of long-term investments and Circle B the subject matter of business combinations, there is an overlap or intersection between the two circles. Including this intersection, three separate areas are created. These areas can be described as follows:

Area I   This area represents long-term investments that have not resulted in an economic unification of the investor and investee companies. Stated alternatively, these are the long-term investment situations where the investor and investee companies have retained both their separate legal identities as well as their separate economic status. In practical terms both portfolio investments (i.e., investments where no control is involved) and investments involving significant influence would be found in this area. However, situations where the investor company has acquired control (subsidiaries) would be excluded.

Area II   This area represents business combinations in which there is no continuing long-term investment relationship between the combining companies. Stated alternatively, these are the business combination transactions where the assets and liabilities of the two companies have been combined into a single legal entity. In general, this would involve situations where one company has acquired the assets of the other company or, alternatively, the assets of both companies have been transferred to a new company. In either case, all of the assets of both companies will be on the books of a single legal entity, resulting in a situation in which the legal and economic entities coincide.

Area III (Overlap) In Areas I and II, there is no conflict between the legal and economic entities involved. In Area III, this situation changes. Area III involves situations where the two companies have achieved economic unification by one company acquiring a controlling interest in the shares of the other company. This means that we are dealing with two separate legal entities (i.e., a parent and its subsidiary) that are being operated as a single economic unit. When accountants are confronted with a conflict between the economic entity and the legal entity, we have noted that the entity assumption requires that attention be directed to the economic entity. The two separate legal entities will have to be accounted for as a single unified business entity, a goal that is achieved through the preparation of consolidated financial statements.

Canadian Pronouncements

Handbook Recommendations

1-31. Given the broadly based nature of the subjects of long-term investments and business combinations, it is necessary to refer to a large number of the Recommendations contained in the *CICA Handbook*. However, the following Sections are of particular relevance to these subjects.

Section 1581: "Business Combinations" This Section replaces Section 1580 and is effective for business combinations on or after July 1, 2001. As we have noted, it requires that all business combination transactions be accounted for by the purchase method. In addition, it provides guidance with respect to the application of this method of accounting for business combinations.

Section 1590: "Subsidiaries" This brief Section was added to the *CICA Handbook* in 1991. It defines a subsidiary as an enterprise controlled by another enterprise and defines control as the continuing power of an enterprise to determine operating, investing and financing policies of the controlled enteprise. The Section also specifies that all subsidiaries must be consolidated.

Section 1600: "Consolidated Financial Statements" This Section was first added to the *CICA Handbook* in 1975, with a major revision occurring in 1991. It contains detailed rules for both the preparation of consolidated financial statements, as well as the application of the equity method to long-term investments.

Section 1625: "Comprehensive Revaluation Of Assets And Liabilities" This Section was added to the *CICA Handbook* in 1992. It deals with recording revised asset and liability amounts in two different situations. The one that is relevant in this material involves an investor acquiring control over an investee (subsidiary). In these circumstances, there will be differences between the fair values of the subsidiary's assets and liabilities and the carrying values in the subsidiary's records. As the purchase price of the subsidiary will be based on fair values, it is the fair value amounts that must be included in the consolidated financial statements. While this can be done through the consolidation procedures, it can be more convenient to record the fair values of the subsidiary's assets on its books at the time of acquisition. This procedure is called "push down" accounting and it is dealt with in Section 1625.

Section 3050: "Long-term Investments" This Section was first added to the *CICA Handbook* in 1972 and has been subject to several revisions. As it presently stands, it contains rules with respect to, the accounting methods to be used for portfolio investments and significantly influenced companies, procedures for the application of the cost and equity methods of accounting for long-term investments, and disclosure requirements applicable to situations in which non-consolidated financial statements are presented for subsidiaries. It also requires the write down of long-term investments in some circumstances and specifies the use of average values for the cost of long term investments that are being sold.

Section 3055: "Interests In Joint Ventures"   This Section was added to the *CICA Handbook* in 1977 and was subject to a significant revision in 1994. It defines joint ventures, requires the use of proportionate consolidation to account for joint venture arrangements, and provides specific procedural rules which reflect the unique nature of joint venture arrangements.

Section 3062: "Goodwill and Other Intangibles"   Prior to the introduction of Section 1581, goodwill was covered by the superseded Section 1580 while other intangibles were dealt with in Section 3060, "Capital Assets". Concurrently with the introduction of Section 1581, this Section was created to provide coverage of all types of intangibles in a single Section.

Other References

1-32.   The preceding pronouncements constitute a comprehensive set of guidelines for dealing with the subjects of business combinations, long-term investments and the preparation of consolidated financial statements. Because of the great importance of these topics there is a significant amount of other material that deals with these subjects. In addition to many articles in professional journals, a large number of Emerging Issues Committee (EIC) Abstracts deal with issues pertinent to one or more of these areas.

1-33.   We will be referring to many of these other references as we move through this material. However, many of them involve issues that are of interest only to those who specialize in this field and, as a consequence, we will not provide coverage of these materials. For anyone with a more detailed interest in this subject, we would refer you to our *Guide to Canadian Financial Reporting* which is included on the CD-ROM which accompanies this text. There is a Chapter in that source for each *CICA Handbook* Section and, at the end of each of these Chapters, there is a comprehensive list of additional readings, including relevant EIC Abstracts.

Long-Term Investments and Business Combinations in Canadian Practice

1-34.   Both business combinations and long-term investments are important areas in Canadian practice. The 2001 edition of *Financial Reporting In Canada* states that, for 2000, 197 of the 200 companies included in the survey indicated that the statements presented were on a consolidated basis. This, of course, indicates the presence of one or more subsidiaries. Also for 2000, 123 of the 200 companies reported the presence of long-term investments other than subsidiaries and joint ventures, and 76 of the companies reported the presence of joint ventures.

1-35.   With respect to business combinations, statistics on the number of these 200 companies disclosing business combination transactions occurring during the current year are as follows:

Year	2000	1999
Purchase Method Used	104	99
Pooling Of Interests Method Used	1	2
Other Method Used	4	1

1-36.   As can be seen in these statistics, the use of the pooling of interests method was rare. As the new Section 1581 becomes effective, its complete disappearance is expected.

Approaching The Subject

1-37.   With the completion of this brief introductory Chapter, Chapters 2 through 8 will provide a systematic and detailed presentation of the concepts and procedures associated with long-term investments, business combinations, and the preparation of consolidated financial statements. Chapters 2 and 3 will be largely conceptual in their content, dealing with the pronouncements contained in Sections 1581, 1590, 1625, and 3050 of the *CICA Handbook*. With these concepts in hand, we will then be in a position to turn our attention to the procedures that are required in the preparation of consolidated financial statements.

1-38.   Chapter 4 will introduce this subject by dealing with the preparation of the consolidated Balance Sheet at the date of acquisition of a subsidiary. This will include material on the conceptual alternatives in consolidation, as well as on the allocation of the investment cost to fair value changes and goodwill.

1-39.   Chapter 5 extends the analysis to cover consolidation in periods subsequent to the acquisition and covers the preparation of the consolidated Income Statement, the consolidated Statements Of Retained Earnings, and the consolidated Statement of Cash Flows. Procedures dealt with here include write offs of fair value changes, recognition of goodwill impairment, elimination of intercompany assets and liabilities, elimination of intercompany expenses and revenues and the elimination of intercompany dividends.

1-40.   Chapter 6 further expands the coverage of basic consolidation procedures by providing a comprehensive analysis of unrealized intercompany profits. The analysis includes consideration of unrealized profits in opening and closing inventories, unrealized profits on the sale of non-depreciable capital assets, and unrealized profits on the sale of depreciable capital assets. Additional coverage of the equity method of accounting for long-term investments is also included in this Chapter.

1-41.   Chapters 2 through 6 provide in depth coverage of basic consolidation procedures, including some material on conceptual alternatives in the preparation of consolidated financial statements. In some advanced financial accounting courses, this may be viewed as adequate coverage of this subject, with no consideration being given to joint ventures or more advanced consolidation procedures.

1-42.   A new feature of the 4th edition of this text is the inclusion of a separate Chapter 7 dealing with joint ventures and the Recommendations contained in Section 3055 of the *CICA Handbook*. In previous editions, material on joint ventures was covered initially in Chapter 2, with more detailed coverage of proportionate consolidation found in Chapter 6. Given the increased importance of this subject and the relatively complex nature of the required procedures, we have concluded that it would be more appropriate to devote a separate Chapter to this material.

1-43.   There are a number of more advanced topics that relate to the preparation of consolidated financial statements. While it is unlikely that an instructor would choose to cover all of these advanced topics, there does not appear to be a consensus as to which subjects are the most important. In order to deal with this situation, we have relegated coverage of all of these topics to a separate Chapter 8. In addition, the problem material which accompanies this Chapter is clearly segregated by subject matter. This will allow instructors to choose to cover as many or as few of these topics as they wish.

1-44.   As a final point, we would note that we have dealt with the subject of income taxes related to business combination transactions and consolidated financial statements in a separate Chapter 12. This reflects the fact that Section 3465 of the *CICA Handbook*, "Income Taxes", contains a significant number of Recommendations dealing with these issues.

Chapter 2

Long-Term Investments

Introduction

Subject Matter

Temporary Investments

2-1. Canadian companies make investments in income producing assets for a variety of reasons. The least complicated situations are those in which the enterprise has a temporary excess of funds and uses these funds to acquire the securities of other companies. Debt securities that mature in less than one year would clearly represent temporary holdings. However, equity securities and debt securities with a maturity of more than one year, may also be classified as temporary. The key factor is the intent of management. If the intent is to dispose of these securities in less than one year, the holding will be considered temporary in nature. Alternatively, if the intent of management is to retain the securities beyond the end of the current operating cycle, they should be classified as long-term investments.

2-2. Temporary investments are classified as current assets and accounted for as per the Recommendations of Section 3010 of the *CICA Handbook*. Coverage of the issues associated with temporary investments can be found in any standard intermediate accounting text.

Long-Term Investments

2-3. The *CICA Handbook* does not provide a definition of long-term investments. As a consequence, the term can be applied to almost any non-current asset other than those that fall within the definitions for property, plant, and equipment (see Paragraph 3061.04 of the *CICA Handbook*), or goodwill and other intangible assets (see Paragraph 3062.05 of the *CICA Handbook*). However, in this Chapter, our focus will be on situations in which a corporation has long-term holdings of securities that have been acquired as part of the overall business strategy of the investor company. We will not give significant attention to other types of long-term investments such as income producing real estate or investments in partnerships or other unincorporated businesses.

2-4. As was pointed out in Chapter 1, long-term investment situations are distinguished by the presence of two separate and distinct legal entities. One of these legal entities (the investor) will be holding the securities issued by the other legal entity (the investee). While various types of securities are included within this framework, we will be largely concerned with long-term investments in equity securities. Some attention will, however, be given to long-term investments in debt securities.

Branch Accounting

2-5.   If an enterprise was interested in starting operations in a different jurisdiction, an alternative to establishing a new corporate entity to carry out those operations would be the establishment of a branch. This represents a fairly simple way to begin operating in the other location as no new legal entity is required.

2-6.   Such a branch may keep a separate set of accounts, recording assets, liabilities, revenues and expenses in much the same fashion as would an incorporated subsidiary. However, unlike the subsidiary, a branch is not a separate legal entity. This means that it will not be required to prepare separate financial statements for external users. The accounting procedures to be used by such a branch are an internal matter and not subject to the constraints created by *CICA Handbook* recommendations. As the focus of this text is on external financial reporting under generally accepted accounting principles, no further attention will be given to branch accounting.

Issues To Be Covered

2-7.   The material in Section 1590, "Subsidiaries", Section 3050 "Long-Term Investments", and Section 3055 "Interests In Joint Ventures" can be grouped into coverage of three broad issues, accompanied by material on a number of more detailed problems. In very general terms, these broad issues can be outlined as follows:

1. **Classification**   The *CICA Handbook*'s classification of long-term investments is largely in terms of the degree of control involved. The types of long-term investments that are identified are as follows:

   - subsidiaries
   - significantly influenced companies
   - portfolio investments
   - joint ventures

   While this Chapter will provide coverage of classification issues related to subsidiaries, significantly influenced companies, and portfolio investments, the characteristics associated with joint ventures will be dealt with in Chapter 7.

2. **Accounting Methods**   The *Handbook* Recommendations also identify the various methods of accounting to be used for long-term investments. They are as follows:

   - cost method
   - equity method
   - proportionate consolidation
   - full consolidation

   This Chapter will provide complete coverage of the cost method as well as a general introduction to the equity method and proportionate consolidation. However, both the application of the equity method and the use of proportionate consolidation require an understanding of the procedures that are used in full consolidation. As a consequence, additional coverage of the equity method will be found in Chapters 5 and 6, while proportionate consolidation will be given detailed coverage in Chapter 7.

3. **Recommended Methods For Specific Investment Classifications**   Given the types of long-term investments identified in the preceding item 1 and the accounting methods identified in item 2, the third broad issue that is dealt with in the *CICA Handbook* Recommendations under consideration here is the determination of which methods should be used with each of the investment types that have been defined.

4. **Other Problems**   Sections 1590, 3050, and 3055 deal with a number of other issues. Coverage in this Chapter will include:

- Non-temporary declines in the value of long-term investments.
- Gains and losses on the sale of long-term investments.
- Disclosure requirements applicable to subsidiaries, significantly influenced companies, and portfolio investments.

Other issues, for example procedures to be used when non-monetary assets are transferred to joint ventures, will be covered in later Chapters.

Classification Of Long-Term Investments

An Overview

2-8.   Long-term investments are those investments that management intends to hold for more than one year after the Balance Sheet date. As noted in Chapter 1, the classification of such long-term investments is based largely on the degree of influence that can be exercised by the investor company. In general, the degree of influence is related to the portion of the investor company voting shares which are held by the investor company. This means that we can depict long-term investment classifications in terms of the following Figure 2-1:

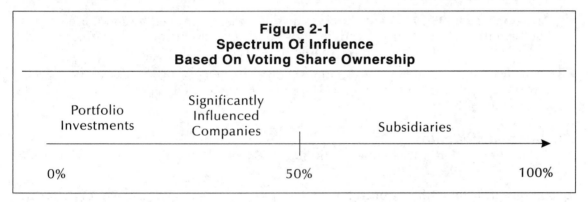

Figure 2-1
Spectrum Of Influence
Based On Voting Share Ownership

Portfolio Investments

Significantly Influenced Companies

Subsidiaries

0%   50%   100%

2-9.   As shown in Figure 2-1, the long-term investment classification involving the highest degree of influence is subsidiaries. In general, this type of long-term investment involves situations where the investor company owns more than 50 percent of the outstanding voting shares of the investee company. However, as will be subsequently pointed out, such majority ownership is no longer a required part of the definition of a subsidiary.

2-10.   At the other extreme we find the classification of portfolio investments. These are long-term investment situations in which the investor company has little or no influence over the affairs of the investee company and, as can be seen in Figure 2-1, this situation normally involves proportionately small holdings of investee voting shares.

2-11.   We have referred to the third classification of long-term investments as significantly influenced companies. The basic idea here is that the investor company has the ability to influence the operating, financing, and investing decisions of the investee, but does not have control over these matters. This would generally require a substantial holding of investee common shares, but less than the 50 percent plus one share that would give the investor company majority control over the investee.

2-12.   We have not shown investments in joint ventures in Figure 2-1 as they are identified by the presence of joint control over the investee. While this issue will be discussed more completely in Chapter 7, we would note that a joint venture is established through a management agreement which may override the percentage of shares held by the individual investors. As a consequence, this type of situation cannot be depicted in Figure 2-1 which classifies investments on the basis of share ownership.

2-13.   This overview provides a somewhat simplified picture of the long-term investment classifications that are found in the Recommendations of the *CICA Handbook*. With this in hand, we can now turn to a more detailed consideration of the individual categories.

Subsidiaries
Defined
2-14.   At one point in time, the *CICA Handbook* defined a subsidiary as an investee for which the investor held a majority of the outstanding voting shares. In general, this was a reasonable definition because majority ownership usually means that an investor company would be able to elect a majority of the investee company's board of directors and, thereby, exercise control over the operating, investing, and financing policies of the investee. However, there was a problem in that, under this definition, no recognition was given to situations in which the investor company was able to exercise control without having majority ownership. The failure to recognize this possibility resulted in situations where an investor company which did in fact have full control of the investee company would account for its long-term investment using methods that were intended for situations involving only significant influence. In other words, the original *Handbook* Recommendation represented an emphasis on legal form, rather than economic substance.

2-15.   The current Section 1590 corrects this situation. The definition of a subsidiary found in this Section is as follows:

> **Paragraph 1590.03(a)**   A **subsidiary** is an enterprise controlled by another enterprise (the parent) that has the right and ability to obtain future economic benefits from the resources of the enterprise and is exposed to the related risks.

2-16.   This represents an improved definition in that it places an emphasis on economic substance (the ability to control the investee) rather than on legal form (ownership of the majority of voting shares).

The Concept Of Control
2-17.   In conjunction with the definition of a subsidiary, Section 1590 defines control as follows:

> **Paragraph 1590.03(b)**   **Control** of an enterprise is the continuing power to determine its strategic operating, investing and financing policies without the co-operation of others.

2-18.   While this definition appears to be very straightforward, it is subject to varying interpretations. The most restrictive interpretation of this definition would be that control requires ownership of 100 percent of the outstanding shares of the investee. This is based on the fact that, as long as there are any shareholders in the investee company other than the controlling investor, corporate legislation will prevent the investor company from undertaking transactions that are harmful to the interests of that group. For example, if the investor owns 100 percent of the outstanding shares, there is nothing to prevent the investor from selling products to the investee at prices in excess of fair market value. However, if there is a non-controlling (minority) interest present in the investee company, this type of transaction could not take place because it would be detrimental to the economic position of these shareholders.

2-19.   While this very restrictive interpretation of control has some appeal from a legal point of view, it fails to recognize that control over the great majority of operating and financing decisions can be achieved with less than 100 percent ownership. This suggests the use of a less restrictive interpretation of control in practical situations.

2-20.   An alternative interpretation of control could be based on the fact that corporate legislation generally requires a two-thirds majority vote for passage of special resolutions. Such transactions as changes in the corporate objectives, amalgamations with other companies, and other changes in the corporate charter would require such a super majority. This means that an interpretation of control based on two-thirds ownership of voting shares would have some appeal from a legal point of view. Again, however, this interpretation is too restrictive in that many of the operating and financing decisions could be controlled with less than two-thirds ownership of the investee company's voting shares.

2-21.   A more practical interpretation of control is based on the idea that, in terms of economic substance, the key factor is the ability of the investor company to determine policy for the great majority of operating and financing decisions that are made by the investee company. This ability is generally associated with simple majority ownership of outstanding voting shares. It is this interpretation of control that is contained in the *CICA Handbook* which states:

> **Paragraph 1590.08**   The level of equity interest in one enterprise held by another leads to a presumption regarding control. An enterprise is presumed to control another enterprise when it owns, directly or indirectly, an equity interest that carries the right to elect the majority of the members of the other enterprise's board of directors, and is presumed not to control the other enterprise without such ownership. In a particular situation, these presumptions may be overcome by other factors that clearly demonstrate that control exists or does not exist. The greater the difference in an enterprise's voting interest from the 50% level, the more persuasive these other factors must be in overcoming the applicable presumption.

2-22.   While this statement clearly establishes voting share ownership as the primary measure of control, it leaves open the possibility of other measures being used. Two examples of such other measures are cited:

> **Paragraph 1590.13(a)**   Ownership of less than the majority of voting shares combined with an irrevocable agreement with other owners to exercise voting rights may result in majority voting power and may, therefore, confer control.

> **Paragraph 1590.13(b)**   Control may exist when an enterprise does not own the majority voting interest if it has the continuing ability to elect the majority of the members of the board of directors through ownership of rights, options, warrants, convertible debt, convertible non-voting equity such as preferred shares, or other similar instruments that, if converted or exercised, would give the enterprise the majority voting interest.

2-23.   An investor may find situations where its use of the resources of the investee company are subject to certain restrictions. Examples of this would be debt covenants which restrict the investee company's ability to pay dividends or regulatory restrictions which control the prices that can be charged by the investee company. Such normal business restrictions do not preclude control by the investor and the classification of the investee as a subsidiary. However, in some cases the restrictions may involve a transfer of voting rights and this could result in the investor no longer being able to exercise control.

2-24.   Section 1590 also notes that a brief interruption of the power to determine strategic policies is not a loss of control. An example of this would be the appointment of a receiver to seize a specific group of assets in order to satisfy a creditor claim. Also noted is the fact that the investor company can have control without choosing to exercise it on a day to day basis. In addition, control can be exercised in situations where the investor has obligations related to the investee that exceed the investee's resources. None of these conditions would prevent the investor's holding from being classified as a subsidiary.

2-25.   However, there are situations in which the restrictions on the investor company's ability to exercise its ownership rights are so severe that control can no longer be considered present. An example of this would be a foreign investee operating in a country which places severe restrictions on the repatriation of earnings. In such cases, the investment would no longer be classified as a subsidiary, despite the presence of majority ownership of voting shares.

2-26.   Another situation where majority ownership of voting shares would not result in a parent/subsidiary relationship arises when there is a demonstrable intent to dispose of the investment in the foreseeable future. Section 1590 notes that when the investor/investee relationship is established for a short term, or where it can be terminated other than by a decision of the acquiring enterprise, the investment should be classified as temporary and accounted for by the methods specified in Section 3010 of the *CICA Handbook*.

Indirect Ownership

2-27.   The preceding discussion of control dealt only with situations in which the investor company had direct ownership of the investee company's outstanding voting shares. However, an investor company can have indirect control of another company, even in situations where the investor company owns none of the shares of that company. Two examples of such indirect control are provided in Figure 2-2.

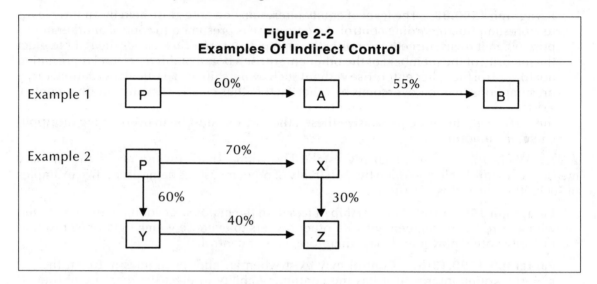

Figure 2-2
Examples Of Indirect Control

2-28.   In Example 1, P owns 60 percent of A. This would give P control over A and make this company a subsidiary. In turn, A owns 55 percent of B, giving A control and making B a subsidiary of A. In addition, P's control of A gives P indirect control over B, making B a subsidiary of P as well as a subsidiary of A.

2-29.   In Example 2, P controls both X and Y. Between them, these two companies own 70 percent of Z, giving them joint control over this company. Because P controls both X and Y, P has indirect control over Z. This means that Z, as well as X and Y are subsidiaries of P.

2-30.   Both of the examples in Figure 2-2 would be referred to as multi-level affiliations. Even more complex relationships can develop if companies acquire shares of other companies that are above them in the chain of control. For example, Z might acquire some of the shares of X or P in Example 2. Shareholdings of this type are referred to as reciprocal shareholdings. The procedures to be used in dealing with both multi-level affiliations and reciprocal shareholdings are dealt with in Chapter 8.

2-31.   A final point here relates to measurement based on indirect interests. Returning to Example 1, when we measure P's indirect interest in B, the resulting value will be based on the product of the ownership percentages. For example, P's interest in B's earnings is based on 33 percent [(60%)(55%)] of those earnings. While such percentages must be used in measurement calculations, they have nothing to do with determining the existence of control. In general, control is based on majority ownership at each stage in the chain of ownership. The fact that an equitable interest, as established by the product of the ownership percentages, is less than 50 percent has nothing to do with whether an indirect interest represents control.

Exercise Two-1 deals with indirect ownership.

Exercise Two-1

Morton Ltd. owns 60 percent of the voting shares of Salt Inc. and 40 percent of the voting shares of Backy Inc. In addition, Salt Inc. owns 15 percent of the shares of Backy Inc.

Required: Briefly explain how Morton Ltd. should classify and account for its investments in Salt Inc. and Backy Inc.

Significantly Influenced Companies

2-32.   The *CICA Handbook* does not provide a specific definition of the category of long-term investments known as significantly influenced companies. However, the basic idea is that they are investees in which an investor company is able to exercise a significant degree of influence without actually having achieved control of the investee company. These situations are described as follows:

> **Paragraph 3050.04**   Significant influence differs from control and joint control. An investor may be able to exercise significant influence over the strategic operating, investing and financing policies of an investee even though the investor does not control or jointly control the investee. The ability to exercise significant influence may be indicated by, for example, representation on the board of directors, participation in policy-making processes, material intercompany transactions, interchange of managerial personnel or provision of technical information. If the investor holds less than 20% of the voting interest in the investee, it is presumed that the investor does not have the ability to exercise significant influence, unless such influence is clearly demonstrated. On the other hand, the holding of 20% or more of the voting interest in the investee does not in itself confirm the ability to exercise significant influence. A substantial or majority ownership by another investor would not necessarily preclude an investor from exercising significant influence.

2-33.   At first glance, the preceding would appear to make the determination of significant influence a matter of professional judgment. However, the inclusion of a specific percentage of share ownership will, almost certainly, be used by many accountants as an administratively convenient guideline for the determination of significant influence. In view of the fact that the determination of significant influence is clearly something that must be determined through the application of judgment on a situation by situation basis it seems unfortunate that any particular percentage of share ownership was even mentioned. There is no logical reason to believe that 20 percent will be more effective in the determination of significant influence than any other arbitrarily determined percentage of share ownership. Therefore, it is possible to make a case that the exercise of judgment would have received more encouragement had this 20 percent guideline been omitted.

2-34.   In applying professional judgment, representation on the board of directors is probably the most reliable indicator of the ability of the investor corporation to exercise significant influence. If the investor company is able to elect one or more members to the investee's board, it would generally be clear that influence is present. The ability to get this representation is a function of the percentage of shares owned and the number of positions on the board. It is also dependent on the type of voting that is used by the investee company. For example, assume an investor owns 10 percent of the shares and there are 10 directors on the board. If the investee corporation uses cumulative voting, the investor will be in a position to elect one director. If the investee corporation uses non-cumulative voting, a majority group of shareholders can, in fact, elect the director that will fill each of the ten positions.

Portfolio Investments

2-35.   The *CICA Handbook* presents a definition of portfolio investments as follows:

> **Paragraph 3050.02(b)   Portfolio investments** are long-term investments that are not interests in joint ventures or partnerships of the reporting enterprise, nor investments in companies that are subject to significant influence by the reporting enterprise.

2-36.   The preceding definition is, of course, straightforward and noncontroversial. The statement is in terms of what a portfolio investment is not. However, it is clear that what is being described is those long-term investment situations in which the investor is not in a position to exert influence over, or become involved in, the affairs of the investee. This would include all long-term holdings of debt securities, as well as long-term holdings of equity securities where the investor company cannot exercise significant influence. As our earlier discussion should have made clear, distinguishing equity investments in which significant influence is present from those in which it is not, will sometimes involve the exercise of considerable professional judgment.

2-37. It should also be noted that the 1984 CICA Research Study, *Accounting For Portfolio Investments*, recommends a somewhat different approach to defining portfolio investments. The definition found in this Study is as follows:

> Portfolio investments are investments that are intended to fulfill a long-term investment strategy of an enterprise and that are generally passive in nature. Portfolio investments include both fixed term and equity investments, but exclude non-passive investments such as investments in subsidiaries, joint ventures, partnerships, and companies subject to significant influence by the investor.

2-38. This definition provides a description of portfolio investments based on their passive nature. We believe that it is preferable to the existing definition in that it defines portfolio investments in terms of what they are, rather than in terms of what they are not.

Joint Ventures

2-39. As we noted earlier in this Chapter, the subject of joint ventures will be given comprehensive treatment in Chapter 7. We would note here that, in somewhat simplified terms, joint venture investments are distinguished by the fact that their operating, financing, and investing activities are subject to joint control by the two or more venturers.

Methods Of Accounting For Long-Term Investments

General Description

2-40. As was indicated earlier, the *CICA Handbook* refers to four methods of accounting for long-term investments. These are the cost method, the equity method, full consolidation, and proportionate consolidation. Of these methods, the cost method is defined and described completely in Section 3050. In addition, the general requirements for the application of the equity method are provided in Section 3050. However, one of the requirements specified in Section 3050 is that, if the equity method is used, it must produce the same investor net income amount that would have been calculated if the investee had been consolidated. This means that a complete understanding of consolidation procedures is required in order to fully implement the equity method. Similarly, proportionate consolidation is given a general definition in Section 3055 but its application in more complex situations requires an understanding of full consolidation procedures.

2-41. As Chapters 4 to 6 are required to provide a presentation of consolidation procedures, it is clear that the only method that can be dealt with in a comprehensive fashion in this Chapter is the cost method. However, in order to understand the relevant Recommendations on which methods should be used for the various identified classifications of long-term investments, a general description of all methods is provided. In addition, this Chapter will also present simple examples of the application of the equity method, full consolidation, and proportionate consolidation. More complex applications of the equity method will be presented in Chapters 5 and 6. Chapter 7 will include a comprehensive presentation of the procedures used in proportionate consolidation.

2-42. Before leaving this general description, you should note that there is no mention in Section 3050 or Section 3055 of the use of market or lower of cost or market as a general method of accounting for long-term investments. While these methods are used in accounting for temporary investments, they are not acceptable for long-term investment holdings. The reason for this is that market values reflect the amount that would be received if the investment was liquidated. Such values are relevant in the case of temporary investments because there is an intent to liquidate. However, in the case of investments that management intends to hold for the long-term, such values are clearly not appropriate as a basis for valuation.

Cost Method Defined

General Procedures

2-43.   The cost method of accounting for long-term investments is a specific application of the general procedures used in accounting for most non current assets. It is based on the historical cost principle and the fact that an equity investor company's only legal claim to income is based on the amount of dividends declared by the investee company. The *Handbook* defines the method as follows:

> **Paragraph 3050.02(c)**   The **cost method** is a basis of accounting for long-term investments whereby the investment is initially recorded at cost; earnings from such investments are recognized only to the extent received or receivable. When the investment is in the form of shares, dividends received in excess of the investor's pro rata share of post acquisition income are recorded as a reduction of the amount of the investment.

2-44.   As stated in the preceding Paragraph, the cost method records the investment at its cost and, in most circumstances, the investor company will continue to carry the asset at this value until it is disposed of. In general, the investor will recognize income only when the investee declares dividends ("extent received or receivable"). No recognition is given to increases or decreases in the Retained Earnings of the investee company, nor is any disclosure provided to indicate that the investee has recorded extraordinary items, results of discontinued operations, or prior period adjustments.

Return Of Capital

2-45.   An exception to the preceding general rules occurs when the dividends declared by the investee represent a return of capital to the investor. This happens when the investee's cumulative dividends since the date of the investor's acquisition of shares exceed the cumulative Net Income of the investee since that date. Stated alternatively, this happens when an investee pays dividends out of Retained Earnings that were present when the investor acquired its shares. A simple example will serve to illustrate this situation:

> **Example**   On December 31, 2002, the Fastee Company has the following Shareholders' Equity:

Common Stock - No Par	$3,400,000
Retained Earnings	4,600,000
Total Shareholders' Equity	$8,000,000

> On this date, the Fastor Company acquires 10 percent of Fastee's outstanding voting shares at a cost of $800,000. During 2003, Fastee has Net Income of nil and declares dividends of $400,000.

2-46.   As Fastee had no Net Income in 2003, the 2003 dividends are being paid out of the December 31, 2002 Retained Earnings balance. From the point of view of Fastee this is not a liquidating dividend. It is an ordinary dividend being paid on the basis of a Retained Earnings balance that is legally available for this purpose. However, from the point of view of Fastor, the $40,000 dividend that they receive from Fastee represents a return of capital. This position is based on the fact that, when they paid $800,000 for their 10 percent share of Fastee, they acquired a 10 percent share of the $4,600,000 Retained Earnings balance that was present in Fastee's December 31, 2002 Balance Sheet. As this balance is being used by Fastee as the basis for the 2003 dividend payment, the $40,000 received by Fastor constitutes a return of part of the original investment and not investment income. The journal entry to record the receipt of the dividend is as follows:

Cash	$40,000	
Investment In Fastee		$40,000

Equity Method Defined
Basic Procedures

2-47. The equity method is defined in the *CICA Handbook* as follows:

> **Paragraph 3050.02(a)** The **equity method** is a basis of accounting for long-term investments whereby the investment is initially recorded at cost and the carrying value adjusted thereafter to include the investor's pro rata share of post-acquisition earnings of the investee, computed by the consolidation method. The amount of the adjustment is included in the determination of net income by the investor and the investment account of the investor is also increased or decreased to reflect the investor's share of capital transactions and changes in accounting policies and corrections of errors relating to prior period financial statements applicable to post-acquisition periods. Profit distributions received or receivable from an investee reduce the carrying value of the investment.

2-48. Ignoring for the moment special disclosure requirements and the need for consolidation adjustments, we can describe the equity method either in terms of asset value or income amounts. These descriptions are as follows:

> **Investment (Asset) Value** The investment account is initially recorded at cost. In each subsequent accounting period, it is adjusted up or down to reflect the investor company's share of the change in Retained Earnings of the investee company. This adjustment could also be described as a two stage process in which the investment account is increased (decreased) by the investor's share of the investee's Net Income (Net Loss) and decreased by the investor's share of the investee's dividends declared.

> **Investment Income** Investment Income under the equity method is simply the investor company's share of the reported Net Income of the investee company.

Special Disclosure Requirements

2-49. When an investee that is to be accounted for by the equity method has recorded results of discontinued operations, extraordinary items, capital transactions, or prior period adjustments related to accounting changes or errors, the *CICA Handbook* makes the following Recommendation:

> **Paragraph 3050.09** *In accounting for an investment by the equity method, the investor's proportionate share of the investee's discontinued operations, extraordinary items, changes in accounting policy, corrections of errors relating to prior period financial statements and capital transactions should be disclosed in the investor's financial statements according to their nature.* (April, 1996)

2-50. This means that if, for example, an investee company has an extraordinary gain, the investor company's share of this gain will be disclosed as an extraordinary gain in the financial statements of the investor company. This provision will be illustrated in an example of the application of the equity method later in this Chapter.

2-51. A second equity method disclosure Recommendation is as follows:

> **Paragraph 3050.10** *When the fiscal periods of an investor and an investee, the investment in which is accounted for by the equity method, are not coterminous, events relating to, or transactions of, the investee that have occurred during the intervening period and significantly affect the financial position or results of operations of the investor should be recorded or disclosed, as appropriate.* (August, 1978)

2-52. This Recommendation would be applicable only when the investor's year end is later than the year end that is reflected in the investee figures used. The appropriate disclosure for the relevant events would follow the pattern required for subsequent events in general (See Section 3820 of the *CICA Handbook*). This Recommendation will not be illustrated in the examples contained in this Chapter.

2-53. Disclosure is also required under the equity method of the treatment given to any difference between the cost of the investment and the investor's share of the underlying net book value of the investee's assets as follows:

> **Paragraph 3050.32** *When investments are accounted for by the equity method, disclosure should be made, in the notes to the financial statements, of the amount of any difference between the cost and the underlying net book value of the investee's assets at the date of purchase, as well as the accounting treatment of the components of such difference.* (January, 1973)

2-54.   This disclosure relates to the need to incorporate various consolidation adjustments into the equity method. As will be explained in the following paragraphs, these consolidation adjustments are covered in Chapters 5 and 6.

Consolidation Adjustments

2-55.   The need to incorporate consolidation adjustments into equity method procedures is clearly established in the following Recommendation:

> **Paragraph 3050.08** *Investment income as calculated by the equity method should be that amount necessary to increase or decrease the investor's income to that which would have been recognized if the results of the investee's operations had been consolidated with those of the investor.* (August, 1978)

2-56.   This requirement means that investment income under the equity method must be adjusted for all of the same factors that influence consolidation procedures. While these terms will not mean very much to you at this stage, adjustments would be required for fair value amortization, goodwill impairment, upstream unrealized profits, and downstream unrealized profits. These consolidation adjustments will be covered in Chapters 5 and 6 and, as a consequence, the equity method examples in this Chapter will involve simple situations where such adjustments are not required. This means that we will have to return to the equity method in Chapters 5 and 6 in order to fully illustrate this method of accounting for long-term investments.

Consolidation Defined

2-57.   We have previously noted that long-term investments sometimes involve situations in which the investor company has complete control over the affairs of the investee company. In such situations, the two companies are being operated as if they were a single business or economic entity and, as a consequence, accounting should focus on the economic resources and operations of the combined companies. Consolidation is an accounting method which accomplishes this goal. It accounts for the investor and investee companies as if they were a single entity, adding together all of the assets, liabilities, expenses and revenues of the two companies. However, these procedures always begin with the single entity accounting records of the two companies. Given this, the procedures required to adjust various asset values and to eliminate the effects of the different intercompany transactions are quite complex. As a consequence, only a very elementary example of the application of consolidated procedures will be presented in this Chapter.

2-58.   We would note, however, that when consolidation procedures are applied, the account which reflects the investment in the investee to be consolidated will always be replaced by the investee's individual assets and liabilities. This means that no investment account will be included in the consolidated financial statements presented by the investor company. As a result, investor companies use a variety of different methods to account for the investment account in their single entity records. Since the investment account will not be disclosed in the consolidated financial statements, the method by which this balance will be accounted for in the single entity records of the investee company is not subject to generally accepted accounting principles. In turn, this means that the investment account that reflects the investment in the investee to be consolidated can be carried by either the cost method or the equity method.

Proportionate Consolidation Defined

2-59.   Under this modified version of consolidation, only the investor's share of the investee's assets, liabilities, expenses, and revenues are added to those of the investor. This is in contrast to full consolidation where 100 percent of the investee's assets, liabilities, expenses, and revenues are added to those of the investor company, with the non-controlling interest in these items being disclosed as a separate item in the financial statements. When the investor company owns 100 percent of the investee company's shares, there is no difference between full and proportionate consolidation.

2-60.   While a complete application of proportionate consolidation requires the same adjustments as those required by full consolidation, we will provide a simple example to illustrate this procedure in this Chapter.   A more complete presentation of proportionate consolidation is included in Chapter 7, Interests In Joint Ventures.

Application Of The Cost And Equity Methods
Example One
2-61.   The example which follows involves no fair value changes, goodwill, or intercompany transactions.   It will serve to fully illustrate the cost method and to introduce the equity method of accounting for long-term investments.

Example One   On December 31, 2002, the Stor Company purchases 30 percent of the outstanding voting shares of the Stee Company for $6 million in cash. On this date, the carrying value of the net identifiable assets of the Stee Company total $20 million. All of the Stee Company's identifiable assets and liabilities have fair values that are equal to their carrying values.   There are no intercompany transactions other than dividend payments during the three years subsequent to December 31, 2002.   Dividends are declared on November 1 of each year and paid on December 1 of the same year. The Stee Company's Net Income and Dividend Declared and Paid for this period are as follows:

Year	Net Income	Dividends Declared and Paid
2003	$2,000,000	$1,500,000
2004	500,000	1,500,000
2005	3,500,000	1,700,000

The Net Income of the Stee Company does not include any extraordinary items in any of the years under consideration.   In terms of bookkeeping procedures to be used, we will assume that Stor records the Stee dividends when received and, in applying the equity method, adjusts accounts for its share of Stee's Net Income at the end of each year.

Required   Provide the journal entries for the Stor Company related to its investment in the Stee Company for the years 2002 through 2005. They should be prepared under the assumption that the Stor Company accounts for its Investment In Stee using (a) the cost method and (b) the equity method.

Example One Solution - Cost Method Journal Entries
2-62.   The journal entry required to record the initial investment on December 31, 2002 is as follows:

Investment In Stee	$6,000,000	
Cash		$6,000,000

2-63.   The journal entry required for the 2003 receipt of dividends is as follows:

Cash	$450,000	
Investment Income		$450,000

(To record the receipt of 30 percent of the Stee Company's $1,500,000 dividends declared.)

2-64.   The journal entry required for the 2004 receipt of dividends is as follows:

Cash $450,000
      Investment In Stee $150,000
      Investment Income   300,000
(To record the receipt of 30 percent of the Stee Company's dividends and the resulting decrease in the investment account due to a return of capital.)

Note   At this point the Stee Company has paid dividends of $3,000,000 but has only earned $2,500,000 since the Stor Company acquired the Stee Company shares. This means that, from the point of view of Stor Company, there has been a return of capital. To reflect this fact, Stor Company will write down its investment account by $150,000 (30 percent of $500,000). The Investment Income totals $750,000 for the two years since acquisition ($450,000 + $300,000) and this is equal to 30 percent of the sum of the Stee Company's income for the two years ($2,000,000 for 2003 plus $500,000 for 2004).

2-65.   The journal entry required for the 2005 receipt of dividends is as follows:

Cash $510,000
      Investment Income $510,000
(To record the receipt of 30 percent of the Stee Company's dividends of $1,700,000.)

Note   This entry leaves the balance in the Investment In Stee account at $5,850,000 ($6,000,000 - $150,000). It could be argued that since the Stee Company has retained sufficient earnings in 2005 to replace the pre-acquisition retained earnings that were disbursed in 2004, the investment account should be restored to its original balance of $6,000,000. This would be accomplished with a debit to the Investment In Stee and a credit to Investment Income of $150,000. This would bring the total Investment Income for the three years to $1,410,000 ($450,000 + $300,000 + $510,000 + $150,000) which is equal to 30 percent of the $4,700,000 in dividends that have been paid by the Stee Company during the three years since Stor Company acquired its shares. We would note that, while the *CICA Handbook* does not deal with this issue, practitioners appear to leave the investment account at its reduced value in these situations.

Exercise Two-2

On January 1, 2002, Placor Inc. acquires 20 percent of the outstanding voting shares of Placee Inc. at a price that was equal to 20 percent of that Company's net assets. During the year ending December 31, 2002, Placee had Net Income of $150,000 and paid dividends of $100,000. In the year ending December 31, 2003, the Company had a net loss of $40,000 and paid dividends of $50,000. For the year ending December 31, 2004, Placee's Net Income was $90,000 and it paid dividends of $80,000. The investment does not give Placor significant influence over Placee.

> Exercise Two-2 deals with the application of the cost method.

Required: Provide Placor's journal entries related to its Investment in Placee for the three years ending December 31, 2002, 2003, and 2004.

Example One Solution - Equity Method Journal Entries

2-66.   The journal entry required to record the initial investment on December 31, 2002 is the same as under the cost method:

Investment In Stee $6,000,000
      Cash $6,000,000

2-67.   Under the procedures that we are using, two entries are required during 2003. The first entry records the receipt of the Stee dividends. The second makes the year end adjustment to record Stor's share of Stee's Net Income as an increase in the Investment in Stee account. If Stee had a Net Loss, Stor's share of the loss would be recorded as an Investment Loss and a decrease in the Investment in Stee account.

Cash	$450,000	
Investment In Stee		$450,000

(To record the receipt of 30 percent of the Stee Company's $1,500,000 of dividends declared as a reduction in Stor's equity interest in Stee.)

Investment In Stee	$600,000	
Investment Income		$600,000

(To record Stor's 30 percent share of Stee's $2,000,000 Net Income as an increase in Stor's equity interest in Stee and as a revenue)

Note It is possible to accomplish the same result with a single net entry as follows:

Cash	$450,000	
Investment In Stee	150,000	
Investment Income		$600,000

The difference in these two approaches is a matter of preference. The two entry approach reflects the way the entries would normally be recorded in practice since dividends are paid during the year and the Net Income figure would not be available until after the year end. However, the single net entry approach is sometimes used as a shortcut in textbook examples.

2-68. For 2004, two entries would again be required under the equity method:

Cash	$450,000	
Investment In Stee		$450,000

(To record the receipt of 30 percent of the Stee Company's $1,500,000 of dividends declared as a reduction in Stor's equity interest in Stee. Note that under the equity method, as all dividends are recorded as a reduction in the investment account, there is no need to track whether the dividends were paid from retained earnings that were present at acquisition.)

Investment In Stee	$150,000	
Investment Income		$150,000

(To record Stor's 30 percent share of Stee's $500,000 Net Income as an increase in Stor's equity interest in Stee and as a revenue.)

2-69. For 2005, two entries would again be required under the equity method:

Cash	$510,000	
Investment In Stee		$510,000

(To record the receipt of 30 percent of the Stee Company's $1,700,000 of dividends declared as a reduction in Stor's equity interest in Stee.)

Investment In Stee	$1,050,000	
Investment Income		$1,050,000

(To record Stor's 30 percent share of Stee's $3,500,000 Net Income as an increase in Stor's equity interest in Stee and as a revenue.)

Exercise Two-3 deals with the application of the equity method.

Exercise Two-3

On January 1, 2002, Placor Inc. acquires 20 percent of the outstanding voting shares of Placee Inc. at a price that was equal to 20 percent of that Company's net assets. During the year ending December 31, 2002, Placee had Net Income of $150,000 and paid dividends of $100,000. In the year ending December 31, 2003, the Company had a net loss of $40,000 and paid dividends of $50,000. For the year ending December 31, 2004, Placee's Net Income was $90,000 and it paid dividends of $80,000. The investment gives Placor significant influence over Placee.

Required: Provide Placor's journal entries related to its Investment in Placee for the three years ending December 31, 2002, 2003, and 2004.

Application Of The Equity Method
Example Two
2-70.   It was noted previously that the equity method requires special disclosure when the investee has results of discontinued operations, extraordinary items, capital transactions or prior period adjustments.   This recommendation can be illustrated by extending the preceding example (the basic data is repeated for your convenience).

Example Two   On December 31, 2002, the Stor Company purchases 30 percent of the outstanding voting shares of the Stee Company for $6 million in cash. On this date, the carrying value of the net identifiable assets of the Stee Company total $20 million. All of the Stee Company's identifiable assets and liabilities have fair values that are equal to their carrying values.

The Stor Company uses the equity method to account for its investment in the Stee Company. We have examined the Stor Company's accounting for 2003, 2004, and 2005 under the equity method. The 2006 condensed Income Statements of the two companies are as follows:

	Stor Company	Stee Company
Sales	$3,500,000	$750,000
Expenses	3,000,000	550,000
Income Before Extraordinary Items	$ 500,000	$200,000
Extraordinary Loss	-0-	(80,000)
Net Income	$ 500,000	$120,000

There are no intercompany transactions between the Stee Company and the Stor Company during 2006.

Required: Prepare the condensed Income Statement of the Stor Company for 2006.

Example Two Solution
2-71.   The Stor Company's 2006 Income Statement using the equity method of accounting would be as follows:

Sales	$3,500,000
Ordinary Investment Income (30% of $200,000)	60,000
Total Revenues	$3,560,000
Expenses	3,000,000
Income Before Extraordinary Items	$ 560,000
Extraordinary Investment Loss (30% of $80,000)	(24,000)
Net Income	$ 536,000

2-72.   As can be seen in the preceding Income Statement, the investee's extraordinary item would be disclosed as an extraordinary item in the Income Statement of the investor enterprise. This would be true, even if some or all of the items were ordinary transactions from the point of view of the investor company. This is because they remain extraordinary transactions from the point of view of the investee and the related investment income.

> Exercise Two-4 deals with disclosure under the equity method.

Exercise Two-4

On January 1, 2002, Clearly Inc. acquires 15 percent of the outstanding shares of Muddle Ltd. The consideration for the investment was $1,000,000 in cash plus Clearly Inc. shares with a fair market value of $500,000. At the time of this investment, the net book value of Muddle Ltd. was $10,000,000 and all of the Company's assets and liabilities had fair values that were equal to their carrying values. Both Companies have a December 31 year end.

During the year ending December 31, 2002, Muddle Ltd. has Net Income of $20,000 and pays no dividends.

During the year ending December 31, 2003, Muddle Ltd. has Income Before Discontinued Operations of $346,000. However, a loss on discontinued operations reduces Net Income to $46,000. Based on its recent history of profits, Muddle declares and pays dividends which total $103,000 during the year ending December 31, 2003.

Required: Provide any journal entry that would be required on Clearly's books to account for its Investment in Muddle Ltd. for the year ending December 31, 2003 assuming that Clearly accounts for its investment in Muddle Ltd. using:

A.   the cost method.

B.   the equity method.

Application Of The Equity Method, Proportionate Consolidation and Full Consolidation

Example Three

2-73.   An additional example of accounting methods for long-term investments will provide a simple illustration of the application of the equity method, proportionate consolidation, and full consolidation. The example is as follows:

Example Three   On January 1, 2002, Marker Ltd. acquires 60 percent of the outstanding voting shares of Markee Inc. for $250,000. On this date, Markee Inc. has Common Stock - No Par of $400,000 and Retained Earnings of $600,000. Note that the investment cost of $600,000 is equal to 60 percent of Markee Inc.'s book value of $1,000,000. The identifiable assets and liabilities of Markee Inc. have fair values that are equal to their carrying values on this date. Both Companies have a December 31 year end.

During the year ending December 31, 2002, Markee Inc. has Net Income of $80,000 and declares and pays dividends of $30,000. Other than the payment of dividends, there are no intercompany transactions during the year and Markee has no results of discontinued operations, extraordinary items, capital transactions or accounting changes or errors requiring prior period adjustments.

Equity Method Solution

2-74.   Normally, a 60 percent investment would give Marker Ltd. control, with Markee Inc. being classified as a subsidiary. This would suggest that consolidated statements should be prepared. However, in this first version of our example, we will assume that Marker Ltd. has restrictions on its ability to control Markee Inc. and, as a consequence, will use the equity method to account for this investment. Given this, Marker Ltd.'s journal entries to record its share of Markee's 2002 Dividends Declared and Markee's 2002 Net Income would be as follows:

Cash [(60%)($30,000)]	$18,000	
Investment In Markee		$18,000
Investment In Markee [(60%)($80,000)]	$48,000	
Investment Income		$48,000

The Balance Sheets of the two Companies as at December 31, 2002 and the Income Statements for the year ending December 31, 2002 would be as follows:

Marker Ltd. And Markee Inc.
Equity Method Balance Sheets
As At December 31, 2002

	Marker Ltd.	Markee Inc.
Cash	$ 175,000	$ 105,000
Accounts Receivable	425,000	220,000
Inventories	970,000	550,000
Investment In Markee (At Equity)	630,000	-0-
Plant And Equipment (Net)	2,700,000	725,000
Total Assets	$4,900,000	$1,600,000
Current Liabilities	$ 250,000	$ 125,000
Long-Term Liabilities	750,000	425,000
Common Stock - No Par	1,200,000	400,000
Retained Earnings	2,700,000	650,000
Total Equities	$4,900,000	$1,600,000

Marker Ltd. And Markee Inc.
Equity Method Income Statements
For Year Ending December 31, 2002

	Marker Ltd.	Markee Inc.
Sales	$4,172,000	$1,500,000
Investment Income (Equity Method)	48,000	-0-
Total Revenues	$4,220,000	$1,500,000
Cost Of Goods Sold	$2,700,000	$ 975,000
Other Expenses	1,200,000	445,000
Total Expenses	$3,900,000	$1,420,000
Net Income	$ 320,000	$ 80,000

Proportionate Consolidation Solution

2-75.   If we assume that, despite its ownership of 60 percent of the voting shares, Marker Ltd. must share control with another shareholder, Markee Inc. would be classified as a joint venture. This means that proportionate consolidation procedures must be applied.

2-76.   The preceding financial statements reflect the application of the equity method to this situation. Note that in this simple example, the $630,000 equity value of the Investment In Markee is exactly equal to 60 percent of the net assets of Markee [(60%)($1,600,000 - $125,000 - $425,000)]. Proportionate consolidation would simply replace this $630,000 with 60 percent of the individual assets and liabilities of Markee Inc. This will result in the following Balance Sheet and Income Statement:

Marker Ltd. And Markee Inc.
Proportionate Consolidation Balance Sheet
As At December 31, 2002

Cash [$175,000 + (60%)($105,000)]	$ 238,000
Accounts Receivable [$425,000 + (60%)($220,000)]	557,000
Inventories [$970,000 + (60%)($550,000)]	1,300,000
Investment In Markee	
(Replaced By Marker's Share Of Markee's Net Assets)	-0-
Plant And Equipment (Net) [$2,700,000 + (60%)($725,000)]	3,135,000
Total Assets	$5,230,000
Current Liabilities [$250,000 + (60%)($125,000)]	$ 325,000
Long-Term Liabilities [$750,000 + (60%)($425,000)]	1,005,000
Common Stock - No Par (Marker's Only)	1,200,000
Retained Earnings (Marker's Only)	2,700,000
Total Equities	$5,230,000

Marker Ltd. And Markee Inc.
Proportionate Consolidation Income Statement
For Year Ending December 31, 2002

Sales [$4,172,000 + (60%)($1,500,000)]	$5,072,000
Cost Of Goods Sold [$2,700,000 + (60%)($975,000)]	$3,285,000
Other Expenses [$1,200,000 + (60%)($445,000)]	1,467,000
Total Expenses	$4,752,000
Net Income	$ 320,000

2-77.   Note that the Net Income under proportionate consolidation is $320,000, the same figure that we arrived at for Marker Ltd. as a single entity using the equity method to account for its investment in Markee Inc. This makes clear that the basic difference between these two methods is one of disclosure. Under the equity method, Marker records $48,000 or 60 percent of Markee's Net Income as a single line item called Investment Income. In contrast, proportionate consolidation incorporates 60 percent of all of Markee's Revenues and Expenses into the Income Statement. While the detail contained in the statements looks very different, the bottom line figure of $320,000 is not changed.

Full Consolidation Solution

2-78.   In this last version of this example, we will assume that Marker's 60 percent holding of voting shares provides it with unrestricted control over Markee. With Markee Inc. classified as a subsidiary, consolidated financial statements will be required.

2-79.   It is somewhat more difficult to explain the appearance of the statements that result from using full consolidation procedures. Under these procedures, 100 percent of the assets, liabilities, expenses, and revenues of Markee will be added to those of Marker. However, since Marker does not own 100 percent of these amounts, a new equity interest will have to be disclosed in both the Income Statement and the Balance Sheet.

2-80.   This new equity interest reflects the 40 percent share of assets and income that belong to the minority shareholders. The examples in the *CICA Handbook* refer to this as a "non-controlling interest", reflecting the fact that in certain very limited circumstances it may not be a "minority interest" (e.g., where the investor obtains control without owning a majority of the voting shares). However, in practice the term minority interest is still widely used.

2-81. In the consolidated Balance Sheet, this Non-Controlling Interest is simply 40 percent of the net assets of Markee. Correspondingly, in the consolidated Income Statement, the Non-Controlling Interest is 40 percent of Markee's Net Income. The required financial statements are as follows:

Marker Ltd. And Markee Inc.
Full Consolidation Balance Sheet
As At December 31, 2002

Cash ($175,000 + $105,000)	$ 280,000
Accounts Receivable ($425,000 + $220,000)	645,000
Inventories ($970,000 + $550,000)	1,520,000
Investment In Markee (Replaced By Markee's Net Assets)	-0-
Plant And Equipment ($2,700,000 + $725,000)	3,425,000
Total Assets	$5,870,000

Current Liabilities ($250,000 + $125,000)	$ 375,000
Long-Term Liabilities ($750,000 + $425,000)	1,175,000
Non-Controlling Interest [(40%)($400,000 + $650,000)]	420,000
Common Stock - No Par (Marker's Only)	1,200,000
Retained Earnings (Marker's Only)	2,700,000
Total Equities	$5,870,000

Marker Ltd. And Markee Inc.
Full Consolidation Income Statement
For Year Ending December 31, 2002

Sales ($4,172,000 + $1,500,000)	$5,672,000
Cost Of Goods Sold ($2,700,000 + $975,000)	$3,675,000
Other Expenses ($1,200,000 + $445,000)	1,645,000
Total Expenses	$5,320,000
Total Income	$ 352,000
Non-Controlling Interest [(40%)($80,000)]	(32,000)
Consolidated Net Income	$ 320,000

2-82. Note that this is the same $320,000 of Net Income that resulted from the application of both the equity method and proportionate consolidation.

2-83. As a final point on the examples of proportionate and full consolidation, you should not be concerned if you find these examples somewhat confusing at this point in the text. They are, in fact, fairly simple examples that will be easily understood once you have completed the work in Chapter 5. They were introduced at this point simply to give you a general idea of the approach that is taken when these procedures are applied. You should not, at this stage of the text, spend a great deal of time trying to achieve a full understanding of these procedures.

Application Of The Equity Method - EIC Abstract No. 8
Example Four
2-84. A final example will be used to illustrate a further aspect of the general application of the equity method:

Example Four On January 1, 2002, Duster Ltd. acquires 35 percent of the outstanding voting shares of Dustee Ltd. for $3,500,000 in cash. At the time of this acquisition, the net book value of Dustee Ltd. was $50 million. Duster Ltd. was able to acquire these shares at this price because it was anticipated that Dustee Ltd. was going to experience severe losses during the next two years. This expectation appears to be correct in that Dustee Ltd.'s loss for the year ending December 31, 2002 is $12 million.

Example Four Solution

2-85. Under the usual equity method procedures, the journal entry to reflect this result would be as follows:

Investment Loss [(35%)($12,000,000)]	$4,200,000	
Investment In Dustee		$4,200,000

2-86. The problem here is that this entry would create a credit balance of $700,000 in the Investment In Dustee account and this balance would have to be reported as a liability. Since equity investments in corporations are generally protected by limited liability, the recording of a liability in these circumstances would not be appropriate in normal circumstances. As a consequence, an investor company would usually stop recording further equity method losses when the related asset balance reaches nil.

2-87. However, the Emerging Issues Committee (EIC) was asked if there were any circumstances in which it would be appropriate to continue recording losses after an equity investment balance reached nil. Their response is reflected in EIC Abstract No. 8 in which they indicate that continuing to record such losses would be appropriate if the investor was likely to share in them. In their view, this would be the case if any of the following conditions are present:

- the investor has guaranteed obligations of the investee; or
- the investor is otherwise committed to provide further financial support for the investee; or
- the investee seems assured of imminently returning to profitability.

2-88. The other issue dealt with in this EIC Abstract was the question of what disclosure should be provided in those cases where the investor does not continue to record equity method losses. In general, they indicated that the information to be disclosed would be a matter of professional judgment but could include:

- disclosure of unrecognized losses for the period and accumulated to date; and
- the investor's accounting policies with respect to the investment, including the policy to be followed should the investee return to profitability.

2-89. The Committee also indicated that, when losses have not been recorded on an investee that later returns to profitability, the investor should resume recognizing its share of those profits only after its share of the profits equals its share of the losses not recognized.

Exercise Two-5 deals with deficits in equity method investment accounts.

Exercise Two-5

On January 1, 2002, Ausser Ltd. acquires 40 percent of the outstanding voting shares of Aussee Inc. for $400,000. During the year ending December 31, 2002, Aussee experiences a Net Loss of $1,500,000. During the subsequent year ending December 31, 2003, Aussee has Net Income of $800,000. Ausser accounts for its investment in Aussee using the equity method.

Required: Provide the journal entries to record Ausser's Investment Income (Loss) for the years ending December 31, 2002 and December 31, 2003.

Application Of The Cost Method To Debt Securities

Example

2-90. As previously indicated, long-term investments in debt securities would be classified as portfolio investments. While procedures for dealing with these securities are given extensive treatment in most intermediate accounting texts, a simple example is useful in the context of our general discussion of long-term investments:

> **Example** On January 1, 2002, Barton Inc. acquires debt securities with a par value of $2,000,000 at a cost of $2,250,000. The bonds mature in 10 years and pay interest annually on December 31 at a coupon rate of 8 percent. It is the intent of management to hold these securities until their maturity.

Solution

2-91. The acquisition of the bonds would be recorded as follows:

Bonds Receivable - Par Value	$2,000,000	
Bonds Receivable - Premium	250,000	
Cash		$2,250,000

2-92. As we are dealing with a long-term investment in debt securities, it is appropriate to amortize the premium on the bonds. For the sake of simplicity, we will assume straight line amortization of this amount, resulting in an annual write off of $25,000 ($250,000 ÷ 10 years). The following annual entry would be required to record interest received and the premium amortization:

Cash [(8%)($2,000,000)]	$160,000	
Bonds Receivable - Premium		$ 25,000
Interest Revenue		135,000

2-93. If the bonds are held, as intended, until their maturity, the premium will have been eliminated through amortization. The following entry would be required to record the receipt of the par value amount:

Cash	$2,000,000	
Bonds Receivable - Par Value		$2,000,000

2-94. Alternatively, if the bonds are sold prior to maturity, the proceeds of disposition will be compared to the book value of the debt securities including the unamortized premium. The difference will then be recorded as a gain or loss.

Exercise Two-6

On January 1, 2002, Larson Ltd. acquires debt securities with a par value of $3,000,000 at a cost of $2,840,000. The bonds mature in eight years and pay interest annually on December 31 at a coupon rate of 6 percent. The bond discount or premium is amortized using the straight line method.

Larson Ltd. has a December 31 year end. While the original intent of management was to hold these bonds to maturity, they are sold on January 1, 2005 for $3,050,000.

Required: Provide the journal entry to record the disposition of the bonds on January 1, 2005.

> Exercise Two-6 deals with long-term investments in debt securities.

Evaluation Of Cost And Equity Methods

2-95. If an individual who was familiar with the accounting procedures used for most of the long-term assets of an enterprise were asked to develop an accounting method to be used for long-term investments, the individual would probably arrive at a set of procedures that look very much like the cost method. This method uses acquisition cost as its basic measure of value. Income is subsequently recognized only when there is a clear legal basis for such recognition. In the case of long-term investments in equity securities, this legal basis would require a dividend declaration. In contrast, the equity method records as income and includes in asset values the investor's claim to the undistributed earnings of the investee. From a legal point of view, the investor has no real claim to these balances and, in many situations, will never realize the amounts that have been recorded.

2-96.   The preceding analysis suggests that the cost method is more consistent with general accounting procedures than the equity method in situations where there is less than full control over the investee. Unfortunately there is a problem with this conclusion. Under the cost method, Investment Income is based on the dividend declarations of the investee. This income is the investor's share of the investee's dividends declared, without regard to the GAAP determined earnings of the investee. While economic reality requires that there be a long-run relationship between reported income and dividend declarations, the directors of the investee have great discretion in determining short-run variations in the percentage of GAAP based earnings paid out as dividends. This does not create a problem when the investor company is not in a position to influence the board of directors. However, there are many situations short of full control of the investee, where the investor is able to exercise considerable influence on the actions of the investee's directors. In these cases, the use of the cost method would allow the investor company to have significant influence over its own Investment Income.

2-97.   For this reason, the equity method is required in situations where the investor company has influence over the investee. This would generally include all long-term investments in significantly influenced investees. In requiring the equity method in these circumstances, a further potential problem is also dealt with. This is the possibility that the investor company could influence the terms of intercompany transactions between the investor and investee enterprises. As was noted previously and as will be illustrated in subsequent chapters, the application of the equity method requires the elimination of all intercompany profits, both those of the investor and those of the investee, from the reported Investment Income.

2-98.   As we have noted, the cost method is used for dealing with portfolio investments. While the cost method approach is consistent with our treatment of most other non-current assets, some feel that more consideration should be given to the market value of such investments. The 1984 CICA Research Study, *Accounting For Portfolio Investments*, concluded that the use of market values for these investments would provide the most useful information for decision making purposes. Further, the study group recommended that gains or losses should be recognized as they occur on the basis of market related values. This is in contrast to the current situation in which gains and losses are recorded when there is a long-term investment disposition, a transaction over which the investor company has complete discretion as to timing.

Evaluation Of Consolidation
Proportionate Consolidation

2-99.   Prior to the October, 1994 revision of Section 3055, joint ventures were most commonly accounted for by the equity method. The previous version of Section 3055 indicated that, if a substantial portion of the investor's operations were in the form of joint ventures, it was permissible to use proportionate consolidation. However, the use of this method was never required.

2-100.   In general, the use of the equity method for joint ventures was a reasonable approach. The cost method had to be rejected because, by the very definition of a joint venture investment, the investor had to be involved in the management of the investee. The definition of joint venture investments also precluded any investor having the complete control over the investee that would justify the use of the full consolidation method. With the elimination of both the cost method and full consolidation for joint ventures, the use of the equity method was an almost inevitable choice.

2-101.   However, there was a problem with the application of the equity method in some joint venture situations. Companies existed which had no real economic activity other than their investment in joint ventures. For such companies, the use of the equity method would result in a one line Balance Sheet (Investment In Joint Ventures) and a one line Income Statement (Investment Income From Joint Ventures). This was clearly an inadequate form of disclosure and, given this problem, the use of proportionate consolidation provided an effective solution.

2-102. In response to this problem, the Accounting Standards Board concluded that proportionate consolidation was the appropriate method to be used for all joint venture situations. This is stated as follows:

> **Paragraph 3055.17** *Interests in joint ventures should be recognized in the financial statements of the venturer using the proportionate consolidation method.* (January, 1995)

2-103. In our opinion, this Recommendation requires the general use of proportionate consolidation in order to correct a problem that arises in only limited circumstances (e.g., where a major portion of the enterprise activities take the form of joint ventures). We do not think that this is an appropriate solution to the problem. A Special Report by the G4 + 1 Group reached a similar conclusion (*Reporting Interest In Joint ventures And Similar Arrangements*, FASB, September, 1999). As is discussed more completely in Chapter 7, this report completely rejects the use of proportionate consolidation, recommending an alternative method for joint ventures which is known as the "expanded equity method".

Full Consolidation

2-104. There is general agreement that, when an investor company has achieved sufficient control over an investee that resources are freely interchangeable and the two entities can be operated as a single economic unit, the application of full consolidation procedures is appropriate. At one point in time, the *CICA Handbook* listed a limited number of situations where subsidiaries could be excluded from consolidation. However, current *Handbook* Recommendations in this area leave no choice. If control over an investee exists, the investee is a subsidiary and must be consolidated with the financial statements of the parent or investor company.

2-105. While there is general agreement on the usefulness of consolidated financial statements for measuring the financial position and results of operations for a controlled group of companies, there is criticism of the fact that these are normally the only financial statements presented by the parent company. For a large multi-national conglomerate, these consolidated statements might aggregate financial data for a hundred or more separate companies. Further, these companies could be involved in dozens of different lines of business or in many different geographic locations around the world.

2-106. To some extent, the segmented information requirements of Section 1701, "Segment Disclosures", alleviate this problem by providing for disclosure of reportable operating segments. However, segmented information fails to take into account the legally defined interests of creditors, tax authorities, and non-controlling (minority) interest shareholders. Creditors can only take legal action against individual legal entities. In fact, an individual company can be in bankruptcy without threatening the overall health of the consolidated group. Further, tax returns must be filed by each individual corporation and non-controlling interest shareholders must look to the individual corporation in which they hold shares for their expected return on investment.

2-107. This leads some to argue that consolidated statements should be presented in conjunction with the single entity statements of the companies which comprise the consolidated group. This, in fact, is the approach that is taken in many industrialized countries other than Canada and the United States. As the whole area of consolidated financial statements is currently under comprehensive review in the United States, we may see changes in this situation in the next few years.

Recommended Accounting Methods For Long-Term Investments

Overview

2-108. We have completed our presentation of the classification of long-term investments and the description of the methods that are available to account for them. We are now in a position to consider which of the methods described is most appropriate for each of the long-term investment classifications that have been defined. The alternative classification choices that are available to companies eligible for differential reporting are covered beginning at Paragraph 2-130.

Portfolio Investments

2-109.   The least complex Recommendation in this area pertains to portfolio investments. With respect to these investments, the *CICA Handbook* states the following:

> **Paragraph 3050.18**   *The cost method should be used in accounting for portfolio investments.* (August, 1978)

2-110.   This Recommendation reflects the fact that the investor company is not in a position to exercise significant influence or control over the investee. While it is consistent with other Recommendations for dealing with the valuation of long-term assets, there is some question as to its usefulness for decision making purposes.

2-111.   There are no exceptions to this accounting treatment for portfolio investments. However, as noted previously, the cost of the investment can be reduced in situations where there is a return of the investor company's capital. In addition, investments that have experienced a non-temporary decline in value must be written down, without regard to the method being used to account for them (see the discussion which begins at Paragraph 2-139). There are no circumstances under which the value of portfolio investments would be written up to a value in excess of cost.

2-112.   As we have noted, all long-term investments in debt securities are considered to be portfolio investments. Given this, the *CICA Handbook* notes the following:

> **Paragraph 3050.19**   In the case of fixed term securities, it would be appropriate to amortize any discount or premium arising on purchase over the period to maturity. As a result of the amortization, earnings from the investment would reflect a yield based on purchase costs, not on coupon rates, and the carrying value of the investment would be adjusted systematically, during the period it is held, toward the amount expected to be realized at maturity or an earlier call date.

2-113.   While this suggests that discount or premium on long-term debt should be amortized, it does not specify the method to be used for this amortization. The statement that the "carrying value of the investment would be adjusted systematically" would permit the use of either the straight line or the effective yield approach.

Significantly Influenced Companies

2-114.   As was noted in our evaluation of the equity method, if investors in significantly influenced companies were allowed to use the cost method, it would be possible for them to manipulate investment income via their influence over the investee's dividend policy. Given this possibility, the *CICA Handbook* makes the following Recommendation:

> **Paragraph 3050.06**   *An investor that is able to exercise significant influence over an investee that is neither a subsidiary as defined in* "Subsidiaries", *Section 1590, nor a joint venture as defined in* "Interests In Joint Ventures", *Section 3055, should account for the investment by the equity method.* (January, 1995)

2-115.   The equity method would continue to be used until such time as significant influence is no longer present and significantly influenced company is no longer the appropriate classification for the investee. While this is not specifically dealt with in the *Handbook*, in some situations significant influence may evolve into control over the investee. This would normally follow the acquisition of additional voting shares and would result in the investee being classified as a subsidiary. In such situations, the investor company would switch from using the equity method to using consolidation procedures.

2-116. It is also possible that an investor company will lose its ability to exercise significant influence. If this occurs, the following Recommendation is applicable:

> **Paragraph 3050.07** *When an investor ceases to be able to exercise significant influence over an investee, the investment should be accounted for by the cost method.* (January, 1992)

2-117. You should note that there are alternative approaches to the application of this Recommendation. This reflects the fact that, when an investor has applied the equity method to an investment, the investment account will no longer be carried at its original cost. In most cases it will be at a value in excess of original cost, reflecting the investor's share of the investee's Retained Earnings since acquisition. In switching over to the cost method, the accounting change could be applied on either a retroactive or prospective basis.

> **Example** On January 1, 2002, Phosphor Inc. acquired 25 percent of the outstanding shares of Latlee Ltd. for $2,000,000. This investment provided Phosphor Inc. with significant influence over the affairs of Latlee Ltd. By December 31, 2002, the Investment In Latlee account had been increased to $2,500,000 to reflects Phosphor's share of Latlee Ltd.'s increase in Retained Earnings. On January 1, 2003, because of a bylaw change which revised the rules by which Latlee's Board Of Directors were elected, Phosphor Inc. loses its ability to influence the affairs of Latlee Ltd.

2-118. On January 1, 2003, Phosphor will have to switch from accounting for its investment in Latlee by the equity method, to accounting for this asset by the cost method. If the change were applied retroactively, the investment would have to be restored to its original cost of $2,000,000. This would require the investment to be written down, resulting in the recognition of a loss. In contrast, prospective treatment would use the $2,500,000 equity value at the date of the change as the deemed cost, applying cost method procedures to those accounting periods subsequent to the change. Under this prospective treatment, no loss or gain would be recognized at the time of the accounting change.

2-119. While not a formal Recommendation, Paragraph 3050.16 notes that cost is deemed to be the carrying value (equity value) at the time of the switch from the equity method to the cost method. This suggests the use of prospective treatment when an investor is no longer able to exercise significant influence over an investee. This Paragraph also notes that this might be an appropriate time to consider whether there has been an impairment in the value of the investment that would require a write down under Paragraph 3050.20 (see our Paragraph 2-139).

2-120. The use of prospective treatment in these situations creates an additional problem in the application of the cost method. As cost is deemed to be the equity value at the time of the change from the equity method to the cost method, the investment account will reflect the Retained Earnings of the investee up to the time of the change. This is in contrast to the usual cost procedures in which the investment account reflects the investee Retained Earnings only to the date on which the investment was made. This difference has an influence on the determination of whether some portion of an investee's dividend represents a return of capital to the investor. In this situation, a return of capital occurs when the cumulative amount of dividends exceeds income in the period subsequent to the date of the accounting change. Continuing the example from Paragraph 2-117, if Latlee had 2003 earnings of $500,000, but paid dividends of $1,000,000, half of the $250,000 dividend received by Phosphor would have to be accounted for as a return of capital, despite the fact that Phosphor's share of Latlee's increase in Retained Earnings was equal to $500,000 in 2002.

Joint Ventures

2-121. The general Recommendation here is as follows:

> **Paragraph 3055.17** *Interests in joint ventures should be recognized in the financial statements of the venturer using the proportionate consolidation method.* (January, 1995)

2-122.   The complications associated with the implementation of this Recommendation are given detailed consideration in Chapter 7, along with our coverage of other issues related to interests in joint ventures.

Subsidiaries

2-123.   When an investor company has control over the operating, investing, and financing activities of an investee company, the two companies can normally be considered a single economic entity. In such circumstances, it is a well established practice for accountants to concentrate on the single economic entity, rather than on the separate investor and investee legal entities. As the definition of a subsidiary is based on control, it is not surprising that consolidation is the required accounting method. The *CICA Handbook* makes the following Recommendation with respect to the accounting treatment of subsidiaries:

> **Paragraph 1590.16**   *An enterprise should consolidate all of its subsidiaries.* (January, 1992)

2-124.   This is a very restrictive rule which provides no flexibility with respect to the consolidation of investments that are classified as subsidiaries. This reflects the fact that, under earlier rules which were less rigid, it appeared that investor companies used the available flexibility to enhance their consolidated statements by excluding certain subsidiaries (e.g., subsidiaries with large debt loads).

Accounting Methods Summarized

2-125.   The conclusions reached in Sections 1590, 3050, and 3055 on the appropriate accounting methods to be used for each investment classification can be summarized in Figure 2-3 which follows:

Figure 2-3 Accounting Methods Summarized		
Investment Classification	**Degree Of Control**	**Accounting Method**
Portfolio Investments	No Influence Or Control	Cost Method
Significantly Influenced Companies	Significant Influence, But No Control	Equity Method*
Joint Ventures	Shared Control	Proportionate Consolidation*
Subsidiaries	Complete Control	Consolidation*

    * See differential reporting exemptions coverage starting at Paragraph 2-130.

2-126.   As is clear from Figure 2-3, the cost method is only used in those cases where the investor is not in a position to exercise significant influence over the affairs of the investee. As was previously explained, this prevents the investor company from manipulating investment income in those situations where it is in a position to control the dividend policy of the investee.

2-127.   Correspondingly, the equity method is required in the cases where the investor can exercise significant influence. As applied under Canadian accounting standards, the income and asset values recorded under this method must be adjusted for all of the same factors that would require adjustments if the consolidation method were applied (e.g., unrealized intercompany profits). This prevents the investor company from manipulating investment income via intercompany transactions using arbitrary transfer prices.

2-128. In the case of joint ventures, proportionate consolidation is required. This reflects the fact that the investor company will have influence over the investee through its joint control of that enterprise

2-129. Finally, in those cases where the investor company has control over the investee, the investor and investee companies are accounted for as a single economic unit. This is accomplished through the preparation of consolidated financial statements.

Differential Reporting and Long-Term Investments
Qualifying Enterprises
2-130. In January, 2002, a new Section 1300, "Differential Reporting", was added to the *CICA Handbook*. This new Section exempts qualifying enterprises from a group of specified *Handbook* Recommendations. A qualifying enterprise is defined as follows:

> **Paragraph 1300.06** *An enterprise is a qualifying enterprise for purposes of the differential reporting options set out in an Accounting Recommendation, Accounting Guideline or Abstract of Issue Discussed by the Emerging Issues Committee when and only when:*
>
> *(a) it is a non-publicly accountable enterprise; and*
> *(b) its owners unanimously consent to the application of differential reporting options in accordance with paragraph 1300.13. (January, 2002)*

Subsidiaries
2-131. Among the exemptions are certain Recommendations related to the methods of accounting to be used for long-term investments. With respect to subsidiaries, Section 1590 includes the following Recommendation:

> **Paragraph 1590.27** *An enterprise that qualifies under "Differential Reporting", Section 1300, may elect to use either the equity method or the cost method to account for subsidiaries that would otherwise be consolidated in accordance with paragraph 1590.16. All subsidiaries should be accounted for using the same method. (January, 2002)*

2-132. When qualifying enterprises use this exemption, several other Recommendations are applicable:

> **Paragraph 1590.27** *A loss in value of an investment in a non-consolidated subsidiary that is other than a temporary decline should be accounted for in accordance with the requirements of "Long-Term Investments", paragraphs 3050.20-.26. (January, 2002)*

> **Paragraph 1590.28** *When an enterprise applies one of the alternative methods permitted by paragraph 1590.26, the financial statements should be described as being prepared on a non-consolidated basis and each statement should be labelled accordingly. (January, 2002)*

> **Paragraph 1590.29** *Investments in non-consolidated subsidiaries should be presented separately in the balance sheet. Income or loss from those investments should be presented separately in the income statement. (January, 2002)*

> **Paragraph 1590.30** *An enterprise that has applied one of the alternative methods permitted by paragraph 1590.26 should disclose:*
>
> *(a) the basis used to account for subsidiaries; and*
> *(b) the particulars of any shares or other securities issued by the enterprise that are owned by non-consolidated subsidiaries. (January, 2002)*

2-133. It is also noted that when subsidiaries are not consolidated, Section 3840, "Related Party Transactions", applies to those intercompany transactions that would have been eliminated on consolidation.

Significantly Influenced Companies

2-134.   Section 3050 contains the following exemption for significantly influenced companies:

> **Paragraph 3050.39**   *An enterprise that qualifies under "Differential Reporting", Section 1300, may elect to use the cost method to account for its investments in companies subject to significant influence that would otherwise be accounted for by the equity method in accordance with paragraph 3050.06. All investments in companies subject to significant influence should be accounted for using the same method.* (January, 2002)

2-135.   When this exemption is used, Section 3050 contains two additional disclosure Recommendations:

> **Paragraph 3050.40**   *Investments in companies subject to significant influence accounted for using the cost method should be presented separately in the balance sheet. Income from those investments should be presented separately in the income statement.* (January, 2002)

> **Paragraph 3050.41**   *An enterprise that has applied the alternative method permitted by paragraph 3050.39 should disclose the basis of accounting used to account for investments in companies subject to significant influence.* (January, 2002)

Joint Ventures

2-136.   An exemption is also provided in Section 3055 with respect to accounting for joint ventures:

> **Paragraph 3055.47**   *An enterprise that qualifies under "Differential Reporting", Section 1300, may elect to use either the equity method or the cost method to account for its interests in joint ventures that would otherwise be accounted for using the proportionate consolidation method in accordance with paragraph 3055.17. All interests in joint ventures should be accounted for using the same method.* (January, 2002)

2-137.   Here again, when the exemption is used, additional disclosure is required as follows:

> **Paragraph 3055.47**   *An enterprise that qualifies under "Differential Reporting", Section 1300, may elect to use either the equity method or the cost method to account for its interests in joint ventures that would otherwise be accounted for using the proportionate consolidation method in accordance with paragraph 3055.17. All interests in joint ventures should be accounted for using the same method.* (January, 2002)

> **Paragraph 3055.48**   *A loss in value of an interest in a joint venture not proportionately consolidated that is other than a temporary decline should be accounted for in accordance with the requirements of "Long-Term Investments", paragraphs 3050.20-.26.* (January, 2002)

> **Paragraph 3055.49**   *Interests in joint ventures not proportionately consolidated should be presented separately in the balance sheet. Income or loss from those interests should be presented separately in the income statement.* (January, 2002)

> **Paragraph 3055.50**   *An enterprise that has applied one of the alternative methods permitted by paragraph 3055.47 should disclose the basis used to account for interests in joint ventures.* (January, 2002)

2-138.   Note that these are basically the same Recommendations that apply when the differential reporting exemptions are used to exclude subsidiaries from the consolidated financial statements. Also noted here is that Recommendations of Section 3840, "Related Party Transactions" are applicable to the intercompany transactions that would have been eliminated in the preparation of proportionately consolidated financial statements.

Declines In The Value Of Long-Term Investments

General Provisions

2-139.   The general *Handbook* provision dealing with the question of when a long-term investment should be written down is as follows:

> **Paragraph 3050.20**   *When there has been a loss in value of an investment that is other than a temporary decline, the investment should be written down to recognize the loss.* The write-down would be included in the determination of income and may or may not be an extraordinary item. (See "Extraordinary Items", Section 3480) (January 1973)

2-140.   This provision would apply, regardless of the method that was being used to account for the investment. In those cases where the investment is carried by the cost or equity method, the *CICA Handbook* notes:

> **Paragraph 3050.25**   When either the equity method or the cost method is used, a decline in value that is other than temporary would be recognized by writing down the investment.

2-141.   While you will not fully understand this point until we have covered consolidation procedures, the investment account for subsidiaries is always eliminated and replaced by the net assets of the subsidiaries. Given this, the write down of an investment in a subsidiary will take the form of a reduction in the value of specific assets in the consolidated Balance Sheet. The usual choice for this write down would be any Goodwill that was recognized when the subsidiary was acquired.

Debt Securities

2-142.   The implementation of Paragraph 3050.20 to holdings of debt securities does not present any major problems. The only possibilities that would lead an investor to conclude that an investment in debt securities should be written down are:

- the securities might be disposed of before they mature at a value that is less than their carrying value; or

- the debt issuer might default on some part of the interest or principal prior to the maturity of the securities.

2-143.   Changes in the market value of debt securities are not of significance in those cases where the investor intends to hold the investment to its maturity date, provided such changes do not reflect the possibility that the debt issuer will default on its obligations under the debt agreement.

Equity Securities

2-144.   The implementation of Paragraph 3050.20 with respect to securities that do not have either a fixed maturity date or a fixed maturity value will generally be more difficult than is the case with holdings of debt securities. There are some fairly obvious situations that indicate there has been a non-temporary loss in value, such as an investee in bankruptcy or one for which there is an agreement to sell at a price which will result in a loss. However, in the majority of situations, the investor will have to examine a number of factors to determine if a write down is appropriate. Paragraph 3050.24 suggests that the following be taken into consideration:

- a prolonged period during which the quoted market value of the investment is less than its carrying value;
- severe losses by the investee in the current year or current and prior years;
- continued losses by the investee for a period of years;
- suspension of trading in the securities;
- liquidity or going concern problems of the investee;
- the current fair value of the investment (an appraisal) is less than its carrying value.

2-145. This Paragraph goes on to note the following with respect to the use of these factors:

> ... when a condition, indicating that an impairment in value of an investment may have occurred, has persisted for a period of three or four years, there is a general presumption that there has been a loss in value which is other than a temporary decline. This presumption can only be rebutted by persuasive evidence to the contrary.

Subsequent Increase In Value

2-146. It is possible that, after a long-term investment has been written down, the fortunes of the investee will improve and the investment will increase in value. This, of course, raises the question of whether the investment should be written back up to its original value. The *CICA Handbook* takes the position that, once an investment has been reduced in value, this new value should be viewed as the cost for subsequent accounting purposes. This view is reflected in the following Recommendation:

> **Paragraph 3050.21**   *A write-down of an investment to reflect a loss in value should not be reversed if there is a subsequent increase in value.* (August, 1978)

2-147. This Recommendation can only be defended on grounds of conservatism. It is difficult to understand why the same kind of evidence that was used to support a write down of the long-term investment could not be used to support a reversal of such a write down. However, this approach is consistent with the treatment given to write downs of property, plant, and equipment under the Recommendations of Section 3061 (see Paragraph 3061.39), as well as the treatment of write downs or impairment of goodwill and other intangible assets under Section 3062 (see Paragraph 3062.21 and 3062.25).

Gains And Losses On The Sale Of Investments

2-148. A long-term investment may consist of a group of identical securities which have been acquired at different points in time and, as a consequence, at different prices. When part of such a group is disposed of, some assumption must be made as to the flow of costs to be allocated to the sale. The normal alternatives would be specific identification, LIFO (last-in, first-out), FIFO (first-in, first-out), or average cost. The *CICA Handbook* takes the position that average cost best reflects the gain or loss that would be recognized if the entire investment were disposed of. This is reflected in the following Recommendation:

> **Paragraph 3050.27**   *For the purposes of calculating a gain or loss on the sale of an investment, the cost of the investment sold should be calculated on the basis of the average carrying value.* (January, 1973)

2-149. This Recommendation is consistent with the required income tax treatment of gains and losses on such identical properties (See Section 47 of the *Income Tax Act*).

Exercise Two-7 deals with gains and losses on the sale of long-term investments.

Exercise Two-7

Salson Inc. has acquired shares in Tofal Ltd. over a number of years. The total portfolio is as follows:

	Number Of Shares	Total Cost
1st Purchase	2,400	$27,600
2nd Purchase	3,450	42,600
3rd Purchase	1,740	22,450
4th Purchase	4,360	72,400

During the current year, Salson Inc. sells 5,250 of its Tofal Ltd. shares at a price of $28 per share.

Required: Determine the gain or loss that would be recorded by Salson Inc. on its sale of Tofal Ltd. shares.

Additional Disclosure Requirements

Subsidiaries

2-150.   We have previously noted that control will normally be identified by the presence of majority ownership of voting shares. However, Section 1590 recognizes that this is not always the case. Control can exist without majority ownership and lack of control may occur where there is majority ownership. As these situations are not the usual ones, Paragraphs 1590.22 and 1590.23 specify additional disclosure requirements:

> **Paragraph 1590.22**   *When a reporting enterprise does not own, directly or indirectly through subsidiaries, an equity interest carrying the right to elect the majority of the members of the board of directors of a subsidiary, the reporting enterprise should disclose (i) the basis for the determination that a parent-subsidiary relationship exists, (ii) the name of the subsidiary, and (iii) the percentage ownership (if any). (January, 1992)*

> **Paragraph 1590.23**   *When a reporting enterprise owns, directly or indirectly through subsidiaries, an equity interest carrying the right to elect the majority of the members of the board of directors of an investee that is not a subsidiary, the reporting enterprise should disclose (i) the basis for the determination that a parent-subsidiary relationship does not exist, (ii) the name of the investee, (iii) the percentage ownership, and (iv) either separate financial statements of the investee, combined financial statements of similar investees or, provided all information significant to the consolidated financial statements is disclosed, condensed financial statements (including notes) of the investee. (January, 1992)*

Portfolio Investments And Significantly Influenced Companies

2-151.   Section 3050 contains several Recommendations with respect to the disclosure of portfolio investments and significantly influenced companies. They are as follows:

> **Paragraph 3050.29**   *The basis of valuation of long-term investments should be disclosed. (January, 1973)*

> **Paragraph 3050.30**   *Investments in companies subject to significant influence, other affiliated companies and other long-term investments should each be shown separately. (January, 1992)*

> **Paragraph 3050.31**   *Income from investments in companies subject to significant influence, other affiliated companies and other long-term investments should each be shown separately. Income calculated by the equity method should be disclosed separately. (January, 1992)*

> **Paragraph 3050.32**   *When investments are accounted for by the equity method, disclosure should be made, in the notes to the financial statements, of the amount of any difference between the cost and the underlying net book value of the investee's assets at the date of purchase, as well as the accounting treatment of the components of such difference. (January, 1973)*

> **Paragraph 3050.33**   *When portfolio investments include marketable securities, the quoted market value of such securities as well as their carrying value should be disclosed. (January, 1973)*

Long-Term Investments In Canadian Practice

Statistics From Financial Reporting In Canada

2-152.   Of the 200 companies surveyed for the 2001 edition of *Financial Reporting in Canada*, 123 disclosed the presence of long-term investments other than joint ventures in their 2000 annual reports. With respect to the valuation of these investments, 48 companies used both cost and equity, 31 used cost only, and 25 used equity only. The remaining 19 companies either did not disclose the basis of valuation or, alternatively, used some method other than cost or equity.

2-153.   Again looking at the 123 companies that disclosed the presence of long-term investments other than joint ventures, 91 segregated investment assets by type of investment, and 54 provided investment income segregated by type.

2-154.   If you would like more detailed information on Canadian practice statistics, the complete 2001 edition of *Financial Reporting in Canada* is on the CD-ROM which accompanies this text. The material on long-term investments is in Chapter 23.

Example From Canadian Practice

2-155.   The following example is from the annual report of Bema Gold Corporation for the reporting period ending December 31, 2000. This example illustrates disclosure of long term investments carried on an equity basis and a write down of carrying value. This example illustrates disclosure of long-term investments carried on an equity basis and on a cost basis.

Balance Sheet Disclosure

The account "Investments" (US$2,694,000 for 2000 and US$30,274,000 for 1999) refers to Note 5. Total Assets are US$175,950,000 for 2000 and US$204,202,000 for 1999.

Income Statement Disclosure

(in thousands of United States dollars)

for the years ended December 31	2000	1999	1998
Loss before the undernoted items	5,443	1,682	10,278
Equity in losses of associated companies	779	601	1,069
Investment losses (Note 5)	9,331	–	–
Write-down of investments (Notes 4 and 5)	11,773	–	–
Write-down of mineral properties (Note 6)	22,565	1,765	32,738
Write-down of notes receivable (Note 4)	1,248	–	2,042
Net loss for the year	$51,139	$ 4,048	$46,127

Notes To Financial Statements

(in thousands of United States dollars)

Note 2   Summary of significant accounting policies (in part)

Principles of consolidation (in part)

Prior to November 15, 2000, the Company consolidated the accounts of Victoria Resource Corporation ("Victoria"); since this date, the Company accounts for its investment in Victoria on an equity basis as the Company's shareholding in Victoria fell below 50%.

Investments

Investments in companies over which the Company can exercise significant influence are accounted for using the equity method. The excess cost of these investments over the related underlying equity in the net assets of the investee companies at the time of purchase relates to specific mineral exploration properties. Other long-term investments are carried at the lower of cost or estimated net realizable value.

Note 4   Assets Held For Sale (in part)

Effective February 26, 2001, pursuant to a "lock-up" agreement dated September 12, 2000, the Company tendered 20.7 million El Callao Mining Corp. ("El Callao") shares to a Crystallex International Corporation ("Crystallex") takeover bid. The Company has received 1.38 million Crystallex shares valued at approximately $1.2 million for its El Callao shares.

During the year ended 2000, the Company wrote-down its investment in and receivable from El Callao by $10.3 million and $1.2 million respectively, to their estimated net recoverable amounts. In connection with the sale, the Company will pay to its financing consultant and advisor, Endeavour Financial Corporation ("Endeavour Financial"), a transaction fee of 2% of the value paid by Crystallex. Endeavour Financial is related to a director of the Company.

Note 5   Investments

2000		Carrying Value	Market	Ownership
Equity:	Victoria	$1,083	$775	42%
	El Callao (Note 4)	–	–	
	Other	154	292	
Cost:	Arizona Star	1,457	961	5%
		$2,694	$2,028	

1999		Carrying Value	Market	Ownership
Equity:	Victoria	$ –	$ –	
	El Callao (Note 4)	11,759	1,150	45%
	Other	258	370	
Cost:	Arizona Star	18,257	6,700	32%
		$30,274	$8,220	

During the year ended December 31, 2000, the Company sold 10.5 million shares of Arizona Star Resource Corp. ("Arizona Star") for net proceeds of $5.7 million, reducing the Company's ownership interest from 32% to 5%. This resulted in a loss on disposal of $9.4 million. Effective November 20, 2000, the Company changed its method of accounting for its investment in Arizona Star from an equity basis to a cost basis. Due to the continued depressed gold market, the carrying value of the Company's remaining investment in Arizona Star was written down by $1.5 million at December 31, 2000.

On November 15, 2000, the Company began accounting for its investment in Victoria on an equity basis (Note 2). Due to this change in accounting method the following assets and liabilities were excluded from the consolidated accounts: current assets $11,000, exploration property $1,393,000, current liabilities $109,000 and non-controlling interest $231,000.

Included in other investments are Consolidated Puma Minerals Corp. and Consolidated Westview Resource Corp.

Additional Readings

2-156.   In writing the material in the text, we have incorporated all of the relevant *CICA Handbook* Recommendations, as well as material from other sources that we felt to be of importance. This includes some, but not all, of the EIC Abstracts that relate to long-term investments, as well as material from U.S. accounting pronouncements and ideas put forward in articles published in professional accounting journals.

2-157.   While this approach meets the needs of the great majority of accounting students, some of you may wish to pursue this subject in greater depth. To facilitate this, you will find a fairly comprehensive bibliography of materials on the subject of long-term investments in Chapter 27 of our *Guide to Canadian Financial Reporting*. Chapter 27 of the *Guide* also contains summaries of the EIC Abstracts that are directly related to this subject. The Abstracts that are summarized as an appendix to Chapter 27 are as follows:

- EIC Abstract No. 8 - Paragraph 27-121 (Recognition Of An Equity Accounted Investee's Losses In Excess Of The Investment)
- EIC Abstract No. 56 - Paragraph 27-122 (Exchangeable Debentures)
- EIC Abstract No. 102 - Paragraph 27-123 (Accounting For Shares Received From The Demutualization Of A Mutual Insurance Enterprise)

2-158.   The complete *Guide to Canadian Financial Reporting* is available on the CD-ROM which accompanies this text.

Problems For Self Study

(The solutions for these problems can be found following Chapter 16 of the text.)

Self Study Problem Two - 1

Carson Investments is a manufacturing company with a variety of investments in Canadian companies. These investments can be described as follows:

Best Parts Inc. Carson Investments owns 45 percent of the outstanding common shares of Best Parts Inc. Over 90 percent of this company's sales are made to Carson Investments. In addition to the holding of common shares, Carson owns 60 percent of the outstanding 12 percent, cumulative preferred shares of Best Parts Inc.

Research Tech Ltd. Carson owns 25 percent of the outstanding common shares of Research Tech Ltd., a company established with three other investors to do research on a new manufacturing process. The other investors each have 25 percent of the outstanding common shares. However, two of these investors do not participate in the management of the Company, leaving all operating decisions in the hands of Carson and one other investor.

Entell Ltd. Carson owns 46 percent of the outstanding voting shares of Entell Ltd. Included in the assets of Entell is an investment in 18 percent of the outstanding common shares of Chelsea Distributors Inc. In recent years, Chelsea has experienced adverse operating results and there is some question as to whether it will be able to continue as a going concern.

Chelsea Distributors Inc. Carson owns directly 37 percent of the outstanding common shares of Chelsea Distributors Inc. In addition, Chelsea owns 3 percent of the outstanding voting shares of Carson Investments Ltd.

Required: Describe and justify the recommended accounting treatment for each of the intercorporate investments, including those made by Carson Investments' investees.

Self Study Problem Two - 2

On July 1, 2002, the Miser Company purchased 25 percent of the outstanding voting shares of the Mercy Company for $4 million in cash. On the acquisition date, all of the net identifiable assets of the Mercy Company had fair values that were equal to their carrying values. The carrying value of Mercy Company's net assets was $16 million. Net Income and dividends declared and paid of the Mercy Company for the year of acquisition and the three subsequent years are as follows:

Year	Net Income (Net Loss)	Dividends Declared and Paid
2002	$ 600,000	$ 600,000
2003	(2,000,000)	400,000
2004	1,500,000	500,000
2005	3,000,000	1,000,000

Net Income accrued uniformly over the year 2002 and one-half of that year's dividends were declared between July 1 and December 31. Both Companies close their books on December 31. The 2005 Net Income figure of the Mercy Company includes an Extraordinary Loss of $800,000. There were no intercompany transactions, other than dividend payments, during any of the four years.

Required: Provide the Miser Company's dated journal entries to account for its investment in the Mercy Company for each of the four years assuming:

A. that its 25 percent shareholding does not result in significant influence over the Mercy Company;

B. that its 25 percent shareholding does result in significant influence over the Mercy Company.

Self Study Problem Two - 3

On January 1, 2002, the Buy Company purchased 25 percent of the outstanding voting shares of the Sell Company for cash of $1,500,000. On this date, the Sell Company had net assets of $6,000,000. This was reflected in the Sell Company's Shareholders' Equity which consisted of No Par Common Stock of $7,000,000 and a deficit or debit balance in Retained Earnings of $1,000,000. On the acquisition date, all of the identifiable assets and liabilities of the Sell Company had fair values that were equal to their carrying values.

Between January 1, 2002 and December 31, 2004, the Sell Company had a total Net Income of $3,000,000 and paid dividends which totalled $2,000,000. During this period, dividend payments were the only intercompany transactions.

For the year ending December 31, 2005, prior to the Buy Company taking into account any amounts for Investment Income from the Sell Company, the two Companies have the following Income Statements:

Buy and Sell Companies
Income Statements
For the Year Ending December 31, 2005

	Buy	Sell
Sales	$5,000,000	$2,000,000
Cost of Goods Sold	(3,000,000)	(1,800,000)
Other Expenses	(800,000)	(400,000)
Income (Loss) Before Investment Income and Extraordinary Items	$1,200,000	($ 200,000)
Extraordinary Gain (Net of $400,000 in Taxes)	-0-	600,000
Income Before Investment Income	$1,200,000	$ 400,000

On January 1, 2005, the Retained Earnings balance of the Buy Company was $15,000,000. This balance included the investment income calculated by the equity method for Buy's Investment In Sell during the period January 1, 2002 through December 31, 2004. During the year ending December 31, 2005, the Buy Company declares and pays dividends in the amount of $500,000 while the corresponding dividend figure for the Sell Company is $150,000.

Also during 2005, the Sell Company discovers an expense which was overlooked in 2004 for tax and accounting purposes of $50,000 (net of taxes of $20,000). This error is deducted in the Sell Company's Statement of Retained Earnings.

Required:

A. Assume that the Buy Company's 25 percent investment in the shares of the Sell Company gives it significant influence over the Sell Company. Prepare the Buy Company's Income Statement and Statement of Retained Earnings for the year ending December 31, 2005, assuming that the equity method has been used to account for its Investment In Sell.

B. Assume that the Buy Company's 25 percent investment in the shares of the Sell Company does not give it significant influence over the Sell Company. Prepare the Buy Company's

Income Statement and Statement of Retained Earnings for the year ending December 31, 2005, assuming that the cost method has been used to account for its Investment In Sell since the acquisition date. (This will require a recalculation of the Buy Company's January 1, 2005 Retained Earnings balance.)

C. Calculate the balance in the Investment In Sell account as at December 31, 2005, under the Part A assumptions.

Assignment Problems

(The solutions for these problems are only available in
the solutions manual that has been provided to your instructor.)

Assignment Problem Two - 1
On January 1, the Lestor Company purchased 20 percent of the outstanding voting shares of the Rapone Company. The purchase price, all of which was paid in cash, amounted to $5 million. On the acquisition date, the fair value of the Rapone Company's net assets was $25 million. During the three years following the acquisition date the Rapone Company had Net Income and paid dividends as follows:

Year	Net Income (Net Loss)	Dividends
1	$1,500,000	$1,000,000
2	(1,000,000)	1,000,000
3	4,000,000	1,000,000

All dividends were paid in the year in which they were declared. That is, there were no Dividends Payable at the end of any of the three years. There were no intercompany transactions, other than dividend payments, during any of the years under consideration. Both Companies close their books on December 31.

Required:

A. Assume that the Lestor Company's 20 percent shareholding does not result in significant influence over the Rapone Company. Provide the Lestor Company's dated journal entries to account for its investment in the Rapone Company for each of the three years.

B. Assume that the Lestor Company's 20 percent shareholding does result in significant influence over the Rapone Company. Provide the Lestor Company's dated journal entries to account for its investment in the Rapone Company for each of the three years.

C. Calculate the balance in the Investment In Rapone account as at December 31 of the third year for both Part A and Part B of this problem.

Assignment Problem Two - 2

On January 1, 1999, the Bronson Company purchased 18 percent of the outstanding shares of the Somerset Company. The purchase price, all of which was paid in cash, amounted to $1.8 million. On the acquisition date, the fair value of the Somerset Company's net assets was $10 million and all of the assets and liabilities had fair values that were equal to their carrying values. Both Companies have a fiscal year which ends on December 31.

During the four years following the Bronson Company's acquisition of the Somerset Company's shares, the Somerset Company had income and declared and paid dividends as follows:

Year	Net Income (Net Loss)	Dividends
1999	$ 950,000	$350,000
2000	(1,140,000)	140,000
2001	750,000	160,000
2002	840,000	320,000

Other Information:

1. The Somerset Company's 2001 Net Income includes an Extraordinary Loss of $163,000.

2. During 2002, the Company changed its accounting policy with respect to the calculation of Depreciation Expense. The change was accounted for retroactively, resulting in an addition to Retained Earnings of $246,000 to reflect the effects of this change on prior periods.

3. There were no intercompany transactions between Bronson and Somerset, other than dividend payments, during any of the years under consideration.

Required:

A. Assume that the Bronson Company's 18 percent shareholding does not result in significant influence over the Somerset Company. Provide the Bronson Company's dated journal entries to account for its Investment In Somerset for the years 1999 through 2002.

B. Assume that the Bronson Company's 18 percent shareholding does result in significant influence over the Somerset Company. Provide the Bronson Company's dated journal entries to account for its Investment In Somerset for the years 1999 through 2002.

Assignment Problem Two - 3

The Fostor Company purchased 30 percent of the outstanding voting shares of the Festee Company for $1,200,000 in cash on January 1, 2000. On that date, the Festee Company's Shareholders' Equity was made up of Common Stock ($50 par, $2 million issued and outstanding), other Contributed Capital of $500,000 and Retained Earnings of $1.5 million. There were no differences between the carrying values and the fair values of any of its identifiable assets or liabilities. The net income and dividends declared and paid by the Festee Company for the two years subsequent to its acquisition were as follows:

	2000	2001
Net Income (Loss)	($100,000)	$160,000
Dividends	40,000	50,000

The Income Statements for the year ending December 31, 2002, prior to the recognition of any Investment Income, for the Fostor and Festee Companies are as follows:

Foster and Festee Companies
Income Statements
Year Ending December 31, 2002

	Fostor	Festee
Sales	$2,000,000	$550,000
Other Revenues	100,000	-0-
Total Revenue	$2,100,000	$550,000
Cost Of Goods Sold	$1,000,000	$300,000
Other Expenses	200,000	50,000
Total Expenses	$1,200,000	$350,000
Income Before Extraordinary Items	$ 900,000	$200,000
Extraordinary Loss	-0-	30,000
Net Income	$ 900,000	$170,000

During 2002, the Fostor Company declared and paid dividends of $100,000 while Festee Company declared and paid dividends of $70,000. The Festee Company declares and pays its dividends on December 31 of each year.

Required:

A. Assume that the Fostor Company cannot exercise significant influence over the affairs of the Festee Company. Provide the journal entry of the Fostor Company related to its investment in the Festee Company for the year ending December 31, 2002.

B. Assume that the Fostor Company can exercise significant influence over the affairs of the Festee Company. Provide the following:

1. The dated journal entries of the Fostor Company related to its investment in Festee Company for the years ending December 31, 2000, 2001 and 2002.

2. The Income Statement of the Fostor Company, including recognition of any investment income or loss, for the year ending December 31, 2002.

3. The balance in the Investment In Festee account as it would appear on the December 31, 2002 Balance Sheet of the Fostor Company.

Assignment Problem Two - 4
On January 1, 1999, Tribble Company purchased 40 percent of the outstanding voting shares of the Marcus Company for $320,000 in cash. On that date, Marcus had Common Stock - No Par of $500,000, Retained Earnings of $300,000 and all of its identifiable assets and liabilities had fair values that were equal to their carrying values. Between January 1, 1999 and December 31, 2001, Marcus had Net Income and paid dividends as follows:

	1999	2000	2001
Net Income (Loss)	$300,000	($400,000)	$320,000
Dividends	100,000	50,000	70,000

There were no extraordinary items or prior period adjustments for Marcus in the three years 1999 through 2001. For the year ending December 31, 2002, the Income Statements of the Tribble and Marcus Companies, before recognition of any investment income, were as follows:

Tribble and Marcus Companies
Income Statements
For the Year Ending December 31, 2002

	Tribble	Marcus
Sales	$2,300,000	$850,000
Other Revenues	200,000	-0-
Total Revenues	$2,500,000	$850,000
Cost Of Goods Sold	$1,000,000	$500,000
Other Expenses	500,000	80,000
Total Expenses	$1,500,000	$580,000
Income Before Extraordinary Items	$1,000,000	$270,000
Extraordinary Loss	-0-	20,000
Net Income	$1,000,000	$250,000

Assuming the use of the cost method to account for its Investment in Marcus, Tribble had a Retained Earnings balance of $4,600,000 on January 1, 2002. Tribble declared $150,000 in dividends in that year. Marcus declared and paid dividends of $120,000 in 2002.

During 2002, Marcus initiated a change in accounting policy. The change was accounted for retroactively, resulting in a prior period addition to the Company's Retained Earnings balance in the amount of $700,000.

Required:

A. Assume that the Tribble Company carries its investment in Marcus by the cost method. Prepare the dated journal entries for the Tribble Company related to its investment in the Marcus Company for the years 1999 through 2002, the Income Statement for the Tribble Company for the year ending December 31, 2002, and the Statement of Retained Earnings for the Tribble Company for the year ending December 31, 2002.

B. Assume that, since its acquisition, the Tribble Company has carried its investment in Marcus by the equity method. Prepare the dated journal entries for the Tribble Company related to its investment in the Marcus Company for the years 1999 through 2002, the Income Statement for the Tribble Company for the year ending December 31, 2002, and the Statement Of Retained Earnings for the Tribble Company for the year ending December 31, 2002. (Note that the Retained Earnings balance of the Tribble Company given in the problem is based on the assumption that the cost method has been used since the acquisition and must be recalculated.)

Assignment Problem Two - 5

On January 1, 2002, Flor Company acquires 650,000 of the outstanding common shares of Flee Company at a cost of $20,800,000. On this date, the Shareholders' Equity of Flee Company was as follows:

Common Stock - No Par (1,000,000 Shares)	$10,000,000
Retained Earnings	22,000,000
Total Shareholders' Equity	$32,000,000

At this time, all of the identifiable assets and liabilities of Flee Company have fair values that are equal to their carrying values. Both Companies have a December 31 year end.

During the year ending December 31, 2002, Flee Company has Net Income of $1,800,000, and declares and pays dividends of $600,000. For 2002, Flee Company does not report any results of discontinued operations, extraordinary items or capital transactions. Other than Flee's Dividends Declared, there are no transactions between the two Companies during the year. Flor Company carries its Investment In Flee Company using the equity method.

The single entity Balance Sheets for the two companies as at December 31, 2002 and the Income Statements for the year ending December 31, 2002, are as follows:

Flor And Flee Companies
Balance Sheets As At December 31, 2002

	Flor Company	Flee Company
Cash	$ 7,400,000	$ 1,300,000
Accounts Receivable	12,600,000	7,700,000
Inventories	27,600,000	12,600,000
Investment In Flee (Note One)	21,580,000	-0-
Plant And Equipment (Net)	15,820,000	20,400,000
Total Assets	$85,000,000	$42,000,000
Current Liabilities	$17,800,000	$ 1,620,000
Long-Term Liabilities	23,400,000	7,180,000
Common Stock - No Par	12,500,000	10,000,000
Retained Earnings	31,300,000	23,200,000
Total Equities	$85,000,000	$42,000,000

Note One   The value of the Investment In Flee under equity method procedures would be calculated as follows:

Initial Cost Of Investment	$20,800,000
Equity In Flee Earnings [(65%)($1,800,000)]	1,170,000
Dividends Received [(65%)($600,000)]	(390,000)
Investment At Equity - December 31, 2002	$21,580,000

Flor and Flee Companies
Income Statements For The Year Ending December 31, 2002

	Flor Company	Flee Company
Sales	$14,600,000	$7,260,000
Investment Income [(65%)($1,800,000)]	1,170,000	-0-
Total Revenues	$15,770,000	$7,260,000
Cost Of Sales	$ 8,240,000	$2,780,000
Depreciation Expense	4,260,000	1,260,000
Other Expenses	1,100,000	1,420,000
Total Expenses	$13,600,000	$5,460,000
Net Income	$ 2,170,000	$1,800,000

Required:

A. Assume that Flor Company intends to account for its Investment In Flee Company using proportionate consolidation. Prepare the Balance Sheet as at December 31, 2002 and the Income Statement for the year ending December 31, 2002 for the Flor Company.

B. Assume that Flor Company intends to account for its Investment In Flee Company using full consolidation. Prepare the consolidated Balance Sheet as at December 31, 2002 and the consolidated Income Statement for the year ending December 31, 2002 for the Flor Company and its investee.

Case Two - 1

Small World Limited owns a chain of retail stores which sell children's books and toys. The President of Small World, Ted Kidd, hopes that his company will eventually achieve vertical integration with many of its suppliers. At the moment, Small World owns 55 percent of the outstanding common shares of Blocks N Things, a toy wholesaler.

Blocks N Things owns 22 percent of the outstanding common shares and 53 percent of the outstanding non cumulative, non participating preferred shares of Craftco Limited, a manufacturer of wooden toys. No other Craftco shareholder or group of related shareholders holds preferred or common shares to the same extent as Blocks N Things.

Craftco currently owns 13 percent of the outstanding common shares of Delta Inc., a major Canadian pulp and paper company. The market value of Delta's shares has decreased substantially since acquisition.

Small World Limited also owns 40 percent of the outstanding common shares of Delta Inc.

Required: Describe and justify the recommended accounting treatment for each of the above intercorporate investments.

(SMA adapted)

Chapter 3

Business Combinations

Note On Current Developments (May, 2002)

During the last two years, there have been dramatic changes in the *CICA Handbook* Recommendations on accounting for business combination transactions. In September, 2001, a new Section 1581, "Business Combinations", was added to replace the now superseded Section 1580. Also at that time, Section 3060, "Capital Assets", was significantly revised and divided into two Sections — Section 3061, "Property, Plant, and Equipment", and Section 3062, "Goodwill and Other Intangible Assets". The changes contained in these new Sections were the result of extensive deliberations, as well as collaboration and consultation with standard setters in other countries. In particular, this process has served to harmonize Canadian standards on business combinations with those in the United States. This was a fairly unusual harmonization process in that the changes in U.S. standards were much more significant than the changes in Canadian standards.

The changes introduced in these new *Handbook* Sections, to the extent that they relate to business combination transactions, will be covered in detail in this Chapter. However, in order to give you some perspective on the nature of these revisions, we will provide a general description of the major changes at this point. They are as follows:

- Section 1581 requires the use of the purchase method of accounting for all business combination transactions. Previously, the pooling-of-interests method could be used in limited circumstances. Now it is completely prohibited in Canada. A similar prohibition was introduced in the U.S. with much more dramatic effects. As pooling-of-interests accounting was widely used in the U.S., its elimination was much more significant with respect to U.S. financial reporting.

- Prior to these changes, goodwill was subject to amortization over a maximum period of 40 years. With the introduction of Section 3062, amortization of goodwill is no longer permitted. Goodwill is now subject to an annual test for impairment, with the test being applied at the reporting unit level. If, as a result of this annual test, goodwill is found to be impaired, it must be written down with an impairment loss included as as separate line item in the Income Statement.

- It appears that, in the past, accountants did not always identify separately all of the intangibles that were acquired in business combination transactions, particularly if those intangibles had not been recorded on the books of the acquiree. The new Section 1581 requires that all acquiree intangibles that meet certain criteria must be recognized on the books of the acquired company.

There are many other more detailed changes, including new presentation and disclosure Recommendations. However, the preceding items are the major changes that have been introduced.

Introduction

Business Combinations Defined

3-1.   The *CICA Handbook* defines a business combination transaction in the following manner:

> **Paragraph 1581.06(a)**   A **business combination** occurs when an enterprise acquires net assets that constitute a business, or acquires equity interests of one or more other enterprises and obtains control over that enterprise or enterprises.

3-2.   The economic concept that underlies the term business combination is that you have two or more independent and viable economic entities that are joined together for future operations as a single economic or business entity. The original economic entities can be corporations, unincorporated entities, or even a separable portion of a larger economic entity. The key factor is that each could be operated as a single, viable, business entity.

3-3.   The matter is complicated by the fact that there are many legal avenues to achieving the goal of combination. The least complex arrangements involve situations where one enterprise acquires the assets of the other, either through payment of cash or, if a corporation is involved, through the issuance of shares. In other situations, one enterprise acquires control of the other through an acquisition of shares, again either using cash as consideration or, alternatively, using newly issued shares as consideration. Other combinations involve transferring the assets of both predecessor entities into a new corporation or having a new corporation acquire the shares of both predecessor entities.

3-4.   Examples of some of these combinations include the following:

- A corporation acquires all of the net assets of a second corporation for cash.
- A corporation issues shares to the owners of an unincorporated business in return for all of their net assets.
- A corporation issues new shares as consideration for all of the outstanding shares of a second corporation.
- A new corporation is formed and issues shares to the owners of two separate unincorporated businesses in return for all of the net assets of the two enterprises.

3-5.   There are, of course, a number of other possibilities.

3-6.   In reviewing this definition of what constitutes a business combination, it is important to note what is not included in the definition. Excluded from this concept would be:

- The acquisition of a single asset or a group of assets that do not constitute a business entity.

- A transfer or exchange of assets between a parent and one of its subsidiaries. The parent and subsidiary are already a combined entity from an accounting point of view and any further transactions between them would not change the economic substance of the situation.

- A transfer or exchange of assets or shares between two subsidiaries of the same parent. Similar to the preceding example, the two subsidiaries are already part of a combined entity and any further transactions between them would not change the economic substance of the situation.

- The acquisition of a significantly influenced company.

3-7.   While the formation of a joint venture might, in fact, involve a business combination, the *Handbook* notes specifically that this type of transaction is not covered by Section 1581.

Legal Avenues To Combination

The Problem

3-8.   As noted in Paragraph 3-3, there are many different legal forms that could be used to combine the operations of two independent business entities. The choice among these forms involves a great many issues, including tax considerations, the desire to retain the name of one of the enterprises, the ability to access the capital markets in a particular manner, or simply various contractual arrangements that one or both of the enterprises have with suppliers, employees, or customers.

3-9.   This is an important issue for accountants as the legal form used can, in some circumstances, obscure the actual economic substance of a transaction. An outstanding example of this type of situation would be transactions that are referred to as reverse takeovers. An example of this would be to have Company X, with 100,000 shares outstanding, issue 400,000 shares to acquire all of the shares of Company Y. Legally Company X is the parent company and it has acquired Company Y as a subsidiary. However, from an economic point of view, the former shareholders of Company Y now own a controlling interest in Company X. This means that, in actual fact, the subsidiary Company X has acquired the parent Company Y.

3-10.   As an accountant's mandate is to focus on economic substance, it is important to have some understanding of the legal forms that can be used to implement a business combination transaction. This section is directed towards a presentation of the basic forms that can be used. Note, however, this is an extremely complex area, particularly when consideration is given to tax factors. A full discussion of legal forms for business combinations goes beyond the scope of this text.

Example

3-11.   Our discussion of legal form will use a simple example to illustrate the various possible alternatives. Assume that two corporations, the Alpha Company and the Beta Company have, for a variety of reasons, decided to come together in a business combination transaction and continue their operations as a single economic entity. The date of the combination transaction is December 31, 2002 and, on that date the Balance Sheets of the two companies are as follows:

Alpha And Beta Companies
Balance Sheets As At December 31, 2002

	Alpha Company	Beta Company
Current Assets	$153,000	$ 35,000
Non-Current Assets	82,000	85,000
Total Assets	$235,000	$120,000
Liabilities	$ 65,000	$ 42,000
Common Stock:		
(5,000 Shares Issued And Outstanding)	95,000	—
(10,000 Shares Issued And Outstanding)	—	53,000
Retained Earnings	75,000	25,000
Total Equities	$235,000	$120,000

3-12.   In order to simplify the use of this Balance Sheet information in the examples which follow, we will assume that all of the identifiable assets and liabilities of the two companies have fair values that are equal to their carrying values. In addition, we will assume that the shares of the two Companies are trading at their book values. This would be $34.00 per share for Alpha [($95,000 + $75,000) ÷ 5,000] and $7.80 per share for Beta [($53,000 + $25,000) ÷ 10,000]. This indicates total market values for Alpha Company and Beta Company of $170,000 and $78,000, respectively.

Basic Alternatives

3-13.   We will consider four basic alternatives in our discussion of the legal forms for implementing business combination transactions. They can be described as follows:

1.   Alpha Company could acquire the net assets of Beta Company through a direct purchase from that Company. The consideration paid to Beta could be cash, other assets, or Alpha Company debt or equity securities.
2.   A new organization, Sigma Company, could be formed. Sigma Company could then issue shares to both Alpha Company and Beta Company in return for their net assets. The proportion of shares issued would likely be based on their respective market values, 68.55% [$170,000 ÷ ($170,000 + $78,000)] for Alpha and the remaining 31.45% for Beta. As the newly formed Sigma Company would not have any assets to use as consideration in this transaction, Alpha and Beta would receive debt or equity securities of Sigma Company.
3.   Alpha could acquire the shares of Beta Company directly from the shareholders of that Company. The consideration paid to the Beta shareholders could be cash, other assets, or Alpha Company debt or equity securities.
4.   A new organization, Sigma Company, could be formed. Sigma Company could then issue its debt or equity securities directly to the shareholders of Alpha Company and Beta Company in return for the shares of the two Companies.

3-14.   There are other possibilities here. For example, if Alpha had a subsidiary, Alpha could gain control over Beta by having the subsidiary acquire the Beta Company shares from the Beta shareholders. In addition, most corporate legislation provides for what is referred to as a statutory amalgamation. This involves a process whereby two corporations become a single corporation that is, in effect, a continuation of the predecessor corporations. However, an understanding of the four basic approaches listed above is adequate for the purposes of this material. These basic alternatives will be discussed and illustrated in the Paragraphs which follow.

Acquisition Of Assets By Alpha Company

3-15.   Perhaps the most straightforward way in which the Alpha and Beta Companies could be combined would be to have one of the Companies simply acquire the net identifiable assets of the other. Using our basic example, assume that the Alpha Company gives Beta Company cash of $78,000 (Beta's net book value) to acquire the assets and liabilities of Beta Company. This approach is depicted in Figure 3-1.

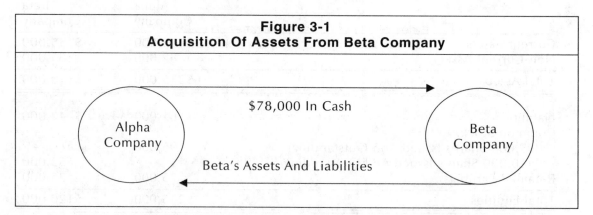

Figure 3-1
Acquisition Of Assets From Beta Company

3-16.   At this point, it is likely that the Beta Company would go through a windup operation by distributing the cash received from Alpha Company to its shareholders in return for the outstanding Beta Company shares. If this were to happen, the Beta Company shares would be canceled and the Beta Company would cease to exist as a separate legal entity. However, no matter what course of action is taken by Beta Company after the sale of its net assets, all of the assets and liabilities of the combined Companies will be recorded on Alpha Company's books and the accounting for the combined Companies will take place as a continuation of this

Company's records. This means that the business combination transaction has been carried out in such a fashion that both Companies' operations have been transferred to a single continuing legal entity. Alpha Company's Balance Sheet subsequent to the business combination transaction would be as follows:

Alpha Company
Balance Sheet As At December 31, 2002
Acquisition Of Beta Assets For Cash

Current Assets ($153,000 - $78,000 + $35,000)	$110,000
Non-Current Assets ($82,000 + $85,000)	167,000
Total Assets	$277,000
Liabilities ($65,000 + $42,000)	$107,000
Common Stock (Alpha's 5,000 Shares Issued And Outstanding)	95,000
Retained Earnings (Alpha's Balance)	75,000
Total Equities	$277,000

3-17. It would not be necessary for Alpha to acquire 100 percent of the net assets of Beta in order to have the transaction qualify as a business combination transaction. If Alpha were to acquire, for example, the manufacturing division of Beta, this transaction would be subject to the accounting rules for business combinations. The key point is that Alpha must acquire a group of assets sufficient to be viewed as a separate economic or business entity. As was noted previously, the acquisition of a single asset or group of assets that does not constitute a business entity would be outside the coverage of Section 1581 of the *CICA Handbook*.

3-18. You should also note that this business combination transaction could have been carried out using Alpha Company shares rather than cash. While the economic outcome would be the same unification of the two Companies, the resulting Alpha Company Balance Sheet would be somewhat different. More specifically, the Current Assets would not have been reduced by the $78,000 outflow of cash and there would be an additional $78,000 in Common Stock outstanding. If the new shares were issued at their December 31, 2002 market value of $34.00 per share, this transaction would have required 2,294 new Alpha shares to be issued ($78,000 ÷ $34.00). This alternative Balance Sheet would be as follows:

Alpha Company
Balance Sheet As At December 31, 2002
Acquisition Of Beta Assets For Shares

Current Assets ($153,000 + $35,000)	$188,000
Non-Current Assets ($82,000 + $85,000)	167,000
Total Assets	$355,000
Liabilities ($65,000 + $42,000)	$107,000
Common Stock (7,294 Shares Issued And Outstanding)	173,000
Retained Earnings	75,000
Total Equities	$355,000

Acquisition Of Assets By Sigma Company

3-19. The acquisition of assets approach could be implemented through the use of a new corporation. Continuing to use our basic example, assume that a new Company, the Sigma Company, is formed and the new Company decides to issue shares with a fair market value of $10 per share. Based on this value and the respective market values of the two companies, Sigma will issue 17,000 shares to Alpha Company ($170,000 ÷ $10) and 7,800 shares to Beta Company ($78,000 ÷ $10) in return for the assets and liabilities of the two Companies.

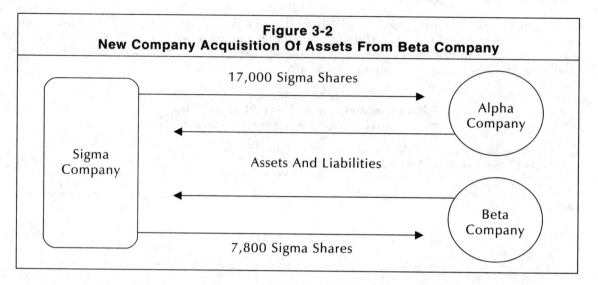

Figure 3-2
New Company Acquisition Of Assets From Beta Company

17,000 Sigma Shares

Alpha Company

Sigma Company

Assets And Liabilities

Beta Company

7,800 Sigma Shares

3-20.   You should note that any value could have been used for the Sigma Company shares as long as the number of shares issued to Alpha and Beta was proportionate to the market values of the two companies. For example, a value of $5 could have been used for the Sigma shares, provided 34,000 shares shares were issued to Alpha and 15,600 shares to Beta (34,000 shares at $5 equals the $170,000 fair market value for Alpha, while 15,600 shares at $5 equals the $78,000 fair market value for Beta). This approach to bringing the two companies together is depicted in Figure 3-2.

3-21.   Under this approach, Sigma Company acquires the net assets of both Alpha and Beta Companies. As Sigma is a new company, the only consideration that can be used would be newly issued Sigma shares. Sigma Company's Balance Sheet subsequent to the business combination transaction would be as follows:

Sigma Company
Balance Sheet As At December 31, 2002

Current Assets ($153,000 + $35,000)	$188,000
Non-Current Assets ($82,000 + $85,000)	167,000
Total Assets	$355,000
Liabilities ($65,000 + $42,000)	$107,000
Common Stock (24,800 Shares Issued And Outstanding)	248,000
Total Equities	$355,000

3-22.   As was the case when Alpha acquired the net assets of Beta on a direct basis, the result of the business combination is that both Companies' operations have been transferred to a single continuing legal entity. The only difference here is that the continuing legal entity is a new company rather than one of the combining Companies. The resulting Sigma Company Balance Sheet is fundamentally the same as would have resulted from Alpha Company acquiring the net assets of Beta using Alpha shares as consideration. The only difference is that, because Sigma is a new Company, all of the Shareholders' Equity must be allocated to Common Stock, rather than being split between Common Stock and Retained Earnings.

Acquisition Of Shares By Alpha Company

3-23.   Another legal route to the combination of Alpha and Beta would be to have one of the two Companies acquire a majority of the outstanding voting shares of the other Company. Continuing to use our basic example, the Alpha Company will give $78,000 in cash to the Beta shareholders in return for 100 percent of the outstanding shares of the Beta Company. This

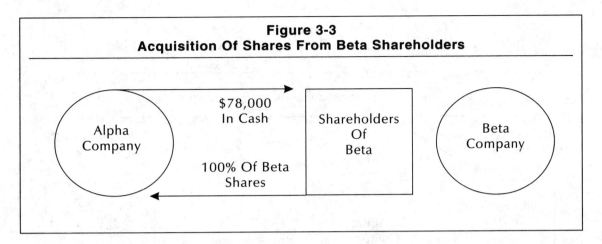

Figure 3-3
Acquisition Of Shares From Beta Shareholders

approach is depicted in Figure 3-3.

3-24.   While in this example we have assumed that Alpha acquired 100 percent of the shares of Beta, a business combination would have occurred as long as Alpha acquired sufficient shares to achieve control over Beta. In general, this would require acquisition of a majority of Beta's voting shares. The acquisition of shares could be carried out in a variety of ways. Alpha could simply acquire the shares in the open market. Alternatively, they could be acquired from a majority shareholder, through a public tender offer to all shareholders, or through some combination of these methods.

3-25.   Regardless of the method used, acquisition of a majority of the outstanding voting shares of Beta Company would mean that Alpha Company was in a position to exercise complete control over the affairs of the Beta Company. As a result of this fact, the two Companies could be viewed as a single economic entity and a business combination could be said to have occurred. This would be the case despite the fact that the two Companies have retained their separate legal identities. In this situation, in order to reflect the economic unification of the two Companies, consolidated financial statements would have to be prepared. While we have not yet covered the detailed procedures for preparing consolidated financial statements, the basic idea is that the investee's (subsidiary's) assets and liabilities will be added to those of the investor (parent). The resulting consolidated Balance Sheet would be as follows:

Alpha Company And Subsidiary
Consolidated Balance Sheet As At December 31, 2002

Current Assets ($153,000 - $78,000 + $35,000)	$110,000
Non-Current Assets ($82,000 + $85,000)	167,000
Total Assets	$277,000
Liabilities ($65,000 + $42,000)	$107,000
Common Stock (5,000 Shares Issued And Outstanding)	95,000
Retained Earnings	75,000
Total Equities	$277,000

3-26.   There are a number of advantages that can be associated with acquiring shares rather than assets to effect the business combination transaction. First, the acquisition of shares can be a method of going around a company's management if they are hostile to the idea of being acquired. In addition, less financing is needed as only a majority share ownership is required for control over 100 percent of the net assets. Also in the area of financing, if the purchase is timed properly, it may be possible to acquire shares when the stock market is depressed, thereby paying less than the fair values of the identifiable assets of the business.

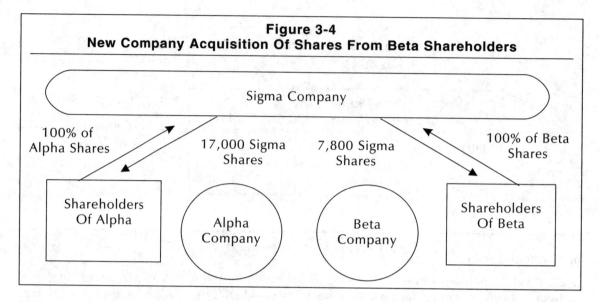

Figure 3-4
New Company Acquisition Of Shares From Beta Shareholders

3-27.   Another advantage would arise should the acquiring company ever wish to dispose of its investment. Shares, particularly if they are publicly traded, are a much more liquid asset than would be the individual assets of an operating company. Finally, this form of business combination provides for the continuation of the acquired company in unaltered legal form. This means it retains its identity for marketing purposes, the tax basis of all of its assets remain unchanged, and there is no interruption of the business relationships that have been built up by the acquired company. As a result of all of these advantages, the majority of business combinations involving large, publicly traded companies will be implemented using a legal form which involves an acquisition of shares.

Acquisition Of Shares By Sigma Company

3-28.   As was the case with business combinations based on an acquisition of assets, an alternative to having one entity acquire the shares of the other is to establish a new company to acquire the shares of both predecessor companies. As in our earlier example, we will call the new company Sigma Company. We will assume that it issues 17,000 of its shares to the shareholders of Alpha Company in return for all of their outstanding shares. Correspondingly, 7,800 shares will be issued to the shareholders of Beta Company in return for all of their outstanding shares. This business combination transaction is depicted in Figure 3-4.

3-29.   In this case, there will be three ongoing legal entities. These would be the parent Sigma Company, as well as Alpha Company and Beta Company, which have now become subsidiaries. Once again we are faced with a situation in which, despite the presence of more than one separate legal entity, the underlying economic fact is that we have a single unified economic entity. This requires the information for these three Companies to be presented in a single consolidated Balance Sheet as follows:

Sigma Company And Subsidiaries
Consolidated Balance Sheet As At December 31, 2002

Current Assets ($153,000 + $35,000)	$188,000
Non-Current Assets ($82,000 + $85,000)	167,000
Total Assets	**$355,000**
Liabilities ($65,000 + $42,000)	$107,000
Common Stock (24,800 Shares Issued And Outstanding)	248,000
Total Equities	**$355,000**

3-30.   You will note that the only differences between this consolidated Balance Sheet and the one that was prepared when Alpha acquired the shares of Beta are:

- Current Assets are $78,000 higher because Alpha used cash as consideration where Sigma issued Common Stock.

- Shareholders' Equity consists only of Common Stock with no Retained Earnings balance because Sigma is a new Company.

Exercise Three-1

Two corporations, Blocker Company and Blockee Company, have decided to combine and continue their operations as a single economic entity. The date of the business combination transaction is December 31, 2002 and, on that date the Balance Sheets of the two companies are as follows:

Blocker and Blockee Companies
Balance Sheets As At December 31, 2002

	Blocker Company	Blockee Company
Current Assets	$1,406,000	$ 987,000
Non-Current Assets	2,476,000	1,762,000
Total Assets	$3,882,000	$2,749,000
Liabilities	$ 822,000	$ 454,000
Common Stock:		
(180,000 Shares Issued And Outstanding)	1,800,000	N/A
(51,000 Shares Issued And Outstanding)	N/A	1,145,000
Retained Earnings	1,260,000	1,150,000
Total Equities	$3,882,000	$2,749,000

All of the identifiable assets and liabilities of the two companies have fair values that are equal to their carrying values. The shares of the two Companies are trading at their book values. This would be $17 per share for Blocker [($1,800,000 + $1,260,000) ÷ 180,000] and $45 per share for Blockee [($1,145,000 + $1,150,000) ÷ 51,000]. This indicates total market values for Alpha Company and Beta Company of $3,060,000 and $2,295,000, respectively.

Required: Prepare the Balance Sheet for the economic entity that results from the following business combinations:

A. Blocker acquires 100 percent of the net assets of Blockee in return for $795,000 in cash and debt securities with a maturity value of $1,500,000.

B. Blocker acquires 100 percent of the outstanding shares of Blockee by issuing to the Blockee shareholders 135,000 new Blocker shares.

C. A new Company, Blockbuster Inc. is formed. The new company decides to issue shares with a fair market value of $15 per share. The shareholders of Blocker receive 204,000 of the new shares in return for their Blocker shares, while the shareholders of Blockee receive 153,000 of the new shares in return for their Blockee shares.

End of Exercise Exercise Three-1

> Exercise Three-1 deals with legal forms for business combinations.

Legal Avenues And Tax Considerations
Acquisition Of Assets

3-31.   While it would not be appropriate in financial reporting material to provide a comprehensive discussion of the tax provisions that are associated with the various legal avenues to combination, these matters are of sufficient importance that a brief description of major tax aspects is required. Looking first at combinations involving the acquisition of assets, there is a need to distinguish between situations in which cash and/or other assets are the consideration and those situations in which new shares are issued. If a company acquires the assets of another business through the payment of cash or other assets, the acquired assets will have a completely new tax base, established by the amount of non-share consideration given. There would be no carry over of any of the tax values (i.e., adjusted cost base or undepreciated capital cost) that are associated with the business which gave up the assets.

3-32.   The same analysis could apply to situations in which shares are issued to acquire the assets of another business. However, while the transfer might take place at new tax values, there is also the possibility that different values might be used. As long as the transferor of the assets is a Canadian corporation, the parties to the combination can use the *Income Tax Act* Section 85 rollover provisions. In simplified terms, ITA Section 85 allows assets to be transferred at an elected value that could be anywhere between the fair market value of the assets and their tax values in the hands of the transferor.

3-33.   In general, investors will prefer to acquire assets rather than shares. In most situations, the value of the acquired assets will exceed their carrying values and, if the investor acquires assets, these higher values can be recorded and become the basis for future capital cost allowance (CCA) deductions. In contrast, if the investor acquires shares, the investee company will continue to use the lower carrying values as the basis for CCA, resulting in higher taxable income and taxes payable. In addition, if the investor acquires shares, any problems involving the investee's tax returns for earlier years are acquired along with the shares. When the investor company acquires assets, it simply has a group of assets with a new adjusted cost base and any investee tax problems are left with the selling entity.

3-34.   From the point of view of a person selling an existing business, they will generally have a preference for selling shares. If shares are sold, any resulting income will be taxed as a capital gain, only one-half of which will be taxable. In the alternative sale of assets, income will include capital gains, but may also include fully taxable recapture of CCA. Further, for the seller to have access to the funds resulting from the sale, it may be necessary to go through a complex windup procedure.

3-35.   If the corporation being sold is a qualified small business corporation, there is an additional advantage to selling shares rather than assets. Gains on the sale of shares of this type of corporation may be eligible for the special $500,000 lifetime capital gains deduction.

Acquisition Of Shares

3-36.   In looking at situations in which the combination is carried out through an acquisition of shares, the type of consideration used also has some influence. If shares are acquired through the payment of cash or other assets, the shares will have a new tax base equal to their fair market value as evidenced by the amount of consideration given. In addition, any excess of consideration over the adjusted cost base of the shares given up will create an immediate capital gain in the hands of the transferor. However, if new shares are issued to acquire the target shares, Section 85.1 of the *Income Tax Act* can be used. This Section provides that in a share for share exchange, any gain on the shares being transferred can effectively be deferred. Under the provisions of this Section, the old shares are deemed to have been transferred at their adjusted cost base and, in turn, the adjusted cost base of the old shares becomes the adjusted cost base of the new shares that have been received.

3-37.   While the type of consideration used to effect the business combination can make a significant difference to the transferor of the shares, it does not influence the tax status of the assets that have been indirectly acquired through share ownership. As this legal form of combination results in both parties continuing to operate as separate legal and taxable entities, the assets remain on the books of the separate companies and their tax bases are not affected in any way by the transaction. As noted previously, in most cases these tax bases will be lower than the fair market values of the assets and, as a result, lower than the tax bases that would normally arise if the assets were acquired directly.

Alternative Accounting Methods

Basic Example

3-38.   The appropriate accounting methods to be used for business combination transactions has been a controversial issue in financial reporting for over 40 years. To knowledgeable individuals, the solution to the controversy has been apparent for most of this period. However, this is an area where the selection of method can have an enormous influence on the reported earnings of the companies that are involved. As a consequence, resolving the business combination problem has proved difficult, particularly in the United States.

3-39.   A simple example will serve to illustrate the nature of the problem.

Example   On December 31, 2002, Sigma Company has 50,000 common shares outstanding. On this date, Sigma Company acquires all of the outstanding shares of Chi Company by issuing 10,000 Sigma Company shares to the shareholders of Chi Company in return for all of their outstanding shares. At this time the shares of Sigma Company are trading at $50 per share, resulting in a total investment cost of $500,000. On this date, prior to the business combination, the condensed Balance Sheets of the two companies are as follows:

	Sigma Company	Chi Company
Net Assets	$2,500,000	$300,000
Common Shares	$1,500,000	$100,000
Retained Earnings	1,000,000	200,000
Total Equities	$2,500,000	$300,000

On this date, the fair values of the Sigma Company net identifiable assets is $2,800,000. The corresponding figure for Chi is $350,000.

Investment Analysis   Sigma has paid $500,000 for net assets with a carrying value of $300,000. The payment can be analyzed as follows:

Investment Cost	$500,000
Book Value	(300,000)
Differential (Excess of Cost Over Book Value)	$200,000
Fair Value Change on Identifiable Assets	(50,000)
Goodwill	$150,000

Note   The use of this schedule will be explained in more detail when we examine a more complex example later in this Chapter.

The Purchase Method

3-40.   Accountants generally attempt to concentrate on the economic substance of transactions rather than their form. This fact is particularly important in accounting for business combinations. As previously described, these combination transactions can assume a great variety of legal forms. However, these forms should not be allowed to obscure the fact that, in the great majority of business combinations, one of the combining business entities will have a dominant or controlling interest in the combined business entity. This certainly appears to be the case in the preceding example. After the issuance of new shares, the original Sigma shareholders will hold 50,000 out of a total of 60,000 shares outstanding.

3-41.   Sigma, which is the dominant or controlling company in our example can be viewed as the acquiring company and, given this analysis, the business combination transaction can then be thought of as an acquisition of assets. The economic substance of this transaction is simply that Sigma (the acquirer) is purchasing the net assets of Chi (the acquiree). It would follow that Sigma should account for this business combination transaction in a manner that is analogous to the treatment which is accorded to other acquisitions of assets. The only unique feature involved in a business combination transaction is that it always involves a basket purchase of assets. While Section 3061, Property, Plant, and Equipment, suggests that, in general, the cost of a basket should be prorated on the basis of the relative fair values of the assets acquired, Section 1581 requires somewhat more complex allocation procedures when there is a business combination transaction.

3-42.   The purchase method of accounting for business combinations is based on the view that a business combination transaction is simply an acquisition of assets that should be accounted for in a manner similar to any other acquisition of assets. The assets of the acquiring company are not affected by the acquisition and the acquired assets would be recorded at their cost to the acquirer (fair value). Given this, the combined net assets of Sigma and its subsidiary would be as follows:

Net Identifiable Assets ($2,500,000 + $350,000)	$2,850,000
Goodwill	150,000
Net Assets	$3,000,000

The Pooling-Of-Interests Method

3-43.   While in our example, the Sigma Company is clearly the acquiring company, the analysis is not always so obvious. If Sigma had issued 50,000 shares to acquire Chi, both shareholder groups would have an equal number of Sigma shares and it would not be clear as to which of the companies was, in fact, the acquirer. In these circumstances, it would be possible to argue that the business combination transaction is not an acquisition of assets, but rather a joining together of two enterprises into a combined business enterprise. There are two accounting methods that could be identified with this interpretation:

- **Pooling-of-Interests** Under this approach, the assets of the combining companies are left at their carrying values, with no recognition of either fair value changes or goodwill. In the application of this method a retroactive approach is used, accounting for the combining enterprises as through they had always been combined. Applying this method to our example would result in the following net assets:

Net Assets ($2,500,000 + $300,000)	$2,800,000

- **New Entity Approach (a.k.a., Fair Value Pooling)**   Under this approach, the combined company is viewed as a new entity that requires a new basis of accounting for both companies. Carrying values would be replaced by fair values, not just for one of the enterprises, but rather for both of the combining enterprises. Applying this method to our example would result in the following net assets:

Net Assets ($2,800,000 + $350,000)	$3,150,000

3-44.   For many years, most analysts have been in agreement that an acquirer can be identified in the great majority of business combination transactions and, as a consequence, the purchase method would the appropriate method. This view was reflected in the superseded Section 1580 of the *CICA Handbook* which required the use of the purchase method except for "those rare transactions where no acquirer can be identified". When an acquirer could not be identified, the use of the pooling-of-interests method was required. Under no circumstances was the new entity approach acceptable. With this Recommendation in place, the use of the pooling-of-interests method in Canada was, in fact, rare.

3-45.   This was not the case in the United States. The accounting rules in that country were such that pooling-of-interests accounting could be used for almost any business combination transaction that involved an exchange of shares. As a result, pooling-of-interests accounting was widely used. Further, there was strong resistance to any change in the applicable rules that would serve to limit the use of this method.

3-46. The basis for this resistance was due to a very practical consideration. This was the fact that the purchase method requires the recording of the acquiree's fair value changes and goodwill on the books of the combined enterprise. In our example, there would be a 66-2/3 percent increase in the recorded values of Chi's assets, from $300,000 to $500,000 ($350,000 + $150,000). To the extent that this increase involved assets with limited lives, this extra $200,000 would have to be amortized and charged to income. In contrast, pooling-of-interests accounting retained the old carrying values for the acquired company, resulting in lower amortization charges and higher net income figures in the years subsequent to the combination transaction. Given the fact that the potential differences resulting from the choice between the two methods were often very significant, it is not surprising that the battle to eliminate this method was fiercely fought.

CICA Conclusion

3-47. In a harmonized effort, standard setters in both the U.S. and Canada agreed that the pooling-of-interests method should be eliminated as an acceptable method of accounting for business combination transactions. In Canada, this is reflected in the following Recommendation in Section 1581:

> **Paragraph 1581.09** *The purchase method of accounting should be used to account for all business combinations.* (July, 2001)

3-48. This Recommendation is based on the view that an acquirer can be identified in all business combination transactions. This is probably not an appropriate conclusion. Under the superseded Section 1580, accountants did find situations where an acquirer could not be identified. Such transactions were rare but they did occur. Further, the resulting financial statements were audited and approved by accountants that we must assume were acting in good faith. This suggests the preceding requirement for uniform application of the purchase method to all business combination transactions will not reflect the economic substance of a limited number of business combination transactions. Given this, it is surprising that the Accounting Standards Board did not retain its previous Recommendation in this area. The fact that it was changed may have resulted from an effort to harmonize U.S. and Canadian standards in this area. Certainly, the complete elimination of pooling-of-interests accounting is preferable to the misuse of that method that was occurring in U.S. practice.

Application of the Purchase Method

Acquisition Date

3-49. Business combinations are usually very complex transactions supported by detailed legal agreements involving the transfer of assets or equity interest and control to the acquiring business entity. While in some cases a single date may be involved, it is not uncommon for more than one date to be specified for the various components of the transaction. When more than one date is involved, Section 1581 provides the following suggestion:

> **Paragraph 1581.19** The date of acquisition is either:
>
> (a) the date on which the net assets or equity interests are received and the consideration is given; or
> (b) the date of a written agreement, or a later date designated therein, which provides that control of the acquired enterprise is effectively transferred to the acquirer on that date, subject only to those conditions required to protect the interests of the parties involved.

3-50. In those cases where the parties to the combination designate an effective date other than the date on which assets are received and consideration given, the cost of the purchase should be reduced by imputed interest at an appropriate current rate for the intervening period. This imputed interest would also reduce the income of the acquirer.

Identification Of An Acquirer
General Rules

3-51.   The fact that Section 1581 requires the use of the purchase method for all business combination transactions means that an acquirer must always be identified. This is a more complex process under this new Section than it was under the superseded Section 1580. As we have noted, under that Section, accountants were able to identify a small number of business combination transactions where no acquirer was present. While it is virtually certain that such situations still exist, the Section 1581 Recommendations make no exceptions to the rule that an acquirer must be identified. Given this, it is not surprising that Section 1581 provides additional guidance in this area.

3-52.   Prior to examining this more detailed guidance, we will look at some situations where the identification process presents no problems. Referring to the various cases that we considered in the discussion of legal forms, assume that Alpha Company gives cash to either Beta Company in order to acquire the net assets of that Company, or to the Beta Company shareholders in order to acquire a controlling interest in its voting shares. Where the cash is given to Beta Company to acquire net assets, all of the assets and liabilities of both companies are now on the books of Alpha Company. Since neither Beta Company nor its shareholders have received any of the shares of Alpha Company as part of the combination transaction, they have no continuing participation in the combined company. Clearly Alpha Company is the acquirer. If the cash had gone to the Beta Company shareholders, a similar situation would exist. While in this case Beta Company would continue as a legal entity after the combination transaction, its former shareholders would not participate in its ownership. As was the case when the assets were acquired for cash, we would conclude that Alpha Company is the acquirer.

3-53.   The situation becomes more complex when voting shares are used as consideration. This reflects the fact that voting shares allow the pre-combination equity interests in both of the combining companies to have a continuing equity interest in the combined company. This would be the case without regard to whether the shares were issued to acquire assets or, alternatively, to acquire shares.

3-54.   Conceptually, the solution to the problem is fairly simple. Assuming that the combining enterprises are both corporations, the acquirer is the company whose shareholders, as a group, wind up with more than 50 percent of the voting shares in the combined company. While the preceding guideline sounds fairly simple, its implementation can be somewhat confusing. Consider, for example, the case depicted in Figure 3-5.

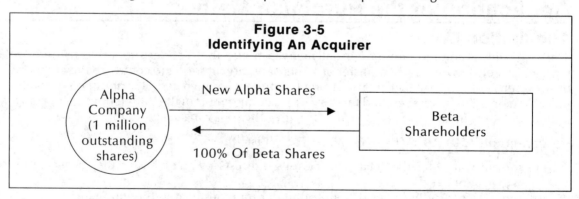

Figure 3-5
Identifying An Acquirer

Alpha Company (1 million outstanding shares)

New Alpha Shares →

← 100% Of Beta Shares

Beta Shareholders

3-55.   In this legal form, the combined entity will be the consolidated enterprise consisting of Alpha Company and its subsidiary Beta Company. The Alpha shareholder group will consist of both the original Alpha shareholders and the new Alpha shareholders who were formerly Beta shareholders. In the usual case, fewer than one million shares would have been issued to the Beta shareholders and, as a consequence, the original Alpha shareholders will be in a majority position. This means that, generally, Alpha Company will be identified as the acquirer.

3-56.   There are, however, other possibilities. If Alpha issued more than 1 million shares to the shareholders of Beta, the Beta shareholders would then own the majority of the voting shares of Alpha and this means that Beta Company would have to be considered the acquirer. This type of situation is referred to as a reverse takeover and will be given more attention later in this section.

Additional Handbook Guidance

3-57.   Continuing with our example, a further possibility would be that Alpha would issue exactly 1 million shares to the Beta shareholders. In this case, neither shareholder group has a majority of voting shares. This is an example of a type of situation where simply looking at the post-combination holdings of voting shares will not serve to clearly identify an acquirer. Because of the possibility of such complications, Section 1581 provides a list of factors that should be considered in identifying an acquirer. The list includes both voting shares and other factors as follows:

- The relative voting rights in the combined enterprise after the combination — all else being equal, the acquirer is the combining enterprise whose owners as a group retained or received the larger portion of the voting rights in the combined enterprise. In determining which group of owners retained or received the larger portion of the voting rights in the combined enterprise, the existence of any unusual or special voting arrangements, and options, warrants, or convertible securities is considered.

- The existence of a large non-controlling interest in the combined enterprise when no other owner or organized group of owners has a significant interest — all else being equal, the acquirer is the combining enterprise whose single owner or organized group of owners holds the largest non-controlling interest in the combined enterprise.

- The composition of the governing body of the combined enterprise — all else being equal, the acquirer is the combining enterprise whose owners or governing body has the ability to elect or appoint a voting majority of the governing body of the combined enterprise.

- The composition of the senior management of the combined enterprise — all else being equal, the acquirer is the combining enterprise whose senior management dominates that of the combined enterprise. Senior management generally consists of the executive committee, when one exists, or the chair of the board, the chief executive officer, the chief operating officer, the chief financial officer, and those divisional heads that report directly to the officers.

- The payment of a premium over market value — all else being equal, the acquirer is the combining enterprise that pays a premium over the market value of the equity instruments of the other combining enterprise or enterprises. This criteria would only be applicable in the case of publicly traded shares.

3-58.   When a new enterprise is formed and issues equity interests to the combining enterprises in order to effect the combination, one of the predecessor enterprises will have to be designated as the acquired. The preceding factors are likely to be useful in this process.

3-59.   A further complication arises in situations where the combination involves more than two enterprises. In such situations, it is unlikely that any of the preceding criteria will serve to identify an acquirer. When this happens, the *Handbook* suggests giving consideration to the enterprises that initiated the combination, and to whether the assets or earnings of one of the combining enterprises significantly exceed those of the others. The requirement to identify an acquirer remains in place in such situations, regardless of the difficulty in applying the concept.

Reverse Takeovers

3-60.   As we have noted, in some business combination transactions a "reverse takeover" may occur. Referring back to Figure 3-5, we noted that if Alpha Company were to issue more than 1 million new shares to the shareholders of Beta Company in return for their shares, these former Beta Company shareholders would now be the majority shareholders in the combined company. This means that, while Beta Company has been legally acquired and has become a subsidiary, it would be identified as the acquirer for accounting purposes. You should note that such reverse takeovers can only occur in those situations where the legal acquirer uses its own shares to obtain either the assets or shares of the legal acquiree.

3-61.   Continuing the example from Figure 3-5, if Alpha has issued 2,000,000 new shares to the former shareholders of Beta, they now hold two-thirds (2,000,000/3,000,000) of the outstanding shares of Alpha. From a legal point of view, Alpha has acquired control of Beta through ownership of 100 percent of Beta's outstanding voting shares. Stated alternatively, Alpha is the parent company and Beta is its subsidiary. If you were to discuss this situation with a lawyer, there would be no question from a legal viewpoint that Alpha Company is the acquiring company.

3-62.   However, this is in conflict with the economic picture. As a group, the Beta share-holders own a majority of shares in the combined economic entity and, under the requirements of the *CICA Handbook*, Beta is deemed to be the acquirer. In other words, the economic outcome is the "reverse" of the legal result.

3-63.   Reverse takeovers are surprisingly common in practice and are used to accomplish a variety of objectives. One of the more common, however, is to obtain a listing on a public stock exchange. Referring to the example just presented, assume that Alpha is an inactive public company that is listed on a Canadian stock exchange. It is being used purely as a holding company for a group of relatively liquid investments. In contrast, Beta is a very active private company that would like to be listed on a public stock exchange. Through the reverse takeover procedure that we have just described, the shareholders of Beta have retained control over Beta. However, the shares that they hold to exercise that control are those of Alpha and these shares can be traded on a public stock exchange. The transaction could be further extended by having Alpha divest itself of its investment holdings and change its name to Beta Company. If this happens, Beta has, in effect, acquired a listing on a public stock exchange through a procedure that may be less costly and time consuming than going through the usual listing procedures.

3-64.   As noted previously, reverse takeovers are surprisingly common in practice, usually involving situations like the one described in the preceding paragraph. For a number of years EIC Abstract No. 10, "Reverse Takeover Accounting", has provided guidance on accounting for reverse takeovers. None of this material was incorporated into the new Section 1581 so that this Abstract remains the primary reference to this subject. We will not give additional attention to reverse takeovers in this Chapter. However, in Chapter 4, as part of our discussion of preparing consolidated Balance Sheets at the acquisition date, we will provide a more detailed consideration of these transactions.

Exercise Three-2 deals with the identification of acquirers.

Exercise Three-2
For each of the following independent cases, indicate which of the combining companies should be designated as the acquirer.

A.   Delta has 100,000 shares of common stock outstanding. In order to acquire 100 percent of the voting shares of Epsilon, it issues 150,000 new shares of common stock.

B.   Delta has 100,000 shares of common stock outstanding. It pays cash of $1,500,000 in order to acquire 48 percent of the voting shares of Epsilon. No other Epsilon shareholder owns more than 5 percent of the voting shares.

C.   Delta, Epsilon, Zeta, and Gamma transfer all of their net assets to a new corporation, Alphamega. In return, Gamma receives 40 percent of the shares in Alphamega, while the other three companies each receive 20 percent of the Alphamega shares.

D.   Delta has 100,000 shares of common stock outstanding. Delta issues 105,000 shares to the sole shareholder of Epsilon in return for all of his outstanding shares. As it is the intention of this shareholder to retire from business activities, the management of Delta will be in charge of the operations of the combined company.

End Of Exercise Three-2

Recognition of Assets and Income

3-65.   With respect to the recognition of assets and liabilities acquired in a business combination transaction, Section 1581 contains the following Recommendation:

> **Paragraph 1581.11**   *The acquirer in a business combination should recognize the assets acquired and liabilities assumed from the date of acquisition, including any assets and liabilities that may not have been recognized on the balance sheet of the acquired enterprise.* (July, 2001)

3-66.   The reference to "assets and liabilities that may not have been recognized on the balance sheet of the acquired enterprise" reflects the fact that, prior to the introduction of Section 1581, in many business combination transactions, the acquiree's unrecognized intangible assets were simply included in the goodwill figure.   As we shall see later in this Chapter, Section 1581 requires separate recognition of all intangible assets that meet specific recognition criteria.   This new requirement, in conjunction with the preceding Recommendation, should serve to limit this practice.

3-67.   The second recognition Recommendation in Section 1581 relates to the income of the acquirer:

> **Paragraph 1581.12**   *The financial statements of the acquirer for the period in which a business combination occurs should include the earnings and cash flows of the acquired enterprise from the date of acquisition only.* (July, 2001)

3-68.   As we have indicated previously, the purchase method treats the business combination transaction as an ordinary acquisition of assets.   It is consistent with this view that earnings from the acquired assets would only be included in the income of the combined company from the date on which they are acquired.

Determining the Cost of the Purchase
General Rules

3-69.   The basic measurement Recommendation in Section 1581 is as follows:

> **Paragraph 1581.21**   *Assets acquired and liabilities assumed in a business combination should be measured initially based on the cost of the purchase to the acquirer, determined as of the date of acquisition.* (July, 2001)

3-70.   The key factor in implementing this rule is, of course, determining the cost of the purchase.   Section 1581's general Recommendation on this issue is as follows:

> **Paragraph 1581.22**   *The cost of the purchase to the acquirer should be determined by the fair value of the consideration given or the acquirer's share of the fair value of the net assets or equity interests acquired, whichever is more reliably measurable, except when the transaction does not represent the culmination of the earnings process (see "Non-Monetary Transactions", paragraph 3830.08).* (July, 2001)

3-71.   The problems involved in implementing this Recommendation would vary with the nature of the consideration given.   The following guidelines would cover most situations:

- If the acquirer pays cash there is no significant problem.

- If the acquirer gives other assets, the fair value of the assets provided may be used as the purchase price.   However, if the assets being given are productive assets not held for sale in the ordinary course of business, and they are being exchanged for similar productive assets, Paragraph 1581.22 would require that the exchange take place at the carrying values of these assets on the books of the acquirer.   This is noted through the reference to Paragraph 3830.08 of the *CICA Handbook* Section, "Non-Monetary Transactions" that is contained in Paragraph 1581.22.   This means that, if the acquiring company gave equipment with a carrying value on its books of $500,000 in return for similar equipment of the acquiree, the newly acquired equipment would be recorded at $500,000, without regard to the fair values of either the equipment given up or the equipment acquired.

- If shares with a quoted market price are issued by the acquirer, this market price will normally be used as the primary measure of the purchase price. Section 1581 notes that, if preferred shares are used as consideration, their value might be assessed by reference to debt securities with similar characteristics. It is likely that this guidance only applies when the preferred shares do not have a quoted market price.

- If the acquirer issues shares that do not have a market price or if it is agreed that the market price of the shares issued is not indicative of their fair value, the fair value of the net assets acquired would serve as the purchase price in the application of this method of accounting for business combinations. Section 1581 notes that the values of all of the net assets acquired, including any goodwill, should be assessed in this process.

- In general, no gain or loss would be recognized by the acquirer as part of the business combination transaction. Exceptions to this would be situations where non-cash assets are used as consideration and the fair value differs from their carrying value (see preceding discussion of non-monetary transactions), or in situations where the fair value of the net assets acquired exceeds the cost of the purchase (see our later discussion of negative goodwill).

3-72.   The preceding represents an application of the familiar idea that assets are recorded at the fair value of the consideration given or, if there are significant problems in determining the fair value of that consideration, the fair value of the assets acquired.

Direct Costs Of Combination - General Rules

3-73.   Another familiar idea is that all of the direct costs related to the acquisition of a particular asset should be included as a part of the cost of the acquisition. This general rule would, of course, apply to the assets acquired in a business combination that is accounted for by the purchase method of accounting. This is reflected in the *Handbook* as follows:

Paragraph 1581.27   *The cost of the purchase includes the direct costs of the business combination. Costs of registering and issuing shares issued to effect a business combination should be treated as a capital transaction (see "Capital Transactions", Section 3610). Indirect and general expenses related to business combinations should be recognized as expenses when incurred.*

3-74.   The costs to be capitalized must be incremental and would include finder's fees and other amounts paid to lawyers, accountants, appraisers and other consultants. However, allocations of internal costs, including the costs of maintaining an acquisitions department, are not incremental costs and should be recognized as an expense as incurred. This issue is dealt with in detail in EIC Abstract No. 42, "Costs Incurred on Business Combinations".

Contingent Consideration

3-75.   It is possible for a business combination agreement to provide for the payment of additional consideration if some specified event or transaction occurs in future accounting periods. The issue that is created by such contingent consideration is whether the consideration should be recorded at the time of the combination transaction or only when the contingency is resolved and the additional amounts are issued or become payable. The *CICA Handbook* contains the following Recommendation:

Paragraph 1581.29   *When the amount of any contingent consideration can be reasonably estimated at the date of acquisition and the outcome of the contingency can be determined beyond reasonable doubt, the contingent consideration should be recognized at that date as part of the cost of the purchase. When the amount of contingent consideration cannot be reasonably estimated or the outcome of the contingency cannot be determined without reasonable doubt, details of the contingency should be disclosed. Neither a liability nor outstanding equity instruments are recognized until the contingency is resolved and consideration is issued or becomes issuable.* (July, 2001)

3-76.   Additional Recommendations provide more detailed guidance for two particular forms of contingency payments. Specific statements are made with respect to contingency payments related to earnings performance of the acquiree and payments related to the future market prices of shares issued to effect a combination transaction.

Payments Contingent On Earnings

3-77.   It is not uncommon for the owners of an acquiree to make the argument that the enterprise is really worth more than is being offered by the acquirer and that the earnings of some future period will support this contention. A way of dealing with this possibility is for the acquirer to agree to pay additional consideration should the acquiree's belief about the future earnings prove to be correct. This results in a situation where there is contingent consideration based on the acquiree's future earnings.

3-78.   When additional payment is contingent on the future earnings of the acquiree, the *Handbook* states the following:

> **Paragraph 1581.31** *When additional consideration is contingent on maintaining or achieving specified earnings levels in future periods, the acquirer should recognize the current fair value of the consideration issued or issuable as an additional cost of the purchase when the contingency is resolved and the additional consideration is issued or becomes issuable.* (Paragraph 1581.52 addresses the accounting for contingent consideration in a business combination when the fair value of the net assets acquired exceeds the cost of the acquired enterprise.) (July, 2001)

3-79.   The accounting treatment of contingent consideration based on earnings can be illustrated by the following simple example:

Example   On January 1, 2002, the Mor Company issues 3 million of its no par value voting shares in return for all of the outstanding voting shares of the Mee Company. On this date the Mor Company shares have a fair value of $25 per share or $75 million in total. In addition to the current payment, the Mor Company agrees that, if the 2002 earnings per share of the Mee Company is in excess of $3.50, the Mor Company will pay an additional $10 million in cash to the former shareholders of the Mee Company.   The appropriate entry on January 1, 2002 would be as follows:

Investment In Mee	$75,000,000	
No Par Common Stock		$75,000,000

If at the end of 2002, the Mee Company's earnings per share has exceeded the contingency level of $3.50, the following entry to record the contingency payment would be required:

Investment In Mee	$10,000,000	
Cash		$10,000,000

Alternatively, if the earnings per share do not exceed $3.50 per share, no additional payment would be made and no journal entry would be required.

3-80.   Given that all of the identifiable assets have been assigned fair value (see our later discussion titled "Allocation of the Purchase Price"), this additional $10 million would have to be allocated to goodwill (or an adjustment of the allocation of negative goodwill) in the preparation of the consolidated financial statements.

Exercise Three-3

On June 30, 2002, Lor Inc. issues 1,250,000 of its no par value voting shares in return for all of the outstanding voting shares of Lee Ltd. At this time the Lor shares are trading at $11 per share. Negotiators for Lee have argued that this price is too low because it does not reflect the large increase in Earnings Per Share that is expected for their year ending December 31, 2002.

In order to resolve this dispute, Lor agrees to issue an additional 250,000 shares on March 1, 2003, provided Lee's Earnings Per Share for the year ending December 31, 2002 reach or exceed $1.90 per share.

Exercise Three-3 deals with consideration that is contingent on acquiree earnings.

This is a continuation of Exercise Three-3.

Lee's Earnings Per Share for the year are reported as $2.05 and, on March 1, 2003, Lor issues the required shares. At this time the Lor shares are trading at $11.50 per share.

Required: Provide the journal entry that would be required to record the issuance of Lor shares on June 30, 2002, and the additional issuance of Lor shares on March 1, 2003.

End Of Exercise Three-3

Payments Contingent On Share Prices

3-81. When shares are used as consideration in a business combination transaction, the acquirer is likely to be making the argument that the shares being offered are worth more than their current market value and that this view will be supported by some future market price for the stock. In this case, the acquirer may agree to pay additional amounts or issue additional shares if the market value of the shares does not reach a certain price at some future point in time.

3-82. In situations where additional payments are contingent on future price performance of the acquirer's shares, the *Handbook* Recommends the following:

> **Paragraph 1581.32** *Any consideration that will be payable if the market price of the shares issued to effect the combination does not reach at least a specified value by a specified future date should not change the amount recognized as the cost of the purchase. When additional consideration becomes payable, the current fair value of such consideration should be offset by a simultaneous reduction in the value placed on the shares issued at the date of acquisition to their lower current fair value.* (July, 2001)

3-83. The accounting treatment of contingencies based on share prices can be illustrated by extending the previous example used to illustrate the accounting treatment of contingencies based on earnings. The revised example is as follows:

> **Example** On January 1, 2002, the Mor Company issues 3 million of its no par value voting shares in return for all of the outstanding voting shares of the Mee Company. On this date the Mor Company shares have a fair value of $25 per share or $75 million in total. In this case we will assume that the Mor Company has agreed to pay an additional $15 million if, on December 31, 2002, the market price of the Mor Company shares is not equal to at least $30 per share. In this situation, the Mor Company has, in effect, guaranteed the Mee Company shareholders a value of $30 per share for the Mor Company shares. If the market price does not move from its current $25 per share up to at least $30 per share, the Mor Company will provide the difference by paying $15 million (3 million shares at $5 per share). In view of this fact, the purchase price should include this contingency payment and the required journal entry would be as follows:

Investment In Mee	$90,000,000	
No Par Common Stock		$90,000,000

If the Mor Company shares reach $30 by the end of 2002, no further entries will be required and the No Par Common Stock will remain at $90,000,000. On the other hand, if they fail to achieve the specified level and the contingency payment must be made, the No Par Common Stock will be reduced by the following entry:

No Par Common Stock	$15,000,000	
Cash		$15,000,000

Note that the payment of contingent consideration does not affect the cost of the purchase of the Mee Company.

Exercise Three-4

Exercise Three-4 deals with consideration that is contingent on the acquirer's share price.

On June 30, 2002, Lor Inc. issues 1,250,000 of its no par value voting shares in return for all of the outstanding voting shares of Lee Ltd. At this time the Lor shares are trading at $11 per share. Negotiators for Lor have argued that this number of shares is appropriate because current market conditions have kept the share price of Lor below their real value.

In order to resolve this dispute, Lor has agreed to issue an additional 250,000 shares on March 1, 2003 if the market value of its shares is not at least $12.50 per share on December 31, 2002.

On December 31, 2002, the Lor shares are trading at $11.75 per share and, as a consequence, Lor must issue an additional 250,000 shares on March 1, 2003. At this time the Lor shares are trading at $11.50 per share.

Required: Provide the journal entry that would be required to record the issuance of Lor shares on June 30, 2002, and the additional issuance of Lor shares on March 1, 2003.

End Of Exercise Three-4

Stock Options

3-84.   By way of background, we would note that Section 3870, "Stock-Based Compensation And Other Stock-Based Payments", encourages the use of fair value accounting for stock options, but permits the use of the intrinsic value approach. However, when options are involved in a business combination transaction, the rules are more restrictive. While not in the form of Recommendations, the Appendix to Section 1581 provides the following guidance with respect to how stock options should be dealt with in the context of business combination transactions:

- Stock options may be granted by the acquiring enterprise in a business combination transaction. In determining the cost of the purchase, any stock options granted as part of the purchase consideration should be measured at their fair value, consistent with paragraph 1581.22, even if this is not the enterprise's existing policy for accounting for stock options. New grants of unvested options made to employees at the time of the business combination are not part of the purchase consideration.

- When the acquired enterprise has outstanding stock options, granted to employees or to non-employees, the acquiring enterprise may exchange these for options on its own stock (or that of an affiliated enterprise). The options granted by the acquiring enterprise are valued at fair value, consistent with paragraph 1581.22, even if this is not the enterprise's existing policy for accounting for stock options. The fair value of the options forms part of the purchase consideration.

- When an acquiring enterprise that has adopted a method of accounting for stock-based compensation other than the fair value based method, such as the intrinsic value based method, exchanges outstanding stock options granted by an acquired enterprise, to the extent that service is required subsequent to the consummation date of the acquisition in order to vest in the replacement awards, a portion of the unearned compensation for service to be rendered in the future is calculated using the enterprise's normal accounting policy, and is allocated to unearned compensation and recognized as compensation cost over the remaining future vesting (service) period. The allocated unearned compensation cost is deducted from the fair value of the awards for purposes of the allocation of the purchase price to the other assets acquired.

3-85.   It can be noted that, in general, when stock options are issued as part of a business combination transaction, the use of the fair value approach is required, even in those situations where the intrinsic value approach is being used for other options that have been issued.

Allocation Of The Purchase Price to Fair Values
General Rules

3-86.   It was previously noted that the purchase method of accounting for business combinations is simply a way of treating these transactions in a manner that is analogous to other asset acquisition transactions. The only real complicating factor is the fact that a single purchase price must be allocated over a large group of identifiable assets, identifiable liabilities, and goodwill. The general guidelines for this allocation process are found in the *CICA Handbook* as follows:

> **Paragraph 1581.40**   *The cost of purchase should be allocated as follows:*
>
> (a) *all assets acquired and liabilities assumed in a business combination, whether or not recognized in the financial statements of the acquired enterprise, except goodwill and future income taxes recognized by an acquired enterprise before its acquisition, should be assigned a portion of the total cost of the purchase based on their fair values at the date of acquisition; and*
>
> (b) *the excess of the cost of the purchase over the net of the amounts assigned to assets acquired and liabilities assumed should be recognized as an asset referred to as goodwill.* (July, 2001)

3-87.   An understanding of the procedures that are implicit in this Recommendation is essential, not just to be able to deal with business combination transactions, but also to able to properly prepare consolidated financial statements. For example, as clarification of this Recommendation, Paragraph 1541.45 specifically states that neither goodwill nor future income tax assets and liabilities previously recognized by an acquired enterprise are recognized in the consolidated financial statements of the acquirer. The acquisition of a subsidiary is a business combination transaction and, since all subsidiaries must be included in the consolidated financial statements, the allocation process described in Paragraph 1581.40 is required whenever consolidated financial statements are prepared.

3-88.   This allocation process can be described as a two-step procedure as follows:

Step A   Determine the fair values of the acquiree's identifiable assets and liabilities. This includes both tangible and intangible assets acquired, without regard to whether they were recorded on the books of the acquiree. In practical situations, this is a complex process which will involve considerable effort on the part of both accountants and appraisers. This process is discussed in more detail in the Section titled "Determination Of Fair Values".

Step B   It is unlikely that the purchase price will be equal to the acquirer's share of the sum of the fair values of the identifiable assets and liabilities of the acquiree. As a consequence, it is necessary to compare the purchase price with the investor's share of the fair values of the identifiable net assets that have been acquired. This comparison can have two possible outcomes:

1.   If the purchase price is the larger figure, the excess will be allocated to goodwill. This possibility will be discussed in the Section titled "Goodwill".

2.   If the purchase price is less than the acquirer's share of the fair values, the deficiency is referred to as negative goodwill. The disposition of this balance will be discussed in the Section titled "Negative Goodwill".

Determination Of Fair Values - Tangible Assets and Liabilities

3-89.   Section 1581 defines fair value as follows:

> **Paragraph 1581.06(b)**   **Fair value** is the amount of the consideration that would be agreed upon in an arm's length transaction between knowledgeable, willing parties who are under no compulsion to act.

3-90.   Section 1581 makes several general points with respect to the process of determining fair value:

- In determining these amounts, independent appraisals and actuarial or other valuations may be used as an aid.
- When an asset or liability is valued based on estimated future cash flows, discounting should be used.
- In those situations where assets, including cash, are subject to particular restrictions, consideration should be given to these restrictions in the valuation process.
- Any goodwill previously recognized by the acquiree should not be recognized in the financial statements of the combined company.

3-91.   Paragraph 1581.43 provides general guidance for assigning amounts to particular tangible assets acquired and liabilities assumed. It contains the following:

(a) Marketable securities at current net realizable values.

(b) Receivables at present values of amounts to be received determined at appropriate current interest rates, less allowances for uncollectibility and collection costs, if necessary.

(c) Inventories:

(i) Finished goods and merchandise at estimated selling prices less the sum of:
— costs of disposal; and
— a reasonable profit allowance for the selling effort of the acquirer;

(ii) Work in process at estimated selling prices of finished goods less the sum of:
— costs to complete;
— costs of disposal; and
— a reasonable profit allowance for the completing and selling effort of the acquirer based on profit for similar finished goods; and

(iii) Raw materials at current replacement costs.

(d) Plant and equipment:

(i) to be used, at the current replacement cost for similar capacity unless the expected future use of the assets indicates a lower value to the acquirer; and

(ii) to be sold, at fair value less cost to sell.

Replacement cost may be determined directly when a used asset market exists. Otherwise, an estimate of depreciated replacement cost is used. The acquirer does not carry forward the accumulated depreciation of the acquired enterprise.

(e) Intangible assets that meet the criteria in paragraph 1581.48, at estimated or appraised values.

(f) Other assets, including land, natural resources, and non-marketable securities, at estimated or appraised values.

(g) Accounts and notes payable, long-term debt, and other claims payable, at present values of amounts to be paid determined at appropriate current interest rates.

(h) Accrued benefit assets or accrued benefit liabilities for defined benefit plans for employee future benefits:

(i) When the plan is to continue in operation, the accrued benefit obligation is calculated using best estimate assumptions and plan assets are valued at fair value, in accordance with "Employee Future Benefits", Section 3461. Any previously existing unamortized net actuarial gain (loss), unamortized past service cost, unamortized transitional obligation or unamortized transitional asset is eliminated with the result that the accrued benefit asset or accrued benefit liability is the difference between the accrued benefit obligation and the fair value of plan assets. The carrying amount of an accrued benefit asset in the acquired enterprise's financial statements may need to be reduced when the acquirer expects limitations on its ability to access a plan surplus as a result of existing regulations of the relevant jurisdiction and the plan.

(ii) When the plan is to be wound up, the accrued benefit asset or accrued benefit liability is valued based on the amount expected to be received or paid on settlement.

(iii) When the plan of the acquired enterprise is amended as a condition of the business combination (for example, when the change is required by the seller as part of the transaction), the effects of any improvements attributed to services rendered by the employees of the acquired enterprise's plan prior to the date of the business combination are accounted for in valuing the accrued benefit obligation of the acquired enterprise. Otherwise, when improvements to the plan of the acquired enterprise are not a condition of the business combination, credit granted for past service is recognized as a plan amendment by the acquirer. When the acquirer has developed a formal plan to terminate or curtail the plan, the effects of those actions are considered in measuring the accrued benefit obligation. Otherwise, no future changes to the plan are anticipated.

(i) Liabilities and accruals, such as accruals for warranties, vacation pay, and deferred compensation — at present values of amounts to be paid determined at appropriate current interest rates.

(j) Other liabilities and commitments, such as unfavourable leases, contracts, and commitments and plant closing expense incident to the acquisition — at present values of amounts to be paid determined at appropriate current interest rates.

Determination of Fair Values - Temporary Differences

3-92. If a business combination involves an acquisition of assets, the newly acquired assets will generally have a tax basis equal to their carrying value and no temporary differences will be present. This means that the existing future income asset or liability values (FITAL values) of the acquiree will not be carried forward and no additional FITAL values will be recorded as a result of the business combination transaction.

3-93. However, in many business combination transactions, the fair values of acquired assets will differ from their tax values on the books of the acquired company. This situation can result from two possible causes:

- In situations where assets have been acquired to effect the business combination, the transfer of assets may involve a rollover provision (e.g., ITA 85) under which assets are transferred at elected values without regard to their fair values at the time of the business combination.

- In situations where shares have been acquired to effect the business combination, the acquired subsidiary will continue as a separate legal entity and will retain old tax values for its assets, without regard to their fair values at the time of the business combination.

3-94. Prior to the 1997 introduction of Section 3465, "Income Taxes", to the *CICA Handbook*, Section 1580 indicated that these alternative tax values should be taken into consideration in the determination of fair values. Consider, for example, an item of equipment for which fair value is determined on the basis of its replacement cost. If its tax value is less than its normal replacement cost, its fair value would have to be reduced to reflect the fact that the tax deductions associated with the acquired asset are less than those associated with a purchase of a new asset at full replacement cost.

3-95. The introduction of Section 3465 has changed this situation as is reflected in the following guidance from Section 1581:

Paragraph 1581.46 The values placed by an acquirer on the assets and liabilities of an acquired enterprise are determined based on their fair values, without reference to their values for tax purposes, or tax bases.

3-96. A simple example will serve to clarify this point.

Example Meta Inc. acquires all of the outstanding shares of Acta Ltd. At that time, Acta Ltd. has depreciable assets with an original cost of $540,000, a replacement cost of $500,000, a carrying value on the books of Acta Ltd. of $400,000 and an undepreciated capital cost (UCC) of $200,000. Both companies are subject to a tax rate of 40 percent.

Solution On the books of Acta Ltd., there would be a Future Income Tax Liability of $80,000 [(40%)($400,000 - $200,000)]. This amount would not be carried forward to the consolidated financial statements.

The depreciable assets would be recorded in the consolidated financial statements at their full replacement cost of $500,000, without regard to the fact that their deductibility is limited to the UCC amount of $200,000. The temporary difference would be reflected in a Future Income Tax Liability of $120,000 [(40%)($500,000 - $200,000)], to be included in the consolidated financial statements.

3-97.   Further attention will be given to this issue in Chapter 12, which provides detailed coverage of the tax aspects of business combination transactions and the preparation of consolidated financial statements.

Exercise Three-5

Gor Inc. completes a business combination with Gee Ltd. at the end of the current year. At the time of this business combination, Gee Ltd. has property, plant, and equipment with an original cost of $2,432,000, a replacement cost of $1,863,000, and a net book value of $1,578,000. The undepreciated capital cost (UCC) of the various Classes to which this equipment has been allocated is $842,000. As Gee Ltd. has been subject to a tax rate of 35 percent, the $736,000 ($1,578,000 - $842,000) temporary difference is reflected in a Future Income Tax Liability of $257,600.

Required: Indicate the Future Income Tax Liability that will be disclosed in the books of the combined company under the following alternative assumptions.

A.   The legal form of the combination is such that Gor acquired the shares of Gee.
B.   The legal form of the combination is such that Gor acquired the assets of Gee.

End Of Exercise Three-5

> Exercise Three-5 deals with temporary differences in business combination transactions.

Determination of Fair Values - Loss Carry Forwards

3-98.   A further tax related consideration involves loss carry forward benefits. Under the provisions of Section 3465, the benefit of a loss carry forward can only be recognized as an asset when it is more likely than not that the benefit will be realized. The implementation of this concept involves a number of difficulties in the context of accounting for business combinations.

3-99.   The first of these problems is the question of whether the loss carry forward can be transferred to the combined company. If the combination involves an acquisition of assets, it is likely that the loss carry forward will not be available to the combined company. If no rollover provision is used, the benefit of the carry forward will certainly be lost if this format is used. However, some rollover provisions (e.g., ITA 87) provide for a transfer of loss carry forward benefits in the context of an acquisition of assets.

3-100.   If shares are acquired, the loss carry over will continue on the books of the subsidiary company. However, its availability may be limited by the acquisition of control rules [see ITA 111(4)].

3-101.   A full discussion of these issues extends well beyond the scope of this text. What can be said here is this:

- If the loss carry forward benefit is legally available to the combined company; and

- if it is more likely than not that the benefit will be realized by the combined company; then

- its fair value is equal to the amount of the carry forward multiplied by the appropriate tax rate; and

- this amount should be recognized in the financial statements of the combined company, without regard to whether it has been recognized by the acquiree (the combined company may be able to claim that realization is more likely than not, even if the acquiree could not make this claim).

Determination of Fair Values - Identifiable Intangible Assets

3-102.   Section 1581 defines an intangible asset as follows:

> **Paragraph 1581.06(d)**   An intangible asset is an asset, other than a financial asset, that lacks physical substance.

3-103.   As such, this term encompasses both goodwill, as well as other intangible assets whose source of value can be identified (e.g., a patent). However, a terminology problem arises when one refers to the content of Section 3062, "Goodwill and Other Intangible Assets". In that Section, the term "intangible asset" is used to refer to intangible assets other than goodwill. In order to avoid confusion, as well as the somewhat awkward designation "intangible assets other than goodwill", we will use the term "identifiable intangible assets" to refer to those intangible assets other than goodwill.

3-104.   Prior to the issuance of Section 1581, it was believed that, in practice, identifiable intangible assets acquired in business combination transactions were not being recognized, particularly in situations where they had not been recognized on the books of the acquiree. For example, the acquiree might have incurred significant costs in the development of a manufacturing process. As such costs are usually charged to income as they are incurred, this process would not appear as an asset on the books of the acquiree. However, if the company is acquired in a business combination transaction, some portion of the cost of the purchase could represent a payment for this process.

3-105.   Given that such intangibles were not recognized on the books of the acquiree, it is likely that the acquirer made little effort to attach a fair value to this process and, as a consequence, no separate asset value would be recognized. This meant that the value of the process would be included in the total value assigned to goodwill. When there was a requirement to amortize the resulting goodwill balance, this was not a serious problem. While the cost of the process might be amortized over an incorrect useful life, it would, in fact, be amortized and charged to income over some limited period. However, the prohibition against amortizing goodwill in Section 3062 created the possibility that identifiable intangible assets with limited lives would not be amortized in situations where their value was allocated to goodwill. To deal with this possibility, Section 1581 makes the following Recommendation:

> **Paragraph 1581.48**   *An intangible asset should be recognized apart from goodwill when:*
>
> (a) *the asset results from contractual or other legal rights (regardless of whether those rights are transferable or separable from the acquired enterprise or from other rights and obligations); or*
> (b) *the asset is capable of being separated or divided from the acquired enterprise and sold, transferred, licensed, rented, or exchanged (regardless of whether there is an intent to do so).*
>
> *Otherwise it should be included in the amount recognized as goodwill.* (July, 2001)

3-106.   This Recommendation is intended to ensure that an effort is made to record a fair value for all identifiable intangible assets that meet the specified conditions. With respect to the implementation of this provision, several points should be noted:

• Paragraph 1581.48(a) requires an intangible asset acquired in a business combination to be recognized apart from goodwill when it arises from contractual or other legal rights. Intangible assets that meet that criterion are recognized apart from goodwill even when the asset is not transferable or separable from the acquired enterprise or from other rights and obligations. Examples of this type of situation would include:

(a) An acquired enterprise leases a manufacturing facility under an operating lease that has terms that are favourable relative to market prices. The lease terms explicitly prohibit transfer of the lease (through either sale or sublease). The value arising from that operating lease contract is an intangible asset that meets the criterion for recognition apart from goodwill in paragraph 1581.48(a), even though the lease contract cannot be sold or otherwise transferred.

(b) An acquired enterprise owns and operates a nuclear power plant. The license to operate that power plant is an intangible asset that meets the criterion for recognition apart from goodwill in paragraph 1581.48(a), even when it cannot be sold or transferred separately from the acquired power plant.

(c) An acquired enterprise owns a technology patent. It has licensed that patent to others for their exclusive use outside Canada in exchange for which the enterprise receives a specified percentage of future non-Canadian revenue. Both the technology patent and the related license agreement meet the criterion for recognition apart from goodwill in paragraph 1581.48(a) even when it is not practical to sell or exchange the patent and the related license agreement separately from one another.

- When an intangible asset acquired in a business combination does not arise from contractual or other legal rights, paragraph 1581.48(b) requires that it be recognized apart from goodwill only when it is separable — that is, when it is capable of being separated or divided from the acquired enterprise and sold, transferred, licensed, rented or exchanged. Exchange transactions provide evidence that an intangible asset is separable from the acquired enterprise and might provide information that can be used to estimate its fair value. An acquired intangible asset meets the criterion in paragraph 1581.48(b) if there is evidence of exchange transactions for that type of asset or for an asset of a similar type. For example, customer and subscriber lists are frequently leased and thus meet the criterion.

- An intangible asset that meets the criterion in paragraph 1581.48(b) is recognized apart from goodwill even when the acquired enterprise does not intend to sell, lease, or otherwise exchange that asset.

- An intangible asset that is not separable from the enterprise individually still meets the criterion in paragraph 1581.48(b) when it is separable from the acquired enterprise in combination with a related contract, asset, or liability. Examples of this would include:

(a) Deposit liabilities and related depositor relationship intangible assets are exchanged in observable exchange transactions. Therefore, the depositor relationship intangible asset is recognized apart from goodwill.

(b) An acquired enterprise owns a United States registered trademark, a related secret formula, and non-patented technical expertise used to manufacture the trademarked product. To transfer ownership of a trademark in the United States, the owner is also required to transfer everything else necessary for the new owner to produce a product or service indistinguishable from that produced by the former owner. The non-patented technical expertise meets the criterion in paragraph 1581.48(b) because it must be separated from the enterprise and sold if the related trademark is sold.

3-107.   An Appendix to Section 1581 contains an extensive listing of the types of assets that would meet the Paragraph 1581.48 criteria. (A complete reproduction of this listing goes beyond the scope of this text. However, if you are interested in this subject, the complete Appendix can be found in Chapter 13 of our *Guide to Canadian Financial Reporting*. This *Guide* is included on the CD-ROM which comes with this text.) The list includes:

- market related intangibles (e.g., trademarks),
- customer related intangibles (e.g., customer lists),
- artistic related intangible assets (e.g., books or musical works),
- contract based intangible assets (e.g., leasing arrangements), and
- technology based intangible assets (e.g., computer software).

Goodwill

The Concept

3-108.   In order to record the business combination transaction, the fair values of the identifiable assets and liabilities of the acquiree are determined on an individual basis. When these assets are put together as a business enterprise, it is unlikely that the sum of these fair values will be equal to the value of the business as an operating economic entity. If the assets were used in an effective and efficient manner, it is possible for the business to be worth considerably more than the sum of its individual asset values. Alternatively, ineffectual management or other factors can depress the value of a business well below the sum of the fair values of its assets. Note that this is not a clear indication that the assets should be liquidated on an individual basis. Fair values are based on the value of an asset to a going concern and, while in some cases they may be equal to liquidation values, this is not likely to be the case for most non-current assets.

3-109. If the business is worth more than the sum of its individual asset values, this will be reflected in the prices paid by an acquirer in a business combination. In this situation, when the acquisition cost exceeds the acquirer's share of the fair values of the acquiree's identifiable net assets, the excess is generally referred to as goodwill. From a conceptual point of view, goodwill is the capitalized expected value of enterprise earning power in excess of a normal rate of return for the particular industry in which it operates. As an example of this concept, consider the following:

> **Example**: Ryerson Ltd. has net identifiable assets with a current fair value of $1 million. Its annual income has been $150,000 for many years and it is anticipated that this level of earnings will continue indefinitely. A normal rate of return in Ryerson's industry is 10 percent as reflected in business values that are typically 10 times reported earnings.

3-110. Given this information, it is clear that Ryerson has goodwill. Normal earnings on Ryerson's $1 million in net assets would be $100,000, well below the Company's $150,000. Based on these earnings and a valuation benchmark of 10 times earnings, the value of Ryerson as a going concern would be $1.5 million. This would suggest the presence of goodwill as follows:

Value Of Ryerson As A Going Concern	$1,500,000
Fair Value Of Ryerson's Net Identifiable Assets	(1,000,000)
Goodwill	$ 500,000

3-111. While it is clear that, in this simplified example, Ryerson has goodwill, it is unlikely that it will be recorded in the Company's Balance Sheet. Even in situations where an enterprise has incurred significant costs for the creation of goodwill (e.g., management training or advertising directed at enhancing the image of the enterprise), GAAP does not permit the recognition of internally generated goodwill. This reflects the belief that there is no reliable procedure for the measurement of such amounts. In a more general context, this belief prevents the recognition of most internally generated intangibles. The only exception to this is the recognition of certain development costs as assets under the provisions of Section 3450 of the *CICA Handbook*, "Research and Development Costs".

Measurement In Practice

3-112. While it is not possible under GAAP to recognize internally generated goodwill, we often find goodwill in corporate balance sheets. In fact, in many cases, it can be a very significant item. However, these amounts usually reflect goodwill that has been recognized as the result of a business combination transaction.

3-113. In practical terms, the only useful definition of goodwill under GAAP is the excess of the purchase price over the acquirer's proportionate share of the fair values of the acquiree's net identifiable assets at the date of a business combination. This is reflected in the following *CICA Handbook* definition of goodwill:

> **Paragraph 3062.05(b)** **Goodwill** is the excess of the cost of an acquired enterprise over the net of the amounts assigned to assets acquired and liabilities assumed. The amount recognized as goodwill includes acquired intangible assets that do not meet the criteria in "Business Combinations", Section 1581, for recognition as an asset apart from goodwill.

3-114. Returning to our example involving Ryerson Ltd., if another enterprise were to purchase either the net assets or the shares of this enterprise for the suggested value of $1,500,000, the acquirer would record the goodwill of $500,000 that was calculated in the example.

3-115. In general, this is the only basis for recording significant amounts of goodwill. One sometimes sees nominal amounts of goodwill added to corporate Balance Sheets without the purchase of another enterprise. However, this is a procedure that is acceptable only if the amount involved is immaterial.

General Accounting Procedures

3-116. As noted in the previous section, the excess of the cost of an acquisition over the fair values of the identifiable assets acquired is recorded as goodwill. Prior to 2001, all of the *Handbook* Recommendations related to goodwill were found in Section 1580, "Business Combinations". Under these Recommendations, no attempt was made to segregate any unrecorded intangibles other than goodwill that might have been acquired in the business combination transaction and included in this total excess. Once recorded, the goodwill balance was subject to straight-line amortization over a period not exceeding forty years. There was no requirement that the amount recorded be subsequently tested for impairment. In addition, there was a prohibition against any non-systematic write-off of the balance unless there was some clearly identifiable reason for believing that the goodwill was no longer present.

3-117. The revision of the *Handbook* Section on Business Combinations, along with the introduction of a new *Handbook* Section 3062, "Goodwill and Other Intangible Assets", will result in dramatic changes in the way we account for goodwill. The first of these Recommendations is as follows:

> **Paragraph 3062.22** *Goodwill should be recognized on an enterprise's balance sheet at the amount initially recognized, less any write-down for impairment.* (January, 2002)

3-118. While not explicitly stated, it is clear from the wording of this Recommendation that the amount recorded as goodwill will not be subject to amortization. Rather, it will be the subject of a periodic impairment test which may or may not result in a write-down of any amount that is recorded.

3-119. Any goodwill balance that is recognized will generally be tested on an annual basis for impairment. As specified in the following Recommendation, the annual test can sometimes be omitted:

> **Paragraph 3062.39** *Goodwill of a reporting unit should be tested for impairment on an annual basis, unless all of the following criteria have been met:*
>
> (a) *The assets and liabilities that make up the reporting unit have not changed significantly since the most recent fair value determination.*
> (b) *The most recent fair value determination resulted in an amount that exceeded the carrying amount of the reporting unit by a substantial margin.*
> (c) *Based on an analysis of events that have occurred and circumstances that have changed since the most recent fair value determination, the likelihood that a current fair value determination would be less than the current carrying amount of the reporting unit is remote.* (January, 2002)

3-120. Alternatively, more frequent testing may be required under some circumstances:

> **Paragraph 3062.42** *Goodwill of a reporting unit should be tested for impairment between annual tests when an event or circumstance occurs that more likely than not reduces the fair value of a reporting unit below its carrying amount.* (January, 2002)

3-121. Examples of such events or circumstances are as follows:

(a) a significant adverse change in legal factors or in the business climate;

(b) an adverse action or assessment by a regulator;

(c) unanticipated competition;

(d) a loss of key personnel;

(e) a more-likely-than-not expectation that a significant portion or all of a reporting unit will be sold or otherwise disposed of;

(f) the testing for write-down or impairment of a significant asset group within a reporting unit; or

(g) the recognition of a goodwill impairment loss in its separate financial statements by a subsidiary that is a component of the reporting unit.

3-122.   Consistent with other *Handbook* Sections which require asset write-downs (e.g., Section 3050, "Long-Term Investments"), once a goodwill impairment loss is recognized, it cannot be reversed in a subsequent period.

Goodwill Impairment Losses

3-123.   Section 3062 requires that the goodwill impairment losses be measured at the reporting unit level. For this purpose, reporting units are defined as follows:

> A **reporting unit** is the level of reporting at which goodwill is tested for impairment and is either an operating segment (see "Segment Disclosure", Section 1701), or one level below (referred to as a component).

3-124.   In practice, this requirement presents significant difficulties. When there is a business combination transaction, any amount recognized as goodwill must be allocated to individual reporting units. In order to accomplish this, all of the other net assets acquired must also be assigned to segments. Further complicating the situation is that, when these new requirements are first adopted, they must be applied retroactively to all previous business combination transactions.

3-125.   A full discussion of the implementation of this requirement goes beyond the needs of general accounting students and, as a consequence, will not be given further attention in this text. However, if it is a subject that is of interest to you, Chapter 30 of our *Guide to Canadian Financial Reporting* provides more detailed coverage of impairment losses. This *Guide* can be found on the CD-ROM which accompanies this text.

Goodwill Presentation and Disclosure

3-126.   With respect to presentation of goodwill in the financial statements, the following two Recommendations are relevant:

> **Paragraph 3062.48**   *The aggregate amount of goodwill should be presented as a separate line item in an enterprise's balance sheet.* (January, 2002)

> **Paragraph 3062.49**   *The aggregate amount of goodwill impairment losses should be presented as a separate line item in the income statement before extraordinary items and discontinued operations, unless a goodwill impairment loss is associated with a discontinued operation. A goodwill impairment loss associated with a discontinued operation should be included on a net-of-tax basis within the results of discontinued operations.* (January, 2002)

3-127.   With respect to the disclosure of goodwill, the following Recommendations are relevant:

> **Paragraph 3062.51**   *The financial statements should disclose the following information:*
>
> (a) *The changes in the carrying amount of goodwill during the period including:*
>   (i) *the aggregate amount of goodwill acquired;*
>   (ii) *the aggregate amount of impairment losses recognized; and*
>   (iii) *the amount of goodwill included in the gain or loss on disposal of all or a portion of a reporting unit.*

Enterprises that report segment information in accordance with "Segment Disclosures", Section 1701, should provide the above information about goodwill in total and for each reportable segment and should disclose any significant changes in the allocation of goodwill by reportable segment. When any portion of goodwill has not yet been allocated to a reporting unit at the date the financial statements are issued, the unallocated amount and the reasons for not allocating that amount should be disclosed.

(b) and (c) [These additional paragraphs refer to intangibles other than goodwill.]

Paragraph 3062.53 *For each goodwill impairment loss recognized, the following information should be disclosed in the financial statements that include the period in which the impairment loss is recognized:*

(a) a description of the facts and circumstances leading to the impairment;

(b) the amount of the impairment loss; and

(c) when a recognized impairment loss is an estimate that has not yet been finalized, that fact and the reasons therefor and, in subsequent periods, the nature and amount of any significant adjustments made to the initial estimate of the impairment loss.

When the carrying amount of a reporting unit exceeds its fair value, but the second step of the impairment test is not complete and a reasonable estimate of the goodwill impairment loss cannot be determined (see paragraph 3062.28), that fact and the reasons therefor should be disclosed. (January, 2002)

Evaluation of Goodwill Procedures

3-128.   The changes in the procedures for accounting for goodwill appear to be related to the changes in the rules for business combination transactions. For some time, it has been recognized that the pooling-of-interests method of accounting for business combinations was not a sound accounting procedure. While it was not widely used in Canada, its use was pervasive in the United States. As this method did not require the recognition or amortization of goodwill, its application had a very favourable effect on earnings, when compared to the results under the purchase method of accounting for business combinations. Given this, there was significant resistance to the elimination of this method, despite the fact that it had few knowledgeable supporters.

3-129.   Fortunately, reason prevailed and standard setters in both the U.S. and in Canada have achieved the total elimination of this badly flawed method of accounting. While many other factors were involved, it is likely that their ability to accomplish this goal was facilitated by the simultaneous elimination of the requirement to amortize goodwill.

3-130.   When there is a business combination transaction we have an objective measure of the amount of goodwill that is present at that time. However, we do not attempt to identify the specific reasons that this value exists. Given the lack of any specific explanation for the presence of goodwill, it is extremely difficult to arrive at a rational estimate of its useful life. For many years we used an arbitrary solution to the problem — amortization over a period not to exceed 40 years. At one point in time, there appeared to be a belief that this maximum was too long and that goodwill should be written off over a shorter period. In 1993, International Accounting Standard No. 22 recommended that goodwill arising in business combination transactions should be written off over a period not exceeding five years.

3-131.   Standard setters in the U.S. and Canada considered similar changes. However, with the possibility of having to use purchase accounting for all business combinations on the horizon, the view that goodwill had an indefinite life moved to the forefront. While it would perhaps be overly cynical to suggest this change was necessary in order to muster the required support for the elimination of the pooling-of-interests method, it certainly facilitated this process. If goodwill had an indefinite life, it would not have to be amortized, thereby eliminating a major depressant of post-combination earnings when the purchase method was applied.

3-132. In concluding that goodwill would no longer be subject to amortization, a further problem was created. As we have noted, when the acquired company had intangible assets that were not recorded on the books of the acquiree, it is likely that they often became part of the total amount allocated to goodwill. The fact that these intangibles often had a limited life was not a problem when amortization of goodwill was required. However, with the elimination of this requirement, it was apparent that there was a need to use greater care in identifying and recognizing all of the intangibles that were acquired as part of the business combination transaction. For this reason, the elimination of the requirement to amortize goodwill was accompanied by a new Recommendation specifically requiring that an effort be made to identify and recognize all of the intangibles acquired in the combination transaction.

Negative Goodwill
Basic Rules
3-133. Fair values for the identifiable assets of the acquiree are determined on a going concern basis. As these values are, in general, in excess of the liquidation values of the assets, it is possible that an enterprise will be sold for less than the sum of the fair value of its net assets.

> **Example** Loser Inc. has net assets with a carrying value of $650,000 and fair values totaling $900,000. These net assets are acquired in a business combination transaction for $725,000 in cash, resulting in negative goodwill of $175,000. Note that the $900,000 figure reflects fair values and these these are not equal to liquidation values. If the sum of the liquidation values of these assets exceeded $725,000, it is likely that Loser Inc. would have been liquidated, rather than sold as a going concern.

3-134. In recording this business combination transaction, the acquired assets will require a debit of $900,000, while the cash payment will be recognized with a credit of $725,000. We are left in need of an additional credit of $175,000, the amount that we have referred to as negative goodwill. There are various possibilities for this credit, depending on how we analyze the reason for its existence. The various possibilities that are considered in the literature on this subject are as follows:

> **Overstated Fair Values** One view would be that an adequate job of determining the fair values of the identifiable assets was not done and, as a result, they are overstated. If this view is adopted, the appropriate credit would be to one or more of the identifiable assets acquired in the business combination transaction. In general, we would assume that the assets to be reduced would be non-monetary items.

> **Bargain Purchase** A second view would be that a bargain purchase was involved. The suggestion would be that, perhaps because of poor operating results, the acquiree enterprise is being sold under some form of duress and this has resulted in an artificially low price. Consistent with this view would be a credit to some type of gain on the transaction.

> **Inadequate Rate of Return** A third interpretation, one that is more consistent with the view of positive goodwill, is that the discount reflects the fact that the acquired enterprise is not earning a normal rate of return on its assets, resulting in a going concern value that is less than the sum of the fair values of the identifiable net assets. This interpretation would suggest the use of a general valuation account that would be shown as a contra to the total assets balance.

3-135. It is the first of these views that takes precedence in the Section 1581 Recommendation on negative goodwill:

> **Paragraph 1581.50** *When the net of the amounts assigned to assets acquired and liabilities assumed exceeds the cost of the purchase ("excess" — sometimes referred to as negative goodwill):*

> (a) *that excess should be allocated as a pro rata reduction of the amounts that otherwise would be assigned to all of the acquired assets except:*

(i) financial assets other than investments accounted for by the equity method;

(ii) assets to be disposed of by sale;

(iii) future income tax assets;

(iv) prepaid assets relating to employee future benefit plans; and

(v) any other current assets, to the extent the excess is eliminated; and

(b) any remaining excess should be presented as an extraordinary gain. (July, 2001)

3-136.   As indicated, this Recommendation relies largely on the overstated fair values interpretation of the negative goodwill balance. If the fair values assigned to the various eligible assets was reduced to nil, then any remaining balance would be credited to an extraordinary gain. We would expect this to be a fairly rare situation. Note, however, that when it occurs, the gain is treated as extraordinary, without regard to the general criteria found in Section 3480 for this classification.

3-137.   An additional problem arises when there is negative goodwill in a situation where contingent consideration is involved. In this case, the settlement of the contingency, could result in the negative amount being reduced or eliminated. Given this possibility, Section 1581 makes the following Recommendation:

Paragraph 1581.52   *When a business combination involves a contingent consideration agreement that might result in recognition of an additional element of cost of the purchase on resolving the contingency, an amount equal to the lesser of the maximum amount of contingent consideration and the excess should be recognized as if it were a liability. When the contingency is resolved and the consideration is issued or becomes issuable, any excess of the fair value of the contingent consideration issued or issuable over the amount initially recognized should be recognized as an additional cost of the purchase. Any excess of the amount initially recognized as if it were a liability over the fair value of the contingent consideration issued or issuable should first be allocated as a pro rata reduction of the amounts assigned to assets acquired in accordance with paragraph 1581.50(a). Any amount that remains should be accounted for in accordance with paragraph 1581.50(b). (July, 2001)*

3-138.   In effect, this Recommendation provides for deferring the allocation of any negative goodwill until such time as all possible contingent consideration has been issued.

Exercise Three-6

On December 31, 2002, the assets and liabilities of Manee Ltd. have the following fair values:

Cash	$ 265,000
Accounts Receivable	340,000
Inventories	855,000
Property, Plant, and Equipment	1,340,000
Liabilities	(425,000)
Net Assets At Fair Values	$2,375,000

On this date, 100 percent of the shares of Manee Ltd. are acquired by another corporation for $1,850,000 in cash.

Required: Calculate the values that will be recorded in the acquirer's consolidated financial statements to reflect the acquisition of Manee Ltd.

End Of Exercise Three-6

> Exercise Three-6 deals with negative goodwill.

Treatment Of Shareholders' Equity

3-139.   As the purchase method of accounting for business combinations takes the position that the transaction is simply an acquisition of assets, the acquiring company's shareholders' equity would only be changed to the extent that new shares were issued as consideration to the acquired company or its shareholders. However, under some of the legal forms of combination this may be in violation of relevant corporate legislation. For example, if the net assets of two existing companies are transferred to a newly established corporation, the *Canada Business Corporations Act* would require that all of the shareholders' equity of the new corporation be classified as contributed capital. A further problem would arise if the combination were implemented using a statutory amalgamation provision. In this type of transaction, corporate legislation usually requires that the contributed capital of the amalgamated company be equal to the aggregate of the contributed capital of the amalgamating enterprises.

3-140.   This is, of course, in conflict with the purchase accounting requirement that the shareholders' equity of the combined company have the same amounts of contributed capital and retained earnings as the acquiring company. When conflicts of this sort arise, the relevant corporate legislation would be the determining factor in the presentation of the combined company's shareholders' equity. In the case of statutory amalgamations, the *Handbook* suggests that the additional capital be allocated to a contributed surplus account.

Intercompany Transactions

3-141.   If the legal form of the business combination is such that the combining companies remain legally separate, there may be intercompany transactions subsequent to the combination transaction. The effects of transactions such as purchases and sales between the combining companies subsequent to the combination would be removed from all accounts. The necessary adjustments are covered in Chapter 5 (no unrealized intercompany profits) and Chapter 6 (with unrealized intercompany profits). However, for transactions between the two companies that take place prior to the combination, no adjustments would be required as they are viewed as arm's length transactions.

Purchase Method Example

Basic Data

3-142.   The preceding material has provided a discussion and description of the various procedures that are required in the application of the purchase method of accounting for business combinations. The example which follows will serve to illustrate the application of these procedures. We have ignored tax considerations in this example.

Example   On December 31, 2002, the Balance Sheets of the Dor and Dee Companies, prior to any business combination transaction, are as follows:

Balance Sheets
As At December 31, 2002

	Dor Company	Dee Company
Cash	$ 1,200,000	$ 600,000
Accounts Receivable	2,400,000	800,000
Inventories	3,800,000	1,200,000
Plant And Equipment (Net)	4,600,000	2,400,000
Total Assets	$12,000,000	$5,000,000
Liabilities	$ 1,500,000	$ 700,000
Common Stock - No Par*	6,000,000	2,500,000
Retained Earnings	4,500,000	1,800,000
Total Equities	$12,000,000	$5,000,000

*On this date, prior to the transactions described in the following paragraphs, each Company has 450,000 common shares outstanding.

On December 31, 2002, the Dor Company issues 204,000 shares of its No Par Common Stock to the Dee Company in return for 100 percent of its net assets. On this date the shares of the Dor Company are trading at $25 per share. All of the identifiable assets and liabilities of the Dee Company have fair values that are equal to their carrying values except for the Plant And Equipment which has a fair value of $2,700,000 and a remaining useful life of ten years. Both Companies have a December 31 year end and, for the year ending December 31, 2002, Dor reported Net Income of $800,000 and Dee reported Net Income of $250,000.

Identification Of An Acquirer

3-143.   Since the Dor Company issued fewer shares (204,000) to the Dee Company than it had outstanding prior to the business combination (450,000), the shareholders of the Dor Company would be the majority shareholders in the combined company and the Dor Company would be identified as the acquirer.

Determination Of Purchase Price

3-144.   With a market value of $25 per share, the 204,000 shares issued to effect the business combination would have a total market value in the amount of $5,100,000. This would be the purchase price of the Dee Company.

Investment Analysis

3-145.   Whenever the purchase method of accounting for business combination transactions is used, it will be necessary to allocate the cost of the purchase to the fair values of identifiable assets and liabilities and to establish a value for either a positive or negative goodwill. This will require an analysis of the total cost of the investment in any situation where the purchase method is being used to account for a business combination transaction. In those cases where the legal form of the combination requires the preparation of consolidated financial statements, this investment analysis can be fairly complex. However, in a simple problem such as the one under consideration, there is no need to have a detailed schedule. It is sufficient to simply calculate the total fair value of the Dee Company's net assets and then compare this value with the purchase price to determine the amount of Goodwill.

3-146.   The total fair values would be calculated as follows:

Carrying Values - Dee's Net Assets ($5,000,000 - $700,000)	$4,300,000
Fair Value Change On Plant ($2,700,000 - $2,400,000)	300,000
Fair Values - Dee's Net Assets	$4,600,000

3-147.   Given the purchase price and the fair values, the Goodwill that will be recognized from this business combination can be calculated in the following manner:

Purchase Price	$5,100,000
Fair Values - Dee's Net Assets	(4,600,000)
Goodwill To Be Recognized	$ 500,000

Schedule For Investment Analysis

3-148.   As noted previously, we are normally required to prepare consolidated financial statements in more complex situations, usually involving a large number of fair value changes. The calculations are further complicated in that, if the parent does not acquire 100 percent of the subsidiary's shares, only the parent's proportionate interest in the fair value changes will be recognized. This means that a more systematic approach to the investment analysis is required.

3-149.   There are many different approaches that can be used to analyze the investment account, all of which will provide a correct solution to the problem. The investment analysis approach that we will use throughout this text is as follows:

- Subtract the subsidiary's book value (or, in those cases where the acquiring company purchases less than 100 percent of the subsidiary's shares, the investor's proportionate interest in this book value) from the cost of the investment. We will refer to the resulting balance as a differential (other terms used for this balance are "purchase price discrepancy" and "excess of cost over book value"). If it is a positive number, it indicates that the investor is paying more than his proportionate share of the subsidiary's book values and that there is a debit amount to be allocated. A negative number reflects a credit balance to be allocated. Note that, as the differential reflects the total of all fair value changes and goodwill to be recognized, a positive balance does not necessarily indicate the presence of goodwill.

- Once the differential has been established, we will then add or subtract the various fair value changes that have been determined for the subsidiary's identifiable assets and liabilities. As a positive differential reflects a debit balance to be allocated, we will subtract any fair value changes which require allocation of debits (increases in assets or decreases in liabilities). Correspondingly, we will add any fair value changes that require credits (decreases in assets or increases in liabilities).

- The resulting balance will be allocated to goodwill if it is positive. If the balance is negative, it will be allocated as per the Recommendation in Paragraph 1581.50.

3-150.   Applying these rules to Dor Company's purchase of Dee Company's net assets results in the following analysis:

Investment Cost	$5,100,000
Book Value - Dee's Net Assets ($5,000,000 - $700,000)	(4,300,000)
Differential	$ 800,000
Fair Value Increase On Plant ($2,700,000 - $2,400,000)	(300,000)
Goodwill	$ 500,000

3-151.   In a simple case such as this, the use of this schedule is not particularly useful. However, in dealing with more complex situations involving the preparation of consolidated financial statements, this approach will provide for an orderly and systematic approach to the allocation of the investment cost.

Journal Entry

3-152.   Using the preceding investment analysis, we are now in a position to record the business combination. It would be recorded on the books of the Dor Company as a simple acquisition of net assets. Except for Dee's Plant And Equipment and the Goodwill to be recorded as a result of the business combination, the carrying values from the books of the Dee Company would be used. The entry is as follows:

Cash	$ 600,000	
Accounts Receivable	800,000	
Inventories	1,200,000	
Plant And Equipment (Fair Value)	2,700,000	
Goodwill (Arising From The Acquisition)	500,000	
Liabilities		$ 700,000
Common Stock - No Par (Dor)		5,100,000

Combined Balance Sheet

3-153.   The resulting December 31, 2002 Balance Sheet for the Dor Company, which now includes all of the assets and liabilities of the Dee Company, would be as follows:

Dor Company
Balance Sheet
As At December 31, 2002

Cash ($1,200,000 + $600,000)	$ 1,800,000
Accounts Receivable ($2,400,000 + $800,000)	3,200,000
Inventories ($3,800,000 + $1,200,000)	5,000,000
Plant And Equipment ($4,600,000 + $2,700,000)	7,300,000
Goodwill	500,000
Total Assets	$17,800,000

Liabilities ($1,500,000 + $700,000)	$ 2,200,000
Common Stock - No Par ($6,000,000 + $5,100,000)	11,100,000
Retained Earnings (Dor's Only)	4,500,000
Total Equities	$17,800,000

Combined Income and Earnings Per Share

3-154.   We noted previously that Paragraph 1581.12 indicates that the income of the acquired company is only included in the combined companies' income from the date of acquisition. As the date of acquisition was December 31, 2002, none of Dee's 2002 Net Income would be included in the Net Income of the combined company. This means that Dor's reported Net Income for the year ending December 31, 2002 will be $800,000.

3-155.   With respect to Earnings Per Share, Dor Company would have 654,000 shares outstanding at the end of the year (450,000 original shares, plus the 204,000 shares issued to acquire the net assets of Dee Company). However, the additional 204,000 shares were issued on December 31, 2002 and, in the basic Earnings Per Share calculation, they would have a weight of nil. This means that basic Earnings Per Share for the combined company would be $1.78 ($800,000 ÷ 450,000).

Exercise Three-7

On December 31, 2002, the Balance Sheets of the Saller and Sallee Companies, prior to any business combination transaction, are as follows:

Exercise Three-7 deals with the application of the purchase method.

Balance Sheets
As At December 31, 2002

	Saller Company	Sallee Company
Cash	$ 1,876,000	$ 564,000
Accounts Receivable	3,432,000	1,232,000
Inventories	5,262,000	2,485,000
Property, Plant, and Equipment (Net)	6,485,000	4,672,000
Total Assets	$17,055,000	$8,953,000
Liabilities	$ 4,843,000	$2,237,000
Common Shares		
Saller (423,000 Shares Issued And Outstanding)	9,306,000	N/A
Sallee (185,000 Shares Issued And Outstanding)	N/A	3,885,000
Retained Earnings	2,906,000	2,831,000
Total Equities	$17,055,000	$8,953,000

> This is a continuation of Exercise Three-7.

On December 31, 2002, the Saller Company issues 135,000 shares of its Common Stock to the Sallee Company in return for 100 percent of its net assets. On this date the shares of the Saller Company are trading at $52 per share. Sallee's Cash and Accounts Receivable have fair values that are equal to their carrying values. With respect to Sallee's other assets and liabilities, the Inventories have a fair value of $2,732,000, the Property, Plant and Equipment has a fair value of $4,512,000, and the liabilities have a fair value of $2,115,000. Both Companies have a December 31 year end and, for the year ending December 31, 2002, Saller reported Net Income of $1,465,000 and Sallee reported Net Income of $372,000.

Required: Prepare the combined Balance Sheet that would be presented by Saller Company on December 31, 2002. In addition, determine the Net Income and Earnings Per Share of the Saller Company that would be reported for the year ending December 31, 2002.

End Of Exercise Three-7

Disclosure

Recommendations

3-156. Section 1581 contains the following disclosure Recommendation for business combinations completed during the period:

Paragraph 1581.55 *For each material business combination completed during the period, the combined enterprise should disclose the following:*

(a) *the name and a brief description of the acquired enterprise and, when shares are acquired, the percentage of voting shares acquired;*

(b) *the period for which the earnings of the acquired enterprise are included in the income statement of the combined enterprise;*

(c) *the cost of the purchase and, when applicable, the number of equity instruments issued or issuable, the value assigned to those equity instruments, and the basis for determining that value;*

(d) *a condensed balance sheet disclosing the amount assigned to each major class of asset and liability of the acquired enterprise at the date of acquisition;*

(e) *contingent payments, options, or commitments specified in the acquisition agreement and the accounting treatment that will be followed should any such contingency occur; and*

(f) *for any purchase price allocation that has not been finalized, that fact and the reasons therefor and, in subsequent periods, the nature and amount of any material adjustments made to the initial allocation of the purchase price. (July, 2001)*

3-157. A further disclosure Recommendation is applicable when goodwill and other intangible assets acquired are significant:

Paragraph 1581.56 *When the amounts assigned to goodwill or other intangible assets acquired are significant in relation to the total cost of the purchase, the combined enterprise should disclose the following:*

(a) *for intangible assets subject to amortization, the total amount assigned and the amount assigned to each major intangible asset class;*

(b) *for intangible assets not subject to amortization, the total amount assigned and the amount assigned to each major intangible asset class; and*

(c) *for goodwill:*

   (i) *the total amount of goodwill and the amount that is expected to be deductible for tax purposes; and*

   (ii) *for enterprises that are required to disclose segment information in accordance with "Segment Disclosures", Section 1701, the amount of goodwill by reportable segment. (July, 2001)*

3-158.   There is also a disclosure Recommendation for situations where a number of imma-terial business combinations are, in the aggregate, material:

Paragraph 1581.57   *When a series of individually immaterial business combinations are completed during the period that are material in the aggregate, the combined enterprise should disclose the following:*

(a) *the number of enterprises acquired and a brief description of those enterprises;*
(b) *the aggregate cost of the acquired enterprises, the number of equity instruments issued or issuable, and the value assigned to those equity instruments;*
(c) *the aggregate amount of any contingent payments, options, or commitments and the accounting treatment that will be followed should any such contingency occur (when potentially significant in relation to the aggregate cost of the purchases); and*
(d) *the information described in paragraph 1581.56, when the aggregate amount assigned to goodwill or to other intangible assets acquired is significant in relation to the aggre-gate cost of the purchases. (July, 2001)*

Disclosure Examples

3-159.   Appendix B of Section 1581 contains examples of the disclosure that should accom-pany business combination transactions. The first example illustrates the disclosure of a material business combination in the year of acquisition. It is as follows:

Note C: Acquisitions

On June 30, 20X2, Alpha acquired 100 percent of the outstanding common shares of Beta. The results of Beta's operations have been included in the consolidated financial statements since that date. Beta is a provider of data networking products and services in Canada and Mexico.

The aggregate purchase price was $9,400,000, including $7,000,000 of cash and common stock valued at $2,400,000. The value of the 100,000 common shares issued was determined based on the average market price of Alpha's common shares over the two-day period before and after the terms of the acquisition were agreed to and announced.

The following table summarizes the estimated fair value of the assets acquired and liabili-ties assumed at the date of acquisition. Alpha is in the process of obtaining third-party valuations of certain intangible assets; thus, the allocation of the purchase price is subject to refinement.

As at June 30, 20X2

Current assets	$2,400,000	
Property, plant and equipment	1,500,000	
Intangible assets	4,900,000	
Goodwill	2,200,000	
Total assets acquired		$11,000,000
Current liabilities	($ 500,000)	
Long-term debt	(1,100,000)	
Total liabilities assumed		(1,600,000)
Net assets acquired		$ 9,400,000

Of the $4,900,000 of acquired intangible assets, $2,400,000 was assigned to registered trademarks that are not subject to amortization. The remaining intangible assets include computer software of $1,500,000, patents of $800,000, and other assets of $200,000.

The $2,200,000 of goodwill was assigned to the technology and communications segments in the amounts of $1,300,000 and $900,000, respectively. Of that total amount, $250,000 is expected to be deductible for tax purposes.

3-160. The second example involves the acquisition of several individually immaterial business combinations that are material in the aggregate. It is as follows:

Note C: Acquisitions

In 20X3, Alpha acquired the following four enterprises for a total cost of $1,000,000, which was paid primarily in cash:

- Omega Consulting, based in Zurich, Switzerland, a leading provider of telecommunications consulting services;
- Gamma Systems, based in London, England, a producer of digital networking technology;
- Delta Communications, Inc., based in Portland, USA, a start-up data networking company; and
- Kappa Networks, Inc., based in Atlanta, USA, a designer and manufacturer of wireless communications networks.

Goodwill recognized in those transactions amounted to $300,000, and that amount is expected to be fully deductible for tax purposes. Goodwill was assigned to the communication and technology segments in the amounts of $120,000 and $180,000, respectively.

Subsequent Events

3-161. Business combinations may occur after the Balance Sheet date but prior to the issuance of financial statements. As such transactions may be very significant with respect to the acquiring enterprise, Section 1581 makes the following Recommendation:

Paragraph 1581.59 *The information in paragraphs 1581.55-.56 should be disclosed, to the extent practical, for each material business combination completed after the balance sheet date but before the financial statements are completed.* (July, 2001)

Transitional Provisions

3-162. The Recommendations that we have discussed in this Chapter apply to all business combinations initiated on or after July 1, 2001. The Section contains a fairly complex set of transitional Recommendations which call for a mix of retroactive and prospective treatment. As an understanding of these procedures will not be necessary after a brief transitional period, we do not believe that they should be covered this text. However, if you are interested in more detailed coverage of these provisions, they can be found in Chapter 13 of our *Guide to Canadian Financial Reporting*. This *Guide* is included on the CD-ROM which comes with this text.

Business Combinations In Canadian Practice

Statistics From Financial Reporting In Canada

3-163. Of the 200 companies surveyed for the 2001 edition of *Financial Reporting in Canada*, 109 companies disclosed one or more business combination transactions in their 2000 annual reports. Only one of these companies disclosed the use of the pooling-of-interests method.

3-164. With respect to the disclosure provided by the companies disclosing the use of the purchase method, the survey results included the following:

- 96 companies provided the name of the acquiree.
- 96 companies provided details of the assets acquired.
- 96 companies provided details of the consideration given.
- 89 companies indicated the date of the acquisition.
- 79 companies provided a description of the business acquired.

- 70 companies indicated the period for which results of operations of the acquired business are included.
- 13 companies provided details of contingent consideration.

Example From Practice

3-165.   The following example is from the annual report of Maax Inc. for the reporting period ending February 29, 2000. This example illustrates the application of the purchase method of accounting to a business combination transaction. It contains disclosure of net assets acquired.

Notes To Financial Statements

(in thousands of dollars)

Note 2   Business Acquisitions

On March 1, 1999 and on August 1, 1999, the Company acquired all shares of Novax Modular Group Inc. and Imperial Woodcraft, which are specialized in the manufacturing and distribution of kitchen cabinets and kitchen cabinet doors respectively.

On January 1, 2000, the Company acquired, through a subsidiary, all outstanding shares of SaniNova B.V., a Netherlands company specialized in the design, development, manufacturing and distribution of bathroom products.

During the past year, the Company also acquired the assets of Shostal Ltd. and Novi, which are specialized in the design, development, manufacturing and distribution of bathroom products.

Furthermore, it acquired the shares of Savannah Spa Manufacturing and Coleman Spas, Inc., which are specialized in the design, development, manufacturing and distribution of spas.

These acquisitions have been accounted for using the purchase method and the results of operations are included from the dates of acquisitions. The fair value of net assets acquired is as follows:

	2000	1999
Net operating working capital	$ 14,143	$ 11,470
Fixed assets	17,589	11,440
Other assets	521	153
Goodwill	39,462	33,639
Bank overdrafts	(3,262)	(3,643)
	68,453	53,059
Bank loans	(1,570)	–
Long-term debt	(13,227)	(1,101)
Fair value on net assets acquired	$ 53,656	$ 51,958
Consideration:		
Cash	$ 50,160	$ 40,995
Note payable without interest (NLG 4,000)	2,637	–
Balance payable in shares on business acquisition (note 9)	1,200	–
Debenture, 4%	–	6,000
Note payable (US $1,200), 7.5%	–	1,843
Issuance of shares	–	3,120
	53,997	51,958
Deemed interest on purchase price	(341)	–
	$ 53,656	$ 51,958

Note 16   Commitments And Contingencies

a) Business acquisitions:

The acquisition agreements of Novi and Coleman Spas, Inc. both include a price adjustment clause based on the final value of net assets acquired on a $1 for a $1 basis if these net assets are different from the amount stipulated in the contracts. The parties to these agreements are in the final phase of arbitration.

b) Contingent payment:

Some business purchase agreements provide for a contingent payment of a maximum amount of $19,271,000 based on future income of the business acquired until February, 2005.

Additional Readings

3-166.   In writing the material in the text, we have incorporated all of the relevant *CICA Handbook* Recommendations, as well as material from other sources that we felt to be of importance. This includes some, but not all, of the EIC Abstracts that relate to business combinations, as well as material from U.S. accounting pronouncements and ideas put forward in articles published in professional accounting journals.

3-167.   While this approach meets the needs of the great majority of accounting students, some of you may wish to pursue this subject in greater depth. To facilitate this, you will find a fairly comprehensive bibliography of materials on the subject of business combinations in Chapter 13 of our *Guide to Canadian Financial Reporting*. Chapter 13 of the *Guide* also contains summaries of the EIC Abstracts that are directly related to this subject. The abstracts that are summarized as an appendix to Chapter 13 are as follows:

- EIC Abstract No. 10 - Paragraph 13-156 (Reverse Takeover Accounting)
- EIC Abstract No. 12 - Paragraph 13-157 (Capitalization Of Interest Costs On Investments In Potential Takeover Targets)
- EIC Abstract No. 14 - Paragraph 13-158 (Adjustments To The Purchase Equation Subsequent To The Acquisition Date)
- EIC Abstract No. 42 - Paragraph 13-159 (Costs Incurred On Business Combinations)
- EIC Abstract No. 55 - Paragraph 13-160 (Identifiable Assets Acquired In A Business Combination)
- EIC Abstract No. 62 - Paragraph 13-161 (Measurement Of Cost Of A Business Acquisition Effected By Issuing Shares)
- EIC Abstract No. 66 - Paragraph 13-162 (Transfer Of A Business Between Entities Under Common Control)
- EIC Abstract No. 73 - Paragraph 13-163 (Buy Out Transactions)
- EIC Abstract No. 114 - Paragraph 13-164 (Liability Recognition For Costs Incurred On Purchase Business Combinations)
- EIC Abstract No. 119 - Paragraph 13-165 (The Date of Acquisition In A Business Combination)

3-168.   The complete *Guide to Canadian Financial Reporting* is available on the CD-ROM which accompanies this text.

Problems For Self Study

(The solutions for these problems can be found following Chapter 16 of the text.)

Self Study Problem Three - 1

On December 31, 2002, the Balance Sheets of the Graber and the Grabee Companies are as follows:

Graber and Grabee Companies
Balance Sheets
As At December 31, 2002

	Graber	Grabee
Cash	$ 50,000	$ 70,000
Accounts Receivable	250,000	330,000
Inventories	400,000	300,000
Plant and Equipment (Net)	1,200,000	600,000
Land	800,000	400,000
Goodwill	150,000	50,000
Total Assets	$2,850,000	$1,750,000
Current Liabilities	$ 75,000	$ 50,000
Long Term Liabilities	800,000	400,000
Future Income Tax Liabilities	200,000	100,000
Common Stock - Par $20	800,000	-0-
Common Stock - Par $100	-0-	560,000
Contributed Surplus	400,000	340,000
Retained Earnings	575,000	300,000
Total Equities	$2,850,000	$1,750,000

On December 31, 2002, the Graber Company issues 40,000 of its Par $20 common shares to the Grabee Company in return for 100 percent of its net assets. The December 31, 2002 market price of the Graber Company shares is $35 per share while the Grabee shares are trading at $250 per share on this date. After selling its net assets, the Grabee Company distributes the Graber shares to its shareholders in return for their shares. The Grabee shares are then cancelled and the Company ceases to exist as a separate legal entity. The direct expenses of carrying out this business combination transaction amount to $10,000 and are paid in cash.

Other Information

1. All of the net identifiable assets of the two Companies have fair values that are equal to their carrying values except for the Grabee Company's Goodwill and Future Income Tax Liabilities and the following other accounts:

	Fair Values	
	Graber	Grabee
Plant and Equipment (Net)	$1,800,000	$800,000
Land	1,000,000	300,000
Long Term Liabilities	750,000	450,000

2. The Net Income of the Graber Company for the year ending December 31, 2002 was $125,000 while that of the Grabee Company amounted to $200,000.

3. The 2002 Net Income of the Graber Company included a $20,000 gain resulting from the sale of land to the Grabee Company on July 8, 2002.

4. The 2002 Net Income of the Grabee Company included a $50,000 gain on sales of merchandise in November to the Graber Company. All of this merchandise remained in the December 31, 2002 Inventories of the Graber Company.

5. Subsequent to the business combination transaction, the combined company will be under the direction of the Graber management team.

Required: Prepare the combined company's Balance Sheet as at December 31, 2002 and calculate the combined company's Net Income and Earnings Per Share for the year ending December 31, 2002.

Self Study Problem Three - 2

On December 31, 2002, the condensed Balance Sheets of the Ero Company and the Tick Company are as follows:

Ero and Tick Company
Condensed Balance Sheets
As At December 31, 2002

	Ero	Tick
Monetary Assets	$ 200,000	$1,000,000
Non-Monetary Assets	3,800,000	4,000,000
Total Assets	$4,000,000	$5,000,000
Monetary Liabilities	$ 100,000	$ 800,000
Common Stock (200,000 Shares Issued)	2,500,000	-0-
Common Stock (100,000 Shares Issued)	-0-	3,000,000
Retained Earnings	1,400,000	1,200,000
Total Equities	$4,000,000	$5,000,000

On December 31, 2002, the Monetary Assets and Liabilities of both Companies have fair values that are equal to their carrying values. The fair values of Ero's Non-Monetary Assets are $400,000 greater than their carrying values while Tick's Non-Monetary Assets are $600,000 less than their carrying values. For both Companies, the Non-Monetary Assets have an estimated remaining useful life of 4 years. Both Companies use the straight line method for all depreciation and amortization calculations. Neither Company owns any intangible assets that result from contractual or other legal rights, or are capable of being separated or divided and sold, transferred, licensed, rented, or exchanged.

The Net Income of the Ero Company for the year ending December 31, 2002 is $400,000 and the Net Income of the Tick Company for the year ending December 31, 2002 is $600,000. If there had been no business combination on December 31, 2002, the 2003 Net Income of Ero would have been $700,000 and that of Tick would have been $800,000. There are no intercompany transactions or dividends declared in 2002 or 2003. Goodwill impairment was determined to be nil for the year ended December 31, 2003.

These two Companies can effect a business combination by different legal avenues. Both of the following cases assumes that a business combination takes place on December 31, 2002. As the problem is designed to illustrate the concepts involved in the application of purchase accounting, your solutions should be consistent with the associated concepts and should ignore any effects that corporate legislation might have on the shareholders' equity of the combined company.

A. Ero issues 100,000 of its shares to Tick in return for 100 percent of Tick's net assets. The shares of Tick are cancelled and Ero is the sole survivor of the combination. Ero shares are trading at $40 per share on this date.

B. Ero Company and Tick Company cease to exist as separate legal and economic entities. A new Company, the Erotick Company is formed which issues 300,000 no par value common shares. Of these new shares, Tick receives 180,000 in return for 100 percent of its net assets and Ero receives 120,000 shares in return for 100 percent of its net assets. On the date of the combination, Ero shares are trading at $24 per share and Tick shares are trading at $72 per share.

Required: For both of the preceding cases, prepare the appropriate combined Balance Sheet as at December 31, 2002. In addition, compute Net Income and Basic Earnings Per Share figures for the business entity resulting from the combination for both 2002 and 2003. Your solution should comply with Sections 1581 and 3062 of the *CICA Handbook*.

Self Study Problem Three - 3

On December 31, 2002, the condensed Balance Sheets of the Gold Company and the Medal Company are as follows:

Gold and Medal Companies
Balance Sheets
As At December 31, 2002

	Gold	Medal
Monetary Assets	$ 500,000	$ 300,000
Non-Monetary Assets	5,500,000	3,200,000
Total Assets	$6,000,000	$3,500,000
Monetary Liabilities	$ 300,000	$ 100,000
Common Stock (100,000 Shares Outstanding)	4,200,000	-0-
Common Stock (100,000 Shares Outstanding)	-0-	2,000,000
Retained Earnings	1,500,000	1,400,000
Total Equities	$6,000,000	$3,500,000

During 2002, the Net Income of the Gold Company was $1 million while the Net Income of the Medal Company was $200,000. For 2003, if we assume that there is no business combination on December 31, 2002, the corresponding Net Income figures would be $1.5 million and $500,000. No dividends were paid by either Company in 2002 or 2003. No intercompany transactions occurred during 2003.

The Monetary Assets and Liabilities of both Companies have fair values that are equal to their carrying values. The fair values of the Non-Monetary Assets are $6 million for Gold and $3 million for Medal. The Non-Monetary Assets consist of Plant And Equipment with an estimated useful life of 5 years with no anticipated net salvage value. Both Companies use the straight line method for all depreciation and amortization calculations. There are no intercompany transactions or dividends declared in 2002 or 2003. Goodwill impairment was determined to be nil for the year ended December 31, 2003.

On December 31, 2002, there are several different legal avenues that the two Companies can use to effect a business combination. Three different possibilities are as follows:

A. Medal issues 90,000 of its shares in return for the net assets of Gold. At the date of the combination the shares of Medal are trading at $65 per share. Gold continues to exist as a separate legal entity.

B. Gold issues 80,000 of its shares in return for the net assets of Medal. The shares of Medal are cancelled and Medal ceases to exist as a legal entity. At the date of the combination the shares of Gold are trading at $50 per share.

C. A new Company, the Goldmedal Company, is formed and issues 50,000 no par value common shares to Gold in return for all of its net assets and 30,000 shares to Medal in return for all of its net assets. The Gold Company and the Medal Company distribute the Goldmedal shares to their shareholders and cease to exist as separate legal and economic entities. At the date of the combination, the Gold Company shares are trading at $75 and the Medal Company shares are trading at $45 per share.

Required: For each of the preceding independent cases, prepare the combined Balance Sheet as at December 31, 2002. In addition, compute Net Income and Earnings Per Share figures for the business entity resulting from the combination for both the year ending December 31, 2002 and the year ending December 31, 2003. Your solutions should be prepared based on the *CICA Handbook* Recommendations, without regard to any corporate legislation requirements that may be applicable.

Assignment Problems

(The solutions for these problems are only available in
the solutions manual that has been provided to your instructor.)

Assignment Problem Three - 1

On December 31, 2002, the condensed Balance Sheets of the Hyper Company and the Tension Company are as follows:

Hyper and Tension Companies
Condensed Balance Sheets
At December 31, 2002

	Hyper	Tension
Monetary Assets	$1,400,000	$ 800,000
Non-Monetary Assets	4,600,000	2,200,000
Total Assets	$6,000,000	$3,000,000
Monetary Liabilities	$ 500,000	$ 200,000
Common Stock (100,000 Shares Outstanding)	3,000,000	-0-
Common Stock (10,000 Shares Outstanding)	-0-	2,000,000
Retained Earnings	2,500,000	800,000
Total Equities	$6,000,000	$3,000,000

The Monetary Assets of both Companies have fair values that are equal to their carrying values. The fair value of the Hyper Company's Non-Monetary Assets is $4 million and the fair value of its Monetary Liabilities is $400,000. The fair value of the Tension Company's Non-Monetary Assets is $2 million and the fair value of its Monetary Liabilities is $250,000. Neither Company owns any intangible assets that result from contractual or other legal rights, or are capable of being separated or divided and sold, transferred, licensed, rented, or exchanged.

These two Companies can effect a business combination by several different legal avenues. Each of the following cases assumes that one of these available avenues has been chosen and that a business combination takes place on December 31, 2002. The cases are completely independent and in selecting the accounting method to be used, assume that the Company whose shareholders have majority share ownership in the combined business entity is deemed to be the acquiring Company. As the problem is designed to illustrate the concepts involved in the application of purchase accounting, your solutions should be consistent with the concepts associated with these procedures and should ignore any effects that corporate legislation might have on the shareholders' equity of the combined company.

A. The Hyper Company issues 70,000 of its shares in return for the net assets of the Tension Company. The shares of Tension are cancelled and Tension ceases to exist as a separate legal entity. At the date of the combination the shares of the Hyper Company are trading at $45 per share.

B. The Tension Company issues 15,000 of its shares in return for the net assets of the Hyper Company. The shares of the Hyper Company are cancelled and the Hyper Company ceases to exist as a separate legal entity. At the date of the combination, the shares of the Hyper Company are trading at $75 per share and the shares of the Tension Company are trading at $500 per share.

C. A new Company, the Hypertension Company, is formed. This new Company issues 15,000 no par value shares to the Hyper Company in return for all of its net assets and 10,000 no par value shares to the Tension Company in return for all of its net assets. Both the Hyper Company and the Tension Company distribute the Hypertension Company shares to their shareholders in return for all of their outstanding shares. The Hyper Company and Tension Company shares are cancelled and the two Companies cease to exist as separate legal entities. At the date of the combination, the Hyper Company shares are trading at $90 per share and the Tension Company shares are trading at $600 per share.

Required: For each of the preceding cases, prepare the appropriate combined Balance Sheet as at December 31, 2002.

Assignment Problem Three - 2

On December 31, 2002, the assets and liabilities of the Davis Company and the Jones Company have fair values and book values as follows:

Davis and Jones Companies
Balance Sheets
At December 31, 2002

	Davis		Jones	
	Book Value	Fair Value	Book Value	Fair Value
Cash	$ 450,000	$ 450,000	$ 375,000	$ 375,000
Accounts Receivable	560,000	545,000	420,000	405,000
Inventories	1,200,000	1,150,000	875,000	950,000
Net Plant And Equipment	2,800,000	3,200,000	1,450,000	1,250,000
Goodwill	-0-	-0-	125,000	-0-
Total Assets	$5,010,000	$5,345,000	$3,245,000	$2,980,000
Current Liabilities	$ 325,000	$ 325,000	$ 295,000	$ 295,000
Bonds Payable	1,200,000	1,400,000	870,000	910,000
Future Income Tax Liability	780,000	N/A	430,000	N/A
No Par Common Stock	2,100,000	N/A	1,200,000	N/A
Retained Earnings	605,000	N/A	450,000	N/A
Total Equities	$5,010,000		$3,245,000	

On December 31, 2002, the Davis Company issues 30,000 shares of its No Par Common Stock in return for all of the assets and liabilities of the Jones Company. On this date the Davis Company shares are trading at $65 per share while the Jones Company shares are trading at $32.50 per share.

Other Information:

1. The No Par Common Stock of the Davis Company, prior to the business combination, consists of 42,000 shares issued at an average price of $50 per share. The No Par Common Stock of the Jones Company consists of 60,000 shares issued at an average price of $20 per share.

2. The Jones Company has an unrecognized loss carry forward of $300,000. Both Companies are subject to a combined provincial and federal tax rate of 40 percent. The two Companies feel that there is reasonable assurance that the carry forward benefit will be realized if they are brought together in a business combination transaction.

Required: Prepare the December 31, 2002 Balance Sheet that would be required for the combined company resulting from the business combination transaction.

Assignment Problem Three - 3

As at December 31, 2002, the condensed Balance Sheets of Monson Ltd., Barrister Ltd., and Flex Ltd. are as follows:

Monson Ltd.
Condensed Balance Sheet
At December 31, 2002

	Book Values	Fair Values
Current Assets	$ 24,200	$ 25,000
Non-Current Assets	186,500	193,200
Total Assets	$210,700	
Liabilities	$ 78,400	$ 75,600
No Par Common Stock (11,000 Shares)	93,500	
Retained Earnings	38,800	
Total Equities	$210,700	

Barrister Ltd.
Condensed Balance Sheet
At December 31, 2002

	Book Values	Fair Values
Current Assets	$ 35,800	$ 34,500
Non-Current Assets	220,600	168,400
Total Assets	$256,400	
Liabilities	$ 56,300	$ 58,200
No Par Common Stock (5,500 Shares)	66,000	
Retained Earnings	134,100	
Total Equities	$256,400	

Flex Ltd.
Condensed Balance Sheet
At December 31, 2002

	Book Values	Fair Values
Current Assets	$ 46,300	$ 47,300
Non-Current Assets	152,200	156,600
Total Assets	$198,500	
Liabilities	$ 62,400	$ 59,800
No Par Common Stock (18,000 Shares)	45,000	
Retained Earnings	91,100	
Total Equities	$198,500	

The three companies intend to combine their activities and are considering a variety of approaches. Three possible approaches are as follows:

Approach One   Flex Ltd. would borrow $303,000. Using the loan proceeds, Flex Ltd. would pay cash of $160,000 to Monson Ltd. and cash of $143,000 to Barrister

Ltd., in return for all of the assets and liabilities of the two companies. There will be a wind up of the operations of both Monson Ltd. and Barrister Ltd.

Approach Two   Barrister Ltd. would borrow $326,000. Using the loan proceeds, Barrister Ltd. would pay cash of $170,000 to the shareholders of Monson Ltd. and cash of $156,000 to the shareholders of Flex Ltd., in return for all of the outstanding shares of these two companies.

Approach Three   Monson Ltd. will issue 11,000 new common shares to Barrister Ltd. and 11,000 new common shares to Flex Ltd. In return, Monson Ltd. will receive all of the assets and liabilities of the two companies. There would be a wind up of the activities of the two companies. At this time, the common stock of Monson Ltd. is trading at $13.50 per share. Neither Barrister Ltd. nor Flex Ltd. are given representation on the Monson Ltd. Board Of Directors.

Required: Prepare the December 31, 2002 Balance Sheet for the combined company that would result from each of the three approaches described.

Assignment Problem Three - 4

On December 31, 2002, Public Ltd. acquires all of the outstanding shares of Private Inc. The consideration consists of 100,000 Public Ltd. shares plus $1,200,000 in cash. At the time of issue, the Public Ltd. shares are trading at $10.50. As part of the acquisition contract, Public Ltd. agrees that, if by the end of 2003 their shares are not trading at a price of $12.00 or more, it will pay an additional $150,000 in cash to the former shareholders of Private Inc.

On December 31, 2002, the pre business combination Balance Sheets of the two Companies are as follows:

Public Ltd. and Private Inc.
Balance Sheets
As At December 31, 2002

	Public Ltd.	Private Inc.
Cash	$1,892,000	$ 342,000
Accounts Receivable	767,000	-0-
Inventories	1,606,000	641,000
Land	462,000	107,000
Plant And Equipment - Cost	3,272,000	2,727,000
Accumulated Depreciation	(1,203,000)	(776,000)
Patent	-0-	103,000
Goodwill	372,000	-0-
Total Assets	$7,168,000	$3,144,000
Current Liabilities	$ 458,000	$ -0-
Bonds Payable - Par	1,507,000	800,000
Bond Payable - Premium	48,000	23,000
Public Common Stock - No Par (250,000 Shares)	2,500,000	N/A
Private Common Stock - No Par	N/A	1,200,000
Retained Earnings	2,655,000	1,121,000
Total Equities	$7,168,000	$3,144,000

Other Information:

1.   The stock of Public Ltd. is traded on a national stock exchange. As a consequence, they are required to prepare audited financial statements. Private Inc. is a Canadian controlled private corporation and has never needed audited financial statements.

2. As there has been no need for Private Inc. to comply with generally accepted accounting principles (GAAP), the Company records revenues and current expenses on a cash basis. After some investigation, it is determined that on January 1, 2002, Private Inc. had unrecorded Accounts Receivable of $220,000 and unrecorded Accounts Payable of $273,000. The corresponding balances on December 31, 2002 are $326,000 for Accounts Receivable and $473,000 for Accounts Payable.

3. Public Ltd. records Inventories at lower of cost and market. Private Inc.'s Inventories are carried at cost. On December 31, 2002, the net realizable value of Private Inc.'s Inventories was $607,000.

4. On December 31, 2002, the appraised value of Private Inc.'s Land was $93,000.

5. The December 31, 2002 fair value of Private Inc.'s Plant And Equipment is $2,103,000.

6. The Patent on Private Inc.'s books was purchased on January 1, 1997 and is being amortized over what was expected to be its useful life, ten years. However, the process that is covered by the Patent has been replaced by a less costly procedure, and is no longer used by the Company. Private Inc. does not own any other intangible assets.

7. Private Inc.'s Bonds Payable were privately placed with a large Insurance Company. At current market rates of interest they have a present value of $790,000. However, they can only be retired by paying the Insurance Company a premium of 10 percent over their par value.

Required: Prepare the December 31, 2002 Balance Sheet for the combined companies Public Ltd. and its subsidiary, Private Inc. Your solution should comply with Sections 1581 and 3062 of the *CICA Handbook*.

Case Three - 1

The Haggard Corporation Limited (Haggard, hereafter), a federally chartered Canadian company, has concluded negotiations with the Jones Corporation Limited (Jones, hereafter) for the purchase of all of the latter corporation's assets at fair market value, effective January 1, 2002. Jones Corporation Limited operates a restaurant and a catering business.

An examination at that date by independent experts disclosed that the fair market value of Jones' inventories was $150,000, and of its machinery and equipment was $160,000. The original costs of the machinery and equipment was $140,000. It was determined that accounts receivable were fairly valued at book value.

Jones held 1,000 of the common shares of Haggard and the fair market value of these shares was $62,000. This value corresponds with the value of Haggard's common shares in the open market and would be expected to hold for transactions involving a substantially larger number of shares.

The purchase agreement provides that the total purchase price of all assets will be $490,000, payable as follows:

1. Assumption of the current liabilities of Jones at their book value;

2. Settlement of the Jones debenture debt at its current value in a form acceptable to Jones debenture holders;

3. Haggard shares held by Jones and acquired by Haggard as a result of the transaction would be subsequently returned to Jones at fair market value as part of the consideration;

4. Haggard holds 1,000 shares of Jones and these would be returned to Jones. The value to be ascribed to these shares is 1/10 of the difference between the total purchase price of all assets stated above ($490,000) less the current value of its liabilities.

5. The balance of the purchase consideration was to be entirely in Haggard common shares, except for a possible fractional share element which would be paid in cash.

The Jones debenture holders, who are neither shareholders of Haggard nor Jones, have agreed to accept Haggard bonds in an amount equal to the current value of the Jones debentures which are yielding 10 percent. The Haggard bonds carry a 12 percent coupon and trade at par. The face value of each bond is $1,000.

Any amounts assigned to goodwill in this business combination will be deductible for tax purposes as cumulative eligible capital up to a maximum of 75 percent.

Jones, upon conclusion of the agreement, would be wound up. The Balance Sheets of both corporations, as at the date of implementation of the purchase agreement (January 1, 2002), are as follows:

Balance Sheets
As At January 1, 2002

	Haggard	Jones
Cash	$ 100,000	$ -0-
Accounts Receivable	288,000	112,000
Inventories At Cost	250,000	124,000
Investment In Jones (1,000 Shares)	20,000	-0-
Investment In Haggard (1,000 Shares)	-0-	40,000
Machinery And Equipment - Net	412,000	100,000
Total Assets	$1,070,000	$376,000
Current Liabilities	$ 60,000	$ 35,000
7% Percent Debentures -		
Due December 31, 2006 (Note One)	-0-	100,000
12% Percent Bonds -		
Due December 31, 2006 (Note One)	500,000	-0-
Premium On Bonds	20,000	-0-
Common Stock (Note Two)	200,000	100,000
Retained Earnings	290,000	141,000
Total Equities	$1,070,000	$376,000

Note One   Interest is paid annually.

Note Two   Each company has issued 10,000 shares.

Both corporations have fiscal years that are identical to the calendar year.

The present value of an annuity of $1 for 5 periods at 10 percent is $3.7908. The present value of $1 to be received at the end of 5 periods at 10 percent is $.6209.

Required:

A. Prepare Haggard's pro-forma Balance Sheet as at January 1, 2002.

B. Draft a note to the 2002 financial statements disclosing the purchase of Jones' net assets.

C. Indicate how this purchase would be presented in Haggard's 2002 Cash Flow Statement.

D. Assume that Jones had a non-capital loss carry forward for tax purposes of $500,000. Should the form of the purchase of Jones differ? Explain your conclusion.

(CICA Adapted)

Case Three - 2

You have just started work as a management accountant with Aristotle Capital Corporation (ACC), a well capitalized, privately held holding company, with a wide variety of investment holdings in Canada. Your first project relates to the proposed acquisition of a significant interest in the common shares of General Chisel Limited (GCL).

GCL has recently gone public, and has shown rapid growth. Its operations include the Canadian manufacture of small hand tools as well as the importation of tools from several Pacific Rim countries. All products are packaged under the GCL label, a registered trademark, and sold to independent retailers and a number of smaller hardware chains.

Comparative draft financial statements for GCL for the years 2002 and 2003 are attached as Exhibit 1 and drafts of several of the notes to the financial statements are shown in Exhibit 2.

You have been asked to prepare a report for the acquisitions committee. Your objectives are to develop a list of potential problem areas and risks which may affect the proposed acquisition decision. Each of the items identified should be briefly analyzed.

Required: Based on the information provided, prepare a report for the acquisitions committee regarding GCL.

(SMA Adapted)

Exhibit 1
General Chisel Limited
Comparative Financial Statements

Draft Consolidated Balance Sheet
As At December 31
('000s)

	2003	2002
Current assets		
Cash	$ 1,075	$ 3,712
Accounts receivable	14,140	10,770
Inventories	22,543	17,125
Other	836	528
Current assets	$38,594	$32,135
Property, plant and equipment	12,834	11,515
Intangible assets	2,178	1,854
Other long-term assets	876	724
Total Assets	$54,482	$46,228
Current liabilities		
Bank debt	$ 4,705	$ 3,802
Accounts payable	9,013	7,697
Dividends payable	169	169
Current portion of long-term debt	3,355	2,067
Taxes payable	1,768	833
Current Liabilities	$19,010	$14,568
Long-term debt		
Mortgage and notes	$ 8,867	$ 6,466
Convertible debentures (8%)	6,000	6,000
Long Term Liabilities	$14,867	$12,466
Future Income Tax Liabilities	$ 1,568	$ 1,302
Shareholders' equity		
Common shares	$ 6,375	$ 6,270
Retained earnings	12,953	11,881
Cumulative translation loss	(291)	(259)
Shareholders' Equity	$19,037	$17,892
Total Equities	$54,482	$46,228

Draft Consolidated Income Statement
For The Year Ended December 31
('000s)

	2003	2002
Sales	$98,703	$76,021
Cost of goods sold and operating expenses	91,620	70,356
Operating income	$ 7,083	$ 5,665
Expenses:		
Depreciation	$ 1,614	$ 1,377
Amortization	184	102
Interest	1,734	1,619
Foreign currency gain	(33)	(92)
Expenses Other Than Operating	$ 3,499	$ 3,006
Earnings before tax	$ 3,584	$ 2,659
Income tax:		
Current	$ 1,526	$ 707
Future	309	511
Income Tax Expense	$ 1,835	$ 1,218
Net income	$ 1,749	$ 1,441
Earnings per share:		
Basic	$0.13	$0.11
Diluted	$0.11	$0.10

Draft Consolidated Statement Of Retained Earnings
For The Year Ended December 31
('000s)

	2003	2002
Opening balance as previously reported	$10,418	$ 9,828
Change in accounting policy (Note 2)	1,463	1,215
Opening balance as restated	$11,881	$11,043
Add: Net income	1,749	1,441
Balance Available For Dividends	$13,630	$12,484
Deduct: Dividends	677	603
Closing balance	$12,953	$11,881

Exhibit 2
General Chisel Limited
Excerpts From The Notes To The
Comparative Financial Statements

1. **Accounting Policies: Foreign Currency Translation**   All foreign operations are considered self-sustaining. Assets, liabilities, revenues and expenses are translated using the current rate method, in accordance with the recommendations of the *CICA Handbook*.

2. **Change in Accounting Policy**   During 2003, the company decided to change its method of revenue recognition for sales to new wholesale customers from the installment sales method to recognition of all revenue at the point of sale. The amounts reported reflect the cumulative effect on income of that change.

4. **Earnings per share**   These amounts are based on the weighted average common shares outstanding. Diluted earnings per share reflect the dilutive effect which would have resulted had all convertible securities been converted into common shares as of the beginning of the current year.

7. **Contingencies**   There are several outstanding claims and legal actions involving the company and its subsidiaries. In the opinion of management, the outcome of these matters should not have a material effect on the financial position of the company.

Chapter 4

Consolidated Balance Sheet At Acquisition

Introduction To Consolidations

The Objective Of Consolidation

4-1.   As noted in the previous Chapter, in some business combinations, the combining entities maintain their separate legal existence. This means that each of the companies will maintain a separate, single entity, set of books. However, since there has been a business combination, it is necessary to prepare a combined set of financial statements to present to the investors in the acquiring or parent company. This follows from the view that when two or more companies are being operated as a single economic entity, the accounting records should reflect that fact. Consolidated financial statements are designed to accomplish that goal. The objective in preparing consolidated financial statements is to account for the parent and its subsidiaries as if they were a single economic entity. This form of accounting will essentially ignore the separate legal existence of these combined companies.

Consolidated Financial Statements And User Needs

4-2.   General purpose financial statements find their way into the hands of a wide variety of users. Investors, creditors, government organizations and consumer interest groups would constitute only a partial list of the individuals and organizations that are interested in the external financial reports of Canadian business organizations. Because consolidated financial statements do not reflect the activities of a real legal entity, users of such statements should have a clear understanding of the limits that this situation places on the usefulness of these statements. As was implied in the preceding paragraph, consolidated financial statements are prepared primarily to meet the needs of the shareholders of the parent or acquiring company. There are other groups that have some interest in one or more of the combining companies. For the most part, however, these groups will not receive a significant benefit from consolidated financial statements.

4-3.   Consolidated financial statements are of primary interest to the group which is in a position to control the consolidated entity, the majority shareholders of the parent company. The legal position of other interested parties is as follows:

Creditors Since the consolidated entity has no status as a legal entity, it cannot have creditors. The liabilities that are disclosed in the consolidated Balance Sheet are those of the individual legal entities (parent and subsidiary companies) and creditor claims must be satisfied out of the assets of these legal entities. This conclusion may be modified by the presence of intercompany guarantees on debt obligations.

Taxation Authorities In Canada, there is no legal basis for filing a consolidated tax return. The parent and each of its subsidiaries must file separate tax returns and the consolidated financial statements are essentially ignored by the taxation authorities. Since the *CICA Handbook* requires income tax allocation, this means that consolidated income will generally be different than the aggregate taxable income of the combined companies. This situation is given detailed consideration in Chapter 12.

Non-Controlling Shareholders If there are non-controlling shareholders in one or more of the subsidiary companies, their primary interest will be in the single entity statements of the subsidiary. They have no real way in which to participate in the operating results of the combined company.

4-4. The position of other potentially interested groups could be analyzed in a similar manner.

Consolidation Policy

4-5. Most published consolidated financial statements provide a note regarding consolidation policy (i.e., which investees are included in the consolidated financial statements). Since the objective of consolidation is to treat a group of legally separate companies that are being operated as a single entity as a single accounting entity, consolidation would be conceptually appropriate for investees where the investor has control, has the right and ability to obtain future economic benefits from the resources of the enterprise, and is exposed to related risks. As noted in Chapter 2, investees that fit this description are called subsidiaries and this means that consolidation is only appropriate for those investees that can be classified as subsidiaries.

4-6. Despite the fact that companies have no real alternatives with respect to the consolidation of subsidiaries, it remains common to have the basis of consolidation discussed in the Statement Of Accounting Policies. In the survey of the 2000 annual reports of 200 companies in the 2001 edition of *Financial Reporting In Canada*, 191 of these companies discussed their basis of consolidation in their Statement of Accounting Policies. This discussion usually includes a listing of the principal subsidiaries, with the percentage of ownership.

4-7. A fairly typical example of such disclosure, taken from the 2000 annual report of Cogeco Inc., is as follows:

Note 1 Significant Accounting Policies (in part)

Consolidation Principles

The consolidated financial statements include the accounts of the Company and its subsidiaries. Business acquisitions are accounted for under the purchase method and operating results are included in the consolidated financial statements as of the date of the acquisition of control. Other investments are recorded at cost, except for an investment of 20% in a general partnership, Canal Indigo, and an investment of 49% in Stornaway Productions Inc., by Cogeco Radio-Television Inc., which are accounted for under the equity method.

Business segments and percentage in interest of the main subsidiaries are as follows:

Segment	Principal subsidiary	Percentage of Interest
Cable	Cogeco Cable Inc.	46.7% (90% of voting rights)
Media	Cogeco Radio-Television Inc.	100% (100% of voting rights)

A Note On Terminology

4-8.   When a parent company owns less than 100 percent of the outstanding shares of a subsidiary, disclosure will have to be given to the interests of shareholders other than the parent company. At one point in time, subsidiaries were defined in terms of majority ownership and, as a consequence, it was always appropriate to refer to the interests of non-controlling shareholders as a minority interest.

4-9.   With the 1991 change in the definition of a subsidiary, it is now possible for a parent's control to be based on less than a majority of the voting shares of that subsidiary. This means that there can be situations in which the non-controlling interest is not, in fact, a minority interest. Reflecting this possibility, all of the *CICA Handbook* references consistently use the term "Non-Controlling Interest".

4-10.   While practice has been slow to change, there is a clear trend towards the use of the term Non-Controlling Interest. Referring to statistics on 200 companies collected in *Financial Reporting in Canada*, in 1995, 74 companies provided disclosure of this interest in their Income Statement, with 39 using the term Minority Interest and only 19 using the term Non-Controlling Interest. In 2000, 83 companies provided disclosure of this interest, with 39 using the term Non-Controlling Interest and 32 using the term Minority Interest.

4-11.   In keeping with both the *CICA Handbook* references and the trend in practice, we will use the term Non-Controlling Interest throughout the remainder of this text. Note, however, that in almost all of our examples, the controlling interest is also the majority interest. This means that the term Minority Interest could appropriately be substituted for our use of the term Non-Controlling Interest.

Conceptual Alternatives In Consolidation

Basis For Alternatives

4-12.   When consolidated financial statements are being prepared with subsidiaries in which the parent company has 100 percent ownership of the outstanding shares, there is no controversy as to the procedures that are to be used. However, the presence of less than 100 percent ownership introduces non-controlling shareholders into the consolidation process. As there are a variety of views as to the nature of the relationship between the non-controlling shareholders and the consolidated entity, it follows that there are several ways in which this group's interest in the consolidated net income and net assets could be dealt with.

4-13.   The literature on consolidations generally makes reference to three different views of the nature of the non-controlling interest and, correspondingly, presents three conceptual alternatives in the preparation of consolidated financial statements. These three approaches are normally referred to as the entity approach, the proprietary approach, and the parent company approach. You should note that what is referred to here as the proprietary conceptual approach is, in fact, the basis for proportionate consolidation procedures. As noted previously, proportionate consolidation is the required method for dealing with joint ventures.

4-14.   For a variety of reasons, we believe that you should have some understanding of these three conceptual alternatives. The reasons for this view include:

- An understanding of these conceptual alternatives will enhance your ability to understand the specific procedures that are required in Canada.

- An understanding of these conceptual alternatives will allow you to evaluate proposed changes that are likely to take place in this area.

- Canadian consolidation requirements do not adopt a consistent conceptual approach. An understanding of the available alternatives will facilitate your understanding of the inconsistencies found in current CICA Recommendations.

4-15.   This Chapter will provide you with a description of the view of the non-controlling interest that is inherent in each of the three conceptual alternatives. This will be followed by a description of the consolidation procedures that would be consistent with the view of the non-controlling interest that is inherent in each of the alternatives. A simple example will be used to illustrate the alternatives as they apply to the valuation of subsidiary assets.

4-16.   When the three alternatives have been described, the associated procedures listed, and asset valuation procedures illustrated, there will be an evaluation of the three different concepts. Subsequent to this evaluation will be a summary of the procedures that have been adopted in Section 1600 of the *CICA Handbook*. This additional listing is necessitated by the fact that Section 1600 does not consistently recommend a single conceptual alternative.

4-17.   In reviewing the procedures that are listed under each conceptual alternative, do not be disturbed if you do not fully understand what is being described. They are listed at this point only to give you an overall picture of the relevant conceptual alternatives. You may, however, wish to return to these lists periodically as you develop a more complete understanding of specific consolidation procedures. We will return to the list of Section 1600 Recommendations at the end of Chapter 6, after we have completed our survey of basic consolidation procedures. At that point, you should have a full understanding of the consolidation procedures that are required in Canada.

The Entity Concept
Nature Of The Entity Concept
4-18.   This conceptual approach to consolidation is based on the view that the non-controlling shareholders are simply part of another class of residual ownership interest and they differ from the controlling shareholders only in the size of their holdings. We have found it helpful to think of the non-controlling interest under the entity concept as being analogous to the position of preferred shareholders in a non-consolidated situation. That is, the non-controlling interest is still clearly part of the residual equity of the business even though its claim may differ somewhat from that of the majority or controlling shareholders.

Associated Procedures
4-19.   The following procedures and disclosure would be consistent with the adoption of the entity concept of the nature of the non-controlling interest:

Asset Valuation   Both the parent's and the non-controlling interest's share of the fair values, as determined at the acquisition date, of the subsidiary's net identifiable assets would be recorded on the consolidated Balance Sheet. The same would be true for any goodwill that is being recognized as part of the business combination transaction.

Non-Controlling Interest In The Balance Sheet

- **Disclosure**   The Non-Controlling Interest would be a component of total shareholders' equity.

- **Calculation**   The Non-Controlling Interest in the consolidated Balance Sheet would consist of its proportionate share of the fair values of the subsidiary's net identifiable assets and goodwill, adjusted for all of the same factors that require adjustments to be made to the majority interest. These factors would include amortization of fair value changes, recognition of goodwill impairment, and the elimination of all of the unrealized intercompany profits of the subsidiary company.

Non-Controlling Interest In The Income Statement

- **Disclosure**   Since the non-controlling shareholders are viewed as a residual ownership interest, their proportionate share of subsidiary income would not be deducted in the computation of consolidated net income. Rather, their share would be viewed as a distribution of income in the consolidated Statement Of Retained Earnings. Note the similarity of the treatment given to the non-controlling shareholders to that given to preferred shareholders in non consolidated situations. The income applicable to both groups would be disclosed as a distribution of income in the Statement Of Retained Earnings, not as a determinant of net income.

- **Calculation** The Non-Controlling Interest in the consolidated Income Statement would consist of its proportionate share of the reported income of the subsidiary, adjusted for all of the same factors that require adjustments to be made to the parent's share. These factors would include the current charge for amortization of fair value changes, recognition of goodwill impairment, the elimination of current subsidiary intercompany profits that are still unrealized from the consolidated point of view, and the addition of subsidiary intercompany profits from previous years that have become realized for consolidation purposes during the current year.

Unrealized Intercompany Profits Of The Subsidiary The entity concept's view that the non-controlling shareholders occupy a residual ownership position would mean that both the parent's and the non-controlling interest's share of unrealized intercompany profits of the subsidiary be treated in a similar fashion. This would require the elimination of all such subsidiary profits with the amounts being charged proportionately to the parent and the non-controlling interest. This approach is sometimes referred to as 100 percent pro rata elimination of unrealized intercompany profits of the subsidiary company.

Asset Valuation Illustrated
4-20.   The only consolidation procedure that is relevant to this Chapter's subject of the consolidated Balance Sheet at acquisition is asset valuation. A simple example will be used to illustrate asset valuation procedures under the three conceptual alternatives:

Example Acker Inc. acquires 60 percent of Bloom Ltd. Acker has Land with a carrying value of $2,300,000. At the time of acquisition, Bloom has Land with a carrying value of $400,000 and a fair value of $450,000.

4-21.   Under the entity approach, the value for Land that would be included in the consolidated Balance Sheet would be calculated as follows:

Acker Inc. - Carrying Value	$2,300,000
Bloom Ltd. - 100 Percent Of Fair Value	450,000
Consolidated Land	$2,750,000

The Proprietary Concept
Nature Of The Proprietary Concept
4-22.   This conceptual approach is based on the view that the non-controlling shareholders are complete outsiders to the consolidated entity. Their interest in the subsidiary's assets, liabilities, expenses, and revenues would not even be considered in the preparation of consolidated financial statements. Stated another way, the proprietary approach is based on the somewhat legalistic view that, with respect to the subsidiary's assets, liabilities, expenses, and revenues, the consolidated entity includes only the parent company's proportionate share of these balances.

Associated Procedures
4-23.   The following procedures and disclosure would be consistent with the adoption of the proprietary concept of the nature of the non-controlling interest:

Asset Valuation Only the majority share of fair values, as determined at the acquisition date, of the subsidiary's net identifiable assets and goodwill would be recorded in the consolidated Balance Sheet.

Non-Controlling Interest In The Balance Sheet Since the proprietary approach excludes the non-controlling interest's share of the subsidiary's net identifiable assets from the consolidated balances, no Non-Controlling Interest would be included in the consolidated Balance Sheet.

Non-Controlling Interest In The Income Statement As this approach excludes the non-controlling interest's share of the subsidiary's expenses and revenues from the consolidated balances, no Non-Controlling Interest would be disclosed in the consolidated Income Statement.

Unrealized Intercompany Profits Of The Subsidiary As the proprietary approach does not include the non-controlling interest's share of any of the subsidiary balances in the consolidated account balances, it would only be necessary to eliminate the parent's share of the subsidiary's unrealized intercompany profits. This is sometimes referred to as fractional elimination of unrealized intercompany profits of the subsidiary.

Asset Valuation Illustrated

4-24. The same example that was used to illustrate the entity approach to asset valuation will be used here. It is repeated for your convenience:

Example Acker Inc. acquires 60 percent of Bloom Ltd. Acker has Land with a carrying value of $2,300,000. At the time of acquisition, Bloom has Land with a carrying value of $400,000 and a fair value of $450,000.

4-25. Under the proprietary approach, the value for Land that would be included in the consolidated Balance Sheet would be calculated as follows:

Acker Inc. - Carrying Value	$2,300,000
Bloom Ltd. - 60 Percent of $450,000 Fair Value	270,000
Consolidated Land	$2,570,000

The Parent Company Concept

Nature Of The Parent Company Concept

4-26. Like the entity approach, the parent company approach takes the view that the non-controlling interest's share of assets, liabilities, expenses, and revenues are a part of the consolidated economic entity. The difference from the entity approach is that the non-controlling participation is perceived as being a fixed, creditor-like claim. This would lead to the conclusion that the non-controlling interest will not be affected by any of the adjustments or eliminations that are required by the parent in the preparation of consolidated financial statements. In other words, the non-controlling shareholders participate in the net assets and results of operations of the consolidated entity, but only to the extent of the book values from the single entity financial statements of the subsidiary.

Associated Procedures

4-27. The following procedures and disclosure would be consistent with the adoption of the parent company concept of the nature of the non-controlling interest:

Asset Valuation The consolidated net identifiable assets would include 100 percent of the subsidiary's carrying values but only the parent's share of any fair value changes and/or goodwill that was present at the acquisition date.

Non-Controlling Interest In The Balance Sheet

- **Disclosure** As the parent company approach views the Non-Controlling Interest as an outside interest analogous to creditors in non consolidated statements, it would follow that the Non-Controlling Interest would be grouped with long-term liabilities in the consolidated Balance Sheet.

- **Calculation** The Non-Controlling Interest in the consolidated Balance Sheet would be based on the non-controlling shareholders' proportionate share of the carrying values of the net identifiable assets of the subsidiary company. As this interest is viewed as a fixed or creditor like claim, no adjustments to the single entity records of the subsidiary would be required in the determination of the Non-Controlling Interest that would be disclosed in the consolidated Balance Sheet.

Non-Controlling Interest In The Income Statement

- **Disclosure**   As this approach views the non-controlling shareholders as an outside interest similar to creditors, the Non-Controlling Interest would be treated in the same manner as interest charges. That is, it would be deducted in the computation of consolidated Net Income. Note that it would be deducted as a single figure, not from the individual expenses and revenues as in the proprietary approach.

- **Calculation**   The Non-Controlling Interest in the consolidated Income Statement would be based on the non-controlling shareholders' proportionate share of the reported net income of the subsidiary company. As this interest is viewed as a fixed or creditor like claim, no adjustments to the single entity records of the subsidiary would be required in the determination of the Non-Controlling Interest in the consolidated Income Statement.

Unrealized Intercompany Profits Of The Subsidiary   As the parent company approach views the Non-Controlling Interest as an outside claim that is based on the single entity records of the subsidiary, the non-controlling interest's share of subsidiary unrealized intercompany profits would not be eliminated. In other words, only the parent's share of the subsidiary's unrealized intercompany profits would be eliminated. This is referred to as fractional elimination.

Asset Valuation Illustrated

4-28.   The same example that was used to illustrate the entity and proprietary approaches to asset valuation will be used here. The example is repeated for your convenience:

Example   Acker Inc. acquires 60 percent of Bloom Ltd. Acker has Land with a carrying value of $2,300,000. At the time of acquisition, Bloom has Land with a carrying value of $400,000 and a fair value of $450,000.

4-29.   One way in which the required consolidated Land value could be calculated under the parent company approach is as follows:

Acker Inc. - Carrying Value	$2,300,000
Bloom Ltd.:	
40 Percent Of Carrying Value ($400,000)	160,000
60 Percent Of Fair Value ($450,000)	270,000
Consolidated Land	$2,730,000

4-30.   While the preceding calculation reflects the concept underlying the parent company approach (i.e., assets valued at the non-controlling interest's share of carrying value and the parent's share of fair value), an alternative calculation is often more convenient to use. This alternative approach starts with 100 percent of the subsidiary's carrying value. This amount is then increased or decreased for the parent company's share of any fair value change. This alternative calculation is as follows:

Acker Inc. - Carrying Value		$2,300,000
Bloom Ltd.:		
100 Percent Of Carrying Value	$400,000	
[(60%)($450,000 - $400,000)]	30,000	430,000
Consolidated Land		$2,730,000

Exercise Four-1 deals with the valuation of consolidated assets under the three conceptual alternatives.

Exercise Four-1

On December 31, 2002, Placard Ltd. acquires 75 percent of the outstanding voting shares of Sign Inc. At that time, Placard has Plant and Equipment that cost $2,500,000 and has Accumulated Amortization of $1,000,000. Sign's Plant and Equipment cost $700,000, has Accumulated Amortization of $300,000, and a fair value of $520,000.

Required: Determine the value that would be shown as consolidated Plant and Equipment (Net) for Placard and its subsidiary Sign as of December 31, 2002 under:

A.   the entity conceptual approach;
B.   the proprietary conceptual approach; and
C.   the parent company conceptual approach.

End Of Exercise Four-1

Evaluation Of The Conceptual Alternatives
Proprietary Concept
4-31.   The preceding paragraphs have provided you with a general description of the procedures and disclosure that would be required under the three major conceptual alternatives in the preparation of consolidated financial statements. With respect to the proprietary approach, there is little support for this concept as a general solution to the problem of preparing consolidated financial statements. It is not difficult to understand the reason for this. The objective that is being satisfied in the preparation of consolidated financial statements is the portrayal of the financial position and the results of operations of the parent and its various subsidiaries as if they were a single economic entity. This is based on the assumption that all of the net assets of the entire group of affiliated companies is under the control of the parent company's management. It is not some legalistically determined fraction of subsidiary net assets that is under common control, it is 100 percent of such assets. In view of this fact, the proprietary concept's procedures, which only include the parent company's share of the subsidiary's assets, liabilities, expenses, and revenues in the consolidated financial statements, does not seem to be an appropriate solution. An exception to this would be its application as the proportionate consolidation method used in accounting for joint ventures.

Parent Company Concept
4-32.   If the proprietary concept is rejected as a general solution to the problem of preparing consolidated financial statements, one is left with a choice between the parent company concept and the entity concept. Both of these concepts are the same in that they see the non-controlling shareholders as having an interest in the net assets and income of the consolidated entity. The difference is their divergent views on the nature of that interest. As a consequence, the choice between the procedures and disclosures inherent in the two methods should be based on an analysis of the nature of the claims of the non-controlling shareholders.

4-33.   The parent company concept views the interest of the non-controlling shareholders as being a creditor like interest. For this to be a reasonable position, the non-controlling shareholders would possess rights similar to those which are associated with other creditor claims. The rights that we normally associate with creditor claims are (1) a contractually specified claim to income, (2) a contractually specified claim to principal and (3) the right to receive this principal sum on a contractually specified future date. It is clear that the relationship of the non-controlling shareholders to the consolidated entity does not have any of these characteristics. Given this fact, it is difficult to support the parent company concept.

Entity Concept
4-34.   In our opinion, the non-controlling shareholders have a claim that is best described as a residual equity position. The shares held by this group do not mature, they do not promise any specified return, nor do they purport to return to the investor any specified principal

amount under any circumstances that might be encountered by the firm. These characteristics describe an equity relationship and they describe the position of the non-controlling shareholders. This leads us to the conclusion that the entity concept and its associated procedures and disclosures is the most appropriate approach to the preparation of consolidated financial statements.

The Conceptual Approach Of Section 1600

4-35. The preceding paragraph presents a case for the adoption of the entity concept in the preparation of consolidated financial statements. We believe that Section 1600 of the *CICA Handbook* should have adopted this approach in its entirety. If it was decided that one of the other concepts was a better alternative, we would have hoped that the recommendations would have applied the concept in a consistent manner. Unfortunately, this did not happen. In one area or another of Section 1600, we find examples of all of the previously described conceptual approaches. These inconsistencies are one of the major sources of difficulty in the process of learning to prepare consolidated financial statements. As an initial step towards helping you deal with this difficulty, the following paragraph provides a summary list of the approaches that were adopted with respect to each of the major issues in the preparation of consolidated financial statements. In this and subsequent Chapters, we will provide detailed illustrations of all the procedures described in this list.

4-36. The following procedures reflect the recommendations of the *CICA Handbook* with respect to the preparation of consolidated financial statements:

Asset Valuation The recommended approach to asset valuation is the parent company concept. That is, only the parent's share of any fair value changes and goodwill is recognized at the time of acquisition or combination. As a consequence, only the parent's share of the amortization of these values or recognition of their impairment is recorded in subsequent periods.

Non-Controlling Interest In The Balance Sheet

- **Disclosure** Section 1600 is not explicit on this issue. It simply states that the Non-Controlling Interest in the consolidated net assets of the subsidiary companies should be shown separately from shareholders' equity. This eliminates the entity approach and the fact that a non-controlling interest is present eliminates the proprietary approach. This seems to leave the parent company approach. However, in the absence of a clear statement that the Non-Controlling Interest should be disclosed as a part of long-term liabilities, it often ends up presented in a somewhat ambiguous fashion between the long-term liabilities and the consolidated shareholders' equity.

- **Calculation** The inconsistencies of Section 1600 become apparent in the calculation of the Non-Controlling Interest on the Balance Sheet. In general, this computation follows the parent company approach and bases the Non-Controlling Interest on the non-controlling shareholders' proportionate share of the carrying values of the subsidiary. However, because the entity approach is used for the elimination of unrealized subsidiary profits, these transactions must be taken into account in determining the appropriate balance. Stated generally, the Non-Controlling Interest in the consolidated Balance Sheet would be computed by taking the non-controlling shareholders' proportionate interest in the net book value of the subsidiary's assets after they have been adjusted for any unrealized intercompany profits of the subsidiary company.

Non-Controlling Interest In The Income Statement

- **Disclosure** With respect to income before extraordinary items and the results of discontinued operations, Section 1600 requires that Non-Controlling Interest be given disclosure as a separate line item in the consolidated Income Statement. This, of course, reflects an adoption of the parent company approach. For no apparent reason, extraordinary items and the results of discontinued operations are dealt with by a different conceptual alternative. Only the parent company's proportionate interest in these items is disclosed which is an application of the proprietary concept.

- **Calculation** As was the case with the computation of the Non-Controlling Interest for purposes of disclosure in the consolidated Balance Sheet, the computation here is complicated by the presence of inconsistencies in the Recommendations of Section 1600. Generally, the Non-Controlling Interest in the consolidated Income Statement is based on the reported income of the subsidiary. Once again, however, adjustments must be made for the adoption of the entity approach in dealing with unrealized subsidiary profits. Stated generally, the Non-Controlling Interest in the consolidated Income Statement is calculated by taking the non-controlling shareholders' proportionate interest in the reported income of the subsidiary with the elimination of current subsidiary intercompany profits that are still unrealized from the consolidated point of view and the addition of subsidiary intercompany profits from previous years that have become realized for consolidation purposes during the year.

Unrealized Intercompany Profits Of The Subsidiary As already noted, Section 1600 adopts the entity approach here and requires 100 percent pro rata elimination of unrealized intercompany subsidiary profits.

Conceptual Alternatives In Text Material
Chapter 4
4-37. Conceptual alternatives are relevant to the material in this Chapter only with respect to the procedures used for the valuation of consolidated assets and the disclosure of the Non-Controlling Interest in the consolidated Balance Sheet. In our discussion of the three conceptual alternatives, we used a simple example to illustrate the alternative procedures with respect to the valuation of consolidated assets. As a consequence, we will not give further attention to that issue in this Chapter. We will, however, give some further attention to disclosure of the Non-Controlling Interest in the consolidated Balance Sheet.

4-38. This means that, in the remainder of this Chapter, the consolidation procedures that will be developed are based on the parent company approach to asset valuation. That is, the values recorded in the consolidated financial statements for the various assets and liabilities of the subsidiary will include the parent's share of their fair values, plus the non-controlling interest's share of their book values. As was noted, this is the approach to the valuation of consolidated assets that is required by the Recommendations of the *CICA Handbook*.

Chapters 5 And 6
4-39. Chapter 5 will contain a brief example of the income statement disclosure associated with the three conceptual alternatives. Correspondingly, Chapter 6 will use an example to illustrate the alternative approaches to dealing with unrealized intercompany profits. The remainder of these Chapters will focus on the consolidation procedures that are required by the Recommendations of the *CICA Handbook*.

A Procedural Approach To Preparing Consolidated Financial Statements

Use Of Worksheets
4-40. With the preceding survey of the conceptual alternatives completed, we can now turn our attention to the development of a procedural approach to the preparation of consolidated financial statements. Some textbooks rely on the use of a worksheet as the basis for the development of consolidation procedures. Under this approach, the various Income Statement and Balance Sheet accounts are listed in the first columns of the work sheet, followed by columns for adjustments, eliminations, Non-Controlling Interest, consolidated Balance Sheet, and consolidated Income Statement.

4-41.   While this may be justified by the complex situations encountered in practice, it has very little utility to the student preparing for university or professional examinations. In the context of an examination situation, the mere preparation of the worksheet format would absorb most of the time available for completing a consolidation problem. This would be unfortunate in that preparing the worksheet format is basically a copying process and it would generally not provide even a partial contribution to the total marks allocated to the question.

4-42.   Perhaps of even greater importance is the fact that we have consistently found that students whose only exposure to consolidations is through the use of a worksheet do not usually achieve a level of understanding that extends beyond the procedures that are involved in this type of process. They very quickly learn to fill in the appropriate boxes as required by this mechanical approach. However, if they are asked, for example, to determine or explain consolidated Net Income, they might not be able to provide this information. This means that, unless a consolidation problem is presented in worksheet form, students can have difficulty solving it. This is further complicated in that there are alternative worksheet formats and the ability to manipulate one does not guarantee an ability to deal with alternative formats.

4-43.   As a consequence of these factors, we do not cover the worksheet approach to the preparation of consolidated financial statements in this material.

Direct Definitional Calculations And Journal Entries

4-44.   If you have a thorough understanding of the consolidation process, the most efficient method of preparing consolidated financial statements is to be in a position to make an independent computation of each of the consolidated account balances. However, it would be very difficult to teach this type of approach directly and, as a reflection of this fact, we will develop a set of procedures using journal entries to adjust the existing account balances. These journal entries will be added to or subtracted from the account balances given in the problem in order to arrive at the correct balances for inclusion in the consolidated financial statements.

4-45.   Two points should be made with respect to these journal entries. First, we view them largely as an interim teaching device. We encourage you to discontinue using them as soon as you feel that you understand the concepts well enough to make direct computations of the balances that are required for inclusion in the consolidated financial statements.

4-46.   This is of particular importance when you are preparing to write examinations on this material. In this context, you will generally not have sufficient time to work through all of the journal entries that are required in a comprehensive, multi-statement consolidation problem. As grading marks are usually allocated to the required financial statements, it is essential that you focus on their preparation, rather than spending valuable time writing out a long series of journal entries.

4-47.   To the extent that you continue using journal entries, a second point relates to the nature of the journal entries that are being made. They are only working paper entries and are not recorded in the single entity records of either the parent or subsidiary companies (there would be some exceptions to this if push-down accounting is used). It is particularly important to keep this fact in mind when dealing with consolidation subsequent to acquisition. You must recognize that any entries that were made in preparing the 2002 consolidated financial statements were not entered in the accounts and, to the extent that are still applicable, they will have to be repeated in preparing the 2003 statements.

General Approach Outlined

4-48.   Anticipating the material which follows, our procedures will use three Steps in the development of consolidation procedures. These will be referred to as Steps A, B, and C, and they can be described as follows:

Step A   This Step will involve the elimination of the investment account against the subsidiary shareholders' equity at the time of acquisition. Also included in this Step will be the establishment of the Non-Controlling Interest for the Balance Sheet at acquisition, as well as the allocation of the excess of the investment cost over the carrying values of the assets acquired to the various fair value changes and goodwill that have been established by the purchase price. The procedures involved in this Step are given complete coverage in this Chapter.

Step B   This Step involves a number of adjustments and eliminations for such things as intercompany assets and liabilities, recognition of goodwill impairment losses, intercompany expenses and revenues, and the elimination of unrealized intercompany profits. As these adjustments and eliminations are only required in periods subsequent to acquisition, they will be dealt with in Chapters 5 and 6.

Step C   This final Step will allocate any remaining balance in the Retained Earnings of the subsidiary between the Non-Controlling Interest in the consolidated Balance Sheet and the consolidated Retained Earnings. As was the case with the Step B procedures, the Step C procedures are only required in periods subsequent to acquisition. This means that the Step C procedures will also be dealt with in Chapters 5 and 6.

Consolidated Balance Sheet At Acquisition

Consolidations And Business Combinations

4-49.   While we have made this point several times before, we would like to remind you again that, in all cases where a parent has acquired control over a subsidiary, a business combination transaction has occurred. As with business combinations that use other legal forms, combinations involving the acquisition of the shares must be accounted for by the purchase method. As a consequence, all of the consolidation examples in this and following Chapters, you should keep in mind that the purchase method procedures are applicable to the preparation of the required consolidated financial statements.

4-50.   In Chapter 3 we discussed that one of the features of the purchase method is that the identifiable assets and liabilities of the acquiree must be recorded at fair values. In the great majority of subsidiary acquisitions, the parent is the acquirer and the subsidiary is the acquiree. As a consequence, the fair values of the identifiable assets and liabilities of the subsidiary must be determined and recorded in the consolidated financial statements. In addition, if the investment cost (purchase price) exceeds the parent's share of these fair values, goodwill must also be recorded in the consolidated financial statements. This feature of the purchase method of accounting will be reflected in the development of procedures to be used in preparing a consolidated Balance Sheet at acquisition.

Examples To Be Used

4-51.   The least complex type of consolidation problem involves the preparation of a consolidated Balance Sheet as at the date of acquisition. The presentation of the procedures required to prepare a consolidated Balance Sheet as at the date of acquisition will use four examples. They can be briefly described as follows:

Example One   This very simple example will have the parent company owning 100 percent of the subsidiary company's shares with the investment cost equal to book value and no fair value changes or goodwill present.

Example Two   This will also involve 100 percent ownership. However, the investment cost will differ from book value. This differential will be allocated to fair value changes and goodwill.

Example Three   We will return to our first assumption of the investment cost being equal to book value with no fair value changes. However, the investor's proportionate share of the subsidiary's shares will be less than 100 percent.

Example Four   The final example will involve less than 100 percent ownership of the subsidiary's outstanding shares and will also incorporate fair value changes and a differential between cost and book value.

Example One -
100 Percent Ownership With No Fair Value Changes
Example
4-52.   In this Example, the parent will own 100 percent of the outstanding shares of the subsidiary. There are no fair value changes on any of the subsidiary's identifiable assets or liabilities and the investment cost will be equal to book value.

On December 31, 2002, the Pert Company purchases 100 percent of the outstanding voting shares of the Sert Company for $5 million in cash. On that date, subsequent to the business combination transaction, the Balance Sheets of the two companies are as follows:

Pert and Sert Companies
Balance Sheets
As At December 31, 2002

	Pert	Sert
Cash	$ 800,000	$ 500,000
Accounts Receivable	1,500,000	1,100,000
Inventories	3,400,000	2,500,000
Investment In Sert	5,000,000	-0-
Plant And Equipment (Net)	6,300,000	3,900,000
Total Assets	$17,000,000	$8,000,000
Current Liabilities	$ 800,000	$1,000,000
Long-Term Liabilities	2,200,000	2,000,000
No Par Common Stock	8,000,000	2,000,000
Retained Earnings	6,000,000	3,000,000
Total Equities	$17,000,000	$8,000,000

Other Information:

1.   All of the net identifiable assets of the Sert Company have fair values that are equal to the carrying values that are presented in the preceding Balance Sheet.

2.   During 2002, the Sert Company sold merchandise to the Pert Company for $100,000 and recognized a gross profit on these sales of $40,000. On December 31, 2002, one half of this merchandise remains in the inventories of the Pert Company.

3.   On December 31, 2002, the Pert Company owes the Sert Company $25,000 on open account for merchandise purchased during the year.

Required: Prepare a consolidated Balance Sheet for the Pert Company and its subsidiary, the Sert Company, as at December 31, 2002.

Procedures
4-53.   In somewhat simplified terms, preparation of the consolidated Balance Sheet at acquisition involves adding together all of the assets and equities of the parent and subsidiary companies. However, special procedures are required for certain of these balances. Specifically, these procedures relate to the Pert Company's Investment In Sert account and to the Sert Company's shareholders' equity. In addition, in this example it is also necessary to deal with the intercompany receivable and the intercompany profit.

Investment In Sert
4-54.   The Investment In Sert account on the books of the Pert Company reflects the ownership of the net identifiable assets of the Sert Company. Since in preparing consolidated financial statements we are trying to show the two companies as if they were a single

economic entity, the net identifiable assets of the Sert Company will be included in the consolidated net identifiable assets. If, in addition, we include the Investment In Sert account, we will be counting these net identifiable assets twice. Therefore, it will always be necessary to eliminate 100 percent of the investment account. This will remain the case under our procedures even as the problems become more complex and begin to deal with preparing consolidated financial statements subsequent to acquisition.

Subsidiary Shareholders' Equity

4-55. From the point of view of the consolidated entity, the Sert Company has no shares outstanding. That is, no individual or organization outside of the consolidated entity is holding any of the common shares of the Sert Company. This would mean that in the consolidated financial statements, any Contributed Capital of Sert that is present at the time of acquisition should be eliminated. With respect to Retained Earnings, the purchase method of accounting only includes the income of the acquiree from the date of acquisition forward. As a consequence, none of the Retained Earnings of an acquired company that is present at the time of acquisition would be included in the combined or consolidated company's Retained Earnings. This is reflected in the following *CICA Handbook* Recommendation:

> **Paragraph 1600.22** *The retained earnings or deficit of a subsidiary company at the date(s) of acquisition by the parent should not be included in consolidated retained earnings.* (April, 1975)

4-56. This would necessitate the elimination of any subsidiary Retained Earnings that are present at the time of acquisition. As a general conclusion, it follows that we will always eliminate 100 percent of the subsidiary shareholders' equity at acquisition. Under the procedures that we are developing, this will remain the case even as the problems become more complex and deal with fractional ownership and consolidation subsequent to the date of acquisition.

Elimination Entry

4-57. In the preceding paragraphs, we have developed our first two procedures for preparing consolidated financial statements. As these two procedures are a part of Step A in our general approach to preparing consolidated financial statements, we will designate these procedures as Step A-1 and A-2, respectively.

> **Step A-1 Procedure** Always eliminate 100 percent of the Investment In Subsidiary account.

> **Step A-2 Procedure** Always eliminate 100 percent of all the balances in the subsidiary's shareholders' equity that are present on the acquisition date.

4-58. The journal entry required to carry out these two Steps is as follows:

No Par Common Stock (Sert)	$2,000,000	
Retained Earnings (Sert)	3,000,000	
Investment In Sert		$5,000,000

Intercompany Asset And Liability

4-59. In preparing consolidated financial statements, the Pert Company and the Sert Company are viewed as constituting a single economic entity. From this point of view, any intercompany asset and liability balances do not exist and must be eliminated. The following *CICA Handbook* Recommendation is applicable:

> **Paragraph 1600.19** *Intercompany balances should be eliminated upon consolidation.* (April, 1975)

4-60. This provides the basis for a third procedure in preparing consolidated financial statements. However, we will be required to eliminate intercompany asset and liability balances in years subsequent to acquisition as well as at acquisition. As a consequence, it will become part of Step B in our general approach to consolidations. Given this, we will designate this procedure as Step B-1.

Step B-1 Procedure   Always eliminate 100 percent of intercompany assets and liabilities.

4-61.   In our example, Pert Company owes Sert Company $25,000 on open account. Given this, the entry that is required to implement Step B-1 is as follows:

Current Liabilities	$25,000	
Accounts Receivable		$25,000

Intercompany Gains And Losses

4-62.   In contrast to the intercompany asset and liability balances which are still present at the time of the acquisition, intercompany expense and revenue transactions, as well as any resulting profits, are events which occurred prior to the combination transaction. Further, at the time they occurred, they were not intercompany transactions but, rather, transactions between two independent companies dealing at arm's length. Given this, it is not appropriate to eliminate these amounts or to even think of them as intercompany transactions. This is reflected in the following Recommendation:

> **Paragraph 1600.24**   *Where the carrying value of the assets of the parent company or a subsidiary company include gains or losses arising from intercompany transactions which took place prior to the date of acquisition, such gains or losses should not be eliminated unless the transactions were made in contemplation of acquisition.* (April, 1975)

4-63.   Since there is no indication in the problem that the 2002 transactions were in contemplation of the business combination, no entry is required for these events.

Preparing The Consolidated Balance Sheet

4-64.   As indicated in our discussion of the procedural approach to be used, the preparation of the consolidated Balance Sheet involves adding together the asset and equity balances from the individual Balance Sheets of the two companies and then adjusting these amounts for the various journal entries that have been made. In this Example, the resulting consolidated Balance Sheet, with all of the calculations shown parenthetically, is as follows:

Pert Company And Subsidiary
Consolidated Balance Sheet
As At December 31, 2002

Cash ($800,000 + $500,000)	$ 1,300,000
Accounts Receivable ($1,500,000 + $1,100,000 - $25,000)	2,575,000
Inventories ($3,400,000 + $2,500,000)	5,900,000
Investment In Sert ($5,000,000 - $5,000,000)	-0-
Plant And Equipment ($6,300,000 + $3,900,000)	10,200,000
Total Assets	$19,975,000

Current Liabilities ($800,000 + $1,000,000 - $25,000)	$ 1,775,000
Long-Term Liabilities ($2,200,000 + $2,000,000)	4,200,000
No Par Common Stock (Pert's Only)	8,000,000
Retained Earnings (Pert's Only)	6,000,000
Total Equities	$19,975,000

Notes On Example One   Two points are relevant with respect to the procedures and disclosure for Example One:

- In the actual presentation of the consolidated Balance Sheet, the Investment In Sert account would simply not be shown. It is included here to call your attention to the fact that the account was there on the Pert Company's books and has been eliminated.

- Both components of the consolidated shareholders' equity are identical to those of the parent company. This will always be the case in the consolidated Balance Sheet as at the date of acquisition, a result that follows from the rules that are generally applicable in the purchase method of accounting for business combinations. This will not be the case in periods subsequent to the acquisition date unless the parent company carries the investment by the equity method.

<table>
<tr><td>Exercise Four-2 deals with a consolidated Balance Sheet at acquisition (100% ownership and no fair value changes).</td></tr>
</table>

Exercise Four-2

On December 31, 2002, Pan Inc. acquires 100 percent of the outstanding voting shares of San Ltd. for $2,630,000 in cash. At that time, all of the identifiable assets and liabilities of San Ltd. have fair values that are equal to their carrying values. The Balance Sheets of the two companies on this date, subsequent to the business combination, are as follows:

Pan and San Companies
Balance Sheets
As At December 31, 2002

	Pan Inc.	San Ltd.
Cash	$ 426,000	$ 345,000
Accounts Receivable	727,000	623,000
Inventories	1,753,000	1,265,000
Investment In San	2,630,000	-0-
Plant And Equipment (Net)	3,259,000	2,234,000
Total Assets	$8,795,000	$4,467,000
Current Liabilities	$ 398,000	$ 362,000
Long-Term Liabilities	1,272,000	1,475,000
No Par Common Stock	4,450,000	1,250,000
Retained Earnings	2,675,000	1,380,000
Total Equities	$8,795,000	$4,467,000

Required: Prepare a consolidated Balance Sheet for the Pan Inc. and its subsidiary, San Ltd., as at December 31, 2002. Include the investment elimination journal entry in your solution.

End Of Exercise Four-2

Example Two - 100 Percent Ownership With Fair Value Changes And Goodwill

Example

4-65.   As was the case in Example One, the parent in this Example will own 100 percent of the outstanding shares of the subsidiary. However, in this Example we have added fair value changes on the subsidiary assets as well as a goodwill balance. As a consequence, we will have to use the procedures developed in Chapter 3 to analyze the investment cost and allocate the appropriate amounts to fair value changes and goodwill. The basic data for Example Two is as follows:

On December 31, 2002, the Pend Company purchases 100 percent of the outstanding voting shares of the Send Company for $3,500,000 in cash. On that date, subsequent to the business combination transaction, the Balance Sheets of the two companies are as follows:

Pend and Send Companies
Balance Sheets
As At December 31, 2002

	Pend	Send
Cash	$ 500,000	$ 300,000
Accounts Receivable	1,200,000	800,000
Inventories	1,800,000	1,200,000
Investment In Send	3,500,000	-0-
Plant And Equipment (Net)	3,000,000	2,700,000
Total Assets	$10,000,000	$5,000,000
Current Liabilities	$ 800,000	$ 500,000
Long-Term Liabilities	1,700,000	1,500,000
No Par Common Stock	4,000,000	1,000,000
Retained Earnings	3,500,000	2,000,000
Total Equities	$10,000,000	$5,000,000

Other Information:

1. All of the net identifiable assets of the Send Company have fair values that are equal to their carrying values except for Plant And Equipment which has a fair value that is $300,000 more than its carrying value and the Long-Term Liabilities which have fair values that are $100,000 less than their carrying values.

2. Prior to the business combination, there were no intercompany transactions between the two companies. On the date of the combination, there are no intercompany asset and liability balances.

Required: Prepare a consolidated Balance Sheet for the Pend Company and its subsidiary, the Send Company, as at December 31, 2002.

Procedures

4-66. As described in Example One, Steps A-1 and A-2 are used to eliminate 100 percent of the Investment In Subsidiary account and 100 percent of the subsidiary's shareholders' equity at acquisition. Applying these procedures in this Example results in the following journal entry:

No Par Common Stock (Send)	$1,000,000	
Retained Earnings (Send)	2,000,000	
Differential	500,000	
Investment In Send		$3,500,000

4-67. The application of Steps A-1 and A-2 in this Example results in a journal entry that does not balance, a situation that we have corrected by adding a $500,000 debit that has been temporarily designated Differential (this amount is also referred to the Purchase Price Discrepancy, or simply Excess of Cost Over Book Value). This is a typical result. In most consolidation problems, there will be a difference between the cost of the investment and the investor's share of the book value of the subsidiary that has been acquired. This means that eliminating the investment account against the subsidiary shareholders' equity will result in an imbalance that requires an additional debit or credit. If a debit Differential is required, it reflects an excess of investment cost over the investor's share of subsidiary book value. A credit Differential indicates that the investment cost was less than the investor's share of subsidiary book value. Learning to deal with these differentials is the next step in our development of consolidation procedures.

Treatment Of Differentials

4-68.   The first thing to understand about such differentials is that they will not disappear. The preceding $500,000 must be included somewhere in the consolidated Balance Sheet. Further, it must be allocated to one or more specific accounts. It cannot simply be included in the consolidated Balance Sheet with the account title Differential or Excess Of Cost Over Book Value.

4-69.   In attempting to allocate such differentials to specific asset and liability accounts, it is essential to understand why they exist.   That is, what factors contributed to the Pend Company's decision to pay $500,000 more than the book value of the Send Company's net assets in order to acquire 100 percent of its outstanding shares? From a conceptual point of view, three possible explanations for this situation can be developed. Note that these explanations are not mutually exclusive and, in fact, would usually occur in various combinations. The three possibilities are as follows:

Specific Identifiable Assets   Specific identifiable assets and identifiable liabilities of the Send Company may have fair values that are different from their carrying values. For example, the $500,000 excess of cost over book value in the present example could be explained if the Send Company's Plant And Equipment had a fair value of $3,200,000 or $500,000 more than the carrying value of $2,700,000.

Note that this could include intangibles other than goodwill that have not been recognized on the books of the subsidiary. You may recall from Chapter 3 that the Recommendations on purchase accounting require the recognition of any intangible of the acquiree that (1) results from contractual or other legal rights , or (2) is capable of being separated or divided from the acquired enterprise and sold, transferred, licensed, rented, or exchanged (Paragraph 1581.48).

Subsidiary Goodwill   A second possible explanation of a difference between investment cost and book value relates to how successfully the enterprise is being operated. As was discussed in Chapter 3, if the enterprise is being operated in an unusually successful manner, it is likely that the enterprise as a going concern will have a fair value that is in excess of the sum of the fair values of its identifiable net assets. Such an excess would be allocated to goodwill and could be the explanation of the $500,000 excess in the problem that is under consideration. A similar analysis would apply to situations in which the enterprise is being operated at a less than average level of success, resulting in the need to deal with a differential with a credit balance (negative goodwill).

Consolidated Goodwill   A final possibility is that extra value is created in the business combination process.   There may be so many advantages associated with bringing a particular subsidiary into a combination with a parent company that the parent is prepared to pay more than the net identifiable assets and goodwill of the subsidiary are worth as a single entity. This excess is sometimes referred to as consolidated goodwill and could be the explanation of the $500,000 excess in the problem under consideration. Note that, unlike the two previous explanations for differentials, the consolidated goodwill argument could not be used to explain a credit differential. It is very difficult to believe that the shareholders of the subsidiary would be willing to sell their shares for less than the value of the enterprise simply because there are so many disadvantages associated with affiliation.

4-70.   We would note that while there is clearly a conceptual distinction between subsidiary goodwill and consolidated goodwill, it is of no practical significance. In the application of the purchase method of accounting for business combination transactions, goodwill is measured as the excess (deficiency) of the investment cost over the acquirer's share of the fair values of the acquiree's net identifiable assets. No attempt is made to segregate this total goodwill into a component that was present prior to the business combination transaction and a component that results from the business combination transaction.

4-71. Based on the preceding analysis of the reasons for the existence of debit or credit differentials, it is clear that the *CICA Handbook* Recommendations on accounting for business combinations require that such balances be allocated to fair value changes on identifiable assets, fair value changes on identifiable liabilities, and to positive or negative goodwill. This provides the basis for an additional procedure in the preparation of consolidated financial statements. As this procedure is part of Step A in our general approach to preparing consolidated financial statements, it will be designated Step A-3.

Step A-3 Procedure The total amount of any debit or credit Differential must be allocated to the parent company's share of fair value changes on identifiable assets, fair value changes on identifiable liabilities, and to positive or negative goodwill. Note that we will only recognize the parent company's share of any fair value changes or goodwill. This reflects the fact that the *CICA Handbook* requires the use of the parent company approach for the valuation of subsidiary assets.

Investment Analysis Schedule

4-72. As was noted in Chapter 3, in more complex problems it is useful to have a systematic approach to the allocation of fair value changes and goodwill. While it is was not really necessary in the relatively simple example that was presented in that Chapter, we introduced such a systematic approach in the form of an investment analysis schedule. The rules that were presented in Chapter 3 for the preparation of such schedules are repeated here for your convenience:

Calculating The Differential Subtract the subsidiary's book value (or the parent company's proportionate interest therein in cases where the parent company owns less than 100 percent of the subsidiary shares), from the investment cost. This results in a balance that we will refer to as a Differential. If it is a positive number, it indicates that the investor is paying more than his proportionate share of subsidiary book values and that there is a debit amount to be allocated. A negative number reflects a credit balance to be allocated. Note that, as the Differential reflects the total of all fair value changes and goodwill to be recognized, a positive balance does not clearly indicate the presence of goodwill.

Allocating The Differential Once the Differential has been established, we will then add or subtract the various fair value changes that have been determined for the subsidiary's identifiable assets. As a positive differential reflects a debit balance to be allocated, we will subtract any fair value changes which require the allocation of debits (increase in assets or decreases in liabilities). Correspondingly, we will add any fair value changes that require credits (decreases in assets or increases in liabilities). In this example, both the $300,000 fair value increase on Plant And Equipment and the $100,000 fair value decrease on Long-Term Liabilities involve debits and will be subtracted.

Dealing With Goodwill The resulting balance will be allocated to goodwill if it is positive. If the balance is negative or a credit amount, it will first be allocated to a pro rata reduction in the acquired assets (there are certain exceptions such as financial assets and assets that are to be sold as discussed in Chapter 3). If a credit balance remains after these assets are eliminated, the balance would be treated as an extraordinary gain.

4-73. For this Example, involving the Pend Company and its subsidiary, the Send Company, the investment analysis schedule would be prepared as follows:

Investment Cost	$3,500,000
Book Value Of The Send Company ($1,000,000 + $2,000,000)	(3,000,000)
Differential	$ 500,000
Fair Value Changes:	
Increase On Plant And Equipment	(300,000)
Decrease On Long-Term Liabilities	(100,000)
Goodwill	$ 100,000

4-74. This goodwill balance can be verified in order to check the computations in the schedule. Goodwill is defined as the excess of the investment cost over the investor's share of the fair values of the net identifiable assets of the investee. In this Example, the investment cost was $3,500,000 while the investor's share of the fair values of the investee's net identifiable assets was $3,400,000. This is calculated by taking the carrying values of $3,000,000, plus the fair value increase of $300,000 on the Plant And Equipment plus the fair value decrease of $100,000 on Long-Term Liabilities. Thus, the investment cost, less the investor's 100 percent share of fair values is equal to $100,000 ($3,500,000 - $3,400,000), which verifies the amount of goodwill determined in the investment analysis schedule.

Journal Entry

4-75. Using the information provided by the preceding investment analysis schedule, we can now complete the journal entry needed for the preparation of the required consolidated Balance Sheet at acquisition. In this entry, we will combine Step A-1 (elimination of the investment account), Step A-2 (elimination of the subsidiary shareholders' equity at acquisition), and Step A-3 (allocation of the Differential to fair value changes and goodwill). The entry is as follows:

No Par Common Stock	$1,000,000	
Retained Earnings	2,000,000	
Plant And Equipment (Net)	300,000	
Long-Term Liabilities	100,000	
Goodwill	100,000	
Investment In Send		$3,500,000

4-76. Note that this entry still eliminates 100 percent of both the Investment In Send and the shareholders' equity of the Send Company. In addition, the $500,000 balance which we temporarily designated Differential has been allocated to identifiable assets, identifiable liabilities, and goodwill.

Consolidated Balance Sheet

4-77. Using the same procedures as in Example One, the Example Two consolidated Balance Sheet can be prepared as follows:

Pend Company And Subsidiary
Consolidated Balance Sheet
As At December 31, 2002

Cash ($500,000 + $300,000)	$ 800,000
Accounts Receivable ($1,200,000 + $800,000)	2,000,000
Inventories ($1,800,000 + $1,200,000)	3,000,000
Investment In Send ($3,500,000 - $3,500,000)	Nil
Plant And Equipment (Net) ($3,000,000 + $2,700,000 + $300,000)	6,000,000
Goodwill	100,000
Total Assets	$11,900,000
Current Liabilities ($800,000 + $500,000)	$ 1,300,000
Long-Term Liabilities ($1,700,000 + $1,500,000 - $100,000)	3,100,000
No Par Common Stock (Pend's Only)	4,000,000
Retained Earnings (Pend's Only)	3,500,000
Total Equities	$11,900,000

4-78. The only difference between the procedures used in preparing this consolidated Balance Sheet and those used in preparing the Example One consolidated Balance Sheet is that allocations are made for the fair value changes and goodwill. Note that the consolidated shareholders' equity is still simply the shareholders' equity of the parent company.

Exercise Four-3

On December 31, 2002, Partial Ltd. acquires 100 percent of the outstanding voting shares of Sum Inc. for $2,508,000 in cash. On that date, all of the net identifiable assets of the Sum Inc. have fair values that are equal to their carrying values except for Inventories which have a fair value that is $35,000 less that their carrying value and the Long-Term Liabilities which have fair values that are $57,000 more than their carrying values. The Balance Sheets of the two companies on this date, subsequent to the business combination, are as follows:

Exercise Four-3 deals with a consolidated Balance Sheet at acquisition (100% ownership fair value changes and goodwill).

Partial and Sum Companies
Balance Sheets
As At December 31, 2002

	Partial	Sum
Cash	$ 612,000	$ 256,000
Accounts Receivable	1,346,000	632,000
Inventories	2,111,000	943,000
Investment In Sum	2,508,000	Nil
Plant And Equipment (Net)	3,562,000	1,866,000
Total Assets	$10,139,000	$3,697,000
Current Liabilities	$ 726,000	$ 396,000
Long-Term Liabilities	2,212,000	784,000
No Par Common Stock	3,970,000	830,000
Retained Earnings	3,231,000	1,687,000
Total Equities	$10,139,000	$3,697,000

Required: Prepare a consolidated Balance Sheet for the Partial Ltd. and its subsidiary, Sum Inc., as at December 31, 2002. Include the investment analysis in your solution.

End Of Exercise Four-3

Example Three - Fractional Ownership With No Fair Value Changes Or Goodwill

Example

4-79.   This Example introduces a situation where the parent company owns less than 100 percent of the subsidiary shares (fractional ownership). As a result of this change, we will have to consider the calculation and disclosure of the Non-Controlling Interest in the consolidated Balance Sheet. The basic data for this Example is as follows:

On December 31, 2002, the Pack Company purchases 80 percent of the outstanding voting shares of the Sack Company for $3,200,000 in cash. On that date, subsequent to the business combination transaction, the Balance Sheets of the two Companies are as follows:

Pack and Sack Companies
Balance Sheets
As At December 31, 2002

	Pack	Sack
Cash	$ 600,000	$ 400,000
Accounts Receivable	1,500,000	1,100,000
Inventories	2,100,000	1,400,000
Investment In Sack	3,200,000	-0-
Plant And Equipment (Net)	5,600,000	2,100,000
Total Assets	$13,000,000	$5,000,000

	Pack	Sack
Current Liabilities	$1,200,000	$ 400,000
Long-Term Liabilities	2,800,000	600,000
No Par Common Stock	5,000,000	1,000,000
Retained Earnings	4,000,000	3,000,000
Total Equities	$13,000,000	$5,000,000

Other Information:

1. All of the identifiable assets and liabilities of the Sack Company have fair values that are equal to the carrying values that are presented in the preceding Balance Sheet.

2. Prior to the business combination, there were no intercompany transactions between the two companies. It follows that on the date of the combination there are no intercompany asset and liability balances.

Required: Prepare a consolidated Balance Sheet for the Pack Company and its subsidiary, the Sack Company, as at December 31, 2002.

Procedures

4-80.   With no fair value changes, no goodwill, and no intercompany balances, Steps B-1 and A-3 are not relevant in this Example. However, Steps A-1 and A-2 are still required, even with the presence of a non-controlling interest. You will have no difficulty in understanding the continued need for Step A-1, the requirement that we eliminate 100 percent of the Investment In Subsidiary account. However, with some of the subsidiary's shares held by investors outside the consolidated entity, Step A-2's requirement that we eliminate 100 percent of the subsidiary's shareholders' equity does not seem reasonable. In this Example Three, 20 percent of Sack Company's shares are in the hands of such outsiders and, in the preparation of both the entity and parent company approach consolidated Balance Sheets, the interest of these shareholders in Sack Company's shareholders' equity must be included in the consolidated Balance Sheet.

4-81.   The reason for this seemingly unreasonable requirement is a procedural one. It is true that the non-controlling interest's 20 percent share of Sack Company's shareholders' equity will be included in the parent company and entity approach consolidated Balance Sheets. However, this interest will not be disclosed as No Par Common Stock or Retained Earnings. Rather, it will be disclosed as a Non-Controlling Interest. Therefore, in our approach to preparing consolidated financial statements, we will continue to eliminate 100 percent of the subsidiary's shareholders' equity at acquisition (Step A-2), but we will add a further procedure. As this new procedure is part of Step A in our general approach to consolidated financial statements, it will be designated Step A-4.

Step A-4 Procedure   The non-controlling interest's share of the book value of the subsidiary Shareholders' Equity at acquisition must be allocated to a Non-Controlling Interest account in the consolidated Balance Sheet.

4-82.   The fact that we base the Non-Controlling Interest on the book value of the subsidiary's net assets means that we are not recognizing the non-controlling interest's share of either fair value changes or goodwill. This follows from the fact that the *CICA Handbook* requires the use of the parent company approach to asset valuation.

Investment Analysis Schedule

4-83.   Given that there are no fair value changes or goodwill in this Example, no investment analysis schedule is required.

Journal Entry

4-84.   Based on the preceding analysis, we can complete the journal entry needed to prepare the consolidated Balance Sheet. In this entry we will use Step A-1 (elimination of the investment account), Step A-2 (elimination of 100 percent of the subsidiary shareholders' equity at acquisition), and the new Step A-4 (allocation of 20 percent of Sack Company's shareholders' equity to the Balance Sheet account Non-Controlling Interest).

No Par Common Stock	$1,000,000	
Retained Earnings	3,000,000	
Investment In Sack		$3,200,000
Non-Controlling Interest (20% Of $4,000,000)		800,000

Treatment Of The Non-Controlling Interest

4-85.   The preceding journal entry creates an account titled Non-Controlling Interest. Unless the subsidiary has accumulated a deficit sufficiently large to create a negative balance in shareholders' equity, this account will have a credit balance and, as a consequence, it will be allocated to the equity side of the consolidated Balance Sheet. Some further discussion, however, is required with respect to both the computation and disclosure of this balance.

Computation   With respect to computation, the Non-Controlling Interest in the consolidated Balance Sheet is simply the non-controlling shareholders' proportionate share of the carrying values of the net assets of the subsidiary. This is the approach that is required by the *CICA Handbook*:

> **Paragraph 1600.15**   *The non-controlling interest in the subsidiary's assets and liabilities should be reflected in terms of carrying values recorded in the accounting records of the subsidiary company.* (April, 1975)

If the subsidiary has goodwill on its books, Paragraph 1581.40 indicates that none of the cost of the purchase should be allocated to goodwill of the acquiree that is present at acquisition. The combined effect of Paragraphs 1600.15 and 1581.40 is to require that the parent's share of the subsidiary's recorded goodwill be eliminated against the cost of the investment, while the non-controlling interest's share of this balance be included in the consolidated Balance Sheet.

Disclosure   With respect to the disclosure of the Non-Controlling Interest in the consolidated Balance Sheet, the *CICA Handbook* makes the following somewhat ambiguous Recommendation:

> **Paragraph 1600.69**   *Non-controlling interest in consolidated subsidiary companies should be shown separately from shareholders' equity.* (April, 1975)

While this Recommendation would allow the Non-Controlling Interest to be shown as part of the long-term liabilities, it is most commonly disclosed in practice as a separate item between the long-term liabilities and shareholders' equity. The 2001 edition of *Financial Reporting in Canada* found that, of the 87 companies that disclosed a non-controlling or minority interest in their Balance Sheets, all but one disclosed it as a separate item outside of shareholders' equity.

Other Factors   You should understand that, in real world situations, the Non-Controlling Interest in the consolidated Balance Sheet is a highly aggregated piece of information. If the parent company has fractional ownership of a large number of subsidiary enterprises, all of the interests of the various non-controlling shareholder groups would be included in a single Non-Controlling Interest figure. Further, for those subsidiaries with different classes of non-voting or preferred shares outstanding, these additional equity interests would also become part of the Non-Controlling Interest in the consolidated Balance Sheet. It would be unusual for outstanding subsidiary preferred shares to be disclosed as a separate item in a consolidated Balance Sheet.

Consolidated Balance Sheet

4-86.   Using the same procedures as in Examples One and Two, the Example Three consolidated Balance Sheet would be prepared as follows:

Pack Company And Subsidiary
Consolidated Balance Sheet
As At December 31, 2002

Cash ($600,000 + $400,000)	$ 1,000,000
Accounts Receivable ($1,500,000 + $1,100,000)	2,600,000
Inventories ($2,100,000 + $1,400,000)	3,500,000
Investment In Sack ($3,200,000 - $3,200,000)	Nil
Plant And Equipment (Net) ($5,600,000 + $2,100,000)	7,700,000
Total Assets	$14,800,000

Current Liabilities ($1,200,000 + $400,000)		$ 1,600,000
Long-Term Liabilities ($2,800,000 + $600,000)		3,400,000
Total Liabilities		$5,000,000
Non-Controlling Interest [(20%)($4,000,000)]		800,000
Shareholders' Equity:		
No Par Common Stock (Pack's Only)	$5,000,000	
Retained Earnings (Pack's Only)	4,000,000	9,000,000
Total Equities		$14,800,000

4-87.   Note that we have disclosed the Non-Controlling Interest as a separate item between the Total Liabilities and Shareholders' Equity.

Exercise Four-4 deals with a consolidated Balance Sheet at acquisition (80% ownership and no fair value changes).

Exercise Four-4

On December 31, 2002, Pock Inc. acquires 80 percent of the outstanding voting shares of Sock Ltd. for $2,440,000 in cash. On that date, all of the net identifiable assets of the Sock Inc. have fair values that are equal to their carrying values. The Balance Sheets of the two companies on this date, subsequent to the business combination, are as follows:

Pock and Sock Companies
Balance Sheets
As At December 31, 2002

	Pock	Sock
Cash	$ 943,000	$ 347,000
Accounts Receivable	1,712,000	963,000
Inventories	3,463,000	1,876,000
Investment In Sock	2,440,000	Nil
Plant And Equipment (Net)	4,692,000	1,921,000
Total Assets	$13,250,000	$5,107,000

	Pock	Sock
Current Liabilities	$ 987,000	$ 784,000
Long-Term Liabilities	3,462,000	1,273,000
No Par Common Stock	5,460,000	1,215,000
Retained Earnings	3,341,000	1,835,000
Total Equities	$13,250,000	$5,107,000

Required: Prepare a consolidated Balance Sheet for Pock Inc. and its subsidiary, Sock Ltd., as at December 31, 2002.   Include the investment analysis and the investment elimination journal entry in your solution.

End Of Exercise Four-4

Example Four - Fractional Ownership With Fair Value Changes And Goodwill

Example

4-88.   In this final example, we will continue to have fractional ownership. However, we will add fair value changes and goodwill. The basic data for this Example is as follows:

On December 31, 2002, the Peak Company purchases 90 percent of the outstanding voting shares of the Seek Company for $5,220,000 in cash. On that date, subsequent to the business combination transaction, the Balance Sheets of the two companies are as follows:

Peak and Seek Companies
Balance Sheets
As At December 31, 2002

	Peak	Seek
Cash	$ 1,000,000	$ 700,000
Accounts Receivable	2,100,000	1,200,000
Inventories	3,440,000	2,500,000
Investment In Seek	5,220,000	-0-
Plant And Equipment (Net)	4,240,000	4,600,000
Total Assets	$16,000,000	$9,000,000
Current Liabilities	$ 1,200,000	$1,000,000
Long-Term Liabilities	2,800,000	2,000,000
No Par Common Stock	7,000,000	2,000,000
Retained Earnings	5,000,000	4,000,000
Total Equities	$16,000,000	$9,000,000

Other Information:

1.   All of the identifiable assets of the Seek Company have fair values that are equal to their carrying values except for Plant And Equipment which has a fair value that is $600,000 less than its carrying value and Inventories with fair values that are $100,000 more than their carrying values.

2.   Prior to the business combination, there were no intercompany transactions between the two companies. It follows that on the date of the combination, there are no intercompany asset and liability balances.

Required: Prepare a consolidated Balance Sheet for the Peak Company and its subsidiary, the Seek Company, as at December 31, 2002.

Procedures

4-89.   This final Example provides a complete illustration of the procedures that are required in preparing a consolidated Balance Sheet as at the date of acquisition. However, no new procedures are required. As with all of the preceding examples, we will continue to use Step A-1 (eliminate the investment account) and Step A-2 (eliminate 100 percent of the subsidiary's shareholders' equity at acquisition). As in Example Three, we will need Step A-4 to establish a Non-Controlling Interest to be included in the consolidated Balance Sheet. In addition, we will need Step A-3 from Example Two to allocate the Differential to fair value changes and goodwill.

Investment Analysis Schedule

4-90.   The investment analysis schedule that will be used in this Example is as follows:

	90 Percent	100 Percent
Investment Cost	$5,220,000	$5,800,000*
Book Value Of The Seek Company	(5,400,000)	(6,000,000)
Differential	($ 180,000)	($ 200,000)
Fair Value Changes:		
Decrease On Plant And Equipment	540,000	600,000
Increase On Inventories	(90,000)	(100,000)
Goodwill	$ 270,000	$ 300,000

*The 100 percent figure for the investment cost is the total value for the business that is implied by the price paid for 90 percent of the business ($5,220,000 equals 90 percent of $5,800,000).

4-91.   In general terms, this schedule operates exactly as it did in the 100 percent ownership case. However, because we are only going to recognize the parent company's share of fair value changes and goodwill, all of the information has to be calculated on a 90 percent basis.

4-92.   You will note that, in our schedule, we have retained the 100 percent figures along with the 90 percent figures. As only the fractional calculations are required in preparing a consolidated Balance Sheet at acquisition, it is not really necessary to calculate both the fractional and 100 percent amounts. However, we would urge you to do so, at least in the early stages of your work on consolidations. In most consolidation problems, some of the information is given on a fractional basis (investment cost) while other data is given on a 100 percent basis (fair value changes). As a result, one of the most common errors made in solving consolidation problems is to add or subtract a fractional figure to or from a 100 percent figure. This two column analysis will virtually eliminate this type of error, particularly if the final goodwill figure is verified using a definitional calculation. In this Example, the investment cost is $5,220,000 and the investor's share of the subsidiary's fair values is $4,950,000 [(90%)($6,000,000 - $600,000 + $100,000)]. This verifies the 90 percent goodwill figure of $270,000 ($5,220,000 - $4,950,000).

Journal Entry

4-93.   The required journal entry would be as follows:

No Par Common Stock	$2,000,000	
Retained Earnings	4,000,000	
Inventories	90,000	
Goodwill	270,000	
Plant And Equipment (Net)		$ 540,000
Non-Controlling Interest [(10%)($6,000,000)]		600,000
Investment In Seek		5,220,000

4-94.   This journal entry uses Step A-1 (elimination of 100 percent of the investment account) and A-2 (elimination of 100 percent of the subsidiary shareholders' equity at acquisition). In addition, under Step A-3, it uses the figure from the 90 percent column in the investment analysis schedule to allocate the investor's proportionate share of fair value changes and goodwill. Finally, under Step A-4, it establishes a Non-Controlling Interest to be included in the consolidated Balance Sheet at acquisition. This Non-Controlling Interest is based on the $6,000,000 ($2,000,000 + $4,000,000) book value of Seek Company's Shareholders' Equity.

Consolidated Balance Sheet

4-95.   The required consolidated Balance Sheet is as follows:

Peak Company And Subsidiary
Consolidated Balance Sheet
As At December 31, 2002

Cash ($1,000,000 + $700,000)		$ 1,700,000
Accounts Receivable ($2,100,000 + $1,200,000)		3,300,000
Inventories ($3,440,000 + $2,500,000 + $90,000)		6,030,000
Investment In Seek ($5,220,000 - $5,220,000)		Nil
Plant And Equipment (Net) ($4,240,000 + $4,600,000 - $540,000)		8,300,000
Goodwill		270,000
Total Assets		$19,600,000
Current Liabilities ($1,200,000 + $1,000,000)		$ 2,200,000
Long-Term Liabilities ($2,800,000 + $2,000,000)		4,800,000
Total Liabilities		$ 7,000,000
Non-Controlling Interest [(10%)($6,000,000)]		600,000
Shareholders' Equity:		
No Par Common Stock (Peak's Only)	$7,000,000	
Retained Earnings (Peak's Only)	5,000,000	12,000,000
Total Equities		$19,600,000

Note On Asset Valuation   The consolidated asset and liability balances that are required under the Recommendations of the *CICA Handbook* can be calculated in two different ways. One approach is to take 100 percent of the parent company's carrying values, the non-controlling interest's 10 percent share of subsidiary carrying values, and the parent company's 90 percent share of subsidiary fair values. Applying this to the Inventories in the preceding example gives $6,030,00 [$3,440,000 + (10%)($2,500,000) + (90%)($2,500,000 + $100,000)]. An alternative approach takes 100 percent of the carrying values of the parent company's individual assets and liabilities, plus 100 percent of the carrying values of the subsidiary's individual assets and liabilities, plus or minus the parent company's 90 percent interest in the fair value changes on the subsidiary's individual assets and liabilities. This would give the same $6,030,000 [$3,440,000 + $2,500,000 + (90%)($2,600,000 - $2,500,000)]. While either of these approaches will produce the required solution, we believe the latter approach is more efficient and less error prone, especially since the fair value changes are calculated on the investment analysis schedule. As a consequence, it will be used throughout the remainder of this text. Given this, we would suggest that you use this approach in solving assignment and self study problems.

Note On Non-Controlling Interest   The Non-Controlling Interest has been disclosed as a separate item between the Total Liabilities and Shareholders' Equity.

Exercise Four-5

On December 31, 2002, the Pickle Company purchases 90 percent of the outstanding voting shares of the Sickle Company for $1,480,000 in cash. On that date, most of the net identifiable assets of the Sickle Company have fair values that are equal to their carrying values. However, the Plant and Equipment (Net) has a fair value that is $160,000 less than its carrying value. In addition, Sickle has unrecorded identifiable intangibles that have a fair value of $230,000. These intangibles meet the Paragraph 1581.48 criteria for recognition.

On December 31, 2002, subsequent to the business combination transaction, the Balance Sheets of the two companies are as follows:

> Exercise Four-5 deals with a consolidated Balance Sheet at acquisition (90% ownership with fair value changes).

This is a continuation of Exercise Four-5.

Pickle and Sickle Companies
Balance Sheets
As At December 31, 2002

	Pickle	Sickle
Cash	$ 1,365,000	$ 264,000
Accounts Receivable	2,789,000	657,000
Inventories	2,126,000	1,206,000
Investment In Sickle	1,480,000	-0-
Plant And Equipment (Net)	3,972,000	1,249,000
Total Assets	$11,732,000	$3,376,000
Current Liabilities	$ 1,349,000	$ 764,000
Long-Term Liabilities	2,718,000	1,112,000
No Par Common Stock	5,420,000	490,000
Retained Earnings	2,245,000	1,010,000
Total Equities	$11,732,000	$3,376,000

Required: Prepare a consolidated Balance Sheet for the Pickle Company and its subsidiary, Sickle Company, as at December 31, 2002.

End Of Exercise Four-5

Push-Down Accounting

General Concepts

4-96.   Throughout the preceding discussion of the consolidated Balance Sheet at the time of acquisition, no adjustments were made to the subsidiary's accounting records as a result of its being acquired. As was noted in Chapter 3, the acquisition of majority ownership in a subsidiary is a business combination transaction which is accounted for by the purchase method. Push-down accounting represents an alternative to the procedures that we have described throughout this Chapter, in that it allows fair value changes to be recorded on the books of the subsidiary. In those situations where it is applicable, normally situations involving the ownership of 90 percent or more of the outstanding voting shares of the subsidiary, the use of push-down accounting will significantly simplify the procedures required in the preparation of consolidated financial statements. Section 1625 of the *CICA Handbook*, "Comprehensive Revaluation Of Assets and Liabilities", permits the use of push-down accounting if:

> **Paragraph 1625.04(a)**   *All or virtually all of the equity interests in the enterprise have been acquired, in one or more transactions between non-related parties, by an acquirer who controls the enterprise after the transaction or transactions.*

Example
Basic Data

4-97.   As we noted in the preceding Chapter, an understanding of push-down accounting requires some familiarity with basic consolidation procedures. Now that we have examined consolidation procedures, at least to the extent they apply at the time of acquisition, we can present an example of the push-down accounting procedures. As 90 percent ownership was involved in the preceding Example Four (Paragraph 4-88), we will use the same data to illustrate push-down accounting. This will give you an opportunity to compare the procedures that will be used when push-down accounting is applied, with those used in situations where push-down accounting is not applied. The Example Four data is repeated here for your convenience:

Example On December 31, 2002, the Peak Company purchases 90 percent of the outstanding voting shares of the Seek Company for $5,220,000 in cash. On that date, subsequent to the business combination transaction, the Balance Sheets of the two Companies are as follows:

Pear and Seek Companies
Balance Sheets
As At December 31, 2002

	Peak	Seek
Cash	$ 1,000,000	$ 700,000
Accounts Receivable	2,100,000	1,200,000
Inventories	3,440,000	2,500,000
Investment In Seek	5,220,000	-0-
Plant And Equipment (Net)	4,240,000	4,600,000
Total Assets	$16,000,000	$9,000,000
Current Liabilities	$ 1,200,000	$1,000,000
Long-Term Liabilities	2,800,000	2,000,000
No Par Common Stock	7,000,000	2,000,000
Retained Earnings	5,000,000	4,000,000
Total Equities	$16,000,000	$9,000,000

Other Information:

1. All of the identifiable assets of the Seek Company have fair values that are equal to their carrying values except for Plant And Equipment which has a fair value that is $600,000 less than its carrying value and Inventories with fair values that are $100,000 more than their carrying values.

2. Prior to the business combination there were no intercompany transactions between the two Companies. It follows that on the date of the combination there are no intercompany asset and liability balances.

Required: Prepare a push-down accounting Balance Sheet for the Seek Company as at December 31, 2002. Using this Balance Sheet as a basis for your procedures, prepare a consolidated Balance Sheet for the Peak Company and its subsidiary, the Seek Company, as at December 31, 2002.

CICA Handbook Recommendations

4-98. In applying push-down accounting to this example, three Recommendations of Section 1625 are relevant. The first is as follows:

Paragraph 1625.23 *When a comprehensive revaluation of an enterprise's assets and liabilities is undertaken as a result of a transaction or transactions as described in 1625.04(a), push-down accounting should be applied. The portion of the assets and liabilities related to non-controlling interests should be reflected at the carrying amounts previously recorded by the acquired enterprise.* (January, 1993)

4-99. This Recommendation reflects the fact that the parent company approach to asset valuation at the time of acquisition is required in the preparation of consolidated financial statements. By indicating that the non-controlling interest must be based on carrying values, it is made clear that asset and liability values can include only the acquiring company's share of fair value changes and goodwill. This means that the 90 percent column in the Example Four investment analysis can also be used here.

4-100. The second relevant Recommendation on the application of push-down accounting is as follows:

Paragraph 1625.29   *When a comprehensive revaluation of an enterprise's assets and liabilities is undertaken as a result of a transaction or transactions as described in 1625.04(a),
that portion of retained earnings which has not been included in the consolidated retained
earnings of the acquirer or is not related to any continuing non-controlling interests in the
enterprise should be reclassified to either share capital, contributed surplus, or a separately identified account within shareholders' equity.* (January, 1993)

4-101.   The Paragraph 1625.29 Recommendation requires that, with the exception of two
types of items, the Retained Earnings of the subsidiary at acquisition must be reclassified in
the application of push-down accounting. The two exceptions are:

- Amounts belonging to a non-controlling interest.
- Amounts that have been included in the calculation of Retained Earnings of the acquirer
  as the result of an equity interest which existed prior to obtaining control over the
  subsidiary.

4-102.   The amounts which are reclassified can be allocated to share capital, contributed
surplus, or a separately identified account within shareholders' equity. While the Recommendation is flexible in this regard, we would be inclined to allocate the acquirer's share of
the subsidiary's retained earnings to a separately identified account within shareholders'
equity. This would serve to distinguish this balance from the usual types of shareholders'
equity balances.

4-103.   The third relevant *Handbook* Recommendation is as follows:

Paragraph 1625.30   *The revaluation adjustment arising from a comprehensive revaluation of an enterprise's assets and liabilities undertaken as a result of a transaction or transactions as described in 1625.04(a) should be accounted for as a capital transaction,* (see
CAPITAL TRANSACTIONS, *Section 3610), and recorded as either share capital, contributed surplus, or a separately identified account within shareholders' equity.* (January,
1993)

4-104.   With respect to the revaluation adjustment arising from altered asset and liability
values, Paragraph 1625.30 also provides for alternative disclosure. Our preference in this
case would be to again use a separate account for this amount. An appropriate title would be
Capital Arising On Comprehensive Revaluation Of Assets.

Journal Entry - Push-Down Accounting

4-105.   The journal entry required to implement push-down accounting on the books of the
Seek Company as at December 31, 2002 would be as follows:

Retained Earnings [(90%)($4,000,000)]	$3,600,000	
Inventories	90,000	
Goodwill	270,000	
Capital Arising On Comprehensive		
Revaluation Of Assets (Differential)	180,000	
Plant And Equipment (Net)		$ 540,000
Contributed Surplus [(90%)($4,000,000)]		3,600,000

4-106.   This entry reclassifies the parent's share of Retained Earnings as Contributed
Surplus, records Peak's proportionate share of the fair value changes on Inventories and Plant
And Equipment on Seek's books, records Peak's share of the Goodwill on Seek's books, and
establishes a capital revaluation account for the excess of the cost of the investment over
Seek's book value. (This is the Differential from the Example Four investment analysis
schedule - see Paragraph 4-90.)

Subsidiary Balance Sheet - Push-Down Accounting

4-107.   Given the preceding journal entry, the push-down accounting Balance Sheet of Seek
Company on December 31, 2002 would be prepared as follows:

Seek Company
Push-Down Accounting Balance Sheet
As At December 31, 2002

Cash	$ 700,000
Accounts Receivable	1,200,000
Inventories ($2,500,000 + $90,000)	2,590,000
Plant And Equipment (Net) ($4,600,000 - $540,000)	4,060,000
Goodwill	270,000
Total Assets	$8,820,000

Current Liabilities	$1,000,000
Long-Term Liabilities	2,000,000
No Par Common Stock	2,000,000
Contributed Surplus	3,600,000
Capital Arising On Comprehensive Revaluation Of Assets	(180,000)
Retained Earnings (Non-Controlling Interest)	400,000
Total Equities	$8,820,000

4-108.   Given this push-down accounting Balance Sheet, the procedures for preparing the required consolidated Balance Sheet are simplified. The required journal entry would be as follows:

No Par Common Stock (Seek's)	$2,000,000	
Contributed Surplus (Seek's)	3,600,000	
Retained Earnings (Seek's)	400,000	
Capital Arising On Comprehensive Revaluation Of Assets		$ 180,000
Investment In Seek		5,220,000
Non-Controlling Interest		600,000

4-109.   This entry eliminates all of the subsidiary's Shareholders' Equity balances, eliminates Peak's Investment In Seek, and establishes the Non-Controlling Interest at acquisition. This Non-Controlling Interest balance is equal to their $200,000 [(10%)($2,000,000)] share of No Par Common Stock, plus the $400,000 Retained Earnings Balance. In keeping with the Paragraph 1625.23 requirement that the Non-Controlling Interest must be based on carrying values, the $600,000 can also be calculated by taking 10 percent of the $6,000,000 in Shareholders' Equity from the pre acquisition Balance Sheet of Seek. Given this entry, the required consolidated Balance Sheet is identical to the parent company approach Balance Sheet presented in Example Four:

Peak Company And Subsidiary
Consolidated Balance Sheet
As At December 31, 2002

Cash ($1,000,000 + $700,000)	$ 1,700,000
Accounts Receivable ($2,100,000 + $1,200,000)	3,300,000
Inventories ($3,440,000 + $2,590,000)	6,030,000
Investment In Seek ($5,220,000 - $5,220,000)	Nil
Plant And Equipment (Net) ($4,240,000 + $4,060,000)	8,300,000
Goodwill	270,000
Total Assets	$19,600,000

Current Liabilities ($1,200,000 + $1,000,000)		$ 2,200,000
Long-Term Liabilities ($2,800,000 + $2,000,000)		4,800,000
Total Liabilities		$ 7,000,000
Non-Controlling Interest [(10%)($6,000,000)]		600,000
Shareholders' Equity:		
No Par Common Stock (Peak's Only)	7,000,000	
Retained Earnings (Peak's Only)	5,000,000	12,000,000
Total Equities		$19,600,000

<table>
<tr><td>Exercise Four-6 deals with push-down accounting.</td></tr>
</table>

Exercise Four-6
This is an extension of Exercise Four-5.

On December 31, 2002, the Pickle Company purchases 90 percent of the outstanding voting shares of the Sickle Company for $1,480,000 in cash. On that date, most of the net identifiable assets of the Sum Inc. have fair values that are equal to their carrying values. However, the Plant and Equipment (Net) has a fair value that is $160,000 less than its carrying value. In addition, Sickle has unrecorded identifiable intangibles that have a fair value of $230,000. These intangibles meet the Paragraph 1581.48 criteria for recognition.

On December 31, 2002, subsequent to the business combination transaction, the Balance Sheets of the two companies are as follows:

Pickle and Sickle Companies
Balance Sheets
As At December 31, 2002

	Pickle	Sickle
Cash	$ 1,365,000	$ 264,000
Accounts Receivable	2,789,000	657,000
Inventories	2,126,000	1,206,000
Investment In Sickle	1,480,000	-0-
Plant And Equipment (Net)	3,972,000	1,249,000
Total Assets	$11,732,000	$3,376,000
Current Liabilities	$ 1,349,000	$ 764,000
Long-Term Liabilities	2,718,000	1,112,000
No Par Common Stock	5,420,000	490,000
Retained Earnings	2,245,000	1,010,000
Total Equities	$11,732,000	$3,376,000

Required: Prepare a push-down accounting Balance Sheet for the Sickle Company as at December 31, 2002. Using this Balance Sheet as the basis for your procedures, prepare a consolidated Balance Sheet for the Pickle Company and its subsidiary, the Sickle Company, as at December 31, 2002.

End Of Exercise Four-6

Disclosure Requirements

4-110.   Before leaving the subject of push-down accounting, we would note that the *CICA Handbook* has several disclosure Recommendations that are applicable when this method is used. These are as follows:

Paragraph 1625.34   *In the period that push-down accounting has been first applied the financial statements should disclose the following:*

(a) *the date push-down accounting was applied, and the date or dates of the purchase transaction or transactions that led to the application of push-down accounting;*

(b) *a description of the situation resulting in the application of push-down accounting; and*

(c) *the amount of the change in each major class of assets, liabilities and shareholders' equity arising from the application of push-down accounting. (January, 1993)*

Paragraph 1625.35   *For a period of at least three years following the application of push-down accounting the financial statements should disclose:*

(a) *the date push-down accounting was applied;*

(b) *the amount of the revaluation adjustment and the shareholders' equity account in which the revaluation adjustment was recorded; and*

(c) *the amount of retained earnings reclassified and the shareholders' equity account to which it was reclassified. (January, 1993)*

Reverse Takeovers

EIC Abstract No. 10 - Reverse Takeover Accounting

4-111.   As discussed in Chapter 3, Paragraphs 3-60 to 3-64, there are business combination transactions in which the acquiring company, from a legal point of view is, in fact, the acquiree from an economic point of view. This can only happen when the legal acquirer uses its own shares to obtain either the assets or shares of the legal acquiree. If, for example, an acquirer issues such a large block of shares to the shareholders of an acquiree that, subsequent to the business combination transaction, the acquiree shareholders hold a majority of shares in the acquirer, we have a reverse takeover. Although the concept of reverse takeovers was introduced in Chapter 3, detailed consideration of this topic could not be done until the consolidation procedures covered in this Chapter were completed.

4-112.   We noted in the preceding Chapter that the concepts involved in reverse takeover accounting are no different than those involved in other business combinations where an acquirer can be identified. However, there are sufficient complications in the application of these concepts that the Emerging Issues Committee has issued Abstract No. 10, "Reverse Takeover Accounting". In this Abstract, the Committee reaches a consensus on six specific issues related to reverse takeovers. The issues, as well as the consensus reached, are as follows:

Issue One   In what circumstances is it appropriate to apply reverse takeover accounting principles?

Consensus On Issue One   Paragraph 1581.17 identifies the circumstances in which reverse takeover accounting should be applied. It is as follows:

Paragraph 1581.17   Occasionally, an enterprise obtains ownership of the shares of another enterprise but, as part of the transaction, issues enough voting shares as consideration that control of the combined enterprise passes to the shareholders of the acquired enterprise (commonly referred to as a "reverse takeover"). Although legally the enterprise that issues the shares is regarded as the parent or continuing enterprise, the enterprise whose former shareholders now control the combined enterprise is treated as the acquirer. As a result, the issuing enterprise is deemed to be a continuation of the acquirer and the acquirer is deemed to have acquired control of the assets and business of the issuing enterprise in consideration for the issue of capital.

In identifying the acquirer and thereby determining whether a reverse takeover has occurred, the following factors (set out in Paragraphs 1581.14 and .15) would be considered:

- the relative voting rights in the combined enterprise after the combination
- the existence of a large non-controlling interest in the combined enterprise when no other owner or organized group of owners has a significant interest
- the composition of the governing body of the combined enterprise
- the composition of the senior management of the combined enterprise

Reverse takeover accounting should not normally occur unless a business combination transaction takes place. A business combination excludes an exchange of shares between companies under common control and hence the accounting for such exchanges is not dealt with in this discussion.

Issue Two How should the consolidated financial statements prepared following a reverse takeover be described and what financial statements should be presented as comparative statements?

Consensus On Issue Two The consolidated financial statements (or the financial statements of the company resulting from a legal amalgamation of the two companies after the exchange of shares) should be issued under the name of the legal parent but described in the notes or elsewhere as a continuation of the financial statements of the legal subsidiary and not of the legal parent. As stated in Paragraph 1581.17 (see Issue One), in a reverse takeover situation, the legal parent is deemed to be a continuation of the acquiring company, i.e., the legal subsidiary. The control of the assets and business of the legal parent is deemed to have been acquired in consideration for the issue of capital by the legal subsidiary. In many cases, a reverse takeover transaction will be accompanied by a name change such that the name of the legal parent becomes similar to the name of the legal subsidiary.

The comparative figures presented in the consolidated financial statements prepared after a reverse takeover should be those of the legal subsidiary. The fact that the capital structure of the consolidated entity, being the capital structure of the legal parent, is different from that appearing in the financial statements of the legal subsidiary in earlier periods due to reverse takeover accounting should be explained in the notes to the consolidated financial statements.

Issue Three How should the cost of the purchase be determined and allocated in a reverse takeover transaction?

Consensus On Issue Three The general principle in Section 1581 is that the cost of the purchase should be determined by the fair value of the consideration given or the acquirer's share of the fair value of the net assets acquired, whichever is more reliably measurable. In a reverse takeover, the consideration is given not by the legal parent but is deemed to be given by the legal subsidiary through the issue of capital.

If the fair value of the shares of the legal subsidiary is used to determine the cost of the purchase, a calculation has to be made to determine the number of shares the legal subsidiary would have had to issue in order to provide the same percentage of ownership of the combined company to the shareholders of the legal parent as they have in the combined company as a result of the reverse takeover transaction. The fair value of the number of shares so calculated would be used as the cost of the purchase.

If the quoted market price (as adjusted, where appropriate) of the shares of the legal subsidiary is not indicative of the fair value of the shares that the legal subsidiary would have had to issue, or the fair value is not otherwise reliably measureable, it would be appropriate to use the total fair value of all the issued shares of the legal parent prior to the exchange of shares as a basis for the determination of the cost of the purchase. It may be appropriate to use the quoted market price of the shares of the legal parent traded in the market, after recognizing the possible effects of the price fluctuations, quantities traded, issue costs and similar items, in order to establish the fair value of such shares.

The cost of the purchase determined on an appropriate basis would be allocated to the assets and liabilities of the legal parent on the basis of their fair value as set out in Section

1581. If the cost of the purchase exceeds the fair values assigned to identifiable assets and liabilities, the excess would be recorded as goodwill in the consolidated financial statements.

The consolidated financial statements following a reverse takeover would reflect the fair values of the assets and liabilities of the legal parent while the assets and liabilities of the legal subsidiary would continue to be carried at their book values..

Issue Four   How should the shareholders' equity be determined and presented in the consolidated balance sheet following a reverse takeover transaction?

Consensus On Issue Four   Shareholders' equity should be determined and presented on the consolidated balance sheet as if the consolidated financial statements are a continuation of the legal subsidiary. This means that the retained earnings (or deficit) and other surplus accounts in the consolidated financial statements immediately after the reverse takeover would be the same as the accounts of the legal subsidiary at that date. The retained earnings (or deficit) and any other surplus accounts of the legal parent at the date of the legal combination would be eliminated in consolidation.

The amount shown as issued capital in the consolidated balance sheet would be calculated by adding to the issued capital of the legal subsidiary the amount of the cost of the purchase determined as described above, excluding any costs incurred in cash. However, the capital structure, i.e., the number and type of shares issued, appearing in the consolidated balance sheet would reflect that of the legal parent, including the shares issued to effect the reverse takeover.

In many cases, a reverse takeover transaction will be accompanied by a legal amalgamation. Legislation may require that the amount shown as issued share capital of the amalgamated company is to be equal to the aggregate of the issued share capitals of each of the amalgamating companies prior to the amalgamation (as adjusted for any intercompany shareholdings). In such circumstances, any excess of the share capital legally required to be shown in the balance sheet of the amalgamated company over the value attributed to the shares for accounting purposes should be included as a separate debit in shareholders' equity. There should be a description thereof disclosed either in the balance sheet or in the notes to the financial statements.

Issue Five   How should the earnings per share be determined for a fiscal year during which a reverse takeover occurs and for the years for which comparative statements are presented?

Consensus On Issue Five   For the purpose of computing earnings per share, the number of shares outstanding for the period from the beginning of the fiscal year to the date of the reverse takeover is deemed to be the number of shares issued by the legal parent to the shareholders of the legal subsidiary. For the period from the date of the reverse takeover to the end of the fiscal year, the number of shares to be used in the calculation of the earnings per share would be the actual number of shares of the legal parent outstanding in that period. The weighted average number of shares to be used in computing the earnings per share would be calculated on the basis of the numbers determined for the two periods as described above. The earnings per share to be disclosed for the comparative periods would be computed by dividing the earnings of the legal subsidiary by the number of shares of the legal parent issued in the reverse takeover transaction.

Issue Six   When not all the shareholders of the legal subsidiary exchange their shares for shares in the legal parent, how should the interest of such shareholders be accounted for in the consolidated financial statements?

Consensus On Issue Six   In such a situation, the shareholders who do not exchange their shares become a minority interest in the legal subsidiary. Although from an accounting viewpoint, the company in which they owned shares acquired another company, i.e., the legal parent, they would be treated as minority shareholders of a subsidiary company in the consolidated financial statements prepared after a reverse takeover transaction. Since the assets and liabilities of the legal subsidiary would be included in the consolidated balance sheet at their book values, the minority interest appearing on the consolidated balance sheet would reflect the minority shareholders' proportionate interest in the book value of the net assets of the legal subsidiary.

Examples

Example With No Non-Controlling Interest

4-113. EIC Abstract No. 10 includes two examples which illustrate the various conclusions reached on reverse takeover accounting issues. The first of these examples involve a situation in which all of the subsidiary shares are acquired and there is no non-controlling interest:

Alpha Company - Balance Sheets

	December 31 2002	September 30 2003
Current Assets	$ 400	$ 500
Fixed Assets	1,200	1,300
Total Assets	$1,600	$1,800
Current Liabilities	$ 200	$ 300
Long-Term Liabilities	300	200
Future Income Tax Liability	100	100
Redeemable Preferred Shares (100 Shares)	100	100
Common Shares (100 Shares)	300	300
Retained Earnings	600	800
Total Equities	$1,600	$1,800

Beta Company - Balance Sheets

	December 31 2002	September 30 2003
Current Assets	$1,000	$ 700
Fixed Assets	2,000	3,000
Total Assets	$3,000	$3,700
Current Liabilities	$ 500	$ 600
Long-Term Liabilities	700	800
Future Income Tax Liability	200	300
Common Shares (60 Shares)	600	600
Retained Earnings	1,000	1,400
Total Equities	$3,000	$3,700

Other Information:

1. For the nine months ended September 30, 2003, Alpha Company had Net Income of $200 while Beta had Net Income of $400. No dividends were declared by either Company during the period. Neither company had any Extraordinary Items or Results Of Discontinued Operations during this period.

2. At September 30, 2003, the fair value of Alpha's common shares was $12 per share while that of Beta's shares was $40 per share.

3. On September 30, 2003, the fair values of Alpha's identifiable assets and liabilities are the same as their book values except for fixed assets which have a fair value of $1,500.

4. On September 30, 2003, Alpha issues 150 common shares in exchange for all 60 of the outstanding common shares of Beta.

Investment Analysis

4-114. As the former Beta shareholders now own 60 percent [150 ÷ (100 + 150)] of the outstanding Alpha shares as compared to 40 percent (100 ÷ 250) for the ongoing Alpha share-holders, we are dealing with a reverse takeover. Had this combination been carried out through an issue of Beta shares, Beta would have had to issue 40 additional shares to Alpha in order to give the Alpha shareholders the same 40 percent interest [40 ÷ (60 + 40)] in the combined company. Using the fair value of Beta shares as the basis for determination, this gives a purchase cost of $1,600 [(40 Shares)($40)] and Goodwill can be calculated as follows:

Purchase Price	$1,600
Alpha's Book Value ($300 + $800)	(1,100)
Differential	$ 500
Fair Value Change On Alpha's Fixed Assets ($1,500 - $1,300)	(200)
Goodwill	$ 300

Consolidated Balance Sheet

4-115. Based on these calculations, the required consolidated Balance Sheet can be prepared as follows:

Alpha Company And Subsidiary
Consolidated Balance
As At September 30, 2003

Current Assets ($700 + $500)		$1,200
Fixed Assets ($3,000 + $1,300 + $200)		4,500
Goodwill (See Preceding Calculation)		300
Total Assets		$6,000
Current Liabilities ($600 + $300)		$ 900
Long-Term Liabilities ($800 + $200)		1,000
Future Income Tax Liability ($300 + $100)		400
Shareholders' Equity:		
Redeemable Preferred Shares (100)	$ 100	
Common Shares (Note One)	2,200	
Retained Earnings (Beta's)	1,400	3,700
Total Equities		$6,000

Note One While the number of shares outstanding is Alpha's 250, the $2,200 is made up of Beta's original contributed capital of $600, plus the $1,600 resulting from the deemed issue of 40 additional shares in the reverse takeover.

Consolidated Net Income

4-116. In calculating consolidated Net Income for the year ending December 31, 2003, Alpha's income for the nine month period ending September 30, 2003 would be excluded. On this basis, assume that the consolidated Net Income for combined entity's first full year ending December 31, 2003 is $800. This would be divided by a weighted average of the Alpha Company shares outstanding using 150 shares (the number issued to Beta in the reverse takeover transaction) for the first nine months of 2003 and 250 (the actual number outstanding for this period) for the remaining three months. The weighted average would be calculated as follows:

First Nine Months [(150 Shares)(9/12)]	112.5
Remaining Three Months [(250 Shares)(3/12)]	62.5
Weighted Average Shares Outstanding	175.0

4-117.   Given this weighted average for shares outstanding, the 2003 earnings per share would be calculated as follows:

$$\frac{\text{Consolidated Net Income}}{\text{Weighted Average Shares Outstanding}} = \frac{\$800}{175} = \$4.57$$

If we assume that Beta's Net Income for 2002 was $600, the corresponding comparative figure for 2002 would be calculated as follows:

$$\frac{\text{Consolidated Net Income}}{\text{Weighted Average Shares Outstanding}} = \frac{\$600}{150} = \$4.00$$

Example With Minority Interest

4-118.   The preceding example assumed that all of the Beta shareholders exchanged their shares for those of Alpha. As noted in EIC Abstract No. 10's Issue Six, this may not always be the case and, when it is not, a non-controlling interest is created. Note, however, that this is not the usual non-controlling interest. While it is an interest in the subsidiary, it is not an interest in the acquiree. Rather, it is a minority or non-controlling interest in the acquirer. This means that its presence will not influence the cost of the purchase or the amounts to be allocated to fair value changes or goodwill.

Investment Analysis And Consolidated Balance Sheet

4-119.   To illustrate this possibility, we will modify the original example. The example will be altered by assuming that 150 Alpha shares are offered for the full 60 shares of Beta (2.5 Alpha shares for each Beta share). However, in this version of the example only 56 shares of Beta are tendered for exchange, resulting in the issue of only 140 Alpha shares. This means that the former Beta shareholders own 58.3 percent (140 ÷ 240) of the Alpha shares that are outstanding after the reverse takeover. If the combination had been carried out by issuing Beta shares, the issuance of 40 Beta shares would have resulted in the Beta shareholders retaining their 58.3 percent ownership interest (56 ÷ [56 + 40]) in the combined company. This means that the $1,600 purchase price [(40 Shares)($40 Per Share)] would be the same as in the previous example, as would the amount of Goodwill to be recorded in the consolidated Balance Sheet. Given this, the consolidated Balance Sheet would be as follows:

Alpha Company And Subsidiary
Consolidated Balance Sheet
As At December 31, 2003

Current Assets ($700 + $500)	$1,200
Fixed Assets ($3,000 + $1,300 + $200)	4,500
Goodwill	300
Total Assets	$6,000

Current Liabilities ($600 + $300)		$ 900
Long-Term Liabilities ($800 + $200)		1,000
Future Income Tax Liability ($300 + $100)		400
Total Liabilities		$2,300
Non-Controlling Interest (Note One)		134
Shareholders' Equity:		
Redeemable Preferred Shares (100)	$ 100	
Common Shares (Note Two)	2,160	
Retained Earnings (Note Three)	1,306	3,566
Total Equities		$6,000

Note One   The $134 Non-Controlling Interest is based on 6.7 percent (4 Shares ÷ 60 Shares) of the carrying value of Beta's net assets ($600 + $1,400) prior to the reverse takeover.

Note Two   This note would disclose that there are 240 Alpha shares outstanding. The total amount of $2,160 is made up of the $560 associated with 56 of Beta's pre acquisition shares, plus the $1,600 associated with the 40 shares deemed to be issued in the reverse takeover transaction.

Note Three   The Retained Earnings reflects the majority's 93.3 percent share (56 Shares ÷ 60 Shares) of the $1,400 in Beta Retained Earnings at the time of the reverse takeover.

Exercise Four-7

As of December 31, 2002, Revco Inc. issues 115,000 of its common shares to the shareholders of Marco Ltd. in return for all 25,000 of the outstanding Marco Ltd. shares. On this date, the condensed Balance Sheets of the Revco Inc. and Marco Ltd. are as follows:

> Exercise Four-7 deals with reverse takeovers.

Revco and Marco Companies
Condensed Balance Sheets
As At December 31, 2002

	Revco Inc.	Marco Ltd.
Net Identifiable Assets	$2,465,000	$3,898,000
No Par Common Stock		
Revco (85,000 Shares Outstanding)	$1,275,000	
Marco (25,000 Shares Outstanding)		$2,625,000
Retained Earnings	1,190,000	1,273,000
Total Shareholders' Equity	$2,465,000	$3,898,000

Other Information:

1. At this time, all of the identifiable assets of both companies have fair values that are equal to their carrying values.

2. On December 31, 2002, prior to the business combination transaction, the shares of Marco are trading at $160 per share. The shares of Revco are trading at $34 per share at this time.

3. For the 12 months ending December 31, 2002, Revco Inc. had Net Income of $240,000, while Marco Ltd. had Net Income of $378,000.

Required: Prepare the condensed consolidated Balance Sheet for the combined companies as of December 31, 2002. Calculate consolidated Net Income and consolidated Earnings Per Share for the year ending December 31, 2002.

End Of Exercise Four-7

Summary Of Consolidation Procedures

4-120.   As described in this Chapter, we are developing a set of consolidation procedures involving three steps. This Chapter has focused on Step A and has introduced all of the procedures required to complete this Step. In addition, one procedure from Step B has been introduced. The procedures introduced in this Chapter are as follows:

Step A-1 Procedure   Eliminate 100 percent of the Investment In Subsidiary account.

Step A-2 Procedure   Eliminate 100 percent of all the acquisition date balances in the subsidiary's shareholders' equity (includes both contributed capital and retained earnings).

Step A-3 Procedure   Allocate any debit or credit Differential that is present at acquisition to the investor's share of fair value changes on identifiable assets, fair value changes on identifiable liabilities, and positive or negative goodwill.

Step A-4 Procedure   Allocate to a Non-Controlling Interest account in the consolidated Balance Sheet, the non-controlling interest's share of the at acquisition book value of the total shareholders' equity of the subsidiary (includes both contributed capital and retained earnings).

Step B-1 Procedure   Eliminate 100 percent of all intercompany assets and liabilities.

4-121.   The preceding list includes all of the procedures that are required in Step A. These four Procedures will be used in all subsequent consolidation problems. We will also continue to use Step B-1. However, in Chapters 5 and 6, a number of additional procedures will be added to Step B and the Step C procedures will be introduced.

Summary Of Definitional Calculations

4-122.   You may recall from our discussion of the procedural approach to be used in preparing consolidated financial statements, that we encouraged you to work towards preparing the required balances in these statements by using direct definitional calculations. To assist you in this work, we offer the following definitions that have been developed in the course of this Chapter.

Identifiable Assets And Liabilities   The amount to be included in the consolidated Balance Sheet for any identifiable asset or liability is calculated as follows:

- 100 percent of the carrying value of the identifiable asset (liability) on the books of the parent company at the Balance Sheet date; *plus*

- 100 percent of the carrying value of the identifiable asset (liability) on the books of the subsidiary company at the Balance Sheet date; *plus (minus)*

- the parent company's share of the fair value increase (decrease) on the asset (liability) (i.e., the parent company's share of the difference between the fair value of the subsidiary's asset or liability at time of acquisition and the carrying value of that asset or liability at the time of acquisition).

Goodwill   The Goodwill to be recorded in the consolidated balance sheet is equal to the excess of the cost of the investment over the parent company's share of the fair values of the subsidiary's net identifiable assets as at the time of acquisition.

Non-Controlling Interest - Balance Sheet   The Non-Controlling Interest to be recorded in the consolidated Balance Sheet is an amount equal to the non-controlling interest's ownership percentage of the book value of the subsidiary's common stock equity at the Balance Sheet date.

Contributed Capital   The Contributed Capital to be recorded in the consolidated Balance Sheet is equal to the contributed capital from the single entity Balance Sheet of the parent company.

Retained Earnings   Consolidated Retained Earnings will be equal to the Retained Earnings balance that is included in the Balance Sheet of the parent company.

4-123.   We would note that these definitions reflect the current Recommendations of the *CICA Handbook*. As you might expect, some of these definitions will have to be modified as new consolidation procedures are developed in subsequent Chapters.

Additional Readings

4-127.   In writing the material in the text, we have incorporated all of the relevant *CICA Handbook* Recommendations, as well as material from other sources that we felt to be of importance. This includes some, but not all, of the EIC Abstracts that relate to the preparation of consolidated financial statements, material from U.S. accounting pronouncements, and ideas put forward in articles published in professional accounting journals.

4-128.   While this approach meets the needs of the great majority of accounting students, some of you may wish to pursue this subject in greater depth. To facilitate this, you will find a fairly comprehensive bibliography of materials on subsidiaries and the preparation of consolidated financial statements in our *Guide to Canadian Financial Reporting*. Chapter 12 contains additional readings related to Section 1590 on subsidiaries, while Chapter 13 contains additional readings related to Section 1600 on the preparation of consolidated financial statements.

4-129.   The complete *Guide to Canadian Financial Reporting* is available on the CD-ROM which accompanies this text.

Walk Through Problem

Note This is the first example of what we refer to as walk through problems. In these walk through problems you are provided with a fill-in-the-blank solution format to assist you in solving the problem. This solution format begins on the following page and a complete solution to the problem follows the solution format. These problems are designed to be an easy way to get started with solving the type of problem illustrated in the Chapter. Having completed this problem, you should proceed to the Problems For Self Study which you will have to work without the assistance of a solution format. Also note that this same problem will be continued and extended in Chapters 5 and 6. This is to provide you with a basis for comparison as you move into more difficult procedures that are introduced in these subsequent Chapters.

Basic Data On December 31, 2002, the Puff Company purchased 60 percent of the outstanding voting shares of the Snuff Company for $720,000 in cash. On that date, subsequent to the completion of the business combination, the Balance Sheets of the Puff and Snuff Companies and the fair values of Snuff's identifiable assets and liabilities were as follows:

| | Balance Sheets | | Fair Values |
	Puff	Snuff	Snuff
Cash And Accounts Receivable	$ 350,000	$ 200,000	$200,000
Inventories	950,000	500,000	450,000
Investment In Snuff	720,000	-0-	N/A
Plant And Equipment (Net)	2,400,000	700,000	800,000
Total Assets	$4,420,000	$1,400,000	
Current Liabilities	$ 400,000	$ 100,000	$100,000
Long-Term Liabilities	1,000,000	400,000	360,000
No Par Common Stock	1,000,000	800,000	N/A
Retained Earnings	2,020,000	100,000	N/A
Total Equities	$4,420,000	$1,400,000	

Required: Prepare a consolidated Balance Sheet for the Puff Company and its subsidiary, the Snuff Company, as at December 31, 2002. Your answer should comply with the Recommendations of the *CICA Handbook*.

Walk Through Problem Solution Format

Investment Analysis

	60 Percent	100 Percent
Purchase Price	$	$
Book Value	($)	($)
Differential	$	$
Fair Value Change:		
On Inventories	$	$
On Plant And Equipment	($)	($)
On Long-Term Liabilities	($)	($)
Goodwill	$	$

Investment Elimination Entry

No Par Common Stock	$	
Retained Earnings	$	
Long-Term Liabilities	$	
Plant and Equipment (Net)	$	
Goodwill	$	
Inventories		$
Investment in Snuff		$
Non-Controlling Interest		$

Puff Company And Subsidiary
Consolidated Balance Sheet
As At December 31, 2002

Cash And Accounts Receivable	$
Inventories	$
Investment in Snuff	$
Plant And Equipment (Net)	$
Goodwill	$
Total Assets	$
Current Liabilities	$
Long-Term Liabilities	$
Non-Controlling Interest	$
No Par Common Stock	$
Retained Earnings	$
Total Equities	$

Walk Through Problem Solution

Investment Analysis

	60 Percent	100 Percent
Purchase Price	$720,000	$1,200,000
Book Value	(540,000)	(900,000)
Differential	$180,000	$ 300,000
Fair Value Changes:		
Decrease On Inventories	30,000	50,000
Increase On Plant And Equipment	(60,000)	(100,000)
Decrease On Long-Term Liabilities	(24,000)	(40,000)
Goodwill	$126,000	$ 210,000

Investment Elimination Entry

No Par Common Stock	$800,000	
Retained Earnings	100,000	
Long-Term Liabilities	24,000	
Plant and Equipment (Net)	60,000	
Goodwill	126,000	
Inventories		$ 30,000
Investment in Snuff		720,000
Non Controlling Interest (40% of $900,000)		360,000

Puff Company and Subsidiary
Consolidated Balance Sheet
As At December 31, 2002

Cash and Accounts Receivable ($350,000 + $200,000)	$ 550,000
Inventories ($950,000 + $500,000 - $30,000)	1,420,000
Investment in Snuff	-0-
Plant And Equipment (Net) ($2,400,000 + $700,000 + $60,000)	3,160,000
Goodwill	126,000
Total Assets	$5,256,000

Current Liabilities ($400,000 + $100,000)	$ 500,000
Long-Term Liabilities ($1,000,000 + $400,000 - $24,000)	1,376,000
Non-Controlling Interest	360,000
No Par Common Stock (Puff's Only)	1,000,000
Retained Earnings (Puff's Only)	2,020,000
Total Equities	$5,256,000

Problems For Self Study

(The solutions for these problems can be found following Chapter 16 of the text.)

Self Study Problem Four - 1

On December 31, 2002, the Shark Company pays cash to acquire 70 percent of the outstanding voting shares of the Peril Company. On that date, subsequent to the acquisition transaction, the Balance Sheets of the two Companies are as follows:

Shark and Peril Companies
Balance Sheets
As At December 31, 2002

	Shark	Peril
Cash	$ 590,000	$ 200,000
Accounts Receivable	2,000,000	300,000
Inventories	2,500,000	500,000
Investment In Peril (At Cost)	910,000	-0-
Plant And Equipment (Net)	4,000,000	1,000,000
Total Assets	$10,000,000	$2,000,000
Liabilities	$ 2,000,000	$ 400,000
Common Stock (No Par)	4,000,000	400,000
Retained Earnings	4,000,000	1,200,000
Total Equities	$10,000,000	$2,000,000

On the acquisition date, the fair values of the Peril Company's identifiable assets and liabilities are as follows:

Cash	$ 200,000
Accounts Receivable	250,000
Inventories	550,000
Plant And Equipment (Net)	700,000
Liabilities	(500,000)
Net Fair Values	$1,200,000

Required: Prepare a consolidated Balance Sheet for the Shark Company and its subsidiary the Peril Company as at December 31, 2002. Your solution should comply with the Recommendations of the *CICA Handbook*.

Self Study Problem Four - 2

On December 31, 2002, the Potvin Distributing Company purchased 60 percent of the outstanding voting shares of the Shroder Company. On that date, subsequent to the acquisition transaction, the Balance Sheets of the two Companies were as follows:

Potvin and Shroder Companies
Balance Sheets
As At December 31, 2002

	Potvin	Shroder
Cash	$ 300,000	$ 100,000
Accounts Receivable	2,000,000	200,000
Inventories	3,000,000	400,000
Investment In Shroder (At Cost)	1,200,000	-0-
Plant And Equipment (At Cost)	6,000,000	1,300,000
Accumulated Depreciation	(2,000,000)	(500,000)
Total Assets	$10,500,000	$1,500,000
Accounts Payable	$ 1,500,000	$ 200,000
Long-Term Liabilities	2,000,000	300,000
Common Stock (No Par)	3,000,000	1,500,000
Retained Earnings (Deficit)	4,000,000	(500,000)
Total Equities	$10,500,000	$1,500,000

On December 31, 2002, all of the identifiable assets and liabilities of both Companies have carrying values that are equal to their fair values except for the following:

Fair Values	Potvin	Shroder
Inventories	$2,800,000	$450,000
Plant and Equipment	$4,500,000	$550,000
Long-Term Liabilities	$1,600,000	$400,000

In addition to the preceding information, Shroder holds a copyright which was developed by its employees, but is not recorded on its books. On December 31, 2002, the copyright held by Shroder has a fair value of $200,000 and a remaining useful life of 5 years.

During 2002, the Shroder Company sold merchandise to the Potvin Company for a total amount of $100,000. On December 31, 2002, all of this merchandise has been resold by the Potvin Company, but Potvin still owes Shroder $10,000 on open account for these merchandise purchases.

Required: Prepare a consolidated Balance Sheet for the Potvin Distributing Company and its subsidiary, the Shroder Company as at December 31, 2002. Your solution should comply with the Recommendations of the *CICA Handbook*.

Self Study Problem Four - 3

On December 31, 2002, the Pentogram Company purchased 70 percent of the outstanding voting shares of the Square Company for $875,000 in cash. The Balance Sheets of the Pentogram Company and the Square Company, before the business combination transaction on December 31, 2002, were as follows:

Pentogram and Square Companies
Balance Sheets
As At December 31, 2002

	Pentogram	Square
Cash	$1,200,000	$ 50,000
Accounts Receivable	400,000	250,000
Inventories	2,000,000	500,000
Plant And Equipment	4,000,000	1,400,000
Accumulated Depreciation	(1,000,000)	(300,000)
Total Assets	$6,600,000	$1,900,000
Current Liabilities	$ 200,000	$ 150,000
Long-Term Liabilities	1,000,000	350,000
No Par Common Stock	2,000,000	1,000,000
Retained Earnings	3,400,000	400,000
Total Equities	$6,600,000	$1,900,000

All of the Square Company's identifiable assets and liabilities have carrying values that are equal to their fair values except for Plant and Equipment which has a fair value of $800,000, Inventories which have a fair value of $600,000 and Long-Term Liabilities which have a fair value of $400,000.

Square Company does not own any intangible assets that result from contractual or other legal rights, or are capable of being separated or divided and sold, transferred, licensed, rented, or exchanged.

Required: Prepare a consolidated Balance Sheet for the Pentogram Company and its subsidiary, the Square Company as at December 31, 2002, subsequent to the business combination. Your solution should comply with all of the requirements of the *CICA Handbook*.

Self Study Problem Four - 4

On December 31, 2002, the Shareholders' Equity section of the Balance Sheets of the Revok Company and the Taken Company are as follows:

	Revok	Taken
Contributed Capital:		
Preferred Shares	$100,000	Nil
Common Shares	450,000	$500,000
Retained Earnings	375,000	340,000
Total Shareholders' Equity	$925,000	$840,000

Other Information:

1. There has been no change in the number of shares outstanding for either company during the year ending December 31, 2002.

2. Revok has 40,000 Preferred Shares outstanding and 150,000 Common Shares outstanding. On December 31, 2002, the Common Shares are trading at $9 per share.

3. Taken has 200,000 Common Shares outstanding. On December 31, 2002, these shares are trading at $4 per share.

4. Both Companies have a December 31 year end and, during the year ending December 31, 2002, Revok had Net Income of $56,000 and Taken had Net Income of $34,000. Neither Company declared any dividends during the year ending December 31, 2002. Revok's Preferred Shares are non cumulative.

5. On December 31, 2002, all of the fair values of the net identifiable assets and liabilities of both Companies were equal to their carrying values except:

   - Revok has Land with a carrying value of $50,000 and a fair value of $65,000.
   - Taken has Land with a carrying value of $20,000 and a fair value of $32,000.

6. On December 31, 2002, Taken Company issues 300,000 of its common shares to the shareholders of Revok Company, in return for all of their outstanding common shares.

Required:

A. Calculate the amount of goodwill that will be recorded in the December 31, 2002 consolidated Balance Sheet of Taken Company and its subsidiary Revok Company.

B. Prepare the Shareholders' Equity section of the December 31, 2002 consolidated Balance Sheet of Taken Company and its subsidiary Revok Company.

C. Calculate the 2002 consolidated Net Income for Taken Company and its subsidiary Revok Company.

D. Calculate the 2002 Earnings Per Share for Taken Company and its subsidiary Revok Company.

Assignment Problems

(The solutions for these problems are only available in
the solutions manual that has been provided to your instructor.)

Assignment Problem Four - 1

The Excelsior Company purchased 80 percent of the outstanding voting shares of the Excelsiee Company for $120,000 in cash. On the acquisition date, after the business combination transaction, the Balance Sheets of the two Companies and the fair values of the Excelsiee Company's identifiable assets and liabilities were as follows:

Excelsior and Excelsiee Companies
Balance Sheets

	Book Values Excelsior	Book Values Excelsiee	Fair Values Excelsiee
Cash	$ 100,000	$ 120,000	$ 120,000
Accounts Receivable	1,500,000	500,000	490,000
Inventories	2,300,000	400,000	350,000
Investment in Excelsiee (At Cost)	120,000	-0-	-0-
Plant and Equipment (Net)	3,980,000	1,100,000	1,120,000
Total Assets	$8,000,000	$2,120,000	

	Book Values Excelsior	Book Values Excelsiee	Fair Values Excelsiee
Accounts Payable	$1,000,000	$ 400,000	$ 400,000
Mortgage Payable	-0-	120,000	120,000
Long-Term Liabilities	2,000,000	1,400,000	1,500,000
Common Stock No Par	2,000,000	150,000	
Retained Earnings	3,000,000	50,000	
Total Equities	$8,000,000	$2,120,000	

Required: Prepare a consolidated Balance Sheet for the Excelsior Company and its subsidiary the Excelsiee Company as at the acquisition date. Your answer should comply with the Recommendations of the *CICA Handbook*.

Assignment Problem Four - 2

On December 31, 2002, before the business combination transaction, the Balance Sheets of the Pike Company and the Stirling Company were as follows:

Pike and Stirling Companies
Balances Sheets
As At December 31, 2002

	Pike	Stirling
Cash	$ 195,000	$ 118,500
Accounts Receivable (Net)	472,500	253,500
Inventories	883,500	596,700
Plant And Equipment (Net)	4,050,000	2,251,500
Goodwill	142,500	45,000
Total Assets	$5,743,500	$3,265,200
Current Liabilities	$ 13,500	$ 45,000
Long-Term Liabilities	1,080,000	1,673,700
Preferred Stock - Par $100	-0-	30,000
Common Stock - No Par	2,550,000	1,500,000
Retained Earnings	2,100,000	16,500
Total Equities	$5,743,500	$3,265,200

On December 31, 2002, Pike Company issues 37,500 of its shares in return for 75 percent of the outstanding shares of Stirling. On this same date, Pike purchased one-half of the issue of Stirling Preferred Stock for $15,000 in cash.

On the combination date, the identifiable assets and liabilities of Stirling Company had fair values that were equal to their carrying values except for the following fair values:

Accounts Receivable	$ 237,000
Inventories	571,500
Long-Term Liabilities	1,823,700

The Pike Company has 50,000 No Par Common Shares outstanding with a current market price of $36 per share. The Stirling Company has 20,000 No Par Common Shares outstanding. The Preferred Shares of the Stirling Company are cumulative, non-participating, and have no dividends in arrears. There have been no intercompany transactions prior to December 31, 2002.

Required: Prepare, in accordance with the Recommendations of the *CICA Handbook*, the consolidated Balance Sheet as at December 31, 2002, for Pike Company and its subsidiary, Stirling Company.

Assignment Problem Four - 3

On December 31, 2002, the closed Trial Balances of the Pass Company and the Sass Company, before the business combination transaction, were as follows:

	Pass	Sass
Cash and Receivables	$ 100,000	$ 10,000
Inventories	3,300,000	290,000
Plant And Equipment (At Cost)	9,000,000	3,000,000
Accumulated Depreciation	(3,400,000)	(1,200,000)
Total Assets	$9,000,000	$2,100,000
Current Liabilities	$ 300,000	$ 200,000
Long-Term Liabilities	3,500,000	800,000
Mortgage Payable	-0-	300,000
Common Stock - No Par	1,000,000	-0-
Common Stock - Par $50	-0-	900,000
Contributed Surplus	-0-	300,000
Retained Earnings (Deficit)	4,200,000	(400,000)
Total Equities	$9,000,000	$2,100,000

The Pass Company has 25,000 shares outstanding on December 31, 2002 which are trading at $50 per share on this date. On December 31, 2002, the identifiable assets and liabilities of both Companies had fair values that were equal to their carrying values except for the following fair values:

Fair Values	Pass	Sass
Plant and Equipment (Net)	$7,000,000	$1,500,000
Long-Term Liabilities	3,000,000	900,000

It was also determined that on December 31, 2002, Sass Company had a registered trademark with a fair value of $120,000 that was not recorded on its books.

Prior to the business combination, in 2002, Pass sold merchandise to Sass for $200,000 and Sass sold Pass merchandise for $100,000. On December 31, 2002, one-half of these intercompany purchases had been resold to parties outside the consolidated entity. These sales provide both Companies with a 20 percent gross margin on sales prices. On December 31, 2002, Sass owed Pass $50,000 on its intercompany merchandise purchases.

On December 31, 2002, Pass issued 15,000 of its shares to acquire 75 percent of the outstanding shares of Sass.

Required: Prepare the combined companies' Balance Sheet as at December 31, 2002. Your solution should comply with the Recommendations of the *CICA Handbook*, including Sections 1581 and 3062.

Assignment Problem Four - 4

The Peretti Company and the Blakelock Company are two successful Canadian companies operating on Prince Edward Island. On December 31, 2002, the condensed Balance Sheets and the identifiable fair values of the Peretti Company and the Blakelock Company are as follows:

Peretti Company
December 31, 2002

	Balance Sheet	Fair Values
Current Assets	$2,220,000	$2,340,000
Non-Current Assets (Net)	3,600,000	3,900,000
Total Assets	$5,820,000	
Current Liabilities	$ 420,000	$ 420,000
Long-Term Liabilities	1,500,000	1,440,000
Common Stock - No Par	1,800,000	
Retained Earnings	2,100,000	
Total Equities	$5,820,000	

Blakelock Company
December 31, 2002

	Balance Sheet	Fair Values
Current Assets	$1,800,000	$1,980,000
Non-Current Assets (Net)	3,540,000	2,400,000
Total Assets	$5,340,000	
Current Liabilities	$ 720,000	$ 720,000
Long-Term Liabilities	2,400,000	2,520,000
Common Stock - No Par	1,200,000	
Retained Earnings	1,020,000	
Total Equities	$5,340,000	

The Peretti Company has 300,000 common shares outstanding with a market price of $12 per share. The Blakelock Company has 60,000 common shares outstanding with a market price of $23 per share. On December 31, 2002, Peretti owes Blakelock $48,000 for the use of Blakelock's accounting staff during 2002.

Required: Assume that on December 31, 2002, subsequent to the preparation of the preceding single entity Balance Sheets, the Peretti and Blakelock Companies enter into a business combination. The following two independent cases are based on differing assumptions with respect to how the combination was effected. In both cases, prepare the appropriate Balance Sheet for the combined business entity as at December 31, 2002, subsequent to the business combination.

A.   The Peretti Company purchases 60 percent of the outstanding shares of the Blakelock Company for $900,000 in cash. The consolidated Balance Sheet will be prepared using the entity approach to consolidated financial statements.

B.   The Peretti Company issues 75,000 of its shares and uses them to acquire 60 percent of the Blakelock Company shares. The consolidated Balance Sheet will be prepared in compliance with the recommendations of the *CICA Handbook*.

Assignment Problem Four - 5

On December 31, 2002, the Poplin Company acquires 95 percent of the outstanding shares of Silk Company in return for cash of $1,235,000. The remaining 5 percent of the Silk Company shares remain in the hands of the public.

Immediately after this acquisition transaction, the Balance Sheets of the two Companies were as follows:

Poplin And Silk Companies
Balance Sheets
As At December 31, 2002

	Poplin	Silk
Cash	$ 220,000	$ 78,000
Accounts Receivable	1,140,000	125,000
Inventories	2,560,000	972,000
Investment In Silk	1,235,000	N/A
Land	665,000	137,000
Plant And Equipment (Net)	2,750,000	430,000
Total Assets	$8,570,000	$1,742,000
Current Liabilities	$ 560,000	$ 225,000
Long Term Liabilities	1,340,000	517,000
Common Stock - No Par	2,800,000	450,000
Retained Earnings	3,870,000	550,000
Total Equities	$8,570,000	$1,742,000

At the time of this acquisition, all of the identifiable assets and liabilities of Silk Company had fair values that were equal to their carrying values except the Land which had a fair value of $337,000, and the Plant And Equipment which had a fair value of $380,000. Poplin Company will use push down-accounting, as described in Section 1625 of the *CICA Handbook* to account for its Investment in Silk.

Required:

A. Prepare the Silk Company's Balance Sheet that is to be used in preparing the December 31, 2002 consolidated Balance Sheet.

B. Prepare the consolidated Balance Sheet for Poplin Company and its subsidiary Silk as at December 31, 2002.

Assignment Problem Four - 6

The Balance Sheets of the Fortune Company and the Gold Company as at December 31, 2002 and July 1, 2003 prior to any business combination transaction, were as follows:

	Fortune Company		Gold Company	
	1/7/03	31/12/02	1/7/03	31/12/02
Current Assets	$ 420,000	$ 410,000	$ 620,000	$ 604,000
Fixed Assets (Net)	1,320,000	1,400,000	2,920,000	2,996,000
Total Assets	$1,740,000	$1,810,000	$3,540,000	$3,600,000
Current Liabilities	$ 220,000	$ 230,000	$ 350,000	$ 360,000
Long-Term Liabilities	430,000	680,000	520,000	930,000
Contributed Capital:				
Redeemable Preferred Shares	200,000	200,000	-0-	-0-
Common Shares	500,000	500,000	1,200,000	1,200,000
Retained Earnings	390,000	200,000	1,470,000	1,110,000
Total Equities	$1,740,000	$1,810,000	$3,540,000	$3,600,000

Other Information:

1. For the six month period ending July 1, 2003, the Fortune Company had Net Income of $190,000 and the Gold Company had Net Income of $360,000. These figures did not contain any Extraordinary Items or Results Of Discontinued Operations. Neither Company declared any dividends during this period.

2. On both Balance Sheet dates, the Fortune Company had 20,000 Redeemable Preferred Shares and 50,000 Common Shares outstanding. On July 1, 2003, the Common Shares were trading at $22 per share.

3. On both Balance Sheet dates, the Gold Company had 40,000 Common Shares outstanding. On July 1, 2003, these shares were trading at $75 per share.

4. On July 1, 2003, all of the fair values of Fortune Company's and Gold Company's identifiable assets and liabilities had book values that were equal to their fair values, except for Fixed Assets. Fortune's Fixed Assets had a fair value of $1,900,000, while Gold's Fixed Assets had a fair value of $2,800,000.

5. Neither Company owns any intangible assets that result from contractual or other legal rights, or are capable of being separated or divided and sold, transferred, licensed, rented, or exchanged.

Required: For the following two independent cases, use the guidelines provided by the Emerging Issues Committee (EIC) Abstract No. 10 to prepare the July 1, 2003 Consolidated Balance Sheet for Fortune Company and its subsidiary Gold Company. In addition, calculate Consolidated Net Income and Earnings Per Share for the six month period ending July 1, 2003. Your solution should comply with Sections 1581 and 3062 of the *CICA Handbook*.

A. On July 1, 2003, Fortune Company issues 100,000 additional Common Shares in exchange for all of the outstanding Common Shares of Gold Company.

B. On July 1, 2003, Fortune Company issues 85,000 additional Common Shares in exchange for 36,000 of the outstanding Common Shares of Gold Company.

Chapter 5

Consolidation Subsequent To Acquisition (No Unrealized Intercompany Profits)

Procedures Subsequent To Acquisition

5-1.   Once we move beyond the date on which the parent acquired its controlling interest in the subsidiary shares, the preparation of consolidated financial statements becomes much more complex. We will have to deal with the concept of consolidated Net Income and the preparation of a consolidated Income Statement. Further, both the Statement Of Retained Earnings and the Cash Flow Statement will have to be prepared on a consolidated basis. Even the preparation of a consolidated Balance Sheet in the periods subsequent to the date of acquisition will become more complex as we have to write off fair value changes, recognize any goodwill impairment losses, eliminate intercompany assets and liabilities, and allocate the retained earnings of the subsidiary since acquisition.

5-2.   We will begin this Chapter with a simple example of the conceptual alternatives in the presentation of the consolidated Income Statement. While we will find that the *CICA Handbook* requires the use of the parent company approach in preparing a consolidated Income Statement for a parent company and its subsidiaries, this example will also illustrate other alternatives. In addition, you should note that the proprietary approach consolidated Income Statements illustrated do have a practical application. They are identical to the Income Statements that would be prepared when proportionate consolidation is used to account for joint ventures.

Conceptual Alternatives For The Consolidated Income Statement

Example

5-3.   In order to provide an illustration of the various possible approaches to the preparation of the consolidated Income Statement, we will use the following example:

The Pick Company owns 60 percent of the outstanding shares of the Stick Company. The purchase was made at a time when all of the identifiable assets and liabilities of the Stick Company had carrying values that were equal to their fair values. The purchase price was equal to 60 percent of the carrying values of the Stick Company's net identifiable assets. In a subsequent year the condensed Income Statements of the two Companies are as follows:

Pick and Stick Companies
Income Statements

	Pick	Stick
Sales	$4,000,000	$2,000,000
Cost of Goods Sold	$2,500,000	$1,000,000
Other Expenses	700,000	400,000
Total Expenses	$3,200,000	$1,400,000
Net Income	$ 800,000	$ 600,000

Proprietary Concept Solution

5-4.   Under this conceptual approach, the expenses and revenues that are disclosed in the consolidated Income Statement consist of 100 percent of the parent company's expenses and revenues plus a share of the subsidiary's expenses and revenues that is based on the parent company's ownership interest (60 percent in this example). The resulting Income Statement is as follows:

Pick Company and Subsidiary
Consolidated Income Statement
Proprietary Approach

Sales ($4,000,000 + $1,200,000)	$5,200,000
Cost Of Goods Sold ($2,500,000 + $600,000)	$3,100,000
Other Expenses ($700,000 + $240,000)	940,000
Total Expenses	$4,040,000
Consolidated Net Income	$1,160,000

5-5.   Since the consolidation procedures remove the non-controlling interest's share of the individual subsidiary expenses and revenues, there is no necessity to disclose a separate Non-Controlling Interest in the consolidated Income Statement. This, of course, is analogous to the procedures that were used in preparing the consolidated Balance Sheet under the proprietary concept. You might also note that the consolidated Net Income of $1,160,000 is equal to the sum of the Pick Company's Net Income of $800,000, plus 60 percent of the Stick Company's Net Income of $600,000.

Parent Company Concept Solution

5-6.   This conceptual approach views the non-controlling interest as a part of the consolidated entity and, as a consequence, the consolidated Income Statement includes 100 percent of the expenses and revenues of both the parent and the subsidiary company. With respect to the nature of the non-controlling interest's participation in the consolidated entity, the parent company approach views these shareholders as having a creditor-like interest. Given this view, the non-controlling interest in the income of the consolidated entity would be viewed as a claim analogous to interest charges on creditor interests. This would require that the Non-Controlling Interest be deducted in the computation of consolidated Net Income. The resulting consolidated Income Statement would appear as follows:

Pick Company and Subsidiary
Consolidated Income Statement
Parent Company Approach

Sales ($4,000,000 + $2,000,000)	$6,000,000
Cost Of Goods Sold ($2,500,000 + $1,000,000)	$3,500,000
Other Expenses ($700,000 + $400,000)	1,100,000
Total Expenses	$4,600,000
Combined Income	$1,400,000
Non-Controlling Interest [(40%)($600,000)]	240,000
Consolidated Net Income	$1,160,000

5-7.   There are several aspects of this presentation that you should note. First, in our disclosure we have calculated a separate subtotal for Combined Income. This has been done for illustrative purposes only. Normal disclosure would have the Non-Controlling Interest grouped and deducted with the other expenses of the consolidated entity (note that if the subsidiary has a Net Loss, the Non-Controlling Interest will be an addition rather than a deduction). Referring to the 2001 edition of *Financial Reporting in Canada*, this publication's survey of large Canadian companies found that the Non-Controlling Interest was most commonly shown as a separate item following the disclosure of current and future income taxes.

5-8.   As a second point, note that the Non-Controlling Interest is based on the reported income of the subsidiary. Consistent with the view that the non-controlling shareholders have a creditor-like interest, there is no recognition of their share of the adjustments required in the application of consolidation procedures (e.g., fair value changes). As a consequence, the Non-Controlling Interest in the consolidated Income Statement is simply their 40 percent share of Stick Company's reported Net Income of $600,000.

5-9.   Finally, note that the consolidated Net Income is the same figure that we arrived at using the proprietary approach. This will always be the case as both the proprietary and the parent company approach ignore the non-controlling interest's share of the various adjustments required in applying consolidation procedures. The difference between these two approaches is one of disclosure, with the parent company approach including the Non-Controlling Interest in the consolidated Income Statement while the proprietary approach excludes this amount.

Entity Concept Solution

5-10.   As was the case with the parent company approach, the entity approach views the non-controlling interest as being a part of the consolidated entity. This would mean that the consolidated expenses and revenues would again include 100 percent of the reported expenses and revenues of both the parent company and the subsidiary company. The difference is that the entity approach views the non-controlling interest as an additional class of owner's equity. Given this, the non-controlling interest in the income of the consolidated entity must be treated in a manner analogous to the treatment of dividends on preferred shares. That is, it will be viewed as a distribution of Net Income rather than as a determinant of Net Income. As a result, instead of being a deduction in the computation of consolidated Net Income, the Non-Controlling Interest under the entity concept would be shown as a distribution of income in the consolidated Statement of Retained Earnings. The entity approach consolidated Income Statement would be as follows:

Pick Company and Subsidiary
Consolidated Income Statement
Entity Approach

Sales ($4,000,000 + $2,000,000)	$6,000,000
Cost Of Goods Sold ($2,500,000 + $1,000,000)	$3,500,000
Other Expenses ($700,000 + $400,000)	1,100,000
Total Expenses	$4,600,000
Consolidated Net Income	$1,400,000

5-11.   Note that the figure that was designated Combined Income under the parent company approach has become consolidated Net Income.   Further, it is equal to the combined Net Incomes of the individual entities ($800,000 for Pick and $600,000 for Stick). In this example, with no fair value changes or goodwill, the Non-Controlling Interest would still be $240,000 or 40 percent of the reported income of the subsidiary. As can be seen in the example, however, it would not be disclosed in the consolidated Income Statement. Rather, it would be shown as a deduction in the consolidated Statement Of Retained Earnings in a manner analogous to the disclosure accorded dividends on preferred stock.

CICA Handbook Requirements

5-12.   The position of the *CICA Handbook* on the choice of conceptual approaches to be used in the preparation of the consolidated Income Statement is not internally consistent. With respect to the treatment of the Non-Controlling Interest in Income Before Discontinued Operations And Extraordinary Items, the *Handbook* makes the following Recommendation:

> **Paragraph 1600.67**   *The non-controlling interest in the income or loss before discontinued operations and extraordinary items for the period should be disclosed separately in the consolidated income statement.* (January, 1990)

5-13.   This position reflects the parent company approach in that it requires a Non-Controlling Interest (thus, rejecting the proprietary approach) to be deducted in the consolidated Income Statement, prior to reaching the bottom line figure for Net Income (thus, rejecting the entity approach). However, with respect to the treatment of subsidiary results of discontinued operations and extraordinary items, the Recommendation continues as follows:

> **Paragraph 1600.67**   *Where there are discontinued operations or extraordinary items, the parent company's portion of such items should be disclosed.* (January, 1990)

5-14.   This, of course, is a reflection of the proprietary conceptual approach to consolidations. There is no explanation offered for this apparent inconsistency.

Exercise Five-1 deals with disclosure requirements in the consolidated Income Statement.

Exercise Five-1

On January 1, 2002, Part Company acquires 65 percent of the outstanding shares of Seam Company. At this time, all of the identifiable assets and liabilities of Seam had fair values that were equal to the carrying values. The cost of the shares was equal to 65 percent of the net asset value of Seam. The single entity Income Statements for Part Company and Seam Company, for the year ending December 31, 2002, are as follows:

Part and Seam Companies
Income Statements
Year Ending December 31, 2002

This is a continuation of Exercise Five-1.

	Part Company	Seam Company
Revenues	$982,000	$463,000
Expenses:		
Cost of Goods Sold	$448,000	$219,000
Other Expenses	374,000	115,000
Total Expenses	$822,000	$334,000
Income Before Results Of Discontinued Operations	$160,000	$129,000
Loss From Discontinued Operations	Nil	(63,000)
Net Income	$160,000	$ 66,000

Required: Prepare the consolidated Income Statement for Part Company and its subsidiary Seam Company, for the year ending December 31, 2002. You answer should comply with the Recommendations found in the *CICA Handbook*.

End of Exercise Five-1

General Approach To Problem Solving

The Problem With Consolidation Procedures

5-15.   The preparation of consolidated financial statements, to an extent not approached by any other area of financial accounting, has seen a tremendous amount of attention devoted to the development of detailed and extensive technical procedures. In addition to several alternative worksheet approaches, consolidation problems have been solved using a variety of computerized approaches involving spreadsheets and linear programming. Indeed, it seems that anyone who has ever taught this subject has reached the conclusion that they have found a "better way" to deal with such problems.

5-16.   In our opinion, there are two basic drawbacks with relying on any set of consolidation procedures, including those that will be used in this text:

1. You can develop great facility with any of the available detailed procedural approaches, without acquiring any real understanding of the content of consolidated financial statements. We have often encountered situations where a student, having developed lightning-like speed in manipulating a work sheet, will be completely at a loss when asked to do a simple calculation of consolidated Net Income or the amount of the Non-Controlling Interest to be included in a consolidated Balance Sheet. It appears that focusing on detailed procedures does little to facilitate an understanding of the real content of consolidated financial statements.

2. An equally serious problem with detailed procedural approaches is that they only work when the data for a consolidation problem is presented in the format for which the procedural approach was developed. For example, if you develop a set of procedures that will work when the investment in the subsidiary is carried in the underlying records of the parent company by the cost method, these procedures will not work if the investment is carried by the equity method. Similarly, if procedures are developed for problems which require both a consolidated Income Statement and a consolidated Balance Sheet, they will not work when only a consolidated Balance Sheet is required. If detailed procedures are to be relied on, the only solution to this problem is to develop a full blown set of procedures for every possible problem format.

15-17. As we noted in Chapter 4, it is our belief that if you develop a thorough understanding of the consolidation process, the most efficient method of preparing consolidated financial statements is to be in a position to make an independent computation of each of the consolidated account balances. This approach does not rely on detailed worksheet or journal entry procedures and, as a consequence, there is no need to learn alternative sets of consolidation procedures.

15-18. The problem remains, however, of getting you to the stage where you can efficiently make definitional calculations of the various balances that may be required in a consolidation problem. This requires some type of organized procedural approach and, as we indicated in Chapter 4, we will base our procedures on the use of journal entries applied to the balances that are given in the basic problem data. We would stress that we view these procedures as an interim teaching device. We encourage you to discontinue using them as soon as you feel that you understand the concepts well enough to make direct computations of the balances that are required for inclusion in the consolidated financial statements.

Classification Of Problems
Problem Requirements

5-19. As was indicated in the preceding Section, consolidation problems can be presented in a variety of formats. While there is an almost unlimited number of possibilities in this area, we have found it useful to classify problems in terms of:

1. problem requirements and
2. the method of carrying the investment.

5-20. With respect to problem requirements, there are two basic types of problems. We have designated these two types as open trial balance problems and closed trial balance problems. The two types of problems can be described as follows:

Open Trial Balance Problems   This is the designation that we use for any problem that requires the preparation of any consolidated statement or the calculation of any consolidated information, other than all or part of a consolidated Balance Sheet. The use of this designation reflects the fact that such problems are often, but not always, presented as an open trial balance (i.e., a trial balance prepared before expenses and revenues have been closed to retained earnings). A typical problem of this variety would require the preparation of a consolidated Income Statement, a consolidated Statement Of Retained Earnings, and a consolidated Balance Sheet. Procedures are required here to deal with both the beginning of the year balance in subsidiary Retained Earnings, as well as items of expense or revenue that occur during the year.

Closed Trial Balance Problems   This is the designation that we use for problems which require only the preparation of all or part of a consolidated Balance Sheet. The use of this designation reflects the fact that such problems are often, but not always, presented as a closed trial balance (i.e., a trial balance prepared after expenses and revenues have been closed to retained earnings.) The procedures developed for this type of problem do not have to deal with either the opening Retained Earnings or expense and revenue items that occur during the year.

Accounting Method

5-21. When consolidated financial statements are prepared, the parent's Investment In Subsidiary account will be eliminated and replaced by the various assets and liabilities of the subsidiary. This means that the parent company can carry this Investment In Subsidiary account by any method they choose. As the account will not be included in the published consolidated financial statements, *CICA Handbook* Recommendations are not applicable.

5-22. While it is not possible to establish this from published financial statements, it is likely that most companies carry their Investment In Subsidiary accounts at cost. It is a less complicated method and, in addition, cost is generally the tax basis for such assets. However, it is possible that a problem will be presented with the investment carried at equity. This results in a second approach to the classification of problems — problems in which the Investment In Subsidiary is accounted for by the cost method or problems where the Investment In Subsidiary is carried by the equity method.

Classifications To Be Covered

5-23.   Given the two types of problem requirements that we have designated and the two methods by which the investment may be carried, we can identify the following general types of problems:

1. **Open** Trial Balance with the investment at **Cost**
2. **Closed** Trial Balance with the investment at **Cost**
3. **Open** Trial Balance with the investment at **Equity**
4. **Closed** Trial Balance with the investment at **Equity**

5-24.   In previous editions of this book we have developed procedures to deal with each of these possible problem formats. Our experience has been that this does not enhance your understanding of consolidated financial statements, nor does it assist in arriving at the ultimate goal of preparing consolidated financial statements by using direct definitional calculations.

5-25.   In particular, there seemed to be difficulty in understanding the somewhat awkward procedures that are required when the Investment In Subsidiary account is carried by the equity method. It is our impression that few students ever really mastered these procedures. Further, we do not believe that it is a useful expenditure of your time to make the effort that would be required to fully understand these procedures.

5-26.   Given this situation, the comprehensive example that will be used in this Chapter, as well as in Chapter 6, will illustrate only the two types of problems where the Investment In Subsidiary is carried by the cost method. We will not, in either this Chapter or Chapter 6, develop procedures to be used when the investment is carried by the equity method. Note, however, we have included coverage of these procedures in Chapter 8 which deals with a variety of advanced topics in consolidations. Because of the limited interest in these advanced topics, we have provided Chapter 8 and the related problem material on the CD-ROM which accompanies this text, rather than in the main body of the text.

The Procedures

5-27.   As was indicated in Chapter 4, we are going to develop a set of procedures which use the basic data of the problem, adjust and eliminate parts of this basic data using journal entries, and use this information to arrive at final figures to be included in the consolidated financial statements. As outlined in that Chapter, there are three basic Steps involved in these procedures and they can be described as follows:

> **Step A - Investment Elimination**   This first Step will eliminate 100 percent of the investment account against the subsidiary shareholders' equity at the time of acquisition. As a part of this Step, entries will also be made to record the investor's share of the acquisition date fair value changes and goodwill of the subsidiary. In addition, a Non-Controlling Interest will be established, representing the non-controlling shareholders' interest in carrying values of the net identifiable assets of the subsidiary as at the date of acquisition.

> This Step was dealt with in a comprehensive fashion in Chapter 4 and was codified into a set of four specific procedures to be used. These procedures are repeated here for your convenience:

Step A-1 Procedure Eliminate 100 percent of the Investment In Subsidiary account.

Step A-2 Procedure Eliminate 100 percent of all the balances in the subsidiary's shareholders' equity that are present on the acquisition date.

Step A-3 Procedure Allocate any debit or credit Differential that is present at acquisition to the investor's share of fair value changes on identifiable assets, fair value changes on identifiable liabilities, and positive or negative goodwill.

Step A-4 Procedure Allocate to a Non-Controlling Interest account in the consolidated Balance Sheet, the non-controlling interest's share of the book value of the total Shareholders' Equity of the subsidiary at acquisition.

Note that these procedures will have to be implemented, even in periods subsequent to the year of acquisition. This reflects the fact that consolidation entries are only working paper entries and are not entered on the books of the individual legal entities. An exception to this would be when push-down accounting is used (see Chapter 4). However, unless push-down accounting is used, the Step A entries required in the year of acquisition will have to be repeated in each subsequent year.

Step B - Adjustments And Eliminations This Step involves making adjustments and eliminations to the various accounts that will be included in the consolidated information. At this stage of the development of our consolidation procedures, we can identify four types of adjustments and eliminations that we must be prepared to deal with. They are as follows:

1. If intercompany asset and liability balances are present, they must be eliminated. This procedure was discussed and illustrated in Chapter 4. It was also stated in terms of a specific procedure as follows:

    Step B-1 Procedure Eliminate 100 percent of all intercompany assets and liabilities.

2. In Step A, the parent company's share of all of the acquisition date fair value changes on the subsidiary's assets and liabilities was recorded. To the extent that these fair value changes were recorded on assets with an unlimited economic life, the recorded fair value changes can be left in place until such time as the assets are sold. If such assets are sold, there will be a need to adjust any resulting gain or loss recorded on the books of the subsidiary to reflect the realization of the fair value change.

    When the fair value changes are recorded on assets or liabilities with a limited life, the subsidiary will record amortization, depletion, or depreciation on these assets based on their carrying values. As a consequence, there will be a need to adjust these amortization, depletion, or depreciation amounts to reflect the realization of the fair value changes on these assets and liabilities. If such assets are sold prior to the end of their economic life, the resulting gain or loss must be adjusted for the unrealized balance of the fair value change.

    In addition to the preceding adjustments, the consolidation procedures that will be used subsequent to acquisition will require adjustments to recognize any Goodwill Impairment Loss that has occurred in the post acquisition period.

3. If intercompany expenses and revenues are present, they must be eliminated. Note that, in this Chapter, we are dealing only with intercompany expenses and revenues, not unrealized intercompany profits. For example, if there is an intercompany sale of merchandise and the goods have been resold to an arm's length party, the profit on the original sale is realized and the only elimination will be for the intercompany sale and purchase. However, if the goods remain in the inventories of the purchasing company, the profit on the sale is unrealized because the merchandise remains within the consolidated entity. This unrealized

intercompany profit must be eliminated. The procedures for dealing with this type of situation will be dealt with in Chapter 6.

4. If intercompany dividends have been declared, they must be removed from the revenues and dividends declared account.

Step C - Distribution Of Subsidiary Retained Earnings   Step A eliminated only the at acquisition balance of the subsidiary's retained earnings. In periods subsequent to acquisition, this leaves a balance in the retained earnings of the subsidiary. This balance represents the retained earnings of the subsidiary that have been accumulated since the date of acquisition. If the parent owned 100 percent of the subsidiary and there were no Step B adjustments or eliminations, the subsidiary's retained earnings since acquisition balance would simply become a part of consolidated Retained Earnings.

However, these assumptions are usually not applicable. In most situations there will be less than 100 percent ownership and a portion of the subsidiary retained earnings since acquisition will have to be allocated to the Non-Controlling Interest in the consolidated Balance Sheet. Further, there will almost always be Step B adjustments and eliminations, some of which will alter the subsidiary's retained earnings since acquisition balance. This is further complicated by the fact that some of these Step B changes will apply only to the parent's share of subsidiary retained earnings since acquisition, while others will alter both the parent's and the non-controlling interest's shares of this balance. (This latter situation does not turn up until Chapter 6 when we introduce unrealized intercompany profits.) As a consequence, it is not possible to allocate the parent's and non-controlling interest's shares of the subsidiary's retained earnings since acquisition until we have completed the Step B adjustments and eliminations.

This brings us to Step C. At this point, our one remaining task will be to take the subsidiary's retained earnings since acquisition balance, as adjusted by the Step B adjustments and eliminations, and allocate it between the Non-Controlling Interest in the consolidated Balance Sheet and consolidated Retained Earnings.

5-28.   Given this general outline of the procedures to be followed, we can now turn our attention to the application of these three Steps to the open and closed trial balance versions of a comprehensive problem.

Comprehensive Example - Open Trial Balance With Investment At Cost

Basic Data

5-29.   Our first example involves a problem in which you are asked to prepare more than just a consolidated Balance Sheet. While a consolidated Cash Flow Statement is not required, a consolidated Income Statement and a consolidated Statement of Retained Earnings are required, in addition to a consolidated Balance Sheet. This means that this problem would be classified as an open trial balance problem. As will always be the case in this Chapter, the Investment In Subsidiary is carried at cost.

Example On January 1, 2002, the Pleigh Company purchases 80 percent of the outstanding shares of the Sleigh Company for $3,200,000 in cash. On that date, the Sleigh Company had No Par Common Stock of $2,000,000 and Retained Earnings of $1,500,000. On December 31, 2006, the adjusted trial balances of the Pleigh Company and its subsidiary, the Sleigh Company are as follows:

	Pleigh	Sleigh
Cash	$ 500,000	$ 300,000
Current Receivables	800,000	400,000
Inventories	2,500,000	1,700,000
Long-Term Note Receivable	200,000	-0-
Investment In Sleigh - At Cost	3,200,000	-0-
Land	1,500,000	1,000,000
Plant And Equipment (Net)	4,500,000	1,900,000
Cost Of Goods Sold	2,800,000	1,500,000
Depreciation Expense	200,000	100,000
Other Expenses	364,000	616,000
Interest Expense	240,000	84,000
Dividends Declared	350,000	100,000
Total Debits	$17,154,000	$7,700,000
Current Liabilities	$ 500,000	$ 200,000
Long-Term Liabilities	2,000,000	700,000
No Par Common Stock	8,000,000	2,000,000
Retained Earnings (January 1)	2,550,000	2,300,000
Sales	4,000,000	2,500,000
Interest Revenue	24,000	-0-
Dividend Revenue	80,000	-0-
Total Credits	$17,154,000	$7,700,000
2006 Net Income	$ 500,000	$ 200,000
December 31, 2006 Retained Earnings	$ 2,700,000	$2,400,000

Other Information:

1. At the date of Pleigh Company's acquisition of the Sleigh Company's shares, all of the identifiable assets and liabilities of the Sleigh Company had fair values that were equal to their carrying values except Inventories which had fair values that were $100,000 more than their carrying values, Land with a fair value that was $150,000 less than its carrying value and Plant And Equipment which had a fair value that was $250,000 greater than its carrying value. The Plant And Equipment had a remaining useful life on the acquisition date of 20 years while the Inventories that were present on the acquisition date were sold during the year ending December 31, 2006. The Land is still on the books of the Sleigh Company on December 31, 2006. Both companies use the straight line method to calculate depreciation and amortization.

2. In each of the years since Pleigh acquired control over Sleigh, the goodwill arising on this business combination transaction has been tested for impairment. No impairment was found in any of the years since acquisition.

3. Sleigh Company's Sales during 2006 include sales of $300,000 to Pleigh Company. All of this merchandise has been resold by the Pleigh Company.

4. On December 31, 2006, the Pleigh Company is holding Sleigh Company's long-term note payable in the amount of $200,000. Interest at 12 percent is payable on July 1 of each year. Pleigh Company has been holding this note since July 1, 2004.

Required Prepare a consolidated Income Statement and a consolidated Statement Of Retained Earnings for the year ending December 31, 2006 and a consolidated Balance Sheet as at December 31, 2006 for the Pleigh Company and its subsidiary, the Sleigh Company.

Step A Procedures
Investment Analysis

5-30. As indicated in Chapters 3 and 4, in business combination transactions it is generally useful to prepare an analysis of the investment cost. Using the procedures developed in those Chapters, the analysis of the Pleigh Company's investment in the Sleigh Company is as follows:

	80 Percent	100 Percent
Investment Cost	$3,200,000	$4,000,000
Book Value At Acquisition	(2,800,000)	(3,500,000)
Differential	$ 400,000	$ 500,000
Fair Value Changes:		
Increase On Inventories	(80,000)	(100,000)
Decrease On Land	120,000	150,000
Increase On Plant And Equipment (Net)	(200,000)	(250,000)
Goodwill	$ 240,000	$ 300,000

5-31. Note that this analysis is based on the values for Sleigh Company's assets at the time of acquisition. This reflects the fact that fair value and goodwill amounts to be recognized are established at this time.

5-32. At acquisition, the total fair value of the net assets of the Sleigh Company is $3,700,000 ($3,500,000 + $100,000 - $150,000 + $250,000). The Goodwill of $240,000 can be verified by comparing the investment cost of $3,200,000 to $2,960,000, the investor's 80 percent share of the fair values of $3,700,000.

Investment Elimination

5-33. Based on the preceding analysis and using the procedures developed in Chapter 4, the journal entry to eliminate the investment account is as follows:

No Par Common Stock	$2,000,000	
Retained Earnings	1,500,000	
Plant And Equipment (Net)	200,000	
Inventories	80,000	
Goodwill	240,000	
Land		$ 120,000
Non-Controlling Interest [(20%)($3,500,000)]		700,000
Investment In Sleigh		3,200,000

Step B(1) - Intercompany Assets And Liabilities
Procedure

5-34. The first type of adjustment or elimination that is required in Step B involves the elimination of intercompany assets and liabilities. As was noted in Chapter 4, it is not uncommon for intercompany debts to arise between a parent and a subsidiary. When these two legal entities are viewed as a single economic entity, such intercompany debt has no real economic existence and should be eliminated. The appropriate procedure for this was described in Chapter 4 and codified as Step B-1.

Comprehensive Example

5-35.   There are two such items in this problem. The most obvious is the $200,000 long-term note payable from Sleigh to Pleigh. An additional intercompany balance relates to the fact that the last interest payment on this note was July 1, 2006. This would mean that on December 31, 2006, Sleigh would have recorded interest payable and Pleigh would have recorded interest receivable of $12,000 [(6/12)(12%)($200,000)]. The required elimination entries would be as follows:

Long-Term Liabilities	$200,000	
Long-Term Note Receivable		$200,000
Current Liabilities	$ 12,000	
Current Receivables		$ 12,000

5-36.   You should note that the purpose of this entry is to avoid the overstatement of the total consolidated assets and equities. The elimination of such intercompany liabilities will never have any influence on either the Non-Controlling Interest in the consolidated Balance Sheet or the amount of consolidated Retained Earnings.

Step B(2) - Realization Of Fair Value Changes
General Procedures

5-37.   In Step A, we recorded the parent company's share of fair value changes on the subsidiary's identifiable assets and liabilities. In making the Step A entry, you should have noticed that despite the fact that we are several years past acquisition, the amounts that were recorded were the same as those that would have been recorded at the time of acquisition. This procedure follows from the fact that we are eliminating an investment that is carried at cost, an amount which reflects the fair values that were present at acquisition. Given that the fair value changes recorded in Step A were those at acquisition, we need a further procedure to recognize the extent to which these fair value changes have been realized in the period subsequent to acquisition.

5-38.   Realization of these amounts can take place in one of two ways. In the case of non-current assets with limited lives (Plant And Equipment in our example), realization will occur as the asset is used up. On the books of the subsidiary, the carrying values of the Plant And Equipment would be charged to depreciation or amortization expense on the basis of their carrying values in the subsidiary's single entity records. In the consolidated financial statements, these depreciation or amortization amounts must be adjusted to reflect the depreciation or amortization of the related fair value changes. A similar analysis can be made of liabilities with limited lives.

5-39.   The alternative way in which a fair value change can be realized is through disposal of the asset by the subsidiary. In the case of current assets (Inventories in our example), this will take place in the normal course of business operations in the one year period following acquisition. On the books of the subsidiary, the sale of the current asset will result in the carrying value of the current asset being charged to expense. In a manner analogous to the adjustment of depreciation or amortization expense on depreciable assets, the expense to which the current asset was charged must be adjusted for the realization of the fair value change. In the case of Inventories, the adjustment would be to the consolidated cost of goods sold.

5-40.   It is also possible that a non-current asset with a limited life might be sold prior to the end of that life. This would usually result in the recognition of a gain or loss by the subsidiary with the amount being calculated on the basis of the carrying value of the asset. In this situation, the unamortized portion of the fair value change would be considered realized and, in preparing consolidated financial statements, would be treated as an adjustment of the gain or loss recognized by the subsidiary.

5-41.   For fair value changes on non-current assets with an unlimited life (Land in our example), it may not be necessary to record any adjustment in Step B. If the asset is still owned by the consolidated entity, the fair value change has become a part of its consolidated carrying value. This adjustment would be recorded as part of Step A. As the asset has an unlimited life, there is generally no need to amortize either the asset or the related fair value change in Step B. However, if the asset is sold in a period subsequent to acquisition, any gain or loss recorded by the subsidiary will have to be adjusted to reflect the fact that all of the fair value change that was recognized in the consolidated financial statements has become realized.

5-42.   A further complication in dealing with the adjustments required by the realization of fair value changes is caused by the fact that such realization may occur in either the current period or in an earlier period subsequent to the acquisition date. As all of the subsidiary's expenses and revenues that relate to prior periods would now be accumulated in the subsidiary's Retained Earnings, adjustments for fair value realizations that relate to prior periods will have to be recorded as adjustments of that balance. In contrast, the adjustments for fair value realizations during the current period are made to current expenses or revenues.

5-43.   All of the preceding can be stated as Step B-2 as follows:

Step B-2 Procedure   Give recognition to the post-acquisition realization of acquisition date fair value changes on assets and liabilities that have been used up or sold during the post-acquisition period. To the extent that this realization occurred in prior periods, this recognition will require an adjustment of the opening Retained Earnings of the subsidiary. Alternatively, if the realization occurred in the current period, the adjustment will be to the subsidiary's current period expenses, revenues, gains, or losses. Note that, in closed trial balance problems, there will be no expenses, revenues, gains, or losses to adjust. This means that, in closed trial balance problems, all of the adjustments will be to the closing Retained Earnings.

5-44.   We will now turn our attention to applying this procedure to the fair value changes in our comprehensive example.

Inventories

5-45.   With respect to the Inventories, these were charged at their carrying value to the Cost Of Goods Sold of the Sleigh Company during 2002. This means that all of Sleigh Company's $80,000 share of the fair value increase on Inventories was realized during that prior year. As the subsidiary would have recorded Cost Of Goods Sold on the basis of the $1,700,000 carrying value of the Inventories, an $80,000 addition to this expense is required. In addition, as the Inventories are no longer the property of the subsidiary, it is necessary to reverse that $80,000 increase in Inventories that was recorded in Step A. The entry required in 2002 is as follows:

Cost Of Goods Sold	$80,000	
Inventories		$80,000

5-46.   Since this entry was not recorded on the books of the Sleigh Company, the Retained Earnings of the Sleigh Company will be $80,000 too high in all subsequent years. This would mean that in these subsequent years, including the current 2006 period, the following adjustment will be required in the preparation of consolidated financial statements:

Retained Earnings - Sleigh's Opening	$80,000	
Inventories		$80,000

5-47.   While the preceding debit is to the Retained Earnings of Sleigh, you should note that because we are only recognizing the investor's share of the fair value change, this adjustment would only affect the Pleigh Company's share of the Retained Earnings of Sleigh. This would be true of all of the adjustments of depreciation, depletion and amortization of fair value changes that are required in the process of preparing consolidated financial statements.

Plant And Equipment

5-48.   When a fair value change has been recorded on an asset or liability that is being allocated to income over several accounting periods, this Step B-2 in the consolidation procedures is somewhat more complex. This is due to the fact that different adjustments are required for each accounting period in which income is influenced by the presence of the asset. In the problem under consideration, we allocated a fair value change of $200,000 [(80%)($250,000)] to Plant And Equipment which had a useful life of 20 years at the time of the acquisition on January 1, 2002. This will require a $10,000 ($200,000 ÷ 20) adjustment to Depreciation Expense in each year for the 20 years subsequent to the acquisition date. For example, the required entry for 2002 would be as follows:

Depreciation Expense	$10,000	
Plant And Equipment (Net)		$10,000

5-49. This entry serves to increase Depreciation Expense by $10,000 and to reverse 1/20 of the fair value change that was recorded in Step A. In each subsequent year, the credit to Plant And Equipment (Net) will increase by $10,000. However, the debit to Depreciation Expense will remain at $10,000 and will be accompanied by a debit to Retained Earnings for adjustments to Depreciation Expense for prior periods. Note that in this "open trial balance" version of the problem, any adjustments that are made to Sleigh's Retained Earnings are to the opening balance in this account.

5-50. Based on this analysis, the entries that would have been required in 2003, 2004, and 2005 are as follows:

2003

Retained Earnings - Sleigh's Opening	$10,000	
Depreciation Expense	10,000	
Plant And Equipment (Net)		$20,000

2004

Retained Earnings - Sleigh's Opening	$20,000	
Depreciation Expense	10,000	
Plant And Equipment (Net)		$30,000

2005

Retained Earnings - Sleigh's Opening	$30,000	
Depreciation Expense	10,000	
Plant And Equipment (Net)		$40,000

5-51. The entry specifically required in this problem would adjust Sleigh's opening Retained Earnings for the four years 2002 through 2005 and the Depreciation Expense for the current year. This entry would be as follows:

Required Entry

Retained Earnings - Sleigh's Opening	$40,000	
Depreciation Expense	10,000	
Plant And Equipment (Net)		$50,000

5-52. Here again, the adjustment to the Retained Earnings of the Sleigh Company will only affect the parent company's share of this balance, a reflection of the parent company conceptual approach to the asset valuation problem in the preparation of consolidated financial statements.

Land

5-53. This problem also involves a fair value change on a piece of land which was owned by the Sleigh Company on the acquisition date. This fair value change was recorded in Step A and, since land is not normally subject to depreciation or depletion, no further entry is required here as long as the Sleigh Company still owns the land. Since the problem indicates that Sleigh is still holding the land on December 31, 2006, no Step B entry is required for the land.

Summary

5-54. The preceding illustrates the procedures required by the three different types of fair value changes that you might encounter. These are fair value changes on current assets, fair value changes on assets with unlimited lives and fair value changes on long-term assets and liabilities with limited lives. We remind you that under the parent company approach to asset valuation, these adjustments have no effect on the interest of the non-controlling share-holders, either in the consolidated Balance Sheet or in the consolidated Income Statement.

Step B(3) - Goodwill Impairment

5-55. In Step A, we recognized Goodwill in the amount of $240,000. Prior to 2002, the *CICA Handbook* required that this balance be amortized over a period not exceeding 40 years. Under these rules, the Step B treatment of Goodwill was analogous to the treatment given to fair value changes on depreciable assets. That is, in each period subsequent acquisition, an adjustment would be required to reflect the amortization of this balance. Given this, goodwill could be dealt with under Step B(2), with no need for specifying a separate procedure.

5-56. This is no longer the case. Under the provisions of Section 3062, "Goodwill And Other Intangible Assets", the amortization of goodwill is not permitted. In many cases this will mean that we can treat goodwill like we treat fair value changes on non-depreciable assets such as land. That is, the appropriate amount of goodwill will be recorded in Step A, with no Step B adjustment required in subsequent years.

5-57. This, however, will not always be the case. As you will recall from our discussion of goodwill in Chapter 3, Section 3062 requires that the goodwill balance be tested each year to determine if it has been impaired. If it is determined that impairment has occurred, the balance must be written down and the amount of impairment charged to income as an impairment loss. This will require a consolidation adjustment to recognize a loss in any year in which it is determined that impairment has occurred. This entry will require a debit to Goodwill Impairment Loss and a credit to the Goodwill balance that was recorded in Step A.

5-58. As is the case with other types of fair value write-offs, the Goodwill Impairment Loss that is recorded in the consolidated financial statements will not be recorded in the records of the subsidiary. This means that, from the point of view of the consolidated financial state-ments, the subsidiary's Retained Earnings will be overstated at the end of the write-off period and in all subsequent years. As a consequence, in all of the years subsequent to the recogni-tion of the first consolidated Goodwill Impairment Loss, there will have to be an adjustment to Retained Earnings to reduce this balance for the cumulative Goodwill Impairment Losses of previous years.

5-59. Stated as a procedure, the required adjustment is as follows:

Step B-3 Procedure Recognize current and cumulative goodwill impairment losses that have been measured since the acquisition of the subsidiary and the initial recog-nition of the goodwill balance. To the extent that the impairment took place during the current period, the measured amount will be charged to Goodwill Impairment Loss. To the extent that it occurred in prior periods, it will be charged to Retained Earnings. Note that, in closed trial balance problems, you will not be recording a Goodwill Impairment Loss. This means that, in this type of problem, both the current amount of Goodwill Impairment Loss and the amount recognized in all previous periods subsequent to the acquisition, will be charged to the closing Retained Earnings.

5-60. The Other Information in our comprehensive problem notes that, while goodwill has been tested for impairment in each year since the acquisition of Sleigh Company, no impair-ment has been found. As a consequence, no Step B-3 entry is required in this problem.

Step B(4) - Intercompany Expenses And Revenues
General Procedure

5-61. The fourth type of adjustment or elimination that is required in Step B involves the elimination of intercompany expenses and revenues. The principles that are involved here are identical to those involved in intercompany asset-liability situations. If we view a parent company and its subsidiaries as a single accounting entity, intercompany expenses and revenues reflect transactions which have no real economic existence. Stated as a procedure, the required elimination is as follows:

> **Step B-4 Procedure**   Eliminate 100 percent of all intercompany expenses and revenues.

5-62.   Note that in both Step B-1 which deals with the elimination of intercompany assets and liabilities and with this new Step B-4, we eliminate 100 percent of the relevant items, without regard to the percentage of subsidiary shares which are owned by the parent company.

Intercompany Sales

5-63.   In this problem, Sleigh Company sells merchandise to the Pleigh Company for $300,000. Assume (this information is not part of the basic problem) that Sleigh purchased this merchandise for $180,000 and Pleigh resold it for $350,000. If we simply added together the single entity results for this transaction, the result would be as follows:

Sales ($300,000 + $350,000)	$650,000
Cost Of Goods Sold ($180,000 + $300,000)	(480,000)
Gross Margin	$170,000

5-64.   From the perspective of the two Companies as a single consolidated entity, the correct figures would be a revenue from sales outside the consolidated entity of $350,000 and an expense resulting from purchases outside the consolidated entity of $180,000. To achieve this result we must eliminate both the intercompany expense and intercompany revenue. The required entry is as follows:

Sales	$300,000	
Cost Of Goods Sold		$300,000

5-65.   The effect of this entry is to reduce total expenses and total revenues. It has no influence on gross margin which will remain at $170,000 ($350,000 - $180,000). Further, it will not influence either the non-controlling interest's share or the parent's portion of that income.

5-66.   You should also note that this entry is based on the fact that all of the merchandise that Pleigh has acquired from Sleigh has been resold. If this were not the case, any profit resulting from the sale would be viewed as unrealized and the procedures here would have to be altered. We will deal with this issue in Chapter 6.

Intercompany Interest Expense And Revenue

5-67.   There is a second item in this problem to which this general procedure applies. This is the interest of $24,000 [(12%)($200,000)] on the intercompany note payable. The entry to eliminate this item is as follows:

Interest Revenue	$24,000	
Interest Expense		$24,000

5-68.   As was the case with the intercompany sales entry, the purpose of the preceding entry is to reduce total revenues and expenses. Neither the non-controlling interest's nor the parent's share of Net Income is influenced by this elimination.

Step B(5) - Intercompany Dividends

5-69.   The final Step B elimination in this problem involves the intercompany dividends. The Sleigh Company declared and paid $100,000 in dividends during 2006 and the Pleigh Company recorded the $80,000 of these which it received as a dividend revenue. Obviously, some type of elimination is required.

5-70. To understand this elimination, recall that under the requirements of the *CICA Handbook*, consolidated Net Income is defined using the parent company concept. This means that consolidated Net Income does not include the non-controlling shareholders' share of subsidiary income. As a consequence, in the consolidated Statement Of Retained Earnings, when we show distributions of consolidated Net Income in the form of dividends, the dividends to be disclosed will be those of the parent company only. Since the consolidated Statement Of Retained Earnings discloses only the parent company's dividends, we will have to eliminate 100 percent of the Dividends Declared of the subsidiary. Of this total, the parent company's share will be eliminated from the Dividend Revenues of the parent company while the remainder will be treated as a direct reduction of the Non-Controlling Interest in the Balance Sheet. This analysis can be expressed in the form of Step B-5 as follows:

> **Step B-5 Procedure** Eliminate 100 percent of subsidiary dividends declared. The controlling share of this amount will be deducted from the revenues of the parent company and the non-controlling share of this amount will be deducted from the Non-Controlling Interest in the consolidated Balance Sheet.

5-71. Using this procedure, the required entry is as follows:

Dividend Revenue	$80,000	
Non-Controlling Interest (Balance Sheet)	20,000	
Dividends Declared		$100,000

5-72. With the $20,000 in dividends to the non-controlling shareholders being charged directly to the Non-Controlling Interest account on the consolidated Balance Sheet, the only separate disclosure of this $20,000 item will be in the consolidated Cash Flow Statement.

5-73. As a final point, you should note that there is no need to make any adjustments for dividends paid by the subsidiary in earlier periods. In periods after the dividends are declared, the $80,000 parent's share will be included in the Retained Earnings of the parent company and will become a component of consolidated Retained Earnings. This is appropriate in that these resources are still within the consolidated entity.

Summary Of Step B Adjustments And Eliminations

5-74. The preceding paragraphs have demonstrated and explained the five basic adjustments that are required in Step B for this problem. An additional adjustment will be introduced in Chapter 6 which deals with unrealized intercompany profits. All of these adjustments are common to the great majority of consolidation problems that you will encounter and are, as a consequence, of considerable significance. We will now turn our attention to the final Step of our consolidation procedures, Step C.

Step C - Distribution Of The Subsidiary Retained Earnings
The Problem

5-75. At this point, our one remaining task is to determine the appropriate distribution of the balance that is left in the Retained Earnings account of the Sleigh Company. In the original trial balance, the January 1, 2006 balance in this account was $2,300,000. The remaining balance in this account can be calculated as follows:

Balance - January 1, 2006	$2,300,000
Step A Elimination (Balance At Acquisition)	(1,500,000)
Step B Adjustments:	
Fair Value Increase On Inventories	(80,000)
Fair Value Increase On Plant And Equipment (Net)	(40,000)
Balance After Step A And B Procedures	$ 680,000

5-76. As this remaining balance represents Sleigh earnings that have accrued subsequent to the business combination transaction in which Pleigh acquired Sleigh, a portion of this will be included in the Retained Earnings of the consolidated entity. However, we must also allocate an appropriate portion of this amount to the Non-Controlling Interest in the consolidated Balance Sheet.

5-77.   As more factors enter into our consolidation problems, the computation involved in this distribution becomes fairly complex. A good deal of this complexity results from the fact that the *CICA Handbook* is not consistent with respect to the conceptual approach that is required in the preparation of consolidated financial statements. However, in this Section the only adjustments that have an effect on this distribution are related to fair value changes and goodwill and, as we have previously noted, these adjustments follow the approach that is used for the valuation of consolidated net assets. This is the parent company approach.

5-78.   It follows that none of the Step B adjustments affect the non-controlling interest's share of these Retained Earnings. This means that the non-controlling interest's share of the subsidiary's Retained Earnings since acquisition can simply be based on the carrying value of the subsidiary's Retained Earnings. Despite this simplicity, we will introduce an approach to this computation that can be applied without regard to how complex the problem becomes. While this approach and schedule are not really essential at this stage, it will serve us well when we introduce unrealized intercompany profits in Chapter 6.

Retained Earnings Distribution Schedule

5-79.   This schedule begins with the opening Retained Earnings balance of the subsidiary and immediately removes the portion of this balance that was present at the time of acquisition. In more complex situations, the next step would be to adjust the remaining amount for unrealized upstream profits, the only adjustment which has an effect on the non-controlling interest in subsidiary Retained Earnings. Since there are no unrealized intercompany profits in this problem, we can proceed immediately to the computation and deduction of the non-controlling interest in the Retained Earnings of the subsidiary since acquisition. All other Step B adjustments are then accounted for to arrive at the amount which represents the parent company's share of the adjusted Retained Earnings of the subsidiary since acquisition. This amount, often referred to as an equity pickup, will then be allocated to consolidated Retained Earnings. Stated as a procedure, this allocation can be described as follows:

> **Step C-1 Procedure**   Determine the appropriate allocation of the subsidiary's adjusted Retained Earnings since acquisition. The non-controlling interest's share will be based on book value. In contrast, the allocation to consolidated Retained Earnings will be the parent company's share of book values, adjusted for the realization of fair value changes and any goodwill impairment losses that have occurred since acquisition.

5-80.   Based on this Step, the required schedule can be completed as follows:

Retained Earnings Distribution Schedule

Balance As Per The Trial Balance	$2,300,000
Balance At Acquisition	(1,500,000)
Balance Since Acquisition	$ 800,000
Non-Controlling Interest [(20%)($800,000)]	(160,000)
Available To The Controlling Interest	$ 640,000
Step B Adjustments:	
Inventories	(80,000)
Plant And Equipment (4 Years At $10,000)	(40,000)
To Consolidated Retained Earnings	$ 520,000

5-81.   Note that the Step B adjustments in this schedule reflect the journal entries that were made in the Step B procedures.

5-82.   With the information from this schedule, we can now make the Step C distribution entry to distribute the subsidiary's retained earnings since acquisition balance.

Retained Earnings Distribution Entry

5-83.   The final procedure can be stated as follows:

Step C-2 Procedure   Eliminate the subsidiary's adjusted Retained Earnings since acquisition. This amount will be allocated to the Non-Controlling Interest in the consolidated Balance Sheet and to consolidated Retained Earnings as determined in Step C-1.

5-84.   The entry required to distribute the Sleigh Company's retained earnings since acquisition is as follows:

Retained Earnings - Sleigh	$680,000	
Non-Controlling Interest (Balance Sheet)		$160,000
Consolidated Retained Earnings		520,000

5-85.   This journal entry reduces the Sleigh Company's Retained Earnings balance to zero, distributing the remaining balance to the parent and non-controlling interest. With this entry completed we have established the opening balance for consolidated Retained Earnings. It is simply the Pleigh Company's January 1, 2006 balance of $2,550,000 plus the $520,000 allocation resulting from the preceding journal entry, for a total of $3,070,000.

Preparation Of Consolidated Financial Statements

5-86.   With the addition of the Step C distribution entry, we have completed all of the procedures necessary for the preparation of consolidated financial statements. We will now take the individual account balances from the original trial balance, add and subtract the adjustments that have been made in Steps A, B, and C of our procedures, thereby arriving at the figures to be included in the consolidated financial statements. These computations will be disclosed parenthetically, a method of disclosure that we would recommend for use on examinations. We remind you again that, if your grasp of the procedures which we are using is sufficiently solid, the most efficient approach to the preparation of consolidated financial statements is the direct computation of the individual statement items without taking the time to prepare the preceding working paper journal entries.

Consolidated Income Statement

Statement Disclosure

5-87.   The consolidated Income Statement of the Pleigh Company and its subsidiary for 2006 would be prepared as follows:

Pleigh Company And Subsidiary
Consolidated Income Statement
Year Ending December 31, 2006

Sales ($4,000,000 + $2,500,000 - $300,000)	$6,200,000
Interest Revenue ($24,000 - $24,000)	-0-
Dividend Revenue ($80,000 - $80,000)	-0-
Total Revenues	$6,200,000
Cost Of Goods Sold ($2,800,000 + $1,500,000 - $300,000)	$4,000,000
Depreciation Expense ($200,000 + $100,000 + $10,000)	310,000
Interest Expense ($240,000 + $84,000 - $24,000)	300,000
Other Expenses ($364,000 + $616,000)	980,000
Total Expenses	$5,590,000
Combined Income	$ 610,000
Non-Controlling Interest [(20 Percent)($200,000)]	40,000
Consolidated Net Income	$ 570,000

5-88. We note again that the subtotal for Combined Income is not normal disclosure. It has been included only for computational purposes. Normal disclosure under the required parent company approach would have the Non-Controlling Interest included among the other deductions from revenue. Similarly, there would not be disclosure of either Interest Revenue or Dividend Revenue in an actual consolidated Income Statement. We have included these items here to emphasize that procedures were required to remove them.

Definitional Calculation

5-89. In addition to being able to prepare a consolidated Income Statement in the manner illustrated, it is useful to know how to prepare an independent calculation of the final consolidated Net Income figure. This calculation can be used to verify the consolidated Net Income figure which results from the preparation of a consolidated Income Statement or, in those problems that only require a final consolidated Net Income figure and not a complete statement, this calculation can save you the time that would be required to calculate individual consolidated expenses and revenues. Further, there are some problems which ask for this calculation, without providing you with individual expense and revenue information. When this is the case, it is essential that you know how to make such calculations.

5-90. There are a variety of ways in which this calculation can be made. However, we have found that the approach which is sometimes referred to as the definitional calculation seems to be the easiest to understand. This calculation is as follows:

Pleigh Company's Net Income	$500,000
Intercompany Dividend Revenues	(80,000)
Pleigh's Net Income Less Dividends	$420,000
Pleigh's Equity In The Net Income Of Sleigh [(80%)($200,000)]	160,000
Income Before Adjustments	$580,000
Adjustment For Fair Value Depreciation	(10,000)
Consolidated Net Income	$570,000

Consolidated Statement Of Retained Earnings

Statement Disclosure

5-91. Using the preceding Net Income data, we can now prepare the consolidated Statement Of Retained Earnings for 2006 of the Pleigh Company and its subsidiary. It would be as follows:

Pleigh Company And Subsidiary
Consolidated Statement Of Retained Earnings
Year Ending December 31, 2006

Balance - January 1, 2006 ($2,550,000 + $520,000)	$3,070,000
2006 Net Income	570,000
2006 Dividends (Pleigh's Only)	(350,000)
Balance - December 31, 2006	$3,290,000

Definitional Calculation

5-92. As was the case with consolidated Net Income, you will frequently find it useful to be able to make an independent computation of the end of the year balance in the Retained Earnings account. Here again, this independent computation can be used to verify the figure that was arrived at in the preparation of the consolidated Statement Of Retained Earnings or as a more efficient method of determining this balance when the complete Statement Of Retained Earnings is not required. The definitional approach to the computation of this amount is as follows:

Pleigh's Closing Balance	$2,700,000
Pleigh's Share Of Sleigh's Retained Earnings Since Acquisition [(80%)($2,400,000 - $1,500,000)]	720,000
Adjustments:	
Inventories	(80,000)
Plant (5 Years At $10,000)	(50,000)
Consolidated Retained Earnings As At December 31, 2006	$3,290,000

5-93.   Note that, in this calculation, the calculation of Pleigh's share of Sleigh's Retained Earnings since acquisition is based on that company's book figures ($2,400,000 - $1,500,000 + $900,000) with no adjustments. This reflects the fact that, to this point, all of our consolidation procedures are based on the parent company approach, with all of the adjustments being charged against the parent's share of Retained Earnings. This will change when we introduce unrealized intercompany profits in Chapter 6. Also note that, because we are dealing with end of the period Retained Earnings, the fair value adjustments are for five years. This is in contrast to our earlier adjustments to the opening Retained Earnings which were for only four years.

5-94.   If you are required to prepare a consolidated Statement of Retained Earnings, you have the option of calculating the opening balance first or the closing balance (which should agree with the figure in the Balance Sheet) and working backwards to the opening balance. If the consolidated Statement of Retained Earnings is not required, there may be no need to calculate the opening balance except for verification purposes. The procedures we are using in this problem calculate the opening balance first. If this is done correctly and you have the appropriate figures for both Net Income and Dividends Declared, then the statement itself will calculate the correct closing balance. However, an error in the opening balance calculation, in Net Income or in Dividends Declared will produce an incorrect closing balance. We would suggest that you make an independent verification of the closing balance whenever possible and time permits.

Consolidated Balance Sheet

Non-Controlling Interest

5-95.   While it is not the most efficient way to solve this problem, we can use the procedures that we have just developed to calculate the Non-Controlling Interest on the Balance Sheet. Using this approach, the calculation would be as follows:

Step A Allocation (Balance At Acquisition)	$700,000
Step B Adjustment For Dividends	(20,000)
Step C Allocation (Retained Earnings Since Acquisition)	160,000
Non-Controlling Interest In Income (From Income Statement)	40,000
Non-Controlling Interest (Balance Sheet)	$880,000

5-96.   A more conceptual approach would be based on the fact that the December 31, 2006 Sleigh Company's Shareholders' Equity consists of $2,000,000 in No Par Common Stock and $2,400,000 in Retained Earnings.   This means that the subsidiary's net assets total $4,400,000 and since, in this problem, none of the adjustments or eliminations have any influence on the Non-Controlling Interest, this interest can be calculated by simply taking the non-controlling interest's share of these net assets. That is, 20 percent of $4,400,000 is the required $880,000.

Statement Disclosure

5-97.   With the Non-Controlling Interest established, the consolidated Balance Sheet as at December 31, 2006 of the Pleigh Company and its subsidiary would be prepared as follows:

Pleigh Company And Subsidiary
Consolidated Balance Sheet
As At December 31, 2006

Cash ($500,000 + $300,000)	$ 800,000
Current Receivables ($800,000 + $400,000 - $12,000)	1,188,000
Inventories ($2,500,000 + $1,700,000 + $80,000 -$80,000)	4,200,000
Long-Term Note Receivable ($200,000 - $200,000)	-0-
Investment In Sleigh ($3,200,000 - $3,200,000)	-0-
Land ($1,500,000 + $1,000,000 - $120,000)	2,380,000
Plant And Equipment (Net)	
($4,500,000 + $1,900,000 + $200,000 - $50,000)	6,550,000
Goodwill	240,000
Total Assets	$15,358,000

Current Liabilities ($500,000 + $200,000 - $12,000)	$ 688,000
Long-Term Liabilities ($2,000,000 + $700,000 - $200,000)	2,500,000
Non-Controlling Interest (See Preceding Discussion)	880,000
No Par Common Stock (Pleigh's Balance)	8,000,000
Retained Earnings (See Retained Earnings Statement)	3,290,000
Total Equities	$15,358,000

5-98. Most of the preceding computations follow directly from the trial balance data adjusted by the various journal entries that we have made. The exceptions to this are the Retained Earnings balance and the Non-Controlling Interest which were computed in the preceding sections. Note that the Investment In Sleigh and Long-Term Note Receivable accounts would not be disclosed in actual consolidated financial statements. They have been included in this presentation simply to show the disposition of all of the balances included in the problem data.

Exercise Five-2

Exercise Five-2 deals with open trial balance problems with the investment carried at cost.

On January 1, 2002, the Parker Company purchases 65 percent of the outstanding shares of the Schaffer Company for $1,350,000 in cash. On that date, the Schaffer Company had No Par Common Stock of $700,000 and Retained Earnings of $1,000,000. On December 31, 2006, the adjusted trial balances of the Parker Company and its subsidiary, the Schaffer Company are as follows:

	Parker	Schaffer
Monetary Assets	$ 2,850,000	$ 725,000
Investment In Schaffer - At Cost	1,350,000	Nil
Non-Monetary Assets	6,475,000	2,045,000
Total Expenses	2,940,000	530,000
Dividends Declared	250,000	50,000
Total Debits	$13,865,000	$3,350,000
Liabilities	$ 1,712,500	$ 425,000
No Par Common Stock	3,000,000	700,000
Retained Earnings (January 1)	5,895,000	1,550,000
Sales	3,225,000	675,000
Dividend Revenue	32,500	Nil
Total Credits	$13,865,000	$3,350,000
2006 Net Income	$ 317,500	$ 145,000
December 31, 2006 Retained Earnings	$ 5,962,500	$1,645,000

Other Information:

1. At the date of Parker Company's acquisition of the Schaffer Company's shares, all of the identifiable assets and liabilities of the Schaffer Company had fair values that were equal to their carrying values except for a group of non-monetary assets that had a fair value that was $150,000 greater than its carrying value. These non-monetary assets had a remaining useful life of 15 years. Both companies use the straight-line method for all amortization calculations.

2. In each of the years since Parker acquired control over Schaffer, the goodwill arising on this business combination transaction has been tested for impairment. In 2004, a Goodwill Impairment Loss of $35,000 was recognized. In addition, the impairment test for 2006 found a further impairment of $25,000.

3. Schaffer Company's Sales during 2006 include sales of $85,000 to Parker Company. All of this merchandise has been resold by the Pleigh Company. However, as a result of these sales, on December 31, 2006, Parker still owes Schaffer $15,000 on open account.

Required Prepare a consolidated Income Statement and a consolidated Statement Of Retained Earnings for the year ending December 31, 2006 and a consolidated Balance Sheet as at December 31, 2006 for the Parker Company and its subsidiary, the Schaffer Company.

This is a continuation of Exercise Five-2.

End of Exercise Five-2

Comprehensive Example - Closed Trial Balance With Investment At Cost

Basic Data

5-99.   In this second version of the comprehensive example, the only requirement is the preparation of a consolidated Balance Sheet. As a consequence, the data is presented in the form of a closed trial balance.

On January 1, 2002, the Pleigh Company purchases 80 percent of the outstanding voting shares of the Sleigh Company for $3,200,000 in cash. On that date the Sleigh Company had No Par Common Stock of $2,000,000 and Retained Earnings of $1,500,000. On December 31, 2006, the adjusted trial balances of the Pleigh Company and its subsidiary, the Sleigh Company are as follows:

	Pleigh	Sleigh
Cash	$ 500,000	$ 300,000
Current Receivables	800,000	400,000
Inventories	2,500,000	1,700,000
Long-Term Note Receivable	200,000	-0-
Investment In Sleigh - At Cost	3,200,000	-0-
Land	1,500,000	1,000,000
Plant And Equipment (Net)	4,500,000	1,900,000
Total Debits	$13,200,000	$5,300,000
Current Liabilities	$ 500,000	$ 200,000
Long-Term Liabilities	2,000,000	700,000
No Par Common Stock	8,000,000	2,000,000
Retained Earnings	2,700,000	2,400,000
Total Credits	$13,200,000	$5,300,000

Other Information:

1. At the date of Pleigh Company's acquisition of the Sleigh Company's shares, all of the identifiable assets and liabilities of the Sleigh Company had fair values that were equal to their carrying values except Inventories which had fair values that were $100,000 more than their carrying values, Land with a fair value that was $150,000 less than its carrying value and Plant And Equipment which had a fair value that was $250,000 greater than its carrying value. The Plant And Equipment had a remaining useful life on the acquisition date of 20 years while the Inventories that were present on the acquisition date were sold during the year ending December 31, 2006. The Land is still on the books of the Sleigh Company on December 31, 2006. Both companies use the straight line method to calculate depreciation and amortization.

2. In each of the years since Pleigh acquired control over Sleigh, the goodwill arising on this business combination transaction has been tested for impairment. No impairment was found in any of the years since acquisition.

3. Sleigh Company's Sales during 2006 include sales of $300,000 to Pleigh Company. All of this merchandise has been resold by the Pleigh Company.

4. On December 31, 2006, the Pleigh Company is holding Sleigh Company's long-term note payable in the amount of $200,000. Interest at 12 percent is payable on July 1 of each year. Pleigh Company has been holding this note since July 1, 2004.

Required: Prepare a consolidated Balance Sheet as at December 31, 2006 for the Pleigh Company and its subsidiary, the Sleigh Company.

Procedural Approach

5-100.   The procedural approach here is similar to that used in our first version of this problem. The basic differences can be described as follows:

- All of the Step B fair value write-off entries will now be made to Sleigh's closing Retained Earnings account.

- The Step C entry will involve distributing the December 31, 2006 retained earnings, rather than the January 1, 2006 balance.

- As no consolidated Income Statement is being prepared, there is no need to adjust or eliminate any expense or revenue items.

- As all dividends received have been closed to Retained Earnings, there is no need to eliminate intercompany dividends declared.

Step A Procedures

Investment Analysis

5-101.   The analysis of the investment in Sleigh is identical to the one used in the "open trial balance" version of this problem. It is as follows:

	80 Percent	100 Percent
Investment Cost	$3,200,000	$4,000,000
Book Value	(2,800,000)	(3,500,000)
Differential	$ 400,000	$ 500,000
Fair Value Changes:		
Increase On Inventories	(80,000)	(100,000)
Decrease On Land	120,000	150,000
Increase On Plant And Equipment (Net)	(200,000)	(250,000)
Goodwill	$ 240,000	$ 300,000

Investment Elimination

5-102.   As was the case with the investment analysis, the journal entry here will be the same as in the "open trial balance" version of the problem. It is as follows:

No Par Common Stock	$2,000,000	
Retained Earnings	1,500,000	
Plant And Equipment (Net)	200,000	
Inventories	80,000	
Goodwill	240,000	
Land		$ 120,000
Non-Controlling Interest [(20%)($3,500,000)]		700,000
Investment In Sleigh		3,200,000

Step B(1) - Intercompany Assets And Liabilities

5-103.   The elimination of intercompany asset and liability balances is also the same as in the "open trial balance" version of this problem. The required entries are:

Long-Term Liabilities	$200,000	
Long-Term Note Receivable		$200,000
Current Liabilities	$ 12,000	
Current Receivables		$ 12,000

Step B(2) - Realization Of Fair Value Changes

General Procedures

5-104.   With the investment at cost, recognition will have to be given to realization of fair value changes for the entire period since acquisition. This means that the entries in this version of the problem will have the same effect on the asset and liability accounts as did the entries which were made in the first version of this comprehensive problem. The only difference in the entries is that, since we are working with a closed trial balance, it is no longer possible to adjust expense and revenue accounts. These accounts have been closed into Sleigh's ending Retained Earnings balance and, as a consequence, the portion of the adjustments that were allocated to expenses and revenues in the open trial balance versions of this problem will now go to Retained Earnings.

Inventories

5-105.   Since the fair value change on Inventories had no effect on the 2006 expenses or revenues, the entry here will be the same as it was in the open trial balance version of this problem. It is as follows:

Retained Earnings - Sleigh's Closing	$80,000	
Inventories		$80,000

Plant And Equipment

5-106.   As was the case in the previous version of this problem, we will credit the Plant And Equipment account for 5 years (January 1, 2002 through December 31, 2006) of additional amortization expense on the fair value change. However, instead of splitting the debits between Retained Earnings and the current Depreciation Expense, the entire amount will go to Retained Earnings. The entry would be as follows:

Retained Earnings - Sleigh's Closing	$50,000	
Plant And Equipment (Net)		$50,000

Land

5-107.   As the Land is still on the books of the Sleigh Company, no entry is required to adjust the fair value change on this account.

Step B(3) - Goodwill Impairment

5-108.   As there has been no impairment of goodwill in any of the years since Pleigh acquired Sleigh, no entry is required for this step in our procedures.

Step B(4) - Intercompany Expenses And Revenues

5-109.   In the "open trial balance" version of this problem, we made an entry here to eliminate intercompany expenses and revenues. We noted that this entry was simply to avoid overstating expenses and revenues. Since all of the expenses and revenues are now closed to retained earnings, no entry is required in this closed trial balance version of the problem.

Step B(5) - Intercompany Dividends

5-110.   In the "open trial balance" version of this problem, we made an entry here to eliminate intercompany dividend payments. The entry involved reducing Dividend Revenue or Investment Income and Dividends Declared. Since all of these accounts have been closed to Retained Earnings, no entry is required for intercompany dividends in this closed trial balance version of the problem. The Non-Controlling Interest in consolidated net assets in the previous version of this problem was reduced to the extent of dividend payments to non-controlling shareholders. This effect will be automatically picked up in Step C when we base the allocation to the Non-Controlling Interest on the end of the year Retained Earnings balance of the Sleigh Company. This end of year balance has, of course, had all of the Sleigh Company's 2006 dividends deducted as part of the closing entries.

Step C - Distribution Of The Subsidiary Retained Earnings

Retained Earnings Balance

5-111.   Our one remaining task at this point is to determine the appropriate distribution of the balance that is left in the Retained Earnings account of the Sleigh Company. Note that, in this closed trial balance version of our comprehensive problem, we are concerned with the closing balance of Sleigh's Retained Earnings. The balance that is left in this account can be calculated as follows:

Balance - December 31, 2006	$2,400,000
Step A Elimination (Balance At Acquisition)	(1,500,000)
Balance Since Acquisition	$ 900,000
Step B Adjustments:	
Inventories	(80,000)
Plant And Equipment (5 Years At $10,000)	(50,000)
Balance To Be Distributed	$ 770,000

5-112.   Since we are dealing with Sleigh's closing Retained Earnings balance, all of the Step B adjustments are for five years, rather than for four years as was the case in the open trial balance version of this comprehensive problem.

Retained Earnings Distribution Schedule

5-113.   As indicated in the preceding calculation, $770,000 remains in the Retained Earnings account of the Sleigh Company. We will use the same type of schedule that was introduced in the "open trial balance" version of this problem to analyze the distribution of this amount. It is as follows:

Retained Earnings Distribution Schedule

Balance As Per The Trial Balance	$2,400,000
Balance At Acquisition	(1,500,000)
Balance Since Acquisition	$ 900,000
Non-Controlling Interest [(20%)($900,000)]	(180,000)
Available To The Controlling Interest	$ 720,000
Step B Adjustments:	
Inventories	(80,000)
Plant And Equipment (5 Years At $10,000)	(50,000)
To Consolidated Retained Earnings	$ 590,000

Retained Earnings Distribution Entry

5-114. Using this schedule, we can now make the required Step C distribution entry. The journal entry required to distribute the Sleigh Company's Retained Earnings since acquisition is as follows:

Retained Earnings - Sleigh	$770,000	
Non-Controlling Interest		$180,000
Consolidated Retained Earnings		590,000

5-115. When the $590,000 from the preceding entry is added to the balance of $2,700,000 that is in the Pleigh Company's Retained Earnings account, we have the December 31, 2006 consolidated Retained Earnings figure of $3,290,000.

Consolidated Balance Sheet

Non-Controlling Interest

5-116. Here again, the easiest way to compute the Non-Controlling Interest is to take 20 percent of the end of the year net assets of the Sleigh Company. This 20 percent of $4,400,000 ($2,000,000 + $2,400,000) gives the required Non-Controlling Interest of $880,000. Alternatively, the procedures can be used to arrive at the same result. This calculation would be as follows:

Step A Allocation	$700,000
Step C Allocation	180,000
Non-Controlling Interest	$880,000

Statement Disclosure

5-117. We are now in a position to complete the required consolidated Balance Sheet as at December 31, 2006 of the Pleigh Company and its subsidiary. It would be prepared as follows:

Pleigh Company And Subsidiary
Consolidated Balance Sheet
As At December 31, 2006

Cash ($500,000 + $300,000)	$ 800,000
Current Receivables ($800,000 + $400,000 - $12,000)	1,188,000
Inventories ($2,500,000 + $1,700,000 + $80,000 - $80,000)	4,200,000
Long-Term Note Receivable ($200,000 - $200,000)	-0-
Investment In Sleigh ($3,200,000 - $3,200,000)	-0-
Land ($1,500,000 + $1,000,000 - $120,000)	2,380,000
Plant And Equipment (Net)	
($4,500,000 + $1,900,000 + $200,000 - $50,000)	6,550,000
Goodwill	240,000
Total Assets	$15,358,000

Current Liabilities ($500,000 + $200,000 - $12,000)	$	688,000
Long-Term Liabilities ($2,000,000 + $700,000 - $200,000)		2,500,000
Non-Controlling Interest (See Preceding Discussion)		880,000
No Par Common Stock (Pleigh's Balance)		8,000,000
Retained Earnings (See Retained Earnings Distribution)		3,290,000
Total Equities		$15,358,000

<table>
<tr><td>Exercise
Five-3 deals
with closed
trial balance
problems
with the
investment
carried at
cost.</td></tr>
</table>

Exercise Five-3

(This is identical to Exercise Five-2 except it is a closed trial balance version.)

On January 1, 2002, the Parker Company purchases 65 percent of the outstanding shares of the Schaffer Company for $1,350,000 in cash. On that date, the Schaffer Company had No Par Common Stock of $700,000 and Retained Earnings of $1,000,000. On December 31, 2006, the adjusted trial balances of the Parker Company and its subsidiary, the Schaffer Company are as follows:

	Parker	Schaffer
Monetary Assets	$ 2,850,000	$ 725,000
Investment In Schaffer - At Cost	1,350,000	Nil
Non-Monetary Assets	6,475,000	2,045,000
Total Debits	$10,675,000	$2,770,000
Liabilities	$ 1,712,500	$ 425,000
No Par Common Stock	3,000,000	700,000
Retained Earnings	5,962,500	1,645,000
Total Credits	$10,675,000	$2,770,000

Other Information:

1. At the date of Parker Company's acquisition of the Schaffer Company's shares, all of the identifiable assets and liabilities of the Schaffer Company had fair values that were equal to their carrying values except for a group of non-monetary assets that had a fair value that was $150,000 greater than its carrying value. These non-monetary assets had a remaining useful life of 15 years. Both companies use the straight-line method for all amortization calculations.

2. In each of the years since Parker acquired control over Schaffer, the goodwill arising on this business combination transaction has been tested for impairment. In 2004, a Goodwill Impairment Loss of $35,000 was recognized. In addition, the impairment test for 2006 found a further impairment of $25,000.

3. Schaffer Company's Sales during 2006 include sales of $85,000 to Parker Company. All of this merchandise has been resold by the Pleigh Company. However, as a result of these sales, on December 31, 2006, Parker still owes Schaffer $15,000 on open account.

Required Prepare a consolidated Balance Sheet as at December 31, 2006 for the Parker Company and its subsidiary, the Schaffer Company.

End of Exercise Five-3

Application Of The Equity Method

Basic Concepts

5-118.   In Chapter 2, we indicated that the Net Income of an investor using the equity method for an investee had to be equal to the consolidated Net Income that would result from the consolidation of that investee.   This requirement is based on the following Recommendation:

> **Paragraph 3050.08**   *Investment income as calculated by the equity method should be that amount necessary to increase or decrease the investor's income to that which would have been recognized if the results of the investee's operations had been consolidated with those of the investor.* (August, 1978)

5-119.   With respect to this Chapter, this means that all of the adjustments for fair value changes and goodwill impairment that would be required in the consolidation process, are also required in the application of the equity method. There is, however, a major difference in the disclosure of these adjustments. In consolidation, the various adjustments are included in specific consolidated account balances. For example, if a fair value change on a depreciable asset is recorded in the consolidated Balance Sheet, the related write-off will be disclosed as an addition to Amortization Expense in the consolidated Income Statement. In contrast, the equity method deals with all of these adjustments as modifications of the Investment Asset and Investment Income accounts. This means that an investor using the equity method would not record the fair value change in its single entity Balance Sheet, nor would such an investor record the related write-off as an addition to Amortization Expense. Rather, the fair value amortization amount would be calculated and deducted from Investment Income and from the equity pickup which is added to the Investment Asset account. This is why the application of the equity method is sometimes referred to as a "one line consolidation".

Comprehensive Example

Income Statement

5-120.   To illustrate the basic procedures under the equity method, we will use the same comprehensive example that we have been working with throughout this Chapter. The basic data for this problem is presented in Paragraph 5-29 and will not be repeated here. The only change is that we will assume that Pleigh Company's majority ownership does not give it control over the Sleigh Company and, as a consequence, the investment cannot be consolidated and must be accounted for by the equity method. The Dividend Revenue of $80,000 which represents the dividends received from Sleigh under the cost method would be nil under the equity method.

5-121.   From our previous experience with the Pleigh Company problem, we know that consolidated Net Income for 2006 amounts to $570,000. Since the Pleigh Company's net income without the inclusion of any revenues from its Investment In Sleigh amounts to $420,000 ($500,000 cost method income less $80,000 dividend revenue), the only Investment Income that would satisfy the requirement stated in Paragraph 3050.08 is $150,000.

5-122.   Using this Investment Income, the Income Statement of the Pleigh Company with the Investment In Sleigh carried by the equity method would be as follows:

Pleigh Company
Income Statement
Year Ending December 31, 2006

Sales	$4,000,000
Interest Revenue	24,000
Investment Income	150,000
Total Revenues	$4,174,000
Cost Of Goods Sold	$2,800,000
Depreciation Expense	200,000
Interest Expense	240,000
Other Expenses	364,000
Total Expenses	$3,604,000
Net Income	$ 570,000

5-123.   Under this approach, we have determined Investment Income as a "plug" figure which serves as an amount that will result in Pleigh Company's Net Income satisfying the condition that it must be equal to the amount that would result from the application of consolidation procedures. Note, however, that this amount can be calculated directly as follows:

Pleigh's Interest In Sleigh's Income [(80%)($200,000)]	$160,000
Fair Value Depreciation	(10,000)
Pleigh's Equity Method Investment Income	$150,000

Balance Sheet

5-124.   If Pleigh was not consolidating its investment in Sleigh, and used the equity method in its single entity statements, the Balance Sheet account Investment In Sleigh would have to be increased to reflect Pleigh's equity in this investee. As is the case with Investment Income under the equity method, this Balance Sheet account would be subject to the same types of adjustments that would be required in the preparation of consolidated financial statements. The required balance would be calculated as follows:

Investment In Sleigh At Cost		$3,200,000
Equity Pickup:		
Sleigh's December 31 Retained Earnings	$2,400,000	
Balance At Acquisition	(1,500,000)	
Balance Since Acquisition	$ 900,000	
Pleigh's Share	80%	720,000
Fair Value Adjustments:		
Inventories		(80,000)
Plant And Equipment [(5 Years)($10,000)]		(50,000)
Investment In Sleigh At Equity		$3,790,000

5-125.   If this amount is used on the asset side of Pleigh's single entity Balance Sheet, there will have to be a corresponding $590,000 ($3,890,000 - $3,200,000) adjustment to Retained Earnings on the equity side of the single entity Balance Sheet resulting in Retained Earnings of $3,290,000 ($2,700,000 + $590,000). This will leave Pleigh with the following single entity Balance Sheet under the equity method:

Pleigh Company
Comparison Of Single Entity and Consolidated Balance Sheet
As At December 31, 2006

	Equity Method	Consolidated
Cash	$ 500,000	$ 800,000
Current Receivables	800,000	1,188,000
Inventories	2,500,000	4,200,000
Long-Term Note Receivable	200,000	Nil
Investment In Sleigh (At Equity)	3,790,000	Nil
Land	1,500,000	2,380,000
Plant And Equipment (Net)	4,500,000	6,550,000
Goodwill	Nil	240,000
Total Assets	$13,790,000	$15,358,000
Current Liabilities	$ 500,000	$ 688,000
Long-Term Liabilities	2,000,000	2,500,000
Non-Controlling Interest	Nil	880,000
No Par Common Stock	8,000,000	8,000,000
Retained Earnings	3,290,000	3,290,000
Total Equities	$13,790,000	$15,358,000

5-126.   Note that, when the equity method is used, the resulting Retained Earnings figure in Pleigh's single entity Balance Sheet is equal to the consolidated Retained Earnings figure resulting from the application of consolidation procedures. This result follows from the Paragraph 3050.08 requirement that investment income as calculated by the equity method must be the amount necessary to increase or decrease the investor's income to that which would have been recognized if the results of the investee's operations had been consolidated with those of the investor.

Exercise Five-4

(This is identical to Exercise Five-2 except for the Required.)

On January 1, 2002, the Parker Company purchases 65 percent of the outstanding shares of the Schaffer Company for $1,350,000 in cash. On that date, the Schaffer Company had No Par Common Stock of $700,000 and Retained Earnings of $1,000,000. On December 31, 2006, the adjusted trial balances of the Parker Company and its subsidiary, the Schaffer Company are as follows:

> Exercise Five-4 deals with the application of the equity method.

	Parker	Schaffer
Monetary Assets	$ 2,850,000	$ 725,000
Investment In Schaffer - At Cost	1,350,000	Nil
Non-Monetary Assets	6,475,000	2,045,000
Total Expenses	2,940,000	530,000
Dividends Declared	250,000	50,000
Total Debits	$13,865,000	$3,350,000
Liabilities	$ 1,712,500	$ 425,000
No Par Common Stock	3,000,000	700,000
Retained Earnings (January 1)	5,895,000	1,550,000
Sales	3,225,000	675,000
Dividend Revenue	32,500	Nil
Total Credits	$13,865,000	$3,350,000

This is a continuation of Exercise Five-4.

	Parker	Schaffer
2006 Net Income	$ 317,500	$ 145,000
December 31, 2006 Retained Earnings	$ 5,962,500	$1,645,000

Other Information:

1. At the date of Parker Company's acquisition of the Schaffer Company's shares, all of the identifiable assets and liabilities of the Schaffer Company had fair values that were equal to their carrying values except for a group of non-monetary assets that had a fair value that was $150,000 greater than its carrying value. These non-monetary assets had a remaining useful life of 15 years. Both companies use the straight-line method for all amortization calculations.

2. In each of the years since Parker acquired control over Schaffer, the goodwill arising on this business combination transaction has been tested for impairment. In 2004, a Goodwill Impairment Loss of $35,000 was recognized. In addition, the impairment test for 2006 found a further impairment of $25,000.

3. Schaffer Company's Sales during 2006 include sales of $85,000 to Parker Company. All of this merchandise has been resold by the Pleigh Company. However, as a result of these sales, on December 31, 2006, Parker still owes Schaffer $15,000 on open account.

Required: Assume that the Parker Company's majority ownership of Schaffer shares has never provided control over that Company and, as a consequence, consolidated financial statements cannot be prepared. Provide the Parker Company's single entity Income Statement for the year ending December 31, 2006, and its single entity Balance Sheet as at December 31, 2006 assuming the Investment in Schaffer is accounted for by the equity method since its acquisition. Note that the Parker Company's trial balance given in the problem accounts for the Investment In Schaffer using the cost method.

End Of Exercise Five-4

Consolidated Cash Flow Statement

Differences In Procedures

5-127. In general, the procedures for preparing a consolidated Cash Flow Statement are very similar to those required for a single entity Cash Flow Statement (specific differences are described in the paragraphs which follow).

5-128. In most circumstances, it is not necessary to prepare a complete set of consolidated financial statements in order to complete a consolidated Cash Flow Statement. However, as a minimum, the data for consolidated Net Income, the change in consolidated cash, and the change in other working capital items is needed. In addition, some of the consolidated expenses and revenues will have to be determined in order to provide an appropriate conversion of consolidated Net Income into consolidated Cash Flows From Operating Activities.

5-129. As was indicated, most of the procedures are the same, without regard to whether a consolidated or a single entity Cash Flow Statement is being prepared. The basic procedures for preparing this financial statement are covered in a number of texts and, as a consequence will not be presented in this material. (Detailed coverage of this subject can be found in Chapter 12 of our *Guide To Canadian Financial Reporting*. This *Guide* is included on the CD-ROM which accompanies this text.) There are, however, some procedures that are unique to preparing the consolidated statement. They are as follows:

- Consolidated Net Income is defined in Section 1600 as being after the deduction of the Non-Controlling Interest. Since this deduction does not involve an outflow of consolidated cash, it will be treated in a manner similar to amortization and other expenses which do not involve cash outflows. That is, it will be added back to consolidated Net Income in order to arrive at consolidated Cash Flows From Operating Activities.

- In a single entity Cash Flow Statement, the dividends shown will be the same amount as shown in the Statement Of Retained Earnings. This will not be the case here. The consolidated Cash Flow Statement would disclose all dividends which involve an outflow of consolidated cash. This would include both the dividends declared by the parent company and the dividends declared by the subsidiary and payable to the non-controlling shareholders. You will recall that in the consolidated Statement Of Retained Earnings, we deducted only the dividends declared by the parent company.

- Also unique to the consolidation situation is the possibility that the parent may acquire additional subsidiary shares. Two possible situations can be identified here:

    1. If the shares are acquired for cash directly from the subsidiary, it is an intercompany transaction that would be eliminated and would not appear in the consolidated Cash Flow Statement.

    2. If the shares are acquired for cash from the non-controlling shareholders, the transaction would be disclosed as an outflow of consolidated cash.

A similar analysis can be made when a part of the subsidiary shares are sold.

Section 1540 On Business Combinations
5-130.   In addition to providing general guidelines for the preparation of the Cash Flow Statement, Section 1540, "Cash Flow Statements", also provides specific guidance in the area of business combinations. With respect to a purchase method acquisition and disposal of subsidiaries, the following Recommendations are provided:

Paragraph 1540.42   *The aggregate cash flows arising from each of business combinations accounted for using the purchase method and disposals of business units should be presented separately and classified as cash flows from investing activities.* (August, 1998)

Paragraph 1540.43   *An enterprise should disclose, in aggregate, in respect of both business combinations accounted for using the purchase method and disposals of business units during the period each of the following:*

(a) *the total purchase or disposal consideration;*
(b) *the portion of the purchase or disposal consideration composed of cash and cash equivalents;*
(c) *the amount of cash and cash equivalents acquired or disposed of; and*
(d) *the total assets, other than cash or cash equivalents, and total liabilities acquired or disposed of.* (August, 1998)

Example - Consolidated Cash Flow Statement
Basic Data
5-131.   In order to illustrate the procedures and concepts related to business combinations, a simple example of a consolidated Cash Flow Statement will be presented. The basic data is as follows:

On December 31, 2002, the Pam Company acquired 80 percent of the outstanding shares of the Sam Company for $3,600,000 in cash. On this date, all of the Sam Company's identifiable assets and liabilities had carrying values that were equal to their fair values. The carrying values of the Sam Company's net identifiable assets amounted to $4,000,000.

On December 31, 2005, the Pam Company acquired 100 percent of the outstanding shares of the Tam Company for cash in the amount of $2,200,000. On that date, the Tam Company had cash of $100,000, net non-cash current assets of $400,000, identifiable non-current assets of $2,000,000 and liabilities of $500,000. All of the Tam Company's identifiable assets and liabilities had carrying values that were equal to their fair values.

The comparative condensed Balance Sheets of the Pam Company and its subsidiary, the Sam Company, on December 31, 2004 and December 31, 2005 are as follows:

Pam And Sam Companies
Balance Sheets
As At December 31, 2004

	Pam	Sam
Cash	$ 400,000	$ 300,000
Net Non-Cash Current Assets	5,600,000	1,700,000
Investment In Sam (At Cost)	3,600,000	-0-
Plant And Equipment	12,000,000	8,000,000
Accumulated Depreciation	(5,600,000)	(2,000,000)
Total Assets	$16,000,000	$8,000,000
Long-Term Liabilities	$ 3,000,000	$2,000,000
No Par Common Stock	5,000,000	2,000,000
Retained Earnings	8,000,000	4,000,000
Total Equities	$16,000,000	$8,000,000

Pam And Sam Companies
Balance Sheets
As At December 31, 2005

	Pam	Sam
Cash	$ 800,000	$ 600,000
Net Non-Cash Current Assets	4,800,000	2,200,000
Investment In Sam (Cost)	3,600,000	-0-
Investment In Tam (Cost)	2,200,000	-0-
Plant And Equipment	13,000,000	8,400,000
Accumulated Depreciation	(6,400,000)	(2,200,000)
Total Assets	$18,000,000	$9,000,000
Long-Term Liabilities	$ 3,000,000	$2,500,000
No Par Common Stock	6,000,000	2,000,000
Retained Earnings	9,000,000	4,500,000
Total Equities	$18,000,000	$9,000,000

Other Information:

1. During 2005, the Sam Company issued $500,000 in Long-Term Liabilities for cash.

2. During 2005, the Sam Company purchased Plant And Equipment for $800,000 in cash and sold Plant And Equipment with a cost of $400,000 and a net book value of $200,000 for cash of $60,000.

3. The 2005 Net Income and Dividends Paid for the three Companies are as follows:

	Pam	Sam	Tam
Net Income	$2,000,000	$1,000,000	$300,000
Dividends Paid	1,000,000	500,000	100,000

4. All Companies comply with Section 3062, "Goodwill And Other Intangible Assets", for all the years under consideration.   It was determined that there was a goodwill

impairment loss for 2005 of $40,000 related to Pam Company's purchase of Sam Company shares.

Required: For the year ending December 31, 2005, prepare a consolidated Cash Flow Statement for the Pam Company and its subsidiaries, the Sam Company and the Tam Company.

Preliminary Computations

5-132. Before proceeding directly to the preparation of the consolidated Cash Flow Statement, it will be useful to provide computations for consolidated Net Income and the change in the consolidated working capital and cash position. These calculations are contained in the material which follows.

5-133. We will calculate the consolidated Net Income using the definitional approach. You should note that the Tam Company's Net Income does not have a place in this calculation. This reflects the fact that its acquisition date was December 31, 2005 and the Tam Company's income would only accrue to the consolidated entity subsequent to the acquisition date. Given this, the calculation of the 2005 consolidated Net Income is as follows:

Pam Company's Net Income	$2,000,000
Intercompany Dividends - Sam To Pam [(80%)($500,000)]	(400,000)
Pam's Net Income Exclusive Of Subsidiary Dividends	$1,600,000
Equity Pickup - 80 Percent Of Sam's Net Income	800,000
Income Before Adjustments	$2,400,000
Goodwill Impairment Loss	(40,000)
Consolidated Net Income	$2,360,000

5-134. On December 31, 2005, the $1,500,000 consolidated cash was made up of Pam Company's $800,000, Sam Company's $600,000, plus the newly acquired Tam Company's cash of $100,000. On December 31, 2004, Pam Company had cash of $400,000 while the Sam Company's balance was $300,000. On this earlier date, the Tam Company had not yet been acquired so that its cash does not have a place in the consolidated cash which totals $700,000 on December 31, 2004. The increase in consolidated cash for the year ending December 31, 2005 is equal to $800,000 ($1,500,000 - $700,000).

5-135. On December 31, 2005, the consolidated Net Non-Cash Current Assets were made up of the Pam Company's $4,800,000, the Sam Company's $2,200,000, and the newly acquired Tam Company's Net Non-Cash Current Assets of $400,000, which totals $7,400,000. On December 31, 2004, the Pam Company had Net Non-Cash Current Assets of $5,600,000 while the Sam Company's balance was $1,700,000. On this earlier date, the Tam Company had not yet been acquired so that its balance does not have a place in the December 31, 2004 consolidated Net Non-Cash Current Assets of $7,300,000. The increase in consolidated Net Non-Cash Current Assets for the year ending December 31, 2005 is $100,000 ($7,400,000 - $7,300,000).

Consolidated Cash Flow Statement

5-136. As this example was designed to illustrate the acquisition of a subsidiary, it does not contain all of the information needed to provide the disclosure required by Section 1540 (e.g., cash paid for income taxes).

5-137. In any Cash Flow Statement, the most difficult figure to compute is usually Cash Flows From Operating Activities. It can be calculated by starting at zero, adding operating revenues that generate cash and deducting operating expenses that involve outflows of cash. However, in this example, we have started with Net Income and adjusted this figure for non-cash expense and revenue items.

Consolidated Net Income	$2,360,000
Depreciation Expense (Note One)	1,200,000
Non-Controlling Interest [(20%)($1,000,000)]	200,000
Loss On Sale Of Equipment ($400,000 - $200,000 - $60,000)	140,000
Goodwill Impairment Loss	40,000
Consolidated Working Capital From Operating Activities	$3,940,000
Decrease In Consolidated Net Non-Cash Current Assets (Note Two)	300,000
Consolidated Cash Flows From Operating Activities	$4,240,000

Note One   The Depreciation Expense is equal to the increase in Pam's Accumulated Depreciation of $800,000 ($6,400,000 - $5,600,000), the increase in Sam's Accumulated Depreciation of $200,000 ($2,200,000 - $2,000,000), plus the accumulated depreciation of $200,000 on the Plant And Equipment which was retired.

Note Two   Note that, while there was an overall increase in Net Non-Cash Current Assets of $100,000, this was net of the $400,000 increase which resulted from the acquisition of the Tam Company. As this increase did not relate to operating activities of the consolidated group, it would be removed from the adjustment required to arrive at Cash Flows From Operating Activities, leaving a decrease of $300,000 (an increase of $100,000, less the $400,000 from the Tam Company acquisition).

5-138.   The consolidated Cash Flow Statement for the year ending December 31, 2005 would be prepared as follows:

Pam Company And Subsidiaries
Consolidated Cash Flow Statement
Year Ending December 31, 2005

Cash Flows From (Used In):

Operating Activities

Cash Flows From Operating Activities (Preceding Calculation)		$4,240,000

Financing Activities

Issuance Of Long-Term Debt For Cash	$ 500,000	
Dividends Paid By Pam	(1,000,000)	
Dividends Paid By Subsidiaries To Non		
Controlling Interests (20% of $500,000)	(100,000)	(600,000)

Investing Activities

Acquisition Of Subsidiary (Note One)	($2,100,000)	
Proceeds From The Sale Of Plant	60,000	
Acquisition Of Plant For Cash	(800,000)	(2,840,000)
Increase In Cash		$ 800,000
Cash At Beginning Of Year (Excluding Tam)		700,000
Cash At End Of Year (Including Tam)		$1,500,000

Note One   There are a variety of ways in which the acquisition of the Tam Company could be disclosed in a note to the Cash Flow Statement. One way of accomplishing this is as follows:

Tam Company's Cash Acquired	$ 100,000
Tam's Net Non-Cash Current Assets Acquired	400,000
Tam's Identifiable Non-Current Assets Acquired	2,000,000
Tam's Liabilities Assumed	(500,000)
Tam's Goodwill Acquired (Balancing Figure)	200,000
Cash Paid For Tam Company Shares	$2,200,000

Exercise Five-5

On January 1, 2002, the Parco Company acquires 80 percent of the outstanding voting shares of the Subco Company for $1,000,000 in cash. At this time the Subco Company has No Par Common Stock of $1,000,000 and Retained Earnings of $200,000. Also on this acquisition date, all of the identifiable assets and liabilities of Subco Company had fair values that were equal to their carrying values except for Inventories which had a fair value that was $400,000 less than its carrying value and Equipment which had a fair value that was $300,000 more than its carrying value. The Inventories were sold during the year ending December 31, 2002, while the Equipment had a remaining useful life on January 1, 2002 of ten years with no antici-pated salvage value. Both the Parco Company and the Subco Company use the straight line method for all amortization calculations. Comparative Balance Sheets for the two companies as at December 31, 2006 and December 31, 2007 are as follows:

> Exercise Five-5 deals with consolidated cash flow statements.

	Parco (000's)		Subco (000's)	
	2007	2006	2007	2006
Cash	$ 800	$ 400	$ 365	$ 270
Accounts Receivable	1,500	1,800	900	650
Inventories	2,000	2,600	800	500
Investment In Subco (At Cost)	1,000	1,000	Nil	Nil
Land	1,000	800	450	850
Plant And Equipment (Net)	4,800	6,400	600	800
Total	$11,100	$13,000	$3,115	$3,070
Accounts Payable	$ 400	$ 1,000	$ 700	$ 750
Bonds Payable - Par	3,000	4,000	800	800
Bonds Payable - Premium	Nil	Nil	15	20
Common Stock - No Par	4,000	4,000	1,000	1,000
Retained Earnings	3,700	4,000	600	500
Total	$11,100	$13,000	$3,115	$3,070

Other Information:

1. During 2007, the Parco Company retires outstanding debt with a par value of $1,000,000 for $1,000,000 in cash.

2. During 2007, the Parco Company experiences a Net Loss of $300,000 and does not declare any dividends. This Net Loss includes an $800,000 write-down of Plant And Equipment to reflect the fact that its net carrying amount exceeded its net recoverable amount.

3. During 2007, the Subco Company earns Net Income of $500,000 and declares dividends of $400,000. All of the dividends declared are paid prior to December 31, 2007.

4. The goodwill measured at the time Parco acquired Subco has been tested for impairment in each subsequent year. No impairment has been found.

5. The changes in the Land accounts reflect purchases of land for cash and sales of land for cash. The proceeds from the land sales were equal to the carrying value of the land sold. There were no purchases or sales of Plant and Equipment.

Required:

A. Calculate consolidated Net Income for the Parco Company and its subsidiary, the Subco Company, for the year ending December 31, 2007.

B. Prepare a consolidated Cash Flow Statement for the Parco Company and its subsidiary, the Subco Company, for the year ending December 31, 2007. Your solution should comply with all of the requirements of the *CICA Handbook*.

End of Exercise Five-5

Step-By-Step Acquisitions

Definition And Accounting Recommendations

5-139.   A step-by-step acquisition involves a situation in which an investor acquires control of an investee in a sequence of two or more purchases. Several purchases and a considerable period of time might elapse before a particular investee becomes a subsidiary. However, when control is achieved, the accounting procedures are not conceptually different than those used in dealing with a single step acquisition of a subsidiary. This is reflected in the following *CICA Handbook* Recommendation:

> **Paragraph 1600.13**   *Where an investment in a subsidiary is acquired through two or more purchases, the parent company's interest in the subsidiary's identifiable assets and liabilities should be determined as follows:*
>
> (a) *the assignable costs of the subsidiary's identifiable assets and liabilities should be determined as at each date on which an investment was required;*
>
> (b) *the parent company's interest in the subsidiary's identifiable assets and liabilities acquired at each step in the purchase should be based on the assignable costs of all such assets and liabilities at that date.* (April, 1975)

5-140.   The meaning of assignable costs in the preceding Recommendation is fair values adjusted, if applicable, for any excess of such values assigned over the cost of the purchase. This means that this Recommendation calls for the establishment and allocation of fair values at each purchase date. While these are the same procedures that would be used in the case of a single step acquisition, implementation difficulties may arise as a result of the step-by-step acquisition process.

Implementation Problems

5-141.   As indicated in the previous paragraph, the appropriate solution to accounting for this type of situation would require the determination and allocation of fair value changes and goodwill at each step of the acquisition. However, there are situations in which, at the time of one or more of the early share acquisitions, there is no intent to acquire controlling ownership. If these initial investments are classified as portfolio investments, they will be accounted for by the cost method. Since under the cost method there is no requirement that fair values or goodwill be determined, this information may not be available when it becomes appropriate to consolidate or apply the equity method. In view of this problem, the following suggestion is made:

> **Paragraph 1600.11**   For practical purposes, assignable costs will normally be determined as at the time the first use of equity accounting becomes appropriate (or as at the time the first use of consolidation becomes appropriate, if equity accounting has not previously been appropriate) and at each further major purchase.

5-142.   For those purchases where fair value data is not available, there will still be a differential between investment cost and the investor's proportionate share of book values. This differential, if a debit amount, will have to be allocated to goodwill. If a credit is involved, it will be deducted from identifiable non-monetary assets.

5-143.   An additional modification of general procedures is also suggested. This involves situations in which there are a large number of small purchases. It is stated as follows:

> **Paragraph 1600.11**   Where there are numerous small purchases, it is appropriate to group a series of such purchases into one step, in order to treat the series in the same way as a major purchase.

Example - Step-By-Step Acquisition

Basic Data

5-144.   While the concepts involved in step-by-step acquisitions are identical to those used in single step acquisitions, the procedures involved are sufficiently different to warrant the presentation of a simple illustration of this situation. The basic data for this example is as follows:

Example   On December 31, 2002, the Alpha Company purchases 30 percent of the outstanding shares of the Morgan Company for $2,250,000. On this date, the carrying value of the Morgan Company's net identifiable assets amounts to $5,000,000. All of the fair values of the individual identifiable assets and liabilities of the Morgan Company have carrying values that are equal to their fair values except for an item of Plant And Equipment. This item has a remaining useful life of six years and a fair value that exceeds its carrying value by $1,000,000. Both companies use the straight line method to calculate depreciation and amortization.

On December 31, 2003, the Alpha Company purchases an additional 40 percent of the outstanding shares of the Morgan Company for $3,500,000. On this date, the carrying value of the Morgan Company's net identifiable assets totals $6,000,000. All of the fair values of the identifiable assets and liabilities of the Morgan Company have carrying values that are equal to their fair values except for the item of Plant And Equipment. This is the same item on which there was a fair value change on December 31, 2002. However, the fair value change has increased to a total of $1,500,000 on December 31, 2003. The remaining useful life of this asset is now five years.

The Goodwill measured in each of the purchase transactions has been tested for impairment in each subsequent year. These tests have found no impairment in either 2003 or 2004.

During the years 2002, 2003, and 2004 there are no intercompany transactions between the Alpha Company and its subsidiary the Morgan Company. Also during this period, the Morgan Company's contributed capital remains unchanged. The Alpha Company carries its investments in the Morgan Company using the cost method. On December 31, 2004, the condensed Balance Sheets of the Alpha Company and its subsidiary the Morgan Company are as follows:

Alpha and Morgan Companies
Condensed Balance Sheets
As At December 31, 2004

	Alpha	Morgan
Investment In Morgan Company	$5,750,000	$ -0-
Other Net Identifiable Assets	4,150,000	6,500,000
Total Assets	$9,900,000	$6,500,000
No Par Common Stock	$5,000,000	$2,000,000
Retained Earnings	4,900,000	4,500,000
Total Equities	$9,900,000	$6,500,000

Required: Prepare a consolidated Balance Sheet for the Alpha Company and its subsidiary, the Morgan Company, as at December 31, 2004.

Procedures

5-145.   In a problem such as this, the easiest solution usually involves direct computations of the balances to be included in the consolidated Balance Sheet. While the journal entries used in our general procedures can be used in step-by-step acquisitions, we have found this approach to be very awkward.   As a consequence, we would encourage you to solve step-by-step problems by using direct calculations of the required items, an approach that will be illustrated with this example.

Analysis Of Investments

5-146.   Before proceeding to the direct computation of the various accounts for inclusion in the consolidated Balance Sheet, it is useful to analyze the two investment transactions through which the Alpha Company acquired control of the Morgan Company. The analysis of the first transaction is as follows:

	30 Percent	100 Percent
Investment Cost	$2,250,000	$7,500,000
Book Value - Net Assets	(1,500,000)	(5,000,000)
Differential	$ 750,000	$2,500,000
Fair Value Increase On Plant	(300,000)	(1,000,000)
Goodwill	$ 450,000	$1,500,000

5-147.   In similar fashion, the analysis of the second investment transaction would appear as follows:

	40 Percent	100 Percent
Investment Cost	$3,500,000	$8,750,000
Book Value - Net Assets	(2,400,000)	(6,000,000)
Differential	$1,100,000	$2,750,000
Fair Value Increase On Plant	(600,000)	(1,500,000)
Goodwill	$ 500,000	$1,250,000

Consolidated Net Identifiable Assets

5-148.   At the end of Chapter 4 we provided the following definitional calculation for identifiable assets and liabilities:

Identifiable Assets And Liabilities   The consolidated balance for any identifiable asset or liability is calculated as follows:

- 100 percent of the carrying value of the identifiable asset or liability on the books of the parent company; *plus*

- 100 percent of the carrying value of the identifiable asset or liability on the books of the subsidiary company; *plus (minus)*

- the parent company's share of the increase (decrease) in the fair value of the subsidiary's asset (liability) balance.

5-149.   As we are now in a period subsequent to acquisition, a further component must be added to this definition to recognize that parts of the fair value changes have been realized and must be charged to income. This further component could be stated as follows:

- *minus (plus)* the portion of the fair value increase (decrease) that has become realized since acquisition through usage of the asset, or through its disposal.

5-150.   This definition can be used in dealing with this step-by-step acquisition. The only difference here is that there are two acquisition dates and fair values must be picked up with respect to both of them. The calculation, including accumulated amortization on the fair value changes to December 31, 2004, would be as follows:

December 31, 2004 Book Values:		
Alpha Company's		$ 4,150,000
Morgan Company's		6,500,000
Total Book Values - December 31, 2004		$10,650,000
Fair Value Changes:		
December 31, 2002 Purchase	$300,000	
Amortization [(2)($300,000 ÷ 6)]	(100,000)	200,000
December 31, 2003 Purchase	$600,000	
Amortization ($600,000 ÷ 5)	(120,000)	480,000
Consolidated Net Identifiable Assets		$11,330,000

5-151.   Note carefully that fair value changes are only included to the extent that they are purchased. Changes in fair values that occur subsequent to a particular purchase are not retroactively picked up. As an example, in this situation you would not record the first purchase's 30 percent share of the increase in the fair value change on the Plant And Equipment item from $1,000,000 on December 31, 2002 to $1,500,000 on December 31, 2003. This is, of course, consistent with the general approach under the parent company concept in that only the investor's purchased share of fair value changes and goodwill is recognized.

Goodwill

5-152.   As the first purchase date is after January 1, 2002, the goodwill that was measured in the two purchases cannot be amortized. Further, the problem indicates that there has been no measured impairment of these balances. As a consequence, the consolidated goodwill will simply be $950,000 ($450,000 + $500,000), the sum of the values measured at the two purchase dates.

Consolidated Retained Earnings

5-153.   A definitional calculation can be made here of the required balance for the consolidated Retained Earnings as at December 31, 2004. The only difference that is created by the multiple steps in the acquisition is that multiple equity pickups will be recorded. The calculation is as follows:

Alpha Company's Retained Earnings		$4,900,000
Equity Pickups:		
First Purchase [(30%)($4,500,000 - $3,000,000)]	$450,000	
Second Purchase [(40%)($4,500,000 - $4,000,000)]	200,000	650,000
Amortization Of Fair Value Change		(220,000)
Consolidated Retained Earnings		$5,330,000

5-154.   There is an alternative approach to the calculation of the total equity pickup of $650,000. It is as follows:

First Purchase [(30%)($4,000,000 - $3,000,000)]	$300,000
Second Purchase [(70%)($4,500,000 - $4,000,000)]	350,000
Total Equity Pickup	$650,000

5-155.   While either approach will provide a consistently correct answer, we would suggest you try to use one or the other on a consistent basis.

Consolidated Balance Sheet

5-156. Using the preceding information, the consolidated Balance Sheet would be prepared as follows:

Alpha Company And Subsidiary
Consolidated Balance Sheet
As At December 31, 2004

Net Identifiable Assets (Paragraph 5-150)	$11,330,000
Goodwill ($450,000 + $500,000)	950,000
Total Assets	$12,280,000
Non-Controlling Interest (30 Percent Of $6,500,000)	$ 1,950,000
No Par Common Stock (Alpha Company's Balance)	5,000,000
Retained Earnings (Paragraph 5-153)	5,330,000
Total Equities	$12,280,000

Exercise Five-6

> Exercise Five-6 deals with step-by-step acquisitions.

On December 31, 2002, the Best Company purchases 40 percent of the outstanding shares of the Worst Company for $1,875,000. On this date, the carrying values of the Worst Company's net identifiable assets amount to $3,250,000 (Common Stock of $2,000,000, plus Retained Earnings of $1,250,000). All of the fair values of the individual identifiable assets and liabilities of the Worst Company have carrying values that are equal to their fair values except for Plant And Equipment. Specialized machinery with a remaining useful life of four years has a carrying value of $2,000,000 and a fair value of $2,725,000.

On December 31, 2003, the Best Company purchases an additional 15 percent of the outstanding shares of the Worst Company for $3,500,000. On this date, the carrying values of the Worst Company's net identifiable assets total $4,250,000 (Common Stock of $2,000,000, plus Retained Earnings of $2,250,000). All of the fair values of the identifiable assets and liabilities of the Worst Company have carrying values that are equal to their fair values except for Plant And Equipment. The specialized machinery now has a useful life of three years, a carrying value of $1,600,000, and a fair value of $2,300,00.

There has been no impairment of goodwill in either 2003 or 2004.

On December 31, 2004, the carrying values for Best's and Worst's Plant And Equipment are $3,520,000 and $1,600,000, respectively. The Retained Earnings balance of Best on December 31, 2004 is $4,275,000 while Worst's Retained Earnings balance is $2,450,000.

Required:

A. Calculate consolidated Plant And Equipment as of December 31, 2004.

B. Calculate the amount of Goodwill that would be shown on the December 31, 2004 Balance Sheet.

C. Calculate consolidated Retained Earnings as of December 31, 2004.

End of Exercise Five-6

Summary Of Consolidation Procedures

5-156.   In Chapter 4, we began the development of a set of procedures that could be used in the preparation of a consolidated Balance Sheet at the date of the subsidiary's acquisition. As this Chapter begins to deal with the preparation of a complete set of consolidated financial statements for periods subsequent to acquisition, it contains a significant expansion of these procedures. Further, some modifications of the procedures developed in Chapter 4 were required in order to deal with periods subsequent to acquisition and the need to prepare additional types of consolidated statements. Specifically we have added Steps B-2 to C-2 to deal with procedures required subsequent to the acquisition of the subsidiary. At this point, we will provide you with a complete summary of the procedures developed in Chapters 4 and 5. This summary is as follows:

Step A-1 Procedure   Eliminate 100 percent of the Investment In Subsidiary account.

Step A-2 Procedure   Eliminate 100 percent of all the acquisition date balances in the subsidiary's shareholders' equity (includes both contributed capital and retained earnings).

Step A-3 Procedure   Allocate any debit or credit Differential that is present at acquisition to the investor's share of fair value changes on identifiable assets, fair value changes on identifiable liabilities, and positive or negative goodwill.

Step A-4 Procedure   Allocate to a Non-Controlling Interest account in the consolidated Balance Sheet, the non-controlling interest's share of the at acquisition book value of the total shareholders' equity of the subsidiary (includes both contributed capital and retained earnings).

Step B-1 Procedure   Eliminate 100 percent of all intercompany assets and liabilities.

Step B-2 Procedure   Give recognition to the post-acquisition realization of acquisition date fair value changes on assets and liabilities that have been used up or sold during the post-acquisition period. To the extent that this realization occurred in prior periods, recognition will require an adjustment of the opening retained earnings of the subsidiary. Alternatively, if the realization occurred in the current period, the adjustment will be to the subsidiary's current period expenses, revenues, gains, or losses.

Step B-3 Procedure   Recognize current and cumulative goodwill impairment losses that have been measured since the acquisition of the subsidiary and the initial recognition of the goodwill balance. To the extent that the impairment took place during the current period, the measured amount will be charged to Goodwill Impairment Loss. To the extent that it occurred in prior periods, it will be charged to retained earnings.

Step B-4 Procedure   Eliminate 100 percent of all intercompany expenses and revenues.

Step B-5 Procedure   Eliminate 100 percent of subsidiary dividends declared. The parent's share of this amount will be deducted from the revenues of the parent company and the non-controlling interest's share of this amount will be deducted from the Non-Controlling Interest in the Balance Sheet.

Step C-1 Procedure   Determine the appropriate allocation of the subsidiary's adjusted retained earnings since acquisition. The Non-Controlling Interest's share will be based on book value. After the non-controlling interest is subtracted, the resulting balance will be adjusted for the fair value write-offs called for in Step B(2), as well as any goodwill impairment as described in Step B(3). The balance remaining after these adjustments will be allocated to consolidated retained earnings.

Step C-2 Procedure Eliminate the subsidiary's adjusted Retained Earnings since acquisition. This amount will be allocated to the Non-Controlling Interest in the consolidated Balance Sheet and to consolidated retained earnings as determined in Step C-1.

5-157. The preceding represents a complete set of consolidation procedures for dealing with problems that do not have unrealized intercompany profits. The development of the procedures for dealing with unrealized intercompany profits will be found in Chapter 6.

5-158. We would call your attention to the fact that, as stated, the listed procedures apply to open trial balance problems in which the investment is carried at cost. In other types of problems, modifications will be required. For example, in applying Step B-2 in a closed trial balance problem, there will be no adjustments to current expenses, revenues, gains, or losses as these amounts have been closed to the subsidiary's Retained Earnings account. Such required modifications were illustrated in the closed trial balance version of our comprehensive example.

Summary Of Definitional Calculations

5-159. We continue to encourage you to work towards preparing the required balances in consolidated financial statements by using direct definitional calculations. To assist you in this work, we offer the following definitions that have been developed in the course of Chapters 4 and 5.

Identifiable Assets And Liabilities The amount to be included in the consolidated Balance Sheet for any identifiable asset or liability is calculated as follows:

- 100 percent of the carrying value of the identifiable asset (liability) on the books of the parent company at the Balance Sheet date; *plus*

- 100 percent of the carrying value of the identifiable asset (liability) on the books of the subsidiary company at the Balance Sheet date; *plus (minus)*

- the parent company's share of the fair value increase (decrease) on the asset (liability) (i.e., the parent company's share of the difference between the fair value of the subsidiary's asset or liability at time of acquisition and the carrying value of that asset or liability at the time of acquisition); *minus (plus)*

- amortization of the parent company's share of the fair value increase (decrease) on the asset (liability) for the period since acquisition to the current Balance Sheet date.

Goodwill The Goodwill to be recorded in the consolidated Balance Sheet is equal to:

- the excess of the cost of the investment over the parent company's share of the fair values of the subsidiary's net assets at the time of acquisition; *minus*

- the amount of any goodwill impairment that has been recognized in the period since the acquisition to the current Balance Sheet date.

Non-Controlling Interest - Balance Sheet The Non-Controlling Interest to be recorded in the consolidated Balance Sheet is an amount equal to the non-controlling interest's ownership percentage of the book value of the subsidiary's common stock equity at the Balance Sheet date.

Contributed Capital The Contributed Capital to be recorded in the consolidated Balance Sheet is equal to the contributed capital from the single entity Balance Sheet of the parent company.

Retained Earnings   The Retained Earnings amount to be included in the consolidated Balance Sheet is calculated as follows:

- 100 percent of the Retained Earnings of the parent company; *plus (minus)*

- the parent company's share of the subsidiary's Retained Earnings (Deficit) since acquisition; *plus (minus)*

- 100 percent of the adjustments to consolidated expenses, revenues, gains, and losses for realized fair value changes during the period since acquisition to the current Balance Sheet date; *minus*

- 100 percent of any goodwill impairment that has been recognized since the acquisition to the current Balance Sheet date.

Revenue   The amount of any revenue to be included in the consolidated Income Statement is calculated as follows:

- 100 percent of the amount reported in the parent company's financial statements; *plus*

- 100 percent of the amount reported in the subsidiary's financial statements; *minus*

- 100 percent of any intercompany amounts included in the parent or subsidiary figures; *plus (minus)*

- the parent's share of any fair value changes realized during the period through usage or sale of subsidiary assets (fair value amortization, depreciation, or depletion and amounts realized through the sale of subsidiary assets prior to the end of their economic life). It would be unusual for fair value realizations to be related to revenues. However, it could happen. For example, amortization of a fair value change on a long-term receivable would be treated as an adjustment of interest revenue. An additional example could result from the sale of an asset on which a fair value change has been recorded in the consolidated financial statements. If there was a gain (revenue) on the transaction, it would have to be adjusted for the realized fair value change.

Expense   The amount of any expense to be included in the consolidated Income Statement is calculated as follows:

- 100 percent of the amount reported in the parent company's financial statements; *plus*

- 100 percent of the amount reported in the subsidiary's financial statements; *minus*

- 100 percent of any intercompany amounts included in the parent or subsidiary figures; *plus (minus)*

- the parent's share of any fair value changes realized during the period through usage or sale of subsidiary assets (fair value amortization, depreciation, or depletion and amounts realized through the sale of subsidiary assets prior to the end of their economic life).

Goodwill Impairment Loss   If the required annual test of goodwill for impairment determines that any impairment has occurred during the current period, this amount will be recorded as a Goodwill Impairment Loss.

Non-Controlling Interest - Income Statement   The non-controlling interest in the consolidated Income Statement is an amount equal to the non-controlling interest's ownership percentage of the reported Net Income. Note that, if the subsidiary has extraordinary items or results from discontinued operations, this Non-Controlling Interest will be based on the subsidiary's Income Before Extraordinary Items And

Discontinued Operations. Also note that, in situations where there are preferred shares with a prior claim on the income of the subsidiary, the Non-Controlling Interest to be disclosed in the consolidated Income Statement will include such claims.

Consolidated Net Income   Consolidated Net Income can be calculated as follows:

- 100 percent of the parent company's Net Income, excluding dividends received from the subsidiary; *plus (minus)*
- the parent's share of the subsidiary's reported Net Income (Net Loss); *plus (minus)*
- the parent's share of any fair value changes realized during the period through usage or sale of subsidiary assets (fair value amortization, depreciation, or depletion and amounts realized through the sale of subsidiary assets prior to the end of their economic life); *minus*
- any Goodwill Impairment Loss that is recognized during the period.

5-160.   These definitions are applicable to problems which do not involve the presence of unrealized intercompany profits. When we introduce unrealized intercompany profits in the next Chapter, these definitions will require significant modification.

Walk Through Problem

Note This problem is an extension of the Walk Through Problem that was presented at the end of Chapter 4. As was explained in that Chapter, these problems provide you with a fill-in-the-blank solution format to assist you in solving the problem. These problems are designed to be an easy introduction to solving the type of problem illustrated in the Chapter.

Basic Data On December 31, 2002, the Puff Company purchased 60 percent of the outstanding voting shares of the Snuff Company for $720,000 in cash. On that date, subsequent to the completion of the business combination, the Balance Sheets of the Puff and Snuff Companies and the fair values of Snuff's identifiable assets and liabilities were as follows:

| | December 31, 2002 Balance Sheets | | Fair Values |
	Puff	Snuff	For Snuff
Cash And Accounts Receivable	$ 350,000	$ 200,000	$200,000
Inventories	950,000	500,000	450,000
Investment In Snuff	720,000	-0-	N/A
Plant And Equipment (Net)	2,400,000	700,000	800,000
Total Assets	$4,420,000	$1,400,000	
Current Liabilities	$ 400,000	$ 100,000	$100,000
Long-Term Liabilities	1,000,000	400,000	360,000
No Par Common Stock	1,000,000	800,000	N/A
Retained Earnings	2,020,000	100,000	N/A
Total Equities	$4,420,000	$1,400,000	

The December 31, 2002 Inventories of Snuff are sold during 2003. The Plant And Equipment of Snuff on December 31, 2002 has an estimated useful life of 10 years while the Long-Term Liabilities that were present on that date mature on December 31, 2005. Both Companies use the straight line method of amortization. Puff carries its Investment In Snuff by the cost method.

The Income Statements for the year ending December 31, 2004 and the Balance Sheets as at December 31, 2004 of the Puff and Snuff Companies are as follows:

Puff and Snuff Companies
Income Statements
For The Year Ending December 31, 2004

	Puff Company	Snuff Company
Sales	$2,500,000	$1,300,000
Other Revenues	100,000	30,000
Total Revenues	$2,600,000	$1,330,000
Cost Of Goods Sold	$1,200,000	$ 750,000
Depreciation Expense	400,000	250,000
Other Expenses	800,000	180,000
Total Expenses	$2,400,000	$1,180,000
Net Income	$ 200,000	$ 150,000

Balance Sheets
As At December 31, 2004

	Puff Company	Snuff Company
Cash	$ 100,000	$ 70,000
Accounts Receivable	430,000	180,000
Inventories	1,150,000	400,000
Investment In Snuff	720,000	-0-
Plant And Equipment (Net)	2,150,000	850,000
Total Assets	$4,550,000	$1,500,000
Current Liabilities	$ 300,000	$ 40,000
Long-Term Liabilities	1,000,000	400,000
No Par Common Stock	1,000,000	800,000
Retained Earnings	2,250,000	260,000
Total Equities	$4,550,000	$1,500,000

Other Information:

1. During 2004, the Puff Company declared and paid $100,000 in dividends while the Snuff Company declared and paid $40,000.

2. Included in the 2004 Sales of the Snuff Company are sales of $200,000 to the Puff Company. The Puff Company has resold all of this merchandise to purchasers outside of the consolidated entity. Puff owes Snuff $100,000 on December 31, 2004 for the merchandise purchases.

3. On December 31, 2004, Snuff still owes Puff for management fees earned during 2004. Fees of $25,000 have been charged by Puff and none of this amount has been paid by Snuff in 2004.

4. Goodwill has been tested for impairment in both 2003 and 2004. The test procedures found impairment of $16,000 in 2003, an amount that was recognized as a Goodwill Impairment Loss in that year. A further impairment of $20,000 was found in 2004.

Required: For the Puff Company and its subsidiary the Snuff Company, prepare:

A. A consolidated Income Statement for the year ending December 31, 2004.

B. A consolidated Statement Of Retained Earnings for the year ending December 31, 2004.

C. A consolidated Balance Sheet as at December 31, 2004.

In addition, provide calculations which verify consolidated Net Income for the year ending December 31, 2004, the December 31, 2004 consolidated Retained Earnings, and the December 31, 2004 Non-Controlling Interest in net assets.

Walk Through Problem Solution Format

Step A - Investment Analysis

	60 Percent	100 Percent
Purchase Price	$	$
Book Value	($)	($)
Differential	$	$
Fair Value Decrease On Inventories	$	$
Fair Value Increase On Plant And Equipment	($)	($)
Fair Value Decrease On Long-Term Liabilities	($)	($)
Goodwill	$	$

Step A - Investment Elimination Entry

No Par Common Stock	$	
Retained Earnings	$	
Plant And Equipment (Net)	$	
Long-Term Liabilities	$	
Goodwill	$	
Investment In Snuff		$
Inventories		$
Non-Controlling Interest (Balance Sheet)		$

Step B(1) - Intercompany Assets And Liabilities

Current Liabilities	$	
Accounts Receivable		$
Current Liabilities	$	
Accounts Receivable		$

Step B(2) - Fair Value Adjustment On The Inventories

Inventories	$	
Retained Earnings		$

Step B(2) - Fair Value Adjustment On Plant And Equipment

Retained Earnings - Snuff	$	
Depreciation Expense	$	
Plant and Equipment (Net)		$

Step B(2) - Fair Value Adjustment On Long-Term Liabilities

Retained Earnings - Snuff	$	
Other Expenses	$	
Long-Term Liabilities		$

Step B(3) - Goodwill Impairment

Retained Earnings - Snuff	$	
Goodwill Impairment Loss	$	
Goodwill		$

Step B(4) - Intercompany Expenses And Revenues

Sales	$	
Cost Of Goods Sold		$
Other Revenues	$	
Other Expenses		$

Step B(5) - Intercompany Dividends

Other Revenues	$	
Non-Controlling Interest	$	
Dividends Declared		$

Step C - Retained Earnings Distribution Schedule

Snuff's January 1, 2004 Balance	$	
Snuff's Balance At Acquisition	($	)
Balance Since Acquisition	$	
Non-Controlling Interest [(40%)( )]	($	)
Available To The Controlling Interest	$	
Step B Adjustments:		
Fair Value Decrease On Inventories	$	
Fair Value Increase On Plant and Equipment	($	)
Fair Value Decrease On Long-Term Liabilities	($	)
Goodwill Impairment Loss	($	)
To Consolidated Retained Earnings	$	

Step C - Retained Earnings Distribution Entry

Retained Earnings - Snuff	$	
Non-Controlling Interest	$	
Consolidated Retained Earnings		$

Puff Company And Subsidiary
Consolidated Income Statement
For The Year Ending December 31, 2004

Sales	$
Other Revenues	$
Total Revenues	$
Cost Of Goods Sold	$
Depreciation Expense	$
Other Expenses	$
Goodwill Impairment Loss	$
Non-Controlling Interest	$
Total Expenses	$
Consolidated Net Income	$

Verification Of Consolidated Net Income

Puff Company's Net Income	$
Intercompany Dividend Revenues	($)
Puff's Net Income Less Dividends	$
Puff's Equity In The Net Income Of Snuff	$
Income Before Adjustments	$
Step B Adjustments:	
Fair Value Increase On Plant and Equipment	($)
Fair Value Decrease On Long-Term Liabilities	($)
Goodwill Impairment Loss	($)
Consolidated Net Income	$

Puff Company And Subsidiary
Consolidated Statement Of Retained Earnings
For The Year Ending December 31, 2004

Balance - January 1, 2004	$
Consolidated Net Income	$
Available For Distribution	$
Dividends Declared	$
Balance - December 31, 2004	$

Verification Of Consolidated Retained Earnings

Puff's Closing Balance	$	
Puff's Share Of Snuff's Retained Earnings Since Acquisition	$	
Step B Adjustments:		
Fair Value Decrease On Inventories	$	
Fair Value Increase On Plant and Equipment	($	)
Fair Value Decrease On Long-Term Liabilities	($	)
Goodwill Impairment Losses	($	)
Consolidated Retained Earnings As At December 31, 2004	$	

Puff Company And Subsidiary
Consolidated Balance Sheet
As At December 31, 2004

Cash	$
Accounts Receivable	$
Inventories	$
Investment In Snuff	$
Plant And Equipment (Net)	$
Goodwill	$
Total Assets	$
Current Liabilities	$
Long-Term Liabilities	$
Non-Controlling Interest	$
No Par Common Stock	$
Retained Earnings	$
Total Equities	$

Verification Of The Non-Controlling Interest In Consolidated Net Assets

At Acquisition (Step A)	$
Dividends Declared By Snuff (Step B)	($)
Retained Earnings Distribution (Step C)	$
From Consolidated Net Income	$
Non-Controlling Interest As At December 31, 2004	$

Walk Through Problem Solution

Step A - Investment Analysis

	60 Percent	100 Percent
Purchase Price	$720,000	$1,200,000
Book Value	(540,000)	(900,000)
Differential	$180,000	$ 300,000
Fair Value Decrease On Inventories	30,000	50,000
Fair Value Increase On Plant And Equipment	(60,000)	(100,000)
Fair Value Decrease On Long-Term Liabilities	(24,000)	(40,000)
Goodwill	$126,000	$ 210,000

Step A - Investment Elimination Entry

No Par Common Stock	$800,000	
Retained Earnings	100,000	
Plant And Equipment (Net)	60,000	
Long-Term Liabilities	24,000	
Goodwill	126,000	
Investment In Snuff		$720,000
Inventories		30,000
Non-Controlling Interest (Balance Sheet)		360,000

Step B(1) - Intercompany Assets And Liabilities

Current Liabilities	$100,000	
Accounts Receivable		$100,000
(Intercompany Merchandise Sales)		

Current Liabilities	$25,000	
Accounts Receivable		$25,000
(Management Fees)		

Step B(2) - Fair Value Adjustment On The Inventories

Inventories	$30,000	
Retained Earnings - Snuff		$30,000

Step B(2) - Fair Value Adjustment On Plant And Equipment

Retained Earnings - Snuff's Opening	$6,000	
Depreciation Expense	6,000	
Plant And Equipment (Net)		$12,000
(Annual Adjustment = $60,000/10 = $6,000/Year)		

Step B(2) - Fair Value Adjustment On Long-Term Liabilities

Retained Earnings - Snuff's Opening	$8,000	
Other Expenses	8,000	
Long-Term Liabilities		$16,000
(Annual Adjustment = $24,000/3 = $8,000/Year)		

Step B(3) - Goodwill Impairment

Retained Earnings - Snuff	$16,000	
Goodwill Impairment Loss	20,000	
Goodwill		$36,000

Step B(4) - Intercompany Expenses And Revenues

Sales	$200,000	
Cost Of Goods Sold		$200,000
(Intercompany Merchandise Sales)		
Other Revenues	$25,000	
Other Expenses		$25,000
(Management Fees)		

Step B(5) - Intercompany Dividends

Other Revenues (60% of $40,000)	$24,000	
Non-Controlling Interest (Balance Sheet)	16,000	
Dividends Declared		$40,000

Step C - Retained Earnings Distribution Schedule

Snuff's January 1, 2004 Balance ($260,000 - $150,000 + $40,000)	$150,000
Snuff's Balance At Acquisition	(100,000)
Balance Since Acquisition	$ 50,000
Non-Controlling Interest [(40%)($50,000)]	(20,000)
Available To The Controlling Interest	$30,000
Step B Adjustments:	
Fair Value Increase On Inventory	30,000
Fair Value Decrease On Plant And Equipment	(6,000)
Fair Value Increase On Long-Term Liabilities	(8,000)
Goodwill Impairment Loss	(16,000)
To Consolidated Retained Earnings	$30,000

Step C - Retained Earnings Distribution Entry

Retained Earnings - Snuff	$50,000	
Non-Controlling Interest (Balance Sheet)		$20,000
Consolidated Retained Earnings		30,000

Puff Company And Subsidiary
Consolidated Income Statement
For The Year Ending December 31, 2004

Sales ($2,500,000 + $1,300,000 - $200,000)	$3,600,000
Other Revenues ($100,000 + $30,000 - $25,000 - $24,000)	81,000
Total Revenues	$3,681,000
Cost Of Goods Sold ($1,200,000 + $750,000 - $200,000)	$1,750,000
Depreciation Expense ($400,000 + $250,000 + $6,000)	656,000
Other Expenses ($800,000 + $180,000 + $8,000 - $25,000)	963,000
Goodwill Impairment Loss	20,000
Non-Controlling Interest [(40%)($150,000)]	60,000
Total Expenses	$3,449,000
Consolidated Net Income	$ 232,000

Verification Of Consolidated Net Income

Puff Company's Net Income	$200,000
Intercompany Dividend Revenues	(24,000)
Puff's Net Income Less Dividends	$176,000
Puff's Equity In The Net Income Of Snuff (60% of $150,000)	90,000
Income Before Adjustments	$266,000
Step B Adjustments:	
Fair Value Increase On Plant and Equipment	(6,000)
Fair Value Decrease On Long-Term Liabilities	(8,000)
Goodwill Impairment Loss	(20,000)
Consolidated Net Income	$232,000

Puff Company And Subsidiary
Consolidated Statement Of Retained Earnings
For The Year Ending December 31, 2004

Opening Balance ($2,150,000 + $30,000)	$2,180,000
Consolidated Net Income	232,000
Available For Distribution	$2,412,000
Dividends Declared (Puff's Only)	(100,000)
Closing Balance	$2,312,000

Verification Of Consolidated Retained Earnings

Puff's Closing Balance	$2,250,000
Puff's Share Of Snuff's Retained Earnings Since Acquisition	
[(60%)($260,000 - $100,000)]	96,000
Step B Adjustments:	
Inventories	30,000
Plant (2 Years At $6,000)	(12,000)
Long-Term Liabilities (2 Years At $8,000)	(16,000)
Goodwill ($16,000 + $20,000)	(36,000)
Consolidated Retained Earnings As At December 31, 2004	$2,312,000

Puff Company And Subsidiary
Consolidated Balance Sheet
As At December 31, 2004

Cash ($100,000 + $70,000)	$ 170,000
Accounts Receivable ($430,000 + $180,000 - $100,000 - $25,000)	485,000
Inventories ($1,150,000 + $400,000 - $30,000 + $30,000)	1,550,000
Investment In Snuff ($720,000 - $720,000)	Nil
Plant And Equipment (Net) ($2,150,000 + $850,000 + $60,000 - $12,000)	3,048,000
Goodwill ($126,000 - $36,000)	90,000
Total Assets	$5,343,000

Current Liabilities ($300,000 + $40,000 - $100,000 - $25,000)	$ 215,000
Long-Term Liabilities ($1,000,000 + $400,000 - $24,000 + $16,000)	1,392,000
Non-Controlling Interest [(40%)($1,060,000)]	424,000
Common Stock (Puff's Only)	1,000,000
Retained Earnings (See Statement)	2,312,000
Total Equities	$5,343,000

Verification Of The Non-Controlling Interest In Consolidated Net Assets

At Acquisition (Step A)	$360,000
Dividends Declared By Snuff (Step B)	(16,000)
Retained Earnings Distribution (Step C)	20,000
From Consolidated Net Income	60,000
Non-Controlling Interest As At December 31, 2004	$424,000

Problems For Self Study

(The solutions for these problems can be found following Chapter 16 of the text.)

Self Study Problem Five - 1

On December 31, 2002, the Pastel Company purchased 90 percent of the outstanding voting shares of the Shade Company for $5,175,000 in cash. On that date, the Shade Company had No Par Common Stock of $2,000,000 and Retained Earnings of $4,000,000. All of the Shade Company's identifiable assets and liabilities had carrying values that were equal to their fair values except for:

1. Equipment which had fair values that were $1,000,000 less than their carrying values and a remaining useful life of 10 years.

2. Land which had a fair value that was $100,000 greater than its carrying value.

3. Accounts Receivable with fair values that were $50,000 less than their carrying values.

4. Long-Term Liabilities which had fair values that were $200,000 less than their carrying values and mature on December 31, 2007.

The Balance Sheets of the Pastel Company and the Shade Company as at December 31, 2007 were as follows:

Pastel and Shade Companies
Balance Sheets
As At December 31, 2007

	Pastel	Shade
Cash and Current Receivables	$ 2,625,000	$ 800,000
Inventories	8,000,000	2,000,000
Equipment (Net)	24,000,000	4,000,000
Buildings (Net)	10,000,000	2,000,000
Investment in Shade (Cost)	5,175,000	-0-
Land	2,000,000	1,200,000
Total Assets	**$51,800,000**	**$10,000,000**
Dividends Payable	$ -0-	$ 100,000
Current Liabilities	1,800,000	900,000
Long-Term Liabilities	10,000,000	1,000,000
No Par Common Stock	20,000,000	2,000,000
Retained Earnings	20,000,000	6,000,000
Total Equities	**$51,800,000**	**$10,000,000**

The Income Statements of the Pastel and Shade Companies for the year ending December 31, 2007 were as follows:

Pastel and Shade Companies
Income Statements
For The Year Ending December 31, 2007

	Pastel	Shade
Sales	$8,000,000	$2,000,000
Gain on Sale of Land	500,000	-0-
Other Revenues	800,000	100,000
Total Revenues	$9,300,000	$2,100,000
Cost of Goods Sold	$3,800,000	$ 800,000
Depreciation Expense	1,400,000	300,000
Other Expenses	2,000,000	400,000
Total Expenses	$7,200,000	$1,500,000
Net Income	$2,100,000	$ 600,000

Other Information:

1. In each of the years since Pastel acquired control over Shade, the goodwill arising on this business combination transaction has been tested for impairment. After completing the annual impairment test, it was determined that the goodwill impairment loss for 2007 was $15,000. No impairment was found in any of the other years since acquisition.

2. Both Companies use the straight line method to calculate all depreciation and amortization charges and the First-In, First-Out inventory flow assumption.

3. Pastel uses the cost method to carry its Investment In Shade.

4. The Sales account in the Pastel Company's Income Statement includes only sales of merchandise. All other income is accounted for in Other Revenues.

5. During 2007, Pastel charged Shade $100,000 for management fees. None of this amount has been paid during 2007.

6. During 2007, dividends of $200,000 were declared and paid by Pastel and dividends of $100,000 were declared by Shade. On December 31, 2007, the dividends that were declared by the Shade Company during 2007 had not yet been paid.

7. During 2007, Shade sold to Pastel $500,000 worth of merchandise which was totally resold by Pastel in 2007. Pastel owes Shade $75,000 on December 31, 2007 due to these purchases.

8. During 2007, Pastel sold merchandise to Shade for $150,000. All of this merchandise was resold in 2007. Shade has not paid for these purchases as at December 31, 2007.

Required   Prepare, for the Pastel Company and its subsidiary, the Shade Company:

A. The consolidated Income Statement for the year ending December 31, 2007.

B. The consolidated Statement Of Retained Earnings for the year ending December 31, 2007.

C. The consolidated Balance Sheet as at December 31, 2007.

Self Study Problem Five - 2

On January 1, 2002 the Prude Company purchased 60 percent of the outstanding voting shares of the Sybarite Company for $750,000 in cash. On that date, the Balance Sheet of the Sybarite Company and the fair values of its identifiable assets and liabilities were as follows:

Sybarite Company
Balance Sheet
As At January 1, 2002

	Carrying Values	Fair Values
Cash	$ 10,000	$ 10,000
Current Receivables	200,000	150,000
Inventories	1,090,000	640,000
Plant and Equipment	1,000,000	1,050,000
Accumulated Depreciation	(300,000)	-0-
Total Assets	$2,000,000	
Current Liabilities	$ 200,000	$ 200,000
Long-Term Liabilities	500,000	600,000
No Par Common Stock	1,000,000	
Retained Earnings	300,000	
Total Equities	$2,000,000	

The difference between the carrying value and fair value of the Plant and Equipment relates to a building with a remaining useful life of 14 years. The Long-Term Liabilities all mature on January 1, 2007.

On December 31, 2008, the Balance Sheets of the Prude Company and its subsidiary, the Sybarite Company are as follows:

Prude and Sybarite Companies
Balance Sheets
As At December 31, 2008

	Prude	Sybarite
Cash	$ 50,000	$ 300,000
Current Receivables	300,000	400,000
Inventories	700,000	1,750,000
Investment in Sybarite (Cost)	750,000	-0-
Plant and Equipment	9,000,000	1,000,000
Accumulated Depreciation	(3,000,000)	(650,000)
Total Assets	$7,800,000	$2,800,000
Current Liabilities	$ 300,000	$ 100,000
Long-Term Liabilities	1,000,000	300,000
No Par Common Stock	4,000,000	1,000,000
Retained Earnings	2,500,000	1,400,000
Total Equities	$7,800,000	$2,800,000

Other Information:

1. Both Companies use the straight line method for the calculation of all depreciation and amortization.

2. The Prude Company's Sales include sales of $50,000 to the Sybarite Company. Although this merchandise has been sold by Sybarite, it has not paid Prude for any of this

merchandise during the year. Prude has levied an interest charge of $5,000 on this unpaid amount which is also outstanding on December 31, 2008.

3. There have been no additions or disposals of Plant and Equipment by Sybarite since January 1, 2002.

4. During 2008, Prude had Net Income of $1,000,000 and declared dividends of $200,000, while Sybarite had Net Income of $600,000 and declared and paid dividends of $100,000.

5. In each of the years since Prude acquired control over Sybarite, the goodwill arising on this business combination transaction has been tested for impairment. In 2005, a Goodwill Impairment Loss of $42,000 was recognized. No impairment was found in any of the other years since acquisition.

Required: Prepare a consolidated Balance Sheet as at December 31, 2008 for the Prude Company and its subsidiary, the Sybarite Company.

Self Study Problem Five - 3

On December 31, 2002, the Port Company acquired 30 percent of the outstanding voting shares of the Ship Company for $3,000,000. On December 31, 2003, the Port Company acquired an additional 30 percent of the Ship Company's outstanding voting shares for $3,600,000. The Ship Company's Balance Sheets as at December 31, 2002 and December 31, 2003 were as follows:

Ship Company
Balance Sheets
As At December 31

	2002	2003
Net Monetary Assets	$2,000,000	$3,500,000
Plant and Equipment (Net)	5,000,000	4,500,000
Total Assets	$7,000,000	$8,000,000
Common Stock - No Par	$4,000,000	$4,000,000
Retained Earnings	3,000,000	4,000,000
Total Equities	$7,000,000	$8,000,000

All of the Ship Company's identifiable assets and liabilities had carrying values that were equal to their fair values at both acquisition dates except for a building included in Plant and Equipment. On December 31, 2002, the fair value of the Ship Company's Building was $2 million greater than its carrying value and its remaining useful life on that date was 10 years. At the time of the second purchase the fair value of the Ship Company's Building was $3 million greater than its carrying value. There had been no additions to the account during the year.

All depreciation and amortization charges are calculated on a straight line basis for both Companies.

In each of the years since Port acquired shares of the Ship Company, the goodwill arising from the share purchases has been tested for impairment. No impairment was found in any of the years.

On December 31, 2004, the Balance Sheets of the two Companies were as follows:

Port and Ship Companies
Balance Sheets
As At December 31, 2004

	Port	Ship
Net Monetary Assets	$ 3,400,000	$4,500,000
Investment in Ship (Cost)	6,600,000	-0-
Plant and Equipment (Net)	10,000,000	4,000,000
Total Assets	$20,000,000	$8,500,000
Common Stock - No Par	$10,000,000	$4,000,000
Retained Earnings	10,000,000	4,500,000
Total Equities	$20,000,000	$8,500,000

Required: Prepare, for the Port Company and its subsidiary the Ship Company, a consolidated Balance Sheet as at December 31, 2004.

Self Study Problem Five - 4

On January 1, 2002, the Puberty Company acquired 80 percent of the outstanding voting shares of the Senile Company for $4,000,000 in cash. On that date, the Senile Company had no par value common shares of $1 million outstanding and Retained Earnings of $2 million. At the acquisition date, all identifiable assets and liabilities of the Senile Company had fair values equal to their carrying values except for a building with a remaining useful life of 25 years which had a fair value that was $4,000,000 greater than its carrying value and an issue of 20 year bonds that had a fair value that was $2,000,000 greater than the value at which they were carried on Senile's books. The bonds were issued on January 1, 1998. In addition, on January 1, 2002, Senile had Goodwill of $1,000,000 on its books.

On December 31, 2008, the adjusted trial balances of the Puberty Company and its subsidiary, the Senile Company are as follows:

	Puberty	Senile
Cash and Current Receivables	$ 1,100,000	$ 400,000
Long-Term Receivables	1,000,000	200,000
Inventories	4,000,000	1,300,000
Plant and Equipment (Net)	6,000,000	4,000,000
Goodwill	-0-	1,000,000
Investment in Senile (Cost)	4,000,000	-0-
Cost of Goods Sold	5,000,000	1,500,000
Other Expenses	3,000,000	1,800,000
Dividends Declared	400,000	300,000
Total Debits	$24,500,000	$10,500,000
Current Liabilities	$ 300,000	$ 400,000
Notes Payable	200,000	600,000
Long-Term Liabilities	2,000,000	2,500,000
Common Stock - No Par Value	4,000,000	1,000,000
Retained Earnings	8,000,000	3,200,000
Sales	9,000,000	2,500,000
Other Revenues	1,000,000	300,000
Total Credits	$24,500,000	$10,500,000

Other Information:

1. Puberty carries its investment in Senile by the cost method. In each of the years since Puberty acquired control over Senile, the goodwill arising on this business combination transaction has been tested for impairment. After completing the annual impairment test, it was determined that the goodwill impairment loss for 2008 was $140,000 due to the current year's loss. No impairment was found in any of the other years since acquisition. The goodwill on Senile's books has suffered no impairment in any year.

2. Both Companies use the straight line method to calculate all amortization and depreciation charges.

3. Puberty's 2008 Sales include $1,000,000 in sales to Senile which were priced to provide Puberty with a gross profit of 30 percent of the sales price. This merchandise has been resold by Senile in 2008.

4. Puberty holds a 12 percent, $500,000 Note which is payable by Senile in 2012. Interest is payable April 1 and October 1 on the principal. Puberty has been holding this Note since July 1, 2008.

5. Puberty's Other Revenues include any Investment Income received, as well as $100,000 in management fees which are payable by Senile in 2009.

Required: Prepare, for the Puberty Company and its subsidiary, the Senile Company:

A. the consolidated Income Statement for the year ending December 31, 2008;

B. the consolidated Statement of Retained Earnings for the year ending December 31, 2008; and

C. the consolidated Balance Sheet as at December 31, 2008.

Self Study Problem Five - 5

For the year ending December 31, 2007, the comparative Balance Sheets for the Primate Company and its subsidiary the Savage Company are as follows:

Primate and Savage Companies
Comparative Balance Sheets

	December 31, 2007		December 31, 2006	
	Primate	Savage	Primate	Savage
Cash	$ 660,000	$ 400,000	$1,000,000	$ 200,000
Accounts Receivable	700,000	250,000	500,000	200,000
Inventories	900,000	500,000	1,000,000	400,000
Investments:				
Savage (At Cost)	900,000	-0-	900,000	-0-
Mastodon (At Equity)	250,000	-0-	235,000	-0-
Saber T. (At Cost)	1,500,000	-0-	-0-	-0-
Plant & Equipment (Net)	1,590,000	750,000	1,490,000	700,000
Land	1,000,000	400,000	875,000	500,000
Total Assets	$7,500,000	$2,300,000	$6,000,000	$2,000,000
Current Liabilities	$1,300,000	$ 600,000	$1,000,000	$ 500,000
Long-Term Liabilities	-0-	100,000	-0-	-0-
Common Stock - No Par	3,000,000	500,000	2,000,000	500,000
Retained Earnings	3,200,000	1,100,000	3,000,000	1,000,000
Total Equities	$7,500,000	$2,300,000	$6,000,000	$2,000,000

Other Information:

1. The Primate Company purchased 80 percent of the outstanding voting shares of the Savage Company on January 1, 2002 for $800,000 in cash. On that date, Savage had Retained Earnings of $500,000 and Common Stock - No Par of $500,000. The fair values of the identifiable assets and liabilities of Savage were equal to their carrying values.

2. The Investment in Mastodon was made in 2001 and constitutes a holding of 30 percent of the outstanding voting shares of the Mastodon Company. The Investment was acquired at book value and there have been no intercompany transactions, other than dividend payments between Primate and Mastodon. Since Primate exercises significant influence over the affairs of Mastodon, it is carried at equity. During 2007, Mastodon had net income of $100,000 and paid dividends of $50,000.

3. On December 31, 2007, Primate acquired 100 percent of the outstanding voting shares of the Saber T. Company. The consideration consisted of $500,000 in cash and Primate Company shares with a fair value of $1,000,000. At the date of the acquisition, the Plant and Equipment of the Saber T. Company had a fair value that was $200,000 in excess of its carrying value. The Plant and Equipment had a remaining useful life of 10 years on this date. On the acquisition date, the Saber T. Company's Balance Sheet was as follows:

Saber T Company
Balance Sheet
As At December 31, 2007

Cash	$ 200,000
Accounts Receivable	200,000
Inventories	400,000
Plant and Equipment (Net)	500,000
Total Assets	$1,300,000
Current Liabilities	$ 100,000
Common Stock - No Par	500,000
Retained Earnings	700,000
Total Equities	$1,300,000

4. During 2007, information on Net Income and dividends paid for the Primate Company and its subsidiaries is as follows:

	Primate	Savage	Saber T.
Net Income	$400,000	$200,000	$225,000
Dividends	200,000	100,000	150,000

5. During 2007, Savage issued long-term bonds with a fair value of $100,000 in return for Plant and Equipment. Savage had no other acquisitions or retirements of Plant and Equipment during 2007.

6. During 2007, Primate acquired Plant and Equipment for cash of $400,000. Plant and Equipment with an original cost of $300,000 and Accumulated Depreciation of $200,000 was sold for $200,000.

7. During 2007, Savage sold Land for cash in an arm's length transaction for its carrying value of $100,000. Also during 2007, Primate acquired Land for cash of $125,000.

8. During 2007, $200,000 of the Primate Company's sales were made to the Savage Company. None of this merchandise remains in the December 31, 2007 Inventories of Savage Company. There were no other intercompany inventory sales in 2006 or 2007.

Required:

A. Compute consolidated Net Income for the year ending December 31, 2007 and prepare the consolidated Statement of Retained Earnings for the year ending December 31, 2007 for the Primate Company and its subsidiaries.

B. Prepare the consolidated Cash Flow Statement for the year ending December 31, 2007 for the Primate Company and its subsidiaries.

Assignment Problems

(The solutions for these problems are only available in the solutions manual that has been provided to your instructor.)

Assignment Problem Five - 1

On December 31, 2002, the Percy Company purchased 75 percent of the outstanding voting shares of the Stern Company for $3 million in cash. On that date, Stern had Common Stock - No Par of $2 million and Retained Earnings of $1 million. On December 31, 2002 all of the identifiable assets and liabilities of Stern had fair values that were equal to their carrying values with the following exceptions:

1. Inventories with fair values that were $400,000 less than their carrying values.

2. Land with a fair value that was $800,000 greater than its carrying value.

3. Long-Term Liabilities, maturing on January 1, 2008, with fair values that were $200,000 less than their carrying values.

Both Companies use the straight line method to calculate all depreciation and amortization. The land which was on the books of the Stern Company on December 31, 2002 has not been sold as at December 31, 2007. The Percy Company accounts for its investment in Stern Company using the cost method.

Other data for the year ending December 31, 2007 is as follows:

Income Statements
For The Year Ending December 31, 2007

	Percy	Stern
Merchandise Sales	$5,000,000	$2,000,000
Other Revenues	1,000,000	500,000
Total Revenues	$6,000,000	$2,500,000
Cost of Goods Sold	$2,000,000	$1,000,000
Depreciation Expense	400,000	300,000
Other Expenses	600,000	400,000
Total Expenses	$3,000,000	$1,700,000
Net Income	$3,000,000	$ 800,000

Statements Of Retained Earnings
For The Year Ending December 31, 2007

	Percy	Stern
Opening Balance	$10,000,000	$1,600,000
Net Income	3,000,000	800,000
Balance Available	$13,000,000	$2,400,000
Dividends Declared	1,000,000	400,000
Closing Balance	$12,000,000	$2,000,000

Balance Sheets
as at December 31, 2007

	Percy	Stern
Cash and Current Receivables	$ 1,500,000	$1,200,000
Note Receivable	1,000,000	-0-
Inventories	4,500,000	1,000,000
Investment in Stern (At Cost)	3,000,000	-0-
Plant and Equipment (Net)	9,000,000	3,000,000
Land	2,000,000	800,000
Total Assets	$21,000,000	$6,000,000
Current Liabilities	$ 500,000	$ 200,000
Long-Term Liabilities	3,500,000	1,800,000
Common Stock - No Par	5,000,000	2,000,000
Retained Earnings	12,000,000	2,000,000
Total Equities	$21,000,000	$6,000,000

Other Information:

1. The Long-Term Liabilities of the Stern Company include a $1 million note that is payable to the Percy Company. During 2007, interest expense on this note was $110,000 and on December 31, 2007, $100,000 of this interest had not been paid by Stern. The note is to be paid on December 31, 2010.

2. In each of the years since Percy acquired control over Stern, the goodwill arising on this business combination transaction has been tested for impairment. In 2004, a Goodwill Impairment Loss of $50,000 was recognized. No impairment was found in any of the other years since acquisition.

3. During 2007, Stern had sales of $1,500,000 to Percy while Percy had $500,000 in sales to Stern. All of the merchandise which was transferred in these intercompany sales has been resold during 2007 to companies outside of the consolidated entity.

Required: Prepare, for the Percy Company and its subsidiary, the Stern Company, the following:

A. The consolidated Income Statement for the year ending December 31, 2007.

B. The consolidated Statement of Retained Earnings for the year ending December 31, 2007.

C. The consolidated Balance Sheet as at December 31, 2007.

Assignment Problem Five - 2

On January 1, 2002, the Perry Company purchased 72 percent of the outstanding voting shares of the Styan Company for $3,975,000 in cash. On that date, the Styan Company had No Par Common Stock of $1,680,000 and Retained Earnings of $3,570,000. All of the Styan Company's identifiable assets and liabilities had carrying values that were equal to their fair values except for:

1. Inventories which had fair values of $1,806,000 and book values of $2,037,000.

2. Buildings which had fair values that were $175,000 more than their carrying values and a remaining useful life of 20 years.

3. Land which had a fair value of $1,596,000 and a carrying value of $1,400,000.

4. A Patent with a nil book value and a fair value of $154,000. The patent has a remaining life of two years.

5. Long-Term Liabilities which had fair values that were $210,000 more than their carrying values and mature on December 31, 2011.

The Balance Sheets of the Perry Company and the Styan Company as at December 31, 2004 were as follows:

Perry and Styan Companies
Balance Sheets
As At December 31, 2004

	Perry	Styan
Cash	$ 175,000	$ 17,500
Current Receivables	910,000	140,000
Inventories	1,709,750	1,050,000
Equipment (Net)	3,584,000	2,248,750
Buildings (Net)	3,727,500	2,187,500
Investment in Styan (Cost)	3,975,000	-0-
Land	1,406,250	1,400,000
Total Assets	$15,487,500	$7,043,750
Dividends Payable	$ -0-	$ 70,000
Current Liabilities	840,000	350,000
Long-Term Liabilities	3,587,500	3,064,000
Preferred Stock	280,000	-0-
No Par Common Stock	9,100,000	1,680,000
Retained Earnings	1,680,000	1,879,750
Total Equities	$15,487,500	$7,043,750

The Income Statements of the Perry and Styan Companies for the year ending December 31, 2004 were as follows:

Perry and Styan Companies
Income Statements
For The Year Ending December 31, 2004

	Perry	Styan
Sales	$3,800,000	$1,120,000
Other Revenues	62,400	200,000
Total Revenues	$3,862,400	$1,320,000
Cost of Goods Sold	$1,412,000	$ 623,000
Depreciation Expense	525,000	175,000
Other Expenses	1,567,000	235,000
Total Expenses	$3,504,000	$1,033,000
Income Before Extraordinary Items	$ 358,400	$ 287,000
Extraordinary Loss (Net of Taxes of $1,300,000)	-0-	(2,052,500)
Net Income (Loss)	$ 358,400	($1,765,500)

Other Information:

1. In both of the years since Perry acquired control over Styan, the goodwill arising on this business combination transaction has been tested for impairment. No impairment was found in the prior year. However, due to the large loss for 2004, the goodwill related to the purchase of Styan shares has a nil fair value on December 31, 2004.

2. Both Companies use the straight line method to calculate all depreciation and amortization charges and the First-In, First-Out inventory flow assumption.

3. Perry uses the cost method to carry its Investment In Styan.

4. The Sales account in both Companies' Income Statements include only sales of merchandise. All other income is accounted for in Other Revenues.

5. The Styan Company has sold no Land since January 1, 2002.

6. During 2004, dividends of $175,000 were declared and paid by Perry and dividends of $70,000 were declared by Styan.

7. During 2004, Perry sold to Styan merchandise worth $217,000 which was resold by Styan for a gross profit of $162,000 outside of the consolidated entity in 2004. Styan owes Perry $84,000 on December 31, 2004 due to these purchases.

8. During October, 2004, Styan charged the Perry Company $70,000 for the services of a team of computer programmers. The wages paid to the programmers for this work totalled $58,500. Perry still has a balance of $3,500 outstanding for this charge on December 31, 2004.

Required:

A. Prepare the consolidated Income Statement for the year ending December 31, 2004 of the Perry Company and its subsidiary, the Styan Company.

B. Prepare the consolidated Statement Of Retained Earnings for the year ending December 31, 2004 of the Perry Company and its subsidiary, the Styan Company.

C. Prepare the consolidated Balance Sheet as at December 31, 2004 of the Perry Company and its subsidiary, the Styan Company.

D. Assume that the Perry Company, despite its majority ownership, does not have control over Styan and carries its Investment In Styan using the equity method. Calculate and disclose the amount(s) of investment income that would be shown in the Perry Company's Income Statement under this assumption. (An Income Statement is not required.)

E.   Discuss the factors that should be considered when reviewing the issue of whether the Investment in Styan account should be written down on the single entity financial statements of Perry Company.

Assignment Problem Five - 3

On January 1, 2002, the Prospect Company purchases 80 percent of the outstanding voting shares of the Suspect Company for $1,760,000 in cash. On that date, the Shareholders' Equity of the Suspect Company is as follows:

Common Stock - No Par	$1,050,000
Retained Earnings - Unrestricted	560,000
Reserve For Contingencies	140,000
Total	$1,750,000

On the acquisition date, all of the identifiable assets and liabilities of the Suspect Company have fair values that are equal to their carrying values except for a patent. The patent is carried on Suspect's books at $500,000. Its fair value on the acquisition date is $1,100,000 and its remaining useful life on that date is 10 years.

Between January 1, 2002 and December 31, 2007, the Suspect Company earns $980,000 and pays dividends of $280,000. The Company's Reserve For Contingencies is unchanged during this period.

During the year ending December 31, 2007 the Prospect Company has Net Income of $300,000 and Suspect has Net Income of $100,000. Prospect pays no dividends during 2007 while Suspect pays $50,000. On December 31, 2007, the Prospect Company has Retained Earnings of $2,000,000.

Prospect carries the Investment In Suspect at cost and its Net Income includes Investment Income calculated by this method. Both Companies calculate all depreciation and amortization charges using the straight line method and, during 2007, there are no intercompany transactions other than dividend payments.

Required:

A.   Calculate the consolidated Net Income for the year ending December 31, 2007 for the Prospect Company and its subsidiary the Suspect Company.

B.   Calculate the amount of Goodwill, the carrying value of the Patent, the Non-Controlling Interest, and the Retained Earnings balance that would be shown on the consolidated Balance Sheet of the Prospect Company and its subsidiary the Suspect Company, as at December 31, 2007.

Assignment Problem Five - 4

On April 1, 2002, the Perle Company acquired 70 percent of the outstanding voting shares of the Thane Company for $1,785,000 in cash. On this date the book value of the Thane Company's Shareholders' Equity was $2,600,000 and all of the Thane Company's identifiable assets and liabilities had fair values that were equal to their carrying values except for the following:

	Carrying Value	Fair Value
Marketable Securities	$ 28,000	$ 35,000
Fleet of Trucks	324,000	365,000
Division F - Building and Equipment (Net)	631,000	453,000
Land	96,000	118,000
Long-Term Liabilities - Par $2,000,000	1,983,000	2,010,000

The Marketable Securities were sold on March 17, 2003 for $33,000. The fleet of trucks have an estimated remaining useful life of four years on April 1, 2002 and no anticipated salvage value. The Division F Building and Equipment was purchased on April 1, 1990 and had an estimated useful life of 20 years on that date. When purchased they had an anticipated salvage value of $80,000 and there is no change in the estimates of salvage value or total useful life on April 1, 2002. The parcel of Land is being held in anticipation of expansion in 2008. The Long-Term Liabilities are scheduled to mature on December 31, 2007.

Both Companies use the straight line method for all depreciation and amortization calculations and the Perle Company carries its investment in Thane Company using the cost method. The Perle Company's investment income consists of $5,000 in interest revenue and its income from the Thane Company. During the period April 1, 2002 until December 31, 2004, neither the Perle Company nor the Thane Company issue or retire shares of common stock.

For the year ending December 31, 2004, the Income Statements for the Perle Company and the Thane Company are as follows:

Perle and Thane Companies
Income Statements
For The Year Ending December 31, 2004

	Perle	Thane
Sales Revenue	$4,887,000	$1,450,000
Investment Income	29,500	12,000
Total Revenues	$4,916,500	$1,462,000
Cost Of Goods Sold	$2,117,000	$ 829,000
Depreciation Expense	935,000	135,000
Other Expenses and Losses	1,284,000	246,000
Total Expenses	$4,336,000	$1,210,000
Net Income	$ 580,500	$ 252,000

Other Information:

1. On January 1, 2004, the Retained Earnings balance of the Perle Company was $8,463,000. During 2004, the Perle Company paid dividends totalling $115,000.

2. Between April 1, 2002 and December 31, 2003, Thane earned Net Income of $192,000 and declared dividends totalling $46,000.

3. In each of the years since Perle acquired control over Thane, the goodwill arising on this business combination transaction has been tested for impairment. No impairment was found in any of the years since acquisition.

4. During 2004, the Thane Company used the services of several of the Perle Company's accountants and agreed to pay a fee of $5,600 for these services. On December 31, 2004, this fee remains unpaid. This amount is included in the Sales Revenues of the Perle Company and in the Other Expenses of the Thane Company. The salaries paid to the accountants by the Perle Company for the work done on the Thane Company amount to $4,200 and are included in the Other Expenses of the Perle Company.

5. On January 1, 2004, the Perle Company rented a building from the Thane Company for a monthly rent of $2,000. On December 31, 2004, the Perle Company owed three months rent. The rent is included in the Sales Revenues of the Thane Company and in the Other Expenses of the Perle Company.

Required:

A. For the year ending December 31, 2004, prepare the consolidated Income Statement and the consolidated Statement Of Retained Earnings of the Perle Company and its subsidiary, the Thane Company.

B. Calculate the Non-Controlling Interest that would be shown in the December 31, 2004 consolidated Balance Sheet of the Perle Company and its subsidiary, the Thane Company.

C. Assume that on December 31, 2004, the Thane Company sold the Division F assets to someone outside the consolidated entity for $380,000, creating a loss of $61,594 on Thane Company's books. The sale consisted of the Building and Equipment which had the fair value change on April 1, 2002. Provide the journal entries to record the effect of the loss on the consolidated Income Statement of the Perle Company and its subsidiary, the Thane Company for the year ending December 31, 2004 assuming:

    i.   The loss is included in the Other Expenses and Losses of Thane.
    ii. The loss is classified as a Loss From Discontinued Operations on the Income Statement of Thane.

Assignment Problem Five - 5

The book value and fair value of the net identifiable assets of the Slice Company are as follows:

	Book Value	Fair Value
December 31, 2002	$4,265,000	$4,365,000
December 31, 2003	$4,865,000	$5,065,000

On December 31, 2002, the Piece Company acquires 20 percent of the outstanding voting shares of the Slice Company for cash of $904,000. The remaining useful life of the Slice Company assets on which the fair value changes exist is 10 years and no salvage value is anticipated.

On December 31, 2003, the Piece Company acquires an additional 50 percent of the outstanding voting shares of the Slice Company for cash of $2,873,000. The remaining life of the Slice Company assets on which the fair value changes exist is 9 years.

On December 31, 2004, the book values of the net identifiable assets of the Piece Company and the Slice Company are as follows:

	Piece	Slice
Total Net Identifiable Assets	$8,973,000	$5,653,000

On December 31, 2004, the Retained Earnings balance of the Piece Company is $4,235,000.

Other Information:

1. Both Companies amortize all assets and liabilities using the straight line method.

2. In both 2003 and 2004, the goodwill arising on the Slice share purchases has been tested for impairment. In 2004, a Goodwill Impairment Loss of $40,250 was recognized. No impairment of the Goodwill was found in 2003.

3. During the period January 1, 2002 through December 31, 2004, neither the Piece Company nor the Slice Company issues or retires any of their shares of common stock.

4. During the period January 1, 2002 through December 31, 2004, the only intercompany transactions were dividends declared and paid to the Piece Company by the Slice Company.

5. The Piece Company carries its Investment In Slice Company using the cost method.

6. There is no Goodwill on the single entity books of either the Piece Company or the Slice Company.

Required: Calculate the amounts that would be shown in the consolidated Balance Sheet of the Piece Company and its subsidiary the Slice Company on December 31, 2004 for the following accounts:

A. Net identifiable assets

B. Goodwill

C. Non-Controlling Interest

D. Retained Earnings.

Assignment Problem Five - 6

The ledger account balances for the Pump Company and the Slump Company on December 31, 2002 and 2003 are as follows:

	December 31, 2003		December 31, 2002	
	Pump	Slump	Pump	Slump
Cash	$ 42,200	$ 69,400	$ 113,400	$ 19,600
Accounts Receivable	99,400	128,400	108,400	63,000
Other Current Receivables	82,600	44,800	64,600	49,000
Inventories	93,200	128,800	99,600	96,800
Investment in Slump (Cost)	356,800	-0-	356,800	-0-
Other Long-Term Investments	21,600	66,800	185,600	66,800
Land	36,400	30,000	57,400	30,000
Buildings	271,600	174,000	213,400	130,000
Equipment	122,000	90,000	96,000	90,000
Total Debits	$1,125,800	$732,200	$1,295,200	$545,200

Bad Debt Allowance	$ 9,000	$ 7,800	$ 8,200	$ 7,400
Accumulated Depreciation	139,000	101,200	82,600	62,400
Accounts Payable	45,800	91,800	62,400	73,600
Notes Payable	82,000	50,000	176,800	-0-
Dividends Payable	-0-	28,000	-0-	-0-
Other Accruals	11,800	41,600	25,400	25,200
Taxes Payable	39,200	38,800	73,000	24,600
Bonds Payable	-0-	-0-	60,000	-0-
Capital Stock - No Par	584,000	226,400	584,000	226,400
Opening Retained Earnings	174,800	97,600	124,600	77,400
Net Income	40,200	49,000	98,200	48,200
Total Credits	$1,125,800	$732,200	$1,295,200	$545,200

Other Information:

1. On January 2, 2002, the Pump Company acquired from the shareholders of the Slump Company, 90 percent of the Slump Company's outstanding voting shares for the following consideration:

500 Shares of Pump Common Stock - No Par	$200,000
Note Payable - Due June 30, 2005	156,800
Total Consideration	$356,800

   On that date, the Slump Company's identifiable assets and liabilities had carrying values that were equal to their fair values. The difference between the purchase price and the acquirer's share of the fair values has been allocated to Land. The Note Payable was unexpectedly paid in advance on June 30, 2003. All other Notes Payable present on both December 31, 2002 and 2003 are current.

2. On January 1, 2003, Pump sold Other Investments for proceeds of $202,600. These investments had been carried at a cost of $170,800. Pump also sold Land which had cost $21,000, for proceeds of $37,600.

3. On June 30, 2003, Pump demolished an unneeded Building which had cost $37,800 and had a net book value of $10,800.

4. During 2003, Pump declared and paid cash dividends of $48,000. On December 1, 2003, Slump declared a $28,000 cash dividend. This dividend was payable on January 15, 2004, to holders of record on December 20, 2003. Pump has recorded the dividends in Other Current Receivables. Slump declared no other dividends during 2003.

5. The Pump Company's Bonds Payable were retired in 2003. Cash of $65,000 was paid which included $60,000 in par value, $1,200 in accrued interest and a $3,800 penalty for early retirement.

6. On December 31, 2003, Pump Company's Other Current Receivables include a $50,000 non-interest bearing Note Payable by Slump. Slump Company's December 31, 2003 Accounts Receivable includes $37,000 due from Pump for merchandise purchases. Slump had sold the merchandise to Pump for an amount equal to the cost of the merchandise to Slump. There are no intercompany receivables or payables on December 31, 2002.

Required: Prepare a consolidated Cash Flow Statement for the Pump Company and its subsidiary, the Slump Company for the year ending December 31, 2003. Your solution should comply with the Recommendations of Section 1540.

Chapter 6

Consolidation Subsequent To Acquisition (Including Unrealized Intercompany Profits)

Unrealized Intercompany Profits

Basic Concepts

6-1.   From the point of view of the consolidated entity, profits on intercompany transactions are said to be unrealized until verified by an arm's-length transaction with an individual or organization that is outside or independent of the consolidated entity. For example, if a subsidiary sells merchandise to a parent company and recognizes a profit on the transaction, the profit of the subsidiary is said to be unrealized until such time as the parent resells the merchandise outside of the consolidated entity. Correspondingly, if there is an intercompany sale of a capital asset, any gain or loss recognized by the vendor is unrealized until such time as the purchaser either sells the asset or uses it up.

6-2.   To say that these profits are unrealized from the point of view of the consolidated entity is the equivalent of saying that they do not exist from the consolidated point of view. This problem is the major focus of Chapter 6. We will be concerned with introducing procedures for the elimination of these unrealized intercompany profits in the preparation of consolidated financial statements. We would also note the possibility of unrealized intercompany losses. Similar procedures will be required when such losses arise. The required procedures will involve adjustments to both expenses and revenues in the consolidated Income Statement, as well as to assets and liabilities in the consolidated Balance Sheet.

6-3.   The problem of unrealized intercompany profits should not be confused with the problem of intercompany expenses and revenues. While they are often related, they should be dealt with as two separate and distinct issues. For example, if there is an intercompany payment of interest on a note that is carried on both companies' books at face value, there is an intercompany expense and revenue but no unrealized intercompany profit or loss. In other situations, an unrealized profit may arise at the time of an intercompany expense and revenue. This would be the case, for example, if there was an intercompany sale of merchandise. Note, however, if the purchasing company has resold the merchandise to parties outside the consolidated entity, there will still be an intercompany expense and revenue to be eliminated. However, there will not be an intercompany unrealized profit.

6-4. A final point here is that a profit that is unrealized in one accounting period may become realized in a subsequent period. If, for example, the ending inventories of a subsidiary contained goods purchased from the parent, any profit recorded by the parent on the sale of these goods is unrealized and must not be included in the consolidated figures. However, the ending inventories that contained the unrealized profit are likely to be sold during the following accounting period. If the goods are sold to a party outside of the consolidated entity, the parent company's profit becomes realized at that point and should be included in the consolidated income figures. The point being made here is that the procedures that will be developed in this Chapter must deal with both the removal of unrealized intercompany profits, and with adding them back when they become realized in some future period or periods.

Types Of Unrealized Intercompany Profits

6-5. From a conceptual point of view, all types of unrealized intercompany profits are the same. However, in terms of the procedures to be used in preparing consolidated financial statements, we will find it useful to classify such profits into three groups. These groups are as follows:

1. Unrealized profits on intercompany sales of assets with unlimited lives. The primary example of this situation would be intercompany sales of land.

2. Unrealized profits on intercompany sales of assets that are subject to depreciation, depletion, or amortization. This would include plant and equipment, intangibles with limited lives and natural resources.

3. Unrealized profits on intercompany sales of current assets. The most common example of this situation would be intercompany sales of merchandise or manufactured items that are being held for resale.

6-6. In this Chapter's comprehensive example we will find that the procedures are somewhat different for each of these categories.

Conceptual Alternatives In The Consolidated Income Statement

Downstream Unrealized Profits

6-7. With respect to downstream profits (those resulting from the parent recording a profit on a sale to a subsidiary), there are no conceptual alternatives. Since the profit is that of the parent company, there is no non-controlling interest in it. As a consequence, all such profits will be subject to 100 percent elimination. The elimination will, of course, be charged against consolidated Net Income and consolidated Retained Earnings.

Upstream Unrealized Profits

6-8. With upstream profits (those resulting from the subsidiary recording a profit on a sale to the parent), there is the possibility of a non-controlling interest being present. Such a non-controlling interest would have a claim on the profits of the subsidiary and, as was the case with other consolidation procedures, this would raises the question of how this non-controlling interest should be dealt with in the consolidated financial statements. A simple example will be used to illustrate these conceptual alternatives. The basic data for this example is as follows:

Example The Play Company owns 70 percent of the outstanding voting shares of the Stay Company. The purchase was made at a time when all of the identifiable assets and liabilities of the Stay Company had carrying values that were equal to their fair values. The purchase price was equal to 70 percent of the carrying value of the Stay Company's net identifiable assets. In a subsequent year the Income Statements of the two Companies are as follows:

Play And Stay Companies
Condensed Income Statements

	Play	Stay
Sales Revenue	$7,500,000	$2,200,000
Gain On Sale Of Land To Play Company	-0-	400,000
Total Revenues	$7,500,000	$2,600,000
Expenses	5,600,000	1,900,000
Net Income	$1,900,000	$ 700,000

Proprietary Concept Solution

6-9.   You will recall that under the proprietary conceptual approach, the expenses and revenues that are disclosed in the consolidated Income Statement consist of 100 percent of the parent company's expenses and revenues plus a share of the subsidiary's expenses and revenues that is based on the parent company's ownership interest (70 percent in this example). In addition, because the Gain On Sale Of Land is an unrealized intercompany profit, the parent's share of this item would also be removed. The resulting consolidated Income Statement would appear as follows:

Play Company And Subsidiary
Consolidated Income Statement
(Proprietary Approach)

Sales Revenue ($7,500,000 + $2,200,000 - $660,000)	$9,040,000
Gain On Sale Of Land To Play Company ($400,000 - $120,000 - $280,000)	Nil
Total Revenues	$9,040,000
Expenses ($5,600,000 + $1,900,000 - $570,000)	6,930,000
Consolidated Net Income	$2,110,000

6-10.   As was the case when this concept was illustrated in Chapter 5, the removal of the non-controlling interest's share of the individual expenses and revenues eliminates the need to disclose a Non-Controlling Interest in the consolidated Income Statement. With respect to the treatment of the unrealized intercompany profit, we eliminated the non-controlling interest's share as part of the general application of the proprietary concept. The balance or parent company's share was removed because it was unrealized. This procedure is sometimes referred to as fractional elimination of the unrealized intercompany profit. The consolidated Net Income of $2,110,000 can be verified by taking Play Company's Net Income of $1,900,000 plus $210,000 or 70 percent of Stay Company's realized income of $300,000 ($700,000 - $400,000).

Parent Company Concept Solution

6-11.   This conceptual approach views the non-controlling interest as a part of the consolidated entity and, as a consequence, the consolidated Income Statement would include 100 percent of the expenses and revenues of both the parent and the subsidiary company. With respect to the nature of the non-controlling interest's participation in the consolidated entity, it is viewed as being a creditor-like interest, somewhat akin to an issue of long-term debt. Given this view, the Non-Controlling Interest in the income of the consolidated entity would be viewed as a claim analogous to interest charges on creditor interests and would be deducted in the computation of consolidated Net Income. The resulting consolidated Income Statement would appear as follows:

Play Company And Subsidiary
Consolidated Income Statement
(Parent Company Approach)

Sales Revenue ($7,500,000 + $2,200,000)	$9,700,000
Gain On Sale Of Land To Play Company ($400,000 - $280,000)	120,000
Total Revenues	$9,820,000
Total Expenses ($5,600,000 + $1,900,000)	7,500,000
Combined Income	$2,320,000
Non-Controlling Interest [(30%)($700,000)]	210,000
Consolidated Net Income	$2,110,000

6-12. Note that this is the same consolidated Net Income that we arrived at under the proprietary approach, indicating that in some respects, the parent company approach is simply a modified version of the proprietary approach.

6-13. Also note that the Non-Controlling Interest continues to be based on the reported income of the subsidiary. This result, which is inherent in the application of the parent company approach, could only be achieved in this situation by leaving the non-controlling interest's share of the unrealized intercompany profit in the consolidated revenues.

Entity Concept Solution

6-14. You will recall that under the entity approach, the non-controlling interest is viewed as a part of the consolidated entity. However, in contrast to the parent company approach, the non-controlling interest here is viewed as an additional class of owner's equity. It would follow that the non-controlling interest should be dealt with in a manner that is equivalent to the treatment accorded the controlling interest. With respect to unrealized intercompany profits of the subsidiary company, this view would require the elimination of both the non-controlling and the controlling interests' shares of such profits with the reduction in income being charged in a proportionate manner to the two respective interests. This approach is normally referred to as 100 percent pro rata elimination of subsidiary unrealized profits. It is illustrated in the following consolidated Income Statement:

Play Company And Subsidiary
Consolidated Income Statement
(Entity Approach)

Sales Revenue ($7,500,000 + $2,200,000)	$9,700,000
Gain On Sale Of Land To Play Company ($400,000 - $400,000)	-0-
Total Revenues	$9,700,000
Expenses ($5,600,000 + $1,900,000)	7,500,000
Consolidated Net Income	$2,200,000

6-15. Note that the consolidated Net Income is equal to the sum of the two Companies' Net Incomes ($1,900,000 + $700,000), less the $400,000 unrealized intercompany profit. No Non-Controlling Interest is shown in the preceding Income Statement. Rather, it would be shown in the consolidated Statement Of Retained Earnings as a distribution of consolidated Net Income. Note that this treatment is analogous to the treatment that would be given to dividends on preferred shares and that this is consistent with the entity concept view that the non-controlling interest is an equity interest. Because we have eliminated 100 percent of the unrealized intercompany profit, the non-controlling interest in the consolidated Statement Of Retained Earnings would be $90,000. This is 30 percent of $300,000 (the reported income of the Stay Company of $700,000, less the unrealized intercompany profit of $400,000).

CICA Handbook Requirements

6-16.   The Canadian requirements for dealing with unrealized intercompany profits in consolidated financial statements can be found in two Paragraphs of the *CICA Handbook*. The first is as follows:

> **Paragraph 1600.30**   *Unrealized intercompany gains or losses arising subsequent to the date of an acquisition on assets remaining within the consolidated group should be eliminated. The amount of elimination from assets should not be affected by the existence of a non-controlling interest.* (April, 1975)

6-17.   This calls for 100 percent elimination of all unrealized intercompany profits but does not indicate specifically whose interest should be charged with the elimination. This latter question is clarified as follows:

> **Paragraph 1600.32**   *Where there is an unrealized intercompany gain or loss recognized by a subsidiary company in which there is a non-controlling interest, such gain or loss should be eliminated proportionately between the parent and non-controlling interest in that company's income.* (April, 1975)

6-18.   Taken together, these two Paragraphs call for 100 percent, pro rata elimination of unrealized intercompany profits. This, of course, is an adoption of the entity approach for dealing with this issue. It is somewhat difficult to understand this Recommendation as, in dealing with most of the other issues in consolidation, the *CICA Handbook* has taken the view that the parent company approach is the most appropriate conceptual alternative. While we have already noted our disagreement with the parent company view of the nature of the non-controlling interest, we would have found its adoption considerably more acceptable had it been applied in a consistent manner. However, this is not the case and this inconsistency in dealing with unrealized intercompany profits is one of the major sources of confusion and difficulty in the preparation of consolidated financial statements.

6-19.   Using the data for the example that was previously presented, the consolidated Income Statement of the Play Company and its subsidiary which would comply with all of the requirements of the *CICA Handbook* would be as follows:

Play Company And Subsidiary
Consolidated Income Statement
(As Per CICA Recommendations)

Sales Revenue ($7,500,000 + $2,200,000)	$9,700,000
Gain On The Sale Of Land To Play Company ($400,000 - $400,000)	Nil
Total Revenues	$ 9,700,000
Expenses ($5,600,000 + $1,900,000)	7,500,000
Combined Income	$2,200,000
Non-Controlling Interest [(30%)($700,000 - $400,000)]	90,000
Consolidated Net Income	$2,110,000

6-20.   This is the same consolidated Net Income that was computed under the parent company approach. However, the non-controlling share of the unrealized profit has been removed from both Total Revenues and the Non-Controlling Interest.

Exercise Six-1 deals with unrealized profits in the consolidated Income Statement.

Exercise Six-1

(This is identical to Exercise Five-1 except for the intercompany sales.)

On January 1, 2002, Part Company acquires 65 percent of the outstanding shares of Seam Company. At this time, all of the identifiable assets and liabilities of Seam had fair values that were equal to the carrying values. The cost of the shares was equal to 65 percent of the net asset value of Seam. The single entity Income Statements for Part Company and Seam Company, for the year ending December 31, 2002, are as follows:

Part and Seam Companies
Income Statements
Year Ending December 31, 2002

	Part Company	Seam Company
Revenues	$982,000	$463,000
Expenses:		
Cost of Goods Sold	$448,000	$219,000
Other Expenses	374,000	115,000
Total Expenses	$822,000	$334,000
Income Before Results Of Discontinued Operations	$160,000	$129,000
Loss From Discontinued Operations	Nil	(63,000)
Net Income	$160,000	$ 66,000

The 2002 Revenues of Seam Company include a $75,000 gain resulting from the sale of land to Part Company. Also included in Seam's Revenue are $82,000 in merchandise sales to Part Company. The goods are priced to provide a gross margin of 40 percent on sales prices and have all been resold by Part Company during 2002.

Required: Prepare the consolidated Income Statement for Part Company and its subsidiary Seam Company, for the year ending December 31, 2002. Your answer should comply with the Recommendations contained in the *CICA Handbook*.

End Of Exercise Six-1

Comprehensive Example - Open Trial Balance With Investment At Cost

Basic Data

6-21. We will now turn our attention to a comprehensive example that will illustrate in greater detail the treatment of unrealized intercompany profits. We will use the same basic problem that was used in the comprehensive example in Chapter 5. However, in this Chapter, unrealized intercompany profits have been added. Also, as was the case in Chapter 5, we will deal with two versions of this problem, both with the investment in the subsidiary being carried by the cost method on the books of the parent company.

6-22. The basic data for this open trial balance version of our comprehensive problem is as follows:

On January 1, 2002, the Pleigh Company purchases 80 percent of the outstanding voting shares of the Sleigh Company for $3,200,000 in cash. On that date the Sleigh Company had No Par Common Stock of $2,000,000 and Retained Earnings of $1,500,000. On

December 31, 2006, the adjusted trial balances of the Pleigh Company and its subsidiary, the Sleigh Company are as follows:

	Pleigh	Sleigh
Cash	$ 500,000	$ 300,000
Current Receivables	800,000	400,000
Inventories	2,500,000	1,700,000
Long-Term Note Receivable	200,000	-0-
Investment In Sleigh - At Cost	3,200,000	-0-
Land	1,500,000	1,000,000
Plant And Equipment (Net)	4,500,000	1,900,000
Cost Of Goods Sold	2,800,000	1,500,000
Depreciation Expense	200,000	100,000
Other Expenses	364,000	616,000
Interest Expense	240,000	84,000
Dividends Declared	350,000	100,000
Total Debits	$17,154,000	$7,700,000
Current Liabilities	$ 500,000	$ 200,000
Long-Term Liabilities	2,000,000	700,000
No Par Common Stock	8,000,000	2,000,000
Retained Earnings (January 1)	2,550,000	2,300,000
Sales	4,000,000	2,500,000
Interest Revenue	24,000	-0-
Dividend Revenue	80,000	-0-
Total Credits	$17,154,000	$7,700,000
2006 Net Income	$ 500,000	$ 200,000
December 31, 2006 Retained Earnings	$ 2,700,000	$2,400,000

Other Information:

1. At the date of Pleigh Company's acquisition of the Sleigh Company's shares, all of the identifiable assets and liabilities of the Sleigh Company had fair values that were equal to their carrying values except Inventories which had fair values that were $100,000 more than their carrying values, Land with a fair value that was $150,000 less than its carrying value and Plant And Equipment which had a fair value that was $250,000 greater than its carrying value. The Plant And Equipment had a remaining useful life on the acquisition date of 20 years while the inventories that were present on the acquisition date were sold during the year ending December 31, 2002. The Land is still on the books of the Sleigh Company on December 31, 2006. Both Companies use the straight line method to calculate depreciation and amortization.

2. In each of the years since Pleigh acquired control over Sleigh, the goodwill arising on this business combination transaction has been tested for impairment. No impairment was found in any of the years since acquisition.

3. Sleigh Company's Sales include sales of $300,000 to Pleigh Company. The December 31, 2006 Inventories of the Pleigh Company contain $100,000 of this merchandise purchased from Sleigh Company during 2006. In addition, the January 1, 2006 Inventories of the Pleigh Company contained $70,000 in merchandise purchased from Sleigh Company during 2005. All intercompany sales are priced to provide the selling company a gross margin on sales price of 40 percent.

4. On December 31, 2006, the Pleigh Company is holding Sleigh Company's long-term

note payable in the amount of $200,000. Interest at 12 percent is payable on July 1 of each year. Pleigh Company has been holding this note since July 1, 2004.

5. During 2004, the Pleigh Company sold Land to the Sleigh Company for $100,000 in cash. The Land had a carrying value on the books of the Pleigh Company of $75,000.

6. During 2005, the Sleigh Company sold Land to the Pleigh Company for $150,000. This Land had a carrying value on the books of the Sleigh Company of $110,000.

7. On December 31, 2004, the Sleigh Company sold Equipment to the Pleigh Company for $600,000. The Equipment had originally cost the Sleigh Company $800,000 and, at the time of the intercompany sale, had accumulated depreciation of $350,000. On this date, it was estimated that the remaining useful life of the Equipment was three years with no net salvage value.

Required: Prepare a consolidated Income Statement and a consolidated Statement Of Retained Earnings for the year ending December 31, 2006 and a consolidated Balance Sheet as at December 31, 2006 for the Pleigh Company and its subsidiary, the Sleigh Company.

Procedural Approach

6-23. The same basic approach that was used in solving the comprehensive problem in Chapter 5 will be used here. Some modifications will be generated by the presence of unrealized intercompany profits. These modifications will be mentioned briefly here and described in detail in the solution which follows:

Step A This step will not be changed by the inclusion of unrealized intercompany profits.

Step B The adjustments and eliminations that were introduced in this Step in Chapter 5 will remain the same. However, the presence of unrealized intercompany profits will require that additional eliminations be made.

Step C From a conceptual point of view, this Step is unchanged from Chapter 5. However, the fact that the *CICA Handbook* requires the use of the entity approach for the elimination of unrealized intercompany profits creates significant complications in determining the appropriate distribution of the subsidiary's retained earnings since acquisition.

Step A Procedures
Investment Analysis

6-24. The following investment analysis is unchanged from its presentation of this comprehensive problem in Chapter 5:

	80 Percent	100 Percent
Investment Cost	$3,200,000	$4,000,000
Book Value	(2,800,000)	(3,500,000)
Differential	$ 400,000	$ 500,000
Fair Value Changes:		
Increase On Inventories	(80,000)	(100,000)
Decrease On Land	120,000	150,000
Increase On Plant And Equipment	(200,000)	(250,000)
Goodwill	$ 240,000	$ 300,000

Investment Elimination

6-25. The investment elimination entry would also be unchanged. It is as follows:

No Par Common Stock	$2,000,000	
Retained Earnings	1,500,000	
Plant And Equipment (Net)	200,000	
Inventories	80,000	
Goodwill	240,000	
Land		$ 120,000
Non-Controlling Interest		700,000
Investment In Sleigh		3,200,000

Step B(1) - Intercompany Assets And Liabilities

6-26.   The entries for the elimination of intercompany assets and liabilities are unchanged from Chapter 5. They are as follows:

Long-Term Liabilities	$200,000	
Long-Term Note Receivable		$200,000
Current Liabilities	$12,000	
Current Receivables		$12,000

Step B(2) - Fair Value Write Offs

6-27.   The entries required for the realization or amortization of fair value changes are unchanged from the Chapter 5 version of this comprehensive problem. As the Land is still on the books of Sleigh, no entry is required to adjust the fair value change on this account. The entries are as follows:

Retained Earnings - Sleigh's Opening	$80,000	
Inventories		$80,000
Retained Earnings - Sleigh's Opening	$40,000	
Depreciation Expense	10,000	
Plant And Equipment (Net)		$50,000

Step B(3) - Goodwill Impairment

6-28.   The Other Information in our comprehensive problem notes that, while goodwill has been tested for impairment in each year since the acquisition of Pleigh Company occurred, no impairment has been found. As a consequence, no Step B-3 entry is required in this problem.

Step B(4) - Intercompany Expenses And Revenues

6-29.   The entries for the elimination of intercompany expenses and revenues are unchanged from Chapter 5. They are as follows:

Sales	$300,000	
Cost Of Goods Sold		$300,000
Interest Revenue	$ 24,000	
Interest Expense		$ 24,000

6-30.   Note that under our procedures, the entry for eliminating the intercompany expense and revenue related to the sale of merchandise has not been affected by the fact that a part of the goods remain in the inventories of the purchasing company. That is, we continue to eliminate 100 percent of the intercompany amount. While there are other approaches to dealing with intercompany merchandise sales, we believe that it is best to leave the intercompany expense and revenue procedure unchanged by the presence of an intercompany inventory profit. Using this approach, an additional entry will be required to remove the unrealized profit from the ending inventories of the Pleigh Company. This, however, will not alter the fact that we always eliminate 100 percent of intercompany expenses and revenues. This procedure will be discussed more fully in the material which follows.

Step B(5) - Intercompany Dividends

6-31.   The entry to eliminate the effects of intercompany dividends is unchanged from the Chapter 5 example. It is as follows:

Dividend Revenue	$80,000	
Non-Controlling Interest (Balance Sheet)	20,000	
Dividends Declared		$100,000

Step B(6) - Unrealized Intercompany Profits
Elimination Of Unrealized Profits

6-32.   The only new material in this problem is the addition of unrealized intercompany profits. Four such items have been added:

- There is a downstream unrealized profit resulting from Pleigh Company's 2004 sale of Land to Sleigh Company.

- There is an upstream unrealized profit resulting from Sleigh Company's 2005 sale of Land to Pleigh Company.

- There are unrealized upstream profits in both the opening and closing inventories of Pleigh, resulting from Sleigh's sales of merchandise to that company in 2005 and 2006. Recognition will also have to be given to the fact that the opening inventory profit that was unrealized at the beginning of 2006 has become realized during 2006.

- There is an upstream unrealized profit resulting from Sleigh Company's 2004 sale of Plant And Equipment to Pleigh Company. Recognition will also have to be given to the fact that a portion of this profit has become realized in each year subsequent to the year of the sale.

6-33.   The presence of these unrealized intercompany profits creates the need to introduce the final procedures that are required in the preparation of basic consolidated financial statements. The first of these procedures involves the elimination of any unrealized profits that are present at the end of the current period and can be stated as follows:

Step B-6(a) Procedure   Eliminate 100 percent of all unrealized intercompany profits (losses) that are present in the single entity financial statements. There are three groups of such profits to consider:

1. Profits that were recognized in the single entity statements of the parent or subsidiary in a previous period, remain unrealized at the beginning of the current period and are realized during the current period. Such profits will be deducted from the opening retained earnings of the company that recognized them in their single entity financial statements (unrealized losses would be added back).

2. Profits that were recognized in the single entity statement of the parent or subsidiary in the current period and remain unrealized at the end of the current period (for example, unrealized profits on inventory sales). These profits will be removed from current income through an adjustment of the current expenses or revenues. Note that 100 percent of the profit will be removed, without regard to whether it is an upstream profit or a downstream profit. If it is an upstream profit, its removal will reduce both consolidated Net Income and the Non-Controlling Interest that is included in the consolidated Income Statement.

3. Profits that were recognized in the single entity statement of the parent or subsidiary in the current or a previous period, and remain unrealized at the end of the current period (for example, an unrealized profit in the previous year on the sale of a machine with a four year life). These profits will be removed from the closing retained earnings of the company that recognized them in their single entity financial statements (unrealized losses would be added back).

Realization Of Previously Unrealized Profits

6-34.   We have noted previously that profits that are unrealized from a consolidated point of view in one period, may become realized in subsequent periods. If a parent sells merchandise to a subsidiary during 2002 and that merchandise remains in the December 31, 2002 Inventories of the subsidiary, the profit is unrealized and must be eliminated in the preparation of the 2002 consolidated financial statements. However, in most situations, the subsidiary will sell this merchandise during 2003, thereby realizing the profit from the point of view of the consolidated entity. As the profit will not be included in the 2003 single entity income records of the parent company, it must be added back in the preparation of consolidated financial statements. In other words, unrealized intercompany profits and losses must be eliminated in the preparation of the 2002 consolidated financial statements, with these amounts normally being added back in the preparation of the 2003 consolidated financial statements. While Step B-5(a) can be used to eliminate the 2002 profit, we need an additional procedure to record the 2003 realization of this profit. This procedure can be described as follows:

> **Step B-6(b) Procedure**   Recognize the amount of previously unrealized intercompany profits or losses that have become realized during the period, either through the sale of the related asset or through usage of that asset. The amount that was previously unrealized from the consolidated point of view would be a deduction from the opening single entity retained earnings of the parent or subsidiary company. To the extent the profit has become realized during the period, it will be included in the current consolidated Net Income through an adjustment of an expense or revenue. Any amount of the profit that remains unrealized at the end of the period will be deducted from the closing retained earnings of the relevant parent or subsidiary. As was the case with Step B-6(a), 100 percent of the previously unrealized profit will be recognized, without regard to whether it is upstream or downstream. If it is an upstream profit, the addition will increase both consolidated Net Income and the Non-Controlling Interest in the Income Statement.

6-35.   In the case of intercompany profits on inventories or non-depreciable assets, the realization will take place through a sale transaction that occurs in a single accounting period. This means that Step B-6(a) will be first implemented in the period in which the parent or subsidiary records the unrealized profit and will continue to be applied until the relevant asset is sold. In the period of sale, Step B-6(b) will be used to recognize the realization of the profit in the consolidated financial statements. In other words, for these types of unrealized intercompany profits, Steps B-6(a) and B-6(b) will be applied separately.

6-36.   In contrast, when the unrealized profit is related to the sale of a depreciable asset, the profit becomes realized through usage of the asset. Perhaps the best way to understand this is to think of a depreciable asset as a bundle of economic services. In effect, these services are being sold on a piecemeal basis as the asset is used. This means that the intercompany profit will become realized as the asset is being amortized. Because this realization process is carried out over several accounting periods, we have generally found it easier to net Steps B-6(a) and B-6(b). That is, when dealing with unrealized profits resulting from the intercompany sale of depreciable assets, we will not use separate entries to record the unrealized amount and the amount realized during subsequent periods. Rather, we will use a single net entry that reflects the amount realized during the current period and the remaining unrealized amount at the beginning of the current period.

Presentation Of Material

6-37.   In presenting this material on unrealized intercompany profits, we will often provide you with the entries that were recorded in the single entity records of the parent or subsidiary companies. Such entries are certainly not a required part of the consolidation procedures. However, we believe that the best way to understand this difficult material is to compare the values that are contained in the underlying records of the individual companies with the amounts that are required for consolidation purposes. Once these amounts are carefully established, the appropriate adjustment or elimination becomes a relatively simple bookkeeping problem.

Step B(6) - Downstream Profit On Land
Year Of Sale Procedures

6-38. In 2004, Pleigh Company sold Land with a carrying value of $75,000 to Sleigh Company for $100,000. To record this transaction, the following entry was made in Pleigh's single entity records:

Cash	$100,000	
Land		$75,000
Gain On Sale Of Land		25,000

6-39. At the same time, the Sleigh Company would have recorded the purchase of Land in its single entity records as follows:

Land	$100,000	
Cash		$100,000

6-40. From the point of view of the consolidated entity, this transaction did not occur. This would mean that the Land should still be in the consolidated statements at the old value of $75,000 and that no Gain On Sale should be included in consolidated income. The Step B-6(a) elimination entry which would have accomplished this result in 2004 would be as follows:

Gain On Sale Of Land	$25,000	
Land		$25,000

6-41. This restores the Land value to $75,000 and removes the gain from the records of the Pleigh Company. While this entry would have been made in the process of preparing consolidated financial statements in 2004, it was a working paper entry and the unadjusted values would still remain in the records of the two Companies. That is, the Land would still be on the Sleigh Company's books at $100,000 and the $25,000 Gain would be included in the Retained Earnings of the Pleigh Company. Consequently, in every year subsequent to 2004 (including the current year), the following elimination entry would be required:

Retained Earnings - Pleigh's Opening	$25,000	
Land		$25,000

6-42. You should note that since this is a downstream profit, this elimination will have no effect on the Non-Controlling Interest in either the consolidated Income Statement or the consolidated Balance Sheet.

Future Periods

6-43. Consolidation procedures would require that this entry be continued until the Land is sold by the Sleigh Company to someone outside of the consolidated entity. In the year in which such a sale takes place, separate entries would be required for Steps B-6(a) and B-6(b). They would be as follows:

Retained Earnings - Pleigh's Opening	$25,000	
Land		$25,000
Land	$25,000	
Gain On Sale Of Land		$25,000

6-44. This Gain would be added to any additional gain recorded on the sale by Sleigh in its single entity records and the total would be disclosed in the consolidated Income Statement. If, for example, Sleigh had sold the Land for $130,000, they would have recorded a gain of $30,000 ($130,000 - $100,000) in their records. This adjustment would result in a total gain of $55,000 being shown in the consolidated Income Statement.

6-45. Subsequent to a sale of the Land, no further entries would be required and the Gain would become a legitimate part of the consolidated Retained Earnings.

Step B(6) - Upstream Profit On Land
Year Of Sale Procedures
6-46.   With respect to the 2005 transaction in which Sleigh sold Land with a carrying value of $110,000 to Pleigh for $150,000, the procedures are basically the same as those required on the downstream sale. In the underlying records of the two Companies, Sleigh would have recorded the sale of Land and Pleigh would have recorded the purchase as follows:

Cash	$150,000	
Land		$110,000
Gain On Sale Of Land		40,000
Land	$150,000	
Cash		$150,000

6-47.   The 2005 Step B-6(a) entry to eliminate this Gain and reduce the Land value to the appropriate $110,000, is as follows:

Gain On Sale Of Land	$40,000	
Land		$40,000

6-48.   In contrast to the previous case, this elimination is charged on a pro rata basis to the non-controlling and controlling interests in income. More specifically, the 2005 Non-Controlling Interest in the consolidated Income Statement is reduced by $8,000 [(20%)($40,000)] and consolidated Net Income is reduced by $32,000 [(80%)($40,000)]. This allocation is required because the unrealized intercompany profit is an upstream one and relates to the income of the subsidiary.

6-49.   As we have noted previously, the fact that the elimination of this profit is split on a pro rata basis does not alter the fact that 100 percent of the profit must be removed from the consolidated revenues. The consolidated expenses and revenues include 100 percent of the parent and subsidiary expenses and revenues and, under the *CICA Handbook* requirements, 100 percent of both upstream and downstream profits must be removed from these figures. When a non-controlling interest is involved, the effect of this elimination must be split between that interest and the parent. However, this does not take place in the calculation or disclosure of consolidated expenses and revenues. This pro rata split takes place only in the calculation of the Non-Controlling Interest and consolidated Net Income.

Future Periods
6-50.   Because the 2005 entry was only recorded in the consolidation working papers, it will be necessary to reduce the Land account and remove the profit from the Retained Earnings of the subsidiary in 2006 and all subsequent years the Land is on the consolidated books. The entry to accomplish this is as follows:

Retained Earnings - Sleigh's Opening	$40,000	
Land		$40,000

6-51.   Here again, the effect of this entry will be split between the non-controlling and controlling interests in the consolidated entity. The Non-Controlling Interest in the consolidated Balance Sheet will be reduced $8,000 while consolidated Retained Earnings will be reduced by $32,000.

Step B(6) - Upstream Inventory Profits
Determining The Amount
6-52.   Most problems you encounter will give you the amount of sales that remain in the inventories of the purchasing company. For example, in this problem we know that the Sleigh Company sold $300,000 in merchandise to the Pleigh Company and that $100,000 of this merchandise is still in the closing inventories of the parent company. However, the amount to be eliminated is not the sales price of the merchandise that is still in the inventories of the purchasing company. Rather, it is the amount of gross profit that was recognized by the selling company when these goods were sold. The amount of this gross profit can be communicated

by the problem in a variety of ways. The more common ones are as follows:

- The most straightforward situation is when the amount of the profit is simply stated. For example, this problem could have indicated that the amount of gross profit on the goods that were sold to Pleigh Company and remain in its inventories was $40,000.

- A common approach is the one used in this comprehensive problem. That is, to provide you with a gross margin percentage based on sales prices. This problem states that intercompany transfers are priced to provide the selling company with a gross margin of 40 percent. We then multiply this 40 percent times the $100,000 in merchandise that is still on hand at the end of 2006 to arrive at the unrealized intercompany profit in the ending inventories of $40,000.

- Some problems will state a gross margin percentage that is based on cost rather than selling prices. For example, our problem could have stated that intercompany transfers are priced to provide the selling company with a gross margin equal to two-thirds of cost. We would then have to solve the following simple equation:

[(Cost)(166-2/3%)] = $100,000

Cost = ($100,000 ÷ 166-2/3%)

Cost = $60,000

Subtracting this cost from the sales price of $100,000 would give us the same $40,000 gross profit to be eliminated.

- While we avoid using this approach, we have seen problems where nothing is explicitly stated with respect to profit amounts or percentages. In these cases, a gross margin percentage must be extracted from the income statement data. The Sleigh Company had Sales Revenue of $2,500,000 and a Cost Of Goods Sold of $1,500,000. Its gross margin of $1,000,000 is equal to 40 percent of Sales Revenue. Applying this 40 percent to the merchandise in the inventories of the Pleigh Company gives an unrealized profit in the ending inventories of $40,000. The application of the same percentage to the Sleigh Company sales in the opening inventories of the Pleigh Company gives $28,000 [(40%)($70,000)]. We would note that this approach relies on the somewhat unreasonable assumption that the gross margin percentage on intercompany sales is the same as the gross margin percentage on all other sales.

6-53. Part 3 of the Other Information in our comprehensive example stated that the January 1, 2006 Inventories of Pleigh contained merchandise purchases from Sleigh in the amount of $70,000, with the corresponding figure for the December 31, 2006 Inventories at $100,000. This means that the upstream profits to be eliminated from the opening inventories is $28,000 [(40%)($70,000)], while the corresponding figure for the closing inventories is $40,000 [(40%)($100,000)].

Procedures - Ending Inventory Profits

6-54. In Step B-4 we noted that we would continue to eliminate 100 percent of intercompany sales, even in those cases where some of the transferred merchandise remained in the closing inventories of the purchasing company. This point requires some additional explanation.

6-55. During 2006, Sleigh sold merchandise to Pleigh for $300,000. Based on a 40 percent gross margin, the cost of this merchandise to Sleigh and the real cost of the merchandise to the consolidated entity is $180,000. If Pleigh had resold all of this merchandise, the $300,000 transfer price would have been included in that Company's Cost Of Goods Sold and the elimination of $300,000 of both Sales and Cost Of Goods Sold is an obvious requirement. This leaves the consolidated Cost Of Goods Sold equal to the appropriate $180,000 as recorded in Sleigh's single entity statements.

6-56. In the actual data of the problem, $100,000 of this merchandise remains in Pleigh's Inventories and only $200,000 has been included in Pleigh's Costs Of Goods Sold. This would suggest that only $200,000 of Pleigh's Cost Of Goods Sold should be eliminated. Further, the $40,000 profit that was recorded on this intercompany transfer would have to be removed from Pleigh's Inventories and, since from the point of view of the consolidated entity this merchandise has not been sold, its original $60,000 cost would have to be removed from Sleigh's Cost Of Goods Sold. This would suggest the use of the following elimination entry:

Sales	$300,000	
Cost Of Goods Sold (Pleigh's)		$200,000
Cost Of Goods Sold (Sleigh's)		60,000
Inventories (Pleigh's)		40,000

6-57.   This approach has logical appeal and will, of course, provide you with a correct solution. However, we have found it preferable to keep separate the individual consolidation procedures and will use an alternative, but equivalent approach. This alternative approach uses the basic Cost Of Goods Sold equation which is as follows:

Cost Of Goods Sold = Opening Inventories + Purchases - Closing Inventories

6-58.   Under our alternative procedure, separate entries are made to reflect the need for adjustments to Purchases and to Closing Inventories. Continuing with the data from the comprehensive problem, the full $300,000 of intercompany sales would be included in the Purchases component of the equation and this means we will eliminate 100 percent of this amount. This is consistent with the entry that we made in Step B-4 which is repeated here for your convenience:

Sales	$300,000	
Cost Of Goods Sold		$300,000

6-59.   A second entry will then be used to reflect the fact that the Closing Inventories contained a $40,000 unrealized profit. Removing this from the Closing Inventories figure in the preceding equation requires an increase in Cost Of Goods Sold. The entry to accomplish this and to remove the profit from the Inventories figure in the consolidated Balance Sheet is as follows:

Cost Of Goods Sold	$40,000	
Inventories		$40,000

6-60.   As you can see, the net effect of these two entries is identical to that of the single entry used in the alternative analysis. This latter approach has the advantage of clearly separating Step B-4 from Step B-6 and we have found it to be somewhat easier to understand. As a consequence, this two entry approach will be used in all of the problem solutions that follow.

6-61.   Note that since the increase in the Cost Of Goods Sold is related to the elimination of an unrealized upstream profit, the effect will be shared pro rata by the controlling and the non-controlling interests. The Non-Controlling Interest in the consolidated Income Statement will be reduced by $8,000, while consolidated Net Income will be reduced by the balancing $32,000.

Procedures - Opening Inventories

6-62.   The profits that were unrealized in the opening inventories were included in the income of the selling company in the previous year and would be included in the opening balance of that company's Retained Earnings for the current year. This would mean that our elimination would have to take these profits out of the opening Retained Earnings of the selling company. In addition, the selling company would have calculated the current year's Cost Of Goods Sold using the overstated opening inventory figure and this would result in a Cost Of Goods Sold figure that would be overstated in a corresponding manner. Consequently, our elimination entry would have to reduce the current year's Cost Of Goods Sold. The resulting increase in income would reflect the fact that any unrealized inventory profits that were present at the beginning of the current year would normally be realized by the end of the year. This means that we need to apply Step B-6(b) using the following journal entry:

Retained Earnings - Sleigh's Opening	$28,000	
Cost Of Goods Sold		$28,000

6-63.   Since we are again dealing with an upstream profit, the effect of the $28,000 reduction in the Cost Of Goods Sold would be split between the parent and the non-controlling interest. That is, the Non-Controlling Interest in the consolidated Income Statement would increase by $5,600 [(20%)($28,000)] and consolidated Net Income would increase by $22,400 [(80%)($28,000)].

Step B(6) - Upstream Profit On Depreciable Assets
Basic Concepts
6-64.   Within the context of preparing consolidated financial statements, we have defined realization in terms of transactions with individuals or enterprises that are outside the consolidated entity. That is, an intercompany profit is said to be unrealized until such time as it is verified by a transaction with some entity that is independent of the consolidated group. This idea is very easy to grasp in the case of intercompany profits on the sale of land or inventories. As we have seen, these profits are treated as unrealized until such time as the land or inventories are resold outside of the consolidated entity. The same general principles apply in the case of assets with limited lives of more than one accounting period. In fact, if such assets were resold to an outsider subsequent to an intercompany sale, any unrealized profit that is present at the time of the sale would be considered to be realized at that point in time.

6-65.   However, depreciable assets are normally used in the business rather than sold. Further, any unrealized profits resulting from intercompany sales of these assets will become realized through the use of such assets. As we noted earlier, the best way to visualize this process is to think of a depreciable asset as a bundle of economic services that is being sold on a piecemeal basis as the asset is used over its economic life. While alternative approaches could be justified, the normal procedure is to recognize the realization of the unrealized intercompany profit on depreciable assets using the same allocation pattern that is being used to depreciate the asset. As a consequence, this recognition will take the form of an adjustment of consolidated Depreciation Expense.

6-66.   Consider the intercompany sale in our comprehensive example (Other Information item 7). In this example, Sleigh sold an item of Plant And Equipment with a carrying value of $450,000 ($800,000 - $350,000) to Pleigh for $600,000. As a result of this transaction, Sleigh recorded a gain of $150,000 and Pleigh recorded the Plant And Equipment at a value of $600,000.

6-67.   Using the straight line method, Pleigh will record depreciation on this asset at a rate of $200,000 per year. From the point of view of the consolidated entity, the correct depreciation base is $450,000 (Sleigh's old carrying value) and this amount would be depreciated over the three year remaining life at a rate of $150,000 per year. The required $50,000 per year reduction of consolidated Depreciation Expense ($200,000 - $150,000) would increase combined income by $50,000. This, in effect, would represent the realization of one-third of the $150,000 intercompany profit that the Sleigh Company recorded on this sale. Over the three year life of the asset, the $50,000 per year reduction in Depreciation Expense would reflect realization of the entire intercompany profit on this transaction.

Presentation
6-68.   As we noted earlier, in dealing with depreciable assets, the fact that realization of the intercompany profit takes place over a number of accounting periods means that it is generally easier to combine Steps B-6(a) and B-6(b) into a single net entry for each year. We will follow that approach in the presentation which follows.

6-69.   We also believe that it is useful to discuss all of the annual entries that would have been made since the time of the intercompany asset sale. As a consequence, the following presentation includes entries for 2004, 2005, 2006, and 2007. We remind you that the 2004, 2005, and 2007 entries are for discussion purposes only and are not required to complete the solution. Only the entry for 2006 is needed to prepare the consolidated financial statements for that year.

Profit On Depreciable Asset - Required Entry For 2004 (Year Of Sale)

6-70.   When the intercompany sale took place on December 31, 2004, the Sleigh Company would have made the following entry on its books:

Cash	$600,000	
Plant And Equipment (Net)		$450,000
Gain On Sale		150,000

6-71.   At the same time, the Pleigh Company would have recorded the acquisition of the asset as follows:

Plant And Equipment (Net)	$600,000	
Cash		$600,000

6-72.   As this sale is not a real transaction from the point of view of the combined business entity, the Plant And Equipment is $150,000 too high for inclusion in the consolidated Balance Sheet and the Sleigh Company has recorded a $150,000 Gain On Sale which should not be included in consolidated Net Income. To remedy this situation, the following elimination entry is required:

Gain On Sale	$150,000	
Plant And Equipment (Net)		$150,000

6-73.   This entry leaves Plant And Equipment at the correct figure of $450,000 and eliminates the unrealized intercompany Gain On Sale.   You should note that none of the intercompany profit becomes realized during 2004 as there would have been no usage of the asset subsequent to the December 31 transfer date. As a consequence, there is no adjustment of the 2004 Depreciation Expense.

Profit On Depreciable Asset - Required Entry For 2005

6-74.   The entry for 2005 would be more complex in that additional accounts would require adjustment. On the books of the Pleigh Company, the Plant And Equipment is written down to $400,000 ($600,000 - $200,000).   As the appropriate figure for consolidation purposes is $300,000 ($450,000 - $150,000), this balance will require adjustment. As previously indicated, the current year's Depreciation Expense will have to be adjusted downward by $50,000 ($200,000 - $150,000). Finally, the entire 2004 unrealized profit of $150,000 has been recorded in the Retained Earnings of the Sleigh Company. Since on January 1, 2005, none of this profit had been realized through reduced depreciation expense, the full $150,000 must be removed from Sleigh's opening Retained Earnings. The entry to accomplish all of the preceding would be as follows:

Retained Earnings - Sleigh's Opening	$150,000	
Depreciation Expense		$ 50,000
Plant And Equipment (Net)		100,000

6-75.   Since we are dealing with an upstream profit, all of the effects of this entry will be reflected in pro rata adjustments of the parent's and the non-controlling interest's share of income and net assets. That is, the $150,000 debit to Retained Earnings will reduce the beginning of the year Non-Controlling Interest in net assets (Balance Sheet) by $30,000 [(20%)($150,000)] and the opening consolidated Retained Earnings by $120,000 [(80%)($150,000)].   The $50,000 reduction in Depreciation Expense will increase the Non-Controlling Interest in the 2005 consolidated Income Statement by $10,000 [(20%)($50,000)] and consolidated Net Income by $40,000 [(80%)($50,000)]. Note that, at the end of the year, the net adjustment would be $100,000, the original unrealized amount of $150,000, less the $50,000 realization which took place during 2005. If end of the period figures were being calculated, the elimination of this $100,000 would reduce the Non-Controlling Interest in the consolidated Balance Sheet by $20,000 [(20%)($100,000)] and consolidated Retained Earnings by $80,000 [(80%)($100,000)].

Profit On Depreciable Asset - Required Entry For 2006

6-76. For the problem under consideration, the relevant entry is the one for 2006. This entry would be as follows:

Retained Earnings - Sleigh's Opening	$100,000	
Depreciation Expense		$50,000
Plant And Equipment (Net)		50,000

6-77. On the books of the Pleigh Company, the Plant And Equipment has been written down to a value of $200,000 ($600,000 - $400,000) while the correct figure for consolidation purposes is $150,000 ($450,000 - $300,000). The $50,000 credit to Plant And Equipment provides the adjustment for this difference. As at January 1, 2006, the Retained Earnings balance of the Sleigh Company contains the full $150,000 of intercompany profit that was recognized on the sale of the depreciable asset. Since $50,000 of this was realized through reduced Depreciation Expense in 2005, the remaining unrealized balance on January 1, 2006 is $100,000. It is this amount that the preceding journal entry removes from the Retained Earnings of the Sleigh Company. The credit to Depreciation Expense serves to reduce the 2006 Depreciation Expense from the $200,000 that is on the books of the Pleigh Company to the appropriate $150,000 for consolidation purposes.

6-78. As was explained in conjunction with the 2005 entry, both the reduction in the Retained Earnings of the Sleigh Company and the increase in current income resulting from the reduced depreciation expense will be reflected on a pro rata basis in both the parent's and the non-controlling interest's share of net assets and income.

Profit On Depreciable Asset - Required Entry For 2007

6-79. As was the case with the 2004 and 2005 entries, the 2007 entry is not a necessary part of the solution. However, it will be presented in order to provide a complete illustration of the treatment of a profit on the intercompany sale of a depreciable asset. The entry is as follows:

Retained Earnings - Sleigh's Opening	$50,000	
Depreciation Expense		$50,000

6-80. The debit to the Retained Earnings of the Sleigh Company reflects the fact that of the original unrealized profit of $150,000, $100,000 was realized through reduced depreciation expense in 2005 and 2006, leaving an unrealized balance of $50,000. The $50,000 credit to Depreciation Expense is the usual reduction in this expense from $200,000 to $150,000. Note that the credit to Plant And Equipment is no longer present since the asset would now be fully depreciated. It would have a net book value of zero in the records of the Pleigh Company and this is the appropriate figure for consolidation purposes.

6-81. As in the entries for the previous two years, the effects of the reduced Retained Earnings and Other Expenses would be allocated on a pro rata basis to the parent and the non-controlling interest.

6-82. One additional point needs to be made in this final year of the asset's life. In 2004, the year of the intercompany sale, we removed the $150,000 Gain On Sale from income in the process of preparing consolidated financial statements. In the subsequent three years, we reversed this elimination by increasing income at a rate of $50,000 per year. As at December 31, 2007, these two effects will have netted out and no further adjustments or eliminations will be required in subsequent years.

6-83. Note that this is contrast to the situation with fair value changes. When the cost method is used to carry the investment, the fair value changes will always be recorded as part of the investment elimination and, to the extent that they have been realized through amortization or sale, adjusted for presentation in the Balance Sheet of the current year. Based on the procedures that we are using, these adjustments will continue to be necessary, even if the relevant asset is no longer included in the consolidated Balance Sheet.

Step C - Distribution Of The Subsidiary Retained Earnings
The Problem
6-84.   At this point, our one remaining task is to determine the appropriate distribution of the balance that is left in the Retained Earnings account of the Sleigh Company. The amount of this balance, as adjusted by the Step A and Step B procedures, can be determined as follows:

Sleigh's Opening Balance	$2,300,000
Step A Elimination	(1,500,000)
Balance Since Acquisition	$ 800,000
Step B Adjustments:	
Fair Value on Inventories	(80,000)
Plant (4 Years At $10,000)	(40,000)
Unrealized Upstream Profit On Land Sale	(40,000)
Unrealized Upstream Profit In Opening Inventories	(28,000)
Unrealized Upstream Profit On Equipment	(100,000)
Balance After Adjustments	$ 512,000

6-85.   As this schedule indicates, we are left with $512,000 as the January 1, 2006 adjusted balance of the Sleigh Company's Retained Earnings since acquisition. We must now determine the appropriate distribution between the Non-Controlling Interest in consolidated net assets and consolidated Retained Earnings. We will find that the presence of unrealized upstream profits will significantly complicate this process.

6-86.   If we were consistently using the entity conceptual approach, all of the Step B adjustments would be reflected proportionately in both the non-controlling interest and the controlling interest. The distribution of the remaining balance would be a simple matter of allocating it in proportion to the two respective ownership interests. That is, we could split the remaining $512,000 on a 20 percent, 80 percent basis.

6-87.   Correspondingly, if we were applying the parent company concept in a consistent manner, none of the Step B adjustments would have any influence on the amount of the non-controlling interest in net assets. We could calculate the non-controlling interest in Retained Earnings since acquisition by multiplying the non-controlling percent times the unadjusted Retained Earnings of the subsidiary since acquisition. Then all of the Step B adjustments and eliminations would be charged against the parent company's share of the subsidiary's Retained Earnings since acquisition. In this example, the non-controlling interest in Sleigh's Retained Earnings since acquisition would be $160,000 [(20%)($800,000)], and all of the Step B adjustments for the realization of fair value changes and unrealized intercompany profits would be deducted from the controlling interest.

6-88.   Unfortunately, the *CICA Handbook* did not adopt a consistent conceptual approach to the preparation of consolidated financial statements. While most of the Recommendations are based on the parent company concept, there is one important exception. This is the fact that the entity approach is used in the elimination of unrealized intercompany profits. This means that, unlike the adjustments for the realization of fair value changes, the adjustments for unrealized upstream profits will influence the calculation of the non-controlling interest. As a consequence, we will need a two stage distribution schedule in which unrealized upstream profits are dealt with separately from the other Step B adjustments related to the realization of fair value changes and any goodwill impairment losses.

Retained Earnings Distribution Schedule
6-89.   As was the case in Chapter 5, this schedule begins with the Retained Earnings balance of the subsidiary and, using Step A procedures, removes the portion of this balance that was present at the time of acquisition. As indicated in the preceding section, the presence of unrealized upstream profits means that we cannot calculate the non-controlling interest as a percentage of total retained earnings since acquisition. We must first modify this total for all

of the Step B adjustments and eliminations that involve upstream profits which are unrealized at the beginning of the year. Note that we are concerned with the beginning of the year unrealized profits because, in this open trial balance problem, we are distributing the opening Retained Earnings since acquisition balance.

6-90.   After the removal of the non-controlling interest from the modified balance, all other Step B adjustments and eliminations are added or subtracted to arrive at the appropriate allocation to consolidated Retained Earnings. This two stage schedule reflects a combination of entity and parent company procedures and would appear as follows:

Balance As Per The Trial Balance	$2,300,000
Balance At Acquisition	(1,500,000)
Balance Since Acquisition	$ 800,000
Unrealized Upstream Profits:	
Land	(40,000)
Opening Inventories	(28,000)
Equipment - Beginning Of The Year	(100,000)
Adjusted Balance Since Acquisition	$ 632,000
Non-Controlling Interest [(20%)($632,000)]	(126,400)
Available To The Controlling Interest	$ 505,600
Other Step B Adjustments:	
Fair Value Change On Inventories	(80,000)
Fair Value Change On Plant And Equipment	(40,000)
To Consolidated Retained Earnings	$ 385,600

Retained Earnings Distribution Entry

6-91.   Using the information from the preceding schedule, the journal entry to distribute Sleigh's Retained Earnings since acquisition is as follows:

Retained Earnings - Sleigh's Opening	$512,000	
Non-Controlling Interest (Balance Sheet)		$126,400
Consolidated Retained Earnings		385,600

6-92.   This entry reduces the Sleigh Company's Retained Earnings balance to zero and distributes the total to the controlling and non-controlling interests. With this entry completed we have established the opening balance for consolidated Retained Earnings. It is simply the Pleigh Company's January 1, 2006 balance of $2,550,000, less the $25,000 downstream profit on land, plus the $385,600 allocation resulting from the preceding journal entry, for a total of $2,910,600.

Consolidated Income Statement
Non-Controlling Interest Computation

6-93.   With the addition of the Step C distribution entry, we have completed all of the procedures necessary for the preparation of consolidated financial statements. As was the case in Chapter 5 we will begin with the consolidated Income Statement.

6-94.   In Chapter 5, the calculation of the Non-Controlling Interest in the consolidated Income Statement was simply a matter of multiplying the reported income of the subsidiary by the non-controlling ownership percentage. With the introduction of upstream unrealized profits, the calculation becomes more complex. The reason for this is, of course, the fact that the elimination of these profits is being dealt with using entity concept procedures. This means that we must adjust the reported income of the subsidiary for included profits that have not been realized during the year (e.g., closing inventory profits), as well as for previously unrealized profits that have become realized during the year (e.g., opening inventory profits). Only then can we calculate the appropriate Non-Controlling Interest for inclusion in the consolidated Income Statement. The required calculation would be as follows:

Sleigh Company's Reported Income	$200,000
Realized Gain On Equipment	50,000
Profits In Opening Inventories	28,000
Profits In Ending Inventories	(40,000)
Sleigh's Adjusted Income	$238,000
Non-Controlling Percent	20%
Non-Controlling Interest	$ 47,600

6-95.   In presenting this calculation, we stress the fact that upstream unrealized profits are the only adjustments or eliminations that have any influence on the amount of the Non-Controlling Interest.   This statement is always true and would apply to both the Non-Controlling Interest in the consolidated Income Statement and the Non-Controlling Interest in the consolidated Balance Sheet.

Statement Disclosure

6-96.   The consolidated Income Statement would be prepared as follows:

Pleigh Company And Subsidiary
Consolidated Income Statement
Year Ending December 31, 2006

Sales ($4,000,000 + $2,500,000 - $300,000)	$6,200,000
Interest Revenue ($24,000 - $24,000)	-0-
Dividend Revenue ($80,000 - $80,000)	-0-
Total Revenues	$6,200,000
Cost Of Goods Sold ($2,800,000 + $1,500,000 - $300,000 + $40,000 - $28,000)	$4,012,000
Depreciation Expense ($200,000 + $100,000 + $10,000 - $50,000)	260,000
Interest Expense ($240,000 + $84,000 - $24,000)	300,000
Other Expenses ($364,000 + $616,000)	980,000
Total Expenses	$5,552,000
Combined Income	$ 648,000
Non-Controlling Interest (See previous calculation)	47,600
Consolidated Net Income	$ 600,400

6-97.   Note again that the subtotal for Combined Income is not normal disclosure. Rather, it has been included for computational purposes.   Normal disclosure would have the Non-Controlling Interest included among the other deductions from revenue.

Verification Of Consolidated Net Income

6-98.   As was explained in Chapter 5, it is often useful to be able to make a schedular calculation of consolidated Net Income.   In this version of the comprehensive problem, the schedular calculation of consolidated Net Income is as follows:

Pleigh Company's Net Income	$500,000
Intercompany Dividend Revenues	(80,000)
Pleigh's Net Income Less Dividends	$420,000
Pleigh's Equity In Sleigh's Adjusted Net Income [(80%)($238,000)]	190,400
Income Before Adjustments	$610,400
Adjustment For Fair Value Depreciation	(10,000)
Consolidated Net Income	$600,400

6-99. Note that Pleigh's interest in the income of the Sleigh Company is not based on the reported income of the Sleigh Company. Rather, it is based on the same $238,000 adjusted subsidiary income figure that was used in the computation of the Non-Controlling Interest in consolidated Net Income (see Paragraph 6-94).

Consolidated Statement Of Retained Earnings
Statement Disclosure

6-100. Using the Net Income data, we can now prepare a consolidated Statement Of Retained Earnings. It would be as follows:

Pleigh Company And Subsidiary
Consolidated Statement Of Retained Earnings
Year Ending December 31, 2006

Balance - January 1, 2006 (See Discussion In Step C)	$2,910,600
2006 Net Income (See Income Statement)	600,400
2006 Dividends Declared (Pleigh's Only)	(350,000)
Balance - December 31, 2006	$3,161,000

Verification Of Consolidated Retained Earnings

6-101. As was the case with consolidated Net Income, you will often find it useful to be able to make an independent computation of the end of the year balance in the consolidated Retained Earnings account. In picking up Pleigh's share of the Retained Earnings of the Sleigh Company since acquisition, we must remove the effects of unrealized intercompany profits. The equity pickup included in the verification of consolidated Retained Earnings would be calculated as follows:

Sleigh's Closing Retained Earnings		$2,400,000
Balance At Acquisition		(1,500,000)
Balance Since Acquisition		$ 900,000
Unrealized Upstream Profits:		
Land	($40,000)	
Ending Inventories	(40,000)	
Equipment	(50,000)	(130,000)
Adjusted Balance		$ 770,000
Controlling Percent		80%
Equity Pickup		$ 616,000

6-102. The definitional approach to the computation of the year end consolidated Retained Earnings is as follows:

Pleigh's Closing Balance	$2,700,000
Pleigh's Share Of Sleigh's Retained Earnings Since Acquisition	
(Equity Pickup From Paragraph 6-101)	616,000
Adjustments	
Inventories	(80,000)
Plant (5 Years At $10,000)	(50,000)
Downstream Profit On Land	(25,000)
December 31, 2006 Consolidated Retained Earnings	$3,161,000

Consolidated Balance Sheet

Non-Controlling Interest

6-103. There are two basic ways to determine the Non-Controlling Interest that is shown on the Balance Sheet. One approach would be to use the Sleigh Company's book values adjusted for upstream unrealized profits. This calculation would be as follows:

December 31, 2006 - No Par Common Stock		$2,000,000
December 31, 2006 - Retained Earnings		2,400,000
Unrealized Upstream Profits:		
Land	($40,000)	
Ending Inventories	(40,000)	
Equipment	(50,000)	(130,000)
Sleigh's Adjusted Book Values		$4,270,000
Non-Controlling Percent		20%
Non-Controlling Interest		$ 854,000

6-104. An alternative calculation of the Non-Controlling Interest would start with the Step A allocation of $700,000, deduct the $20,000 Step B adjustment for dividends to non-controlling shareholders and add the Step C allocation of $126,400 and the Non-Controlling Interest of $47,600 from the consolidated Income Statement.

Statement Disclosure

6-105. The consolidated Balance Sheet of the Pleigh Company and its subsidiary would be prepared as follows:

Pleigh Company And Subsidiary
Consolidated Balance Sheet
As At December 31, 2006

Cash ($500,000 + $300,000)	$ 800,000
Current Receivables ($800,000 + $400,000 - $12,000)	1,188,000
Inventories ($2,500,000 + $1,700,000	
+ $80,000 - $80,000 - $40,000)	4,160,000
Long-Term Note Receivable ($200,000 - $200,000)	-0-
Investment In Sleigh ($3,200,000 - $3,200,000)	-0-
Land ($1,500,000 + $1,000,000 - $120,000 - $40,000 - $25,000)	2,315,000
Plant And Equipment ($4,500,000 + $1,900,000	
+ $200,000 - $50,000 - $50,000)	6,500,000
Goodwill	240,000
Total Assets	$15,203,000

Current Liabilities ($500,000 + $200,000 - $12,000)	$ 688,000
Long-Term Liabilities ($2,000,000 + $700,000 - $200,000)	2,500,000
Non-Controlling Interest (See previous calculation)	854,000
No Par Common Stock (Pleigh's Balance)	8,000,000
Retained Earnings (See previous calculation)	3,161,000
Total Equities	$15,203,000

6-106. Most of the preceding computations follow directly from the trial balance data adjusted by the various journal entries that we have made. The exceptions to this are the Retained Earnings balance which was computed in the consolidated Statement Of Retained Earnings, and the Non-Controlling Interest which was previously calculated (see Paragraphs 6-100 and 6-103).

Exercise Six-2 deals with open trial balance problems with the investment carried at cost.

Exercise Six-2

(This is identical to Exercise Five-2 except for Parts 3 and 4.)

On January 1, 2002, the Parker Company purchases 65 percent of the outstanding shares of the Schaffer Company for $1,350,000 in cash. On that date, the Schaffer Company had No Par Common Stock of $700,000 and Retained Earnings of $1,000,000. On December 31, 2006, the adjusted trial balances of the Parker Company and its subsidiary, the Schaffer Company are as follows:

	Parker	Schaffer
Monetary Assets	$ 2,850,000	$ 725,000
Investment In Schaffer - At Cost	1,350,000	Nil
Non-Monetary Assets	6,475,000	2,045,000
Total Expenses	2,940,000	530,000
Dividends Declared	250,000	50,000
Total Debits	$13,865,000	$3,350,000
Liabilities	$ 1,712,500	$ 425,000
No Par Common Stock	3,000,000	700,000
Retained Earnings (January 1)	5,895,000	1,550,000
Sales	3,225,000	675,000
Dividend Revenue	32,500	Nil
Total Credits	$13,865,000	$3,350,000
2006 Net Income	$ 317,500	$ 145,000
December 31, 2006 Retained Earnings	$ 5,962,500	$1,645,000

Other Information:

1. At the date of Parker Company's acquisition of the Schaffer Company's shares, all of the identifiable assets and liabilities of the Schaffer Company had fair values that were equal to their carrying values except for a group of non-monetary assets that had a fair value that was $150,000 greater than its carrying value. These non-monetary assets had a remaining useful life of 15 years. Both companies use the straight-line method for all amortization calculations.

2. In each of the years since Parker acquired control over Schaffer, the goodwill arising on this business combination transaction has been tested for impairment. In 2004, a Goodwill Impairment Loss of $35,000 was recognized. In addition, the impairment test for 2006 found a further impairment of $25,000.

3. Schaffer Company's Sales during 2006 include sales of $85,000 to Parker Company. One-half of the merchandise remains in the December 31, 2006 Inventories of Parker Company. The pricing on these sales provided Schaffer with a 30 percent gross margin based on sales price. In addition, as a result of these sales, on December 31, 2006, Parker still owes Schaffer $15,000 on open account. There were no intercompany sales in 2005.

4. On January 1, 2005, Schaffer sells a piece of equipment to Parker for $120,000 in cash. At this time, the carrying value of the machine on Schaffer's books is $100,000 and it has a remaining useful life of four years.

Required Prepare a consolidated Income Statement and a consolidated Statement Of Retained Earnings for the year ending December 31, 2006 and a consolidated Balance Sheet as at December 31, 2006 for the Parker Company and its subsidiary, the Schaffer Company.

End Of Exercise Six-2

Comprehensive Example - Closed Trial Balance With Investment At Cost

Basic Data

6-107.   In this version of the problem, Investment In Sleigh will continue to be carried at cost. However, the data will be presented in the form of a closed trial balance and only a consolidated Balance Sheet will be required. The data is as follows:

On January 1, 2002, the Pleigh Company purchases 80 percent of the outstanding voting shares of the Sleigh Company for $3,200,000 in cash. On that date the Sleigh Company had No Par Common Stock in the amount of $2,000,000 and Retained Earnings of $1,500,000. On December 31, 2006, the adjusted trial balances of the Pleigh Company and its subsidiary, the Sleigh Company are as follows:

	Pleigh	Sleigh
Cash	$ 500,000	$ 300,000
Current Receivables	800,000	400,000
Inventories	2,500,000	1,700,000
Long-Term Note Receivable	200,000	-0-
Investment In Sleigh - At Cost	3,200,000	-0-
Land	1,500,000	1,000,000
Plant And Equipment (Net)	4,500,000	1,900,000
Total Debits	$13,200,000	$5,300,000
Current Liabilities	$ 500,000	$ 200,000
Long-Term Liabilities	2,000,000	700,000
No Par Common Stock	8,000,000	2,000,000
Retained Earnings	2,700,000	2,400,000
Total Credits	$13,200,000	$5,300,000

Other Information:

1.   At the date of Pleigh Company's acquisition of the Sleigh Company's shares, all of the identifiable assets and liabilities of the Sleigh Company had fair values that were equal to their carrying values except Inventories which had fair values that were $100,000 more than their carrying values, Land with a fair value that was $150,000 less than its carrying value and Plant And Equipment which had a fair value that was $250,000 greater than its carrying value. The Plant And Equipment had a remaining useful life on the acquisition date of 20 years while the inventories that were present on the acquisition date were sold during the year ending December 31, 2002. The Land is still on the books of the Sleigh Company on December 31, 2006. Both Companies use the straight line method to calculate depreciation and amortization.

2.   In each of the years since Pleigh acquired control over Sleigh, the goodwill arising on this business combination transaction has been tested for impairment. No impairment was found in any of the years since acquisition.

3.   Sleigh Company's Sales include sales of $300,000 to Pleigh Company.   The December 31, 2006 Inventories of the Pleigh Company contain $100,000 of this merchandise purchased from Sleigh Company during 2006. In addition, the January 1, 2006 Inventories of the Pleigh Company contained $70,000 in merchandise purchased from Sleigh Company during 2005. All intercompany sales are priced to provide the selling company a gross margin on sales price of 40 percent.

4.   On December 31, 2006, the Pleigh Company is holding Sleigh Company's long-term note payable in the amount of $200,000. Interest at 12 percent is payable on July 1 of each year. Pleigh Company has been holding this note since July 1, 2004.

5. During 2004, the Pleigh Company sold Land to the Sleigh Company for $100,000 in cash. The Land had a carrying value on the books of the Pleigh Company of $75,000.

6. During 2005, the Sleigh Company sold Land to the Pleigh Company for $150,000. This Land had a carrying value on the books of the Sleigh Company of $110,000.

7. On December 31, 2004, the Sleigh Company sold Equipment to the Pleigh Company for $600,000. The Equipment had originally cost the Sleigh Company $800,000 and, at the time of the intercompany sale, had accumulated depreciation of $350,000. On this date, it was estimated that the remaining useful life of the Equipment was three years with no net salvage value.

Required: Prepare a consolidated Balance Sheet as at December 31, 2006 for the Pleigh Company and its subsidiary, the Sleigh Company.

Procedural Approach

6-108.   The procedural approach here is similar to that used in the open trial balance, cost method version of this problem. The basic difference is that all of the Step B adjustments to expenses and revenues will now be made to Sleigh's Retained Earnings account and the Step C entry will involve distributing the December 31, 2006 Retained Earnings, rather than the January 1, 2006 balance.

Step A Procedures
Investment Analysis
6-109.   The analysis of the investment will be identical to the one used in the open trial balance, cost method version of this problem. It is as follows:

	80 Percent	100 Percent
Investment Cost	$3,200,000	$4,000,000
Book Value	(2,800,000)	(3,500,000)
Differential	$ 400,000	$ 500,000
Fair Value Changes:		
Increase On Inventories	(80,000)	(100,000)
Decrease On Land	120,000	150,000
Increase On Plant And Equipment	(200,000)	(250,000)
Goodwill	$ 240,000	$ 300,000

Investment Elimination
6-110.   Based on the preceding analysis, the journal entry to eliminate the Investment In Sleigh account is as follows:

No Par Common Stock	$2,000,000	
Retained Earnings	1,500,000	
Plant And Equipment (Net)	200,000	
Inventories	80,000	
Goodwill	240,000	
Land		$ 120,000
Non-Controlling Interest		700,000
Investment In Sleigh		3,200,000

Step B(1) - Intercompany Assets And Liabilities
6-111.   The elimination of intercompany asset and liability balances is the same in both open trial balance and closed trial balance versions of this problem. The entries are:

Long-Term Liabilities	$200,000	
Long-Term Note Receivable		$200,000

| Current Liabilities | $ 12,000 | |
| Current Receivables | | $ 12,000 |

Step B(2) - Fair Value Write Offs

6-112.   The entries in this version of the problem will have the same effect on the asset and liability accounts as did the entries in the first version of this problem. The only difference is that since we are working with a closed trial balance it is no longer possible to adjust expense and revenue accounts. As these accounts have been closed into the ending retained earnings balances, adjustments will now go to the Retained Earnings account of the Sleigh Company.

6-113.   Since the fair value change on Inventories had no effect on the 2006 expenses or revenues, the entry here will be the same as it was in the first version of this problem. It is as follows:

| Retained Earnings - Sleigh's Closing | $80,000 | |
| Inventories | | $80,000 |

6-114.   As was the case in the first version of this problem, we will credit Plant And Equipment for 5 years (January 1, 2002 through December 31, 2006) of additional depreciation expense on the fair value change. However, instead of splitting the debits between Retained Earnings and the current Depreciation Expense, the entire amount will go to Retained Earnings. The entry is as follows:

| Retained Earnings - Sleigh's Closing | $50,000 | |
| Plant And Equipment (Net) | | $50,000 |

6-115.   As the Land is still on the books of Sleigh, no entry is required to adjust the fair value change on this account.

Step B(3) - Goodwill Impairment

6-116.   The Other Information in our comprehensive problem notes that, while goodwill has been tested for impairment in each year since the acquisition of Pleigh Company occurred, no impairment has been found. As a consequence, no Step B-3 entry is required in this problem.

Step B(4) - Intercompany Expenses And Revenues

6-117.   In the open trial balance versions of this problem, we made an entry here to eliminate intercompany expenses and revenues. We noted that this entry was simply to avoid overstating expenses and revenues. Since all of the expenses and revenues are now closed to retained earnings, no entry is required in this closed trial balance version of the problem.

Step B(5) - Intercompany Dividends

6-118.   In the open trial balance version of this problem we made an entry here to eliminate dividend payments. The entry involved reducing Pleigh's revenues, Dividends Declared and the Non-Controlling Interest in the consolidated Balance Sheet. As Pleigh's revenues and the Dividends Declared accounts have been closed to retained earnings, no entry is required for these adjustments. With respect to the reduction of the Non-Controlling Interest in the consolidated Balance Sheet, this effect will be automatically picked up in Step C when we base our allocation to this account on the end of the year Retained Earnings balance of the Sleigh Company. This end of year balance has, of course, had all of the Sleigh Company's 2006 dividends taken out as part of the closing entries.

Step B(6) - Unrealized Intercompany Profits

6-119.   In the open trial balance version of this problem, our adjustments and eliminations for unrealized intercompany profits had to take into consideration such profits in the opening consolidated Retained Earnings balance, the current period's consolidated expenses and revenues, and the closing balances for inclusion in the consolidated Balance Sheet. In this closed trial balance version of the problem, we are only concerned with unrealized intercompany profits to the extent that they have an effect on the accounts to be included in the December 31, 2006 consolidated Balance Sheet. We will find that this will simplify and, in the case of profits in the opening inventories, eliminate the entries that are required in dealing with unrealized intercompany profits.

Downstream And Upstream Profits On Land

6-120. This problem contains a 2004 intercompany profit of $25,000 on the sale of Land from Pleigh Company to Sleigh and a similar 2005 profit of $40,000 on the sale of Land from Sleigh to Pleigh. The amounts of these profits are unchanged from the beginning of the current accounting period and, as a consequence, the appropriate elimination entries to be used here are the same as those that were required in the open trial balance version of this problem. The entry for the downstream profit is as follows:

Retained Earnings - Pleigh's Closing	$25,000	
Land		$25,000

6-121. For the upstream profit, the entry is:

Retained Earnings - Sleigh's Closing	$40,000	
Land		$40,000

Upstream Inventory Profits

6-122. In this problem there are Sleigh Company profits in the opening Inventories of the Pleigh Company in the amount of $28,000 and a similar balance in the closing Inventories of the Pleigh Company of $40,000.

6-123. With respect to the $28,000 opening inventory profit, in the open trial balance version of this problem we found it necessary to reduce the opening Retained Earnings of the Sleigh Company and increase the 2006 income figures by reducing the 2006 consolidated Cost Of Goods Sold. The combined effect of these two adjustments on the December 31, 2006 Retained Earnings of Sleigh would be zero as the reduction in the January 1, 2006 Retained Earnings would be offset by the increase in 2006 income created by the decrease in Cost Of Goods Sold. As a reflection of this situation, no entry is required for opening inventory profits in closed trial balance, investment at cost type problems. An additional way of looking at this situation would be to note that the Inventories that Pleigh was holding at the beginning of 2006 have been sold and the Sleigh Company's unrealized opening inventory profit has now been realized. Therefore, no elimination entry is required.

6-124. The unrealized profit in the closing Inventories of the Pleigh Company does, however, require an adjustment. The consolidated Inventories must be reduced as was the case in the open trial balance version of the problem. However, the accompanying debit can no longer go to the Cost Of Goods Sold account. Since this account has been closed into the ending Retained Earnings, the adjustment must be to Retained Earnings and would appear as follows:

Retained Earnings - Sleigh's Closing	$40,000	
Inventories		$40,000

Upstream Profit On Equipment

6-125. On December 31, 2004, there was a profit of $150,000 recognized by the Sleigh Company on the sale of a depreciable asset with a three year life to the Pleigh Company. During 2005, $50,000 of this profit was realized through a reduction in consolidated Depreciation Expense. This left $100,000 to be removed from the January 1, 2006 Retained Earnings of the Sleigh Company in the open trial balance version of this problem. Now that we are dealing with a closed trial balance, we must account for the fact that an additional profit realization of $50,000 occurred during 2006. This means that at the end of 2006, the only adjustment will be for the remaining $50,000 which is still unrealized on this date. The entry would be as follows:

| Retained Earnings - Sleigh's Closing | $50,000 | |
| Plant And Equipment (Net) | | $50,000 |

6-126.   Note that, as with the other intercompany profit eliminations, there is no adjustment of the current year's expenses or revenues as they have been closed to Retained Earnings in this closed trial balance problem.

Step C - Distribution Of The Subsidiary Retained Earnings

Retained Earnings Balance

6-127.   The Retained Earnings account of the Sleigh Company in the trial balance for this problem was $2,400,000. In Step A we removed $1,500,000 of this amount, leaving a balance in the amount of $900,000 which had accrued between the acquisition date of January 1, 2002 and the current date of December 31, 2006. Our one remaining task in this problem is to determine how much of this balance is left after the Step B adjustments and to distribute this balance to the parent and non controlling interest. The remaining balance can be determined as follows:

Balance Since Acquisition	$ 900,000
Step B Adjustments:	
Fair Value on Inventories	(80,000)
Plant (5 Years At $10,000)	(50,000)
Unrealized Upstream Profit On Land Sale	(40,000)
Unrealized Upstream Profit In Closing Inventories	(40,000)
Unrealized Upstream Profit On Equipment	(50,000)
Balance After Adjustments	$ 640,000

Retained Earnings Distribution Schedule

6-128.   The schedule for allocating the balance from the preceding Paragraph would be as follows:

Sleigh's Closing Retained Earnings	$2,400,000
Balance At Acquisition	(1,500,000)
Balance Since Acquisition	$ 900,000
Unrealized Upstream Profits:	
Land	(40,000)
Closing Inventories	(40,000)
Plant	(50,000)
Adjusted Balance Since Acquisition	$ 770,000
Non-Controlling Interest [(20%)($770,000)]	(154,000)
Available To The Controlling Interest	$ 616,000
Other Step B Adjustments:	
Fair Value Change On Inventories	(80,000)
Fair Value Change On Plant and Equipment	(50,000)
To Consolidated Retained Earnings	$ 486,000

6-129.   With the information from this schedule, we can now make the required Step C distribution entry.

Retained Earnings Distribution Entry

6-130.   Using the information from the preceding schedule, the journal entry to distribute Sleigh's Retained Earnings since acquisition is as follows:

Retained Earnings - Sleigh	$640,000	
Non-Controlling Interest (Balance Sheet)		$154,000
Consolidated Retained Earnings		486,000

6-131.   This entry reduces the Sleigh Company's Retained Earnings balance to zero and distributes the total to the parent and non-controlling interest. When the credit of $154,000 to the Non-Controlling Interest is added to the Step A credit to this account of $700,000, we have established the appropriate balance of $854,000 for inclusion in the consolidated Balance Sheet as at December 31, 2006. Further, if we take the Pleigh Company's Retained Earnings balance of $2,700,000 from the trial balance, subtract the downstream profit on the intercompany sale of land of $25,000 and add the allocation from above of $486,000, we arrive at a figure of $3,161,000. This figure is the correct figure for consolidated Retained Earnings to be included in the December 31, 2006 Balance Sheet.

Consolidated Balance Sheet

6-132.   With the addition of the Step C distribution entry, we have completed all of the procedures necessary for the preparation of the consolidated Balance Sheet. As expected, this closed trial balance version of the problem produces a Balance Sheet that is identical to the one in the open trial balance version. All of the balances flow directly from the preceding journal entries, resulting in the consolidated Balance Sheet which is presented as follows:

Pleigh Company And Subsidiary
Consolidated Balance Sheet
As At December 31, 2006

Cash ($500,000 + $300,000)	$ 800,000
Current Receivables ($800,000 + $400,000 - $12,000)	1,188,000
Inventories ($2,500,000 + $1,700,000 + $80,000 - $80,000 - $40,000)	4,160,000
Long-Term Note Receivable ($200,000 - $200,000)	-0-
Investment In Sleigh ($3,200,000 - $3,200,000)	-0-
Land ($1,500,000 + $1,000,000 - $120,000 - $40,000 - $25,000)	2,315,000
Plant And Equipment ($4,500,000 + $1,900,000 + $200,0000 - $50,000 - $50,000)	6,500,000
Goodwill	240,000
Total Assets	$15,083,000

Current Liabilities ($500,000 + $200,000 - $12,000)	$ 688,000
Long-Term Liabilities ($2,000,000 + $700,000 - $200,000)	2,500,000
Non-Controlling Interest	854,000
No Par Common Stock	8,000,000
Retained Earnings	3,161,000
Total Equities	$15,083,000

<table>
<tr><td>Exercise Six-3 deals with closed trial balance problems with the investment carried at cost.</td><td>

Exercise Six-3

(This is identical to Exercise Six-2 except it is a closed trial balance version.)

On January 1, 2002, the Parker Company purchases 65 percent of the outstanding shares of the Schaffer Company for $1,350,000 in cash. On that date, the Schaffer Company had No Par Common Stock of $700,000 and Retained Earnings of $1,000,000. On December 31, 2006, the adjusted trial balances of the Parker Company and its subsidiary, the Schaffer Company are as follows:
</td></tr>
</table>

	Parker	Schaffer
Monetary Assets	$ 2,850,000	$ 725,000
Investment In Schaffer - At Cost	1,350,000	Nil
Non-Monetary Assets	6,475,000	2,045,000
Total Debits	$10,675,000	$2,770,000
Liabilities	$ 1,712,500	$ 425,000
No Par Common Stock	3,000,000	700,000
Retained Earnings	5,962,500	1,645,000
Total Credits	$10,675,000	$2,770,000

This is a continuation of Exercise Six-3.

Other Information:

1. At the date of Parker Company's acquisition of the Schaffer Company's shares, all of the identifiable assets and liabilities of the Schaffer Company had fair values that were equal to their carrying values except for a group of non-monetary assets that had a fair value that was $150,000 greater than its carrying value. These non-monetary assets had a remaining useful life of 15 years. Both companies use the straight-line method for all amortization calculations.

2. In each of the years since Parker acquired control over Schaffer, the goodwill arising on this business combination transaction has been tested for impairment. In 2004, a Goodwill Impairment Loss of $35,000 was recognized. In addition, the impairment test for 2006 found a further impairment of $25,000.

3. Schaffer Company's Sales during 2006 include sales of $85,000 to Parker Company. One-half of the merchandise remains in the December 31, 2006 Inventories of Parker Company. The pricing on these sales provided Schaffer with a 30 percent gross margin based on sales price. In addition, as a result of these sales, on December 31, 2006, Parker still owes Schaffer $15,000 on open account. There were no intercompany sales in 2005.

4. On January 1, 2005, Schaffer sells a piece of equipment to Parker for $120,000 in cash. At this time, the carrying value of the machine on Schaffer's books is $100,000 and it has a remaining useful life of four years.

Required   Prepare a consolidated Balance Sheet as at December 31, 2006 for the Parker Company and its subsidiary, the Schaffer Company.

End Of Exercise Six-3

Review Of The Conceptual Alternatives Adopted By Section 1600

6-133.   Now that you have an understanding of all of the basic consolidation procedures, including unrealized intercompany profits, the summary of the conceptual alternatives that was originally presented in Chapter 4 is repeated here for your convenience. The following procedures reflect the recommendations of the *CICA Handbook* with respect to the preparation of consolidated financial statements:

Asset Valuation   The recommended approach to asset valuation is the parent company concept. That is, only the parent's share of any fair value changes and goodwill is recognized at the time of acquisition or combination. As a consequence, only the parent's share of the amortization of these values or recognition of their impairment is recorded in subsequent periods.

Non-Controlling Interest In The Balance Sheet

- **Disclosure**   Section 1600 is not explicit on this issue. It simply states that the Non-Controlling Interest in the consolidated net assets of the subsidiary companies should be shown separately from shareholders' equity. This eliminates the entity approach and the fact that a non-controlling interest is present eliminates the proprietary approach. This seems to leave the parent company approach. However, in the absence of a clear statement that the Non-Controlling Interest should be disclosed as a part of long-term liabilities, it often ends up presented in a somewhat ambiguous fashion between the long-term liabilities and the consolidated shareholders' equity.

- **Calculation**   The inconsistencies of Section 1600 become apparent in the calculation of the Non-Controlling Interest on the Balance Sheet. In general, this computation follows the parent company approach and bases the Non-Controlling Interest on the non-controlling shareholders' proportionate share of the carrying values of the subsidiary. However, because the entity approach is used for the elimination of unrealized subsidiary profits, these transactions must be taken into account in determining the appropriate balance. Stated generally, the Non-Controlling Interest in the consolidated Balance Sheet would be computed by taking the non-controlling shareholders' proportionate interest in the net book value of the subsidiary's assets after they have been adjusted for any unrealized intercompany profits of the subsidiary company.

Non-Controlling Interest In The Income Statement

- **Disclosure**   With respect to income before extraordinary items and the results of discontinued operations, Section 1600 requires that Non-Controlling Interest be given disclosure as a separate line item in the consolidated Income Statement. This, of course, reflects an adoption of the parent company approach. For no apparent reason, extraordinary items and the results of discontinued operations are dealt with by a different conceptual alternative. Only the parent company's proportionate interest in these items is disclosed which is an application of the proprietary concept.

- **Calculation**   As was the case with the computation of the Non-Controlling Interest for purposes of disclosure in the consolidated Balance Sheet, the computation here is complicated by the presence of inconsistencies in the Recommendations of Section 1600. Generally, the Non-Controlling Interest in the consolidated Income Statement is based on the reported income of the subsidiary. Once again, however, adjustments must be made for the adoption of the entity approach in dealing with unrealized subsidiary profits. Stated generally, the Non-Controlling Interest in the consolidated Income Statement is calculated by taking the non-controlling shareholders' proportionate interest in the reported income of the subsidiary with the elimination of current subsidiary intercompany profits that are still unrealized from the consolidated point of view and the addition of subsidiary intercompany profits from previous years that have become realized for consolidation purposes during the year.

Unrealized Intercompany Profits Of The Subsidiary   As already noted, Section 1600 adopts the entity approach here and requires 100 percent pro rata elimination of unrealized intercompany subsidiary profits.

Application Of The Equity Method

Basic Concepts

6-134. In Chapter 5, we indicated that the Net Income of an investor using the equity method for an investee had to be equal to the consolidated Net Income that would result from the consolidation of that investee. This requirement was based on the following Recommendation:

> **Paragraph 3050.08** *Investment income as calculated by the equity method should be that amount necessary to increase or decrease the investor's income to that which would have been recognized if the results of the investee's operations had been consolidated with those of the investor.* (August, 1978)

6-135. In Chapter 5 this meant that all of the adjustments for fair value write offs and any goodwill impairment losses that would be required in the consolidation process, are also required in the application of the equity method. As you would expect, similar adjustments are required for the unrealized intercompany profits that were introduced in this Chapter. As was noted in Chapter 5, however, there is a major difference in the disclosure of these adjustments when the equity method is applied. In consolidation, the various adjustments are included in specific consolidated account balances. In contrast, the equity method deals with all of these adjustments as modifications of the Investment Asset and Investment Income accounts.

Comprehensive Example

Income Statement

6-136. As we did in Chapter 5, we will use the comprehensive example that we have been working with throughout this Chapter to illustrate the application of the equity method. The basic data for this problem was presented in Paragraph 6-21 and will not be repeated here. The only change is that we will assume that Pleigh Company's majority ownership does not give it control over the Sleigh Company and, as a consequence, the investment cannot be consolidated.

6-137. From our previous experience with the Pleigh Company problem, we know that consolidated Net Income for 2006 amounts to $600,400 (Paragraph 6-96). Since the Pleigh Company's net income without the inclusion of any revenues from its Investment In Sleigh amounts to $420,000 ($500,000 cost method income less $80,000 dividend revenue), the only Investment Income that would satisfy the requirement stated in Paragraph 3050.08 is $180,400. This figure can be verified as follows:

Pleigh's Interest In Sleigh's Income:		
Sleigh's Reported Net Income	$200,000	
Realized Gain On Equipment	50,000	
Profits In Opening Inventories	28,000	
Profits In Ending Inventories	(40,000)	
Sleigh's Adjusted Income	$238,000	
Pleigh's Proportionate Interest	80%	$190,400
Fair Value Adjustment For Fair Value Depreciation		(10,000)
Pleigh's Equity Method Investment Income		$180,400

6-138. Sleigh's Adjusted Income of $238,000 is also used to calculate the Non-Controlling Interest disclosed on the consolidated Income Statement (see Paragraph 6-94). Using the equity method Investment Income, the Income Statement of the Pleigh Company with the Investment In Sleigh carried by the equity method would be as follows:

Pleigh Company
Income Statement
Year Ending December 31, 2006

Sales	$4,000,000
Interest Revenue	24,000
Investment Income	180,400
Total Revenues	$4,204,400
Cost Of Goods Sold	$2,800,000
Depreciation Expense	200,000
Interest Expense	240,000
Other Expenses	364,000
Total Expenses	$3,604,000
Net Income	$ 600,400

Balance Sheet

6-139.   If Pleigh was not consolidating its investment in Sleigh, and used the equity method in its single entity statements, the Balance Sheet account Investment In Sleigh would have to be increased to reflect Pleigh's equity in this investee. As is the case with Investment Income under the equity method, this Balance Sheet account would be subject to the same types of adjustments that would be required in the preparation of consolidated financial statements. The following equity pickup uses the same $770,000 Adjusted (Retained Earnings) Balance Since Acquisition as was used in the Retained Earnings distribution schedule in Paragraph 6-128. The required balance would be calculated as follows:

Investment In Sleigh At Cost		$3,200,000
Equity Pickup:		
Sleigh's December 31 Retained Earnings	$2,400,000	
Balance At Acquisition	(1,500,000)	
Balance Since Acquisition	$ 900,000	
Unrealized Upstream Profits:		
Land	(40,000)	
Closing Inventories	(40,000)	
Equipment	(50,000)	
Adjusted Balance Since Acquisition	$ 770,000	
Pleigh's Share	80%	616,000
Adjustments:		
Inventories		(80,000)
Plant And Equipment [(5 Years)($10,000)]		(50,000)
Downstream Profit On Land		(25,000)
Investment In Sleigh At Equity		$3,661,000

6-140.   If this amount is used on the asset side of Pleigh's single entity Balance Sheet, there will have to be a corresponding $461,000 ($3,661,000 - $3,200,000) adjustment to Retained Earnings on the equity side of the single entity Balance Sheet. This will leave Pleigh with the following single entity Balance Sheet under the equity method:

Pleigh Company
Single Entity Balance Sheet
As At December 31, 2006

Cash	$ 500,000
Current Receivables	800,000
Inventories	2,500,000
Long-Term Note Receivable	200,000
Investment In Sleigh (At Equity)	3,661,000
Land	1,500,000
Plant And Equipment (Net)	4,500,000
Total Assets	$13,661,000

Current Liabilities	$ 500,000
Long-Term Liabilities	2,000,000
No Par Common Stock	8,000,000
Retained Earnings ($2,700,000 + $461,000)	3,161,000
Total Equities	$13,661,000

6-141.   Note that, when the equity method is used, the resulting Retained Earnings figure in Pleigh's single entity Balance Sheet is equal to the consolidated Retained Earnings figure resulting from the application of consolidation procedures (see Paragraph 6-132). This result follows from the Paragraph 3050.08 requirement that investment income as calculated by the equity method must be the amount necessary to increase or decrease the investor's income to that which would have been recognized if the results of the investee's operations had been consolidated with those of the investor.

Alternative Disclosure

6-142.   In the example we have just considered, there were no downstream intercompany profits in the 2006 Net Income of the Pleigh Company. If such profits had been present, it would have been acceptable under the requirements of the *CICA Handbook* to simply deduct them from the Investment Income total. In view of the fact that such downstream profits are not included in the reported income of the Sleigh Company, this does not seem to be a particularly desirable form of disclosure. This inappropriateness is recognized in the *CICA Handbook* which provides for alternative disclosure of unrealized downstream profits. The relevant provision is as follows:

Paragraph 3050.15   The elimination of an unrealized intercompany gain or loss has the same effect on net income whether the consolidation or equity method is used. However, in consolidated financial statements, the elimination of a gain or loss may affect sales and cost of sales otherwise to be reported. In the application of the equity method, the gain or loss is eliminated by adjustment of investment income from the investee or by separate provision in the investor's financial statements, as is appropriate in the circumstances.

6-143.   This Paragraph permits the disclosure of unrealized downstream profits as a separate item in the Income Statement of the investor company which is applying the equity method. It would be our view that such disclosure would be preferable to the deduction of such profits from the Investment Income account.

Exercise Six-4
(This is identical to Exercise Six-2 except for the Required.)

On January 1, 2002, the Parker Company purchases 65 percent of the outstanding shares of the Schaffer Company for $1,350,000 in cash. On that date, the Schaffer Company had No Par Common Stock of $700,000 and Retained Earnings of $1,000,000. On December 31,

Exercise Six-4 deals with the application of the equity method.

This is a continuation of Exercise Six-4.

2006, the adjusted trial balances of the Parker Company and its subsidiary, the Schaffer Company are as follows:

	Parker	Schaffer
Monetary Assets	$ 2,850,000	$ 725,000
Investment In Schaffer - At Cost	1,350,000	Nil
Non-Monetary Assets	6,475,000	2,045,000
Total Expenses	2,940,000	530,000
Dividends Declared	250,000	50,000
Total Debits	**$13,865,000**	**$3,350,000**
Liabilities	$ 1,712,500	$ 425,000
No Par Common Stock	3,000,000	700,000
Retained Earnings (January 1)	5,895,000	1,550,000
Sales	3,225,000	675,000
Dividend Revenue	32,500	Nil
Total Credits	**$13,865,000**	**$3,350,000**
2006 Net Income	$ 317,500	$ 145,000
December 31, 2006 Retained Earnings	$ 5,962,500	$1,645,000

Other Information:

1. At the date of Parker Company's acquisition of the Schaffer Company's shares, all of the identifiable assets and liabilities of the Schaffer Company had fair values that were equal to their carrying values except for a group of non-monetary assets that had a fair value that was $150,000 greater than its carrying value. These non-monetary assets had a remaining useful life of 15 years. Both companies use the straight-line method for all amortization calculations.

2. In each of the years since Parker acquired control over Schaffer, the goodwill arising on this business combination transaction has been tested for impairment. In 2004, a Goodwill Impairment Loss of $35,000 was recognized. In addition, the impairment test for 2006 found a further impairment of $25,000.

3. Schaffer Company's Sales during 2006 include sales of $85,000 to Parker Company. One-half of the merchandise remains in the December 31, 2006 Inventories of Parker Company. The pricing on these sales provided Schaffer with a 30 percent gross margin based on sales price. In addition, as a result of these sales, on December 31, 2006, Parker still owes Schaffer $15,000 on open account. There were no intercompany sales in 2005.

4. On January 1, 2005, Schaffer sells a piece of equipment to Parker for $120,000 in cash. At this time, the carrying value of the machine on Schaffer's books is $100,000 and it has a remaining useful life of four years.

Required: Assume that the Parker Company's majority ownership of Schaffer shares has never provided control over that Company and, as a consequence, consolidated financial statements cannot be prepared. Provide the Parker Company's single entity Income Statement for the year ending December 31, 2006, and its single entity Balance Sheet as at December 31, 2006 assuming the Investment in Schaffer is accounted for by the equity method since its acquisition. Note that the Parker Company's trial balance given in the problem accounts for the Investment In Schaffer using the cost method.

End Of Exercise Six-4

Consolidated Cash Flow Statement

6-144.   The preparation of a consolidated Cash Flow Statement was covered in Chapter 5. While this Chapter has added coverage of unrealized intercompany profits, this new material does not alter the procedures used to prepare the consolidated Cash Flow Statement. This means that there is no requirement for further discussion of this important financial statement in this Chapter. However, to facilitate your understanding of the procedures involved with the preparation of consolidated Cash Flow Statements, we are including an exercise which illustrates this process.

Exercise Six-5

(This is identical to Exercise Five-5 except for Parts 5 and 6.)

> Exercise Six-5 deals with the preparation of consolidated Cash Flow Statements.

On January 1, 2002, the Parco Company acquires 80 percent of the outstanding voting shares of the Subco Company for $1,000,000 in cash. At this time the Subco Company has No Par Common Stock of $1,000,000 and Retained Earnings of $200,000. Also on this acquisition date, all of the identifiable assets and liabilities of Subco Company had fair values that were equal to their carrying values except for Inventories which had a fair value that was $400,000 less than its carrying value and Equipment which had a fair value that was $300,000 more than its carrying value. The Inventories were sold during the year ending December 31, 2002, while the Equipment had a remaining useful life on January 1, 2002 of ten years with no antici- pated salvage value. Both the Parco Company and the Subco Company use the straight line method for all amortization calculations. Comparative Balance Sheets for the two companies as at December 31, 2006 and December 31, 2007 are as follows:

	Parco (000's)		Subco (000's)	
	2007	2006	2007	2006
Cash	$ 800	$ 400	$ 365	$ 270
Accounts Receivable	1,500	1,800	900	650
Inventories	2,000	2,600	800	500
Investment In Subco (At Cost)	1,000	1,000	Nil	Nil
Land	1,000	800	450	850
Plant And Equipment (Net)	4,800	6,400	600	800
Total	$11,100	$13,000	$3,115	$3,070
Accounts Payable	$ 400	$ 1,000	$ 700	$ 750
Bonds Payable - Par	3,000	4,000	800	800
Bonds Payable - Premium	Nil	Nil	15	20
Common Stock - No Par	4,000	4,000	1,000	1,000
Retained Earnings	3,700	4,000	600	500
Total	$11,100	$13,000	$3,115	$3,070

Other Information:

1.   During 2007, the Parco Company retires outstanding debt with a par value of $1,000,000 for $1,000,000 in cash.

2.   During 2007, the Parco Company experiences a Net Loss of $300,000 and does not declare any dividends. This Net Loss includes an $800,000 write-down of Plant And Equipment to reflect the fact that its net carrying amount exceeded its net recoverable amount.

3.   During 2007, the Subco Company earns Net Income of $500,000 and declares dividends of $400,000. All of the dividends declared are paid prior to December 31, 2007.

This is a continuation of Exercise Six-5.

4. The goodwill measured at the time Parco acquired Subco has been tested for impairment in each subsequent year. No impairment has been found.

5. During 2007, the Subco Company sells Land to the Parco Company for cash of $200,000. The carrying value of this Land on the books of the Subco Company was $400,000. There were no purchases or sales of Plant and Equipment.

6. During 2007, the Subco Company sells merchandise to the Parco Company at a sales price of $400,000. On December 31, 2007, $100,000 of this merchandise is in the Inventories of the Parco Company and this merchandise contains a gross profit in the amount of $40,000. In addition, at this year end date, Parco Company still owes Subco Company $100,000 on open account. During 2006, there were no intercompany sales of merchandise.

Required:

A. Calculate consolidated Net Income for the Parco Company and its subsidiary, the Subco Company, for the year ending December 31, 2007.

B. Prepare a consolidated Cash Flow Statement for the Parco Company and its subsidiary, the Subco Company, for the year ending December 31, 2007. Your solution should comply with all of the requirements of the *CICA Handbook*.

End Of Exercise Six-5

Step-By-Step Acquisitions

6-145.   As was the case with the consolidated Cash Flow Statement, basic procedures for step-by-step acquisitions were covered in Chapter 5. While there is no need for further discussion of this type of acquisition in this Chapter, we believe that it is useful to include an Exercise to illustrate the required procedures when unrealized intercompany profits are included. As with the other Exercises in this Chapter, Exercise Six-6 is an extension of the similar Exercise in Chapter 5.

Exercise Six-6 deals with step-by-step acquisitions.

Exercise Six-6

(This is identical to Exercise Five-6 except for the unrealized intercompany profits.)

On December 31, 2002, the Best Company purchases 40 percent of the outstanding shares of the Worst Company for $1,875,000. On this date, the carrying values of the Worst Company's net identifiable assets amount to $3,250,000 (Common Stock of $2,000,000, plus Retained Earnings of $1,250,000). All of the fair values of the individual identifiable assets and liabilities of the Worst Company have carrying values that are equal to their fair values except for Plant And Equipment. Specialized machinery with a remaining useful life of four years has a carrying value of $2,000,000 and a fair value of $2,725,000.

On December 31, 2003, the Best Company purchases an additional 15 percent of the outstanding shares of the Worst Company for $3,500,000. On this date, the carrying values of the Worst Company's net identifiable assets total $4,250,000 (Common Stock of $2,000,000, plus Retained Earnings of $2,250,000). All of the fair values of the identifiable assets and liabilities of the Worst Company have carrying values that are equal to their fair values except for Plant And Equipment. The specialized machinery now has a useful life of three years, a carrying value of $1,600,000, and a fair value of $2,300,00.

There has been no impairment of goodwill in either 2003 or 2004.

During 2003, Worst sold Land to Best for $250,000. The carrying value of the Land on Worst's books was $200,000.

During 2004, Worst sold merchandise to Best for $450,000. The sales were priced to provide Worst with a gross margin of 25 percent on the sales price. One-third of this merchandise remains in the December 31, 2004 inventories of Best.

This is a continuation of Exercise Six-6.

On December 31, 2004, the carrying values for Best's and Worst's Plant And Equipment are $3,520,000 and $1,600,000, respectively. The Retained Earnings balance of Best on December 31, 2004 is $4,275,000 while Worst's Retained Earnings balance is $2,450,000.

Required:

A. Calculate consolidated Plant And Equipment as of December 31, 2004.

B. Calculate the amount of Goodwill that would be shown on the December 31, 2004 Balance Sheet.

C. Calculate consolidated Retained Earnings as of December 31, 2004.

End Of Exercise Six-6

Summary Of Consolidation Procedures

6-146. In Chapter 4, we began the development of a set of procedures that could be used in the preparation of a consolidated Balance Sheet at the date of the subsidiary's acquisition. In Chapter 5 we made substantial additions to this list involving intercompany expenses and revenues, fair value amortization, and the distribution of subsidiary retained earnings since acquisition. In this Chapter, in addition to modifying some of the Chapter 5 procedures to reflect the presence of unrealized intercompany profits, we added new Step B procedures for eliminating and restoring such items. Specifically we have added Step B-6 and modified Step C-1 to deal with unrealized intercompany profits. We are now in a position to provide a complete summary of basic consolidation procedures as developed in this text. This summary is as follows:

Step A-1 Procedure Eliminate 100 percent of the Investment In Subsidiary account.

Step A-2 Procedure Eliminate 100 percent of all the acquisition date balances in the subsidiary's shareholders' equity (includes both contributed capital and retained earnings).

Step A-3 Procedure Allocate any debit or credit Differential that is present at acquisition to the investor's share of fair value changes on identifiable assets, fair value changes on identifiable liabilities, and positive or negative goodwill.

Step A-4 Procedure Allocate to a Non-Controlling Interest account in the consolidated Balance Sheet, the non-controlling interest's share of the at acquisition book value of the total shareholders' equity of the subsidiary (includes both contributed capital and retained earnings).

Step B-1 Procedure Eliminate 100 percent of all intercompany assets and liabilities.

Step B-2 Procedure Give recognition to the post-acquisition realization of acquisition date fair value changes on assets and liabilities that have been used up or sold during the post-acquisition period. To the extent that this realization occurred in prior periods, recognition will require an adjustment of the opening retained earnings of the subsidiary. Alternatively, if the realization occurred in the current period, the adjustment will be to the subsidiary's current period expenses, revenues, gains, or losses.

Step B-3 Procedure   Recognize current and cumulative goodwill impairment losses that have been measured since the acquisition of the subsidiary and the initial recognition of the goodwill balance. To the extent that the impairment took place during the current period, the measured amount will be charged to Goodwill Impairment Loss. To the extent that it occurred in prior periods, it will be charged to retained earnings.

Step B-4 Procedure   Eliminate 100 percent of all intercompany expenses and revenues.

Step B-5 Procedure   Eliminate 100 percent of subsidiary dividends declared. The parent's share of this amount will be deducted from the revenues of the parent company and the non-controlling interest's share of this amount will be deducted from the Non-Controlling Interest in the Balance Sheet.

Step B-6(a) Procedure   Eliminate 100 percent of all unrealized intercompany profits (losses) that are present in the single entity financial statements. There are three groups of such profits to consider:

1.   Profits that were recognized in the single entity statements of the parent or subsidiary in a previous period, remain unrealized at the beginning of the current period and are realized during the current period. Such profits will be deducted from the opening retained earnings of the company that recognized them in their single entity financial statements (unrealized losses would be added back).

2.   Profits that were recognized in the single entity statement of the parent or subsidiary in the current period and remain unrealized at the end of the current period (for example, unrealized profits on inventory sales). These profits will be removed from current income through an adjustment of the current expenses or revenues. Note that 100 percent of the profit will be removed, without regard to whether it is an upstream profit or a downstream profit. If it is an upstream profit, its removal will reduce both consolidated Net Income and the Non-Controlling Interest that is included in the consolidated Income Statement.

3.   Profits that were recognized in the single entity statement of the parent or subsidiary in the current or a previous period, and remain unrealized at the end of the current period (for example, an unrealized profit in the previous year on the sale of a machine with a four year life). These profits will be removed from the closing retained earnings of the company that recognized them in their single entity financial statements (unrealized losses would be added back).

Step B-6(b) Procedure   Recognize the amount of previously unrealized intercompany profits or losses that have become realized during the period, either through the sale of the related asset or through usage of that asset. The amount that was previously unrealized from the consolidated point of view would be a deduction from the opening single entity retained earnings of the parent or subsidiary companies. To the extent the profit has become realized during the period, it will be included in the current consolidated Net Income through an adjustment of an expense or revenue. Any amount of the profit that remains unrealized at the end of the period will be deducted from the closing retained earnings of the relevant parent or subsidiary. As was the case with Step B-6(a), 100 percent of the previously unrealized profit will be recognized, without regard to whether it is upstream or downstream. If it is an upstream profit, the addition will increase both consolidated Net Income and the Non-Controlling Interest in the Income Statement.

Step C-1 Procedure   Determine the appropriate allocation of the subsidiary's adjusted retained earnings since acquisition. The book value of the subsidiary retained earnings since acquisition will first be adjusted for upstream profits that are unrealized as of the date applicable to the retained earnings balance (opening retained earnings in open trial balance problems). This adjusted balance will be multiplied by the ownership percentage of the non-controlling interest, with the product being allocated to the non-controlling interest. After the non-controlling interest is subtracted, the resulting balance will be adjusted for the fair value write-offs called for in Step B(2), as well as any goodwill impairment as described in Step B(3). The balance remaining after these adjustments will be allocated to consolidated retained earnings.

Step C-2 Procedure Eliminate the subsidiary's adjusted retained earnings since acquisition. This amount will be allocated to the Non-Controlling Interest in the consolidated Balance Sheet and to consolidated retained earnings as determined in Step C-1.

6-147. As we did in Chapter 5, we would remind you that, as stated, the listed procedures apply to open trial balance problems with the investment in the subsidiary carried by the cost method. In dealing with closed trial balance problems these procedures will need to be modified. Such required modifications were illustrated in the closed trial balance version of our comprehensive example.

Summary Of Definitional Calculations

6-148. With this Chapter's coverage of the procedures required to deal with unrealized intercompany profits, we can now provide you with a comprehensive list of the definitions to be used in preparing consolidated financial statements. We continue to encourage you to work towards preparing the required balances in consolidated financial statements by using these direct definitional calculations. The list is as follows:

Identifiable Assets And Liabilities The amount to be included in the consolidated Balance Sheet for any identifiable asset or liability is calculated as follows:

- 100 percent of the carrying value of the identifiable asset (liability) on the books of the parent company at the Balance Sheet date; *plus*

- 100 percent of the carrying value of the identifiable asset (liability) on the books of the subsidiary company at the Balance Sheet date; *plus (minus)*

- the parent company's share of the fair value increase (decrease) on the asset (liability) (i.e., the parent company's share of the difference between the fair value of the subsidiary's asset or liability at time of acquisition and the carrying value of that asset or liability at the time of acquisition); *minus (plus)*

- amortization of the parent company's share of the fair value increase (decrease) on the asset (liability) for the period since acquisition to the current Balance Sheet date; *minus (plus)*

- upstream and downstream intercompany profits (losses) that are unrealized as of the Balance Sheet date.

Goodwill The Goodwill to be recorded in the consolidated Balance Sheet is equal to:

- the excess of the cost of the investment over the parent company's share of the fair values of the subsidiary's net assets at the time of acquisition; *minus*

- the amount of any goodwill impairment that has been recognized in the period since the acquisition to the current Balance Sheet date.

Non-Controlling Interest - Balance Sheet The Non-Controlling Interest to be recorded in the consolidated Balance Sheet is an amount equal to the non-controlling interest's ownership percentage multiplied by:

- the book value of the subsidiary's common stock equity at the Balance Sheet date; *minus (plus)*

- upstream intercompany profits (losses) that are unrealized as of the Balance Sheet date.

Contributed Capital   The Contributed Capital to be recorded in the consolidated Balance Sheet is equal to the contributed capital from the single entity Balance Sheet of the parent company.

Retained Earnings   The Retained Earnings amount to be included in the consolidated Balance Sheet is calculated as follows:

- 100 percent of the Retained Earnings of the parent company; *plus (minus)*

- the parent company's share of the subsidiary's Retained Earnings (Deficit) since acquisition, adjusted for upstream profits (losses) that are unrealized as of the Balance Sheet date; *plus (minus)*

- 100 percent of the adjustments to consolidated expenses, revenues, gains, and losses for realized fair value changes during the period since acquisition to the current Balance Sheet date; *minus*

- 100 percent of any goodwill impairment that has been recognized since the acquisition to the current Balance Sheet date.

- downstream intercompany profits (losses) that are unrealized as of the Balance Sheet date.

Revenue   The amount of any revenue to be included in the consolidated Income Statement is calculated as follows:

- 100 percent of the amount reported in the parent company's financial statements; *plus*

- 100 percent of the amount reported in the subsidiary's financial statements; *minus*

- 100 percent of any intercompany amounts included in the parent or subsidiary figures; *minus (plus)*

- the parent's share of any fair value changes realized during the period through usage or sale of subsidiary assets (fair value amortization, depreciation, or depletion and amounts realized through the sale of subsidiary assets prior to the end of their economic life). It would be unusual for fair value realizations to be related to revenues. However, it could happen. For example, amortization of a fair value change on a long-term receivable would be treated as an adjustment of interest revenue. An additional example could result from the sale of an asset on which a fair value change has been recorded in the consolidated financial statements. If there was a gain (revenue) on the transaction, it would have to be adjusted for the realized fair value change; *minus (plus)*

- 100 percent of any upstream or downstream unrealized profits (losses) that are included in the parent or subsidiary company revenues (e.g., gain on an intercompany sale of land during the current year); *plus (minus)*

- 100 percent of any upstream or downstream unrealized profits (losses) that were unrealized in a previous period, but have become realized during the current period (e.g., gain on an intercompany sale of land in a previous year, with the land being resold outside the consolidated entity during the current year).

Expense   The amount of any expense to be included in the consolidated Income Statement is calculated as follows:

- 100 percent of the amount reported in the parent company's financial statements; *plus*

- 100 percent of the amount reported in the subsidiary's financial statements; *minus*

- 100 percent of any intercompany amounts included in the parent or subsidiary figures; *plus (minus)*

- the parent's share of any fair value changes realized during the period through usage or sale of subsidiary assets (fair value amortization, depreciation, or depletion and amounts realized through the sale of subsidiary assets prior to the end of their economic life).

- 100 percent of any upstream or downstream unrealized profits (losses) that are included in the parent or subsidiary company expenses (e.g., unrealized intercompany profits in the closing inventories would be added to the consolidated Cost Of Goods Sold); *minus (plus)*

- 100 percent of any upstream or downstream unrealized profits (losses) that were unrealized in a previous period, but have become realized during the current period (e.g., unrealized intercompany profits in the opening inventories would be subtracted from the consolidated Cost Of Goods Sold).

Goodwill Impairment Loss   If the required annual test of goodwill for impairment determines that any impairment has occurred during the current period, this amount will be recorded as a Goodwill Impairment Loss.

Non-Controlling Interest - Income Statement   The Non-Controlling Interest to be recorded in the consolidated Income Statement will be an amount equal to the non-controlling interest's ownership percentage multiplied by:

- the reported Net Income of the subsidiary; *minus (plus)*

- 100 percent of upstream unrealized intercompany profits (losses) that are included in the Net Income of the subsidiary (e.g., upstream unrealized profits in the closing inventories); *plus (minus)*

- 100 percent of upstream profits that were eliminated in a previous period because they were unrealized, but that have become realized during the current period (e.g., upstream unrealized profits in the opening inventories).

Note that, if the subsidiary has extraordinary items or results from discontinued operations, this Non-Controlling Interest will be based on the subsidiary's Income Before Extraordinary Items And Discontinued Operations. Also note that, in situations where there are preferred shares with a prior claim on the income of the subsidiary, the Non-Controlling Interest to be disclosed in the consolidated Income Statement will include such claims.

Consolidated Net Income   Consolidated Net Income can be calculated as follows:

- 100 percent of the parent company's Net Income, excluding dividends received from the subsidiary; *plus (minus)*

- the parent's share of the sum of:

   - the subsidiary's reported Net Income (Net Loss); *minus (plus)*

   - upstream unrealized intercompany profits (losses) that are included in the Net Income of the subsidiary (e.g., upstream unrealized profits in the closing inventories); *plus (minus)*

   - upstream profits that were eliminated in a previous period because they were unrealized, but that have become realized during the current period (e.g., upstream unrealized profits in the opening inventories).

   minus (plus)

- the parent's share of any fair value changes realized during the period through usage or sale of subsidiary assets (fair value amortization, depreciation, or depletion and amounts realized through the sale of subsidiary assets prior to the end of their economic life); *minus*

- any Goodwill Impairment Loss that is recognized during the period; *minus (plus)*

- 100 percent of downstream profits (losses) that are included in the Net Income of the parent (e.g., downstream unrealized profits in the closing inventories); *plus (minus)*

- 100 percent of downstream profits that were eliminated in a previous period because they were unrealized, but that have become realized during the current period (e.g., downstream unrealized profits in the opening inventories).

6-149.   This comprehensive list of definitions can be used to solve any basic consolidation problem in which the investment in the subsidiary is carried by the cost method. We would encourage the use of them in solving the problems which accompany this Chapter.

Walk Through Problem

Note   This problem is an extension of the Walk Through Problem that was presented at the end of Chapters Four and Five. As previously explained, these problems provide you with a fill-in-the-blank solution format to assist you in solving the problem. These problems are designed to be an easy introduction to solving the type of problem illustrated in the Chapter.

Basic Data   On December 31, 2002, the Puff Company purchased 60 percent of the outstanding voting shares of the Snuff Company for $720,000 in cash. On that date, subsequent to the completion of the business combination, the Balance Sheets of the Puff and Snuff Companies and the fair values of Snuff's identifiable assets and liabilities were as follows:

| | December 31, 2002 Balance Sheets | | Fair Values |
	Puff	Snuff	For Snuff
Cash And Accounts Receivable	$ 350,000	$ 200,000	$200,000
Inventories	950,000	500,000	450,000
Investment In Snuff	720,000	-0-	N/A
Plant And Equipment (Net)	2,400,000	700,000	800,000
Total Assets	$4,420,000	$1,400,000	
Current Liabilities	$ 400,000	$ 100,000	$100,000
Long-Term Liabilities	1,000,000	400,000	360,000
No Par Common Stock	1,000,000	800,000	N/A
Retained Earnings	2,020,000	100,000	N/A
Total Equities	$4,420,000	$1,400,000	

The December 31, 2002 Inventories of Snuff are sold during 2003. The Plant And Equipment of Snuff on December 31, 2002 has an estimated useful life of 10 years while the Long-Term Liabilities that were present on that date mature on December 31, 2005. Both Companies use the straight line method of amortization. Puff carries its Investment In Snuff by the cost method.

The Income Statements for the year ending December 31, 2006 and the Balance Sheets as at December 31, 2006 of the Puff and Snuff Companies are as follows:

Income Statements
For The Year Ending December 31, 2006

	Puff Company	Snuff Company
Sales	$3,700,000	$2,000,000
Other Revenues	200,000	50,000
Total Revenues	$3,900,000	$2,050,000
Cost Of Goods Sold	$2,000,000	$1,100,000
Depreciation Expense	600,000	400,000
Other Expenses	900,000	350,000
Total Expenses	$3,500,000	$1,850,000
Net Income	$ 400,000	$ 200,000

Balance Sheets
As At December 31, 2006

	Puff Company	Snuff Company
Cash	$ 80,000	$ 75,000
Accounts Receivable	500,000	325,000
Inventories	1,375,000	750,000
Investment In Snuff	720,000	-0-
Plant And Equipment (Net)	2,325,000	1,100,000
Total Assets	$5,000,000	$2,250,000
Current Liabilities	$ 400,000	$ 220,000
Long Term Liabilities	1,000,000	750,000
No Par Common Stock	1,000,000	800,000
Retained Earnings	2,600,000	480,000
Total Equities	$5,000,000	$2,250,000

Other Information:

1. During 2006, Puff declared and paid $150,000 in dividends while Snuff declared and paid $75,000 in dividends.

2. Included in the 2006 Sales of Snuff are sales of $300,000 to Puff on which Snuff earned a gross profit of $125,000. Of these sales, $60,000 remain in the December 31, 2006 inventories of Puff. The January 1, 2006 inventories of Puff contained merchandise purchased from Snuff for $75,000 on which Snuff had earned a gross profit of $35,000. Puff owes Snuff $45,000 on December 31, 2006 for the merchandise purchases.

3. During 2006, Puff had sales of $175,000 to Snuff. Of these sales, $80,000 are on hand in the December 31, 2006 inventories of Snuff. Of the $250,000 of sales from Puff to Snuff in 2005, $110,000 were not resold in 2005. Puff's intercompany sales are priced to provide a gross margin of 40 percent of sales price.

4. Goodwill has been tested for impairment in the years 2003 through 2006. The test procedures found impairment or $16,000 in 2003, an amount that was recognized as a Goodwill Impairment Loss in that year. A further impairment loss of $20,000 was found and recognized in 2004. No impairment was found in 2005 or 2006.

5. On January 1, 2003, the Snuff Company sold the Puff Company a machine for $250,000. The machine had been purchased by Snuff on January 1, 2002 for $360,000 and had an estimated useful life on that date of six years with no salvage value expected. On December 31, 2002, the date of the business combination, this machine had a fair value that was equal to its carrying value.

5. On December 12, 2006, the Snuff Company sold a piece of land that it had purchased for $15,000 on July 21, 2002 to Puff for $33,000. This price is to be paid on February 24, 2007.

Required: For the Puff Company and its subsidiary the Snuff Company, prepare:

A. A consolidated Income Statement for the year ending December 31, 2006.

B. A consolidated Statement Of Retained Earnings for the year ending December 31, 2006.

C. A consolidated Balance Sheet as at December 31, 2006.

In addition, provide calculations which verify consolidated Net Income for the year ending December 31, 2006, the December 31, 2006 consolidated Retained Earnings, and the December 31, 2006 Non-Controlling Interest in net assets.

Walk Through Problem Solution Format

Step A - Investment Analysis

	60 Percent	100 Percent
Purchase Price	$	$
Book Value	($)	($)
Differential	$	$
Fair Value Decrease On Inventories	$	$
Fair Value Increase On Plant And Equipment	($)	($)
Fair Value Decrease On Long-Term Liabilities	($)	($)
Goodwill	$	$

Step A - Investment Elimination Entry

No Par Common Stock	$	
Retained Earnings	$	
Plant And Equipment (Net)	$	
Long-Term Liabilities	$	
Goodwill	$	
Investment In Snuff		$
Inventories		$
Non-Controlling Interest (Balance Sheet)		$

Step B(1) - Intercompany Assets And Liabilities

Current Liabilities	$	
Accounts Receivable		$
Current Liabilities	$	
Accounts Receivable		$

Step B(2) - Fair Value Adjustment On The Inventories

Inventories	$	
Retained Earnings		$

Step B(2) - Fair Value Adjustment On Plant And Equipment

Retained Earnings - Snuff	$	
Depreciation Expense	$	
Plant and Equipment (Net)		$

Step B(2) - Fair Value Adjustment On Long-Term Liabilities

Retained Earnings - Snuff	$	
Other Expenses	$	
Long-Term Liabilities		$

Step B(3) - Goodwill Impairment

Retained Earnings - Snuff	$	
Goodwill Impairment Loss	$	
Goodwill		$

Step B(4) - Intercompany Expenses And Revenues

Sales	$	
Cost Of Goods Sold		$
Other Revenues	$	
Other Expenses		$

Step B(5) - Intercompany Dividends

Other Revenues	$	
Non-Controlling Interest	$	
Dividends Declared		$

Step B(6) - Upstream Intercompany Inventory Profits

Cost Of Goods Sold $

       Inventories $

Retained Earnings - Snuff $

       Cost Of Goods Sold $

Step B(6) - Downstream Intercompany Inventory Profits

Cost Of Goods Sold $

       Inventories $

Retained Earnings - Puff $

       Cost Of Goods Sold $

Step B(6) - Upstream Sale Of Machine

Plant And Equipment $

Depreciation Expense $

       Retained Earnings - Snuff $

Step B(6) - Upstream Sale Of Land

Other Revenues $

       Plant And Equipment (Net) $

Step C - Retained Earnings Distribution Schedule

Snuff's January 1, 2006 Balance	$	
Snuff's Balance At Acquisition	($	)
Balance Since Acquisition	$	
Upstream Profits:		
Inventories	($	)
Equipment	$	
Adjusted Balance Since Acquisition	$	
Non-Controlling Interest		%
Available To The Controlling Interest	$	
Step B Adjustments:		
Fair Value Decrease On Inventories	$	
Fair Value Increase On Plant and Equipment	($	)
Fair Value Decrease On Long-Term Liabilities	($	)
Goodwill Impairment Losses	($	)
To Consolidated Retained Earnings	$	

Step C - Retained Earnings Distribution Entry

Retained Earnings - Snuff	$	
Non-Controlling Interest	$	
Consolidated Retained Earnings		$

Puff Company And Subsidiary
Consolidated Income Statement
For The Year Ending December 31, 2006

Sales	$
Other Revenues	$
Total Revenues	$
Cost Of Goods Sold	$
Depreciation Expense	$
Other Expenses	$
Non-Controlling Interest	$
Total Expenses	$
Consolidated Net Income	$

Puff Company And Subsidiary
Consolidated Statement Of Retained Earnings
For The Year Ending December 31, 2006

Balance - January 1, 2006	$
Consolidated Net Income	$
Available For Distribution	$
Dividends Declared	$
Balance - December 31, 2006	$

Verification Of Consolidated Net Income

Puff Company's Net Income		$
Intercompany Dividend Revenues		($)
Puff's Net Income Less Dividends		$
Snuff Company's Reported Income	$	
Upstream Adjustments:		
Profits In Ending Inventories	($)	
Profits In Opening Inventories	$	
Realized Loss On Equipment	($)	
Upstream Gain on Land Sale	($)	
Adjusted Subsidiary Income	$	
Controlling Percent		%
Equity Pickup		$
Step B Adjustments:		
Fair Value Increase On Plant and Equipment		($)
Fair Value Decrease On Long-Term Liabilities		($)
Downstream Adjustments:		
Profits in Ending Inventories		($)
Profits in Opening Inventories		$
Consolidated Net Income		$

Verification Of Consolidated Retained Earnings

Puff's Closing Balance		$
Snuff's Closing Balance	$	
Balance At Acquisition	($)	

Balance Since Acquisition	$	
Upstream Adjustments:		
Profits in Ending Inventories	($)	
Unrealized Loss on Equipment	$	
Unrealized Gain on Land Sale	($)	

Adjusted Balance Since Acquisition	$	
Controlling Percent	%	

Equity Pickup		$
Step B Adjustments:		
Fair Value Decrease On Inventories		$
Fair Value Increase On Plant and Equipment		($)
Fair Value Decrease On Long-Term Liabilities		($)
Goodwill Impairment Losses		($)
Downstream Closing Inventory Profits		($)

Consolidated Retained Earnings As At December 31, 2006		$

Puff Company And Subsidiary
Consolidated Balance Sheet
As At December 31, 2006

Cash	$
Accounts Receivable	$
Inventories	$
Investment In Snuff	$
Plant And Equipment (Net)	$
Goodwill	$
Total Assets	$
Current Liabilities	$
Long-Term Liabilities	$
Non-Controlling Interest	$
No Par Common Stock	$
Retained Earnings	$
Total Equities	$

Verification Of The Non-Controlling Interest In Consolidated Net Assets

At Acquisition (Step A)	$
Dividends Declared By Snuff (Step B)	($)
Retained Earnings Distribution (Step C)	$
From Consolidated Net Income	$
Non-Controlling Interest As At December 31, 2006	$

Walk Through Problem Solution

Step A - Investment Analysis

	60 Percent	100 Percent
Purchase Price	$720,000	$1,200,000
Book Value	(540,000)	(900,000)
Differential	$180,000	$ 300,000
Fair Value Decrease On Inventories	30,000	50,000
Fair Value Increase On Plant And Equipment	(60,000)	(100,000)
Fair Value Decrease On Long-Term Liabilities	(24,000)	(40,000)
Goodwill	$126,000	$ 210,000

Step A - Investment Elimination Entry

No Par Common Stock	$800,000	
Retained Earnings	100,000	
Plant And Equipment	60,000	
Long-Term Liabilities	24,000	
Goodwill	126,000	
Investment In Snuff		$720,000
Inventories		30,000
Non-Controlling Interest		360,000

Step B(1) - Intercompany Assets And Liabilities

Current Liabilities	$45,000	
Accounts Receivable		$45,000

(Intercompany Merchandise Sales)

Current Liabilities	$33,000	
Accounts Receivable		$33,000

(Intercompany Land Sale)

Step B(2) - Fair Value Adjustment On The Inventories

Inventories	$30,000	
Retained Earnings - Snuff		$30,000

Step B(2) - Fair Value Adjustment On Plant And Equipment

Retained Earnings - Snuff	$18,000	
Depreciation Expense	6,000	
Plant And Equipment (Net)		$24,000

(Annual Adjustment = $60,000/10 = $6,000/Year)

Step B(2) - Fair Value Adjustment On Long Term Liabilities

Retained Earnings - Snuff	$24,000	
Other Expenses	-0-	
Long-Term Liabilities		$24,000

(There is no effect on consolidated Net Income
since the Long-Term Liabilities have matured.)

Step B(3) - Goodwill Impairment

Retained Earnings - Snuff ($16,000 + $20,000)	$36,000	
Goodwill		$36,000

Step B(4) - Intercompany Expenses And Revenues

Sales ($300,000 + $175,000)	$475,000	
Cost Of Goods Sold		$475,000

Step B(5) - Intercompany Dividends

Other Revenues [(60%)($75,000)]	$45,000	
Non-Controlling Interest (Balance Sheet)	30,000	
Dividends Declared		$75,000

Step B(5) - Upstream Intercompany Inventory Profits

Cost Of Goods Sold	$25,000	
Inventories		$25,000

(Unrealized Intercompany Profits in Closing Inventories = [($60,000/$300,000)($125,000)])

Retained Earnings - Snuff	$35,000	
Cost Of Goods Sold		$35,000

(Unrealized Profits in Opening Inventories - Given)

Step B(5) - Downstream Inventory Profits

Cost Of Goods Sold	$32,000	
Inventories		$32,000

(Unrealized Profits in Closing Inventories = 40% of $80,000)

Retained Earnings - Puff	$44,000	
Cost Of Goods Sold		$44,000

(Unrealized Profits in Opening Inventories = 40% of $110,000)

Step B(5) - Upstream Sale Of Machine

Plant And Equipment (Net)	$10,000	
Depreciation Expense	10,000	
Retained Earnings - Snuff		$20,000

(Annual Adjustment = [$360,000 - $60,000 - $250,000]/5 years = $10,000/Year)

Step B(5) - Upstream Sale Of Land

Other Revenues ($33,000 - $15,000)	$18,000	
Plant And Equipment (Net)		$18,000

Step C - Retained Earnings Distribution Schedule

Snuff's January 1, 2006 Balance ($480,000 - $200,000 + $75,000)	$355,000
Snuff's Balance At Acquisition	(100,000)
Balance Since Acquisition	$255,000
Opening Upstream Profits:	
Inventories	(35,000)
Equipment	20,000
Adjusted Balance Since Acquisition	$240,000
Non-Controlling Interest [(40%)($240,000)]	(96,000)
Available To The Controlling Interest	$144,000
Step B Adjustments:	
Fair Value Decrease On Inventory	30,000
Fair Value Increase On Plant And Equipment	(18,000)
Fair Value Decrease On Long-Term Liabilities	(24,000)
Goodwill Impairment Losses	(36,000)
To Consolidated Retained Earnings	$ 96,000

Step C - Retained Earnings Distribution Entry

Retained Earnings - Snuff	$192,000	
Non-Controlling Interest		$ 96,000
Consolidated Retained Earnings		96,000

Puff Company And Subsidiary
Consolidated Income Statement
For The Year Ending December 31, 2006

Sales ($3,700,000 + $2,000,000 - $475,000)	$5,225,000
Other Revenues ($200,000 + $50,000 - $45,000 - $18,000)	187,000
Total Revenues	$5,412,000
Cost Of Goods Sold ($2,000,000 + $1,100,000 - $475,000	
+ $25,000 - $35,000 + $32,000 - $44,000)	$2,603,000
Depreciation Expense ($600,000 + $400,000 + $6,000 + $10,000)	1,016,000
Other Expenses ($900,000 + $350,000)	1,250,000
Non-Controlling Interest	
[(40%)($200,000 - $25,000 + $35,000 - $18,000 - $10,000)]	72,800
Total Expenses	$4,941,800
Consolidated Net Income	$ 470,200

Puff Company And Subsidiary
Consolidated Statement Of Retained Earnings
For The Year Ending December 31, 2006

Opening Balance (See Note)	$2,402,000
Consolidated Net Income	470,200
Available For Distribution	$2,872,200
Dividends Declared (Puff's Only)	(150,000)
Closing Balance	$2,722,200

Note - The opening consolidated Retained Earnings consists of Puff's opening balance of $2,350,000 ($2,600,000 - $400,000 + $150,000) plus the Step C allocation of $96,000 less the opening unrealized downstream inventory profits of $44,000.

Verification Of Consolidated Net Income

Puff Company's Net Income		$400,000
Intercompany Dividend Revenues		(45,000)
Puff's Net Income Less Dividends		$355,000
Snuff Company's Reported Income	$200,000	
Upstream Adjustments:		
Profits In Ending Inventories	(25,000)	
Profits In Opening Inventories	35,000	
Realized Loss On Equipment	(10,000)	
Upstream Gain on Land Sale	(18,000)	
Adjusted Subsidiary Income	$182,000	
Controlling Percent	60%	109,200
Step B Adjustments:		
Fair Value Depreciation		(6,000)
Liability Amortization		-0-
Downstream Adjustments:		
Profits in Ending Inventories		(32,000)
Profits in Opening Inventories		44,000
Consolidated Net Income		$470,200

Verification Of Consolidated Retained Earnings

Puff's Closing Balance		$2,600,000
Snuff's Closing Balance	$480,000	
Balance At Acquisition	(100,000)	
Balance Since Acquisition	$380,000	
Upstream Adjustments:		
Profits in Ending Inventories	(25,000)	
Unrealized Loss on Equipment	10,000	
Unrealized Gain on Land Sale	(18,000)	
Realized Balance Since Acquisition	$347,000	
Controlling Percent	60%	208,200
Step B Adjustments:		
Inventories		30,000
Plant (4 Years At $6,000)		(24,000)
Long-Term Liabilities (Matured)		(24,000)
Goodwill ($16,000 + $20,000)		(36,000)
Downstream Closing Inventory Profits		(32,000)
Consolidated Retained Earnings As At December 31, 2006		$2,722,200

Puff Company And Subsidiary
Consolidated Balance Sheet
As At December 31, 2006

Cash ($80,000 + $75,000)	$ 155,000
Accounts Receivable ($500,000 + $325,000 - $45,000 - $33,000)	747,000
Inventories ($1,375,000 + $750,000	
- $30,000 + $30,000 - $25,000 - $32,000)	2,068,000
Investment In Snuff ($720,000 - $720,000)	Nil
Plant And Equipment (Net) ($2,325,000 + $1,100,000	
+ $60,000 - $24,000 + $10,000 - $18,000)	3,453,000
Goodwill ($126,000 - $36,000)	90,000
Total Assets	$6,513,000

Current Liabilities ($400,000 + $220,000 - $45,000 - $33,000)	$ 542,000
Long Term Liabilities ($1,000,000 + $750,000 - $24,000 + $24,000)	1,750,000
Non-Controlling Interest	
[(40%)($1,280,000 - $25,000 + $10,000 - $18,000)]	498,800
Common Stock (Puff's Only)	1,000,000
Retained Earnings (See Statement)	2,722,200
Total Equities	$6,513,000

Verification Of The Non-Controlling Interest In Consolidated Net Assets

At Acquisition (Step A)	$360,000
Dividends Declared By Snuff (Step B)	(30,000)
Retained Earnings Distribution (Step C)	96,000
From Consolidated Net Income	72,800
Non-Controlling Interest As At December 31, 2006	$498,800

Problems For Self Study

(The solutions for these problems can be found following Chapter 16 of the text.)

Self Study Problem Six - 1

(This is an extension of Self Study Problem Five-1)

On December 31, 2002, the Pastel Company purchased 90 percent of the outstanding voting shares of the Shade Company for $5,175,000 in cash. On that date, the Shade Company had No Par Common Stock of $2,000,000 and Retained Earnings of $4,000,000. All of the Shade Company's identifiable assets and liabilities had carrying values that were equal to their fair values except for:

1. Equipment which had fair values that were $1,000,000 less than their carrying values and a remaining useful life of 10 years.

2. Land which had a fair value that was $100,000 greater than its carrying value.

3. Accounts Receivable with fair values that were $50,000 less than their carrying values.

4. Long-Term Liabilities which had fair values that were $200,000 less than their carrying values and mature on December 31, 2007.

The Balance Sheets of the Pastel Company and the Shade Company as at December 31, 2007 were as follows:

Pastel and Shade Companies
Balance Sheets
As At December 31, 2007

	Pastel	Shade
Cash and Current Receivables	$ 2,625,000	$ 800,000
Inventories	8,000,000	2,000,000
Equipment (Net)	24,000,000	4,000,000
Buildings (Net)	10,000,000	2,000,000
Investment in Shade (Cost)	5,175,000	-0-
Land	2,000,000	1,200,000
Total Assets	$51,800,000	$10,000,000
Dividends Payable	$ -0-	$ 100,000
Current Liabilities	1,800,000	900,000
Long-Term Liabilities	10,000,000	1,000,000
No Par Common Stock	20,000,000	2,000,000
Retained Earnings	20,000,000	6,000,000
Total Equities	$51,800,000	$10,000,000

The Income Statements of the Pastel and Shade Companies for the year ending December 31, 2007 were as follows:

Pastel and Shade Companies
Income Statements
For The Year Ending December 31, 2007

	Pastel	Shade
Sales	$8,000,000	$2,000,000
Gain on Sale of Land	500,000	-0-
Other Revenues	800,000	100,000
Total Revenues	$9,300,000	$2,100,000
Cost of Goods Sold	$3,800,000	$ 800,000
Depreciation Expense	1,400,000	300,000
Other Expenses	2,000,000	400,000
Total Expenses	$7,200,000	$1,500,000
Net Income	$2,100,000	$ 600,000

Other Information:

1. In each of the years since Pastel acquired control over Shade, the goodwill arising on this business combination transaction has been tested for impairment. After completing the annual impairment test, it was determined that the goodwill impairment loss for 2007 was $15,000. No impairment was found in any of the other years since acquisition.

2. Both Companies use the straight line method to calculate all depreciation and amortization charges and the First-In, First-Out inventory flow assumption.

3. Pastel uses the cost method to carry its Investment in Shade.

4. The Sales account in the Pastel Company's Income Statement includes only sales of merchandise. All other income is accounted for in Other Revenues.

5. During 2007, Pastel charged Shade $100,000 for management fees. None of this amount has been paid during 2007.

6. During 2007, dividends of $200,000 were declared and paid by Pastel and dividends of $100,000 were declared by Shade. On December 31, 2007, the dividends that were declared by the Shade Company had not yet been paid.

7. During 2007, Shade sold to Pastel $500,000 worth of merchandise of which 75 percent had been resold by Pastel in 2007. Pastel owes Shade $75,000 on December 31, 2007 due to these purchases. The December 31, 2006 Inventories of Pastel contained $300,000 of merchandise purchased from Shade in 2006. The Shade Company's sales are priced to provide it with a 60 percent gross margin on its sales price.

8. During 2006, Pastel sold $300,000 of merchandise to the Shade Company and earned a total gross profit of $120,000 on these sales. On December 31, 2006, $150,000 of this merchandise is still in the inventories of Shade. During 2007, Pastel sold merchandise which had cost it $60,000 to Shade for $150,000. None of this merchandise was resold in 2007. Shade has not paid for these 2007 purchases as at December 31, 2007.

9. On January 1, 2004, Shade sold a piece of equipment that it had purchased on January 1, 2001 for $180,000 to Pastel for $120,000. On January 1, 2001, the machine had an estimated useful life of 18 years with no net salvage value and there is no change in these estimates at the time of the sale to Pastel.

10. On December 30, 2007, Pastel sold to Shade for cash of $1,500,000, a Building with a net book value of $800,000 and the Land it was situated on which had originally cost $200,000. Shade allocated $1,100,000 of the purchase price to the Building and the remainder to the Land. The Building has an estimated remaining useful life of 25 years on this date. The gain on this sale is disclosed separately for reporting purposes on Pastel's books.

Required: Prepare, for the Pastel Company and its subsidiary, the Shade Company:

A. The consolidated Income Statement for the year ending December 31, 2007.

B. The consolidated Statement of Retained Earnings for the year ending December 31, 2007.

C. The consolidated Balance Sheet as at December 31, 2007.

Self Study Problem Six - 2

On December 31, 2002, the Plate Company purchased 80 percent of the outstanding shares of the Stone Company for $7,800,000 in cash. On this date, the identifiable assets and liabilities of the Stone Company had carrying values and fair values as follows:

	Carrying Values	Fair Values
Cash	$ 500,000	$ 500,000
Accounts Receivable	1,500,000	1,500,000
Inventories	3,000,000	4,000,000
Land	1,500,000	1,000,000
Plant and Equipment	9,000,000	8,000,000
Accumulated Depreciation	(3,000,000)	-0-
Software Programs	-0-	500,000
Total Assets	$12,500,000	
Current Liabilities	$ 1,000,000	$ 1,000,000
Long-Term Liabilities	4,500,000	6,000,000
Common Stock - No Par	3,000,000	
Unrestricted Retained Earnings	3,000,000	
Reserve for Contingencies	1,000,000	
Total Equities	$12,500,000	

On December 31, 2002, the Plant and Equipment of the Stone Company had a remaining useful life of 20 years. The December 31, 2002 Inventories of Stone were sold in 2003. On December 31, 2002, the Stone Company had internally developed software that was patent protected. The asset was written off by Stone in 2004 when technological advances made the software obsolete.

On December 31, 2007, the adjusted trial balances for the Plate Company and the Stone Company are as follows:

	Plate	Stone
Cash	$ 3,000,000	$ 700,000
Accounts Receivable	7,500,000	2,100,000
Inventories	14,300,000	5,600,000
Land	9,000,000	2,500,000
Plant and Equipment	26,400,000	12,000,000
Patents	1,400,000	-0-
Investment in Stone (At Cost)	7,800,000	-0-
Cost of Goods Sold	6,400,000	3,400,000
Other Expenses	3,800,000	1,600,000
Dividends Declared	2,000,000	1,000,000
Total Debits	$81,600,000	$28,900,000
Accumulated Depreciation	$10,600,000	$ 6,500,000
Current Liabilities	8,500,000	1,200,000
Long-Term Liabilities	15,000,000	4,500,000
Common Stock - No Par	20,000,000	3,000,000
Reserve for Contingencies	-0-	500,000
Unrestricted Retained Earnings	11,000,000	6,200,000
Total Revenues	16,500,000	7,000,000
Total Credits	$81,600,000	$28,900,000

Other Information:

1. There have been no additions or disposals of Plant and Equipment by the Stone Company between December 31, 2002 and December 31, 2007. The land on the books of the Stone Company on December 31, 2002 has not been sold.

2. In each of the years since Plate acquired control over Stone, the goodwill arising on this business combination transaction has been tested for impairment. No impairment was found in any of the years since acquisition.

3. All of the Long-Term Liabilities of the Stone Company mature on December 31, 2011.

4. On January 1, 2004, the Stone Company purchased a Patent for $1,100,000. On that date, the remaining legal life of the Patent was 11 years. On January 1, 2005 the Patent had a carrying value on the Stone Company's books of $1,000,000. At this time, the Patent was sold to the Plate Company for $2,000,000.

5. During 2007, the Plate Company sold Land to the Stone Company for $1,000,000. The carrying value of the Land on the books of the Plate Company was $500,000.

6. During 2007, $2,000,000 of the Stone Company's Sales were made to the Plate Company. A total of $500,000 of this merchandise remains in the December 31, 2007 Inventories of the Plate Company. The December 31, 2006 Inventories of the Plate Company contained merchandise purchased from the Stone Company for $800,000. All intercompany sales are priced to provide the selling Company with a gross profit margin on sales price of 30 percent.

7. Both Companies use the straight line method to calculate all amortization.

Required:

A. Prepare a consolidated Income Statement for the Plate Company and its subsidiary, the

Stone Company, for the year ending December 31, 2007.

B. Prepare a consolidated Statement of Retained Earnings for the Plate Company and its subsidiary, the Stone Company, for the year ending December 31, 2007.

C. Prepare a consolidated Balance Sheet for the Plate Company and its subsidiary, the Stone Company, as at December 31, 2007.

Self Study Problem Six - 3

On January 1, 2002, the Prime Company acquired 60 percent of the outstanding voting shares of the Sublime Company for $3 million in cash. On this date, the Sublime Company had No Par Common Stock of $3 million and Retained Earnings of $2 million. All of Sublime's identifiable assets and liabilities had fair values that were equal to their carrying values except for the Accounts Receivable which had a total net realizable value that was $100,000 less than its stated value and a piece of equipment with a fair value that was $400,000 less than its carrying value and had a remaining useful life of 3 years.

Both Companies use the straight line method to calculate all depreciation and amortization expenses. Prime carries its investment in Sublime by the cost method.

On December 31, 2003, the Balance Sheets of the Prime Company and its subsidiary, the Sublime Company, are as follows:

Balance Sheets
As At December 31, 2003

	Prime	Sublime
Cash and Current Receivables	$ 1,600,000	$ 1,000,000
Inventories	2,400,000	1,500,000
Investment in Sublime (At Cost)	3,000,000	-0-
Long-Term Receivables	1,500,000	-0-
Plant and Equipment (Net)	14,000,000	8,500,000
Land	5,000,000	2,000,000
Total Assets	$27,500,000	$13,000,000
Current Liabilities	$ 4,500,000	$ 2,000,000
Long-Term Liabilities	5,000,000	3,000,000
No Par Common Stock	6,000,000	3,000,000
Retained Earnings	12,000,000	5,000,000
Total Equities	$27,500,000	$13,000,000

Other Information:

1. The Prime Company sold merchandise to the Sublime Company in 2002 of which $300,000 remained in the December 31, 2002 Inventories of Sublime. This merchandise was sold in 2003 and Prime made no further sales of inventories to Sublime in 2003. Prime's sales are priced to provide it with a 40 percent gross margin on cost.

2. Sublime's Sales in 2003 included $500,000 in sales to Prime. Of these sales, $200,000 remain in the December 31, 2003 Inventories of Prime. Prime's January 1, 2003 inventories contained $400,000 of merchandise purchased from Sublime of which $300,000 was purchased in 2002 and sold in 2003. The remaining $100,000 was specialized merchandise purchased in 2001, prior to the business combination and $50,000 of this specialized merchandise remains in Prime's December 31, 2003 Inventories. Sublime's sales are priced to provide it with a 25 percent gross margin on cost.

3. On July 1, 2003, the Sublime Company sold a machine it had built for a cost of $200,000 to the Prime Company for $150,000. The machine had an estimated useful life on July 1, 2003 of 5 years. On December 31, 2003, the Prime Company has a liability outstanding of 80 percent of the purchase price and this will be paid in 2004.

4. The Sublime Company purchased Land for $2 million from Prime on November 1, 2002. The land was originally purchased by Prime for $1 million. The purchase price is to be paid in 5 equal installments of $400,000 on January 1 of each year subsequent to the sale.

5. During 2003, Prime earned Net Income of $2,000,000 and paid dividends of $400,000 and Sublime earned Net Income of $500,000 and paid dividends of $100,000.

6. In each of the years since Prime acquired control over Sublime, the goodwill arising on this business combination transaction has been tested for impairment. No impairment was found in any of the years since acquisition.

Required: Prepare a consolidated Balance Sheet for the Prime Company and its subsidiary, the Sublime Company, as at December 31, 2003.

Self Study Problem Six - 4

On January 1, 2002, the Pork Company purchased 80 percent of the outstanding voting shares of the Salt Company for $1 million in cash. At the acquisition date, the carrying value of the net assets of Salt was equal to $1 million and all of its identifiable assets and liabilities had fair values that were equal to their carrying values, except for an issue of 10 percent coupon Bonds Payable which had a fair value which was $100,000 less than its carrying value. The bonds mature on January 1, 2012.

Salt Company does not own any intangible asset that results from contractual or other legal rights, or is capable of being separated or divided and sold, transferred, licensed, rented, or exchanged at any time.

The condensed Income Statements for the two companies for the year ending December 31, 2005 are as follows:

Pork and Salt Companies
Income Statements
For The Year Ending December 31, 2005

	Pork	Salt
Sales	$600,000	$400,000
Cost of Goods Sold	$250,000	$300,000
Other Expenses	300,000	150,000
Total Expenses	$550,000	$450,000
Income (Loss) Before Extraordinary Items	$ 50,000	($ 50,000)
Extraordinary Gain (Loss)	100,000	(200,000)
Net Income (Loss)	$150,000	($250,000)

Other Information

1. In each of the years since Pork acquired the shares of Salt, the goodwill arising on this business combination transaction has been tested for impairment. In 2005, a Goodwill Impairment Loss of $40,000 was recognized. No impairment was found in any of the other years since the shares were acquired.

2. On January 1, 2004, the Salt Company sold a building to the Pork Company for $4,500,000. When Salt purchased the building on January 1, 1999 for $5,500,000, it had an estimated useful life of 20 years.

3. During 2005, Pork paid $100,000 in dividends and no dividends were paid by Salt.

4. Both Companies use the straight line method to calculate depreciation and amortization.

Required:

A. Prepare a consolidated Income Statement for the Pork Company and its subsidiary, the Salt Company, for the year ending December 31, 2005.

B. Assume that the Pork Company does not classify the Salt Company as a subsidiary. Prepare an Income Statement for the Pork Company for the year ending December 31, 2005 assuming it uses the equity method to account for its investment in the Salt Company.

Self Study Problem Six - 5

On December 31, 2002, the Rosebud Company purchased 20 percent of the outstanding voting shares of the Ginko Company for $600,000 in cash. On that date, the Ginko Company's Balance Sheet and the fair values of its identifiable assets and liabilities were as follows:

	Carrying Values	Fair Values
Cash And Current Receivables	$ 300,000	$ 300,000
Inventories	1,000,000	800,000
Plant And Equipment (Net)	2,000,000	2,400,000
Total Assets	$3,300,000	
Current Liabilities	$ 200,000	$ 200,000
Long-Term Liabilities	600,000	600,000
Common Stock - No Par	1,000,000	
Retained Earnings	1,500,000	
Total Equities	$3,300,000	

On this date, the remaining useful life of the Ginko Company's Plant And Equipment is estimated to be 10 years.

On December 31, 2005, the Rosebud Company purchased an additional 55 percent of the outstanding voting shares of the Ginko Company for $1,705,000 in cash. This increases its total percentage of ownership to 75 percent. On that date, the Ginko Company's Balance Sheet and the fair values of its identifiable assets and liabilities were as follows:

	Carrying Values	Fair Values
Cash And Current Receivables	$ 500,000	$ 500,000
Inventories	1,375,000	1,375,000
Land	425,000	475,000
Plant And Equipment (Net)	1,400,000	1,600,000
Total Assets	$3,700,000	
Current Liabilities	$ 300,000	$ 300,000
Long-Term Liabilities	600,000	700,000
Common Stock - No Par	1,000,000	
Retained Earnings	1,800,000	
Total Equities	$3,700,000	

There has been no purchase or sale of Plant And Equipment by the Ginko Company during the years 2003 through 2005. The Long-Term Liabilities mature on December 31, 2025. The Rosebud Company accounts for its Investment In Ginko by the cost method.

The Income Statements and Statements of Retained Earnings of the Rosebud and Ginko Companies for the year ending December 31, 2010, and their Balance Sheets as at December 31, 2010 were as follows:

Balance Sheets
As At December 31, 2010

	Rosebud	Ginko
Cash And Current Receivables	$ 500,000	$ 600,000
Inventories	600,000	1,200,000
Investment In Ginko	2,305,000	-0-
Land	795,000	500,000
Plant And Equipment (Net)	2,900,000	2,200,000
Total Assets	$7,100,000	$4,500,000
Current Liabilities	$ 500,000	$ 400,000
Long-Term Liabilities	1,000,000	600,000
Common Stock - No Par	2,000,000	1,000,000
Retained Earnings	3,600,000	2,500,000
Total Equities	$7,100,000	$4,500,000

Income Statements
For The Year Ending December 31, 2010

	Rosebud	Ginko
Sales Of Merchandise	$5,000,000	$2,000,000
Other Revenues	200,000	100,000
Total Revenues	$5,200,000	$2,100,000
Cost Of Goods Sold	$2,500,000	$ 800,000
Other Expenses and Losses	1,000,000	900,000
Total Expenses and Losses	$3,500,000	$1,700,000
Net Income	$1,700,000	$ 400,000

Statements Of Retained Earnings
For The Year Ending December 31, 2010

	Rosebud	Ginko
Opening Balance	$2,500,000	$2,200,000
Net Income	1,700,000	400,000
Balance Available	$4,200,000	$2,600,000
Dividends Declared	600,000	100,000
Closing Balance	$3,600,000	$2,500,000

Other Information:

1. In each of the years since Rosebud acquired control over Ginko, the goodwill arising on this business combination transaction has been tested for impairment. No impairment was found in any of the years since acquisition.

2. There has been no sale of Plant And Equipment or Land by the Ginko Company during the years under consideration except for a piece of equipment which was purchased on January 1, 2006 for $300,000. On that date, it had an expected useful life of 6 years. The piece of equipment was sold to Rosebud for $100,000 on January 1, 2008.

3. During 2009, Rosebud had sales of $400,000 to Ginko of which $150,000 were not resold by Ginko until 2010. In 2010, of the $550,000 in total sales from Rosebud to Ginko, $220,000 remained in the December 31, 2010 inventories of Ginko. On December 31, 2010, Ginko still owes Rosebud $175,000 for 2010 merchandise purchases. All of Rosebud's sales to Ginko are priced to provide a gross margin on sales prices of 50 percent.

4. In 2009, Ginko had sales of $160,000 to Rosebud of which all but $20,000 was resold by Rosebud during 2009. During 2010, Rosebud purchased $190,000 of merchandise from Ginko of which $45,000 remained in the December 31, 2010 inventories of Rosebud. All of Ginko's sales to Rosebud are priced to provide a gross margin on sales prices of 60 percent.

5. The Rosebud Company and the Ginko Company account for inventories on a first-in, first-out basis. Both Companies use the straight line method to calculate all depreciation and amortization.

6. On December 15, 2010, the Rosebud Company sold a parcel of Land to the Ginko Company for $75,000, payable in two equal installments on December 15, 2010 and January 15, 2011. The Rosebud Company had purchased this parcel of land for $118,000 in 2004.

Required: Prepare a consolidated Income Statement and Statement of Retained Earnings for the year ending December 31, 2010, and a consolidated Balance Sheet as at December 31, 2010 for the Rosebud Company and its subsidiary the Ginko Company.

Self Study Problem Six - 6

On July 1, 2002, the Patco Company paid $720,000 in cash to acquire 80 percent of the outstanding voting shares of the Stand Company. At this date the fair values of all of Stand Company's identifiable assets and liabilities had fair values that were equal to their carrying values except for a group of fixed assets and a copyright. The fixed assets had a carrying value that exceeded their fair value by $120,000. These assets have a remaining useful life on July 1, 2002 of four years. The copyright is the only intangible asset owned by Stand and it has a fair value of $90,000 on July 1, 2002.

The following condensed financial statements for the two Companies have been provided by the chief accountant for Patco:

2002 Balance Sheets

	January 1 Patco	July 1 Stand	December 31 Patco	December 31 Stand
Cash	$ 25,000	$ 10,000	$ 12,000	$ 6,000
Non-Cash Current Assets	1,000,000	140,000	663,000	84,000
Investment In Stand	-0-	-0-	720,000	-0-
Fixed Assets (Net)	1,500,000	900,000	1,680,000	1,050,000
Intangible Assets	700,000	60,000	525,000	54,000
Total Assets	$3,225,000	$1,110,000	$3,600,000	$1,194,000
Current Liabilities	$ 450,000	$ 60,000	$ 450,000	$ 75,000
Long-Term Liabilities	600,000	300,000	675,000	300,000
Common Stock	1,500,000	225,000	1,500,000	225,000
Retained Earnings	675,000	525,000	975,000	594,000
Total Equities	$3,225,000	$1,110,000	$3,600,000	$1,194,000

2002 Income Statements

	Patco Year Ended December 31	Stand Six Months Ended December 31
Sales	$4,600,000	$600,000
Cost Of Goods Sold	$2,700,000	$375,000
Depreciation Expense	525,000	120,000
Amortization Of Intangibles	175,000	6,000
Other Expenses	900,000	30,000
Total Expenses	$4,300,000	$531,000
Net Income	$ 300,000	$ 69,000

In addition to the preceding single entity financial statements, Patco's accountant also provides the following consolidated Balance Sheet for Patco Company and its subsidiary Stand Company:

Consolidated Balance Sheet
As At December 31, 2002

Cash	$ 18,000
Non-Cash Current Assets	730,000
Fixed Assets	2,659,650
Intangible Assets	792,600
Total Assets	$4,200,250
Current Liabilities	$ 525,000
Long-Term Liabilities	975,000
Non-Controlling Interest	163,130
Common Stock	1,500,000
Retained Earnings	1,037,120
Total Equities	$4,200,250

Other Information:

1. The Patco Company carries its Investment In Stand by the cost method. Both Companies use the straight line method for all depreciation and amortization calculations.

2. During the period July 1, 2002 through December 31, 2002, Stand sells merchandise to Patco in the total amount of $170,000. One-half of this merchandise is in the closing Inventories of Patco. The intercompany sales are priced to provide a markup of 25 percent on its invoice cost.

3. On October 1, 2002, Stand sold equipment to Patco for $98,000. The Equipment had a carrying value on the books of Stand of $112,000 and, at the time of the sale, its remaining useful life was estimated to be 10 years. On July 1, 2002, the carrying value of this equipment was equal to its fair value.

4. On March 1, 2002, Patco purchased a Building for $218,000. The vendor accepted a $75,000, 5 year mortgage from Patco and the remainder of the purchase price was paid in cash.

5. All intangible assets are tested annually for impairment by both companies. No impairment was found in any year.

Required:

A. Calculate consolidated Net Income for Patco Company and its subsidiary Stand Company for the year ending December 31, 2002.

B. Verify the calculations used by the Patco Company accountant in establishing the consolidated Balance Sheet values for:

   1. Intangible Assets
   2. Non-Controlling Interest
   3. Retained Earnings

C. Prepare a consolidated Cash Flow Statement for the Patco Company and its subsidiary Stand Company for the year ending December 31, 2002.

Assignment Problems

(The solutions for these problems are only available in
the solutions manual that has been provided to your instructor.)

Assignment Problem Six - 1

(This is an extension of Assignment Problem Five-1)

On December 31, 2002, the Percy Company purchased 75 percent of the outstanding voting shares of the Stern Company for $3 million in cash. On that date, Stern had Common Stock - No Par of $2 million and Retained Earnings of $1 million. On December 31, 2002 all of the identifiable assets and liabilities of Stern had fair values that were equal to their carrying values with the following exceptions:

1. Inventories with fair values that were $400,000 less than their carrying values.

2. Land with a fair value that was $800,000 greater than its carrying value.

3. Long-Term Liabilities, maturing on January 1, 2008, with fair values that were $200,000 less than their carrying values.

Both Companies use the straight line method to calculate all depreciation and amortization. The land which was on the books of the Stern Company on December 31, 2002 has not been sold as at December 31, 2007. The Percy Company accounts for its investment in Stern Company using the cost method.

Other data for the year ending December 31, 2007 is as follows:

Income Statements
For The Year Ending December 31, 2007

	Percy	Stern
Merchandise Sales	$5,000,000	$2,000,000
Other Revenues	1,000,000	500,000
Total Revenues	$6,000,000	$2,500,000
Cost of Goods Sold	$2,000,000	$1,000,000
Depreciation Expense	400,000	300,000
Other Expenses	600,000	400,000
Total Expenses	$3,000,000	$1,700,000
Net Income	$3,000,000	$ 800,000

Statements Of Retained Earnings
For The Year Ending December 31, 2007

	Percy	Stern
Opening Balance	$10,000,000	$1,600,000
Net Income	3,000,000	800,000
Balance Available	$13,000,000	$2,400,000
Dividends Declared	1,000,000	400,000
Closing Balance	$12,000,000	$2,000,000

Balance Sheets
as at December 31, 2007

	Percy	Stern
Cash and Current Receivables	$ 1,500,000	$1,200,000
Note Receivable	1,000,000	-0-
Inventories	4,500,000	1,000,000
Investment in Stern (At Cost)	3,000,000	-0-
Plant and Equipment (Net)	9,000,000	3,000,000
Land	2,000,000	800,000
Total Assets	$21,000,000	$6,000,000
Current Liabilities	$ 500,000	$ 200,000
Long-Term Liabilities	3,500,000	1,800,000
Common Stock - No Par	5,000,000	2,000,000
Retained Earnings	12,000,000	2,000,000
Total Equities	$21,000,000	$6,000,000

Other Information:

1. The Long-Term Liabilities of the Stern Company include a $1 million note that is payable to the Percy Company. During 2007, interest expense on this note was $110,000 and on December 31, 2007, $100,000 of this interest had not been paid by Stern. The note is to be paid on December 31, 2010.

2. In each of the years since Percy acquired control over Stern, the goodwill arising on this business combination transaction has been tested for impairment. In 2004, a Goodwill Impairment Loss of $50,000 was recognized. No impairment was found in any of the other years since acquisition.

3. Stern had sales of $1,500,000 to Percy during 2007 of which $400,000 remained in the December 31, 2007 inventories of Percy. The 2006 sales of $2,000,000 from Stern to Percy left $800,000 of merchandise in the December 31, 2006 inventories of Percy.

4. Stern's purchases for 2007 included $500,000 of merchandise from Percy. Of these purchases, 60 percent remained in the December 31, 2007 inventories of Stern. There had been no purchases from Percy remaining in the December 31, 2006 inventories of Stern. All intercompany sales and purchases are priced to provide the selling company with a gross margin of 50 percent of the sales price.

5. On January 1, 2005, Stern sold a machine with a net book value of $250,000 to Percy for $350,000. At that time, the machine had a remaining useful life of 5 years.

6. On September 1, 2007, Percy sold a parcel of land which was purchased in 2003 for $100,000, to Stern for $350,000. The gain on this sale is included in Other Revenues.

Required: Prepare, for the Percy Company and its subsidiary, the Stern Company, the following:

A. The consolidated Income Statement for the year ending December 31, 2007.

B. The consolidated Statement of Retained Earnings for the year ending December 31, 2007.

C. The consolidated Balance Sheet as at December 31, 2007.

Assignment Problem Six - 2

On December 31, 2002, the Pumpkin Company purchased 75 percent of the outstanding voting shares of the Squash Company for $4,200,000 in cash. On that date, the Squash Company had No Par Common Stock of $3,900,000 and Retained Earnings of $600,000. All of the Squash Company's identifiable assets and liabilities had carrying values that were equal to their fair values except for:

1. Equipment which had a fair value of $270,000 more that its carrying value and a useful life of 20 years when purchased by Squash on December 31, 1997.

2. Land which had a fair value that was $300,000 greater than its carrying value.

3. Inventories with fair values that were $60,000 more than their carrying values.

4. Long-Term Liabilities which had fair values that were $90,000 more than their carrying values and mature on December 31, 2008.

The Balance Sheets of the Pumpkin Company and the Squash Company as at December 31, 2006 were as follows:

Pumpkin and Squash Companies
Balance Sheets
As At December 31, 2006

	Pumpkin	Squash
Cash and Current Receivables	$ 1,620,000	$ 930,000
Inventories	1,800,000	660,000
Long-Term Receivables	840,000	300,000
Plant and Equipment (Net)	4,500,000	2,700,000
Investment in Squash (Cost)	4,200,000	-0-
Land	2,400,000	1,200,000
Total Assets	$15,360,000	$5,790,000
Current Liabilities	$ 480,000	$ 240,000
Long-Term Liabilities	660,000	390,000
No Par Common Stock	10,200,000	3,900,000
Retained Earnings	4,020,000	1,260,000
Total Equities	$15,360,000	$5,790,000

The Income Statements of the Pumpkin and Squash Companies for the year ending December 31, 2006 were as follows:

Pumpkin and Squash Companies
Income Statements
For The Year Ending December 31, 2006

	Pumpkin	Squash
Sales	$5,610,000	$1,770,000
Interest Revenue	84,000	30,000
Other Revenues	90,000	-0-
Total Revenues	$5,784,000	$1,800,000
Cost of Goods Sold	$3,900,000	$1,260,000
Interest Expense	66,000	45,000
Other Expenses	690,000	240,000
Total Expenses	$4,656,000	$1,545,000
Net Income	$1,128,000	$ 255,000

Other Information:

1. In each of the years since Pumpkin acquired control over Squash, the goodwill arising on this business combination transaction has been tested for impairment. In 2004, a Goodwill Impairment Loss of $84,000 was recognized. No impairment was found in any of the other years since acquisition.

2. Both Companies use the straight line method to calculate all depreciation and amortization charges and the First-In, First-Out inventory flow assumption.

3. Pumpkin uses the cost method to carry its Investment in Squash.

4. During 2006, dividends of $360,000 were declared and paid by Pumpkin and dividends of $120,000 were declared and paid by Squash.

5. The Pumpkin Company manufactures machines with a five year life. Its Sales total in the Income Statement includes only sales of these machines. Intercompany sales of these machines are priced to provide Pumpkin with a 20 percent gross profit on sales prices in all the years under consideration. On December 31, 2004, Pumpkin sold machines it had manufactured to Squash for $150,000. Squash uses the machines in its production process. On January 1, 2006, Pumpkin sold an additional $300,000 of these machines to the Squash Company. There were no other intercompany sales of these machines in any of the years under consideration.

6. The Squash Company manufactures paper products used in offices. During 2005, Squash sold to Pumpkin $18,000 worth of office supplies of which all but $3,000 were used by Pumpkin in 2005. During 2006, Pumpkin purchased $15,000 worth of merchandise from Squash. During 2006, the Pumpkin Company used $9,000 worth of the paper products purchased from Squash. Squash's intercompany sales are priced to provide it with a 50 percent gross margin on its sales price.

7. On January 1, 2004, Squash sold a piece of equipment to Pumpkin that it had purchased on January 1, 1999. On January 1, 1999, the machine had an estimated useful life of 13 years with no net salvage value and there is no change in this estimate at the time of the sale to Pumpkin. Pumpkin paid 20 percent more than the $300,000 carrying value of the equipment on Squash's books on January 1, 2004.

8. During 2005, Squash sold land that had a carrying value of $240,000 to Pumpkin for a profit of $30,000. One-half of the proceeds was paid at that date and the remainder is due on July 1, 2007. The Land that had the fair value increase on December 31, 2002 is still on the books of Squash.

9. On December 31, 2006, Squash had current receivables of $6,000 from Pumpkin and Pumpkin is owed $18,000 by Squash. Intercompany interest which was paid during 2006 on outstanding intercompany payables totalled $1,000 for Squash and $1,400 for Pumpkin.

Required:

A. Prepare the consolidated Income Statement for the year ending December 31, 2006 of the Pumpkin Company and its subsidiary, the Squash Company.

B. Prepare the consolidated Statement of Retained Earnings for the year ending December 31, 2006, of the Pumpkin Company and its subsidiary, the Squash Company.

C. Prepare the consolidated Balance Sheet as at December 31, 2006 of the Pumpkin Company and its subsidiary, the Squash Company.

Assignment Problem Six - 3

On January 1, 2002, the Paul Company acquired 75 percent of the outstanding voting shares of the Saul Company for $6,000,000 in cash. On this date the Saul Company had No Par Common Stock of $6,200,000 and Retained Earnings of $2,800,000. At this acquisition date, the Saul Company had Plant And Equipment that had a fair value that was $600,000 less than its carrying value, Long-Term Liabilities that had a fair value that was $200,000 more than their carrying values and Inventories with a fair value that was less than their carrying values in the amount of $800,000. All of the other identifiable assets and liabilities of the Saul Company had fair values that were equal to their carrying values on the date of acquisition. The remaining useful life of the Plant And Equipment was 12 years with no anticipated salvage value. The Long-Term Liabilities were issued at par of $4,000,000 and mature on January 1, 2012.

On January 1, 2005, the Saul Company sells a broadcast licence to the Paul Company for $900,000. On this date the carrying value of this broadcast licence on the books of the Saul Company was $1,000,000 and the remaining useful life was five years. All depreciation and amortization is accounted for on a straight line basis by both companies.

Between January 1, 2002 and January 1, 2007, the Saul Company had Net Income of $2,200,000 and paid dividends of $800,000. On January 1, 2007, the Retained Earnings of the Paul Company were $30,000,000. During 2007, the Paul Company declared and paid dividends of $200,000 and the Saul Company declared and paid dividends of $100,000. The Paul Company carries its Investment in Saul by the cost method.

The condensed Income Statements of the two Companies for the year ending December 31, 2007 are as follows:

Paul and Saul Companies
Income Statements
For The Year Ending December 31, 2007

	Paul	Saul
Total Revenues	$5,000,000	$2,000,000
Cost Of Goods Sold	$3,000,000	$1,200,000
Other Expenses	1,500,000	600,000
Total Expenses	$4,500,000	$1,800,000
Net Income	$ 500,000	$ 200,000

During 2007, 40 percent of the Saul Company's Revenues resulted from sales to the Paul Company. Half of this merchandise remains in the ending inventories of the Paul Company and has not yet been paid for. The December 31, 2007 inventory balances for the Paul and Saul Companies are $950,000 and $380,000 respectively.

On January 1, 2007, the inventories of the Paul Company contained purchases from the Saul Company of $500,000. All intercompany merchandise transactions are priced to provide Saul with a gross margin on sales prices of 40 percent.

The Saul Company has not issued any additional Common Stock or Long-Term Liabilities since the date of its acquisition by the Paul Company. On December 31, 2007, the Paul Company had $15,000,000 in Long-Term Liabilities.

In each of the years since Paul purchased the shares of Saul, the goodwill arising from this share purchase has been tested for impairment. No impairment was found in any of the years since acquisition.

Required:

A. Prepare the consolidated Income Statement for the year ending December 31, 2007 for the Paul Company and its subsidiary, the Saul Company, in compliance with the Recommendations of the *CICA Handbook*.

B. Calculate the amounts, showing all computations, that would be included in the consolidated Balance Sheet as at December 31, 2007 of the Paul Company and its subsidiary, the Saul Company for the following accounts:

   1. Retained Earnings
   2. Non-Controlling Interest
   3. Inventories
   4. Broadcast Licence
   5. Long-Term Liabilities

Assignment Problem Six - 4

On January 1, 2002, the Plantor Company purchased 75 percent of the outstanding voting shares of the Plantee Company for $850,000 in cash. This amount was $100,000 greater than the Plantor Company's share of the carrying values of the Plantee Company's net identifiable assets. The entire $100,000 is allocated to a building and will be charged to income over a 20 year period.

No dividends were paid by either Company in 2004. Plantor Company carries its investment in Plantee Company using the cost method. The Income Statements of the two Companies for the year ending December 31, 2004 are as follows:

Income Statements
For The Year Ending December 31, 2004

	Plantor	Plantee
Sales	$500,000	$200,000
Cost of Goods Sold	$300,000	$100,000
Other Expenses	140,000	76,000
Total Expenses	$440,000	$176,000
Income Before Extraordinary Items	$ 60,000	$ 24,000
Extraordinary Gain	-0-	6,000
Net Income	$ 60,000	$ 30,000

Other Information:

1. During 2004, the Plantor Company sold $100,000 in merchandise to the Plantee Company. Of these sales, $15,000 remains in the December 31, 2004 Inventories of the Plantee Company. All intercompany purchases are priced to provide the selling Company with a normal gross profit.

2. During 2004, the Plantee Company sold $50,000 in merchandise to the Plantor Company. Of these sales, $20,000 remains in the December 31, 2004 Inventories of the Plantor Company. There were no intercompany inventory sales prior to 2004.

3. On January 2, 2002, the Plantee Company sold equipment to the Plantor Company for $100,000. On that date the equipment was carried on the Plantee Company's books at $135,000 and had a remaining useful life of 5 years.

4. Both Companies use the straight line method to calculate all depreciation and amortization.

Required:

A. Prepare a consolidated Income Statement for the Plantor Company and its subsidiary the Plantee Company for the year ending December 31, 2004.

B. Assume that the Plantor Company cannot classify the Plantee Company as a subsidiary. Prepare the Plantor Company's Income Statement for the year ending December 31, 2004 assuming it uses the equity method to account for its investment in the Plantee Company.

Assignment Problem Six - 5

On December 31, 2002, the Plain Company acquired 25 percent of the outstanding voting shares of the Steppe Company for $1,250,000. On December 31, 2004, the Plain Company acquired an additional 40 percent of the outstanding voting shares of the Steppe Company for $1,680,000. The fair values of the identifiable assets and liabilities of the Steppe Company were equal to their carrying values except for Current Assets and Long-Term Liabilities. The condensed Balance Sheets and the fair values of the Steppe Company on the acquisition dates were as follows:

Balance Sheets
As At December 31

	2004	2002
Current Assets	$ 800,000	$1,200,000
Plant and Equipment (Net)	5,400,000	5,300,000
Total Assets	$6,200,000	$6,500,000
Current Liabilities	$ 300,000	$ 500,000
Long-Term Liabilities	2,000,000	2,000,000
Common Stock - No Par	3,000,000	3,000,000
Retained Earnings	900,000	1,000,000
Total Equities	$6,200,000	$6,500,000

Fair Values

	2004	2002
Current Assets	$ 600,000	$ 800,000
Long-Term Liabilities	$1,700,000	$1,800,000

The Long-Term Liabilities were issued on December 31, 1992 and mature on December 31, 2012. The Plain Company carries its investment in the Steppe Company by the cost method. Both Companies use the straight line method to calculate all depreciation and amortization.

The condensed Balance Sheets of the Plain Company and the Steppe Company as at December 31, 2005 are as follows:

Balance Sheets
As At December 31, 2005

	Plain	Steppe
Current Assets	$ 2,070,000	$1,400,000
Investment in Steppe	2,930,000	-0-
Plant and Equipment (Net)	9,000,000	6,200,000
Total Assets	$14,000,000	$7,600,000
Current Liabilities	$ 1,000,000	$ 600,000
Long-Term Liabilities	5,000,000	2,000,000
Common Stock - No Par	3,000,000	3,000,000
Retained Earnings	5,000,000	2,000,000
Total Equities	$14,000,000	$7,600,000

In each of the years since Plain acquired shares of the Steppe Company, the goodwill arising from the share purchases has been tested for impairment. No impairment was found in any of the years.

During 2005, the Steppe Company declared and paid $100,000 in dividends and the Plain Company declared $150,000 in dividends which were not paid until January, 2006.

The Steppe Company sold $300,000 of merchandise to the Plain Company during 2005. Of these sales, merchandise which contained a $50,000 gross profit for the Steppe Company remained in the December 31, 2005 inventories of the Plain Company. Merchandise containing a gross profit of $75,000 for the Steppe Company had been included in the December 31, 2004 inventories of the Plain Company. There were no intercompany inventory sales prior to 2004.

Required: Prepare a consolidated Balance Sheet for the Plain Company and its subsidiary, the Steppe Company as at December 31, 2005.

Assignment Problem Six - 6

The Norwood Company purchased 75 percent of the outstanding voting shares of the Sollip Company on January 1, 2002 for $2,000,000 in cash. On that date, the Sollip Company's identifiable assets and liabilities had fair values that were equal to their carrying values except for Plant and Equipment, which had a fair value that was $40,000 more than carrying value and Long-Term Liabilities with a fair value that was $80,000 less than carrying value. The Plant and Equipment had a remaining life of 10 years with no anticipated salvage value and the Long-Term Liabilities mature on January 1, 2012. On the acquisition date, Sollip had Retained Earnings of $1,400,000 and Common Stock of $600,000.

The Norwood Company carries its investment in Sollip by the cost method. Both Companies use the straight line method to calculate depreciation and amortization.

The comparative Balance Sheets and the condensed Statement of Income and Change in Retained Earnings for the year ending December 31, 2005 of the Norwood Company and its subsidiary, the Sollip Company are as follows:

Balance Sheets
As At December 31

	Norwood 2005	Norwood 2004	Sollip 2005	Sollip 2004
Cash	$1,009,988	$ 360,000	$1,200,000	$ 600,000
Accounts Receivable	1,394,000	64,000	780,000	200,000
Inventories	310,000	170,000	480,000	320,000
Investment in Sollip (At Cost)	2,000,000	2,000,000	-0-	-0-
Plant and Equipment	6,240,000	6,000,000	4,000,000	4,000,000
Accumulated Depreciation	(3,045,667)	(2,800,000)	(1,988,000)	(1,600,000)
Land	120,000	120,000	60,000	-0-
Total Assets	$8,028,321	$5,914,000	$4,532,000	$3,520,000
Current Liabilities	$2,468,321	$ 714,000	$1,452,000	$ 760,000
Long-Term Liabilities	900,000	800,000	560,000	360,000
Common Stock - No Par	2,020,000	2,000,000	600,000	600,000
Retained Earnings	2,640,000	2,400,000	1,920,000	1,800,000
Total Equities	$8,028,321	$5,914,000	$4,532,000	$3,520,000

Income Statements
Year Ending December 31, 2005

	Norwood	Sollip
Total Revenues	$2,760,000	$2,000,000
Cost of Goods Sold	$1,200,000	$ 790,000
Depreciation Expense	410,667	548,000
Other Expenses and Losses	849,333	342,000
Total Expenses and Losses	$2,460,000	$1,680,000
Net Income	$ 300,000	$ 320,000
Retained Earnings, January 1	2,400,000	1,800,000
Balance Available	$2,700,000	$2,120,000
Dividends	60,000	200,000
Balance, December 31	$2,640,000	$1,920,000

Other Information:

1. On January 1, 2003, the Sollip Company sold furniture to the Norwood Company for $31,000. The furniture had a net book value of $85,000 and an estimated life on this date of four years with no anticipated salvage value.

2. On December 31, 2004, the Norwood Company had in its inventories $35,000 of merchandise that it had purchased from Sollip during 2004. During 2005, Norwood purchased $200,000 of merchandise from Sollip of which $75,000 remain in the December 31, 2005 inventories of Norwood. The Norwood Company sold $120,000 of merchandise to Sollip during 2005 which was resold during the year for $165,000. Intercompany inventory sales are priced to provide the selling company with a 30 percent gross profit on sales price.

3. On December 31, 2005 due to the intercompany inventory sales, the Norwood Company owed the Sollip Company $60,000 and the Sollip Company owed the Norwood Company

$80,000. There were no intercompany accounts payable balances on December 31, 2004.

4. On January 1, 2005, to raise cash, the Norwood Company took out a $100,000 second mortgage on its assets. In addition, it sold office equipment that had cost $195,000 and had accumulated depreciation of $165,000 for $20,000.

5. On December 31, 2005, the Sollip Company sold a machine to the Norwood Company for $55,000. The machine had been purchased on January 1, 2002 for $200,000 and had an expected life at that date of 5 years with no anticipated salvage value. The Sollip Company had taken depreciation for 2005 on the machine before the sale. The only Plant and Equipment acquisition of the Sollip Company was a $200,000 machine to replace the one sold to Norwood.

6. On June 30, 2005, the Norwood Company also purchased other Equipment for a combination of $360,000 in cash and 4,000 No Par common shares. The stock was trading at $5 per share on this date.

7. On April 1, 2005, the Sollip Company issued 20 year, 14 percent bonds for $200,000 and used part of the proceeds to purchase a parcel of land.

8. In the year of acquisition of Sollip, a Goodwill Impairment Loss of $200,000 was recognized due to an unfavourable ruling in a court case. No impairment was found in any of the other years since acquisition.

Required: (Note that in Parts A, B and C, financial statements are not required.)

A. Compute consolidated Net Income for the year ending December 31, 2005 for the Norwood Company and its subsidiary, the Sollip Company.

B. Calculate consolidated Retained Earnings as at December 31, 2005 for the Norwood Company and its subsidiary, the Sollip Company.

C. Compute the Non-Controlling Interest that would be disclosed on the consolidated Balance Sheet of the Norwood Company and its subsidiary, the Sollip Company as at December 31, 2005.

D. Prepare the consolidated Cash Flow Statement for the year ending December 31, 2005 for the Norwood Company and its subsidiary, the Sollip Company.

Assignment Problem Six - 7

The single entity and consolidated Balance Sheets and Income Statements for the Pomp Company and its subsidiary, the Sircumstance Company, for the year ending December 31, 2006, are as follows:

Balance Sheets
As At December 31, 2006

	Pomp	Sircumstance	Consolidated
Cash	$ 20,000	$ 15,000	$ 35,000
Accounts Receivable	400,000	250,000	520,000
Inventories	380,000	335,000	635,000
Investment in Sircumstance	1,500,000	-0-	-0-
Land	800,000	1,200,000	2,100,000
Plant and Equipment (Net)	3,000,000	2,300,000	5,500,000
Goodwill	-0-	-0-	190,000
Total Assets	$6,100,000	$4,100,000	$8,980,000
Current Liabilities	$ 200,000	$ 100,000	$ 190,000
Dividends Payable	50,000	25,000	55,000
Bonds Payable	2,000,000	1,475,000	3,475,000
Non-Controlling Interest	-0-	-0-	524,000
Common Stock (No Par)	3,000,000	1,000,000	3,000,000
Retained Earnings	850,000	1,500,000	1,736,000
Total Equities	$6,100,000	$4,100,000	$8,980,000

Income Statements
For The Year Ending December 31, 2006

	Pomp	Sircumstance	Consolidated
Sales	$3,200,000	$2,500,000	$5,400,000
Cost of Goods Sold	(2,000,000)	(1,000,000)	(2,720,000)
Other Expenses	(800,000)	(1,400,000)	(2,310,000)
Goodwill Impairment Loss	-0-	-0-	10,000
Investment Income	40,000	-0-	-0-
Non-Controlling Interest	-0-	-0-	4,000
Net Income	$ 440,000	$ 100,000	$ 374,000
Dividends Declared	(200,000)	(50,000)	(200,000)
Increase in Retained Earnings	$ 240,000	$ 50,000	$ 174,000

Other Information: Pomp Company acquired its investment in the Common Stock of the Sircumstance Company on January 1, 2002. At that time, all of the identifiable assets and liabilities of the Sircumstance Company had fair values that were equal to their carrying values except for Land which had a fair value that was $125,000 in excess of its carrying value. The Land is still on the books of the Sircumstance Company on December 31, 2006.

In each of the years since Pomp acquired control over Sircumstance, the goodwill arising on this business combination transaction has been tested for impairment. No impairment was found in any year prior to 2006.

Both Companies calculate depreciation and amortization using the straight line method.

The Sircumstance Company regularly sells merchandise to the Pomp Company and, after further processing, the merchandise is resold by the Pomp Company. On January 1, 2004, the Sircumstance Company sold Equipment to the Pomp Company at a loss. At the time, the remaining useful life of this Equipment was five years. Since the Pomp Company acquired its investment in the Sircumstance Company, there has been no change in the number of Sircumstance Company common shares outstanding.

Required: On the basis of the information you can develop from an analysis of the preceding individual and consolidated financial statements, provide answers to the following questions.

A.   What percentage of the outstanding common shares of the Sircumstance Company were purchased by the Pomp Company on January 1, 2002?

B.   Does the Pomp Company carry its investment in the Common Stock of the Sircumstance Company by the cost method or the equity method? Explain the basis for your conclusion.

C.   Assume that $1,500,000 was the cost of the Pomp Company's investment in the Common Stock of the Sircumstance Company. What was the balance in the Retained Earnings account of the Sircumstance Company on January 1, 2002?

D.   What is the amount of intercompany inventory sales that the Sircumstance Company made to the Pomp Company during 2006?

E.   What is the explanation for the difference between the consolidated Cost of Goods Sold and the combined Cost of Goods Sold of the two affiliated companies?

F.   On January 1, 2004, what was the amount of unrealized loss on the intercompany sale of Plant and Equipment by Sircumstance Company to the Pomp Company?

G.   Prepare a schedule of intercompany debts and, if possible, indicate which company is the creditor and which is the debtor.

H.   Show how the $4,000 Non-Controlling Interest in consolidated Net Income was determined.

I.   Show how the Non-Controlling Interest of $524,000 in the consolidated Balance Sheet was determined.

J.   Prepare a schedule in which you derive the $1,736,000 balance in consolidated Retained Earnings on December 31, 2006.

K.   Prepare a schedule in which you derive the $374,000 in consolidated Net Income for the year ending December 31, 2006.

Chapter 7

Interests In Joint Ventures

Introduction

A New Chapter

7-1.   A joint venture is a type of long-term investment. In fact, at one point in time, the accounting Recommendations relevant to such affiliates were covered in Section 3050, the *CICA Handbook* Section that provides general coverage of long-term investments. However, in 1977, the material related to joint ventures was removed from Section 3050 and allocated to Section 3055, "Interests In Joint Ventures".

7-2.   Through the previous (third) edition of this text, we continued to provide our coverage of joint ventures as part of Chapter 2, our general Chapter on Long-Term Investments. However, with the major revision and expansion of Section 3055 that took place in 1995, the rules related to this type of investment became sufficiently complex that the Chapter 2 coverage had to be supplemented extensively in Chapter 6. This was required in order to deal with unrealized intercompany profits and the detailed application of proportionate consolidation procedures.

7-3.   Given the increased complexity associated with interests in joint ventures, we have concluded that it would be best to have the material on this type of long-term investment allocated to a separate Chapter. While Chapter 2 continues to provide a very general description of joint venture arrangements, as well as an elementary example of proportionate consolidation procedures, detailed coverage of joint ventures is now found in this Chapter 7. This approach has two advantages. First, the amalgamation of this material into a single Chapter should make it easier to understand the overall nature of the procedures that are associated with this type of investment. A second advantage, particularly with the growing trend towards one-semester advanced financial accounting courses, relates to the fact that some instructors feel that material on joint ventures is not important enough to warrant coverage. By relegating all of the detailed material on joint ventures to a single Chapter, it can be omitted without the need for a listing of omitted page numbers or problems with text continuity.

7-4.   We would note, however, that we continue to attach considerable importance to this material. Joint venture arrangements are very common in the business world. Further, the Recommendations associated with joint ventures are distinctly different from those that apply to any other type of long-term investment. An understanding of these Recommendations is necessary for any accountant wishing to deal with long-term investments in a reasonably comprehensive fashion.

Purpose And Scope Of Section 3055

7-5.   Section 3055 deals with accounting for interests in joint ventures in the general purpose financial statements of profit oriented enterprises. It covers the reporting of joint venture assets, liabilities, revenues and expenses in the financial statements of venturers, regardless of the legal structure under which the joint venture activity takes place. However, the Section does not deal with the accounting to be used by the joint venture itself.

7-6.   Joint venture accounting is only applicable in the economic circumstances outlined in Section 3055. There may be situations which fall within these circumstances that are not referred to as joint ventures. Section 3055 would be applicable in these situations, regardless of the term used by the venturer to identify the interest. In contrast, there may be situations that are referred to as joint venture arrangements that do not fall within the circumstances outlined in Section 3055. Section 3055 would not be applicable in these situations.

7-7.   Accounting for interests in joint ventures that are not included in the consolidated financial statements of the venturer is dealt with in Section 3050 (see Chapter 2). Accounting for interests in joint ventures in the financial statements of not-for-profit enterprises is covered in Section 4450 (see Chapter 14).

Joint Ventures Defined

General Rules

7-8.   A considerable amount of difficulty has been experienced in establishing a clear cut definition of what constitutes a joint venture. This reflects the fact that it is often difficult to distinguish this type of long-term investment from other long-term investment situations where the investor has the ability to exercise significant influence. The basic *Handbook* definition of a joint venture is as follows:

> **Paragraph 3055.03(c)**   A **joint venture** is an economic activity resulting from a contractual arrangement whereby two or more venturers jointly control the economic activity.

7-9.   This definition contains a number of terms that require further clarification. This clarification is provided in two additional Section 3055 definitions:

> **Paragraph 3055.03(b)**   **Joint control** of an economic activity is the contractually agreed sharing of the continuing power to determine its strategic operating, investing and financing policies.

> **Paragraph 3055.03(e)**   A **venturer** is a party to a joint venture, has joint control over that joint venture, has the right and ability to obtain future economic benefits from the resources of the joint venture and is exposed to the related risks.

7-10.   With respect to the meaning of control, it can be assumed that the definition of control that is provided in Section 1590 is equally applicable in this context.

> **Paragraph 1590.03(b)**   **Control** of an enterprise is the continuing power to determine its strategic operating, investing and financing policies without the co-operation of others.

7-11.   From the preceding definitions it can be concluded that the most important distinguishing feature of a joint venture is that its economic activity is subject to joint control by two or more venturers. Such joint control would preclude any one of the venturers from having unilateral control over the venture's economic activity. If the control agreement that is in place allows any one of the investors to exercise unilateral control, none of the investors will be able to classify their interest as a joint venture. The investor with unilateral control would classify its investment as a subsidiary, while the other investors would classify their interests as either portfolio investments or significantly influenced investees, as appropriate.

7-12.   There may be investors with an economic interest in a joint venture who do not partic- ipate under the agreement for joint control. This does not preclude the investors who do participate under the control agreement from classifying their investment as a joint venture. However, investors who do not participate under the agreement would not be able to use this classification and would have to classify their investment as either a portfolio investment or a significantly influenced investee, as appropriate.

7-13.   From the point of view of an individual interest in a joint venture, the venturer must have the right and ability to obtain future economic benefits from the resources of the joint venture and must be exposed to the risks related to the use of these resources. If the interest does not involve such risk and reward sharing, it should be viewed as a loan rather than as an equity interest in a joint venture. Long-term loan arrangements are normally classified as portfolio investments.

7-14.   The control agreement may take a variety of different forms. It may involve a contract between the various venturers or, alternatively, the agreement may be incorporated in the articles of incorporation or by-laws of the joint venture. The arrangement will normally be in writing and cover such matters as the activities, duration, policies and procedures of the joint venture, the allocation of ownership, the decision making process, the capital contributions by the venturers and the sharing by the venturers of the output, revenue, expenses or results of the joint venture.

7-15.   The joint venture definitions do not prevent one of the venturers from acting as the manager for the enterprise. As long as this manager is acting within policies that have been agreed on under the terms of the contractual agreement for the venture, the enterprise can be viewed as a joint venture arrangement. However, if the manager has the continuing power to determine the strategic operating, investing, and financing policies of the enterprise, without review by the other equity interests, then the manager is in control of the venture and should classify the investment as a subsidiary.

Forms Of Organization

7-16.   Section 3055 provides a discussion of the various forms and structures that can be used to carry out joint venture operations. Three basic forms are identified and they can be described as follows:

1. **Jointly Controlled Operations**   This form involves the use of the assets and other resources of the individual venturers, rather than the establishment of a corporation, partnership or other enterprise, or a financial structure that is separate from the venturers themselves. Characteristics of this form would include:

    - Each venturer uses its own property, plant and equipment, and carries its own inventories for purposes of the joint venture activities.
    - Assets remain under the individual ownership and control of each venturer.
    - Each venturer incurs its own expenses and liabilities and raises its own financing.
    - The arrangement will provide for the sharing of revenues and of common expenses among the various venturers.

    An example of this form might involve several venturers combining their efforts to manufacture a product. In this situation, different parts of the manufacturing opera- tion might be carried out by each of the venturers using their own assets and other resources. While each venturer would incur their own costs, they would receive a share of the revenues from the product, as per the terms of the joint venture agreement.

2. **Jointly Controlled Assets**   In this situation, the joint venture involves the joint control and possible joint ownership by the venturers, of one or more assets contrib- uted to or acquired for the use of the joint venture. Each venturer will take a share of the output from the assets and each will be responsible for a share of the expenses incurred. As was the case with jointly controlled operations, this type of joint venture

does not involve the establishment of a corporation, partnership, or other enterprise, or a financial structure that is separate from the venturers themselves.

Examples of this form of operation could involve the joint control of a rental property or the joint development of a natural resource property.

3. **Jointly Controlled Enterprise** This form of joint venture involves establishing a separate corporation or partnership in which each venturer has an investment interest. The separately established entity would operate much like other investment entities, except for the fact that it would be subject to the joint control of the various venturers. Characteristics of this form would include:

- While each venturer contributes cash or other resources to the joint venture, the venture itself will own the assets, assume the liabilities, receive the revenues, and incur the expenses of the joint venture operations.

- The venture may enter into contracts in its own name and raise financing for the purposes of joint venture activity.

- In most cases, each venturer will share in the income of the jointly controlled enterprise. In a minority of cases, the venturers will share in the output of the enterprise, rather than the income.

Examples of this form would include any situation where two or more venturers transfer relevant assets into a separate corporation or partnership.

Classification Example

7-17. The following simple example illustrates the classification of joint ventures in the context of other types of long-term investments. Note that, in terms of form of organization, the example involves a jointly controlled enterprise.

Example A new company, the Venture Company, is formed and all of the shares are acquired by four investor Companies. These Companies and their proportionate ownership interests are as follows:

- Company A holds 60 percent of the shares.
- Company B holds 20 percent of the shares.
- Company C holds 15 percent of the shares.
- Company D holds 5 percent of the shares.

The four investor Companies sign an agreement that stipulates that Company A and Company D will not participate in the affairs or operations of the business. The agreement further specifies that in all areas essential to the operation of the business, decisions will be made by and require the consent of both Company B and Company C. The classification of the investment in the Venture Company by each of the investor Companies would be as follows:

Company A While Company A holds a majority of the voting shares in the Venture Company, the joint venture agreement prevents the Company from exercising the control that we normally associate with majority ownership. Further, it does not appear that Company A will have any real influence on the affairs of Venture Company. As a consequence, Company A would classify Venture Company as a portfolio investment.

Companies B and **C** There is a contractual agreement in place under which two or more venturers control the enterprise. Further, under this agreement, B and C have joint control. Given their participation under the agreement and the fact that no single investor has unilateral control, Companies B and C would classify their long-term investments in Venture Company as joint venture investments.

Company D This investor, because of its exclusion from any share of joint control, would classify the investment as a portfolio investment.

Accounting Methods

Long-Term Investments In General

7-18.   Chapter 2 indicates that there are four possible methods of accounting for long-term investments. These are:

- the cost method;
- the equity method;
- full consolidation; and
- proportionate consolidation.

7-19.   These methods are discussed, evaluated in general terms, and illustrated with relatively simple examples in Chapter 2.

Joint Venture Recommendations

7-20.   As is noted in the Section "Joint Ventures Defined", an investor must participate in the management of an investee in order for the investment to be classified as a joint venture. This means that such investors will be in a position to influence the policies of the investee, including decisions related to the declaration of dividends. As is noted in Chapter 2, the cost method defines investment income in terms of investee dividends declared, without regard to the actual performance of the investee. In view of this, it would not be appropriate to allow joint venture investors to use the cost method.

7-21.   The definition of a joint venture also specifies that none of the participant investors can have unilateral control. As full consolidation is only appropriate in situations where the investor has control over the investee, we can conclude that full consolidation is never appropriate for a joint venture investment.

7-22.   This process of elimination appears to suggest that joint ventures be accounted for by the equity method, the method that is used with other long-term investments where the investor has influence but not control. However, in some situations there is a serious problem with the use of the equity method for joint ventures. There are Canadian companies whose total economic activity consists of investments in a variety of joint venture arrangements. If such investor companies use the equity method, their financial statements would consist of a Balance Sheet in which there is only a single asset (Investments In Joint Ventures) and an Income Statement made up of a single revenue (Investment Income).

7-23.   In situations such as this, the equity method would not constitute effective disclosure and, as a consequence of this problem, Section 3055 specifies the use of proportionate consolidation:

> **Paragraph 3055.17**   *Interests in joint ventures should be recognized in the financial statements of the venturer using the proportionate consolidation method.* (January, 1995)

7-24.   In making this Recommendation, the Accounting Standards Board argues that it is essential that each venturer reflect the substance and underlying economic reality of its interest, without regard to the structures or forms under which the joint venture activities take place. By providing financial statement users with the most appropriate information about the resources, obligations and operations of a venturer that conducts business through one or more joint ventures, the Accounting Standards Board has indicated that it believes the proportionate consolidation method achieves this essential objective.

7-25.   We are inclined to agree with this conclusion in situations where the majority of an enterprise's economic activity consists of investments in joint ventures. However, we do not feel that the use of proportionate consolidation is appropriate for all joint ventures. This method includes a portion of investee assets, liabilities, expenses, and revenues that are not under the control of the investor company. This is not consistent with the general reasoning that supports the preparation of consolidated financial statements. Further, it puts Canada out of line with most other countries, as well as the relevant international accounting standard. For example, International Accounting Standard No. 31, "Financial Reporting Of

Interests In Joint Ventures", encourages the use of proportionate consolidation, but permits the use of the equity method.

Proportionate Consolidation In Alternative Legal Forms
Joint Venture As A Separate Enterprise
7-26.   A simple example presented in Chapter 2 illustrates the application of proportionate consolidation. In addition, a more comprehensive example will be presented later in this Chapter. Both of these examples are based on the legal form of the joint venture being an investment in a separate incorporated enterprise. The application of proportionate consolidation in this type of situation results in the venturer recognizing:

1. in its balance sheet, its share of the assets and its share of the liabilities of the jointly controlled enterprise; and

2. in its income statement, its share of the revenue and its share of the expenses of the jointly controlled enterprise.

7-27.   While this separate enterprise arrangement is, for most of us, the most familiar type of joint venture arrangement, other forms and structures exist. These alternative forms are given brief attention in the material which follows.

Other Forms
7-28.   Joint venture activities may be undertaken without establishing a separate enterprise through arrangements involving jointly controlled operations (see Paragraph 7-16). When this is the case, the *Handbook* indicates that using the proportionate consolidation method results in the venturer recognizing:

1. in its balance sheet, the assets that it controls and the liabilities that it incurs; and

2. in its income statement, its share of the revenue of the joint venture and its share of the expenses incurred by the joint venture.

7-29.   A further alternative involves carrying on joint venture activities through arrangements involving only jointly controlled assets (see Paragraph 7-13). In this situation, the *Handbook* indicates that use of the proportionate consolidation method results in the venturer recognizing:

1. in its balance sheet, its share of the jointly controlled assets and its share of any liabilities incurred jointly with the other venturers in relation to the joint venture; and

2. in its income statement, any revenue from the sale or use of its share of the output of the joint venture, and its share of any expenses incurred by the joint venture.

7-30.   While recognizing the existence of alternative approaches to organizing joint venture activities, the more complex examples of joint venture procedures that are presented later in this Chapter will be based on situations in which the joint venture activities are carried out through a separate enterprise.

Cessation Of Joint Control
7-31.   In situations where a separate enterprise has been established to carry out joint venture activities, proportionate consolidation will be required as long as the joint venture agreement is in effect. However, if joint control ceases to exist, other methods will have to be used.

7-32.   If joint control has been lost because one investor has acquired unilateral control over the enterprise, the enterprise that has gained unilateral control will become subject to the Recommendations of Section 1590, "Subsidiaries". In general, this will result in this investor using full consolidation procedures.

7-33.   An individual investor may cease to participate in joint control for a variety of reasons. This could happen through one of the other investors acquiring unilateral control or, alternatively, through a change in the joint venture agreement such that the particular investor no longer participates in the control mechanism. For investors in this position, the requirements of Section 3050, "Long-Term Investments", becomes applicable. This would result in the application of either the cost method or the equity method, depending on how the investment was classified.

7-34. A further possibility here is that joint venture operations would be discontinued. In this situation, the provisions of Section 3475, "Discontinued Operations" would be applicable.

Differential Reporting

7-35. Differential reporting, as it applies to various types of long-term investments, was discussed in Chapter 2. You may recall from Chapter 2 that enterprises qualifying for differential reporting are allowed to use either the cost or equity method to account for interests in joint ventures. Also noted was that, when these alternative methods are used, additional disclosure requirements are applicable. As the relevant Recommendations were covered beginning in Paragraph 2-136, they will not be repeated in this Chapter.

Exercise Seven-1

Mason Enterprises Inc. is a new corporation. It is owned by four corporations and their interests can be described as follows:

Company 1 This company owns 40 percent of the outstanding voting shares, but does not participate in the management of the joint venture.

Company 2 This company owns 25 percent of the outstanding voting shares and shares management control with Company 3.

Company 3 This company owns 25 percent of the outstanding voting shares and shares management control with Company 2.

Company 4 This company owns 10 percent of the outstanding voting shares, but does not participate in the management of the joint venture.

Required: Indicate how Companies 1 through 4 would classify and account for their investment in Mason Enterprises Inc.

End Of Exercise Seven-1

> Exercise Seven-1 deals with classification and accounting methods for long-term investments.

Non-Cash Capital Contributions

The Problem

7-36. In making a long-term investment in the shares or debt securities of an investee company, the consideration used by the investor company could be cash, shares or debt of the investor company, or non-cash assets owned by the investor company. While non-cash assets could be used to acquire any type of investment, this does not appear to be a common occurrence in the case of subsidiaries, portfolio investments, or significantly influenced companies. As a consequence, the *CICA Handbook* has not given any attention to this issue in Section 3050.

7-37. However, contributions of non-cash assets to joint ventures are sufficiently common that attention has been given to the problems associated with such contributions, both by the Accounting Standards Board and by the Emerging Issues Committee.

7-38. Problems arise with non-cash investment contributions when the assets contributed are carried, on the venturer's books, at values other than current fair market value. For example, a venturer might contribute land with a carrying value of $500,000 and a current fair market value of $1,000,000. The issues that arise in this type of situation are as follows:

- To what extent, if any, should gains be recognized on the transfer of non-cash assets to a joint venture in return for an equity interest in that venture?

- To what extent, if any, should losses be recognized on the transfer of non-cash assets to a joint venture in return for an equity interest in that venture?

- How are these conclusions altered when the venturer receives cash or other assets in addition to an equity interest in the joint venture?

- If a gain or loss is to be recognized on the transfer of non-cash assets to a joint venture, how is the amount of gain or loss to be determined?

Relevant Pronouncements
Section 3055
7-39.   The basic rules for dealing with transfers of non-cash assets to joint ventures are in Section 3055. However, all or part of such transfers may be non-monetary in nature, thereby making Section 3830, "Non-Monetary Transactions", relevant (see Chapter 50 in our *Guide To Canadian Financial Reporting* which can be found on the CD-ROM which accompanies this text). In addition, Sections 3061, "Property, Plant, and Equipment" (covered in Chapter 29 of our *Guide To Canadian Financial Reporting*) and 3062, "Goodwill and Other Intangible Assets" (covered in Chapter 30 of our *Guide To Canadian Financial Reporting*), also contain Recommendations that may have influence on such transactions. Given this, we will examine the relevant provisions of these three *Handbook* Sections, prior to looking at the Recommendations of Section 3055 on this subject.

Section 3830 - Non-Monetary Transactions
7-40.   Consider the following example:

Example   Company A and Company B form a joint venture. Company A's capital contribution consists of a factory with a fair market value of $1,000,000 and a carrying value of $200,000. Company B's capital contribution consists of equipment with a fair market value of $1,000,000 and a carrying value of $350,000. Each venturer receives a 50 percent equity interest in the joint venture.

7-41.   From the point of view of both venturers, they have exchanged ownership of productive assets for an interest in similar productive assets. The assets are not assets that are held for resale and no monetary consideration is involved.

7-42.   The following Recommendation is relevant here:

Paragraph 3830.08   *Non-monetary exchanges that do not represent the culmination of the earnings process should be recorded at the carrying value of the asset or service given up in the exchange adjusted by any monetary consideration received or given.* (January, 1990)

7-43.   An example of a transaction that would not represent the culmination of the earnings process is as follows:

Paragraph 3830.09(b)   An exchange of productive assets not held for sale in the ordinary course of business for similar productive assets or for an equivalent interest in the same or similar productive assets.

7-44.   A contribution of non-cash assets to a joint venture in return for an equity interest in the joint venture, all of the assets of which consist of similar assets, would be a transaction described by Paragraph 3830.09(b). As a result, such a transaction would not involve the culmination of an earnings process and Paragraph 3830.08 would require that the transaction be recorded at the carrying value of the assets transferred. This leads us to the conclusion that, when non-cash assets are transferred to a joint venture in return for nothing other than an equity interest in that joint venture, the transfer should be made at the carrying value of the assets transferred with no income amount being recorded. Note, however, Paragraph 3830.08 indicates that the carrying value can be adjusted for any monetary consideration received and this provides for the possibility of recognizing some amount of income on the transfer. Section 3055 reflects this analysis of the applicability of Section 3830 to non-cash asset contributions to joint ventures.

Exercise Seven-2

As its only capital contribution to a joint venture, Hardy Ltd. contributes Property, Plant, and Equipment with a fair value of $950,000 and a carrying value of $600,000. In return, Hardy receives a 30 percent interest in the joint venture.

Required: Provide the journal entry to record Hardy Ltd.'s investment in the joint venture.

End Of Exercise Seven-2

> Exercise Seven-2 deals with non-monetary transactions.

Sections 3061 and 3062 - Tangible and Intangible Capital Assets

7-45.   Section 3830 requires that transfers of non-cash assets in return for an interest in similar assets be recorded at the carrying value of the assets transferred. This clearly prohibits a venturer from recognizing his share of any gain on assets transferred to a joint venture in return for an equity interest in that venture. In turn, it would seem to suggest that losses would be similarly prohibited on such transfers. However, the loss situation is also influenced by the requirements of Section 3061, "Property, Plant, and Equipment", and Section 3062, "Goodwill and Other Intangible Assets". Consider the following example:

Example   Company X and Company Y form a joint venture. Company X's capital contribution consists of a factory with a fair market value of $500,000 and a carrying value of $900,000. Company Y's capital contribution consists of equipment with a fair market value of $500,000 and a carrying value of $350,000. Each venturer receives a 50 percent equity interest in the joint venture.

7-46.   Company X, in dealing with an arm's length party, has agreed to accept an equity interest that is worth $500,000 in return for an asset with a carrying value of $900,000. This is clear and objective evidence that the asset is worth less than its carrying value. Both Sections 3061 and Section 3062 contain Recommendations requiring the write-down of assets in such situations:

Paragraph 3061.38   *When the net carrying amount of an item of property, plant and equipment, less related accumulated provision for future removal and site restoration costs and future income taxes, exceeds the net recoverable amount, the excess should be charged to income.* (December, 1990)

Paragraph 3062.18   *An intangible asset that is subject to amortization should be tested for impairment in accordance with the write-down provisions of "Property, Plant, and Equipment", Section 3061.* (January, 2002)

Paragraph 3062.19   *An intangible asset that is not subject to amortization should be tested for impairment annually, or more frequently if events or changes in circumstances indicate that the asset might be impaired. The impairment test should consist of a comparison of the fair value of the intangible asset with its carrying amount. When the carrying amount of the intangible asset exceeds its fair value, an impairment loss should be recognized in an amount equal to the excess.* (January, 2002)

7-47.   If we believe that the transfer of an asset to a joint venture in return for an equity interest with a value that is less than the carrying value of the asset, is evidence of a decline in the recoverable amount or fair value of the asset, then the quoted Paragraphs would require recognition of the loss on such assets prior to their transfer. Subsequent to the write-down under these Recommendations, the assets could be transferred at their carrying value as per the provisions of Paragraph 3830.08 for exchanges of non-monetary assets. In effect, this requires that losses on investment contributions of non-cash assets to joint ventures in exchange for an equity interest must be recognized.

General Approach For Transfers

7-48.   When a venturer transfers an asset to a joint venture in return for an equity interest in the venture, he has given up unilateral control of the asset in exchange for participation in joint control of the asset by the various parties to the joint venture agreement. Provided the venturer making the transfer is dealing at arm's length with the other parties to the joint venture agreement, the asset transfer can be viewed as an arm's length transaction. This is important in that it creates a presumption that the transfer was made at the asset's fair value and this, in turn, provides a basis for recognizing some portion of any gain or loss arising on the transfer.

Losses On Transfers

7-49.   We will use the following simple example to illustrate the Recommendations of Section 3055 with respect to losses on asset transfers.

> **Example**   A venturer has land with a current fair market value of $400,000 and an original cost of $500,000. The venturer intends to transfer this land to a joint venture in which he will have a 25 percent equity interest.

7-50.   One possibility here would be that, after acquiring his 25 percent interest through an investment of cash, the land is transferred to the joint venture in return for cash equal to its fair value of $400,000. While Section 3055 does not deal explicitly with this situation, the Section's view that such transfers are arm's length transactions would suggest that the entire loss of $100,000 would be taken into income at the time of transfer. As cash is involved, Section 3830 would not be applicable and, as a consequence, there would be no constraint on the venturer's ability to recognize losses or gains. In addition, the transfer would be evidence of a non-temporary decline in value, resulting in a need to write down the entire value of the asset under the provisions of Section 3061.

7-51.   The situation becomes more complex if the asset is exchanged for an equity interest in the venture, rather than for cash or other monetary assets. This situation is covered in Section 3055 as follows:

> **Paragraph 3055.26**   *When a venturer transfers assets to a joint venture and receives in exchange an interest in the joint venture, any loss that occurs should be charged to income at the time of the transfer to the extent of the interests of the other non-related venturers. When such a transaction provides evidence of a decline that is other than temporary in the carrying amount of the relevant assets, the venturer should recognize this decline by writing down that portion of the assets retained through its interest in the joint venture.* (January, 1995)

7-52.   Returning to the preceding example, Paragraph 3055.26 would require that at least $75,000 of the total loss of $100,000 ($400,000 - $500,000) be taken into income at the time of transfer. With the venturer in our example having a 25 percent equity interest in the joint venture, the $75,000 would represent the 75 percent interest of the other non-related venturers.

7-53.   While at least $75,000 of the loss must be taken into income because of the Recommendation in Paragraph 3055.26, we would expect that, in most situations, the value established by the terms of the transfer to the joint venture would provide a strong indication that there has been a non-temporary decline in value. This would mean that Paragraph 3055.26, as reinforced by the Recommendation in Paragraph 3061.38, would require a full write down of the asset to its fair value. Such a write down would mean that the full $100,000 loss would have to be taken into income.

Exercise Seven-3 deals with losses on assets transferred as capital contributions.

Exercise Seven-3

As its capital contribution to a joint venture, Gravel Ltd. contributes capital assets with a fair value of $480,000 and a carrying value of $840,000. In return, Gravel receives a 25 percent interest in the joint venture and $380,000 in cash.

Required: Provide the journal entry to record Gravel Ltd.'s investment in the joint venture.

End Of Exercise Seven-3

Gains On Transfers

General Rules

7-54. With respect to the recognition of gains, the general Recommendation is as follows:

> **Paragraph 3055.27** *When a venturer transfers assets to a joint venture and receives in exchange an interest in the joint venture, any gain that occurs should be recognized in the financial statements of the venturer only to the extent of the interests of the other non-related venturers, and accounted for in accordance with paragraphs 3055.28 and 3055.29. (January, 1995)*

7-55. Note carefully the difference between this Recommendation on gains and the Paragraph 3055.26 Recommendation on losses. The Paragraph 3055.26 Recommendation requires that losses be taken into income, not just recognized in the financial statements. The Paragraph 3055.27 Recommendation on gains refers only to recognition in the financial statements. When we examine Paragraphs 3055.28 and 3055.29, we will find that, in some situations, none of the recognized gain will be taken into income at the time the asset is transferred to the joint venture. This would be accomplished by setting up a Deferred Gain account in the joint venturer's proportionately consolidated Balance Sheet.

7-56. While it is possible that no gain will be taken into income at the time the asset is transferred to the joint venture, the portion of the gain that must be recognized as a result of the Recommendation in Paragraph 3055.26 will eventually be included in income. To the extent that this gain is not taken into income at the transfer date, it will be taken into income in some later accounting period. The timing of this income inclusion is governed by the following two Recommendations:

> **Paragraph 3055.28** *When the contributing venturer receives cash or other assets that do not represent a claim on the assets of the joint venture, only that portion of the gain that relates to the amount of cash received or the fair value of the other assets received should be taken to income at the time of the transfer. (January, 1995)*

> **Paragraph 3055.29** *Any remaining portion of the gain that does not meet the conditions in paragraph 3055.28 should be deferred and amortized to income in a rational and systematic manner over the life of the contributed assets. If the contributed assets are non-depreciable, the deferred gain should be taken to income on a basis appropriate to the expected revenue or service to be obtained from their use by the joint venture. If the contributed assets are disposed of by the joint venture, any unamortized portion of the deferred gain should be taken to income. (January, 1995)*

7-57. In situations where the contributing venturer receives only an equity interest in the joint venture, Paragraph 3055.27 would require that the other joint venturer's interest in the gain be recognized at the time the asset is transferred by the contributing venture. However, Paragraph 3055.28 would prevent any portion of this recognized gain from being included in the contributing venturer's income at the time of transfer. The recognized portion of the gain would have to be included in income in subsequent periods as per the Recommendation in Paragraph 3055.29.

Exercise Seven-4 deals with gains on assets transferred as capital contributions.

Exercise Seven-4

As its capital contribution to a joint venture, Lorty Ltd. contributes capital assets with a fair value of $325,000 in return for a 25 percent equity interest in the new enterprise. The assets have a carrying value on the books of Lorty of $264,000.

Required: Provide the journal entry to record Lorty Ltd.'s investment in the joint venture.

End Of Exercise Seven-4

7-58.   If the contributing venturer receives cash or other assets in addition to an equity interest, all or part of the recognized gain can be included in the contributing venturer's income at the time of transfer. Note, however, in applying Paragraph 3055.28, the amount of cash or other assets received must be reduced to the extent that they have been financed by the borrowing of the joint venture. This requirement is reflected in the following Recommendation:

Paragraph 3055.30   *For purposes of paragraph 3055.28, in determining the portion of the gain that should be taken to income, the amount of cash received or the fair value of the other assets received should be reduced by the contributing venturer's proportionate interest in cash or other assets derived from, or financed by, borrowings of the joint venture and by any obligation assumed by the contributing venturer that would in substance reverse or negate the original receipt of cash or other assets.* (January, 1995)

7-59.   The process of calculating the gain to be recognized under Paragraph 3055.28 is described as follows:

Paragraph 3055.34   Where the contributing venturer concurrently receives in exchange cash or other assets that do not represent in any way an investment in, or a claim on, the assets of the joint venture and where the venturer has no commitments to reinvest such consideration received in the joint venture, the portion of the gain that would be taken to income referred to in paragraph 3055.28 would be the difference between:

(a) the fair value of the consideration received, i.e. the amount of cash received or the fair value of the other assets received less the portion of cash or other assets represented by the contributing venturer's proportionate interest in cash or other assets derived from, or financed by, borrowings of the joint venture and less any obligation assumed by the contributing venturer that in substance would reverse or negate the original receipt of cash or other assets; and

(b) the net carrying value of the assets considered to be partly sold, i.e. that portion of the aggregate carrying value of those assets determined by applying the ratio of the fair value of the consideration received over the fair value of the assets transferred.

7-60.   After we have recognized the portion of the total gain specified in Paragraph 3055.27 and taken all or part of this gain into income as required by Paragraph 3055.28, we may be left with a Deferred Gain. This Deferred Gain will be taken into income in accordance with Paragraph 3055.29. For depreciable assets, this will be in a rational and systematic manner over their remaining life. For non-depreciable assets, Paragraph 3055.29 requires that the Deferred Gain be taken into income on a basis appropriate to the expected revenues that the asset will produce. Paragraph 3055.29 also requires that, if the transferred asset is sold by the joint venture, any portion of the Deferred Gain that has not been taken into income in previous periods, should be taken into income when the sale occurs.

Example One - No Bank Financing

7-61.   As an example of the application of Section 3055 Recommendations in situations where the contributing venturer receives cash or other assets that do not represent an equity interest in the venture, consider the following arrangement from the point of view of Alpha Company:

Example   Alpha Company and Beta Company, two unrelated companies, form a joint venture. Alpha contributes a manufacturing plant with an estimated fair value of $700 and a carrying value of $300. Alpha receives cash of $100 from the joint venture and a 40 percent interest in the joint venture. Alpha is not obligated to reinvest the cash or make further contributions. Beta contributes cash of $900 to the joint venture in return for a 60 percent interest in the joint venture.

7-62.   Applying Paragraph 3055.27, Alpha is able to recognize Beta's 60 percent share of the total gain. The maximum gain that can be recognized and the portion of this total gain that is taken into income at the time of the transfer would be calculated as follows:

Fair Value At Transfer	$700
Carrying Value At Transfer	(300)
Total Gain	$400
Alpha's Share (40 Percent)	(160)
Gain That Can Be Recognized	$240
Proceeds Of Disposition (All Unencumbered)	$100
Cost Of Assets Considered To Be Sold [($100 ÷ $700)($300)]	(43)
Gain To Be Taken Into Income At Time Of Transfer	$ 57

7-63.   Notice that, in this case, no bank financing was involved and, as a consequence, the proceeds of disposition are unencumbered and equal to the full amount of the cash received.

7-64.   Alpha's initial investment in the joint venture, before the application of proportionate consolidation procedures, would be as follows:

Carrying Value Of Plant	$300
Total Gain Recognized	240
Value Of Capital Contribution	$540
Equity Returned	(100)
Initial Investment	$440

Exercise Seven-5

Barco Inc. has entered into a joint venture agreement with two other corporations. As its capital contribution, the Company contributes capital assets with a fair value of $426,000 and a carrying value of $310,000. In return, Barco receives a 20 percent equity interest in the joint venture and $176,000 in cash. The other two corporations each contribute cash in return for a 40 percent interest in the joint venture.

Required: Provide the journal entry to record Barco Inc.'s investment in the joint venture.

End Of Exercise Seven-5

> Exercise Seven-5 deals with assets transferred for cash (no bank financing).

Example Two - Bank Financing

7-65.   In the previous example, all of the cash received by Alpha came from the funds invested by Beta. In this second example, we will assume the joint venture requires bank financing in order to make the payment to Alpha:

Example   Alpha Company and Beta Company, two unrelated corporations, form a joint venture. Alpha contributes a manufacturing plant with an estimated fair value of $1,000 and a net carrying value of $250. Alpha receives cash of $800 and a 40 percent interest in the joint venture. Alpha is not obligated to reinvest the cash or make further contributions. Beta contributes cash of $300 to the joint venture in return for a 60 percent interest in the joint venture. The joint venture borrows $650 from a bank.

7-66. Paragraph 3055.27 requires that Alpha give recognition to Beta's 60 percent share of the gain. The maximum gain that can be recognized and the portion of this total gain that is taken into income at the time of the transfer would be calculated as follows:

Fair Value At Transfer	$1,000
Carrying Value At Transfer	(250)
Total Gain	$ 750
Alpha's Share (40 Percent)	(300)
Gain That Can Be Recognized	$ 450
Gross Proceeds	$ 800
Share Of Cash Borrowed [(40%)($800 - $300)]	(200)
Net Proceeds	$ 600
Cost Of Assets Considered To Be Sold [($600 ÷ $1,000)($250)]	(150)
Gain To Be Taken Into Income At Time Of Transfer	$ 450

7-67. Note that in the calculation of the net proceeds, recognition is given to the fact that only $300 of the $800 in cash received by Alpha came from Beta. The remaining $500 came from the proceeds of the bank loan and Alpha is responsible for 40 percent of this amount. This serves to illustrate the application of Paragraph 3055.30.

7-68. Also note that the gain to be taken into income is the same amount as the total gain to be recognized. This results from the fact that the $600 Net Proceeds is equal to 60 percent of the fair value of the asset transferred, the same percentage as Beta's share of the joint venture. Given this situation, there is no further gain to be taken into income in subsequent periods.

7-69. The carrying value for Alpha's initial investment in the joint venture, before the application of proportionate consolidation procedures, would be calculated as follows:

Carrying Value Of Plant	$250
Gain Recognized	450
Value Of Capital Contribution	$700
Equity Returned	(800)
Initial Investment	($100)

7-70. Based on the fact that the amount received by Alpha from the joint venture ($800) exceeds the value of its contribution as measured under Section 3055 ($700), the interest in the joint venture is a liability rather than an asset.

Exercise Seven-6

Exercise Seven-6 deals with assets transferred for cash (with bank financing).

Tortly Ltd. has entered into a joint venture agreement with two other corporations. Tortly contributes assets with a fair value of $723,000 and a carrying value of $487,000. In return, Tortly receives a one-third interest in the joint venture and $123,000 in cash. Each of the other venturers contribute $50,000 in cash and capital assets with a fair market value of $550,000. The joint venture arranges a bank loan for $350,000 in order to finance its cash requirements.

Required: Provide the journal entry to record Tortly Ltd.'s investment in the joint venture.

End Of Exercise Seven-6

Transactions Between A Venturer And A Joint Venture

General Rules

7-71. Section 3055 of the *CICA Handbook* requires that interests in joint ventures be accounted for by the proportionate consolidation method. This would suggest that joint venture accounting requires the usual full consolidation adjustments for fair value write-offs and upstream and downstream unrealized intercompany profits. However, the fact that joint ventures are defined in a manner which creates a special relationship between its venturers has led the Accounting Standards Board to make a different Recommendation for dealing with profits arising on the intercompany transactions between a joint venture and its venturers.

7-72. To illustrate the differences, we will use an example in which an investee sells merchandise with a cost of $80,000 to one of its investor companies for $100,000, recording a profit of $20,000 which has not been realized through a subsequent resale by the investor company. Consider the differences in how this situation would be dealt with if the investee were a subsidiary, a significantly influenced company accounted for by the equity method or, alternatively, a joint venture accounted for by proportionate consolidation:

Subsidiary If the investee were a subsidiary, consolidation procedures would require that both the intercompany expense and revenue of $100,000 and the unrealized intercompany profit of $20,000 be eliminated. This conclusion results from the view that the parent and subsidiary are components of a single accounting entity and, as a consequence, a real sales transaction did not occur.

Significantly Influenced Company - Equity Method Under the equity method, the investor and investee are accounted for as separate entities and a real transaction did take place. As a consequence, there would be no elimination of the $100,000 intercompany expense and revenue. However, the presence of significant influence makes this a non-arm's length transaction, raising questions about the reliability of any profit figures that are reported. Given this, the *Handbook* Recommendations require the elimination of 100 percent of any unrealized intercompany profits in the application of the equity method. This is accomplished by a reduction in the Investment Income account, rather than through adjustments of specific expenses and revenues.

Joint Ventures - Proportionate Consolidation As any investor who classifies an investment as a joint venture must participate in its management, venturers clearly have influence over the joint venture. As a consequence, transactions between venturers and the joint venture appear to be on a non-arm's length basis. However, there is a difference from a situation where the equity method is appropriate because the investor has significant influence over the investee. In joint ventures, all of the venturers participate under the management agreement and are likely to pay careful attention to transactions that take place between the joint venture and other venturers. In fact, it would be unusual to find a joint venture agreement that does not specify the terms and conditions under which intercompany transactions can take place. Given this, it is usually reasonable to view transactions between a joint venture and its venturers as being arm's length in the sense that they are controlled by the relationship established in the joint venture arrangement or by an informal agreement among the joint venturers.

However, there is a problem. To the extent that the venturer has an equity interest in the joint venture, the intercompany transaction is, in effect, a transaction between the venturer and itself as represented by its interest in the joint venture. As a consequence, recognition of the particular venturer's share of the profit or loss does not appear to be appropriate.

The preceding discussion would suggest that, in the application of proportionate consolidation in joint venture situations, only the individual venturer's share of intercompany expenses, revenues, and unrealized profits would be eliminated. As will be discussed in the following Section, this is the position taken in Section 3055 of the *CICA Handbook*.

Section 3055 Recommendations
Downstream Transactions

7-73.   When there is a sale in the normal course of business operations from the venturer to the joint venture, commonly referred to as a downstream sale, Section 3055 makes the following Recommendation:

Paragraph 3055.36   *When a venturer sells assets to a joint venture in the normal course of operations and a gain or loss occurs, the venturer should recognize the gain or loss in income to the extent of the interests of the other non-related venturers. When such a transaction provides evidence of a reduction in the net realizable value, or a decline in the value, of the relevant assets, the venturer should recognize the full amount of any loss in income.* (January, 1995)

7-74.   To illustrate this provision, consider the following:

Example   On January 1, 2002, a group of joint venturers form Jointly Ltd.(JL) with a total investment of $1,000 in cash. One of the investors, Nordwell Inc. (NI), has received a 30 percent interest in return for $300 in cash. NI is a holding Company formed for this investment transaction and, on this date, the Company has no other assets or liabilities. The Balance Sheets of the two Companies on January 1, 2002 would be as follows:

Balance Sheets
As At January 1, 2002

	Nordwell	Jointly
Cash	Nil	$1,000
Investment In JL	$300	Nil
Total Assets	$300	$1,000
Common Stock (Total Equities)	$300	$1,000

During the year ending December 31, 2002, NI purchases merchandise on credit for $100 and sells it to JL for $160 in cash. The merchandise has not been resold at year end. Neither Company had other transactions during the year ending December 31, 2002. The Balance Sheets for the two Companies as at December 31, 2002 and the Income Statements for the year ending December 31, 2002 are as follows:

Balance Sheets
As At December 31, 2002

	Nordwell	Jointly
Cash	$160	$ 840
Inventory	Nil	160
Investment In JL	300	Nil
Total Assets	$460	$1,000
Accounts Payable	$100	Nil
Common Stock	300	$1,000
Retained Earnings	60	Nil
Total Equities	$460	$1,000

Income Statements
Year Ending December 31, 2002

	Nordwell	Jointly
Sales	$160	Nil
Cost Of Sales	100	Nil
Net Income	$ 60	Nil

7-75.   The first step in the consolidation procedures would be to eliminate the Investment In JL, JL's Common Stock and, because we are using proportionate consolidation, the 70 percent interest of the other joint venturers in Jointly's assets. The entry would be as follows:

Common Stock (JL)	$1,000	
Cash [(70%)($840)]		$588
Inventory [(70%)($160)]		112
Investment In JL		300

7-76.   As JL had no Income Statement items, there is no need for an entry to eliminate the interest of the other joint venturers in expenses or revenues. This means that the only other elimination entry is the one required to deal with the downstream sale. As NI can recognize this transaction to the extent of the interests of the other joint venturers, only NI's shares of the Sales, Costs Of Sales, and unrealized profit will have to be eliminated. The required entry is as follows:

Sales [(30%)($160)]	$48	
Inventory [(30%)($160 - $100)]		$18
Cost Of Sales [(30%)($100)]		30

7-77.   Given the preceding eliminations, the proportionate consolidation Balance Sheet and Income Statement can be prepared as follows:

Nordwell Inc.
Proportionate Consolidation Balance Sheet (Downstream Profits)
As At December 31, 2002

Cash ($160 + $840 - $588)	$412
Inventory (Nil + $160 - $112 - $18)	30
Investment In JL ($300 - $300)	Nil
Total Assets	$442
Accounts Payable	$100
Common Stock	300
Retained Earnings ($60 - $18)	42
Total Equities	$442

Nordwell Inc.
Proportionate Consolidation Income Statement (Downstream Profits)
Year Ending December 31, 2002

Sales ($160 - $48)	$112
Cost Of Sales ($100 - $30)	70
Net Income	$ 42

7-78.   Note that, if full consolidation procedures had been applied, the entire intercompany transaction would have been eliminated and there would have been no content in the consolidated Income Statement for the year ending December 31, 2002.

7-79.   As a final point on downstream transactions, note that the Paragraph 3055.36 Recommendation contemplates the possibility of recognizing 100 percent of a loss when the transaction provides evidence of a reduction in net realizable value. This is consistent with the Paragraph 3055.26 Recommendation on capital contributions to joint ventures, which also permitted full recognition of a loss under these circumstances.

<table>
<tr><td>Exercise Seven-7 deals with downstream inter-company profits.</td></tr>
</table>

Exercise Seven-7

On January 1, 2002, a group of joint venturers form Combo Inc. (CI) with a total investment of $465,000 in cash. One of the investors, Bonder Ltd. (BL), has received a 25 percent interest in return for $116,250 in cash. BL is a holding Company formed for this investment transaction and, on this date, the Company has no other assets or liabilities. The Balance Sheets of the two Companies on January 1, 2002 would be as follows:

Balance Sheets As At January 1, 2002

	Bonder	Combo
Cash	Nil	$465,000
Investment In Combo	$116,250	Nil
Total Assets	$116,250	$465,000
Common Stock (Total Equities)	$116,250	$465,000

During the year ending December 31, 2002, BL purchases merchandise on credit for $56,000 and sells it to CI for $84,000 in cash. None of the merchandise has been resold at year end. Neither Company had any other transactions during the year ending December 31, 2002. The Balance Sheets for the two Companies as at December 31, 2002 and the Income Statements for the year ending December 31, 2002 are as follows:

Balance Sheets As At December 31, 2002

	Bonder	Combo
Cash	$ 84,000	$381,000
Inventory	Nil	84,000
Investment In Combo	116,250	Nil
Total Assets	$200,250	$465,000
Accounts Payable	$ 56,000	Nil
Common Stock	116,250	$465,000
Retained Earnings	28,000	Nil
Total Equities	$200,250	$465,000

Income Statements
Year Ending December 31, 2002

	Bonder	Combo
Sales	$84,000	Nil
Cost Of Sales	56,000	Nil
Net Income	$28,000	Nil

Required: For Bonder Ltd., and its investee Combo Inc., prepare a proportionate consolidation Balance Sheet as at December 31, 2002, and a proportionate consolidation Income Statement for the year ending December 31, 2002.

End Of Exercise Seven-7

Upstream Transactions

7-80. When there is a sale from the joint venture to one of the venturers, commonly referred to as an upstream sale, the following Recommendation applies:

Paragraph 3055.37 *When a venturer purchases assets from a joint venture in the normal course of operations, the venturer should not recognize its share of the profit or loss of the joint venture on the transaction until the assets are sold to a third party. However, when the transaction provides evidence of a reduction in the net realizable value, or a decline in the value of the relevant assets, the venturer should recognize its share of the loss in income immediately.* (January, 1995)

7-81. In order to illustrate this provision, we will use the same basic example that was presented in Paragraph 7-74, modified to include an upstream rather than a downstream transaction. The example is as follows:

Example On January 1, 2002, a group of joint venturers form Jointly Ltd.(JL) with a total investment of $1,000 in cash. One of the investors, Nordwell Inc. (NI), has received a 30 percent interest in return for $300 in cash. NI is a holding Company formed for this investment transaction and, on this date, its only other asset or liability is cash of $220. The Balance Sheets of the two Companies on January 1, 2002 would be as follows:

Balance Sheets
As At January 1, 2002

	Nordwell	Jointly
Cash	$220	$1,000
Investment In JL	300	Nil
Total Assets	$520	$1,000
Common Stock	$520	$1,000

During the year ending December 31, 2002, JL purchases merchandise for $150 in cash and sells it to NI for $220 in cash. The merchandise has not been resold at year end. Neither Company had other transactions during the year ending December 31, 2002. The Balance Sheets for the two Companies as at December 31, 2002 and the Income Statements for the year ending December 31, 2002 are as follows:

Balance Sheets
As At December 31, 2002

	Nordwell	Jointly
Cash	Nil	$1,070
Inventory	$220	Nil
Investment In JL	300	Nil
Total Assets	$520	$1,070
Common Stock	$520	$1,000
Retained Earnings	Nil	70
Total Equities	$520	$1,070

Income Statements
Year Ending December 31, 2002

	Nordwell	Jointly
Sales	Nil	$220
Cost Of Sales	Nil	150
Net Income	Nil	$ 70

7-82.   A first entry is required to eliminate NI's Investment in JL, JL's Common Stock, and the other venturers' interest in the assets, liabilities, expenses, and revenues of JL:

Common Stock (JL)	$1,000	
Sales [(70%)($220)]	154	
Cost Of Sales [(70%)($150)]		$105
Cash [(70%)($1,070)]		749
Investment In JL		300

7-83.   If there had been an opening balance in JL's Retained Earnings, the preceding entry would have also eliminated that balance.

7-84.   A second entry is required to eliminate NI's share of the intercompany Sales, Cost Of Sales, and the unrealized profit in the ending Inventory:

Sales [(30%)($220)]	$66	
Inventory [(30%)($220 - $150)]		$21
Cost Of Sales [(30%)($150)]		45

7-85.   Using the preceding journal entries, the proportionate consolidation Balance Sheet and Income Statement can be prepared as follows:

Nordwell Inc.
Proportionate Consolidation Balance Sheet (Upstream Profits)
As At December 31, 2002

Cash (Nil + $1,070 - $749)	$321
Inventory ($220 + Nil - $21)	199
Investment In JL ($300 - $300)	Nil
Total Assets	$520
Common Stock	$520
Retained Earnings	Nil
Total Equities	$520

Nordwell Inc.
Proportionate Consolidation Income Statement (Upstream Profits)
Year Ending December 31, 2002

Sales (Nil + $220 - $154 - $66)	Nil
Cost Of Sales (Nil + $150 - $105 - $45)	Nil
Net Income	Nil

7-86.   With respect to the proportionate consolidation Income Statement, we have not included any disclosure of the intercompany transaction. This reflects the fact that, while we can recognize the other venturers' share of the intercompany profit, it is not disclosed in the proportionate consolidation Income Statement.

7-87.   Note that, in this example, the preceding consolidated Income Statement is the same as that which would result from the application of full consolidation procedures. That is, 100 percent of JL's expenses and revenues have been eliminated. There is, however, a different reason for the elimination of the other venturers' share of these expenses and revenues. In the preceding statement, these amounts were eliminated because we are using proportionate consolidation procedures. In full consolidation, these amounts would be eliminated because they were intercompany and the transactions which they reflect did not occur from a consolidated point of view.

Exercise Seven-8

On January 1, 2002, a group of joint venturers form Combo Inc. (CI) with a total investment of $465,000 in cash. One of the investors, Bonder Ltd. (BL), has received a 25 percent interest in return for $116,250 in cash. BL is a holding Company formed for this investment transaction and, on this date, the Company has no other assets or liabilities. The Balance Sheets of the two Companies on January 1, 2002 would be as follows:

> Exercise Seven-8 deals with upstream inter-company profits.

Balance Sheets
As At January 1, 2002

	Bonder	Combo
Cash	Nil	$465,000
Investment In Combo	$116,250	Nil
Total Assets	$116,250	$465,000
Common Stock (Total Equities)	$116,250	$465,000

During the year ending December 31, 2002, CI purchases merchandise for $32,000 in cash and sells it to BL on account for $48,000. None of the merchandise has been resold at year end. Neither Company had any other transactions during the year ending December 31, 2002. The Balance Sheets for the two Companies as at December 31, 2002 and the Income Statements for the year ending December 31, 2002 are as follows:

Balance Sheets
As At December 31, 2002

	Bonder	Combo
Cash	Nil	$433,000
Accounts Receivable	Nil	48,000
Inventory	$ 48,000	Nil
Investment In Combo	116,250	Nil
Total Assets	$164,250	$481,000
Accounts Payable	$ 48,000	Nil
Common Stock	116,250	$465,000
Retained Earnings	Nil	16,000
Total Equities	$164,250	$481,000

Income Statements
Year Ending December 31, 2002

	Bonder	Combo
Sales	Nil	$48,000
Cost Of Sales	Nil	32,000
Net Income	Nil	$16,000

This is a continuation of Exercise Seven-8.

Required: For Bonder Ltd., and its investee Combo Inc., prepare a proportionate consolidation Balance Sheet as at December 31, 2002, and a proportionate consolidation Income Statement for the year ending December 31, 2002.

End Of Exercise Seven-8

Upstream And Downstream Transactions Compared

7-88.   With both upstream and downstream intercompany profits, the venturer is allowed to recognize the share of such profits that belongs to the other non-affiliated venturers in its consolidated financial statements. However, because proportionate consolidation is being used, the resulting disclosure is somewhat confusing.

7-89.   In the consolidated Balance Sheet for the downstream profits example (Paragraph 7-77), none of the $60 intercompany profit is included in the Inventory balance. The $30 balance in this account is simply NI's 30 percent share of the $100 original cost of the Inventory. This does not mean, however, that we have not recognized the other venturers' 70 percent share of the profit. This is clear from the proportionate consolidation Income Statement which shows a profit equal to $42 (70 percent of $60). The reason that this $42 does not show up in the Inventory figure is that the Inventory belongs to JL and this means that proportionate consolidation procedures have removed 70 percent of all of JL's accounts. The $42 has been removed here, not because it is intercompany, but because proportionate consolidation procedures remove all values that belong to the other joint venturers.

7-90.   The Inventory figure in the proportionate consolidation Balance Sheet in the upstream profits example in Paragraph 7-85 includes the 70 percent share of the $70 intercompany profit that belongs to the other joint venturers {$199 = [$150 cost to JL + (70%)($70)]}. The reason that the profit is included in the consolidated Inventory figure in this case is that the Inventory is on the books of NI. This means that it will not be eliminated by proportionate consolidation procedures.

7-91.   However, the $49 profit is not included in the proportionate consolidation Income Statement. This reflects the fact that, in upstream transactions, the Sales and Cost Of Sales figures are from the books of JL. This means that 70 percent of these figures are eliminated through proportionate consolidation procedures, thereby eliminating in the proportionate consolidation Income Statement, the $49 profit that is included in the proportionate consolidation Balance Sheet. The investor, NI, had Sales and Cost Of Sales of nil and the joint venture's only sale was to NI. The fact that the total profit on this sale was unrealized results in a proportionate consolidation Income Statement where the Sales and the Cost Of Sales are also nil.

Comprehensive Example

Basic Data

7-92.   The following comprehensive example will serve to illustrate the application of proportionate consolidation procedures:

On January 1, 2002, Laroo Ltd. (LL) and Rotan Inc. (RI) establish a new corporation which will market products that both companies produce. LL has no affiliation with RI other than their common ownership of the new corporation. The new corporation is called Cooperative Enterprises Inc. (CEI).

LL's capital contribution consists of a Building with a carrying value of $1,500,000 and a fair value of $2,000,000. The building is situated on leased land. The lease payments are at current fair market value and the lease is transferred to CEI at the time of its incorporation. On January 1, 2002, the remaining term of the lease is 20 years and this is also the remaining economic life of the building. In return for the building, LL receives 60 percent of CEI's voting shares and $200,000 in cash. LL records a gain of $500,000 on the transfer of the building.

RI's capital contribution consists of $1,200,000 in cash. In return, RI receives 40 percent of CEI's voting shares.

LL and RI sign an agreement which provides for joint control over CEI. All significant operating and financing decisions must be approved by both of the investor companies.

For the year ending December 31, 2002, the single entity Balance Sheets and Income Statements for LL and CEI are as follows:

Balance Sheets
As At December 31, 2002

	LL	CEI
Cash And Receivables	$ 1,500,000	$ 300,000
Inventories	4,800,000	1,500,000
Investment In CEI (At Cost)	1,800,000	-0-
Land	1,100,000	-0-
Building	3,500,000	2,000,000
Accumulated Depreciation	(1,200,000)	(100,000)
Total Assets	$11,500,000	$3,700,000
Liabilities	$ 2,200,000	$ 200,000
Common Stock - No Par	5,000,000	3,000,000
Retained Earnings	4,300,000	500,000
Total Equities	$11,500,000	$3,700,000

Income Statements
For The Year Ending December 31, 2002

	LL	CEI
Sales	$ 4,200,000	$ 2,800,000
Gain On Sale Of Building	500,000	-0-
Cost Of Goods Sold	(2,500,000)	(1,500,000)
Depreciation Expense	(700,000)	(100,000)
Other Expenses	(400,000)	(700,000)
Net Income	$ 1,100,000	$ 500,000

Other Information:

1. During the year ending December 31, 2002, CEI sells merchandise to LL for $420,000. This merchandise had cost CEI $350,000 and none of it has been resold by LL.

2. During the year ending December 31, 2002, LL sells merchandise to CEI for $860,000. This merchandise had cost LL $740,000 and one-half of it has been resold by CEI.

3. Neither LL nor CEI declare or pay dividends during the year ending December 31, 2002.

Required: Using proportionate consolidation procedures, prepare a consolidated Balance Sheet as at December 31, 2002 and a consolidated Income Statement for the year ending December 31, 2002, for LL and its investee CEI.

Investment Elimination

7-93.   The journal entry to eliminate the Investment In CEI, CEI's Common Stock - No Par, CEI's Retained Earnings (At Acquisition), and the other venturer's (RI's) 40 percent share of the individual assets, liabilities, expenses, and revenues of CEI would be as follows:

Common Stock - No Par (CEI's)	$3,000,000	
Retained Earnings (At Acquisition)	Nil	
Accumulated Depreciation (40%)	40,000	
Liabilities (40%)	80,000	
Sales (40%)	1,120,000	
Cash And Receivables (40%)		$ 120,000
Inventories (40%)		600,000
Building (40%)		800,000
Cost Of Goods Sold (40%)		600,000
Depreciation Expense (40%)		40,000
Other Expenses (40%)		280,000
Investment In CEI		1,800,000

7-94.   Note that, at this point, we are left with 60 percent of the carrying values of CEI's assets, liabilities, expenses, and revenues. Because we are using proportionate consolidation, there is no non-controlling interest to reflect RI's interest in the assets, liabilities, expenses, and revenues of CEI.

Analysis Of Gain

7-95.   In transferring the Building to CEI, LL recognized a gain of $500,000 ($2,000,000 - $1,500,000). Under the provisions of Section 3055, this gain can only be recognized to the extent of the interest of the other non-affiliated venturer. This provides the following analysis:

Total Gain	$500,000
LL's Share (60 Percent)	(300,000)
Gain To Be Recognized	$200,000

7-96.   To the extent that LL received cash or assets other than an equity interest in NVI, this gain can be taken into income at the time of transfer. The calculation of the amount to be taken into income at the time of transfer is as follows:

Cash Received At Transfer	$200,000
Cost Of Asset Considered To Be Sold:	
[($200,000 ÷ $2,000,000)($1,500,000)]	(150,000)
Gain To Be Taken Into Income At Transfer	$ 50,000

7-97.   The remaining $150,000 ($200,000 - $50,000) of the gain that can be recognized, will be taken into income over the 20 year life of the Building. This will be at a rate of $7,500 per year.

7-98.   As the $300,000 unrecognized gain will have to be removed from the consolidated carrying value of the Building, the consolidated Depreciation Expense will have to be decreased annually by $15,000 ($300,000 ÷ 20 Years).

Gain Adjustment - Building

7-99.   An entry is required to deal with the total gain recognized by LL on the transfer of the Building. The entry will leave the $50,000 of the gain that can be taken into income at transfer in the Gain On Sale Of Building account. The $300,000 of the gain that cannot be recognized will be removed from the Building account, while the $150,000 portion of the gain that will be recognized over the life of the Building will be allocated to a Deferred Gain account. The required entry is as follows:

Gain On Sale Of Building ($500,000 - $50,000)	$450,000	
Building (Unrecognized Portion)		$300,000
Deferred Gain		150,000

7-100. This entry, when combined with the earlier elimination of RI's 40 percent share of the Building, leaves a balance of $900,000 ($2,000,000 - $800,000 - $300,000). As would be expected, this is equal to LL's 60 percent share of the original $1,500,000 carrying value for the Building.

Deferred Gain Amortization

7-101. As one year has passed since the Building was transferred to CEI, one-twentieth of the Deferred Gain has been realized and can be taken into income. The appropriate entry is as follows:

| Deferred Gain | $7,500 | |
| Gain On Sale Of Building | | $7,500 |

7-102. As CEI has recorded depreciation on the $2,000,000 fair value of the Building, this must be adjusted to reflect the removal of the $300,000 unrecognized gain from this asset. This will require an annual adjustment of $15,000 ($300,000 ÷ 20 Years) as follows:

| Accumulated Depreciation | $15,000 | |
| Depreciation Expense | | $15,000 |

7-103. This entry, when combined with the earlier elimination of RI's 40 percent share of the Building, leaves Accumulated Depreciation and Depreciation Expense at $45,000. As was the case with the Building account, this is equal to depreciation at 5 percent on LL's $900,000 [(60%)($1,500,000)] share of the original carrying value of the building.

7-104. There are intercompany expenses and revenues arising from both upstream ($420,000) and downstream ($860,000) sales of merchandise. In the case of joint ventures, intercompany sales and any related intercompany profit can be recognized to the extent of the share of the other non-affiliated venturers (Paragraphs 3055.36 and 3055.37). In the case of downstream transactions, this means that we must eliminate the selling venturer's share of the sale and any unrealized profit resulting from the transaction. The remainder of the downstream sale and the related profit will remain in the proportionate consolidation results. When an upstream transaction is involved, all of the sale and unrealized profit must be eliminated. While we can recognize the other non-related venturer's share of the profit in the consolidated Balance Sheet (it is included in an asset on the books of the venturer and not subject to proportionate consolidation procedures), the sale and profit belong to the other non-related venturer and will be removed by the proportionate consolidation procedures.

7-105. With respect to the entry to eliminate the intercompany sales, RI's 40 percent share of the upstream sale was eliminated in our first journal entry. This means that we will only need to eliminate $1,112,000 [(60%)($420,000) + $860,000] of these sales. The required entry is as follows:

| Sales | $1,112,000 | |
| Cost Of Goods Sold | | $1,112,000 |

7-106. As some of the merchandise has not been resold, there are also unrealized intercompany profits to be eliminated. The upstream amount is $70,000 [(100%)($420,000 - $350,000)] and the downstream amount is $60,000 [(50%)($860,000 - $740,000)]. As was the case with upstream intercompany sales, we have already eliminated RI's 40 percent share of all of CEI's profits and, as a consequence, we only need to eliminate $42,000 [(60%)($70,000)] of the unrealized upstream profit of $70,000. With respect to the downstream profit, we will need to eliminate 60 percent of this total, an amount of $36,000 [(60%)(50%)($860,000 - $740,000)]. The entry to eliminate this total of $78,000 ($42,000 + $36,000) is as follows:

Cost Of Goods Sold
($42,000 upstream + $36,000 downstream) $78,000
    Inventories $78,000

7-107.   Given these entries, the required consolidated Balance Sheet can be prepared as follows:

LL And Investee CEI
Consolidated Balance Sheet (Proportionate Basis)
As At December 31, 2002

Cash And Receivables ($1,500,000 + $300,000 - $120,000)	$ 1,680,000
Inventories ($4,800,000 + $1,500,000 - $600,000 - $78,000)	5,622,000
Investment In CEI ($1,800,000 - $1,800,000)	-0-
Land (LL's Only)	1,100,000
Building ($3,500,000 + $2,000,000 - $800,000 - $300,000)	4,400,000
Accumulated Depreciation ($1,200,000 + $100,000 - $40,000 - $15,000)	(1,245,000)
Total Assets	$11,557,000
Liabilities ($2,200,000 + $200,000 - $80,000)	$ 2,320,000
Deferred Gain ($150,000 - $7,500)	142,500
Common Stock - No Par (LL's Only)	5,000,000
Retained Earnings (See Note)	4,094,500
Total Equities	$11,557,000

Note   The balance in consolidated Retained Earnings can be verified with the following calculation:

LL's Balance - December 31, 2002	$4,300,000
Unrecognized Gain On Building Transfer	(300,000)
Deferred Gain On Building Transfer	(150,000)
Gain Realized During 2002	7,500
Depreciation Adjustment	15,000
Downstream Inventory Profit [(60%)($60,000)]	(36,000)
BL's Adjusted Balance	$3,836,500
Equity Pickup [(60%)($500,000 - $70,000)]	258,000
Consolidated Retained Earnings	$4,094,500

7-108.   The required consolidated Income Statement would be prepared as follows:

LL And Investee CEI
Consolidated Income Statement (Proportionate Basis)
Year Ending December 31, 2002

Sales ($4,200,000 + $2,800,000 - $1,120,000 - $1,112,000)	$4,768,000
Gain On Sale Of Building ($500,000 - $450,000 + $7,500)	57,500
Cost Of Goods Sold ($2,500,000 + $1,500,000 - $600,000 - $1,112,000 + $78,000)	(2,366,000)
Depreciation Expense ($700,000 + $100,000 - $40,000 - $15,000)	(745,000)
Other Expenses ($400,000 + $700,000 - $280,000)	(820,000)
Consolidated Net Income	$ 894,500

7-109.   The consolidated Net Income figure can be verified with the following calculation:

LL's 2002 Net Income	$1,100,000
Unrecognized Gain On Building Transfer	(300,000)
Deferred Gain On Building Transfer	(150,000)
Gain Realized During 2002	7,500
Depreciation Adjustment	15,000
Downstream Inventory Profit [(60%)($60,000)]	(36,000)
BL's Adjusted Balance	$ 636,500
Equity Pickup [(60%)($500,000 - $70,000)]	258,000
Consolidated Net Income	$ 894,500

7-110.   Note that the preceding adjustments to LL's Net Income are the same as the adjustments in the verification of consolidated Retained Earnings. This is because it is the first year of operations of CEI.

Disclosure

7-111.   In order to give investors a better understanding of the extent to which the venturer's activities are carried out in the form of joint ventures, separate disclosure of the venturer's share of assets, liabilities, revenues, expenses, net income, and cash flows of the joint venture are required. This is reflected in the following Recommendation:

> **Paragraph 3055.41**   *A venturer should disclose the total amounts and the major components of each of the following related to its interests in joint ventures:*
>
> *(a) current assets and long-term assets;*
> *(b) current liabilities and long-term liabilities;*
> *(c) revenues, expenses and net income;*
> *(d) cash flows resulting from operating activities;*
> *(e) cash flows resulting from financing activities; and*
> *(f) cash flows resulting from investing activities. (January, 1995)*

7-112.   This information would normally be presented on a combined basis for all of the venturer's joint venture activities. In those situations where substantially all of the activities of a venturer are carried out through joint ventures, a statement that this is the case would be sufficient disclosure.

7-113.   Joint venture arrangements involve contingencies and commitments, even to the extent of an individual venturer becoming responsible for other venturers' shares of joint venture obligations. The need for disclosure in this type of situation is reflected in the following Recommendation:

> **Paragraph 3055.42**   *A venturer should disclose its share of any contingencies and commitments of joint ventures and those contingencies that exist when the venturer is contingently liable for the liabilities of the other venturers of the joint ventures. (January, 1995)*

7-114.   Paragraph 3055.44 indicates that it is generally desirable to disclose a listing and description of significant interests in joint ventures, including the names and the proportion of ownership interest held in particular ventures. Other disclosure requirements may arise for joint ventures as the result of the application of other *CICA Handbook* Sections. For example, some of the Recommendations of Section 3840, "Related Party Transactions" would often be applicable to joint ventures.

Joint Ventures In Canadian Practice

Statistics From Financial Reporting In Canada

7-115. Of the 200 companies surveyed for the 2001 edition of *Financial Reporting in Canada*, 76 companies indicated in their 2000 annual reports that they participated in one or more joint venture arrangements. Of the 76 companies, 69 accounted for these arrangements using proportionate consolidation. Of the remaining companies, 3 used other methods (cost or equity) and 4 did not disclose the method that they used.

7-116. With respect to other types of disclosure, the following additional statistics are included for the 200 companies surveyed for the 2001 edition of *Financial Reporting in Canada:*

- 50 companies provided separate disclosure of the current and non-current assets of their joint ventures;
- 45 companies provided separate disclosure of the current and long-term liabilities of their joint ventures; and
- 53 companies disclosed the operating, financing, and investing cash flows of their joint venture arrangements.

Example From Practice

7-117. The following example is from the annual report of Domtar Inc. for the reporting period ending December 31, 2000. It illustrates disclosure of joint venture investments in both the Accounting Policies and in a separate note to the financial statements. It provides fairly detailed disclosure of joint venture financial information.

Notes To Financial Statements
(millions of Canadian dollars)

Note 1   Summary of Significant Accounting Policies (in part)
Basis Of Consolidation
The consolidated financial statements include the accounts of Domtar Inc. (the Corporation) and all its subsidiaries and joint ventures (collectively Domtar). Investments over which the Corporation exercises significant influence are accounted for by the equity method. The Corporation's interest in joint ventures is accounted for by the proportionate consolidation method.

Note 3   Business Acquisitions (in part)
Armor-Box
In October 2000, Norampac (a 50-50 joint venture with Cascades Inc.) acquired all of the assets of the Armor-Box Corporation, a corrugated products converting plant in the United States, for cash consideration of $20 million (the Corporation's proportionate share being $10 million).

Note 11   Long-Term Debt (in part)

	Maturity	2000	1999
Norampac			
Unsecured notes			
9.5% Notes (2000 and 1999 – U.S. $75)	2008	113	108
9.375% Notes	2008	50	50
Reducing revolving credit facility(secured)			
(2000 – FF33; 1999 – U.S. $9; FF33; Cdn $13)	2003	7	33
Other		7	11
		177	202

Note 16   Interest In A Joint Venture

Effective December 30, 1997, the Corporation and Cascades Inc. merged their respective packaging businesses to form Norampac, a 50-50 joint venture.

The following amounts represent Domtar's proportionate interest in Norampac:

	2000	1999
	$	$
Assets		
Current assets	157	136
Long-term assets	396	365
Liabilities		
Current liabilities	75	78
Long-term liabilities	250	216

	2000	1999	1998
	$	$	$
Earnings			
Net sales	524	453	434
Operating profit	100	59	29
Financing expenses	18	21	22
Net earnings	56	22	3
Cash flows			
Cash flows provided from operating activities	111	38	24
Cash flows provided from (used for) investing activities	(50)	(14)	2
Cash flows used for financing activities	(42)	(24)	(26)

7-118.   Additional examples of joint venture disclosure in published annual reports can be found in Chapter 24 of our *Financial Reporting In Canada*. This publication is available on the CD-ROM which accompanies this text.

Additional Readings

7-119.   In writing the material in the text, we have incorporated all of the relevant *CICA Handbook* Recommendations, as well as material from other sources that we felt to be of importance. This includes ideas put forward in articles published in professional accounting journals.

7-120.   While this approach meets the needs of the great majority of accounting students, some of you may wish to pursue this subject in greater depth. To facilitate this, you will find a fairly comprehensive bibliography of materials on the subject of interests in joint ventures in Chapter 28 of our *Guide to Canadian Financial Reporting*. Chapter 28 of the *Guide* also contains a summary of EIC Abstract No. 38, "Accounting By Newly Formed Joint Ventures". This is the only current EIC Abstract that provides significant guidance on joint ventures.

7-121.   The complete *Guide to Canadian Financial Reporting* is available on the CD-ROM which accompanies this text.

Problems For Self Study

(The solutions for these problems can be found following Chapter 16 of the text.)

Self Study Problem Seven - 1

Each of the following independent cases involves three companies which deal with each other at arm's length. They are Acres Ltd. (AL), Barrus Ltd. (BL), and Caron Ltd. (CL). In all cases presented, the three companies are forming a joint venture called Collusive Ventures Ltd. (CVL) and the joint venture agreement gives them the following equity interests in this new enterprise:

Venturer	AL	BL	CL
Equity Interest In CVL	25 Percent	35 Percent	40 Percent

We will be concerned with accounting for the capital contribution being made by AL and, as a consequence, the capital contributions of BL and CL will be the same in all cases. They are as follows:

BL This venturer contributes cash of $600,000 and other assets with a fair value of $450,000. The carrying value of these assets on BL's books is $220,000.

CL This venturer contributes cash of $400,000 and other assets with a fair value of $800,000. The carrying value of these assets on CL's books is $1,115,000.

Case One In return for its 25 percent equity interest in CVL, AL contributes non-monetary assets with a fair value of $750,000 and a carrying value of $1,000,000. AL receives no other assets from CVL and CVL does not assume any additional debt at the time of its incorporation.

Case Two In return for its 25 percent equity interest in CVL, AL contributes non-monetary assets with a fair value of $1,100,000 and a carrying value on AL's books of $600,000. In addition to its 25 percent equity interest, AL receives $350,000 in cash. CVL does not assume any additional debt at the time of its incorporation.

Case Three In return for its 25 percent equity interest in CVL, AL contributes cash of $350,000 and non-monetary assets with a fair value of $400,000. The carrying value of these non-monetary assets on the books of AL is $250,000. AL receives no other assets from CVL and CVL does not assume any additional debt at the time of its incorporation.

Case Four In return for its 25 percent equity interest in CVL, AL contributes non-monetary assets with a fair value of $1,400,000 and a carrying value on AL's books of $1,100,000. In addition to its 25 percent equity interest, AL receives $650,000 in cash. At the time of incorporation, CVL borrows $1,000,000. The three venturers are responsible for this debt in proportion to their equity interests in CVL.

Case Five In return for its 25 percent equity interest in CVL, AL contributes non-monetary assets with a fair value of $2,500,000 and a carrying value on AL's books of $2,000,000. In addition to its 25 percent equity interest, AL receives $1,750,000 in cash. At the time of incorporation, CVL borrows $1,000,000. The three venturers are responsible for this debt in proportion to their equity interests in CVL.

Required: Following the Recommendations of Section 3055 of the *CICA Handbook*, determine the amount of the gain or loss that would be recognized by AL at the time it makes its capital contribution to CVL.

Self Study Problem Seven - 2

On April 1, 2002, Sentinel Resources Ltd. and the Molar Oil Company jointly purchase Numa Inc. The enterprise will be operated as a joint venture and fits the joint venture definition contained in Section 3055 of the *CICA Handbook*. The main objective of Numa Inc. will be to develop oil fields in northern Alberta. Sentinel Resources contributes $450,000 in cash for 45 percent of Numa Inc.'s outstanding voting shares while Molar Oil purchases the remaining 55 percent for $550,000. Other than the joint venture agreement, there is no affiliation of any sort between the two investor companies.

On April 1, 2002, after the purchase of Numa Inc., the condensed Balance Sheets of the three companies and the fair values of the identifiable non-current assets are as follows:

Condensed Balance Sheets
As At April 1, 2002

	Sentinel	Molar	Numa
Net Current Assets	$1,050,000	$ 950,000	$100,000
Investment in Numa	450,000	550,000	-0-
Other Non-Current Assets	5,300,000	7,600,000	840,000
Total Assets	$6,800,000	$9,100,000	$940,000
Common Stock - No Par	$4,000,000	$5,000,000	$940,000
Retained Earnings	2,800,000	4,100,000	-0-
Total Equities	$6,800,000	$9,100,000	$940,000
Non-Current Assets - Fair Values	$5,700,000	$9,800,000	$900,000

The fair values of the net current assets are equal to their carrying values. In each of the three companies, the difference between the fair values and carrying values of the non-current assets arises from Land.

For the year ending March 31, 2003, the condensed Income Statements, before the recognition of any investment income, and the dividends declared of the three Companies are as follows:

Condensed Income Statements
For The Year Ending March 31, 2003

	Sentinel	Molar	Numa
Revenues	$7,800,000	$9,600,000	$660,000
Expenses and Losses	6,400,000	8,500,000	480,000
Net Income	$1,400,000	$1,100,000	$180,000
Dividends Declared	$ 300,000	$ 500,000	$ 40,000

Also during the year ending March 31, 2003, the following transactions occurred between Numa Inc. and its investor companies:

1. On March 1, 2003, Molar Oil purchased crude oil from Numa Inc. for $390,000. The cost allocated to the oil by Numa Inc. is $314,000. All of this oil is being stored by Molar Oil and it will be sold in April, 2003.

2. On March 31, 2003, Sentinel Resources purchased Equipment from Numa Inc. for $95,000. The Equipment had been carried on the books of Numa Inc. at a net book value of $175,000. The resulting $80,000 loss is included in the Expenses And Losses of Numa.

Required: Using the Recommendations of Section 3055 of the CICA Handbook:

A. Prepare the condensed proportionate consolidation Balance Sheet of Sentinel Resources as at April 1, 2002, after the acquisition of 45 percent of Numa Inc.

B. Prepare the condensed proportionate consolidation Income Statement of Sentinel Resources Ltd. for the year ending March 31, 2003.

C. Prepare the condensed proportionate consolidation Income Statement of Molar Oil Company for the year ending March 31, 2003.

Self Study Problem Seven - 3

On January 1, 2002, the Daunton Company, Etna Company, and Lerner Company establish DEL Ltd. The three companies sign an agreement which specifies that in all areas essential to the operation of DEL Ltd., decisions must be made by and require the consent of each of the three companies. Other than this agreement, there is no affiliation of any sort between the three investor companies. The new company is organized to do pharmaceutical research. The Daunton Company and the Etna Company each hold 40 percent of DEL Ltd's outstanding voting shares while the Lerner Company holds the remaining 20 percent.

During the year ending December 31, 2002, DEL Ltd. had Net Income of $475,000 and declared dividends of $75,000. On November 1, 2002, the Daunton Company purchased excess laboratory chemicals from DEL Ltd. for $16,000. They had been purchased by DEL Ltd. for $52,000 and had a limited shelf life. On December 31, 2002, the Etna Company purchased a patented process from DEL Ltd. for $183,000. The cost allocated to this process by DEL Ltd. was $100,000.

On December 31, 2002, the Joffry Company, which has no affiliation with the original investors, purchases all of the outstanding voting shares of DEL Ltd. held by the Daunton Company and the Etna Company. On that date, the condensed Balance Sheets of the Joffry Company and DEL Ltd. and the fair values of DEL Ltd.'s assets and liabilities are as follows:

Balance Sheets
As At December 31, 2002

	Joffry Book Value	DEL Ltd. Book Value	DEL Ltd. Fair Value
Current Assets	$ 780,000	$ 300,000	$320,000
Non-Current Assets	1,500,000	700,000	$650,000
Investment In DEL (At Cost)	720,000	-0-	
Total Assets	$3,000,000	$1,000,000	
Liabilities	$ 500,000	$ 200,000	$160,000
Common Stock (No Par)	1,000,000	400,000	
Retained Earnings	1,500,000	400,000	
Total Equities	$3,000,000	$1,000,000	

Required:

A. Assume that the Joffry Company signs an agreement which specifies that in all areas essential to the operation of DEL Ltd., decisions must be made by and require the consent of both the Lerner Company and the Joffry Company. Prepare the Balance Sheet for the Joffry Company as at December 31, 2002 assuming the Joffry Company uses proportionate consolidation to account for its Investment in DEL Ltd.

B. Assume that there is no agreement that provides for participation in the affairs or operations of DEL Ltd. by the Lerner Company. Prepare the consolidated Balance Sheet for the Joffry Company and its subsidiary DEL Ltd. as at December 31, 2002.

C. Provide the journal entries related to the Etna Company's income and dividends from its Investment in DEL Ltd. for the year ending December 31, 2002, prior to the sale of DEL Ltd. Etna Company uses the equity method to account for its investment in DEL Ltd. in its single entity records. Your solution should show the calculation of Investment Income and comply with all of the requirements of the *CICA Handbook*.

Self Study Problem Seven - 4

On January 1, 2002, Barton Ltd. (BL) and Systems Inc. (SI) establish a new corporation which will market products that both companies produce. BL has no affiliation with SI other than their common ownership of the new corporation. The new corporation will be called New Venture Inc. (NVI). BL and SI signed an agreement which provides for joint control over NVI. All significant operating and financing decisions must be approved by both of the investor companies.

BL's capital contribution consists of a Building with a carrying value of $400,000 and a fair value of $1,200,000. The building is situated on leased land. The lease payments are at current fair market value and the lease is transferred to NVI at the time of its incorporation. On January 1, 2002, the remaining term of the lease is 10 years and this is also the remaining economic life of the building. In return for the building, BL receives 45 percent of NVI's voting shares and $300,000 in cash. BL records a gain of $800,000 on the transfer of the building.

SI's capital contribution consists of $1,100,000 in cash. In return, SI receives 55 percent of NVI's voting shares.

For the year ending December 31, 2002, the single entity Balance Sheets and Income Statements for BL and NVI are as follows:

Balance Sheets
As At December 31, 2002

	BL	NVI
Cash And Receivables	$1,600,000	$ 420,000
Inventories	3,420,000	1,160,000
Investment In NVI (At Cost)	900,000	-0-
Land	620,000	-0-
Building	2,120,000	1,200,000
Accumulated Depreciation	(630,000)	(120,000)
Total Assets	$8,030,000	$2,660,000
Liabilities	$ 470,000	$ 120,000
Common Stock - No Par	4,800,000	2,000,000
Retained Earnings	2,760,000	540,000
Total Equities	$8,030,000	$2,660,000

Income Statements
For The Year Ending December 31, 2002

	BL	NVI
Sales	$3,500,000	$2,300,000
Gain On Sale Of Building	800,000	-0-
Total Revenues	$4,300,000	$2,300,000
Cost Of Goods Sold	$2,200,000	$1,490,000
Depreciation Expense	220,000	120,000
Other Expenses	340,000	150,000
Total Expenses	$2,760,000	$1,760,000
Net Income	$1,540,000	$ 540,000

Other Information:

1. During the year ending December 31, 2002, NVI sells merchandise to BL for $250,000. This merchandise had cost NVI $200,000 and none of it has been resold by BL.

2. During the year ending December 31, 2002, BL sells merchandise to NVI for $940,000. This merchandise had cost BL $860,000 and one-half of it has been resold by NVI.

3. Neither BL nor NVI declare or pay dividends during the year ending December 31, 2002.

Required: Using proportionate consolidation procedures, prepare a consolidated Balance Sheet as at December 31, 2002 and a consolidated Income Statement for the year ending December 31, 2002, for BL and its investee, NVI. Your solution should comply with the Recommendations of Section 3055 of the *CICA Handbook*.

Assignment Problems

(The solutions for these problems are only available in
the solutions manual that has been provided to your instructor.)

Assignment Problem Seven - 1

Each of the following Cases involves two companies which deal with each other at arm's length. The two companies are Boom Boom Ltd. (BBL) and Yum Yum Inc. (YYI). Boom Boom Ltd. is involved in processing popcorn products, while Yum Yum Inc. manufactures luxury ice cream products. They have decided to form a new company, Paradise Ventures Ltd. (PVL), in order to do research on the use of popcorn in ice cream products. The new company will be subject to a management agreement which gives BBL and YYI joint control of the investing, financing, and operating activities of the company.

The two cases which follow describe the capital contributions made by BBL and YYI in the organization of PVL. They are independent of each other.

Case One BBL contributes cash of $1,500,000, one item of manufacturing equipment with a fair value of $560,000 and a carrying value of $450,000, and a second item of manufacturing equipment with a fair value of $740,000 and a carrying value of $860,000. The transfer of the second item of equipment to PVL is considered to be evidence of a non-temporary decline in the value of the equipment. In return for these capital contributions, BBL receives a 56 percent equity interest in PVL. YYI contributes $2,200,000 in cash in return for a 44 percent equity interest in PVL.

Case Two BBL contributes a manufacturing plant with a fair value of $1,840,000 and a carrying value of $1,320,000. In return for this plant, BBL receives cash of $1,000,000 and a 42 percent equity interest in PVL. BBL is not obligated to reinvest the cash. YYI contributes $600,000 in cash and other assets with a fair value of $560,000 and a carrying value of $423,000. In return for this capital contribution, YYI receives a 58 percent equity interest in PVL. PVL borrows $2,300,000 from the Royal Bank.

Required: For both of the preceding independent Cases, assume that in BBL's single entity financial statements, the Investment In PVL will be accounted for by the equity method and that, in determining the gain or loss on the transfer of the manufacturing plant to PVL, BBL will follow the Recommendations contained in Section 3055 of the *CICA Handbook*. Determine the following for each Case.

A. Determine the total gain or loss to be recognized by BBL on its transfer of the manufacturing plant and equipment to PVL. In addition, indicate the amount of this gain or loss that can be taken into income at the time of transfer.

B. Determine the value to be recorded in BBL's single entity financial statements as the initial Investment In PVL.

C. Provide the journal entry that would be used by BBL to record the investment transaction.

Assignment Problem Seven - 2

High Venture Ltd. (HVL, hereafter) is a research and development company with 1,000,000 outstanding voting shares that are held by three sponsoring corporations. When the Company was formed on January 1, 2002, Alpha Company invested $1,500,000 in cash in return for 300,000 of the HVL shares and Beta Company paid $2,000,000 in cash for 400,000 HVL shares. Chi Company provided an office building and the land on which it is situated in return for the remaining 300,000 HVL shares. The land was on Chi's books at a carrying value of $450,000 while the building was carried at a net book value of $650,000 and has a remaining useful life of ten years. At the time of the transfer, the fair value of the land was $500,000 and the fair value of the building was $1,000,000. Chi recognizes a gain of $400,000 on the transfer of this property to HVL.

Other Information:

1. During the year ending December 31, 2002, HVL reports a Net Income of $250,000. Included in this figure is a gain of $30,000 resulting from the December 31, 2002 sale of unused equipment to Alpha Company. HVL does not declare any dividends during this year.

2. For the year ending December 31, 2002 and without including any investment income related to HVL, Alpha reports a Net Income of $350,000, Beta reports a Net Income of $675,000, and Chi reports a Net Income of $852,000. Alpha's Net Income includes a $20,000 gain resulting from the sale of merchandise to HVL. This merchandise is still in the December 31, 2002 inventories of HVL. Beta's 2002 Net Income includes a $60,000 gain on the sale of land to HVL at the end of 2002.

3. The joint venture agreement which governs the activities of HVL gives joint control of the operation to Alpha and Chi and prohibits Beta from exercising any influence over the affairs of HVL. Other than the joint venture agreement, there is no affiliation of any sort between the three investor companies. The joint venture agreement covers the terms of all intercompany transactions.

Required:

A. Indicate the accounting method that should be used by each of the three investor companies for dealing with their investment in HVL. Explain your conclusions.

B. For each of the three investor Companies, calculate 2002 Net Income, including their appropriate share of the earnings of HVL.

Your answer should comply with the Recommendations of Section 3055 of the *CICA Handbook*.

Assignment Problem Seven - 3

On January 1, 2002, Saytor Ltd. acquires 35 percent of the outstanding common shares of Saytee Inc. at a cost of $3,066,000. On this date, the Shareholders' Equity of Saytee Inc. was as follows:

Common Stock - No Par	$4,500,000
Retained Earnings	3,700,000
Total Shareholders' Equity	$8,200,000

At this time, all of the identifiable assets and liabilities of Saytee Inc. have fair values that are equal to their carrying values. This means that the $196,000 excess of the purchase price ($3,066,000) over Saytor's 35 percent share of Saytee's book value ($2,870,000) will be allocated to Goodwill.

The remaining 65 percent of the shares of Saytee are owned by Paytor Ltd. Saytor has no affiliation with Paytor other than their common ownership of Saytee. Saytor and Paytor sign an agreement which provides for joint control over Saytee. All significant operating and financing decisions must be approved by both of the investor companies.

During the year ending December 31, 2002, Saytee Inc. has Net Income of $462,000 and declares and pays dividends of $250,000. For 2002, Saytee does not report any results of discontinued operations, extraordinary items or capital transactions. Other than Saytee's Dividends Declared, there are no transactions between the two Companies during the year. Saytor Ltd. carries its Investment In Saytee using the equity method. Both Companies have a December 31 year end.

The Balance Sheets for the two companies as at December 31, 2002 and the Income Statements for the year ending December 31, 2002, are as follows:

Saytor And Saytee Companies
Balance Sheets
As At December 31, 2002

	Saytor Ltd.	Saytee Inc.
Cash	$ 420,000	$ 270,000
Accounts Receivable	1,340,000	896,000
Inventories	2,370,000	3,560,000
Investment In Saytee (Note)	3,140,200	-0-
Plant And Equipment (Net)	3,170,000	5,708,000
Total Assets	$10,440,200	$10,434,000
Current Liabilities	$ 872,000	$ 462,000
Long-Term Liabilities	2,100,000	1,560,000
Common Stock - No Par	3,700,000	4,500,000
Retained Earnings	3,768,200	3,912,000
Total Equities	$10,440,200	$10,434,000

Note The equity value for the Investment In Saytee would be calculated as follows:

Cost On January 1, 2002	$3,066,000
Equity Pickup For 2002 ([35%][$462,000 - $250,000])	74,200
Investment At Equity	$3,140,200

Saytor And Saytee Companies
Income Statements
Year Ending December 31, 2002

	Saytor Ltd.	Saytee Inc.
Sales	$12,572,300	$8,623,000
Investment Income [(35%)($462,000)]	161,700	-0-
Total Revenues	$12,734,000	$8,623,000
Cost Of Sales	$ 7,926,000	$5,824,000
Depreciation Expense	3,116,000	1,326,000
Other Expenses	1,132,000	1,011,000
Total Expenses	$12,174,000	$8,161,000
Net Income	$ 560,000	$ 462,000

Required: Using proportionate consolidation procedures, prepare the consolidated Balance Sheet as at December 31, 2002 and the consolidated Income Statement for the year ending December 31, 2002 for Saytor Ltd. and its investee, Saytee Inc. Your solution should comply with the Recommendations of Section 3055 of the *CICA Handbook*.

Assignment Problem Seven - 4

On January 1, 2002, Sparkling Ltd. (SL) and Raindrop Inc. (RI) formed a new corporation to market water fountains to be sold to local shopping malls. This new corporation will be called Fountain Venture Inc. (FVI). SL and RI have no affiliation with each other except for their joint ownership in FVI. SL and RI signed an agreement which provides for joint control over FVI. All significant operating and financing decisions must be approved by both of the investor companies.

SL's capital contribution is a warehouse with a carrying value of $600,000 and a fair value of $2,000,000. The building is located on leased land, with lease payments that are at current market values. On January 1, 2002, there are 10 years remaining on the lease. This is also the remaining economic life of the building. The lease is transferred to FVI at the time of incorporation. SL receives 48 percent of FVI's voting shares and $500,000 in cash. A gain of $1,400,000 is recorded by SL on the transfer of the building.

RI's capital contribution is $1,625,000 in cash, in return for which, RI receives 52 percent of FVI's voting shares.

For the year ending December 31, 2002, the single entity Balance Sheets and Income Statements for SL and FVI are as follows:

Balance Sheets
As At December 31, 2002

	SL	FVI
Cash And Receivables	$ 2,600,000	$ 670,000
Inventories	5,480,000	1,850,000
Investment in FVI (At Cost)	1,500,000	-0-
Land	990,000	-0-
Building	3,400,000	2,000,000
Accumulated Depreciation	(1,010,000)	(200,000)
Total Assets	$12,960,000	$ 4,320,000
Liabilities	$ 850,000	$ 405,000
Common Stock - No Par	7,680,000	3,125,000
Retained Earnings	4,430,000	790,000
Total Equities	$12,960,000	$ 4,320,000

Income Statements
For The Year Ending December 31, 2002

	SL	FVI
Sales	$5,600,000	$3,600,000
Gain On Sale Of Building	1,400,000	-0-
Total Revenues	$7,000,000	$3,600,000
Cost Of Goods Sold	3,500,000	2,380,000
Depreciation Expense	340,000	200,000
Other Expenses	540,000	230,000
Total Expenses	$4,380,000	$2,810,000
Net Income	$2,620,000	$ 790,000

Other Information:

1. During the year ending December 31, 2002, FVI sells merchandise to SL for $400,000.

This merchandise had cost FVI $300,000 and 50 percent of it has been resold by SL.

2. During the year ending December 31, 2002, SL sells merchandise to FVI for $1,500,000. This merchandise had cost $1,380,000 and none of it has been resold by FVI.

3. Neither SL nor FVI declare or pay dividends during the year ending December 31, 2002.

Required: Prepare a consolidated Balance Sheet as at December 31, 2002 and a consolidated Income Statement for the year ending December 31, 2002, for SL and its investee, FVI. Your solution should comply with the Recommendations of the *CICA Handbook*.

Chapter 8

Advanced Topics In Consolidations

Introduction To Advanced Topics

8-1.   A full treatment of the subject of preparing consolidated statements could easily require a full one semester course to cover the many procedures that are inherent in this complex process. As a result of the work we do for professional accountants through the Canadian Institute of Chartered Accountants, we have prepared materials covering most of these procedures, including both text material and supporting problems.

8-2.   In previous editions of this text, we have included this material on advanced topics as a separate Chapter in the text. However, we have found that few instructors make use of this material and, even in those cases where they do, they cover only one or two of these difficult topics. Given the limited amount to which this material is used, we have decided not to include this Chapter in the paper version of the text.

8-3.   As this may create a problem for those instructors that assign one or more of these advanced topics in their courses, as well as for those individuals who use this book as a comprehensive reference on the preparation of consolidated financial statements, we have accommodated their needs by including this Chapter 8 on the CD-ROM that accompanies this text. This makes this material available to those interested in material on advanced consolidation topics, while not expanding an already large book with material that is of limited interest to the majority of its users.

8-4.   The topics covered in this Chapter on the CD-ROM in the form of a pdf file are as follows:

- Multi-Level Affiliations
- Reciprocal Shareholdings
- Intercompany Bondholdings
- Subsidiary Preferred Stock
- Transactions Involving Subsidiary Shares
- Consolidation With Investment At Equity

8-5.   Each of these subjects is supported by problem material. The problems related to each subject are found at the end of the appropriate section.

Chapter 9

Translation of Foreign Currency Transactions

Introduction To Foreign Currency Translation

The Need For Translation

9-1.   Virtually every Canadian business has some involvement with foreign currency translation. Even small enterprises will find themselves occasionally ordering some product from a U.S. supplier and, in most cases, this product will have to be paid for in U.S. dollars. In order to incorporate the cost of this product into Canadian dollar financial statements, the amount must be converted from U.S. currency into Canadian dollars.

9-2.   For large, publicly traded companies, such enterprises will not only be engaged in purchase and sale transactions, in many cases they will often go to foreign capital markets in order to obtain needed financing. This financing will usually be obtained and repaid in a currency other than the Canadian dollar, again creating a need to convert the foreign currency into the domestic currency in order to prepare the required Canadian dollar financial statements. Further, these larger enterprises often operate in one or more foreign countries. As these operations are usually carried out through a separate legal entity such as a subsidiary, it becomes necessary to translate complete financial statements of this separate entity in order for them to be included in the Canadian dollar financial statements of the parent company.

9-3.   While a great variety of business events result in a need to translate foreign currency, they can be categorized into two broad groups:

Foreign Currency Transactions   Business enterprises may find themselves engaged in foreign currency transactions. That is, they may be buying or selling goods or services with the prices denominated in a foreign currency, borrowing or lending money with the amounts that are payable or receivable denominated in some foreign currency, or acquiring foreign currency assets, liabilities, revenue streams, or forward exchange contracts which serve as a hedge of some other foreign currency transaction or balance. In these situations, foreign currency translation is required in order to convert individual assets, liabilities, expenses or revenues into Canadian dollars so that they can be included as an integral part of the financial statements of the domestic enterprise.

Foreign Currency Financial Statements   A second situation which requires that domestic enterprises deal with the translation of foreign currencies arises when a Canadian investor company has subsidiaries, significantly influenced companies, or joint ventures that carry on their operations in a foreign country. Generally, the financial statements of these investees will be expressed in the currency of the country in which they operate. Thus, in order to either apply consolidation procedures or the equity method of accounting, the statements of these investees will have to first be translated into Canadian dollars. Note, however, that there is no need to translate the financial statements of investees that are accounted for by the cost method. As such assets are carried at cost, with only dividends declared being recorded by the investor as Investment Income, only these two accounts require translation. In contrast, consolidation requires translation of the full set of investee foreign currency statements, while application of the equity method requires translation of Net Income of the investee in order to determine Investment Income.

9-4. This Chapter deals with conceptual and procedural issues associated with foreign currency transactions. We will find that the issues associated with translating purchase, sale, and capital transactions are fairly easy to deal with. However, accounting for hedging transactions has proved to be an extremely difficult area, with some issues still under discussion at the time this text is being written (May, 2002).

9-5. In Chapter 10, we complete our coverage of foreign currency translation by dealing with the translation of foreign currency financial statements. The issues here tend to be somewhat more complex. However, unlike the situation with accounting for hedges, the procedures to be used are well established and no longer subject to significant discussion or controversy.

Foreign Exchange Rate Terminology

9-6. A foreign exchange rate is essentially a ratio of the values of two currencies. As such, they can be expressed in terms of either currency. For example, the statement that the U.S. dollar is worth $1.60 Canadian is the equivalent of stating that the Canadian dollar is worth $0.625 U.S. ($1 ÷ $1.60). While we will usually express rates in terms of the currency's value in Canadian dollars (e.g., US$1 = C$1.60), you should be able to deal with either format and, in addition, be able to convert one format to the other.

9-7. Exchange rates are market determined and, because of this, they are constantly changing. A rate quoted on May 1 will likely be different on May 2. Indeed, for large transactions, the rate at 8:00 a.m. on May 1 may be different at 9:00 a.m. on May 1. Such day-to-day fluctuations reflect the volume of transactions in world-wide markets involving the two currencies that are reflected in a particular exchange rate.

9-8. There are also long-term trends in exchange rates. For example, many world currencies, including the Canadian dollar and the Japanese yen, have experienced a multi-year decline in their value relative to the U.S. dollar. While there are many factors involved in such trends, the most important is relative rates of inflation. If a country has a very high rate of inflation relative to another country, there will almost certainly be a decline in the value of the currency of the country with the high rate of inflation relative to the currency of the country with little or no inflation. The high correlation between exchange rates and relative rates of inflation has been demonstrated in a number of empirical studies.

9-9. The fact that exchange rates change over time means that the accountant has to choose the rate that is appropriate for the translation of each item in the financial statements. While average rates may be used to simplify the translation when a large volume of transactions is involved, the basic choice is whether to translate using the spot rate at the Balance Sheet date or, alternatively, using what is referred to as the historic rate. These rates can be described as follows:

> **Spot Or Current Exchange Rate** The term spot rate is used to refer to the exchange rate at a particular point in time. In accounting literature, the most relevant spot rate is the one which prevails at the Balance Sheet date and, in this context, it is generally referred to as the current rate. For the purposes of translating a December 31, 2003 Balance Sheet, the December 31, 2003 exchange rate would be used as the current exchange rate. Note that, when comparative statements are presented, there would

be a different current exchange rate for each Balance Sheet date.

Historic Exchange Rate This term is used to refer to the exchange rate that prevailed at the time particular Balance Sheet item was acquired (asset) or incurred (liability). If an item of equipment was acquired on January 1, 2003, the historic rate would be the exchange rate that prevailed on that date, without regard to the date of the Balance Sheet in which the item of equipment is included.

9-10. In textbook examples, we generally assume that there is a single exchange rate at any point in time. In the real world, this is clearly not the case. As anyone who has exchanged currencies for travel outside of Canada is aware, financial institutions have different rates for buying a currency vs. selling the same currency. For example, you might find that, if you are buying U.S. dollars, the exchange rate is $1.59 Canadian, but if you are selling U.S. dollars, the exchange rate is $1.55 Canadian.

9-11. As illustrated in the preceding paragraph, at any given point in time, there will be at least two rates for a particular currency — the rate for selling the currency and the rate for buying the currency. These rates are sometimes referred to as the bid and ask rates. In addition, these rates will vary between financial institutions, as well as with the size of the transaction (e.g., better rates are usually available on larger transactions). Further, in less developed countries or countries where the government controls currency exchange, there may be a wide variety of rates depending on the type of transaction involved (e.g., a better rate for export proceeds, as opposed to import costs).

9-12. We will not illustrate the problem of multiple exchange rates in the material which follows. However, you should be aware that our references to a single exchange rate on a particular date are, in fact, a simplification of real world conditions.

A Note On Current Developments

9-13. Canadian accounting standards for foreign currency translation are found in Section 1650 of the *CICA Handbook*, "Foreign Currency Translation". This *Handbook* Section was originally issued in 1983 and, given the changes that have taken place in the international business environment since it was issued, it has been in need of revision for some time.

9-14. This has proved to be difficult process. An Exposure Draft, "Foreign Currency Translation", was issued by the Accounting Standards Board in September, 1993. For largely technical reasons, this Exposure Draft was replaced by a May, 1996 Re-Exposure Draft. However, work was suspended on this Re-Exposure Draft in 1999 and in March, 2001, a new Exposure Draft was released. In December, 2001, a revised Section 1650 was issued. The two major changes were as follows:

- Under the old Section 1650, exchange gains and losses on long-term monetary items were deferred and amortized over the remaining life of the items. Canada was the only country in the world that followed this practice. The current Section 1650 is harmonized with the standards of other countries as it now requires that such exchange gains and losses be taken into income immediately.

- Under the old Section 1650, there was no requirement that separate disclosure be given to the amount of exchange gain or loss that is included in the income of the current period. The current Section 1650 recommends that separate disclosure be given to this amount.

9-15. This revised Section 1650 did not serve to resolve all of the issues related to foreign currency translation. More specifically, the revision did not deal with the issues associated with hedge accounting. As you are likely aware, this is an extremely difficult and controversial area of accounting practice. Further, hedge accounting has many important applications other than those associated with foreign currency and, because of this situation, it was not possible to resolve the foreign currency hedging issues until there was a more general solution to the problems associated with these procedures. As the subject of hedge accounting is a component of the larger project dealing with financial instruments, work on this material is ongoing.

9-16.   However, the Accounting Standards Board recognized that there was considerable variation in the application of hedge accounting in Canadian practice. Given this situation, the Accounting Standards Board has concluded that, pending completion of internationally harmonized standards applicable to hedging activities, it was desirable to provide additional guidance for applying the hedge accounting requirements that are currently included in Section 1650. As a result, in December, 2001, the Accounting Standards Board issued Accounting Guideline No. 13 titled "Hedging Relationships". This Accounting Guideline is directed at improving the consistency with which existing hedging Recommendations are implemented.

Temporal Method of Translation

Alternative Methods

9-17.   At various points in time, four different translation methods have been used in Canadian practice. These methods differ in terms of which accounts are translated at current rates and which accounts are translated at historic rates. Briefly described, these methods are as follows:

- **Current/Non-Current Method**   Under this method, current assets and liabilities are translated at current exchange rates, while non-current assets and liabilities are translated at historic exchange rates.

- **Monetary/Non-Monetary Method**   Under this method, monetary assets and liabilities are translated at current exchange rates, while non-monetary assets and liabilities are translated at historic exchange rates.

- **Temporal Method**   Under this method, assets and liabilities that are measured at current values are translated at current rates, while assets and liabilities that are measured at historic values are translated at historic rates.

- **Current Rate Method**   Under this method, all assets and liabilities are translated at current rates.

9-18.   Until the 1980's, the current/non-current method was the required method in both Canada and the United States. However, it is now recognized to be an inappropriate approach to translation and is no longer used. The monetary/non-monetary method is also flawed and, at this point in time, there is no knowledgeable support for or usage of this method. However, it is sufficiently similar to the temporal method that some confusion exists as to its applicability. As a consequence, we will provide a brief section that clarifies the difference between these two methods.

9-19.   This leaves the temporal method and the current rate method. Depending on the circumstances, both of these methods are conceptually sound and specified as appropriate in *CICA Handbook* Recommendations. However, this Chapter is directed at the translation of foreign currency transactions. For this purpose, the temporal method is the only acceptable method and, reflecting this fact, we will focus our attention on the application of this method. The use of the current rate method is limited to situations involving self-sustaining foreign operations. As this material is covered in Chapter 10, we will defer our discussion of the conceptual basis for, and the application of, the current rate method until that Chapter.

Temporal Method

9-20.   The basic feature of the temporal method is that the exchange rate used for the translation of a particular item is based on the manner in which the item is valued. More specifically with respect to Balance Sheet items:

- Items valued at current values are translated using current exchange rates (e.g., Accounts Receivable or Inventories carried at their current replacement cost).

- Items valued at historic values are translated using historic exchange rates (e.g., Land or Plant and Equipment).

9-21.   Consider the following example:

Example   As at December 31, 2002, the records of Trader Inc. indicate the following balances resulting from foreign currency transactions denominated in Euros (€):

Accounts Receivable	€ 500,000
Inventories (At Replacement Cost)	€ 600,000
Equipment - Cost	€1,000,000

On December 31, 2002, the exchange rate between the Canadian dollar (C$) and the Euro is €1 = C$1.40. The Equipment was purchased on June 30, 2002 when the exchange rate was €1 = C$1.35.

Solution   Using the temporal method, the translated value of these balances would be as follows:

Accounts Receivable [(€500,000)(C$1.40)]	$ 700,000
Inventories [(€600,000)(C$1.40)]	$ 840,000
Equipment - Cost [(€1,00,000)(C$1.35)]	$1,350,000

Note that, because they are carried at a current value (replacement cost), the inventories are translated using the current rate at the Balance Sheet date. Because equipment is carried at historical cost under GAAP, it is translated at the historic exchange rate of $1.35, resulting in a value of $1,350,000. Regardless of future movements in the value of the Euro, the cost of this equipment will remain unchanged at $1,350,000. As our basic accounting model uses historic cost for most capital assets, this is an appropriate result. The fact that the translated "historical cost" of this asset does not change over time is the basis for the claim that the temporal method retains the Canadian dollar as the unit of measure.

9-22.   We have noted that we sometimes encounter confusion between the temporal method and the monetary/non-monetary methods of translation. Before discussing this issue, we would note that Section 1650 defines monetary items as follows:

Paragraph 1650.03   Money and claims to money the value of which, in terms of the monetary unit, whether foreign or domestic, is fixed by contract or otherwise. Future income tax liabilities and assets are classified as monetary items.

9-23.   With this definition in place, the confusion between the two translation methods can be clarified by noting the types of items to which the two methods apply current and historic exchange rates:

Current Rates   The temporal method applies current rates to items valued at current values, while the monetary/non-monetary method applies current rates to monetary items.

Historic Rates   The temporal method applies historic rates to items valued at historic values, while the monetary/non-monetary method applies historic rates to non-monetary items.

9-24.   If you give careful consideration to these rules, it becomes clear that, with respect to the treatment of the majority of assets and liabilities, these two methods will produce identical results. This is based on the following:

- All monetary assets are valued at current values and, as a consequence, would be translated by the current exchange rate under either translation method.

- Most non-monetary assets are carried at historic values and, as a consequence, would be translated using historic exchange rates under either translation method.

9-25.   The only time a difference arises in the application of the two translation methods is in situations where you have a non-monetary asset valued at a current value. As you aware, this is fairly unusual under GAAP, with the most common example being inventories (a non-monetary asset) carried at net realizable value or replacement cost. As it would translate this current value using an historic rate, the use of the pure monetary/non-monetary approach is not appropriate in this type of situation. This view is reflected in the *CICA Handbook*'s definition of the temporal method.

Paragraph 1650.03 Temporal Method A method of translation which translates assets, liabilities, revenues and expenses in a manner that retains their bases of measurement in terms of the Canadian dollar (i.e., it uses the Canadian dollar as the unit of measure). In particular:

(i) monetary items are translated at the rate of exchange in effect at the balance sheet date;

(ii) non-monetary items are translated at historical exchange rates, unless such items are carried at market, in which case they are translated at the rate of exchange in effect at the balance sheet date;

(iii) ... [the remainder of this definition deals with revenues and expenses of foreign operations, a subject that is covered in Chapter 10].

9-26. It would be our opinion that it would have been preferable to drop the references to monetary and non-monetary items from this definition. However, with the exception that is included in item (ii), it is an appropriate expression of the temporal method.

9-27. With the focus of this Chapter being on foreign currency transactions, we will not extend our discussion of the temporal method to cover expenses and revenues. However, we would note that a literal application of the temporal method rules to transactions such as purchases would require the translation of each item acquired at the rate which prevailed on the transaction date. When a large volume of such transactions is involved, the following guidance is appropriate:

Paragraph 1650.61 Literal application of the Recommendations in this Section might require a degree of detail in record keeping and computations that would be burdensome as well as unnecessary to produce reasonable approximations of the results. Accordingly, it is acceptable to use averages or other methods of approximation. For example, translation of the numerous revenues, expenses, gains and losses at the exchange rates at the dates such items are recognized is generally impractical, and an appropriately weighted average exchange rate for the period would normally be used to translate such items.

9-28. In many cases, it will be acceptable to use a simple average based on dividing the sum of the beginning of the period and end of the period exchange rates by two. However, the use of this unweighted calculation is based on two assumptions. First, the purchases or sales of the item being translated must have occurred uniformly over the averaging period, and second, the change in the exchange rate must have occurred uniformly over the averaging period. If either of these assumptions is not appropriate, then some type of weighted average must be used.

Exercise Nine-1 deals with the application of the temporal method.

Exercise Nine-1

The following items are commonly found in corporate Balance Sheets.

1. Accounts Receivable
2. Inventories (At Cost)
3. Inventories (At Net Realizable Value)
4. Prepaid Rent
5. Long-Term Notes Receivable
6. Land
7. Goodwill
8. Taxes Payable
9. Estimated Liability For Warranties

10. Bonds Payable
11. Future Income Tax Liability
12. Preferred Shares

This is a continuation of Exercise Nine-1.

Required: If these items were denominated in a foreign currency, they would be translated using either the current exchange rate at the Balance Sheet date or, alternatively, the appropriate historic rate. For each item, indicate whether it should be translated using the current rate or the historic rate in the application of the temporal method.

End Of Exercise Nine-1

Accounting Recommendations

9-29. As noted previously, Section 1650 of the *CICA Handbook* requires the use of the temporal method for the translation of all aspects of foreign currency transactions. With respect to the transactions per se, the following Recommendation is applicable:

> **Paragraph 1650.14** *At the transaction date, each asset, liability, revenue or expense arising from a foreign currency transaction of the reporting enterprise should be translated into Canadian dollars by the use of the exchange rate in effect at that date, except when the transaction is hedged, in which case the rate established by the terms of the hedge should be used.* (July, 1983)

9-30. As will be discussed in the Section of this Chapter that deals with hedging, the reference to "the rate established by the terms of the hedge" involves situations where an anticipated future transaction has been hedged, not situations in which an exposed monetary position has been hedged.

9-31. As foreign currency transactions commonly involve balances which are not settled by the Balance Sheet date, Paragraphs 1650.16 and 1650.18 provide Recommendations for translating Balance Sheet accounts. These Paragraphs are as follows:

> **Paragraph 1650.16** *At each balance sheet date, monetary items denominated in a foreign currency should be adjusted to reflect the exchange rate in effect at the balance sheet date.* (July, 1983)

> **Paragraph 1650.18** *At each balance sheet date, for non-monetary assets of the reporting enterprise that are carried at market, the Canadian dollar equivalent should be determined by applying the exchange rate in effect at the balance sheet date to the foreign currency market price.* (July, 1983)

9-32. While not stated explicitly, the preceding two Recommendations imply that any non-monetary items carried at historical values will be translated at historical rates.

Exchange Gains And Losses

Nature Of Exchange Gains And Losses

9-33. Every method of translation applies the current exchange rate to at least some of the Balance Sheet items subject to translation. In the case of the temporal method, this rate is applied to any item that is carried in the Balance Sheet at current value. As exchange rates are constantly changing, the process of translating an item at current rates means that, even in cases where there is no change in the underlying foreign currency value, there will be changes in the translated balance. In the context of accounting for foreign currency transactions, these changes in value are generally referred to as exchange gains or losses.

9-34. As an example, assume that during the current calendar year, we had a liability of 1,000,000 British Pounds (£). If the exchange rate increases from £1 = $2.25 on January 1 to £1 = $2.35 on December 31, the translated balances would be as follows:

December 31 Liability (£1,000,000 @ $2.35)	$2,350,000
January 1 Liability (£1,000,000 @ $2.25)	(2,250,000)
Increase In Canadian Dollar Value	$ 100,000

9-35.   As a liability is involved, this $100,000 increase in the translated balance from $2,250,000 to $2,350,000 is an exchange loss. If the £1,000,000 balance had been an asset, the increase in value would have been an exchange gain. Correspondingly, when the translation process decreases a liability it creates an exchange gain and when the process decreases an asset, the result is an exchange loss.

9-36.   There is some discussion in the accounting literature with respect to alternative treatments of these amounts. For example, when the payable related to the acquisition of an asset is subject to an increase or decrease in value resulting from the translation process, there is a view that suggests that this increase or decrease should be added to or subtracted from the acquired asset. A similar argument arises when translation requires the adjustment of an interest bearing receivable or payable. It has been suggested that this adjustment should be applied to the amount of interest revenue or expense that will be recorded on the Balance Sheet item. However, no accounting standards use this approach and, as a consequence, we will give it no further attention.

9-37.   In this Chapter we are dealing exclusively with foreign currency transactions. This means that, in most cases, the foreign currency amounts that are being translated will actually be converted into Canadian dollars. For example, if a Canadian company borrows in U.S. dollars, the amount borrowed will normally be repaid by buying U.S. dollars with Canadian dollars. If the value of the U.S. dollar increases between the time of the borrowing and the point in time when the liability is repaid, there is a real out-of-pocket loss. Given this, it is difficult to support any treatment of the required adjustment as anything other than a loss.

9-38.   However, in Chapter 10, when we are dealing with translating foreign currency financial statements, a different analysis may be appropriate. If a U.S. subsidiary of a Canadian company borrows in U.S. dollars, it may be able to repay the liability with U.S. dollars generated through its U.S. operations. If this is the case, the fact that the value of the U.S. dollar increases or decreases relative to the Canadian dollar has no real economic impact. Reflecting this view, we will find that, when these conditions prevail, the *CICA Handbook* does not require that adjustments resulting from the translation of items at current rates be included in income. Rather these adjustments are treated as a separate component of shareholders' equity.

Allocation Of Exchange Gains And Losses To Income

9-39.   As we have noted, exchange gains and losses result whenever an item is translated using the current rate of exchange. As the spot rate of exchange is constantly changing, exchange gains and losses are accruing throughout the year. However, they are measured only at Balance Sheet dates, using the current spot rate of exchange on those dates.

9-40.   While exchange gains and losses are measured as of Balance Sheet dates, there is still the question of how they should be allocated to income. While this issue appears to be settled at this point in time, it has been the subject of considerable controversy over many years. At various times, four different approaches were advocated and/or used. They are illustrated in the example which follows:

Example   On January 1, 2002, a Canadian company borrowed €1,000,000 which will be repaid on January 1, 2007. The exchange rate on January 1, 2002 was €1 = C$1.40. It remains at that level until January 1, 2004. On January 1, 2004, the rate goes to €1 = C$1.45. It remains at this level until the debt is repaid on January 1, 2007. This results in an exchange loss of $50,000 [(€1,000,000)(C$1.40 - C$1.45)].

The four different approaches to allocating this $50,000 loss to income would be as follows:

- **No Deferral**   Under this approach, the entire $50,000 would be charged to income in 2004, the year in which the exchange rate change took place.

- **Deferral Until Realization**   If the cash approach to realization is used, the entire $50,000 loss would be deferred until 2007, the year in which the liability is settled.

- **Allocation Over The Total Life Of The Liability**   Under this approach, the loss would be allocated to income over the entire five year life of the liability at the rate of $10,000 per year. This solution would also raise the question of the appropriate treatment for the amounts allocated to 2002 and 2003, the years prior to the actual exchange rate change.

- **Allocation Over The Remaining Life Of The Liability**   Under this alternative, the $50,000 would be allocated to 2004, 2005, and 2006 at the rate of $16,667 ($50,000/3) per year.

9-41.   In analyzing this issue, it is useful to refer to Section 1000, "Financial Statement Concepts". In dealing with questions of recognition, this Section provide the following guidance:

Paragraph 1000.44   The recognition criteria are as follows:

(a) the item has an appropriate basis of measurement and a reasonable estimate can be made of the amount involved; and

(b) for items involving obtaining or giving up future economic benefits, it is probable that such benefits will be obtained or given up.

9-42.   In the case of exchange gains and losses, there is no controversy over whether there is an appropriate basis of measurement which can be used to provide a reasonable estimate of the amount involved. In the example that is under consideration, no one would suggest that the liability not be written up to C$1,450,000 on January 1, 2004 when the exchange rate changes to C$1.45. Exchange rates are market determined and C$1,450,000 is clearly an objective measure of the amount of the liability.

9-43.   Given that criterion (a) is easily satisfied, arguments for any sort of deferral must be based on criterion (b), the question of whether it is probable that such benefits will be obtained or given up. In other words, while the changes in value must be recognized in the Balance Sheet, there may still be an argument for deferring the inclusion of the change in value in the Income Statement. In this regard, it could be noted that the only point in time at which there is certainty as to the amount that will be given up to pay the liability is when it is settled on January 1, 2007. This provides a fairly weak argument for deferral of all gains and losses until this point in time.

9-44.   However, criterion (b) refers to probability, not certainty. Despite the possibility that future exchange rate changes will alter the amount that will ultimately be paid, the January 1, 2004 value of C$1,450,000 represents our best measure of the amount that will probably be given up. Stated alternatively, it is the most probable estimate after January 1, 2004 of the amount that will ultimately be given up. This leads to the conclusion that the entire $50,000 loss should not be deferred beyond 2004.

9-45.   As to allocation over either the total life of the liability or to the remaining life of the liability, the only defence for these approaches is that they smooth income by spreading the exchange gain or loss over the life of the liability. While management may favour accounting procedures that reduce fluctuations, smoothing income is not a goal that is acceptable as a basis for selecting accounting principles. As a consequence, both of these deferral approaches must be rejected.

9-46.   Given the preceding analysis, it seems clear that recognition of any gain or loss in income should occur in the same period as its measurement in the Balance Sheet. Supporting this view is a further problem associated with all of the deferral approaches. When, in our example, we must credit the liability for the $50,000 increase in its translated value, if we defer the resulting loss, it must be set up as an asset in the Balance Sheet. In other words, under this approach, an unfavorable movement in exchange rates that will require more dollars to extinguish a foreign currency liability is being treated as an asset. This clearly is in conflict with the definition of assets that is found in Section 1000 of the *CICA Handbook*.

Accounting Recommendations

9-47.   Until 2002, the *CICA Handbook* required that exchanges gains and losses on long-term monetary items be deferred and amortized over the remaining life of the item. While, at one time, this approach was widely used throughout the world, it had been discarded in every industrialized country except Canada. This was widely recognized as something of an embarrassment for our country and, for some period of time, it was the intent of the Accounting Standards Board to revise this Recommendation. However, because uncertainties about hedge accounting standards resulted in continued delays in the revision of Section 1650, this deferral and amortization approach remained in effect until December, 2001.

9-48.   In December, 2001, the Accounting Standards Board issued a minor revision to Section 1650, largely to eliminate this deferral and amortization approach to exchange gains and losses. The revised Section contains the following Recommendation on this issue:

> **Paragraph 1650.20**   *An exchange gain or loss of the reporting enterprise that arises on translation or settlement of a foreign currency denominated monetary item or a non-monetary item carried at market should be included in the determination of net income for the current period.*

9-49.   This Recommendation adopts the no deferral approach and requires that all exchange gains and losses be taken into income in the year in which they occur. Given the discussion of this issue in the preceding section, this change clearly represents an improvement in Canadian accounting standards.

9-50.   The Section 1650 revision also included a new disclosure Recommendation with respect to exchange gains and losses:

> **Paragraph 1650.44**   *The amount of exchange gain or loss included in income should be disclosed. Exchange gains or losses from dealer transactions of certain enterprises, primarily banks, that are dealers in foreign exchange may be disclosed as dealer gains or losses rather than as exchange gains or losses.* (January, 2002)

9-51.   This Recommendation is reinforced by what is essentially an equivalent Recommendation in Section 1520, "Income Statement". This Section lists the items that must be given separate disclosure in the Income Statement. The list includes the following:

> **Paragraph 1520.03(l)**   *The amount of exchange gain or loss included in income, except for exchange gains and losses of a dealer in foreign exchange that are disclosed as dealer gains or losses.* (January, 2002)

Credit Sales Of Goods Or Services

Conceptual Alternatives

9-52.   When a Canadian company buys (sells) goods or services in a foreign country, the transaction will usually give rise to a foreign currency denominated payable (receivable). Applying the temporal method of translation will require that the payable (receivable) balance be translated at the current rate of exchange as of the Balance Sheet date, resulting in adjustments of any payables (receivables) that are outstanding as of that date.

As noted in the *Handbook*, there are two views as to the disposition of any adjustment that may be required by changes in the dollar value of the payable (receivable) prior to its settlement. These two views are generally referred to as the one transaction perspective and the two transaction perspective and can be described as follows:

One Transaction Perspective   Under this view, when a Canadian company purchases or sells merchandise, the transaction is incomplete until the amount of Canadian dollars required to settle the related payable or receivable is determined. This means that any adjustment of the foreign currency receivable or payable that is required between the transaction date and the settlement date would be viewed as part of the cost of the merchandise purchased or the sales price of the merchandise sold.

Two Transaction Perspective   Under this alternative view, the purchase or sale of merchandise is viewed as a separate and distinct transaction from the ultimate settlement of the related receivable or payable balance. This means that the merchandise cost or sales price is firmly established as at the date of the transaction and any subsequent adjustment of the resulting receivable or payable would be viewed as an exchange gain or loss resulting from the decision to carry exposed foreign currency balances.

Example - One Transaction vs. Two Transaction Perspective

9-53.   The following simple example will serve to illustrate the difference between the one transaction and two transaction perspectives.

Example   The Emp Company has a fiscal year end of December 31. It purchases merchandise in Trinidad for resale in Canada. The merchandise must be paid for in Trinidad-Tobago dollars (TT$, hereafter) on February 1 of the year subsequent to its purchase. In Canada, the merchandise is sold for cash of $11 per unit. All of the merchandise purchased in a year is sold on April 1 of the following year. Purchases, which occur on November 1 of each year, are as follows:

Date Of Purchase	Quantity	Unit Price	Total Price
November 1, 2002	10,000	TT$ 20	TT$200,000
November 1, 2003	12,000	16	192,000
November 1, 2004	-0-	14	-0-

Between January 1, 2002 and December 30, 2003, the exchange rate for the Trinidad-Tobago dollar is TT$1 = C$0.20. On December 31, 2003, the exchange rate goes to TT$1 = C$0.25. It remains at this level throughout 2004.

Example Solution   The following entry to record the first purchase of merchandise on November 1, 2002 is the same for both perspectives.

Merchandise (TT$200,000 At C$0.20)	C$40,000	
Accounts Payable		C$40,000

Since there has been no movement in the exchange rate, the following February 1, 2003 entry to record the payment for the merchandise is the same for both perspectives.

Accounts Payable (TT$200,000 At C$0.20)	C$40,000	
Cash		C$40,000

The following April 1, 2003 entries to record sales and the related Cost Of Goods Sold would also be the same under both perspectives.

Cash (10,000 Units At C$11)	C$110,000	
Sales		C$110,000
Cost Of Goods Sold (TT$200,000 At C$0.20)	C$ 40,000	
Merchandise		C$40,000

The following entry to record the purchase of merchandise on November 1, 2003 would be the same under both perspectives.

Merchandise (TT$192,000 At C$0.20)   C$38,400
    Accounts Payable   C$38,400

An entry is required on December 31, 2003 to adjust the Accounts Payable to reflect the change in the exchange rate. Under the one transaction perspective this adjustment would be added to the cost of Merchandise with the following entry:

Merchandise - One Transaction
   [(TT$192,000)(C$0.25 - C$.020)]   C$9,600
    Accounts Payable   C$9,600

Alternatively, under the two transaction perspective, the adjustment would be treated as an exchange loss to be included in the computation of the current year's income. The entry under this perspective would be as follows:

Exchange Loss - Two Transaction
   [(TT$192,000)(C$0.25 - C$.020)]   C$9,600
    Accounts Payable   C$9,600

The following entry to record the payment of the Accounts Payable on February 1, 2004 would be the same under both perspectives.

Accounts Payable (TT$192,000 At C$0.25)   C$48,000
    Cash   C$48,000

The following entry to record Sales on April 1, 2004 would be the same under both perspectives.

Cash (12,000 Units At C$11)   C$132,000
    Sales   C$132,000

The Cost Of Goods Sold entry would vary between the two perspectives. Under the one transaction perspective, the exchange adjustment has been added to the cost of the merchandise and the Cost Of Goods Sold entry would be as follows:

Cost Of Goods Sold (TT$192,000 At C$0.25)   C$48,000
    Merchandise - One Transaction   C$48,000

Alternatively, under the two transaction perspective, the adjustment was charged to income in 2003 and will not affect the amount shown as Cost Of Goods Sold:

Cost Of Goods Sold (TT$192,000 At C$0.20)   C$38,400
    Merchandise - Two Transaction   C$38,400

Summary Of Results

9-54.   The results of the preceding journal entries can be summarized in the following condensed Income Statements:

One Transaction Perspective Results

	2003	2004	Cumulative
Sales	$110,000	$132,000	$242,000
Cost Of Goods Sold	40,000	48,000	88,000
Net Income	$ 70,000	$ 84,000	$154,000

Two Transaction Perspective Results

	2003	2004	Cumulative
Sales	$110,000	$132,000	$242,000
Cost Of Goods Sold	40,000	38,400	78,400
Operating Income	$ 70,000	$ 93,600	$163,600
Exchange Loss	9,600	-0-	9,600
Net Income	$ 60,400	$ 93,600	$154,000

9-55.   You will note that the cumulative income for the two years is $154,000 regardless of the perspective that is adopted. However, the choice between the two perspectives does affect both the timing and the disclosure of the exchange adjustment.

Evaluation Of Perspectives

9-56.   There appears to be general agreement that the two transaction perspective is the more appropriate interpretation of the economic factors involved in foreign currency merchandise transactions. It would seem clear that in the preceding situation, the Emp Company could have avoided having an exposed payable position by paying the liability at the transaction date, by purchasing sufficient foreign currency at the transaction date to pay the liability at the settlement date, or by entering into a forward exchange contract to hedge the exposed position. The fact that it chose not to do this and that an exchange loss resulted is really a separate decision and it should not be allowed to affect the translated value of the merchandise that was acquired. This view is reflected in the *CICA Handbook* as follows:

> **Paragraph 1650.13**   In the opinion of the Committee, once foreign currency purchases and sales, or inventories, fixed assets and other non-monetary items obtained through foreign currency transactions, have been translated and recorded, any subsequent changes in the exchange rate will not affect those recorded amounts.

Exercise Nine-2

Exportit Ltd. has a fiscal year end of December 31. It purchases merchandise in Canada for resale in Europe. In Europe, the merchandise is sold for cash of €8 per unit. All of the merchandise purchased in a given year is sold on June 30 of the following year. However, the resulting receivable is not collected until June 30 of the following year. Purchases, which occur on November 1 of each year, are as follows:

> Exercise Nine-2 deals with sales of merchandise with the receivable denominated in a foreign currency.

Date Of Purchase	Quantity	Unit Price	Total Price
November 1, 2002	50,000	$5	$250,000
November 1, 2003	75,000	$6	450,000
November 1, 2004	-0-	$7	-0-

Between January 1, 2002 and December 31, 2003, the exchange rate for the Euro is €1 = $1.38. On January 1, 2004, the exchange rate goes to €1 = C$1.42 and remains at this level throughout the remainder of the year.

Required: Provide condensed Income Statements for both of the two years ending December 31, 2003 and December 31, 2004, as well as a cumulative Income Statement for two years using:

A.   The one transaction approach to recording foreign currency transactions.

B.   The two transaction approach to recording foreign currency transactions.

End Of Exercise Nine-2

Capital Transactions

Background

9-57.   When a Canadian company borrows (lends) funds and the resulting liability (asset) is denominated in a foreign currency, the company is certain to experience exchange gains or losses over the life of the liability (asset). The balance resulting from such transactions is a monetary item and will be translated at the current exchange rate prevailing at each Balance Sheet date. As the current rate changes from year to year, the translated balance will increase or decrease, resulting in the need to recognize exchange gains or losses.

9-58.   Prior to 2002, the *CICA Handbook* required that gains and losses on these long-term monetary items be deferred and amortized over the period to maturity of the receivable or payable item. As was noted previously, this approach was unique to Canada and lacked any sort of real conceptual support. Fortunately, this rule has been replaced by the more reasonable requirement that exchange gains and losses be included in income in their entirety in the year in which they occur.

9-59.   We would note that we are not concerned here with capital transactions involving equity instruments. Investments in equity instruments are translated at historic rates and, in many cases involve affiliated foreign operations, a subject that is covered in Chapter 10. Even if no foreign operation is involved, the fact that these investments are recorded at historic exchange rates means that their translation will not result in exchange gains or losses.

9-60.   The same analysis would apply to equity instruments that are issued in return for foreign currency. Again, these instruments are translated at historic rates, with no possibility of exchange gains or losses arising in subsequent periods.

Basic Example

9-61.   The following example illustrates the procedures required in dealing with exchange gains and losses.

Example - Capital Transactions   On December 31, 2002, a Canadian company with a December 31 year end borrows 1,000,000 Foreign Currency units (FC, hereafter). Assume that this liability does not require the payment of interest. The liability will mature on December 31, 2007, five years after it was issued. Exchange rates at December 31 for the years 2002 through 2007 are as follows:

December 31, 2002	FC1 = $2.00
December 31, 2003	FC1 = $2.50
December 31, 2004	FC1 = $2.50
December 31, 2005	FC1 = $1.80
December 31, 2006	FC1 = $1.80
December 31, 2007	FC1 = $2.25

Example Solution   The main feature that you should note in this solution is that exchange gains and losses are only recognized in the accounting periods in which there was a change in the exchange rate for the foreign currency units.

The entry on December 31, 2002 records the liability that has been assumed. It would be as follows:

Cash (FC1,000,000 At $2.00)	$2,000,000	
Long-Term Liability		$2,000,000

By December 31, 2003, the exchange rate has moved to FC1 = $2.50. The resulting exchange loss would be taken into income with the following entry:

Exchange Loss [(FC1,000,000)($2.50 - $2.00)]	$500,000	
Long-Term Liability		$500,000

As the exchange rate did not change during 2004, there is no need for any entry on December 31, 2004. By December 31, 2005, the exchange rate has moved to FC1 = $1.80. The resulting exchange gain would be taken into income with the following entry:

Long-Term Liability [(FC1,000,000)($2.50 - $1.80)] $700,000
    Exchange Gain $700,000

As the exchange rate remained at $1.80 during 2006, no entry is required on December 31, 2006. The first entry on December 31, 2007 would recognize the exchange loss resulting from the increase in the exchange rate to $2.25. It would be as follows:

Exchange Loss [(FC1,000,000)($2.25 - $1.80)] $450,000
    Long-Term Liability $450,000

A final entry would be required to record the payment of the liability. This would be as follows:

Long-Term Liability (FC1,000,000 At $2.25) $2,250,000
    Cash $2,250,000

9-62. Note that this solution reflects Recommendations that are applicable for fiscal years beginning on or after January 1, 2002. In earlier periods, each gain or loss recorded at the Balance Sheet dates would have been amortized over the remaining life of the liability. For example, the 2003 loss would have been recorded as follows:

Exchange Loss [(1/5)($500,000)] $100,000
Deferred Exchange Loss [(4/5)($500,000)]   400,000
    Long-Term Liability $500,000

9-63. The Deferred Exchange Loss would be reported in the Balance Sheet as an asset and, in subsequent periods, it would be charged to income at the rate of $100,000 per year. A similar treatment would have been given to the 2005 exchange gain and the 2007 exchange loss. This was a fairly complex process and will not be missed by either accounting students or professional accountants.

Exercise Nine-3

On January 1, 2002, Candor Inc. borrows 585,000 Euros (€) from a French bank. Interest at 7 percent per annum is to be paid on December 31 of each year during the three year term of the loan. The principal amount must be repaid on the December 31, 2004. At the time of the borrowing, the exchange rate is €1 = $1.40. It remains at this level until January 1, 2003, at which time it increases evenly throughout the year to €1 = $1.45 on December 31, 2003. It remains at this level until December 31, 2004 when it decreases to €1 = $1.42.

Required: Provide all of the journal entries required to account for this loan during the three year period January 1, 2002 through December 31, 2004.

End Of Exercise Nine-3

> Exercise Nine-3 deals with capital transactions.

Hedging Relationships

What Is A Hedging Relationship?

9-64. The unabridged edition of the *Random House Dictionary Of The English Language* defines the verb "to hedge" as follows:

> To protect against a complete loss (of a bet, investment, financial position, etc.) by placing a smaller bet or bets on another contestant or other contestants, by investing in another thing or area in order to compensate for a possible loss, etc.; to mitigate a possible loss by diversifying (one's bets, investments, etc.).

9-65. Hedging is generally accomplished by establishing a hedging relationship, an arrangement that is defined in Accounting Guideline No. 13 (AcG-13) as follows:

A **hedging relationship** is a relationship established by an entity's management between a hedged item and a hedging item, including a synthetic instrument relationship.

9-66. As is often the case, this definition relies on technical terms which require additional definitions. These are provided in AcG-13 as follows:

A **hedged item** is all or a specified portion of an asset, a liability or an anticipated transaction, or a group of similar assets, liabilities or anticipated transactions, having an identified risk exposure that an entity has taken steps to modify.

A **hedging item** is all or a specified portion of an asset, a liability or an anticipated transaction, or a group of assets, liabilities or anticipated transactions, modifying a risk exposure identified in the hedged item, provided that non-derivative items in a group are all similar.

9-67. Hedging occurs in many areas of business. Various types of hedging arrangements are available for commodities, equity securities, and interest rates, as well as for foreign currency situations. While AcG-13 deals with all types of hedges, in this Chapter we will focus on hedging relationships involving foreign currencies.

What Do We Hedge?

9-68. For hedging relationships related to foreign currencies, the two most common types of situations are as follows:

Hedge Of An Anticipated Transaction These transactions are defined in AcG-13 as follows:

An **anticipated transaction** is any transaction expected to occur in the future that has not yet given rise to a recognized asset or liability

If an attempt was made to hedge such an anticipated transaction (e.g., a purchase commitment denominated in a foreign currency), it could be identified as a hedged item. The purpose of any hedge that might be used here would be to establish the cost of the anticipated foreign currency transaction at the then current exchange rate for Canadian dollars. If the hedge is successful, the Canadian dollar value of the anticipated transaction will not be affected by subsequent changes in the exchange rate between the Canadian dollar and the foreign currency.

Hedge Of Monetary Assets And Liabilities Foreign currency transactions often result in a Canadian company carrying monetary assets or liabilities that are denominated in a foreign currency. The purpose of any hedge that might be used here is to counteract the possibility of incurring an exchange gain or loss on the monetary asset or liability at the settlement date or some earlier financial statement preparation date.

9-69. In addition to hedges involving foreign currency transactions, we will give some attention in this Chapter to hedges of investments in self-sustaining foreign operations.

How Do We Hedge?

9-70. Regardless of the foreign currency transaction involved, there are a number of ways that a hedged position can be accomplished. A simple example will serve to make this point clear.

Example On February 1, 2003, a Canadian company purchases merchandise in Germany for 500,000 Euros (€). The merchandise must be paid for in Euros on May 1, 2003. On February 1, 2003, the exchange rate is €1 = $1.40, resulting in a Canadian dollar liability of $700,000. The company wishes to insure that exchange rate movements during the period February 1, 2003 to May 1, 2003 do not result in exchange gains or losses on this liability. This could be accomplished in one of several ways:

- **Purchase Of Euros**   The company could simply purchase €500,000 in currency on February 1, 2003 and hold this amount until it was needed to extinguish the liability. This simple solution would not be commonly used because the foreign currency does not provide any rate of return over the period in which it is held.

- **Purchase Of Monetary Assets**   It will generally be more appropriate for the Canadian company to hedge its position through the purchase of a monetary asset denominated in Euros. For example, if they were to make short term investments in debt securities which were receivable in Euros, this would hedge the €500,000 liability and, at the same time, provide some rate of return on the assets held.

- **Purchase Of Non-Monetary Assets**   It would be possible for the company to hedge its €500,000 liability by purchasing a non-monetary asset denominated in Euros. Such assets as German land, inventories, or equipment could serve in this role. However, the acquisition and disposition of such assets would generally be less convenient than the other alternatives and, in addition, the fact that such assets do not have a fixed Euro value could make them ineffective as a hedge. As a consequence, this would not be a common solution to the hedging problem.

- **Entering A Forward Or Futures Exchange Contract**   Perhaps the most convenient solution to the problem of hedging the €500,000 liability would be to simply enter a forward or futures exchange contract to receive €500,000 on May 1, 2003. Under this approach, the hedging goal is accomplished, no investment of funds is required, and the only cost is the premium required on the contract (see the next Section for an explanation of contract premiums and discounts).

- **Acquiring A Future Income Stream**   A final possibility, in certain circumstances, would be for the company to acquire a foreign currency income stream. If, for example, the Canadian company licensed a German enterprise to produce one of its products, it could anticipate that the Euro royalties on this arrangement will be sufficient to pay the €500,000 liability.

9-71.   In this Section, we will present and discuss the general principles involved in the two types of foreign currency situations which may require hedges and illustrate such hedges as currency, monetary assets, and non-monetary assets. Consideration will also be given to situations involving a hedge of a net investment in a self-sustaining foreign operation. Because of the complexity of forward exchange contracts and the possibility that they may be used for purposes other than hedging, these contracts will be dealt with in a separate Section of this Chapter.

Hedge Accounting
Described
9-72.   In order to understand the importance of being able to identify a particular item as a hedging instrument, it is necessary to understand the concept of "hedge accounting". AcG-13 defines this concept as follows:

> **Hedge accounting** is a method for recognizing the gains, losses, revenues and expenses associated with the items in a hedging relationship, such that those gains, losses, revenues and expenses are recognized in income in the same period when they would otherwise be recognized in different periods.

9-73.   For example, assume a Canadian company acquires 2,000,000 Swiss Francs (SF, hereafter) at a point in time when SF1 = $1.05. If the rate changes to SF1 = $0.95, the Canadian dollar value of this currency will be reduced from $2,100,000 to $1,900,000. If this currency balance is not being used as a hedge, a $200,000 foreign exchange loss would have to be included in the company's income.

9-74. Alternatively, if the SF2,000,000 was serving as a hedge of a SF2,000,000 anticipated purchase of merchandise, hedge accounting would permit the loss on the currency to be deferred until the anticipated transaction takes place. In cases such as this, the question of whether the SF2,000,000 can be identified as a hedge of an anticipated transaction becomes a significant issue in the determination of enterprise income.

The Problem

9-75. In cases where a hedging item is directly related to an outstanding monetary balance, the question of whether or not to use hedge accounting is not an issue. For example, if our SF2,000,000 currency holding was matched with a SF2,000,000 short-term liability, normal accounting procedures would result in the loss on the currency holding being exactly offset by a gain on the liability. The only thing that hedge accounting would add in this case is the possibility that net disclosure would be provided for the offsetting gain and loss. In this case there would be no problem of matching dates as the currency could be used to pay the liability at any point in time. Unfortunately, hedges are seldom this perfect in the real world.

9-76. Consider the fairly simple situation where an short-term monetary asset is being used to hedge a monetary liability. In some cases, the monetary asset may have a different maturity than the related liability. It is also possible that the amounts involved in the two financial instruments may be different. There are even situations where the currencies are different. If you can demonstrate that there is a close correlation in the movements of two currencies, for example the U.S. dollar and the Euro, it would be possible to hedge a Euro liability with a U.S. dollar asset. A further complication would arise in large multinational organizations with operations being carried out in many different currencies. In this type of organization, there may be many natural or internal hedges between financial instruments being issued or held in different parts of the organization. However, accurate tracking of such relationships would be extremely difficult.

9-77. A more difficult problem arises when the hedge is directed, not at an actual foreign currency monetary balance, but at an anticipated future foreign currency transaction. To explain this situation, we will return to our Swiss Franc example where the SF2,000,000 currency holding is designated as a hedge of an anticipated purchase of merchandise that must be paid for in Swiss Francs. As we noted, the question of whether or not hedge accounting can be used for this relationship is of considerable significance in the determination of enterprise income. If the currency cannot be identified as a hedge, exchange gains and losses resulting from changes in the value of the currency holding will have to be taken into income as they occur. Alternatively, if the SF2,000,000 qualifies for hedge accounting, such gains and losses can be deferred until the anticipated transaction takes place.

9-78. The question of where hedge accounting is appropriate cannot be answered in a totally objective manner, particularly in situations involving an anticipated future transaction as the hedged item. This clearly leaves the possibility that, when a hedging instrument experiences losses, management will look for ways to designate the instrument as a hedge in order to avoid recognition of the loss. There is, in fact, considerable evidence that this has happened on more than one occasion. This necessity to judge the intention of management is one of the main reasons that standard setting bodies have had major difficulties in providing comprehensive pronouncements on the subject of hedge accounting and the identification of hedging relationships.

Exercise Nine-4 deals with hedging transactions.

Exercise Nine-4

On June 30, 2002, Numa Ltd. purchases merchandise in the United States for US$275,000. The merchandise must be paid for on December 31, 2002. Also on June 30, 2002, the company purchases a U.S. dollar certificate of deposit with a maturity value of US$300,000. The bill matures on December 31, 2002. On June 30, 2002, the exchange rate is US$1 = C$1.55. It remains at this level until December 31, 2002, at which point the rate changes to US$1 = C$1.60.

Required:

A. Provide the journal entries to record the described transactions, assuming that the certificate of deposit is not designated as a hedge of the US$ liability.

B. Provide the journal entries to record the described transactions, assuming that the certificate of deposit is designated as a hedge of the US$ liability.

In both parts of this question, ignore any interest that accrues on the certificate of deposit.

End Of Exercise Nine-4

This is a continuation of Exercise Nine-4.

Identifying Hedges
CICA Handbook Recommendation

9-79.   As discussed in the preceding section, there are problems with identifying hedges, even in situations involving hedges of outstanding monetary balances. However, the greatest potential for abuse arises when a financial instrument is used to hedge an anticipated foreign currency transaction.

9-80.   As we have noted, the problem here is that management may be tempted to identify a particular financial instrument as a hedge, simply to avoid including losses on that instrument in income. One solution would be to require that such anticipated transactions be supported by some type of contract. That would mean, for example, that to claim that there is an anticipated purchase of merchandise in a foreign currency, the transaction would have to be supported by a firm purchase commitment.

9-81.   While such a legalistic approach would solve the problem of spurious claims about anticipated transactions, the Accounting Standards Board concluded that it would be too restrictive to deal with the types of foreign exchange risk that confront Canadian business. As a consequence, the *Handbook* requires only that management take the responsibility for identifying items that are being used as hedges. This is reflected in the following *CICA Handbook* Recommendation:

> **Paragraph 1650.50**   *If a foreign exchange contract, asset, liability or future revenue stream is to be regarded as a hedge of a specific foreign currency exposure:*
>
> *(a) it should be identified as a hedge of the item(s) to which it relates; and*
>
> *(b) there should be reasonable assurance that it is and will continue to be effective as a hedge. (July, 1983)*

Accounting Guideline No. 13

9-82.   With respect to the actual implementation of the preceding Recommendation, AcG-13 provides guidance on the conditions required for the use of hedge accounting:

> A hedging relationship qualifies for hedge accounting only when all of the following conditions are satisfied:
>
> (a) At the inception of the hedging relationship, the entity should have:
>
> (i) identified the nature of the specific risk exposure or exposures being hedged in accordance with its risk management objective and strategy; and
>
> (ii) designated that hedge accounting will be applied to the hedging relationship.
>
> (b) At the inception of the hedging relationship, the entity should have formal documentation of:
>
> (i) its risk management objective and strategy for establishing the relationship;
>
> (ii) the hedging relationship, identifying the hedged item, the related hedging item, the nature of the specific risk exposure or exposures being hedged and the intended term of the hedging relationship;

(iii) the method for assessing the effectiveness of the hedging relationship; and

(iv) the method of accounting for the hedging relationship, including the income recognition of the gains, losses, revenues and expenses associated with the items in the relationship.

(c) Both at the inception of the hedging relationship and throughout its term, the entity should have reasonable assurance that the relationship will be effective, consistent with the entity's originally documented risk management objective and strategy. Accordingly:

(i) the effectiveness of the hedging relationship should be reliably measurable, which requires that the effects of the risk exposure being modified be reliably measurable for the hedged item and the hedging item;

(ii) the hedging relationship should be assessed on a regular periodic basis over its term to determine that it has remained, and is expected to continue to be, effective; and

(iii) in the case of a hedging relationship involving an anticipated transaction, it should be probable that the transaction will occur and present an exposure to variations in cash flows ultimately affecting income.

9-83. The Guideline also provides guidance on hedging relationships involving anticipated transactions. The basic principle here is that it must be probable that the anticipated transaction will occur at the time and in the amount expected. In evaluating whether anticipated transactions are probable, the Guideline lists the following factors to consider:

a. the existence of a firm commitment to undertake the anticipated transaction;

b. the existence of similar transactions in the past;

c. the financial and operational ability of the entity to carry out the anticipated transaction;

d. the extent of the entity's current commitments of resources to the business activity of which the anticipated transaction is a part;

e. the length of time to the date the anticipated transaction is expected to occur;

f. the extent of loss or disruption to the entity if it does not undertake the anticipated transaction;

g. the likelihood that another transaction might take place to achieve the same business purpose; and

h. the likelihood that another party will be willing and able to undertake the anticipated transaction with the entity.

Accounting For A Hedge Of An Anticipated Transaction

9-84. When an enterprises arranges for a hedge of an anticipated transaction, the goal is to establish the Canadian dollar price of the goods or services to be purchased or sold. In view of this intent, the *CICA Handbook* states the following:

Paragraph 1650.52 *When a purchase or sale of goods or services in a foreign currency is hedged before the transaction, the Canadian dollar price of such goods or services is established by the terms of the hedge.* (July, 1983)

9-85. A simple example will serve to illustrate this type of hedge:

Example On June 1, 2003, a Canadian enterprise agrees to purchase goods in Denmark on September 1, 2003 at a price of 800,000 Danish Krones (DK). Assume that, on this commitment date, the rate of exchange is DK1 = $0.25. On September 1, 2003, the exchange rate is DK1 = $0.22.

9-86. If no hedge was established on the commitment date, the merchandise would be recorded at whatever exchange rate prevailed on September 1, 2003. The cost of the merchandise would be $176,000 (DK800,000 @ $0.22). This would not be the case if the commitment were hedged.

9-87. To illustrate this possibility, assume that at the time of the commitment, the Canadian company purchases DK800,000 in currency at DK1 = $0.25, holds this currency until the September 1, 2003 purchase date, and uses the currency to pay for the merchandise. In this case, the merchandise would be recorded at $200,000 (DK800,000 @ $0.25) and there would be no exchange gain or loss on the currency holding or any other aspect of the transaction. The same analysis would apply if the commitment had been hedged by holding a Danish krone denominated monetary investment, the only difference being the additional income on the investment. In the unusual situation where the hedge consisted of a non-monetary investment, it is not entirely clear what value the Paragraph 1650.52 Recommendation would apply to the merchandise. We would presume that it would continue to be $200,000, not the ultimate Danish krone proceeds of the investment translated at some appropriate rate of exchange.

9-88. Section 1650 also notes that when a hedge of a commitment to purchase or sell goods or services is terminated or ceases to be effective prior to the date of the related purchase or sale, any exchange gain or loss deferred on the hedge up to that date will continue to be deferred and included as part of the Canadian dollar price of the goods purchased or sold when the transaction takes place. Continuing our previous example, assume that the Canadian company had constructed its hedge using a currency holding and that it decides to sell these Danish krones on August 1, 2003. If, on this date, the exchange rate is DK1 = $0.23, the loss of $16,000 [($0.25 - $0.23)(DK800,000)] would be deferred and included as part of the Canadian dollar price of the goods purchased on September 1, 2003. This would result in a merchandise cost of $192,000 ($176,000 + $16,000).

Exercise Nine-5

On September 30, 2002 Britor Ltd. acquires a British short-term money market instrument for £375,000. This money market instrument is sold on December 1, 2002 for £385,000.

> Exercise Nine-5 deals with hedging an anticipated transaction.

Also on September 30, 2002, after reviewing three quotes, Britor Ltd. decides that it will purchase British manufacturing equipment with a total cost of £375,000 from Bulldog Machinery. The equipment will be delivered on December 1, 2002, and will be paid for on December 31, 2002.

Relevant exchange rates are as follows:

September 30, 2002	£1 = $2.30
December 1, 2002	£1 = $2.27
December 31, 2002	£1 = $2.25

Required: Provide the following:

A. The journal entries required to record the acquisition and sale of the short-term investment assuming that Britor Ltd. does not designate the money market instrument as a hedge of the equipment purchase commitment

B. The journal entries required to record the described transactions assuming that Britor Ltd. designates the money market instrument as a hedge of the equipment purchase commitment.

End Of Exercise Nine-5

Accounting For A Hedge Of Monetary Assets Or Liabilities

9-89.   As we have stated earlier, the intent of a hedge of a monetary asset or liability is to counteract the possibility of incurring an exchange gain or loss at the settlement date. As a reflection of this view, Paragraph 1650.54 makes the following Recommendation:

Paragraph 1650.54   *If a foreign currency denominated monetary item is covered by:*

(a) *a hedge that is itself a foreign currency denominated monetary item, any exchange gain or loss on the hedge should be offset against the corresponding exchange loss or gain on the hedged item;*

(b) *a hedge that is a non-monetary item, any exchange loss or gain on the foreign currency denominated monetary item should be deferred until the settlement date of that monetary item.* (July, 1983)

9-90.   Once again, a simple example will serve to illustrate these requirements:

Example   On November 1, 2002, a Canadian company with a December 31 year end, purchases merchandise in Switzerland for 1,000,000 Swiss Francs (SF, hereafter). Assume that, at this time, the exchange rate is SF1 = $0.90 and, as a consequence, both the merchandise and the resulting payable would be recorded at $900,000. The merchandise is paid for on February 1, 2003 when the exchange rate is SF1 = $0.95. On December 31, 2002, the exchange rate is SF1 = $0.92.

9-91.   If, in this situation, no hedge of the exposed Swiss Franc liability was provided, the company would have to accrue a loss of $20,000 [(SF1,000,000)($0.92 - $0.90)] on December 31, 2002. As it would require $950,000 to pay the SF1,000,000 on February 1, 2003, a further exchange loss of $30,000 [(SF1,000,000)($0.95 - $0.92)] would have to be recorded on this settlement date. Alternatively, if the Canadian company hedged its Swiss Franc liability by holding currency or a monetary investment denominated in Swiss Francs, there would be no net gain or loss recorded, either at the December 31 year end or on the February 1 settlement date. While from a technical point of view there would be a loss on the payable on both of these dates, the losses would be exactly offset by a gain on the monetary asset holding. Paragraph 1650.54 requires that these amounts be offset against each other.

9-92.   While we would not expect such a transaction to be normal, a hedge could have been created using a non-monetary asset such as an investment in Swiss Franc denominated equity securities. Assume that this is the case and that equity securities costing SF1,000,000 on November 1, 2002 are sold on February 1, 2003 for SF1,200,000. At the December 31 year end, the Accounts Payable would have to be written up to $920,000 and an exchange loss of $20,000 would have to be recorded. Further, there would be no offsetting gain on the non-monetary investment as it would be translated at the historical rate of $0.90. In this situation, Paragraph 1650.54 requires the deferral of the $20,000 loss until February 1, 2003. On this settlement date, the SF1,000,000 of the SF1,200,000 proceeds from the sale of the non-monetary investments would be applied to the liability, net of the deferred loss, while the remaining SF200,000 would be converted into $190,000 (SF200,000 @ $0.95) and this would be recorded as a gain. The cost of the merchandise would remain at $900,000 and there would be no loss on the Accounts Payable.

Exercise Nine-6 deals with hedging an exposed monetary position.	**Exercise Nine-6** On October 15, 2002, Arlin Inc. purchases merchandise in France at a cost of 425,000 Euros (€). These goods must be paid for on March 1, 2003. At this time, the company also acquires French equity securities at a cost of €425,000. These securities are designated as a hedge of the €425,000 payable and they are sold for €410,000 on March 1, 2003. The Company has a December 31 year end. Relevant exchange rates are as follows:

October 15, 2002	€1 = $1.38
December 31, 2002	€1 = $1.40
March 1, 2003	€1 = $1.43

Required: Provide the journal entries required to record the described transactions.

Discontinuance Of Hedge Accounting

9-93.   Section 1650 does not deal with the discontinuance of hedge accounting. However, AcG-13 states that an entity should discontinue hedge accounting when a hedging relationship ceases to satisfy the conditions for hedge accounting. Those conditions cease to be satisfied when:

(a) the hedging item ceases to exist as a result of its maturity, expiry, sale, termination, cancellation or exercise, unless it is replaced by another hedging item as part of the entity's documented hedging strategy;

(b) the hedged item ceases to exist as a result of its maturity, expiry, sale, termination, cancellation or exercise;

(c) the entity terminates its designation of the hedging relationship;

(d) the hedging relationship ceases to be effective; or

(e) it is no longer probable that the anticipated transaction will occur substantially as and when identified on inception of the hedging relationship.

9-94.   AcG-13 also describes the accounting consequences of ceasing to satisfy the conditions for hedge accounting as follows:

(a) When a hedging item ceases to exist as a result of its maturity, expiry, sale, termination, cancellation or exercise and is not replaced as part of the entity's documented hedging strategy, any gains, losses, revenues or expenses associated with the hedging item that had been deferred previously as a result of applying hedge accounting are carried forward to be recognized in income in the same period as the corresponding gains, losses, revenues or expenses associated with the hedged item.

(b) When a hedged item ceases to exist as a result of its maturity, expiry, sale, termination, cancellation or exercise, any gains, losses, revenues or expenses associated with the hedging item that had been deferred previously as a result of applying hedge accounting are recognized in the current period's income statement along with the corresponding gains, losses, revenues or expenses recognized on the hedged item. This treatment applies when it is no longer probable that an anticipated transaction will occur substantially as and when identified on inception of the hedging relationship.

(c) When an entity terminates its designation of a hedging relationship or a hedging relationship ceases to be effective, hedge accounting is not applied to gains, losses, revenues or expenses arising subsequently. However, the hedge accounting applied to the hedging relationship in prior periods is not reversed. Any gains, losses, revenues or expenses deferred previously as a result of applying hedge accounting continue to be carried forward for subsequent recognition in income in the same period as the corresponding gains, losses, revenues or expenses associated with the hedged item.

Exercise Nine-7

On September 30, 2002, Argent Inc. decides that it will purchase Argentinian merchandise with a total cost of 260,000 Pesos (P). The merchandise will be delivered on January 15, 2003, and must be paid for on March 1, 2003. At the same time, Argent acquires an Argentinian short-term money market instrument for P260,000. Argent has a December 31 year end.

On January 4, 2003, Argent decides that it does not need the Argentinian merchandise and cancels the purchase order. Reflecting this decision, the money market instrument is sold on this date for P270,000.

Relevant exchange rates are as follows:

> Exercise Nine-7 deals with discontinuance of hedge accounting.

This is a continuation of Exercise Nine-7.

September 30, 2002	P1 = $0.50
December 31, 2002	P1 = $0.48
January 4, 2003	P1 = $0.47

Required: Provide the journal entries required to record the described transactions.

End Of Exercise Nine-7

Accounting For A Hedge Of A Net Investment In A Self-Sustaining Foreign Operation

9-95.   We will find in Chapter 10 that, for those operations that are designated as self-sustaining foreign operations, gains or losses arising on the translation of financial statements are not included in income. Rather, as long as the investor company intends to continue the foreign operation, they are allocated to a separate section of shareholders' equity. While this treatment will be explained in detail in Chapter 10, we would note here that a problem may arise when an enterprise decides to hedge its investment in a self-sustaining foreign operation.

9-96.   For example, an investment in a German subsidiary might be hedged by borrowing in Euros and designating the resulting liability as a hedge of the net investment in the foreign operation. The problem here is that, while the gains or losses on the investment in the foreign operation would not be taken into income, the Recommendations of Section 1650 would normally require that the gains or losses on the liability must be taken into income as they occur. To mitigate this anomaly, Section 1650 suggests that when this type of hedging relationship exists, the gains or losses on the hedging item be excluded from income and included with the gains or losses arising on the translation of financial statements, as part of the separate section of shareholders' equity.

Forward Exchange Contracts

Nature Of Forward Exchange Contracts

Terminology

9-97.   A forward exchange contract is an agreement to exchange, on a specified future date, a specified quantity of a particular currency at an exchange rate established at the time of entering into the contract. In order to fully understand the nature of such contracts and the accounting procedures that are used to deal with them, it is necessary to comprehend a number of definitions that are used in connection with such arrangements. These definitions are as follows:

- **Forward Contract Commitment Date**   The date of entering into a forward exchange contract.

- **Spot Rate**   The exchange rates for immediate delivery of currencies exchanged. As we have noted previously, in the real world there will generally be at least two such rates at a given point in time. These rates would include the rate applicable to buying the currency and the rate applicable to selling the currency.

- **Forward Rate**   The exchange rate for future delivery of currencies to be exchanged.

- **Premium Or Discount**   The amount of the forward contract multiplied by the difference between the forward rate and the spot rate at the forward contract commitment date.

Example

9-98.   To illustrate these definitions and to serve as a basis for examples of accounting for forward exchange contracts, a simple example will be used. This example is as follows:

Example On October 1, 2002, Canco Ltd. enters a forward exchange contract to receive 1,000,000 Euros (€) on March 1, 2003 at a rate of €1 = $1.42. The spot rate on October 1, 2002 is €1 = $1.40. On December 31, 2002, when the company closes its books and prepares financial statements, the spot rate is €1 = $1.45 and on March 1, 2003 it is €1 = $1.46.

9-99. Note that the Canadian company is not committed to actually receiving the Euros. The company has simply entered a non-cancelable executory contract agreeing to exchange Canadian dollars for Euros at a future point in time. It is unlikely that Canco will ever take delivery of this currency. If the forward contract is being used as a hedge, the Euros will be used to cover the monetary liability or to make the anticipated purchase. Alternatively, if the contract is not being used as a hedge, Canco would simply pay or receive the difference in value on the settlement date.

9-100. Despite the seeming clarity of this situation, some authors continue to argue that a receivable and payable should be recorded for the amounts of currency specified in the contract ($1,420,000 or €1,000,000 at $1.42). Given that there is no intent to receive or pay these amounts, it is difficult to see the basis for this conclusion. Further, given that this is an executory contract, the recording of a $1,420,000 receivable and payable would not be in keeping with GAAP. The normal treatment of unperformed or executory contracts is to provide only note disclosure. The one important exception to this is in the area of leases and this exception is specifically justified and provided for in Section 3065 of the *CICA Handbook*. No such exception is provided for forward exchange contracts and none would seem advisable.

Premium Or Discount

9-101. The only cost associated with entering the forward exchange contract described in the example is the premium of $20,000 [(€1,000,000)($1.42 - $1.40)]. The amount of such premiums is influenced primarily by two factors. The first of these is expectations with respect to the future movement of the relevant exchange rate. It would appear in this case that the Euro is expected to go up relative to the Canadian dollar. If expectations were weaker or there was some belief that the Euro would decline, the premium would be smaller or could even become a discount.

9-102. Interest rates are also influential here. Forward exchange contracts are a way of taking a position in a foreign currency without a significant investment of funds. For example, if an enterprise had a liability of £1,000,000, a forward exchange contract to take delivery of £1,000,000 represents an approach to hedging the liability. As such, it is an alternative to simply holding the £1,000,000 in currency. In view of this alternative, it is unlikely a company would enter into a forward contract if the premium exceeds the cost of interest on borrowing an equivalent amount of the foreign currency.

9-103. There is some confusion about the appropriate treatment of premium or discount. In our view, the appropriate treatment is dependent on the use of the forward exchange contract:

Hedge Of An Exposed Monetary Position When a contract is entered to hedge an exposed monetary position resulting from a transaction that has already taken place (e.g., a purchase of merchandise), the premium is a cost that is being incurred to avoid having an exchange gain or loss over the period until the monetary position is settled. The appropriate accounting treatment is to charge this cost to income over that period. It is not a cost that should be added to the recorded value of the transaction (e.g., added to the cost of the merchandise purchased). An alternative treatment can be justified on the grounds of materiality, but not on the grounds of accounting principles.

Hedge Of An Anticipated Transaction When a contract is entered to hedge an anticipated transaction, the goal is to establish the Canadian dollar price at which the future transaction will be recorded. In this case the premium should be added to the

Canadian dollar price by recording the future transaction at the contract rate of exchange, rather than the spot rate of exchange at the time the transaction occurs.

9-104. The confusion on this issue results from a misinterpretation of the only *Handbook* Recommendation that relates to this issue:

> **Paragraph 1650.** *When a purchase or sale of goods or services in a foreign currency is hedged before the transaction, the Canadian dollar price of such goods or services is established by the terms of the hedge.* (July, 1983)

9-105. Some writers have interpreted this to mean that all hedged transactions should be recorded using the terms of the hedge. Careful reading shows that this is not the case. The key phrase is "hedged before the transaction", making it clear that this provision only applies to situations where the forward exchange contract is a hedge of anticipated future transactions. It cannot be applied in situations where the forward exchange contract is used to hedge a current or past transaction.

Forward Contracts Vs. Futures Contracts

9-106. While we will not explore this issue fully in this text, you should be aware that there is a difference between forward exchange contracts and futures contracts. The former are individually negotiated agreements in which the amount of currency as well as the settlement date can be tailored to the needs of the parties to the contract. Such contracts cannot usually be traded or sold prior to the settlement date.

9-107. In contrast, futures contracts are standardized in terms of both amounts (typically US$100,000) and settlement dates. Unlike forward exchange contracts, they are traded on organized exchanges and can be bought and sold prior to their settlement date. While we will focus on the accounting procedures to be used for forward exchange contracts, much of our discussion would be equally applicable to futures contracts.

Forward Exchange Contract As A Hedge Of An Anticipated Foreign Currency Commitment

9-108. The forward exchange contract example in Paragraph 9-98 could be extended to illustrate the use of a forward contract as a hedge of a commitment to purchase goods or services:

> **Example** On October 1, 2002, Canco Ltd. enters a forward exchange contract to receive 1,000,000 Euros (€) on March 1, 2003 at a rate of €1 = $1.42. The spot rate on October 1, 2002 is €1 = $1.40. On December 31, 2002, when the company closes its books and prepares financial statements, the spot rate is €1 = $1.45 and on March 1, 2003 it is €1 = $1.46.

Canco anticipates that it will purchase and pay for €1,000,000 in merchandise on March 1, 2003. In this case, the effect of having the forward exchange contract as a hedge is to establish the Canadian dollar price of the merchandise to be purchased. This value is established at $1,420,000 by the contracted forward rate of $1.42. This means that the premium on the contract becomes part of the cost of the merchandise and, given that the Euros received under the contract are used to purchase the merchandise on March 1, 2003, there will be no gain or loss on the contract to be taken into income.

Example Solution Because of the executory nature of the forward exchange contract, no entry would be required on October 1, 2002.

On December 31, 2002, it would be possible to record the forward exchange contract as an asset, with a corresponding credit to a deferred gain. However, if it is still the intent of the company to use the Euros received under the contract to purchase merchandise, we believe that it would be more appropriate to make no entry at this date.

On March 1, 2003, the company would use $1,420,000 in cash to purchase the €1,000,000 in currency. If these Euros were used to purchase the merchandise as planned, the entry would be as follows:

Merchandise	$1,420,000	
Cash		$1,420,000

If, for some reason, the merchandise was not purchased, the Euros could be sold at the March 1, 2003 spot rate of €1 = $1.46 and this would result in a gain as follows:

Cash [(€1,000,000)($1.46 - $1.42)]	$40,000	
Gain		$40,000

Exercise Nine-8

On November 15, 2002, Sellor Inc. enters a forward contract to make delivery of 625,000 Australian dollars (A$) on February 15, 2003, at a rate of A$1 = C$0.88. At this time the spot rate for the Australian dollar is A$1 = C$0.87. Also on this date, the company makes a commitment to sell merchandise to an Australian firm for A$625,000. The merchandise is to be delivered on February 15, 2003, with payment being due on delivery. The company has a December 31 year end.

Relevant exchange rates are as follows:

November 15, 2002	A$1 = C$0.87
December 31, 2002	A$1 = C$0.91
February 15, 2003	A$1 = C$0.93

Required: Provide the journal entries required to record the described transactions.

End Of Exercise Nine-8

> Exercise Nine-8 deals with hedging an anticipated transaction with a forward exchange contract.

Forward Exchange Contract As A Hedge Of A Monetary Asset Or Liability

9-109. The forward exchange contract example in Paragraph 9-98 could be extended to illustrate the use of a forward contract as a hedge of an exposed monetary asset.

Example On October 1, 2002, Canco Ltd. enters a forward exchange contract to receive 1,000,000 Euros (€) on March 1, 2003 at a rate of €1 = $1.42. The spot rate on October 1, 2002 is €1 = $1.40. On December 31, 2002, when the company closes its books and prepares financial statements, the spot rate is €1 = $1.45 and on March 1, 2003 it is €1 = $1.46.

On October 1, 2002, Canco purchases €1,000,000 in German merchandise, with the resulting payable due on March 1, 2003. The forward exchange contract is designated as a hedge of this monetary liability.

Example Solution In this situation, the merchandise would be recorded using the spot rate on October 1, 2002. The $20,000 [(€1,000,000)($1.42 - $1.40)] premium on the contract would become a hedging expense to be recognized over the period in which the forward contract serves as a hedge.

The only entry required on October 1, 2002 would be to record the purchase of merchandise at the spot rate:

Merchandise (€1,000,000 At $1.40)	$1,400,000	
Accounts Payable		$1,400,000

As noted previously, the premium on forward exchange contracts must be recognized as an expense over the life of the hedging arrangement. Since the life of the contract is five months and three months have passed as of December 31, 2002, an entry is required on December 31, 2002 to recognize 3/5 of the premium as an expense:

Hedge Expense [(3/5)(€1,000,000)($1.42 - $1.40)]	$12,000	
Premium Liability		$12,000

Also on this date, it is necessary to adjust the payable to reflect the new spot rate of €1 = $1.45. This entry by itself would result in an exchange loss. However, the forward exchange contract will be used to offset this loss and, as a consequence, this contract should be recognized as an asset at a value which reflects its intended use. These considerations could be recorded with two journal entries as follows:

Exchange Loss [(€1,000,000)($1.45 - $1.40)]	$50,000	
Accounts Payable		$50,000

Forward Exchange Contract [(€1,000,000)($1.45 - $1.40)]	$50,000	
Exchange Gain		$50,000

While the preceding two entries are an accurate solution to the problem, it is clear that the loss and gain will always be equal in a fully hedged situation such as this. As a reflection of this situation, we have previously noted that the *CICA Handbook* suggests that the corresponding gain and loss should be offset for financial statement presentation. Given this suggestion, the more appropriate net entry would be as follows:

Forward Exchange Contract		
[(€1,000,000)($1.45 - $1.40)]	$50,000	
Accounts Payable		$50,000

Prior to recording the settlement of the payable on March 1, 2003, it is useful to illustrate the accrual of the hedge expense for the remaining two months of the contract as well as recognize the increased values of the foreign currency liability and related forward exchange contract. These two entries would be as follows:

Hedge Expense [(2/5)(€1,000,000)($1.42 - $1.40)]	$8,000	
Premium Liability		$8,000

Forward Exchange Contract		
[(€1,000,000)($1.46 - $1.45)]	$10,000	
Accounts Payable		$10,000

With these adjustments in place, the entry to record the settlement of the liability and the forward exchange contract would be as follows:

Accounts Payable	$1,460,000	
Premium Liability	20,000	
Forward Exchange Contract		$ 60,000
Cash [(€1,000,000)($1.42)]		1,420,000

It would, of course, be possible to expand this entry significantly by providing separate entries for the exchange of currencies under the forward exchange contract. However, the preceding entry is a better representation of the manner in which the Canadian dollar cash flows will actually take place.

Exercise Nine-9 deals with hedging an exposed monetary asset with a forward exchange contract.

Exercise Nine-9
This is an extension of Exercise Nine-8.

On November 15, 2002, Sellor Inc. enters a forward contract to make delivery of 625,000 Australian dollars (A$) on February 15, 2003, at a rate of A$1 = C$0.88. At this time the spot rate for the Australian dollar is A$1 = C$0.87. Also on this date, the company sells merchandise to an Australian firm for A$625,000. The merchandise is to be paid for on February 15, 2003. The company has a December 31 year end.

Relevant exchange rates are as follows:

November 15, 2002	A$1 = C$0.87
December 31, 2002	A$1 = C$0.91
February 15, 2003	A$1 = C$0.93

Required: Provide the journal entries required to record the described transactions.

Speculative Forward Exchange Contracts

9-110.   We would expect that the majority of forward exchange contracts entered into by Canadian enterprises serve as hedges of either foreign currency monetary assets or liabilities or, alternatively, anticipated transactions. Without question, however, there are situations in which contracts are entered for purely speculative reasons. In such a situation, hedge accounting cannot be used. When hedge accounting cannot be used, gains and losses on financial instruments cannot be deferred and must be taken into income as they occur. With respect to the measurement of the gain or loss, the amount would be determined by multiplying the foreign currency amount of the forward contract by the difference between the contracted forward rate and the forward rate available for the remaining maturity of the contract. No separate recognition would be given to the discount or premium.

9-111.   The forward exchange contract example in Paragraph 9-98 could be extended to illustrate a speculative forward exchange contract.

> **Example**   On October 1, 2002, Canco Ltd. enters a forward exchange contract to receive 1,000,000 Euros (€) on March 1, 2003 at a rate of €1 = $1.42. The spot rate on October 1, 2002 is €1 = $1.40. On December 31, 2002, when the company closes its books and prepares financial statements, the spot rate is €1 = $1.45 and on March 1, 2003 it is €1 = $1.46.

The forward contract is not serving as a hedge of any other foreign currency transaction or commitment.

> **Example Solution**   No entry would be required on October 1, 2002.

Since the Canadian company is closing its books on December 31, 2002, an entry would be required to recognize a gain on the contract. To determine the amount of the gain, we could use the December 31 spot rate. However, our contract gives us delivery two months after this date and it is probably more appropriate to use the two month forward rate to place a value on the contract. Taking this approach, we will assume that the two month forward rate for the Euro on December 31, 2002 is €1 = $1.48. Given this additional information, the journal entry would be as follows:

Forward Exchange Contract		
[(€1,000,000)($1.48 - $1.42)]	$60,000	
Exchange Gain		$60,000

When the forward exchange contract is settled on March 1, 2003, the cash inflow would be based on €1,000,000 times the difference between the current spot rate of $1.46 and the contract rate of $1.42. Recognition of this inflow of $40,000 and the recognition of the December 31, 2002 to March 1, 2003 loss would be recorded in the following journal entry:

Cash [(€1,000,000)($1.46 - $1.42)]	$40,000	
Exchange Loss [(€1,000,000)($1.48 - $1.46)]	20,000	
Forward Exchange Contract		$60,000

This entry reflects the fact that the forward exchange contract would be settled on a net basis, with the only cash flow based on the difference between the contract rate of $1.42 and the $1.46 spot rate at the settlement date.

Exercise Nine-10 deals with a speculative forward exchange contract.

Exercise Nine-10

This is an extension of Exercises Nine-8 and Nine-9.

On November 15, 2002, Sellor Inc. enters a forward contract to make delivery of 625,000 Australian dollars (A$) on February 15, 2003, at a rate of A$1 = C$0.88. At this time the spot rate for the Australian dollar is A$1 = C$0.87. The contract is not designated as a hedging item. The company has a December 31 year end.

Relevant spot exchange rates are as follows:

November 15, 2002	A$1 = C$0.87
December 31, 2002	A$1 = C$0.91
February 15, 2003	A$1 = C$0.93

In addition, on December 31, 2002, the spot rate for making delivery of Australian dollars on February 15, 2003 is A$1 = $0.94.

Required: Provide the journal entries required to record the described transactions.

End Of Exercise Nine-10

Foreign Currency Translation In Canadian Practice And Additional Readings

9-112. Statistics on foreign currency translation can be found *Financial Reporting In Canada*. There is some discussion of this information in Chapter 10. Chapter 10 also contains comments on the availability of additional readings on foreign currency translation.

Problems For Self Study

(The solutions for these problems can be found following Chapter 16 of the text.)

Self Study Problem Nine - 1

On December 31, 2002, the Jordanian government loans the Canadian Company, Petroteach, 5 million Jordan dinars (D, hereafter) interest-free. This money is to be used to establish a training center for skilled workers in the oil industry. The loan matures on December 31, 2006. Assume that the relevant exchange rates for the next four years are as follows:

December 31, 2002	D1 = $1.80
December 31, 2003	D1 = $2.10
December 31, 2004	D1 = $2.00
December 31, 2005	D1 = $2.00
December 31, 2006	D1 = $1.70

The Petroteach Company closes its books on December 31 of each year and accounts for foreign currency transactions using the recommendations contained in Section 1650 of the *CICA Handbook*.

Required: Prepare the journal entries that would be required to account for the loan on December 31 of each year to maturity.

Self Study Problem Nine - 2

On December 1, 2002, the Canadian Switzcan Company enters into a forward exchange contract to purchase 2,000,000 Swiss francs (SF, hereafter) on March 31, 2003 at a rate of SF1 = $1.00. Assume that the spot rates of exchange on dates relevant to this contract are as follows:

December 1, 2002	SF1 = $0.96
December 31, 2002	SF1 = $0.98
March 31, 2003	SF1 = $1.03

The 3 month forward rate on December 31, 2002 is SF1 = $1.05. The Switzcan Company closes its books on December 31 and accounts for forward exchange contracts using the recommendations of Section 1650 of the *CICA Handbook* and the CICA Accounting Guideline No. 13, "Hedging Relationships".

Required: In the following independent cases, provide the journal entries that would be required on December 1, 2002, December 31, 2002 and March 31, 2003 to account for the forward exchange contract and any other transactions that are included in the individual cases.

A. On December 1, 2002, Switzcan Company makes a commitment to its Swiss supplier to purchase merchandise on March 31, 2003. The cost of the merchandise is SF2,000,000, it will be delivered on March 31, 2003, and the invoice is payable on the delivery date. Management designates that a hedging relationship exists between the commitment and the forward contract.

B. On December 1, 2002, Switzcan purchases merchandise from its Swiss supplier at a cost of SF2,000,000. The invoice must be paid on March 31, 2003. Management designates that a hedging relationship exists between the payable and the forward contract.

C. On December 1, 2002, Switzcan decides to speculate in foreign currency via a forward exchange contract.

Self Study Problem Nine - 3

On November 1, 2002, the Riskless Company, a Canadian based trading company, sells merchandise to a New Zealand distributor for 5 million New Zealand dollars (NZ$, hereafter). The invoice is to be paid in New Zealand dollars by the New Zealand distributor on February 1, 2003. Also on November 1, 2002, the Riskless Company makes a commitment to purchase equipment from a New Zealand manufacturer for NZ$20 million. The equipment is to be delivered on March 1, 2003 and the entire purchase price must be paid on that date in New Zealand dollars.

In view of the preceding transactions, on November 1, 2002 the Riskless Company enters into two forward exchange contracts for hedging purposes. The first contract allows the Company to deliver NZ$5 million on February 1, 2003 at an exchange rate of NZ$1 = C$.69. The second contract permits Riskless to buy NZ$20 million on March 1, 2003 at an exchange rate of NZ$1 = C$.75. In implementing these transactions, the financial vice-president of Riskless becomes very impressed with the profit potential inherent in forward exchange contracts. As a consequence, he enters into an additional contract on November 1, 2002. This final contract, which is purely for speculative purposes, calls for Riskless to deliver NZ$10 million on June 1, 2003 at an exchange rate of NZ$1 = C$.80.

Date	Spot Rate For New Zealand dollars
November 1, 2002	C$.70
December 31, 2002	C$.73
February 1, 2003	C$.74
March 1, 2003	C$.76
June 1, 2003	C$.82

In addition to the preceding spot rates, on December 31, 2002, the 5 month forward rate for delivering New Zealand dollars is NZ$1 = C$.81. The Riskless Company closes its books on December 31.

Required   For each of the following dates, provide the journal entries that would be required to account for the preceding foreign currency transactions:

A. November 1, 2002
B. December 31, 2002
C. February 1, 2003
D. March 1, 2003
E. June 1, 2003

Assignment Problems

(The solutions for these problems are only available in
the solutions manual that has been provided to your instructor.)

Assignment Problem Nine - 1
The following items are commonly found in corporate Balance Sheets.

1. Cash
2. Inventories (At Replacement Cost)
3. Prepaid Insurance
4. Long-Term Receivables
5. Equipment
6. Patents
7. Future Income Tax Assets
8. Taxes Payable
9. Advances From Customers
10. Convertible bonds

Required: If these items were denominated in a foreign currency, they would be translated using either the current exchange rate at the Balance Sheet date or, alternatively, the appropriate historic rate. For each item, indicate whether it should be translated using the current rate or the historic rate.

Assignment Problem Nine - 2
The Svedberg Company begins operations on January 1, 2002. Its only business is the importation of educational chemistry sets from Sweden. The chemistry sets are paid for in Swedish krona (Kr, hereafter). Purchases during the first five years of operation are as follows:

Year	Quantity	Unit Price	Total Price
2002	5,000	Kr 500	Kr 2,500,000
2003	10,000	525	5,250,000
2004	12,000	540	6,480,000
2005	2,000	550	1,100,000
2006	-0-	530	-0-

The Svedberg Company sells the sets in Canada for $200 per set. All of the sets are paid for and sold in the year following purchase. Inventories are accounted for under the first-in, first-out inventory flow assumption. The Svedberg Company closes its books on December 31 of each of year.

Exchange rate data for the period under consideration was as follows:

January 1, 2002 to December 30, 2003	Kr1 = $.22
December 31, 2003 to December 30, 2004	Kr1 = $.25
December 31, 2004 to December 31, 2006	Kr1 = $.24

Required: Prepare the condensed Income Statements for years 2003 through 2006 of the Svedberg Company using:

A. The one transaction approach to recording foreign currency transactions.

B. The two transaction approach to recording foreign currency transactions.

Assignment Problem Nine - 3

On December 31, 2002, the Ferber Company, a Canadian company, borrows 3,000,000 Malaysia ringgitt (R, hereafter) from the Malaysian government to finance the construction of a factory. This liability does not require the payment of interest. It will mature in four years on December 31, 2006. The Ferber Company has a December 31 year end and exchange rates at Balance Sheet dates are as follows:

December 31, 2002	R1 = $0.40
December 31, 2003	R1 = $0.50
December 31, 2004	R1 = $0.30
December 31, 2005	R1 = $0.30
December 31, 2006	R1 = $0.42

The Ferber Company accounts for foreign currency transactions using the recommendations contained in Section 1650 of the *CICA Handbook*.

Required: Prepare the journal entries that would be required to account for the loan on December 31 of each year to maturity.

Assignment Problem Nine - 4

On December 1, 2002, the Hedgor Company, a Canadian based trading company, buys merchandise from a Hong Kong distributor for 2,000,000 Hong Kong dollars (HK$, hereafter). The invoice is to be paid in Hong Kong dollars by the Hedgor Company on April 1, 2003. Also on December 1, 2002, the Hedgor Company receives a commitment from a South Korean customer to purchase merchandise for 5,000,000 South Korean won (W, hereafter). This merchandise is to be delivered on April 1, 2003 and the entire purchase price must be paid on this date. The Hedgor Company, contrary to its normal sales policies, agrees to accept payment in South Korean won.

In view of the preceding transactions, on December 1, 2002, the Hedgor Company enters into two forward exchange contracts for hedging purposes. The first contract allows the Company to buy HK$2,000,000 on April 1, 2003 at an exchange rate of HK$1 = C$.19. The second contract permits Hedgor to deliver W5,000,000 on April 1, 2003 at an exchange rate of W1 = C$.0010.

Relevant data on exchange rates is as follows:

	Spot Rate For	
Date	Hong Kong dollars	South Korean won
December 1, 2002	C$.20	C$.0009
December 31, 2002	C$.17	C$.0011
April 1, 2003	C$.16	C$.0012

In addition to the preceding spot rates, on December 31, 2002, the 3 month forward rate for receiving Hong Kong dollars is HK$1 = C$.18 while the 3 month forward rate for delivering South Korean won is W1 = C$.0013. The Hedgor Company closes its books on December 31 of each year.

Required: For each of the following dates, provide the journal entries that would be required to account for the foreign currency transactions described in the preceding.

A. December 1, 2002
B. December 31, 2002
C. April 1, 2003

Assignment Problem Nine - 5

Over the past ten years, Hartford Ltd. has had Euro (€) denominated revenues from sales to customers in Germany of between €750,000 and €1,250,000 annually. There are no Euro expenditures associated with these revenues.

In order to avoid the foreign exchange risk associated with these revenues, Hartford Ltd. decides to borrow its current debt requirements in Euros.

On January 1, 2002, Hartford Ltd. borrows €3,000,000 at an interest rate of 10 percent per annum. The debt is to be repaid on December 31, 2004. The Company designates the long-term debt as a hedge of Euro revenues expected to be received in the next three years. The estimated and actual revenues received for the three years 2002 through 2004 were as follows:

	Estimated	Actual
Year Ending December 31, 2002	€1,100,000	€1,300,000
Year Ending December 31, 2003	1,150,000	1,000,000
Year Ending December 31, 2004	750,000	900,000
Total	€3,000,000	€3,200,000

Assume that relevant exchange rates are as follows:

January 1, 2002	€1 = $1.40
Average For 2002	€1 = $1.50
December 31, 2002	€1 = $1.60
Average For 2003	€1 = $1.64
December 31, 2003	€1 = $1.68
Average For 2004	€1 = $1.60
December 31, 2004	€1 = $1.52

The revenues were received uniformly over the year, making it appropriate to translate them using average exchange rates. The hedging relationship is judged effective at each year end.

Required: Prepare the Canadian dollar journal entries required to record:

A. the issuance of the Euro debt,
B. the receipt of the Euro revenues,
C. the year end changes in the value of the debt resulting from changes in the exchange rate for the Euro,
D. the retirement of the debt on December 31, 2004.

Do not make the journal entries required to record the interest payments on the debt.

Assignment Problem Nine - 6

In each Case, provide the journal entries required to record the foreign currency transactions described. All of the enterprises involved in these transactions have a December 31 year end.

Case One   On November 15, 2002, Martin Ltd. sells merchandise in South Africa for 250,000 South African rands (R, hereafter). On this date, the spot rate for the rand was R1 = $0.37. Payment for this merchandise is expected on February 15, 2003 and, in order to hedge their position, on November 15, 2002 Martin Ltd. enters a forward exchange contract to deliver R250,000 on February 15, 2003 at a rate of $.34. The spot exchange rate on December 31, 2002 is R1 = $0.38. Management designates that a hedging relationship exists between the receivable and the forward contract. The receivable is collected and the forward contract settled on February 15, 2003. On this date, the spot rate for the Rand is R1 = $0.32.

Case Two   On June 30, 2002, Wilson Inc. makes a commitment to buy Swiss merchandise at a cost of 125,000 Swiss Francs (SF, hereafter). On this date, the spot rate for Swiss francs is SF1 = $.98. The merchandise is to be delivered and paid for on January 1, 2003. The Company decides to hedge this commitment by entering a forward exchange contract to take delivery of SF125,000 at a rate of SF1 = $1.01 on December 1, 2002. On this date, the exchange rate is SF1 = $.99. Management designates that a hedging relationship exists between the commitment and the forward contract. The Company takes delivery of the Swiss francs on December 1, 2002 and purchases a SF125,000 Swiss term deposit that matures on January 1, 2003. This term deposit earns interest of SF1,000 during the the period December 1, 2002 through December 31, 2002. SF125,000 of the proceeds from the maturing term deposit are used to pay for the merchandise on January 1, 2003. The remaining SF1,000 is converted to Canadian dollars on January 1, 2003. The spot exchange rate on both December 31, 2002 and January 1, 2003 is SF1 = $.99.

Case Three   On October 1, 2002, Lalonde Ltd. purchases merchandise in Sweden for 800,000 Swedish krona (K, hereafter). Payment for this merchandise is to be made on February 1, 2003. On October 1, 2002, the spot rate for the krona is K1 = $0.19. Also on October 1, 2002, Lalonde enters a forward exchange contract to take delivery of K2,000,000 at a rate of K1 = $0.19 on February 1, 2003. The spot exchange rate on December 31, 2002 is K1 = $0.17. This is also the one month forward rate on this date. Management designates that a hedging relationship exists between the payable and K800,000 of the forward contract. The payable for the merchandise and the forward exchange contract are settled on February 1, 2003. On this date, the spot rate for the Krona is K1 = $0.16.

Case Four   On January 1, 2002, Fin Min Ltd. is granted a £1,000,000, interest free loan from one of its British suppliers. The exchange rate at this time is £1 = $2.16. The loan matures on December 31, 2004 and, in order to hedge this obligation, Fin Min enters into a forward exchange contract to take delivery of £1,000,000 on December 31, 2004 at £1 = $2.20. Relevant exchange rates are as follows:

Date	Rate
December 31, 2002	£1 = $2.18
December 31, 2003	£1 = $2.15
December 31, 2004	£1 = $2.30

The loan is repaid as scheduled on December 31, 2004.

Chapter 10

Translation Of Foreign Currency Financial Statements

Introduction

Basic Issues

10-1.   In the previous Chapter 9, we provided fairly comprehensive coverage of the concepts and procedures associated with the translation of balances resulting from transactions denominated in a foreign currency. In presenting this material, we had to deal with two basic issues:

- Selecting the appropriate method of of translation.
- Determining the appropriate treatment of exchange gains and losses (i.e., adjustments arising on the translation of items at current rates of exchange on each Balance Sheet date).

10-2.   With respect to the method of translation, we concluded that items resulting from foreign currency denominated transactions should be translated using the temporal method. As documented in Chapter 9, this view is reflected in the Recommendations of the *CICA Handbook*.

10-3.   There are really two aspects related to the treatment of exchange gains and losses. With respect to whether these items should be included in income, we concluded that all of the gains and losses arising from the translation of foreign currency transactions should be included in income. This leaves open the question of when they should be included in income and, our conclusion in this area was, they should be included in income in the period in which they occur. In other words, they should not be deferred and amortized. While until 2002, *CICA Handbook* Recommendations required deferral and amortization of gains and losses on long-term monetary items, this is no longer the case. Given this change, the *Handbook* Recommendations now require that, to the extent they arise on the translation of foreign currency transactions, exchange gains and losses should be included in Net Income in the period in which they arise.

Modified Conclusions

10-4.   As we indicated at the beginning of Chapter 9, the translation of foreign currency financial statements is a more complex process than the translation of foreign currency transactions. This complexity, along with additional conceptual issues that arise with certain types of foreign operations, leads to the need to modify our conclusions with respect to the two basic issues described in the preceding section. However, this is not always the case. With investments that are designated "integrated foreign operations", the conclusions that we use for foreign currency transactions are applicable. However, there is another type of foreign operation, designated "self-sustaining foreign operations", where standard setters throughout the world have concluded that a different method of translation, as well as a different treatment of exchange gains and losses, is required.

10-5.   In addition to the two basic issues that were introduced in Chapter 9, a new issue arises when we translate a full set of financial statements. In translating the various amounts resulting from foreign currency transactions, the items were created within the context of preparing financial statements in Canada using Canadian generally accepted accounting principles (GAAP). The situation is different here. In many cases the financial statements of the foreign investee will be prepared using the GAAP that prevails in the jurisdiction in which the operation is located. To one degree or another, there will be differences from Canadian GAAP. The question then becomes whether the foreign currency financial statements should be converted to Canadian GAAP prior to translation or, alternatively, translated as they were prepared in the foreign country without reconciliation with Canadian GAAP.

Approach

10-6.   Our approach to this material will be organized as follows:

Accounting Principles   As the issue arises with all types of foreign operations, we will deal first with the question of whether foreign currency financial statements should be converted to Canadian GAAP prior to their translation.

Classification Of Foreign Operations   As our conclusions on other issues will be influenced by the type of foreign operation, the next section will consider the basis for classifying foreign operations as either integrated or self-sustaining.

The Temporal Method Re-Visited   We will find that the temporal method will be required for translating the financial statements of integrated foreign operations. While the temporal method was covered in Chapter 9, its application to financial statements requires further clarification and this will be provided in this section.

The Current Rate Method   For the translation of the financial statements of self-sustaining foreign operations, the current rate method of translation will be required. In this section we will discuss the reasons for using a different translation method for this type of foreign operation, as well as the procedures required for the implementation of this method.

Exchange Gains And Losses   For reasons that will be explained in this section, exchange gains and losses accruing to self-sustaining operations are not included in income. Rather they will be allocated to a separate component of the investor company's shareholders' equity.

10-7.   Following these sections dealing with the conceptual and procedural issues related to the translation of foreign currency financial statements, we will present a fairly comprehensive example that illustrates the application of these techniques to both integrated and self-sustaining foreign operations.

Accounting Principles

The Issue

10-8.   The issue here relates to the idea that GAAP are developed in response to the economic conditions which prevail in the environment where such principles are applied. This is often described as the major justification for the differences between the GAAP that continue exist in various countries of the world. A simple example of this idea might involve a country in which social customs are such that individuals do not take their debt obligations very seriously and frequently default on smaller amounts. In such a country, it is likely that revenue recognition would be based on cash collections rather than using accrual accounting for revenues as GAAP.

10-9.   To the extent that there is validity in the view that locally developed GAAP reflect economic conditions in particular environments, it would follow that the performance of an investee operating in a foreign economic environment could best be measured using the GAAP that have been developed in that environment. In such situations, the foreign currency financial statements of the investee will usually be prepared using the GAAP which prevail in the foreign country. If, as the preceding line of reasoning suggests, the application of these foreign principles results in the most meaningful measure of the performance of the investee, it would suggest that these principles should not be altered before or during the translation process.

10-10.   The problem, however, with retaining foreign GAAP in the translated statements of foreign investees is that, under either the equity method or consolidation, the foreign investee's statements are incorporated into the Canadian dollar statements of the investor company. This, of course, would mean that the resulting statements would not be based on the consistent application of a single set of generally accepted accounting principles.

CICA Conclusion

10-11.   The implications of using foreign GAAP for the auditor's report are obvious and lead to the conclusion that either the foreign investee must keep its basic records in terms of Canadian GAAP or, if for statutory or other reasons the foreign currency records must be based on foreign GAAP, such statements must be modified to reflect Canadian GAAP prior to translation. While not in the form of a formal Recommendation, the *CICA Handbook* expresses this view as follows:

> **Paragraph 1650.04**   Conformity with accounting principles generally accepted in Canada is implicit in and basic to all Recommendations issued by the Accounting Standards Committee. Financial statements of foreign operations would be adjusted, if necessary, to conform with accounting principles generally accepted in Canada when incorporating them in the financial statements of the reporting enterprise.

10-12.   Note that this view is applicable, without regard to the type of foreign operation whose financial statements are being translated.

Exercise Ten-1

Foree Ltd. is a wholly owned subsidiary of Faror Inc., a Canadian public company. Foree is located in a country that permits the cash basis of revenue recognition. Using this basis, the Company reports revenues of 926,000 foreign currency units (FC). While not recorded in the Balance Sheet, at the beginning of the current year, Foree has Accounts Receivable of FC48,000, while at the end of the year, there is an Unearned Revenue balance of FC22,000. Throughout the year, the exchange rate is FC1 = $0.40.

Required: Determine the Canadian dollar revenues that would be included in the consolidated financial statements of Faror Inc. as a result of its investment in Foree Ltd.

End Of Exercise Ten-1

Exercise Ten-1 deals with the accounting principles issue.

Classification Of Foreign Operations

10-13.   The conceptual basis for using different translation approaches to foreign currency financial statements can be found in the *Handbook's* stated objective for this process:

> **Paragraph 1650.06**   For **Foreign Operations**, the ultimate objective of translation is to express financial statements of the foreign operation in Canadian dollars in a manner which best reflects the reporting enterprise's exposure to exchange rate changes as determined by the economic facts and circumstances.

10-14.   This general statement opens the door to the possibility that different objectives will be appropriate in different circumstances.   More specifically, Section 1650 distinguishes between integrated foreign operations and self-sustaining foreign operations. These types of foreign operations are given the following general definitions in Paragraph 1650.03:

> (a) **Integrated Foreign Operation**   A foreign operation which is financially or operationally interdependent with the reporting enterprise such that the exposure to exchange rate changes is similar to the exposure which would exist had the transactions and activities of the foreign operation been undertaken by the reporting enterprise.
>
> (b) **Self-Sustaining Foreign Operation**   A foreign operation which is financially and operationally independent of the reporting enterprise such that the exposure to exchange rate changes is limited to the reporting enterprise's net investment in the foreign operation.

10-15.   In simple terms, an integrated operation would take part in transactions with the Canadian investor company involving sales of goods or services from the foreign country to Canadian purchasers, purchases in Canada of merchandise or other goods to be used in the foreign country, or financing in Canadian capital markets. As there will be actual exchanges of Canadian dollars for the relevant foreign currency, there is real economic exposure to exchange rate risk.

10-16.   In similar fashion, a straightforward example of a self-sustaining foreign operation would involve a foreign operation that has most of its transactions in the foreign economy. Sales are made locally, required purchases are made in the foreign country, and financing is obtained through local financial institutions or capital markets. In such situations, there would be no actual exchanges of the foreign currency for Canadian dollars and no real exposure to exchange rate risk.

10-17.   Real world situations will rarely be this straightforward and, as a consequence, professional judgment will commonly be required in making this classification decision. This fact, along with a list of factors to be considered, is presented in the *CICA Handbook* as follows:

> **Paragraph 1650.10**   Whether a foreign operation is classified as integrated or self-sustaining is dependent on the exposure of the reporting enterprise to exchange rate changes as determined by the economic facts and circumstances. Professional judgment is required in evaluating the economic factors which determine the exposure of a reporting enterprise to exchange rate changes. In making this determination, matters which would be taken into consideration include whether:
>
> (a) there are any factors which would indicate that the cash flows of the reporting enterprise are insulated from or are directly affected by the day-to-day activities of the foreign operation;
>
> (b) sales prices for the foreign operation's products or services are determined more by local competition and local government regulations or more by world-wide competition and international prices and whether such sales prices are primarily responsive on a short-term basis to changes in exchange rates or are immune to such changes;

(c) the sales market for the foreign operation's products and services is primarily outside the reporting enterprise's country or within it;

(d) labor, materials and other costs of the foreign operation's products or services are primarily local costs or whether the foreign operation depends on products and services obtained primarily from the country of the reporting enterprise;

(e) the day-to-day activities of the foreign operation are financed primarily from its own operations and local borrowings or primarily by the reporting enterprise or borrowings from the country of the reporting enterprise;

(f) there is very little interrelationship between the day-to-day activities of the foreign operation and those of the reporting enterprise or whether intercompany transactions with the reporting enterprise form a dominant part of the foreign operation's activities.

10-18. It is this distinction between integrated foreign operations and self-sustaining foreign operations that provides the basis used in Section 1650 for establishing both the appropriate method of translation and the treatment to be given to exchange gains and losses.

Exercise Ten-2

A Canadian public company has four subsidiaries, each of which is located in a different country. They can be described as follows:

> Exercise Ten-2 deals with classification of foreign operations.

German Subsidiary   This subsidiary is a merchandising firm with 100 percent of both its buying activity and its selling activity within Germany.

Brazilian Subsidiary   This subsidiary primarily manufactures a subassembly that is shipped to a Canadian plant for inclusion in a product that is sold to customers located in Canada or in different parts of the world.

Swiss Subsidiary   This subsidiary maintains its records in Swiss francs. The majority of the subsidiary's vendors and customers are located in France.

U.S. Subsidiary   This subsidiary has its head office located in the United States and keeps its records in United States dollars. The subsidiary manufactures a product in Mexico with all production being sold and shipped directly to Japan. Financing has been largely provided by borrowing in the United Kingdom.

Required: For each subsidiary, indicate whether it would be classified as an integrated foreign operation or, alternatively, as a self-sustaining foreign operation.

End Of Exercise Ten-2

Methods Of Translation

Integrated Operations

CICA Conclusion

10-19.   In much the same manner as is the case with foreign currency transactions, integrated operations are exposed to exchange rate risk. As these enterprises will engage in actual exchanges of Canadian dollars for the foreign currency, there will be real economic gains and losses resulting from this exposure. Because of this, the Accounting Standards Board requires the same method of translation for integrated operations as that used for foreign currency transactions. That is, it requires the use of the temporal method as described in the following Recommendation:

Paragraph 1650.29   *Financial statements of an integrated foreign operation should be translated as follows:*

(a) *Monetary items should be translated into the reporting currency at the rate of exchange in effect at the balance sheet date.*

(b) *Non-monetary items should be translated at historical exchange rates, unless such items are carried at market, in which case they should be translated at the rate of exchange in effect at the balance sheet date.*

(c) *Revenue and expense items should be translated in a manner that produces substantially the same reporting currency amounts that would have resulted had the underlying transactions been translated on the dates they occurred.*

(d) *Depreciation or amortization of assets translated at historical exchange rates should be translated at the same exchange rates as the assets to which they relate.* (July, 1983)

10-20. The basis for its conclusion is explained as follows:

Paragraph 1650.07 For **Integrated Foreign Operations**, the reporting enterprise's exposure to exchange rate changes is similar to the exposure which would exist had the transactions and activities of the foreign operation been undertaken by the reporting enterprise. Therefore, the financial statements of the foreign operation should be expressed in a manner which is consistent with the measurement of domestic transactions and operations. The translation method which best achieves this objective is the temporal method because it uses the Canadian dollar as the unit of measure.

Temporal Method Redux

10-21. While the temporal method was covered in some detail in Chapter 9, the discussion was solely in terms of foreign currency transactions. As we are now dealing with foreign currency financial statements, some additional issues require attention.

10-22. To begin, Paragraph 1650.07 states that the temporal method is the best method because "it uses the Canadian dollar as the unit of measure". This point can best be understood by noting that our current accounting model is largely based on using historical cost. This means that, if you are using the Canadian dollar as your unit of measure, the Canadian dollar value for assets carried at historical cost should not change from period to period. The temporal method accomplishes this by translating any balances that are carried at historical values in the foreign currency at the historical exchange rate that is applicable to their time of acquisition. For example, if we acquired land in Germany for 500,000 Euros (€), at a time when €1 = \$1.40, the land would be initially translated to \$700,000 [(€500,000)(\$1.40)]. Applying the temporal method of translation in future years, this value will never change, a fact that reflects the application of historical cost accounting using the Canadian dollar as the unit of measure.

10-23. The other new issue in applying the temporal method is the translation of Income Statement items. The general rule from Paragraph 1650.29 is that revenue and expense items should be translated in a manner that produces substantially the same Canadian dollar amounts that would have resulted had the underlying transactions been translated on the dates they occurred.

10-24. A literal application of this Recommendation would, in many cases, result in the need to translate millions of individual transactions, a process that would have costs that could not be justified in the terms of the benefits received. As was noted in Chapter 9, this is not necessary as noted in the following *Handbook* guidance:

Paragraph 1650.61 Literal application of the Recommendations in this Section might require a degree of detail in record keeping and computations that would be burdensome as well as unnecessary to produce reasonable approximations of the results. Accordingly, it is acceptable to use averages or other methods of approximation. For example, translation of the numerous revenues, expenses, gains and losses at the exchange rates at the dates such items are recognized is generally impractical, and an appropriately weighted average exchange rate for the period would normally be used to translate such items.

10-25. This means that many of the expenses and revenues found in the Income Statement of an integrated foreign operation can be translated at an unweighted average exchange rate for the year. However, this is only appropriate when the following assumptions can be made:

- The item in question occurred uniformly over the period. For example, sales could be translated using the average rate, only if monthly or weekly sales were roughly the same throughout the reporting period.

- The change in the exchange rate occurred uniformly over the year. If, for example, the rate remained unchanged during the first 10 months of the year, followed by an increase of 15 percent in the last two months of the year, use of a simple average for the year would not be appropriate.

10-26. If these assumptions are not appropriate, than translation will either require the translation of individual items or the use of some type of weighted average.

10-27. It should also be noted that the use of an average would not be appropriate with items that involve a large inflow or outflow at a particular point in time. For example, dividends would normally be translated using the rate applicable on the declaration date. Note that it is the declaration date, not the payment date, that is relevant for translation purposes. This reflects the fact that this is the point in time when the liability is recognized.

10-28. A final point relates to expenses, gains, or losses that involve items that are translated at historical costs. Examples of this type of item would be as follows:

- **Amortization Expense** would generally reflect the write-off of assets that are carried at historical costs. Given this, this expense would have to be translated at the same historical rate used to translate the assets that are subject to amortization.

- An additional item of this type would be **Cost Of Sales**. This expense reflects an outflow of non-monetary items and, given this, translation of the expense would generally require separate translation of the opening inventory (at historical rates), purchases (at the average for the year, provided the purchases occurred uniformly over the year), less the closing inventory (at historical rates).

- There would also be complications with **Gains** or **Losses** on the disposition of capital assets. The gain or loss cannot be translated using a single rate. Rather, the proceeds will be calculated at the current rate of exchange on the transaction date, while the cost of the asset given up will be translated at the historical rate applicable to its acquisition.

Exercise Ten-3

Temp Company is a wholly owned French subsidiary of a Canadian public company. Temp Company keeps its records in Euros. The average exchange rate for the current year was €1 = $1.40. The Income Statement of this Company for the current year is as follows:

Temp Company
Income Statement
Current Year

Sales	€920,000
Gain On Sale Of Land	50,000
Total Revenues	€970,000
Expenses:	
Cost Of Sales	€470,000
Amortization Expense	132,000
Other Expenses	220,000
Total Expenses	€822,000
Net Income	€148,000

Exercise Ten-3 deals with the translation of an Income Statement for an integrated foreign operation.

> This is a continuation of Exercise 10-3.

Other Information:

1. Sales, Purchases, and Other Expenses occurred uniformly throughout the year.

2. All of the Company's non-monetary assets were acquired when €1 = $1.35.

3. The opening inventories of €50,000 were acquired when €1 = $1.37, while the closing inventories of €70,000 were acquired when the rate was $1.39.

4. The Gain On Sale Of Land resulted from a disposition of Land with a cost of €80,000. The sale occurred on July 1 of the current year.

Required: Given that Temp Company is classified as an integrated foreign operation, prepare its translated Income Statement for the current year.

End Of Exercise Ten-3

Self-Sustaining Foreign Operations
CICA Conclusions

10-29.   We have noted that, with respect to both the translation of foreign currency transactions and the translation of the the financial statements of integrated foreign operations, the *CICA Handbook* requires the use of the temporal method of translation. We have also discussed the reasons for these conclusions, noting that a basic feature of the temporal method of translation is that it maintains the Canadian dollar as the unit of measure. This feature is best explained by the fact that the temporal method leaves the Canadian dollar value of items that are recorded at historical cost unchanged from period to period. If a €100,000 of Land is translated into $140,000 at its acquisition, it will remain at this $140,000 value for as long as it is held by the enterprise.

10-30.   A different conclusion is reached with respect to self-sustaining operations. This conclusion is found in the following Recommendation:

> **Paragraph 1650.33**   *Financial statements of a self-sustaining foreign operation should be translated as follows:*
>
> (a) *Assets and liabilities should be translated into the reporting currency at the rate of exchange in effect at the balance sheet date.*
>
> (b) *Revenue and expense items (including depreciation and amortization) should be translated into the reporting currency at the rate of exchange in effect on the dates on which such items are recognized in income during the period.*
>
> ...   (July, 1983)

10-31.   The basis for this conclusion is described in the *Handbook's* discussion of the objectives of foreign currency translation:

> **Paragraph 1650.08**   For **Self-Sustaining Foreign Operations**, the reporting enterprise's exposure to exchange rate changes is limited to its net investment in the foreign operation. Therefore, measuring such operations as if they had carried out their activities in Canadian dollars is considered to be less relevant than measuring the overall effect of changes in the exchange rate on the net investment in such operations. The financial statements of the foreign operation should be expressed in Canadian dollars in a manner which does not change financial results and relationships of the foreign operation. The translation method which best achieves this objective is the current rate method because it uses the currency of the foreign operation as the unit of measure.

10-32.   After giving attention to the required procedures under the current rate method, we will provide a more detailed discussion of the conceptual basis for using the current rate method for self-sustaining operations.

Current Rate Method

10-33.   In its definitions section, Section 1650 defines the current rate method as follows:

Paragraph 1650.03(b)   A method of translation which translates assets, liabilities, revenues and expenses in a manner that retains their bases of measurement in terms of the foreign currency (i.e., it uses the foreign currency as the unit of measure).   In particular:

(i)   assets and liabilities are translated at the rate of exchange in effect at the balance sheet date;

(ii)   revenue and expense items (including depreciation and amortization) are translated at the rate of exchange in effect on the dates on which such items are recognized in income during the period.

10-34.   The implementation of this definition in the Balance Sheet is very straightforward. As indicated in the definition, all of the assets and liabilities will be translated at the current exchange rate applicable to each Balance Sheet presented. The only problem in the application of the current rate method in the Balance Sheet is related to determining the various components of shareholders' equity.

10-35.   As all of the assets and liabilities are translated at current rates, the total shareholders' equity balance must also reflect the current rate. However, we will find in the next section that, with respect to self-sustaining foreign operations, exchange gains and losses are excluded from income. Rather, they are allocated to the Balance Sheet as a separate section of shareholders' equity, usually with a title such as Cumulative Translation Adjustment. This means that the translated Shareholders' Equity will be made up of three components which can be described as follows:

Cumulative Translation Adjustment   This account will contain the net exchange gain or loss that has resulted from the translation of assets and liabilities since the acquisition of the foreign operation. This amount can be either positive (a net gain) or negative (a net loss) with respect to the total shareholders' equity balance.

Retained Earnings   This balance will reflect the cumulative translated income of the foreign operation, exclusive of exchange gains and losses and reduced by dividends declared.

Common Shares   As all of the exchange gains and losses have been allocated to to the Cumulative Translation Adjustment account, the contributed capital account, Common Shares, will have to be translated at the historic exchange rate applicable to its issue date. This seeming anomaly flows from the definition of the Cumulative Translation Adjustment account and is the only approach that will produce a total Shareholders' Equity that equals the difference between assets and liabilities when these balances are translated at current rates. It is likely that you will have a better grasp of this point after you have completed the comprehensive example that is presented later in this Chapter.

10-36.   With respect to Income Statement accounts, the definition of the current rate method refers to the use of the exchange rate in effect on each transaction date. As was the case with the temporal method, the use of some type of average will be appropriate for dealing with large volumes of a particular type of transaction. However, this is again conditional on taking into consideration the factors listed in Paragraph 10-25. These factors reflect the need to make assumptions about how the transactions occur over the period, as well as how the change in the exchange rate takes place over the period.

10-37.   Also similar to the temporal method, the use of an average rate would not be appropriate for translating large items that occur on a particular date. The most common example of this that you will encounter in the problem material is dividend declaration. For a significant transaction such as this, the rate on the declaration date should be used.

10-38.   The major difference between the temporal method and the current rate method with respect to translating Income Statement items is with those expenses that involve items translated at historic rates under the temporal method. The two most common examples of this would be Amortization Expense and Cost Of Sales when inventories are carried at cost. Under the temporal method, these expenses have to be translated using the historic rates that applied when the items were acquired. In contrast, under the current rate method, these items will usually be translated using an average rate.

10-39.   A further example of an Income Statement item involving historic rates under the temporal method would be gains and losses on the disposition of capital assets. You will recall that, under the temporal method the proceeds of disposition are translated at the current rate on the transaction date, while the cost of the asset is translated at the applicable historic rate. In contrast, under the current rate method, both the proceeds and the cost would be translated at the current rate on the transaction date.

> Exercise Ten-4 deals with with the translation of Income Statement items for a self-sustaining foreign operation.

Exercise Ten-4
This is an extension of Exercise Ten-3.

Temp Company is a wholly owned French subsidiary of a Canadian public company. Temp Company keeps its records in Euros. The average exchange rate for the current year was €1 = $1.40. The Income Statement of this Company for the current year is as follows:

Temp Company
Income Statement
Current Year

Sales	€920,000
Gain On Sale Of Land	50,000
Total Revenues	€970,000
Expenses:	
Cost Of Sales	€470,000
Amortization Expense	132,000
Other Expenses	220,000
Total Expenses	€822,000
Net Income	€148,000

Other Information:

1.   Sales, Purchases, and Other Expenses occurred uniformly throughout the year.

2.   All of the Company's non-monetary assets were acquired when €1 = $1.35.

3.   The opening inventories of €50,000 were acquired when €1 = $1.37, while the closing inventories of €70,000 were acquired when the rate was $1.39.

4.   The Gain On Sale Of Land resulted from a disposition of Land with a cost of €80,000. The sale occurred on July 1 of the current year.

Required: Given that Temp Company is classified as a self-sustaining foreign operation, prepare its translated Income Statement for the current year.

End Of Exercise Ten-4

Why Self-Sustaining Companies Are Treated Differently
10-40.   To this point, we have presented the Recommendation requiring the use of the current rate method for self-sustaining operations and discussed the implementation of this method. We have not, however, explained the basis for using a different method of translation for this type of operation.

10-41.   At first glance, the use of the use of the temporal method, a method which uses the Canadian dollar as the unit of measure, would seem the logical choice for all types of foreign operations. There is, however, a problem with the use of the temporal method in the translation of foreign currency financial statements. Because this method translates some assets and liabilities at current exchange rates and other assets and liabilities at historic exchange rates, the temporal method consistently alters — some would say distorts — economic relationships that were present in the foreign currency financial statements. A simple example will clarify this point:

Example   On January 1, 2002, a Canadian Company establishes a subsidiary in France by investing 3,000,000 Euros (€) at a time when the exchange rate was €1 = $1.40. On this same date, the subsidiary borrows an additional €3,000,000 and invests the entire €6,000,000 in Land. The resulting foreign currency Balance Sheet as at January 1, 2002 would be as follows:

Balance Sheet
As At January 1, 2002 (€)

Land	€6,000,000
Liabilities	€3,000,000
Shareholders' Equity	3,000,000
Total Equities	€6,000,000

Using either the temporal or the current rate method of translation, the translated Balance Sheet on this date would be as follows:

Balance Sheet
As At January 1, 2002 ($)

Land (At $1.40)	$8,400,000
Liabilities (At $1.40)	$4,200,000
Shareholders' Equity (At $1.40)	4,200,000
Total Equities	$8,400,000

During the year ending December 31, 2002, the exchange rate goes to €1 = $1.60. As there is no other economic activity during this year, the December 31 foreign currency Balance Sheet would be unchanged. However, as there has been a change in the exchange rate, the translated Balance Sheet will vary, depending on whether the temporal or current rate method is used. The two alternative Balance Sheets are as follows:

Balance Sheet
As At December 31, 2002 ($)

	Temporal	Current Rate
Land (At $1.40 And $1.60)	$8,400,000	$9,600,000
Liabilities (At $1.60)	$4,800,000	$4,800,000
Shareholders' Equity (As A Residual)	3,600,000	4,800,000
Total Equities	$8,400,000	$9,600,000

10-42.   A significant economic relationship that is often considered by financial statement users is the percentage of debt to total equities. In the untranslated Balance Sheet, this relationship is 50 percent (€3,000,000 ÷ €6,000,000). When the current rate method is used, this 50 percent relationship is maintained ($4,800,000 ÷ $9,600,000).

10-43.   In contrast, when the temporal method is used, this relationship is increased to 57.1 percent ($4,800,000 ÷ $8,400,000). The fact that this method retains the historic rate for the translation of the Land and, at the same time, uses the current rate to translate the monetary Liabilities, results in a Balance Sheet that makes the subsidiary appear to be a more heavily leveraged, and thereby riskier, enterprise.

10-44.   This result is considered appropriate when there is real exposure to exchange rate risk, as could be the case with an integrated foreign operation. If the Euro debt will have to be paid from revenues generated by sales in Canada that are paid for in Canadian dollars, the increased value of the debt relative to the translated value of the land is a real concern. However, if we are dealing with a self-sustaining foreign operation, with revenues generated in Euros, expenses are paid for in Euros, and financing obtained in Euros, there is no real foreign exchange risk. This would suggest that the current rate method, which uses the Euro as the unit of measure, does a better job of measuring the performance of the foreign operation.

10-45.   This is the basis for requiring the use of the current rate method for self-sustaining operations. As such investees are, by definition, carrying on their operations in the relevant foreign currency, it is appropriate that the foreign currency be used as the unit of measure. By using this method, all of the economic relationships (e.g., debt to equity or gross margin on sales) remain unchanged by the translation process. If the operation has a 10 percent rate of return on assets in the foreign currency financial statements, that 10 percent rate of return will be maintained through the translation process.

Self-Sustaining Operations In Highly Inflationary Economies

10-46.   In general, Paragraph 1650.33 requires that the current rate method be used to translate the financial statements of self-sustaining operations. There is an exception to this, however, when the self-sustaining operation is in a highly inflationary economy. You may have noticed that, when we quoted Paragraph 1650.33, the last component of the Recommendation was missing. This component contained the Recommendation as it applied to self-sustaining operations located in highly inflationary economies:

> **Paragraph 1650.33**   *Financial statements of a self-sustaining foreign operation should be translated as follows:*
>
> *(a)* .....
> *(b)* .....
>
> *Where the economic environment of the foreign operation is highly inflationary relative to that of the reporting enterprise, financial statements should be translated in the manner indicated in paragraph 1650.29 (Paragraph 1650.29 requires the use of the temporal method).*

10-47.   The problem here is that the current rate method of translation uses the foreign currency as the unit of measure. If that currency is rapidly losing value because of a high rate of inflation, it may not be an appropriate unit of measure. As an illustration of this problem, consider the following example:

> **Example**   A self-sustaining operation acquires Land for 500,000 Foreign Currency Units (FC, hereafter) at a time when FC1 = $1.00. During the following year, the local economy experiences a 1000 percent inflation. As would be expected, the exchange rate falls to FC1 = $0.10.

10-48.   When the land was acquired, its translated value would have been $500,000 [(FC500,000)($1.00)]. If we continue to use the current rate method of translation, after one year, the translated value would have fallen to $50,000 [(FC500,000)($0.10)]. This approach would have introduced a degree of instability into the translated figures that was found unacceptable by the Accounting Standards Board. As a consequence, they require the use of the temporal method for self-sustaining operations when they operate in an economic environment that is highly inflationary. Stated alternatively, when a foreign currency is subject to high rates of inflation, it is not an appropriate unit of measure and, as a consequence, the Canadian dollar should be used as the unit of measure.

10-49.   We will find in the Section of this Chapter that deals with exchange gains and losses that, in general, self-sustaining operations do not include exchange gains and losses in income. However, as is the case with the method of translation, when the self-sustaining foreign operation is in a highly inflationary economic environment, the rules change. Self-sustaining foreign operations located in such economies must include their exchange gains and losses in income.

10-50.   While the *CICA Handbook* offers no guidance on what constitutes a highly inflationary economic environment, Statement Of Financial Accounting Standards No. 52, "Foreign Currency Translation", in the U.S., suggests a guideline of 100 percent or more over a three year period. In the absence of *Handbook* guidance, it is likely that this guideline will be used in Canada.

U.S. Functional Currency Approach

10-51.   We have, at this point, reviewed the Canadian rules with respect to which method of translation is to used for foreign operations. As noted, the temporal method must be used for integrated foreign operations while the current rate method must be used for self-sustaining foreign operations.

10-52.   While we do not intend to discuss this in detail, we believe that it is important that you be aware that the U.S. has a different approach to this issue. Under Statement Of Financial Accounting Standards No. 52, "Foreign Currency Translation", the financial statement items of foreign operations must be measured using the "functional currency". This concept is defined as follows:

> An entity's functional currency is the currency of the primary economic environment in which the entity operations; normally, that is the currency of the environment in which an entity primarily generates and expends cash.

10-53.   To understand this approach, we need to refer again to the idea that the temporal method uses the Canadian dollar as the unit of measure, while the current rate method uses the relevant foreign currency as the unit of measure. In this context, consider the following two examples:

German Subsidiary   A Canadian company has a German subsidiary that sells all of its products in Canada, acquires most of its raw materials in Canada, and obtains all of its financing in Canadian capital markets. Under U.S. rules, the functional currency would be the Canadian dollar and the statements of the operation would be translated using the temporal method. Note that, under Canadian rules, this subsidiary would be classified as an integrated foreign operation and this approach would also result in the use of the temporal method.

French Subsidiary   A Canadian company has a French subsidiary that sells all of its products in France, acquires most of its merchandise in France, and obtains all of its financing in French capital markets. Under U.S. rules, the functional currency would be the Euro and the statements of the operation would be translated using the current rate method. Note that, under Canadian rules, this subsidiary would be classified as a self-sustaining foreign operation and this approach would also result in the use of the current rate method.

10-54.   As these two cases indicate, the functional currency approach that is used in the U.S. will often result in the same conclusion as the classification approach that is used in Canada. However, in more complex cases, differences between the two approaches would arise. Discussion of such differences goes beyond the scope of this text.

Exchange Gains And Losses

Integrated Foreign Operations

10-55.   As was the case with the choice of translation methods, the exchange gains and losses of integrated foreign operations will be dealt with in the same manner as the translation gains and losses that arise on the translation of foreign currency transactions. This requirement is reflected in the following Recommendation:

> **Paragraph 1650.31**   *Exchange gains and losses arising on the translation of financial statements of an integrated foreign operation should be accounted for in accordance with the Recommendation in paragraph 1650.20 (Paragraph 1650.20 requires that exchange gains and losses be included in income in the period in which they occur). (July, 1983)*

10-56.   This Recommendation reflects the fact that, because of their nature, integrated operations will be involved in actual exchanges of currencies. Given this, the requirement that exchange gains and losses be included in income seems appropriate.

Self-Sustaining Foreign Operations
CICA Conclusion

10-57.   The *CICA Handbook* requires the following treatment of exchange gains and losses arising on the translation of the financial statements of a self-sustaining foreign operation:

> **Paragraph 1650.36**   *Exchange gains and losses arising from the translation of the financial statements of a self-sustaining foreign operation should be deferred and included in a separate component of shareholders' equity, except when the economic environment of the foreign operation is highly inflationary relative to that of the reporting enterprise, in which case such exchange gains and losses would be treated in accordance with the Recommendation in paragraph 1650.20. (July, 1983)*

10-58.   This Recommendation requires that, in general, translation adjustments which arise in the translation of the foreign currency financial statements of a self-sustaining operation, be allocated to a separate section of shareholders' equity. While Paragraph 1650.36 still uses the term exchange gain or loss, in effect it requires that translation adjustments not be treated as exchange gains or losses. Adjustments arising from the translation of foreign currency items at current rates are not to be included in current income. Further, they will never be included in income unless the investor company disposes of all or part of its investment in the self-sustaining operation, the operation ceases to be a self-sustaining operation, or the economy in which it operates becomes highly inflationary. In other words, under normal circumstances, the amounts allocated to this separate component of shareholders' equity will remain there indefinitely.

10-59.   As was noted in our discussion of methods of translation, a different method of dealing with exchange gains and losses is required for a self-sustaining foreign operation when the economic environment in which it operates is highly inflationary. In these circumstances, all exchange gains and losses are taken into income immediately, with no deferral.

Why Self-Sustaining Operations Are Treated Differently

10-60.   Consider a French subsidiary of a Canadian company that borrows €1,000,000 when the exchange rate is €1 = $1.40, resulting in a translated value of $1,400,000. If the exchange rate goes to €1 = $1.50, the new translated value will be $1,500,000.

10-61.   If this French subsidiary was an integrated operation selling its product in Canada, it would have to use its Canadian dollar revenues to purchase the €1,000,000 required to repay the loan. In this case, there is clearly and out-of-pocket loss of $100,000. In contrast, if this was a self-sustaining operation selling its product in France, the Euro revenues could be used to repay the loan. This means that there would be no exchange of currencies and, more importantly, no real economic loss.

10-62.   As, in general, self-sustaining foreign entities tend to operate largely in the foreign currency of the country in which they reside, exchanges of currency do not occur, resulting in the conclusion that such companies do not suffer real economic losses as the result of movements in exchange rates. This provides the basis for allocating these amounts directly to shareholders' equity, without inclusion in the Income Statement.

Cumulative Translation Adjustment Account

10-63.   As discussed, translation of the financial statements of a self-sustaining foreign operation will usually result in exchange gains and losses being allocated to a separate shareholders' equity account. This separate component of shareholders' equity is disclosed under a number of different titles in published financial statements. The survey results included in the 2001 edition of *Financial Reporting In Canada* indicate that the most common titles are Foreign Currency Translation Adjustment and Cumulative Translation Adjustment.

10-64.   In many cases, this separate component of shareholder's equity will contain a substantial balance. Further, it may be made up of a number of different components (e.g., individual components arising from the translation of different foreign currencies). When this is the case, the *CICA Handbook* requires the following disclosure:

> **Paragraph 1650.39**   *Disclosure should be made of the significant elements which give rise to changes in the exchange gains and losses accumulated in the separate component of shareholders' equity during the period.* (July, 1983)

10-65.   Amounts allocated to this separate component of shareholders' equity will normally remain there indefinitely. However, where there is a sale of part or all of the reporting enterprise's interest in the foreign operation or a reduction in the shareholders' equity of the foreign operation as the result of a capital transaction, the *CICA Handbook* requires the following:

> **Paragraph 1650.38**   *An appropriate portion of the exchange gains and losses accumulated in the separate component of shareholders' equity should be included in the determination of net income when there is a reduction in the net investment.* (July, 1983)

10-66.   This Recommendation is not consistent with U.S. accounting standards in that it permits a portion of the separate component of shareholders' equity to be taken into income when there is a partial liquidation or other reduction in the domestic company's investment in the self-sustaining operation. In contrast, U.S. standards only permit this balance to be taken into income when there is a complete liquidation of the investment position.

Calculation Of Exchange Gains And Losses

10-67.   As was noted in Chapter 9, whenever an item is translated at current exchange rates, exchange gains and losses will arise on that item. For integrated operations using the temporal method, exchange gains and losses only arise on items carried at current values. This would include all monetary items and a limited number of non-monetary items that may be carried at current value. For self-sustaining operations using the current rate method, exchange gains and losses arise on all of the items in the financial statements, without regard to how they are valued in the foreign currency financial statements.

10-68.   Calculating exchange gains and losses on foreign currency transactions is a fairly simple process. If you buy something on account for £1,000 when £1 = $2.30, and you pay the account when £1 = $2.35, you have an exchange loss of $50 [(£1,000)($2.35 - $2.30)].

10-69.   The situation is more complex when calculating the exchange gain or loss resulting from the translation of foreign currency financial statements. With respect to the temporal method, you need to prepare a schedule of changes in the items valued at current value (largely monetary items), translating the opening balance and changes at the exchange rate applicable to the opening Balance Sheet and each transaction date. This gives a computed figure for the closing balance that is then compared with the actual balance translated at the closing Balance Sheet date rate. The difference is the exchange gain or loss for the period. For integrated operations using the temporal method, this amount will be charged or credited to income.

10-70.   The process is much the same when the current rate method is used. The difference is that the schedule will be based on all changes in net assets, not just those that are carried at current values in the foreign currency financial statements.

10-71.   These descriptions, however, are not very useful without being supported with numerical examples. Unfortunately, it is not possible to illustrate these procedures outside the context of a comprehensive example. Given this, we will defer further discussion of these calculations until the next section of the Chapter.

Foreign Currency Financial Statements - Example
Translated Financial Statements Of Subsidiary

10-72.   In this Section, we will demonstrate the procedures to be used for both integrated foreign operations and self-sustaining foreign operations. This example is as follows:

On December 31, 2002, the Port Company acquires 100 percent of the outstanding voting shares of the Ship Company for 42.2 million Canadian dollars ($, hereafter). Port Company is a Canadian corporation and Ship Company is a trading company located in Switzerland. On the acquisition date, Ship Company had Common Stock of 20 million Swiss francs (SF, hereafter) and Retained Earnings of SF32 million. The December 31, 2004 and December 31, 2005 Balance Sheets for the two Companies, as well as their Income Statements for the year ending December 31, 2005 are as follows:

Balance Sheets
As At December 31, 2004

	Port ($)	Ship (SF)
Cash	2,000,000	2,000,000
Accounts Receivable	7,600,000	8,000,000
Inventories	30,000,000	40,000,000
Investment In Ship (At Cost)	42,200,000	-0-
Plant And Equipment (Net)	132,000,000	60,000,000
Total Assets	213,800,000	110,000,000
Current Liabilities	43,800,000	6,000,000
Long-Term Liabilities	30,000,000	40,000,000
No Par Common Stock	60,000,000	20,000,000
Retained Earnings	80,000,000	44,000,000
Total Equities	213,800,000	110,000,000

Balance Sheets
As At December 31, 2005

	Port ($)	Ship (SF)
Cash	6,800,000	2,000,000
Accounts Receivable	18,800,000	14,000,000
Inventories	56,000,000	54,000,000
Investment In Ship (At Cost)	42,200,000	-0-
Plant And Equipment (Net)	120,000,000	50,000,000
Total Assets	243,800,000	120,000,000
Current Liabilities	49,800,000	4,000,000
Long-Term Liabilities	30,000,000	40,000,000
No Par Common Stock	60,000,000	20,000,000
Retained Earnings	104,000,000	56,000,000
Total Equities	243,800,000	120,000,000

Income Statements
For Year Ending December 31, 2005

	Port ($)	Ship (SF)
Sales	390,000,000	150,000,000
Cost Of Goods Sold	340,000,000	120,000,000
Amortization Expense	12,000,000	10,000,000
Other Expenses	14,000,000	8,000,000
Total Expenses	366,000,000	138,000,000
Net Income	24,000,000	12,000,000

Other Information:

1. On December 31, 2002, the carrying values of all identifiable assets and liabilities of the Ship Company are equal to their fair values.

2. Port Company carries its Investment In Ship at cost. There is no goodwill impairment loss in any year since acquisition.

3. Neither the Port Company nor the Ship Company declare or pay dividends during 2005.

4. Ship Company has had no additions to its Plant And Equipment account since December 31, 2002.

5. The Ship Company's Long-Term Liabilities were issued at par on December 31, 2000 and mature on December 31, 2010.

6. Exchange rates for the Swiss Franc are as follows:

December 31, 2000	SF1 = $0.60
December 31, 2001	SF1 = $0.70
December 31, 2002	SF1 = $0.80
December 31, 2003	SF1 = $0.75
December 31, 2004	SF1 = $0.90
December 31, 2005	SF1 = $1.00
Average For 2005	SF1 = $0.95

7. The December 31, 2004 Inventories of the Ship Company are acquired when SF1 = $.88 and the December 31, 2005 Inventories are acquired when SF1 = $.99. Both Companies account for their Inventories using a FIFO assumption.

8. The 2005 Sales of Ship Company contain SF40 million that are made to Port Company. These goods are resold by Port Company during 2005. As at December 31, 2005, the Port Company owes the Ship Company $1,000,000 and the Ship Company owes the Port Company SF2,000,000. These loans do not bear interest and they are to be repaid in 2004. There are no intercompany loans outstanding as at December 31, 2004.

9. Sales, Purchases, Other Expenses and intercompany sales and purchases take place evenly throughout the year, making the use of average exchange rates appropriate. Both Companies use the straight line method for computing all amortization charges.

Integrated Foreign Operation

10-73. If we assume that the Ship Company is an integrated foreign operation, the translated comparative Balance Sheets as at December 31, 2004 and December 31, 2005 and the Income Statement for the year ending December 31, 2005 would be as follows:

Ship Company (Integrated Foreign Operation)
Translated Balance Sheet
As At December 31, 2004

	Untranslated	Rate	Translated
Cash	SF 2,000,000	$0.90	$ 1,800,000
Accounts Receivable	8,000,000	$0.90	7,200,000
Inventories	40,000,000	$0.88	35,200,000
Plant And Equipment (Net)	60,000,000	$0.80	48,000,000
Total Assets	SF110,000,000		$92,200,000
Current Liabilities	SF 6,000,000	$0.90	$ 5,400,000
Long-Term Liabilities	40,000,000	$0.90	36,000,000
No Par Common Stock	20,000,000	$0.80	16,000,000
Retained Earnings	44,000,000	N/A	34,800,000
Total Equities	SF110,000,000		$92,200,000

Ship Company (Integrated Foreign Operation)
Translated Balance Sheet
As At December 31, 2005

	Untranslated	Rate	Translated
Cash	SF 2,000,000	$1.00	$ 2,000,000
Accounts Receivable	14,000,000	$1.00	14,000,000
Inventories	54,000,000	$0.99	53,460,000
Plant And Equipment (Net)	50,000,000	$0.80	40,000,000
Total Assets	SF120,000,000		$109,460,000
Current Liabilities	SF 4,000,000	$1.00	$ 4,000,000
Long-Term Liabilities	40,000,000	$1.00	40,000,000
No Par Common Stock	20,000,000	$0.80	16,000,000
Retained Earnings	56,000,000	N/A	49,460,000
Total Equities	SF120,000,000		$109,460,000

Ship Company (Integrated Foreign Operation)
Translated Income Statement
For The Year Ending December 31, 2005

	Untranslated	Rate	Translated
Sales	SF150,000,000	$0.95	$142,500,000
Opening Inventory	SF 40,000,000	$0.88	$ 35,200,000
Purchases	134,000,000	$0.95	127,300,000
Closing Inventory	(54,000,000)	$0.99	(53,460,000)
Amortization Expense	10,000,000	$0.80	8,000,000
Other Expenses	8,000,000	$0.95	7,600,000
Exchange Loss (Note One)	-0-	N/A	3,200,000
Total Expenses	SF138,000,000		$127,840,000
Net Income	SF 12,000,000		$ 14,660,000

Note One As we noted in paragraph 10-69, what is required is a schedule of changes in the items that are carried at current values. As in this example, all of the items carried at current values are monetary, we can begin the schedule with the net monetary balance on December 31, 2004. The net balance is a liability of SF36,000,000 (SF2,000,000 + SF8,000,000 - SF6,000,000 - SF40,000,000).

Schedule Of Change In Net Monetary Balance
(000s Omitted)

	Untranslated	Rate	Translated
Opening NML*	(SF 36,000)	$0.90	($ 32,400)
Sales	150,000	$0.95	142,500
Purchases	(134,000)	$0.95	(127,300)
Other Expenses	(8,000)	$0.95	(7,600)
Computed Closing NML*			($ 24,800)
Less: Actual Closing NML*	(SF 28,000)	$1.00	(28,000)
Exchange Loss			$ 3,200

*NML = Net Monetary Liability

Note that the untranslated column can be verified by checking with the net monetary liability balance in the December 31, 2005 Balance Sheet (SF2,000,000 + SF14,000,000 - SF4,000,000 - SF40,000,000 = SF28,000,000). It is usually a good idea to check this verification as it will provide an indication as to whether or not you have missed an item required by the schedule.

The other point to note here is that the construction of this schedule is such that if it ends in a positive number, a loss is involved. Correspondingly, a negative number will indicated a gain. The only we to restructure this schedule so that a positive number would be gain, is to treat liabilities as a positive number, an approach which is even less intuitive than the preceding.

In terms of understanding the basis for this schedule, you can think of the closing balance of $24,800 as the liability balance that you would have had if all of the items had been converted to Canadian dollars at the beginning of the year and the revenues and expense converted to Canadian dollars as received or paid. As this did not happen and the company continued to hold or owe Swiss francs, their value in Canadian dollars changes, resulting in an actual closing balance that differs from the computed balance. For example, at the beginning of the year, the opening NML could have been paid with $32,400 Canadian dollars. If it is not, at the end of the year its translated amount will have increased to $36,000, resulting in a loss on this item of $3,600. A similar analysis can be made of each of the other items.

Self-Sustaining Foreign Operation

10-74. If we assume that the Ship Company is a self-sustaining foreign operation, the Balance Sheets as at December 31, 2004 and December 31, 2005 and the Income Statement for the year ending December 31, 2005, are as follows:

Ship Company (Self-Sustaining Foreign Operation)
Translated Balance Sheet
As At December 31, 2004

	Untranslated	Rate	Translated
Cash	SF 2,000,000	$0.90	$ 1,800,000
Accounts Receivable	8,000,000	$0.90	7,200,000
Inventories	40,000,000	$0.90	36,000,000
Plant And Equipment (Net)	60,000,000	$0.90	54,000,000
Total Assets	SF110,000,000		$99,000,000
Current Liabilities	SF 6,000,000	$0.90	$ 5,400,000
Long-Term Liabilities	40,000,000	$0.90	36,000,000
No Par Common Stock	20,000,000	$0.80	16,000,000
Cumulative Translation Adjustment	N/A	N/A	6,800,000
Retained Earnings	44,000,000	N/A	34,800,000
Total Equities	SF110,000,000		$99,000,000

Ship Company (Self-Sustaining Foreign Operation)
Translated Balance Sheet
As At December 31, 2005

	Untranslated	Rate	Translated
Cash	SF 2,000,000	$1.00	$ 2,000,000
Accounts Receivable	14,000,000	$1.00	14,000,000
Inventories	54,000,000	$1.00	54,000,000
Plant And Equipment (Net)	50,000,000	$1.00	50,000,000
Total Assets	SF120,000,000		$120,000,000
Current Liabilities	SF 4,000,000	$1.00	$ 4,000,000
Long-Term Liabilities	40,000,000	$1.00	40,000,000
No Par Common Stock	20,000,000	$0.80	16,000,000
Cumulative Translation Adjustment	N/A	N/A	13,800,000
Retained Earnings	56,000,000	N/A	46,200,000
Total Equities	SF120,000,000		$120,000,000

Ship Company (Self-Sustaining Foreign Operation)
Translated Income Statement
For The Year Ending December 31, 2005

	Untranslated	Rate	Translated
Sales	SF150,000,000	$0.95	$142,500,000
Cost Of Goods Sold	SF120,000,000	$0.95	$114,000,000
Amortization Expense	10,000,000	$0.95	9,500,000
Other Expenses	8,000,000	$0.95	7,600,000
Total Expenses	SF138,000,000		$131,100,000
Net Income	SF 12,000,000		$ 11,400,000

10-75.   Given the information in the problem, it is not possible to calculate the balance that should be included in the Cumulative Translation Adjustment account as at December 31, 2004. We do know that this account, when combined with translated Retained Earnings, must total $41,600,000 (Total Assets, less Current Liabilities, Long-Term Liabilities, and No Par Common Stock). However, given the information that is provided in the problem, there is no way of determining the appropriate split between the two accounts. This is a problem that would be encountered by any Canadian enterprise that made the transition to the current rate approach from any other alternative translation method. In this situation, the *CICA Handbook* provides the following guidance:

> **Paragraph 1650.73**   The difference arising on translating the assets and liabilities of self-sustaining foreign operations at the current rate as of the commencement of the year for which these Recommendations are first applied would be reported as the opening balance of the exchange gains and losses included in a separate component of shareholders' equity.

10-76.   While the meaning of this guidance is not entirely clear, it is our opinion that the intent of the preceding Paragraph 1650.73 is that the opening balance of the Cumulative Translation Adjustment account should be based on the difference between net assets calculated by the current rate method and the equivalent total net assets calculated by the method that was previously in use. Assuming the use of the temporal method prior to December 31, 2004, the shareholders' equity would be the $50,800,000 ($16,000,000 + $34,800,000) calculated in the integrated foreign operation example. The December 31, 2004 Cumulative Translation Adjustment would be calculated as follows:

Current Rate Method Shareholders' Equity	
($16,000,000 + $41,600,000)	$57,600,000
Temporal Method Shareholders' Equity	(50,800,000)
Opening Cumulative Translation Adjustment	$ 6,800,000

10-77.   While this approach is often used in textbook problems involving self-sustaining foreign operations, in practice it is a transitional calculation that is not usually required. Normally the current rate method would be applied from the time of the acquisition of a self-sustaining operation. At this time, there would be no opening cumulative adjustment and subsequent changes could be calculated. This means that this calculation would only be used in situations where a company is switching to the current rate method from some other method of translation.

10-78.   Once we have established the opening balance, the calculation of the change for the year follows the procedures used to calculate the exchange gain or loss for integrated foreign operations. There is, however, an important difference. As the temporal method is used for integrated foreign operations, only monetary items and non-monetary items carried at current values are translated at current rates. This means that only these items are taken into account in the calculation of the exchange gain or loss for the year. This is reflected in the fact that the temporal method exchange loss is based on changes in net monetary items (there are no non-monetary items carried at current values in this example).

10-79.   In contrast, the statements of self-sustaining foreign operations are translated using the current rate method. This means that there will be translation adjustments on all of the assets and liabilities. As you would expect, the calculation of the change in the Cumulative Translation Adjustment account is based on changes in all net assets. The schedule begins with the opening net asset balance of SF64,000,0000. The required schedule is as follows:

Schedule Of Change In Net Assets
(000s Omitted)

	Untranslated	Rate	Translated
Opening Net Assets	SF 64,000	$0.90	$ 57,600
Sales	150,000	$0.95	142,500
Cost Of Goods Sold	(120,000)	$0.95	(114,000)
Amortization Expense	(10,000)	$0.95	(9,500)
Other Expenses	(8,000)	$0.95	(7,600)
Computed Closing Net Assets			$ 69,000
Less: Actual Closing Net Assets	SF 76,000	$1.00	76,000
Decrease (Increase) In The Cumulative Translation Adjustment Balance			($ 7,000)

10-80.   As was the case with the similar schedule in the integrated foreign operation example, the final balance of SF76,000,000 can be verified in the December 31, 2005 Balance Sheet (SF120,000,000 - SF4,000,000 - SF40,000,000 = SF76,000,000). Here again, we suggest that it is useful to do this verification in order to insure that one or more items have not been left out of the schedule.

10-81.   In this example, all of the changes in net assets occur uniformly over the year and, as a consequence, average exchange rates can be used. Given this, the computed closing balance could be calculated by translating the change in the net assets of SF12,000,000 (SF76,000,000 - SF64,000,000) by the average rate of $0.95. When this $11,400,000 [($0.95)(SF12,000,000)] is added to the translated opening balance of $57,600,000, it gives the computed closing balance of $69,000,000. You should note, however, that this only works when all of the changes in net assets occur uniformly over the year. If one or more of the changes does not satisfy this criteria, for example, a dividend declared at the year end, it will have to be translated at an exchange rate other than the simple average for the year. When this is the case, the more detailed schedular calculation is required.

Consolidated Financial Statements

10-82.   We are now in a position to prepare consolidated financial statements for the Port Company and its subsidiary, the Ship Company. These consolidated statements will be based on translation in compliance with the Recommendations of Section 1650 of the *CICA Hand-book* for self-sustaining foreign operations. The first step in the process of preparing consolidated financial statements would be to analyze the investment account. This can be done as follows:

Investment Cost	$42,200,000
Translated Book Value At Acquisition [(SF52,000,000)($0.80)]	(41,600,000)
Excess Of Cost Over Book Value	$ 600,000

10-83.   Since there are no fair value changes present on the acquisition date, the entire $600,000 would be allocated to goodwill. As the acquisition transaction took place subsequent to January 1, 2002, this goodwill will not be amortized. It will, however, be tested for impairment in each year and, as noted in Part 2 of the Other Information in the problem, no impairment has been found in any year since acquisition.

10-84.   Given this investment analysis, the consolidated Balance Sheet, as at December 31, 2004, would be prepared as follows:

Port Company And Subsidiary
Consolidated Balance Sheet
As At December 31, 2004

Cash ($2,000,000 + $1,800,000)	$ 3,800,000
Accounts And Other Receivables ($7,600,000 + $7,200,000)	14,800,000
Inventories ($30,000,000 + $36,000,000)	66,000,000
Investment in Ship ($42,200,000 - $42,200,000)	-0-
Plant And Equipment ($132,000,000 + $54,000,000)	186,000,000
Goodwill	600,000
Total Assets	$271,200,000

Current Liabilities ($43,800,000 + $5,400,000)	$ 49,200,000
Long-Term Liabilities ($30,000,000 + $36,000,000)	66,000,000
Common Stock - No Par (Port Company's)	60,000,000
Cumulative Translation Adjustment	6,800,000
Retained Earnings (See Verification)	89,200,000
Total Equities	$271,200,000

10-85.   The December 31, 2004 consolidated Retained Earnings balance can be verified with the following calculation:

Port Company's Balance		$80,000,000
Ship Company's Translated Balance	$34,800,000	
Ship's Balance At Acquisition		
[($0.80)(SF32,000,000)]	(25,600,000)	9,200,000
Balance - December 31, 2004		$ 89,200,000

10-86.   The consolidated Balance Sheet, as at December 31, 2005, would be as follows:

Port Company And Subsidiary
Consolidated Balance Sheet
As At December 31, 2005

Cash ($6,800,000 + $2,000,000)	$ 8,800,000
Accounts And Other Receivables ($18,800,000	
+ $14,000,000 - $1,000,000 - $2,000,000)	29,800,000
Inventories ($56,000,000 + $54,000,000)	110,000,000
Investment in Ship ($42,200,000 - $42,200,000)	-0-
Plant And Equipment (Net) ($120,000,000 + $50,000,000)	170,000,000
Goodwill	600,000
Total Assets	$319,200,000

Current Liabilities ($49,800,000 + $4,000,000	
- $1,000,000 - $2,000,000)	$ 50,800,000
Long-Term Liabilities ($30,000,000 + $40,000,000)	70,000,000
Common Stock - No Par (Port Company's)	60,000,000
Cumulative Translation Adjustment	
($6,800,000 + $7,000,000)	13,800,000
Retained Earnings (See Verification)	124,600,000
Total Equities	$319,200,000

10-87.   The December 31, 2005 consolidated Retained Earnings balance can be verified with the following calculation:

Port Company's Balance		$104,000,000
Ship Company's Translated Balance	$46,200,000	
Ship's Balance At Acquisition		
[($0.80)(SF32,000,000)]	(25,600,000)	20,600,000
Balance - December 31, 2005		$124,600,000

10-88.   The consolidated Income Statement for the year ending December 31, 2005 would be prepared as follows:

Port Company And Subsidiary
Consolidated Income Statement
Year Ending December 31, 2005

Sales {$390,000,000 + $142,500,000 - [($0.95)(SF40,000,000)]}	$494,500,000
Cost Of Goods Sold {$340,000,000 + $114,000,000	
- [($0.95)(SF40,000,000)]}	$416,000,000
Amortization Expense ($12,000,000 + $9,500,000)	21,500,000
Other Expenses ($14,000,000 + $7,600,000)	21,600,000
Total Expenses	$459,100,000
Net Income	$ 35,400,000

Other Issues

Transactions And Operations Of Foreign Operations Which Are Denominated In Another Currency

10-89.   If a foreign operation of a Canadian company has its own foreign currency transactions or foreign currency operations, it will be necessary to translate these amounts and statements into the currency of the Canadian company's foreign operation using the Recommendations of Section 1650. This could involve using either the temporal or the current rate method, depending on the nature of the items and, in the case of a foreign operation with a foreign operation of its own, the classification of this second tier investment. Once this has been accomplished, the Canadian company's foreign operation can be translated into Canadian dollars using either the temporal or current rate method as is appropriate.

Changes In Circumstances Relating To Foreign Operations

10-90.   When a foreign operation is either reclassified from integrated to self-sustaining or from self-sustaining to integrated, Section 1650 makes the following Recommendation:

> **Paragraph 1650.43**   *When there are significant changes in the economic facts and circumstances which require the translation method applied to a particular foreign operation to be changed, the change in method should be accounted for prospectively. Disclosure should be made of the reasons for the change in the translation method.* (July, 1983)

10-91.   This means that if the change is from self-sustaining to integrated, any previously deferred exchange gains and losses will continue to be deferred and the translated amounts for non-monetary items at the end of the period prior to the reclassification will become the historical cost base in the application of the temporal method. Correspondingly, if the change is from integrated to self-sustaining, the exchange gain or loss attributable to the current rate translation of non-monetary items as of the date of the change would become the balance in the separate component of shareholders' equity.

Investments Accounted For By The Equity Method

10-92.   When an investee is accounted for by the equity method, the investment income that is recorded by the investor company is based on the reported income of the investee, subject to the usual consolidation adjustments. In the case of a foreign investee, the statements will have to be translated prior to the application of the equity method. In such situations, the *CICA Handbook* notes the following:

> **Paragraph 1650.45**   The financial statements of a foreign investee accounted for by the equity method (See "Long-Term Investments," Section 3050) first would be translated into Canadian dollars in accordance with the appropriate Recommendations in this Section; then the equity method would be applied.

10-93.   As the equity method could be applicable to either an integrated or a self-sustaining foreign operation, either the temporal or the current rate method may be applicable.

Translation After A Business Combination

10-94.   The acquisition of a foreign investee will normally be classified as a business combination transaction. The rate used to translate non-monetary assets and liabilities at subsequent Balance Sheet dates will depend on whether the foreign operation is integrated, in which case the historical rate which prevailed at the date of the business combination will be used, or self-sustaining, in which case the current rate will be used. Note that, regardless of when the foreign operation acquired the assets that are being translated, the historical rate will be the rate which prevailed when the investor acquired the assets (i.e., the business combination date).

Intercompany Balances
Integrated Foreign Operations

10-95.   It is not uncommon for intercompany asset and liability balances to arise between a domestic investor company and its foreign investees. In such cases, translation of the foreign currency balance will usually result in exchange gains and losses and this raises the question of what is the appropriate treatment of these balances. With respect to balances related to integrated foreign operations, the *CICA Handbook* suggests:

> **Paragraph 1650.57**   With respect to integrated foreign operations, exchange gains and losses relating to intercompany balances recorded by the reporting enterprise or the foreign operation will be treated in the same manner as those relating to other foreign currency receivables or payables in accordance with the Recommendation in paragraph 1650.20.

Self-Sustaining Foreign Operations

10-96.   The situation is more complex when a self-sustaining foreign operation is involved. In this case, the *CICA Handbook* distinguishes between ordinary intercompany balances (e.g., those arising on intercompany sales of merchandise) and intercompany balances that form part of the net investment (e.g., a holding of the foreign investee's redeemable preferred shares). Based on this distinction, the following guidance is provided:

> **Paragraph 1650.58**   With respect to self-sustaining foreign operations, exchange gains and losses on intercompany account balances that are not included as part of the net investment would be treated in the same manner as those relating to normal foreign currency trade balances in accordance with the appropriate Recommendations of this Section. Exchange gains and losses on intercompany account balances that form part of the net investment would be deferred and included in the separate component of shareholders' equity in accordance with paragraph 1650.36. [Paragraph 1650.36 requires allocation to a separate shareholders' equity section.]

Elimination Of Intercompany Profits

10-97. The issue here is related to the elimination of intercompany profits resulting from transactions between a reporting entity and a foreign investee. Specifically, it must be decided whether to make the elimination using the exchange rate which prevailed at the date of the transaction or, alternatively, using the rate which prevails at the balance sheet date. For integrated foreign operations the answer is clearly the use of the transaction date rate. Somewhat surprisingly, the Accounting Standards Board concludes that this is also the most appropriate rate for self-sustaining operations. Note that this will require that the transaction date rate also be used for any subsequent realization of unrealized profits that have been previously eliminated.

Differences In Financial Statement Dates

10-98. A foreign investee can have a different fiscal year end than that of the domestic investor. When this happens, Paragraph 1650.60 provides the following guidance:

Paragraph 1650.60 When the date of the financial statements of the foreign operation differs from that of the reporting enterprise, those assets and liabilities which are translated at the current rate would normally be translated at the rate in effect at the balance sheet date of the foreign operation, not at the rate in effect at the balance sheet date of the reporting enterprise. When there is a major change in exchange rates between the balance sheet dates of the foreign operation and the reporting enterprise, the effect of the change would be disclosed.

Non-Controlling Interest

10-99. In preparing consolidated financial statements, one or more foreign subsidiaries may have a non-controlling interest. In this situation, the *CICA Handbook* indicates the following:

Paragraph 1650.62 The non-controlling interest reported in an enterprise's consolidated financial statements would be based on the financial statements of the foreign operation in which there is a non-controlling interest after they have been translated according to the Recommendations in this Section. In particular, the non-controlling interest reported would include the non-controlling interest's proportionate share of exchange gains and losses.

Preference Shares

10-100. With respect to the treatment of preference shares in translation, the *CICA Handbook* states the following:

Paragraph 1650.63 Preference shares of a foreign operation held by the reporting enterprise would be translated in the same manner as common shares (i.e., at historical rates) unless redemption is either required or imminent, in which case the current rate would be used. Preference shares held by non-controlling shareholders in an integrated foreign operation would also be translated at historical rates unless redemption is either required or imminent, in which case the current rate would be used. Preference shares held by non-controlling shareholders in a self-sustaining foreign operation would be translated at the current rate. (Where the economic environment of a self-sustaining foreign operation is highly inflationary, the preference shares of the foreign operation would be translated in the same manner as preference shares of integrated foreign operations.)

Application Of Lower Of Cost And Market

10-101. The exchange rate used to translate assets of an integrated foreign operation is dependent on the basis of their valuation in the foreign currency financial statements. If they are valued at cost, historical rates will be applicable while if they are valued at market or some other measure of current value, current exchange rates will be used.

10-102. This would be relevant in the application of lower of cost and market to the problem of inventory valuation. As a result, the translation process may result in the need to write down translated values even when there has been no write down in the foreign currency statements. For example, assume that a German subsidiary has inventories purchased for 1,000,000 Euros (€) when the exchange rate was €1 = $1.40. At the Balance Sheet date, these inventories have a market value of €1,100,000. There is clearly no need to write down the Euro value as the market exceeds the cost. However, if we assume that the Balance Sheet date exchange rate has fallen to €1 = $1.25, the translated market value would be $1,375,000 [(€1,100,000)($1.25)]. As this would be lower than the translated cost of $1,400,000, the translated market figure would be used.

10-103. It is also possible for the opposite situation to occur. That is, it may be necessary in the translated financial statements to reverse a write down that has occurred in the foreign currency statements. In addition, Section 1650 notes that once an asset has been written down to market in the translated financial statements, that dollar amount would continue to be the carrying amount in the translated financial statements until the asset is sold or a further write down is required.

Future Income Tax Assets And Liabilities

10-104. Section 3465, "Income Taxes" adopts the future income tax asset/liability approach. As the resulting tax allocation balances are monetary assets and liabilities, they are translated at current exchange rates. This would be the case for balances on the books of either integrated or self-sustaining foreign operations. This view is reflected in Paragraph 1650.68 as follows:

> **Paragraph 1650.68** Future income tax liabilities and assets are monetary items and, as such, would be translated at the current rate.

Cash Flow Statement

10-105. There are a number of problems that arise in the translation of the Cash Flow Statement of a self-sustaining foreign operation. Paragraph 1650.69 of the *CICA Handbook* offers guidance on the following points:

(a) Cash from operations would be translated at the exchange rate at which the respective items are translated for income statement purposes.

(b) Other items would be translated at exchange rates in effect when the related transactions took place.

(c) The effect of subsequent exchange rate changes on the cash flows during the period and on cash and cash equivalents at the commencement of the period would be disclosed, so that cash and cash equivalents at the end of the period are translated at the exchange rate in effect on that date.

Disclosure And Financial Statement Presentation

10-106. The disclosure requirements of Section 1650 of the *CICA Handbook* are not extensive. We have already noted the only specific recommendations found in this Section. These are Paragraph 1650.39's requirement for disclosure of significant elements which give rise to changes in the exchange gains and losses accumulated in the separate component of shareholders' equity, and Paragraph 1650.43's requirement that disclosure be made of the reasons for any change in translation methods used for foreign operations. One other disclosure Recommendation is included in the revised Section 1650:

> **Paragraph 1650.44** *The amount of exchange gain or loss included in income should be disclosed (see paragraphs 1650.20, 1650.31 and 1650.38). Exchange gains or losses from dealer transactions of certain enterprises, primarily banks, that are dealers in foreign exchange may be disclosed as dealer gains or losses rather than as exchange gains or losses.* (January, 2002)

10-107.   This disclosure is also required in Section 1520, "Income Statement", as follows:

Paragraph 1520.03   *In arriving at the income or loss before discontinued operations and extraordinary items, the income statement should distinguish at least the following items:*
...

(l)   The amount of exchange gain or loss included in income, except for exchange gains and losses of a dealer in foreign exchange that are disclosed as dealer gains or losses (see FOREIGN CURRENCY TRANSLATION, *Section 1650). (January, 2002)*

Foreign Currency Translation In Canadian Practice

Statistics From Financial Reporting In Canada

10-108.   Section 1650 leaves few alternatives in its application. Integrated operations and foreign currency transactions must be translated using the temporal method and self-sustaining operations must be translated using the current rate method. Given this lack of alternatives in the translation of foreign currency statements and transactions, the 2001 edition of *Financial Reporting in Canada* does not present a significant amount of data in this area.

10-109.   The now deleted Paragraph 1650.23 required that exchange gains and losses on long-term monetary items be deferred and amortized. This approach is no longer permitted. However, it was in effect during 2000. The 2000 data indicated that 86 of the 200 survey companies disclosed deferred exchange gains or losses. However, for the majority of these companies, the only disclosure was a reference in a note or in the statement on accounting policies. Of the 86 companies that disclosed deferred exchange gains or losses, 24 indicated the method of amortization, while 49 indicated only that they were being amortized over their service lives.

10-110.   With respect to self-sustaining foreign operations, Section 1650 requires that exchange gains and losses be deferred and included in a separate section of shareholders' equity. A total of 110 companies disclosed such a section, of which 36 designated the balance a "foreign currency translation adjustment" and 28 referred to it as a "cumulative translation adjustment". The remaining companies used a wide variety of other terminology. Paragraph 1650.39 requires that disclosure be made of significant elements which gave rise to changes in this shareholders' equity balance. Such disclosure was made by 29 companies.

10-111.   The old Paragraph 1650.44 noted that it was desirable to disclose the amount of exchange gain or loss that is included in income. This disclosure was provided by 51 of the survey companies. It is expected that disclosure of exchange gains and losses will greatly increase now that the disclosure is required and not simply desirable.

10-112.   Although it is not a foreign currency accounting issue, it is interesting to note that of the 200 companies included in the survey, 48 companies presented their 2000 financial statements in U.S. dollars. Reasons for this included the fact that the enterprise did most of its business in that country, and/or the fact that the securities of the enterprise were traded on U.S. stock exchanges.

Example From Practice

10-113.   Disclosure related to foreign currency translation can be found in the statement of accounting policies or, alternatively, in a note to the financial statements. Our example is from the annual report of Gulf Canada Resources Limited for the year ending December 31, 2000 and illustrates both of these forms of disclosure. This example illustrates disclosure of the amortization of deferred foreign exchange losses that is included in Financial Expenses. The deferred foreign exchange loss is included in Note 11. There is a separate note on the foreign currency translation adjustment balance that is disclosed as part of shareholders' equity.

Balance Sheet Disclosure

(millions of dollars)	2000	1999
Retained earnings (deficit)	(633)	(747)
Foreign currency translation adjustment (Note 18)(10)	(20)	
[Shareholders' Equity]	3,009	1,566
[Liabilities and Shareholders' Equity]	$8,931	$5,435

Income Statement Disclosure

The account "Amortization of deferred exchange losses" ($57 million for 2000 and $26 million for 1999) is included as a component of Note 4, "Finance charges, net". Net income is $148 million for 2000 and a net loss of $172 million for 1999.

Notes To Financial Statements
(millions of dollars)

Summary Of Significant Accounting Policies (in part)

Foreign Currency Translation Assets and liabilities of self-sustaining foreign subsidiaries are translated into Canadian dollars at year-end exchange rates. The resulting unrealized exchange gains or losses are reflected in shareholders' equity. Revenues and expenses are translated using the average rates of exchange during the year.

Assets and liabilities of all other foreign subsidiaries and all other transactions in foreign currencies are translated into Canadian dollars at the exchange rates prevailing at the transaction dates. Monetary assets and liabilities denominated in foreign currencies are translated into Canadian dollars at year-end exchange rates. Exchange gains or losses are included in earnings with the exception of the unrealized gains or losses on translation of long-term monetary liabilities, which are deferred and amortized over the remaining terms of such liabilities on a straight-line basis.

Note 11   Investments, Deferred Charges and Other Assets

December 31	2000	1999
Deferred foreign exchange loss on long-term debt	$60	$58
Deferred long-term debt placement costs	72	86
Deferred long-term debt interest costs	13	0
Portfolio investments	24	23
Loans receivable from related companies (Note 22)	0	7
Other	14	15
	$183	$189

Note 18 Foreign Currency Translation Adjustment

Year ended December 31	2000	1999
Balance, beginning of year	$(20)	$69
Current year's deferred translation adjustments	19	(104)
(Reduction) increase in net investment in foreign operations	(9)	15
Balance, end of year	$(10)	$(20)

Additional Readings

10-114.   In writing the material in the text, we have incorporated all of the relevant *CICA Handbook* Recommendations, as well as material from other sources that we felt to be of importance. This includes material from U.S. accounting pronouncements and ideas put forward in articles published in professional accounting journals.

10-115.   While this approach meets the needs of the great majority of accounting students, some of you may wish to pursue this subject in greater depth. To facilitate this, you will find a fairly comprehensive bibliography of materials on the subject of foreign currency translation in Chapter 17 of our *Guide to Canadian Financial Reporting*. Chapter 17 of the *Guide* also contains summaries of the EIC Abstracts that are directly related to this subject. The Abstracts that are summarized as an appendix to Chapter 17 are as follows:

- EIC Abstract No. 11 - Changes In Reporting Currency
- EIC Abstract No. 26 - Reductions In The Net Investment In Self-Sustaining Operations

10-116.   The complete *Guide to Canadian Financial Reporting* is available on the CD-ROM which accompanies this text.

Problems For Self Study

(The solutions for these problems can be found following Chapter 16 of the text.)

Self Study Problem Ten - 1

The Ambivalent Company is a Mexican subsidiary of a Canadian parent company and its accounts are included in the Canadian dollar consolidated financial statements of the parent company. On December 31, 2003, the following selected amount balances were included in the foreign currency Balance Sheet of the Ambivalent Company (all amounts are expressed in Mexican pesos which are designated P hereafter):

	Debits	Credits
Cash	P 500,000	
Long-Term Receivables	1,500,000	
Inventories	2,000,000	
Plant and Equipment	5,000,000	
Accounts Payable		P 700,000
Long-Term Liabilities		1,200,000
Accumulated Depreciation on Plant and Equipment		2,500,000

The Long-Term Receivables and Plant And Equipment were acquired several years ago when P1 = \$.10. The Long-Term Liabilities were also issued at this time. The Inventories were acquired for P2,100,000 when P1 = \$.20. However, they are carried at their net realizable value as measured at December 31, 2003. The exchange rate on December 31, 2003 is P1 = \$.25.

Required: Translate the above account balances using the following approaches:

A. Temporal approach

B. Current rate approach

Self Study Problem Ten - 2

Investco Ltd. is a Canadian real estate and property developer which decided to hold a parcel of land in downtown St. Michael's, Barbados, for speculative purposes. The land, costing 12,000,000 Barbadian dollars (B\$, hereafter) was financed by a five-year bond (B\$9,000,000), which is repayable in Barbadian dollars, and an initial equity injection by Investco of B\$3,000,000. These transactions took place on January 1, 2002, at which time a Barbadian subsidiary company was created to hold the investment.

Investco plans to sell the land at the end of five years and use the Barbadian dollar proceeds to pay off the bond. In the interim, rent is being collected from another company which is using the land as a parking lot. Rental revenue is collected and interest and other expenses are paid at the end of each month. The 2002 year end draft financial statements of the Barbadian subsidiary company are as follows:

Income Statement
For The Year Ended December 31, 2002

Rental Revenue	B\$1,000,000
Interest Expense	(990,000)
Other Expenses	(10,000)
Net Income	B\$ - 0 -

Balance Sheet
As At December 31, 2002

Cash	B$ - 0 -
Land	12,000,000
Total Assets	B$12,000,000
Bond (Due December 31, 2006)	B$ 9,000,000
Common Stock	3,000,000
Total Equities	B$12,000,000

Assume the exchange rates were as follows:

January 1, 2002	B$1 = C$0.75
December 31, 2002	B$1 = C$0.85
Average, 2002	B$1 = C$0.80

Required:

A. Prepare the translated 2002 Income Statements and Balance Sheets at December 31, 2002, following Canadian generally accepted accounting principles and assuming:

   i) the Barbadian subsidiary is an integrated foreign operation as defined in the revised Section 1650 of the *CICA Handbook*; and

  ii) the Barbadian subsidiary is a self-sustaining foreign operation as defined in the revised Section 1650 of the *CICA Handbook*.

B. Which translation method better reflects Investco's economic exposure to exchange rate movements? Explain.

C. Which translation method would Investco be required to use? Explain.

D. Assume that, instead of incorporating a Barbadian subsidiary, Investco carries the investment (land, debt, etc.) directly on its own books. Some accountants would argue that it is inappropriate to reflect any portion of an unrealized exchange gain or loss on the bond in income because the land serves as an effective hedge. Explain the reasoning behind this position. Would this approach be acceptable? Explain.

(SMA Adapted)

Self Study Problem Ten - 3

Sentex Limited of Montreal, Quebec, has an 80% owned subsidiary, Cellular Company Inc., which operates in Erewhon, a small country located in Central America. Cellular was formed on January 1, 2002 by Sentex and Erewhon Development Inc. which is located in Erewhon. Advantages to Sentex of locating in Erewhon are: easy access to raw materials, low operating costs, government incentives, and the fact that the plastics market of Erewhon is not well developed. All management, including the Chief Operating Officer, Mr. V. Globe, has been appointed by Sentex. Top management of Cellular is paid directly by Sentex.

Cellular makes plastic coatings from petrochemical feedstock purchased form Mexico. The process is automated but still uses significant amounts of native Erewhonese labour. The government of Erewhon has determined that this type of development is good for the country, and has underwritten 22,000 cuzos (local currency of Erewhon) of staff training expenses in 2002 by reducing the taxes payable by Cellular. This employment assistance is not expected to continue in the future.

Approximately 75% of total sales by Cellular is made to Sentex which uses the plastic coatings in its Montreal operations. These coatings are generally of a heavy grade and require special set-up by Cellular. The Sentex orders are handled directly by Mr. Globe and his assistant, Mr. A. Oppong, and the price is set on the basis of variable costs of manufacture, plus freight and a

30% markup, less applicable export tax incentives. The export tax incentive received by Cellular has been about 1,000 cuzos per order. Plastic coatings are also sold to both commercial and wholesale outlets in Erewhon, with commercial users constituting 20% of the total sales revenue of Cellular.

Cellular has agreed with the Erewhon government not to pay any dividends out of profits for two years. After that, it is anticipated that the majority of profits will be remitted by Cellular to Sentex and its other major stockholder, Erewhon Development Inc. The opening balance sheet of Cellular Company Inc. at January 1, 2002, was as follows:

Cellular Company Inc.
Balance Sheet As At January 1, 2002 (in cuzos)

Cash	30,000
Fixed Assets	350,000
Total Assets	380,000
Long-Term Debt	180,000
Common Stock	200,000
Total Equities	380,000

All debt financing was provided by Sentex. The debt was incurred on January 1, 2002 in cuzos, and is secured by the assets of Cellular.

Cellular Company Inc.
Income Statement For the Year Ended December 31, 2002
(in cuzos)

Sales		600,000
Cost Of Goods Sold		400,000
Gross Margin		200,000
Selling And Administrative Expenses	70,000	
Interest	20,000	90,000
Net Income Before Taxes		110,000
Local Taxes	33,000	
Less Allowance For:		
Export Incentive	6,500	
Training Costs	22,000	4,500
Net Income After Taxes		105,500

Cellular Company Inc.
Balance Sheet As At December 31, 2002
(in cuzos)

Cash	25,000
Notes Receivable	100,000
Accounts Receivable	65,000
Inventories (at cost)	90,000
Current Assets	280,000
Fixed Assets (at cost less accumulated depreciation of 120,000)	230,000
Land (for future development)	10,000
Total Assets	520,000

Accounts Payable	30,000
Taxes Payable	4,500
Current Liabilities	34,500
Long-Term Liabilities, 10% Bonds Payable Due January 1, 2009	180,000
Total Liabilities	214,500
Common Stock	200,000
Retained Earnings	105,500
Total Equities	520,000

Other Information:

1. Raw material and labour costs were incurred uniformly throughout the year.

2. Sales were made uniformly throughout the year.

3. The fixed assets were acquired on January 1, 2002, and are depreciated using the sum-of-the-years'-digits method over four years.

4. The note receivable is a 90-day non-interest-bearing note received from a customer in exchange for merchandise sold in October.

5. Land was purchased on December 31, 2002, for 10,000 cuzos.

6. The following exchange rates were in effect for the 2002 year:

Rate at January 1, 2002	1 cuzo = $2.00 Canadian
Average rate for the year 2002	1 cuzo = $1.82 Canadian
Rate at December 31, 2002	1 cuzo = $1.65 Canadian

7. Cost of sales and inventory include depreciation of 98,000 cuzos and 22,000 cuzos respectively. The calculation of Cost of Goods Sold in cuzos is as follows:

Material Purchases	300,000
Labour	70,000
Total Purchases	370,000
Depreciation	120,000
Total Goods Available	490,000
Closing Inventory	(90,000)
Cost Of Goods Sold	400,000

Required   Sentex is in the process of preparing consolidated financial statements for the year ended December 31, 2002.

A. Which method of translation should Sentex use, according to Canadian generally accepted accounting principles? Justify your selection, using the information from the question.

B. Calculate the exchange gain or loss on the accounts of Cellular Company Inc.

C. Prepare the translated Balance Sheet as at December 31, 2002 and the translated Income Statement for the year ending December 31, 2002 for Cellular Company Inc.

(SMA Adapted)

Self Study Problem Ten - 4

The comparative Balance Sheets and the 2002 Income Statement of the Brazal Company, in New Cozos (NC, hereafter) are as follows:

Brazal Company
Comparative Balance Sheets
As At December 31

	2002	2001
Cash And Current Receivables	NC11,000,000	NC 6,500,000
Long-Term Receivable	5,000,000	5,000,000
Inventories	8,000,000	9,500,000
Plant And Equipment	23,000,000	17,000,000
Accumulated Depreciation	(5,000,000)	(4,000,000)
Land	6,000,000	3,000,000
Total Assets	NC48,000,000	NC37,000,000
Current Liabilities	NC 3,000,000	NC 5,000,000
Long-Term Liabilities	10,000,000	-0-
No Par Common Stock	20,000,000	18,000,000
Retained Earnings	15,000,000	14,000,000
Total Equities	NC48,000,000	NC37,000,000

Brazal Company
Income Statement
For The Year Ending December 31, 2002

Sales	NC50,000,000
Interest Revenue	1,000,000
Total Revenues	NC51,000,000
Cost of Goods Sold	NC30,000,000
Taxes	10,000,000
Depreciation Expense	2,000,000
Other Expenses	5,000,000
Total Expenses	NC47,000,000
Income Before Extraordinary Items	NC 4,000,000
Extraordinary Loss	2,000,000
Net Income	NC 2,000,000

Other Information:

1. The Brazal Company was formed as the wholly owned subsidiary of a Canadian public company. On the date of incorporation, January 1, 1995, No Par Common Stock was issued for NC18 million and the proceeds were used to purchase Plant And Equipment for NC17 million on the same day. There were no further purchases or disposals of Plant And Equipment from January 1, 1995 to December 31, 2001. The Brazal Company uses the straight line method to calculate depreciation expense.

2. The Long-Term Receivable resulted from a sales transaction on January 1, 2001 and is receivable on December 31, 2005. Interest at a rate of 20 percent per year is paid on the principal and is recorded in Interest Revenue.

3. The December 31, 2001 Inventories were acquired on October 1, 2001. The Inventories in the December 31, 2002 Balance Sheet were acquired on October 1, 2002.

4. On January 1, 2002, Plant And Equipment with an original cost of NC4 million and a Net Book Value of NC3 million was expropriated by the local government for cash of NC1 million. The loss arising from this transaction is considered extraordinary.

5. On January 1, 2002, Long-Term Liabilities with a maturity date of December 31, 2011 and an interest rate of 12 percent were issued for total proceeds of NC10 million. These funds were used to purchase NC10 million in equipment on April 1, 2002. The equipment has an estimated useful life of 10 years.

6. The Land on the books on December 31, 2001 was acquired on January 1, 2001. The 2002 purchase of Land for NC3 million occurred on July 1, 2002.

7. Sales, Interest Revenue, Purchases and Other Expenses occurred evenly throughout the year. This would make the use of average indexes appropriate.

8. Taxes accrued evenly throughout the year and were paid in two equal installments of NC5 million on July 1, 2002 and NC5 million on December 31, 2002.

9. Assume the foreign exchange rate data for the New Cozo and the Canadian dollar is as follows:

January 1, 1995	NC1 = $.100
January 1, 2001	NC1 = $.060
October 1, 2001	NC1 = $.045
December 31, 2001	NC1 = $.040
Average for 2001	NC1 = $.050
April 1, 2002	NC1 = $.038
July 1, 2002	NC1 = $.035
October 1, 2002	NC1 = $.032
December 31, 2002	NC1 = $.030
Average for 2002	NC1 = $.035

10. Dividends of NC1 million were declared and paid on October 1, 2002.

11. The new issue of NC2 million in No Par Common Stock occurred on April 1, 2002.

12. The inventory is accounted for on the First-In, First-Out cost flow assumption.

Required:

A. Assume that the Brazal Company is classified as an integrated foreign operation. Prepare in Canadian dollars a Balance Sheet as at December 31, 2001, a Balance Sheet as at December 31, 2002, and a Statement of Income and Change in Retained Earnings for the year ending December 31, 2002.

B. Assume that the Brazal Company is classified as a self sustaining foreign operation. Assume that prior to the year ending December 31, 2002 the Brazal Company was classified and accounted for as an integrated foreign operation. Prepare in Canadian dollars a Balance Sheet as at December 31, 2001, a Balance Sheet as at December 31, 2002, and a Statement of Income and Change in Retained Earnings for the year ending December 31, 2002.

Assignment Problems

(The solutions for these problems are only available in
the solutions manual that has been provided to your instructor.)

Assignment Problem Ten - 1

Telemark Inc., a manufacturer of cross-country ski equipment, has incorporated a wholly owned Norwegian operating subsidiary, Suomi Inc. All of the subsidiary's capital results from the issuance of a 25 year, 11 percent mortgage for 3,500,000 Norwegian krone (K, hereafter) on April 1, 2002. Suomi Inc. uses the total proceeds to finance the purchase of an office building on that date. The first interest payment of K385,000 and the first principal repayment of K140,000 are payable on April 1, 2003.

The total cost of the real estate has been allocated 80 percent to the building and 20 percent to the land. The building has an estimated useful life of 25 years and no net salvage value. Both Telemark Inc. and Suomi Inc. use the straight line method to calculate depreciation expense.

Assume the exchange rate for the Norwegian krone had the following values:

April 1, 2002	K1 = $0.29
March 31, 2003	K1 = $0.25

The exchange rate changed uniformly over the year ending March 31, 2003.

Required:

A. Suomi Inc. can be classified as an integrated foreign operation or a self-sustaining foreign operation by Telemark Inc. For both cases, calculate the effect of the building purchase and related mortgage on the consolidated financial statements of Telemark Inc. for the year ending March 31, 2003. Specifically, translate the Balance Sheet and Income Statement accounts of Suomi Inc. affected by the building purchase, mortgage and any translation adjustments.

B. What is the principal determinant of whether a foreign operation is classified as integrated or self-sustaining? Provide one example of the factors that should be considered in the analysis. Using your calculations in Part A, briefly discuss which method would provide more favorable results for the shareholders of Telemark Inc. in the current year and in the future.

(SMA Adapted)

Assignment Problem Ten - 2

On December 31, 2001, the Maple Leaf Company, a Canadian company, buys $7,000,000 worth of Euros (€, hereafter) at a rate of €1 = $1.40. The resulting €5,000,000 is used to establish a new German subsidiary company, the Rhine Company, on this same date. Also on this date, the Rhine Company borrows, at an annual rate of 10 percent, an additional €5,000,000 in Germany. The debt must be repaid after ten years. The Rhine Company then invests the entire cash balance of €10,000,000 in a tract of land. The land is immediately leased for a period of ten years with the lessee agreeing to pay the Rhine Company €1,000,000 at the end of each year.

During the subsequent year, the only activities of the Rhine Company are the collection of the lease payment and the payment of the interest on the Long-Term Debt. To simplify the problem, all other expenses and revenues of the Company have been ignored.

The Rhine Company's Income Statement for the year ending December 31, 2002 and its Balance Sheet as at December 31, 2002 in Euros are as follows:

Income Statement
Year Ending December 31, 2002

Lease Revenue	€1,000,000
Interest Expense	500,000
Net Income	€ 500,000

Balance Sheet
As At December 31, 2002

Cash	€ 500,000
Land	10,000,000
Total Assets	€10,500,000
Long-Term Debt	€ 5,000,000
Contributed Capital	5,000,000
Retained Earnings	500,000
Total Equities	€10,500,000

The exchange rate increased to €1 = $1.60 on January 1, 2002 and remained unchanged at that level until January 1, 2003.

Required: Prepare the Rhine Company's translated Income Statement for the year ending December 31, 2002 and the Company's translated Balance Sheet as at December 31, 2002 in Canadian dollars using the alternative methods described in the following three Cases.

Case One Assume that the temporal method is used for the translation of all assets and liabilities and that exchange adjustments are included in income in the year in which the exchange rate change occurs.

Case Two Assume that the temporal method is used for the translation of all assets and liabilities and that exchange adjustments are treated as an adjustment of the shareholders' equity of the Rhine Company.

Case Three Assume that the current rate method is used for the translation of all assets and liabilities and that exchange adjustments are treated as an adjustment of the shareholders' equity of the Rhine Company.

Assignment Problem Ten - 3

The Chinese Company, Jo Sun Inc., is a wholly owned subsidiary of the Canadian company, Goodnite Inc. Goodnite Inc. acquired its investment in the shares of Jo Sun Inc. on January 1, 1989. The Statement Of Income And Change In Retained Earnings for Jo Sun Inc. in Chinese renminbi (R, hereafter) for the year ending December 31, 2002 is as follows:

Jo Sun Company
Statement of Income and Change in Retained Earnings
Year Ending December 31, 2002

Sales Revenue	R4,500,000
Cost Of Goods Sold	R1,500,000
Depreciation Expense	225,000
Interest Expense	150,000
Selling And Administrative Expense	375,000
Taxes (At 30 Percent)	675,000
Total Expenses	R2,925,000
Income Before Extraordinary Items	R1,575,000
Extraordinary Loss On Expropriation Of Land (Net Of R45,000 In Taxes)	255,000
Net Income	R1,320,000
Dividends Declared	120,000
Increase In Retained Earnings	R1,200,000

Other Information:

1. The Sales Revenue arises from sales of mattresses and bedding. Sales occur evenly throughout the year.

2. The inventory on hand on January 1, 2002 was purchased on September 30, 2001 for R450,000. Purchases during 2002 of R1,800,000 occurred evenly over the first three quarters. The inventory on hand on December 31, 2002 was purchased on September 30, 2002. Inventory is accounted for on a first-in, first-out inventory flow assumption.

3. The Depreciation Expense pertains to a building which was purchased on January 1, 1992.

4. The Interest Expense relates to the 10 percent, 20 year bonds which were issued for R1,500,000 on January 1, 2002.

5. The Selling And Administrative Expenses occurred evenly over the year.

6. Income Taxes on ordinary income accrued evenly over the year.

7. The Extraordinary Loss arises from the expropriation of a parcel of land which was purchased on January 1, 1992 for R750,000. This land was expropriated by the local government on December 31, 2002 for proceeds of R450,000.

8. The dividends of Jo Sun Inc. were declared on September 30, 2002 and paid on December 31, 2002.

9. The net monetary assets of Jo Sun Inc. on January 1, 2002, before the issuance of the R1,500,000 in bonds (see Part 4), totalled R2,250,000.

10. Changes in the exchange rate occurred uniformly over the year 2002. The relationship between the Chinese renminbi and the Canadian dollar on relevant dates was as follows:

January 1, 1992	R1 = $.20
September 30, 2001	R1 = $.24
January 1, 2002	R1 = $.25
March 31, 2002	R1 = $.27
June 30, 2002	R1 = $.29
September 30, 2002	R1 = $.31
December 31, 2002	R1 = $.33
Average For 2002	R1 = $.29

Required: Translate the Statement Of Income And Change In Retained Earnings of the Jo Sun Company for use in the preparation of the 2002 consolidated financial statements of the Goodnite Company assuming:

A. the Jo Sun Company is an integrated foreign operation.

B. the Jo Sun Company is a self sustaining foreign operation.

Assignment Problem Ten - 4

Royce Ltd. is a British company with all of its facilities located in Manchester, England. The Company was founded on December 31, 1998. However, on December 31, 1999, all of its outstanding shares were acquired by Beaver Inc., a publicly traded Canadian company. You have been assigned the task of translating Royce's financial statements from U.K. pounds (£) into Canadian dollars for inclusion in the consolidated financial statements of Beaver Inc.

Royce Ltd.'s Balance Sheets as at December 31, 2002 and December 31, 2003, as well as its Statement Of Income And Change In Retained Earnings for the year ending December 31, 2003, are as follows:

Royce Ltd.
Balance Sheets
As At December 31

	2003	2002
Cash	£ 212,000	£ 187,000
Accounts Receivable	350,000	327,000
Inventories	1,856,000	1,528,000
Plant And Equipment (Net)	4,900,000	5,320,000
Land	600,000	800,000
Total Assets	£7,918,000	£8,162,000
Current Liabilities	£ 87,000	£ 143,000
Long-Term Liabilities	700,000	1,000,000
Common Stock - No Par	5,600,000	5,600,000
Retained Earnings	1,531,000	1,419,000
Total Equities	£7,918,000	£8,162,000

Royce Ltd.
Statement Of Income And Change In Retained Earnings
Year Ending December 31, 2003

Sales	£6,611,000
Gain On Sale Of Land	125,000
Total Revenues	£6,736,000
Cost Of Goods Sold	£4,672,000
Depreciation Expense	420,000
Selling And Administrative Expenses	1,230,000
Interest Expense	84,000
Loss On Debt Retirement	50,000
Total Expenses	£6,456,000
Net Income	£ 280,000
Less: Dividends On Common Shares	168,000
Increase In Retained Earnings	£ 112,000

Other Information:

1. All £5,600,000 of Royce's Common Stock - No Par was issued when the Company was founded on December 31, 1998. With respect to the proceeds, £800,000 was used to acquire the Land which is shown in the December 31, 2002 Balance Sheet. Of the remaining proceeds, £4,400,000 was used to acquire Plant And Equipment with an estimated useful life of 20 years. This Plant And Equipment is being depreciated on a straight line basis.

2. One-quarter of the Land which was acquired when Royce was founded was sold on July 1, 2003. The proceeds of disposition were £325,000, resulting in a reported gain on the sale of £125,000.

3. Royce still owns all of the Plant And Equipment that was acquired when the Company was founded. In addition, a further £2,000,000 of Plant And Equipment was acquired on January 1, 2002. This more recently acquired Plant And Equipment was estimated to have a useful life of 10 years at the time of its acquisition and is being depreciated by the straight line method over this period.

4. The acquisition of Plant And Equipment described in Item 3 was financed with £1,000,000 of internally generated funds along with £1,000,000 of debt financing. The stated rate of interest on the debt is 12 percent per annum, with payments required on July 1 and January 1 of each year. The debt was issued on January 1, 2002 at its maturity value and is scheduled to mature on December 31, 2011. However, on January 1, 2003, 30 percent of this debt was retired through a payment of £350,000 in cash, resulting in a loss of £50,000.

5. The December 31, 2002 Inventories were acquired on October 1, 2002 and the December 31, 2003 Inventories were acquired on July 1, 2003. The 2003 Sales and Purchases occurred uniformly over the year. The cost of Inventories is determined on a FIFO basis.

6. Because of the nature of Royce's business, a majority of the 2003 Selling And Administrative Expenses were incurred in the second half of the year. Specifically, it is estimated that two-thirds of these expenses were in the second half of 2003 with only one-third being incurred in the first half of the year.

7. The 2003 dividends were declared on October 1, 2003 and paid on December 31, 2003.

8. Selected spot rates for the U.K. Pound are as follows:

December 31, 1998	£1 = $2.20
December 31, 1999	£1 = $2.18
January 1, 2002	£1 = $2.15
October 1, 2002	£1 = $2.11
December 31, 2002	£1 = $2.08
July 1, 2003	£1 = $2.04
October 1, 2003	£1 = $2.02
December 31, 2003	£1 = $2.00

During 2003, the exchange rate moved uniformly downward throughout the year.

Required: To assist in the preparation of Beaver Inc.'s consolidated financial statements, prepare Royce Ltd.'s translated Balance Sheets as at December 31, 2002 and December 31, 2003, as well as its translated Statement Of Income And Changes In Retained Earnings for the year ending December 31, 2003 assuming:

A. Beaver Inc. has classified Royce Ltd. as an integrated foreign operation.

B. Beaver Inc. has classified Royce Ltd. as a self sustaining foreign operation. To assist in the preparation of these statements, you have been provided with the information that the correct December 31, 2002 balance in the Cumulative Translation Adjustment account is a credit of $772,000.

Assignment Problem Ten - 5

On December 31, 2000, the Olaf Company, a Danish retail operation, was acquired by a Canadian company. On this acquisition date, the carrying values of all of the identifiable assets and liabilities of the Olaf Company equalled their fair values and the Canadian parent purchased 100 percent of the voting shares of Olaf at their book value. On December 31, 2000, the Olaf Company had the following account balances in krone (Kr, hereafter):

Retained Earnings	Kr 192,000
No Par Common Stock	Kr1,200,000
Land	Kr 600,000
Equipment	Kr 510,000
Accumulated Depreciation - Equipment	Kr 70,000
Building	Kr2,100,000
Accumulated Depreciation - Building	Kr 320,000

The adjusted Trial Balance of the Olaf Company for the year ending December 31, 2002 is as follows:

Cash	Kr 150,000
Accounts Receivable	255,000
Inventory	510,000
Building	2,100,000
Equipment	690,000
Land	600,000
Cost of Goods Sold	2,400,000
Depreciation Expense	240,000
Other Expenses	960,000
Dividends Declared	600,000
Total Debits	Kr8,505,000

Accounts Payable	Kr 450,000
Long-Term Note Payable	900,000
No Par Common Stock	1,200,000
Retained Earnings	600,000
Sales	4,500,000
Accumulated Depreciation	840,000
Allowance For Doubtful Accounts	15,000
Total Credits	Kr8,505,000

Other Information:

1. Sales and inventory Purchases occurred uniformly over the year. The Other Expenses include Kr6,000 of bad debts which were credited to the Allowance For Doubtful Accounts on December 31, 2002. Also on December 31, 2002, Kr9,000 in bad debts were written off against the Allowance For Doubtful Accounts. The remainder of the Other Expenses occurred uniformly over the year.

2. The exchange rate for the Danish krone and the Canadian dollar is as follows:

December 31, 2000	Kr1 = $0.1000
December 31, 2001	Kr1 = $0.1600
Average for the 2001 fourth quarter	Kr1 = $0.1525
December 31, 2002	Kr1 = $0.2000
Average for 2002	Kr1 = $0.1800
Average for the 2002 fourth quarter	Kr1 = $0.1950

3. The dividends were declared on January 1, 2002.

4. Year end Inventories are purchased uniformly over the last quarter of each year. On December 31, 2001 the Inventories totalled Kr750,000 and on December 31, 2002 they totalled Kr510,000.

5. On January 1, 2002, equipment was purchased for Kr180,000. It has an estimated useful life of six years with no anticipated net salvage value. The Olaf Company uses the straight line method to calculate depreciation expense.

6. The December 31, 2002 Accumulated Depreciation balance is allocated Kr240,000 to the Equipment and Kr600,000 to the Building.

7. The Long-Term Note Payable was issued on January 1, 2001 and is due on January 1, 2007.

8. The Olaf Company had current monetary assets of Kr230,000 and current monetary liabilities of Kr890,000 as at December 31, 2001.

Required: The Olaf Company is classified as an integrated foreign operation by its Canadian parent. Its financial statements are translated to be included in the consolidated financial statements of the Canadian parent. Prepare the following in accordance with the recommendations of the *CICA Handbook*:

A. The translated Income Statement of the Olaf Company for the year ending December 31, 2002.

B. The translated Balance Sheet of the Olaf Company as at December 31, 2002.

C. An independent calculation of the foreign exchange gain or loss.

Assignment Problem Ten - 6

The Statement of Income and Change in Retained Earnings and the comparative Balance Sheets for the year ending March 31, 2003, of the Bulgar Company, a Bulgarian company, in Bulgarian lev (L, hereafter) are as follows:

Bulgar Company
Statement Of Income And Change In Retained Earnings
For The Year Ending March 31, 2003

Sales	L67,263,750
Total Revenues	L67,263,750
Cost of Goods Sold	L45,000,000
Depreciation Expense	2,700,000
Other Expenses	13,725,500
Taxes	1,650,000
Total Expenses	L63,075,500
Net Income	L 4,188,250
Dividends On Common Stock	1,500,000
Increase in Retained Earnings	L 2,688,250

Bulgar Company
Balance Sheets As At March 31

	2003	2002
Cash And Current Receivables	L 4,938,250	L 2,900,000
Inventories	3,450,000	3,750,000
Plant And Equipment	27,000,000	27,000,000
Accumulated Depreciation	(7,200,000)	(4,500,000)
Land	7,500,000	4,500,000
Total Assets	L35,688,250	L33,650,000
Current Liabilities	L 1,150,000	L 1,800,000
Long-Term Liabilities	9,000,000	9,000,000
No Par Common Stock	22,500,000	22,500,000
Retained Earnings	3,038,250	350,000
Total Equities	L 35,688,250	L33,650,000

Other Information:

1. On April 1, 2000, the date of incorporation of the Bulgar Company, No Par Common Stock was issued for L22.5 million. The proceeds were used to purchase Plant And Equipment for L18,000,000 and Land for L4,500,000 on the same day. The Plant and Equipment had an estimated service life of ten years with no anticipated salvage value. The Bulgar Company uses the straight line method to calculate depreciation expense.

2. On April 1, 2001, additional Plant and Equipment was purchased with the proceeds from a L9 million issue of bonds maturing on April 1, 2011. These additions also have a ten year estimated service life with no anticipated salvage value.

3. The March 31, 2002 Inventories were acquired on January 1, 2002. The Inventories in the March 31, 2003 Balance Sheet were acquired on January 1, 2003. The Bulgar

Company uses the first-in, first-out inventory flow assumption.

4. Sales, Purchases and Other Expenses occurred evenly throughout the year. The taxes were paid quarterly in equal installments.

5. On October 1, 2002, Land was purchased for cash of L3 million.

6. The dividends on common stock were declared on January 1, 2003 updated and paid on February 1, 2003.

7. The exchange rate movements occurred evenly throughout the year. The average exchange rate for the year ending March 31, 2003 was L1 = $.84. Other foreign exchange rate data for the lev and the Canadian dollar was as follows:

April 1, 2000	L1 = $.75
April 1, 2001	L1 = $.78
January 1, 2002	L1 = $.78
March 31, 2002	L1 = $.82
July 1, 2002	L1 = $.85
October 1, 2002	L1 = $.84
January 1, 2003	L1 = $.83
March 31, 2003	L1 = $.85

Required: Prepare, in Canadian dollars, a Statement of Income and Change in Retained Earnings for the year ending March 31, 2003 and comparative Balance Sheets as at March 31, 2002 and March 31, 2003 assuming that under the definitions contained in Section 1650 of the *CICA Handbook*, the Bulgar Company is classified:

A. As an integrated foreign operation.

B. As a self-sustaining foreign operation. Assume that prior to the year ending March 31, 2002 the Bulgar Company was classified and accounted for as an integrated foreign operation.

Assignment Problem Ten - 7

Canco is a Canadian corporation that specializes in the selling of men's and women's pants. In an attempt to diversify its product line, it acquired 80 percent of the outstanding voting shares of the Forco Company on December 31, 2002 for $10 million in cash. Forco is a Hong Kong based company that is famous for the extensive line of sweaters that it sells. Because of the extensive use of common distribution channels that will be possible after this business combination, Forco is classified as an integrated foreign operation.

The comparative Balance Sheets of the two Companies as at December 31, 2002 and December 31, 2003 and the Income Statements of the two Companies for the year ending December 31, 2003 are as follows:

Balance Sheets
As At December 31, 2002

	Canco (Canadian$)	Forco (Hong Kong$)
Cash	1,000,000	8,000,000
Accounts Receivable	1,000,000	10,000,000
Inventories	3,000,000	7,000,000
Investment In Forco (Cost)	10,000,000	-0-
Plant And Equipment (Net)	5,000,000	6,000,000
Land	-0-	2,000,000
Total Assets	20,000,000	33,000,000
Current Liabilities	1,000,000	3,000,000
Long-Term Liabilities	5,000,000	5,000,000
No Par Common Stock	5,000,000	15,000,000
Retained Earnings	9,000,000	10,000,000
Total Equities	20,000,000	33,000,000

Balance Sheets
As At December 31, 2003

	Canco (Canadian$)	Forco (Hong Kong$)
Cash	2,000,000	10,000,000
Accounts Receivable	3,100,000	11,200,000
Inventories	4,000,000	9,000,000
Investment In Forco (Cost)	10,000,000	-0-
Plant And Equipment (Net)	4,400,000	4,300,000
Land	-0-	3,000,000
Total Assets	23,500,000	37,500,000
Current Liabilities	1,500,000	3,500,000
Long-Term Liabilities	5,000,000	5,000,000
No Par Common Stock	5,000,000	15,000,000
Retained Earnings	12,000,000	14,000,000
Total Equities	23,500,000	37,500,000

Canco And Forco Companies
Income Statements
For The Year Ending December 31, 2003

	Canco (Canadian$)	Forco (Hong Kong$)
Sales	35,000,000	40,000,000
Cost Of Goods Sold	28,000,000	32,000,000
Depreciation Expense	1,000,000	500,000
Selling And Administrative Expenses	1,600,000	1,500,000
Other Expenses and Losses	600,000	1,000,000
Tax Expense	800,000	1,000,000
Total Expenses	32,000,000	36,000,000
Net Income	3,000,000	4,000,000

Other Information:

1. Assume that selected exchange rates between the Hong Kong dollar (HK$) and the Canadian dollar (C$) are as follows:

January 1, 1997	HK$1 = C$.210
March 1, 1997	HK$1 = C$.220
July 1, 2002	HK$1 = C$.230
December 31, 2002	HK$1 = C$.240
Average For 2002	HK$1 = C$.230
May 1, 2003	HK$1 = C$.250
July 1, 2003	HK$1 = C$.255
September 1, 2003	HK$1 = C$.260
December 31, 2003	HK$1 = C$.270
Average For 2003	HK$1 = C$.255

   The exchange rate changed uniformly throughout the period under consideration.

2. At the time Canco acquired its interest in Forco, all of the identifiable assets and liabilities of Forco had carrying values that were equal to their fair values except for Equipment which had a fair value that was HK$1,500,000 greater than its carrying value. The remaining useful life of this Equipment on December 31, 2002 was twelve years. Forco's Plant And Equipment was acquired on March 1, 1997. Both Companies use straight line calculations for all depreciation and amortization charges.

3. During 2003 there was no impairment of the goodwill arising from the purchase of the Forco Company shares.

4. Selling And Administration Expenses occurred uniformly over the second half of 2003. Sales, Purchases, Other Expenses, and Tax Expense took place evenly throughout the year.

5. The December 31, 2002 Inventories of Forco were purchased on July 1, 2002. The December 31, 2003 Inventories of Forco were purchased on September 1, 2003.

6. The Long-Term Liabilities of the Forco Company were issued on January 1, 1997 and mature on January 1, 2007. Forco's No Par Common Stock was also issued on January 1, 1997.

7. Neither of the two companies declared or paid dividends during 2003.

8. Forco's Land consists of two parcels. One was acquired on July 1, 2002 for HK$2,000,000 and the second was purchased for HK$1,000,000 on September 1, 2003.

9. On May 1, 2003 Canco purchases Equipment from Forco at a price of $250,000. The Equipment has a carrying value of HK$1,200,000 on the books of Forco and a remaining useful life at the time of the sale of four years. This is not the Equipment on which there was a fair value change at the time Canco acquired Forco.

10. On May 1, 2003, Forco sold HK$5,000,000 in merchandise to Canco. Of this sale, Canco had HK$2,000,000 remaining in the December 31, 2003 Inventories. Sales are priced to provide a gross profit of 20 percent on the sales price. Both Companies account for Inventories on a First In, First Out basis.

Required: Prepare translated Balance Sheets as at December 31, 2002 and December 31, 2003, and a translated 2003 Income Statement for the Forco Company. Using these translated financial statements, prepare consolidated Balance Sheets as at December 31, 2002 and December 31, 2003, and a consolidated Income Statement for the year ending December 31, 2003, for the Canco Company and its subsidiary, the Forco Company. Ignore the effect of intercompany transactions on the consolidated Tax Expense.

Chapter 11

Accounting For Income Taxes: Basic Issues and Procedures

Introduction

Basic Issues

11-1.   This Chapter and Chapter 12 deal with one of the most complex and controversial areas in financial reporting — the concepts and procedures involved in accounting for income taxes. In general terms, this subject matter can be divided into two broad areas:

Interperiod Tax Allocation   As will be discussed in this Chapter, there are significant differences between the assets, liabilities, expenses and revenues that will be included in an enterprise's financial statements, and the corresponding figures that will be included in its tax records. Given this situation, Canadian accounting standards require recognition of some parts of taxes payable in periods other than those in which they fall due under the rules established by the CCRA (Canada Customs and Revenue Agency). This process is referred to as interperiod tax allocation. Under the superseded Section 3470, this process focused on timing differences and resulted in the recognition of deferred tax debit and credit balances. In contrast, under Section 3465, this process focuses on temporary differences in the Balance Sheet and results in the recognition of Future Income Tax Assets and Future Income Tax Liabilities (FITAL). It is this area of accounting for income taxes that has generated the most controversy.

Intraperiod Tax Allocation (a.k.a., Intrastatement Tax Allocation)   Once the amount of income taxes to be included in the financial statements has been determined, the question of where it should be disclosed within the statements remains. This is the subject matter of intraperiod tax allocation (a.k.a., intrastatement allocation). Recommendations here include a requirement to disclose the income taxes related to extraordinary items with those items, the requirement to disclose income taxes related to capital transactions in the statement of shareholders' equity, as well as a number of other such Recommendations. Little controversy is associated with these procedures.

11-2.   Coverage of both of these areas will be found in this Chapter.

Recent Developments

11-3.   For many years, interperiod tax allocation procedures were based on the Recommendations of Section 3470 of the *CICA Handbook*.   These Recommendations required interperiod allocation which reflected timing differences between the accounting income reported in the Income Statement of the enterprise, and the corresponding figures that were reported in its tax return. Timing differences were defined in terms of revenues and expenses that would have the same total over the life of the enterprise, but that were being charged or credited to income in different periods for tax and accounting purposes. For example, a capital asset with a cost of $100,000 will result in both tax and accounting deductions of this amount.   However, the amounts deducted in particular time periods for Depreciation Expense will usually be different from the amounts deducted in that period for Capital Cost Allowance (CCA). The resulting Balance Sheet amounts were referred to as Deferred Income Taxes and, as they reflected a deferred charge to income, they were not adjusted for changing tax rates. This approach was referred to as the deferred charge approach to interperiod tax allocation.

11-4.   Until the late 1980s, this approach was consistent with the procedures used for dealing with income taxes under the accounting standards of most of Canada's trading partners.   However, this deferred charge approach has been gradually discredited, with most other countries opting for the alternative Future Income Tax Asset And Liability (FITAL) approach to interperiod tax allocation. This latter approach was adopted in 1992 in the U. S. when the FASB issued Statement Of Financial Accounting Standards No. 109, *Accounting For Income Taxes*. It is also the approach used in International Accounting Standard No. 12, "Income Taxes" which was revised to reflect this approach in 1996. This left Canada with an accounting standard on accounting for taxes that was not only out of line with those of its major trading partner, but also with most of the rest of the world.

11-5.   This was not a situation that could be allowed to continue. Such a major difference between Canadian and International GAAP can only survive when there is a sound conceptual reason for the Canadian position. This is clearly not the case with the deferred charge approach to interperiod tax allocation and, as a consequence, the Accounting Standards Board issued an Exposure Draft for a revised Section 3470 of the *CICA Handbook* in March, 1996. The proposals of this Exposure Draft, most importantly the adoption of the FITAL approach for dealing with temporary differences, were incorporated into a new Section 3465 which was added to the *CICA Handbook* in December, 1997.

11-6.   Section 3465 establishes standards for the recognition, measurement, presentation and disclosure of income and refundable taxes in an enterprise's financial statements. Exceptions to some of the Recommendations are made for certain rate regulated enterprises. In addition, special considerations related to the accounting for investment tax credits are dealt with in "Investment Tax Credits", Section 3805. While the Section consistently refers to "enterprises", it is clear that its primary applicability is to corporations.

11-7.   As an indication of just how controversial the Section 3465 Recommendations are, the effective date of this Section is not until fiscal years beginning on or after January 1, 2000 for public enterprises. A further deferral until January 1, 2002 for non-public enterprises.

11-8.   This deferral for non-public enterprises was effectively extended indefinitely by the introduction of Section 1300, "Differential Reporting". This new *Handbook* Section exempts qualifying "non-publicly accountable enterprises" from a number of reporting requirements, the most important of which are probably the Recommendations related to interperiod tax allocation. In effect, qualifying enterprises can ignore tax allocation procedures and report the income taxes on a taxes payable basis. If you would like more information on this important new *CICA Handbook* Section, see Chapter 3 of our *Guide To Canadian Financial Reporting*. This Guide is available on the CD-ROM which accompanies this text.

Approach To The Subject

11-9.   In the first part of this Chapter, we will focus on basic concepts and procedures involved in the implementation of interperiod and intraperiod tax allocation. This will provide you with a thorough understanding of these subjects, including their applicability to loss carry overs and refundable taxes. Subsequent to this coverage of basic concepts and procedures, we will turn to some of the more detailed Recommendations included in Section 3465. Section 3465 also provides fairly detailed guidance in areas such as income tax considerations related to business combination transactions. The income tax issues associated with business combinations are dealt with in Chapter 12.

11-10.   We will begin our coverage of interperiod tax allocation with a discussion of alternative approaches to dealing with differences between accounting and tax information. The basic alternatives are the taxes payable approach (available to enterprises that qualify for differential reporting), the deferred charge approach (used in superseded Section 3470), and the asset/liability approach (required by Section 3465). A simple example will be used to illustrate these alternatives and their relative merits will be evaluated.

Differences Between Accounting/Tax Information: Alternative Approaches

GAAP Vs. Tax

11-11.   Most publicly traded corporations must prepare financial statements in accordance with the generally accepted accounting principles (GAAP) that are presented in the *CICA Handbook*. In addition, other organizations that have a need for audited financial statements must also comply with these principles. This means that the great majority of larger Canadian corporations will produce GAAP based financial statements.

11-12.   With respect to the objective of these financial statements, the *CICA Handbook* notes the following:

> **Paragraph 1000.15**   The objective of financial statements is to communicate information that is useful to investors, members, contributors, creditors and other users ("users") in making their resource allocation decisions and/or assessing management stewardship. Consequently, financial statements provide information about:
>
> (a) an entity's economic resources, obligations and equity/net assets;
> (b) changes in an entity's economic resources, obligations and equity/net assets; and
> (c) the economic performance of the entity.

11-13.   These same corporations will also have to prepare a corporate income tax return and, in the preparation of this tax return, they will be required to prepare a Schedule 1 which calculates Net Income For Tax Purposes. This Net Income For Tax Purposes figure provides the basis for Taxable Income. In preparing these tax figures, the corporation's objective is very different from that cited in Paragraph 1000.15 of the *CICA Handbook*. Stated simply, the objective that is usually served in determining Net Income For Tax Purposes and Taxable Income is to minimize the payment of federal and provincial income taxes.

11-14.   Given these alternative objectives, it is not surprising that there are significant differences between Accounting Net Income and Taxable Income. Some of the more common of these differences can be described as follows:

- Accounting Depreciation Expense is typically less than the amount deducted for CCA in the determination of Net Income For Tax Purposes. In terms of the frequency of occurrence, as well as amounts involved, this is easily the most important of the differences between accounting income before taxes and Net Income For Tax Purposes.

- Accounting gains and losses on the disposal of capital assets are determined by deducting the net book value of individual assets from the resulting proceeds of disposition. For tax purposes, such disposals may result in capital gains, recapture of CCA, or terminal losses,

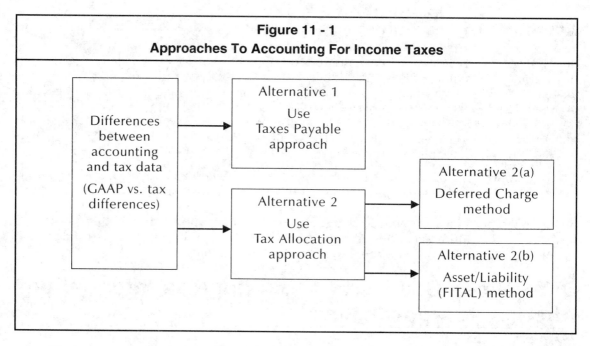

Figure 11 - 1
Approaches To Accounting For Income Taxes

with the amounts determined by deducting the lesser of the proceeds of disposition and the capital cost of the individual assets from the UCC of the asset's class.

- Some accounting expenses cannot be deducted or may be only partially deducted for tax purposes. Examples of this would include certain automobile costs, the costs of club dues and recreational facilities, and the cost of business meals and entertainment.

- Dividends from other taxable Canadian corporations are included in accounting revenues but are deducted in the determination of Taxable Income.

- Some accounting expenses which are determined on an accrual basis must be deducted for tax purposes on a cash basis. Examples of this would be warranty costs and pension costs.

- The benefits associated with tax loss carry forwards may be recognized for accounting purposes, prior to their realization for tax purposes.

11-15.   There are, of course, many other differences between Accounting Net Income and Taxable Income. However, these are among the most common and, as a consequence, they will be the most frequently used in the examples presented in the remainder of this Chapter.

Alternative Approaches Described
Classification Of GAAP Vs. Tax Differences

11-16.   The two basic alternatives used to accounting for differences between accounting Net Income and Net Income For Tax Purposes are the taxes payable approach and the tax allocation approach. Under the taxes payable approach, taxes are accounted for on the basis of the relevant tax legislation, with no attention being given to how this legislation differs from GAAP. Alternatively, tax allocation takes these differences into consideration. This can be implemented in a variety of ways of which two will be considered here. These are the deferred charge method and future income tax asset/liability (FITAL) approach.

11-17.   Figure 11-1 begins by indicating a situation where differences exist between accounting and tax data. While we have not outlined this problem in Figure 11-1 , one of the first difficulties that we will encounter in this Chapter is the fact that there are different approaches to the classification of these differences.

11-18.   Under the superseded Section 3470, classification of GAAP/tax differences was based on income differences. Interperiod tax allocation was used when there were "timing differences" between accounting income and taxable income. Timing differences were defined as situations in which a given cost or revenue is being allocated to accounting income on a different basis than it is being allocated to taxable income. It is expected that over the life of the enterprise, the total amount of the expense (deduction) or revenue (inclusion) will be the same for both tax and accounting records. However, differences arise as a result of alternative methods being used for the allocation of the relevant total to the income of particular accounting or tax years. The classic example of a timing difference situation would be the expenses (deductions) related to the cost of a capital asset. Over the life of the asset, the total depreciation expense subtracted in the determination of accounting Net Income will be equal to the total CCA deducted in calculating Net Income For Tax Purposes. However, because depreciation expense and CCA are often based on different allocation patterns, the two amounts are not likely to be equal in any given year.

11-19.   Under Section 3465, the focus of GAAP/tax differences is on the Balance Sheet. Whenever there is a difference between the tax basis of an asset or liability, and its carrying amount in the Balance Sheet, it is referred to as a "temporary difference". Consider the capital asset situation referred to in the preceding paragraph. At the Balance Sheet date, a temporary difference would exist if there was a difference between the carrying value of the asset in the accounting records (cost, less accumulated depreciation) and the undepreciated capital cost balance (cost, less accumulated CCA).

11-20.   In many situations, the two concepts are related in an obvious manner. Considering again the capital asset situation, the temporary difference at any Balance Sheet date would simply be the sum of all previous timing differences recorded in periods prior to the Balance Sheet date. However, despite the existence of such relationships, the two concepts are different. Section 3470's timing differences are related to income figures, while Section 3465's temporary differences are related to Balance Sheet items. In practical terms, the two approaches can produce different results (e.g., fair value changes recorded in a business combination transaction create a temporary difference, but do not generally produce timing differences). However, a more complete discussion of the determination of temporary differences will be deferred until a later point in this Chapter.

Alternative 1: Taxes Payable Method
11-21.   Whether GAAP/tax differences are classified as timing differences under Section 3470 or as temporary differences under Section 3465, the next issue becomes whether or not to use interperiod allocation procedures. When tax allocation is not used, all differences between GAAP and tax figures are simply ignored. This approach is referred to as the taxes payable method.

11-22.   Under this taxes payable approach, the Tax Expense or Tax Benefit to be included in the current period's Income Statement is simply the amount of taxes that are payable for the current taxation year. This statement assumes the accounting and taxation years are the same. If this is not the case, the taxes payable amount will have to be pro rated to fit the accounting year. However, the Income Statement item will still be based exclusively on the amount of taxes that are legally required to be paid.

11-23.   With the Tax Expense or Tax Benefit based on tax return figures, the only tax related item that will be disclosed in the Balance Sheet will be the actual amount of taxes that are payable or receivable as a result of filing the current year's tax return. There will be no deferred tax debits or credits, and no Future Income Tax Assets or Future Income Tax Liabilities.

Alternative 2(a): Deferred Charge Approach
11-24.   When the deferred charge approach is used, the Tax Expense or Tax Benefit to be disclosed in the current period's Income Statement includes the amount of taxes that are currently payable. However, in order to be consistent with the other revenues and expenses included in the accounting income figure, this amount is increased (when accounting income is larger than taxable income because of timing differences) or decreased (when accounting

income is less than taxable income because of timing differences) by an amount equal to the current tax rate multiplied by the current period's timing differences. This amount would be referred to as the deferred portion of the current Tax Expense (Benefit).

11-25.   In the Balance Sheet, the deferrals would be accumulated in an account normally referred to as Deferred Income Taxes. A credit balance would reflect a cumulative excess of accounting income over taxable income, while a debit balance would reflect a cumulative excess of taxable income over accounting income. The normal balance would be a credit, reflecting the efforts of the enterprise to minimize taxes.

11-26.   As these Balance Sheet items arise as the result of deferring a charge or credit to income, they are viewed as "deferred charges", not as assets and liabilities. As a result, they are not adjusted for changes in the applicable tax rates. This means that deferred income tax balances often reflect a wide variety of tax rates.

11-27.   We have mentioned this approach as, until the end of 2001, it was still GAAP in Canada for non-public companies (1999 was the last year of applicability for public companies). However, it is no longer used in Canada or in any other industrialized country. Given this we will not make any further references to the deferred charge approach.

Alternative 2(b): Future Income Tax Asset/Liability (FITAL) Method

11-28.   Under this alternative, at each Balance Sheet date, the enterprise determines the amount of temporary differences between the tax basis of its assets and liabilities, and their respective carrying values in the accounting records. If the tax basis of its assets is less than their carrying value (or the tax basis of its liabilities exceeds their carrying value), a Future Income Tax Liability is recorded. Similarly, if the tax basis of its assets is more than their carrying value (or the tax basis of its liabilities is less than their carrying value), a Future Income Tax Asset results. The amounts to be recorded would be the amount of the temporary difference, multiplied by the tax rate which is expected to be applicable when the asset is realized or the liability settled. In most cases, the tax rate used would be the current rate. However, if different rates have been enacted for the relevant future periods, these future rates would be used.

11-29.   As the Balance Sheet items which arise under this method are viewed as assets and liabilities, rather than as deferred charges or credits to income, it follows that they should be adjusted as tax rates change. The guiding valuation principle is that, at each Balance Sheet date, the amount reported as Future Income Tax Assets or Future Income Tax Liabilities should reflect the tax rates that will be applicable when they are realized or settled. This means that they must be adjusted whenever current rates change or applicable future rates are expected to change.

11-30.   Unlike the deferred charge method where the Balance Sheet items arise from procedures applied in the Income Statement, under the asset/liability method, the Income Statement inclusion follows from the procedures that have been applied in the Balance Sheet. As was the case with the deferred charge method, the Tax Expense (Benefit) begins with the amount of taxes that are currently payable (receivable). We will then add to (subtract from) this amount the difference between the Future Income Tax Liability (Asset) at the end of the period and the Future Income Tax Liability (Asset) at the beginning of the period. This adjustment will reflect both the change in the temporary differences that took place during the year, as well as any changes in tax rates that have been applied to the balance at the beginning of the year.

Basic Example
Data
11-31.   We will use a very simple example to illustrate the taxes payable and FITAL approaches to accounting for income taxes. As the taxes payable approach can be used by enterprises that qualify for differential reporting, both this method, as well as the generally required FITAL approach, can be encountered in practice. The data that will be used to illustrate these approaches is as follows:

Example   Interpro Inc. is established on January 1, 2002 through the investment of $100,000 by its shareholders. The entire $100,000 is used to acquire a capital asset with an estimated useful life of two years. It will be written off on a straight line basis over that period. For income tax purposes, the entire cost of the asset can be deducted in the year of acquisition. The Company has a December 31 year end.

During the year ending December 31, 2002, the asset produces revenues of $110,000. There are no other revenues and the only expense other than income taxes is for depreciation of the asset. The results for the year ending December 31, 2003 are identical to those for 2002. No dividends are paid in either year.

The Company is subject to tax rates of 45 percent in 2002 and 50 percent in 2003. At the end of 2002, the Company knew that its 2003 tax rate would be 50 percent.

Income Statements for the two years 2002 and 2003, and Balance Sheets for the years ending December 31, 2002 and December 31, 2003, before tax factors are taken into consideration, are as follows:

Income Statements	Year 2002	Year 2003
Revenues	$110,000	$110,000
Depreciation Expense	(50,000)	(50,000)
Pre Tax Income	$ 60,000	$ 60,000

Balance Sheets As At December 31	2002	2003
Cash (Pre Tax)	$110,000	$220,000
Capital Asset (Net)	50,000	Nil
Total Assets	$160,000	$220,000
Common Stock	$100,000	$100,000
Retained Earnings (Pre Tax)	60,000	120,000
Total Equities	$160,000	$220,000

Taxes Payable Method Example

11-32.   If the taxes payable method is used, the Tax Expense will be based on the current taxes payable. For 2002 the amount would be $4,500 [($110,000 - $100,000)(45%)]. For 2003 the figure would be $55,000 [($110,000 - Nil)(50%)]. If we assume that these amounts are paid in cash prior to the year end, the resulting financial statements under this method would be as follows:

Income Statements	Year 2002	Year 2003
Revenues	$110,000	$110,000
Depreciation Expense	(50,000)	(50,000)
Tax Expense	(4,500)	(55,000)
Net Income	$ 55,500	$ 5,000

Balance Sheets As At December 31	2002	2003
Cash	$105,500	$160,500
Capital Asset (Net)	50,000	Nil
Total Assets	$155,500	$160,500
Common Stock	$100,000	$100,000
Retained Earnings	55,500	60,500
Total Equities	$155,500	$160,500

Evaluation Of Taxes Payable Method

11-33.   Despite the fact that the taxes payable method was not acceptable under GAAP prior to 2002, there were a number of arguments in its favour presented in the now superseded Paragraph 3470.09 of the *CICA Handbook*. They include the following:

(a) since it is taxable income and not accounting income that attracts taxation, the taxes actually payable for the period represent the appropriate cost to be allocated to that period;

(b) it is unnecessary to provide for income taxes for which there is no legal liability at the end of the financial period;

(c) while timing differences in one period may give rise to the reverse situation in some future period, the date of the reversal may be indefinitely postponed, and accordingly there is no necessity to provide for an amount which may never become payable;

(d) even where the taxes may become payable in some future period, it is usually difficult to estimate the future tax effects with any degree of accuracy.

11-34.   As noted previously, the new Section 1300, Differential Reporting, permits the use of the taxes payable method for qualifying non-publicly accountable entities.

11-35.   Prior to the issuance of Section 1300, the taxes payable method had always been rejected in favour of some form of tax allocation. Under the now superseded Section 3470 and its focus on timing differences related to accounting vs. taxable income, the major argument against the taxes payable method was that it was not consistent with the matching principle. That is, under the taxes payable method, the Tax Expense is not based on the revenues and other expenses that are included in accounting Net Income. This can clearly be seen in our example. In 2002, the Tax Expense is only $4,500, despite Pre Tax Income of $60,000. In a similar fashion, the 2003 Tax Expense is $55,000 on a Pre Tax Income of the same amount.

11-36.   Under Section 3465, the argument against the taxes payable method shifts to Balance Sheet items. The concern here is that the capital asset that is recorded at a net book value of $50,000 in the December 31, 2002 Balance Sheet has a tax basis of nil. This means that if the carrying value is realized there will be a tax obligation which is not reflected in that Balance Sheet.

11-37.   Other arguments against the taxes payable method include:

• the fact that, because the taxes payable calculation involves many discretionary items (e.g., amount of CCA deducted), use of this figure in financial statements could be subject to manipulation; and

• the fact that, because taxes payable are not based on the accounting figures included in the Income Statement, the resulting after tax income figures will be more volatile.

Asset/Liability (FITAL) Method Example

11-38.   This approach recognizes Future Income Tax Assets and Liabilities on the basis of temporary differences on assets and liabilities in the Balance Sheet. Such temporary differences are based on differences between the tax basis and the carrying values of assets and liabilities included in the Balance Sheet. In this example, the temporary differences on the capital asset, as well as the related Future Income Tax Liability, would be calculated as follows:

December 31	2002	2003
Carrying Value Of Capital Assets	$50,000	Nil
Tax Basis	Nil	Nil
Temporary Difference	$50,000	Nil
Tax Rate*	50%	50%
Future Income Tax Liability	$25,000	Nil

*As the 2003 rate is known at the end of 2002, the Future Income Tax Liability would be adjusted to reflect that rate in the December 31, 2002 Balance Sheet.

11-39.   The Tax Expense for the two years would include the amount of taxes currently payable (as per the taxes payable method), adjusted for changes in the Future Income Tax Liability. Given this, the resulting financial statements for the two years are as follows:

Income Statements	Year 2002	Year 2003
Revenues	$110,000	$110,000
Depreciation Expense	(50,000)	(50,000)
Pre Tax Income	$ 60,000	$ 60,000
Tax Expense:		
Current	(4,500)	(55,000)
Future	(25,000)	25,000
Net Income	$ 30,500	$ 30,000

Balance Sheets As At December 31	2002	2003
Cash	$105,500	$160,500
Capital Asset (Net)	50,000	Nil
Total Assets	$155,500	$160,500
Future Income Tax Liability	$ 25,000	Nil
Common Stock	100,000	$100,000
Retained Earnings	30,500	60,500
Total Equities	$155,500	$160,500

11-40.   You should note that this method produces $60,500 in cumulative income over the two year period, the same amount as we recorded under the taxes payable approach. However, this method produces a fairly even pattern over the two years, with $30,500 in 2002 and $30,000 in 2003. In contrast, the taxes payable alternative records $55,500 of income in 2002, followed by only $5,000 in 2003.

Evaluation Of FITAL Method
11-41.   There is, of course, widespread support for this asset/liability method of tax allocation. This is evidenced by the fact that standard setting bodies throughout the world have adopted this approach. The basic arguments which support this approach are found in the *CICA Handbook* as follows:

Paragraph 3465.02   A fundamental principle in the preparation of financial statements is that an asset will be realized for at least its carrying amount in the form of future economic benefits. In some cases, realization of the carrying amount from sale or use of the asset will give rise to an increase or reduction in income taxes payable in the period of realization or later. For example, an asset with a carrying amount of $1,000 may have a tax basis of $600, such that realization of the carrying amount of $1,000 will give rise to income of $400 that is subject to tax, and an increase in income taxes otherwise payable.

Paragraph 3465.03   Similarly, a fundamental principle in the preparation of financial statements is that a liability will be settled for its carrying amount through the future transfer or use of assets, provision of services or other yielding of economic benefits. In some cases, settlement of the liability for the carrying amount will give rise to a decrease or an increase in income taxes payable in the year of settlement or later. For example, an accrued pension liability of $1,000 might be deductible for tax purposes only when an amount is actually paid. Payment of the accrued amount will give rise to a deduction of

$1,000 in computing income that is subject to tax, and a reduction in income taxes otherwise payable.

Paragraph 3465.04   The resultant future tax outflows or inflows from the realization of assets and settlement of liabilities at their carrying amounts meet the conceptual definitions of assets and liabilities. Therefore, a future income tax asset or future income tax liability would be recognized for the tax effects that will arise if an asset is realized or a liability is settled for its carrying amount.

11-42.   Without elaborating on this point, we are not comfortable with this reasoning. As the normal result of applying these procedures will be large Future Income Tax Liabilities, the question of whether these balances really are liabilities is relevant. Liabilities are defined in the *CICA Handbook* as follows:

Paragraph 1000.32   Liabilities are obligations of an entity arising from past transactions or events, the settlement of which may result in the transfer or use of assets, provision of services or other yielding of economic benefits in the future.

Paragraph 1000.33   Liabilities have three essential characteristics:

(a) they embody a duty or responsibility to others that entails settlement by future transfer or use of assets, provision of services or other yielding of economic benefits, at a specified or determinable date, on occurrence of a specified event, or on demand;
(b) the duty or responsibility obligates the entity leaving it little or no discretion to avoid it; and
(c) the transaction or event obligating the entity has already occurred.

Paragraph 1000.34   Liabilities do not have to be legally enforceable provided that they otherwise meet the definition of liabilities; they can be based on equitable or constructive obligations. An equitable obligation is a duty based on ethical or moral considerations. A constructive obligation is one that can be inferred from the facts in a particular situation as opposed to a contractually based obligation.

11-43.   We are of the opinion that the Future Income Tax Liabilities that are recorded under the application of Section 3465 are not consistent with this definition. We would note that, in most cases, there is no probable outflow of resources. Further, as it is the earning of taxable income that creates taxes payable, the transaction or event which might cause a Future Income Tax Liability to exist has not, in fact, taken place.

11-44.   Our view is that the taxes payable approach is the conceptually sound solution to this problem. While this view is shared by a fairly large number of analysts, it is clear that tax allocation on the basis of the asset/liability approach will continue to be required of all entities that do not qualify for differential reporting.

Exercise Eleven-1 deals with comparing the taxes payable approach to the tax allocation approach.

Exercise Eleven-1

Note   This exercise will be very difficult for students who have had no previous exposure to this material. If this is the case, it can be skipped without affecting your understanding of the remainder of the Chapter.

Marston Inc. is established on January 1, 2002 through the investment of $240,000 by its shareholders. The entire $240,000 is used to acquire a capital asset with an estimated useful life of three years. It will be written off on a straight line basis over that period. For income tax purposes, CCA will be calculated using a straight-line rate of 50 percent. The Company has a December 31 year end.

During each of the fiscal years 2002, 2003, and 2004, the asset produces revenues of $155,000. During these three years, there are no other revenues and the only expense other than income taxes is for depreciation of the asset. No dividends are paid in any of the years.

The Company is subject to tax rates of 60 percent in 2002 and 2003. This is unexpectedly reduced to 40 percent at the beginning of 2004.

This is a continuation of Exercise Eleven-1.

Income Statements for the three years 2002, 2003, and 2004, and Balance Sheets for the years ending December 31, 2002, 2003, 2004, before tax factors are taken into consideration, are as follows:

Income Statement	Year 2002	Year 2003	Year 2004
Revenues	$155,000	$155,000	$155,000
Depreciation Expense	(80,000)	(80,000)	(80,000)
Pre Tax Income	$ 75,000	$ 75,000	$ 75,000

Balance Sheet - December 31	2002	2003	2004
Cash Pre-Tax)	$155,000	$310,000	$465,000
Capital Asset (Net)	160,000	80,000	Nil
Total Assets	$315,000	$390,000	$465,000
Common Stock	$240,000	$240,000	$240,000
Retained Earnings (Pre-Tax)	75,000	150,000	225,000
Total Equities	$315,000	$390,000	$465,000

Required: Prepare the Company's Income Statements for the three years ending December 31, 2002, 2003, and 2004, as well as the Balance Sheets at December 31, 2002, 2003, and 2004, using:

A. The taxes payable approach.
B. The FITAL approach.

End Of Exercise Eleven-1

Other Ideas
Partial Allocation - A Compromise Position

11-45. To this point, we have been discussing comprehensive tax allocation. That is, the use of allocation procedures for all timing or temporary differences which arise during the period. There is also a compromise solution involving what is commonly referred to as partial allocation. Under this approach, tax allocation procedures would be applied to some, but not all, timing or temporary differences.

11-46. Several different criterion have been suggested for the implementation of this partial allocation approach. They include the likelihood that the timing difference will be reversed, the type of transaction which gives rise to the timing or temporary difference, and the one which was adopted in the United Kingdom, the time period in which reversal of the timing difference will occur. While there would be variations in which timing or temporary differences were subject to allocation procedures under these various criteria, all of the proposed criteria would eliminate tax allocation procedures for differences between depreciation and CCA.

11-47. This elimination of tax allocation procedures for differences between depreciation and CCA would serve to significantly reduce the amount of deferred taxes or Future Income Tax Assets and Liabilities included in published Income Statements and Balance Sheets. However, there does not seem to be much conceptual support for this alternative, particularly in view of the fact that allocation procedures are now going to be based on temporary differences rather than timing differences. In addition, after the long battles required to implement new standards in both Canada and the United States, it is difficult to imagine that standard setters will be eager to revisit this issue in the near future.

Net Of Tax Approach

11-48.   While most of the discussion of tax allocation procedures is now in terms of the Balance Sheet items being assets and liabilities, a less well known approach to dealing with interperiod tax allocation is sometimes referred to as the net of tax approach. Proponents of this approach argue that tax allocation balances should be treated as adjustments of the assets or liabilities to which the timing differences relate. For example, when the tax allocation balances relate to the fact that more capital cost allowance than depreciation expense was taken on certain of our limited life assets, proponents of the net of tax view would argue that the resulting tax allocation balances should be subtracted from these assets.

11-49.   The most obvious practical problem with this net of tax view is that not all temporary differences relate to specific assets and liabilities and this would prevent the net of tax approach from being a general solution to the problem. More importantly, it is not our present practice to value assets and liabilities on a net of tax basis. Until such time as net of tax valuation becomes a general practice in accounting, the use of this approach to tax allocation would not be a consistent or acceptable solution to the problem.

Future Income Tax Assets And Liabilities (FITAL)

Note On Terminology

11-50.   As we have noted, Canada has followed the lead of the U.S. in switching from the deferred charge approach to interperiod tax allocation, to what we have been calling the asset/liability approach to interperiod tax allocation. In adopting this approach, the FASB continued the use of the term Deferred Income Taxes to describe the balances resulting from its application. Continued use of this terminology is also found in International Accounting Standard No. 12, as well as in the standards issued on this subject in most other countries.

11-51. Somewhat surprisingly, the Accounting Standards Board decided to part ways with its international trading partners, adopting the terms Future Income Tax Assets and Future Income Tax Liabilities to replace the use of Deferred Income Taxes (this term is commonly used for both debit and credit balances). Because of this, the Canadian approach is commonly referred to as the "Future Income Tax Asset And Liability" approach. We will use this terminology throughout the remainder of this Chapter, usually using the acronym "FITAL".

Introduction To Basic Concepts

11-52.   A fundamental difference between the new Section 3465 and the now superseded Section 3470 is the switch from tax allocation based on timing differences to tax allocation based on temporary differences. Timing differences focused on the Income Statement and were defined in terms of amounts that would be charged or credited to Accounting Income on a different timing basis than they would be charged or credited to Taxable Income, but would total the same amount over the life of the enterprise. As we have noted several times, the classic example of such an item is the annual difference between Depreciation Expense and CCA. Over the life of the enterprise, the total amount deducted for both accounting and tax purposes would be equal to the cost of the asset, less any proceeds resulting from its disposition. However, when these amounts are included in the determination of Accounting Income, the result could be very different from when they are included in the determination of Taxable Income.

11-53.   In keeping with the FITAL approach to interperiod tax allocation, Section 3465 shifts the focus of these procedures to the Balance Sheet. Instead of applying tax allocation procedures to timing differences, the procedures are applied to temporary differences. These differences are defined as follows:

Paragraph 3465.09(c) Temporary differences are differences between the tax basis of an asset or liability and its carrying amount in the balance sheet. Temporary differences may be either:

(i) **Deductible temporary differences**, which are temporary differences that will result in deductible amounts in determining taxable income of future periods when the carrying amount of the asset or liability is recovered or settled; or

(ii) **Taxable temporary differences**, which are temporary differences that will result in taxable amounts in determining taxable income of future periods when the carrying amount of the asset or liability is recovered or settled.

11-54.   While the terms "tax basis of assets" and "tax basis of liabilities" are not included in Section 3465's list of definitions, it is essential to understand what is meant by the tax basis of assets and liabilities. As informally described elsewhere in Section 3465, these items can be defined as follows:

Tax Basis Of Assets   The tax basis of an asset is the amount that, under the rules established by taxation authorities, could be deducted in the determination of taxable income if the asset were recovered for its carrying amount.

Tax Basis Of Liabilities   The tax basis of a liability is its carrying value, less any amount that will be deductible for income tax purposes with respect of that liability in future periods. If the liability is for the future delivery of goods or services, its tax basis is its carrying value, less any amounts that will not be taxed in future periods.

11-55.   In terms of the Balance Sheet, deductible temporary differences fall into two categories:

Deductible Temporary Differences On Assets   These differences would arise when the tax basis of the asset (deductible amount) exceeds its carrying value (e.g., a term investment that has been written down to recognize a non-temporary decline in value).

Deductible Temporary Differences On Liabilities   These differences would arise when the tax basis of a liability (carrying value, less deductible amount) is less than its carrying value (e.g., estimated warranty liabilities).

11-56.   Again in terms of Balance Sheet items, taxable temporary differences would arise as follows:

Taxable Temporary Differences On Assets   These differences would arise when the tax basis of the asset (deductible amount) is less than its carrying value (e.g., a depreciable asset with a UCC that is less than its net book value).

Taxable Temporary Differences On Liabilities   While this possibility is not listed in Section 3465 (see Paragraph 3465.14), the tax basis of a liability could exceed its carrying value, resulting in a taxable temporary difference. This would occur, for example, when long-term bonds are sold at a premium over their face value. As premium amortization is not recognized for tax purposes, the tax basis would remain at the original issue price while the carrying value declines.

11-57.   Summarizing these rules from a different perspective, temporary differences on assets are taxable when the tax basis of the asset is less than its carrying value, and deductible when the tax basis of the asset exceeds its carrying value. With respect to liabilities, temporary differences are deductible when the tax basis of the liability is less than its carrying value, and taxable when the tax basis of the liability is greater than its carrying value.

11-58.   Future Income Tax Assets and Liabilities generally result from the presence of deductible and taxable temporary differences. As a consequence, Section 3465 defines such assets and liabilities in terms of temporary differences:

Paragraph 3465.09(d)   Future income tax assets are the amounts of income tax benefits arising in respect of:

(i)   deductible temporary differences;

(ii)   the carryforward of unused tax losses; and

(iii)   the carryforward of unused income tax reductions, except for investment tax credits.

Paragraph 3465.09(e)   Future income tax liabilities are the amounts of income taxes arising from taxable temporary differences.

11-59.   As is clear from the preceding, the determination of Future Income Tax Assets and Liabilities is a fairly complex process, requiring a full understanding of the tax basis of assets and liabilities, as well as the meaning of deductible temporary differences and taxable temporary differences.   Given this complexity, the remainder of this section will provide a full discussion of the concepts involved in determining Future Income Tax Assets and Future Income Tax Liabilities.

Tax Basis Of Assets And Liabilities
Basic Problem
11-60.   One of the major difficulties with Section 3465 is the fact that the term "tax basis" is not clearly defined, either in the Section or in tax legislation.   Section 248 of the *Income Tax Act* does define "cost amount" for assets as being equal to original cost with respect to non-depreciable capital property and equal to UCC for depreciable property.   There is no similar legislative basis for measuring liabilities.

11-61.   In Section 3465, the tax basis of an asset is informally described (i.e., not specifically defined) as the amount that could be deducted in the determination of taxable income if the asset were recovered for an amount equal to its carrying value.   While this is often consistent with the "cost amount" of assets for tax purposes, there are differences.   A fairly general problem here involves situations where there are capital gains or losses.   Consider a long-term investment with a cost of $100,000, but carried at an equity value of $140,000.   Under the *Income Tax Act*, the cost amount of this asset is $100,000.   However, this is not the amount that could be deducted if the asset were recovered at its $140,000 carrying value.   The amount that could be deducted would be the cost amount of $100,000, plus the non-taxable one-half of the $40,000 capital gain that would arise on the sale of the investment.   This gives a tax basis of $120,000.

11-62.   There are other problems with assets such as goodwill and high cost passenger vehicles.   Additional problems also arise with respect to liabilities (e.g., redeemable preferred stock that has been classified as a liability).   However, the fundamental problem is that Section 3465's tax basis is not a defined concept.   Unlike the situation under Section 3470 where differences between accounting and tax income components were clearly defined, lack of clarity with respect to the tax basis of assets and liabilities makes applying Section 3465 a more difficult process.   These difficulties will be discussed and illustrated as we proceed through this material.

Assets
11-63.   As noted, Section 3465 defines the tax basis of an asset is the amount that could be deducted in the determination of taxable income if the asset were recovered for an amount equal to its carrying value.   Applying this concept to the usual types of items found on the asset side of the Balance Sheet:

Cash And Cash Equivalents   These assets would invariably have a tax basis equal to their carrying value.

Temporary Investments   The tax basis of Temporary Investments would be their cost.   This could be different than their carrying value if the investments were carried at a value other than cost in the accounting records.   As the difference would be a potential capital gain or loss, the tax basis of these assets would be their cost, plus or minus the non-taxable portion of the capital gain or loss.

Accounts Receivable   In the accounting records, Accounts Receivable are carried at their face value, less an allowance for bad debts.   As any tax reserve for bad debts is normally equal to the accounting estimate for bad debts, the tax basis of Accounts Receivable will normally be equal to their carrying value.   An exception could occur if accounting revenues were on an accrual basis, with a reserve for unpaid amounts deducted for tax purposes [(ITA 20(1)(n)]. In this situation, the tax basis would be less than the carrying value by the amount of the reserve.

Inventories In general, inventory valuation methods and inventory cost determination methods are the same for both accounting and tax purposes. This means that the tax basis of inventories would usually be equal to their carrying value. An exception would occur if the enterprise used the LIFO cost determination method for accounting purposes. This method cannot be used for tax purposes and, as a consequence, its use would result in a tax basis that is different than the carrying value for Inventories.

Prepayments The tax basis of prepayments would normally be equal to their carrying value.

Long-Term Investments In Debt Securities The tax basis of long-term investments in debt securities would be their cost, without amortization of any premium over or discount from maturity value. If such premium or discount is amortized in the accounting records, the tax basis of these investments would be different than their carrying value. These differences may involve capital gains or losses.

Long-Term Investments In Equity Securities The tax basis of long-term investments in equity securities is their cost. If such investments are carried in the accounting records at cost, the tax basis will equal the carrying value. If such investments are carried by the equity method, the situation becomes more complex. As the equity method cannot be used for tax purposes, a temporary difference will arise. Here again, the difference will involve a capital gain.

Land Both the tax basis and the carrying value of land will normally be its original cost.

Depreciable Tangible Assets The tax basis of depreciable assets will generally be their UCC. Their carrying value will be their net book value (cost less accumulated Depreciation Expense), a value that will normally exceed the tax basis of the assets.

Different conclusions may be applicable to certain types of depreciable tangible assets where there are special tax rules. For example, the cost of a passenger vehicle in excess of a specified amount ($30,000 for 2001 and 2002) cannot be deducted for tax purposes. Going with this restriction is the fact that, if the vehicle is sold for its carrying value, there are no tax consequences. In effect, for tax purposes, the carrying value can be deducted if the vehicle is disposed of for its carrying value. This means that the tax basis of the vehicle is its carrying value.

Intangible Capital Assets When a company incurs costs in order to develop an intangible asset internally, such costs are usually charged to expense for both tax and accounting purposes. This means that both the carrying value of any resulting asset, as well as its tax basis will be nil. An exception to this may be certain types of development costs which can be capitalized under Section 3450 of the *CICA Handbook*, "Research and Development Costs". This will result in an accounting asset with a positive carrying value. However, such development costs will usually be deducted for tax purposes, resulting in a tax basis for the asset of nil.

With respect to purchased intangible assets, if they have a limited life, their cost will be allocated to either Class 14 or Class 44 (patents). The initial carrying value and tax basis for such assets will be equal to their cost. However, as the pattern of Amortization Expense may be different than the pattern of CCA deductions, the tax basis (UCC) of the assets may be different than their carrying value in future periods.

For tax purposes, purchased intangible assets without a specified life (goodwill for example) will have 75 percent of their cost allocated to the cumulative eligible capital balance. As only 75 percent of the proceeds from the disposition of such assets will be considered for tax purposes, the tax basis of such assets includes the non-taxable 25 percent of the carrying value that could be received without tax consequences. This means that, at the time of acquisition, the tax basis and the carrying value of such assets would be equal. However, in accordance with the Recommendations of Section 3062, Goodwill and Other Intangible Assets, these assets are tested for impairment annually and not amortized. As a result, the tax basis and the carrying value would diverge as the asset is written off for tax purposes and possibly written down for impairment losses. The tax basis of intangible capital assets, at inception, would be 4/3 of the balance in the cumulative eligible capital account.

11-64.   While there are other difficulties in the determination of the tax basis of assets, the preceding analysis deals with those that will be most commonly encountered.

<table>
<tr><td>

Exercise Eleven-2 deals with the tax basis of assets.

</td><td>

Exercise Eleven-2
The following situations describe transactions and events related to particular assets. For each situation, indicate the tax basis of the asset described.

A. The enterprise has Accounts Receivable with a face value of $262,000. In the accounting records, an allowance for bad debts of $18,000 has been deducted.

B. The enterprise costs its Inventories on a LIFO basis. Using this costing method, the Inventories are recorded in the accounting records at a value of $164,000. If the enterprise had used FIFO, the value would be $7,500 higher.

C. The enterprise has Temporary Investments that cost $46,000. They are carried in the accounting records at a value of $44,500.

D. The enterprise has Land that cost $50,000 and is carried in the accounting records at this value.

E. The enterprise has Long-Term Investments that cost $210,000. They are being accounted for by the equity method and are currently carried in the accounting records at a value of $230,000.

F. The enterprise has Class 8 assets with a cost of $230,000 and a net book value of $143,000. The UCC for Class 8 is $132,000.

G. The enterprise owns a luxury passenger vehicle that cost $125,000. It currently has a net book value of $72,000. The UCC for its Class 10.1 is $14,000.

H. The enterprise acquired a Patent at a cost of $23,000. The net book value of the Patent is $18,000 and the balance in Class 44 is $11,000. There are no other assets in Class 44.

I. The enterprise has capitalized development costs of $42,000. All of these amounts have been deducted for tax purposes.

J. The enterprise has just acquired the assets of another company including Goodwill with a value of $143,000.

</td></tr>
</table>

End Of Exercise Eleven-2

Liabilities
11-65.   As we have previously noted, the tax basis of a liability is defined as its carrying value, less any amount that will be deductible for income tax purposes with respect to that liability in future periods. In similar fashion, if the liability is for the future delivery of goods or services, its tax basis is its carrying value, less any amounts that will not be taxed in future periods. While not mentioned in Section 3465, the definition should also include situations where an amount is added to the carrying value because it will be taxable when the liability is settled in a future period (e.g., settlement of bonds that were originally issued at a premium). The different applications of this concept can be described as follows:

Liabilities For Assets Acquired Or Deductible Expenses Incurred   The majority of accounting liabilities result either from the acquisition of assets or from the incurrence of costs that have been both deducted for tax purposes and charged to expense for accounting purposes.   In either case the settlement of the liability would not generate an item to be included in the determination of accounting income. Examples of this would be liabilities for salaries and liabilities related to the purchase of inventories or capital assets. When such liabilities have also created either tax assets or tax deductions, their settlement would have no tax consequences. This means that their tax basis would be equal to their carrying value and no temporary difference would arise. The previous examples related to salaries and inventories would fall into this classification.

Liabilities For Non-Deductible Expenses   Certain liabilities reflect items that can be charged to expense for accounting purposes, but that can never be deducted for tax purposes. Examples of this would be liabilities for non-deductible fines and penalties, and liabilities for club dues or recreational facilities. As with liabilities incurred for deductible expenses, no amount can be deducted for tax purposes when such liabilities are settled. Their tax basis would be equal to their carrying value and no temporary difference would arise.

Liabilities For Expenses To Be Deducted Or Taxed In Future Periods   Certain liabilities reflect items that can be charged to expense prior to their deduction for tax purposes. Examples of this would be liabilities for estimated warranty costs and accrued but unfunded pension costs. In both of these cases, the relevant amount can only be deducted for tax purposes when the costs are actually incurred. As the payment of such liabilities will result in a deductible expense for tax purposes, the tax basis of such liabilities is nil (carrying value, less the amount that can be deducted on the payment of the carrying amount). There would be a temporary difference in this situation.

A less common problem can arise when there is a taxable amount related to the liability. As noted in Paragraph 11-56, tax authorities do not recognize premium amortization on long-term bonds, resulting in a situation in where the original premium on the sale of the issue will be a taxable item when the bonds are retired. In this case, the tax basis of the liability exceeds its carrying value and there is a temporary difference.

Liabilities To Deliver Goods Or Services   As unearned revenues are involved, the settlement of this type of liability will result in an accounting revenue. In most cases, the enterprise will have deducted a reserve for tax purposes for the unearned revenue [ITA 20(1)(m)] and the settlement of the liability would also result in a tax inclusion accounting revenue. This means that the tax basis of the liability is equal to its carrying value. If, however, no reserve has been deducted, the settlement will not result in a revenue and the tax basis of the liability is nil (carrying value, less the amount that will not be taxed when the goods or services are delivered).

11-66.   As was the case with assets, there are other difficulties in the determination of the tax basis of liabilities. However, the preceding analysis deals with those that will be most commonly encountered.

Exercise Eleven-3

The following situations describe transactions and events related to particular liabilities. For each situation, indicate the tax basis of the liability described.

A.   The enterprise has an outstanding bank loan in the amount of $326,000.

B.   The enterprise has trade Accounts Payable of $54,000. These accounts relate to merchandise, all of which is still on hand.

C.   The enterprise owes $18,000 for membership fees at a local golf and country club.

> Exercise Eleven-3 deals with the tax basis of liabilities.

> This is a
> continuation
> of Exercise
> Eleven-3.

D. The enterprise has received $31,000 as advance payment on merchandise to be delivered in the next year. This is shown as a liability in the accounting records.

E. The enterprise has recorded a liability for estimated warranty costs in the amount of $11,000. The liability at the beginning of the year was $13,000.

F. The enterprise has a liability of $15,000 for Wages Payable to construction workers. These costs have been added to the asset value of a new office building that is under construction.

G. The enterprise has issued long-term bonds with a maturity value of $1,200,000. The bonds were originally sold for $1,250,000 and have a current carrying value of $1,240,000.

H. The enterprise has redeemable preferred shares outstanding that were issued for $860,000. This is also the redemption price of the shares. Under the provisions of Section 3860 of the *CICA Handbook*, "Financial Instruments - Disclosure And Presentation", these shares have been classified as long-term debt in the Balance Sheet of the enterprise.

End Of Exercise Eleven-3

Temporary Differences
Introduction
11-67.   As noted in Paragraph 11-53, temporary differences are defined as any difference between the tax basis of an asset or liability, and its carrying value in the GAAP based Balance Sheet. Once the tax basis of an asset or liability is established, the calculation of the associated temporary difference presents no real problems. The determination of the tax basis of assets and liabilities was given detailed treatment in the previous section.

11-68.   While further discussion of the determination of temporary differences is not required here, your understanding of this subject will be enhanced by reviewing examples of temporary differences. To this end, we are providing a fairly long selection of examples of the types of temporary differences that you are likely to encounter. While we will come back to this subject in the next section of this Chapter, we would remind you that taxable temporary differences form the basis for Future Income Tax Liabilities, while deductible temporary differences indicate the presence of Future Income Tax Assets.

Taxable Temporary Differences (Basis For Future Income Tax Liabilities)
11-69.   The following are examples of taxable temporary differences. The amounts indicated will be multiplied by the relevant tax rate, with the product recorded as a Future Income Tax Liability.

Accounts Receivable   The enterprise has recorded Accounts Receivable on the delivery of goods in the amount of $75,000. As the amounts are not collectible until the following year, a reserve for unpaid amounts has been deducted for tax purposes under ITA 20(1)(n), leaving the tax basis of the Accounts Receivable as nil. As the carrying value of the asset is greater than its tax basis, there is a taxable temporary difference of $75,000.

Prepaid Pension Costs   The enterprise has made advance funding payments to its registered pension plan, thereby creating an accounting asset with a value of $1,000,000. As these payments have already been deducted for tax purposes, the tax basis of this asset is nil. As the carrying value of the asset is greater than its tax basis, there is a $1,000,000 taxable temporary difference.

Long-Term Investments At Equity   The enterprise acquired a long-term investment at a cost $1,350,000. As they have significant influence over the investee, the investment is accounted for using the equity method. While the current carrying value of the investment has been increased to $1,560,000, the cost amount remains at

$1,350,000. This means that the tax basis of the asset is $1,455,000, the cost of $1,350,000, plus the $105,000 non-taxable half of the capital gain that would arise if the asset were sold. As the carrying value of the investment exceeds its tax basis, there is a taxable temporary difference of $105,000 ($1,560,000 - $1,455,000).

Land   Land with a cost of $400,000 is sold for $700,000, resulting in an accounting gain of $300,000. Of the total sale price, $350,000 is still receivable at the end of the year. A capital gains reserve of $75,000 [($350,000 ÷ $700,000)] [(½)($700,000 - $400,000)] is deducted for tax purposes. With respect to the receivable, its carrying value is $350,000. As the $75,000 reserve will have to be added back to taxable income when the $350,000 receivable is collected, the tax basis of the receivable is $275,000 ($350,000 - $75,000). As the carrying value of the receivable is greater than its tax basis, there is a $75,000 taxable temporary difference.

Depreciable Capital Assets   The enterprise has depreciable capital assets with a net book value of $1,250,000. The tax basis of these assets is $675,000, the total UCC for the various CCA classes to which these assets have been allocated. As the carrying value of the assets is greater than their tax basis, there is a taxable temporary difference of $575,000 ($1,250,000 - $675,000).

Development Costs   The enterprise has incurred development costs of $420,000 which, because they meet the conditions specified in Section 3450 for capitalization, have been recorded as an asset. These costs have been deducted for tax purposes which means that the tax basis of this asset is nil. As the carrying value of the asset is greater than its tax basis, there is a taxable temporary difference of $420,000.

Deductible Temporary Differences (Basis For Future Income Tax Assets)
11-70.   The following are examples of deductible temporary differences. The amounts indicated will be multiplied by the relevant tax rate, with the product recorded as a Future Income Tax Asset.

Temporary Investments   Temporary Investments of equity securities are carried at the lower of cost or market. The enterprise currently holds such securities with a cost of $125,000 and a market value of $115,000. If the investments were realized at their market value of $115,000, the result would be a capital loss of $10,000, only one-half of which would be deductible. This means that the tax basis of the Temporary Investments is $120,000 (the cost of $125,000, less the non-deductible one-half of the capital loss), and that there is a deductible temporary difference of $5,000 ($120,000 - $115,000).

Inventories   In the accounting records, Inventories are carried at cost as determined on a LIFO basis. Their carrying value is $550,000. Cost as determined on a FIFO basis is $575,000 and this is the tax basis of the Inventories. As the carrying value of the asset is less than its tax basis, there is a deductible temporary difference of $25,000 ($575,000 - $550,000).

Portfolio Investments   The enterprise has long-term portfolio investments with a cost of $325,000. Because these investments have experienced a non-temporary decline in value, they have been written down to their net realizable value of $215,000. Realization of this carrying value would result in a capital loss of $110,000, only one-half of which would be deductible. This means that the tax basis of the investments is $270,000 (the cost of $325,000, less the non-deductible one-half of the capital loss), and that there is a deductible temporary difference of $55,000 ($270,000 - $215,000).

Goodwill (Eligible Capital Expenditures)   In a business combination transaction involving a cash acquisition of assets, the enterprise has paid $620,000 for the goodwill of the acquiree. In the accounting records, it will be tested annually for impairment. For tax purposes, 75 percent of this amount or $465,000 has been added to the cumulative eligible capital account (CEC). This balance will be amortized at a rate of seven percent per year, applied to the amortized balance.

At any point in time, if the asset was disposed of for its carrying value, 25 percent of this amount would not be taxable (on a disposition of an eligible capital expenditure, only 75 percent of the proceeds are subtracted from the CEC balance). This means that, at acquisition, the tax basis of the goodwill would be equal to the $620,000 carrying value (the CEC balance of $465,000, plus $155,000 which is 25 percent of the $620,000 carrying value).

Accounting and tax values will diverge in subsequent periods. For example, assume that after one year, the goodwill has suffered an impairment loss of $62,000. The accounting carrying value would be $558,000 ($620,000 - $62,000). In contrast, the CEC balance would be $432,450 ($465,000, less 7 percent or $32,550). The tax basis of the asset would be $571,950 [$432,450 + (25%)($558,000)]. As the carrying value of the asset is less than its tax basis, there would be a deductible temporary difference of $13,950 ($571,950 - $558,000).

Product Warranty Costs   The enterprise has recorded a warranty expense and an estimated liability for warranty cost of $25,000. This amount will be deductible for tax purposes when actual warranty costs are incurred. This means that the tax basis of this liability is nil (carrying value of $25,000, less the $25,000 that will be deductible when the warranty liability is settled by delivering warranty services). As the carrying value of these liabilities is greater than their tax basis, there is a deductible temporary difference of $25,000.

Long-Term Bonds   Several years ago, the enterprise issued long-term bonds with a maturity value of $3,000,000. They were sold for $2,900,000 and, in the accounting records, the $100,000 discount is being amortized over the life of the bonds. The current carrying value of the liability is $2,962,000. However, as discount amortization is not recognized for tax purposes, the tax basis of the bonds is $2,900,000 (the carrying value of $2,962,000, less the $62,000 that could be deducted if the liability were settled at its carrying value). As the carrying value of these liabilities exceeds their tax basis, there is a deductible temporary difference of $62,000.

Future Site Restoration Costs   In accordance with the provisions of Section 3061 of the *CICA Handbook*, "Property, Plant and Equipment", the enterprise has recorded a $900,000 liability for future site restoration costs. As these amounts will only be deductible for tax purposes when the expenses are incurred, the tax basis of the liability is nil ($900,000 carrying value, less the $900,000 that will be deductible when the liability is settled). As the carrying value of the liability is greater than its tax basis, there is a deductible temporary difference of $900,000.

Pension Liabilities   The enterprise has accrued a liability for unfunded pension costs of $860,000. For tax purposes, these amounts will be deducted when funding payments are made. This means that the tax basis of this liability is nil ($860,000 carrying value, less the $860,000 that will be deductible when the liability is settled). As the carrying value of the liability is greater than its tax basis, there is a deductible temporary difference of $860,000.

> **Exercise Eleven-4 deals with the determination of temporary differences.**

Exercise Eleven-4

The following situations describe a taxable temporary difference, a deductible temporary difference or no temporary differences. For each situation indicate the amount of any taxable or deductible temporary differences.

A. The enterprise has Inventories carried at LIFO cost of $124,000. Under the average cost approach, the value would be $133,000.

B. The enterprise has recorded a $72,000 liability for non-deductible fines related to environmental pollution.

C. The enterprise has funded all of its $1,650,000 past service pension liability. Only $200,000 of this amount has been charged to expense for accounting purposes.

This is a continuation of Exercise Eleven-4.

D. Several years ago the enterprise issued long-term bonds for $3,200,000. The face value of the bonds is $3,000,000 and their current carrying value in the accounting records is $3,110,000.

E. The enterprise signed a lease that, because the present value of the lease payments exceed 90 percent of the fair value of the leased asset, was capitalized. The asset and liability were initially recorded at $420,000. The current carrying value of the asset is $252,000, while the current carrying value of the liability is $276,000. The lease is treated as an operating lease for tax purposes.

F. Several years ago, the enterprise invested $1,200,000 in specialized scientific research capital assets. Accounting depreciation of $288,000 has been deducted, resulting in a net book value for the assets of $912,000. For tax purposes, the cost of the assets was deducted in the year of their acquisition.

G. The enterprise has depreciable assets with an original cost of $3,400,000, a net book value of $2,150,000, and a UCC of $1,000,000.

H. The enterprise has Temporary Investments with a cost of $56,000. They are recorded in the accounting records at their market value of $53,000.

End Of Exercise Eleven-4

Temporary Differences Vs. Timing Differences

11-71.   As we have noted, the Recommendations of Section 3465 are based on temporary differences that are measured in terms of Balance Sheet accounts. In contrast, the now super-seded Section 3470 made its Recommendations on the basis of timing differences which were measured in terms of Income Statement effects. In the great majority of tax allocation calculations, this conceptual change will have no influence on the numbers that will be produced.

11-72.   For example, assume that at the beginning of the fiscal year, January 1, 2002, a company that is subject to a combined federal/provincial tax rate of 40 percent acquires Class 8 assets with a cost of $200,000, and an estimated service life of 20 years. As of this point in time, both the carrying value and the tax basis of these assets is $200,000. Using the straight line method of amortization, the carrying value of the assets on December 31, 2002 would be $190,000 [($200,000 - (5%)($200,000)]. On this same date, the tax basis of the assets would be $180,000 [$200,000 - (20%)(½)($200,000)]. Using the alternative terminologies of Sections 3465 and 3470, this situation would be described as follows:

Beginning Of The Year   Using Section 3465 terminology, we would state that at the beginning of the year, there are no temporary differences and no Future Income Tax Assets or Liabilities related to these assets. Alternatively, under Section 3470's terminology, we would state that there are no accumulated timing differences and no deferred tax debits or credits related to these assets.

During The Year   Under the Section 3465 approach, there would be a change in temporary differences of $10,000 [nil at the beginning of the year, increasing to ($190,000 - $180,000) at the end of the year]. This amount would be multiplied by the tax rate of 40 percent, with the resulting $4,000 recorded as a Future Tax Expense for the year. Under Section 3470, there would be a timing difference of $10,000 (depreciation expense of $10,000 vs. CCA of $20,000). This amount would be multiplied by the tax rate of 40 percent, with the resulting $4,000 recorded as a Deferred Tax Expense for the year.

End Of The Year   Under Section 3465, we would state that there was a taxable temporary difference at the end of the year of $10,000 ($190,000 - $180,000). This difference would be reflected in a Future Income Tax Liability of $4,000 [(40%)($10,000)]. Under Section 3470, we would state that, at the end of the year, there are accumulated timing differences of $10,000. These timing differences would be reflected in a deferred income tax credit of $4,000.

11-73.   As the preceding example makes clear, this two approaches result in the same amount being shown in both the Income Statement and the Balance Sheet. The only difference is in the terminology used to describe the balances. It would appear that this would be the case for most of the items that can be described as temporary differences.

11-74.   We are discussing these similarities, despite the fact that Section 3470 is no longer relevant, because most authors have found that the concept of timing differences is still useful in analyzing complex problems involving a large number of differences between accounting and taxable income. In our later discussion of how to solve such problems, you will find that that the schedule which we use is based on the concept of timing differences. We will also use the concept of permanent differences. Unlike timing differences, where any current amount will be offset in current or future periods, permanent differences are items in which the difference between the tax and accounting figures will not change over the life of the enterprise. An example of this would be one-half of all capital gains. While 100 percent of capital gains will be included in accounting income, one-half of such amounts will never be taxed.

Converting Temporary Differences To Future Income Tax Assets And Liabilities

11-75.   The definition of Future Income Tax Assets and Future Income Tax Liabilities was presented in Paragraph 11-58. With respect to liabilities there are no problems. It would appear that all Future Income Tax Liabilities can be related to particular assets and liabilities that are presented in the accounting Balance Sheet. This means that once you have determined all of your taxable temporary differences, Future Income Tax Liabilities are simply those amounts multiplied by the relevant tax rate. While this issue will be discussed further at a later point in this Chapter, the relevant rate would normally be the rate in effect at the Balance Sheet date.

11-76.   The situation is more complex with respect to the recording of Future Income Tax Assets. For those Future Income Tax Assets which relate to assets or liabilities in the accounting Balance Sheet, there will be deductible temporary differences. In cases such as this, the Future Income Tax Assets will simply be the amount of the deductible temporary difference, multiplied by the relevant tax rate. Here again, the relevant rate will normally be the rate in effect as at the end of the year.

11-77.   As noted in the definition of Future Income Tax Assets, there are other Future Income Tax Assets which do not relate to assets and liabilities found in the accounting Balance Sheet. The most obvious of these Future Income Tax Assets involves unused tax loss carry forwards. If an enterprise has a $1,000,000 non-capital loss in the current period and, if this loss cannot be carried back to any of the three preceding taxation years, it becomes a loss carry forward. If we assume that the enterprise has a combined federal/provincial tax rate of 40 percent, there is a potential tax benefit of $400,000. While there is no accounting asset related to this potential benefit, it will be recorded as a Future Income Tax Asset if it is more likely than not that it can be realized in the applicable future period.

11-78.   The other type of Future Income Tax Asset referred to in the definition of these items relates to the carry forward of unused income tax reductions other than investment tax credits. Section 3465 contains the following examples of such items:

Paragraph 3465.15   ...

(a) a certain percentage of expenditures for mineral property exploration and development may be allowed as an additional deduction for income tax purposes ("earned depletion"). There may be no related asset for financial statement purposes. The difference between the tax basis of the earned depletion base and the carrying amount of nil is a deductible temporary difference which gives rise to a future income tax asset;

(b) research costs are recognized as an expense in the financial statements in the period in which they are incurred but might not be deducted in determining taxable income until a later period. The difference between the tax basis of the research costs, being the amount the taxation authorities will permit as a deduction in the future, and the carrying amount of nil is a deductible temporary difference which gives rise to a future income tax asset;

(c) for financial statement purposes, an enterprise might recognize profits on a long-term contract using the percentage of completion method but use the completed contract method when determining taxable income. Income is therefore being deferred for tax purposes, with no corresponding amount being deferred for accounting purposes. The income deferred for tax purposes represents a taxable temporary difference.

11-79. While no Balance Sheet item would be present for these items, Future Income Tax Assets would still be recorded.

Purpose And Scope Of Section 3465

11-80. The purpose of Section 3465 is to establish standards for the recognition, measurement, presentation, and disclosure of income and refundable taxes in the general purpose financial statements of Canadian enterprises. It is based on the principle that comprehensive tax allocation procedures should be applied in order to record Future Income Tax Assets and Liabilities related to deductible and taxable temporary differences. It is not applicable to the special considerations related to accounting for investment tax credits. These considerations are covered in Section 3805 of the *CICA Handbook*.

11-81. For purposes of this Section, income taxes are defined as follows:

Paragraph 3465.09(a) **Income taxes** include:

(i) all domestic and foreign taxes that are based on taxable income;

(ii) taxes, such as mining taxes, that are based on a measure of revenue less certain specified expenses;

(iii) alternative minimum income taxes, including taxes based on measures other than income and that may be used to reduce income taxes of another period; and

(iv) taxes, such as withholding taxes, that are based on amounts paid to the enterprise.

11-82. The position of rate regulated enterprises is different in that, in many cases, future income tax payments will be included in the rates that are charged to customers. In such cases, the future taxes are claims on the resources of the particular enterprise and should not be recorded as liabilities of the enterprise. Given this, Section 3465 includes the following exception to its general scope provision:

Paragraph 3465.102 *A rate regulated enterprise need not recognize future income taxes in accordance with the Recommendations of this Section to the extent that future income taxes are expected to be included in the approved rate charged to customers in the future and are expected to be recovered from future customers. If future income taxes are not recognized in accordance with the Recommendations of this Section, the rate regulated enterprise should disclose the following, in addition to the information to be disclosed in accordance with paragraphs 3465.91 and 3465.92:*

(a) the reason why future income tax liabilities and future income tax assets have not been recognized; and

(b) the amount of future income tax liabilities, future income tax assets and future income tax expense that have not been recognized. (January, 2000)

11-83. Note that this exception only applies to the extent that future income taxes are expected to be recovered from rates charged to future customers. Otherwise, the provisions of the Section apply and the recording of Future Income Tax Assets and Liabilities is required. Rate regulated enterprises are defined in the Section as follows:

> **Paragraph 3465.09(k)** A **rate regulated enterprise** is an enterprise which meets all of the following criteria:
>
> (i) the rates for regulated services or products provided to customers are established by or are subject to approval by a regulator or a governing body empowered by statute or contract to establish rates to be charged for services or products;
>
> (ii) the regulated rates are designed to recover the cost of providing the services or products; and
>
> (iii) it is reasonable to assume that rates set at levels that will recover the cost can be charged to and collected from customers in view of the demand for the services or products and the level of direct and indirect competition. This criterion requires consideration of expected changes in levels of demand or competition during the recovery period for amounts recorded as recoverable under the rate formula.

Exercise Eleven-5

Exercise Eleven-5 deals with the scope of Section 3465.

Listed below are a number of different taxes that might be assessed on an enterprise. Indicate which of these taxes fall within the scope of Section 3465.

- Part IV tax on dividends received by a private corporation.
- A provincial capital tax that must be paid in full without regard to the amount of income related taxes paid.
- The federal goods and services tax (GST).
- The harmonized sales tax (HST) assessed in New Brunswick, Nova Scotia, and Newfoundland.
- Part I federal income tax assessed on an enterprise in a regulated industry.
- The federal large corporations tax (Part I.3 tax).

End Of Exercise Eleven-5

Current Income Tax Assets And Liabilities

11-84.   The cost or benefit of current income taxes is defined in Section 3465 as follows:

> **Paragraph 3465.09(g)**   The **cost (benefit) of current income taxes** is the amount of income taxes payable (recoverable) in respect of the period.

11-85.   The reference here is to taxes that must be paid or that can be recovered as a result of information that is included in the tax return of the enterprise for the current year. Most commonly, this would be the taxes payable as a result of the inclusions and deductions reported for the current taxation year. However, if the current tax return reports a loss, this can be carried back to the three previous years in order to claim a refund of taxes paid in those years. Such a carry back will result in taxes that are currently receivable.

11-86.   This means that, at the end of any taxation year, there will be either taxes that are currently payable or taxes that are currently receivable. The current amount payable will reflect taxes that must be paid because of taxable activities during the current or preceding taxation years. Any current amount receivable will reflect taxes paid in previous years that are being recovered because of a loss carry back.

11-87.   With respect to these current income tax assets and liabilities, the following Recommendations are applicable:

Paragraph 3465.19   *Current income taxes, to the extent unpaid or recoverable, should be recognized as a liability or asset and should not be included in future income tax liabilities or future income tax assets.* (January, 2000)

Paragraph 3465.20   *The benefit relating to a tax loss arising in the current period that will be carried back to recover income taxes of a previous period should be recognized as a current asset and not included in future income tax liabilities or future income tax assets.* (January, 2000)

11-88.   The use of the term current in the context of the phrase "current income taxes" should not be confused with the use of this term in the classification of assets and liabilities. "Current income taxes", to the extent that they have not been paid or received will be classified as current assets and liabilities. However, current assets and liabilities could also include "future income taxes", provided the amounts would be received or settled within one year of the Balance Sheet date.

Exercise Eleven-6

During its first year of operations, the year ending December 31, 2002, Salin Ltd. has Net Income and Taxable Income of $125,000.

During the year ending December 31, 2003, the Company experienced a Net Loss for accounting and tax purposes of $85,000.

In both years, the Company was subject to a combined federal/provincial tax rate of 23 percent.

Required: Provide the journal entry to record the Company's Tax Expense (Benefit) for the year ending December 31, 2003. Indicate the disclosure that would be required in the Company's December 31, 2003 Balance Sheet.

End Of Exercise Eleven-6

> Exercise Eleven-6 deals with current income taxes.

Basic Tax Allocation Procedures

Introduction

11-89.   At the heart of Section 3465, is the requirement that Future Income Tax Assets and Liabilities must be recognized for all temporary differences. This reflects an adoption of comprehensive tax allocation procedures, implemented with the asset/liability approach.

11-90.   In this section, we will present the specific Section 3465 Recommendations that support this approach. We will also discuss possible analytical approaches to implementing these Recommendations. In addition, an example will be presented to illustrate the application of the suggested analytical approach.

11-91.   Our concern here will be with basic tax allocation Recommendations. There are a number of more technical issues associated with these Recommendations which, if presented on a simultaneous basis, would tend to obscure the general approach that is being adopted by Section 3465. These more technical issues will be dealt with at a later point in this Chapter and in Chapter 12.

Tax Allocation Recommendations
Balance Sheet Amounts

11-92.   The Recommendations of Section 3465 require the recognition of Future Income Tax Assets and Future Income Tax Liabilities at each Balance Sheet date. These Recommendation are as follows:

Paragraph 3465.22   *At each balance sheet date, except as provided in paragraphs 3465.33, 3465.35 and 3465.37, a future income tax liability should be recognized for all taxable temporary differences other than those arising from any portion of goodwill which is not deductible for tax purposes. (January, 2000)*

Paragraph 3465.24   *At each balance sheet date, except as provided in paragraphs 3465.33, 3465.35 and 3465.37, a future income tax asset should be recognized for all deductible temporary differences, unused tax losses and income tax reductions. The amount recognized should be limited to the amount that is more likely than not to be realized. (January, 2000)*

Note   The complications referred to in Paragraph 3465.33, 3465.35, and 3465.37 relate to integrated foreign operations, intra group transfers, and investments that are to be consolidated. These Paragraphs will be considered at a later point in this Chapter.

Measurement

11-93.   With respect to the measurement of the Future Income Tax Assets and Liabilities, Section 3465 makes the following Recommendation:

Paragraph 3465.56   *Income tax liabilities and income tax assets should be measured using the income tax rates and income tax laws that, at the balance sheet date, are expected to apply when the liability is settled or the asset is realized, which would normally be those enacted at the balance sheet date. (January, 2000)*

11-94.   In some situations, there may be announced changes in the tax rates which are expected to apply when Future Income Tax Assets are realized or Future Income Tax Liabilities are settled. It would be appropriate to use a substantially enacted future tax rate or future tax law only when there is persuasive evidence that:

- the government is able and committed to enacting the proposed change in the foreseeable future; and

- where the change relates to the current year, the enterprise expects to be assessed based on the announced tax rates or tax laws.

11-95.   The rates used should reflect the expected values of any special tax incentives that are available to the enterprise. This would include such provisions as the small business deduction, the manufacturing and processing profits deduction, and the resource allowance deduction.

11-96.   When different rates apply to different levels of income (e.g., the small business deduction is only available on the first $200,000 of active business income), the tax rate that is expected to apply to taxable income in the period in which temporary differences are expected to reverse should be used. When allocations of incentives must be made to individual companies (e.g, the associated companies rules for the small business deduction), the tax rates should reflect these allocations.

Exercise Eleven-7 deals with measurement of FITAL.

Exercise Eleven-7

Note   This exercise should not be attempted by students who have not had a course in corporate taxation.

Caldwell Inc. is a Canadian controlled private corporation. It is not associated with any other corporation. It has permanent establishments in both Alberta and Saskatchewan. It is expected that, for the next several years, the formula provided in the *Income Tax Regulations* will result in 40 percent of the Company's Taxable Income being allocated to Alberta and 60 percent being allocated to Saskatchewan. The regular and small business rates in Alberta are 15.5 percent and 6.0 percent respectively, while the corresponding rates in Saskatchewan are 17.0 percent and 8.0 percent.

While the Company's Taxable Income is expected to vary from year to year, management believes that it will average $300,000 per year over the next five to ten years. All of the Company's income results from active business activities, none of which involve manufacturing and processing.

This is a continuation of Exercise Eleven-7.

Required: Determine the tax rate that the Company should use in converting temporary differences to FITAL balances. Ignore the general and accelerated rate reduction.

End Of Exercise Eleven-7

Discounting

11-97.   As future amounts are involved, it would seem that discounting would be an appropriate procedure to be used in the measurement of Future Income Tax Assets and Liabilities. However, because of the many problems associated with the application of present value concepts, Section 3465 rejects this possibility:

> **Paragraph 3465.57**   *Future income tax liabilities and future income tax assets should not be discounted.* (January, 2000)

11-98.   This conclusion is consistent with Statement Of Financial Accounting Standards No. 109 in the United States.

Income Statement Amounts

11-99.   With respect to amounts to be included in the Income Statement, the following two Recommendations are applicable:

> **Paragraph 3465.63**   *The cost (benefit) of current and future income taxes should be recognized as income tax expense included in the determination of net income or loss for the period before discontinued operations and extraordinary items, ...* (January, 2000)

> **Paragraph 3465.64**   *Changes in future income tax balances recognized in accordance with paragraph 3465.56 as a result of changes in tax laws or rates should be included in future income tax expense reported in income before discontinued operations and extraordinary items.* (January, 2000)

11-100.   Paragraph 3465.63 makes it clear that the current Income Tax Expense or Income Tax Benefit should include both current and future income taxes. The amount of future income taxes to be included would be equal to the change in the net Future Income Tax Liability (Asset). The change in this net balance would, in turn, be dependent on changes in taxable (deductible) temporary differences during the period. However, Paragraph 3465.64 indicates that this amount would also include changes in the net Future Income Tax Liability (Asset) related to changes in tax laws or rates.

11-101.   To make these points clear, consider the following simple example:

> **Example**   An enterprise has net taxable temporary differences on December 31, 2001 of $1,000,000. At that point in time, the enterprise is subject to a combined statutory tax rate of 40 percent. At December 31, 2002, the net taxable temporary differences total $1,200,000 and the tax rate has increased to 45 percent. The enterprise has a December 31 year end.

11-102.   The amount that will added to the 2002 Income Tax Expense for future income taxes would be calculated as follows:

Ending Future Income Tax Liability [(45%)($1,200,000)]	$540,000
Beginning Future Income Tax Liability [(40%)($1,000,000)]	(400,000)
Addition To Future Income Tax Expense	$140,000

11-103.   This addition is made up of two components. Of the total of $140,000, $90,000 [(45%)($1,200,000 - $1,000,000)] relates to the increase in taxable temporary differences. The remaining $50,000 results from the 5 percent increase in the tax rate applied to the beginning Future Income Tax Liability of $1,000,000.

Tax Allocation Disclosure

Income Statement

11-104.   **Segregation Of Tax Expense**   Section 3465 requires fairly detailed disclosure of amounts related to its basic tax allocation Recommendations. With respect to the general disclosure of Income Tax Expense, the Recommendation is as follows:

> **Paragraph 3465.85**   *Income tax expense included in the determination of net income or loss before discontinued operations and extraordinary items should be presented on the face of the income statement.* (January, 2000)

11-105.   This Recommendation is reinforced by a similar requirement in Section 1520, "Income Statement".

11-106.   **Current Vs. Future Amounts**   In most situations, the Income Tax Expense figure will include both taxes that are currently payable, and amounts that will be payable at some future date. When this is the case, the following Recommendation is applicable:

> **Paragraph 3465.91**   *The following should be disclosed separately:*
>
> (a) *current income tax expense or benefit included in the determination of income or loss before discontinued operations and extraordinary items;*
>
> (b) *future income tax expense or benefit included in the determination of income or loss before discontinued operations and extraordinary items;*
>
> (c) ...

11-107.   There are several ways in which the disclosure called for in Paragraph 3465.91 could be implemented. Alternatives are as follows:

• The current and future portions of Income Tax Expense could be segregated in the Income Statement.

• A single total for Income Tax Expense could be shown in the Income Statement, accompanied by note disclosure of the current and future portions.

• A single total for Income Tax Expense could be shown in the Income Statement, accompanied by disclosure of the future portion as an adjustment to cash from operating activities in the Cash Flow Statement.

11-108.   **Limited Applicability**   Paragraph .92 of Section 3465 contains several additional Recommendations related to Income Tax Expense that are only applicable to public enterprises, life insurance enterprises, deposit taking institutions, or co-operative businesses. For this purpose, the Section defines a public enterprise as follows:

> **Paragraph 3465.09(j)**   A **public enterprise** is an enterprise that:
>
> (i)   has issued debt or equity securities that are traded in a public market (a domestic or foreign stock exchange or an over-the-counter market, including local or regional markets);
>
> (ii) is required to file financial statements with a securities commission; or
>
> (iii) provides financial statements for the purpose of issuing any class of securities in a public market.

11-109. Nature And Effect Of Temporary Differences The first of the Recommendations that are applicable only to public enterprises, life insurance enterprises, deposit taking institutions, or co-operative businesses requires disclosure of:

Paragraph 3465.92(a) *the nature and tax effect of the temporary differences, unused tax losses and income tax reductions that give rise to future income tax assets and future income tax liabilities. Significant offsetting items included in future income tax assets and liabilities balances should be disclosed;* (January, 2000)

11-110. What is called for here is a description of the items that are creating the future income tax component of Income Tax Expense. This would include such things as differences between depreciation expense and CCA, other major types of temporary differences, as well as information about unused loss carry forwards.

11-111. Components Of Income Tax Expense A second Recommendation applicable only to public enterprises, life insurance enterprises, deposit taking institutions, or co-operative businesses requires disclosure of:

Paragraph 3465.92(b) *the major components of income tax expense included in the determination of income or loss for the period before discontinued operations and extraordinary items;* (January, 2000)

11-112. This requirement would suggest that the current component of Income Tax Expense should be segregated between taxes that are payable on current taxable income, and taxes that are currently recoverable because of loss carry backs from a subsequent year. The future component of Income Tax Expense would also be segregated. Possible disclosure here would include:

- future tax amounts related to changes in temporary differences during the period;
- future tax amounts related to changes in tax rates;
- future tax amounts resulting from the recognition of previously unrecognized loss carry forwards; and
- future tax amounts resulting from the write down of future tax assets.

11-113. Reconciliation With Statutory Rate A final Recommendation applicable only to public enterprises, life insurance enterprises, deposit taking institutions, or co-operative businesses requires disclosure of:

Paragraph 3465.92(c) *a reconciliation of the income tax rate or expense, related to income or loss for the period before discontinued operations and extraordinary items, to the statutory income tax rate or dollar amount, including the nature and amount using percentages or dollar amounts of each significant reconciling item. Significant offsetting items included in the income tax expense should be disclosed even when there is no variation from the statutory income tax rate.* (January, 2000)

11-114. In addition to temporary differences to which tax allocation procedures are applied, there are many other differences between Accounting Income and Taxable Income. Examples of such differences would include non-taxable intercompany dividend revenues, and non-deductible amounts related to automobile costs. Under the now superseded Section 3470, such differences were referred to as permanent differences. While Section 3465 has not retained this terminology, such "permanent" differences continue to be present. As no tax allocation procedures are used for permanent differences, their presence can mean that the reported Income Tax Expense does not reflect the statutory rate of taxation. A simple example will make this point clear:

Example A corporation has Accounting Income Before Taxes for the current year of $500,000. As the Accounting Income figure includes $200,000 in dividends from other taxable Canadian corporations, Taxable Income for the year is equal to

$300,000. The corporation is subject to a statutory tax rate of 45 percent, resulting in current taxes payable of $135,000.

As the non-taxable dividends do not involve a temporary difference, tax allocation procedures would not be applied and the corporation's condensed Income Statement would be as follows:

Accounting Income Before Taxes	$500,000
Income Tax Expense - Current Amount	(135,000)
Accounting Net Income	$365,000

11-115.   As this example illustrates, differences such as non-taxable dividends can result in an Income Tax Expense which could easily mislead investors and other users as to the statutory tax rate applicable to the enterprise. In such situations, Paragraph 3465.92(c) requires a reconciliation between the actual Income Tax Expense, as compared to the Expense that would result from the application of the statutory income tax rate. The reconciliation that would be required in our simple example would be as follows:

Taxes At Statutory Rate of 45 Percent [(45%)($500,000)]	$225,000
Tax Savings From Non-Taxable Dividends [(45%)($200,000)]	(90,000)
Income Tax Expense Reported	$135,000

11-116.   In practice, such reconciliations can be very complex, particularly for enterprises involved with mining or other natural resource operations. We have seen such income tax reconciliation notes occupy a full page of an annual report.

Balance Sheet

11-117.   **Segregation And Classification**   In the Balance Sheet, Section 3465 requires that income tax assets and liabilities be segregated from other assets and liabilities:

Paragraph 3465.86   *Income tax liabilities and income tax assets should be presented separately from other liabilities and assets. Current income tax liabilities and current income tax assets should be presented separately from future income tax liabilities and future income tax assets.* (January, 2000)

11-118.   Most enterprises segregate current assets from non-current assets, and current liabilities from non-current liabilities. The following Recommendations are applicable to such enterprises:

Paragraph 3465.87   *When an enterprise segregates assets and liabilities between current and non-current assets and liabilities, the current and non-current portions of future income tax liabilities and future income tax assets should also be segregated. The classification between current and non-current should be based on the classification of the liabilities and assets to which the future income tax liabilities and future income tax assets relate. A future income tax liability or future income tax asset that is not related to a liability or asset recognized for accounting purposes, should be classified according to the expected reversal date of the temporary difference. Future income tax assets related to unused tax losses and income tax reductions should be classified according to the date on which the benefit is expected to be realized.* (January, 2000)

11-119.   Note that, in general, the classification of income tax assets and liabilities between current and non-current is based on the classification of the asset or liability to which the tax item relates. For example, income tax liabilities resulting from non-current depreciable assets having a net book value in excess of their UCC would be classified as non-current. Income tax assets and liabilities that do not relate to particular Balance Sheet items would be classified as current or non-current on the basis of when the temporary difference is expected to reverse. The same approach applies to income tax assets related to tax loss carry forwards. The assets would be classified on the basis of when the benefit of the carry forward is expected to be realized. We would expect that, in most cases, income tax assets and liabilities that do not relate to specific Balance Sheet items will be classified as non-current, reflecting the uncertainty associated with the timing of the reversal of the related temporary difference or the realization of the future benefit.

11-120.   **Offsetting**   Section 3465 also deals with the problem of offsetting Future Income Tax Liabilities against Future Income Tax Assets. There is a prohibition against offsetting current amounts against non-current amounts, provided the enterprise uses such classifications in its Balance Sheet.

11-121.   Section 3465 recognizes that it is not appropriate to offset Future Income Tax Liabilities in one tax jurisdiction against Future Income Tax Assets in a different tax jurisdiction. For example, it would not be appropriate to offset a Future Income Tax Liability that, when settled, will result in taxes payable in Canada, against a Future Income Tax Asset that, when realized, will result in tax deductions in a foreign country.

11-122.   Also noted in Section 3465 is the fact that the Future Income Tax Liabilities of one taxable entity cannot be eliminated by applying the Future Income Tax Assets of a different taxable entity. As there is no statutory provision for filing a consolidated tax return in Canada, the parent and each subsidiary company in a consolidated group are separate taxable entities. In such situations, some companies may have net income tax liabilities, while others may have net income tax assets. Clearly, the income tax assets of one taxable entity cannot be used to eliminate the income tax liabilities of a different taxable entity.

11-123.   In general, Section 3465 Recommends offsetting current income tax assets against current income tax liabilities, and offsetting non-current income tax assets against non-current income tax liabilities. However, this is only permitted if the assets and liabilities relate to the same taxable entity and to the same tax jurisdiction. The relevant Recommendation is as follows:

> **Paragraph 3465.88**   *Current income tax liabilities and current income tax assets should be offset if they relate to the same taxable entity and the same taxation authority. Future income tax liabilities and future income tax assets should be offset if they relate to the same taxable entity and the same taxation authority. However, when an enterprise classifies assets and liabilities as current and non-current, the current portion of future income tax balances should not offset any future income tax balances classified as non-current. (January, 2000)*

11-124.   In implementing this Recommendation, Section 3465 recognizes the possibility that tax planning strategies can be used to utilize inter entity income tax assets and liabilities (e.g., transfers of profitable assets from an entity with Future Income Tax Liabilities to an entity with Future Income Tax Assets resulting from loss carry forwards). In this type of situation, offsetting is permitted:

> **Paragraph 3465.89**   *When enterprises in a group are taxed separately by the same taxation authority, a future income tax asset recognized by one enterprise in the group should not be offset against a future income tax liability of another enterprise in the group unless tax planning strategies could be implemented to satisfy the requirements of paragraph 3465.88 when the future income tax liability becomes payable. (January, 2000)*

Solving Tax Allocation Problems
Example
11-125.   As the accounting for tax problems become more complex, you are required to deal with temporary differences, as well as other differences between accounting and tax information. In such cases, it is essential that you have some type of analytical format for dealing with the large amount of information that may be involved.

11-126.   For many years, two alternative formats have been used to assist in preparing financial statements involving income taxes. The first involves a three column schedule in which the bottom line in each column provides the amounts required for the tax journal entry. An alternative approach uses a sequential calculation to move from Financial Statement Income to what is designated Accounting Income, and finally to Taxable Income. The former approach appears to be more widely used and, as a consequence, it will be used in this Chapter and the related problem material.

11-127.   The replacement of Section 3470 with Section 3465 has shifted the focus of tax allocation from timing differences in the Income Statement, to temporary differences in the Balance Sheet. As a reflection of this, the major example of tax allocation presented in the Appendix to Section 3465 (Example 2) based its analysis on Balance Sheet changes. We found this approach to be somewhat awkward and difficult to understand. Further, at this point we have found that the traditional three column approach provided the same results in a manner that was much easier to implement. Given this, we will continue to work with this format.

11-128.   In order to illustrate the three column format in the context of a basic tax allocation problem, we will use the following example:

> **Example**   On December 31, 2001, the Maxin Company had taxable temporary differences of $210,000. As the statutory combined tax rate on this date is 40 percent, the Company's Balance Sheet contains a Future Income Tax Liability of $84,000 [(40%)($210,000)]. The Company's year end is December 31.
>
> During 2002, the Company has Accounting Income Before Taxes of $200,000. In computing this figure, the Company's accountant included $25,000 in Dividend Revenue from taxable Canadian corporations and deducted $10,000 for membership dues in the Inland Golf And Country Club. In addition, the Depreciation Expense deducted in the computation of 2002 accounting income was $50,000 while the maximum capital cost allowance of $75,000 is claimed for tax purposes. For 2002, the Company's statutory combined tax rate is 42 percent. This increase in the tax rate was not anticipated at the end of 2001.

Problem Solving Format

11-129.   Our problem solving format begins by setting up three columns and entering Accounting Income Before Taxes in the first two of these columns as follows:

	Accounting Income	Taxable Income	Change In Temporary Differences
Income Before Taxes	$200,000	$200,000	

11-130.   Before considering the mechanical aspects of this schedule, it is worthwhile to consider what will be contained in each of the three columns. The first column provides the basis for calculating the Income Tax Expense or Income Tax Benefit that will be included in the Company's Income Statement. As we are using comprehensive tax allocation procedures, it will not be adjusted for changes in temporary differences. However, it will be adjusted for all other differences between the current period's Accounting Income and current year's Taxable Income. This would include such items as non-taxable dividends received and non-deductible membership dues.

11-131.   When this column total is multiplied by the current tax rate, it will give the Current Tax Expense or Tax Benefit for the period, as well as the Future Tax Expense or Future Tax Benefit for the period, to the extent that this future item relates to changes in temporary differences that occurred during the current period. A new feature in this analytical format relates to the fact that Section 3465 requires the total balance of Future Income Tax Assets and Liabilities to be adjusted for changes in tax rates. Since this adjustment must be included in the current period's Future Tax Expense or Future Tax Benefit, the required adjustment will have to be added to the total of this Accounting Income column in order to arrive at the appropriate figure for inclusion in the Income Statement.

11-132.   The Taxable Income column will be used to convert Accounting Income Before Taxes to Taxable Income and will be adjusted for both temporary and other differences between Accounting Income Before Taxes and Taxable Income. The final figure in this column will provide the basis for the calculation of taxes payable using the current tax rate. It will not be altered by adjustments of Future Income Tax Assets and Liabilities for changes in tax rates. For those of you familiar with corporate tax returns, this column contains the same information that will be included in the required Schedule 1.

11-133. As the name implies, the Change In Temporary Differences column will then be used to accumulate the changes that took place during the period in taxable and deductible temporary differences. Recognizing that taxable temporary differences are more common than deductible differences, changes in taxable differences are added to this column and changes in deductible differences are subtracted. As was the case with the Accounting Income column, adjustments related to the effect of changing tax rates on Future Income Tax Assets and Liabilities will have to be added to or subtracted from this column. The final figure in this column will become the basis for calculating additions to Future Income Tax Liabilities or Future Income Tax Assets. A positive number will result in an addition to liabilities or a reduction in assets, while a negative number will be an addition to assets or a reduction in liabilities.

11-134. Given the preceding analysis of the individual columns, rules for dealing with entries that will be made are as follows:

- Differences between current period Accounting Income Before Taxes and current period Taxable Income that reflect changes in temporary differences are added or deducted from both the Taxable Income column and the Change In Temporary Differences column, with the opposite arithmetic signs being applied.

- Other differences (formerly known as permanent differences) between the current period Accounting Income Before Taxes and current period Taxable Income are added or deducted from both the Accounting Income column and the Taxable Income column, with the same arithmetic signs being applied.

- Tax rate adjustments to the opening balance of Future Income Tax Assets and/or Future Income Tax Liabilities will be added or deducted from both the Accounting Income column and the Temporary Differences column, with the same arithmetic sign being applied. This adjustment is done after the current period totals have been multiplied by the current period tax rate.

11-135. The completed schedule would appear as follows:

	Accounting Income	Taxable Income	Change In Temporary Differences
Income Before Taxes	$200,000	$200,000	
Membership Fees	10,000	10,000	
Dividend Revenue	(25,000)	(25,000)	
Depreciation		50,000	($50,000)
Capital Cost Allowance		(75,000)	75,000
Balances	$185,000	$160,000	$25,000
Tax Rate	42%	42%	42%
Current Tax Balances	$ 77,700	$ 67,200	$10,500
Effect Of Change In Tax Rate [(42% - 40%)($210,000)]	4,200	N/A	4,200
Total Tax Balances	$ 81,900	$67,200	$14,700

11-136. As was previously indicated, the bottom line of the preceding schedule provides the required information for preparing the 2002 journal entry to record the Maxin Company's tax balances. Note that the first column, which provides the required debit, will always be equal to the sum of the remaining two columns in which positive balances will be reflected in credit entries. The appropriate journal entry is as follows:

Tax Expense	$81,900	
Taxes Payable		$67,200
Future Income Tax Liability		14,700

11-137. The Income Statement for 2002, including disclosure of the split between current and future Tax Expense, would be as follows:

Income Before Taxes		$200,000
Tax Expense:		
Current	$67,200	
Future	14,700	81,900
Net Income		$118,100

11-138. As the reported tax expense does not reflect the current tax rate of 42 percent, additional disclosure is required under Paragraph 3465.92(c) to reconcile these amounts. Appropriate disclosure would be as follows:

Taxes At Statutory Rate [(42%)($200,000)]	$84,000
Tax Savings From Non-Taxable Dividends [(42%)($25,000)]	(10,500)
Tax Cost Of Non-Deductible Dues [(42%)($10,000)]	4,200
Adjustment of Future Income Tax Liability [(42% - 40%)($210,000)]	4,200
Income Tax Expense Reported	$81,900

> Exercise Eleven-8 deals with the format for solving tax allocation problems.

Exercise Eleven-8

On December 31, 2001, the Saxon Ltd. had taxable temporary differences of $560,000. As the statutory combined tax rate on this date is 41 percent, the Company's Balance Sheet contains a Future Income Tax Liability of $229,600 [(41%)($560,000)]. The Company's year end is December 31.

During 2002, the Company has Accounting Income Before Taxes of $325,000. In computing this figure, the Company's accountant included a gain on the sale of land of $50,000. This land was a capital asset. In addition, the Depreciation Expense deducted in the computation of 2002 accounting income was $92,000 while the maximum capital cost allowance of $71,000 is claimed for tax purposes. For 2002, the Company's statutory combined tax rate is 37 percent. This increase in the tax rate was not anticipated at the end of 2001.

Required: Prepare the journal entry to record taxes for the year ending December 31, 2002. In addition, prepare the Income Statement for that year. Your answer should include all of the disclosure required for public companies by the the *CICA Handbook*.

End Of Exercise Eleven-8

Intraperiod Allocation

Basic Concept

11-139. Terms such as "extraordinary items", "results of discontinued operations", "capital transaction", "correction of an accounting error", and "adjustment resulting from a change in accounting policy", are accounting terms which have no meaning in the context of calculating Taxable Income. However, under GAAP, special disclosure requirements require segregated presentation of these various types of changes in the net assets of the enterprise. For example, adjustments related to changes in accounting policy are charged directly to Retained Earnings, rather than being disclosed as an inclusion or deduction in the Income Statement.

11-140.   In contrast, current and future Taxes Payable are single figures that do not segregate the components which make up their respective totals. The idea that we are concerned with here is that, for financial reporting purposes, taxes which relate to items subject to special disclosure requirements under GAAP should be segregated and given disclosure consistent with the item to which they relate. The basic Recommendation which requires such segregation is as follows:

Paragraph 3465.63   *The cost (benefit) of current and future income taxes should be recognized as income tax expense included in the determination of net income or loss for the period before discontinued operations and extraordinary items, except that:*

(a) *any portion of the cost (benefit) of current and future income taxes related to discontinued operations or extraordinary items of the current period should be included in the income statement with the results of discontinued operations or extraordinary items, respectively;*

(b) *any portion of the cost (benefit) of current and future income taxes relating to capital transactions in the current period, or relating to items that are credited or charged directly to equity in the current period, should be charged or credited directly to equity;*

(c) *any portion of the cost (benefit) of current and future income taxes arising at the time of changes in shareholder status should be treated as a capital transaction (see "Capital Transactions", Section 3610);*

(d) *any portion of the cost of future income taxes arising at the time an enterprise renounces the deductibility of expenditures to an investor should be treated as a cost of issuing the security to the investor;*

(e) *any portion of the cost (benefit) of future income taxes arising at the time of acquisition of an asset, other than an asset acquired in a business combination, should be recognized in accordance with paragraph 3465.43;*

(f) *any portion of the cost (benefit) of current and future income taxes recognized at the time of a business combination should be included in the allocation of the cost of the purchase (see paragraphs 3465.17 and 3465.46);*

(g) *any other portion of the cost (benefit) of future income taxes related to a business combination, investment in a significantly influenced investee, interest in a joint venture or comprehensive revaluation of assets and liabilities should be recognized in accordance with paragraphs 3465.48, 3465.51, and 3465.52;*

(h) *any refundable taxes should be recognized in accordance with paragraphs 3465.71, 3465.72, 3465.73 and 3465.79.*

(i) *any portion of the cost (benefit) of current and future income taxes relating to the correction of an error or a change in accounting policy should be recognized in a manner consistent with the underlying item (see "Accounting Changes", Section 1506). (January, 2000)*

11-141.   While the preceding Recommendation requires that taxes be allocated to the accounting item to which they relate (e.g., taxes related to an extraordinary item should be disclosed with the extraordinary item), it does not specifically require that the amount of such taxes be separately disclosed. However, for most of the items listed, separate disclosure of the amount of the tax is required as follows:

Paragraph 3465.91   *The following should be disclosed separately:*

(a) *current income tax expense or benefit included in the determination of income or loss before discontinued operations and extraordinary items;*

(b) *future income tax expense or benefit included in the determination of income or loss before discontinued operations and extraordinary items;*

(c) income tax expense or benefit related to discontinued operations;

(d) income tax expense or benefit related to extraordinary items recognized during the period;

(e) the portion of the cost of current and future income taxes related to capital transactions or other items that are charged or credited to equity; and

(f) the amount and expiry date of unused tax losses and income tax reductions, and the amount of deductible temporary differences, for which no future income tax asset has been recognized. (January, 2000)

Example

11-142.   A simple example will illustrate the concept described in the preceding Section:

Example   During the current year, Intra Inc. has income before taxes and extraordinary items of $1,000,000, as well as an extraordinary gain of $250,000 before taxes. There are no differences between these Accounting Income figures and the amounts that will be included in Taxable Income. The Company is subject to a tax rate of 35 percent.

11-143.   In this case, Taxable Income will be $1,250,000 and Taxes Payable will be $437,500 [(35%)($1,250,000)]. For financial reporting purposes, this single figure must be segregated into two components. These would be the $350,000 in Taxes Payable that relate to the $1,000,000 in income before taxes and extraordinary items, and the $87,500 that relates to the Extraordinary Gain. This information would be presented in a condensed Income Statement as follows:

Intra Inc.
Condensed Income Statement
Current Year

Income Before Taxes And Extraordinary Item		$1,000,000
Income Tax Expense (All Current)		(350,000)
Income Before Extraordinary Item		$ 650,000
Extraordinary Gain	$250,000	
Related Taxes (All Current)	(87,500)	162,500
Net Income		$ 812,500

11-144.   Similar treatment would be given to the other types of items listed in Paragraph 3465.63.

A More Complex Example

11-145.   A somewhat more complex example will serve to illustrate situations which involve both interperiod and intraperiod income tax allocation:

Example   At the end of 2001, The Hatch Company has net taxable temporary differences of $900,000. As the tax rate in effect at that point in time was 35 percent, these differences were reflected in a Future Income Tax Liability of $315,000. At the beginning of 2002, the government changed the tax rate to 40 percent. This change was not anticipated at the end of 2001.

The 2002 accounting Income Before Taxes And Extraordinary Items for the Hatch Company is $500,000. The computation of this figure included $25,000 in dividends received from taxable Canadian corporations. The capital cost allowance deducted in the calculation of taxable income was $300,000 while the Depreciation Expense charged in the calculation of accounting income was $200,000.

During 2002, the Company experienced an Extraordinary Gain amounting to $37,500 before taxes. This gain qualified as a capital gain for tax purposes.

In addition, there was a change in accounting policy which was applied retroactively. This change involved a change in the amortization method applied to depreciable assets. It increased the accumulated amortization by $75,000, and this amount was deducted from the opening balance of retained earnings. This change did not alter the tax basis of the depreciable assets.

The Company had a December 31, 2001 Retained Earnings balance of $2,000,000. No dividends were declared or paid in 2002.

11-146. The analysis of the Hatch Company's tax balances for 2002 would be as follows:

	Accounting Income	Taxable Income	Change In Temporary Differences
Income Before Taxes	$500,000	$500,000	
Dividend Revenue	(25,000)	(25,000)	
Depreciation		200,000	($200,000)
Capital Cost Allowance		(300,000)	300,000
Ordinary Balance	$475,000	$375,000	$100,000
Tax Rate	40%	40%	40%
Tax Balances Before Rate Change	$190,000	$150,000	$ 40,000
Rate Change [($900,000)(40% - 35%)]	45,000	N/A	45,000
Tax Balances - Ordinary Income	$235,000	$150,000	$ 85,000
Extraordinary Gain	$37,500	$37,500	
Non-Taxable One-Half	(18,750)	(18,750)	
Extraordinary Balance	$18,750	$18,750	Nil
Tax Rate	40%	40%	
Tax Balances - Extraordinary Item	$ 7,500	$ 7,500	Nil
Prior Period Adjustment	($75,000)	($75,000)	
Non-Deductible Increase In Accumulated Amortization		75,000	($75,000)
Prior Period Balance	($75,000)	Nil	($75,000)
Tax Rate	40%		40%
Tax Balances - Prior Period Adjustment	($30,000)	Nil	($30,000)

11-147. Based on the preceding schedule, the journal entry to record taxes would be as follows:

Income Tax Expense - Ordinary	$235,000	
Income Tax Expense - Extraordinary	7,500	
Future Income Tax Asset - Non-Current	30,000	
Income Tax Benefit - Prior Period Adjustment		$ 30,000
Future Income Tax Liability - Non-Current		85,000
Taxes Payable ($150,000 + $7,500)		157,500

11-148. Based on this entry, Hatch Company's Income Statement would be as follows:

Hatch Company
Condensed Income Statement
Year Ending December 31, 2002

Income Before Taxes And Extraordinary Items		$500,000
Income Tax Expense (Note One):		
Current (From Schedule)	($150,000)	
Future (From Schedule)	(85,000)	(235,000)
Income Before Extraordinary Items		$265,000
Extraordinary Gain	$ 37,500	
Applicable Taxes (All Current - Note Two)	(7,500)	30,000
Net Income		$295,000

Note One The required reconciliation (Paragraph 3465.92) between the actual Income Tax Expense and the expense at the statutory rate would be as follows:

Taxes At Statutory Rate Of 40 Percent [(40%)($500,000)]	$200,000
Tax Savings From Non-Taxable Dividends [(40%)($25,000)]	(10,000)
Change In Future Income Tax Liability Resulting From	
Rate Change [(40% - 35%)($900,000)]	45,000
Income Tax Expense Reported	$235,000

Note Two All of the taxes on the Extraordinary Gain are currently payable. The reason that the effective tax rate is 20 percent rather than the statutory rate of 40 percent is that the item is a capital gain and only 50 percent of the amount is taxed.

11-149. The Hatch Company's Statement of Retained Earnings would be as follows:

Opening Balance - As Previously Reported		$2,000,000
Prior Period Adjustment	($75,000)	
Applicable Taxes (All Future)	30,000	(45,000)
Opening Balance - As Restated		$1,955,000
Net Income		295,000
Closing Balance		$2,250,000

Exercise Eleven-9 deals with intraperiod and interperiod tax allocation.

Exercise Eleven-9

On December 31, 2001, Ondine Inc. has taxable temporary differences of $670,000, all related to differences between the net book value and the UCC of its depreciable assets. These differences are reflected in a Future Income Tax Liability of $134,000. This amount is calculated at the enacted tax rate of 20 percent that is applicable to the Company. This rate reflects the fact that Ondine is a Canadian controlled private corporation (CCPC). On this date, the Company's Retained Earnings balance is $2,896,000.

During the year ending December 31, 2002, the Company's Income Before Taxes And Extraordinary Items, calculated in accordance with generally accepted accounting principles, is $423,000. This amount is after the deduction of $93,000 in Depreciation Expense. In its 2002 tax return, the Company deducted the maximum CCA of $134,000. Other information applicable to this year is as follows:

1. As the result of an expropriation of Land, the Company experiences an Extraordinary Loss of $92,000. The loss is a capital loss for tax purposes. While the Company has no capital gains in the current year or the three previous years, the Company believes that it is more likely than not to have sufficient capital gains in future years to be able to use the loss.

2. On January 1, 2002, the Company's shares are listed on a recognized stock exchange, resulting in the Company losing its status as a CCPC. This means that the effective tax rate for the company increases to 42 percent.

This is a continuation of Exercise Eleven-9.

3. Early in 2002, the Company decides to change its accounting policy with respect to depreciation. This accounting change increases the 2002 Depreciation Expense by $36,000, an amount that has been incorporated into the $93,000 that was deducted in the determination of Income Before Taxes And Extraordinary Items. The effect of this change on the Depreciation Expense of prior years was an increase of $73,000.

4. The Company paid no dividends during the year ending December 31, 2002.

5. At December 31, 2002, the Company's only temporary differences are those related to the difference between the net book value and the UCC of the Company's depreciable assets.

Required:

A. Prepare the journal entries to record current and future income taxes for Ondine Inc. for the year ending December 31, 2002.

B. Prepare a combined Statement Of Income And Change In Retained Earnings for the year ending December 31, 2002.

End Of Exercise Eleven-9

Treatment Of Losses

The Nature Of The Problem
What The Law Allows
11-150.   The rules for loss carry overs as specified in the *Income Tax Act* are as follows:

Non-Capital (Operating) Losses   Current period non-capital losses can be carried back to be applied against Taxable Income in the three preceding taxation years and carried forward to be applied against Taxable Income in the seven subsequent taxation years. To the extent that such losses relate to farm operations, the carry forward period is extended to ten years. If the farm loss carry overs are restricted by Section 31 of the *Income Tax Act*, they can only be deducted to the extent that there is farm income in the current period.

Net Capital Losses   Current period net allowable capital losses can be carried back to be applied against Taxable Income in the preceding three years and carried forward to be applied against Taxable Income in any subsequent year. However, net capital losses can only be deducted to the extent that there are taxable capital gains in the current period.

11-151.   Loss carry backs are applied to the taxable income of previous years in order to claim a refund of taxes paid during those years. The refund will be at the rates which prevailed during the relevant preceding years. With respect to the carry forwards, these are applied against the taxable income of future periods to reduce the amount of taxes payable in those years. As you would expect, the benefits will be realized at the rates in effect in the relevant future years.

Accounting Problems With Loss Carry Backs
11-152.   With respect to loss carry backs, the accounting problem is not significant. The preceding years' taxable incomes and taxes paid are known quantities and, as a result, there is generally no uncertainty associated with either the amount of the current period loss that can be carried back or the amount of tax refund that will result from this carry back. Since we are certain of realizing (receiving in cash or reducing a tax liability) the loss carry back benefit, it is

clear that the benefit should be included in income in the year the loss occurs. This means that an Income Tax Benefit will be included in income, thereby reducing the amount of the Net Loss for the period.

Accounting Problems With Loss Carry Forwards

11-153.   With respect to the benefits associated with loss carry forwards, we are confronted with a significantly more difficult issue. This relates to the fact that the benefit is not certain but, rather, is dependent on the enterprise's ability to generate sufficient income within the loss carry forward period to make use of the benefit. In the case of net capital loss carry forwards, there is an additional restriction in that the required future income must be in the form of taxable capital gains.

11-154.   If sufficient Taxable Income is not generated, the loss carry forward on non-capital losses can expire and the potential benefit will be lost. While net capital loss carry forwards do not expire, the inability of the enterprise to generate taxable capital gains may create a situation where the benefit will not be used in the foreseeable future.

11-155.   This uncertainty raises the question of when a benefit related to a loss carry forward should be recognized. Two possible answers to this question include:

1. The carry forward benefit can be recognized in the period in which the loss which engendered it occurred. This assumes that the enterprise will generate sufficient Taxable Income of the appropriate type to be able to make use of the potential loss carry forward benefit. As the loss is related to items included and deducted in the current period, this solution would be consistent with the matching principal.

2. Recognition of the carry forward benefit can be deferred until sufficient income is generated to allow the enterprise to actually experience a reduction in future taxes payable. This solution assumes that there is sufficient uncertainty with respect to the realization of the loss carry forward benefit to warrant the deferral of its recognition.

11-156.   There is also the possibility of recognizing part, but not all, of the benefit in the period of loss or, alternatively, recognizing the benefit in a period subsequent to the loss but prior to its application against future taxes payable. This latter alternative would be appropriate when the earnings outlook of the enterprise improves in a period that is after the loss, but before the benefit is actually realized. Alternatively, there may be a need for de-recognition of previously recognized amounts in situations where the company's prospects have deteriorated.

11-157.   These issues make the dealing with loss carry forward benefits a fairly complex area of financial reporting. Subsequent to reviewing the specific Recommendations of Section 3465, we will present a number of different examples to illustrate some of these complexities.

Section 3465 Recommendations

Loss Carry Backs

11-158.   As was noted in the previous section, there is no uncertainty with respect to the benefit associated with a loss carry back. As a consequence, this benefit will be treated as a receivable, a view that is reflected in the following Section 3465 Recommendation:

> **Paragraph 3465.20**   *The benefit relating to a tax loss arising in the current period that will be carried back to recover income taxes of a previous period should be recognized as a current asset and not included in future income tax liabilities or future income tax assets.* (January, 2000)

11-159.   When this receivable is recorded, a corresponding amount will be included in the loss period's Income Statement as part of the current component of Income Tax Expense or Income Tax Benefit.

Loss Carry Forwards

11-160.   As noted previously, the situation here is more complex. The basic Recommendation is as follows:

> **Paragraph 3465.24**   *At each balance sheet date, except as provided in paragraphs 3465.33, 3465.35 and 3465.37, a future income tax asset should be recognized for all deductible temporary differences, unused tax losses and income tax reductions. The amount recognized should be limited to the amount that is more likely than not to be realized.* (January, 2000)

> Paragraph 3465.33, 3465.35, and 3465. 37 refer to specialized situations, some of which will be covered in Chapter 12. They are not of concern in this Chapter.]

11-161.   For this purpose, "more likely than not" is defined as follows:

> **Paragraph 3465.09(i)**   An event is **more likely than not** when the probability that it will occur is greater than 50%.

11-162.   To begin, you should note that Section 3465 makes it much easier to recognize a loss carry forward benefit than it was under the Recommendations of Section 3470. Under the now superseded Section 3470, loss carry forward benefits could generally be recognized as an asset only if there was "virtual certainty" that they would be realized in future periods. The definition of "virtual certainty" included a requirement that there must be assurance beyond a reasonable doubt that the loss carry forward benefit would be realized. In practical terms, it was unusual for an enterprise to be able to make this claim.

11-163.   Under Section 3465, the enterprise is only required to claim that there is a probability greater than 50 percent that the loss carry forward benefit will be realized. As this is a less stringent test than virtual certainty, recognition of Future Income Tax Assets in the period of a loss is likely to become more common.

11-164.   Section 3465 provides considerable guidance with respect to assessing whether it is more likely than not that a loss carry forward benefit will be realized. The relevant paragraphs are as follows:

> **Paragraph 3465.25**   Future realization of the tax benefit of an existing deductible temporary difference, unused tax loss or unused income tax reduction ultimately depends on the existence of sufficient taxable income of an appropriate nature, relating to the same taxable entity and the same taxation authority, within the carryback/carryforward periods available under the tax law. The following sources of taxable income may be available under the tax law to realize a tax benefit for deductible temporary differences, unused tax losses or income tax reductions:

> (a) future reversals of existing taxable temporary differences;

> (b) future taxable income before the effects of reversing temporary differences, unused tax losses and income tax reductions;

> (c) taxable income in prior year(s) if carryback is permitted under the tax law; and

> (d) tax-planning strategies that would, if necessary, be implemented to realize a future income tax asset.

> **Paragraph 3465.26**   An enterprise would consider tax-planning strategies in determining the extent to which it is more likely than not that a future income tax asset will be realized. Tax planning strategies are actions that:

> (a) are prudent and feasible;

> (b) an enterprise ordinarily might not take, but would take to prevent a tax loss or income tax reduction from expiring unused; and

> (c) would result in realization of future income tax assets.

The carrying amount of any future income tax asset recognized as a result of a tax planning strategy would reflect the cost of implementing that strategy.

Paragraph 3465.27   Forming a conclusion that it is appropriate to recognize a future income tax asset is difficult when there is unfavourable evidence such as cumulative losses in recent years. Other examples of unfavourable evidence include:

(a) a history of tax losses or income tax reductions expiring unused;

(b) losses expected in early future years (by a currently profitable enterprise);

(c) unsettled circumstances that, if unfavourably resolved, would adversely affect future operations and profit levels on a continuing basis in future years; and

(d) a carryback or carryforward period that is so brief that it would limit realization of tax benefits, particularly if the enterprise operates in a traditionally cyclical business.

Paragraph 3465.28   Examples of favourable evidence that might support a conclusion that recognition of a future income tax asset is appropriate despite the existence of unfavourable evidence include:

(a) existing sufficient taxable temporary differences relating to the same taxable entity and the same taxation authority which would result in taxable amounts against which the unused tax losses or income tax reductions can be utilized;

(b) existing contracts or firm sales backlog that will produce more than enough taxable income to realize the future income tax asset based on existing sales prices and cost structures;

(c) an excess of fair value over the tax basis of the enterprise's net assets in an amount sufficient to realize the future income tax asset; or

(d) a strong earnings history exclusive of the loss that created the future deductible amount (unused tax loss carryforward or deductible temporary difference) together with evidence indicating that the loss (for example, an extraordinary item) is an aberration rather than a continuing condition.

Paragraph 3465.29   An enterprise must use judgment in considering the relative impact of unfavourable and favourable evidence on the recognition of a future income tax asset. The weight given to the potential effect of unfavourable and favourable evidence would be commensurate with the extent to which it can be verified objectively. The more unfavourable evidence that exists, the more favourable evidence is necessary and the more difficult it is to support a conclusion that recognition of some portion or all of the future income tax asset is appropriate.

Disclosure Of Unrecognized Benefits

11-165.   When an enterprise is not able to recognize the benefit of a tax loss carry forward, the amount of the unused tax loss must be disclosed along with its expiry date, if applicable. This Recommendation is as follows:

Paragraph 3465.91(f)   *The following should be disclosed separately:*

(a) through (e) .....
(f) the amount and expiry date of unused tax losses and income tax reductions, and the amount of deductible temporary differences, for which no future income tax asset has been recognized. (January, 2000)

11-166.   Note carefully that there is no general disclosure requirement for loss carry forwards. Disclosure is required only if all or part of the associated benefit cannot be recognized. As long as the full benefit of the loss has been recognized, either as a carry back or a carry forward, disclosure of the presence of a carry forward is not required. Also note that it is the loss carry forward amount, not the expected benefit, that is to be disclosed.

11-167.   The other issue here is how to make this required disclosure. While dislosure in a note to the financial statements would satisfy this requirement, the *Handbook* also notes the following:

Paragraph 3465.30   An enterprise could recognize a future income tax asset for all deductible temporary differences, unused tax losses and income tax reductions, reduced by a valuation allowance to the extent that it is more likely than not that some portion or all of the assets will not be realized. The valuation allowance would be sufficient to reduce the future income tax asset to the amount that is more likely than not to be realized. This would result in the same net asset as that determined in accordance with paragraph 3465.24 and after applying the considerations described in paragraphs 3465.25-.29 in determining the amount of the valuation allowance.

11-168.   This suggests that the full benefit available be set up as an asset, with any amount that cannot be currently recognized included in a valuation allowance that will be deducted from the asset. Note, however, this is not an italicized Recommendation, only a suggested alternative to note disclosure.

11-169.   In contrast, this "valuation allowance" approach is required in the United States under the provisions of FASB Statement No. 109, "Foreign Currency Translation". We would expect that, given the ongoing desire to harmonize U.S. and Canadian accounting practices, many Canadian enterprises would adopt this approach on a voluntary basis. Statistics from the 2001 edition of *Financial Reporting In Canada* support this view, with the great majority of companies that disclosed unrecognized loss carry forward benefits using the valuation allowance approach. Given this trend, we will use this approach in our examples.

Reassessment Of Future Income Tax Assets

11-170.   Section 3465 requires the annual reassessment of Future Income Tax Assets. It may be necessary to write down assets that have been set up to recognize loss carry forward benefits, or, alternatively, set up assets for loss carry forward benefits that have not been previously recognized. This Recommendation is as follows:

Paragraph 3465.31   *At each balance sheet date:*

(a) to the extent that it is no longer more likely than not that a recognized future income tax asset will be realized, the carrying amount of the asset should be reduced; or

(b) to the extent that it is more likely than not that an unrecognized future income tax asset will be realized, a future income tax asset should be recognized. (January, 2000)

11-171.   Both parts of this Recommendation will be illustrated in the following example.

Loss Carry Over Examples
Basic Example

11-172.   In this Section, we will present several cases designed to illustrate the various Recommendations of Section 3465 with respect to loss carry overs. All of these cases will be based on the following example:

Example   Carrier Ltd. has a December 31 year end. During the year ending December 31, 2002, it experiences an Accounting Loss Before Taxes of $1,000,000. The Company has no temporary differences at either the beginning or the end of 2002 and, for the year, its Taxable Loss is equal to its $1,000,000 Accounting Loss Before Taxes. The statutory combined tax rate in effect for 2002 is 45 percent.

Case One - Loss Carry Back

11-173.   In this case, we will assume that in the year ending December 31, 2001, Carrier Ltd. had Accounting Income and Taxable Income in excess of $1,000,000, all of which was taxed at a rate of 50 percent. Given this, the entire 2002 loss of $1,000,000 can be carried back to 2001 and a refund claimed. The relevant journal entry would be as follows:

Current Taxes Receivable [(50%)($1,000,000)]	$500,000	
Income Tax Benefit		$500,000

11-174.   Based on this entry, the condensed Income Statement for Carrier Ltd. for the year ending December 31, 2002 would be as follows:

Carrier Ltd.
Condensed Income Statement (100% Carry Back)
Year Ending December 31, 2002

Loss Before Income Taxes	($1,000,000)
Income Tax Benefit (All Current)	500,000
Net Loss	($ 500,000)

11-175.   Additional disclosure would be required to explain why the Income Tax Benefit does not reflect the statutory rate of 45 percent. This is due to the fact that the tax rate applicable to the tax refund is 50 percent.

Case Two - Loss Carry Forward Benefit More Likely Than Not To Be Realized

11-176.   In this case, we will assume that Carrier Ltd. has had no Taxable Income in the three years prior to 2002. However, in 2002, they are able to claim that it is more likely than not that the benefit of the 2002 loss carry forward will be realized. The required journal entry for 2002 would be as follows:

Future Income Tax Asset [(45%)($1,000,000)]	$450,000	
Income Tax Benefit		$450,000

11-177.   Based on this entry, the condensed Income Statement for Carrier Ltd for the year ending December 31, 2002 would be as follows:

Carrier Ltd.
Condensed Income Statement (100% Recognized)
Year Ending December 31, 2002

Loss Before Income Taxes	($1,000,000)
Income Tax Benefit (All Future)	450,000
Net Loss	($ 550,000)

11-178.   In 2003, the Company's Accounting Income Before Taxes and Taxable Income are equal to $1,500,000. The tax rate in effect for 2003 is 50 percent. The Company was not aware of the 2003 tax rate increase at the end of 2002. Given this, the journal entry for the year ending December 31, 2003 would be as follows:

Income Tax Expense	$700,000	
Future Income Tax Asset (Balance)		$450,000
Current Taxes Payable [(50%)($1,500,000 - $1,000,000)]		250,000

11-179.   Based on this entry, the condensed Income Statement for Carrier Ltd. for the year ending December 31, 2003 would be as follows:

Carrier Ltd.
Condensed Income Statement
Year Ending December 31, 2003

Income Before Income Taxes		$1,500,000
Income Tax Expense:		
Current	($250,000)	
Future	(450,000)	(700,000)
Net Income		$ 800,000

11-180.   Additional disclosure would be required to explain why the Income Tax Expense does not reflect the current rate of 50 percent.

Case Three -
Part Of The Loss Carry Forward Benefit More Likely Than Not To Be Realized

11-181.   In this case, we will again assume that Carrier Ltd. has had no Taxable Income in the three years prior to 2002. In 2002, they are able to claim that they are more likely than not to realize the benefit associated with $600,000 of the $1,000,000 loss carry forward. Assuming that disclosure is based on the valuation allowance approach, the required journal entry for 2002 would be as follows:

Future Income Tax Asset [(45%)($1,000,000)]	$450,000	
Income Tax Benefit [(45%)($600,000)]		$270,000
Future Income Tax Asset - Allowance For		
Non-Realization Of Loss Carry Forward Benefit		
[(45%)($1,000,000 - $600,000)]		180,000

11-182.   Based on this entry, the condensed Income Statement for Carrier Ltd. for the year ending December 31, 2002 would be as follows:

Carrier Ltd.
Condensed Income Statement (Part Recognized)
Year Ending December 31, 2002

Loss Before Income Taxes	($1,000,000)
Income Tax Benefit (All Future)	270,000
Net Loss	($ 730,000)

11-183.   In the December 31, 2002 Balance Sheet, the Allowance would be deducted from the Future Income Tax Asset, leaving a net balance of $270,000 [(45%)(600,000)].

11-184.   Additional disclosure would be required in this year to indicate that there is a loss carry forward of $400,000 for which the benefit has not been recognized and that it expires in the year ending December 31, 2009. In addition, the Income Tax Benefit would have to be reconciled with the statutory rate of 45 percent.

11-185.   In 2003, the Company's Accounting Income and Taxable Income are equal to $1,500,000. The tax rate in effect for 2003 remains at 45 percent. For the year ending December 31, 2003, the required journal entry would be as follows:

Income Tax Expense	$495,000	
Future Income Tax Asset - Allowance For		
Non-Realization Of Loss Carry Forward Benefit	180,000	
Future Income Tax Asset		$450,000
Current Taxes Payable [(45%)($1,500,000 - $1,000,000)]		225,000

11-186.   Based on this entry, the condensed Income Statement for Carrier Ltd. for the year ending December 31, 2003 would be as follows:

Carrier Ltd.
Condensed Income Statement
Year Ending December 31, 2003

Income Before Income Taxes		$1,500,000
Income Tax Expense:		
Current	($225,000)	
Future	(270,000)	(495,000)
Net Income		$1,005,000

11-187.   Additional disclosure would be required to explain why the Income Tax Expense does not reflect the current rate of 45 percent.

Case Four -
Loss Carry Forward Benefit Recognized And Subsequently Written Off

11-188.   In this case, we will assume that Carrier Ltd. has had no Taxable Income in the three years prior to 2002. However, as in Case Two, in 2002 they are able to claim that it is more likely than not that the benefit of the 2002 loss carry forward will be realized. The required journal entry for 2002 would be as follows:

Future Income Tax Asset [(45%)($1,000,000)]	$450,000	
Income Tax Benefit		$450,000

11-189.   Based on this entry, the condensed Income Statement for Carrier Ltd. for the year ending December 31, 2002 would be as follows:

Carrier Ltd.
Condensed Income Statement (100% Recognized)
Year Ending December 31, 2002

Loss Before Income Taxes	($1,000,000)
Income Tax Benefit (All Future)	450,000
Net Loss	($ 550,000)

11-190.   In 2003, the Company has Accounting Income Before Taxes and Taxable Income of $100,000, leading management to conclude that it is no longer more likely than not that the benefit of the remaining $900,000 loss carry forward will be realized. The tax rate in 2003 remains unchanged at 45 percent. The journal entry for the year ending December 31, 2003 would be as follows:

Income Tax Expense		
[(45%)($100,000) + ($450,000 - $45,000)]	$450,000	
Future Income Tax Asset (Balance)		$450,000

11-191.   Based on this journal entry, the condensed Income Statement for Carrier Ltd. for the year ending December 31, 2003 would be as follows:

Carrier Ltd.
Condensed Income Statement
Year Ending December 31, 2003

Income Before Taxes	$100,000
Income Tax Expense (All Future)	(450,000)
Net Loss	($350,000)

11-192.   Additional disclosure would be required to indicate that the benefit associated with an unused loss carry forward of $900,000 has not been recognized, and that this carry forward will expire in the year ending December 31, 2009. The Income Tax Expense would also have to be reconciled with the rate in effect of 45 percent.

Case Five - Loss Carry Forward Benefit Recognized
After Year Of Loss But Before Realization

11-193.   In this case, we will assume that Carrier Ltd. has had no Taxable Income in the three years prior to 2002. In 2002, they are unable to claim that any of the benefit associated with the $1,000,000 loss carry forward is more likely than not to be realized. In the year ending December 31, 2003, they have Accounting Income Before Taxes and Taxable Income equal to $200,000. This improved performance allows management to claim that it is now more likely than not that the benefit associated with the remaining $800,000 loss carry forward will be realized. The tax rate in effect for 2003 remains at 45 percent.

11-194.   There would be no tax related journal entry in the year ending December 31, 2002. The condensed Income Statement for Carrier Ltd. for that year would be as follows:

Carrier Ltd.
Condensed Income Statement (None Recognized)
Year Ending December 31, 2002

Loss Before Income Taxes	($1,000,000)
Income Tax Benefit	Nil
Net Loss	($1,000,000)

11-195.   Additional disclosure would be required in this year to indicate that there is a loss carry forward of $1,000,000 for which the benefit has not been recognized and that it expires in the year ending December 31, 2009. In addition, the Income Tax Benefit would have to be reconciled with the rate in effect of 45 percent.

11-196.   The required journal entry for the year ending December 31, 2003 would be as follows:

Future Income Tax Asset		
[(45%)($1,000,000 - $200,000)]	$360,000	
Income Tax Benefit		$360,000

11-197.   The condensed Income Statement for Carrier Ltd. for the year ending December 31, 2003 would be as follows:

Carrier Ltd.
Condensed Income Statement
Year Ending December 31, 2003

Income Before Income Taxes	$200,000
Income Tax Benefit (All Future)	360,000
Net Income	$560,000

11-198.   Additional disclosure would be required to reconcile the Income Tax Benefit with the rate in effect of 45 percent.

Exercise Eleven-10

Finder Inc. has a December 31 year end. During the year ending December 31, 2002, it experiences an Accounting Loss Before Taxes of $375,000. The Company has no temporary differences at either the beginning or the end of 2002 and, for the year, its Taxable Loss is equal to its $375,000 Accounting Loss Before Taxes. Finder Inc. has had no Taxable Income in the three years prior to 2002.

> Exercise Eleven-10 deals with loss carry forwards.

The statutory combined tax rate in effect for 2002 is 43 percent. At the beginning of 2003 the Company's combined tax rate is unexpectedly reduced to 41 percent.

Required: For each of the following independent cases, prepare the journal entries to record taxes for 2002 and 2003. Also, provide a condensed Income Statement for both years. Your answer should include all of the disclosure required for a public company.

A. Assume that, in 2002, Finder Inc. is able to claim that it is more likely than not that the benefit of the 2002 loss carry forward will be realized. In 2003, the Company has accounting and taxable income of $420,000.

B. Assume that, in 2002, Finder Inc. is able to claim that only $200,000 of the loss is more likely than not to be realized. In 2003, the Company has accounting and taxable income of $420,000.

C. Assume that, in 2002, Finder Inc. is able to claim that it is more likely than not that the benefit of the 2002 loss carry forward will be realized. In 2003, the Company has accounting and taxable income of only $10,000. This leads management to conclude that it is no longer more likely than not that the remaining $365,000 of the loss carry forward will be realized.

End Of Exercise Eleven-10

Temporary Differences On Assets Acquired Other Than In A Business Combination

Background

11-199.   In the great majority of situations, when an asset is acquired it will have an initial tax basis that is equal to its initial carrying value. For accounting purposes, the asset will be recorded at its cost and, at that point in time, its adjusted cost base or capital cost for tax purposes will be the same amount. The most common exceptions to this general rule are assets acquired in certain types of business combination transactions that are accounted for by the purchase method. For accounting purposes, these assets are recorded at their fair value which is, in effect, their cost to the acquirer. However, if a tax rollover provision is utilized or if the business combination involves an acquisition of shares, different values can be used for tax purposes. The procedures required in such situations are dealt with in Chapter 12.

11-200.   In addition, there are situations, other than those involving business combination transactions, in which a newly acquired asset will have an initial carrying value that is different than its initial tax basis. These situations may involve cases where the tax basis of the asset is greater than its cost, as well as cases where the tax basis is less than cost. The following Recommendation deals with both of these possibilities:

> **Paragraph 3465.43**   *When an asset is acquired other than in a business combination and the tax basis of that asset is less than its cost, the cost of future income taxes recognized at the time of acquisition should be added to the cost of the asset. When an asset is acquired other than in a business combination and the tax basis of that asset is greater than its cost, the benefit related to future income taxes recognized at the time of acquisition should be deducted from the cost of the asset.* (January, 2000)

Cost Greater Than Tax Basis

11-201.   As an example of the application of Paragraph 3465.43 to a situation where cost exceeds the tax basis of an acquired asset, consider the following:

> **Example**   A corporation acquires a depreciable asset outside of a business combination for cash of $20,000 plus $30,000 in no par value common shares. Because it has been acquired under the provisions of ITA Section 85, its elected tax basis is the UCC of $20,000. The asset had an original cost of $90,000. The corporation is subject to a tax rate of 40 percent.

11-202.   The economic concept which underlies Paragraph 3465.43 is that, because the amount paid for the asset in the example is not fully deductible to the purchaser, the $50,000 paid for the asset is less than the corporation would have paid for the same asset if the cost was fully deductible. Given this, the recorded value for the asset will be increased to reflect the Future Income Tax Liability that exists when the asset is acquired.

11-203.   At first glance, one is inclined to say that the Future Income Tax Liability is equal to $12,000, the corporation's 40 percent tax rate multiplied by the $30,000 difference between the cost of $50,000 and the tax basis of $20,000. This, however, does not work. Adding this amount to the carrying value of the asset results in an amount of $62,000. If the asset were sold for $62,000, the tax liability would be $16,800. This amount is 40 percent of the $42,000 ($62,000 - $20,000) recapture of CCA.

11-204.   What has to be established here is a new carrying value for the asset, such that when the corporation's tax rate is multiplied by the difference between this new carrying value and the $20,000 tax basis of the asset, the product is equal to the difference between the new carrying value and the $50,000 acquisition cost. If we let X equal this new carrying value, the correct amount can be determined as follows:

$$X = \$50,000 + [(40\%)(X - \$20,000)]$$
$$X = \$70,000$$

11-205.   Using this value, the entry to record the acquisition of the asset would be as follows:

Asset	$70,000	
Future Income Tax Liability		$20,000
Cash		20,000
No Par Value Common Stock		30,000

11-206.   The logic of this approach is illustrated by the fact that, if the asset were sold for $70,000, there would be a tax liability of $20,000 [(40%)($70,000 - $20,000)]. In other words, instead of showing the asset at its tax reduced value of $50,000, it will be shown at its full $70,000 value, accompanied by the Future Income Tax Liability that would have to be paid if this value was realized.

Cost Less Than Tax Basis

11-207.   A simple example will also be used to illustrate the application of Paragraph 3465.43 to a situation where the cost of a newly acquired asset is less than its tax basis:

> **Example**   A corporation acquires an asset in an arm's length transaction for $100,000 in cash. As an inducement to make this investment in a particular industry, it gains the right to deduct 125 percent of its cost for tax purposes. The corporation's tax rate is 45 percent. The legislation also stipulates that, if the asset is sold for more than its $100,000 cost, the resulting gain will be treated as fully taxable business income, not as a one-half taxable capital gain.

11-208.   The economic interpretation here is that the corporation paid a higher than normal amount for this asset because of its associated tax benefits. While we are dealing with a Future Income Tax Asset, as opposed to a Future Income Tax Liability in the previous case, the basic idea is unchanged. We need to establish a new carrying value for the asset, such that when the corporation's tax rate is multiplied by the difference between this new carrying value and the $125,000 tax basis of the asset, the product is equal to the difference between the new carrying value and the $100,000 in cash paid. If we let X equal this new carrying value, the correct amount can be determined as follows:

$$X = \$100,000 + [(45\%)(X - \$125,000)]$$
$$X = \$79,545$$

11-209.   The entry to record this value would be as follows:

Asset	$79,545	
Future Income Tax Asset	20,455	
Cash		$100,000

11-210.   The logic of this approach is illustrated by the fact that, if the asset were sold for $79,545, there would be a tax deduction of $20,455 [(45%)($79,545 - $125,000)].

Exercise Eleven-11 deals with temporary differences at time of acquisition.

Exercise Eleven-11

For both of the following cases, prepare the journal entry that would be required to record the acquisition of the asset.

A. A corporation acquires a depreciable asset outside of a business combination for cash of $95,000 plus $135,000 in no par value common shares. Because it has been acquired under the provisions of ITA Section 85, its elected tax basis is the UCC of $95,000. The asset had an original cost of $350,000. The corporation is subject to a tax rate of 35 percent.

B. A corporation acquires an asset in an arm's length transaction for $285,000 in cash. As an inducement to make this investment in a particular industry, it gains the right to deduct 150 percent of its cost for tax purposes. The corporation's tax rate is 40 percent. The legislation also stipulates that, if the asset is sold for more than its $285,000 cost, the resulting gain will be treated as fully taxable business income, not as a one-half taxable capital gain.

End Of Exercise Eleven-11

Income Taxes In Canadian Practice

Statistics From Financial Reporting In Canada

11-211. The 2001 edition of *Financial Reporting In Canada* surveyed annual reports for the four years 1997 through 2000. While Section 3465 was introduced into the *CICA Handbook* in December, 1997, its effective date for public enterprises was for fiscal years beginning on or after January 1, 2000. Of the 200 companies surveyed, 152 companies disclosed that the FITAL method was used, 27 disclosed that the deferred charge method was used, 7 disclosed that both the FITAL method and taxes payable method was used and 14 did not disclose the method used. Of these 14, it appeared that 6 were using the FITAL method and the remaining 6 were using the deferred charge method.

11-212. Most of the survey companies disclosed the amount by which the current tax expense had been increased or decreased by future income taxes or deferred taxes. Of the 200 companies, 109 companies included this disclosure in a note, 58 included this amount as a separate item in the Income Statement and 15 had no disclosure of future or deferred taxes. For the remaining 18, the amount was only evident from the Cash Flow Statement.

11-213. A reconciliation of the actual tax expense or benefit rate with the company's statutory income tax rate was provided by 194 companies. This was provided in dollar form (129 companies), in percentage form (48 companies), both in dollar and percentage form (14 companies) and in narrative form (3 companies)

11-214. Of the 165 companies using the FITAL method, 149 companies disclosed Balance Sheet accounts related to income taxes. Of these 149 companies, 62 disclosed only future income tax liabilities, 15 disclosed only future income tax assets, and 72 disclosed both future income tax assets and liabilities.

11-215. Of the 165 companies using the FITAL method, a total of 87 companies provided some disclosure of unrecognized loss carry forward benefits. Of these 87 companies, 78 disclosed both the amount of the loss and its expiry date.

Example From Practice

11-216. This relatively short example is from the annual report of Abitibi-Consolidated Inc. for the reporting period ending December 31, 2000. This Company has adopted the reporting requirements of Section 3465 during the year. The example includes a reconciliation of the actual tax provision with applicable statutory rates, as well as disclosure of the components of future income tax assets and liabilities.

Balance Sheet Disclosure

The non current liability "Future income taxes" ($875 million for 2000 and $424 million for 1999) refers to Note 5. Total Assets are equal to $11,255 million for 2000 and $3,714 million for 1999.

Income Statement Disclosure
(in millions of Canadian dollars)

	2000	1999	1998
Earnings before the under-noted items	604	293	383
Income tax expense (note 5)	191	57	129
Non-controlling interests	16	10	15
Earnings before goodwill amortization	397	226	239

Notes To Financial Statements
Note 1   Summary Of Significant Accounting Policies (in part)

k) Income taxes
Future income tax assets and liabilities are recognized for the future income tax consequences of events that have been included in the financial statements or income tax returns of the Company. Future income taxes are provided for using the liability method. Under the liability method, future income taxes are recognized for all significant temporary differences between the tax and financial statement bases of assets, liabilities and certain carry forward items.

Future income tax assets are recognized only to the extent that, in the opinion of management, it is more likely than not that the future income tax assets will be realized. Future income tax assets and liabilities are adjusted for the effects of changes in tax laws and rates on the date of enactment or substantive enactment.

n) Change in accounting policies (in part)
Effective January 1, 2000, the Company adopted, retroactively with restatement, the Canadian Institute of Chartered Accountants ("CICA") recommendations for the accounting of income taxes which requires the asset and liability method. As a result of these recommendations, capital assets increased by $35 million, goodwill increased by $141 million, retained earnings on December 31, 1999 increased by $2 million, net future income tax liability increased by $174 million. The restatement of prior years statement of earnings resulted in an increase in net earnings reported for the year ended December 31, 1999 of $4 million (1998 – $1 million).

Note 5   Income Taxes
(in millions of Canadian dollars)
The differences between the effective tax rate reflected in the provision for income taxes and the combined statutory income tax rate are as follows:

	2000	1999	1998
Average combined income tax rate	39%	40%	40%
Manufacturing and processing allowances	(7)	(7)	(7)
Recovery from disposal of a joint venture	–	(7)	–
Canadian large corporations tax	2	(5)	1
Other	(2)	–	–
Effective income tax rate	32%	21%	34%

The temporary differences that give rise to future tax assets and liabilities at December 31 consist of the following:

	2000	1999
Non-current future income tax assets		
Loss carry forwards	$315	$58
Other	12	21
	$327	$79
Non-current future income tax liabilities		
Capital assets	$1,189	$503
Other	13	–
	$1,202	$503
	$875	$424

Significant components of the income tax expense are as follows:

	2000	1999	1998
Current income tax expense	$ 75	$47	$146
Future income tax expense relating to origination and reversal of temporal differences	138	15	(14)
Future income tax benefit resulting from rate change	(22)	(5)	(3)
Income tax expense	$191	$57	$129

Management believes that all future income tax assets will more likely be realized than not and accordingly no valuation allowance has been made.

Additional Readings

11-217.   In writing the material in the text, we have incorporated all of the relevant *CICA Handbook* Recommendations, as well as material from other sources that we felt to be of importance. This includes some, but not all, of the EIC Abstracts that relate to accounting for taxes, as well as material from U.S. accounting pronouncements and ideas put forward in articles published in professional accounting journals.

11-218.   While this approach meets the needs of the great majority of accounting students, some of you may wish to pursue this subject in greater depth. To facilitate this, you will find a fairly comprehensive bibliography of materials on the subject of accounting for taxes in Chapter 42 of our *Guide to Canadian Financial Reporting*. The complete *Guide to Canadian Financial Reporting* is available on the CD-ROM which accompanies this text. Chapter 42 of the *Guide* also contains summaries of the EIC Abstracts that are directly related to this subject. The Abstracts that are summarized as an appendix to Chapter 42 are as follows:

- EIC Abstract No. 99 - "Future Income Taxes In Business Combinations That Do Not Involve The Recognition Of Goodwill As An Intangible Asset Presented Separately On The Balance Sheet"
- EIC Abstract No. 104 - "Impact Of Refundable Taxes On Future Income Tax Calculations"
- EIC Abstract No. 106 - "Application Of CICA 3465 To Investments Accounted For By The Equity Method"
- EIC Abstract No. 107 - "Application Of CICA 3465 To Mutual Fund Trusts, Real Estate Investment Trusts, Royalty Trusts And Income Trusts"
- EIC Abstract No. 108 - "CICA 3465 Transitional Provisions"
- EIC Abstract No. 109 - "Accounting For Resource Allowance Under CICA 3465"
- EIC Abstract No. 110 - "Accounting For Acquired Future Tax Benefits In Certain Purchase Transactions That Are Not Business Combinations"
- EIC Abstract No. 111 - "Determination of Substantively Enacted Tax Rates Under CICA 3465"
- EIC Abstract No. 120 - "CICA 3465 - Future Income Taxes Related To Intangible Assets Acquired In A Business Combination"

Problems For Self Study

(The solutions for these problems can be found following Chapter 16 of the text.)

Self Study Problem Eleven - 1

BLM Inc., a Canadian public company, begins operations on January 1, 2002. Its Balance Sheet on that date, as well as the comparative figures for December 31, 2002, are as follows:

BLM Inc.
Balance Sheets

	January 1 2002	December 31 2002
Cash And Receivables	$ 50,000	$ 96,000
Inventory	220,000	323,000
Deferred Development Costs	Nil	20,000
Investments	35,000	35,000
Land	25,000	25,000
Depreciable Capital Assets (Net)	295,000	279,000
Total Assets	$625,000	$778,000
Accounts Payable	$ 20,000	$ 36,000
Provision For Warranties	Nil	6,000
Fine Payable	Nil	45,000
Accrued Post Retirement Benefits	Nil	8,000
Long-Term Debt	255,000	255,000
Common Stock	350,000	350,000
Retained Earnings	Nil	78,000
Total Equities	$625,000	$778,000

These statements have been prepared without any consideration of current or future income tax obligations. This includes the need to recognize and pay for current income tax liabilities.

Other Information:

1. Income Before Taxes for the year ending December 31, 2002 is $78,000. The Company does not pay any dividends during the year.

2. For the taxation year ending December 31, 2002, the Company's combined federal/provincial tax rate is 40 percent.

3. As at January 1, 2002, the tax basis of all of the Company's assets and liabilities is equal to their carrying values.

4. The Company has an accounting policy of deferring certain types of development costs. These deferred costs totaled $20,000 for 2002. For tax purposes, they are deducted as incurred.

5. During 2002, the Company does not acquire additional capital assets and does not dispose of any of the capital assets held on January 1, 2002. On January 1, 2002, the UCC of the depreciable capital assets was equal to their carrying value of $295,000.

   During 2002, the Company deducted accounting depreciation of $16,000. For tax purposes, they deducted CCA of $28,000, leaving an ending UCC of $267,000.

6. The Company accrues a liability for warranty obligations in the year in which the product is sold. These amounts are not deductible for tax purposes until the warranty services are actually provided and paid for by the Company. This usually occurs several years after the product is sold.

7. During 2002, the Company was fined $45,000 for the violation of certain environmental regulations. This fine is not deductible for tax purposes. The fine does not have to be paid until December 31, 2007.

8. During 2002, the Company entered into an agreement to provide certain post retirement benefits to its employees. For accounting purposes, a liability for these costs is accrued on the basis of actuarial estimates. For tax purposes, these amounts cannot be deducted until they are actually paid. For 2002, $8,000 of such benefits were accrued in the accounting records.

9. The Company has determined that it is more likely than not that taxable income will be available against which any resulting deductible temporary difference can be utilized.

Required: For BLM, prepare a condensed Income Statement for the year ending December 31, 2002, as well as a Balance Sheet as at December 31, 2002. Your solution should comply with the Recommendations of Section 3465 of the *CICA Handbook*, including those related to disclosure.

Self Study Problem Eleven - 2

For the year ending December 31, 2002, the GAAP based condensed Income Statement of Curton Inc., a public company, was as follows:

Curton Inc.
Condensed Income Statement
Year Ending December 31, 2002

Sales And Other Revenues	$2,600,000
Cost Of Goods Sold	$1,400,000
Depreciation Expense	350,000
Other Expenses Except Taxes	650,000
Total Expenses Except Taxes	$2,400,000
Income Before Taxes And The Results	
Of Discontinued Operations	$ 200,000

Other Information:

1. The maximum CCA for the taxation year ending December 31, 2002 is $425,000. This amount is deducted by the Company.

2. The Company began operations in 2001. During the taxation year ending December 31, 2001, the Company had Accounting Income of $250,000 and Taxable Income of $200,000. Taxes for the year were assessed at a 35 percent rate, resulting in payments of $70,000.

3. During the taxation year ending December 31, 2002, the Company closed a business division, resulting in a loss from discontinued operations of $800,000. This is fully deductible for tax purposes.

4. For the taxation year ending December 31, 2002, the Company's tax rate was 40 percent. The 2002 rate increase from 35 percent to 40 percent was not anticipated in 2001.

5. On July 1, 2002, the Company sold depreciable assets with a capital cost of $90,000, for proceeds of disposition of $105,000. The Net Book Value of the assets sold was $80,000, resulting in an accounting gain of $25,000. These were not the last assets in their Class and, after their Capital Cost was deducted from the Class, a positive balance remains.

6. For accounting purposes, the Company deducts a Reserve For Warranties. The balance in this Reserve on January 1, 2002 was $25,000. This balance increased to $40,000 on December 31, 2002.

7. On December 31, 2001, the Company had taxable temporary differences of $50,000. These were reflected in a Future Income Tax Liability of $17,500.

8. Because of its short track record as a company, Curton Inc. is not able to claim that it is more likely than not to realize any loss carry forward benefit.

Required: Provide the journal entry to record the taxes for Curton Inc. for 2002. In addition, prepare the Income Statement and all related disclosure for Curton Inc. for the year ending December 31, 2002. Your answer should comply with the Recommendations of Section 3465 of the *CICA Handbook*.

Self Study Problem Eleven - 3

On December 31, 2002, Quern Inc. has taxable temporary differences of $2,200,000, with this balance reflected in a Future Income Tax Liability of $924,000. The Company is publicly traded and has a December 31 year end.

Until December 31, 2002, the Company had always been subject to a tax rate of 42 percent. On January 1, 2003, the applicable rate is unexpectedly increased to 44 percent.

For the year ending December 31, 2003, Quern Inc. has Accounting Income Before Taxes And The Results Of Discontinued Operations in the amount of $546,000. This amount does not include any taxable capital gains.

Other Information:

1. Depreciation charged to accounting income was $87,000 for the year ending December 31, 2003. Maximum CCA, which was taken by the Company, totalled $111,000 for this year.

2. The Company incurred $38,000 for business meals and entertainment during the year ending December 31, 2003.

3. During the three years ending December 31, 2002, the Company had Taxable Income of $123,000 and Taxes Payable of $51,660. There were no capital gains during this period.

4. During 2003, the Company recorded estimated warranty costs of $31,000. These estimated costs are not likely to be incurred until 2008.

5. During the year ending December 31, 2003, the Company had a Loss From Discontinued Operations of $1,200,000. For tax purposes, $1,050,000 of this loss was a fully deductible terminal loss on depreciable assets, while the $150,000 balance was a capital loss on land (one-half deductible).

6. When the Company has loss carry forwards, it is their policy to assume that one-half of such amounts is more likely than not to be realized. This applies to both capital and non-capital amounts.

Required: Provide the journal entry to record Quern Inc.'s 2003 taxes. Use separate debits and/or credits for each component of the total Tax Expense, as well as for each Balance Sheet item. In addition, prepare the condensed Income Statement of Quern Inc. for the year ending December 31, 2003, including any required notes to the financial statements. Your solution should comply with the Recommendations of Section 3465 of the *CICA Handbook*.

Self Study Problem Eleven - 4

At the beginning of 2002, the Martin Company, a Canadian public company, has a Future Income Tax Liability of $1,260,000, all relating to an excess of Capital Cost Allowance claimed over Depreciation Expense recorded. The Company's tax rate in all previous years was 40 percent and both taxable and accounting income were equal to zero in 1999, 2000, and 2001.

During 2003, the Martin Company has accounting Income Before Taxes of $5,000,000 and this is equal to the 2003 Taxable Income (before consideration of any loss carry overs). The tax rate remains at 40 percent during 2002 and 2003.

These facts provide an initial starting point for each of the three independent cases which follow:

Case A   Assume that during 2002, the Martin Company has a Loss Before Taxes of $2,000,000, records Depreciation Expense of $1,500,000, claims Capital Cost Allowance of $800,000 and can claim that the benefit of any loss carry forward arising in this year is more likely than not to be realized.

Case B   Assume that during 2002, the Martin Company has a Loss Before Taxes of $2,000,000, records Depreciation Expense of $1,500,000, claims Capital Cost Allowance of $800,000 and is unable to claim that it is more likely than not that any loss carry forward arising in this year will be realized.

Case C   Assume that during 2002, the Martin Company has a Loss Before Taxes of $2,000,000, records Depreciation Expense of $1,500,000 and claims no Capital Cost Allowance. At the end of 2002, the Company can claim that it is more likely than not that one-half of any loss carry forward arising in the year will be realized.

Required: For each of the preceding cases provide the journal entry to record taxes, as well as a condensed Income Statement, for the two years 2002 and 2003. Your answer should include all disclosure, including footnotes, that would be required by tax factors in the years 2002 and 2003.

Self Study Problem Eleven - 5

The following data relate to the Loser Company, a Canadian public company, for the years 2000 through 2003:

Year	Income (Loss) Before Taxes	Depreciation Expense	Capital Cost Allowance	Tax Rate
2000	($ 75,000)	$100,000	$100,000	40%
2001	(1,000,000)	100,000	-0-	40%
2002	250,000	100,000	-0-	50%
2003	1,800,000	100,000	250,000	50%

Other Information:

1. In 1999, the Loser Company had accounting income of $100,000, taxable income of $50,000, and paid taxes at a rate of 40 percent or $20,000 in total. The Loser Company had no accounting or taxable income or loss in 1997 and 1998. At the end of 1999, the Loser Company had taxable temporary differences of $700,000, all related to an excess of capital cost allowance taken over depreciation. This was reflected in a December 31, 1999 balance in the Future Income Tax Liability account of $280,000.

2. During both 2000 and 2001, annual dues of $15,000 were paid for membership in the Kelly Lake Yacht Club. The Company discontinued its membership at the end of 2001 and no dues were paid in 2002 and 2003.

3. In 2002 and 2003, the Loser Company's income includes dividends from taxable Canadian companies in the amount of $35,000 per year, a total of $70,000 for the two years.

4. In 2002, the Loser Company incurs a gain of $10,000 from the sale of long-term investments. For tax purposes the $10,000 qualifies as a capital gain.

5. There are no extraordinary items in any of the years under consideration.

6. There is no amendment of any previous year's capital cost allowance. It is expected that depreciation expense under generally accepted accounting principles will remain at $100,000 per year until at least the year 2011.

7. With respect to the benefits associated with unused losses, management indicates that they are "more likely than not" to be realized only to the extent that income would result from the reversal of temporary differences that are present in the year of the loss.

8. The tax rate increase for 2002 was not anticipated at the end of 2001.

Required: For each of the four years under consideration, prepare journal entries to record income taxes and a condensed Income Statement. Your solution should comply with all of the Recommendations of Section 3465 of the *CICA Handbook* and include any required note disclosure.

Assignment Problems

(The solutions for these problems are only available in
the solutions manual that has been provided to your instructor.)

Assignment Problem Eleven - 1

The examples which follow describe various situations in which there may be either a Future Income Tax Asset or a Future Income Tax Liability. For each example, indicate the amount of any Future Income Tax Asset or Future Income Tax Liability. In all of the examples, the enterprise is subject to a combined federal/provincial tax rate of 33 percent.

A. At the end of the current year, the enterprise has inventories carried at LIFO cost. On a FIFO basis the value would be $23,000 higher.

B. At the end of the current year, the enterprise has depreciable assets with a net book value of $2,325,000 and a UCC of $1,642,000.

C. The enterprise has a long-term investment which is accounted for by the equity method. While its original cost was $2,300,000, the accrual of investee losses has reduced the carrying value of the investment to $1,745,000.

D. The enterprise has a 100 percent owned subsidiary which cost $4,200,000. Since acquisition, the subsidiary has earned $456,000 and paid dividends of $193,000.

E. Several years ago, the enterprise signed a long-term lease which, under the requirements of the *CICA Handbook*, was capitalized at its present value of $1,350,000. For tax purposes, the lease was considered to be an operating lease. At the end of the present year, the capitalized asset has a net carrying value of $810,000 and the lease liability has been reduced to $726,000.

F. At the end of the current year, the enterprise has a liability for estimated warranty costs with a carrying value of $123,000. The corresponding value at the beginning of the year was $146,000.

G. At the end of the current year, the enterprise has a liability for pension costs with a carrying value of $2,320,000. While all of this amount has been charged to expense, only $853,000 of the total has been funded.

Assignment Problem Eleven - 2

The partial Income Statement of the Compliance Company, a Canadian public company, for the year ending December 31, 2002 is as follows:

Compliance Company
Income Statement
Year Ending December 31, 2002

Sales	$1,500,000
Other Revenue	150,000
Total Revenue	$1,650,000
Cost Of Goods Sold	$ 800,000
Other Expenses	300,000
Total Expenses Excluding Taxes	$1,100,000
Income Before Taxes And Extraordinary Items	$ 550,000

The Compliance Company's tax rate is 40 percent. The Other Revenue consists of dividends received from taxable Canadian corporations. Cost Of Goods Sold includes straight line depreciation of $500,000.

Other Information:

1. The balance in the Compliance Company's Retained Earnings at January 1, 2002 was $6 million. During 2002, the Compliance Company declared and paid dividends of $200,000.

2. The Compliance Company claimed $750,000 in Capital Cost Allowance for 2002.

3. During 2002, the Compliance Company discovered an expense of $100,000 which related to 2001 that had not been deducted for accounting or tax purposes. This expense is fully deductible for tax purposes at the Company's regular rate. Although the *Income Tax Act* would require an amended tax return to be filed, assume that Compliance Company does not do so. The error correction is included in the 2002 income tax return instead.

4. On April 1, 2002, the municipal government expropriated a warehouse owned by the Compliance Company. The building had been purchased for $420,000 of which $120,000 was allocated to the land. The Company received a total of $960,000 of which $720,000 was allocated to the land. The net book value of the building at the time of the expropriation was $240,000. This gain qualifies as an extraordinary item under Section 3480 of the *CICA Handbook*. The building was not the last one in the class and the sale did not create a negative balance in the class. It was not replaced during the current year.

Required: Prepare the journal entry related to taxes for the Compliance Company for the year ending December 31, 2002. In addition, prepare the Income Statement and Statement Of Retained Earnings for the Compliance Company for the year ending December 31, 2002. Your solution should comply with the recommendations of Section 3465 of the *CICA Handbook* and include any required notes.

Assignment Problem Eleven - 3

The following information relates to the Evasive Company, a Canadian public company, for the year ending December 31, 2002:

1. On January 1, 2002, the Evasive Company had total taxable temporary differences, all related to the difference between the carrying value and the tax basis of the Company's depreciable assets, of $8,000,000. The related Future Income Tax Liability was $3,600,000, reflecting the Company's December 31, 2001 tax rate of 45 percent.

2. The Company's 2002 accounting income before taxes was $850,000. As of January 1, 2002, the Company's effective tax rate unexpectedly increased to 55 percent. The Evasive Company has a January 1, 2002 balance in its Retained Earnings account of $35,000,000. Dividends totalling $250,000 were declared and paid during 2002.

3. Depreciation Expense for 2002 under generally accepted accounting principles was $700,000. The Company takes maximum Capital Cost Allowance for tax purposes and in 2002, this amounted to $950,000.

4. The 2002 accounting income contains dividends received from other taxable Canadian corporations in the amount of $100,000. The 2002 accounting income was reduced by $35,000 by a provision for the termination of redundant employees. This amount will not be paid until 2003.

5. The Company has a long-term investment which has been carried at its original cost of $2,500,000. During 2002, it is decided that this long term investment has experienced a loss in value that is other than a temporary decline. As a result, it is written down to its current market value of $2,000,000. For tax purposes, the loss will qualify as a capital loss when the investment is sold. As the Company has no taxable capital gains in the current year and no taxable capital gains during the previous three years, this loss must be carried forward. Management believes that it is more likely than not that the Company will have adequate taxable capital gains to use this carry forward in future years.

6. During 2002, the Evasive Company discovered an error that overstated a 2001 expense by $105,000 for both accounting and tax records. The resulting increase in income is subject to taxation at the Company's regular rate. Although the *Income Tax Act* would require an amended tax return to be filed, assume that Evasive Company does not do so. The error correction is included in the 2002 income tax return instead.

Required: Provide the journal entry to record the Evasive Company's 2002 taxes with separate debits and/or credits for each component of the total Tax Expense. In addition, prepare the condensed Income Statement and Statement Of Retained Earnings of the Evasive Company for the year ending December 31, 2002, including any required notes to the financial statements. Indicate the tax related balances that would be shown on the December 31, 2002 Balance Sheet. Your solution should comply with the Recommendations of Section 3465 of the *CICA Handbook*.

Assignment Problem Eleven - 4

At the beginning of 2002 the True Blue Company has a Future Income Tax Liability in its accounts of $2,240,000, all relating to an excess of Capital Cost Allowance claimed over Depreciation Expense recorded. The Company's tax rate in all previous years was 40 percent and both taxable and accounting income were equal to zero in 1999, 2000 and 2001. The Company uses a December 31 year end. These facts provide the starting point for each of the following six independent cases.

Case One   Assume that during 2002, the True Blue Company has a Loss Before Taxes of $2,200,000, records Depreciation Expense of $1,800,000, claims Capital Cost Allowance of $800,000, and can claim that it is more likely than not that it will be able to realize the full amount of any loss carry forward benefit. During 2002, the Company's tax rate remains unchanged at 40 percent.

Case Two   Assume that during 2002, the True Blue Company has a Loss Before Taxes of $2,200,000, records Depreciation Expense of $1,800,000, claims Capital Cost Allowance of $800,000, and can claim that it is more likely than not that it will be able to realize the full amount of any loss carry forward benefit. On January 1, 2002, the Company's tax rate increases to 45 percent.

Case Three   Assume that during 2002, the True Blue Company has a Loss Before Taxes of $2,200,000, records Depreciation Expense of $1,800,000, and claims Capital Cost Allowance of $800,000. Management believes that it is more likely than not that they will only be able to realize the benefit associated with $500,000 of any loss carry forward. On January 1, 2002, the Company's tax rate declines to 35 percent.

Case Four   Assume that during 2002, the True Blue Company has a Loss Before Taxes of $2,200,000, records Depreciation Expense of $1,800,000, claims no Capital Cost Allowance, and cannot claim that it is more likely than not that they will be able to realize any part of the benefit of a loss carry forward arising in the year. During 2002, the Company's tax rate remains unchanged at 40 percent.

Case Five   Assume that during 2002, the True Blue Company has a Loss Before Taxes of $2,000,000, but that in 2003 it has Income Before Taxes of $2,400,000. Depreciation Expense is $200,000 per year for both 2002 and 2003. No Capital Cost Allowance is taken in 2002 and $400,000 in Capital Cost Allowance is claimed in 2003. At the end of 2002 the Company can claim that it is more likely than not that it will be able to realize the full amount of any loss carry forward benefit. During 2002 and 2003, the Company's tax rate remains unchanged at 40 percent.

Case Six   Assume that during 2002, the True Blue Company has a Loss Before Taxes of $2,000,000, but that in 2003 it has Income Before Taxes of $2,400,000. Depreciation Expense is $200,000 per year for both 2002 and 2003. No Capital Cost Allowance is taken in 2002 and $400,000 in Capital Cost Allowance is claimed in 2003. At the end of 2002 the Company cannot claim that it is more likely than not that it will able to realize any of the loss carry forward benefit. During 2002, the Company's tax rate remains unchanged at 40 percent. On January 1, 2003, the Company's tax rate increases to 45 percent.

Required: Provide the journal entries required to record taxes and a condensed Income Statement for each year that is under consideration in each of the preceding cases. Your answer should include all required note disclosure and comply with the recommendations of Section 3465 of the *CICA Handbook*.

Assignment Problem Eleven - 5
The following data relate to the Assessed Company, a public Canadian company, for the taxation years 1999 through 2002:

Taxation Year	Ordinary Income (Loss) Before Taxes	Depreciation	Capital Cost Allowance
1999	$ 200,000	$ 50,000	$150,000
2000	(2,800,000)	50,000	-0-
2001	350,000	40,000	-0-
2002	3,000,000	150,000	300,000

Other Information:

1. The tax rate for the Assessed Company is 30 percent for all years prior to 2001 and 60 percent for 2001 and 2002. At the end of 2000, the company is not able to claim that any unused tax loss is more likely than not to be realized. However, at the end of 2001, a change in the Company's competitive position allows them to claim that any remaining unused loss is more likely than not to be realized.

2. There was no taxable income or loss in 1997 or 1998. The Assessed Company will not amend any previous year's capital cost allowance. The Assessed Company's December 31, 1998 Balance Sheet contained temporary differences of $300,000, all of which were related to an excess of capital cost allowance taken over depreciation. This was reflected in a December 31, 1998 Future Income Tax Liability of $90,000.

3. In 1999, the Assessed Company pays bribes totalling $100,000 to officials in the country of Graftland. These bribes are not deductible for tax purposes.

4. In both 2000 and 2002, the Assessed Company's income contains dividends from taxable Canadian corporations of $30,000, a total of $60,000 for the two years.

5. There are no Extraordinary Items in 1999, 2000, or in 2002. In 2001, the Assessed Company incurs an Extraordinary Loss of $100,000 from the expropriation of a parcel of

land. This loss is a capital loss for tax purposes and it can be deducted in 2001 as the Company's 2001 ordinary income contains a $100,000 capital gain from the sale of a long term investment. The relevant capital gains inclusion rate is one-half.

Required: For each of the years under consideration, prepare journal entries to record income taxes for the year. Using this information, prepare a condensed Income Statement for each of the four years. Your solution should comply with Section 3465 of the *CICA Handbook* and include any required notes.

Assignment Problem Eleven - 6

The following two independent cases involve the acquisition of an asset in a transaction other than a business combination. In both cases, the initial tax basis of the asset is different from its cost.

Case A A corporation acquires a new building at a cash cost of $341,000. As a special tax incentive, it will be allowed to deduct CCA on 150 percent of its cost. The corporation is subject to a tax rate of 48 percent. The incentive legislation indicates that the 150 percent figure will be deemed to be the capital cost of the building, and that any loss on its disposition will be a fully deductible business loss.

Case B An individual transfers a depreciable asset with a capital cost of $450,000 and a fair market value of $267,000 to a corporation, using the provisions of Section 85(1) of the *Income Tax Act*. It is the last asset in its CCA Class and the balance in the class is $132,000. The value elected for the transfer is the Class UCC of $132,000. In return for the asset, the corporation issues a note with a fair market value of $132,000 and common shares with a fair market value of $135,000. The corporation is subject to a tax rate of 51 percent.

Required: In both of the preceding cases, provide the journal entry to record the acquisition of the asset on the books of the acquiring corporation. Your entries should comply with all of the Recommendations of Section 3465 of the *CICA Handbook*.

Chapter 12

Accounting For Taxes: Business Combinations And Other Issues

Business Combinations

Introduction

12-1.   The tax considerations that arise in a business combination transaction depend on the legal form of the combination. Some business combinations are legally structured as an acquisition of assets. If no rollover provision is used, the acquired assets will have an initial tax basis equal to their initial carrying value and no unique accounting for tax problems occur. However, if a rollover provision is used, temporary differences will be present at the time the assets are acquired.

12-2.   If the form of the business combination is such that shares are acquired, the situation becomes more complex. This legal form of business combination gives rise to the need to prepare consolidated financial statements. As there is no Canadian statutory provision for filing a consolidated tax return, the individual legal entities that are party to the business combination transaction will continue to file separate tax returns. This means that there will be ongoing temporary differences between the information presented in the consolidated financial statements, and the information presented in the corporate tax returns.

12-3.   Section 3465 contains detailed Recommendations for accounting for taxes in the context of business combinations in general and for consolidated financial statements in particular.

Temporary Differences At Time Of Combination
Influence Of Legal Form
12-4.   Section 1581 requires that the identifiable assets and liabilities acquired in a business combination transaction be recorded at their fair values at the time of acquisition, and that any excess of the purchase price over the acquirer's share of these fair values be recorded as goodwill. Depending on the legal form of the combination and the type of tax planning used, this process may or may not create temporary differences at the time of the business combination transaction. With respect to this issue, there appear to be three different possibilities:

> **Acquisition Of Assets - No Rollover**   In this situation, the acquiring enterprise pays cash or issues shares in order to acquire the assets and liabilities of the acquiree and does not apply a rollover provision. For both tax and accounting purposes, the cost of

the acquisition will be allocated to the fair values of the identifiable asset and liabilities acquired, and to goodwill. These values will then be the carrying values for accounting purposes and the tax basis for income tax purposes. There will be no temporary differences arising at the time of the business combination transaction.

Acquisition Of Assets - Rollover Used   In this situation, the acquiring enterprise pays cash or issues shares in order to acquire the assets and liabilities of the acquiree and makes use of a rollover provision on the transfer of the assets (e.g., ITA Section 85 or 85.1). For accounting purposes, the carrying values will be the fair values of the various assets and liabilities acquired. However, in order to minimize or eliminate taxes for the acquiree, it is likely that some or all of the old tax values will be elected under the rollover provision. This means that, for the acquirer, these old values will be the tax basis of these assets and liabilities acquired. In this situation, temporary differences will arise at the time of the business combination transaction.

Acquisition Of Shares   If the business combination is carried out through an acquisition of shares, the acquiree will continue to exist as a separate legal entity and the tax basis of its assets and liabilities will remain unchanged. This would be the case even if push down accounting were applied. However, in the consolidated financial statements that will be prepared for the combined company, the purchase method of accounting will require that these assets and liabilities be recorded at their fair values. Here again, temporary differences will occur as a result of the business combination transaction.

12-5.   In this Section, we will present examples which illustrate these three possibilities. The appropriate procedures will be considered both at the time of the business combination transaction (acquisition date) and in periods subsequent to acquisition. However, before proceeding to these examples, we will give more detailed consideration to the treatment that is given to the temporary differences that occur at the time of a business combination transaction. In addition, we will have to consider the fact that fair value increases on capital assets may result in capital gains, only a portion of which will be taxable.

Treatment Of Temporary Differences

12-6.   Section 1581, Business Combinations, contains the following guidance on the treatment of temporary differences when allocating the cost of the purchase:

Paragraph 1581.46   The values placed by an acquirer on the assets and liabilities of an acquired enterprise are determined based on their fair values, without reference to their values for tax purposes, or tax bases.

Paragraph 1581.47   Income Taxes, Section 3465, requires that the tax effects of differences between the assigned values of the identifiable assets and liabilities acquired and their tax bases be recognized as future income tax assets and liabilities and included in the allocation of the cost of the purchase. ...

12-7.   Under this approach, if an asset had a replacement cost of $150,000, this amount would be recorded as its fair value without regard to its tax basis. If the tax basis of the asset was $80,000, there would be a taxable temporary difference of $70,000 and a Future Income Tax Liability would have to be accrued at the appropriate tax rate. If, for example, the appropriate rate was 30 percent, the Future Income Tax Liability would be recorded at $21,000.

12-8.   Temporary differences arising on a business combination transaction will normally be given the same treatment as other temporary differences. There is, however, an exception for goodwill. This is noted in the following general *CICA Handbook* Recommendation on taxable temporary differences:

Paragraph 3465.22   *At each balance sheet date, except as provided in paragraphs 3465.33, 3465.35 and 3465.37, a future income tax liability should be recognized for all taxable temporary differences other than those arising from any portion of goodwill which is not deductible for tax purposes.* (January, 2000)

12-9. The *Handbook* continues, justifying the exclusion of goodwill as follows:

Paragraph 3465.23 Any difference between the carrying amount of goodwill and its tax basis is a taxable temporary difference that would usually result in a future income tax liability. This Section does not permit the recognition of such a future income tax liability because goodwill itself is a residual and the recognition of the future income tax liability would merely increase the carrying amount of that residual.

12-10. The Recommendations in Section 3465 will result in temporary differences which arise at the time of a business combination generally being treated like other temporary differences. To the extent they are taxable, they will result in Future Income Tax Liabilities. To the extent they are deductible, they will result in Future Income Tax Assets. The exception to this is temporary differences between the carrying value and tax basis of goodwill. No liability will be recorded to reflect this type of difference. All of these procedures will be illustrated in the examples which follow.

Procedures At Time Of Acquisition
Basic Example

12-11. As previously noted, when the purchase method is used to account for a business combination transaction, temporary differences may arise, resulting in a need to record a Future Income Tax Asset or Future Income Tax Liability. We will use one example to illustrate the procedures associated with the following three cases:

Case 1: An acquisition of assets with no rollover election;
Case 2: An acquisition of assets with the use of a rollover election; and
Case 3: An acquisition of shares with consolidated financial statements being prepared.

12-12. The information that will be used in all three of these cases is as follows:

Example On December 31, 2002, the Balance Sheets of Monson Inc. and Little Ltd., including the fair values for the balances of Little Ltd., are as follows:

Balance Sheets
As At December 31, 2002

	Monson Inc. Carrying Values	Little Ltd. Carrying Values	Little Ltd. Fair Values
Cash	$ 500,000	$ 250,000	$ 250,000
Accounts Receivable	1,600,000	650,000	650,000
Inventories	2,300,000	1,200,000	1,200,000
Land	800,000	450,000	500,000
Plant And Equipment (Net)	4,400,000	2,400,000	2,600,000
Total Assets	$9,600,000	$4,950,000	$5,200,000
Current Liabilities	$ 700,000	$ 340,000	$ 340,000
Long-Term Liabilities	1,200,000	910,000	910,000
Future Income Tax Liability	400,000	160,000	N/A
Common Stock - No Par	4,300,000	2,500,000	N/A
Retained Earnings	3,000,000	1,040,000	N/A
Total Equities	$9,600,000	$4,950,000	

Little Ltd. does not own any unrecorded intangible assets that relate to contractual or other legal rights, or that are capable of being separated or divided and sold, transferred, licensed, rented, or exchanged at any time.

Both companies are taxed in the same jurisdictions and are subject to a rate of 40 percent on all of their income. The Future Income Tax Liability accounts on the books of the two companies reflect an excess of the carrying value of Plant And Equipment over its UCC balance. The balances are recorded at the current tax rate of 40 percent.

Little Ltd.'s Plant And Equipment has an original cost of $3,000,000 and is being depreciated over 10 years at a rate of $300,000 per year. The UCC on December 31, 2002 is $2,000,000, $400,000 less than the net carrying value of $2,400,000. This UCC balance is subject to a declining balance rate of 20 percent.

Case One - Acquisition Of Assets - No Rollover

12-13.   In this first Case, we will assume that, on December 31, 2002, Monson Inc. issues Common Stock - No Par with a fair market value of $4,100,000, in return for all of the assets and liabilities of Little Ltd. Note that in this case, as no rollover provision is being used, all of the assets and liabilities that have been transferred to Monson Inc. will have a tax basis equal to their carrying value. Given this, the analysis of the investment is as follows:

Investment Cost	$4,100,000
Fair Values Of Net Identifiable Assets	
($5,200,000 - $340,000 - $910,000)	(3,950,000)
Goodwill	$ 150,000

12-14.   Note that the tax basis of the goodwill will also be $150,000. For tax purposes, three-quarters of this amount will be added to Monson's Cumulative Eligible Capital (CEC) balance. However, because the other one-quarter of this amount can be realized without tax consequences, the tax basis of Cumulative Eligible Capital is $150,000 (the $112,500 balance in CEC, plus the $37,500 portion of the capital gain that would not be taxed on the realization of the $150,000 fair value).

12-15.   Given this analysis, the Balance Sheet of Monson Inc. subsequent to the business combination transaction would be as follows:

Monson Inc. Balance Sheet
As At December 31, 2002

Cash ($500,000 + $250,000)	$ 750,000
Accounts Receivable ($1,600,000 + $650,000)	2,250,000
Inventories ($2,300,000 + $1,200,000)	3,500,000
Land ($800,000 + $500,000)	1,300,000
Plant And Equipment (Net) ($4,400,000 + $2,600,000)	7,000,000
Goodwill	150,000
Total Assets	$14,950,000
Current Liabilities ($700,000 + $340,000)	$ 1,040,000
Long-Term Liabilities ($1,200,000 + $910,000)	2,110,000
Future Income Tax Liability (Monson's Only)	400,000
Common Stock - No Par ($4,300,000 + $4,100,000)	8,400,000
Retained Earnings (Monson's Only)	3,000,000
Total Equities	$14,950,000

Case Two - Acquisition Of Assets - With Rollover

12-16.   In the previous Case, we assumed that Monson Inc. was prepared to pay $4,100,000 for the assets and liabilities of Little Ltd. when no rollover provision is used. This price was based on the fair values of the identifiable assets and liabilities of Little Ltd., and the belief that this acquiree had above normal earning power that was worth an additional payment of

$150,000 for Goodwill. It was also based on the assumption that all of these items would have a tax basis equal to their carrying value.

12-17.   In this Case, we will assume that Section 85(1) of the *Income Tax Act* is used to transfer the assets of Little Ltd. with fair values in excess of their tax values (Land, Plant And Equipment, and Goodwill). Assuming that minimum tax values will be elected under ITA 85(1), Monson Inc. will have lower future tax deductions from these assets. As a consequence, Monson Inc. would pay a lower price as the assets are clearly less valuable due to their lower tax values. If we ignore the time value of money, the reduction in value of Little Ltd. would be based on the Future Income Tax Liability associated with these lost tax deductions. This amount can be calculated as follows:

	Fair Value From No Rollover Case	Election: Minimum Tax Value	Reduction In Tax Value
Land*	$ 500,000	$ 450,000	$ 25,000
Plant And Equipment	2,600,000	2,000,000	600,000
Goodwill*	150,000	Nil	75,000
			$700,000
Effective Tax Rate			40%
Reduced Asset Value			$280,000

*In the case of Land and Goodwill, the fact that the elected value is lower than the fair value reduces a potential capital gain. This means that the reduction in the tax value of the assets is only one-half of the difference that is created by the ITA 85(1) election.

Those of you with a more in-depth understanding of tax will understand that the $75,000 amount on the goodwill is not a capital gain. Rather, it is an adjustment of the ITA 14(1) income inclusion. The correct calculation would be [($150,000 - Nil)(3/4)(2/3)]. The result, however, is identical to capital gains treatment.

12-18.   The preceding calculation would suggest that, with the use of the rollover provision, Little Ltd. is worth $280,000 less to Monson Inc. than in the previous example. Based on this, we will assume that, on December 31, 2002, Monson Inc. issues Common Stock - No Par with a fair market value of $3,820,000 ($4,100,000 - $280,000) in return for the assets and liabilities of Little Ltd. transferred under the provisions of ITA Section 85(1).

12-19.   While the preceding calculations reflect the economics of the described transaction, Paragraph 3465.22 introduces a significant complication by prohibiting the recognition of a Future Income Tax Liability based on temporary differences related to Goodwill (see our Paragraph 12-8). Given this, the Future Income Tax Liability to be recorded will be $250,000 ($10,000 on Land and $240,000 on Plant And Equipment). It follows from this that the amount of Goodwill to be recorded in the Balance Sheet of the combined company would be as follows:

Investment Cost	$3,820,000
Fair Values Of Net Identifiable Assets	
($5,200,000 - $340,000 - $910,000 - $250,000)	(3,700,000)
Goodwill	$ 120,000

12-20.   What this Case makes clear is that, under the Recommendations of Section 3465, Goodwill is recorded net of its associated Future Income Tax Liability. The $120,000 to be recorded in the Balance Sheet is the original $150,000, less $30,000 [(3/4)(2/3)($150,000 - Nil)(40%)] in future income taxes.

12-21. Based on the preceding calculations, the Balance Sheet for Monson Inc. subsequent to the business combination would be prepared as follows:

Monson Inc.
Balance Sheet
As At December 31, 2002

Cash ($500,000 + $250,000)	$ 750,000
Accounts Receivable ($1,600,000 + $650,000)	2,250,000
Inventories ($2,300,000 + $1,200,000)	3,500,000
Land ($800,000 + $500,000)	1,300,000
Plant And Equipment (Net) ($4,400,000 + $2,600,000)	7,000,000
Goodwill	120,000
Total Assets	$14,920,000

Current Liabilities ($700,000 + $340,000)	$ 1,040,000
Long-Term Liabilities ($1,200,000 + $910,000)	2,110,000
Future Income Tax Liability ($400,000 + $250,000)	650,000
Common Stock - No Par ($4,300,000 + $3,820,000)	8,120,000
Retained Earnings (Monson's Only)	3,000,000
Total Equities	$14,920,000

Case Three - Acquisition Of Shares

12-22. In this Case, we will assume that Monson Inc. acquires all of the shares of Little Ltd. Use of this legal form means that Little Ltd. will continue to operate as a separate legal entity. This, in turn, means that the tax basis of its assets will be unchanged. In effect, the tax values for Little Ltd.'s assets in this case will be the same as in the previous case where the assets were acquired using an ITA 85(1) rollover.

12-23. As we used Little's underlying tax values as our elected values in Case Two, the tax values here will be the same. As a consequence, we will use the same $3,820,000 purchase price. Monson Inc. will issue Common Stock - No Par shares with a fair market value of $3,820,000 in return for all of the outstanding shares of Little Ltd. We would note, however, that in actual practice, the price might be lower. There are factors which provide incentives to the vendor of a corporation to sell shares rather than assets (e.g., the lifetime capital gains deduction on shares of a qualified small business corporation). These factors could lead to a lower price for Little Ltd.

12-24. As the temporary differences in this Case Three are the same as in Case Two, the same amounts for the Goodwill and Future Income Tax Liability will be recorded. Given this, the Balance Sheet subsequent to the business combination is as follows:

Monson Inc.
Consolidated Balance Sheet
As At December 31, 2002

Cash ($500,000 + $250,000)	$ 750,000
Accounts Receivable ($1,600,000 + $650,000)	2,250,000
Inventories ($2,300,000 + $1,200,000)	3,500,000
Investment In Little Ltd. ($3,820,000 - $3,820,000)	Nil
Land ($800,000 + $500,000)	1,300,000
Plant And Equipment (Net) ($4,400,000 + $2,600,000)	7,000,000
Goodwill	120,000
Total Assets	$14,920,000

Current Liabilities ($700,000 + $340,000)	$ 1,040,000
Long-Term Liabilities ($1,200,000 + $910,000)	2,110,000
Future Income Tax Liability ($400,000 + $250,000)	650,000
Common Stock - No Par ($4,300,000 + $3,820,000)	8,120,000
Retained Earnings (Monson's Only)	3,000,000
Total Equities	$14,920,000

12-25.   This Balance Sheet is identical to the one which was prepared in the previous case. The only difference is that we have indicated that Monson Inc. had a $3,820,000 Investment In Little Ltd. that had to be eliminated in the consolidation procedures. This fact would not, of course, be disclosed in the actual financial statements.

12-26.   We would also note that the $250,000 addition to the Future Income Tax Liability includes the $160,000 that is included in Little's single entity Balance Sheet. Our calculation of this amount included all temporary differences, including those that apply to Little Ltd. as a separate legal entity.

Procedures Subsequent To Acquisition
Dealing With The Equity Pickup
12-27.   In this Section, we will extend Case Three of the Monson Inc./Little Ltd. example to illustrate the appropriate accounting for tax procedures in periods subsequent to acquisition. However, before proceeding to this issue we have to deal with the treatment of something that is commonly referred to as the equity pickup. When full consolidation procedures, proportionate consolidation procedures, or the equity method of accounting are applied to a long-term investment, the financial statements of the investor will reflect its share of the retained earnings of the investee since the acquisition of the investment. This investor's share of the unremitted earnings of the investee is commonly referred to as the equity pickup.

12-28.   This equity pickup is not a recognized value in current tax legislation and, as a consequence, the tax basis of such investments remains their cost. This means that, whenever an investor company recognizes an equity pickup in their financial statements, there will be a temporary difference between carrying values and tax basis values.

12-29.   While this type of temporary difference has some of the same characteristics as other temporary differences, it also has some different properties which have led the Accounting Standards Board to give equity pickup temporary differences the special attention that is contained in the following Recommendation:

Paragraph 3465.37　*At each balance sheet date, a future income tax liability or future income tax asset should be recognized for all temporary differences arising from investments in subsidiaries and interests in joint ventures, except with respect to the difference between the carrying amount of the investment and the tax basis of the investment when it is apparent that this difference will not reverse in the foreseeable future. Any future income tax asset should be recognized only to the extent that it is more likely than not that the benefit will be realized.* (January, 2000)

12-30.   Section 3465 goes on to describe such differences as follows:

Paragraph 3465.38　Temporary differences may arise from investments in subsidiaries and interests in joint ventures in a number of different circumstances, for example:

(a) differences between the carrying amounts (in the consolidated financial statements) of individual assets and liabilities of subsidiaries and joint ventures and their tax basis ("inside basis differences"); or

(b) differences between the carrying amount of an investment in a subsidiary or an interest in a joint venture and its tax basis ("outside basis differences") because of items such as:

(i)   the existence of undistributed income of subsidiaries and joint ventures; or

(ii)   changes in foreign exchange rates when a parent and its subsidiary are based in different countries.

12-31.   The meaning of this material is not completely clear to us. In particular, we have not encountered the terms "inside basis" and "outside basis" in any other source. Further, Section 3465 does not provide any definition of these terms. Accordingly, what follows is our interpretation of these terms.

12-32.   It would appear to us that the differences referred to in Paragraph 3465.38(a) are the fair value changes and goodwill that exist at the time of a subsidiary's acquisition. As other Recommendations make it clear that Future Income Tax Assets and Liabilities should be recognized for these types of temporary differences, we would assume that these items are not covered by the Paragraph 3465.37 Recommendation.

12-33.   The differences referred to in Paragraph 3465.38(b)(i) are what we have referred to as the equity pickup. As we have noted, this type of situation results in a temporary difference between the accounting basis of the investment and the corresponding tax basis.

12-34.   The concern here is that the amount of this difference will be determined by the amount of dividends paid by the investee and, in the case of both subsidiaries and joint ventures, the investor company is in a position to influence this policy. Further, the investor in the subsidiary or joint venture often views this interest in undistributed profits as an additional permanent investment in the investee.

12-35.   Given an investor's ability to control the reversal of such temporary differences, as well as the fact that there may be no intention to implement such a reversal, a Future Income Tax Liability will not be recognized unless it is apparent that all or part of the related temporary difference will reverse in the foreseeable future.

12-36.   Temporary differences like those just described for subsidiaries and joint ventures also exist for investments subject to significant influence and accounted for by the equity method. Section 3465 indicates that a Future Income Tax Liability should be recorded in this case since the investor is not normally able to control the timing of the reversal of temporary differences. We are not in complete agreement with this conclusion in that the degree of influence here may be equal to or greater than the degree of influence that is present with an investment in a joint venture. This would suggest similar treatment for these two types of investees.

12-37.   A further problem arises if we do record Future Income Tax Liabilities on temporary differences resulting from equity pickups on significantly influenced companies. Such differences could be realized either through the sale of the investment or through dividend distributions by the investee. In the former case, the result would be a capital gain, only a portion of which would be taxable. If dividends are distributed, taxation will vary depending on the status of the recipient (e.g., dividends from taxable Canadian corporations paid to a public corporation would not be taxed). These alternatives create complications with respect to the amount of the Future Income Tax Liability to be recorded.

12-38.   There is an additional reference in Paragraph 3465.38(b)(ii) to differences resulting from changes in foreign exchange rates when a parent and its subsidiary are based in different countries. It would appear that this is a reference to the special shareholders' equity balance that is used to accumulate the exchange gains and losses of self sustaining foreign operations. In this case, the Paragraph 3465.37 Recommendation would prohibit the recognition of a Future Income Tax Asset or Liability related to a temporary difference on this Balance Sheet item, except where there is an intent to liquidate the self sustaining foreign operation.

Example - Subsequent To Acquisition

12-39. In order to illustrate income tax procedures in the years subsequent to a business combination transaction, we will extend the Monson Inc./Little Ltd. example that was presented in Paragraph 12-12 assuming shares were acquired.

Example Continued After completing the annual impairment test on Little Ltd.'s goodwill, Monson determined that there was no goodwill impairment loss for 2003. The single entity Statements Of Income And Retained Earnings for the year ending December 31, 2003, along with the single entity Balance Sheets as at December 31, 2003, for these two companies are as follows:

Statements Of Income And Retained Earnings
Year Ending December 31, 2003

	Monson Inc.	Little Ltd.
Revenues	$1,460,000	$ 872,000
Expenses Other Than Taxes	(1,060,000)	(662,000)
Pre Tax Income	$ 400,000	$ 210,000
Income Tax Expense (Note One)		
Current	(110,000)	(44,000)
Future	(50,000)	(40,000)
Net Income	$ 240,000	$ 126,000
Retained Earnings - January 1, 2003	3,000,000	1,040,000
Dividends	(75,000)	Nil
Retained Earnings - December 31, 2003	$3,165,000	$1,166,000

Note One All of the Income Tax Expense of both companies have been accrued at a rate of 40 percent. The Future component of this expense results from an increase in taxable temporary differences on Plant And Equipment. For Little Ltd., these differences increased from $400,000 ($2,400,000 - $2,000,000) at the beginning of the year, to $500,000 ($2,100,000 - $1,600,000) at the end of the year.

Balance Sheets
As At December 31, 2003

	Monson Inc.	Little Ltd.
Cash	$ 610,000	$ 280,000
Accounts Receivable	1,840,000	830,000
Inventories	2,265,000	1,516,000
Investment In Little Ltd.	3,820,000	N/A
Land	820,000	450,000
Plant And Equipment (Net)	4,500,000	2,100,000
Total Assets	$13,855,000	$5,176,000
Current Liabilities	$ 770,000	$ 420,000
Long-Term Liabilities	1,350,000	890,000
Future Income Tax Liability	450,000	200,000
Common Stock - No Par*	8,120,000	2,500,000
Retained Earnings	3,165,000	1,166,000
Total Equities	$13,855,000	$5,176,000

*As we are looking at an extension of Case Three, Monson's Common Stock - No Par includes the $3,820,000 in shares that were issued to acquire the Little Ltd. shares. When added to the original balance of $4,300,000, we have the total of $8,120,000.

Case Three Extended - Acquisition Of Shares

12-40.   The required consolidated Statement Of Income And Retained Earnings would be prepared as follows:

Monson Inc. And Subsidiary
Consolidated Statement Of Income And Retained Earnings
Year Ending December 31, 2003

Revenues ($1,460,000 + $872,000)		$2,332,000
Expenses Other Than Taxes (Note One)		(1,742,000)
Pre Tax Income		$ 590,000
Income Tax Expense: (Note Two)		
Current ($110,000 + $44,000)	($ 154,000)	
Future (Note Three)	(82,000)	(236,000)
Net Income (Note Four)		$ 354,000
Consolidated Retained Earnings - January 1, 2003 (Monson's Only)		3,000,000
Dividends		(75,000)
Consolidated Retained Earnings - December 31, 2003		$3,279,000

Note One   The consolidated Expenses Other Than Taxes would be calculated as follows:

Monson's Single Entity Expenses	$1,060,000
Little's Single Entity Expenses	662,000
Fair Value Depreciation On Plant And Equipment ($200,000 ÷ 10)	20,000
Total Expenses Other Than Taxes	$1,742,000

Note Two   The statutory rate of 40 percent applied to the $590,000 of Income Before Taxes would give the reported Income Tax Expense of $236,000.

Note Three   The consolidated Future Income Tax Expense would be as follows:

Monson's Single Entity Expense	$50,000
Little's Single Entity Expense	40,000
Reduction In Temporary Differences Resulting From Fair Value Depreciation [(40%)($200,000 ÷10)]	(8,000)
Total Consolidated Future Income Tax Expense	$82,000

Note Four   The consolidated Net Income Figure can be verified as follows:

Monson' Net Income	$240,000
Equity Pickup [(100%)($126,000)]	126,000
Fair Value Depreciation On Plant	(20,000)
Future Income Tax Expense Reduction - Fair Value Depreciation	8,000
Consolidated Net Income	$354,000

12-41.   The required consolidated Balance Sheet would be prepared as follows:

Monson Inc. And Subsidiary
Consolidated Balance Sheet
As At December 31, 2003

Cash ($610,000 + $280,000)	$ 890,000
Accounts Receivable ($1,840,000 + $830,000)	2,670,000
Inventories ($2,265,000 + $1,516,000)	3,781,000
Investment In Little Ltd. ($3,820,000 - $3,820,000)	Nil
Land ($820,000 + $500,000)	1,320,000
Plant And Equipment (Net) (Note Five)	6,780,000
Goodwill	120,000
Total Assets	$15,561,000
Current Liabilities ($770,000 + $420,000)	$ 1,190,000
Long-Term Liabilities ($1,350,000 + $890,000)	2,240,000
Future Income Tax Liability (Note Six)	732,000
Common Stock - No Par (No Change)	8,120,000
Retained Earnings (From Statement)	3,279,000
Total Equities	$15,561,000

Note Five The consolidated Plant And Equipment (Net) would be calculated as follows:

Monson's Plant And Equipment	$4,500,000
Little's Plant And Equipment	2,100,000
Fair Value Increase	200,000
Amortization Of Fair Value Increase	(20,000)
Total Consolidated Plant And Equipment	$6,780,000

Note Six The consolidated Future Income Tax Liability would be calculated as follows:

Monson's Future Income Tax Liability	$450,000
Little's Future Income Tax Liability	200,000
Liability On Land [(40%)(1/2)($50,000)]	10,000
Liability On Plant And Equipment Fair Value Change [(40%)($200,000 - $20,000)]	72,000
Total Future Income Tax Liability	$732,000

This amount could also be calculated by adding the $82,000 change for the year (see Income Statement) to the opening consolidated balance of $650,000.

Goodwill Impairment Loss

12-42.   If there had been a goodwill impairment loss, a reconciliation of the reported income tax rate and the statutory rate would be required. For example, if there had been a goodwill impairment loss of $24,000, the Pre Tax Income would have been $566,000 ($590,000 - $24,000). The statutory rate of 40 percent applied to this $566,000 would give an Income Tax Expense of $226,400. The reported Income Tax Expense of $236,000 would remain the same and it exceeds this amount by $9,600. The difference reflects the fact that in accordance with Paragraph 3465.22 (our Paragraph 12-8) no reduction in Future Income Tax Expense is recognized for the $24,000 goodwill impairment loss.

Unrealized Intercompany Profits

12-43.   While this is not illustrated in the preceding example, the preparation of consolidated financial statements normally involves the elimination of unrealized intercompany profits. These are profits on transfers between companies within a consolidated group that have not been realized through a subsequent transfer to an entity outside the consolidated group. From a purely accounting point of view, without considering income taxes, we gave this subject comprehensive coverage in Chapter 6. However, as tax returns are not filed on the basis of consolidated information, there are tax implications associated with the elimination of unrealized intercompany profits.

12-44.   In order to discuss the tax implications of unrealized intercompany profits, consider the following simple example:

Example   A parent company sells merchandise with a cost of $45,000 to a 100 percent owned subsidiary for $60,000. At the end of the period, the merchandise is still in the inventories of the subsidiary. Both companies are subject to a tax rate of 40 percent.

12-45.   From a tax point of view, the parent company has $15,000 of income as a result of this transaction, and the subsidiary has acquired merchandise with a tax basis of $60,000.

12-46.   The problem here is that, in the preparation of consolidated financial statements, unrealized intercompany profits must be eliminated, leaving the carrying value of the asset at the original $45,000. This means that there is a deductible temporary difference between the carrying value of the merchandise and its tax basis of $60,000, a situation which would normally result in the recording of a Future Income Tax Asset of $6,000 [(40%)($60,000 - $45,000)]. In dealing with this situation, Section 3465 makes the following Recommendation:

Paragraph 3465.35   *When an asset is transferred between enterprises within a consolidated group, a future income tax liability or asset should not be recognized in the consolidated financial statements for a temporary difference arising between the tax basis of the asset in the buyer's tax jurisdiction and its cost as reported in the consolidated financial statements. Any taxes paid or recovered by the transferor as a result of the transfer should be recorded as an asset or liability in the consolidated financial statements until the gain or loss is recognized by the consolidated entity.* (January, 2000)

12-47.   This approach is supported as follows:

Paragraph 3465.36   *Although the difference between the buyer's tax basis and the cost of transferred assets as reported in the consolidated financial statements technically meets the definition of a temporary difference, the substance of accounting for it as such would be to recognize income taxes related to inter company gains or losses that are not recognized under "Consolidated Financial Statements", Section 1600. Similar principles would apply to investments subject to significant influence and interests in joint ventures.*

12-48.   We find these statements to be somewhat confusing as can be illustrated by extending our simple example. On the books of the purchasing company, the merchandise would be recorded at $60,000, an amount that would be fully deductible to that company. The entries on the books of the selling company would be as follows:

Cash or Accounts Receivable	$60,000	
Sales		$60,000
Cost Of Goods Sold	$45,000	
Inventories		$45,000
Income Tax Expense [(40%)($60,000 - $45,000)]	$6,000	
Taxes Payable Or Cash		$6,000

12-49.   The normal elimination entries for the sale and profit would be as follows:

| Sales | $60,000 | |
| Cost Of Goods Sold | | $60,000 |

| Cost Of Goods Sold | $15,000 | |
| Inventories | | $15,000 |

12-50.   In conflict with the statements made in Paragraph 3465.35 and 3465.36, if we do not recognize a Future Income Tax Asset, we will be leaving a $6,000 Income Tax Expense on the selling companies, for which there is no corresponding amount of taxable income. In our opinion it is essential that an additional entry be made as follows:

| Future Income Tax Asset | $6,000 | |
| Tax Expense | | $6,000 |

12-51.   In the following period, when the merchandise is sold and the profit realized, the $6,000 Future Income Tax Asset would be charged to Tax Expense. While this is in conflict with the Paragraph 3465.35 statement that "a future income tax liability or asset should not be recognized in the consolidated financial statements for a temporary difference arising between the tax basis of the asset in the buyer's tax jurisdiction and its cost as reported in the consolidated financial statements", it would appear to us to be the only reasonable solution to this problem. Further, it is supported by the Paragraph 3465.35 statement that "Any taxes paid or recovered by the transferor as a result of the transfer should be recorded as an asset or liability in the consolidated financial statements until the gain or loss is recognized by the consolidated entity". In short, it would appear to us that Paragraph 3465.35 contains contra-dictory advice and, in our view, the second position taken in this Recommendation is the correct one.

12-52.   Unrealized intercompany profits are also eliminated in the application of the equity method for significantly influenced investments, and in the application of proportionate consolidation to joint venture investments. The same principles would be applicable to any taxes related to these eliminations.

Loss Carry Overs
Business Combinations

12-53.   In a business combination, the acquiree may have unused tax loss carry forwards. Depending on the legal form of the business combination, as well as the applicability of the acquisition of control rules, some or all of these losses may be available to the combined company. When this is the case, the following Recommendation is applicable:

Paragraph 3465.46   *When, at the time of a business combination, the acquirer considers it more likely than not that it will realize a future income tax asset of its own that was previously unrecognized, it should include a future income tax asset as an identifiable asset when allocating the cost of the acquisition.* (January, 2000)

12-54.   A simple example will serve to illustrate the application of this provision:

Example   On December 31, 2002, Bondor Ltd. pays $1,200,000 in cash to acquire 100 percent of the outstanding shares of Bondee Inc. Both Companies have a December 31 year end and are subject to a tax rate of 35 percent.

At the time of the business combination, Bondee Inc. has net identifiable assets with a carrying value and tax basis of $600,000. The fair value of these assets is $850,000. In addition, the Company has an unused non-capital loss carry forward of $200,000. This loss carry forward has not been recognized on Bondee Inc.'s books.

12-55.   If Bondor Ltd. is able to claim that it is more likely than not that the benefit of the $200,000 loss carry forward will be realized, the $1,200,000 purchase price will be allocated as follows:

Investment Cost	$1,200,000
Fair Value Of Identifiable Assets	(850,000)
Excess Of Cost Over Fair Values	$ 350,000
Future Income Tax Asset [(35%)($200,000)]	(70,000)
Future Income Tax Liability [(35%)($850,000 - $600,000)]	87,500
Goodwill (Residual)	$ 367,500

12-56.   As specified in Section 3465, no Future Income Tax Liability has been recognized for the temporary difference associated with the goodwill.

12-57.   In contrast to the preceding analysis, if Bondor Ltd. was not able to claim that it is more likely than not that the benefit of the $200,000 loss carry forward will be realized, the allocation would be altered as follows:

Investment Cost	$1,200,000
Fair Value Of Identifiable Assets	(850,000)
Excess Of Cost Over Fair Values	$ 350,000
Future Income Tax Liability [(35%)($850,000 - $600,000)]	87,500
Goodwill (Residual)	$ 437,500

12-58.   As can be seen in the preceding allocation schedule, if the loss carry forward benefit is not recognized at the time of acquisition, it effectively becomes part of the goodwill balance. To some degree, this explains the basis for the following Recommendation:

Paragraph 3465.48   *When a future income tax asset acquired in a business combination that was not recognized as an identifiable asset by the acquirer at the date of the acquisition is subsequently recognized by the acquirer, the benefit should be applied:*

(a) *first to reduce to zero any unamortized goodwill related to the acquisition; then*

(b) *to reduce to zero any unamortized intangible assets (see "Goodwill And Other Intangible Assets", Section 3062) related to the acquisition; and then*

(c) *to reduce income tax expense. (January, 2000)*

12-59.   Continuing the simple example that we have presented, assume that the allocation of the purchase price was as presented in Paragraph 12-57. If, in a subsequent accounting period, the management of Bondor Ltd. concluded that Bondee Inc.'s loss carry forward benefit was more likely than not to be realized, a Future Income Tax Asset of $70,000 would be recorded, along with a corresponding reduction in the amount of goodwill to be disclosed.

12-60.   Similar problems with the recognition of acquired loss carry forward benefits arise in a number of other situations. These are covered by the following additional Recommendations:

Paragraph 3465.51   *The principles in paragraphs 3465.46 and 3465.48 should be applied:*

(a) *when accounting for an investment subject to significant influence or an interest in a joint venture; and*

(b) *when recognizing future income tax assets in periods subsequent to the application of push down accounting (see "Comprehensive Revaluation Of Assets And Liabilities", Section 1625). (January, 2000)*

Paragraph 3465.52   *When a future income tax asset that was not recognized at the date of a comprehensive revaluation as a result of a financial reorganization (see "Comprehensive Revaluation Of Assets And Liabilities", Section 1625) is subsequently recognized, the benefit should be applied:*

(a) *first to reduce to zero any unamortized intangible assets (see "Goodwill And Other Intangible Assets", Section 3062) that were recorded at the date of the comprehensive revaluation; and then*

(b) *in a manner consistent with the revaluation adjustment recorded at the date of the comprehensive revaluation.* (January, 2000)

Other Income Tax Issues

Integrated Foreign Operations

12-61.   We have previously noted that Section 3465 generally requires the recognition of Future Income Tax Liabilities for taxable temporary differences, and Future Income Tax Assets for deductible temporary differences. Earlier in this Chapter we have discussed exceptions to this general rule for temporary differences related to Goodwill, and for temporary differences related to the equity pickup in the application of consolidation procedures. A further exception occurs with respect to integrated foreign operations.

12-62.   As described in Section 1650 of the *CICA Handbook*, "Foreign Currency Translation", integrated foreign operations are foreign operations which are financially or operationally interdependent with the reporting enterprise such that the exposure to exchange rate changes is similar to the exposure which would exist had the transactions and activities of the foreign operation been undertaken by the reporting enterprise. As they essentially operate in Canadian dollars, the Canadian dollar is considered to be the appropriate currency of measurement. This view is implemented by translating the foreign currency financial statements using the temporal method of translation.

12-63.   Under the temporal method, most non-monetary assets are translated at historical rates of exchange. Consider, for example, a Canadian company with a German subsidiary classified as an integrated foreign operation. If that subsidiary acquired Land at a cost of 1,000,000 Euros (€) at a point in time when €1 = $1.40, the Land would be recorded in the consolidated financial statements at $1,400,000. If, at a later point in time, the rate for the Euro changed to €1 = $1.50, the Land would continue to be disclosed in the consolidated financial statements at its historic cost of $1,400,000. The problem is that its tax basis in Germany is still €1,000,000 and, at current exchange rates, the cost of €1,000,000 is $1,500,000. In other words, there is a deductible temporary difference between the $1,400,000 carrying value of the asset, and its $1,500,000 tax basis.

12-64.   The situation described in the preceding paragraph would normally require recognition of a Future Income Tax Asset based on the deductible temporary difference. However, in this situation, the following Recommendation is applicable:

Paragraph 3465.33   *A future income tax asset or liability should not be recognized for a temporary difference arising from the difference between the historical exchange rate and the current exchange rate translations of the cost of non-monetary assets or liabilities of integrated foreign operations.* (January, 2000)

12-65.   Section 3465 justifies this position as follows:

Paragraph 3465.34   ... Although that difference technically meets the definition of a temporary difference, the substance of accounting for it as such would be to recognize future income taxes on exchange gains and losses that are not recognized under Section 1650. In order to resolve that conflict and to reduce complexity by eliminating cross-currency (Canadian dollar cost versus foreign tax basis) computations of future income taxes, recognition of future income tax assets and future income tax liabilities for those differences is prohibited.

Refundable Taxes

General Application

12-66.   Section 3465 provides the following definition of refundable taxes:

Paragraph 3465.09(b)   **Refundable taxes** are taxes that are based on certain types of income and that are refundable when certain amounts are paid to shareholders.

12-67.   Without going into great detail, a certain portion of the Part I tax that must be paid on investment income earned by Canadian controlled private corporations is designated as refundable. In addition, a refundable Part IV tax is assessed on certain types of intercorporate dividends received by private companies. These taxes are refundable on the basis of $1 for each $3 of dividends distributed by the corporation paying the dividends.

12-68.   With respect to the accrual of such taxes, the following Recommendation is made:

Paragraph 3465.73   *Refundable taxes should be accrued with respect to all related elements of income recognized in the period, whether the taxes with respect to such amounts are payable currently or in the future.* (January, 2000)

12-69.   With respect to the treatment of taxes paid but not, as yet, refunded, the basic accounting issue is whether they should be treated as a Future Income Tax Asset, an increase in the Income Tax Expense, or as a reduction in Shareholders' Equity. General guidance on this issue is in the form of the following two non-italicized paragraphs:

Paragraph 3465.75   Any taxes that will be refundable on payment of an amount related to an item classified as equity would not be treated as an asset since they do not represent a potential economic benefit - the benefit could only be realized by a decrease in net assets.

Paragraph 3465.76   Any taxes that would be refundable on payment of amounts related to an item classified as a liability represent an advance payment in respect of an expense and would therefore be recorded as an asset.

12-70.   These two paragraphs suggest that refundable taxes related to equity items be treated as a capital transaction while, in contrast, refundable taxes related to liabilities be treated as an asset.

Financial Instruments Recommendations

12-71.   Section 3860, "Financial Instruments - Disclosure And Presentation", has changed the traditional classifications of certain items on the equity side of the Balance Sheet as follows:

- A portion of newly issued convertible bonds must be treated as part of shareholders' equity rather than allocated entirely to liabilities.

- Certain types of preferred shares, those with contractual obligations for the issuers to make cash payments to the holders, must be classified as liabilities.

12-72.   While these changes have been incorporated into the *CICA Handbook*, they have not affected the Canada Customs and Revenue Agency's position on these items. From a tax point of view, convertible bonds do not have an equity component and all preferred shares are equity instruments. This means that there may be refundable taxes on items that are accounted for as liabilities, as well as no refundable taxes related to items that are accounted for as equity. In the context of this somewhat confusing situation, Section 3465 puts forward the following Recommendations:

Paragraph 3465.71   *When a payment related to a component of an instrument classified as a liability under "Financial Instruments - Disclosure And Presentation", Section 3860, will give rise to a refund of income taxes previously paid, the refundable amount should be recognized as a future income tax asset.* (January, 2000)

Paragraph 3465.72 *Refundable taxes that are in the nature of advance distributions related to a component of an instrument classified as equity under "Financial Instruments - Disclosure And Presentation", Section 3860, should be charged to retained earnings when it is more likely than not that such taxes will be recovered in the foreseeable future. The recovery of such refundable taxes should be credited to retained earnings. The charge and the recovery should be disclosed separately. When it is not more likely than not that the taxes will be recovered in the foreseeable future, the taxes should be charged to income.* (January, 2000)

12-73. The treatment of refundable taxes under these two Recommendations can be summarized as follows:

Refundable Taxes As An Asset This would be appropriate when a payment related to an item classified as a liability will give rise to a refund.

Refundable Taxes As A Shareholders' Equity Item This would be appropriate when the taxes paid are in the nature of an advance distribution to holders of an item classified as equity, and it is more likely than not that the taxes will be recovered in the foreseeable future. The taxes will be charged to Retained Earnings when paid, and credited to Retained Earnings when refunded.

Refundable Taxes As An Expense This would be appropriate when the taxes paid are in the nature of an advance distribution to holders of an item classified as equity, and it cannot be claimed that it is more likely than not that the taxes will be recovered in the foreseeable future.

Mutual Fund Corporations

12-74. Mutual fund corporations differ from other corporations in a variety of ways. For one thing, they are generally required to distribute a major part of their earnings in order to retain some of the tax advantages associated with this form of organization.

12-75. In addition, shares in mutual fund corporations are redeemable at the holder's option. The redemptions take place at a net asset value which is determined on a daily basis. To maintain equity between various investors leaving at different points in time, it is necessary to include in this net asset value any refundable taxes that are available on the shares. Given this, it is not surprising that Section 3465 requires that refundable taxes paid by mutual fund corporations be treated as assets:

Paragraph 3465.79 *Refundable taxes on mutual fund corporations should be recorded as an asset.* (January, 2000)

Convertible Debt

12-76. As noted in the preceding section, Section 3860 of the *CICA Handbook* requires that the proceeds from issuing convertible bonds be split between a debt component and an equity component. As this split is not recognized by the Canada Customs and Revenue Agency (formerly Revenue Canada), there will be a temporary difference between the carrying value of the liability and its tax basis. However, the settlement of such liabilities may not have tax consequences for the issuer (e.g., if it is converted). As a consequence, Section 3465 indicates that where the enterprise is able to settle the instrument without the incidence of taxes, the tax basis of the liability component is considered to be the same as its carrying amount and there is no temporary difference.

Alternative Minimum Tax (Capital Taxes)

12-77. Some taxes are levied without regard to the amount of income earned by the enterprise. The most common types of such taxes are provincial capital taxes and the federal large corporations tax. Such taxes sometimes involve some form of carry over provision. For example, the Canadian surtax paid can be applied against the federal large corporations tax, with any excess carried over to prior and future years to be applied against the large corporations tax paid in those years. When this is the case, the following Recommendation is applicable:

> **Paragraph 3465.81** *Any amounts of income tax payable currently that may reduce income taxes of a future period should be recorded as a future income tax asset if it is more likely than not that income taxes will be sufficient to recover the amounts payable currently. Any amounts not more likely than not to be recovered should be included in current income tax expense.* (January, 2000)

Other Disclosure Recommendations

12-78.   For the most part, we have tried to present disclosure requirements as part of the discussion of particular income tax issues. However, a number of disclosure Recommendations do not relate directly to the issues that we have discussed. As a consequence, they are presented in this separate Section.

12-79.   The first two of these Recommendations cover situations where the enterprise is not subject to income taxes. These Recommendations are as follows:

> **Paragraph 3465.98** *An enterprise that is not subject to income taxes because its income is taxed directly to its owners should disclose that fact.* (January, 2000)

> **Paragraph 3465.99** *A public enterprise, life insurance enterprise, deposit taking institution or co-operative business enterprise that is not subject to income taxes because its income is taxed directly to its owners should disclose the net difference between the tax bases and the reported amounts of the enterprise's assets and liabilities.* (January, 2000)

12-80.   While there is no statutory provision under Canadian income tax law that provides for the filing of a consolidated tax return, U. S. tax laws provide for such returns. When a Canadian company is involved in such returns, the following Recommendation applies:

> **Paragraph 3465.101** *If an enterprise is a member of a group that files a consolidated income tax return, the enterprise should disclose in its separately issued financial statements:*
>
> *(a) the aggregate amount of current and future income tax expense for the period and the amount of any tax-related balances due to or from affiliates as of the balance sheet date.*
>
> *(b) the principal provisions of the method by which the consolidated amount of current and future income tax expense is allocated to members of the group and the nature and effect of any changes in that method (and in determining related balances to or from affiliates) during the periods for which the disclosures in (a) above are presented.* (January, 2000)

Additional Readings

12-81.   A reference to sources of additional readings on accounting for taxes can be found at the end of Chapter 11.

Assignment Problems

(The solutions for these problems are only available in
the solutions manual that has been provided to your instructor.)

Assignment Problem Twelve - 1

(This problem is an extension of Self Study Problem Four - 3)

On December 31, 2002, the Pentogram Company purchased 70 percent of the outstanding voting shares of the Square Company for $875,000 in cash.   The Balance Sheets of the Pentogram Company and the Square Company before the business combination transaction on December 31, 2002 were as follows:

**Pentogram And Square Companies
Balance Sheets
As At December 31, 2002**

	Pentogram	Square
Cash	$1,200,000	$ 50,000
Accounts Receivable	400,000	250,000
Inventories	2,000,000	500,000
Plant And Equipment	4,000,000	1,400,000
Accumulated Depreciation	(1,000,000)	(300,000)
Total Assets	$6,600,000	$1,900,000
Current Liabilities	$ 200,000	$ 150,000
Long-Term Liabilities	1,000,000	350,000
No Par Common Stock	2,000,000	1,000,000
Retained Earnings	3,400,000	400,000
Total Equities	$6,600,000	$1,900,000

All of the Square Company's identifiable assets and liabilities have carrying values that are equal to their fair values except for Plant and Equipment which has a fair value of $800,000, Inventories which have a fair value of $600,000 and Long-Term Liabilities which have a fair value of $400,000.

The tax basis of all of the assets and liabilities of both companies are equal to their carrying values. Both the Pentogram Company and the Square Company are taxed at a rate of 38 percent on all of their income. The taxes on the two companies are levied in the same jurisdiction.

Required: Prepare a consolidated Balance Sheet for the Pentogram Company and its subsidiary, the Square Company as at December 31, 2002. Your solution should comply with all of the requirements of the *CICA Handbook*, including Section 3465, "Income Taxes".

Assignment Problem Twelve - 2

(This problem is an extension of Self Study Problem Four - 1)

On December 31, 2002, the Shark Company pays cash to acquire 70 percent of the outstanding voting shares of the Peril Company. On that date the Balance Sheets of the two Companies are as follows:

Shark And Peril Companies
Balance Sheets
As At December 31, 2002

	Shark	Peril
Cash	$ 590,000	$ 200,000
Accounts Receivable	2,000,000	300,000
Inventories	2,500,000	500,000
Investment In Peril (At Cost)	1,050,000	-0-
Plant And Equipment (Net)	4,000,000	1,000,000
Total Assets	$10,140,000	$2,000,000
Liabilities	$ 2,000,000	$ 400,000
Common Stock (No Par)	4,000,000	400,000
Retained Earnings	4,140,000	1,200,000
Total Equities	$10,140,000	$2,000,000

On the acquisition date, the fair values of the Peril Company's assets and liabilities are as follows:

Cash	$ 200,000
Accounts Receivable	250,000
Inventories	550,000
Plant And Equipment (Net)	700,000
Liabilities	(500,000)
Net Fair Values	$1,200,000

The tax basis of all of the assets and liabilities of both companies are equal to their carrying values. Both the Shark Company and the Peril Company are taxed at a rate of 46 percent on all of their income. The taxes on the two companies are levied in the same jurisdiction.

Required: Prepare a consolidated Balance Sheet for the Shark Company and its subsidiary the Peril Company, as at December 31, 2002. Your answer should comply with all of the Recommendations of the *CICA Handbook*, including Section 3465, "Income Taxes".

Assignment Problem Twelve - 3

(This problem is an extension of Assignment Problem Twelve - 2)

On December 31, 2002, the Shark Company pays cash to acquire 70 percent of the outstanding voting shares of the Peril Company at a cost of $1,050,000 in cash. On that date the Peril Company had Common Stock (No Par) outstanding of $400,000 and Retained Earnings of $1,200,000.

On the acquisition date, all of Peril's identifiable assets and liabilities had fair values that were equal to their carrying values except for the following:

	Carrying Value	Fair Value
Accounts Receivable	$ 300,000	$ 250,000
Inventories	500,000	550,000
Plant And Equipment (Net)	1,000,000	700,000
Liabilities	400,000	500,000

At this time, the Plant And Equipment has a remaining useful life of 8 years. The Liabilities mature on December 31, 2007.

On December 31, 2002, the tax basis of all of the assets and liabilities of both companies are equal to their carrying values.

Both the Shark Company and the Peril Company are taxed at a rate of 46 percent on all of their income. The taxes on the two companies are levied in the same jurisdiction. All of the taxable temporary differences in the single entities' books which arise during 2003 are related to an excess of the carrying values of Plant And Equipment over the corresponding UCC value.

The single entity Statements Of Income And Retained Earnings for the year ending December 31, 2003, and the single entity Balance Sheets as at December 31, 2003, for the Shark Company and its subsidiary the Peril Company are as follows:

Shark And Peril Companies
Statement Of Income And Retained Earnings
Year Ending December 31, 2003

	Shark	Peril
Revenues	$4,300,000	$1,411,500
Expenses Other Than Taxes	(3,700,000)	(1,149,000)
Income Before Taxes	$ 600,000	$ 262,500
Tax Expense:		
Current	(207,000)	(86,250)
Future	(69,000)	(34,500)
Net Income	$ 324,000	$ 141,750
Retained Earnings At January 1, 2003	4,140,000	1,200,000
Dividends	(102,000)	Nil
Retained Earnings At December 31, 2003	$4,362,000	$1,341,750

Shark And Peril Companies
Balance Sheets
As At December 31, 2003

	Shark	Peril
Cash	$ 301,000	$ 209,750
Accounts Receivable	2,140,000	327,500
Inventories	2,970,000	514,000
Investment In Peril (At Cost)	1,050,000	-0-
Plant And Equipment (Net)	4,150,000	1,125,000
Total Assets	$10,611,000	$2,176,250
Liabilities	$ 2,180,000	$ 400,000
Future Income Tax Liability - Non-Current	69,000	34,500
Common Stock (No Par)	4,000,000	400,000
Retained Earnings	4,362,000	1,341,750
Total Equities	$10,611,000	$2,176,250

An impairment test on the goodwill arising from the acquisition of Peril determines that there has been a goodwill impairment loss of $8,120 during the year ending December 31, 2003. None of the goodwill is deductible for tax purposes.

Required: Prepare a consolidated Balance Sheet for the Shark Company and its subsidiary the Peril Company, as at December 31, 2003, as well as a consolidated Statement Of Income And Retained Earnings for the year ending December 31, 2003. Your answer should comply with all of the Recommendations of the *CICA Handbook*, including Section 3465, "Income Taxes".

Chapter 13

Accounting For Partnerships

Introduction To Unincorporated Businesses

13-1.   Because of the requirements of provincial securities regulators, companies whose securities are publicly traded must consistently follow the generally accepted accounting principles (GAAP) that are contained in the *CICA Handbook* or other authoritative sources. Failure to do so can lead to modifications to the audit report and, in extreme cases, a suspension of trading in the company's securities.   Even if the corporation's securities are not publicly traded, compliance with *Handbook* Recommendations will generally be required by the federal or provincial corporations act under which the corporation was established.

13-2.   The situation is different with respect to unincorporated businesses. As their ownership interests cannot be publicly traded, they are not subject to the requirements of provincial securities regulation.   Further, the establishment of such businesses does not require the creation of an artificial legal entity and, as a consequence, they are not subject to rules such as those found in corporate enabling statutes. These facts mean that unincorporated businesses are not generally subject to the Recommendations of the *CICA Handbook*.

13-3.   There is, however, often a constraint on the ability of such businesses to avoid *Handbook* Recommendations.   When unincorporated businesses require financing, it is not uncommon for creditors to require audited financial statements. When this is the case, the issuance of an unqualified auditor's report will generally require compliance with GAAP. It should be noted, however, that the introduction of Section 1300, "Differential Reporting", has exempted non-publicly accountable enterprises from a number of *Handbook* requirements.   Most unincorporated businesses would be considered non-publicly accountable enterprises and, as a consequence, exempt from these requirements.

13-4.   For unincorporated enterprises, GAAP also includes a group of Recommendations that are specifically applicable to this type of business. This situation is described in Section 1800 as follows:

> **Paragraph 1800.01**   Minimum standards of disclosure which apply to unincorporated businesses as well as incorporated businesses are dealt with elsewhere in this *Handbook*. Special problems arise, however, in statements of unincorporated businesses because such businesses, unlike limited companies, are not entities separate from their owners. Only these special problems are dealt with in this Section.

13-5.   Unincorporated businesses can be divided into two categories — proprietorships where there is a single owner and partnerships where there are two or more owners (while it is possible to argue that unincorporated joint ventures are a third category, we will view them as a type of partnership for accounting purposes). With respect to those situations where there is a single owner of the business, in the absence of a requirement for audited financial statements, these businesses can use any accounting procedures they wish, including doing no accounting at all except as required by taxation authorities. The objective of financial statements here is to meet the needs of the single owner, with no concern for other equity interests. When creditors advance funds to the business, they may require that their interest be protected by the preparation of audited financial statements, in which case the Recommendations of the *CICA Handbook*, including those contained in Section 1800, come into play. Given this situation, we do not believe that proprietorship accounting requires any discussion beyond that provided with respect to the Recommendations of Section 1800.

13-6. The situation is different with respect to partnerships. As more than one equity interest is involved, financial statements must provide a basis for fair allocation and distribution of partnership resources. This requirement applies not only with respect to income reporting, it applies in a variety of situations, including admittance of a new partner, retirement of an existing partner, and liquidation of the partnership. These problems are not dealt with in Section 1800 or elsewhere in the *Handbook*. As a consequence, this Chapter is largely devoted to the issues associated with accounting for partnerships.

13-7. Our coverage of partnership accounting will follow the discussion of the more general Recommendations that are contained in Section 1800.

Recommendations Of Section 1800

Disclosing The Entity

13-8. A basic problem with accounting for unincorporated businesses relates to the fact that for this type of business, whether it is a proprietorship or a partnership, there is no legal distinction between the business and its owners. However, given the presence of the entity assumption, accountants will generally prepare financial statements which reflect the economic distinction between the business and its owners. To avoid possible confusion that might result from using this approach, Section 1800 makes the following two Recommendations:

> **Paragraph 1800.04** *The financial statements of an unincorporated business should indicate clearly the name under which the business is conducted and, where practicable, the names of the owners.* (January, 1969)

> **Paragraph 1800.05** *It should also be made evident that the business is unincorporated and that the statements do not include all the assets, liabilities, revenues and expenses of the owners.*

Transactions With Owners

13-9. An additional problem arises with unincorporated businesses in that any salaries, interest, or other payments to the owners of the business are not really arm's length transactions. Because of this, Section 1800 requires separate disclosure of these amounts:

> **Paragraph 1800.07** *Any salaries, interest or similar items accruing to owners of an unincorporated business should be clearly indicated by showing such items separately either in the body of the income statement or in a note to the financial statements.*

13-10. In some situations, there are no payments by the unincorporated business to its owner or owners. To avoid any possible confusion in this area, Section 1800 makes the following Recommendation:

> **Paragraph 1800.08** *If no such charges are made in the accounts, this fact should be disclosed in the financial statements.*

13-11. While the issue is not discussed in Section 1800, there is a further issue with respect to the treatment of salary and interest payments to the owners of an unincorporated business.

The issue here is whether such amounts should be disclosed as a distribution of the entity's net income (i.e., deducted after the determination of net income) or, alternatively, disclosed as a determinant of net income (i.e., deducted as an expense in the determination of the entity's net income). This issue will be discussed more completely in our material on partnership accounting.

Income Taxes

13-12.   Under Canadian income tax legislation, proprietorships and partnerships are not taxable entities. This means that, while the owners will be taxed on the income of unincorporated businesses, the businesses are not directly liable for any taxes on their income. While it would be possible to include the personal taxes applicable to the income of the business in the financial statements of the business, the Accounting Standards Board does not feel this to be appropriate and makes the following Recommendation:

> **Paragraph 1800.10**   *No provision for income taxes should be made in the financial statements of businesses for which income is taxed directly to the owners.* (January, 1968)

13-13.   Because of the somewhat unusual nature of this situation as compared to corporate financial statements, Section 1800 makes an additional Recommendation with respect to disclosure:

> **Paragraph 1800.11**   A business that is not subject to tax because its income is taxed directly to its owners would disclose that fact. A public enterprise that is not subject to tax because its income is taxed directly to its owners would also disclose the net difference between the tax bases and the reported amounts of the enterprise's assets and liabilities. (See "Income Taxes", Disclosure, Section 3465.)

Statement Of Owner's Capital Accounts

13-14.   Section 1000 of the *CICA Handbook* indicates that profit oriented enterprises would normally provide a Statement Of Retained Earnings. Section 1800 is more specific in this area in that it requires a Statement Of Owners' Capital Accounts. The Recommendation is as follows:

> **Paragraph 1800.12**   *The financial statements of unincorporated businesses should include a statement setting out the details of the changes in the owners' equity during the period and this statement should set out separately contributions of capital, income or losses, and withdrawals.*

Introduction To Accounting For Partnerships

Partnerships Defined

13-15.   In the case of the corporate form of organization, a separate legal entity is involved and this separate legal entity can be established under either the Canada Business Corporations Act or one of the provincial corporation acts. In contrast, partnerships do not constitute an entity which is legally separate from the owners of the business. Further, there is no national legislation in Canada that is analogous to the Uniform Partnership Act which prevails throughout the United States. As a consequence, we can discuss the legal aspects of partnerships in Canada only within the context of provincial legislation. Fortunately, this does not present significant problems as differences between legislation in the various provinces do not have a significant impact on accounting procedures. In addition, a large part of the legislation is designed to cover situations where some aspects of the partner's rights and obligations have not been covered in the partnership agreement. As a consequence, the contents of the partnership agreement become the dominant consideration in the accounting area.

13-16.   In simple terms, a partnership is an agreement between two or more entities to undertake some business enterprise. A somewhat more formal definition is found in the Ontario Partnerships Act as follows:

Partnership Defined Partnership is the relation that subsists between persons carrying on a business in common with a view to profit, but the relation between the members of a company or association that is incorporated by or under the authority of any special or general Act in force in Ontario or elsewhere, or registered as a corporation under any such Act, is not a partnership within the meaning of this act.

13-17. This more specific definition excludes the possibility of having a partnership with corporate entities as partners and, in effect, restricts the legal meaning of the term to partnerships between individuals. This involves more in the way of legal form than it does substance as, clearly, corporations do form "partnerships" to undertake particular business ventures. However, as a result of this type of definition, in Canada we tend to refer to these corporate "partnerships" as joint ventures.

13-18. Most of the businesses which fall within the legal definition of partnerships are small relative to Canadian public corporations. In terms of the nature of their business activities, the majority would be involved in either merchandising activities or professional activities such as accounting, the provision of legal services, or medicine. The use of the partnership form by such professionals reflects the fact that, in some provinces, professionals such as accountants, lawyers, and doctors are not allowed to incorporate.

13-19. As is implied in the preceding definition, all that is required to establish a partnership is an agreement between the parties that are involved. This agreement could be as simple as a "handshake deal" based purely on oral discussions. However, if significant resources are involved, this type of arrangement is likely to be very unsatisfactory. Even between good friends with the best of intentions, disputes will invariably arise and can seriously disrupt the business activities of the enterprise. As a consequence, partnership agreements should be established in writing, preferably with professional advice, and be designed to cover as many of the possible areas of activity as feasible. A normal agreement would deal with at least the following:

- The names of the partners, the starting date and duration of the agreement, and the amount and type of assets to be contributed by the partners.

- The manner in which profits and losses are to be shared, including any provisions for salaries, interest on drawings, interest on loans from the partnership, and interest on loans to the partnership.

- The nature of the activities that the enterprise will undertake.

- The authority and responsibilities to be vested in each partner.

- The amount of insurance on the lives of the partners to be paid to the surviving partners as beneficiaries.

- The procedures to be used in liquidation, including provisions for dealing with the arbitration of disputes.

13-20. In the absence of a properly drawn up agreement, any one of these items could become the sources of a dispute and, if it cannot be resolved informally, litigation. Making the effort to construct a well thought out partnership agreement is the best defence against such potential conflicts.

Characteristics Of Partnerships

13-21. As with other forms of business organizations, the partnership form of organiation has certain characteristics with which it can be associated. These characteristics are frequently presented as lists of advantages and disadvantages. However, in actual fact, the situation is somewhat more complex than that and, as a reflection of that fact, our discussion will be somewhat broader in nature. The basic characteristics of the partnership form of business organization are described in the Paragraphs which follow:

Limited Life We have previously noted that a partnership does not generally exist as a legal entity separate from the participating partners. As a consequence, the life of a partnership is terminated by the death or retirement of any of the partners. Further, from a strict legal point of view, even the admission of a partner creates a new partnership and terminates the legal life of the previous organization. The continuing and invariable need to create new legal entities is expensive, can be the source of protracted disputes, and may lead to serious disruptions of the normal business activities of the organization. It would seem clear that, relative to the corporate form of organization, this characteristic must be viewed as a disadvantage of partnerships. Note, however, that a well constructed partnership agreement will have provisions for dealing with the addition of new partners and the withdrawal of existing partners.

Unlimited Liability   Also related to the absence of a separate legal existence for the partnership, is the unlimited liability that confronts the participating partners. What this means is that if the partnership encounters serious financial difficulties, creditors can look not only to the assets of the business for satisfaction but, in addition, can lay claim to the personal assets of the partners. Here again, this characteristic is generally cited as a disadvantage relative to the corporate form of organization as it significantly extends the liability of any potential partner, and, thereby, may reduce their interest in investing. Note, however, that this is probably not an accurate analysis when partnership organizations are compared to similar sized corporations. For smaller or owner-managed corporations, creditors will generally require that shareholders provide a personal guarantee for repayment of any amounts extended. This means that, in effect, the shareholders of such corporations do not have unlimited liability.

There is a possible way of avoiding the problem of unlimited liability and this is by establishing a certain number of limited partners. This simply means that any partner that is so designated has his liability limited to some specified amount, generally the amount that has been invested. However, legislation on limited partnerships requires that every such organization have at least one general partner with unlimited liability.

Ease Of Formation   This issue is somewhat less clear cut. In general, it is probably fair to say that a partnership is somewhat easier to form than a corporation. Two people can simply make an informal agreement to undertake some business activity and a partnership is formed. In contrast, the process of incorporation involves complying with a number of legislative requirements and will generally involve legal expenses of at least $500 to $1,000. However, small corporations are constructed along a fairly simple format, with the rights and obligations of the owners clearly established by the relevant enabling legislation. In contrast, partnerships often tend to evolve along more individualized patterns. In this type of situation, the construction of an appropriate and comprehensive partnership agreement may, in fact, be more complex than would be the formation of a corporation.

Mutual Agency   This simply means that each partner has the authority to act for the partnership and to enter into contracts which are binding with respect to all of the partners. Depending on the particular provincial legislation, this may be limited in cases where the partner has acted beyond the normal scope of business operations and without specific authority resulting from the partnership agreement. When this characteristic is viewed in the context of the unlimited liability to which most partners are exposed, it would seem clear that it can be an undesirable feature of the partnership form of business organization. A bad decision on the part of one partner can have seriously adverse effects on the other participants in the partnership.

Co-ownership Of Property And Profits   The individual partners have no claim to any of the specific assets of the business but, rather, acquire an interest in all of the assets. The property becomes jointly owned by all partners and each partner has an ownership interest in the profits of the partnership. The major difficulty with this arrangement is that when partners are admitted or retired, the amount of the new or retiring partner's interest must be established and this may prove to be a difficult and time consuming process.

Taxation   Here again, the lack of a separate legal identity for enterprises organized as partnerships is influential. As a result of this lack of identity, the Income Tax Act contains no definition of what constitutes a partnership. However, the Act requires that partnership income be calculated on the assumption that the partnership is a separate person resident in Canada and that its fiscal period is its taxation year. Each partner's share of the income from the partnership from any business or property and its capital gains (or losses) is treated as his income or gain from such a source whether distributed to the person or not. In considering taxation, there are a number of complex factors that must be taken into consideration. A complete discussion of the taxation of partnerships would not be appropriate in material on financial reporting. However, taxation is an important consideration with respect to the partnership form of organization and, when it is a relevant issue, it is essential to obtain appropriate professional advice.

Regulation Subsequent To Formation   This issue is relatively clear cut. Partnerships have the advantage of being less subject to regulation and supervision by all levels of government than would enterprises which are organized as corporations. This would be particularly true if the corporation were publicly traded and had to comply with the extensive reporting requirements to which such organizations are subjected.

13-22.   A quick review of the preceding list of characteristics makes the position of the partnership form of organization clear. From a legal point of view, partnerships have very few differences from proprietorships. The choice between these two forms will hinge largely on the capital needs of the enterprise. The choice between partnership and corporate forms, however, is more complex. While this is not the case for enterprises which involve professional groups that are prohibited from incorporating, for small businesses the choice may be difficult. Limited life and unlimited liability may not be particularly influential here, and the ease of formation and lack of regulation may push the owners in the direction of the partnership form. As we have noted previously, the tax issue could be extremely important and in actual fact, tax considerations may be the primary consideration in making the choice.

13-23.   As we begin to consider larger enterprises, the issue generally becomes easier to resolve. If the capital requirements of an enterprise are such that a large investor group must be involved, the problems associated with limited life, unlimited liability, and mutual agency become virtually insurmountable. In this type of situation, the corporate form of organization becomes the only reasonable alternative.

Partnerships And The Accounting Entity

13-24.   One of the fundamental assumptions of financial reporting is that accountants should concentrate on providing financial reports for definable business or economic entities. However, much of the accountant's activity takes place in an environment in which various types of legal entities are defined. Since these legal definitions will invariably have some influence on the information needs of financial statement users, the accountant's position is one which involves a potential conflict.

13-25.   In many cases this conflict does not arise. For a simple corporation with no subsidiaries, the legal and economic entities will generally coincide and, as a result, the financial statements prepared to represent the economic entity will be the same as those that would be prepared to meet any of the requirements of the legal entity. However, this is not always the case. The most important example of a conflict between the legal and economic entities is the situation where a parent company has one or more subsidiaries that can be considered a part of the same economic entity as the parent or investor company. In this case, the accountant deals with the conflict by preparing consolidated financial statements which concentrate on the economic entity rather than the separate legal entities that are represented by the parent and subsidiary companies.

13-26.   A similar type of conflict arises in dealing with the financial statements of partnerships. From a legal point of view, the real entities involved in a partnership are the partners themselves. As we have noted, the law does not make a distinction between the status of a partner's personal dwelling and a building in which there is a joint interest with other partners. While the individual partners may wish to have personal financial statements prepared, in judging the performance or position of the partnership as a business entity, it is important to have financial statements which segregate the assets, liabilities, expenses, and revenues of the partnership from those of the partners. In order to accomplish this goal, the accountant must look through the legal form of the organization and prepare statements which reflect the economic substance of the business. This is why we find that, in practice, most accountants are accustomed to viewing partnerships as separate entities with a continuity of life, accounting policies, and asset valuations. It should be noted, however, that the principles and procedures to be used in segregating this accounting entity from its conflicting legal environment, are not nearly as developed and well established as those used in the similar process of preparing consolidated financial statements.

Partnership Owners' Equity Accounts

13-27.   In accounting for a proprietorship, a single owner's equity account is generally adequate as there are no legal or equity apportionment issues which require the segregation of any part of this balance. In contrast, accounting for the owners' equity of a corporation requires, as a minimum, a strict segregation of contributed and earned capital in order to meet the usual legal requirement that dividends can only be paid from earned capital. The situation with partnership owners' equity is less clear cut.

13-28.   From the point of view of general legislation on partnerships, there is no reason to segregate any portion of the owners' equity balance. However, the need to account for the individual equity balances of each partner and information requirements related to implementing the partnership agreement with respect to profit sharing, drawings, and loans, will generally lead to some partitioning of the owners' equity balance. While this may vary from partnership to partnership, the usual pattern will involve three separate types of accounts for each partner. These will normally be:

Capital Accounts   This is the basic account to which each partner's original investment will be credited. In subsequent years, it will be increased by additional investment as well as the partner's share of any net income of the partnership. It will be reduced by any withdrawals by the partner of partnership assets as well as the partner's share of any net losses of the enterprise.

Drawings   In most situations, each partner will have a drawing account. This account will generally be used to account for two types of transactions. First, when a partner withdraws any amounts of salary to which he is entitled, it will be debited to this account. In addition, withdrawals that are made by the partner in anticipation of his annual share of profits would also be debited to this account. This account should not be used for withdrawals of partnership assets that could be viewed as permanent reductions in invested capital, nor should the account be used for loans. At the end of the accounting period, this account will generally be closed to the partner's capital account.

Loans   If it is permitted under the partnership agreement, partners may sometimes borrow funds from the enterprise and, in some situations, a partner may loan funds to the organization. In maintaining equitable relationships between the partners, it is important that this type of transaction be carefully segregated from either drawings against salaries or profits, or increases and decreases in invested capital. To facilitate this segregation, it is the usual practice to set up separate loan receivable and payable accounts for each partner where balances exist. These accounts would not be closed at the end of the period but, rather, would be carried until such time as the balance is paid.

13-29.   The preceding describes a typical set of owners' equity accounts for a partnership. There are, of course, many possible variations, the most common of these being a failure to segregate Drawings accounts from Loans accounts. In addition, if the partnership agreement places any specific restrictions on any or all of the capital balances of the partners, additional accounts may be required to reflect these restrictions.

Partnership Formation

13-30.   The obvious starting point for any discussion of accounting for partnerships would be to consider the transactions required at the inception of the business. If the partnership is not formed from any predecessor organizations, it is simply a matter of recording the assets that have been contributed by the partners. For example, if X and Y form a partnership by each investing $100,000 in cash, the journal entry would be as follows:

Cash	$200,000	
X, Capital		$100,000
Y, Capital		100,000

13-31.   The procedures are only slightly more complex when the assets are other than cash or when the partnership assumes one or more liabilities of a partner. The basic point here is that the assets and liabilities should be recorded at their fair values as at the time the partnership is organized. As an example, assume the same situation as presented in the previous Paragraph, except that X, instead of investing $100,000 in cash, gives the new enterprise a building with a fair value of $150,000 and the enterprise assumes X's mortgage on the building in the amount of $50,000. The required entry would be as follows:

Cash	$100,000	
Building	150,000	
Mortgage Payable		$ 50,000
X, Capital		100,000
Y, Capital		100,000

13-32.   In some situations, partners may be credited with capital balances that are not equal or proportionate to the fair values of the identifiable net assets they are contributing. This would generally reflect the fact that one or more partners is bringing some factor other than identifiable net assets into the business. This could involve special skills, a favorable reputation in the industry, or simply personal assets at a level that enhance the fund raising capacity of the partnership. To illustrate, we can return to the example in Paragraph 13-30. Assume, however, that X is granted an interest equal to that of Y in both capital and income, but that X only contributes $80,000 in cash while Y continues to contribute $100,000. The most reasonable interpretation of this situation is that X has contributed, in addition to the $80,000 in cash, goodwill in the amount of $20,000. Under this interpretation, the appropriate entry would be:

Cash	$180,000	
Goodwill	20,000	
X, Capital		$100,000
Y, Capital		100,000

13-33.   An alternative interpretation that is frequently used in practice would involve the assumption that Y is granting a bonus to X of $10,000. Under this assumption, no Goodwill would be recorded and both capital accounts would be recorded at $90,000. This effectively assumes that Y has paid $100,000 for a one half interest in a business that is worth $180,000. We are of the opinion that this is not a reasonable interpretation of the economic substance of the transaction.

13-34.   It is not uncommon for a partnership to be formed with one or more of the partners contributing an existing proprietorship. This type of transaction is somewhat more complex in that it would be necessary to determine the fair values of all of the identifiable assets and liabilities as well as any existing goodwill for each predecessor enterprise. The guidelines contained in Section 1581 of the *CICA Handbook* for implementing these procedures in business combinations would generally be applicable in this type of partnership formation situation (see Chapter 3 for a discussion of these procedures). Despite these additional complications, the principles involved are no different than in those cases where the partners contribute only identifiable assets. All of the contributed identifiable assets and liabilities and any existing goodwill would be recorded as the new partnership's assets and, at the same time, the partners' capital accounts would be credited for the amounts contributed. If there was a disparity between the net assets contributed and the amount allocated to the various partners' capital accounts, it can be dealt with by recognition of additional goodwill being contributed by one or more partners or on the basis of bonus payments to one or more partners. As we indicated in the previous Paragraph, we believe that the former interpretation is the more reasonable of the two alternatives.

Partnership Income

General Principles

13-35.   The design of an appropriate and equitable system for the allocation of partnership income is one of the more important components of any properly designed partnership agreement. If the agreement fails to specify a plan for sharing the income of the enterprise, most provincial legislation calls for income to be shared equally. As in many cases, such equal sharing would not be considered an equitable arrangement, most partnership agreements devote considerable attention to the problem of income allocation.

13-36.   The partnership income allocation problem is made complex by the fact that partners may contribute a variety of different services to the enterprise. In most cases, all partners will contribute some portion of the partnership capital, either in cash or in the form of some other types of assets. In addition, it would be normal for some or all of the partners to work in the enterprise on an ongoing basis. Beyond this, one or more of the partners may possess very substantial personal financial resources which may enhance the ability of the enterprise to obtain a better credit rating, resulting in either more financing or financing at a more favorable rate. Such partners must also be rewarded for the fact that they may lose considerably more in the event the partnership experiences financial adversity or bankruptcy. All of this means that, in order to provide a completely equitable income sharing arrangement, the partnership agreement should give consideration to amounts of capital contributed, the worth of services provided to the partnership by working partners, and any differential amounts of risk related to the amount of personal assets owned by the various partners.

13-37.   In practice, consideration is not always given to all of these matters. While many variations are possible, four types of income sharing arrangements seem to be the most common. They are as follows:

Fixed Ratios   The simplest type of arrangement would involve simply sharing on the basis of some agreed upon ratio, other than that established by relative capital contributions. The ratio will generally be the same for both profits and losses but may, in particular circumstances, differ depending on whether or not the business is successful.

Capital Contributions   Under this approach, capital balances would be used as a basis for determining each partner's share of partnership profits or losses. When this approach is used, the partnership agreement must make clear which capital balance is to be used in establishing profit sharing ratios. It could be the balance originally invested, the beginning of the year balance, or the end of the year balance. However, the most reasonable approach would seem to be to use the average balance for the year. It would also be necessary to specify the effects of loans and/or drawings on the determination of the relevant capital balance.

Salaries With Ratios For Any Remainder   Here salaries are established for the partners that work in the enterprise and any income or loss balance that remains is allocated on the basis of either fixed or capital contribution ratios. Here again, if fixed ratios are used, they will usually apply to both profits and losses.

Salaries And Interest With Ratios For Any Remainder   In this type of plan, all factors are considered. Partners are given credit for services rendered in the form of salaries, for capital contributed in the form of interest, and for any other risk considerations in the ratios established for distributing any remaining balance of profit or loss. When this approach is used, the partnership agreement must clearly establish the priority of the various types of claims. If earnings are not adequate to cover all three allocations, it becomes important to know whether salary claims take precedence over interest claims, or whether interest claims stand ahead of allocations for the assumption of additional risk.

13-38.   We think that the last approach described will provide the most useful information. There are, of course, difficulties associated with establishing reasonable salary levels in non-arms length situations, as well as some question as to whether capital contributed at risk should be viewed as earning "interest". However, this type of arrangement allows all of the components of the partner's relationship with the business to be given consideration. In addition, it gives a better indication of the performance of the enterprise itself. If, for example, the business is earning less than the fair value of the services rendered by the partners, then a failure to charge enterprise income with salaries will obscure the fact that from an economic point of view the business is losing money.

13-39.   Profit sharing is the most likely source of disputes among the partners. As a consequence, it is important that the partnership agreement not only provide a method for sharing partnership income but that, in addition, the means of determining that income be established as well. The amount of detail required will vary from agreement to agreement. However, at a minimum, the accounting period and the source from which accounting procedures will be adopted should be included as a part of the agreement.

Allocation Procedures

Example

13-40.   In order to illustrate the various types of profit sharing arrangements described in Paragraph 13-37, a simple example will be used:

Example   Two partners, S and T, are involved and the data for the current calendar year is as follows:

	Partner S	Partner T
Original Investment	$40,000	$60,000
Capital Balance, January 1	55,000	65,000
Additional Investment, April 1	5,000	-0-
Drawings, June 30	4,000	6,000
Additional Investment, October 1	-0-	3,000

For the current year ending December 31, the S and T Partnership earned a Net Income of $15,000, before consideration of any salaries to the partners or interest on their capital contributions.

Fixed Ratios

13-41.   This type of arrangement is sufficiently simple that it requires little discussion. If, for example, the agreement called for profits to be shared equally, S and T would be credited with $7,500 each. This amount, reduced by the balances in the Drawings accounts would be closed to the end of the period Capital accounts, leaving S with a balance of $63,500 ($55,000 + $5,000 - $4,000 + $7,500) and T with a balance of $69,500 ($65,000 - $6,000 + $3,000 + $7,500). This type of profit sharing arrangement would, in most circumstances, be very easy to administer. However, it can be criticized for failing to give weight to the varying capital and service contributions that the two partners may be making to the enterprise.

Capital Contributions

13-42.   As we have previously noted, when profit sharing is to be based on the relative capital contributions of the partners, there are various ways in which this approach can be applied. If it were based on original contributions, the income to be allocated to each partner could be calculated as follows:

S's Share = [($15,000)($40,000 ÷ $100,000)] = $6,000

T's Share = [($15,000)($60,000 ÷ $100,000)] = $9,000

13-43.   Alternatively, if unweighted end of the year capital balances, without the inclusion of the year's income were used ($56,000 + $62,000), the relative income shares of the two partners would be calculated as follows:

S's Share = [($15,000)($56,000 ÷ $118,000)] = $7,119

T's Share = [($15,000)($62,000 ÷ $118,000)] = $7,881

13-44.   Probably the most equitable way of using capital contributions as a basis for profit sharing is to use the weighted average capital balance for the year. In using this approach, the partnership agreement should specify what amounts are to be included in the weighted average capital calculation. In our example, we will assume that drawings are treated as reductions of capital when they occur but that income for the year is not included in the calculation. On this basis, the weighted average capital balances for the two partners would be calculated as follows:

Weighted Average Capital Balances
For The Year Ending December 31

	Amount	Weight	Weighted Amount
For Partner S:			
January 1, Balance	$55,000	1.00	$55,000
Added Investment	5,000	.75	3,750
Drawings	(4,000)	.50	(2,000)
Totals	$56,000		$56,750
For Partner T:			
January 1, Balance	$65,000	1.00	$65,000
Added Investment	3,000	.25	750
Drawings	(6,000)	.50	(3,000)
Totals	$62,000		$62,750

13-45.   Given the preceding calculations, the partners' respective shares of income could be calculated as follows:

S's Share = [($15,000)($56,750 ÷ $119,500)] = $7,123

T's Share = [($15,000)($62,750 ÷ $119,500)] = $7,877

Salaries With Ratios For Any Remainder

13-46.   As we move to this somewhat more complex type of profit sharing arrangement, we will assume that both S and T work in the partnership and it is their belief that the fair value of their services would be $5,000 for S and $3,000 for T. The partnership agreement then specifies that any profit or loss after the deduction of these salaries should be split on the basis of 40 percent to S and 60 percent to T. On this basis the profit for the year would be split as follows:

S's Share = [(40%)($15,000 - $5,000 - $3,000)] = $2,800

T's Share = [(60%)($15,000 - $5,000 - $3,000)] = $4,200

13-47.   This means that the total distributions to the two partners would be as follows:

	Partner S	Partner T	Totals
Salaries	$5,000	$3,000	$ 8,000
Profit Shares	2,800	4,200	7,000
Totals	$7,800	$7,200	$15,000

13-48.   In this type of arrangement, it is important for the partnership agreement to specify exactly what happens in the event income is less than the salaries. In this case, if income before the consideration of salaries had only been $5,000, the deduction of salaries would have created a $3,000 loss. Normally, this loss would be split using the same 40 percent, 60 percent ratio and this would have resulted in a reduction in the capital accounts of the two partners. However, there is nothing to prevent the two partners from putting a clause into the partnership agreement which provides for salaries to be accrued only when partnership income is sufficient to provide for them.

Salaries And Interest With Ratios For Any Remainder

13-49.   In this final case, we will assume that the partnership agreement calls for salaries of $5,000 for S and $3,000 for T, interest at 10 percent on the beginning of the year capital balances, and for the remaining profit or loss to be allocated on the basis of 40 percent to S and 60 percent to T. The balance to be distributed on the basis of these ratios can be calculated as follows:

Income Before Salaries Or Interest	$15,000
Salaries ($5,000 + $3,000)	(8,000)
Balance Before Interest	$ 7,000
Interest [(10%)($55,000 + $65,000)]	(12,000)
Balance To Be Distributed	($ 5,000)

13-50.   On the basis of the 40:60 sharing plan in the partnership agreement, this loss would be distributed $2,000 to S and $3,000 to T and this would result in the following total distribution to the two partners:

	Partner S	Partner T	Totals
Salaries	$5,000	$3,000	$ 8,000
Interest	5,500	6,500	12,000
Loss	(2,000)	(3,000)	(5,000)
Totals	$8,500	$6,500	$15,000

13-51.   As was the case when only salaries and fixed ratio sharing was involved, it is important for the partnership agreement to provide a clear indication of what happens when salaries and, in this case, interest on capital balances exceeds income. The normal procedure would be to give priority to salaries, followed by interest on capital contributions, with any remaining profit or loss distributed in agreed upon ratios. Again, however, there is nothing to prevent the partnership agreement from specifying some alternative type of arrangement.

Disclosure

13-52.   In partnership accounting, the meaning of the term Net Income is not entirely clear. If the partnership agreement calls for the payment of salaries to the partners, and these amounts are fairly representative of the fair value of the services rendered by the partners, it would seem appropriate to deduct these amounts as operating expenses before arriving at a Net Income figure. However, if the partnership agreement calls for some form of interest on invested capital, our conventional approach to the calculation of Net Income does not provide for deductions of amounts allocated to the ownership interest of the enterprise. If, however, loans by the partners to the partnership were involved, interest on such liability amounts might be included in the determination of Net Income.

13-53.   Probably as a reflection of the fact that transactions between partners and the partnership are less than fully arms length in nature, the conventional procedure is to disclose Net Income before any distributions to the partners. For example, if we assume that the $15,000 income figure from Paragraph 13-40 was based on Revenues of $40,000 and Expenses of $25,000, and that distributions were as calculated in Paragraph 13-50, the partnership Income Statement could be as follows:

S And T Partnership
Income Statement

Revenues	$40,000
Expenses	25,000
Net Income	$15,000

13-54.   The actual distribution of this income would then be disclosed in a Statement Of Partners' Capital Accounts as follows:

S And T Partnership
Statement Of Partners' Capital Accounts

	Partner S	Partner T	Totals
Balance, January 1	$55,000	$65,000	$120,000
Additional Investment	5,000	3,000	8,000
Balance Before			
Income And Drawings	$60,000	$68,000	$128,000
Net Income	8,500	6,500	15,000
Drawings	(4,000)	(6,000)	(10,000)
Balance, December 31	$64,500	$68,500	$133,000

Changes In The Partnership Group

Conceptual Problems

13-55.   Under most provincial legislation in Canada, any change in the participating group of partners involves a dissolution of the existing partnership agreement and necessitates the preparation of a new one. In the absence of a specific alternative provision in the partnership agreement, this would include all of the following types of events:

- The admission of a new partner.
- The retirement or death of one of the existing partners.
- The transfer of an existing partnership interest to a new owner (note that this differs from U.S. law which would not view this as a termination of the partnership agreement).

13-56.   Since the partnership agreement forms the only legal basis for the existence of a partnership, a legal perspective would view the preceding events as involving the formation of a new business enterprise.

13-57.   Under present generally accepted accounting principles, all of the assets and liabilities transferred to a new business should be recorded at their fair values as at the date the business is formed. This would also include the recording of any goodwill that might be contributed by the investors or their predecessor business organizations. We observed this principle in the examples illustrating the formation of a completely new partnership (Paragraphs 13-30 through 13-34) and there is no question as to its applicability in that type of situation. However, we are now faced with a more difficult question. Should the fact that each ownership change involves the formation of a new legal agreement lead us to the application of the asset and liability revaluation procedures that are generally required in the formation of a new business entity? The alternative would, of course, be to assume a continuity of existence similar to that of a corporation. Under this assumption, a change in the ownership interest has no real effect on the continuity of the accounting records and does not provide a basis for any revaluation of asset or liability balances.

13-58.   While the legal answer is clear, it is not necessarily satisfactory. As we have noted previously, the primary concern of accountants is with economic substance rather than with legal form. Therefore, the real question to be answered is does a change in ownership interest of a partnership involve the creation of a new economic entity or, alternatively, do such changes involve only a change in legal form as represented by the new partnership agreement. In the Paragraphs which follow, this issue is considered in the context of the various types of transactions which can result in changes in the partnership group.

13-59.   In some situations, an exchange of interests takes place outside of the partnership entity. More specifically, there are situations in which an existing partner sells his interest to a new partner, with the consideration being exchanged directly between the individuals. In this type of situation no new assets enter the partnership books, the partnership is generally not directly involved in the negotiations related to the transaction, and the new partner will normally assume exactly the same rights and obligations that were associated with the previous partner. In fact, it is not uncommon for the partnership agreement to provide for the implementation of such transfers without a legal dissolution of the partnership. Given these facts, it would be our view that treating this type of ownership change as the formation of a new business entity would rarely be an appropriate approach. It follows from this position that continuity of the partnership accounting records should be maintained and that no changes would be made in the carrying values of any of the assets or liabilities of the partnership.

13-60.   The situation is less clear cut when a partnership admits a new partner or an existing partner leaves through death or retirement. It is our view that a single solution to the problem does not exist and, in the absence of clear cut guidelines for determining whether a new economic entity has been created, some amount of judgment will have to be applied. For example, in a large public accounting firm with hundreds of partners, the admission and retirement of partners are events which occur with great frequency. Further, these admissions and retirements will generally not have any real influence on the continuity of the business activities in which the firm is engaged. In these circumstances, it would be extremely unreasonable to view the admission or retirement of a partner as the creation of a new economic entity and, as a consequence, no break in the continuity of the accounting records should occur.

13-61.   Alternatively, assume that we are dealing with a partnership involving only two partners operating a retail store at the same location for a period of twenty years. Continuing the example, assume that a new partner is brought in, contributing cash in an amount equal to the fair value of the existing partnership net assets, and that the three partners intend to use this cash to open a new operation in a different line of business. A similar example could involve a situation where two partners have worked together for many years and one decides to leave, taking with him half of the assets and clients of the partnership. In both of these situations, a case can be made for the idea that a new business entity has been created and that this new entity is acquiring a group of identifiable assets, goodwill, and liabilities that should be recorded at new values measured as at the date of the admission of the new partner or the retirement of the old.

13-62.   Unfortunately, many situations are not as clear cut as those described in the preceding two Paragraphs. Further complicating the problem at the present time, is the fact that there are no existing guidelines for the determination of whether the admission or retirement of a partner constitutes the formation of a new economic entity. As a consequence, we find alternative treatments being applied in practice. When it is assumed that the admission or retirement of a partner does not involve the formation of a new business entity, the respective equity interests are allocated on the basis that the newly admitted or retiring partner is either paying a bonus to or receiving a bonus from the other partners in the organization. This approach will be illustrated in the Sections dealing with both admissions and retirements of partners.

13-63.   In contrast, when it is assumed that the admission or retirement of a partner does involve the formation of a new business entity, identifiable assets will be revalued to their fair values and goodwill, if applicable, will be recorded. There is also a compromise solution that is sometimes encountered. There appears to be a continuing reluctance on the part of some accountants to record goodwill in partnership admission and retirement transactions. This leads to procedures under which fair values are recorded for identifiable assets and liabilities, but any goodwill being acquired by the new business is ignored. It would be our position that this compromise position is not appropriate. If the circumstances of the admission or retirement are such that the resulting partnership can be viewed as a new economic entity, then generally accepted accounting principles would require the recording of any goodwill acquired by this new entity. As a consequence, the examples in the Sections on the admissions and retirements of partners will illustrate only the complete procedures that we associate with the formation of a new entity.

Exchange Of Ownership Interests

13-64.   The following is an example of an exchange in ownership interest outside of the partnership structure.

Example   The Balance Sheet of the STU Partnership on December 31 of the current year is as follows:

STU Partnership
Balance Sheet As At December 31

Total Net Assets	$1,500,000
Partner S, Capital	$ 500,000
Partner T, Capital	500,000
Partner U, Capital	500,000
Total	$1,500,000

The partnership agreement calls for all profits and losses to be shared on an equal basis. On this date, Partner U sells his interest to a new partner V for $600,000, who pays this amount of cash directly to Partner U.

13-65.   You will recall our argument that, in this type of situation, there would rarely be justification for the revaluation of partnership assets (Paragraph 13-59). Given this view, the appropriate entry on the partnership books to record the transaction would be as follows:

Partner U, Capital	$500,000	
Partner V, Capital		$500,000

13-66.   This would leave the December 31 Balance Sheet unchanged except for the new name which attaches to one of the capital accounts.

13-67.   You should also note that the entry and the resulting Balance Sheet would not be affected by the amount paid by Partner V for Partner U's proportionate interest. As we have previously noted, it would be very rare for this type of transaction to result in the creation of a new economic entity. As a result, any business valuation information that is implicit in the transfer price of the partnership interest will generally not be used as a basis for any revaluation of assets or recognition of goodwill.

Admission Of New Partners
Basic Example

13-68.   In view of the fact that additions to the partnership's assets are involved and because alternative assumptions as to the nature of the transaction have greater applicability in the case of partnership admissions, accounting for them requires greater elaboration than was the case with an exchange of partnership interests. To facilitate your understanding of the problems involved, a single basic example will be used to illustrate four cases of a partner admission.

Case 1:   Consideration Exceeds Book Value - New Entity Assumption
Case 2:   Consideration Exceeds Book Value - Continuity Assumption
Case 3:   Consideration Below Book Value - New Entity Assumption
Case 4:   Consideration Below Book Value - Continuity Assumption

Example   The Balance Sheet of the AB Partnership as at December 31 of the current year is as follows:

AB Partnership
Balance Sheet As At December 31

Total Net Assets	$500,000
Partner A, Capital	$250,000
Partner B, Capital	250,000
Total	$500,000

The partnership agreement calls for Partners A and B to share all profits and losses equally. In all of the examples which follow, they are admitting Partner C with a one third interest in assets, income and losses. This means that the three partners will each have equal shares after the admission of Partner C. On December 31, before the admission of Partner C, the fair values of the net assets of the AB Partnership are equal to $600,000.

Admission Case One - Consideration Exceeds Book Value - New Entity

13-69.   As a first example, assume that Partner C pays cash of $325,000 to the partnership in return for a one third interest in assets, income, and losses, and that the admission of this partner can be viewed as the creation of a new economic entity. The admission price implies a total value for the new partnership of $975,000 ($325,000 ÷ 1/3) and a value for the combined interest of Partners A and B of $650,000 [($975,000)(2/3)]. Since the total fair values of the net assets of the partnership only amount to $600,000, this would imply the existence of Goodwill in the amount of $50,000. As in this Case we are going to assume that the admission of Partner C creates a new business entity, the following entry will be required to recognize these value changes:

Net Assets	$100,000	
Goodwill	50,000	
Partner A, Capital		$75,000
Partner B, Capital		75,000

13-70.   After this adjustment, the entry to record the admission of Partner C would be as follows:

Cash (Net Assets)	$325,000	
Partner C, Capital		$325,000

13-71.   The resulting Balance Sheet for the new partnership would be as follows:

ABC Partnership
Balance Sheet As At December 31

Net Identifiable Assets	$925,000
Goodwill	50,000
Total	$975,000

Partner A, Capital	$325,000
Partner B, Capital	325,000
Partner C, Capital	325,000
Total	$975,000

Admission Case Two - Consideration Exceeds Book Value - Continuity

13-72.   In this Case, we will assume that Partner C makes the same $325,000 investment which we considered in Case One. However, the circumstances are such that the admission does not break the continuity of the existing business entity and, as a consequence, we would not view C's admission to the Partnership as a basis for revaluing assets. Given this interpretation, we must then assume that C is paying a bonus of $25,000 to each of the existing partners. The total assets will amount to $825,000 ($500,000 + $325,000) and C's one third interest will be valued at $275,000 [($825,000)(1/3)]. The entry to record C's admission to the partnership would be as follows:

Cash	$325,000	
Partner A, Capital		$ 25,000
Partner B, Capital		25,000
Partner C, Capital		275,000

13-73.   The resulting Balance Sheet would appear as follows:

ABC Partnership
Balance Sheet As At December 31

Total Net Assets	$825,000

Partner A, Capital	$275,000
Partner B, Capital	275,000
Partner C, Capital	275,000
Total	$825,000

Admission Case Three - Consideration Below Book Value - New Entity

13-74.   In this Case, we will assume that C is admitted to a one third interest in the Partnership in return for cash of $200,000 and that the admission can be interpreted as resulting in the formation of a new business entity. If we continue to assume that the fair values of the AB Partnership's net assets are $600,000 , this means that the investment cost is below both the book value and the fair values of the interests of either Partner A or Partner B. This could mean one of two things. First, this lower value could imply that the existing partnership has negative goodwill. However, this interpretation is not widely used in present practice. Rather, a second interpretation, that Partner C is bringing goodwill into the business, is used. If there is a reasonable basis for this interpretation, then we believe that the assumption that a new business entity is being formed would still require the recording of the identifiable assets at their fair values. While this would often not be done in practice, the solution which follows adjusts these assets to their fair values. The adjusting entry would be as follows:

Net Assets	$100,000
Partner A, Capital	$50,000
Partner B, Capital	50,000

13-75. With this adjustment completed, the interests of Partners A and B have been increased to $300,000. Assuming that Partner C's interest is also worth $300,000, the fact that he is admitted with a cash payment of only $200,000 implies that he is bringing goodwill with a value of $100,000 to the partnership. Based on this economic interpretation, the entry to record the admission of Partner C would be as follows:

Cash	$200,000
Goodwill	100,000
Partner C, Capital	$300,000

13-76. Note that, if we had not recorded the fair value changes on the Partnership's Net Assets, Partner C would have only been credited with $50,000 in Goodwill and the capital accounts of the three partners would be at $250,000. However, based on the preceding entries, the Balance Sheet of the ABC Partnership would be prepared as follows:

ABC Partnership
Balance Sheet As At December 31

Net Identifiable Assets	$800,000
Goodwill	100,000
Total	$900,000
Partner A, Capital	$300,000
Partner B, Capital	300,000
Partner C, Capital	300,000
Total	$900,000

Admission Case Four - Consideration Below Book Value - Continuity

13-77. In this Case, we will assume that C is admitted to the Partnership in return for a cash payment of $220,000 and that the admission does not constitute the formation of a new business entity. Since the admission of C does not constitute a basis for the revaluation of assets, then we must assume that the existing partners are each granting C a bonus of $10,000. The total assets will amount to $720,000 ($500,000 + $220,000) and C's one third interest will amount to $240,000 ($720,000 ÷ 3). Based on this economic interpretation of the admission, the entry to record C's admission to the partnership would be as follows:

Cash	$220,000
Partner A, Capital	10,000
Partner B, Capital	10,000
Partner C, Capital	$240,000

13-78. The resulting Balance Sheet for the ABC Partnership would be as follows:

ABC Partnership
Balance Sheet As At December 31

Total Net Assets	$720,000
Partner A, Capital	$240,000
Partner B, Capital	240,000
Partner C, Capital	240,000
Total	$720,000

Retirement Of Existing Partners

Basic Example

13-79.   As was the case in our consideration of the admission of new partners, we will use a single basic example for four different Cases illustrating the retirement of partners. The cases are the same as those used with the admission of partners. That is, Case One will involve consideration in excess of book value combined with the new entity assumption, Case Two will involve consideration in excess of book value combined with the continuity assumption, Case Three will involve consideration that is less than book value combined with the new entity assumption, and Case Four will involve consideration that is less than book value combined with the continuity assumption. The basic example is as follows:

Example   The Balance Sheet of the XYZ Partnership as at December 31 of the current year is as follows:

XYZ Partnership
Balance Sheet As At December 31

Total Net Assets	$600,000
Partner X, Capital	$200,000
Partner Y, Capital	200,000
Partner Z, Capital	200,000
Total	$600,000

The partnership agreement calls for Partners X, Y, and Z to share all profits and losses equally. On December 31, it has been determined that the fair values of the identifiable Net Assets of the XYZ Partnership total $690,000. In the Cases which follow, Partner Z is being retired through a payment of partnership cash.

Retirement Case One - Consideration Exceeds Book Value - New Entity

13-80.   In this first Case, we will assume that Partner Z is retired in return for a payment of $250,000 in partnership cash and the circumstances are such that the remaining partnership can be viewed as a new business entity. The $250,000 payment to Partner Z for his one-third interest implies a total value for the business of $750,000. This is $150,000 in excess of the book values of these assets and, given the fact that it has been determined that the identifiable assets have a total fair value of $690,000, this $150,000 excess would be allocated $90,000 to the identifiable assets and $60,000 to Goodwill. The entry to accomplish this allocation is as follows:

Net Identifiable Assets	$90,000	
Goodwill	60,000	
Partner X, Capital		$50,000
Partner Y, Capital		50,000
Partner Z, Capital		50,000

13-81.   Given the preceding adjustment, the entry to retire Partner Z would be as follows:

Partner Z, Capital	$250,000	
Cash (Net Identifiable Assets)		$250,000

13-82.   The resulting Balance Sheet, after the retirement of Partner Z would be as follows:

XY Partnership
Balance Sheet As At December 31

Net Identifiable Assets	$440,000
Goodwill	60,000
Total	$500,000
Partner X, Capital	$250,000
Partner Y, Capital	250,000
Total	$500,000

Retirement Case Two - Consideration Exceeds Book Value - Continuity

13-83.   In this Case, we will again assume that Partner Z is retired in return for partnership cash in the amount of $250,000. However, in this case the interpretation will be that this retirement did not result in a new business entity and a need to revalue assets. As the payment to Z is $50,000 in excess of the book value of his interest, we will have to assume that Partner X and Partner Y are each paying a bonus of $25,000 to Partner Z. The retirement entry which would reflect that assumption is as follows:

Partner X, Capital	$ 25,000	
Partner Y, Capital	25,000	
Partner Z, Capital	200,000	
Cash		$250,000

13-84.   The resulting Balance Sheet for the XY Partnership would be as follows:

XY Partnership
Balance Sheet As At December 31

Total Net Assets	$350,000
Partner X, Capital	$175,000
Partner Y, Capital	175,000
Total	$350,000

Retirement Case Three - Consideration Below Book Value - New Entity

13-85.   We will assume in this situation that Partner Z is retired in return for a payment of $180,000 and that the retirement can be viewed as resulting in the formation of a new business entity. The price paid to Partner Z for his one third interest implies a total value for the enterprise of $540,000 [(3)($180,000)], a value that is $60,000 less than the $600,000 carrying value of the Net Assets and $150,000 less than their fair value of $690,000. This means that either the Partnership has negative goodwill in the amount of $150,000 ($690,000 - $540,000) or that there are factors in Partner Z's personal situation that make him willing to sacrifice a part of his equity in order to retire from the business.

13-86.   If Partner Z has actually made a sacrifice in order to facilitate his retirement, the amount of this sacrifice could be measured by the $20,000 difference between the capital balance of $200,000 and the retirement price of $180,000, and it would be appropriate to credit this amount to the capital accounts of Partners X and Y. This would result in a solution identical to that which would be used if we assume partnership continuity and use the bonus method to retire Z. This solution is illustrated in Case Four.

13-87.   Alternatively, if we assume that the deficiency relates to negative goodwill, present generally accepted accounting principles require such amounts to be charged to specific assets (see our discussion of this issue in Chapter 3). This means that we cannot adjust the Net Assets to their current fair values of $690,000. Rather, we will have to write them down to the $540,000 balance implied in the purchase price. The entry for this adjustment would be as follows:

Partner X, Capital	$20,000	
Partner Y, Capital	20,000	
Partner Z, Capital	20,000	
Net Assets		$60,000

13-88.   After the preceding adjustment, the entry that would be required to retire Partner Z would be as follows:

Partner Z, Capital	$180,000	
Cash		$180,000

13-89.   The resulting Balance Sheet for the XY Partnership would be as follows:

XY Partnership
Balance Sheet As At December 31

Total Net Assets	$360,000
Partner X, Capital	$180,000
Partner Y, Capital	180,000
Total	$360,000

Retirement Case Four - Consideration Below Book Value - Continuity

13-90.   We again assume in this Case that Partner Z is retired in return for a payment of $180,000, but that the transaction did not result in the formation of a new business entity. Since there is no basis for the revaluation of any of the Partnership assets, we will have to assume that Z is paying a bonus of $10,000 each to Partners X and Y. The journal entry to retire Partner Z under this assumption would be as follows:

Partner Z, Capital	$200,000	
Partner X, Capital		$ 10,000
Partner Y, Capital		10,000
Cash		180,000

13-91.   The resulting Balance Sheet for the XY Partnership would be as follows:

XY Partnership
Balance Sheet As At December 31

Total Net Assets	$420,000
Partner X, Capital	$210,000
Partner Y, Capital	210,000
Total	$420,000

Partnership Liquidation

General Procedures

13-92.   In the context of partnership accounting, the term liquidation refers to situations in which the partners agree to terminate their operation of the enterprise, convert the assets to cash, pay off any outstanding liabilities, and distribute the remaining cash to the partners. In some cases, the business may be sold as a unit in a single transaction while, in other cases, the liquidation process may involve individual asset sales over a considerable period of time.

13-93.   Whether sold as a unit or disposed of on a piece by piece basis, the liquidation of the partnership assets will invariably involve gains and losses. While the partnership agreement might have a special provision dealing with gains and losses arising at the time of liquidation, such gains and losses would normally be allocated to the partners on the basis of their usual profit sharing ratios. These gains and losses will then be added or subtracted to the capital accounts of the partners and these capital account balances will serve as the basis for distributing any partnership cash that is left subsequent to the payment of partnership liabilities.

13-94.   If the partnership experiences losses in the liquidation process, one or more partners may end up with a debit or negative balance in their capital account. If this happens, such partners are responsible for eliminating this balance by making additional capital contributions from their personal assets. If, in this process, the concerned partners become personally insolvent and cannot provide the assets necessary to eliminate their debit capital balances, then any remaining debit balance in their accounts will become additional partnership losses to be shared by the remaining partners.

13-95.   If the partnership experiences particularly severe losses in the process of liquidation, it may find itself in a situation in which its liabilities exceed its assets. In this case the partnership is said to be insolvent and one or more of the capital accounts will have debit balances. In fact, it is possible that all of the capital accounts may have such balances. The only statement that can be made with certainty when the partnership is insolvent is that the sum of the debit capital balances exceeds the sum of any credit balances which may exist. As is the case when debit balances develop in the capital accounts of a solvent partnership, the partners in this position must eliminate this debit balance by making additional capital contributions from their personal assets. If they become personally insolvent in the process of making these contributions, any remaining debits must be allocated to other partners, with the process continuing until all of the partners are insolvent or contributions from the partners' personal assets have been sufficient to satisfy all creditor claims.

13-96.   In the Sections which follow, a number of Cases will be presented to illustrate the preceding general procedures. The Cases will cover situations in which there is a single distribution of cash to the partners as well as the somewhat more complex situations in which the cash distributions take the form of a number of installment payments over some period of time.

Single Step Liquidations

13-97.   The following basic example will be used to illustrate three different Cases of single step liquidations:

Example   The Balance Sheet of the JKL Partnership as at December 31 of the current year is as follows:

JKL Partnership
Balance Sheet As At December 31

Total Assets	$680,000

Liabilities	$250,000
Partner J, Capital	180,000
Partner K, Capital	130,000
Partner L, Capital	120,000
Total	$680,000

The partnership agreement calls for all profits and losses, including any which arise in the process of liquidation, to be shared equally between the three partners.

Liquidation Case One -
All Capital Balances Sufficient To Absorb Share Of Liquidation Loss

13-98.   In this first, relatively simple case, we will assume that the assets are sold for $590,000 in cash, resulting in a liquidation loss of $90,000 ($680,000 - $590,000). This would be allocated to the capital balances of the partners as follows:

	Partner J	Partner K	Partner L	Total
Balance Before Liquidation	$180,000	$130,000	$120,000	$430,000
Share Of Liquidation Loss	(30,000)	(30,000)	(30,000)	(90,000)
Adjusted Balance	$150,000	$100,000	$ 90,000	$340,000

13-99.   The adjusted balance would be the amount of cash to be distributed to each partner. This means that of the total of $590,000, the creditors would receive $250,000 and the partners would receive the remaining $340,000 as per the schedule in the preceding Paragraph.

Liquidation Case Two - Some Capital Balances Not Sufficient
To Absorb Share Of Liquidation Loss

13-100.   In this somewhat more complex case, we will assume that the assets are sold for only $260,000 in cash, resulting in a liquidation loss in the amount of $420,000 ($680,000 - $260,000). This loss would be allocated to the capital balances of the partners as follows:

	Partner J	Partner K	Partner L	Total
Balance Before Liquidation	$180,000	$130,000	$120,000	$430,000
Share Of Liquidation Loss	(140,000)	(140,000)	(140,000)	(420,000)
Adjusted Balance	$ 40,000	($ 10,000)	($ 20,000)	$ 10,000

13-101.   At this point, there are a number of possibilities. If Partners K and L are solvent, they will be called on to contribute additional investment funds in the amount of $10,000 and $20,000 respectively. This would give total cash of $290,000 which would be distributed on the basis of $250,000 to the creditors and $40,000 to Partner A.

13-102.   However, things may not go quite so smoothly. Assume, for example, that Partner L has become personally insolvent and is unable to contribute additional funds. Because Partner L has not been able to absorb his full share of the liquidation loss, the additional $20,000 will have to be allocated equally to Partners J and K. This will leave Partner J with a balance of $30,000 and Partner K with a deficit of $20,000. Assuming Partner K to be solvent, he would then have to contribute an additional $20,000 to the partnership, providing a total amount to be distributed of $280,000. This would be distributed on the basis of $250,000 to the creditors and $30,000 to Partner J.

Liquidation Case Three - Partnership Insolvent

13-103.   In this final example of a single step liquidation, we will assume that the assets are sold for only $230,000, resulting in a loss of $450,000. Further, as the cash balance of $230,000 is smaller than the liabilities of the partnership, the enterprise is now said to be insolvent. As we have noted previously, this means that one or more of the partners will now have debit balances in their capital accounts. This is made evident in the following allocation schedule:

	Partner J	Partner K	Partner L	Total
Balance Before Liquidation	$180,000	$130,000	$120,000	$430,000
Liquidation Loss	(150,000)	(150,000)	(150,000)	(450,000)
Adjusted Balance	$ 30,000	($ 20,000)	($ 30,000)	($ 20,000)

13-104.   If both Partner K and Partner L are solvent, this situation presents no real problem. These partners will contribute to the Partnership an additional $20,000 and $30,000, respectively. This will provide a total cash balance of $280,000, of which $250,000 will go to the creditors and $30,000 will be paid to Partner J.

13-105.   Alternatively, if all three of the partners are insolvent, Partner J will not receive his $30,000 adjusted balance and a plan for distributing the $230,000 to the creditors will have to be established.

13-106.   However, a more likely scenario lies between these two extremes. This is that some partners will be solvent while others will be insolvent. To illustrate this possibility, assume that Partner L is insolvent, while Partners J and K remain personally solvent. Partner L's debit balance of $30,000 will be split evenly between Partners J and K, leaving a $15,000 credit for Partner J and a $35,000 debit for Partner K. Partner K will then have to contribute an additional $35,000, giving a total cash balance for the Partnership of $265,000. Of this amount, $250,000 will be distributed to the creditors with the remaining $15,000 going to Partner J.

Installment Liquidations

General Principles

13-107.   In situations where the liquidation of the partnership assets takes place over a considerable period of time, it would be possible to delay any cash distributions to the partners until the entire liquidation process is complete. However, in most cases the partners will prefer to have partial distributions made as the liquidation progresses. If it is decided that such installment distributions are to be made, then it becomes necessary to calculate the amount of each installment that will be distributed to each partner. Two factors complicate this calculation. First, until the liquidation is complete, the partnership does not know what the total amount of the gain or loss on liquidation will be. A second factor relates to the possibility that one or more partners may become insolvent and may not be able to make any payments that might be required to eliminate debit balances in their capital accounts.

13-108.   The two problems are generally dealt with by making the following two assumptions at the time of each installment distribution:

1. After each distribution, assume that the remaining assets will be disposed of for nil proceeds, with no further distributions of cash to the partners as a result of their disposition.

2. Assume that any partner with a capital deficiency subsequent to a distribution will not be able to eliminate it through additional capital contributions to the partnership. This means that there will be no additional funds from this source available for distribution to the partners.

13-109.   In making distributions based on these assumptions, it is likely that a point will be reached where the partners' remaining capital balances are in the same ratios as their profit sharing percentages. At this point, any further distributions can simply be based on the applicable profit sharing percentages.

13-110.   A simple example will be used to illustrate the general principles that have been described.

Example   On December 31 of the current year, the EFG Partnership has the following Balance Sheet:

EFG Partnership
Balance Sheet As At December 31

Total Assets	$900,000

Liabilities	$300,000
Partner E, Capital	300,000
Partner F, Capital	180,000
Partner G, Capital	120,000
Total	$900,000

The partnership agreement calls for the partners to share all profits and losses equally. Cash from the sale of assets becomes available in four installments during the year. The amounts of the installments are as follows:

First Installment	$330,000
Second Installment	150,000
Third Installment	120,000
Fourth Installment	60,000
Total	$660,000

At this point, all of the partnership assets have been sold and there will be no further distributions to the partners.

13-111.   The total assets were $900,000 when the liquidation began and with proceeds of $660,000, this means that, overall, the partners will experience a $240,000 loss. If this were a single step liquidation, the amounts to be paid to the partners could be calculated as follows:

	Partner E	Partner F	Partner G	Total
Balance Before Liquidation	$300,000	$180,000	$120,000	$600,000
Share Of Liquidation Loss	(80,000)	(80,000)	(80,000)	(240,000)
Adjusted Balance	$220,000	$100,000	$ 40,000	$360,000

13-112.   The preceding calculation provides the goal for our installment distributions. The installments must be allocated in such a fashion that the total amounts distributed to each partner will be equal to the amounts calculated in the preceding Paragraph.

13-113.   With respect to the first installment of $330,000, the first $300,000 will have to be paid to the partnership creditors. This leaves only $30,000 for the partners and, if we assume that they will receive no further distributions, their total loss would be $570,000. The loss would be allocated as follows:

	Partner E	Partner F	Partner G	Total
Balance Before Liquidation	$300,000	$180,000	$120,000	$600,000
Share Of Liquidation Loss	(190,000)	(190,000)	(190,000)	(570,000)
Adjusted Balance	$110,000	($ 10,000)	($ 70,000)	$ 30,000

13-114.   As both Partner F and Partner G have negative balances, all of the $30,000 remaining cash would be paid to Partner E, leaving a balance in that partner's capital account of $270,000 ($300,000 - $30,000).

13-115.   The sum of the first and second installments is $480,000. If this second installment were, in fact, the last payment to the partners, the total loss on the $900,000 in assets would be $420,000. Assuming that Partner G is not able to make up the capital deficiency which arises at this stage, the second installment would be distributed on the basis of the following schedule:

	Partner E	Partner F	Partner G	Total
Balance After First Installment	$270,000	$180,000	$120,000	$570,000
Share Of Liquidation Loss	(140,000)	(140,000)	(140,000)	(420,000)
Preliminary Balance	$130,000	$ 40,000	($ 20,000)	$150,000
Distribution Of The Capital				
Deficiency Of Partner G	(10,000)	(10,000)	20,000	Nil
Adjusted Balance	$120,000	$ 30,000	$ -0-	$150,000

13-116.   Thus, the second installment of $150,000 would be distributed $120,000 to Partner E and $30,000 to Partner F. This would leave the capital balance of Partner E at $150,000 ($270,000 - $120,000). Partner F's balance would also be at $150,000 ($180,000 - $30,000). However, both of these balances remain larger than that of Partner G and, as a consequence, it is not yet possible to distribute future installments on the basis of profit sharing ratios.

13-117.   The third installment brings the total proceeds to $600,000. If this were viewed as the last installment, the total loss on the $900,000 in assets would be $300,000 and this would be distributed as per the following schedule:

	Partner E	Partner F	Partner G	Total
Balance After				
Second Installment	$150,000	$150,000	$120,000	$420,000
Share Of Liquidation Loss	(100,000)	(100,000)	(100,000)	(300,000)
Adjusted Balance	$ 50,000	$ 50,000	$ 20,000	$120,000

13-118.   Based on the preceding schedule, the third installment would be distributed $50,000 each to Partners E and F, and $20,000 to Partner G. Also of importance is the fact that at this point, the remaining balance in each of the Partner's capital accounts is $100,000. Since these balances are equal and the profit and loss allocation is based on equal shares, we are now in a position where the Partners' shares of total capital are equal to their income shares. As noted in Paragraph 13-109, when this stage is reached, subsequent distributions of cash can be made on the basis of profit and loss sharing ratios. This means that the fourth installment of $60,000 will simply be distributed $20,000 to each partner.

13-119.   We have now completed the allocation of all four installments. We noted in Paragraph 13-111 that, if the liquidation had taken place in a single step, Partner E would have received $220,000, Partner F, $100,000, and Partner G, $40,000. Since our goal was to achieve an identical result through the various installments, it is useful to verify that this has, in fact, happened. The following schedule provides this verification:

	Partner E	Partner F	Partner G	Total
First Installment	$ 30,000	$ -0-	$ -0-	$ 30,000
Second Installment	120,000	30,000	-0-	150,000
Third Installment	50,000	50,000	20,000	120,000
Fourth Installment	20,000	20,000	20,000	60,000
Total Distribution	$220,000	$100,000	$40,000	$360,000

13-120.   This serves to verify that we have distributed the cash that became available in the installment liquidation steps in a manner that complied with the partnership agreement.

Installment Liquidation Distribution Schedules

13-121. The preceding section illustrated the calculations required to deal with a known schedule of cash distributions as they became available over a period of time. A somewhat different approach to this problem can be involved in administering liquidations. Rather than calculating the allocation of cash distributions as they occur, a schedule of distributions could be required in advance of any specified amounts becoming available. To illustrate the approach to be used in solving this type of problem, the following simple example will be used.

Example On December 31 of the current year, the PQR Partnership has the following Balance Sheet:

PQR Partnership
Balance Sheet As At December 31

Total Net Assets	$2,400,000
Partner P, Capital	$1,400,000
Partner Q, Capital	650,000
Partner R, Capital	350,000
Total	$2,400,000

The partnership agreement calls for all profits and losses, including any which arise in the process of liquidation, to be shared on the basis of 50 percent for P, 30 percent for Q, and 20 percent for R.

13-122. If the respective capital balances were in proportion to the profit sharing ratios, the solution to this problem would be very simple. Distributions would simply be made on the basis of the profit sharing percentages. However, in the preceding example, Partner P's capital balance is more than his 50 percent share of profits while the other partner's capital balances are below their share of profits. This makes it necessary to calculate the loss absorbing capacity of each partner's capital account. These calculations are as follows:

Partner P - ($1,400,000 ÷ 50%) = $ 2,800,000

Partner Q - ($650,000 ÷ 30%) = $ 2,166,667

Partner R - ($350,000 ÷ 20%) = $ 1,750,000

13-123. What we have calculated here is the amount of loss that each partner, given his profit sharing percentage, could absorb without his capital account having a deficit balance. For example, if the loss was $2,800,000, P's share of this loss would be $1,400,000, an amount that would serve to exactly eliminate his capital balance of $1,400,000.

13-124. As Partner P is in a position to absorb his share of a $2,800,000 loss, all cash distributions would go to Partner P until this loss absorbing capacity is reduced to the next highest amount, the $2,166,667 capacity of Partner Q. This would mean that the first $316,667 [($2,800,000 - $2,166,667)(50%)] would go to Partner P, reducing his capital account to $1,083,333. At this point new loss absorbing capacities could be calculated as follows:

Partner P - ($1,083,333 ÷ 50%) = $2,166,667

Partner Q - ($650,000 ÷ 30%) = $2,166,667

Partner R - ($350,000 ÷ 20%) = $1,750,000

13-125. In order to equalize the loss absorbing capacities of all three partners, Partners P and Q will have to receive the next $333,333 in distributions [($2,166,667 - $1,750,000)(80%)] on the basis of a 50:30 ratio. This means that Partner P will receive $208,333 [(50/80)($333,333)] and be left with a balance of $875,000 ($1,083,333 -

$208,333). Correspondingly, Partner Q will receive $125,000 [(30/80)($333,333)], and be left with a balance of $525,000 ($650,000 - $125,000). Subsequent distributions of partnership assets can simply be based on the normal profit sharing ratios of each of the three partners. This is a reflection of the fact that, subsequent to the second distribution, the loss absorbing capacities of the three Partners are now equal as shown in the following calculations:

Partner P - ($875,000 ÷ 50%) = $1,750,000

Partner Q - ($525,000 ÷ 30%) = $1,750,000

Partner R - ($350,000 ÷ 20%) = $1,750,000

13-126.   It also means that the capital balances of the three partners are in proportion to their profit and loss sharing ratios. This can be seen in the following schedule:

	Partner P	Partner Q	Partner R	Total
Original Balance	$1,400,000	$650,000	$350,000	$2,400,000
First Distribution	(316,667)	-0-	-0-	(316,667)
Second Distribution	(208,333)	(125,000)	-0-	(333,333)
Remaining Balance	$ 875,000	$525,000	$350,000	$1,750,000

13-127.   A quick verifying calculation will demonstrate that the capital balances of the three partners are now in the ratio 50:30:20, the same basis on which they share profits and losses.

Incorporation Of A Partnership

13-128.   Under some circumstances, successful partnerships may give consideration to the advantages to be gained from incorporating. These advantages could include an improved tax situation, the ability to raise additional funds more efficiently, or the desire to remove personal assets from the risks associated with participating in a partnership.

13-129.   In such situations, the accounting complications are not particularly significant. The fundamental decision that must be made is to decide whether or not the change in legal form constitutes the creation of a new business entity. While there is room for the application of judgment in this situation, we are of the opinion that the incorporation of a partnership generally creates a new business entity. This will mean that there is a need to adjust all of the assets and liabilities that are being transferred to the corporation at their current fair values. It would also be appropriate to record any partnership goodwill that has been acquired by the newly formed corporation. However, because of valuation problems associated with this intangible asset, this will generally not occur in many practical situations.

13-130.   The accounting records for the corporation could be simply a continuation of the old records of the partnership. In most cases, however, a new set of books will be opened. The appropriate entries will simply involve recording the newly acquired assets at the current fair values and setting up a liability to the partners for the value of the net assets transferred. This liability will then be discharged by the issuance of shares of capital stock.

Problems For Self Study

(The solutions for these problems can be found following Chapter 16 of the text.)

Self Study Problem Thirteen - 1

The partnership of George Brown and Terry Green was formed on February 28 of the current year. At that date the following assets, recorded at their fair values, were contributed:

	George Brown	Terry Green
Cash	$35,000	$ 25,000
Merchandise		45,000
Building		100,000
Furniture And Equipment	15,000	

The building is subject to a mortgage loan of $30,000 which is to be assumed by the partnership. The partnership agreement provides that George and Terry share profits or losses equally.

Required:

A. What are the capital balances of the partners on February 28 of the current year?

B. If the partnership agreement states that the initial capital balances of the partners should be equal, and no recognition should be given to any intangible assets contributed, what are the partners' capital balances on February 28 of the current year?

C. Given the facts stated in requirement B, except that any contributed goodwill should be recognized in the accounts, what are the partners' capital balances on February 28 of the current year? How much goodwill should be recognized?

Self Study Problem Thirteen - 2

Jim Bond and Bob Ray organized the Bond And Ray Partnership on January 1 of the current year. The following entries were made in their capital accounts during the current year:

	Debit	Credit	Balance
Bond Capital:			
January 1		$20,000	$20,000
April 1		5,000	25,000
October 1		5,000	30,000
Ray Capital:			
January 1		40,000	40,000
March 1	$10,000		30,000
September 1	10,000		20,000
November 1		10,000	30,000

Partnership net income, computed without regard to salaries or interest, is $20,000 for the current year.

Required: Indicate the distribution of net income between the partners under the following independent profit-sharing conditions:

A. Interest at 4 percent is allowed on average capital investments, and the remainder is divided equally.

B. A salary of $9,000 is to be credited to Ray; 4 percent interest is allowed to each partner on his ending capital balance; residual profits or losses are divided 60 percent to Bond and 40 percent to Ray.

C. Salaries are allowed to Bond and Ray in amounts of $8,300 and $9,500, respectively, and residual profits or residual losses are divided in the ratio of average capital balances.

D. A bonus of 20 percent of partnership net income is credited to Bond, a salary of $5,000 is allowed to Ray, and residual profits or residual losses are shared equally. (The bonus and salary are regarded as "expenses" for purposes of calculating the amount of the bonus.)

Self Study Problem Thirteen - 3

Allison, Brook, And Carey are partners. Douglas is to be admitted to the partnership at the end of the current fiscal year. On this date, the profit sharing ratios and capital balances of the original partners are as follows:

Partner	Profit Sharing	Capital Balance
Allison	60%	$194,000
Brook	30%	$130,000
Carey	10%	$ 76,000

Required:

A. Assume that Douglas is admitted to the partnership by investing $80,000 for a 20 percent interest in capital and profits. What alternative methods could be used to record the admission of Douglas to the partnership? Provide the journal entries for each method.

B. Assume that Douglas purchases a 20 percent interest in the partnership ratably from the existing partners by paying $84,000 cash directly to the partners. What alternative methods could be used to record the admission of Douglas to the partnership? Provide the journal entries for each method.

Self Study Problem Thirteen - 4

Several years ago, Tom, Dick, and Harry Jones formed a partnership to carry on their professional activities. The partnership agreement calls for profits and losses to be shared according to the following percentages:

Brother	Percent
Tom	20
Dick	30
Harry	50

At the end of the Partnership's current fiscal year, the condensed Balance Sheet of the Partnership was as follows:

The Jones Brothers Partnership
Condensed Balance Sheet

Total Identifiable Assets	$164,000
Liabilities	$ 45,000
Tom Jones, Capital	26,000
Dick Jones, Capital	41,000
Harry Jones, Capital	52,000
Total Equities	$164,000

The brothers estimate that the current fair values of the identifiable assets total $189,000.

Required: The brothers are considering a number of alternatives for expanding, contracting, or liquidating their partnership. Provide the information which is indicated for each of the four independent alternatives that are described in the following paragraphs:

A. Tom Jones is prepared to sell his interest in the Jones Brothers Partnership to his sister Shirley. He would give up his interest in return for $31,500 in cash to be paid directly to him. Provide the journal entry(ies) on the books of the Partnership to record this change in ownership interest.

B. The brothers are prepared to admit their sister Shirley into the Partnership with a 20 percent interest in profits and losses. She will be required to contribute $40,000 in cash to the Partnership in return for this interest. The partners believe that the admission of Shirley would be of sufficient importance to account for the transaction on a new entity basis. Provide the journal entry(ies) on the books of the Partnership to record the admission of Shirley Jones to the Partnership.

C. Dick Jones may wish to retire from the Partnership. If this retirement takes place, the brothers have agreed that Dick should receive a cash payment of $54,000 for his 30 percent interest in the Partnership. The partners do not believe that this retirement is a sufficient change in the business to warrant any revaluation of the Partnership assets. Provide the journal entry(ies) that would be required on the books of the Partnership to record the retirement of Dick Jones.

D. As all three of the brothers have developed separate business interests in recent years, they may decide to liquidate the Partnership. It is their belief that the identifiable assets of the partnership could be sold for their fair values which total $189,000. If the liquidation was carried out and the anticipated amount of cash received for the assets, provide the journal entry(ies) to record the transaction and the distribution of the resulting cash balance.

Self Study Problem Thirteen - 5

Jones, Smith, and Doe are partners in a retailing business which has been operating for a number of years. Their profit sharing and capital balances on December 31 of the current year are as follows:

Partner	Profit Sharing	Capital Balance
Jones	30 Percent	$ 327,000
Smith	45 Percent	482,000
Doe	25 Percent	191,000

Required: The following Cases represent three different and completely independent transactions. In each Case, we will assume that the transaction took place on December 31 of the current year. You are to provide any journal entries that would be required to record the transaction that has been described.

Case 1   Breem is admitted to the partnership with a one-third interest in profits and capital. In return for this interest he makes a cash payment of $540,000 to the partnership. It is determined that the price paid by Breem reflects the fact that the Partnership has unrecorded Goodwill. This Goodwill is to be recorded as part of the admission transaction.

Case 2   Doe gives up his share of the partnership in return for a cash payment of $171,000. The remaining partners decide not to revalue assets to reflect the price that was paid to Doe in this transaction.

Case 3   It is decided that the partnership is to be liquidated. Because of the size of the business, the assets will be liquidated in several groups. After the sale of the first group of Partnership assets, some of the proceeds are used to pay off the creditors of the Partnership. After the payments to the creditors have been made, $100,000 in cash remains and this is distributed to the Partners as per the partnership agreement.

Self Study Problem Thirteen - 6

The condensed Balance Sheet of the Portly, Brawn and Large partnership just prior to liquidation is as follows:

Portly, Brawn and Large Partnership
Condensed Balance Sheet

Total Assets	$1,032,000
Accounts Payable	$ 72,000
Portly, Loan	48,000
Portly, Capital	112,000
Brawn, Capital	320,000
Large, Capital	480,000
Total Equities	$1,032,000

Portly, Brawn, And Large share profits and losses in the ratio of 1 : 4 : 5, respectively.

Required: Construct a systematic plan showing how cash should be distributed to the various equities as it becomes available during the liquidation process.

Assignment Problems

(The solutions for these problems are only available in
the solutions manual that has been provided to your instructor.)

Assignment Problem Thirteen - 1

Journalize the admission of Brown to the partnership of Black and Blue in each of the following independent cases. The capital balances of Black and Blue are $20,000 and $20,000 and they share profits and losses equally.

A.   Brown is admitted to a one-third interest in capital, profits, and losses with a contribution of $20,000.

B.   Brown is admitted to a one-fourth interest in capital, profits, and losses with a contribution of $24,000. Total capital of the new partnership is to be $64,000.

C.   Brown is admitted to a one-fifth interest in capital, profits, and losses upon contributing $6,000. Total capital of the new partnership is to be $50,000.

D.   Brown is admitted to a one-fifth interest in capital, profits, and losses by the purchase of one-fifth of the interests of Black and Blue, paying $2,000 directly to Black and $2,000 directly to Blue. Total capital of the new partnership is to be $40,000.

E.   Brown is admitted to a one-fifth interest in capital, profits, and losses by the purchase of one-fifth of the interests of Black and Blue, paying $9,000 directly to Black and $8,000 directly to Blue. Total capital of the new partnership is to be $55,000.

F.   Brown is admitted to a one-third interest in capital, profits, and losses upon contributing $14,000, after which each partner is to have an equal capital equity in the new partnership.

G.   Brown is admitted to a one-fifth interest in capital, profits, and losses upon contributing $14,000. Total capital of the new partnership is to be $70,000.

Assignment Problem Thirteen - 2

A number of years ago, John, Joseph, Judas, and Jerry Goody formed a partnership to carry on their professional activities. The partnership agreement calls for profits and losses to be shared according to the following percentages:

Brother	Percent
John	18
Joseph	23
Judas	32
Jerry	27

At the end of the Partnership's current fiscal year, the condensed Balance Sheet of the Partnership was as follows:

The Goody Brothers Partnership
Condensed Balance Sheet

Total Identifiable Assets	$978,000
Liabilities	$114,000
John Goody, Capital	162,000
Joseph Goody, Capital	193,000
Judas Goody, Capital	268,000
Jerry Goody, Capital	241,000
Total Equities	$978,000

The brothers estimate that the current fair values of the identifiable assets total $1,200,000.

Required: The brothers are considering a number of alternatives for expanding, contracting, or liquidating their partnership. Provide the information which is indicated for each of the five independent alternatives that are described in the following paragraphs:

A.   John Goody is prepared to sell his interest in the Goody Brothers Partnership to his sister Jill. He would give up his interest in return for $197,000 in cash to be paid directly to him by Jill. Provide the journal entry on the books of the Partnership to record this change in ownership interest.

B.   Because of poor health, Judas Goody wishes to retire from the partnership and move to Rangoon. If the retirement takes place, the other Brothers are prepared to pay Judas $197,000 for his 32 percent interest in the Partnership. The partners do not believe that this retirement is a sufficient change in the business to warrant any revaluation of the

Partnership assets. Provide the journal entry that would be required on the books of the Partnership to record the retirement of Judas Goody.

C. All of the brothers have developed separate business interests in recent years and, as a consequence, they are considering the liquidation of the partnership. It is their belief that the identifiable assets of the Partnership could be sold for their fair values which total $1,200,000. However, to realize this value the assets will have to be sold over an extended period of time. The brothers anticipate that the first sale of assets would bring in cash of $423,000. Provide the journal entry to record the distribution of this $423,000.

D. The brothers are planning to admit their sister Jill into the partnership with a 20 percent interest in profits and losses. She will be required to contribute $312,000 in cash to the Partnership in return for this interest. The partners believe that admission of Jill would be of sufficient importance to account for the transaction on a new entity basis. Provide the journal entry on the books of the Partnership to record the admission of Jill Goody to the Partnership.

E. In order to increase his interest in the partnership, Jerry Goody acquires two percentage points of the interests of each of his brothers. This total of six percentage points will bring his interest to 33 percent and, in order to acquire this additional interest, he pays an additional $96,000 into the partnership. The partners agree that this transaction is not important enough to justify any new basis of accounting for the Partnership's assets. Provide the journal entry to record the change in ownership interests.

Assignment Problem Thirteen - 3

A number of years ago, Ellen, Eileen, Edna, and Edwina Lee formed a partnership to carry on their professional activities. The partnership agreement calls for profits and losses to be shared according to the following percentages:

Sister	Percent
Ellen	13
Eileen	8
Edna	42
Edwina	37

At the end of the Partnership's current fiscal year, the condensed Balance Sheet of the Partnership was as follows:

The Lee Sisters Partnership
Condensed Balance Sheet

Total Identifiable Assets	$4,118,000
Liabilities	$ 226,000
Ellen Lee, Capital	511,000
Ellen Lee, Drawing	(52,000)
Eileen Lee, Capital	342,000
Edna Lee, Capital	1,576,000
Edna Lee, Drawing	(108,000)
Edwina Lee, Capital	1,623,000
Total Equities	$4,118,000

The sisters estimate that the current fair values of the identifiable assets total $4,876,000.

Required: The sisters are considering a number of alternatives for expanding, contracting, or liquidating their partnership. Provide the information which is indicated for each of the five independent alternatives that are described in the following paragraphs:

A. Because of personal differences with the other sisters, Edna Lee would like to retire from the Partnership and move to another city. The other sisters have agreed to pay Edna $1,845,000 of Partnership funds and eliminate her $108,000 drawing in return for her 42 percent interest. They also feel that Edna's departure will improve the operations of the business and therefore it is an appropriate occasion to revalue the Partnership's identifiable assets. Provide the journal entry(ies) that would be required on the books of the Partnership to record the retirement of Edna Lee.

B. The youngest sister of the partners, Elvira Lee, would like to enter the partnership. Eileen Lee is prepared to give up her 8 percent interest if Elvira will pay her $423,000 in cash. Provide the journal entry(ies) on the books of the Partnership to record this change in ownership interest.

C. In order to increase her 8 percent interest in the Partnership, Eileen Lee acquires four percentage points of the interests of each of the other sisters. This brings her total interest in the Partnership to 20 percent and reduces the interests of the other sisters correspondingly. To acquire this additional interest, Eileen pays $642,000 in cash to the Partnership. The partners do not believe that this transaction is of sufficient importance to revalue the partnership assets. Provide the journal entry(ies) to record this transaction on the books of the Partnership.

D. It is the intention of the sisters to liquidate the partnership. In order to get satisfactory prices for the various partnership assets, they have decided to sell them in an orderly fashion over the next twelve months. They anticipate that the first sale of assets should bring in $1,250,000 in cash. Indicate the amounts that would be distributed to the partnership creditors and the four sisters if the first sale does bring in this estimated amount.

E. John Chong is to be admitted to the partnership with a 20 percent interest in profits and losses. He will be required to pay cash of $1,263,000 to the Partnership. The partners believe that this admission is of such significance that the transaction should be accounted for using the new entity approach. Provide the journal entry(ies) required to record this transaction on the books of the Partnership.

Assignment Problem Thirteen - 4

Two years ago, Tammy, Jessica and Donna formed a partnership, FHR Enterprises, to carry on various fundraising and publicity activities. The partnership agreement calls for profits and losses to be shared according to the following ratios:

Partner	Ratio
Tammy	3/6
Jessica	2/6
Donna	1/6

At the end of FHR Enterprises' current fiscal year, its condensed Balance Sheet was as follows:

FHR Enterprises
Condensed Balance Sheet

Current Monetary Assets		$527,000
Furniture and Fixtures (Net)		130,000
Total Identifiable Assets		$657,000
Liabilities		$225,000
Tammy, Capital	$216,000	
Jessica, Capital	144,000	
Donna, Capital	72,000	432,000
Total Equities		$657,000

An independent appraisal estimates the current fair values of the furniture and fixtures total $118,000.

Required: Provide the information which is indicated for each of the independent alternatives that are described in the following paragraphs:

A. Donna retires from the Partnership to pursue a new career as an author. She receives a cash payment of $90,000 for her interest in FHR Enterprises. Tammy and Jessica plan to continue in partnership and maintain the original income sharing ratio. Provide the journal entry(ies) that would be required on the books of the Partnership to record the retirement of Donna assuming:

  i.   Tammy and Jessica do not believe that this retirement is a sufficient change in the business to warrant any revaluation of the Partnership assets.

  ii. Tammy and Jessica believe that this retirement is a sufficient change that the remaining partnership can be viewed as a new business entity.

B. FHR Enterprises admits Ollie into the Partnership. Ollie is given a 25 percent interest in capital, and profits and losses. Tammy, Jessica and Donna will share the remaining 75 percent of the partnership earnings in the same original ratio existing prior to the admission of Ollie.

  i.   FHR Enterprises agrees to admit Ollie into the Partnership for an investment of $120,000 in cash. Before Ollie is admitted, Tammy withdraws $15,000 cash from the partnership. The original partners do not believe that this admission is a sufficient change in the business to warrant any revaluation of the Partnership assets. Provide the journal entry(ies) on the books of the Partnership to record the cash withdrawal and the admission of Ollie to the Partnership.

  ii. FHR Enterprises admits Ollie into the Partnership for an investment of $150,000 in cash. The original partners believe that this admission is a sufficient change that the remaining partnership can be viewed as a new business entity. Provide the journal entry(ies) on the books of the Partnership to record the admission of Ollie to the Partnership.

Assignment Problem Thirteen - 5

Joe Green and his brother Pete have operated as partners in a small greenhouse business for thirty years. They are nearing retirement age and Pete would like to sell his share of the business and move to Florida. Joe's son, Tom, has worked in the greenhouse operation since he was a child and has gradually taken on more responsibility so that he is now acting as manager. He has $20,000 in savings and can borrow $30,000 more to invest in the partnership with his father. Tom would continue as manager and Joe would gradually reduce his involvement, acting as a consultant when required. Tom wants to build a new packing house and implement a hydroponic growing system, but requires more capital to do so.

The Green Partnership currently has a demand loan from the bank with an interest rate of 7 percent. Tom's brother, Robert, a successful doctor, is willing to invest $80,000, but is not sure whether he wants to be a partner in the business.

The partnership Balance Sheet as at December 31, 2002 is as follows:

Green Partnership
Balance Sheet
December 31, 2002

Cash	$ 10,000
Supplies	5,000
Equipment (Net)	30,000
Land And Buildings (Net)	60,000
Total Assets	$105,000
Accounts Payable	$ 5,000
Bank Loan	15,000
Joe, Capital	42,500
Pete, Capital	42,500
Total Equities	$105,000

An independent appraiser has estimated the following fair values at December 31, 2002:

Supplies	$ 4,000
Equipment	$ 46,000
Land and Buildings	$100,000

Required: The following parts are independent cases.

A. Assume that Pete and Joe dissolve their partnership and that Joe, Tom and Robert form a partnership on January 1, 2003.

1. Prepare the new partnership Balance Sheet. Show all calculations and state your assumptions.

2. What items should be specified in the new partnership agreement?

3. Discuss how the income or loss for 2003 could be allocated to the new partners.

4. How would the Balance Sheet and income allocation change if Robert contributes financially, but is not admitted as a partner?

B. Assume that Pete gives up his share of the partnership for a cash payment of $60,000 on January 1, 2003. Joe decides not to revalue the assets to reflect the price that Pete was paid. Provide the journal entry to record Pete's retirement.

C.   Assume that Pete gives up his share of the partnership for a cash payment of $70,000 on January 1, 2003. Joe decides to revalue the assets as he views the resulting enterprise as a new business entity. On that same date, Tom invests $50,000 for a 50 percent share in the partnership and Robert decides to lend the Green partnership $80,000 in the form of a Note Payable. Joe and Tom decide that Tom is bringing goodwill into the partnership.

1.   Provide the journal entries to record the preceding transactions and prepare the Balance Sheet of the new partnership as at January 1, 2003.

2.   On January 2, 2003, Joe contributes an additional $25,000 in capital to the partnership. Later that day, the partners are informed that their greenhouse is situated on a site that has been contaminated by radioactive waste. They decide to liquidate the partnership immediately and receive a total of $22,000 for the Supplies, Equipment, Land and Buildings of the partnership. Calculate the amount of cash that would be distributed to each partner on the liquidation of the partnership.

D.   Assume that Pete gives up his share of the partnership on January 1, 2003 and on that date, both Tom and Robert purchase a one-third share in the partnership. During the year, Joe has drawings of $28,000 and Tom has drawings of $45,000. These withdrawals are equal to the salaries for Joe and Tom, respectively, as stated in the partnership agreement. The agreement also allows each partner a 10 percent interest on his ending capital balance, without inclusion of the year's income or any withdrawals. Any residual profits or losses are shared equally.

The income of the Green Partnership for the year ending December 31, 2003, computed without regard to salaries to the partners or interest on the capital contributions of the partners, was equal to $200,000. The ending capital balances, calculated before consideration of withdrawals or income of the year are equal to $70,000 for Joe, $50,000 for Tom and $80,000 for Robert. Calculate the income share for each partner for the year.

(SMA Adapted)

Assignment Problem Thirteen - 6

At the year end of the current fiscal year, the Balance Sheet of the Norton, Simon, Carly, and Jones Partnership is as follows:

Norton, Simon, Carly, and Jones Partnership
Condensed Balance Sheet

Monetary Assets	$ 573,000
Non-Monetary Assets	1,114,000
Total Assets	**$1,687,000**
Current Liabilities	$ 71,500
Long-Term Liabilities	26,500
Norton, Capital	173,000
Simon, Capital	337,000
Carly, Capital	692,000
Jones, Capital	387,000
Total Equities	**$1,687,000**

The Partnership agreement calls for profit and loss sharing on the following basis:

Norton	10 Percent
Simon	20 Percent
Carly	40 Percent
Jones	30 Percent

Because of irreconcilable differences between the partners, it has been decided that the Partnership will be liquidated as soon as possible. However, the partners are agreed that the assets should be disposed of in an orderly fashion, even if it requires some delay in their ultimate disposition. The cash proceeds of all sales will be distributed as they become available.

Required: Prepare a schedule for the distribution of the cash which will result from the sale of Partnership assets.

Assignment Problem Thirteen - 7
You have been shortlisted for a position as financial consultant for a major Canadian consulting firm. As part of the recruitment procedure, you are asked to demonstrate your basic knowledge of partnerships. Specifically, you are presented with the following four independent partnership scenarios and are asked to write a brief note on each, identifying the relevant issues, concerns and implications of the related circumstances.

The situations are briefly summarized as follows:

1. Partnership A has run into financial difficulty. In discussing the problem, Bert and Ernie, two of the partners, conclude that unless additional financing can be found, the business should be sold or wound up. Oscar, the third partner, joins them and announces that their troubles are over as he has just signed an agreement with Sue making her a full partner in exchange for an investment of $200,000. Neither Bert nor Ernie has ever met Sue.

2. Heather and Bernie have just formed Partnership B. Heather has considerable experience and has made a substantial investment in the business. Bernie, on the other hand, has less experience and has made a smaller investment. Bernie will be working full time in the partnership, while Heather, in the short run, will keep her job outside the partnership and assist Bernie only when needed.

3. Partnership C has run into financial difficulty, and one of the partners has just left town, leaving the other partners to pay off all the debts of the business.

4. Moe and Larry are the sole partners in Partnership D. The partnership has been profitable and has expanded rapidly. Moe is in favor of incorporating the business at this time but Larry would like more information before making a decision.

Required: Prepare the required note for each situation.

(SMA adapted)

Assignment Problem Thirteen - 8
Sally Hart, architect, has operated a sole proprietorship in Guelph since 1995. The practice has become quite successful, in no small part due to Sally's aggressive marketing and excellent reputation in the community.

However, it is now August 2002 and Sally has decided to form a partnership with a recent graduate, Mary Seoul. The new partnership is to take effect immediately after her existing fiscal year, August 31, 2002.

Sally has come to you for assistance in the financial accounting aspects of the new partnership. Specifically, she is interested in how the assets being brought into the partnership will be valued on the opening balance sheet.

According to the new partnership agreement, Sally will be contributing all assets and liabilities used in her existing practice to the new partnership. This includes the capital assets, working capital and long term debt. The working capital consists of accounts receivable, supplies and trade accounts payable. There is an extensive amount of "work-in-progress" (WIP) on Sally's accounts that will also be transferred. In the past, Sally has not recorded WIP on her books of account. The capital assets consist of the single office building used in the practice, desks, chairs and drafting tables.

As Mary has no capital assets and no clients, it was agreed her contribution would be in the form of cash.

The agreement stipulates that they will each own 50% of the new partnership as well as sharing equally in all billings made and expenses incurred, effective September 1, 2002.

Sally has informed you that, due to deflation, the property used as an office has a fair market value below its original cost. Its value is also below the existing mortgage. The mortgage is secured by the property as well as a personal guarantee from Sally.

Finally, Sally informed you that she is being sued by a disgruntled client. The lawsuit implicates Sally as the cause of structural damage in a home she designed in 1997. Sally is concerned since the amount of the lawsuit is in excess of her insurance coverage. While the outcome of the lawsuit is not known at this time, it is expected to be resolved within 12 months.

Required: Advise Sally on how each of the assets and liabilities transferred should be valued on the opening balance sheet of the new partnership. The bank, holding the mortgage, requires the financial statements to be prepared in accordance with generally accepted accounting principles.

(OICA Adapted)

Assignment Problem Thirteen - 9

Length, Width and Hite (LWH) is a firm of architects, with one office in a large Canadian city. The firm has been in operation for over 20 years and, as of September 1, 2002, had 18 partners and a staff of 60. LWH owns a building in which it occupies three floors and it rents out the other three. The firm also has ownership interests of 10% to 50% in several properties. The ownership usually arose because the builders had difficulty paying architects' fees to LWH, and the firm accepted equity interests. Most of these properties have mortgages.

The firm's year end is December 31. Your employer, CA & Co., chartered accountants, has performed compilation engagements, for income tax purposes, for LWH for many years. The last compilation engagement was conducted at December 31, 2001 and you were in charge of the assignment.

On September 2, 2002, the managing partner of LWH, Mr. Lee, informed you that LWH has decided to wind up the practice as of November 30, 2002. Apparently, the partners had several disagreements, so they decided to dissolve the partnership. Mr. Lee and 5 other partners of LWH intend to form a new partnership, Vector and Company (VC), and the others will each choose between forming a new partnership or proceeding on their own. The staff will be divided among the new practices. The clients will choose the partner with whom they wish to remain associated.

Mr. Lee has asked CA & Co. to accept two special engagements:

1. The partners of LWH want to wind up the firm "equitably," and want assurance that each partner receives a "fair share" of the equity. Mr. Lee wants CA & Co. to identify the financial information to be used for the winding up of LWH and to explain why this information is necessary. Furthermore, he would like CA & Co. to indicate how it would substantiate the financial information.

   As part of the dissolution agreement, the partners of LWH agreed to have a report prepared describing the financial information other than financial statements that will be useful to the partners in their new practices. CA & Co. has been asked to prepare this report.

2. Mr. Lee requires CA & Co.'s assistance in selecting significant accounting policies for VC.

The engagement partner, Jim Spinney, has asked you to prepare a memo discussing the nature of the special engagements and work to be performed. The memo should address the issues raised and provide the information required by Mr. Lee. Relevant tax considerations should be identified in the memo.

You have made several inquiries, and have learned the following.

1. At November 30, 2002, LWH will have receivables outstanding and a material amount of work in progress. LWH currently has:

    a. Ownership of its building, which has a mortgage with a 12% interest rate, due in 2005.

    b. Several interests in properties, as stated previously.

    c. A copyright on a design for grocery stores, for which it is entitled to royalties over the next 12 to 15 years.

    d. Leases on computer equipment that expire over the period 2004 through 2005. The lease payments exceed current market rates. LWH is required to make monthly payments to the lessor.

    e. Office equipment and architectural materials and equipment.

    f. Artwork, a library, and miscellaneous assets. Most of the costs were expensed several years ago.

    g. Various pension obligations to a few non-partners who hold or have held administrative positions.

2. The building, property interests, copyright, artwork, library, and miscellaneous assets will be transferred to VC. Some computer leases, some equipment, and some pension obligations will not be transferred to VC but will accompany the non-VC partners. The non-VC partners will be occupying separate premises.

3. All vehicles and some equipment are leased from a company owned by the spouses of the three most senior partners of LWH. The leases extend to 2007 and were set at fair market value at the time that they were signed. However, the lease payments are now well above fair market value. All three partners are becoming partners of VC. The vehicles and equipment are to be assigned to VC, under the proposed terms of the wind-up of LWH.

4. VC will be using a different bank from the one that LWH uses. However, both banks use the same lending formula for maximum loans: 70% of current receivables and 40% of work in progress. LWH's bank has agreed to give the partnership three months after November 30, 2002, to pay the loan that will be outstanding on LWH's wind-up date. Both banks require personal guarantees from each partner. VC's new bank requires the financial statements of VC to be reviewed. Mr. Lee has asked CA & Co. to perform a review of VC as at December 31, 2002, its first fiscal year end.

5. LWH partners who have retired in the past are paid 20% of their equity per year for five years from the date of their retirement.

6. Partners receive interest at the prime rate on their outstanding loans to the LWH partnership. Only some partners have lent funds to LWH.

7. LWH charges each client at a standard cost per hour. This charge to work in progress includes labour, overhead, and a profit element. Generally, the labour cost for non-partners is about 40% of the standard costing rate. Most receivables are invoiced at 80% to 120% of the standard cost shown in the client work in progress account.

Required   Prepare the memo to Jim Spinney.

(CICA Adapted)

Chapter 14

Accounting For Not-For-Profit Organizations

Introduction

14-1.   Until 1989, not-for-profit organizations were not subject to the Recommendations of the *CICA Handbook* and, as a consequence, they were in a position to use virtually any accounting principles that they wished.   Not surprisingly, this led to a situation in which different not-for-profit organizations used a wide variety of procedures, resulting in financial statements that made meaningful interpretation by users extremely difficult.

14-2.   This began to change in 1989.   While recognizing that its Recommendations were not applicable in all areas of not-for-profit accounting, the *CICA Handbook* became applicable to these organizations in general.   This change was accompanied by the addition of Section 4230, "Non-Profit Organizations - Specific Items", to the *Handbook*.   This small Section provided limited guidance on such matters as pledges, donated materials and services, and restricted amounts, and was withdrawn in 1998.

14-3.   Since 1989, the CICA's Accounting Standards Board and its Not-For-Profit Task Force have worked on developing accounting standards to deal with certain areas where these organizations have unique problems.   This process reached fruition with the issuance of six *CICA Handbook* Sections in 1996 and one additional Section in 1997.   These Sections are:

Section 4400   Financial Statement Presentation By Not-For-Profit Organizations

Section 4410   Contributions - Revenue Recognition

Section 4420   Contributions Receivable

Section 4430   Capital Assets Held By Not-For-Profit Organizations

Section 4440   Collections Held By Not-For-Profit Organizations

Section 4450   Reporting Controlled And Related Entities By Not-For-Profit Organizations

Section 4460   Disclosure Of Related Party Transactions By Not-For-Profit Organizations

14-4.   It is likely that these Recommendations have led to improved financial reporting by not-for-profit organizations.   While some not-for-profit organizations may choose not to comply with some or all of these Recommendations, the need to have credibility with the users of their financial statements, particularly those who contribute resources, certainly encourages full or partial compliance.

Not-For-Profit Organizations Defined

14-5.   The definition of not-for-profit organizations does not include government entities. Recommendations applicable to federal, provincial, territorial, and local governments and to other government entities, such as funds, agencies, and corporations are found in the separate *CICA Public Sector Accounting Handbook* issued by the Public Sector Accounting Board (PSAB).

14-6.   All seven of the relevant *CICA Handbook* Sections repeat the same definition of not-for-profit organizations. This definition is as follows:

> **Paragraph 4400.02(a)   Not-for-profit organizations** are entities, normally without transferable ownership interests, organized and operated exclusively for social, educational, professional, religious, health, charitable or any other not-for-profit purpose. A not-for-profit organization's members, contributors and other resource providers do not, in such capacity, receive any financial return directly from the organization.

14-7.   The preceding definition makes it clear that there are three characteristics associated with being a not-for-profit organization. These are:

1.   Not-for-profit organizations normally do not have a transferable ownership interest.

2.   Not-for-profit organizations are operated exclusively for social, educational, professional, religious, health, charitable, or other not-for-profit purposes.

3.   The resource providers, be they members or contributors, do not stand to benefit because of their status as resource providers.

14-8.   In many cases, the application of this definition is very straightforward. For organizations that have no activity other than raising funds and using these funds in achieving not-for-profit goals, there is little question as to their status as a not-for-profit organization. This would apply to such organizations as the Canadian Cancer Society or the United Way.

14-9.   However, the classification of other organizations may be less clear cut. For example, while golf and country clubs are not usually organized to make a profit, use of the facilities generally requires the payment or contribution of a membership fee. This means that the members benefit because of their status as resource providers. Similar problems exist with condominium corporations and various types of agricultural co-ops.

14-10.   There are other problems related to organizations such as hospitals and universities, where a government organization is often the principal contributor. If such organizations are considered to be government agencies, then they are subject to the Recommendations of the Public Sector Accounting Board. Alternatively, if they are considered to be not-for-profit organizations, the *CICA Handbook* Recommendations are applicable.

GAAP For Not-For-Profit Organizations

General Approach

14-11.   One of the major issues considered in the 1980 CICA Research Study, *Financial Reporting For Non-Profit Organizations*, was the question of whether these organizations should be subject to the profit oriented Recommendations of the *CICA Handbook*. One view was that profit and not-for-profit organizations were sufficiently similar that the existing *Handbook* rules could be applied without modification. At the opposite extreme, it was possible to argue that the differences between these two types of organizations were so great that it would be appropriate to establish a completely separate set of generally accepted accounting principles for not-for-profit organizations.

14-12.   After giving the matter considerable attention, the Committee preparing the Research Study decided on a compromise. They concluded that not-for-profit organizations were sufficiently different that some specialized Recommendations were essential. For example, profit oriented enterprises do not usually have to deal with contributions and pledges. In areas such as this, specialized Recommendations were needed. However, in many areas of accounting, not-for-profit organizations were similar to those organizations with a profit making orientation. In these areas, the usual *CICA Handbook* Recommendations would be applicable. An example of this type of situation would be Section 1505, which requires disclosure of accounting policies. Clearly the type of disclosure called for in this Section would be equally applicable to both types of organizations.

14-13.   We previously noted that, in 1989, most of the Recommendations in the *CICA Handbook* became applicable to not-for-profit organizations. In addition, Section 4230 was added to the *CICA Handbook* in that year. (Section 4230 has been subsequently withdrawn.) These events reflect the adoption of the compromise approach suggested by the 1980 CICA Research Study. The *Handbook* Sections that were issued in 1996 and 1997 also reflect this approach.

14-14.   It is interesting to note that a 1980 CICA Research Study on accounting for government organizations reached a very different conclusion. Their recommendation was that a separate body of accounting standards be established for government organizations. This recommendation was implemented with the establishment of the Public Sector Accounting Board (PSAB). The Recommendations of this Board are now found in a separate PSAB *Handbook*.

14-15.   To assist with user understanding of not-for-profit GAAP, *CICA Handbook* Sections 4400 through 4460 have an introduction which describes the current approach. Included in this introduction is an Appendix that sets out the applicability of the various *CICA Handbook* Sections to not-for-profit organizations. As the great majority of *Handbook* Sections are designated as applicable, reproducing the entire Appendix would not be useful. However, we do feel that it is important that you have some awareness of the sections having either limited applicability or no applicability. These Sections are as follows:

Section 1300	Differential Reporting
Section 1501	International Accounting Standards
Section 1520	Income Statement
Section 1540	Cash Flow Statements
Section 1581	Business Combinations*
Section 1590	Subsidiaries*
Section 1625	Comprehensive Revaluation Of Assets And Liabilities
Section 1701	Segment Disclosure
Section 1751	Interim Financial Statements
Section 1800	Unincorporated Businesses
Section 3055	Interests In Joint Ventures*
Section 3061	Property, Plant, And Equipment
Section 3062	Goodwill And Other Intangible Assets
Section 3240	Share Capital
Section 3250	Surplus
Section 3260	Reserves
Section 3465	Income Taxes
Section 3500	Earnings Per Share
Section 3610	Capital Transactions
Section 3800	Accounting For Government Assistance
Section 3805	Investment Tax Credits
Section 3840	Related Party Transactions
Section 3841	Economic Dependence
Section 3870	Stock-Based Compensation And Other Stock-Based Payments
Section 4100	Pension Plans
Section 4210	Life Insurance Enterprises

* These Sections contain guidance that may be relevant to
some not-for-profit organizations.

Overview Of Handbook Sections For Not-For-Profit Organizations

14-16. The material that is contained in the seven *Handbook* Sections presents a number of ideas. Some aspects of these ideas are confusing and, in addition, they are interrelated in a manner that cuts across the boundaries of the individual Sections. Before proceeding to a more detailed consideration of these Sections, we would like to give you a broad overview of their content and the manner in which we intend to present the material.

14-17. A basic issue that is covered in these new Sections is the use of fund accounting. While we will describe fund accounting concepts in more detail in the next section of this Chapter, we would note that this is a form of accounting in which the total entity is disaggregated into a group of components or funds. Though it has no applicability to profit-oriented enterprises, it has been, and continues to be, widely used by both government and not-for-profit organizations.

14-18. Section 4400 establishes that not-for-profit organizations can use fund accounting in any format that they wish. However, there is a constraint. Unless it is used in the form that the Section describes as the "restricted fund method" the organization will be limited in its approach to revenue recognition. This does not become clear until you read Section 4410 which deals specifically with revenue recognition. As a result, our detailed coverage of Section 4410 will precede our in-depth coverage of Section 4400.

14-19. Section 4410 indicates that not-for-profit contributions must be recognized using either the "restricted fund method" or the "deferral method". The restricted fund method allows restricted contributions to be recognized when they are received, as opposed to being deferred until there is compliance with the restrictions, either through making expenditures or through the passage of time (restrictions may require certain types of expenditures or they may require that the funds be used in specified periods of time). This restricted fund method, which provides for earlier recognition of restricted revenues, can only be used in the context of fund accounting. Further, it is only available when the approach to fund accounting is based on classifying funds in terms of their restrictions. It is not available with any other form of fund accounting.

14-20. The combined Recommendations of Sections 4400 and 4410 result in a situation in which a Canadian not-for-profit organization can use its choice of three different approaches to preparing its financial statements. These approaches can be described as follows:

Aggregated (Non-Fund) Accounting   If the organization chooses not to use fund accounting, it will present its financial statements on an aggregate basis. If this approach is used, the deferral method of revenue recognition must be adopted.

Fund Accounting - Restricted Fund Basis   If the organization uses fund accounting and classifies its funds in terms of externally imposed restrictions, it can use the restricted fund method of revenue recognition for contributions received.

Fund Accounting - Other Basis   If the organization uses fund accounting and classifies its funds on any basis other than externally imposed restrictions (for example, funds classified by activity such as providing counselling or meals), it must use the deferral approach to revenue recognition for its contributions.

14-21. The preceding results of the combined reading of Sections 4400 and 4410 provides the basis of accounting for not-for-profit organizations in Canada. The other material in the seven Sections can be described as follows:

Section 4400   In addition to providing for the use of fund accounting, Section 4400 contains Recommendations on the form and content of the four financial statements that should be presented by not-for-profit organizations.

Section 4410   This Section provides detailed guidance on the restricted fund and deferral methods of revenue recognition. Guidance is also provided for not-for-profit revenues other than contributions (e.g., investment income).

Section 4420   This brief Section should have been incorporated into Section 4410. Its only content is a Recommendation with respect to the measurement of contributions receivable. Guidance is also provided on pledges and bequests.

Section 4430   This important Section deals with capital assets held by not-for-profit organizations. Prior to the issuance of Section 4430, most organizations did not recognize their capital assets in their Balance Sheets, charging purchased items to expense in the period acquired and, in many cases, not giving any recognition to contributed capital assets. Section 4430 changes this situation by requiring that both purchased and contributed assets be recorded in the Statement Of Financial Position of the organization. It also deals with related issues such as the amortization of capital assets after they have been recorded in the accounts.

Section 4440   This brief Section deals with collections (e.g., the Henry Moore works held by the Art Gallery Of Ontario). It serves to make this type of capital asset exempt from the Recommendations of Section 4430.

Section 4450   This Section deals with the reporting that is required for controlled, significantly influenced, or other related entities in the financial statements of not-for-profit organizations.

Section 4460   This Section deals with the disclosure standards for related party transactions in the financial statements of not-for-profit organizations. Measurement issues are not dealt with in this Section.

14-22.   In our approach to this material, we will begin by providing a general description of the concepts and procedures that are involved in fund accounting. This will be followed by a detailed discussion of revenue recognition for not-for-profit organizations, including the appropriate procedures for dealing with contributions receivable. This will include consideration of how the type of fund accounting adopted will influence the revenue recognition method used. With this material in hand, we will then present the material contained in Section 4400 on financial statement presentation.

14-23.   At this point an example will be presented to illustrate the three basic approaches that can be used by not-for-profit organizations in preparing their financial statements. In this first example we will not include capital assets. Following this example, we will discuss the material in Sections 4430 and 4440 dealing with the capital assets of not-for-profit organizations. After we have reviewed this material, our first example will be extended to include capital assets, providing a fairly comprehensive illustration of the various methods that can be used by not-for-profit organizations.

14-24.   The remainder of the Chapter will consider the *Handbook* Sections on the reporting entity and related party transactions, as well as a brief description of encumbrance accounting procedures.

Fund Accounting

Basic Concepts

14-25.   As we have noted, fund accounting is widely used by both government organizations and not-for-profit organizations. It involves dividing the reporting entity into a number of pieces that are referred to as funds. As defined by the National Council On Governmental Accounting (a U.S. organization), a fund is defined as follows:

> A fund is defined as a fiscal and accounting entity with a self balancing set of accounts recording cash and other financial resources, together with all related liabilities and residual equities or balances, and changes therein, which are segregated for the purpose of carrying on specific activities or attaining certain objectives in accordance with special regulations, restrictions, or limitations.

14-26.   Some of the typical funds that would be used by a not-for-profit organization would be as follows:

- **Current (Or Operating) Fund - Unrestricted**   Unrestricted contributions such as donations, bequests, grants and other income are reported in this fund, together with the day-to-day operating costs.

- **Current Fund - Restricted**   Current restricted funds are expendable funds restricted by the contributors for special purpose expenditures of a current nature.

- **Endowment (Donor Designated) Fund**   This fund contains assets donated to an organization with the stipulation by the donor that only the income earned can be used, either for the general purposes of the organization or for special purposes. The asset is, therefore, restricted and non-expendable.   Gains and losses realized on endowment investments may be transferable to other funds, depending on the terms of the original gift.

- **Board Designated Fund**   The difference between this fund and a donor designated endowment fund is that, in the latter case, the board does not have access to the principal. Resources allocated for a particular purpose by the board of directors can be used for another purpose if the board wishes to change its previous allocation.

- **Plant Or Capital Asset Fund**   This grouping normally comprises long-term assets such as land, building, furniture and equipment.

- **Custodial Funds**   These are funds held in trust for other organizations.

14-27.   Once the appropriate group of funds has been established, the *CICA Handbook* defines fund accounting as follows:

> **Paragraph 4400.02(c)   Fund accounting** comprises the collective accounting procedures resulting in a self-balancing set of accounts for each fund established by legal, contractual or voluntary actions of an organization. Elements of a fund can include assets, liabilities, net assets, revenues and expenses (and gains and losses, where appropriate). Fund accounting involves an accounting segregation, although not necessarily a physical segregation, of resources.

Example

14-28.   A very simple example can be used to illustrate these ideas:

> **Example**   Community Sports Ltd. is established on December 31 of the current year to encourage hiking in the summer and skiing in the winter. On this date, it receives unrestricted contributions of $500,000. Its Board allocates these contributions as follows:

General Administration	$100,000
Hiking Promotion	250,000
Skiing Promotion	150,000
Total	$500,000

There are no other transactions before the December 31 year end.

14-29.   If we assume that fund accounting is not used, the Statement of Operations for the current year and the Statement of Financial Position as at the year end would be as follows:

Community Sports Ltd.
Statement of Operations For The Current Year

Revenues	$500,000
Expenses	Nil
Excess Of Revenues Over Expenses	$500,000

Community Sports Ltd.
Statement of Financial Position As At December 31

Cash	$500,000
Total Assets	$500,000
Unrestricted Net Assets	$500,000

14-30.   If the organization decides to use fund accounting, it would probably have separate funds for hiking and skiing, as well as an operating fund. In applying fund accounting, Community Sports could either put together three separate sets of financial statements or, alternatively, present all of the funds in a multi column format. The latter approach is illustrated as follows:

Community Sports Ltd.
Statement Of Operations For The Current Year

	Operating Fund	Hiking Fund	Skiing Fund	Total
Revenues	$100,000	$250,000	$150,000	$500,000
Expenses	Nil	Nil	Nil	Nil
Excess Of Revenues Over Expenses	$100,000	$250,000	$150,000	$500,000

Community Sports Ltd.
Statement of Financial Position As At December 31

	Operating Fund	Hiking Fund	Skiing Fund	Total
Cash	$100,000	$250,000	$150,000	$500,000
Total Assets	$100,000	$250,000	$150,000	$500,000
Unrestricted Net Assets	$100,000	$250,000	$150,000	$500,000

14-31.   While this example is far too simple to be generally useful, it does serve to illustrate the basic difference between fund accounting and the more familiar aggregated approach to financial reporting.

The Need For Fund Accounting

14-32.   While fund accounting has been widely used in both government and not-for-profit organization accounting, there are those who question its usefulness. The two basic problems with fund accounting can be described as follows:

Fund Definition   Individual organizations can define the funds that they will use in a totally arbitrary fashion. This means that similar organizations can be made to appear very different through the use of a different group of funds. Further, the use of arbitrarily defined funds can be used to obscure the overall performance of the organization.

Interfund Transfers   Until Section 4400 was added to the *CICA Handbook*, there were no rules governing the reporting of interfund transfers. Such transfers could be made at the discretion of the organization and could be reported in a manner that suggested more activity than the organization was actually experiencing.

14-33. These problems lead some authorities to suggest that fund accounting be eliminated. However, this form of accounting has a long tradition of use. Further, fund accounting has many supporters in the not-for-profit accounting community. These supporters point out that a unique feature of not-for-profit organizations is the fact many of the resources that they receive are subject to various types of restrictions on their use. They argue that fund accounting is a very effective way of disclosing and keeping track of these restrictions. This is probably the primary argument that influenced the Accounting Standards Board in their decision to allow continued use of fund accounting in the not-for-profit area.

CICA Recommendations

14-34. While recognizing that fund accounting has potential difficulties, Section 4400 of the *CICA Handbook* allows the use of this approach in preparing the financial statements of not-for-profit organizations. The Board has, however, made a number of Recommendations that will deal with some of the problems.

14-35. To deal with the potentially arbitrary nature of fund definitions, Section 4400 makes the following Recommendation:

> **Paragraph 4400.06** *An organization that uses fund accounting in its financial statements should provide a brief description of the purpose of each fund reported.* (April, 1997)

14-36. This requires that not-for-profit organizations provide some rationale for the particular array of funds they are using. It is also noted that each fund reported should be presented on a consistent basis from year to year. If there are changes, they will have to be reported as changes in accounting policies.

14-37. With respect to the form of presentation, Section 4400 notes that fund accounting statements can be presented either individually, or in a multi-column format. It is even acceptable to use different formats for different statements of the same organization. The only constraint is that each format used satisfies the Recommendations made in the Section.

14-38. With respect to the problem of reporting interfund transfers, Section 4400 Recommends the following:

> **Paragraph 4400.12** *Interfund transfers should be presented in the statement of changes in net assets.* (April, 1997)

> **Paragraph 4400.13** *The amount and purpose of interfund transfers during the reporting period should be disclosed.* (April, 1997)

> **Paragraph 4400.14** *The amounts, terms and conditions of interfund loans outstanding at the reporting date should be disclosed.* (April, 1997)

14-39. These Recommendations will prevent interfund transfers from being treated as revenues in the Statement Of Operations. In addition, it should discourage the use of interfund transfers to give a false impression of activity, in that it requires a statement as to the purpose of these transactions.

14-40. If the organization uses a multi-column approach to disclosure, interfund loans and advances would be presented in the individual funds, but eliminated from the totals column of the statement. If a single column format is used, the only disclosure of these amounts would be in the notes to the financial statements.

Revenue Recognition - Handbook Section 4410

The Matching Principle Revised

14-41. You are all familiar with the application of the matching principle in profit oriented accounting. The major goal of a profit oriented enterprise is to generate revenues and, hopefully, profits. Revenues are recognized when they are earned and the resulting consideration can be reasonably measured. While this usually occurs when goods are sold, there are variations on this such as the percentage of completion method of recognizing revenue.

14-42. The situation with contributions received by not-for-profit organizations is different. The goal of these organizations is to deliver services. This means that, instead of starting with recognizing revenues, not-for-profit organizations focus on the cost of delivering services. When these costs are determined, the appropriate revenues are matched against the costs of providing services. In other words, the matching process is reversed, as compared to the situation with a profit oriented enterprise.

14-43. Because of this reversal, the usual Section 3400 revenue recognition procedures are not applicable to contributions received by not-for-profit organizations. Given this situation, revenue recognition is one of the areas where not-for-profit organizations need their own accounting standards.

Recognition Alternatives For Not-For-Profit Organizations

14-44. The basic Recommendation on revenue recognition for not-for-profit organizations is as follows:

> **Paragraph 4410.10** *An organization should recognize contributions in accordance with either:*
>
> *(a) the deferral method; or*
>
> *(b) the restricted fund method.* (April, 1997)

14-45. This Recommendation is a bit flawed in that it refers to the recognition of "contributions" under these two methods. As we will find out when we examine the more detailed provisions of Section 4410, these two methods are also applied to revenues other than contributions (e.g., investment income).

14-46. The first of these methods is defined as follows:

> **Paragraph 4410.02(d)** Under the **deferral method** of accounting for contributions, restricted contributions related to expenses of future periods are deferred and recognized as revenue in the period in which the related expenses are incurred. Endowment contributions are reported as direct increases in net assets. All other contributions are reported as revenue of the current period. Organizations that use fund accounting in their financial statements without following the restricted fund method would account for contributions under the deferral method.

14-47. As implied by the name, this method requires that the recognition of revenues that are restricted with respect to their use be deferred until that use actually occurs. For example, if an organization receives contributions of $500,000 during 2002, with the use of the funds being restricted to expenses that will be incurred in 2003, these revenues will not be included in the 2002 Statement Of Operations. Rather, they will be deferred and recognized in the 2003 Statement Of Operations.

14-48. The alternative restricted fund method is defined as follows:

> **Paragraph 4410.02(e)** The **restricted fund method** of accounting for contributions is a specialized type of fund accounting which involves the reporting of details of financial statement elements by fund in such a way that the organization reports total general funds, one or more restricted funds, and an endowment fund, if applicable. Reporting of financial statement elements segregated on a basis other than that of use restrictions (e.g., by program or geographic location) does not constitute the restricted fund method.

14-49. This terminology is somewhat unfortunate in that it really refers to a method of applying fund accounting (i.e., funds established on the basis of restrictions), rather than to a method of revenue recognition. However, if this definition is read in conjunction with other provisions in Section 4410, it becomes clear that what is being referred to here is really the cash basis of revenue recognition. (If the not-for-profit organization records contributions receivable, these would also be included in the revenues of the period, an issue that will be discussed in a later section of this Chapter.) Returning to our example from Paragraph 14-47, if the organization receives contributions in 2002 that are restricted to expenses that will be incurred in 2003, use of the restricted fund method would permit these contributions to be recognized as revenues in 2002.

14-50.   What the definition of the restricted fund method really clarifies is that it can only be used in situations where the not-for-profit organization has the following grouping of funds :

- A general or operating fund.

- One or more restricted funds.

- One or more endowment funds, if applicable.

14-51.   As the restricted fund method allows earlier recognition of revenues from contributions, it is likely that this requirement will encourage not-for-profit organizations to classify their funds in terms of externally imposed restrictions. This would seem appropriate in that the primary argument for the continued use of fund accounting is that it is an effective way of disclosing and keeping track of restrictions on the use of contributions.

14-52.   This is a fairly subtle solution to the problem of fund classification. Organizations are permitted to use any array of funds that they choose. However, if the basis for selection is not restrictions on contributions, they will have to use the deferral method of revenue recognition for contributions. This has the effect of creating two forms of fund accounting:

1.   Fund accounting with funds classified to disclose restrictions.

2.   Fund accounting with funds classified on any other basis (the normal alternative would be to disclose programs).

14-53.   When these two applications of fund accounting are added to the possibility of using aggregated or non-fund accounting, we then have three different approaches to preparing the financial statements of not-for-profit organizations. While these alternatives were described in our overview of the relevant *Handbook* Sections, their description is repeated here to reinforce our discussion of the revenue recognition alternatives presented:

Aggregated (Non-Fund) Accounting   If the organization chooses not to use fund accounting, it will present its financial statements on an aggregate basis. If this approach is used, the deferral method of revenue recognition must be adopted.

Fund Accounting - Restricted Fund Basis   If the organization uses fund accounting and classifies its funds in terms of externally imposed restrictions, it can use the restricted fund method of revenue recognition for contributions received.

Fund Accounting - Other Basis   If the organization uses fund accounting and classifies its funds on any basis other than externally imposed restrictions (i.e., restrictions on the use of funds imposed by donors), it must use the deferral approach to revenue recognition for its contributions.

Revenues Of Not-For-Profit Organizations
Contributions

14-54.   A unique feature of not-for-profit organizations is the fact that they receive a significant portion of the revenues in the form of contributions. Section 4410 defines the various types of contributions received by not-for-profit organizations as follows:

Paragraph 4410.02(b)   A **contribution** is a non-reciprocal transfer to a not-for-profit organization of cash or other assets or a non-reciprocal settlement or cancellation of its liabilities. Government funding provided to a not-for-profit organization is considered to be a contribution.

There are three types of contributions identified for purposes of this Section:

(i) A **restricted contribution** is a contribution subject to externally imposed stipulations that specify the purpose for which the contributed asset is to be used. A contribution restricted for the purchase of a capital asset or a contribution of the capital asset itself is a type of restricted contribution.

(ii) An **endowment contribution** is a type of restricted contribution subject to externally imposed stipulations specifying that the resources contributed be maintained permanently, although the constituent assets may change from time to time.

(iii) An **unrestricted contribution** is a contribution that is neither a restricted contribution nor an endowment contribution.

14-55.   As further elaboration of the preceding definitions, Section 4410 defines restrictions as follows:

Paragraph 4410.02(c)   Restrictions are stipulations imposed that specify how resources must be used. External restrictions are imposed from outside the organization, usually by the contributor of the resources. Internal restrictions are imposed in a formal manner by the organization itself, usually by resolution of the board of directors. Restrictions on contributions may only be externally imposed. Net assets or fund balances may be internally or externally restricted. Internally restricted net assets or fund balances are often referred to as reserves or appropriations.

14-56.   The important point to note here is that, for purposes of applying the revenue recognition rules of Section 4410, only externally imposed restrictions qualify for defining restricted contributions. While the concept of external restrictions can be fairly complex in practice, the basic idea is that a contribution is restricted if the contributor has some type of recourse if the funds are not used in the manner specified. The degree of formality that is associated with the restriction may vary from situation to situation.

Other Not-For-Profit Organization Revenues
14-57.   Because of the diversity of not-for-profit organizations, different organizations receive different types of revenues. Not all of these require special attention in Section 4410. For example, a not-for-profit hospital may operate a tuck shop to sell various consumer products that its clients and their visitors require. This type of operation is analogous to other similar activities found in profit oriented operations (e.g., a hotel may have a similar operation). Revenues of this type would be subject to the usual revenue recognition rules that apply to profit oriented enterprises.

14-58.   Many not-for-profit organizations also have investment income. While some of these revenues may be equivalent to the investment income received by profit oriented enterprises, there is the possibility that contributors of the income earning assets have attached restrictions to the income produced. Because of this possibility, Section 4410 provides Recommendations for dealing with the investment income of not-for-profit organizations.

Application Of The Deferral Method
14-59.   As indicated in the definition of the deferral method, some types of not-for-profit organization revenues must be deferred and only recognized when the related expenses are incurred. In simple terms, this deferral procedure applies directly to amounts that are restricted, whereas, amounts of revenues that are not restricted can be recognized as received. Section 4410 does, however, provide fairly detailed guidance on the application of this method to various types of revenues. This guidance is as follows:

Unrestricted Contributions   These contributions can be recognized in the period in which they are received or become receivable.

Restricted Contributions   The basic idea here is that the recognition of restricted contributions must be deferred until the restriction is fulfilled. The actual implementation of this will depend on the type of restriction that is involved:

Expenses Of Current Period If the restriction is for current period expenses, the contributions should be recognized in the current period.

Expenses Of Future Periods In this case, the contributions should be recognized in the same period or periods in which the related expenses are made.

Purchase Of Capital Assets If the restriction is based on acquiring capital assets that will be amortized, the contributions should be recognized on the same basis that the amortization expense is recorded. Alternatively, if the contributions are restricted to the acquisition of non-amortizable assets, they should be recorded as direct increases in net assets, without being disclosed as a revenue in the Statement Of Operations.

Repayment Of Debt The recognition pattern here will depend on the purpose for which the debt was incurred:

- If the debt was for expenses of one or more periods, the repayment contributions should be recognized when the related expenses are recognized.

- If the debt was for the acquisition of non-amortizable capital assets, the repayment contributions should be added directly to net assets without being recorded as revenues in the Statement Of Operations.

- If the debt was for any other purpose, the repayment contributions should be recognized as revenue in the current period.

Endowment Contributions These contributions should be recorded as direct increases in net assets during the current period. They should not be included in the revenues disclosed in the Statement Of Operations.

Investment Income As was the case with contributions restricted to the repayment of debt, the treatment of investment income amounts is dependent on their nature:

- If the investment income is not subject to external restrictions, it should be recognized as a revenue during the current period.

- If the investment income must be added to the principal amount of resources held for endowment, the net investment income should be recorded as a direct increase or decrease in net assets, not as a revenue in the Statement Of Operations.

- If the investment income is subject to other types of restrictions, it should be allocated to income on the same basis as was used for restricted contributions (e.g., if it is restricted to purchases of amortizable capital assets, it should be recognized as a revenue on the same basis as the amortization expense is recorded).

Application Of The Restricted Fund Method

14-60. In contrast to the deferral method, the restricted fund method generally allows revenues to be recognized in the period in which they are received or become receivable. Here again, however, Section 4410 provides fairly detailed guidance for individual types of revenues:

Unrestricted Contributions These contributions can be recognized in the period in which they are received or become receivable. They should be disclosed in the general fund.

Restricted Contributions The treatment here will depend on whether a restricted fund is being used for the particular type of restriction that is involved. For example, if an organization receives contributions that are restricted to providing food for the homeless, the treatment of these contributions will depend on whether a separate restricted fund has been established for this type of activity.

Contributions With A Corresponding Restricted Fund   In this case, the restricted contributions should be recognized as a revenue of the related fund in the period in which they are received or become receivable.

Contributions With No Corresponding Restricted Fund   These contributions should be recognized on the same basis as they would be under the deferral method (e.g., if they are restricted to purchases of amortizable capital assets, they should be recognized as a revenue on the same basis as the amortization expense is recorded).

Endowment Contributions   These contributions should be recognized as a revenue of the endowment fund in the period in which they are received or become receivable. Note the difference here from the treatment of these amounts under the deferral method. Under the deferral method, endowment contributions are not recorded as revenues, but as direct increases in the endowment fund assets.

Investment Income   As was the case under the deferral method, the treatment of investment income amounts is dependent on their nature:

- If the investment income is not subject to external restrictions, it should be recognized as a revenue during the current period.   It would be included in the general fund.

- If the investment income must be added to the principal amount of resources held for endowment, the net investment income should be recorded as a revenue in the Statement Of Operations of the endowment fund in the period in which it becomes received or receivable.

- If the investment income is subject to a restriction for which there is a corresponding restricted fund, it should be included as a revenue in the Statement Of Operations of that fund in the period in which it becomes received or receivable.   If no corresponding restricted fund exists, it should be recognized on the same basis as under the deferral method.

Contributions Receivable (Section 4420)

14-61.   Not-for-profit organizations often receive promises to make contributions at some future point in time, thereby creating potential assets in the form of contributions receivable. The problem here is that the underlying documentation for such receivables is highly variable. Such documentation ranges from a carefully prepared will that provides a very specific grant of assets to the not-for-profit organization, to a simple pledge card which may have been signed at the end of an emotional fund raiser fueled by large quantities of alcohol or other mind altering substances.   In the former case, recognition of the receivable and the related revenue presents no accounting problems. The latter case is more problematical in that it is certainly not legally enforceable and, depending on the circumstances, may or may not be collectible.

14-62.   Section 1000, "Financial Statement Concepts", provides general criteria for the recognition of items in the financial statements. The Section points out that items should only be recognized if:

- they involve giving up or receiving economic benefits; and
- they have a reasonable basis for measurement.

14-63.   It would be our opinion that this provides adequate guidance for dealing with the contributions that are receivable by not-for-profit organizations. They clearly involve receiving economic benefits and, while the question of having a reasonable basis of measurement is complicated by the lack of a legal claim for some receivables, the underlying concept is little different than that applicable to other receivables.

14-64.   Despite this basic similarity, a separate Section 4420 was added to the *CICA Handbook* to deal with the contributions receivable of not-for-profit organizations. The basic Recommendation of this Section is as follows:

Paragraph 4420.03 *A contribution receivable should be recognized as an asset when it meets the following criteria:*

(a) the amount to be received can be reasonably estimated; and
(b) ultimate collection is reasonably assured. (April, 1997)

14-65. The Section points out that these rules are equally applicable to both pledges and bequests. In addition to this Recommendation with respect to recognition, the Section also makes a Recommendation with respect to the disclosure of contributions receivable:

Paragraph 4420.08 *When a not-for-profit organization has recognized outstanding pledges and bequests in its financial statements, the following should be disclosed:*

(a) the amount recognized as assets at the reporting date; and
(b) the amount recognized as revenue in the period. (April, 1997)

Non-Monetary Contributions

14-66. The great majority of contributions to not-for-profit organizations are in the form of cash or cash equivalents. However, many of these organizations also receive contributions in the form of non-monetary assets. Such contributions range from major works of art that are clearly of significant value, to garbage bags full of discarded clothing that may actually have a negative value in terms of their costs of disposal.

14-67. A similar problem arises with contributed services. Volunteer services can range from an experienced accountant preparing the financial statements of the not-for-profit organization to a local socialite who insists on being at every fund raiser, despite the fact that she manages to offend at least half of the potential contributors who she speaks with.

14-68. The *Handbook* deals with both of these problems with the following Recommendation:

Paragraph 4410.16 *An organization may choose to recognize contributions of materials and services, but should do so only when a fair value can be reasonably estimated and when the materials and services are used in the normal course of the organization's operations and would otherwise have been purchased.* (April, 1997)

14-69. This Recommendation establishes two criteria for the recognition of non-monetary contributions:

- Their value must be subject to reasonable estimation. While this is not explicitly stated, it is likely that many items would not be recognized because the cost of estimation would likely exceed any benefits to be achieved through this process.

- Contributed goods and services would only be recognized if they would have otherwise been purchased. This is likely to eliminate the recognition of a significant portion of the voluntary services received.

Revenue Related Disclosure
Contributions

14-70. Section 4410 requires the following general disclosure related to contributions:

Paragraph 4410.21 *An organization should disclose:*

(a) the policy followed in accounting for endowment contributions; and
(b) the policies followed in accounting for restricted contributions. (April, 1997)

Paragraph 4410.22 *An organization should disclose its contributions by major source.* (April, 1997)

Paragraph 4410.23 *An organization should disclose the policy followed in accounting for contributed materials and services.* (April, 1997)

Paragraph 4410.24   *An organization should disclose the nature and amount of contributed materials and services recognized in the financial statements.* (April, 1997)

Deferral Method

14-71.   Section 4410 makes the following Recommendations with respect to the disclosure of deferred contributions:

Paragraph 4410.52   *Deferred contributions balances should be presented in the statement of financial position outside net assets.* (April, 1997)

Paragraph 4410.53   *An organization should disclose the nature and amount of changes in deferred contributions balances for the period.* (April, 1997)

14-72.   One additional Recommendation for the disclosure of net investment income by organizations using the deferral method is as follows:

Paragraph 4410.55   *An organization should disclose the following related to net investment income earned on resources held for endowment:*

(a) *the amounts recognized in the statement of operations in the period;*

(b) *the amounts deferred in the period;*

(c) *the amounts recognized as direct increases or decreases in net assets in the period; and*

(d) *the total earned in the period.* (April, 1997)

Restricted Fund Method

14-73.   For organizations using the restricted fund method, the following Recommendations are applicable to deferred contributions:

Paragraph 4410.73   *When restricted contributions are recognized in the general fund in accordance with paragraph 4410.65, any deferred contributions balances should be presented in the statement of financial position outside net assets.* (April, 1997)

Paragraph 4410.74   *When restricted contributions are recognized in the general fund in accordance with paragraph 4410.65, the nature and amount of changes in deferred contributions balances for the period should be disclosed.* (April, 1997)

14-74.   One additional disclosure Recommendation deals with the net investment income of organizations using the restricted fund method:

Paragraph 4410.76   *An organization should disclose the following related to net investment income earned on resources held for endowment:*

(a) *the amounts recognized in the general fund in the period;*

(b) *the amounts recognized in each restricted fund in the period;*

(c) *the amounts recognized in the endowment fund in the period;*

(d) *any amounts deferred in the period; and*

(e) *the total earned in the period.* (April, 1997)

Financial Statement Presentation Handbook Section 4400

Required Financial Statements

14-75.   Section 1000 of the *CICA Handbook*, "Financial Statement Concepts", specifies the required financial statements for both profit-oriented and not-for-profit organizations. For not-for-profit organizations, the list is reiterated in Section 4400:

Paragraph 4400.05 Financial statements for a not-for-profit organization normally include:

(a) a statement of financial position;
(b) a statement of operations;
(c) a statement of changes in net assets; and
(d) a statement of cash flows.

14-76. Section 4400 notes that other titles may be used for these statements. In addition, it may be desirable to combine statements. For example, many organizations will combine the Statement Of Operations with the Statement Of Changes In Net Assets.

14-77. Section 4400 also provides a general disclosure requirement with respect to the nature of not-for-profit organizations.

Paragraph 4400.04 *A clear and concise description of a not-for-profit organization's purpose, its intended community of service, its status under income tax legislation and its legal form should be included as an integral part of its financial statements.* (April, 1997)

14-78. The remaining Recommendations of Section 4400 relate to specific financial statements and will be considered in the context of those statements.

Statement Of Financial Position
General Recommendations
14-79. Without regard to whether or not fund accounting is used, a not-for-profit organization must provide all fund totals for each item presented in the Statement Of Financial Position. This is reflected in the following Recommendation:

Paragraph 4400.18 *For each financial statement item, the statement of financial position should present a total that includes all funds reported.* (April, 1997)

14-80. The preparation of this Statement should be based on the general *CICA Handbook* rules, including Section 1510 which provides Recommendations on segregating current assets and current liabilities. However, certain additional disclosure items are unique to not-for-profit organizations. These additional items are as follows:

Paragraph 4400.19 *The statement of financial position should present the following:*

(a) *net assets invested in capital assets;*
(b) *net assets subject to restrictions requiring that they be maintained permanently as endowments;*
(c) *other restricted net assets;*
(d) *unrestricted net assets; and*
(e) *total net assets.* (April, 1997)

14-81. The total net asset figure, a figure analogous to owners' equity for a profit oriented enterprise, may also be referred to as "Fund Balances" or "Accumulated Surplus (Deficit)". Note that this balance does not include deferred contributions.

14-82. With respect to the "net assets invested in capital assets" balance, the amount disclosed should be reduced by related debt. [**Byrd/Chen Note:** This conclusion does not appear in any Recommendation. However, it is implicit in the use of the term net, and reinforced by the example in the Appendix to Section 4400.] When the deferral method is used, the balance does not include any amount of deferred restricted contributions received for the purchase of capital assets.

Disclosure Of External Restrictions
14-83. External restrictions are of significance because they limit the organization's financial flexibility. Given this, Section 4400 has additional disclosure Recommendations for these amounts. For organizations using the deferral method, the Recommendation is as follows:

Paragraph 4400.26   *The following should be disclosed:*

(a) *the amounts of deferred contributions attributable to each major category of external restrictions with a description of the restrictions; and*

(b) *the amount of net assets subject to external restrictions requiring that they be maintained permanently as endowments.* (April, 1997)

14-84.   The corresponding Recommendation for organizations using the restricted fund method is as follows:

Paragraph 4400.28   *The following should be disclosed:*

(a) *the amount of net assets (fund balances) subject to external restrictions requiring that they be maintained permanently as endowments;*

(b) *the amounts of net assets (fund balances) attributable to each major category of other external restrictions with a description of the restrictions; and*

(c) *the amounts of deferred contributions attributable to each major category of external restrictions with a description of the restrictions.* (April, 1997)

Statement Of Operations
General Recommendations
14-85.   The objective of this statement is to communicate information about changes in the organization's economic resources and obligations for the period. The information it contains can be used to evaluate the organization's performance during the period, including its continued ability to provide services. The statement can also be used to evaluate management.

14-86.   Section 4400 does not contain specific Recommendations as to classification of expenses, recognizing that different organizations may classify by object (e.g., wage, rent, advertising), while others may classify by function or program (e.g., feeding the poor, providing shelter for the homeless). To the extent that the organization has any of the items listed in Section 1520 of the *CICA Handbook*, the individual disclosure requirements of that Section would be applicable here.

14-87.   Not-for-profit organizations have a tradition of reporting certain revenue items net of the related expenses. An example of this would be the net proceeds of particular fund raising events. In an effort to limit this type of disclosure, Section 4400 provides the following Recommendation:

Paragraph 4400.37   *Revenues and expenses should be disclosed at their gross amounts.* (April, 1997)

14-88.   This disclosure could either be in the Statement Of Operations or, alternatively, in the notes to the financial statements. To the extent that the items relate to the organization's main, ongoing service delivery activities, disclosure in the Statement Of Operations is preferred.

Deferral Method
14-89.   For those organizations using the deferral method, the following Recommendation is applicable:

Paragraph 4400.33   *The statement of operations should present*

(a) *for each financial statement item, a total that includes all funds reported; and*
(b) *total excess or deficiency of revenues and gains over expenses and losses for the period.* (April, 1997)

14-90.   The first part of the Recommendation applies when some form of fund accounting is being used in conjunction with the deferral method. It ensures that information will be provided for the organization as a whole. The remainder of the Recommendation calls for the presentation of a not-for-profit organization's equivalent to a "bottom line".

Restricted Fund Method

14-91. Section 4400 contains the following Recommendation that is specific to those organizations using the restricted fund method:

Paragraph 4400.35 *The statement of operations should present the following for the period:*

(a) the total for each financial statement item recognized in the general fund;

(b) the total for each financial statement item recognized in the restricted funds, other than the endowment fund;

(c) the total for each financial statement item recognized in the endowment fund; and

(d) excess or deficiency of revenues and gains over expenses and losses for each of the general fund, restricted funds other than the endowment fund and the endowment fund. (April, 1997)

14-92. As was the case with the Recommendation for organizations using the deferral method, this Recommendation insures that information is available for the total organization and that a "bottom line" is presented for the specified fund balances.

Statement Of Changes In Net Assets

14-93. This Statement is the not-for-profit equivalent of the Statement Of Changes In Shareholders' Equity for a profit oriented corporation. For a not-for-profit organization, it will disclose information about changes in the portions of net assets attributable to endowments, to capital assets, and to other external and internal restrictions. It provides information with respect to the organization's overall accumulation or depletion of assets. For those not-for-profit organizations that use fund accounting, this Statement may also be referred to as a Statement Of Changes In Fund Balances.

14-94. Disclosure items that are unique to not-for-profit organizations are specified in the following Recommendation:

Paragraph 4400.41 *The statement of changes in net assets should present changes in the following for the period:*

(a) net assets invested in capital assets;

(b) net assets subject to restrictions requiring that they be maintained permanently as endowments;

(c) other restricted net assets;

(d) unrestricted net assets; and

(e) total net assets. (April, 1997)

Statement Of Cash Flows

14-95. The general rules presented in Section 1540, "Cash Flow Statements" of the *CICA Handbook* are, for the most part, applicable here. In addition, Section 4400 adds two Recommendations that are specific to the Statement Of Cash Flows of not-for-profit organizations. They are as follows:

Paragraph 4400.44 *The statement of cash flows should report the total changes in cash and cash equivalents resulting from the activities of the organization during the period. The components of cash and cash equivalents should be disclosed. (April, 1997)*

Paragraph 4400.45 *The statement of cash flows should distinguish at least the following:*

(a) cash from operations: the components of cash from operations should be disclosed or the excess of revenues over expenses should be reconciled to cash flows from operations; and

(b) the components of cash flows resulting from financing and investing activities, not included in (a) above. (April, 1997)

14-96.   Section 4400 notes that cash receipts from operations would include unrestricted contributions, restricted contributions that are to be used for operations, and other revenues arising from the organization's ordinary activities, such as fees for services, proceeds on the sale of goods and unrestricted investment income. Cash disbursements for operations would comprise expenditures made by the organization in carrying out its service delivery activities.

14-97.   Components of cash flows from financing activities would include cash contributed that is restricted for the purpose of acquiring capital assets and cash contributed for endowment. Cash receipts and disbursements related to the assumption and repayment of debt would also be presented as components of cash flows from financing activities. Components of cash flows from investing activities would include the acquisition of capital assets, the purchase of investments, and the proceeds on disposal of major categories of assets, such as capital assets and investments.

14-98.   Section 4400 notes that non-cash financing and investing transactions (e.g. contributions of capital assets) should be reported as a cash inflow combined with a cash outflow. We would note that Section 1540 would exclude this type of transaction from the Cash Flow Statement.

14-99.   The Section also indicates that, in situations where a Cash Flow Statement would not provide additional useful information, no such Statement need be prepared. This might apply, for example, to an organization with relatively simple operations and few or no significant financing and investing activities.

Example 1 (No Capital Assets)

Basic Data

14-100.   At this point, we would like to present an example that illustrates the three accounting approaches that can be used by a not-for-profit organization (i.e., aggregate accounting, restricted fund accounting, and other basis fund accounting). This example will illustrate a number of the Recommendations for revenue recognition and financial statement presentation. It will not, however, include capital asset considerations. A second version of this example will be presented after we have discussed Sections 4430 (Capital Assets) and 4440 (Collections). This second example will be a continuation of this example with the addition of purchased and contributed capital assets. We will use the data of this example in three different cases in order to illustrate the alternatives that are available in not-for-profit accounting.

14-101.   The basic data for this example is as follows:

Organization And Purpose   On January 1, 2002, the Local Care Society (LCS) is organized as a not-for-profit organization. Its purpose is to serve the needs of its local community in two areas:

- The provision of meals for elderly individuals who are unable to leave their homes (meals activity).

- The provision of winter clothing for children who are living in poverty (clothing activity).

The organization will have a December 31 year end.

Endowment Contributions   Initial funding is provided by a wealthy individual who makes an endowment contribution of $50,000. These funds are invested in debt securities. There are no restrictions on the income that is produced by these investments. During the year ending December 31, 2002, such income amounted to $4,000.

Unrestricted Contributions   The organization solicits and receives unrestricted contributions which are then allocated to both the meals activity and the clothing activity by the organization's Board Of Directors.   During the year ending December 31, 2002,

$400,000 in contributions were received. At year end, an additional $35,000 in contributions were receivable. The receivable is related to the meals activity. The Board believes that this is a reasonable estimate of the amount that will actually be collected. The $435,000 total was allocated $285,000 to the meals activity and $150,000 to the clothing activity.

Restricted Contributions   The organization accepts additional contributions that are restricted to use in the clothing activity. These funds are segregated and a separate report is made to contributors on their usage. During the year ending December 31, 2002, restricted contributions of $125,000 were received. No contributions are receivable at year end.

Expenses   During the year ending December 31, 2002, the organization incurred the following expenses:

	Meals Activity	Clothing Activity
Wages And Salaries	$ 20,000	$ 25,000
Cost Of Materials Provided	180,000	190,000
Transportation Costs	30,000	5,000
Other Expenses	15,000	20,000
Total	$245,000	$240,000

It is estimated that 40 percent ($96,000) of the expenses related to the clothing activity have been made from the restricted contributions.

On December 31, 2002, there were outstanding Accounts Payable related to the meals activity expenses of $30,000.

Case One - No Fund Accounting

14-102.   In this Case, we will assume that LCS is not using fund accounting. This means that they will have to use the deferral method of revenue recognition. It also means that all of the entries required during the year will be recorded in a single journal. In reviewing these journal entries, we would remind you that, for a not-for-profit organization, the Balance Sheet account that is analogous to Shareholders' Equity for a corporation is titled Net Assets. The required entries would be as follows:

Endowment Contributions

Cash	$50,000	
Net Assets - Restricted For Endowment Purposes		$50,000

(Paragraph 4400.19 requires segregation of amounts that are restricted for endowment purposes)

Investment Of Endowment Contributions

Investments	$50,000	
Cash		$50,000

Investment Income

Cash	$4,000	
Revenue - Investment Income		$4,000

(As there are no restrictions on this Investment Income, it can be recognized in the current period.)

Unrestricted Contributions

Cash	$400,000	
Contributions Receivable	35,000	
Revenue - Unrestricted Contributions		$435,000

Restricted Contributions

Cash	$125,000	
Deferred Contributions		$125,000

(Under the deferral method, restricted contributions cannot be recognized until the related expenses are incurred. The Deferred Contributions account is a Balance Sheet account that must be disclosed outside the Net Asset balance.)

Expenses

Wages And Salaries ($20,000 + $25,000)	$ 45,000	
Cost Of Materials Provided ($180,000 + $190,000)	370,000	
Transportation Costs ($30,000 + $5,000)	35,000	
Other Expenses ($15,000 + $20,000)	35,000	
Cash ($245,000 + $240,000 - $30,000)		$455,000
Accounts Payable		30,000

Amortization Of Deferred Contributions

Deferred Contributions [(40%)($240,000)]	$96,000	
Revenue - Amortization Of Deferred Contributions		$96,000

[Contributions that are restricted to expenses for clothing can be recognized as revenue to the extent that such expenses have been incurred. In this case the amount is $96,000, leaving a Deferred Contributions balance of $29,000 ($125,000 - $96,000)].

Closing Entry

Revenue - Unrestricted Contributions	$435,000	
Revenue - Amortization Of Deferred Contributions	96,000	
Revenue - Investment Income	4,000	
Wages And Salaries		$ 45,000
Cost Of Materials Provided		370,000
Transportation Costs		35,000
Other Expenses		35,000
Net Assets - Unrestricted		50,000

(All of the expenses and revenues would be closed to the Net Assets - Unrestricted balance at the end of the fiscal year. The $50,000 is a balancing figure that is also calculated on the Statement of Operations and Fund Balances.)

14-103.   Based on these journal entries required financial statements would be as follows:

LCS Organization
Statement Of Operations And Fund Balances
Year Ending December 31, 2002

Revenues:

Unrestricted Contributions	$435,000
Amortization Of Deferred Contributions	96,000
Investment Income	4,000
Total Revenues	**$535,000**

Expenses:

Wages And Salaries	$ 45,000
Cost Of Materials Provided	370,000
Transportation Costs	35,000
Other Expenses	35,000
Total Expenses	**$485,000**
Excess Of Revenues Over Expenses	$ 50,000
Opening Unrestricted Net Assets	Nil
Closing Unrestricted Net Assets	**$ 50,000**

LCS Organization
Statement Of Cash Flows
Year Ending December 31, 2002

Cash Flows From Operating Activities:

Unrestricted Contributions	$400,000
Restricted Contributions	125,000
Investment Income	4,000
Expenses	(455,000)
Total	**$ 74,000**

Cash Flows From Financing And Investing:

Endowment Contributions	50,000
Investment Of Endowment Contributions	(50,000)
Increase In Cash	$ 74,000
Opening Cash Balance	Nil
Closing Cash Balance	**$ 74,000**

LCS Organization
Statement Of Financial Position
As At December 31, 2002

Cash (From Statement Of Cash Flows)	$ 74,000
Investments	50,000
Contributions Receivable	35,000
Total	**$159,000**

Accounts Payable	$ 30,000
Deferred Contributions	29,000
Net Assets:	
Restricted For Endowment Purposes	50,000
Unrestricted	50,000
Total	**$159,000**

Case Two - Restricted Fund Accounting

14-104. In this Case, we will assume that LCS establishes separate funds for endowment contributions, restricted clothing activity contributions, and a general fund. Given this, the organization will be able to use the restricted fund basis of revenue recognition. Reflecting this, separate journal entries will have to be made for each of the defined funds.

14-105. A further point here is that, when fund accounting is used, the Statement of Financial Position account that we referred to as Net Assets in Case One will be titled Fund Balances. Both of these titles refer to the not-for-profit organization equivalent of Shareholders' Equity for a corporation. While both are acceptable, the *Handbook* tends to use the term Fund Balances in those examples that involve any type of fund accounting.

14-106. The required journal entries are as follows (explanations that are unchanged from Case One will not be repeated here):

Endowment Fund Entries

Endowment Contributions

Cash	$50,000	
Fund Balances - Restricted For Endowment Purposes		$50,000

Investment Of Endowment Contributions

Investments	$50,000	
Cash		$50,000

General Fund Entries

Investment Income

Cash	$4,000	
Revenue - Investment Income		$4,000

(The entry is in the general fund as there are no restrictions on the use of this income)

Unrestricted Contributions

Cash	$400,000	
Contributions Receivable	35,000	
Revenue - Unrestricted Contributions		$435,000

Expenses

Wages And Salaries [$20,000 + (60%)$25,000)]	$ 35,000	
Cost Of Materials Provided [$180,000 + (60%)($190,000)]	294,000	
Transportation Costs [($30,000 + (60%)($5,000)]	33,000	
Other Expenses [$15,000 + (60%)($20,000)]	27,000	
Cash [$245,000 + (60%)($240,000) - $30,000)]		$359,000
Accounts Payable		30,000

Closing Entry - General Fund

Revenue - Unrestricted Contributions	$435,000	
Investment Income	4,000	
Wages And Salaries		$ 35,000
Cost Of Materials Provided		294,000
Transportation Costs		33,000
Other Expenses		27,000
Fund Balances - Unrestricted		50,000

(Note that this is the same $50,000 credit to the unrestricted fund balance (net assets) as was made in Case One)

Restricted Fund Entries

Restricted Contributions

Cash	$125,000	
Revenue - Restricted Contributions		$125,000

(Note that, as the restricted fund method of accounting is being used, all of the restricted contributions can be recorded as revenue, without regard to when the related expenses are incurred.)

Expenses

Wages And Salaries [(40%)($25,000)]	$ 10,000	
Cost Of Materials Provided [(40%)($190,000)]	76,000	
Transportation Costs [(40%)($5,000)]	2,000	
Other Expenses [(40%)($20,000)]	8,000	
Cash [(40%)($240,000)]		$96,000

Closing Entry - Restricted Fund

Revenue - Restricted Contributions	$125,000	
Wages And Salaries		$ 10,000
Cost Of Materials Provided		76,000
Transportation Costs		2,000
Other Expenses		8,000
Fund Balances - Restricted For Clothing		29,000

[Note that the $29,000 of restricted contributions that have not been spent is included in the Fund Balances. This is in contrast to the deferral method where this balance is shown as Deferred Contributions and not included in Fund Balances (Net Assets)].

14-107.   Using the preceding journal entries, the required financial statements would be prepared as follows:

LCS Organization
Statement Of Operations And Fund Balances
Year Ending December 31, 2002

	General Fund	Restricted Fund	Endowment Fund
Revenues:			
Unrestricted Contributions	$435,000		
Restricted Contributions		$125,000	
Investment Income	4,000		
Endowment Contributions			$50,000
Total Revenues	$439,000	$125,000	$50,000
Expenses:			
Wages And Salaries	$ 35,000	$ 10,000	
Cost Of Materials Provided	294,000	76,000	
Transportation Costs	33,000	2,000	
Other Expenses	27,000	8,000	
Total Expenses	$389,000	$ 96,000	Nil
Excess Of Revenues Over Expenses	$ 50,000	$ 29,000	$50,000
Opening Fund Balances	Nil	Nil	Nil
Closing Fund Balances	$ 50,000	$ 29,000	$50,000

LCS Organization
Statement Of Cash Flows
Year Ending December 31, 2002

	General Fund	Restricted Fund	Endowment Fund
Cash Flows From Operating Activities:			
Unrestricted Contributions	$400,000		
Restricted Contributions		$125,000	
Investment Income	4,000		
Expenses	(359,000)	(96,000)	
Total	$ 45,000	$ 29,000	Nil
Cash Flows From Financing And Investing:			
Endowment Contributions			$50,000
Investments Acquired	Nil	Nil	(50,000)
Increase In Cash	$ 45,000	$ 29,000	Nil
Opening Cash Balance	Nil	Nil	Nil
Closing Cash Balance	$ 45,000	$ 29,000	Nil

LCS Organization
Statement Of Financial Position
As At December 31, 2002

	General Fund	Restricted Fund	Endowment Fund	Total
Cash (From Statement Of Cash Flows)	$ 45,000	$ 29,000		$ 74,000
Investments			$ 50,000	50,000
Contributions Receivable	35,000			35,000
Total	$ 80,000	$ 29,000	$ 50,000	$159,000
Accounts Payable	$ 30,000			$ 30,000
Fund Balances:				
Restricted For Clothing		$ 29,000		29,000
Restricted For Endowment			$ 50,000	50,000
Unrestricted	50,000			50,000
Total	$ 80,000	$ 29,000	$ 50,000	$159,000

14-108.   As this example illustrates, when the restricted fund method is used, all-fund totals are not required for either the Statement Of Operations or the Statement Of Cash Flows. However, such totals are always required for the Statement Of Financial Position.

Case Three - Fund Accounting On Other Basis

14-109.   This final version of our Case will also assume that LCS uses fund accounting. However, it will not qualify for the restricted fund method of revenue recognition as it classifies its funds by programs rather than by restrictions. They will use a general fund, a meals activity fund, and a clothing activity fund. Endowment funds will be accounted for through the general fund. As was the situation in Case Two, separate journal entries will have to be made for each of the defined funds. These entries are as follows:

General Fund Entries
Endowment Contributions

Cash	$50,000	
Fund Balances - Restricted For Endowment Purposes		$50,000

(Despite the fact that there is no separate endowment fund, separate disclosure must be given to the portion of the Fund Balances amount that is restricted for endowment purposes.)

Investment Of Endowment Contributions

Investments	$50,000	
Cash		$50,000

Investment Income

Cash	$4,000	
Revenue - Investment Income		$4,000

(The entry is in the general fund as there are no restrictions on the use of this income)

Closing Entry - General Fund

Revenue - Investment Income	$4,000	
Fund Balances - Unrestricted		$4,000

Meals Fund Entries
Unrestricted Contributions

Cash	$250,000	
Contributions Receivable	35,000	
Revenue - Unrestricted Contributions		$285,000

(While the Board has allocated this amount to meal activity, this is not an external restriction and, as a consequence, it can be recognized as a current revenue.)

Expenses

Wages And Salaries	$ 20,000	
Cost Of Materials Provided	180,000	
Transportation Costs	30,000	
Other Expenses	15,000	
Cash ($245,000 - $30,000)		$215,000
Accounts Payable		30,000

Closing Entry - Meal Fund

Revenue - Unrestricted Contributions	$285,000	
Wages And Salaries		$ 20,000
Cost Of Materials Provided		180,000
Transportation Costs		30,000
Other Expenses		15,000
Fund Balances - Unrestricted		40,000

Clothing Fund Entries
Unrestricted Contributions

Cash	$150,000	
Revenue - Unrestricted Contributions		$150,000

(While the Board has allocated this amount to clothing activity, this is not an external restriction and, as a consequence, it can be recognized as a current revenue.)

Restricted Contributions

Cash	$125,000	
Deferred Contributions		$125,000

(As the deferral method is being used, the recognition of these contributions as revenue must be deferred.)

Expenses

Wages And Salaries	$ 25,000	
Cost Of Materials Provided	190,000	
Transportation Costs	5,000	
Other Expenses	20,000	
Cash		$240,000

Amortization Of Deferred Contributions

Deferred Contributions [(40%)($240,000)]	$96,000	
Revenue - Amortization Of Deferred Contributions		$96,000

(As was the situation in Case One, Deferred Contributions can be recognized as revenues to the extent of related expenses.)

Closing Entry - Clothing Fund

Revenue - Unrestricted Contributions	$150,000	
Revenue - Amortization Of Deferred Contributions	96,000	
Wages And Salaries		$ 25,000
Cost Of Materials Provided		190,000
Transportation Costs		5,000
Other Expenses		20,000
Fund Balances - Unrestricted		6,000

{The $6,000 credit to Fund Balances - Unrestricted reflects the unused portion of the $150,000 of unrestricted contributions that was allocated to clothing [$150,000 - (60%)($240,000)]}

14-110.   Using the preceding journal entries, the required financial statements can be prepared as follows:

LCS Organization
Statement Of Operations And Fund Balances
Year Ending December 31, 2002

	General Fund	Meals Activity Fund	Clothing Activity Fund	Total
Revenues:				
Unrestricted Contributions		$285,000	$150,000	$435,000
Restricted Contributions			96,000	96,000
Investment Income	$4,000			4,000
Total Revenues	$4,000	$285,000	$246,000	$535,000
Expenses:				
Wages And Salaries		$ 20,000	$ 25,000	$ 45,000
Cost Of Materials Provided		180,000	190,000	370,000
Transportation Costs		30,000	5,000	35,000
Other Expenses	Nil	15,000	20,000	35,000
Total Expenses	Nil	$245,000	$240,000	$485,000
Excess Of Revenues Over Expenses	$4,000	$ 40,000	$ 6,000	$ 50,000
Opening Fund Balances	Nil	Nil	Nil	Nil
Closing Fund Balances	$4,000	$ 40,000	$ 6,000	$ 50,000

LCS Organization
Statement Of Cash Flows
Year Ending December 31, 2002

	General Fund	Meals Activity Fund	Clothing Activity Fund	Total
Cash Flows From Operating Activities				
Unrestricted Contributions		$250,000	$150,000	$400,000
Restricted Contributions			125,000	125,000
Investment Income	$ 4,000			4,000
Expenses		(215,000)	(240,000)	(455,000)
Total	$ 4,000	$ 35,000	$ 35,000	$ 74,000
Cash Flows From Financing And Investing:				
Endowment Contributions	50,000			50,000
Investments Acquired	(50,000)	Nil	Nil	(50,000)
Increase In Cash	$ 4,000	$ 35,000	$ 35,000	$ 74,000
Opening Cash Balance	Nil	Nil	Nil	Nil
Closing Cash Balance	$ 4,000	$ 35,000	$ 35,000	$ 74,000

LCS Organization
Statement Of Financial Position
As At December 31, 2002

	General Fund	Meals Activity Fund	Clothing Activity Fund	Total
Cash (From Statement of Cash Flows)	$ 4,000	$35,000	$35,000	$ 74,000
Investments	50,000			50,000
Contributions Receivable		35,000		35,000
Total	$54,000	$70,000	$35,000	$159,000
Accounts Payable		$30,000		$ 30,000
Deferred Contributions			$29,000	29,000
Fund Balances:				
Restricted For Endowment	$50,000			50,000
Unrestricted	4,000	40,000	6,000	50,000
Total	$54,000	$70,000	$35,000	$159,000

Capital Assets Of Not-For-Profit Organizations Handbook Sections 4430 And 4440

Background To The Problem

14-111. For both not-for-profit and government organizations, the traditional practice has been not to record assets in the financial statements. In general, such assets were charged to expense when acquired, leaving no balance to be subject to amortization in future periods.

14-112. While there is still support for this type of approach, the great majority of authorities in this area view such practices as inappropriate. As a reflection of this fact, Section 4430 has been added to the *CICA Handbook*. The basic purpose of this Section is to require not-for-profit organizations to deal with their capital assets in basically the same manner as is specified in Section 3061, "Property, Plant, and Equipment", for profit oriented enterprises. In fact, much of Section 4430 duplicates the content of Section 3061.

14-113. As a measure of the controversy surrounding this issue, you should note that the Accounting Standards Board felt obliged to make exceptions to these rules for the capital assets of not-for-profit organizations. These exceptions are dealt with in the next Section.

Exceptions To Capital Assets Rule

Small Organizations

14-114. The first exception relates to smaller organizations. In order to implement this exception, Section 4430 contains the following statement:

> **Paragraph 4430.03** Organizations may limit the application of this Section to the Recommendation in paragraph 4430.40 if the average of annual revenues recognized in the statement of operations for the current and preceding period of the organization and any entities it controls is less than $500,000. When an organization reports some of its revenues net of related expenses, gross revenues would be used for purposes of this calculation.

14-115. The additional disclosures that must be provided in these situations are as follows:

> **Paragraph 4430.40** *Organizations meeting the criterion in paragraph 4430.03 and not following the other Recommendations of this Section should disclose the following:*
>
> *(a) the policy followed in accounting for capital assets;*
>
> *(b) information about major categories of capital assets not recorded in the statement of financial position, including a description of the assets; and*
>
> *(c) if capital assets are expensed when acquired, the amount expensed in the current period. (April, 1997)*

Collections

14-116. Collections are defined in Section 4440 as follows:

> **Paragraph 4440.03(b)** **Collections** are works of art, historical treasures or similar assets that are:
>
> (i) held for public exhibition, education or research;
>
> (ii) protected, cared for and preserved; and
>
> (iii) subject to an organizational policy that requires any proceeds from their sale to be used to acquire other items to be added to the collection or for the direct care of the existing collection.

14-117. A typical example of a collection would be a group of paintings held by a not-for-profit art gallery. Such assets often present significant valuation problems. Perhaps, more importantly, they generally do not depreciate in value. If they do experience a change in value, it is more likely to be in an upward direction. Further, they are not a resource that can be used by the organization for any other purpose.

14-118.   Given these considerations, it is not surprising that the Accounting Standards Board decided not to apply the requirements of Section 4430 to these assets. This is accomplished in a less than straightforward manner. Section 4430 does not simply say that these assets are exempt from its Recommendations. Rather, it provides the following definition of Capital Assets:

> **Paragraph 4430.05(b)   Capital assets**, comprising tangible properties, such as land, buildings and equipment, and intangible properties, are identifiable assets that meet all of the following criteria:
>
> (i)   are held for use in the provision of services, for administrative purposes, for production of goods or for the maintenance, repair, development or construction of other capital assets;
>
> (ii)   have been acquired, constructed or developed with the intention of being used on a continuing basis;
>
> (iii) are not intended for sale in the ordinary course of operations; and
>
> (iv) are not held as part of a collection.

14-119.   By excluding collections from the definition of capital assets, the Accounting Standards Board has, in effect, exempted these assets from the Recommendations of Section 4430.

Recognition And Measurement
Initial Recognition
14-120.   The basic Recommendation here is as follows:

> **Paragraph 4430.06**   *A capital asset should be recorded on the statement of financial position at cost. For a contributed capital asset, cost is considered to be fair value at the date of contribution. In unusual circumstances when fair value cannot be reasonably determined, the capital asset should be recorded at nominal value.* (April, 1997)

14-121.   This Recommendation requires that the capital assets of not-for-profit organizations be recorded at cost and, in addition, it specifies that the cost of a contributed capital asset is its fair value at the time of contribution. Fair value, as defined in Paragraph 4430.05, is the amount of the consideration that would be agreed upon in an arm's length transaction between knowledgeable, willing parties who are under no compulsion to act. Use of nominal values is acceptable when fair value cannot be reasonably determined.

14-122.   The Section makes a number of additional points with respect to capital assets:

- The cost should include all costs necessary to put the asset into use.

- If an asset is acquired by a not-for-profit organization, at a cost that is substantially below fair value, it should be recorded at fair value, with the difference reported as a contribution.

- The cost of a basket purchase should be allocated on the basis of the relative fair values of the assets acquired.

- The cost of self constructed or self developed assets should include direct costs of construction or development, along with any overhead costs directly attributable to the construction or development activity. In the case of self developed intangibles, future benefits may be so uncertain that recording the costs of development as an asset cannot be justified.

- A betterment should be capitalized. These are defined as service enhancements that increase capacity, lower operating costs, extend the useful life, or improve the quality of output of the asset.

14-123.   Other than the possibility of recording a contribution as part of an asset acquisition transaction, all of these suggestions are consistent with the treatment given to the capital assets of profit oriented enterprises.

Amortization

14-124.   With respect to amortization, Section 4430 contains the following Recommendation:

> **Paragraph 4430.16**   *The cost, less any residual value, of a capital asset with a limited life should be amortized over its useful life in a rational and systematic manner appropriate to its nature and use by the organization. Amortization should be recognized as an expense in the organization's statement of operations.* (April, 1997)

14-125.   This Recommendation serves to put the capital assets of not-for-profit organizations on virtually the same footing as those of profit oriented enterprises. The discussion in Section 4430 of this Recommendation is similar to that contained in Section 3061 on this subject, providing for the use of different amortization methods and encouraging the estimation of residual value in determining the amount to be written off. There is a small difference from Section 3061 in that the amortization Recommendation in Section 3061 calls for the write off of the greater of cost less salvage value over the life of the asset, and cost less residual value over the useful life of the asset.

14-126.   Section 4430 points out that, along with land, works of art and historical treasures may have virtually unlimited lives. This would suggest that amortization would not be appropriate in these circumstances. We would remind you that, if the work of art is part of a collection, the Recommendations of Section 4430 are not applicable.

14-127.   When fund accounting is used, the fund to which amortization will be charged is a matter of judgment. The common answers would be to charge these amounts to either the capital asset fund or the general fund.

14-128.   As is the case with Section 3061, Section 4430 requires a periodic review of amortization:

> **Paragraph 4430.23**   *The amortization method and the estimate of the useful life of a capital asset should be reviewed on a regular basis.* (April, 1997)

14-129.   Events that might indicate a need for revision would include the following:

- a change in the extent the capital asset is used;
- a change in the manner in which the capital asset is used;
- removal of the capital asset from service for an extended period of time;
- physical damage;
- significant technological developments; and
- a change in the law or environment affecting the period of time over which the capital asset can be used.

Future Removal And Site Restoration Costs

14-130.   Section 4430 contains a Recommendation that is identical to Section 3061's in this area:

> **Paragraph 4430.25**   *When reasonably determinable, provisions for future removal and site restoration costs, net of expected recoveries, should be recognized as expenses in a rational and systematic manner.* (April, 1997)

14-131.   Given the nature of not-for-profit organizations, we would expect that the application of this Recommendation to this type of enterprise would be relatively rare.

Write Downs

14-132.   Again following the pattern established in Section 3061, Section 4430 makes the following Recommendation in this area:

Paragraph 4430.28   *When a capital asset no longer has any long-term service potential to the organization, the excess of its net carrying amount over any residual value should be recognized as an expense in the statement of operations. A write down should not be reversed.* (April, 1997)

Disposals

14-133.   The difference between the net proceeds of a disposal and the net carrying value of an asset is normally recorded in the Statement Of Operations. If there are unamortized deferred contributions related to the capital asset disposed of, they would be recognized as revenue in the period of disposal, provided that all related restrictions have been complied with.

Presentation And Disclosure

All Capital Assets

14-134.   For all capital assets of not-for-profit organizations, the following disclosure is required:

Paragraph 4430.31   *For each major category of capital assets there should be disclosure of:*

(a) cost;
(b) accumulated amortization, including the amount of any write downs; and
(c) the amortization method used, including the amortization period or rate. (April, 1997)

Paragraph 4430.32   *The net carrying amounts of major categories of capital assets not being amortized should be disclosed.* (April, 1997)

Paragraph 4430.33   *The amount of amortization of capital assets recognized as an expense for the period should be disclosed.* (April, 1997)

Paragraph 4430.34   *The amount of any write downs of capital assets should be disclosed in the financial statements for the period in which the write downs are made.* (April, 1997)

Contributed Capital Assets

14-135.   Further Recommendations are made with respect to contributed capital assets:

Paragraph 4430.37   *The nature and amount of contributed capital assets received in the period and recognized in the financial statements should be disclosed.* (April, 1997)

Paragraph 4430.38   *Information should be disclosed about contributed capital assets recognized at nominal value.* (April, 1997)

Example 2 (Includes Capital Assets)

Basic Data

14-136.   This is an extension of the example that was presented in Paragraph 14-101. It involves the same Local Care Society (LCS) and extends their activities into the year ending December 31, 2003. It is made more complex by the addition of capital assets and their amortization. The basic data for LCS for the year ending December 31, 2003 is as follows:

Endowment Contributions   There are no additional endowment contributions during the year ending December 31, 2003. The endowment investments have income of $3,000 during this period.

Unrestricted Contributions   During the year ending December 31, 2003, $600,000 in unrestricted contributions were received. In addition, the $35,000 in contributions that were receivable at the end of 2002 are collected in full during 2003. At year end, there is an additional $40,000 in contributions that are receivable. The receivable is related to the meals activity. The Board believes that this is a reasonable estimate of the amount that will actually be collected. This $640,000 total was allocated $360,000 to the meals activity, $180,000 to the clothing activity, and $100,000 for the acquisition of a building to be used in the organization's operations.

Capital Assets   On July 1, 2003, the organization acquires a building for a total cost of $100,000. Of this total, $20,000 represents the fair value of the land on which the building is situated and the remaining $80,000 reflects the fair value of the building. The estimated useful life of the building is 10 years and no significant residual value is anticipated. The organization uses straight line amortization, charging only one-half year's amortization in the year in which an asset is acquired.

Restricted Contributions   The organization continues to accept additional contributions that are restricted to use in the clothing activity. During the year ending December 31, 2003, restricted contributions of $175,000 were received. No restricted contributions are receivable at year end.

Expenses   During the year ending December 31, 2003, the organization incurred the following expenses:

	Meals Activity	Clothing Activity
Wages And Salaries	$ 25,000	$ 20,000
Cost Of Materials Provided	210,000	230,000
Transportation Costs	35,000	15,000
Other Expenses	15,000	25,000
Total	$285,000	$290,000

It is estimated that 50 percent of the expenses related to clothing activity have been made from restricted funds. On December 31, 2003, there were outstanding Accounts Payable related to the meals activity expenses of $25,000.

Case One - No Fund Accounting
14-137.   In this Case, we will assume that LCS is not using fund accounting. This means that they will have to use the deferral method of revenue recognition. Based on this approach, the required journal entries are as follows:

Investment Income

Cash	$3,000	
Revenue - Investment Income		$3,000

Unrestricted Contributions

Cash	$35,000	
Contributions Receivable (Opening)		$35,000

Cash	$600,000	
Contributions Receivable (Closing)	40,000	
Revenue - Unrestricted Contributions		$640,000

Acquisition Of Capital Assets

Land	$20,000	
Building	80,000	
Cash		$100,000

Amortization Of Capital Assets

Amortization Expense [($80,000)(1/10)(1/2)]	$4,000	
Accumulated Amortization		$4,000

Restricted Contributions

Cash	$175,000	
Deferred Contributions		$175,000

(As the deferral method is being used, these contributions must be deferred until the related expenses are incurred.)

Expenses

Accounts Payable (Opening)	$30,000	
Cash		$30,000

Wages And Salaries ($25,000 + $20,000)	$ 45,000	
Cost Of Materials Provided ($210,000 + $230,000)	440,000	
Transportation Costs ($35,000 + $15,000)	50,000	
Other Expenses ($15,000 + $25,000)	40,000	
Cash ($285,000 + $290,000 - $25,000)		$550,000
Accounts Payable (Closing)		25,000

Amortization Of Deferred Contributions

Deferred Contributions [(50%)($290,000)]	$145,000	
Revenue - Amortization Of Deferred Contributions		$145,000

(Restricted contributions can be included in revenue to the extent of current expenses related to these contributions.)

Closing Entry

Revenue - Unrestricted Contributions	$640,000	
Revenue - Amortization Of Deferred Contributions	145,000	
Revenue - Investment Income	3,000	
Amortization Expense		$ 4,000
Wages And Salaries		45,000
Cost Of Materials Provided		440,000
Transportation Costs		50,000
Other Expenses		40,000
Net Assets - Invested In Capital Assets ($100,000 - $4,000)		96,000
Net Assets - Unrestricted ($209,000 - $96,000)		113,000

(Paragraph 4400.19 requires separate disclosure of the amount of the Net Asset balance that has been invested in capital assets. Note that the amount is disclosed net of accumulated amortization. All of the expenses and revenues would be closed to the Net Assets - Unrestricted balance at the end of the fiscal year. The $209,000 is a balancing figure that is also calculated on the Statement of Operations and Fund Balances.)

14-138.   Using these journal entries, the required financial statements would be prepared as follows:

LCS Organization
Statement Of Operations And Fund Balances
Year Ending December 31, 2003

Revenues:

Unrestricted Contributions	$640,000
Amortization Of Deferred Contributions	145,000
Investment Income	3,000
Total Revenues	**$788,000**

Expenses:

Wages And Salaries	$ 45,000
Cost Of Materials Provided	440,000
Transportation Costs	50,000
Amortization Expense [($80,000/10)(1/2)]	4,000
Other Expenses	40,000
Total Expenses	**$579,000**

Excess Of Revenues Over Expenses	$209,000
Invested In Capital Assets (Net)	(96,000)
Opening Unrestricted Net Assets	50,000
Closing Unrestricted Net Assets	**$163,000**

LCS Organization
Statement Of Cash Flows
Year Ending December 31, 2003

Cash Flows From Operating Activities:

Unrestricted Contributions ($600,000 + $35,000)	$635,000
Restricted Contributions	175,000
Investment Income	3,000
Expenses ($285,000 + $290,000 + $30,000 - $25,000)	(580,000)
Total	**$233,000**

Cash Flows From Financing And Investing:

Capital Assets Acquired	(100,000)
Increase In Cash	**$133,000**
Opening Cash Balance	74,000
Closing Cash Balance	**$207,000**

LCS Organization
Statement Of Financial Position
As At December 31, 2003

Cash (From Statement Of Cash Flows)		$207,000
Investments		50,000
Contributions Receivable		40,000
Capital Assets:		
Land		20,000
Building	$80,000	
Accumulated Amortization	(4,000)	76,000
Total Assets		**$393,000**

Accounts Payable	$ 25,000
Deferred Contributions*	59,000
Net Assets:	
Restricted For Endowment Purposes	50,000
Invested In Capital Assets	96,000
Unrestricted	163,000
Total Equities	$393,000

*Unamortized deferred contributions amount is calculated as follows:

Balance - December 31, 2002	$ 29,000
Additions	175,000
Expenses Incurred [(50%)($290,000)]	(145,000)
Balance - December 31, 2003	$ 59,000

Case Two - Restricted Fund Accounting

14-139.   In this Case, we will assume that LCS establishes separate funds for endowment contributions, restricted clothing activity contributions, and a general fund. Capital assets will be accounted for in the general fund. Given this classification of funds, the organization will be able to use the restricted fund basis of revenue recognition. With the use of fund accounting, separate journal entries will have to be made for each of the defined funds.

Endowment Fund Entries

No entries are required in the endowment fund as, during 2003, no new contributions were received and no new investments were made.

General Fund Entries

Investment Income

Cash	$3,000	
Revenue - Investment Income		$3,000

(The entry is in the general fund as there are no restrictions on the use of this income)

Unrestricted Contributions

Cash	$35,000	
Contributions Receivable (Opening)		$35,000

Cash	$600,000	
Contributions Receivable (Closing)	40,000	
Revenue - Unrestricted Contributions		$640,000

Acquisition Of Capital Assets

Land	$20,000	
Building	80,000	
Cash		$100,000

Amortization Of Capital Assets

Amortization Expense [($80,000)(1/10)(1/2)]	$4,000	
Accumulated Amortization		$4,000

Expenses

Accounts Payable (Opening)	$30,000	
Cash		$30,000

Wages And Salaries [$25,000 + (50%)$20,000)]	$ 35,000	
Cost Of Materials Provided [$210,000 + (50%)($230,000)]	325,000	
Transportation Costs [($35,000 + (50%)($15,000)]	42,500	
Other Expenses [$15,000 + (50%)($25,000)]	27,500	
Cash [$285,000 + (50%)($290,000) - $25,000)]		$405,000
Accounts Payable (Closing)		25,000

Closing Entry - General Fund

Revenue - Unrestricted Contributions	$640,000	
Revenue - Investment Income	3,000	
Amortization Expense		$ 4,000
Wages And Salaries		35,000
Cost Of Materials Provided		325,000
Transportation Costs		42,500
Other Expenses		27,500
Fund Balances - Invested In Capital Assets		96,000
Fund Balances - Unrestricted		113,000

(As in Case One, the $209,000 increase in the general fund's balance must be allocated to both an unrestricted amount and to an amount invested in capital assets.)

Restricted Fund Entries

Restricted Contributions

Cash	$175,000	
Revenues - Restricted Contributions		$175,000

(As the restricted fund method is being used, all of these contributions can be included in the revenues of the current period.)

Expenses

Wages And Salaries [(50%)($20,000)]	$ 10,000	
Cost Of Materials Provided [(50%)($230,000)]	115,000	
Transportation Costs [(50%)($15,000)]	7,500	
Other Expenses [(50%)($25,000)]	12,500	
Cash [(50%)($290,000)]		$145,000

Closing Entry - Restricted Fund

Revenue - Restricted Contributions	$175,000	
Wages And Salaries		$ 10,000
Cost Of Materials Provided		115,000
Transportation Costs		7,500
Other Expenses		12,500
Fund Balance - Restricted For Clothing		30,000

14-140. Using the preceding journal entries, the required financial statements can be prepared as follows:

LCS Organization
Statement Of Operations And Fund Balances
Year Ending December 31, 2003

	General Fund	Restricted Fund	Endowment Fund
Revenues:			
Unrestricted Contributions	$640,000		
Restricted Contributions		$175,000	
Investment Income	3,000		
Total Revenues	$643,000	$175,000	Nil
Expenses:*			
Wages And Salaries	$ 35,000	$ 10,000	
Cost Of Materials Provided	325,000	115,000	
Transportation Costs	42,500	7,500	
Amortization Expense	4,000	-0-	
Other Expenses	27,500	12,500	
Total Expenses	$434,000	$145,000	Nil
Excess Of Revenues Over Expenses	$209,000	$ 30,000	Nil
Invested In Capital Assets (Net)	(96,000)		
Opening Fund Balances	50,000	29,000	$50,000
Closing Fund Balances	$163,000	$ 59,000	$50,000

*All of the meals activity expenses, plus 50 percent of the clothing activity expenses have been allocated to the general fund. The restricted fund has been allocated 50 percent of the clothing activity expenses.

LCS Organization
Statement Of Cash Flows
Year Ending December 31, 2003

	General Fund	Restricted Fund	Endowment Fund
Cash Flows From Operating Activities:			
Unrestricted Contributions	$635,000		
Restricted Contributions		$175,000	
Investment Income	3,000		
Expenses	(435,000)	(145,000)	
Total	$203,000	$ 30,000	Nil
Cash Flows From Financing And Investing:			
Capital Assets Acquired	(100,000)		
Increase In Cash	$103,000	$ 30,000	Nil
Opening Cash Balance	45,000	29,000	Nil
Closing Cash Balance	$148,000	$ 59,000	Nil

LCS Organization
Statement Of Financial Position
As At December 31, 2003

	General Fund	Restricted Fund	Endowment Fund	Total
Cash (From Statement Of Cash Flows)	$148,000	$59,000		$207,000
Investments			$50,000	50,000
Contributions Receivable	40,000			40,000
Capital Assets:				
Land	20,000			20,000
Building	80,000			80,000
Accumulated Amortization	(4,000)			(4,000)
Total	$284,000	$59,000	$50,000	$393,000
Accounts Payable	$ 25,000			$ 25,000
Fund Balances:				
Restricted For Clothing		$59,000		59,000
Restricted For Endowment			$50,000	50,000
Invested In Capital Assets (Net)	96,000			96,000
Unrestricted	163,000			163,000
Total	$284,000	$59,000	$50,000	$393,000

14-141.   As was noted in our first example, when the restricted fund method is used, all-fund totals are required only in the Statement Of Financial Position.

Case Three - Fund Accounting On Other Basis

14-142.   This final version of our Case will also assume that LCS uses fund accounting. However, it will not qualify for the restricted fund method of revenue recognition as it classifies its funds by programs rather than by restrictions. They will use a general fund, a meals activity fund, and a clothing activity fund. Endowment funds will be accounted for through the general fund.

General Fund Entries

Investment Income

Cash	$3,000	
Revenue - Investment Income		$3,000

(The entry is in the general fund as there are no restrictions on the use of this income)

Unrestricted Contributions

Cash	$100,000	
Revenue - Unrestricted Contributions		$100,000

(The remaining unrestricted contributions, including those that are still receivable, have been allocated to the meals and clothing funds.)

Acquisition Of Capital Assets

Land	$20,000	
Building	80,000	
Cash		$100,000

Amortization Of Capital Assets

Amortization Expense [($80,000)(1/10)(1/2)]	$4,000	
Accumulated Amortization		$4,000

Closing Entry - General Fund

Revenue - Unrestricted Contributions	$100,000	
Revenue - Investment Income	3,000	
Amortization Expense		$ 4,000
Fund Balances - Unrestricted		3,000
Fund Balances - Invested In Capital Assets		96,000

(The increase in the general fund balance from operations is $99,000 and $96,000 of this amount must be allocated to a separate account for investments in capital assets.)

Meals Fund Entries

Unrestricted Contributions

Cash	$35,000	
Contributions Receivable (Opening)		$35,000

Cash	$330,000	
Contributions Receivable (Closing)	30,000	
Revenue - Unrestricted Contributions		$360,000

Expenses

Accounts Payable (Opening)	$30,000	
Cash		$30,000

Wages And Salaries	$ 25,000	
Cost Of Materials Provided	210,000	
Transportation Costs	35,000	
Other Expenses	15,000	
Cash		$260,000
Accounts Payable (Closing)		25,000

Closing Entry - Meals Fund

Revenue - Unrestricted Contributions	$360,000	
Wages And Salaries		$ 25,000
Cost Of Materials Provided		210,000
Transportation Costs		35,000
Other Expenses		15,000
Fund Balances - Unrestricted		75,000

Clothing Fund Entries

Unrestricted Contributions

Cash	$180,000	
Revenue - Unrestricted Contributions		$180,000

Restricted Contributions

Cash	$175,000	
Deferred Contributions		$175,000

(As the deferral method is being used, the recognition of these contributions as revenue must be deferred.)

Expenses

Wages And Salaries	$ 20,000	
Cost Of Materials Provided	230,000	
Transportation Costs	15,000	
Other Expenses	25,000	
Cash		$290,000

Amortization Of Deferred Contributions

Deferred Contributions	$145,000	
Revenue - Restricted Contributions		$145,000

(The deferred contributions can be recognized as revenue to the extent that they have been used in the current period to incur expenses.)

Closing Entry

Revenue - Unrestricted Contributions	$180,000	
Revenue - Restricted Contributions	145,000	
Wages And Salaries		$ 20,000
Cost Of Materials Provided		230,000
Transportation Costs		15,000
Other Expenses		25,000
Fund Balance - Unrestricted		35,000

(The addition to the Fund Balance - Unrestricted reflects the $180,000 in unrestricted contributions, less the $145,000 [($290,000)(50%)] in expenses that were not paid for out of restricted contributions.)

14-143. Using the preceding journal entries, the required financial statements can be prepared as follows:

LCS Organization
Statement Of Operations And Fund Balances
Year Ending December 31, 2003

	General Fund	Meals Activity Fund	Clothing Activity Fund	Total
Revenues:				
Unrestricted Contributions	$100,000	$360,000	$180,000	$640,000
Restricted Contributions			145,000	145,000
Investment Income	3,000			3,000
Total Revenues	$103,000	$360,000	$325,000	$788,000
Expenses:				
Wages And Salaries		$ 25,000	$ 20,000	$ 45,000
Cost Of Materials Provided		210,000	230,000	440,000
Transportation Costs		35,000	15,000	50,000
Amortization Expense	$ 4,000			4,000
Other Expenses		15,000	25,000	40,000
Total Expenses	$ 4,000	$285,000	$290,000	$579,000
Excess Of Revenues				
Over Expenses	$ 99,000	$ 75,000	$ 35,000	$209,000
Invested In Capital Assets	(96,000)			(96,000)
Opening Unrestricted				
Fund Balances	4,000	40,000	6,000	50,000
Closing Unrestricted Fund Balances	$ 7,000	$115,000	$ 41,000	$163,000

LCS Organization
Statement Of Cash Flows
Year Ending December 31, 2003

	General Fund	Meals Activity Fund	Clothing Activity Fund	Total
Cash Flows From Operating Activities				
Unrestricted Contributions*	$100,000	$355,000	$180,000	$635,000
Restricted Contributions			175,000	175,000
Investment Income	3,000			3,000
Expenses*		(290,000)	(290,000)	(580,000)
Total	$103,000	$ 65,000	$ 65,000	$233,000
Cash Flows From Financing And Investing:				
Capital Assets Acquired	(100,000)			(100,000)
Increase In Cash	$ 3,000	$ 65,000	$ 65,000	$133,000
Opening Cash Balance	4,000	35,000	35,000	74,000
Closing Cash Balance	$ 7,000	$100,000	$100,000	$207,000

LCS Organization
Statement Of Financial Position
As At December 31, 2003

	General Fund	Meals Activity Fund	Clothing Activity Fund	Total
Cash (From Statement Of Cash Flows)	$ 7,000	$100,000	$100,000	$207,000
Investments	50,000			50,000
Contributions Receivable*		40,000		40,000
Capital Assets				
Land	20,000			20,000
Building	80,000			80,000
Accumulated Amortization	(4,000)			(4,000)
Total	$153,000	$140,000	$100,000	$393,000
Accounts Payable*		$ 25,000		$ 25,000
Deferred Contributions			$ 59,000	59,000
Fund Balances:				
Restricted For Endowment	$ 50,000			50,000
Invested In Capital Assets	96,000			96,000
Unrestricted	7,000	115,000	41,000	163,000
Total	$153,000	$140,000	$100,000	$393,000

*All of the receivables and payables have been allocated to the meals activity fund. The Unrestricted Contributions of $355,000 have been adjusted for the contributions receivable ($360,000 + $35,000 - $40,000). The expenses of $290,000 allocated to the meals activity fund have been adjusted for the Accounts Payable ($285,000 + $30,000 - $25,000).

14-144. Note that, when fund accounting is used with the deferral method, all-fund totals must be included for all of the financial statements. This is in contrast to fund accounting with the restricted fund method. In this latter case, all-fund totals are only required for the Statement Of Financial Position.

Reporting Controlled And Related Entities
Handbook Section 4450

Background

14-145.   The accounting Recommendations applicable to profit oriented enterprises provide detailed guidance on accounting for various types of related entities. Section 4450 is designed to provide similar guidance for the related entities of not-for-profit organizations. Prior to the introduction of this Section, there was often little or no disclosure of the various related entities that a not-for-profit organization might either control or influence. Further, when disclosure was provided, there was little consistency between organizations as to the type of disclosure that they provided.

14-146.   Section 4450 deals with these issues. While it does not require the consolidation of all controlled affiliates, it specifies the disclosure that is required when consolidation is not used for these entities. It also deals with the presentation and disclosure that is required when a not-for-profit organization participates in joint venture arrangements, or has significant influence over another organization.

Related Entities Defined

14-147.   Section 4450 begins by defining possible relationships between a not-for-profit organization and other related entities. These definitions are found in Paragraph 4450.02 as follows:

Control of an entity is the continuing power to determine its strategic operating, investing and financing policies without the co-operation of others.

Joint control of an economic activity is the contractually agreed sharing of the continuing power to determine its strategic operating, investing and financing policies.

A **joint venture** is an economic activity resulting from a contractual arrangement whereby two or more venturers jointly control the economic activity.

Significant influence over an entity is the ability to affect the strategic operating, investing and financing policies of the entity.

An **economic interest** in another not-for-profit organization exists if:

(i)   the other organization holds resources that must be used to produce revenue or provide services for the reporting organization; or

(ii)   the reporting organization is responsible for the liabilities of the other organization.

14-148.   The definitions related to control, joint control, and significant influence are the same as those used by profit oriented enterprises and, as such, require no further explanation. However, the concept of "economic interest" is unique to the not-for-profit accounting area and, as a consequence, warrants further discussion.

14-150.   While the preceding definition lays out the general rules for determining economic interest, Paragraph 4450.10 provides further guidance by listing possible indicators of such an interest:

(a)   The other organization solicits funds in the name of and with the expressed or implied approval of the reporting organization, and substantially all of the funds solicited are intended by the contributor or are otherwise required to be transferred to the reporting organization or used at its discretion or direction;

(b)   The reporting organization transfers significant resources to the other organization, whose resources are held for the benefit of the reporting organization;

(c) The other organization is required to perform significant functions on behalf of the reporting organization that are integral to the reporting organization's achieving its objectives; or

(d) The reporting organization guarantees significant liabilities of the other organization.

14-151.   The Section also notes that economic interests can exist in varying degrees of significance. There are situations where the relationship is such that the reporting organization would not be able to function in its current form without the organization in which it has an economic interest. In such cases, the existence of the economic interest may be a strong indicator that control exists. In contrast, some economic interests are much more limited and exist without the reporting entity having control or even significant influence.

14-152.   Factors to be considered in the determination of economic interest would include whether the other organization is required to transfer resources or perform functions for the reporting organization. Further, externally imposed restrictions on the other organization's assets could create an economic interest. However, a funding relationship where the other organization is not obliged to provide resources to the reporting organization is usually not considered to be an economic interest. Similarly, a situation where another organization holds fund raising events from time to time for the benefit of the reporting organization does not automatically create an economic interest.

14-153.   With these definitions in mind, we can now deal with Section 4450's specific Recommendations concerning entities that are related to a not-for-profit organization.

Controlled Not-For-Profit Organizations
Basic Recommendation
14-154.   Section 4450 is permissive with respect to the accounting to be used by a not-for-profit organization in accounting for controlled not-for-profit organizations. It allows the reporting entity to choose between three different alternatives:

Paragraph 4450.14   *An organization should report each controlled not-for-profit organization in one of the following ways:*

(a) *by consolidating the controlled organization in its financial statements;*

(b) *by providing the disclosure set out in paragraph 4450.22; or*

(c) *if the controlled organization is one of a large number of individually immaterial organizations, by providing the disclosure set out in paragraph 4450.26. (April, 1997)*

14-155.   The first and probably best choice on this list is consolidation. If the controlling organization rejects this alternative, it must provide the following disclosure for the not-for-profit organization that is controlled:

Paragraph 4450.22   *For each controlled not-for-profit organization or group of similar controlled organizations not consolidated in the reporting organization's financial statements, the following should be disclosed, unless the group of controlled organizations is comprised of a large number of individually immaterial organizations (see paragraph 4450.26):*

(a) *total assets, liabilities and net assets at the reporting date;*

(b) *revenues (including gains), expenses (including losses) and cash flows from operating, financing and investing activities reported in the period;*

(c) *details of any restrictions, by major category, on the resources of the controlled organizations; and*

(d) *significant differences in accounting policies from those followed by the reporting organization. (April, 1997)*

14-156. Note that there is no mention of using the equity method here. As the controlled entity is a not-for-profit organization, it is unlikely to have equity interests outstanding. In the absence of a measurable equity interest, the equity method cannot be used.

14-157. A final possibility for dealing with controlled not-for-profit organizations is as follows:

Paragraph 4450.26 *An organization may exclude a group of controlled organizations from both consolidation and the disclosure set out in paragraph 4450.22, provided that*

(a) *the group of organizations is comprised of a large number of organizations that are individually immaterial; and*

(b) *the reporting organization discloses the reasons why the controlled organizations have been neither consolidated nor included in the disclosure set out in paragraph 4450.22.* (April, 1997)

14-158. This, in effect, allows a not-for-profit organization to provide no disclosure of a group of controlled entities. Judgment would be required in applying this provision. However, it would be applicable in situations where the number of controlled entities is so large that the de facto exercise of control is not practically feasible.

Consolidated Financial Statements

14-159. The preparation of consolidated financial statements is covered in Section 1600 of the *CICA Handbook*. Most of the procedures listed there will be fully applicable to preparing these statements in the context of not-for-profit organizations. However, the fact that not-for-profit organizations usually do not have a transferable ownership interest may necessitate some modification of these procedures.

Other Considerations

14-160. The Section notes that control may or may not be accompanied by an economic interest. If such an interest is present, its nature and extent must be disclosed.

14-161. As an additional point, there is no requirement for consistency in the application of Paragraph 4450.14. A not-for-profit organization could choose to consolidate some controlled entities, while choosing only to provide additional disclosure for other similar controlled entities.

Controlled Profit Oriented Enterprises

14-162. Because profit oriented enterprises will have a transferable ownership interest, the equity method becomes a feasible alternative. For this type of controlled enterprise, the not-for-profit organization can choose between two alternatives:

Paragraph 4450.30 *An organization should report each controlled profit oriented enterprise in either of the following ways:*

(a) *by consolidating the controlled enterprise in its financial statements; or*
(b) *by accounting for its investment in the controlled enterprise using the equity method and providing the disclosure set out in paragraph 4450.32.* (April, 1997)

14-163. Without regard to the method chosen, disclosure is required as follows:

Paragraph 4450.31 *For a controlled profit oriented enterprise, regardless of whether it is consolidated or accounted for using the equity method, the following should be disclosed:*

(a) *the policy followed in reporting the controlled enterprise; and*
(b) *a description of the relationship with the controlled enterprise.* (April, 1997)

14-164. If the equity method is chosen, additional disclosure requirements are applicable:

Paragraph 4450.32   *For each controlled profit oriented enterprise or group of similar controlled enterprises accounted for using the equity method, the following should be disclosed:*

(a) *total assets, liabilities and shareholders' equity at the reporting date; and*
(b) *revenues (including gains), expenses (including losses), net income and cash flows from operating, financing and investing activities reported in the period.* (April, 1997)

Joint Ventures

14-165.   A choice of two methods of accounting is available to not-for-profit organizations that participate in joint venture arrangements:

Paragraph 4450.36   *An organization should report each interest in a joint venture in either of the following ways:*

(a) *by accounting for its interest using the proportionate consolidation method in accordance with "Interests In Joint Ventures", Section 3055; or*
(b) *by accounting for its interest using the equity method and disclosing the information set out in paragraph 4450.38.* (April, 1997)

14-166. Whether the choice is proportionate consolidation or the use of the equity method, the following disclosure must be provided:

Paragraph 4450.37   *For an interest in a joint venture, regardless of whether it is reported using the proportionate consolidation or the equity method, the following should be disclosed:*

(a) *the policy followed in reporting the interest; and*
(b) *a description of the relationship with the joint venture.* (April, 1997)

14-167.   As was the case with controlled profit oriented enterprises, additional disclosure is required when the equity method is used:

Paragraph 4450.38   *For each interest in a joint venture, or group of similar interests, accounted for using the equity method, the following should be disclosed:*

(a) *the reporting organization's share of the joint venture's total assets, liabilities and net assets, or shareholders' equity, at the reporting date;*

(b) *the reporting organization's share of the joint venture's revenues (including gains), expenses (including losses), and cash flows from operating, financing and investing activities reported in the period; and*

(c) *significant differences in accounting policies from those followed by the reporting organization.* (April, 1997)

Significantly Influenced Not-For-Profit Organizations

14-168.   The required presentation and disclosure for this type of related entity is as follows:

Paragraph 4450.40   *When the reporting organization has significant influence in another not-for-profit organization, the following should be disclosed:*

(a) *a description of the relationship with the significantly influenced organization;*
(b) *a clear and concise description of the significantly influenced organization's purpose, its intended community of service, its status under income tax legislation and its legal form; and*
(c) *the nature and extent of any economic interest that the reporting organization has in the significantly influenced organization.* (April, 1997)

14-169.   The fact that the equity method is not required here once again reflects the fact that most not-for-profit organizations do not have a transferable ownership interest.

Significantly Influenced Profit Oriented Enterprises

14-170.   Reflecting the fact that profit oriented enterprises will have a transferable ownership interest, the Section 4450 Recommendation here requires the use of the equity method:

Paragraph 4450.43   *When the reporting organization has significant influence over a profit oriented enterprise, the investment should be accounted for using the equity method in accordance with "Long-Term Investments", Section 3050. (April, 1997)*

Disclosure Of Economic Interest

14-171.   When a not-for-profit organization has an economic interest in a related entity, the following disclosure is required:

Paragraph 4450.45   *When an organization has an economic interest in another not-for-profit organization over which it does not have control or significant influence, the nature and extent of this interest should be disclosed. (April, 1997)*

Information At Different Dates

14-172.   When the financial statements of the not-for-profit organization and the related entity are not based on the same fiscal period, the following disclosure is required:

Paragraph 4450.47   *When the fiscal periods of the reporting organization and the other entity do not substantially coincide, the financial information required to be disclosed in accordance with paragraph 4450.22, .32 or .38 should be as at the other entity's most recent reporting date and the following should be disclosed:*

(a) the reporting period covered by the financial information; and

(b) the details of any events or transactions in the intervening period that are significant to the reporting organization's financial position or results of operations. (April, 1997)

Disclosure Of Related Party Transactions By Not-For-Profit Organizations
Handbook Section 4460

Purpose

14-173.   This final *Handbook* Section on not-for-profit organizations is concerned with the disclosure of related party transactions. It is analogous to Section 3840 which deals with the related party transactions of profit oriented enterprises. As is the case with Section 3840, this Section does not apply to management compensation arrangements, expense allowances, or other payments to individuals in the normal course of operations.

Definitions

14-174.   Section 4460 contains definitions for not-for-profit organizations, control, joint control, significant influence, and economic interest, that are identical to those found in Section 4450, "Reporting Controlled And Related Entities By Not-For-Profit Organizations". It also contains the same definition of fair value as is found in Section 4430, "Capital Assets Held By Not-For-Profit Organizations". These definitions will not be repeated here. Definitions in this Section that have not been previously presented are as follows:

Related parties exist when one party has the ability to exercise, directly or indirectly, control, joint control or significant influence over the other. Two or more parties are related when they are subject to common control, joint control or common significant influence. Two not-for-profit organizations are related parties if one has an economic interest in the other. Related parties also include management and immediate family members.

A **related party transaction** is a transfer of economic resources or obligations between related parties, or the provision of services by one party to a related party, regardless of whether any consideration is exchanged. The parties to the transaction are related prior to the transaction. When the relationship arises as a result of the transaction, the transaction is not one between related parties.

Identification Of Related Parties

14-175. The Section provides guidance with respect to the identification of related parties. It is expressed in terms of commonly encountered related parties:

Paragraph 4460.04 The most commonly encountered related parties of a reporting organization include the following:

(a) an entity that directly, or indirectly through one or more intermediaries, controls, or is controlled by, or is under common control with, the reporting organization;

(b) an individual who directly, or indirectly through one or more intermediaries, controls the reporting organization;

(c) an entity that, directly or indirectly, is significantly influenced by the reporting organization or has significant influence over the reporting organization or is under common significant influence with the reporting organization;

(d) the other organization when one organization has an economic interest in the other;

(e) management: any person(s) having authority and responsibility for planning, directing and controlling the activities of the reporting organization. (Management would include the directors, officers and other persons fulfilling a senior management function.)

(f) an individual that has either significant influence or joint control over the reporting organization;

(g) members of the immediate family of individuals described in paragraphs (b), (e) and (f). (Immediate family comprises an individual's spouse and those dependent on either the individual or the individual's spouse.);

(h) the other party, when a management contract or other management authority exists and the reporting organization is either the managing or managed party; and

(i) any party that is subject to joint control by the reporting organization (In this instance a party subject to joint control is related to each of the venturers that share that joint control. However, the venturers themselves are not related to one another solely by virtue of sharing of joint control.).

14-176. Those of you familiar with Section 3840 which provides Recommendations with respect to the related party transactions of profit oriented enterprises, will recognize that this list is very similar to the list that is found in that Section. If you would like to compare these lists, Chapter 51 of our *Guide To Canadian Financial Reporting* provides comprehensive coverage of that Section. This *Guide* is available on the CD-ROM which accompanies this text.

Disclosure

General Recommendation

14-177. Section 4460 makes the following Recommendation with respect to the disclosure of related party transactions:

Paragraph 4460.07 *An organization should disclose the following information about its transactions with related parties:*

(a) *a description of the relationship between the transacting parties;*

(b) *a description of the transaction(s), including those for which no amount has been recorded;*

(c) *the recorded amount of the transactions classified by financial statement category;*

(d) *the measurement basis used for recognizing the transaction in the financial statements;*

(e) *amounts due to or from related parties and the terms and conditions relating thereto;*

(f) *contractual obligations with related parties, separate from other contractual obligations;*

(g) *contingencies involving related parties, separate from other contingencies.* (April, 1997)

Description Of The Relationship

14-178.   The Section encourages the use of accurate terminology when complying with Paragraph 4460.07(a). Terms such as controlled organization, significantly influenced organization, or organization under common control, are preferable to more general descriptions such as affiliate or associate. Disclosure here should include a description of the manner in which control or influence is exercised.

Description Of Transactions

14-179.   A description of all transactions, including information about the nature of any items exchanged, is required by Paragraph 4460.07(b). As noted in that Paragraph, this would include transactions, for example an exchange of management services, for which no amounts are recorded in the accounting records.

Amounts And Measurement

14-180.   As with Section 3840 for profit oriented enterprises, Section 4460 requires not-for-profit organizations to disclose the aggregate amount of related party transactions, along with the measurement basis used in recording them. This is particularly important here because, unlike Section 3840, Section 4460 does not include Recommendations with respect to how such related party transactions should be measured.

Other Disclosure Considerations

14-181.   Section 4460 makes the following additional points with respect to the disclosure of the related party transactions of not-for-profit organizations:

• When there are amounts due to and from related parties, disclosure includes the relationship between the parties, as well as the nature of the transactions that created the balances.

• When transactions occur between two organizations both of which will be included in the consolidated financial statements, the transactions will be completely eliminated from the financial statements. This means that no disclosure of such transactions will be required. However, when the equity method is used to account for a related party, any profit or loss on the transaction will be eliminated, but the other components of the transaction will remain in the records of the related organizations. As a result, disclosure will be required in this type of situation.

• In disclosing a not-for-profit organization's contractual obligations and contingencies, Section 3280, "Contractual Obligations", and Section 3290, "Contingencies", would be applicable. Separate disclosure is required for the contractual obligations and contingencies of related parties.

Other Concepts

Budgetary Control

14-182.   Budgets are of importance to all types of organizations, whether they are profit oriented, not-for-profit, or government organizations. Reflecting this situation is the fact that a variety of procedures exist to assist management track and control both expenses and revenues. With respect to profit oriented enterprises, these procedures are never reflected in the actual financial statements that are presented to users.

14-183.   However, not-for-profit organizations sometimes record budgeted amounts in their accounting records. For example, an organization with budgeted revenues of $2,500,000 and budgeted expenses of $2,400,000, might make the following entry:

Budgeted Revenues	$2,500,000	
Budgeted Fund Balance		$ 100,000
Budgeted Expenses		2,400,000

14-184.   This entry would establish a sort of fund that could be used to make ongoing comparisons between actual and budgeted figures. In most cases, these amounts would be closed out at the end of the year and would not be included in published financial statements. Given that these amounts do not form a component of the financial reporting process, we do not believe that they warrant further coverage in this text.

Encumbrance System

14-185.   A set of procedures referred to as an encumbrance system is used by some not-for-profit organizations as a control mechanism. Normally, the acquisition of goods and services is not recorded in the accounts until the items are delivered or services received. Under an encumbrance system, and entry is made at the time a purchase order is issued.

> **Example**   On January 10, 2002, Ardvan issues a purchase order for merchandise that is expected to cost $1,850. On January 31, 2002, the goods are received along with an invoice for $1,923.

> **Example Solution**   The journal entry that would be made at the time the purchase order is issued would be as follows:

Encumbrances	$1,850	
Estimated Commitments		$1,850

When the goods are delivered, they would be recorded with the usual entry, followed by a reversal of the encumbrance entry:

Merchandise	$1,923	
Accounts Payable		$1,923
Estimated Commitments	$1,850	
Encumbrances		$1,850

14-186.   The basic idea behind these procedures is to provide control over expenses. It is believed that if the not-for-profit organization records its commitment, it is less likely to go over the amounts that it has budgeted for expenses.

14-187.   A problem arises at the end of the period in that there will usually be outstanding commitments and these will be reflected in the encumbrance system accounts. However, these accounts reflect purchase commitments. Such commitments are executory contracts and should not be recorded in the financial statements (an exception to that is made for certain leasing arrangements under Section 3065 of the *CICA Handbook*).

14-188.   As an encumbrance system balances internal matters that should not be part of the financial reporting process, we will give this subject no further attention in this material.

Example From Practice

14-189.   This example is from the annual report of Canadian Cancer Society for the reporting period ending September 30, 2001. Included are the four financial statements as well as part of the notes to the financial statements.

Consolidated Statement of Resources
(In thousands of dollars)

September 30, 2001, with comparative figures for 2000

	2001	2000
Assets		
Current assets:		
Cash	$ 6,509	$ 8,851
Accounts receivable	2,264	1,647
Prepaid expenses	4,027	1,454
Investments	47,235	34,278
	60,035	46,230
Deferred pension costs	1,187	1,894
Capital assets (note 2)	11,339	11,664
	$72,561	$59,788
Liabilities and Resources		
Current liabilities:		
Accounts payable	$ 3,827	$ 3,485
Research contribution payable to		
National Cancer Institute of Canada	7,964	3,441
Deferred revenue	3,905	2,760
	15,696	9,686
Obligation for post-retirement benefits other than pensions	5,701	4,915
Resources:		
Externally restricted	4,520	2,758
Invested in capital assets	11,339	11,664
Internally restricted	20,308	18,435
Unrestricted	14,997	12,330
	51,164	45,187
Commitments (note 6)		
	$72,561	$59,788

Consolidated Statement of Financial Activities - Operations and Externally Restricted Resources
(In thousands of dollars)

Year ended September 30, 2001, with comparative figures for 2000

	Operations		Externally restricted	
	2001	2000	2001	2000
Revenue:				
Annual giving	$43,902	$42,941	$19	$491
Special events, gross revenue	25,515	22,187	3,932	–
In memoriam	13,526	13,415	9	10
Major and planned gifts	29,678	23,657	584	150
Other income	5,868	5,601	992	178
Investment income	2,968	2,857	147	123
	121,457	110,658	5,683	952
Expenditures:				
Grants and fellowships:				
Research grants - National Cancer Institute of Canada (note 3)	43,194	42,465	–	–
Research grants to other organizations	100	50	252	605
Fellowships and professional education	524	318	23	11
Grants to lodges and health centres	3,394	2,828	–	–
	47,212	45,661	275	616
Functional disbursements:				
Public education	13,641	11,797	604	402
Patient services	19,988	17,074	277	277
Fundraising - general	22,619	20,887	94	34
Fundraising - special events	5,158	4,418	3,323	–
Administration	7,248	6,356	17	18
	68,654	60,532	4,315	731
	115,866	106,193	4,590	1,347
Excess (deficiency) of revenue over expenditures before the undernoted	5,591	4,465	1,093	(395)
Pension expense	707	562	–	–
Increase (decrease) in resources	$4,884	$3,903	$1,093	$(395)

Consolidated Statement of Changes in Resources
(In thousands of dollars)

Year ended September 30, 2001, with comparative figures for 2000

					2001	2000
	Externally restricted	Invested in capital assets	Internally restricted	Unre-stricted	Total	Total
Resource balances, beginning of year	$2,758	$11,664	$18,435	$12,330	$45,187	$41,679
Increase (decrease) in resources	1,093	(2,223)	(402)	7,509	5,977	3,508
Additions to capital assets	–	1,898	(332)	(1,566)	–	–
Appropriations (note 4)	669	–	2,607	(3,276)	–	–
Resource balances, end of year	$4,520	$11,339	$20,308	$14,997	$51,164	$45,187

Consolidated Statement of Cash Flows
(In thousands of dollars)
Year ended September 30, 2001, with comparative figures for 2000

	2001	2000
Cash provided by (used in):		
Operating activities:		
Increase in resources	$ 5,977	$3,508
Items not involving cash:		
Amortization of capital assets	2,223	1,804
Decrease in deferred pension costs	707	562
Increase (decrease) in deferred revenue	1,145	(222)
Increase in obligation for post-retirement benefits other than pensions	786	559
Change in non-cash operating working capital	1,675	2,877
	12,513	9,088
Investing activities:		
Capital asset additions	(1,898)	(2,133)
Increase in investments	(12,957)	(3,924)
	(14,855)	(6,057)
Increase (decrease) in cash	(2,342)	3,031
Cash, beginning of year	8,851	5,820
Cash, end of year	$ 6,509	$ 8,851

Notes To Consolidated Financial Statements

The Canadian Cancer Society is incorporated under the Canada Corporations Act as a non-profit organization without share capital and is a registered charity under the Income Tax Act. The Society is a national, community-based organization of volunteers, whose mission is the eradication of cancer and the enhancement of the quality of life of people living with cancer. The Society, in partnership with the National Cancer Institute of Canada, achieves its mission through programs of research, education, patient services and advocacy for healthy public policy. These efforts are supported by volunteers and staff and funds raised in communities across Canada.

1. Significant accounting policies:

(a) Basis of presentation:

These financial statements include the financial activities and financial position of the 10 provincial Divisions and the National Operations of the Canadian Cancer Society. The presentation of financial statements in conformity with generally accepted accounting principles requires management to make estimates and assumptions that affect the reported amount of assets and liabilities and disclosure of contingent assets and liabilities at the date of the financial statements and revenue and expenses for the year reported. Actual results could differ from those estimates.

(b) Fund accounting:

The Society follows the restricted fund method of accounting for contributions.

Resources are classified as follows:

Externally restricted	Resources in respect of which a donor or testator has specified restrictions as to their use.
Invested in capital assets	Resources which have been invested in capital assets and therefore not available for other purposes.
Internally restricted	Resources which have been allocated for specific purposes by the Society.
Unrestricted	Resources available for general operating purposes, such as program delivery, administration and fundraising activities.

(c) Revenue and expenditures:
(i) Revenue:

Revenue from campaign and in memoriam donations are recognized on a cash basis, with no accrual being made for amounts pledged but not received.

Special events revenue is recognized on completion of the event.

The Society is the beneficiary under various wills and trust agreements. The total realizable amounts are not at present readily determinable. The Society recognizes such bequests when the proceeds are received.

Investment income is recognized on an accrual basis.

Donor payments on life insurance policies and life annuities which vest irrevocably with the Society and which are tax receipted by the Society are recognized as an investment and as deferred revenue until such time when the proceeds are received, at which point, they are recognized as revenue.

(ii) Expenditures:

Fellowships and grants may be awarded and contracts entered into for a period covering more than one fiscal year. The statement of financial activities reflects only that portion of fellowships, grants or contracts payable during the current fiscal year.

Expenditures of a functional nature are charged to public education, patient services, administration or revenue development according to the activity which they benefit. Certain expenditures benefit more than as one functional activity and, accordingly, are pro rated on a predetermined basis. A policy exists that enforces annual review and approval of the basis of allocation for all expenditures. As well, the predetermined basis of allocation may be revised according to circumstance prevailing at any given time.

Expenditures are charged as follows:

(a) Public education:

Expenses incurred to improve knowledge about prevention and early detection of cancer by providing information and skill development through programs, advocacy and collaboration.

(b) Patient services:

Expenses incurred to improve the quality of life of people with cancer, their family and friends. A range of services has evolved to meet the social, spiritual, information and emotional needs of people with cancer. The services provided vary from province to province, but may include emotional support, dissemination of information, transportation and practical assistance.

(c) Fundraising:

Expenses incurred in the generation of donation revenue to provide the means to further the Society's mission. Included in fundraising expenses are costs related to the residential canvass, special events, in memoriam and gift planning activities.

(d) Administration:

Expenses incurred to operate the organization and its programs in a cost-effective manner while maximizing all opportunities to further the Society's mission. Administration costs which relate specifically to public education, patient services or fundraising are allocated to these respective expense categories.

(d) Investments:
Investments are recorded at cost, which approximates market value and consist primarily of banker's acceptances, government bonds, and guaranteed investment certificates.

(e) Capital assets:
Capital assets purchased by the Society are recorded at cost and those donated to the Society are recorded at their fair market value at the date of acquisition when fair market value can be reasonably estimated. Capital assets are amortized on a straight-line basis over the following periods:

Buildings	15 years
Furniture and fixtures	3 years
Office equipment	3 years
Vehicles	3 years
Leasehold improvements	Lease term

(f) Prepaid expenses:
Prepaid expenses consist primarily of pamphlets and educational materials, revenue development and other supplies maintained at the Society and are recorded at cost.

(g) Employee future benefit plans:

The Society maintains employee future benefit plans providing pension, other retirement and post-retirement benefits to most of its employees.

The Society accrues its obligations under a defined benefit employee pension plan and the related costs, net of plan assets.

The Society also accrues the cost of providing benefits other than pension to retired employees and their spouses. The benefits include medical services, life insurance and extended health care benefits. This post-retirement benefit plan is not funded.

The cost of pensions and other retirement benefits earned by employees is actuarially determined using the projected benefit method pro rated on service and management's best estimate of expected plan investment performance, salary escalation, retirement ages of employees and expected health care costs.

For the purpose of calculating the expected return on plan assets, those assets are valued at fair value.

The excess of the net actuarial gain (loss) over 10% of the lesser of the accrued benefit obligation and plan assets at the beginning of the year is amortized over the average remaining service period of active employees. The average remaining service period of the active employees covered by the pension and benefits plans is eight years (2000 - 10.5 years).

(h) Volunteer services:

The Society's programs benefit substantially from services in the form of volunteer time. These invaluable services are not recorded in these financial statements.

3. Economic interest:

The Society has an economic interest in the activities of the National Cancer Institute of Canada ("NCIC") by virtue of significant funds remitted to the NCIC for research in support of the Society's mission. The Society has remitted 34% (2000 - 38%) of its revenue to the NCIC. The remittance for the fiscal year was $43,194 (2000 - $42,465).

The NCIC is incorporated under the Canada Corporations Act as a non-profit organization without share capital and is a registered charity under the Income Tax Act (Canada). The NCIC's mission is to undertake and support cancer research and related programs in Canada that will lead to reductions in the incidence, morbidity and mortality from cancer.

4. Appropriations:

During the year, appropriations amongst unrestricted, internally restricted and externally restricted resources were approved by both the National and Divisional Boards of Directors. The majority of the funds were appropriated from unrestricted resources to internally restricted resources to ensure proper segregation of specific Board approved initiatives.

Additional Readings

14-190.   In writing the material in the text, we have incorporated all of the relevant *CICA Handbook* Recommendations, as well as material from other sources that we felt to be of importance.   While this approach meets the needs of the great majority of accounting students, some of you may wish to pursue this subject in greater depth. To facilitate this, you will find a fairly comprehensive bibliography of materials on the subject of accounting for not-for-profit organizations in Chapter 58 of our *Guide to Canadian Financial Reporting*. Chapter 58 of the *Guide* also contains summaries of the EIC Abstracts that are directly related to this subject. The abstracts that are summarized as an appendix to Chapter 58 are as follows:

- EIC Abstract No. 36 - Accounting For Government Funding To Non-Profit Organizations
- EIC Abstract No. 51 - Accounting By The Recipient For Debenture Payments To Be Financed By Government Funding
- EIC Abstract No. 95 - Accounting For Capital Assets Of A Condominium Corporation
- EIC Abstract No. 105 - Revenue Recognition Of Non-Refundable Initiation Fees In Not-For-Profit Organizations

14-191.   The complete *Guide to Canadian Financial Reporting* is available on the CD-ROM which accompanies this text.

Assignment Problems

(The solutions for these problems are only available in
the solutions manual that has been provided to your instructor.)

Assignment Problem Fourteen - 1

On January 1, 2002, the Environmental Protection Society (EPS) is organized as a not-for-profit organization. Its purpose is to serve two needs in its Province:

- Planting trees in urban areas.
- Cleaning up litter along various secondary roads.

The organization has a December 31 year end.

The initial funding for the organization is provided by a group of wealthy individuals who make an endowment contribution of $132,000. The funds are invested in debt securities. All of the income earned by these endowment funds is restricted to use in the Society's tree planting activities. During the year ending December 31, 2002, the income on the endowment investment totalled $6,450.

The organization solicits and receives unrestricted contributions from a large number of sources. Such contributions are allocated to both tree planting and to litter cleanup by the Board Of Directors of the organization. During the year ending December 31, 2002, $582,000 of such contributions were received and, at the end of the year, an additional $127,000 in contributions were receivable. The Board believes that this is a reasonable estimate of the amount that will actually be collected. The $709,000 total was allocated $490,000 to tree planting and $219,000 to litter cleanup.

The organization accepts additional contributions that are restricted to use in the tree planting activities. These funds are segregated and a separate report is made to contributors on their usage. During the year ending December 31, 2002, restricted contributions of $146,000 were received and, at the end of the year, an additional $23,000 of restricted contributions were receivable.

The organization operates out of fully furnished office space that is rented for $2,500 per month. Three quarters of the space is used for tree planting activities, with the remainder used for litter cleanup activities.

During the year ending December 31, 2002, the organization incurred the following expenses:

	Tree Planting Activities	Litter Cleanup Activities
Wages And Salaries	$328,000	$ 86,000
Cost Of Materials Provided	107,000	32,000
Rent	22,500	7,500
Other Expenses	72,500	36,500
Total	$530,000	$162,000

A total of 20 percent ($106,000) of the expenses related to tree planting activities were paid for out of the restricted contributions bank account.

On December 31, 2002, there were outstanding Accounts Payable related to the litter cleanup activity expenses of $42,000.

EPS uses fund accounting with funds established for endowment contributions and restricted tree planting amounts, in addition to a general fund.

Required:

A. Prepare journal entries, including closing entries, to record the information in the problem.

B. Prepare a Statement Of Operations And Fund Balances, a Statement Of Financial Position, and a Statement Of Cash Flows for the year ending December 31, 2002. Your solution should comply with the Recommendations of the *CICA Handbook*.

Assignment Problem Fourteen - 2

(This is an extension of Assignment Problem Fourteen - 1)

On January 1, 2002, the Environmental Protection Society (EPS) is organized as a not-for-profit organization. Its purpose is to serve two needs in its Province:

- Planting trees in urban areas.
- Cleaning up litter along various secondary roads.

The organization has a December 31 year end.

The initial funding for the organization is provided by a group of wealthy individuals who make an endowment contribution of $132,000. The funds are invested in debt securities. There are no restrictions on the use of the income resulting from this investment. During the year ending December 31, 2002, the income on the endowment investment totaled $6,450.

The organization solicits and receives unrestricted contributions from a large number of sources. Such contributions are allocated to both tree planting and to litter cleanup by the Board Of Directors of the organization. During the year ending December 31, 2002, $582,000 of such contributions were received and, at the end of the year, an additional $127,000 in contributions were receivable. These receivables are allocated to the tree planting fund. The Board believes that this is a reasonable estimate of the amount that will actually be collected. The $709,000 total was allocated $490,000 to tree planting and $219,000 to litter cleanup.

The organization accepts additional contributions that are restricted to use in the tree planting activities. These funds are segregated and a separate report is made to contributors on their usage. During the year ending December 31, 2002, restricted contributions of $146,000 were received and, at the end of the year, an additional $23,000 of restricted contributions were receivable. These receivables were allocated to the tree planting fund.

The organization operates out of fully furnished office space that is rented for $2,500 per month. Three quarters of the space is used for tree planting activities, with the remainder used for litter cleanup activities.

During the year ending December 31, 2002, the organization incurred the following expenses:

	Tree Planting Activities	Litter Cleanup Activities
Wages And Salaries	$328,000	$ 86,000
Cost Of Materials Provided	107,000	32,000
Rent	22,500	7,500
Other Expenses	72,500	36,500
Total	$530,000	$162,000

A total of 20 percent ($106,000) of the expenses related to tree planting activities were paid for out of the restricted contributions bank account.

On December 31, 2002, there were outstanding Accounts Payable related to the litter cleanup activity expenses of $42,000.

EPS uses fund accounting with funds established for tree planting activities and litter cleanup activities, in addition to a general fund. Endowment contributions are accounted for in the general fund.

Required:

A. Prepare journal entries, including closing entries, to record the information in the problem.

B. Prepare a Statement Of Operations And Fund Balances, a Statement Of Financial Position, and a Statement Of Cash Flows for the year ending December 31, 2002. Your solution should comply with the Recommendations of the *CICA Handbook*.

Assignment Problem Fourteen - 3

The Good Samaritan Centre (GSC) was established on January 1, 2002 to provide food to the needy in the local community through a soup kitchen. The soup kitchen provides three meals a day. The GSC also opened a food and clothing cupboard on July 1, 2002 in the basement of the restaurant.

GSC is run by a small number of permanent employees with the help of part-timers and a large group of dedicated volunteers.

Initial funding for the Centre was provided by the estate of Owen Moses in the amount of $800,000. Part of the funds were used to purchase an old restaurant for $220,000, and a used van for $20,000. The purchase price of $220,000 for the restaurant was allocated $100,000 to land and $120,000 to the building. As well, $100,000 represented endowment contributions, $370,000 was restricted for the food and clothing cupboard, and the balance was unrestricted. The restaurant building is amortized over twenty years on a straight-line basis, while the the van is amortized using the declining balance method of amortization at a rate of 20 percent. The van has an expected residual value of $500. Only one-half year's amortization will be taken in the year of acquisition.

The endowment contributions were invested in debt securities. There are no restrictions on the income that is produced by these investments. During the year ending December 31, 2002, investment income relating to these investments totaled $15,970.

Daniel Smith, the Executive Director for the GSC was very proactive in securing support from the local community and the United Way. Contributions for the year totaled $725,000 with $225,000 restricted for use in the food and clothing cupboard. Daniel was able to negotiate with a local radio station to have the advertising for the annual drive to stock the food and clothing cupboard donated rather than paying the $2,100 cost.

During the year ending December 31, 2002, the organization incurred the following expenses:

	Soup Kitchen	Food And Clothing Cupboard
Wages and Salaries	$150,000	$ 30,000
Cost of materials	250,000	100,000
Transportation costs	5,000	3,000
Other expenses	4,200	26,000
Totals	$409,200	$159,000

All of the expenses of the food and clothing cupboard were paid for with restricted contributions.

Required:

A. Prepare journal entries to record the information in the problem, including closing entries for each fund.

B. Prepare the Statement of Operations and Fund Balances for the year ending December 31, 2002, a Cash Flow Statement for the year ending December 31, 2002, and the Statement of Financial Position at December 31, 2002.

Assignment Problem Fourteen - 4

On January 1, 2002, the Winter Sports Society (WSS) is organized as a not-for-profit organization. Its purpose is to serve the needs of its local community in two areas:

• Encouraging children to learn ice skating outside of the arena environment.

• The provision of cross country ski equipment to needy senior citizens.

The organization will have a December 31 year end.

Initial funding is provided by a wealthy individual who makes an endowment contribution of $87,000. These funds are invested in debt securities. There are no restrictions on the income that is produced by these investments. During the year ending December 31, 2002, such income amounted to $4,370.

The organization solicits and receives unrestricted contributions. Such contributions are allocated to both skating promotion and ski equipment provision by the organization's Board Of Directors. During the year ending December 31, 2002, $726,000 in contributions were received. At year end, an additional $56,000 in contributions were receivable. The Board believes that this is a reasonable estimate of the amount that will actually be collected. This total was allocated $410,000 to the skating activity and $372,000 to the skiing activity. All of the receivables are allocated to the skating activity.

The organization accepts additional contributions that are restricted to use in the provision of ski equipment to needy senior citizens. These funds are segregated and a separate report is made to contributors on their usage. During the year ending December 31, 2002, restricted contributions of $242,000 were received. No restricted contributions are receivable at year end. All of these restricted contributions are deposited in a separate bank account.

The organization operates out of a fully furnished office space that is rented for $2,000 per month. The use of the space is split equally between the skating and skiing activities of the organization.

During the year ending December 31, 2002, the organization incurred the following expenses:

	Skating Activity	Skiing Activity
Wages And Salaries	$173,000	$ 71,000
Cost Of Materials Provided	32,000	274,000
Transportation Costs	41,000	33,000
Rent	12,000	12,000
Other Expenses	27,000	31,000
Total	$285,000	$421,000

A total of 50 percent ($210,500) of the expenses related to the skiing activity have been paid for out of the restricted contributions bank account.

On December 31, 2002, there were outstanding Accounts Payable related to the skating activity expenses of $30,000.

Required: Prepare a Statement Of Operations And Fund Balances, a Statement Of Financial Position, and a Statement Of Cash Flows for the year ending December 31, 2002 under each of the following assumptions:

A. WSS does not use fund accounting.

B. WSS uses fund accounting with funds established for endowment contributions and restricted skiing contributions, in addition to a general fund.

C. WSS uses fund accounting with funds established for skating activities and skiing activities, in addition to a general fund. Endowment contributions are dealt with through the general fund.

Journal entries are not required. Your solution should comply with the Recommendations of Sections 4400 and 4410 of the *CICA Handbook*.

Assignment Problem Fourteen - 5

This is an extension of Assignment Problem Fourteen - 4. It involves the same Winter Sports Society (WSS) and extends their activities into the year ending December 31, 2003. It is made more complex by the addition of capital assets and their amortization.

There are no additional endowment contributions during the year ending December 31, 2003. The endowment fund investments have income of $4,820 during this period.

During the year ending December 31, 2003, $842,300 in unrestricted contributions were received. At year end, there is an additional $53,250 in contributions that are receivable. The Board believes that this is a reasonable estimate of the amount that will actually be collected. This total was allocated $510,050 to the skating activity, $243,500 to the skiing activity, and $142,000 for the acquisition of a building to be used in the organization's operations. All of the receivables are allocated to the skating activity.

On July 1, 2003, the organization acquires a building for a total cost of $142,000. Of this total, $37,000 represents the fair value of the land on which the building is situated and the remaining $105,000 reflects the fair value of the building. The estimated useful life of the building is 20 years and no significant residual value is anticipated. The organization uses straight line amortization, charging only one-half year's amortization in the year in which an asset is acquired.

The organization continues to accept additional contributions that are restricted to use in the skiing activity. As in the past, these funds are placed in a separate bank account. During the year ending December 31, 2003, restricted contributions of $317,600 were received. No contributions are receivable at year end.

During the year ending December 31, 2003, the organization incurred the following expenses:

	Skating Activity	Skiing Activity
Wages And Salaries	$345,600	$ 32,400
Cost Of Materials Provided	48,200	362,300
Transportation Costs	19,400	21,600
Rent	6,000	6,000
Other Expenses	23,300	45,900
Total	$442,500	$468,200

The records show that 56 percent of the expenses related to the skiing activity were made from restricted funds.

On December 31, 2003, there were outstanding Accounts Payable related to the skating activities expenses of $32,430.

Required: Prepare a Statement Of Operations And Fund Balances, a Statement Of Financial Position, and a Statement Of Cash Flows for the year end December 31, 2003 under each of the following assumptions:

A. WSS does not use fund accounting.

B. WSS uses fund accounting with funds established for endowment contributions and restricted skiing contributions, in addition to a general fund.

C. WSS uses fund accounting with funds established for skating activities and skiing activities, in addition to a general fund. Endowment contributions are dealt with through the general fund.

Journal entries are not required. Your solution should comply with the Recommendations of Sections 4400 to 4460 of the *CICA Handbook*.

Assignment Problem Fourteen - 6

On August 15, 1998, the European Exchange Club (EEC) was formed in an effort to create a united social group out of several separate regional clubs in the vicinity of the city of Decker, located in central Canada. The purpose of the group is to combine resources to meet the recreational, cultural, and social needs of their collective members. EEC was formed through the collaboration of the following clubs and their memberships:

	Members
The Canadian Russian Society	12,300
The Italian Clubs of Canada	10,800
Portuguese Cultural Foundation	4,100
Association Of Greeks Of The World	2,700
The German Groups	1,100
Other	1,700
Total	32,700

It is now December 2002. EEC's executives have spent the past few years planning and preparing for its operation. The club's community centre is expected to be fully completed next year. The facilities of the club will include the following:

- a multi-purpose building to house banquets, meetings and arts activities
- hiking trails
- indoor/outdoor tennis facilities
- bicycle trails
- baseball diamonds
- an indoor/outdoor pool
- a soccer field

The multi-purpose building is 75 percent complete, and EEC's executives have stated that it is "approximately within budget." Estimated building costs were outlined in a 1998 feasibility study, as follows:

Construction Cost	$2,300,000
Site Preparation Costs	400,000
Furniture And Fixtures	550,000
Consulting Fees	120,000
Miscellaneous	80,000
Total	$3,450,000

The four acres of land on which the facility is built were provided by the provincial government by way of a five-year lease at $1 a year. The adjacent land of 60 acres was contributed to the club by The Italian Clubs of Canada. Previously, this land had been leased to a farmer for $54,000 a year. The 64 acres will be used for the following projects, which will incur the additional costs listed below:

Hiking Trails	$ 595,000
Baseball Diamonds	30,000
Soccer Field	22,000
Bicycle Trails	95,000
Indoor/Outdoor Pool	700,000
Indoor/Outdoor Tennis Facilities	300,000
Total	$1,742,000

In addition to these development costs, the club faces annual operating costs of approximately $740,000, outlined in Exhibit I. John Mendez-Smith, the newly elected president of the club, has approached your firm, Young and Kerr Chartered Accountants, to prepare a report that provides recommendations on accounting. You took the notes appearing in Exhibit II at a meeting with the club's president and executive committee.

Required: Prepare the report.

(CICA Adapted)

Exhibit I
European Exchange Club
Yearly Budget

Operating Revenues

Membership Fees	$ 91,000
Social Rentals	185,000
Meeting Rentals	50,000
Sport Rentals	23,000
Concessions	61,000
Fundraising Events	225,000
Total Operating Revenues	**$635,000**

Operating Costs

Salaries	$363,000
Administrative Costs	39,000
Maintenance	126,000
Utilities	112,000
Educational Scholarships	100,000
Total Operating Costs	**$740,000**

Exhibit II
Notes Taken From Your Meeting With
Mr. Mendez-Smith And The Executive Committee

1. Under the lease agreement with the Province, EEC is responsible for maintenance and all costs of improvements. The lease agreement provides for 20 renewal terms of five years' duration each. Renewal is based on the condition that EEC makes the club's services available to all present and future EEC member-clubs and their membership.

2. EEC has requested an operating grant from the provincial government. Its proposal requests the Province to provide EEC with annual funds to cover 50% of "approved" operating costs incurred to provide services to all club members.

   The City of Decker wishes to construct an arena and a swimming pool and has opposed the proposed operating grant. The City has asked to be the first in line for available provincial funds.

   The committee members suspect that they will have to compromise on their proposal and are having problems determining the minimum annual funds required by the club from the Province.

3. The Russian and Italian clubs have been arguing with other clubs over the equalization payments required from each club. Currently, each club makes payments to EEC based upon their proportionate membership. Payments for each calendar year are made on February 1 of the following year.

   The Russian group performs the administrative functions of EEC and has charged, and will continue to charge, the club only 50% of the market value of these services.

4. The accounting function is a major concern of the member-club representatives. In particular, they have raised the following issues:

   a) Several fund raising events are organized by individual member clubs.

   b) Any donations to EEC are received through the member clubs.

   c) No accounting has been made of services donated to EEC by the members of the individual clubs.

d) EEC has approached a bank to assist in future phases of the club's development. The bank has informed EEC that it is interested in asset values and EEC's ability to repay the loans.

Chapter 15

Financial Instruments

Introduction

Background

15-1.   It seems that you cannot read a professional magazine or the business section of a newspaper without reading something about financial instruments, derivatives, or one of the other complex types of financial instruments. But what are financial instruments? And what do accountants need to know about them? The good news is that accounting for traditional financial instruments, such as accounts receivable, accounts payable and corporate shares is straightforward and is covered in introductory accounting textbooks. The bad news is that there are hundreds of different kinds of financial instruments that have been created in the last two decades and more are being created every day. The complexity of this topic is evident from the sheer volume of material written about financial instruments. One of the most recent publications on accounting for financial instruments, *Financial Instruments and Similar Items*, released by the Joint Working Group of Standard-Setters (JWG) in December 2000, is almost 300 pages long.

15-2.   This Chapter does not cover everything there is to know about financial instruments, but it will review the basics of how the most common instruments work, as well as the most recent recommendations on their proper accounting treatment.

What Is A Financial Instrument?

15-3.   Section 3860 of the *CICA Handbook* defines financial instruments as follows:

Paragraph 3860.05(a)   A **financial instrument** is any contract that gives rise to both a financial asset of one party and a financial liability or equity instrument of another party.

15-4.   As is often the case, this definition includes terms that require their own definitions:

Paragraph 3860.05(b)   A **financial asset** is any asset that is:
(i)   cash;
(ii) a contractual right to receive cash or another financial asset from another party;
(iii) a contractual right to exchange financial instruments with another party under conditions that are potentially favourable; or
(iv) an equity instrument of another entity.

Paragraph 3860.05(c) A **financial liability** is any liability that is a contractual obligation:

(i) to deliver cash or another financial asset to another party; or

(ii) to exchange financial instruments with another party under conditions that are potentially unfavourable.

Paragraph 3860.05(d) An **equity instrument** is any contract that evidences a residual interest in the assets of an entity after deducting all of its liabilities.

15-5. These definitions may appear circular at first. That is because many financial instruments are contracts to transfer other financial instruments in the future. But ultimately, although a chain of exchanges may take place, the end result is that cash or equity shares will change hands.

15-6. Section 3860 also provides useful guidance on items that are *not* financial instruments. Physical assets, such as inventories and equipment, as well as intangible assets, are not financial instruments. Although having control over such assets will help an entity generate future cash flows, they do not by themselves give the holder a contractual right to receive cash or other financial assets. Further, assets or obligations that will lead to exchanges of goods and services, rather than exchanges of financial assets, are not financial instruments. These would include most prepaid expenses, unearned revenues, and warranty obligations. Another useful clarification provided by Section 3860 addresses income taxes payable or recoverable. Although these items *will* result in exchanges of cash, income taxes are imposed by statutory authority. They are not the result of a contract per se, and are therefore *not* considered financial instruments.

15-7. Some financial instruments are not recognized in an entity's financial statements. For example, guaranteeing the loan of a related party is a contractual obligation to pay cash to another party, even though this obligation is contingent on a future event that may or may not occur. Section 3860 states that an entity must disclose information about the extent and nature of all financial instruments, both recognized and unrecognized, in the notes to its financial statements.

Exercise Fifteen-1 deals with identifying and classifying financial instruments.	**Exercise Fifteen-1** The following is a list of Balance Sheet items. Use the definitions in *CICA Handbook* Section 3860 to determine whether each item is a financial instrument or not and, if so, whether it is a financial asset, a financial liability or an equity instrument.

1. Cash and cash equivalents
2. Accounts receivable
3. Inventories
4. Shares in portfolio investments
5. Property, plant and equipment, net
6. Bank loan outstanding
7. Accounts payable and accrued liabilities
8. Current portion of long-term debt
9. Long-term debt
10. Future income taxes
11. Common shares and warrants outstanding
12. Retained earnings

End Of Exercise Fifteen-1

Why Do Companies Get Involved With Financial Instruments?

15-8.   There are three main reasons why companies become involved with financial instruments. They can be described as follows:

1. To raise or invest funds. Entities raise funds by issuing financial liabilities, such as corporate bonds, or equity instruments, such as shares. Entities invest funds by buying financial assets, such as government treasury bills, corporate bonds or shares.

2. To hedge. Hedging is an activity designed to modify an entity's exposure to one or more risks, by creating an offset between changes in the fair value of, or the cash flows attributable to, the hedged item and the hedging item.

3. To speculate. Speculating involves taking on new risk, usually in an area that is not related to the operations of the enterprise, in order to obtain profit or gain.

15-9.   Financial instruments have been around for a long time. For centuries, companies have issued stocks and bonds to raise funds and the financial marketplace has invested in those same stocks and bonds. Although both the issuer and the holder recognized that these instruments involved certain risks on both sides of the contract, the parties for the most part accepted these risks. However, in the last few decades, as more sophisticated risk management practices developed, it became routine for companies to take steps to reduce the risks associated with holding or issuing traditional financial instruments. Buying put options, which give the holder to right to sell shares at a specified price and therefore reduces the risk associated with the price fluctuations of shares held by an entity as an investment, is an example of this type of risk management activity.

What Types Of Risks Do Businesses Typically Face?

15-10.   There are a number of general, non-financial risks that all businesses face. These include sovereign risk (the possibility that a foreign government may take or fail to take an action that affects the business economically) and internal control risk (the possibility that errors or mismanagement may occur when economic activities become difficult to control). General risks such as these cannot be managed with financial instruments and they are not under consideration in this Chapter.

15-11.   The four most relevant types of risk for this discussion can be outlined as follows:

1. **Price Risk**   This type of risk takes several forms. These forms can be described as follows:

    • **Currency risk** is the risk that the value of a financial instrument will fluctuate due to changes in foreign exchange rates.

    • **Interest rate risk** is the risk that the value of a financial instrument will fluctuate due to changes in market interest rates.

    • **Market risk** is the risk that the value of a financial instrument will fluctuate as a result of changes in market prices whether these changes are caused by factors specific to the individual security or its issuer or factors affecting all securities traded in the market.

2. **Credit risk** is the risk that one party to a financial instrument will fail to discharge an obligation and cause the other party to incur a financial loss.

3. **Liquidity risk**, also referred to as funding risk, is the risk that an entity will encounter difficulty in raising funds to meet commitments associated with financial instruments. Liquidity risk may result from an inability to sell a financial asset quickly at close to fair value.

4. **Cash flow risk** is the risk that future cash flows associated with a monetary financial instrument will fluctuate in amount. In the case of a floating rate debt instrument, for

example, such fluctuations result in a change in the effective interest rate of the financial instrument, usually without a corresponding change in its fair value.

15-12.   Different financial instruments have been developed to manage these different types of financial risks. For example, interest-rate swaps are used to manage interest rate risk and forward exchange contracts are used to manage currency risk. When an entity takes an action to reduce its exposure to an existing risk, it is hedging that risk.

15-13.   As hedging instruments such as options and swaps became better known in the financial markets, an interesting trend started to develop. Investors began to view some of these instruments as viable investments in their own right and invested in them not for hedging purposes, but purely for speculation. Unfortunately, because some of these financial instruments were relatively new in the marketplace and, in addition, were extremely complex, many investors did not fully understand the risks associated with them.

15-14.   As a result of this situation, many well-known companies incurred significant losses when they invested heavily in these new financial instruments. For example, Proctor & Gamble lost $130 million. Merrill Lynch, an investment firm, lost $377 million. One of the most spectacular losses resulting from poor control over financial instruments involved the Barings Bank. Barings was a 135-year old English bank that went bankrupt in 1995 when an employee stationed in Singapore accumulated over $1.6 billion in losses over a three-year period from trading futures and options. These newsworthy losses alerted the financial press, as well as the financial industry and the accounting profession, to the risks inherent in financial instruments, and particularly in the newer brand of financial instruments known as derivatives. Derivative use was becoming widespread but they were often poorly understood.

15-15.   The process of controlling the use of financial instruments in an organization is no different from controlling any other aspect of the organization. Establishing objectives, monitoring performance and using a system that includes segregation of duties and independent checks are all important aspects of any good internal control system. Because some instruments are extremely complex and may be new to the organization, ensuring that adequate control exists over their use is particularly important. Most of the articles that appeared in the business press about financial instruments in the 1990s focused on the huge amounts of money that organizations had lost from investing in or issuing them, which made it clear that internal control over financial instruments was frequently weak. For the most part, organizations have taken heed of these well-publicized disasters and, as a result, internal control systems over financial instruments in organizations have improved during the last decade.

What Types Of Financial Instruments Exist?

15-16.   Financial Instruments can be classified into three basic types — primary instruments, hybrid instruments, and derivatives. These basic types, along with examples of hybrids and derivatives, can be described as follows:

1.   **Primary instruments**. These are the traditional instruments that have existed for decades. Examples are receivables, payables and common shares.

2.   **Hybrid instruments**. These are instruments that have the features of more than one primary financial instrument. Examples of such hybrid instruments are as follows:

   • **Convertible bonds** have a debt element and an equity element. Standard-setters have been concerned about how convertible debt should be accounted for since they are not strictly debt or equity. The classification issue is critical as it has an effect on the income statement as well as on the balance sheet. Interest on bonds that have been classified as equity instruments will not be treated as an expense in the income statement, but as a dividend in the retained earnings statement instead. Similarly, the distinction between debt and equity affects the cash flow statement. Interest that has been disclosed as an expense in the income statement will appear in the operating section of the cash flow statement. Interest that has been shown as a dividend in the retained earnings statement will be disclosed as a financing item in the cash flow statement.

- **Term-life preferred shares** also have a debt element and an equity element and standard-setters have been concerned about how shares with a redemption date should be accounted for. As with convertible bonds, the classification issue is critical. Dividends on shares that have been classified as financial liabilities will be treated as expenses in the income statement and as operating items in the cash flow statement.

In classifying such hybrid instruments, Section 3860 makes it clear that the process must be based on economic substance rather than legal form.

3. **Derivative instruments**. Derivatives are contracts that transfer the risks associated with a primary financial instrument (called the underlying interest) to another party. They are called derivatives because their value is *derived* from the value of the underlying interest. Generally, all derivatives are either options or forward contracts. An option is the **right** to buy or sell something in the future, whereas a forward contract is an **obligation** to buy or sell something in the future. The most common examples of derivatives are financial options, futures, forwards, interest rate swaps and currency swaps.

- **Financial Option**: An option is a formal contract that grants the holder the right, but not the obligation, to buy or sell a specified quantity of a specified underlying interest at a specified price within a specified period of time. The other party to the transaction, called the **writer** of the option, has the obligation to honour the contract should the holder exercise his option. The underlying interest can be an equity share, a currency, a debt instrument or a share index. There are two kinds of options:

  - a call option which gives the holder the right to **buy** the underlying interest, and
  - a put option which gives the holder the right to **sell** the underlying interest.

- **Futures**: Futures are exchange-traded contracts to deliver or take delivery of a specified quantity of a currency during a specified future month at a specified price.

- **Forwards**: Forwards are agreements between two parties to exchange a specified currency on a specified date at a specified price. They work like futures but are designed by the two parties and are not traded contracts.

- **Interest rate swaps**: An interest swap is an agreement between two parties to exchange cash flows based on some agreed-to formula. Frequently, the formula is based on a fixed interest rate on one side and a floating rate on the other. No principal is exchanged, only the interest calculated on the agreed-to notional principal amount.

- **Currency swaps**: A foreign exchange swap is an exchange of two currencies with an agreement to re-exchange these same currencies at the same rate at a specified future date.

Options, forwards, futures and swaps also exist for commodities, such as metals, grains and other farm products, but since they are based on commodities, they do not meet the definition of a financial instrument, and they are not discussed further here, although they work the same way as financial contracts.

Examples of how options, futures and swaps work, including how to account for them, appear at the end of this chapter.

Sources of Financial Instruments

15-17.   Companies planning to acquire or issue primary or hybrid financial instruments, such as stocks, bonds and loans, have traditionally used banks and brokerage companies to help them with these investing and financing activities. The market for derivative instruments is more recent but has grown remarkably fast. The Wall Street Journal recently estimated that derivative contracts are currently a $40 trillion market.

15-18.   The market for options and futures is well-developed. Canadian equity options and futures trade on the Montreal and Toronto stock exchanges and trading activity is administered by the Canadian Derivatives Clearing Corporation. Like stock prices, prices for options and forwards are quoted in the business section of daily newspapers.

15-19.   Interest-rate or currency swaps require the services of a financial intermediary. Companies typically make contractual arrangements at the most advantageous terms available to them in their local capital markets. Companies that then wish to change the nature of their existing financial contracts may use commercial bankers to find other parties around the world willing to swap specific terms of their respective contractual arrangements. These institutions do not match companies one-to-one; rather, they form pools of capital that can be swapped. A further advantage of swaps is that swaps give the parties access to capital in other markets (generally foreign markets) that they could not access directly or easily on their own.

15-20.   The financial intermediaries also guarantee the payments, and can also provide quotations on the fair values of existing swap arrangements. These arrangements are very common for large institutions, but they are usually for large amounts and swaps may not be readily available to companies with smaller interests.

Exotic Types of Financial Instruments

15-21.   In the explosive financial environment of the 1980s, innovative financial managers used their creativity to invent a host of new and exotic types of financial instruments. The philosophy at that time seemed to be: if someone wants it and it doesn't already exist, invent it. Theoretically, any instrument can be created if you find both an issuer and a holder who agree to the terms. If an investor doesn't want to buy a bond with interest, strip the interest from the bond and sell the interest stream to another investor. If an issuer doesn't want to issue bonds with a fixed cash maturity value, issue price-index bonds instead, or commodity bonds payable in barrels of oil.

15-22.   This inventive approach resulted in the emergence of a myriad of specialized instruments that are often referred to by acronyms and that have names that run the gamut from A to Z. Over the years, instruments named BUNNIES, COLTS, FLICS, OPPOSSMS and ZECROS have existed. Unpopular instruments have already died off, but new ones are being created virtually every day. It is beyond the scope of this Chapter to explain each one. However, anyone involved with financial instruments should ensure they know the nature of any instrument they are considering becoming a party to, so that they understand the risks involved.

Issues And Standards

Accounting Issues

15-23. As with any accounting problem, issues of recognition (and de-recognition), measurement, presentation, and disclosure exist. With respect to financial instruments, under the issue of recognition, we have questions such as the following:

- Is a contract a transaction?
- What is and is not a financial instrument?
- What kinds of financial instruments are there?
- How do you distinguish one kind from another?
- When should financial instruments be recorded in the books?
- When should they be taken off the books?
- How should gains/losses on financial instruments be treated in the financial statements?

15-24.   Under the issue of measurement, we have questions such as:

- How should we value financial instruments at inception (i.e. at recognition date)?
- How should we value them over their lives?
- If one financial instrument is acquired to hedge another financial instrument, should the valuation method used for the two instruments be the same?

15-25.   Under the issue of presentation, we have questions such as:

- How should financial instruments be classified in the statements?
- Should a financial instrument that is acquired to hedge another financial instrument be offset against that financial instrument in the financial statements?

15-26.   Under the issue of disclosure, we have questions such as:

- How should financial instruments and the risks associated with them be disclosed to the readers of the statements?
- What are the significant characteristics of a financial instrument that must be disclosed in order for a reader to be able to evaluate the company's financial instruments?

Basic Problems

15-27.   Financial instruments developed so quickly and are so complex that the accounting profession was unable to develop appropriate accounting recommendations for them in a timely fashion. By the late 1980s, the following problems became clear:

1.   Certain financial instruments were being accounted for incorrectly due to misunderstandings about their economic substance;

2.   There was too much variability in the way certain items were being treated for accounting purposes.

3.   There was inadequate disclosure to allow readers to fully assess the financial situation of the company and the riskiness of their financial instruments.

The Standard-Setting Process For Financial Instruments

15-28.   Developing comprehensive standards for recognition, de-recognition, fair value measurement, presentation and disclosure of financial instruments has been a concern of the CICA for well over a decade and has been high on its list of priorities.

15-29.   Most accounting standards in developed countries continue to be published by their national accounting boards. Over the years, however, it has become apparent that cooperation among standard-setting bodies around the world is important for the smooth movement of global investment funds and there has been a move towards harmonization of accounting standards as a result of this. Accounting for financial instruments was of particular concern internationally because of the widespread use of these financial instruments in practice and because it was recognized that accounting standards in this area were inadequate.

15-30.   The CICA is committed to facilitating the harmonization of Canadian accounting standards with U.S. and international standards. Consistent with this commitment, the CICA joined forces with the International Accounting Standards Board (IASB) on the topic of financial instruments and the two bodies released a joint Discussion Paper titled *Accounting for Financial Assets and Liabilities* in 1997. In the meantime, the FASB had been addressing the topic on its own. To address concerns that these two groups might be working at cross-purposes, a Joint Working Group Of Standard-Setters (JWG) was created in 1997. The JWG consisted of nominees of accounting standard-setters or other professional organizations in Australia, Canada, France, Germany, Japan, New Zealand, five Nordic countries, the United Kingdom and the United States, as well as the IASC. The CICA/IASC Paper was further amended as a result of deliberations of the JWG members and the amended paper, *Financial Instruments and Similar Items*, was released in December 2000. The positions taken in the Draft Standard reflect the views of a majority of the JWG members. They do not necessarily represent the views of the organizations that nominated the members to the JWG.

15-31.   Each member organization issued the JWG document in its own jurisdiction, and invited comments from its constituents, with a due date for these comments on or around June 30, 2001. The document is approximately 300 pages, and consists of three parts: the Draft Standard itself (70 pages), the Application Supplement (70 pages – which provides further explanation on how certain aspects of the standard would be applied), and the Basis for Conclusions (160 pages – which summarizes factors considered in deliberations and reasons for the decisions).   The members of the JWG have been deliberating on the comments received on its report since the summer of 2001.

15-32.   In its *Invitation to Comment* on the Special Report of the JWG, the CICA acknowledges that "the nature of financial instruments and the accounting issues they raise are such that a single world-wide standard is preferable, if not necessary." Not only does the CICA's collaboration with other countries promote harmonization of standards, it also allows the CICA to play a leadership role in the international standard-setting process. The CICA expects to issue an Exposure Draft of a proposed standard based on the report soon.   International cooperation to ensure that each jurisdiction's standards on these issues are as similar as possible is expected.

15-33.   There are significant differences between the JWG's Draft Standard and the initial position of the FASB on defining financial instruments and measuring them at fair value, which is described in the FASB Preliminary Views *Reporting Financial Instruments and Certain Related Assets and Liabilities at Fair Value*, issued in December 1999. How these differences will be resolved remains to be seen.

Relevant Publications

15-34.   Since 1988, the Accounting Standards Board (AcSB) of the CICA, in collaboration with other accounting bodies around the world, has been involved in developing comprehensive standards for financial instruments. The key publications resulting from this effort are the following:

1. Section 3860 of the *CICA Handbook*, "Financial Instruments – Disclosure and Presentation", issued in 1995. The IASB also released an equivalent standard, IAS 32, at that time. A number of EIC Abstracts were subsequently issued by the AcSB to provide some application guidance on these issues. These publications do not deal with recognition and measurement issues. The content of this *Handbook* Section will be given detailed consideration in a later section of this Chapter.

2. Statement Of Financial Accounting Standards (SFAS) No. 133, "Accounting for Derivative Instruments and Hedging Activities", released by the FASB in June 1998 and subsequently amended by Statement Of Financial Accounting Standards No. 138. This standard promotes a fair value model for derivative instruments. The content of SFAS No. 133 is briefly summarized in this section of the Chapter.

3. International Accounting Standard (IAS) No. 39, "Financial Instruments: Recognition and Measurement", issued by the International Accounting Standards Board (IASB) in December 1998. This standard, like SFAS No. 133, also made a partial move towards fair value accounting for financial instruments.

4. An Invitation to Comment, *Financial Instruments and Similar Items*, released by the Joint Working Group of Standard-Setters (JWG) in December 2000. This draft standard proposes a comprehensive fair value model for all financial instruments. The content of this Invitation To Comment will be briefly summarized in this section of the Chapter.

5. Accounting Guideline No. 13, "Hedging Relationships". This Guideline was issued by the Accounting Standards Board in December 2001. It provides guidance on the application of hedge accounting. This Guideline will be referred to in our discussion of Other Issues. It is also discussed in Chapter 9, "Foreign Currency Transactions", of this text.

6. Section 3870 of the *CICA Handbook*, "Stock-Based Compensation And Other Stock-Based Payments", was issued in January, 2002. Some attention will be given to this new Section in our material on Other Issues. For a more detailed discussion of this Section, we refer you to Chapter 55 of our *Guide To Canadian Financial Reporting*. This *Guide* is available on the CD-ROM that accompanies this text.

Publication Summaries

Statement Of Financial Accounting Standards No. 133

15-35.   The key points of the current recommendations on the recognition and measurement of derivative instruments found in SFAS No. 133 are:

*   All derivatives should be recognized on the balance sheet.

*   All derivatives should be valued at fair market value, both initially and subsequently.

*   Gains and losses as a result of changes in the fair market value of derivatives that are not hedging instruments should be included in the income statement.

*   Gains and losses in the fair market value of derivatives that qualify as hedges should follow the accounting of the hedged item.

JWG Draft Standard

15-36.   The key proposals of the JWG's Draft Standard are:

*   All financial instruments should be measured at fair value when recognized and at each subsequent measurement date (Paragraph 69).

*   Changes in the fair value of financial instruments should be recognized in the income statement (Paragraph 136).

15-37.   The Draft Standard is intended to apply to all enterprises and all financial instruments except:

*   those for which there are currently accounting Recommendations in the Handbook (such as investments in subsidiaries and associates, employee benefits, and equity instruments issued by the reporting entity) or

*   those that are the subject of separate study (such as insurance contracts).

15-38.   Although it proposes the use of fair values, the JWG also recognizes that, in rare circumstances, there are certain private equity instruments for which it is not practicable to make a reliable estimate of fair value. In that situation, the JWG proposes that the instrument be reported at its carrying value at the time the entity determined that a fair value is not estimable, or at its recoverable value if that is less (Paragraphs 122 and 125).

15-39.   The JWG's Draft Standard would also require expanded disclosures about financial risks, management's objectives and policies for managing those risks, and the methods used to estimate fair values. It is expected that, once a final standard is issued on these matters, implementation of the standard will take about two years.

15-40.   Until *CICA Handbook* Recommendations are actually released, and companies begin to apply the new Recommendations, it is difficult to predict how the JWG's Draft Standard on fair values will be implemented in practice. These are complex issues and attempts to over-simplify them for illustrative purposes run the risk of masking how difficult it is in reality to deal with these issues.

15-41.   The members of the JWG have been deliberating on the comments received on its report since the summer of 2001. More than 280 comments were received, with more than 40 from Canada. Financial analysts strongly support the proposals, but preparers are mostly opposed, citing a variety of reasons for their concerns. Other constituent groups, such as auditors and regulators, had mixed responses to the proposals. Many respondents suggested field-testing be undertaken on the proposed fair value model. The Accounting Standards

Board's task now is to address the respondents' concerns and to fill the current gap in Canadian standards. International cooperation to ensure that each jurisdiction's standards on these issues are as similar as possible will continue to be a priority.

15-42.   Despite the mixed responses, the Accounting Standards Board is optimistic that consensus will develop on the JWG proposals and that it will eventually adopt a standard that incorporates them. Thus, it has been looking at, and will continue to address, what new sections will have to be added and what changes will have to be made to existing *Handbook* sections as a result of the proposals. A cursory review of the Table of Contents in the *CICA Handbook* suggests that changes may need to be made to many of the existing sections, namely, those that deal with cash, temporary investments, accounts and notes receivable, impaired loans, long-term investments, long-term debt, share capital, contractual obligations, contingencies, foreign currency translation and the current section on financial instruments.

15-43.   Although the JWG's Draft Standard is still at the comment stage, it is expected that the fair value model will eventually become the status quo for financial instruments. Anticipating the acceptance of the JWG's proposals, the Accounting Standards Board has recently issued a number of amendments to existing *Handbook* sections that move Canadian GAAP closer to the JWG position. In March 2001, the Accounting Standards Board issued Accounting Guideline No. 12, "Transfers of Receivables", to address the fact that these financing arrangements can include put or call options or forward commitments. In December 2001, Section 1650, "Foreign Currency Translation", was amended to eliminate the unique Canadian treatment of deferring and amortizing exchange gains and losses related to foreign currency denominated long-term monetary items. Now these gains and losses will go through the income statement. Also at this time, Accounting Guideline No. 13, "Hedging Relationships", was introduced in order to encourage more consistent application of hedge accounting.

Section 3860: Presentation And Disclosure Of Financial Instruments

Purpose And Scope

15-44.   The continuing process of innovation in domestic and international financial markets has created a need for sound general principles of accounting for financial instruments. Given this situation, the purpose of Section 3860 is to enhance financial statement users' understanding of the significance of recognized and unrecognized financial instruments to an entity's financial position, performance and cash flows.

15-45.   The presentation Recommendations in this Section deal with classification of financial instruments between liabilities and equity, the classification of related interest, dividends, losses, and gains, and the offsetting of assets and liabilities.

15-46.   The disclosure Recommendations of this Section deal with information about factors that affect the amount, timing and certainty of an entity's future cash flows relating to financial instruments. The Section also encourages disclosure about the nature and extent of an entity's use of financial instruments, the business purposes that they serve, the risks associated with them, and management's policies for controlling these risks.

15-47.   Section 3860 should be applied to presentation and disclosure issues associated with all types of financial instruments, except for the following:

(a)   interests in subsidiaries, which are accounted for in accordance with "Subsidiaries", Section 1590;

(b)   interests in entities subject to significant influence, which are accounted for in accordance with "Long Term Investments", Section 3050;

(c)   interests in joint ventures, which are accounted for in accordance with "Interests In Joint Ventures", Section 3055; and

(d) obligations for stock-based compensation to employees and other stock-based payments to non-employees, which are accounted for in accordance with "Stock-Based Compensation And Other Stock-Based Payments", Section 3870;

(e) employers' obligations for employee future benefits and related plan assets, which are accounted for in accordance with "Employee Future Benefits", Section 3461; and

(f) pension obligations of defined benefit pension plans, which are dealt with in "Pension Plans", Section 4100.

15-48.   It is also noted that other *Handbook* Sections may contain additional requirements that are more extensive or explicit for particular financial instruments. Examples of such Sections would be Section 3065, "Leases", and 4100, "Pension Plans".

Liabilities And Equities
The Financial Reporting Issue
15-49.   Canadian practice has traditionally disclosed preferred shares as a component of shareholders' equity in the corporation's Balance Sheet. However, as some of these securities take on more and more of the characteristics of debt, it has become clear that such disclosure is not always appropriate.

15-50.   This issue has important implications both in the Balance Sheet and the Income Statement. Looking at the equity side of the Balance Sheet, the classification of some types of preferred shares as liabilities could result in significant changes in important indicators of financial health such as the debt to equity ratio. Perhaps even more importantly, in the Income Statement, the treatment of preferred shares as debt would mean that the dividends on these shares would be treated like interest. That is, rather than being viewed as a distribution of Net Income, these amounts would be deducted in the determination of Net Income. This could result in a significant reduction in the Net Income of the enterprise. However, earnings per share would not be changed as it is based on the earnings of the common shareholders.

15-51.   We would also note that the problem is made more difficult by the fact that there are various legal and tax constraints associated with the difference between classification as a liability and classification as shareholders' equity.

Section 3860 Recommendation
15-52.   Section 3860 contains the following Recommendation with respect to the classification of liabilities and equity:

Paragraph 3860.18   *The issuer of a financial instrument should classify the instrument, or its component parts, as a liability or as equity in accordance with the substance of the contractual arrangement on initial recognition and the definitions of a financial liability and an equity instrument.* (January, 1996)

15-53.   While we presented these definitions previously, the relevant definitions of financial liabilities and equity instruments are repeated here for your convenience:

Paragraph 3860.05(c)   A **financial liability** is any liability that is a contractual obligation:

(i) to deliver cash or another financial asset to another party; or

(ii) to exchange financial instruments with another party under conditions that are potentially unfavourable.

Paragraph 3860.05(d)   An **equity instrument** is any contract that evidences a residual interest in the assets of an entity after deducting all of its liabilities.

15-54.   In the application of Paragraph 3860.18, the key consideration in these definitions is the existence of a contractual obligation on one party to the financial instrument (the issuer) to either deliver cash or another financial asset to the other party (the holder) or to exchange another financial instrument with the holder under conditions that are potentially unfavourable to the issuer. When this condition is present, the financial instrument clearly meets the definition of a financial liability.

15-55.   With respect to securities commonly referred to as preferred shares, if such securities provide for mandatory redemption by the issuer for a fixed or determinable amount at a fixed or determinable future, or if they give the holder the right to require the issuer to redeem the share at or after a particular date for a fixed or determinable amount, the securities meet the definition of a financial liability and should be classified as such.

15-56.   The *Handbook* notes that even when there is no explicit redemption provision, there may be terms or conditions in the securities that may indirectly have the same result. Examples of this would be:

- A contractually accelerating dividend provision such that, within the foreseeable future, the issuer will be economically compelled to redeem the securities.

- Redemption may be required by some future event that is likely to occur (e.g., an increase in the prime rate to some specified level).

15-57.   Preferred shares that have either an explicit provision or terms and conditions that will lead to their being redeemed on potentially unfavourable terms should be classified as liabilities and disclosed as such on the Balance Sheet of the enterprise. Correspondingly, the dividends on such shares should be treated like interest in the Income Statement. That is, they should be deducted in the determination of the Net Income of the enterprise. The classification should take place at the time the securities are first issued.

15-58.   Several additional points can be made with respect to this classification process:

Preferred Shares   In keeping with the Section 3860 Recommendation, preferred shares with a scheduled redemption date, or with redemption at the option of the holder, should be classified as financial liabilities. However, if redemption is at the option of the issuer, the shares will be classified as equity until such time as the issuer formally notifies the holders of an intention to redeem. When preferred shares are not redeemable, classification depends on other rights. If the issuer is legally required to pay fixed amounts of dividends on specified dates, the shares will be classified as financial liabilities.

Perpetual Debt Instruments   Some debt securities either have no right to receive a return of principal or a right to a return of principal under terms that make it very unlikely. As long as such instruments are legally required to make fixed interest payments on specified debts, they should be classified as financial liabilities.

Co-operative Organizations And Partnerships   Interests in these organizations may be difficult to classify because of the variety of different terms and conditions that may be attached to them. For example, some types of membership shares in co-operative organizations may entitle the holder to a fixed redemption amount payable at a future date that is fixed or determinable by reference to a future event. Other types of membership shares may entitle the holder only to a pro rata share of the residual equity in the co-operative organization determined as of the date at which the holder becomes qualified to withdraw the interest. The first type of share meets the definition of a financial liability because it is a specific obligation of the issuer. The second type of share is considered to be an equity instrument, even though the issuer may have an obligation to redeem it under certain circumstances.

Classification - Interest, Dividends, Gains, Losses

15-59.   The distinction between liability instruments and equity instruments has important implications for income determination. If a financial instrument is classified as a liability, payments made to the holders of the instrument are considered to be interest payments which reduce reported Net Income. In contrast, payments to the holders of equity financial instruments are viewed as dividends which are disclosed as distributions of Net Income and reported in the Statement Of Retained Earnings.

15-60.   There are also important differences when financial instruments are redeemed or otherwise retired. If an instrument is classified as a liability, any difference between the carrying value and the amounts required to eliminate the balance from the accounts will be treated as a gain or loss to be included in the determination of Net Income. In contrast, the elimination of an equity item is viewed as a capital transaction and, as a consequence, differences between the carrying value and the amount of assets given up to retire or redeem the equity balance will not be included in Net Income.

15-61.   The classification of these items will, of course, depend on the classification of the Balance Sheet item to which they relate. This view is reflected in the following Recommendation:

> **Paragraph 3860.31**   *Interest, dividends, losses and gains relating to a financial instrument, or a component part, classified as a financial liability should be reported in the income statement as expense or income. Distributions to holders of a financial instrument classified as an equity instrument should be reported by the issuer directly in equity.* (January, 1996)

15-62.   The Paragraph 3860.31 Recommendation means that dividends declared on preferred shares that are classified as financial liabilities will be measured and disclosed in the same manner as interest payments on bonds. This would include accrual of such dividends prior to their declaration date.

15-63.   In addition to this alternative treatment of dividends on preferred shares classified as liabilities, any gains or losses on the redemption, cancellation, or reissue of such shares will have to be taken into income, rather than treated as a capital transaction.

15-64.   Dividends that are being treated as interest expense can be grouped together with and disclosed as a component of interest expense. However, there may be tax or other reasons for separate disclosure of such dividends.

The Tax Issue

15-65.   Redeemable preferred shares are widely used in tax planning. For example, in an estate freeze, it is a normal procedure for the freezor (i.e., the wealthy individual wishing to freeze the value of his or her estate) to exchange common or growth shares in an operating corporation for non-growth preferred shares. In order to clearly establish the value for these shares, they are often redeemable at the option of the holder. At the time of the freeze, common or growth shares with a nominal value will be issued to the freezor's beneficiaries (e.g., spouse or children). A rollover provision such as that found in Section 86 of the *Income Tax Act* is normally used to implement this plan.

15-66.   The types of preferred shares used in these situations will almost invariably require the issuing corporation to transfer cash to the holder. This means that under the Recommendations of Section 3860, these shares must be classified as liabilities. This has created considerable furor in the tax community and the reasons are not difficult to understand.

15-67.   The reclassification of these preferred shares as liabilities will, in many tax planning situations, create an equity side to the Balance Sheet that is almost entirely debt. In most of these arrangements, the holder of such preferred shares is unlikely to demand redemption of the securities, particularly if it would cause any financial hardship to the issuing corporation. Despite the fact that no change in economic substance is involved, the tax community has expressed their significant concern that bankers and other creditors will be influenced by this reclassification to downgrade the credit rating of the enterprise. This could lead to increased difficulty in obtaining financing for companies that use such preferred shares.

15-68.   This issue has been largely resolved by the introduction of Section 1300, "Differential Reporting". Under the Recommendations of this *Handbook* Section, qualifying non-publicly accountable enterprises will no longer have to classify certain equity-like preferred shares as debt. A more detailed discussion of Section 1300 can be found in Chapter 3 of our *Guide To Canadian Financial Reporting*. This *Guide* is provided on the CD-ROM that accompanies this text.

Exercise Fifteen-2 deals with the classification of preferred stock.

Exercise Fifteen - 2

The condensed Balance Sheet as at December 31, 2002, and a partial Income Statement for the year ending December 31, 2002, for Classify Inc. is as follows:

Condensed Balance Sheet
As At December 31, 2002

Current Assets		$5,000,000
Non-Current Assets		1,000,000
Total Assets		$6,000,000
Current And Long-Term Liabilities		$ 500,000
Preferred Stock - Stated Value (6% Dividend)		4,500,000
Common Stock Equity (Contributed And Earned)		
January 1, 2002	$1,050,000	
2002 Operating Income	220,000	
Payments To Preferred Shareholders*	(270,000)	1,000,000
Total Equities		$6,000,000

*[(6%)($4,500,000)]

Partial Income Statement
Year Ending December 31, 2002

Operating Revenues	$660,000
Operating Expenses	(440,000)
Operating Income	$220,000

No dividends were paid on the Common Stock during 2002.

Required: Ignore tax considerations when solving this problem.

A. Assume that the preferred shares do not have a scheduled redemption date and are not redeemable at the option of the holder. Prepare an Income Statement for the year ending December 31, 2002. In addition, provide the journal entry that would be required on January 1, 2003 if the Company purchased the Preferred Stock in the open market for $4,200,000 in cash.

B. Assume that the preferred shares are redeemable at the option of the holder. Prepare an Income Statement for the year ending December 31, 2002. In addition, provide the journal entry that would be required on January 1, 2003 if the Company purchased the Preferred Stock in the open market for $4,200,000 in cash.

End Of Exercise Fifteen - 2

Compound Financial Instruments

Basic Recommendation

15-69.   The most common example of the types of compound financial instruments under consideration here would be convertible securities. These involve either debt securities or preferred shares that are convertible, at the discretion of the holder, into a specified number of common shares. Stated alternatively, the basic security (debt or preferred shares) is accompanied by an option to acquire common shares.

15-70.   Prior to the introduction of Section 3860, when an enterprise issued such convertible securities, no recognition was given to the value associated with the option to acquire common shares. All of the consideration received by the enterprise was allocated either to the basic debt issue or the basic preferred stock issue. This procedure systematically understated the cost of carrying the debt or preferred shares and the value that had been contributed to the common stock equity of the enterprise.

15-71.   Section 3860 changes this situation dramatically as a result of the following Recommendation:

> **Paragraph 3860.24**   *The issuer of a financial instrument that contains both a liability and an equity element should classify the instrument's component parts separately in accordance with paragraph 3860.18.* (January, 1996)

15-72.   As noted previously, *Handbook* Paragraph 3860.18 requires the classification of financial instruments in accordance with the substance of the contractual arrangement and the definitions of a financial liability and an equity instrument. This would clearly require that proceeds received from the issuance of convertible securities be divided between a financial liability and an equity instrument.

15-73.   A practical problem here is how to split the total proceeds of the convertible issue into the respective debt and equity components. Section 3860 does not deal with measurement issues and, as a consequence, it does not prescribe the use of any particular approach to this problem. However, Paragraph 3860.29 describes two approaches that might be used:

(a) assigning to the less easily measurable component (often an equity instrument) the residual amount after deducting from the instrument as a whole the amount separately determined for the component that is more easily measurable; and

(b) measuring the liability and equity components separately and, to the extent necessary, adjusting these amounts on a pro rata basis so that the sum of the components equals the amount of the instrument as a whole.

Separate Recognition Illustrated

15-74.   A simple example will serve to illustrate the application of these two approaches:

> **Example**   An entity issues 2,000 convertible bonds at the start of Year 1. The bonds have a three year term, and are issued at par with a face value of $1,000 per bond, giving total proceeds of $2,000,000. Interest is payable annually at a coupon rate of 6 percent. Each bond is convertible at any time up to maturity into 250 common shares.
>
> When the bonds are issued, the prevailing market interest rate for similar debt without conversion options is 9 percent. At the issue date, the market price of one common share is $3. The dividends expected over the three year term of the bonds amount to $0.14 per share at the end of each year. The risk free annual interest rate for a three year term is 5 percent.

15-75.   Using the first valuation approach, we would first determine the value of the bond component of the compound instrument on the basis of a simple present value calculation using the 9 percent market rate for non-convertible debt:

PV Principal - $2,000,000 After Three Years	$1,544,367
PV Interest - $120,000 Per Year For Three Years	303,755
Value Of Liability Component	$1,848,122

15-76.   Given the total issue price of $2,000,000, the value of the equity instrument would be calculated as follows:

Total Proceeds	$2,000,000
Market Value - Liability Component	(1,848,122)
Value Of Equity Component	$ 151,878

15-77.   The alternative valuation approach recognizes that it would also be possible to arrive at a separate determination of the fair value of the equity instrument. While this can be done using a variety of option pricing models, Section 3860 refers to the Black-Scholes model. If this model is applied, a value of $144,683 is arrived at for the equity instrument. (Students would not be expected to use the Black-Scholes model to calculate this number. For readers interested in further coverage of option pricing models, see the Appendix to this Chapter.)

15-78.   When this equity instrument value is combined with the present value of the debt instrument, the total value for the issues is as follows:

Value Of Liability Instrument	$1,848,122
Value Of Equity Instrument	144,683
Total Combined Value	$1,992,805

15-79.   This combined value is $7,195 less than the $2,000,000 proceeds from the convertible issue. If this difference is pro rated to the two instruments on the basis of their independently determined values, the result is an allocation of $1,854,794 [$1,848,122 + ($1,848,122/$1,992,805)($7,195)] to the financial liability and $145,206 [$144,683 + ($144,683/$1,992,805)($7,195)] to the equity instrument.

Exercise Fifteen-3

Exercise
Fifteen-3
deals with
compound
financial
instruments.

An entity issues $4,500,000 face value convertible bonds on January 1, 2002. Interest is payable annually at a coupon rate of 8 percent. The bonds have a four year term and are issued for total proceeds of $4,575,360, a price that provides the purchaser with an effective yield of 7.5 percent. Each bond is convertible at any time up to maturity into 10 common shares and, at the time the bonds are issued, the shares are trading at $80. When the bonds are issued, the prevailing market interest rate for similar debt without conversion options is 8 percent.

On January 1, 2006, the shares are trading at $120. After the interest payment that is due on this date, all of the bonds are converted to common shares.

Required: Provide the journal entry required to record the issuance of the bonds on January 1, 2002, as well as the entry to record their conversion on January 1, 2006.

End Of Exercise Fifteen-3

Additional Points On Compound Financial Instruments

15-80.   Several additional points should be made with respect to these compound financial instruments:

Likelihood Of Conversion   Section 3860 notes that classification of the equity and liability components of convertible bonds should not be altered to reflect a change in the likelihood that the conversion option will be exercised. The value of the equity position is established at the time the convertible bonds are issued and, as with other components of Shareholders' Equity, it should not be altered to reflect changes in its value.

Carrying Value: Issuer As the issuer cannot usually transfer its obligation or terminate it prior to maturity or conversion, it will carry the liability component on a cost basis. Interest costs will be based on the effective yield method.

Carrying Value: Holder If the holder carries the components of the compound instrument at fair value, it may be unnecessary for it to account separately for the components. If the components are carried at cost, the components will be accounted for separately. The liability component may have to be reduced if there is an increase in credit risk. Correspondingly, the conversion right is subject to impairment as the time value inherent in the carrying amount decreases over time.

Conversion: Issuer On conversion, the issuer will reclassify the liability component to equity as part of the carrying value of the newly issued common shares. No gain or loss will be recognized on the transaction.

Conversion: Holder The holder will have a new investment in common shares that will be recorded at the aggregate carrying amount of the debt and conversion option components. No gain or loss will be recognized on the conversion.

Compound Commodity Linked Instruments

15-81. A compound commodity linked instrument gives rise to non-financial assets and liabilities as well as financial assets and liabilities, generally by giving the holder an option to exchange a financial asset for a non-financial asset. An oil linked bond, for example, usually gives the holder the right to receive a fixed amount of cash on maturity or earlier redemption, with a stream of fixed periodic interest payments, and the option to exchange the principal amount for a fixed quantity of oil on maturity or redemption.

15-82. This Section applies only to the financial liability of the issuer and financial asset of the holder of a commodity linked or similar type of compound instrument. On initial recognition, the financial and non-financial components are recognized separately, based on an allocation of the total consideration paid or received for the compound instrument.

15-83. Normally, a commodity linked instrument is issued at a price such that the value of the exchange option is small. The option will generally be "out-of-the-money" and will have no intrinsic value. Options are said to be out-of-the-money when the option price is greater than the current fair market value of the related commodity. Even if the commodity's market price increases to the point where the option is "in-the-money", a financial liability continues to exist until the option is exercised. This reflects the fact that the price of the commodity may drop, taking the option "out-of-the-money".

Offsetting Of A Financial Asset And A Financial Liability
Basic Recommendation

15-84. The basic Recommendation in this area is as follows:

Paragraph 3860.34 *A financial asset and a financial liability should be offset and the net amount reported in the balance sheet when an entity:*

(a) *has a legally enforceable right to set off the recognized amounts; and*
(b) *intends either to settle on a net basis, or to realize the asset and settle the liability simultaneously.* (January, 1996)

General Rules

15-85. In general, GAAP does not permit the offsetting of assets and liabilities for the purpose of Balance Sheet disclosure. However, when this procedure reflects the entity's expected future cash flows, Section 3860 requires offsetting.

15-86.   This would generally be the case only when a debtor has the legal right to eliminate all or a portion of an obligation due to a creditor by applying against that obligation an amount due to the debtor. This is referred to as the right to offset the recognized amounts.

15-87.   In addition to having the right to set off, the conditions for offsetting require that the entity actually intends to use that right to settle the liability. If the entity intends to realize the asset and settle the liability separately, offsetting is not permitted. Intent may be influenced by an entity's normal business practice, the requirements of the financial markets in which it operates or other circumstances that may limit its ability to settle net or to settle simultaneously.

15-88.   While it is not a common situation, a debtor may have a legal right to apply an amount due from a third party against the amount due to a creditor. Provided there is an agreement among the three parties that clearly establishes the debtor's right of offset, Paragraph 3860.34 would be applicable.

15-89.   Section 3860 distinguishes between offsetting a recognized financial asset and a recognized financial liability and the removal of a previously recognized item from the Balance Sheet. The basic difference is that with the removal of a previously recognized item, there may be a gain or loss to be recognized. This could not happen with offsetting.

15-90.   Paragraph 3860.41 notes that offsetting is not appropriate in the following circumstances:

(a) several different financial instruments are used to emulate the features of a single financial instrument (i.e., a "synthetic instrument");

(b) financial assets and financial liabilities arise from financial instruments having the same primary risk exposure (for example, assets and liabilities within a portfolio of forward contracts or other derivative instruments) but involve different counterparties;

(c) financial or other assets are pledged as collateral for non-recourse financial liabilities;

(d) financial assets are set aside in trust by a debtor for the purpose of discharging an obligation without those assets having been accepted by the creditor in settlement of the obligation (for example, a sinking fund arrangement); or

(e) obligations incurred as a result of events giving rise to losses are expected to be recovered from a third party by virtue of a claim made under an insurance policy.

15-91.   Section 3860 notes the existence of "master netting arrangements". These arise when an entity undertakes a large number of financial instrument transactions with a single counterparty. Such agreements provide for a single net settlement of all financial instruments covered by the agreement, usually only in the event of default on, or termination of, any one contract. They are used by financial institutions to provide protection against loss in the event of bankruptcy or events that result in a counterparty being unable to meet its obligations. Since these arrangements normally only come into effect in unusual circumstances, there is no intent to settle on a net basis as part of the normal business operations. As a result, these master netting arrangements do not provide a basis for offsetting.

Disclosure
General Requirements
15-92.   The disclosures required by this Section are intended to provide information that will enhance users' understanding of the significance of recognized and unrecognized financial instruments to an entity's financial position, performance and cash flows and to assist in assessing the amounts, timing and certainty of future cash flows associated with those instruments.

15-93.   Beyond providing quantitative information on financial instrument balances and transactions, entities are encouraged to provide a discussion of the extent to which financial instruments are used, the associated risks and the business purposes associated with financial instruments, including policies on matters such as hedging of risk exposures, avoidance of undue concentrations of risk and requirements for collateral to mitigate credit risks.

15-94.   Section 3860 does not prescribe the format of the required disclosures or its location within the financial statements. In the case of recognized financial instruments, balances will be included in the financial statements. There is no requirement that such information be repeated in the notes to the financial statements. In dealing with unrecognized financial instruments, the required disclosures can only be presented in notes or other supplementary types of information.

15-95.   With respect to the level of detail for the required disclosures, it will be necessary to strike a balance between providing excessive detail that is of little value to users and obscuring significant information by using too much aggregation. Such decisions will require the exercise of professional judgment.

15-96.   For disclosure purposes, management will be required to group financial instruments into appropriate classes. Characteristics that will be used in this process would include:

• Whether the instruments are recognized or unrecognized.

• The measurement basis used (cost vs. fair value).

15-97.   When disclosure of a particular instrument or group of instruments is included in both the notes and the financial statements, users should be able to reconcile the information contained in the two locations.

Accounting Policies

15-98.   As there are alternative accounting polices for dealing with financial instruments, Section 1505, "Disclosure Of Accounting Policies", would be applicable. The disclosure required by Section 1505 for financial instruments could include:

(a) the criteria applied in determining when to recognize a financial asset or financial liability on the balance sheet and when to cease to recognize it;

(b) the basis of measurement applied to financial assets and financial liabilities both on initial recognition and subsequently; and

(c) the basis on which income and expense arising from financial assets and financial liabilities is recognized and measured.

15-99.   Section 3860 lists the following as transactions where it may be necessary to disclose accounting policies:

(a) transfers of financial assets when there is a continuing interest in, or involvement with, the assets by the transferor, such as securitizations of financial assets, repurchase agreements and reverse repurchase agreements;

(b) transfers of financial assets to a trust for the purpose of satisfying liabilities when they mature without the obligation of the transferor being discharged at the time of the transfer, such as an in-substance defeasance trust;

(c) acquisition or issuance of separate financial instruments as part of a series of transactions designed to synthesize the effect of acquiring or issuing a single instrument;

(d) acquisition or issuance of financial instruments as hedges of risk exposures; and

(e) acquisition or issuance of monetary financial instruments bearing a stated interest rate that differs from the prevailing market rate at the date of issue.

15-100.   With respect to disclosure of accounting policies for measuring financial instruments, Section 3860 points out that it is not adequate to simply indicate the use of cost or fair value. Additional information is necessary to allow users to understand how the method has been applied. For example, when cost is used, the entity might be required to disclose how it accounts for:

- Costs of acquisition or issuance;

- Premiums and discounts on monetary financial assets and financial liabilities;

- Changes in the estimated amount of determinable future cash flows associated with a monetary financial instrument such as a bond indexed to a commodity price;

- Changes in circumstances that result in significant uncertainty about the timely collection of all contractual amounts due from monetary financial assets;

- Declines in the fair value of financial assets below their carrying amount; and

- Restructured financial liabilities.

15-101.   For instruments carried at fair value, disclosure should include the methods used in determining these amounts (quoted market prices, appraisals, etc.).

15-102.   Accounting policy disclosure would include the basis for reporting in the income statement realized and unrealized gains and losses, interest, and other items of income and expense associated with financial instruments. When income and expense items are netted in the Income Statement and the corresponding Balance Sheet items are not netted, the reason for such presentation should be disclosed.

Terms And Conditions
15-103.   The basic Recommendation in this area is as follows:

Paragraph 3860.52   *For each class of financial asset, financial liability and equity instrument, both recognized and unrecognized, an entity should disclose information about the extent and nature of the financial instruments, including significant terms and conditions that may affect the amount, timing and certainty of future cash flows.* (January, 1996)

15-104.   The Section makes a number of additional points with respect to general disclosure:

Paragraph 3860.54   ... terms and conditions that may warrant disclosure include:

(a) the principal, stated, face or other similar amount which, for some derivative instruments, such as interest rate swaps, may be the amount (referred to as the notional amount) on which future payments are based;

(b) the date of maturity, expiry or execution;

(c) early settlement options held by either party to the instrument, including the period in which, or date at which, the options may be exercised and the exercise price or range of prices;

(d) options held by either party to the instrument to convert the instrument into, or exchange it for, another financial instrument or some other asset or liability, including the period in which, or date at which the options may be exercised and the conversion or exchange ratio(s);

(e) the amount and timing of scheduled future cash receipts or payments of the principal amount of the instrument, including instalment repayments and any sinking fund or similar requirements;

(f)   stated rate or amount of interest, dividend or other periodic return on principal and the timing of the payments;

(g) collateral held, in the case of a financial asset, or pledged, in the case of a financial liability;

(h) in the case of an instrument for which cash flows are denominated in a currency other than the entity's reporting currency, the currency in which receipts or payments are required;

(i) in the case of an instrument that provides for an exchange, information described in items (a) to (h) for the instrument to be acquired in the exchange; and

(j) any condition of the instrument or an associated covenant that, if contravened, would significantly alter any of the other terms (for example, a maximum debt-to-equity ratio in a bond covenant that, if contravened, would make the full principal amount of the bond due and payable immediately).

Individual Vs. Group Disclosure   If no single instrument is individually significant to the future cash flows of the entity, the essential characteristics of the instruments should be described by reference to appropriate groupings of like instruments.

Other Specific Requirements   Other *Handbook* Sections may have specific disclosure requirements for financial instruments (e.g., Section 3050, "Long Term Investments").

Legal Form   When the Balance Sheet presentation of a financial instrument differs from the instrument's legal form (e.g., preferred stock presented as debt), it is desirable for an entity to explain in the notes to the financial statements the nature of the instrument.

Relationships Between Instruments   Disclosure should be made in a manner that indicates the nature and extent of the associated financial risk exposures and any relationships between instruments that alter the entity's overall risk exposure. Examples of this would include the relationship between a hedging instrument and the related hedged position, or the relationship between the components of a synthetic instrument.

Disclosures Concerning Interest Rate Risk

15-105.   The basic Recommendation in this area is as follows:

Paragraph 3860.57   *For each class of financial asset and financial liability, both recognized and unrecognized, an entity should disclose information about its exposure to interest rate risk, including:*

(a) contractual repricing or maturity dates, whichever dates are earlier; and
(b) effective interest rates, when applicable. (January, 1996)

15-106.   This disclosure would include which of the entity's financial assets are exposed to:

(a) **Interest Rate Price Risk**   An example of this would be monetary financial assets or financial liabilities with a fixed interest rate.

(b) **Interest Rate Cash Flow Risk**   An example of this would be a monetary financial asset or financial liability with a floating interest rate that is reset as market rates change.

(c) **Not Exposed To Interest Rate Risk**   An example of this would be some investments in equity securities.

15-107.   In transactions such as securitization, an entity may retain exposure to interest rate risk on financial assets, even when those assets are removed from the Balance Sheet. Correspondingly, it may be exposed to interest rate risk as the result of a transaction where no financial asset or financial liability is recognized. An example of this latter situation would be a commitment to issue funds at a specified rate of interest. Despite the fact that the relevant financial assets or liabilities are not included in the Balance Sheet, disclosure of the nature and extent of the entity's exposure should be provided.

15-108.   Changes in interest rates have a direct impact on the cash flows associated with particular financial assets or financial liabilities. Information about contractual repricing or maturity dates provides users with information as to how long interest rates are fixed. This gives a basis for evaluating interest rate price risk and, thereby, the potential for gain or loss. In the case of instruments that are repriced prior to maturity, the repricing date is clearly more relevant than the maturity date.

15-109. While the basic Recommendation refers to contractually determined repricing or maturity dates, expected repricing or maturity dates may differ from those specified in the legal arrangement. An example of this would be mortgage loans where the creditor can choose to repay prior to maturity. When management is able to predict with reasonable reliability the expected dates on which the loans will be repaid, disclosure of this information can be useful.

15-110. The effective interest rate on a monetary financial instrument is the rate that, when used to discount the future cash flows from the instrument, will equate its value to the carrying amount of the instrument. The future cash flows would extend to the next repricing or maturity date. The rate is a historical one for fixed rate instruments carried at amortized cost and a current market rate for floating rate instruments or instruments carried at fair value.

15-111. This requirement for disclosure of the effective interest rate applies to bonds, notes, and other similar monetary financial instruments that create a return to the holder and a cost to the issuer which reflects the time value of money. It does not apply to financial instruments that do not provide a determinable interest rate. This would include non-monetary financial instruments and most derivative instruments.

15-112. Section 3860 provides a description of several possible formats for providing the required information on interest rate risk:

(a) The carrying amounts of financial instruments exposed to interest rate price risk may be presented in tabular form, grouped by those that are contracted to mature or reprice (i) within one year of the balance sheet date, (ii) more than one year and less than five years from the balance sheet date, and (iii) five years or more from the balance sheet date.

(b) When the performance of an entity is significantly affected by the level of its exposure to interest rate price risk or changes in that exposure, more detailed information is desirable. An entity such as a bank may disclose, for example, separate groupings of the carrying amounts of financial instruments contracted to mature or reprice (i) within one month of the balance sheet date, (ii) more than one and less than three months from the balance sheet date, and (iii) more than three and less than twelve months from the balance sheet date.

(c) Similarly, an entity may indicate its exposure to interest rate cash flow risk through a table indicating the aggregate carrying amount of groups of floating rate financial assets and financial liabilities maturing within various future time periods.

(d) Interest rate information may be disclosed for individual financial instruments or weighted average rates or a range of rates may be presented for each class of financial instrument. An entity groups instruments denominated in different currencies or having substantially different credit risks into separate classes when these factors result in instruments having substantially different effective interest rates.

15-113. Information about interest rate sensitivity may also be useful. This would involve indicating the effect of a hypothetical change in the prevailing level of market interest rates on the fair value of financial instruments and future earnings and cash flows from these instruments.

15-114. In the case of floating rate instruments, this would involve indicating possible changes in interest income or interest expense. In the case of fixed rate instruments, the reporting would involve disclosing potential gains or losses.

15-115. Sensitivity disclosure should include information about the basis on which the information is prepared, including any significant assumptions that have been made. The disclosure may or may not be limited to the direct effects of interest rate changes on the instruments that are on hand on the Balance Sheet date.

Disclosures Concerning Credit Risk

15-116.   The basic Recommendation in this area is as follows:

Paragraph 3860.67   *For each class of financial asset, both recognized and unrecognized, an entity should disclose information about its exposure to credit risk, including:*

(a) the amount that best represents its maximum credit risk exposure at the balance sheet date, without taking account of the fair value of any collateral, in the event other parties fail to perform their obligations under financial instruments; and

(b) significant concentrations of credit risk. (January, 1996)

15-117.   This disclosure Recommendation is designed to assist users in assessing the extent to which failures by counterparties to discharge obligations could reduce the amount of future cash inflows from financial assets on hand at the Balance Sheet date. While such failures will give rise to a financial loss to be included in the entity's Income Statement, the Recommendation does not require an entity to disclose an assessment of the probability of losses arising in the future.

15-118.   Note that this disclosure requirement is for amounts exposed to credit risk, without regard to potential recoveries from collateral. Reasons for this approach are as follows:

(a) to ensure that the users of financial statements have a consistent measure of the amount exposed to that risk for all financial assets, whether the assets are recognized or not; and

(b) to take into account the possibility that the exposure to loss may differ from the carrying amount of a recognized financial asset or the fair value of an unrecognized financial asset that is otherwise disclosed in the financial statements.

15-119.   Section 3860 makes several additional points with respect to the disclosure of credit risk:

Recognized Financial Assets   In the case of recognized financial assets exposed to credit risk, the carrying value of the assets in the Balance Sheet, net of an appropriate provision for loss, usually represents the amount of exposure to credit risk. In situations such as this, no additional disclosure, beyond that provided in the Balance Sheet, is required.

Unrecognized Financial Assets   With unrecognized financial assets, the maximum credit risk exposure may be equal to the principal, stated, face or other similar contractual value for the asset. This value would be disclosed in accordance with Paragraph 3860.52 and no further disclosure is required. Similarly, when the maximum credit risk of an unrecognized financial asset is equal to its fair value, this amount would be disclosed in accordance with Paragraph 3860.78 and no further disclosure is required. However, if the maximum possible loss on an unrecognized financial asset differs from the amounts disclosed in accordance with Paragraph 3860.52 or 3860.78, additional disclosure is required.

Set Off Rights   When an entity has a legally enforceable right to set off a financial asset against a financial liability, the net amount will be reported in the Balance Sheet, provided there is an intent to settle on a net basis. Disclosure under Paragraph 3860.67 should include the existence of the legal right of set off. Further, if the financial liability against which a right of set off exists is due to be settled before the financial asset, the entity is exposed to credit risk on the full carrying amount of the asset if the counterparty defaults after the liability has been settled.

Master Netting Arrangements   An entity may have entered into a master netting arrangement that mitigates exposure to credit loss but does not meet the criteria for offsetting. It is desirable for the entity to disclose the terms of the master netting arrangement. Additional disclosure should indicate that:

- the credit risk associated with financial assets subject to a master netting arrangement is eliminated only to the extent that financial liabilities due to the same counterparty will be settled after the assets are realized; and

- the extent to which an entity's overall exposure to credit risk is reduced through a master netting arrangement may change substantially within a short period following the balance sheet date because the exposure is affected by each transaction subject to the arrangement.

Guarantees   If an entity guarantees an obligation of another party, disclosure is required under Paragraph 3860.67. This would include situations such as securitization transactions in which an entity remains exposed by recourse provisions even after the relevant assets have been removed from its Balance Sheet.

Concentrations Of Credit Risk   These must be disclosed separately when they are not inherent in the business of an entity and not apparent from other disclosures. This disclosure should include a description of the shared characteristic that identifies each concentration and the amount of the maximum possible exposure to loss associated with all recognized and unrecognized financial assets sharing that characteristic.

Concentrations of credit risk may arise from exposures to a single debtor or to a group of debtors having similar characteristics. Such concentrations might also arise if a large portion of an entity's debtors are in a single industry or single geographic area. Section 1700, "Segmented Information" may provide useful guidance in identifying the types of credit risk concentrations that may arise and determining the appropriate degree of disaggregation in general purpose financial statements.

Disclosures Concerning Fair Value

15-120.   The basic Recommendation in this area is as follows:

Paragraph 3860.78   *For each class of financial asset and financial liability, both recognized and unrecognized, an entity should disclose information about fair value. When it is not practicable within constraints of timeliness or cost to determine the fair value of a financial asset or financial liability with sufficient reliability, that fact should be disclosed together with information about the principal characteristics of the underlying financial instrument that are pertinent to its fair value. (January, 1996)*

15-121.   Fair value information is crucial to many types of business decisions. It is a value that reflects the judgment of the financial markets as to the present value of the expected future cash flows associated with an instrument. These values provide a neutral basis for assessing management's stewardship by indicating the effects of its decisions to buy, sell, or hold financial assets and, incur, maintain, or discharge financial liabilities. Fair values are essential for making comparisons of financial instruments as they are not influenced by the purpose for which the instrument is being used, or by when or by whom the instrument was issued or acquired.

15-122.   Additional points made by Section 3860 with respect to the disclosure of fair value information are as follows:

Location Of Disclosure   When an entity does not carry a financial asset or financial liability in its Balance Sheet at fair value, the information will have to be provided through note or other supplementary disclosures.

Methods   As fair value can be determined by a variety of methods, disclosure should be made of the methods used.

Going Concern Assumption   In the determination of fair values, the entity should assume that it is a going concern and that the amount that would be paid or received would not be based on a forced transaction or involuntary liquidation. However, the fair value of a financial asset that is to be sold in the immediate future would be influenced by the depth of the market for the asset.

Instruments Traded In Active Markets For financial instruments traded in active markets, the quoted market price, adjusted for potential transaction costs, would be the best evidence of fair value. When there are separate bid and ask prices, the following would apply:

- For assets held or liabilities to be issued, use the bid price.

- For assets to be acquired or liabilities held, use the ask price.

Instruments Without Usable Market Prices In situations where market prices do not exist or where the volumes of trading are too small to provide reliable values, estimation techniques will be used to determine fair values. These would include references to other similar instruments, discounted cash flow analysis, and option pricing models.

Transaction Costs Fair values should include all costs that would be incurred to exchange or settle the underlying financial instrument. These would include taxes and duties, fees and commissions paid to agents, advisers, brokers or dealers, and levies by regulatory agencies or securities exchanges.

Range Of Values When an instrument is not traded in an active and efficient market, it may be more appropriate to disclose a range in which the fair value is reasonably believed to lie, rather than a single figure.

Inability To Determine Fair Values When disclosure of fair value information is omitted because it is not possible to arrive at a sufficiently reliable figure, disclosure should be provided to assist users of financial statements in making their own judgments. If there is a reasonable basis for doing so, management may give its opinion as to the relationship between the fair value and carrying value of such instruments.

Other Issues For those financial instruments that are carried on the Balance Sheet at other than fair values, the disclosure of fair values should be in a form that permits comparison with the carrying values. With respect to offsetting fair value disclosures, this should happen only to the extent that the related carrying amounts are offset. Fair values for unrecognized financial instruments should be presented separately from the fair values for recognized items.

15-123. As was the case with the provisions related to re-classification of certain types of preferred shares, this disclosure provision was a problem for smaller companies. As a consequence, Section 1300, "Differential Reporting", indicates that non-publicly accountable enterprises will no longer have to provide certain fair value disclosures unless they are "readily obtainable". See Chapter 3 of the *Guide To Canadian Financial Reporting* for a more detailed discussion of this change. The *Guide* is available on the CD-ROM that accompanies this text.

Disclosure Of Financial Assets Carried At An Amount In Excess Of Fair Value

15-124. The basic Recommendation here is as follows:

Paragraph 3860.89 *When an entity carries one or more financial assets at an amount in excess of their fair value, the entity should disclose:*

(a) *the carrying amount and the fair value of either the individual assets, or appropriate groupings of those individual assets; and*

(b) *the reasons for not reducing the carrying amount, including the nature of the evidence that provides the basis for management's belief that the carrying amount will be recovered.* (January, 1996)

15-125. The decision to not write down a financial asset when its carrying value is in excess of its fair value involves an exercise of management judgment. The disclosure that is required here provides users with an understanding of this judgment process and with a basis for assessing the possibility that circumstances may eventually lead to a reduction in the asset's carrying value.

15-126. The entity's approach to dealing with declines in the value of financial assets, should be disclosed as per the Recommendations of Section 1505, "Disclosure Of Accounting Policies". This should include an indication of the evidence specific to the asset that leads management to the conclusion that the asset's carrying amount will be recovered.

Disclosures Concerning Hedges

15-127. In the economic sense, hedging concerns the reduction or elimination of the effects of market risk, interest rate risk or currency risk, some or all of which may be present in a financial instrument. It involves entering into some type of transaction with a view to reducing the entity's exposure to losses due to these types of price risk. In most hedging situations, an additional consequence of the transaction is to reduce the potential for profit associated with a financial instrument.

15-128. A wide variety of hedging instruments are available in today's financial markets. They include forward contracts, futures contracts, interest rate and currency swaps, caps, collars, floors, as well as various types of option arrangements. For the most part, hedging instruments are derivative in nature and designed to transfer one element of the risks inherent in a particular primary instrument.

15-129. Accounting procedures for these instruments are complicated by the fact that they are often used for speculative as well as hedging purposes as can be shown in the following simple example.

> **Example** On January 1, 2002, an enterprise with a December 31 year end enters a forward exchange contract to take delivery of 1,000,000 Foreign Currency Units (FCU, hereafter) on July 1, 2003. If the contract rate is FCU1 = $0.90 (equal to the spot rate on that date), and the spot rate on December 31, 2002 is FCU1 = $0.80, the question of whether or not this contract is serving as a hedge becomes very significant.

> **Example Solution** If the contract was entered for purely speculative purposes, the forward exchange contract would be classified as an operating instrument subject to fair value accounting procedures. This would mean that a loss of $100,000 {[FCU1,000,000)][($0.90 - $0.80)]} would have to be recorded and taken into 2002 Net Income. Alternatively, if the enterprise has a FCU1,000,000 payable that is due on July 1, 2003, the contract is serving as a hedge and hedge accounting becomes appropriate.

15-130. Under hedge accounting procedures, gains and losses on a hedging instrument are recognized on the same basis as the corresponding loss or gain on the hedged position. This means that the $100,000 loss on the forward contract would be exactly offset by a corresponding gain on the FCU1,000,000 payable, resulting in no inclusion in the 2002 Net Income of the enterprise. This somewhat oversimplified example serves to make clear the importance of distinguishing between those financial instruments that are being used as a hedge and those that would be classified as operating transactions.

15-131. Because of the importance of this classification issue, Section 3860 contains the following disclosure Recommendation related to hedging relationships:

> **Paragraph 3860.92** *When an entity has accounted for a financial instrument as a hedge of risks associated with anticipated future transactions, it should disclose:*
>
> *(a) a description of the anticipated transactions, including the period of time until they are expected to occur;*
>
> *(b) a description of the hedging instruments; and*
>
> *(c) the amount of any deferred or unrecognized gain or loss and the expected timing of recognition as income or expense. (January, 1996)*

54-132. The information required in this Recommendation permits the users of an entity's financial statements to understand the nature and effect of a hedge of an anticipated future transaction. This information may be provided on an aggregate basis when a hedged position comprises several anticipated transactions or has been hedged by several financial instruments.

15-133.   The Paragraph 3860.92(c) Recommendation should be applied without regard to whether the gains or losses have been recognized in the financial statements. This Recommendation is complicated by the fact that the accounting for the hedging instrument may take a variety of forms:

- If the hedging instrument is carried at fair value, any gain or loss will be unrealized, but recorded in the entity's Balance Sheet.
- If the hedging instrument is carried at cost, any gain or loss will be unrecognized.
- If the hedging instrument has been sold or settled, the gain or loss will be realized.

15-134.   In all of these cases, the gain or loss will be deferred until such time as the hedged transaction is completed.

15-135.   Further guidance in this area was provided when, in December, 2001, Accounting Guideline No. 13, "Hedging Relationships" was issued. This Guideline is discussed in Chapter 9, Foreign Currency Transactions. Although the Guideline specifically addresses hedges of foreign currency items, it is equally applicable to other types of hedges.

Other Disclosures

15-136.   Paragraph 3860.95 provides examples of other information that may be desirable to disclose:

> **Paragraph 3860.95**   Additional disclosures are encouraged when they are likely to enhance financial statement users' understanding of financial instruments. It may be desirable to disclose such information as:
>
> (a) the total amount of the change in the fair value of financial assets and financial liabilities that has been recognized as income or expense for the period;
>
> (b) the total amount of deferred or unrecognized gain or loss on hedging instruments other than those relating to hedges of anticipated future transactions; and
>
> (c) the average aggregate carrying amount during the year of recognized financial assets and financial liabilities, the average aggregate principal, stated, notional or other similar amount during the year of unrecognized financial assets and financial liabilities and the average aggregate fair value during the year of all financial assets and financial liabilities, particularly when the amounts on hand at the balance sheet date are unrepresentative of amounts on hand during the year.

Other Issues

Recognition and De-recognition

15-137.   Recognition is the process of recording an item in the financial statements of an entity. De-recognition is the process of removing an item from the financial statements. General recognition criteria are provided in Section 1000 of the *CICA Handbook*, "Financial Statement Concepts", and specific guidance on revenue recognition is found in Section 3400, "Revenue". In both of these sections, recognition by an entity requires that two criteria be satisfied. One is that the item must have a reasonable basis of measurement. The second is that the significant risks and rewards of ownership must rest with the entity.

15-138.   The JWG's Draft Standard takes a similar position with respect to financial assets and liabilities. An enterprise should recognize a financial instrument when it has the contractual rights or obligations that result in an asset or liability and de-recognize a financial instrument or a component thereof when it no longer has the pertinent rights or obligations. The proposal requires a components approach to transfers involving financial instruments. The entity must assess the nature of the instrument and its component parts, and examine its involvement in the rights and obligations associated with those component parts. It may be appropriate to treat the instrument as a whole or to disaggregate it and treat its component parts differently, according to circumstances.

15-139.   It is difficult to apply this approach to complex transfers where the transferor has a continuing involvement in the transferred assets, such as securitizations or sale and repurchase arrangements or stock lending arrangements. In these transactions, assessing whether the continuing involvement is significant enough to warrant keeping the assets on the entity's books requires considerable judgment. Generally, the Draft Standard requires that a transferor continue to recognise a transferred financial asset, or its component parts, if the transferor has a conditional or unconditional obligation to repay the consideration received, or if the transferor has a call option over the transferred component that the transferee does not have the practical ability to transfer to a third party.

15-140.   The CICA has provided guidance on a number of these complex areas by means of Accounting Guidelines, such as Accounting Guideline No. 12, "Transfer of Receivables", and Abstracts of Emerging Issues, such as EIC Abstract No. 79 , "Gain Recognition In Arm's Length And Related Party Transactions When The Consideration Received Includes A Claim On The Asset Sold", and EIC Abstract No. 85, "Seller's Retention of Substantial Risk Of Ownership". These topics are very complex and require considerable expertise to interpret and apply. As such, a detailed discussion of these issues is beyond the scope of this chapter.

Determining Fair Values

15-141.   It is generally understood that fair value information is widely used for business purposes. In SFAS No. 133, the FASB stated "fair value is the most relevant measure for financial instruments and the only relevant measure for derivative instruments". Currently, in Canada, if an entity does not carry a financial asset or liability at its fair value in the Balance Sheet, it usually provides fair value information through supplementary disclosures. If the JWG's Draft Standard is accepted, actual recognition of fair values in the financial statements will become the norm.

15-142.   As was discussed in our coverage of that material, Section 3860 provides considerable guidance on the determination of fair values. The JWG's Draft Standard provides further guidance on the use of fair values. Specifically, it states that:

- The fair value of a financial instrument is an estimate of its market exit price in an arm's length transaction.

- Expected costs to complete the transaction should *not* be deducted in estimating the fair value. This is in contrast to the position taken in Section 3860 which indicated that, when market values are used to determine fair values, the quoted values should be adjusted for transaction costs.

- The best market price is an actual transaction price for an identical instrument on the measurement date. If that is not available, prices for similar instruments on dates close to the measurement date may be used and adjusted if necessary. Special considerations are required when certain situations exist, such as infrequent trading or holdings of large blocks that would affect how useful the market exit prices are for estimating fair values.

- When fair values cannot be estimated using market values, valuation techniques should be used. If there is a valuation technique that is commonly used by market participants to price the instrument being measured, the enterprise should use that technique.

Accounting For Derivatives

Background

15-143.   Accounting for primary financial instruments is not covered in this chapter. It is assumed that the readers of this text have studied accounting for receivables, bonds, shares and other primary instruments in other accounting courses. The focus here will be on derivative financial instruments. Derivative instruments, such as financial options, futures and forwards, interest rate swaps and currency swaps, are financial instruments that derive their value through some type of relationship with a primary financial instrument.

15-144.   This subject is complicated by the previously noted fact that there is a long and growing list of such financial instruments. Given this, it would not be possible to provide anything approaching a comprehensive treatment of this subject. Our solution to this problem will be to give primary attention to what is perhaps the commonly used derivative financial instrument — stock rights.

15-145.   Corporations often issue rights that provide the holder with the option to acquire a specified number of company shares under specific conditions and within a specified period of time. Depending on how they are being used, stock rights are also referred to as stock options or stock warrants. The major uses of rights are as follows:

- To honour the pre-emptive rights of existing shareholders when the company is planning a new share issue. In this context, the term stock rights is the normal designation.

- As compensation to officers and employees. In this context, the term stock options is normally used.

- As payment to outside parties for purchased goods and services. The term stock options is also used here.

- As a poison pill to discourage hostile take-overs.   Here again, the normal designation is stock options.

- With other financial instruments being issued to the public to make the issue more attractive. In this context, the normal designation is stock warrants.

15-146.   As previously discussed, Section 3860 addresses accounting for options issued with other debt or equity securities as sweeteners. Whether these options are issued as separate instruments or as conversion privileges built in to other securities, the issue price must be allocated to the component parts and separately recognized in the accounts according to their economic substance.

15-147.   Until December 2001, there were no Canadian pronouncements dealing with the other types of stock rights issues. Because many of these rights were issued for no consideration, or for consideration that was not easily measured, they were typically recorded only by memorandum entry. The new *Handbook* Section 3870 "Stock-Based Compensation and Other Stock-Based Payments" will change that. It provides comprehensive treatment of all types of stock-based compensation, including stock options. This *Handbook* Section is large and complex, involving issues that go beyond the scope of this Chapter. If you have a particular interest in this area, we would refer you to Chapter 55 of our *Guide To Canadian Financial Reporting* which provides comprehensive treatment of this Section.

15-148.   Following our discussion of stock rights, some examples of accounting for other types of derivatives will be provided.

Stock Options
Basic Concepts
15-149.   Assume that an employee is granted an option to buy 5,000 company shares at $20 per share. How should this be accounted for? Generally, non-monetary exchanges should be recorded at the fair value of the consideration given up unless the fair value of the consideration received is more clearly determinable. The benefit received in this case is employee effort, which is difficult to measure. Thus we look at the fair value of the option granted. Is this determinable? Some companies' stock options trade on stock exchanges. Can these values be used? The problem with this approach is that there is no market for options granted as compensation. Employees usually cannot trade such options. They, or their beneficiaries, must either exercise them or allow them to expire. Because of measurement uncertainties, traditional accounting for stock options has relied on a piecemeal approach. Until recently, there was no Canadian accounting pronouncement on this issue, and companies generally followed the guidance of APB No. 25, *Accounting for Stock Issued to Employees*, which was released in the United States in 1972. This pronouncement suggests the use of what is known as the intrinsic value approach to accounting for stock options.

15-150. To illustrate, let's continue with the preceding example. If the option is granted for current or past performance, the option is usually issued in-the-money (e.g., the exercise price is less than the current market price). The excess of current market price of the share over exercise price is called the intrinsic value of the option and this intrinsic value has been used in the past to measure compensation expense. Assuming that the current market price of the shares is $22 on the grant date, traditional accounting practice measured compensation expense as $10,000 [(5,000)($22 - $20)] and the following entry was made:

Compensation Expense [(5,000)($22 - $20)] $10,000
        Stock Options $10,000

15-151. The account Stock Options is shown in the share capital section of shareholder's equity. If the options are later exercised, the company makes the following entry:

Cash [(5,000)($20)] $100,000
Stock Options   10,000
        Common Shares $110,000

15-152. On the other hand, the following entry is made if the options expire:

Stock Options $10,000
        Contributed Capital – Expired Options $10,000

15-153. In the preceding case, the options and the compensation expense are recognized in the company's books because the options have intrinsic value. However, if the option is intended as an incentive for future performance, which is usually the case, the option is normally issued out-of-the-money, that is, the exercise price is higher than the current market price of the share at grant date. Following the above measurement technique, no compensation expense is measured in this case.

15-154. Is this appropriate? Isn't the option still valuable, even if it is out-of-the-money? Since the option is good for a period of time, there is still a chance that the market price of the share will rise above the exercise price before the option expires. The value associated with this potential for future gains is generally referred to as the time value of the option. Thus, the value of an option stems from two aspects — intrinsic value and time value. Is time value measurable?

Section 3870 On Stock Options

15-155. Standard setters have long recognized that a failure to recognize the time value of options represents a major flaw in GAAP. While attempts have been made to require such measurement to be included in the accounts, to date they have not been successful. This alternative approach is generally referred to as the fair value approach and the use of this approach is encouraged in the new Section 3870. However, the Section permits the continued use of the intrinsic value approach to accounting for stock options when they are given as compensation to employees.

15-156. In somewhat simplified terms, Section 3870 identifies three situations in which stock options may be used. These situations, along with the appropriate accounting treatment, are discussed in the paragraphs which follow:

15-157. **Transactions With Non-Employees** There are situations in which an enterprise acquires goods or services from non-employees and pays for these items by issuing stock options. When options are used in these circumstances, the fair value approach must be used. Measurement can be based on either the fair value of the goods or services received or, alternatively, on the fair value of the options issued, whichever is more reliably measurable. This type of transaction is called a reciprocal transfer, since both parties to the contract give up something of value. When these contracts are signed prior to performance or payment, and when they involve contingencies that will be resolved in the future, there has been some uncertainty in the past as to when these transactions should be recognized. The AcSB provides guidance on this issue, specifying that the measurement date should be the earliest of:

- the date at which performance by the counter-party is complete,
- the date at which a performance commitment is reached, or
- the date at which the equity instruments are granted by the entity if they are fully vested and non-forfeitable at that time.

15-158.   Recording the contract at the date of performance commitment, prior to either performance or payment being completed, recognizes the contract relatively early in the process. This is considered appropriate since a commitment implies that performance is probable. Performance is considered probable when the contract specifies a penalty to the counter-party if performance is not forthcoming, a penalty that goes beyond simply forfeiting the right to be paid.

15-159.   Some aspects of the contract may depend on future events, such as a future stock price. When the contract is recognized before all conditions are met, changes to the fair value of the entity's commitment after the initial measurement date are recognized each period until all uncertainties are resolved. However, a cost that has been recognized should not be reversed if a stock option that the counter-party has a right to exercise lapses.

15-160.   If the transaction is a non-reciprocal transfer, such as an entity giving its shares to a charity, the transaction should be recorded at the date at which the terms of the transfer are known or the date of the commitment, whichever is later, using the fair value of the consideration given up.

15-161.   The following example illustrates a reciprocal transfer:

Example   On January 1, 2002, Sushi Company agrees to grant 2,000 stock options to an architect to design its new corporate office. The architect agrees to deliver the plans within one year. The option is exercisable at $20 anytime after the plans are delivered up to December 31, 2005. If at December 31, 2003, the stock price is not above $20, Sushi will grant up to 500 additional stock options. An option-pricing model measures the value of the unconditional options for 2,000 shares at $10,000 and the value of the conditional options at $2,000.

Example Solution   The entry to record the granting of this option would be:

Building* $12,000
      Stock options $12,000

*The cost of architectural services is properly capitalized as part of the cost of the new building.

The date of this entry would follow the recommendations of Paragraph 3870.14 and would likely be made on January 1, 2002, as long as there is evidence that a performance commitment exists at that date.

15-162.   **Non-Compensatory Transactions With Employees**   To be considered non-compensatory, a stock option plan must have the following characteristics:

- It must be available to substantially all full-time employees.
- The options must have a short life (no more than 31 days).
- The discount from market price must be small (less than five percent).

15-163.   Given these characteristics, the goal here is to issue new shares to employees, not to provide incentives for future performance. Such options would have no time value. As a consequence, the accounting is very straightforward. The amount received as payment for the shares is recorded as contributed capital, even if it is less than the market price of the shares at the time of issue.

15-164.   **Compensatory Transactions With Employees**   These are the options that we hear so much about in the financial and popular press. Their issuance is generally limited to a group of key executives, the option price is generally at or above the market price of the shares at time of issue and, because of their longer maturities, they have time value. While the use of fair value accounting is encouraged for this type of option, it is not required. Even through there is considerable pressure from analysts and other user groups to use this approach, the intrinsic value method can still be used for this type of stock option.

15-165. If the fair value approach is used, the fair value of the options issued will be accounted for as compensation expense. This type of option is generally awarded to encourage performance over some period of future service, usually measured as the period of time between the grant date and the date when the options become vested (e.g., no longer conditional on continued employment). Section 3870 requires that any compensation expense that is recognized be allocated over this service period.

15-166. The following example illustrates this type of situation:

Example Talbot Company grants 300 10-year options to each of its 300 employees on January 1, 2002 as part of their compensation. The exercise price is equal to the stock price on the grant date. All options vest at the end of three years to employees still with Talbot at that time. The company expects 3 percent of the options to be forfeited each year due to employee turnover. Actual forfeitures are 5 percent in 2002, but it is not until 2003 that Talbot is convinced that it should change its estimate to 6 percent per year. At the end of 2004, when the options become vested, forfeitures have averaged 6 percent per year. An option-pricing model measures the fair value of the options at grant date to be $12.05 each. The entries to recognize these options are:

2002

Compensation Expense	$329,931	
Stock Options		$329,931

[($12.05)(300)(300)(97%)(97%)(97%)]= $989,793 ÷ 3 years

The actual forfeiture rate of 5 percent in 2002 will not change the above calculation as long as management believes its 3 percent estimate will prevail over the 3-year vesting period. If there was no change in estimate during the vesting period, the same entry for the same amount would be made in both 2003 and 2004. But, in this case, Talbot changes its estimate to 6 percent in 2003. The revised number of options expected to vest is therefore 74,752 [(90,000)(94%)(94%)(94%)] and the new estimate of compensation expense is $900,768 [(74,752)($12.05)]. In 2003, Talbot will recognize compensation cost of $300,256 based on the new calculation ($900,768 ÷ 3) and will adjust the $29,675 ($300,256 - $329,931) over-accrual for last year, as follows:

2003

Stock Options	$29,675	
Compensation Expense		$29,675

Compensation Expense	$300,256	
Stock Options		$300,256

In 2004, since the actual forfeiture rate is 6 percent, no adjustment of the numbers accrued to date is necessary and the third entry is made as follows:

2004

Compensation Expense	$300,256	
Stock Options		$300,256

These options will remain on the balance sheet in the share capital section until exercised or until they expire.

Stock Appreciation Rights

15-167. In another common type of stock plan, the company grants stock appreciation rights (SARs) to selected employees. These rights allow the employee to receive cash, shares or a combination of cash and shares based on the difference between a specified share price and the quoted market price per share at some future date. SAR plans are accounted for the same way as regular stock option plans, except that:

- Compensation expense is not known for certain when it is initially recorded. Estimates are updated based on the quoted market price of the shares at the end of each period and any difference is treated as a change in estimate in the year of the share price change.

- Because SARs are primarily cash-based commitments and not commitments to issue equity, they are often shown as liabilities rather than as stock options in the shareholders' equity section.

15-168.   The following example illustrates the use of stock appreciation rights:

Example   Assume the same facts as in the preceding example on compensatory stock options, except that Talbot gives its employees a choice between receiving 300 stock options or 300 cash SARs. The employee makes the choice at exercise date.

Because the employee can choose a cash settlement, this commitment will be recorded as a liability. If Talbot could choose whether to honour the commitment with either stock or cash, the award would be treated as an equity instrument, unless Talbot's past practice has been to settle such awards with cash.

Relevant share prices are as follows:

At grant date	$50
December 31, 2002	$55
December 31, 2003	$58
December 31, 2004	$56

Example Solution   As noted, Section 3870 recommends that total expected compensation expense be measured on the basis of the difference between the end of the year price of the shares and the price specified in the SAR arrangement, multiplied by the number of SARs expected to vest times the stock price appreciation from grant date to year-end. Based on this approach, the entry will be:

2002

Compensation Expense	$136,901	
Liability Under SAR Plan		$136,901

[(300)(300)(97%)(97%)(97%)($55 - $50)] = $410,703 ÷ 3 years

At the end of each year thereafter, the liability is re-estimated based on the then-current market price and employment turnover experience as follows:

2003

Compensation Expense	$199,340	
Liability Under SAR Plan		$199,340

[(300)(300)(94%)(94%)(94%)($58 - $50)] = $598,020 ÷ 3 years

Compensation Expense	$62,439	
Liability Under SAR Plan		$62,439

To adjust for the 2002 under-accrual ($199,340 - $136,901)

2004

Compensation Expense	$149,505	
Liability Under SAR Plan		$149,505

[(300)(300)(94%)(94%)(94%)($56 - $50)] = $448,515 ÷ 3 years

Liability Under SAR Plan	$99,670	
Compensation Expense		$99,670

To adjust for the 2002 and 2003 over-accruals [($149,505)(2) – ($199,340)(2)]

This adjustment process would continue so that the compensation will ultimately be measured as the intrinsic value of the SARs at the exercise or expiration date. If the employee chooses to exercise the stock options instead of the cash SARs, the shares issued will be measured at the carrying value of the SARs liability at exercise date.

Other Derivative Examples

15-169.   The preceding section provided fairly detailed coverage of stock options. As noted, however, there are many other types of derivative arrangements. While it would not be feasible to attempt coverage of all of these arrangements, some additional examples of common situations are provided in this section.

Interest Rate Swaps

15-170.   The following example will serve to illustrate this type of derivative arrangement:

Example   Company X has a $1,000,000 bank loan with a rate of prime plus 1 percent and fears that interest rates will rise. Company Y has a $1,000,000 bank loan with a rate of 5.5 percent and therefore faces no risk from rising rates. However, Y thinks that rates may decline and so would prefer to have a variable loan. Given this, X and Y enter into an interest rate swap on February 1, 2003, that is, they enter into a contract whereby X will pay Y interest based on a fixed rate and Y will pay X interest at a variable rate. Assume that the prime rate is 4.20 percent in December, 2002, 4.25 percent in January, 2003, 4.33 percent in February, 2003 and 4.80 percent in March, 2003.

By borrowing money at a variable rate, the Company X has exposed itself to interest rate risk. The interest rate swap provides protection against this risk.

Example Solution   The journal entries required are as follows:

	Company X		Company Y	
December 31, 2002				
Interest Expense	$4,333		$4,583	
Cash		$4,333		$4,583
	[($1,000,000)(5.20%)(1/12)]		[($1,000,000)(5.5%)(1/12)]	
January 31, 2003				
Interest Expense	$4,375		$4,583	
Cash		$4,375		$4,583
	[($1,000,000)(5.25%)(1/12)]		[($1,000,000)(5.5%)(1/12)]	
February 28, 2003				
Interest Expense	$4,442		$4,583	
Cash		$4,442		$4,583
	[($1,000,000)(5.33%)(1/12)]		[($1,000,000)(5.5%)(1/12)]	
Interest Expense	$4,583			
Cash*		$4,583		
Cash*			$4,583	
Interest Expense				$4,583
Interest Expense			$4,442	
Cash*				$4,442
Cash*	$4,442			
Interest Expense		$4,442		

* Once the swap is arranged, the cash flows among all the participants will go through the financial intermediary that arranged the swap. Here, the cash is shown as flowing to and from the individual participants for illustrative purposes only. This approach will also be used for the March entries.

	Company X	Company Y
March 31, 2003		
Interest Expense	$4,833	$4,583
Cash	$4,833	$4,583
	[($1,000,000)(5.80%)(1/12)]	[($1,000,000)(5.5%)(1/12)]
Interest Expense	$4,583	
Cash*	$4,583	
Cash*		$4,583
Interest Expense		$4,583
Interest Expense		$4,833
Cash*		$4,833
Cash*	$4,833	
Interest Expense	$4,833	

Notice how the swap has changed the nature of the companies' cash flow streams. X's interest has gone from being fixed to variable and Y's has gone from variable to fixed. In hindsight, and assuming that there are no further changes in interest rates, X made the right decision. Y would have been better off not entering into the swap, but of course, neither company knew for certain at the time of the swap whether interest rates were going to rise or fall and by how much. The situation could still change, depending on what happens to interest rates over the remainder of the loan's life.

Also notice that the swap itself, which is a contract, is not initially recognized in either company's book, since no funds change hands to seal the contract. A critical part of the new proposals of the JWG is that all financial instruments will be marked to fair values at balance sheet dates. Therefore, each company will have to determine the fair value of the swap and the fair value of their loans, given the change in interest rates, and then record these fair values in the next reporting period's balance sheet. If the hedge has been effective, the changes in fair values should be similar and might exactly offset each other. The profession has considered whether these changes in fair values should flow through the income statement and the JWG Draft Standard has suggested that they should.

Currency Swaps

15-171.   The following example will serve to illustrate this type of derivative arrangement:

Example   On January 1, 2002, Maple Leaf Company (MLC) buys a German machine for 125,000 Euros (€) when the current exchange rate is €1 = $1.414. MLC must pay the debt in Euros on March 31, 2002. MLC fears that the Canadian dollar may decline in value before March 31 so, on January 1, MLC enters into a forward exchange contract on January 1 to receive €125,000 on March 31 at the forward exchange rate of €1 = $1.455. The spot rate on March 31 is €1 = $1.420.

In this case, MLC has currency risk because of an exposed monetary liability. It has used the forward exchange contract to hedge this risk.

Example Solution   The required journal entries are as follows:

January 1

Equipment [(€125,000)($1.414)]	$176,750	
Accounts Payable (To Broker)		$176,750

March 31

Accounts Payable [(€125,000)($1.414)]	$176,750	
Hedge Expense [(€125,000)($1.455 - $1.414)]	5,125	
Cash [(€125,000)($1.455)]		$181,875

The comment made about recognition of the derivative in the interest rate swap example applies here as well. The forward contract is a separate contract from the contract to purchase the equipment, but it is not recognized separately under current GAAP. It is treated as off-balance-sheet financing. Since the forward contract is subject to fair value changes as exchange rates fluctuate, changes in the fair value of these contracts would be recognized in the accounts at balance sheet dates under the JWG's Draft Standard.

Put Options With Prices Rising

15-172.   The following example will serve to illustrate this type of derivative arrangement:

Example   Investor Company holds 10,000 shares of TD Bank as a short-term investment. The shares were bought on January 1, 2002 for $40.50 each and are trading on March 1, 2002 at $42. Investor fears that bank stock prices may fall so it buys enough October 31, 2002, $40 put options at $2.20 each to cover its 10,000 shares. Each option gives the gives the holder the right to sell a share for $40, anytime before October 31, 2002 (in the real world, put option contracts are always for 100 shares).

On October 31, 2002, Investor sells the shares for $48 per share and lets the put options expire.

Investor is exposed to market risk, which has been hedged with the option contracts.

Example Solution   The journal entries required are as follows:

January 1

Investment In Shares [(10,000)($40.50)]	$405,000	
Cash		$405,000

March 1

Investment In Options [(10,000)($2.20)]	$22,000	
Cash		$22,000

September 30

Cash	$480,000	
Investment In Options		$ 22,000
Investment In Shares		405,000
Gain On Sale		53,000

In this case, because stock prices increased, the hedging strategy did not pay off. It cost Investor $22,000 to protect its investment from possible price declines that did not occur.

Put Options With Prices Falling

15-173.   The following example will serve to illustrate this type of derivative arrangement:

Example   Assume the same facts as in the previous example, except that the actual share price on October 31, 2002, when Investor decides to sell its shares, is $32.

Example Solution   The journal entries required would be as follows:

January 1

Investment In Shares	$405,000	
Cash		$405,000

March 1

Investment In Options	$22,000	
Cash		$22,000

October 31

Cash	$400,000	
Loss On Sale	27,000	
Investment In Options		$ 22,000
Investment In Shares		405,000

In this case, Investor's strategy, which cost $22,000, paid off. Without the options, Investor would have sold its shares for a loss of $85,000 [(10,000)($40.50 - $32)]. But because Investor was able to exercise its options and sell the shares for $40 each, Investor's loss on the transaction was only $27,000 [($40.50 - $40.00)(10,000) + $22,000]. Hedging strategies are not cheap, but if the stock is volatile, the company may consider such activities to be worthwhile.

Call Options With Prices Rising

15-174.   The following example will serve to illustrate this type of derivative arrangement:

Example   Stacey and Tracey Smith each receive $9,000 from their grandmother. Stacey users her $9,000 to buy 300 shares of Bell Canada when the shares are trading at $30 each. Tracey uses her $9,000 to buy July 31, 2002, $30 Bell call options, which are trading at $2.50 each. The call options give Tracey the right to buy Bell shares at $30 at any time prior to July 31, 2002. Her $9,000 gives her 3,600 options.

Example Solution   If Bell shares rise to $38 by July 31, each sister's gain or loss, ignoring commissions, is as follows:

Stacey's Gain [(300)($38 - $30)]	$2,400
Tracey's Gain [(3,600)($38 - $30) - $9,000]	$19,800

The return on investment for Stacey is 26.7 percent ($2,400 ÷ $9,000), while Tracey's return on investment is 220 percent ($19,800 ÷ $9,000).

Call Options With Prices Falling

15-175.   The following example will serve to illustrate this type of derivative arrangement:

Example   Assume the same facts as in the previous example, except that the Bell shares fall to $28 by July 31.

Example Solution   In this case, each sister's gain or loss, ignoring commissions, is as follows:

Stacey's Loss [(300)($30 - $28)]	$600
Tracey's Loss (Cost Of Options)	$9,000

It is reasonable to assume that Tracey will exercise her options only if it is advantageous for her to do so. Here, the options are worthless on their expiry date since the market value of the shares at that time is less than the exercise price.

The loss on investment for Stacey is 6.7 percent ($600 ÷ $9,000), while Tracey's loss is 100 percent, the full cost of the call options.

From examining the potential gains and losses of each sister's strategy in these examples, it can be seen that although each sister bought a financial instrument with her $9,000 gift, it is Tracey who assumed more risk by buying the derivative instead of the stock itself. This illustrates one of the key elements of options; you can make a lot of money in a short period of time but you can also lose your whole investment very quickly. If this is not clearly understood, it can lead to unexpectedly large losses by those who speculate in derivatives.

Financial Instruments In Canadian Practice

Statistics From Financial Reporting In Canada
General Disclosure

15-176.   Of the 200 companies surveyed in the 2001 edition of *Financial Reporting In Canada*, 196 provided some type of disclosure of financial instruments in their 2000 annual reports. The number of companies providing separate disclosure of individual items is as follows:

Fair value information	189
Extent and nature of financial instruments	186
Terms and conditions	173
Segregation of convertible proceeds	37
Preferred shares as debt	9

Example From Practice

15-177.   The following example is from the annual report of Linamar Corporation for the reporting period ending December 31, 2000. This example illustrates disclosure of financial instruments, including forward exchange contracts.

Notes To Financial Statements
(Thousands of dollars)

Note 11   Financial Instruments
Foreign Currency Risk

The company enters into forward exchange contracts to manage exposure to currency rate fluctuations related primarily to its future net cash inflows of US dollars from operations. The purpose of the company's foreign currency hedging activities is to minimize the effect of exchange rate fluctuations on business decisions and the resulting uncertainty on future financial results. At December 31, 2000, the company was committed to a series of monthly forward exchange contracts to sell US dollars which mature during the following three years as noted below. At December 31, 2000, the net unrecognized loss on these contracts was approximately $12.2 million. As these forward exchange contracts qualify for accounting as hedges, the unrealized gains and losses are deferred and recognized in earnings as the sales and expenses which generate the net cash flow occur.

Year	Amount Hedged (US$)	Average Exchange Rate
2001	131,000,000	1.4651
2002	120,000,000	1.4606
2003	95,000,000	1.4664

The company enters into forward exchange contracts to manage exposure to currency rate fluctuations related primarily to its future cash outflows of Euro from certain capital asset acquisitions. The purpose of the company's foreign currency hedging activities is to minimize the effect of exchange rate fluctuations on business decisions and the resulting uncertainty on future financial results. At December 31, 2000, the company was committed to a series of forward exchange contracts to purchase Euro maturing during the following years as noted below. At December 31, 2000, the net unrecognized gain was approximately $767,887. As these forward exchange contracts qualify for accounting as hedges, the unrealized gains and losses are deferred and recognized as a component of the capital asset acquisition.

Year	Amount Hedged (Euro)	Average Exchange Rate
2001	€32,043,789	1.3976
2002	€6,844,848	1.4074

The Company's short-term bank borrowings are denominated in U.S. dollars and these are not accounted for as hedges.

Credit Risk

A substantial portion of the company's accounts receivable are with large customers in the automotive and truck industry and are subject to normal industry credit risks. At December 31, 2000, the accounts receivable from the company's three largest customers amounted to 29.0%, 4.7% and 3.0% of accounts receivable (1999 - 22.9%, 2.8% and 7.2%).

Interest Rate Risk

At December 31, 2000, the increase or decrease in net earnings for each 1% change in interest rates on the short-term bank borrowings amounts to approximately $1.0 million (1999 - $0.8 million).

Fair Value

Fair value represents the amount that would be exchanged in an arm's length transaction between willing parties and is best evidenced by a quoted market price, if one exists. The company's fair values are management's estimates and are generally determined using market conditions at a specific point in time and may not reflect future fair values. The determinations are subjective in nature, involving uncertainties and matters of significant judgment. At December 31, 2000, the carrying values reported in the balance sheet for cash and short-term investments, accounts receivable, income taxes recoverable and current liabilities approximate fair value, due to the short-term nature of those instruments. The fair values of the investments and the long-term debt are not significantly different from carrying values.

Additional Readings

15-178.   In writing the material in the text, we have incorporated all of the relevant *CICA Handbook* Recommendations, as well as material from other sources that we felt to be of importance. This includes some, but not all, of the EIC Abstracts that relate to financial instruments, as well as material from U.S. accounting pronouncements and ideas put forward in articles published in professional accounting journals.

15-179.   While this approach meets the needs of the great majority of accounting students, some of you may wish to pursue this subject in greater depth. To facilitate this, you will find a fairly comprehensive bibliography of materials on the subject of financial instruments in Chapter 54 of our *Guide to Canadian Financial Reporting*. Indicative of the interest in this subject is the fact that this bibliography runs to four full pages in the paper version of the *Guide*.

15-180.   Chapter 54 of the *Guide* also contains summaries of the EIC Abstracts that are directly related to this subject. The Abstracts that are summarized as an appendix to Chapter 54 are as follows:

* EIC Abstract No. 32 (Gold Loans)
* EIC Abstract No. 39 (Accounting For The Issue Of Certain Derivative Instruments)
* EIC Abstract No. 57 (Spot Deferred Forward Contracts)
* EIC Abstract No. 58 (Accrued Interest Upon Conversion Of Convertible Debt)
* EIC Abstract No. 68 (Patronage Allocations)
* EIC Abstract No. 69 (Recognition And Measurement Of Financial Instruments Presented As Liabilities Or Equity Under CICA 3860)
* EIC Abstract No. 70 (Presentation Of A Financial Instrument When A Future Event Of Circumstance May Affect The Issuer's Obligations)
* EIC Abstract No. 71 (Financial Instruments That May Be Settled At The Issuer's Option In Cash Or Its Own Equity Instruments)
* EIC Abstract No. 72 (Presentation Of Member's Shares In A Co-operative Organization As Liabilities Of Equity)

- EIC Abstract No. 74 (Presentation Of Preferred Shares Requiring The Issuer To Make Repurchases)
- EIC Abstract No. 75 (Scope Of CICA 3860 - Interests In Subsidiaries Presented In Non-Consolidated Financial Statements)
- EIC Abstract No. 82 (Accounting For Dual Currency Bonds)
- EIC Abstract No. 87 (Balance Sheet Classification Of Share Capital Issued By A Split Share Corporation)
- EIC Abstract No. 91 (Offsetting An Obligation By Virtue Of A Claim Against A Third Party)
- EIC Abstract No. 96 (Accounting For The Early Extinguishment Of Convertible Securities Through (1) Early Redemption Or Repurchase And (2) Induced Early Conversion)
- EIC Abstract No. 100 (Accounting For Guaranteed Funds)
- EIC Abstract No. 113 (Accounting By Commodity Producers For Written Call Options)
- EIC Abstract No. 117 (FASB Statement Of Financial Accounting Standards No. 133, Accounting For Derivative Instruments And Hedging Activities)

15-181.   Our *Guide To Canadian Financial Reporting* is available on the CD-ROM which accompanies this text.

Appendix To Chapter Fifteen:
Option Pricing Theory

Since the most recent accounting recommendations on financial instruments are promoting the use of fair values, interest in reliable ways of determining fair values has increased. The markets for traded options, forwards and futures are well-developed and market prices are readily available for them in the financial press, just as they are for publicly-traded shares. The theory of how derivatives are priced by the market in which they trade has been an object of much study in finance for decades. Here, a brief review of the pricing of options is provided.

Put and call options have two elements included in their price:

1. the intrinsic value of the option, and
2. the time value of the option.

A call option has intrinsic value if its exercise price is below the current market price of the stock. A put option has a current value if its exercise price is less than the current market price. In other words, if it would be advantageous to exercise the option today, the option is said to be in-the-money, and therefore has intrinsic value. If an option is out-of-the-money, however, it is still valuable because of the time value of the option.

A number of option-pricing models that address this issue of time value have been developed. In one of the best-known models, it is hypothesized that the time value of an option is related to the factors listed below. The direction of the relationship between these factors and the price of an option is fairly intuitive if you clearly understand the nature of an option.

To test your understanding of the subject, fill in the blanks below from the choices provided. The solutions are provided on the following page.

1. The fair value of a stock option _____ (increases, decreases) as the life of the option increases.

    Hint: The stock market might be selling 30-day, 60-day and 90-day call options for a particular stock. If you buy the 90-day option, you have 90 days for the exercise of the option to become useful to you. If you buy the 30-day option, you have 30 days for it to become useful. Which option is more valuable to you, the 90-day one or the 30-day one?

2. The fair value of a stock option _____ (increases, decreases) as the variability of the price of the stock itself increases.

    Hint: Company A's stock price varies very little. In the last year, its price has ranged from $28 to $30. Company B's stock is more variable; it has ranged from $25 to $35. The stock market is selling 30-day $32 call options for Company A and Company B, when both stocks are trading at $29. The option will be useful if the stock price rises above $32 in the next 30 days. Which stock price has a better chance of rising to $32 in 30 days?

3. The fair value of a stock option _____ (increases, decreases) as the exercise price approaches the current stock price.

    Hint: The stock market is selling 30-day $32 call options for Company A and Company B, when Company A's stock is trading at $29 and Company's B stock is trading at $25. The options will be useful if the stock price rises above $32 in the next 30 days. Which stock price has a better chance of rising to $32 in 30 days?

4. The fair value of a stock option _____ (increases, decreases) as the risk-free interest rate rises.

   Hint: The risk-free interest rate is the rate that a risk-free financial instrument (such as a bond issued by the federal government) pays. The riskier an instrument, the more return a person should expect from holding that instrument. If returns on risk-free assets rise in the marketplace, would you expect the price of a stock option to rise or fall?

5. The fair value of a stock option _____ (increases, decreases) as the expected dividend yield on the stock increases.

   Hint: Since stock prices are a function of future expected dividends, when a dividend is declared on a share, the ex-dividend price of the share decreases. If the price of the stock decreases, what do you expect will happen to the price of a call option on that stock?

Solution

1. The fair value of a stock option increases as the life of the option increases.
2. The fair value of a stock option increases as the variability of the price of the stock itself increases.
3. The fair value of a stock option increases as the exercise price approaches the current stock price.
4. The fair value of a stock option increases as the risk-free interest rate rises.
5. The fair value of a stock option decreases as the expected dividend yield on the stock rises.

Summary: The preceding questions illustrates that the price of a call option is positively correlated with the risk-free rate of return, the riskiness of the underlying stock, the life of the option and the proximity of the option's exercise price to the current stock price and it is negatively correlated with the dividend yield on the stock.

Problems For Self Study

(The solutions for these problems can be found following Chapter 16 of the text.)

Self Study Problem Fifteen - 1
Indicate whether the following statements are true or false.

1. All monetary items qualify as financial assets or liabilities.

2. All financial assets and liabilities are monetary in nature.

3. Derivative instruments do not meet the definition of financial instruments.

4. There are no authoritative pronouncements published yet by the CICA on financial instruments.

5. CICA Handbook Section 3860 on Financial Instruments deals with measurement issues only.

6. There has been significant collaboration among international standard-setters on the issue of accounting for financial instruments.

7. Canadian GAAP requires that financial instruments be disclosed according to their legal form, regardless of their economic substance.

8. Interest on perpetual bonds that have been classified as equities on the balance sheet should be treated as an expense in the income statement.

9. Adoption of the proposals on financial instruments by the JWG will have little effect on current Canadian GAAP.

10. Income taxes due, since they are payable in cash, are financial liabilities.

Self Study Problem Fifteen - 2
Indicate whether the following items found on a typical company's balance sheet are financial instruments or not.

1. Patents

2. Provision for estimated warranties

3. Goodwill

4. Guaranteed investment certificates

5. Option to purchase wheat

6. Computer equipment

7. Last month's rent on deposit with landlord

8. Salaries payable

9. Savings accounts in foreign countries

10. Option to acquire land

11. Inventory held on consignment

12. Estimated liability for contingent loss

13. Leased automobile equipment

14. Obligations under capital leases

15. Pension obligations

16. Notes payable in barrels of oil

17. Non-marketable equity securities
18. Option to acquire equity in a joint venture
19. Taxes payable
20. Revenue received in advance
21. Redeemable preferred shares
22. Accumulated amortization on buildings
23. Future income tax credits
24. Convertible bonds

Self Study Problem Fifteen - 3

Below are a number of common Balance Sheet items:

1. Cash and cash equivalents

2. Accounts receivable

3. Inventories

4. Shares in long-term portfolio investments

5. Property, plant and equipment, net

6. Bank loan outstanding

7. Accounts payable and accrued liabilities

8. Current portion of long-term debt

9. Long-term debt

10. Future income taxes

11. Common shares and warrants outstanding

12. Retained earnings

Methods of valuation that could be used for these items are as follows:

- Face (maturity or future) value
- Present value, calculated by using yield rate at issue date
- Net realizable value
- Historical transaction amount
- Current market value
- Historical cost, net of amortization to date
- Lower of cost and market
- Cumulative balance over time, no fixed valuation method

Required: For each balance sheet item, select the existing generally accepted valuation method for the item from the list provided above.

Self Study Problem Fifteen - 4

Bluenose Corporation issues $10 million 5-year 8 percent bonds on January 1, 2002 at par. Interest is payable annually on December 31. On January 1, 2002, Bluenose enters into a four-year receive-fixed pay-variable interest rate swap with terms (face amount, term and interest date) that match its debt. Interest rates decline to 6.8 percent by the end of 2002 (assume for simplicity that the drop takes place on January 2 and stays in effect until December 31). At December 31, 2002, dealer quotes indicate that the fair value of the swap is $400,000, and the fair value of the debt has increased by $400,000 because of the decline in rates.

Required: Prepare dated journal entries for Bluenose for 2002, including recognizing the changes in the fair values of the financial instruments as proposed by the JWG's Draft Standard.

Self Study Problem Fifteen - 5

Toth Corporation issued $10 million, 8 percent, 20-year convertible bonds on March 31, 2002 for $8,500,000. Interest is payable each March 31 and each $1,000 bond is convertible into 20 shares of common stock, at the option of the investor, anytime between April 1, 2012 and maturity date. The financial intermediary that helped Toth place the bonds estimated that, without the conversion privilege, the bonds would have sold for a price that reflected an 11 percent effective rate. The Company has a December 31 year end.

The present value of $1 to be received after 20 periods discounted at 11 percent is $.12403. The present value of an annuity of $1 for 20 periods discounted at 11 percent is $7.96333.

Required:

A. Prepare journal entries to record the issue of the bonds on March 31, 2002 and the interest expense for 2002 and 2003. Use the effective interest method to amortize any bond discount or premium on the bonds.

B. Repeat the journal entries in part A, assuming that the financial intermediary uses an option-pricing model to determine the value of the conversion option at $1,000,000. Use the proportional method in this case to allocate the issue proceeds.

C. Assume that 10% of the investors elect to convert their bonds at the earliest possible date, when Toth's common shares are trading at $45 each. Prepare the journal entry to record the conversion, assuming that Toth used the figures in part B at inception date and straight-line amortization to amortize the bond discount instead of the effective interest method.

Self Study Problem Fifteen - 6

You have been asked to do the first-time audit for Tripp Limited, a small, privately-held company. Edward Tripp and his wife Linda each own 50 percent of the company's 5,000 shares. When you ask about the account "Advances from owners", you find out that this represents an amount loaned by Ed Tripp to the company 10 years ago. The loan is non-interest bearing and has no maturity date. Ed Tripp, who also manages the company, has no intention of repaying this loan in the foreseeable future. Your examination also shows that the bank loan agreement specifies that the company's debt to equity ratio cannot exceed 1.5:1. The Company's Balance Sheet is as follows:

Tripp Company
Balance Sheet
December 31, 2002

Current assets	$100,000
Long-term assets	400,000
Total assets	$500,000
Current liabilities	$100,000
Long-term bank loan	100,000
Advances from owners	100,000
Common shares	100,000
Retained earnings	100,000
Total liabilities and shareholders' equity	$500,000

Required: How should "Advances from owners" be classified on Tripp's balance sheet? Explain your conclusion.

Self Study Problem Fifteen - 7

On January 1, 2002, Greet Limited issued $100,000 maturity value, 7 percent, 5 year bonds for $104,213. At this time, the market rate of interest was 6 percent. Interest is paid each December 31. Interest rates rose significantly during 2002, and the yield for similar bonds at the end of 2002 and 2003 was 8 percent.

The present value of $1 to be received after 4 periods discounted at 8 percent is $.73503. The present value of an annuity of $1 for 4 periods discounted at 8 percent is $3.31213.

Required: Prepare the dated journal entries for Greet for 2002 and 2003, in accordance with the JWG's Draft Standard regarding the use of fair values for measurement purposes.

Self Study Problem Fifteen - 8

On January 2, 2002, Lilly Corporation granted Erin Patrick, the president, an option to purchase 4,000 of Lilly's common shares at $50 per share. The option becomes exercisable on January 2, 2004, after Patrick has completed two years of service. The market value of Lilly's common shares was $45 on January 2, 2002 and $60 at December 31, 2002. An option-pricing model measures the fair value of the options at grant date to be $4 each and the company expects Ms. Patrick to stay with the company indefinitely. Ms. Patrick exercises half of the options at the earliest possible date, when the shares are trading at $62.

Required: Prepare the journal entries for Lilly Corporation to properly reflect these options from the grant date to the first exercise date.

Assignment Problems

(The solutions for these problems are only available in
the solutions manual that has been provided to your instructor.)

Assignment Problem Fifteen - 1
Indicate whether the following statements are true or false.

1. Accounts receivable are financial instruments.

2. Intangible assets are financial instruments.

3. A perpetual bond is a derivative.

4. All derivatives are financial instruments.

5. Interest on bonds that have been classified as equity instruments will be shown as dividends in the financial statements.

6. A call option gives the holder the right to sell the underlying interest.

7. The fair value of a stock option is derived from the value of the underlying stock.

8. The term speculation means taking actions to reduce risk.

9. Prices of financial instruments can change due to currency risk, interest rate risk and/or market risk.

10. Stock options can be used to hedge the risk associated with holding many corporate shares.

11. Buying stock options is less risky than buying the shares themselves.

12. The price of a stock option decreases as the variability of the underlying stock increases.

13. Interest rate swaps are rarely used in practice.

14. An investor who holds shares and thinks that the share price may fall can hedge her risk by buying put options.

15. An investor who holds a $40 call option when the stock is trading at $45 will likely exercise his option.

16. Many of the staggering losses that well-known companies incurred from holding financial instruments were due to not understanding the risks associated with the instruments.

17. The principles of internal control over financial instruments are similar to those over other types of assets.

18. In December 2000, the CICA issued a new Handbook Section on recognition and measurement of all financial instruments.

19. The CICA has been a marginal player in the international development of accounting standards for financial instruments.

20. The proposal in the Draft Standard of the Joint Working Group of standard-setters that has caused the most controversy is that all risks associated with financial instruments owned by a company must be disclosed in the financial statements.

Assignment Problem Fifteen - 2
Below is a list of items.

1. A temporary investment in Bell Canada shares

2. Accounts receivable

3. Inventory

4. Prepaid rent

5. Computer equipment

6. Bank overdraft

7. Bank loan payable

8. Income taxes payable

9. Long-term bonds payable

10. Common share warrants issued

11. Common shares issued

12. A guarantee on securitized receivables that have been recorded as a sale

Required:

A. Use the definitions in *CICA Handbook* Section 3860 to determine whether each item is a financial instrument or not and, if so, whether it is a financial asset, a financial liability or an equity instrument.

B. Section 3860 requires that the following information be disclosed where appropriate for financial instruments:

  • terms and conditions

  • interest rate risk

  • credit risk

  • fair value

For the items identified in part A as financial instruments, specify which of the disclosures listed above would likely be required.

Assignment Problem Fifteen - 3

Below are a number of common financial instruments.

1. Accounts receivable

2. Guaranteed investment certificate

3. Estimated liability for contingent loss

4. Pension obligations

5. Marketable equity securities

6. Long-term portfolio investments in equity securities

7. Bonds payable

Methods of valuation that could be used for these items are as follows:

  • face value

  • historical cost

  • lower of cost or market

  • fair value at balance sheet date

  • fair value at inception date (i.e., date of initial recognition)

Required: For each of the items numbered 1 to 7, select the existing generally accepted valuation method for this item from the list of choices provided. Comment on whether current GAAP is likely to be affected by the JWG's Draft Standard that promotes a fair value model for all financial instruments.

Assignment Problem Fifteen - 4

At the beginning of 2002, Brown Corporation issued 10,000 convertible preferred shares at $35 per share. The shares are convertible into common shares on a share-for-share basis. During 2002, 2,000 of the preferred shares were converted into common shares. The market price of the preferred shares at the time of conversion was $42 per share; the market price of the common shares was $44 per share.

Required: Prepare journal entries to record the issuance of the preferred shares at the beginning of the year and at the conversion of preferred into common during the year.

Assignment Problem Fifteen - 5

Swathmore Corporation issued $100,000 5-year bonds on January 1, 2002 at par. The bonds bear annual interest at a minimum of 5 percent, which can increase depending on the company's dividend payments. Interest is paid each December 31. The bonds are convertible into common shares anytime up to their maturity date at the company's option.

The present value of $1 to be received after 5 periods discounted at 5 percent is $.78353. The present value of an annuity of $1 for 5 periods discounted at 5 percent is $4.32948.

Required:

A. Use *CICA Handbook* Section 3860 to determine how the bonds should be classified on the company's balance sheet.

B. Prepare journal entries for 2002 to reflect the substance of the bonds, assuming that the company had a good year in 2002 and as a result paid 8 percent interest.

C. Make the entries for 2002, assuming that the interest is paid in common shares.

Assignment Problem Fifteen - 6

Parker Corporation issued 5,000 term preferred shares on July 1, 2002 for $300,000. The shares carry a 10 percent dividend rate payable each July 1 and are redeemable for cash on July 1, 2007. The company has a December 31 year end.

Required:

A. How should the shares be classified on Parker's balance sheet? Explain your conclusion.

B. Prepare journal entries for the year ending December 31, 2002.

Assignment Problem Fifteen - 7

Richardson Exploration Limited issued $1,000,000 in perpetual bonds at face value on January 1, 2002 to finance exploration of a tract of land they own in Argentina. The bonds have no repayment schedule, but are due when the operations in Argentina are wound up. The bonds are also redeemable at any time at the option of the company at 102. The bonds carry annual interest at 8 percent payable at December 31. On December 31, 2005, the company decides to redeem the bonds.

Required:

A. How should the bonds be classified on Richardson's balance sheet? Explain your conclusion.

B. Prepare the journal entries for 2002 and 2005, assuming that the bonds qualify as financial liabilities.

C. Prepare the journal entries for 2002 and 2005, assuming that the bonds (including the interest stream) qualify as equity instruments.

Assignment Problem Fifteen - 8

Duran Limited issued 5-year, $100,000 maturity value, 8 percent bonds on January 1, 2002. Interest is payable on December 31. Duran may settle the principal either by paying cash or by issuing its own common shares to the bondholders. Each $1,000 bond is convertible at the option of the holder into 140 common shares of Duran. The bonds sold at 98. The yield rate for similar non-convertible debt is 8 percent. The fair value of the conversion privilege is estimated to be $5,000.

The present value of an annuity of $1 for 5 periods discounted at 8 percent is $3.9927. Also note that, at an effective annual rate of 10.37 percent, $61,058 will accumulate to $100,000 after five years.

Required:

A. Discuss the appropriate treatment of the bonds in the balance sheet of Duran.

B. Prepare the journal entries for 2002 and 2003.

C. Assuming that the conversion option is never exercised, prepare the entry to retire the bonds at the end of their 5 year life.

Assignment Problem Fifteen - 9

McLeod Limited issued $250,000 maturity value, 8 percent, convertible 10-year debentures on January 1, 2002 at par. Interest is payable semi-annually in cash on June 30 and December 31. The debentures are convertible into common shares at a conversion price of $25 per share. At the date of issue, McLeod could have issued similar non-convertible debt at an effective rate of 10 percent. On January 1, 2007, McLeod makes a tender offer to buy the debt back at the market value of $400,000, which is accepted. On that date, McLeod could have issued 5 year non-convertible debt at 6 percent.

The following present value factors can be used in solving this problem:

Present value of $1 after 20 periods at 5 percent	.37689
Present value of $1 after 10 periods at 5 percent	.61391
Present value of $1 after 10 periods at 3 percent	.74409
Present value of an annuity of $1 for 20 periods at 5 percent	12.46221
Present value of an annuity of $1 for 10 periods at 5 percent	7.72173
Present value of an annuity of $1 for 10 periods at 3 percent	8.53020

Required: Prepare the journal entry to record the debt repurchase.

Assignment Problem Fifteen - 10

Oak Corporation issued 10,000 of its own previously unissued shares for land to be used as a future plant site.

Required: Record the transaction under each of the following independent assumptions:

A. The land was appraised at $900,000 last year. The shares, which were actively traded on the Toronto Stock Exchange, had a market value at the time of the transaction of $750,000.

B. The land was appraised at $600,000; the shares, which were closely held, did not have a readily determinable market value.

C. Neither the fair market value of the land nor the fair market value of the shares was readily determinable.

Assignment Problem Fifteen - 11

At the beginning of 2002, Wicker Corporation had the following account balance:

> Common shares (authorized 5,000,000 shares,
> issued 1,000,000 shares) $12,000,000

Selected transactions during 2002 were as follows:

1. On May 1, Stock Option Plan A was adopted. The plan covers all employees and allows each employee to purchase up to 100 of Wicker common shares at $16 per share, which is $.70 less than the market price of the stock at the date of grant. The options expire on May 31, 2002.

2. 4,000 shares were issued in May under Stock Option Plan A.

3. On July 1, options were granted to five key executives under Stock Option Plan B. Under the plan the executives may purchase up to 3,000 shares each. The shares may be acquired between January 1, 2004 and December 31, 2010 at $18 per share; the market price at the date of the grant was $20. The executives must be in the employ of Wicker when they exercise the options and Wicker believes that all employees will remain with the firm. An option-pricing model estimates the fair value of the options to be $2.50 each at the grant date.

4. One of the five executives covered under Stock Option Plan B left Wicker in March of 2003.

Required:

A. Prepare the journal entries for 2002 related to the above information.

B. Prepare the contributed capital section of Wicker's balance sheet at December 31, 2002.

Assignment Problem Fifteen - 12

At the beginning of 2002, Kruger Corporation granted stock appreciation rights (SARs) to three of its key executives. Under the terms of the SAR plan, each executive was entitled to receive either cash, Kruger common shares or a combination of both cash and shares. The amount to be received was to be determined by the difference between the quoted market price of Kruger's common shares at the date of exercise and the predetermined price of $20 per SAR.

Kruger granted a total of 30,000 SARs, which were exercisable after January 1, 2005, and the executives were required to be in the employ of the company at the date of exercise. The per share market price of Kruger's common shares at the end of each year was as follows:

2002	$34
2003	$39
2004	$49
2005	$45
2006	$48

When the plan was adopted, it was assumed that the executives would select the option to receive cash. Eighty percent of the SARs were exercised on December 31, 2005, and the appropriate amount of cash was paid.

Required: Prepare all journal entries required in connection with the SAR plan for 2002 through 2006.

Chapter 16

Part One: Segment Disclosures

Introduction

The Basic Issue

16-1.   The financial statements of an enterprise are usually prepared on a consolidated or total enterprise basis, aggregating the financial data of the various activities of the enterprise. While investors and creditors recognize the importance of this aggregate data to the process of reporting the overall performance of the enterprise, they have indicated that disaggregated data is also of use to them. They point out that evaluation of the risk and return of a particular enterprise is a central element in making investment and lending decisions. For a diversified enterprise, such an evaluation is not possible without some information on the segments of the business. Various alternatives for such disaggregation include product lines, operating divisions of the enterprise, geographic regions, and major customers.

16-2.   While the preceding Paragraph provides a general explanation of the desirability of segmented information, there are arguments which suggest that such information should not be required. These arguments include:

- Such information is too interpretive to be classified as accounting information and, thus, does not belong in the financial statements.

- Such information may not be subject to the same degree of verifiability as consolidated information.

- Such information is costly to compile.

- Such information may provide information that is useful to a firm's competitors.

16-3.   It is the last of these arguments that engenders the greatest resistance to increased amounts of segment disclosure. Many enterprises have expressed a strong belief that they can be harmed by providing such information.

16-4.   While there is some validity in all of the preceding arguments, standard setters in the U.S., Canada, and much of the rest of the industrialized world, have concluded that the merits of segmented information outweigh the disadvantages that can be associated with requiring its presentation.

16-5.   In the United States, the FASB issued Statement Of Financial Accounting Standards No. 131, "Disclosures About Segments Of An Enterprise And Related Information" in June, 1997. Despite differing titles, Section 1701 and Statement Of Financial Accounting

Standards No. 131 are substantially identical. This is in keeping with the CICA's oft cited goal of harmonizing U. S. and Canadian accounting standards. The only real difference between the two Standards is in their scope. The U. S. Standard limits its scope to publicly traded business enterprises. Section 1701 Recommendations apply not only to public enterprises, but deposit taking institutions and life insurance enterprises as well.

Purpose And Scope

16-6. Section 1701 requires that public enterprises and some other enterprises disclose certain information about operating segments and also about their products and services, the geographic areas in which they operate, and their major customers. The *CICA Handbook* also requires the disclosure of certain information about operating segments in interim financial reports.

16-7. The scope of Section 1701 is described as follows:

Paragraph 1701.08 *This Section should be applied by public enterprises, cooperative business enterprises, deposit-taking institutions and life insurance enterprises. Public enterprises are those enterprises that have issued debt or equity securities that are traded in a public market (a domestic or foreign stock exchange or an over-the-counter market, including local or regional markets), that are required to file financial statements with a securities commission, or that provide financial statements for the purposes of issuing any class of securities in a public market.* (January, 1998)

16-8. While only the entities referred to in Paragraph 1701.08 are required to provide segment disclosures, other types of enterprises are encouraged to provide some or all of the disclosure required by Section 1701.

Objectives Of Segmented Information

16-9. As described in Section 1701, the objective of requiring disclosures about segments of an enterprise and related information is to provide:

Paragraph 1701.02 ... information about the different types of business activities in which an enterprise engages and the different economic environments in which it operates to help users of financial statements:

(a) better understand the enterprise's performance;
(b) better assess its prospects for future net cash flows; and
(c) make more informed judgments about the enterprise as a whole.

That objective is consistent with the objectives of general purpose financial reporting.

16-10. From this description, it is clear that segmented information is directed towards providing information that will be useful in making interperiod comparisons for an individual enterprise. This more detailed disclosure of economic trends should be of significant assistance in projecting the amount, timing and uncertainty associated with prospective future cash flows, as well as understanding the enterprise's performance and making more informed judgments about the enterprise as a whole.

16-11. It must be noted, however, that segmented information cannot be used to make meaningful comparisons between similar segments of two or more companies. As will become clear as we look at the more detailed Recommendations of Section 1701, the parameters of reportable operating segments will depend on the manner in which management organizes the enterprise for purposes of making operating decisions and assessing performance. Given this approach, the Section does not provide definitions of the items to be disclosed (e.g., segment profit or loss). Under these circumstances, most of the segment disclosures provided will be of little use in making comparisons of what appear to be similar segments in different companies.

16-12. To alleviate this problem, Section 1701 requires some disclosure of the revenues that the enterprise derives from each of its products or services. This provides a limited basis for comparability between enterprises.

Management Approach

16-13. The objective described in the preceding Section might be met by providing statements that are disaggregated in several different ways. This could include by products and services, by geography, by legal entity, or by type of customer.

16-14. Section 1701 takes what is referred to as the management approach to segment disclosures. Under this approach, the reportable operating segments are based on the way in which management organizes the segments within the enterprise for making operating decisions and assessing performance. This means that the segments are evident from the structure of the enterprise's internal organizations, and financial statement preparers will be able to provide the required information in a cost effective and timely manner.

Reportable Operating Segments

Operating Segment Defined

16-15. The following was stated in the discussion of segmented information contained in a 1993 position paper issued by the Association For Investment Management And Research:

> ... priority should be given to the production and dissemination of financial data that reflects and reports sensibly the operations of specific enterprises. If we could obtain reports showing the details of how an individual business firm is organized and managed, we would assume more responsibility for making meaningful comparisons of those data to the unlike data of other firms that conduct their business differently.

16-16. This statement is indicative of the type of support that exists for the management approach to segment disclosures. Under the management approach required by Section 1701, the focus of segment disclosures is reportable operating segments. Section 1701 provides the following definition of an operating segment:

Paragraph 1701.10   An operating segment is a component of an enterprise:

(a) that engages in business activities from which it may earn revenues and incur expenses (including revenues and expenses relating to transactions with other components of the same enterprise),

(b) whose operating results are regularly reviewed by the enterprise's chief operating decision maker to make decisions about resources to be allocated to the segment and assess its performance, and

(c) to which discrete financial information is available.

An operating segment may engage in business activities for which it has yet to earn revenues, for example, startup operations may be operating segments before earning revenues.

16-17.   With respect to this definition, Section 1701 makes a number of additional points:

- It is noted that not every part of an enterprise is an operating segment or part of an operating segment. Corporate headquarters and functional departments that do not earn revenues (e.g., accounting) would fall into this category. It is specifically noted that an enterprise's employee future benefit plans should not be considered to be operating segments.

- As the term is used in Paragraph 1701.10, "chief operating decision maker" identifies a function that may be described by a variety of titles. The basic idea is that this individual or group of individuals is responsible for allocating resources and assessing the performance of the operating segments of the enterprise.

- In many cases, the three characteristics described in Paragraph 1701.10 will clearly identify a single set of operating segments. There are, however, situations in which the chief operating decision maker will use more than one set of segmented information. In such cases, other factors may be useful in identifying a single set of components which constitute the operating segments of an enterprise. Such factors might include the nature of the business activities of each component, the existence of managers responsible for them, and the types of information presented to the board of directors.

- In most situations, an operating segment will have a segment manager. Such segment managers are usually accountable to and maintain regular contact with the chief operating decision maker in order to discuss operating activities, financial results, forecasts, or plans for the segment. The chief operating decision maker may also be a segment manager for one or more segments. In addition, a single individual may be a segment manager for more than one segment. In those cases where the characteristics used to identify an operating segment are applicable to more than one set of components of an organization, the set for which segment managers are held responsible should provide the basis for segment disclosures.

- In a matrix form of organization, operating segment characteristics may apply to overlapping sets of components for which managers are held responsible. An example of this would be an organization in which one group of managers is held responsible for certain product or service lines, while a different group is responsible for particular geographic areas. Financial information would be available for both sets of components and the chief operating decision maker would review both sets of information. Section 1701 notes that, in this type of situation, components based on products and services would form the basis for operating segment disclosure.

Reportable Operating Segments Identified

General

16-18.   In the preceding section, we discussed the definition of an operating segment under the management approach to segment disclosure. While this definition allows us to identify the operating segments of an organization, it is unlikely that it will be appropriate to provide disclosure for all of the operating segments identified. This means that the next issue to be considered is which of these operating segments should be considered reportable. Section 1701's general statement on identifying reportable operating segments is as follows:

Paragraph 1701.16   *An enterprise should disclose separately information about each operating segment that:*

(a) has been identified in accordance with paragraphs 1701.10 - .15 or that results from aggregating two or more of those segments in accordance with paragraph 1701.18, and

(b) exceeds the quantitative thresholds in paragraph 1701.19.

Paragraphs 1701.22 - .25 specify other situations in which separate information about an operating segment should be disclosed. (January, 1998)

16-19.   Under this Recommendation, an operating segment or group of aggregated operating segments, is considered to be reportable if it meets a specific quantitative threshold. This means that the process of identifying reportable operating segments begins with consideration of which operating segments can be aggregated. When the aggregation process is completed, the individual and aggregated operating segments will then be evaluated on the basis of the quantitative threshold in order to establish whether they should be considered reportable. The aggregation process and the quantitative threshold will be considered in the sections which follow.

Aggregation Of Operating Segments

16-20.   As the goal of segment disclosure is to provide information on components of an enterprise that have similar economic characteristics, it would seem appropriate to aggregate those operating segments that have similar economic characteristics. Section 1701 notes that operating segments may be aggregated if:

1. aggregation is consistent with the objective and basic principles of Section 1701;

2. the segments have similar economic characteristics; and

3. the segments are similar in each of the following areas:

   - the nature of the products and services;
   - the nature of the production processes;
   - the type or class of customer for their products and services;
   - the methods used to distribute their products or provide their services; and
   - if applicable, the nature of the regulatory environment (for example, banking, insurance, or public utilities).

Quantitative Threshold

16-21.   Once operating segments have been identified and aggregated as appropriate, they will generally be considered reportable if they meet the following quantitative threshold:

Paragraph 1701.19   *An enterprise should disclose separately information about an operating segment that meets any of the following quantitative thresholds:*

(a) *Its reported revenue, including both sales to external customers and intersegment sales or transfers, is 10 percent or more of the combined revenue, internal and external, of all operating segments.*

(b) *The absolute amount of its reported profit or loss is 10 percent or more of the greater, in absolute amount, of:*

   (i) *the combined reported profit of all operating segments that did not report a loss, or*
   (ii) *the combined reported loss of all operating segments that did report a loss.*

(c) *Its assets are 10 percent or more of the combined assets of all operating segments.* (January, 1998)

16-22.   A simple example will serve to illustrate the application of the preceding Recommendation:

Example   A company has identified eight operating segments with reported profits or losses as follows:

Segment	Profit (Loss)
A	$ 63,000
B	210,000
C	50,000
D	277,000
Total	$600,000
E	($239,000)
F	(64,000)
G	(45,000)
H	(302,000)
Total	($650,000)

16-23.   Since the total reported loss of all industry segments that incurred a loss is greater than the total reported profit of all industry segments that earned a profit, a segment would be reportable under Paragraph 1701.19 if its reported profit or loss exceeded $65,000 or 10 percent of $650,000. This would mean that segments B, D, E, and H would be defined as reportable segments under Paragraph 1701.19(b). While segments A, C, F, and G do not qualify as reportable under Paragraph 1701.19(b), they may qualify under either 1701.19(a) or 1701.19(c).

Dominant Segment Disclosure

16-24.   While it is still possible that a particular enterprise could go through the analysis that we have described and conclude that they have only one operating segment, this practice is not encouraged by any specific Recommendation that provides for this approach. The dominant segment approach is further discouraged by a Recommendation that requires a minimum allocation to operating segments. This Recommendation is as follows:

> **Paragraph 1701.22**   *If the total of external revenue reported by operating segments constitutes less than 75 percent of an enterprise's total revenue, additional operating segments should be identified as reportable segments (even if they do not meet the criteria in paragraph 1701.19) until at least 75 percent of the enterprise's total revenue is included in reportable segments.* (January, 1998)

Non-Reportable Operating Segments

16-25.   Even when the minimum segmentation Recommendation of Paragraph 1701.22 is applied, it is likely that there will be other operating activities or segments that will not be given separate disclosure. With respect to these activities and segments, Section 1701 contains the following Recommendation:

> **Paragraph 1701.23**   *Information about other business activities and operating segments that are not reportable should be combined and disclosed in an "all other" category separate from other reconciling items in the reconciliations required by paragraph 1701.35. The sources of the revenue included in the "all other" category should be described.* (January, 1998)

Changes In Reportable Operating Segments

16-26.   It is probable that, from time to time, there will be changes in the group of operating segments that are identified as being reportable. When a reportable operating segment loses that status, the following Recommendation is relevant:

> **Paragraph 1701.24**   *If management judges an operating segment identified as a reportable segment in the immediately preceding period to be of continuing significance, information about that segment should continue to be disclosed separately in the current period even if it no longer meets the criteria for separate disclosure in paragraph 1701.19.* (January, 1998)

16-27.   In the alternative situation, where a previously non-reportable component of the enterprise is identified as a reportable operating segment during the current period, this Recommendation is applicable:

> **Paragraph 1701.25**   *If an operating segment is identified as a reportable segment in the current period due to the quantitative thresholds, prior period segment data presented for comparative purposes should be restated to reflect the newly reportable segment as a separate segment even if that segment did not satisfy the criteria for separate disclosure in paragraph 1701.19 in the prior period unless it is impracticable to do so.* (January, 1998)

Reportable Operating Segment Disclosures
Types Of Disclosure

16-28.   Section 1701 requires disclosure in three separate categories. These categories are described as follows:

- General information.

- Information about reported segment profit or loss, including certain revenues and expenses included in reported segment profit or loss, segment assets, and the basis of measurement for segmented information.

- Reconciliations of the various types of segmented information with the corresponding enterprise amounts.

16-29. There are also disclosure provisions with respect to previously disclosed information for prior periods. These components of required disclosure are discussed in the subsections which follow.

General Information

16-30. The required disclosure here relates to the process by which the enterprise determined its reportable segments, as well as the types of products and services from which the reportable segments derive their revenues. The Recommendation is as follows:

Paragraph 1701.29 *An enterprise should disclose the following general information:*

(a) *Factors used to identify the enterprise's reportable segments, including the basis of organization* (for example, whether management has chosen to organize the enterprise around differences in products and services, geographic areas, regulatory environments, or a combination of factors and whether operating segments have been aggregated).

(b) *Types of products and services from which each reportable segment derives its revenues.* (January, 1998)

16-31. A 1992 CICA Research Study, *Financial Reporting For Segments*, was instrumental in the development of Section 1701. This Research Study contained several examples of appropriate segment disclosures, which will be used in the remainder of this chapter to illustrate the required *Handbook* Recommendations of Section 1701. The following, adapted from the CICA Research Study, is an example of the type of disclosure that would be appropriate under Paragraph 1701.29(a):

Example Diversified Company's reportable segments are strategic business units that offer different products and services. They are managed separately because each business requires different technology and marketing strategies. Most of the businesses were acquired as a unit, and the management at the time of the acquisition was retained.

16-32. The CICA Research Study example also includes the following as an illustration of the disclosure that would be appropriate under Paragraph 1701.29(b):

Example Diversified Company has five reportable segments: auto parts, motor vessels, software, electronics, and finance. The auto parts segment produces replacement parts for sale to auto parts retailers. The motor vessels segment produces small motor vessels to serve the offshore oil industry and similar businesses. The software segment produces application software for sale to computer manufacturers and retailers. The electronics segment produces integrated circuits and related products for sale to computer manufacturers. The finance segment is responsible for portions of the company's financial operations including financing customer purchases of products from other segments and real estate lending operations.

Information About Profit Or Loss And Assets

16-33. Section 1701 specifies a fairly extensive list of items to be disclosed for each reportable operating segment:

Paragraph 1701.30 *An enterprise should disclose a measure of profit or loss and total assets for each reportable segment. An enterprise also should disclose the following about each reportable segment if the specified amounts (i) are included in the measure of segment profit or loss reviewed by the chief operating decision maker or (ii) are otherwise regularly provided to the chief operating decision maker, even if not included in that measure of segment profit or loss:*

(a) *Revenues from external customers.*
(b) *Revenues from transactions with other operating segments of the same enterprise.*
(c) *Interest revenue.*
(d) *Interest expense.*
(e) *Amortization of capital assets.*

(f) *Revenues, expenses, gains or losses resulting from items that do not have all of the characteristics of extraordinary items (see EXTRAORDINARY ITEMS, Section 3480) but result from transactions or events that are not expected to occur frequently over several years, or do not typify normal business activities of the entity.*

(g) *Equity in the net income of investees subject to significant influence.*

(h) *Income tax expense or benefit.*

(i) *Extraordinary items.*

(j) *Significant noncash items other than amortization of capital assets and goodwill.*

An enterprise should disclose interest revenue separately from interest expense for each reportable segment unless a majority of the segment's revenues are from interest and the chief operating decision maker relies primarily on net interest revenue to assess the performance of the segment and make decisions about resources to be allocated to the segment. In that situation, an enterprise may disclose that segment's interest revenue net of its interest expense and disclose that it has done so. (November 1999)

Paragraph 1701.31 *An enterprise should disclose the following about each reportable segment if the specified amounts (i) are included in the determination of segment assets reviewed by the chief operating decision maker or (ii) are otherwise regularly provided to the chief operating decision maker, even if not included in the determination of segment assets:*

(a) *The amount of investment in investees subject to significant influence.*

(b) *Total expenditures for additions to capital assets and goodwill. (November 1999)*

16-34. The Diversified Company example from the CICA Research Study, (see Paragraph 16-31) is extended to illustrate the following disclosure format that could be used to comply with Paragraphs 1701.30 and 1701.31:

	Auto Parts	Motor Vessels	Software	Elec- tronics	Finance	All Other	Totals
Revenues from external customers	$3,000	$5,000	$9,500	$12,000	$5,000	$1,000[a]	$35,500
Intersegment revenues	-	-	3,000	1,500	-	-	4,500
Interest revenue	450	800	1,000	1,500	-	-	3,750
Interest expense	350	600	700	1,100	-	-	2,750
Net interest revenue[b]	-	-	-	-	1,000	-	1,000
Amortization of capital assets	200	100	50	1,500	1,100	-	2,950
Segment profit	200	70	900	2,300	500	100	4,070
Other significant non-cash items: Cost in excess of billing on long-term contracts	-	200	-	-	-	-	200
Segment assets	2,000	5,000	3,000	12,000	57,000	2,000	81,000
Expenditures for segment capital assets	300	700	500	800	600	-	2,900

[a]Revenues from segments below the quantitative thresholds are attributable to four operating segments of Diversified Company. Those segments include a small real estate business, an electronics equipment rental business, a software consulting practice, and a warehouse leasing operation. None of those segments has ever met any of the quantitative thresholds for determining reportable segments.

[b]The finance segment derives a majority of its revenue from interest. In addition, management primarily relies on net interest revenue, not the gross revenue and expense amount, in managing that segment. Therefore, as permitted by paragraph 1701.30, only the net amount is disclosed.

Diversified Company does not allocate income taxes or unusual items to segments. In addition, not all segments have significant noncash items other than amortization of capital assets.

16-35. There are, of course, a number of issues associated with the measurement of the items listed in the preceding Recommendations and illustrated in the Example. These will be discussed in the next section which deals with accounting policies and measurement in segment disclosures.

Reconciliations

16-36. For a variety of reasons (e.g., different accounting policies for segment disclosures), the sum of the operating segment data for a particular financial statement item is not likely to be equal to the amount actually reported in the aggregate financial statements. Given this, Section 1701 makes the following Recommendation with respect to reconciling these alternative amounts:

Paragraph 1701.35 *An enterprise should disclose reconciliations of all of the following:*

(a) The total of the reportable segments' revenues to the enterprise's total revenues.

(b) The total of the reportable segments' measures of profit or loss to the enterprise's income before income taxes, discontinued operations and extraordinary items. However, if an enterprise allocates items such as income taxes and extraordinary items to segments, the enterprise may choose to reconcile the total of the segments' measures of profit or loss to the enterprise's income after those items.

(c) The total of the reportable segments' assets to the enterprise's total assets.

(d) The total of the reportable segments' amounts for every other significant item of information disclosed to the corresponding total amount for the enterprise (for example, an enterprise may choose to disclose liabilities for its reportable segments, in which case the enterprise would reconcile the total of reportable segments' liabilities for each segment to the enterprise's total liabilities if the segment liabilities are significant).

All significant reconciling items should be separately identified and described (for example, the amount of each significant adjustment to reconcile accounting methods used in determining segment profit or loss to the enterprise's total amount would be separately identified and described). (January, 1998)

16-37. The CICA Research Study example is extended here to illustrate the reconciliation disclosures required under Paragraph 1701.35:

Example

Revenues	
Total revenues for reportable segments	$34,500
Other revenues	1,000
Elimination of intersegment revenues	(4,500)
Total enterprise revenues	$31,000

Profit Or Loss	
Total profit or loss for reportable segments	$3,970
Other profit or loss	100
Elimination of intersegment profits	(500)
Unallocated amounts:	
Litigation settlement received	500
Other corporate expenses	(750)
Adjustment to pension expense in consolidation	(250)
Income before income taxes and extraordinary items	$3,070

Assets

Total assets for reportable segments	$79,000
Other assets	2,000
Elimination of receivable from corporation headquarters	(1,000)
Goodwill not allocated to segments	4,000
Other unallocated amounts	1,000
Enterprise total	$85,000

Other Significant Items

	Segment Totals	Adjustments	Enterprise Totals
Interest revenue	$3,750	$ 75	$3,825
Interest expense	2,750	(50)	2,700
Net interest revenue (finance segment only)	1,000	-	1,000
Expenditures for capital assets	2,900	1,000	3,900
Amortization of capital assets	2,950	-	2,950
Cost in excess of billings on long-term contracts	200	-	200

The reconciling item to adjust expenditures for capital assets is the amount incurred for the corporate headquarters building, which is not included in segment information. None of the other adjustments are significant.

Restatement Of Segment Disclosures

16-38.   As we have noted previously, it is likely enterprises will experience year-to-year changes in their group of reportable operating segments. When this happens, Section 1701 favours the retroactive approach as indicated in the following Recommendation:

> **Paragraph 1701.36**   *If an enterprise changes the structure of its internal organization in a manner that causes the composition of its reportable segments to change, the corresponding information for earlier periods should be restated unless it is impracticable to do so. Accordingly, an enterprise should restate those individual items of disclosure that it can practicably restate but need not restate those individual items, if any, that it cannot practicably restate. Following a change in the composition of its reportable segments, an enterprise should disclose whether it has restated the corresponding items of segment information for earlier periods. (January, 1998)*

16-39.   If a retroactive approach is not applied in such situations, the following Recommendation is applicable:

> **Paragraph 1701.37**   *If an enterprise has changed the structure of its internal organization in a manner that causes the composition of its reportable segments to change, and if segment information for earlier periods is not restated to reflect the change, the enterprise should disclose in the year in which the change occurs segment information for the current period under both the old basis and the new basis of segmentation unless it is impracticable to do so. (January, 1998)*

Accounting Principles And Measurement

16-40.   Under Section 1701's management approach to segment disclosures, the basic Recommendation on measurement is as follows:

> **Paragraph 1701.32**   *The amount of each segment item disclosed should be the measure reported to the chief operating decision maker for purposes of making decisions about allocating resources to the segment and assessing its performance. Adjustments and eliminations made in preparing an enterprise's general purpose financial statements and*

allocations of revenues, expenses, and gains or losses should be included in determining reported segment profit or loss only if they are included in the measure of the segments' profit or loss that is used by the chief operating decision maker. Similarly, only those assets that are included in the measure of the segment's assets that is used by the chief operating decision maker should be disclosed for that segment. If amounts are allocated to reported segment profit or loss or assets, those amounts should be allocated on a reasonable basis. (January, 1998)

16-41.   Under this approach, there is no specification of the accounting principles to be used. Further, no definitions of items such as segment revenue, segment expense, or segment profit or loss are required. While the absence of such definitions is consistent with the management approach to segment disclosures, the absence of these definitions is of concern to some. This was the case with James J. Leisenring, a member of the FASB who dissented from the adoption of Statement Of Financial Accounting Standards No. 131 (this Statement is largely identical to Section 1701). A part of his dissent is as follows:

> By not defining segment profit or loss, this Statement allows any measure of perfor-mance to be displayed as segment profit or loss as long as that measure is reviewed by the chief operating decision maker. Items of revenue and expense directly attribut-able to a given segment need not be included in the reported operating results of that segment, and no allocation of items not directly attributable to a given segment is required. As a consequence, an item that results directly from one segment's activi-ties can be excluded from that segment's profit or loss. Mr. Leisenring believes that, minimally, this Statement should require that amounts directly incurred by or directly attributable to a segment be included in that segment's profit or loss and that assets identified with a particular segment be consistent with the measurement of that segment's profit or loss.

> ... Mr. Leisenring supports the management approach for defining reportable segments and supports requiring disclosure of selected segment information in condensed financial statements of interim periods issued to shareholders. Mr. Leisenring believes, however, that the definitions of revenues, operating profit or loss, and identifiable assets should be retained in this Statement and applied to segments identified by the management approach.

16-42.   While both Canadian and U. S. standard setters rejected Mr. Leisenring's view, there is clearly cause for concern with the wide range of approaches that can be used in preparing segment information. To at least partially alleviate that concern, Section 1701 includes a Recommendation requiring fairly extensive disclosure of the manner in which segment profit or loss and segment assets have been determined:

> **Paragraph 1701.34**   *An enterprise should disclose an explanation of the measurements of segment profit or loss and segment assets for each reportable segment. At a minimum, an enterprise should disclose the following:*

> (a) *The basis of accounting for any transactions between reportable segments.*

> (b) *The nature of any differences between the measurements of the reportable segments' profits or losses and the enterprise's income before income taxes, discontinued opera-tions and extraordinary items (if not apparent from the reconciliations described in paragraph 1701.35). Those differences could include accounting policies and policies for allocation of centrally incurred costs that are necessary for an understanding of the segment information disclosed.*

> (c) *The nature of any differences between the measurements of the reportable segments' assets and the enterprise's total assets (if not apparent from the reconciliations described in paragraph 1701.35). Those differences could include accounting policies and policies for allocation of jointly used assets that are necessary for an understanding of the segment information disclosed.*

(d) *The nature of any changes from prior periods in the measurement methods used to determine reported segment profit or loss and the effect, if any, of those changes on the measure of segment profit or loss.*

(e) *The nature and effect of any asymmetrical allocations to segments (for example, an enterprise might allocate amortization expense to a segment without allocating the related capital assets to that segment). (January, 1998)*

16-43.   The CICA Research Study example includes the type of disclosure that would be appropriate under Paragraph 1701.34:

Example   The accounting policies of the segments are the same as those described in the summary of significant accounting policies except that pension expense for each segment is recognized and measured on the basis of cash payments to the pension plan. Diversified Company evaluates performance based on profit or loss from operations before income taxes not including non-recurring gains and losses and foreign exchange gains and losses.

16-44.   As was noted in an earlier section, the chief operating decision maker may use more than one measure of a segment's profit or loss, as well as more than one measure of segment assets. Section 1701 suggests that, in this situation, the measures used for segment disclosure should be those that management believes are determined in accordance with the measurement principles most consistent with those used in measuring the corresponding total amounts in the enterprise's financial statements.

Enterprise Wide Disclosures

General

16-45.   As we have indicated previously in this Chapter, the primary focus of segment disclosures under Section 1701 is on reportable operating segments, with such segments identified on the basis of the organization of the business activities of the enterprise. Unless the enterprise's business activities are organized on the basis of products and services, or geographic regions, we may encounter situations in which:

- an operating segment may report revenues from a range of different products or services;

- different operating segments may report revenues from essentially the same products or services;

- assets may be reported in one geographic area with related revenue being included in different geographic areas; or

- more than one operating segment may carry on activities in the same geographic area.

16-46.   Such results are, of course, consistent with the management approach to segment disclosures. However, users of financial statements are clearly interested in having more detailed information about products and services provided by the enterprise, geographic areas in which the enterprise operates, and major customers. As a consequence, Paragraph 1701.39 through 1701.43 include Recommendations requiring the disclosure of such information. Note, however, that this disclosure need be provided only if it is not provided as part of the reportable operating segment information required elsewhere in Section 1701.

Information About Products And Services

16-47.   In order to provide some basis for comparison with enterprises providing similar products and services, Section 1701 includes the following Recommendation:

Paragraph 1701.39   *An enterprise should disclose the revenues from external customers for each product and service or each group of similar products and services unless it is impracticable to do so. The amounts of revenues disclosed should be based on the financial information used to produce the enterprise's general purpose financial statements. If providing the information is impracticable, that fact should be disclosed. (January, 1998)*

16-48. The Diversified Company example, from the CICA Research Study, has operating segments that are based on different products and services (see Paragraph 16-31). As a consequence, no additional disclosure is required under Paragraph 1701.39.

Information About Geographic Areas

16-49. As was the case with lines of products and services, Section 1701 requires additional information about geographic areas:

> **Paragraph 1701.40** *An enterprise should disclose the following geographic information unless it is impracticable to do so:*
>
> (a) *Revenues from external customers:*
>
> (i) *attributed to the enterprise's country of domicile, and*
> (ii) *attributed to all foreign countries in total from which the enterprise derives revenues.*
>
> *If revenues from external customers attributed to an individual foreign country are material, those revenues should be disclosed separately. An enterprise should disclose the basis for attributing revenues from external customers to individual countries.*
>
> (b) *Capital assets and goodwill:*
>
> (i) *located in the enterprise's country of domicile, and*
> (ii) *located in all foreign countries in total in which the enterprise holds assets.*
>
> *If assets in an individual foreign country are material, those assets should be disclosed separately.*
>
> *The amounts disclosed should be based on the financial information used to produce the general purpose financial statements. If providing the geographic information is impracticable, that fact should be disclosed.* (January, 1998)

16-50. As the Diversified Company example from the CICA Research Study did not have operating segments based on geographic areas, Paragraph 1701.40 is applicable. The illustration of geographic information included in the Example is as follows:

Example
Geographic Information

	Revenues	Capital Assets and Goodwill
Canada	$19,000	$11,000
United States	4,200	-
Taiwan	3,400	6,500
Japan	2,900	3,500
Other foreign countries	1,500	3,000
Total	$31,000	$24,000

Revenues are attributed to countries based on location of customer.

Information About Major Customers

16-51. A final type of enterprise wide disclosure required by Section 1701 is information about major customers:

> **Paragraph 1701.42** *An enterprise should disclose information about the extent of its reliance on its major customers. If revenues from transactions with a single external customer amount to 10 percent or more of an enterprise's revenues, the enterprise should disclose that fact, the total amount of revenues from each such customer, and the identity of the segment or segments reporting the revenues.* (January, 1998)

16-52.   In applying this provision, Section 1701 notes that a group of enterprises under common control should be considered to be a single customer. In contrast, the federal government, a provincial government, a local government, or a foreign government would each be considered to be a single customer.

16-53.   In general, enterprises are reluctant to disclose information about particular customers as such information may be useful to competitors. As a consequence, Section 1701 does not require disclosure of the identity of major customers, or the amount of revenues that each segment receives from such customers.

16-54.   The CICA Research Study example includes the following illustration of disclosure about major customers:

Example
Major Customer Disclosure

Revenues from one customer of Diversified Company's software and electronics segments represent approximately $5,000 of the Company's total revenues.

Segment Disclosures In Canadian Practice

Statistics From Financial Reporting In Canada

16-55.   The 2001 edition of *Financial Reporting in Canada* states that for 2000, 178 of the 200 surveyed companies provided operating and/or geographic segment information, 10 disclosed that their operations had a dominant segment only, and the remaining 12 did not provide information on operating or geographic segments. With respect to the form of segmentation, 51 companies reported information on the basis of operating segments only, 2 companies reported on the basis of geographic segments only, 28 companies provided disclosure of geographic segments with an indication that there was a dominant segment, and 97 companies disclosed both operating and geographic segments.

16-56.   For the 148 companies disclosing information about operating segments, 38 provided information about two segments, 56 provided information about three segments, 29 provided information about four segments, and 25 provided information about five or more segments.

16-57.   For the companies disclosing information about operating segments, the number of companies reporting various types of information was as follows:

Measure of profit or loss	142
Revenues	140
Total assets	135
Amortization of capital assets and goodwill	127
Total expenditures for additions to capital assets and goodwill	119
General description of segment products and services	116

16-58.   For the 127 companies that provided information about geographic segments, 39 reported two segments, 32 reported three segments, 32 reported four segments, and 24 reported five or more segments.

16-59.   For the companies reporting geographic segments, the number of companies reporting various types of information were as follows:

Total assets	114
Revenues	126

16-60.   The great majority of companies providing segment disclosure did so on a comparative basis.

Example From Practice

16-61. The following example is from the annual report of MAAX Inc. for the reporting period ending February 29, 2000. There are three business (operating) segments and the existence of a major customer is disclosed.

Notes To Financial Statements

(in thousands of dollars)

Note 15   Segmented Information

The Company designs, develops, manufactures and distributes products in three business segments, being: bathroom products, spas and kitchen cabinets. Until February 29, 1999, the Company evaluated shower doors and medicine cabinets as a distinct segment. Since that date, this segment is included with the bathroom products segment and comparative figures have been reclassified accordingly. The bathroom products segment includes sales of bathtubs and showers made of acrylic, fiberglass and ABS as well as shower doors and medicine cabinets. The business segments are managed separately because each business requires different technologies and marketing strategies. The management of the Company evaluates the performance of each segment based on income before income taxes and goodwill amortization. The operations are located in Canada, United States and Europe.

The accounting policies used in these business segments are the same as those described in the summary of significant accounting policies. Intersegment sales are recorded at the exchange value, which is the amount agreed to by the parties.

Approximately 25% (23% in 1999) of total sales are attributed to one client.

Reconciliations with the financial statements of revenues and assets by geographic segment and business segment are:

	2000	1999
By geographic segment:		
Net sales, from Canadian facilities:		
Canada	$134,689	$108,758
United States	86,881	43,007
Overseas	2,647	3,433
	224,217	155,198
Net sales, from American facilities:		
Canada	51	94
United States	203,372	156,455
Overseas	954	1,148
	204,377	157,697
Net sales, from European facilities:		
Overseas	3,282	–
	$431,876	$312,895
Fixed assets and goodwill:		
Canada	$126,203	$78,532
United States	82,443	84,264
Europe	28,248	–
	$236,894	$162,796

	2000	1999
By business segment:		
Sales:		
Bathroom products	$ 329,811	$285,594
Spas	61,517	27,362
Kitchen cabinets	40,851	–
	432,179	312,956
Intersegment sales:		
Bathroom products	9	61
Spas	294	–
	303	61
Net sales:		
Bathroom products	329,802	285,533
Spas	61,223	27,362
Kitchen cabinets	40,851	–
	$431,876	$312,895
Income before income taxes and goodwill amortization:		
Bathroom products	$ 28,143	$ 31,942
Spas	(1,388)	338
Kitchen cabinets	3,412	–
	$ 30,167	$ 32,280
Amortization of fixed assets and goodwill:		
Bathroom products	$11,782	$9,860
Spas	1,643	834
Kitchen cabinets	1,070	–
	$14,495	$10,694
Assets:		
Bathroom products	$319,727	$234,330
Spas	45,539	43,466
Kitchen cabinets	31,665	–
	$396,931	$277,796
Additions to fixed assets and goodwill:		
Bathroom products	$28,391	$18,622
Spas	2,108	378
Kitchen cabinets	5,930	–
	$36,429	$19,000

Additional Readings

16-62.   In writing the material in the text, we have incorporated all of the relevant *CICA Handbook* Recommendations, as well as material from other sources that we felt to be of importance. If you wish to pursue this subject in greater depth, you will find a fairly comprehensive bibliography of materials on the subject of segment disclosures in Chapter 18 of our *Guide to Canadian Financial Reporting,* as well as a summary of the following Abstract.

  • EIC Abstract No. 115 - Segment Disclosure - Application of the Aggregate Criteria in CICA 1701

16-63.   The complete *Guide to Canadian Financial Reporting* is available on the CD-ROM that accompanies this text.

Part Two: Interim Financial Statements

Introduction

16-64.   There are a number of possible uses that can be made of interim reports. The most frequently cited of these would be as follows:

- As a basis for estimating annual earnings.
- As a basis for making forward projections for any relevant future period, including annual periods.
- To assist in identifying turning points in the company's earnings or liquidity patterns.
- As a basis for evaluating management performance.
- To supplement the annual report in a continuing process of conveying information on the financial progress of the enterprise.

16-65.   The need for such reports was strongly reinforced by a Toronto Stock Exchange survey of analysts concerning corporate disclosure. The survey indicated that 61 percent of the respondents viewed quarterly financial statements as an essential source of information in making investment decisions. A further 31 percent indicated that the quarterly financial statements are "often useful". However, only 40 percent rated the accuracy and completeness of information in quarterly financial statements as "good" or "very good". Further, an overwhelming majority believed that disclosure in the United States is better than in Canada and cited more detailed quarterly reports as a key reason for this view.

16-66.   It was with a view to correcting this situation that *CICA Handbook* Section 1750 on interim financial reporting was revised in September, 2000. The introduction of Section 1751 should make a significant contribution to changing the opinions of the analysts surveyed in the Toronto Stock Exchange report.

Purpose and Scope

16-67.   The objective of Section 1751 is to establish standards for interim financial statements. The basis for this objective is the belief that timely and reliable interim financial reporting improves the ability of investors, creditors, and others to understand an enterprise's capacity to generate earnings and cash flows and its financial condition and liquidity.

16-68.   The basic requirements for presenting interim reports are established under Canada's various securities laws and regulations. In addition, other enterprises may be required by law, regulation, or contract to provide interim financial statements to shareholder, creditors, regulatory agencies , or other interested parties. There are also situations in which an enterprise simply chooses to provide such reports without having any legal requirement to do so.

16-69.   Given this situation, Section 1751 makes no attempt to specify which enterprises should present interim financial statements. This is consistent with both IAS 34 and Accounting Principles Board (APB) Opinion No. 28. However, if interim financial statements are prepared and presented as being in compliance with GAAP, they must be prepared in accordance with the Recommendations of Section 1751. Note, however, that there is no prohibition against providing non-GAAP interim financial statements, provided that are not presented as being in compliance with GAAP.

16-70.   Some of the Recommendations of Section 1751 could be applied to not-for-profit organizations. However, not-for-profit organizations are excluded from the scope of this Section.

Materiality

16-71.   Section 1000 of the *CICA Handbook* describes materiality as follows:

> **Paragraph 1000.17**   Users are interested in information that may affect their decision making. Materiality is the term used to describe the significance of financial statement information to decision makers. An item of information, or an aggregate of items, is material if it is probable that its omission or misstatement would influence or change a decision. Materiality is a matter of professional judgment in the particular circumstances.

16-72.   The issue here is whether this concept should be applied in relation to the figures in the interim financial statements or, alternatively, in relation to the figures that will be included in the full year or annual results. The AcSB adopted the approach that materiality must be assessed in relation to the interim period financial data.

16-73.   This is not consistent with APB No. 28 in the U.S. That pronouncement indicates that materiality is to be assessed relative to the estimated income for the full fiscal year. However, a new Staff Accounting Bulletin from the Securities and Exchange Commission is likely to change this situation.

Definitions

16-74.   As with most recent additions to the *Handbook*, a group of definitions is included in Section 1751. They are as follows:

> **Paragraph 1751.06**   The following terms are used in this Section with the meanings specified:
> (a) A **fiscal year** is normally a twelve-month period but in some circumstances, such as the establishment of a new entity or a change in fiscal year end, may be more or less than twelve months.
> (b) **Annual financial statements** are financial statements for a fiscal year.
> (c) An **interim period** is a financial reporting period within a fiscal year that is shorter than the fiscal year.
> (d) **Interim financial statements** are financial statements for an interim period.

16-75.   The AcSB's definition of "interim financial statements" makes it clear that the Section does not cover anything beyond the complete set of financial statements that it requires for GAAP compliance. In particular, it excludes any other financial information, such as management discussion and analysis of financial condition and operating results. Without this clarification, the Section could be read as mandating explanatory or analytical disclosures generally considered beyond the scope of financial statements. This change serves to harmonize the Canadian standard more closely with that contained in APB Opinion No. 28.

Content of Interim Financial Statements

Minimum Components

16-76.   With respect to the minimum content of annual financial statements, Section 1500, "General Standards of Financial Statement Presentation", notes the following:

Paragraph 1500.03   Financial statements normally include the balance sheet, income statement, statement of retained earnings and cash flow statement. Notes to financial statements, and supporting schedules to which the financial statements are cross-referenced, are an integral part of such statements; the same does not apply to information set out elsewhere in an annual report, in a prospectus, or in other material attached to or submitted with financial statements.

16-77.   In the following Recommendation, Section 1751 requires essentially the same set of financial statements in interim reports as would be found in annual reports:

Paragraph 1751.10   *Interim financial statements should include, at a minimum, the following components:*

(a) *balance sheet;*
(b) *income statement;*
(c) *statement of retained earnings;*
(d) *cash flow statement; and*
(e) *notes to financial statements providing the disclosures required by paragraph 1751.14.* (January, 2001)

16-78.   Two additional points are made with respect to this Recommendation:

• There is nothing in Section 1751 that is intended to prohibit or discourage disclosures beyond the minimum required. This Recommendation simply specifies the minimum components that must be present.

• This Recommendation, as well as subsequent ones dealing with the content of the required statements and other disclosures, is applicable to all interim financial statements, including those prepared in accordance with requirements for annual financial statements.

Minimum Content of Financial Statements

16-79.   The AcSB concluded that disclosing fewer line items in interim financial statements than are required in annual financial statements would deprive users of important information. Further, there would be little or no reduction in the amount of work required on the part of financial statements preparer. This conclusion is reflected in the following Recommendation:

Paragraph 1751.11   *An enterprise's interim financial statements should include, at a minimum, each of:*

(a) *the headings and subtotals included in its most recent annual financial statements,*
(b) *the line items required by the Recommendations of other Sections in annual financial statements, and*
(c) *the disclosures required by paragraph 1751.14, that are applicable in relation to the enterprise's financial position, results of operations and cash flows for the periods covered.* (January, 2001)

16-80.   A further Recommendation makes it clear that interim financial statements should include Earnings Per Share information:

Paragraph 1751.12   *Basic and diluted earnings per share should be presented on the face of an income statement for an interim period when an enterprise is required to present this information in its annual financial statements.* (January, 2001)

16-81.   There are a number of complications associated with the calculation of Earnings Per Share information for interim periods. If you would like more information on this *CICA Handbook* Section, see Chapter 45, "Earnings Per Share" of our *Guide To Canadian Financial Reporting*. This Guide is available on the CD-ROM that accompanies this text.

Minimum Disclosure

16-82.   In approaching the issue of minimum disclosure requirements, the AcSB believed that it was reasonable to assume that users of interim financial statements generally have access to the most recent annual financial statements. Given this, they felt that it was unnecessary for the notes to interim financial statements to provide immaterial updates to the information that was already reported in the notes to those annual financial statements. In interim reports, users will be most concerned with a description of transactions and events that are significant to an understanding of the changes in an enterprise's financial position and its performance since the end of its most recently completed fiscal year.

16-83.   Given this approach, it becomes very important for users to consult the annual report prior to reaching any important conclusions with respect to the enterprise. In particular, the AcSB was concerned that information about material contingencies might be ignored. Under the approach being used, such contingencies would not have to be reported in a particular interim report if there was no change in its status. To deal with this type of situation, the AcSB added a requirement [Paragraph 1751.14(a)] that, when interim financial statements do not conform in all respects with minimum GAAP for annual statements, there should be a statement to that effect, along with a directive that the interim statements should be read in conjunction with the most recent annual report.

16-84.   The minimum disclosure Recommendations are found in one very long Paragraph as follows:

> **Paragraph 1751.14**   *An enterprise should include at least the following information in its interim financial statements, when applicable:*
>
> (a)   *When the disclosures in the interim financial statements do not conform in all respects to the requirements of generally accepted accounting principles for annual financial statements, the interim financial statements should include a statement to that effect. That statement should also indicate that the interim financial statements should be read in conjunction with the most recent annual financial statements.*
>
> (b)   *The interim financial statements should include a statement that they follow the same accounting policies and methods of their application as the most recent annual financial statements, except for:*
>
> > (i)   *any policy or method that has been changed (including a change made in adopting a new accounting requirement);*
> > (ii)   *any new policy or method that has been adopted for new events or circumstances or new types of transactions;*
> > (iii) *any accounting method applied to address circumstances that affect the preparation of the interim financial statements but have no effect on annual financial statements; or*
> > (iv)   *a special accounting method applied to address temporary inventory costing fluctuations (see paragraph 1751.18).*
>
> *When an enterprise has adopted a new or changed accounting policy or method, the interim financial statements should provide such disclosures concerning those matters as will be required in the annual financial statements for the current fiscal year by other Sections (including "Accounting Changes", Section 1506). When an accounting method has been applied to address circumstances that affect the preparation of the interim financial statements but have no effect on annual financial statements, or a special accounting method has been applied to address temporary inventory costing fluctuations, the enterprise should disclose that*

method in the interim financial statements.

(c) *The interim financial statements should include a description of any seasonality or cyclicality of interim period operations.*

(d) *The interim financial statements should disclose the nature and amount of changes in estimates of:*

  (i)   amounts reported in prior interim periods of the current fiscal year, and
  (ii) amounts reported in prior fiscal years,

  when those changes have a material effect in the current interim period.

(e) *The interim financial statements should disclose the following information about each reportable segment determined according to "Segment Disclosure", Section 1701, when that Section requires an enterprise to provide segment disclosures:*

  (i)   revenues from external customers;
  (ii)   intersegment revenues;
  (iii) a measure of segment profit or loss;
  (iv)   total assets for which there has been a material change from the amount disclosed in the most recent annual financial statements;
  (v)   a description of differences from the most recent annual financial statements in the basis of segmentation or in the basis of measuring segment profit or loss;
  (vi)   a reconciliation of the total of the reportable segments' measures of profit or loss to the enterprise's income or loss before discontinued operations and extraordinary items, in which significant reconciling items should be separately identified and described (however, when an enterprise allocates items such as extraordinary items to segments, the enterprise may choose to reconcile the total of the segments' measures of profit or loss to the enterprise's income after those items); and
  (vii) when an enterprise changes the structure of its internal organization in a manner that causes the composition of its reportable segments to change, information for each prior period presented in the interim financial statements restated in accordance with SEGMENT DISCLOSURES, paragraphs 1701.36-.37.

  The information about reportable segments should be provided for the current interim period and cumulatively for the current fiscal year to date, with comparative information for the comparable interim periods (current and year-to-date) of the immediately preceding fiscal year.

(f) *The interim financial statements should disclose events subsequent to the end of the interim period that have not been reflected in the financial statements for the interim period (see "Subsequent Events", Section 3820).*

(g) *The interim financial statements should include the disclosures required in annual financial statements concerning:*

  (i)   business combinations;
  (ii)   plans to exit an activity, plans for restructuring and integration related to a business combination, financial reorganizations and spin-offs;
  (iii) discontinued operations; and
  (iv)   extraordinary items.

(h) *The interim financial statements should disclose changes in the existence, likelihood or amount of contingencies since the end of the most recently completed fiscal year (see "Contingencies", Section 3290).*

(i) *The interim financial statements should present any other information required for fair presentation of financial position, results of operations or cash flows for the interim period (see "General Standards of Financial Statement Presentation" Section 1500).*

The information specified in (d), (e) and (i) should be reported for both the current interim period and the current fiscal year to date. The information specified in (a) - (c) and (f) - (h) is required only for the current fiscal year to date. (January, 2001)

16-85.   Section 1751 gives several examples of the types of disclosure required by Paragraph 1751.14. They are as follows:

- Changes in the level of commitments for the purchase of capital assets (see "Contractual Obligations", Section 3280).
- Any debt default or any breach of a debt covenant that has not been corrected subsequently (see "Long-Term Debt", Section 3210).
- Related party transactions not in the normal course of operations (see "Related Party Transactions", Section 3840).

Periods to be Presented

16-86.   Section 1751 has the following Recommendation dealing with the periods to be reported in interim financial statements:

Paragraph 1751.16   *Interim financial statements should include:*

(a) *a balance sheet as of the end of the current interim period and a comparative balance sheet as of the end of the immediately preceding fiscal year;*

(b) *income statements for the current interim period and cumulatively for the current fiscal year to date, with comparative statements for the comparable interim periods (current and year-to-date) of the immediately preceding fiscal year;*

(c) *a statement of retained earnings cumulatively for the current fiscal year to date, with a comparative statement for the comparable year-to-date period of the immediately preceding fiscal year; and*

(d) *cash flow statements for the current interim period and cumulatively for the current fiscal year to date, with comparative statements for the comparable interim periods (current and year-to-date) of the immediately preceding fiscal year. (January, 2001)*

16-87.   This Recommendation makes it clear that a full set of financial statements are required in interim financial statements. In addition, both the Income Statement and the Cash Flow Statement must be presented for both the current interim period and for the current fiscal year to date.

16-88.   Under the new Section 1300, "Differential Reporting", qualifying non-publicly accountable enterprises are allowed to present the preceding year's financial statements as comparative information in the preparation of interim financial statements. This new *Handbook* Section exempts qualifying "non-publicly accountable enterprises" from a number of reporting requirements. If you would like more information on this important new *CICA Handbook* Section, see Chapter 3 of our *Guide To Canadian Financial Reporting*. This Guide is available on the CD-ROM that accompanies this text.

Recognition and Measurement

Basic Concepts

Described

16-89.   There are two distinct approaches to the measurement of interim earnings, generally referred to as the discrete approach and the integral approach. These two approaches are described in the CICA Research Report, *Interim Financial Reporting: A Continuous Process*, as follows:

The **discrete** approach recognizes revenues and expenses for the period in question, thus treating that period in isolation (i.e., as if the interim period were an annual accounting period). Under this view, the accruals, deferrals, and estimations at the end of each interim period are determined by following the same principles and judgments which apply to annual periods. In effect:

- expense recognition does not change with the length of the reporting period;
- interim reporting requires only those estimates and allocations required for annual reporting;
- components of financial statements such as assets, liabilities, expenses, and earnings are defined the same as they are for annual statements;
- the shorter the reporting period, the more likely that seasonal influences and discretionary costs will cause fluctuations in period-to-period earnings.

On the contrary, the **integral** approach (which appears to be a modification of the **discrete** approach so that the results for the interim period may better relate to the results of operations for the annual period) has the following characteristics:

- expenses are allocated to interim periods based on estimates of annual revenues and expenses;
- inaccuracies in the above estimates require adjustments in subsequent interim periods;
- earnings fluctuate less than under other approaches;
- components of financial statements such as assets, liabilities, expenses, and earnings may be defined differently for interim periods than for annual;
- unforeseen items such as extraordinary gains/losses are recognized as they arise.

Example

16-90. A somewhat simplified example will serve to illustrate the application of these concepts:

Example The Conmax Company estimates that sales during the current calendar year will total 1 million units at $5 per unit. The Company provides interim reports for each quarter of the calendar year and its sales follow an extremely seasonal pattern. In past years, the pattern has been 20 percent of sales in the first quarter, 20 percent in the second quarter, 50 percent in the July through September quarter and 10 percent in the last quarter. With respect to variable costs, the budget calls for $2.00 per unit in variable manufacturing costs and $.50 per unit in variable selling expenses. Fixed manufacturing costs are estimated at $1 million and fixed selling and administrative costs are anticipated to total $500,000. Both types of fixed costs are incurred in equal quarterly amounts. The total budget for the Conmax Company would appear as follows:

Estimated Sales (1,000,000 At $5.00)		$5,000,000
Variable Costs:		
Manufacturing (1,000,000 At $2.00)	$2,000,000	
Selling (1,000,000 At $.50)	500,000	$2,500,000
Fixed Costs:		
Manufacturing	$1,000,000	
Selling And Administrative	500,000	1,500,000
Total Estimated Costs		$4,000,000
Budgeted Profit		$1,000,000

During the year, all of the revenues and costs occurred exactly as anticipated and units produced were equal to units sold. The resulting dollar figures for quarterly sales are as follows:

Quarter	Units	Dollars
First	200,000	$1,000,000
Second	200,000	1,000,000
Third	500,000	2,500,000
Fourth	100,000	500,000
Total	1,000,000	$5,000,000

Discrete Approach Solution

16-91.   Interim results of the Conmax Company, using the discrete approach are as follows:

Quarter	First	Second	Third	Fourth
Sales (At $5)	$1,000,000	$1,000,000	$2,500,000	$500,000
Variable Cost (At $2.50)	(500,000)	(500,000)	(1,250,000)	(250,000)
Contribution	$ 500,000	$ 500,000	$1,250,000	$250,000
Fixed Costs ($1,500,000/4)	(375,000)	(375,000)	(375,000)	(375,000)
Net Income (Loss)	$ 125,000	$ 125,000	$ 875,000	($125,000)

16-92.   The discrete approach solution produces the budgeted total income figure of $1,000,000. However, by allocating fixed costs to income as they are incurred on a quarterly basis, it has produced interim income figures that are more variable than the sales pattern would suggest (i.e., the percentage changes in income are more than the percentage changes in sales). Further, the interim earnings figures would not provide a basis for predicting annual income if you knew the seasonal pattern of sales. That is, if first quarter sales were normally 20 percent of the annual total, you could not use the above information to predict annual results because the first quarter income of $125,000 is not 20 percent of the annual total. You might also question whether the Company really experienced a loss in the fourth quarter.

Integral Approach Solution

16-93.   Under the integral approach, the contribution for each quarter will be the same as it was under the discrete approach. The difference here is that fixed costs will be allocated on the basis of the number of units sold and produced in each period. As the total fixed costs were $1,500,000 ($1,000,000 + $500,000), they will be allocated over the 1,000,000 estimated units at a rate of $1.50 per unit. The results under this approach are as follows:

Quarter	First	Second	Third	Fourth
Sales (At $5)	$1,000,000	$1,000,000	$2,500,000	$500,000
Variable Cost (At $2.50)	(500,000)	(500,000)	(1,250,000)	(250,000)
Contribution	$ 500,000	$ 500,000	$1,250,000	$250,000
Fixed Costs (At $1.50)	(300,000)	(300,000)	(750,000)	(150,000)
Net Income	$ 200,000	$ 200,000	$ 500,000	$100,000
Deferred Fixed Costs	$ 75,000	$ 150,000	($ 225,000)	$ -0-

16-94.   The integral approach solution also produces the budgeted total income figure of $1,000,000. The Deferred Fixed Costs are calculated by subtracting the cumulative allocated fixed costs from the cumulative actual fixed costs [($1,500,000 ÷ 4) = $375,000 per quarter]. By allocating fixed costs in proportion to sales, we produce interim income figures that are both proportional to sales and useful for predicting annual results. As an example of this latter point, if we knew that 20 percent of the Company's business occurred in the first quarter, we could use the interim income of $200,000 to predict the annual total of $1,000,000. This would appear to suggest that the integral approach is a better solution to this problem. However, there are problems with this approach.

Problems With The Integral Approach Solution

16-95.   The preceding Paragraph presented the results that would be produced by applying the integral approach. This solution was based on the assumption that all revenues and costs for the year were exactly as they were budgeted. Two types of problems can cause difficulty and sometimes produce absurd results in the application of the integral approach. These problems are differences between actual and budgeted costs and/or the volume of sales being more or less than was anticipated. We will illustrate the effects of each of these types of problems separately.

16-96.   To illustrate the problems associated with the difference between actual and budgeted costs, we will assume that all of the Conmax Company's costs were exactly as budgeted except that in the fourth quarter, the actual fixed costs incurred turned out to be nil. Keeping in mind that there was a deferred credit in fixed costs at the end of the third quarter, the fourth quarter integral approach Income Statement would be as follows:

Sales	$500,000
Variable Costs	(250,000)
Contribution Margin	$250,000
Fixed Costs (Credit)	225,000
Net Income	$475,000

16-97.   This result, which presents a Net Income that is equal to 95 percent of sales, is clearly not reasonable. However, it can easily happen under the integral approach when costs are incorrectly estimated. It is even possible to find examples where income exceeds total revenue in the last quarter of the fiscal year.

16-98.   To illustrate the problems associated with variances in sales volume, assume that first quarter costs are exactly as estimated. However, the sales volume is only 100,000 units at $5 for a total of $500,000. If we ignore the effect of this result on the predictions for the year, the first quarter integral approach Income Statement would be as follows:

Sales	$500,000
Variable Costs	(250,000)
Contribution Margin	$250,000
Fixed Costs (At $1.50)	(150,000)
Net Income	$100,000

16-99.   If the first quarter sales volume is a non-recurring shortfall, the preceding result is reasonable. However, if it turns out that the sales of 100,000 units is the usual 20 percent of the annual total, then total sales for the year will only be 500,000 units and the fixed costs will have to be allocated on a different basis. In other words, if the $1,500,000 in fixed costs is to be spread over only 500,000 units rather than the anticipated 1,000,000 units, the per unit charge under the integral approach will be $3.00 instead of the old basis of $1.50. This would result in the following Income Statement for the first quarter:

Sales	$500,000
Variable Costs	(250,000)
Contribution Margin	$250,000
Fixed Costs (At $3.00)	(300,000)
Net Income (Loss)	($ 50,000)

16-100.   This, of course, is a significantly different result than was the case when the estimate of total sales was not adjusted on the basis of the first quarter results. It is indicative of the difficulties that misestimating volume can generate in the application of the integral approach to the computation of interim income.

A Compromise Solution

16-101.   The preceding solutions have presented the discrete and integral approaches in their unmodified form. In practice, the more usual approach would be to use the integral approach for manufacturing costs and the discrete approach for other types of costs. This avoids the problem of treating deferred selling and administrative costs as assets and/or liabilities. Applying this combination approach to the interim results for the Conmax Company produces the following results:

Quarter	First	Second	Third	Fourth
Sales (At $5)	$1,000,000	$1,000,000	$2,500,000	$500,000
Variable Cost (At $2.50)	(500,000) (	500,000) (	1,250,000)	(250,000)
Contribution	$ 500,000	$ 500,000	$1,250,000	$250,000
Fixed Costs:				
Manufacturing (At $1.00)	(200,000) (	200,000) (	500,000)	(100,000)
Selling	(125,000) (	125,000) (	125,000)	(125,000)
Net Income	$ 175,000	$ 175,000	$ 625,000	$ 25,000

Accounting Policies

General Conclusions

16-102.   In general, Section 1751 adopts the discrete approach to the preparation of interim financial statements. This is reflected in the following Recommendation:

> **Paragraph 1751.18**   *An enterprise should apply the same accounting policies and methods of their application in its interim financial statements as it applied in its most recent annual financial statements,....*

16-103. By requiring the use of the same accounting policies in interim financial statements as were used in the most recent annual financial statements, the AcSB has, in general rejected the types of allocations that are required under the integral approach. This conclusion is reinforced by two other Recommendations dealing with particular issues. The first involves revenues which are received seasonally, cyclically, or only occasionally. This would include items such as dividend revenue, royalties, and government grants, as well as revenues for which sales tend to be seasonal. The Recommendation is as follows:

> **Paragraph 1751.27**   *An enterprise should recognize revenues in its interim financial statements on the same basis as in its annual financial statements. Accordingly, revenues received seasonally, cyclically, or occasionally within a fiscal year should be accrued or deferred at the end of an interim period only when that accrual or deferral would be appropriate at the end of a fiscal year.* (January, 2001)

16-104.   A similar Recommendation is made with respect to costs incurred unevenly during the year:

> **Paragraph 1751.29**   *An enterprise should recognize costs in its interim financial statements on the same basis as in its annual financial statements. Accordingly, costs incurred unevenly within a fiscal year should be accrued or deferred at the end of an interim period only when that accrual or deferral would be appropriate at the end of a fiscal year.* (January, 2001)

16-105.   There are several points to be made with respect to these Recommendations:

Use of Estimates   The preparation of interim financial statements will generally require a greater use of estimation than would be the case with annual financial statements. This does not change the principles used for recognizing and measuring losses from inventory write-downs, restructurings, or asset impairments in an interim period. This is the case even when year-to-date measurements involve changes for amounts reported in prior interim periods of the current fiscal year.

Recognition of Elements   In order to be recognized in financial statements, Section 1000 of the *CICA Handbook* requires that they meet the definition of an element. This is of particular relevance here with respect to assets and liabilities. An item that would not be considered an asset or liability at the end of the year cannot be treated as an asset or a liability in an interim period. An example of this might be the costs of a major advertising campaign. If it is the policy of the enterprise to write off such costs in the annual financial statements, they cannot be treated as an asset in the interim financial statements, even if there appears to be justification for doing so (e.g., third quarter advertising for Christmas merchandise to be sold in the fourth quarter).

Costs and Expenses That Benefit More Than One Period   This is similar to the preceding discussion of elements. However, it is given separate consideration because it is a phrase that is used in APB Opinion No. 28. That Opinion permits, but does not require, enterprises to allocate costs and expenses that clearly benefit more than one interim period within the same fiscal year among the interim periods benefited. This is not permitted under Section 1751.

16-106.   An Appendix to Section 1751 provides more detail on the application of these general principles. This material will be given attention in a later section of this Chapter.

Exceptions

16-107.   Paragraph 1751.18 was previously quoted with respect to the general approach to accounting policies that has been adopted for interim financial statements. The complete Paragraph also contains several exceptions to this general approach:

Paragraph 1751.18   *An enterprise should apply the same accounting policies and methods of their application in its interim financial statements as it applied in its most recent annual financial statements, except in the case of:*

(a) *a change in accounting policy or method (including a change made in adopting a new accounting requirement), or a new accounting policy or method, adopted after the end of the most recently completed fiscal year that will be reflected in the next annual financial statements;*

(b) *an accounting method applied to address circumstances that affect the preparation of the interim financial statements but have no effect on annual financial statements; or*

(c) *a special accounting method necessary to avoid the potentially misleading effects on reported interim period income of temporary inventory costing fluctuations from a liquidation of base period LIFO inventory quantities or a planned purchase price, volume or capacity cost variance under a standard cost accounting system.* (January, 2001)

16-108.   The first of these items, changes in accounting policies, is a fairly obvious exception. While the general rule is that accounting policies from the most recent annual financial statements should be used, if there has been a change during the year, it would clearly be more relevant to use the policies that will be in place at the end of the year. Note that this type of situation was subject to a specific disclosure Recommendation in Paragraph 1751.14(b). This Recommendation specifically required interim financial statements to include a statement that they follow the same accounting policies and methods of their application in the most recent annual financial statements except for certain specific events. Changes in accounting policies were included as exceptions.

16-109.   The second exception refers to accounting methods that are applied to address circumstances that affect the preparation of interim financial statements but have no effect on annual financial statements. There is no discussion of what type of transactions and events are contemplated here, either in the Section itself or in the "Background Information and Basis for Conclusions" that was released by the CICA. Given this lack of clarity, this provision appears to provide something of a loophole for the adoption of diverse practices in this area. It is unfortunate that this item was not given a more precise meaning.

16-110. Paragraph 1751.18(c) actually contains two exceptions to the discrete approach to measuring interim earnings. The first of these relates to inventory valuation and is limited to very specific circumstances. One of the unfortunate side effects of using the LIFO approach to inventory costing is that it can retain very old values in the Balance Sheet. The inventory balance that is carried forward may reflect prices that could be 10 or 20 years out of date and, in most cases, significantly undervalued. If, during an interim period, a seasonally low level of inventories results in these values being brought into income, the result can be an unrealistically low cost of sales and an inflated income figure. Section 1751 allows the use of methods to alleviate this distortion, provided that it is temporary in nature.

16-111. You might note that Section 1751 differs from APB Opinion No. 28 in its treatment of inventories. Under that Opinion, if there is a decline in the net realizable value of inventories at the end an interim period, it does not have to be taken into income if it is expected to reverse prior to the end of the year. This exception to the discrete method was not incorporated into the Canadian standard.

16-112. The other item in Paragraph 1751.18(c) is manufacturing cost variances arising under a standard cost accounting system. Standard costing methods based on annual determinations of expected manufacturing costs are intended to deal with expected seasonal fluctuations of certain types of costs, particularly those associated with capacity. If the variances resulting from the application of this type of system were taken into income in each interim period, the result could be very confusing to investors. As a consequence, this exception is provided.

Restatement of Previous Interim Periods

16-113. Under Section 1506, "Accounting Changes", retroactive treatment is given to changes in accounting policy unless the the necessary financial data is not reasonably determinable, the change is made to comply with an Accounting Guideline or an Abstract of an Issue Discussed by the CICA Emerging Issues Committee that permits prospective application, or the change is made in accordance with the Recommendations of another Section that permits or requires application on other than a retroactive basis. Under the retroactive approach, the financial statements of all prior periods are restated to give effect to the new accounting policy.

16-114. With respect to dealing with changes in accounting policy in interim financial statements, the following Recommendation is applicable:

> **Paragraph 1751.31** *A change in accounting policy, other than one for which the transition is specified by a new accounting requirement, should be reflected by restating the financial statements of prior interim periods of the current fiscal year. Unless the financial data necessary for retroactive application is not reasonably determinable, the comparable interim periods of prior fiscal years (see paragraph 1751.16) should also be restated. When a change in accounting policy has been made in the current interim period, an enterprise should disclose its effect on the net income and, when applicable, basic and diluted earnings per share of previous interim periods within the current fiscal year and, unless the financial data necessary for retroactive application is not reasonably determinable, the comparable interim periods of the prior fiscal year. (January, 2001)*

16-115. This Recommendation ensures that financial statements for all interim periods within a particular fiscal year will be prepared using consistent accounting policies. Except in those cases where the necessary financial data is not reasonably determinable, it also provides for consistency with comparable interim periods in previous years. In the absence of this Recommendation, the use of inconsistent policies would complicate the analysis and understandability of interim period information.

Transitional Provisions

16-116.   In general, these Recommendation must be applied to interim financial statements in fiscal years beginning on or after January 1, 2001.   This is noted in the following Recommendation:

Paragraph 1751.34   *The Recommendations of this Section should be applied to interim financial statements for interim periods in fiscal years beginning on or after January 1, 2001.   Earlier application is encouraged. An enterprise adopting these Recommendations in the middle of a fiscal year should do so with effect from the beginning of the fiscal year. Enterprises other than public enterprises, co-operative organizations, deposit-taking institutions and life insurance enterprises may defer application of these Recommendations until interim periods in fiscal years beginning on or after January 1, 2002. Public enterprises are those enterprises that have issued debt or equity securities that are traded in a public market (a domestic or foreign stock exchange or an over-the-counter market, including local or regional markets), that are required to file financial statements with a securities commission, or that provide financial statements for the purpose of issuing any class of securities in a public market.* (January, 2001)

16-117.   Note that the application is required in the first fiscal period, not the first interim period, subsequent to the effective date.   For non-public companies, the application can be deferred to fiscal years beginning on or after January 1, 2002.   In those cases where earlier application is made, it might occur in the middle of a fiscal year.   For example, a company with a September 30, 2001 year end, might first apply these provision in the quarter which begins January 1, 2001.   If this happens, they would have to put these policies into effect from the beginning of the fiscal year on October 1, 2000.

16-118.   When this Section is first implemented, retroactive application is required:

Paragraph 1751.35   *For interim periods in the fiscal year in which the Recommendations of this Section are first applied, comparative information in accordance with paragraph 1751.16 should be provided on a basis consistent with these Recommendations, unless it is impracticable to do so.   When it is impracticable to present prior period information on a basis consistent with these Recommendations, such information as is available should nonetheless be presented and the fact that it has not been prepared in accordance with this Section should be disclosed.* (January, 2001)

Interim Financial Reporting In Canadian Practice

Statistics From Financial Reporting In Canada

16-119.   Our basic source on current Canadian accounting practices has been the CICA's *Financial Reporting in Canada*. This source is devoted to a survey of accounting practices as reflected in the annual reports of major Canadian companies and, as a consequence, it does not provide any information related to interim reports. This makes it impossible to comment on either the number of interim reports that are provided or the accounting practices that are found in those reports that are available.

Examples From Practice

16-120.   As a substitute for more detailed statistical information, the following briefly summarizes the financial reporting information that appeared in the interim reports of two publicly traded Canadian companies.   The statements are listed in the order they are disclosed in the interim reports.

Bombardier Inc. Interim Report for the third quarter which ended October 31, 2001. This report contained:

- A consolidated Balance Sheet with comparative figures as at January 31, 2001.

- Consolidated Statements of Income for the three months ending October 31, 2001, and for the nine months ended October 31, 2001. Comparative figures were provided for October 31, 2000.

- Consolidated Statements of Retained Earnings for the nine months ended October 31, 2001. Comparative figures were provided for October 31, 2000.

- Consolidated Statements of Cash Flows for the three months ending October 31, 2001, and for the nine months ended October 31, 2001. Comparative figures were provided for October 31, 2000.

MDS Inc. Interim Report for the fourth quarter which ended October 31, 2001. This report contained:

- Consolidated Statements of Income for the three months and year ending October 31, 2001 and October 31, 2000.

- Consolidated Statements of Retained Earnings for the three months and year ending October 31, 2001 and October 31, 2000.

- Consolidated Balance Sheets as at October 31, 2001 and October 31, 2000.

- Consolidated Statements of Cash Flows for the three months and year ending October 31, 2001 and October 31, 2000.

16-121. The reports varied considerably in size, style and content. In the case of MDS Inc., the statements were clearly marked as unaudited. The Bombardier statements were mixed in this regard. The results for the third quarter were marked as unaudited. However, because the comparative Balance Sheet information was for the previous year end, these figures appear to have been audited.

Additional Readings

11-122. In writing the material in the text, we have incorporated all of the relevant *CICA Handbook* Recommendations, as well as material from other sources that we felt to be of importance. While this approach meets the needs of the great majority of accounting students, some of you may wish to pursue this subject in greater depth. To facilitate this, you will find a fairly comprehensive bibliography of materials on the subject of interim financial statements in Chapter 19 of our *Guide to Canadian Financial Reporting*. The complete *Guide to Canadian Financial Reporting* is available on the CD-ROM that accompanies this text.

Appendix A - Periods to be Presented

16-123.   This Appendix discusses and illustrates the application of the definitions in paragraph 1751.06 and the principle in paragraph 1751.16.

16-124.   A public enterprise with a fiscal year ending December 31 (calendar year) will present the following information in its quarterly interim financial statements as of June 30, 2001:

Balance sheet:		
At	June 30, 2001	December 31, 2000
Income statement:		
6 months ended	June 30, 2001	June 30, 2000
3 months ended	June 30, 2001	June 30, 2000
Statement of retained earnings:		
6 months ended	June 30, 2001	June 30, 2000
Cash flow statement:		
6 months ended	June 30, 2001	June 30, 2000
3 months ended	June 30, 2001	June 30, 2000

16-125.   An interim period may be of any length, not just three months, as long as it covers a financial reporting period within a fiscal year that is shorter than the fiscal year. A "stub" period may arise within a fiscal year as a result of a requirement, such as a prospectus requirement, to provide information up to a date later than the most recent normal interim period end. A "stub" period constitutes an interim period when financial statements for the period are presented separately.

16-126.   A short fiscal year of less than twelve months is not an interim period. A change in year end that creates a fiscal year longer than twelve months may result in a final interim period that is longer than normal or an additional interim period.

16-127.   Not all interim period financial information is required to be presented in accordance with generally accepted accounting principles. The enterprise in the preceding illustration may, for example, also prepare monthly financial statements for management purposes that are provided to its bankers. In the absence of any statutory, regulatory or contractual requirement that they be prepared in accordance with generally accepted accounting principles, those monthly financial statements are not subject to the requirements of this Section.

Appendix B - Implementation Guidance

Employee Payroll Taxes and Contributions to Government Plans

16-128. When employer payroll taxes or contributions to government plans such as the Canada or Quebec Pension Plan, employment insurance or workers' compensation are assessed on an annual basis, the employer's related expense is recognized in interim periods using an estimated average annual effective payroll tax or contribution rate, even though a large portion of the payments may be made early in the fiscal year. A common example is the employment insurance contribution that is imposed up to a certain maximum level of earnings per employee. For higher income employees, the maximum income is reached before the end of the fiscal year, and the employer makes no further payments up to the end of the year. An estimated average annual effective payroll tax or contribution rate takes into account factors such as employee turnover expected to affect the total amount of an enterprise's annual cost. The purpose of recognizing the cost on this basis is to reflect the cost of an annual charge relative to the provision of service by employees, to which the payroll taxes and contributions pertain, rather than relative to the schedule of payments.

Major Planned Periodic Maintenance or Overhaul

16-129. The cost of a planned major periodic maintenance or overhaul or other seasonal expenditure that is expected to occur late in the year is not accrued for interim reporting purposes unless an event has caused the enterprise to have a legal or constructive obligation. The mere intention or necessity to incur expenditure related to the future is not sufficient to give rise to an obligation.

Liability Accruals

16-130. A liability accrual (provision) is recognized when an enterprise has no realistic alternative but to make a transfer of economic benefits as the result of an event that has created a legal, equitable or constructive obligation. The amount of the obligation is adjusted upward or downward, with a corresponding loss or gain recognized in the income statement, when the enterprise's best estimate of the amount of the obligation changes.

16-131. This Section requires that an enterprise apply the same criteria for recognizing and measuring a liability accrual at the end of an interim period as it does at the end of its fiscal year. The existence or non-existence of an obligation to transfer benefits is not a function of the length of the reporting period. It is a question of fact.

Year End Bonuses

16-132. The nature of year-end bonuses varies widely. Some are earned simply by continued employment during a time period. Others are earned based on a monthly, quarterly, or annual measure of operating results. They may be purely discretionary, contractual, or based on years of historical precedent.

16-133. A bonus is accrued for interim reporting purposes only when (i) the bonus is a legal obligation or past practice makes the bonus a constructive obligation for which the enterprise has no realistic alternative but to make the payments, and (ii) a reliable estimate of the amount of the obligation can be made. The fact that a bonus is determined or paid only on an annual basis does not mean that it is not accrued for interim reporting purposes. The existence of a legal obligation or a constructive obligation is determined for interim reporting purposes on the same basis as for annual reporting purposes. An enterprise can make a reliable estimate of its legal or constructive obligation under a bonus plan only when:

(a) the formal terms of the plan contain a formula for determining the amount of the benefit;

(b) the enterprise determines the amounts to be paid before the financial statements are completed; or

(c) past practice gives clear evidence of the amount of the enterprise's constructive obligation.

16-134. The following guidance and volume rebates or discounts may be helpful in determining the existence or amount of certain types of bonus obligations.

Contingent Lease Payments

16-135. Contingent lease payments may constitute a legal or constructive obligation that is recognized as a liability by the lessee. When, for example, a lease provides for contingent payments based on the lessee achieving a certain level of annual sales, an obligation can arise in interim periods of the fiscal year before the required annual level of sales has been achieved, when it is probable that the required level of sales will be achieved and the enterprise, therefore, has no realistic alternative but to make the future lease payment. However, the lessor recognizes contingent lease revenue only when the contingency has been resolved as a result of the required level of sales having been achieved, which may be in an interim period prior to the final interim period of the fiscal year.

Intangible Assets

16-136. An enterprise applies the definition and recognition criteria for an intangible asset in the same way at the end of an interim period as at the end of a fiscal year. Costs incurred before the recognition criteria for an intangible asset are met are recognized as expenses. Costs incurred after the specific point at which the criteria are met are recognized as part of the cost of an intangible asset. Deferring costs as assets in an interim Balance Sheet in the hope that the recognition criteria will be met later in the fiscal year is not justified.

Pensions

16-137. Pension cost for an interim period is calculated on a year-to-date basis by using the actuarially determined pension cost rate at the end of the most recently completed fiscal year, adjusted for the effects of any remeasurement of plan assets and obligations during the current fiscal year and for curtailments, settlements, or other such one-time events.

Vacations, Holidays, and Other
Short-Term Compensated Absences

16-138. Accumulating compensated absences are those that are carried forward and can be used in future periods when the current period's entitlement is not used in full. "Employee Future Benefits", Section 3461, requires an enterprise to measure the expected cost of, and obligation for, accumulating compensated absences (other than occasional sick days and vacation days that do not vest or accumulate beyond twelve months after the current reporting period) at the amount the enterprise expects to pay as a result of the unused entitlement that has accumulated at the end of a fiscal year. That principle is also applied at the end of an interim period. Conversely, an enterprise recognizes no expense or liability for non-accumulating compensated absences at the end of an interim period, just as it recognizes none at the end of a fiscal year.

Other Planned But Irregularly Occurring Costs

16-139. An enterprise's budget may include certain costs expected to be incurred irregularly during the fiscal year, such as charitable contributions and employee training costs. Those costs generally are discretionary even though they are planned and tend to recur from year to year. Recognizing an obligation at the end of an interim period for such costs that have not yet been incurred is not consistent with the criteria in "Financial Statement Concepts", Section 1000, for recognizing a liability.

Income Taxes

16-140.   Under "Income Taxes", Section 3465, the focus on accounting for income taxes is on recognizing and measuring current and future income tax assets and liabilities, which are normally determined on an annual basis consistent with the requirements of tax legislation. An enterprise's annual income tax expense or benefit is determined on the basis of changes to the balance of income tax assets and liabilities after taking account of cash payments and receipts. This approach is not possible for interim financial reporting purposes, making it necessary for enterprises to estimate their income tax assets, liabilities, expenses and benefits. In general, subject to the following guidance, interim period income tax expense is accrued using the tax rate that is applicable to expected total annual earnings.

16-141.   Interim period income tax expense is calculated by applying to an interim period's pre-tax income the tax rate that is applicable to expected total annual earnings, that is, the estimated average annual effective income tax rate. That estimated average annual rate reflects a blend of any progressive tax rate structure expected to be applicable to the full year's earnings. The estimated average annual income tax rate is re-estimated at the end of each interim period on a year-to-date basis, consistent with paragraph 1751.18. Paragraph 1751.14(d) requires disclosure of the nature and amount of changes in estimates that have a material effect in the current interim period.

16-142.   To the extent practicable, a separate estimated average annual effective income tax rate is determined for each taxing jurisdiction and applied individually to the interim period pre-tax income of each jurisdiction. Similarly, when different income tax rates apply to different categories of income (such as capital gains or income earned in particular industries), to the extent practicable, a separate rate is applied to each individual category of interim period pre-tax income. While that degree of precision is desirable, it may not be achievable in all cases, and a weighted average of rates across jurisdictions or across categories of income may be justified when it is a reasonable approximation of the effect of using more specific rates. In arriving at an estimated average annual effective income tax rate applicable to income before discontinued operations and extraordinary items, an enterprise excludes the effect of the income taxes on any extraordinary item, discontinued operation or other item of income for which the tax effect is presented separately. The tax expense or benefit associated with each such item is determined separately on the basis of the income tax rates applicable to it, and recognized in the income statement of the interim period in which the item itself is recognized.

16-143.   To illustrate the application of the foregoing principle, an enterprise reporting quarterly expects to earn income of $10,000 pre-tax each quarter and operates in a jurisdiction with a tax rate of 20 percent on the first $20,000 of annual earnings and 30 percent on all additional earnings. There are no discontinued operations or extraordinary items. Actual earnings match expectations. This means that $10,000 [(20%)($20,000 + (30%)$(20,000)] of tax is expected to be payable for the full year on $40,000 of pre-tax income. The following income tax expense is reported in each quarter:

	1st Quarter	2nd Quarter	3rd Quarter	4th Quarter	Annual
Tax expense	$2,500	$2,500	$2,500	$2,500	$10,000

16-144.   As another illustration, an enterprise reports quarterly, incurs a pre-tax loss of $5,000 in the first quarter but expects to earn $15,000 pre-tax profit in the second quarter and incur losses of $5,000 in each of the two remaining quarters (thus having zero income for the year), and operates in a jurisdiction in which its average annual income tax rate is estimated to be 20 percent. The following table shows the amount of income tax expense that the enterprise expects to report in each quarter:

	1st Quarter	2nd Quarter	3rd Quarter	4th Quarter	Annual
Tax expense	$(1,000)	$3,000	$(1,000)	$(1,000)	Nil

16-145.   When an enterprise estimates that it will have future tax benefits as of the end of the current fiscal year from deductible temporary differences, unused tax losses or unused tax reductions other than investment tax credits arising in the current year, it assesses whether it is more likely than not to realize that benefit. To the extent that some or all of the tax benefit is not expected to meet the criterion for recognition, it is not reflected in the computation of the enterprise's estimated average annual income tax rate.

16-146.   The effects of new tax legislation, including changes in tax rates, are reflected in income tax expense or benefit and liabilities or assets in accordance with "Income Taxes", Section 3465. The effects of new tax legislation are recognized as follows:

(a)   The effect of a change in income tax laws or rates on taxes currently payable or recoverable for the current year is reflected in the computation of the estimated average annual income tax rate after the date or dates of enactment or substantive enactment, beginning no earlier than the first interim period that includes the date of enactment or substantive enactment of the new income tax laws or rates.

(b)   The effect of a change in income tax laws or rates on future income tax assets and liabilities is included in income before discontinued operations and extraordinary items as a component of future income tax expense or benefit in the interim period that includes the date of enactment or substantive enactment of the change. The effect of a change in income tax laws or rates at the enactment date is recognized immediately rather than allocated to subsequent interim periods by an adjustment of the estimated average annual income tax rate for the remainder of the year. In effect, there is a catch-up adjustment for the effect of the change in income tax laws or rates in the interim period that includes the date of the change.

(c)   When a change in income tax laws or rates is enacted at a date other than an enterprise's fiscal year end, estimates of temporary differences as of the enactment date may be necessary to determine the effect of the change on future income tax assets and liabilities.

Tax Credits

16-147.   Some tax jurisdictions give taxpayers credits against tax payable based on amounts of capital expenditures, exports, research and development expenditures, or other bases (for example, the federal investment tax credit for scientific research expenditures). Tax credits constituting government assistance are accounted for in accordance with "Accounting for Government Assistance", Section 3800. Investment tax credits are accounted for in accordance with "Investment Tax Credits", Section 3805. For other types of tax credits, anticipated tax benefits for the full year are generally reflected in computing the estimated annual effective income tax rate, because those credits are granted and calculated on an annual basis under most tax laws and regulations. On the other hand, tax benefits that relate to a one-time event are recognized in computing income tax expense in the interim period in which the event occurs, in the same way that special tax rates applicable to particular categories of income are not blended into a single effective annual tax rate.

Tax Loss and Tax Credit Carrybacks and Carryforwards

16-148.   The benefits of a tax loss carryback are reflected in the interim period in which the related tax loss occurs. "Income Taxes", Section 3465, provides that the "benefit relating to a tax loss arising in the current period that will be carried back to recover income taxes of a previous period should be recognized as a current asset." A corresponding reduction of tax expense or increase of tax benefit is also recognized.

16-149.   "Income Taxes", Section 3465, provides that "... a future income tax asset should be recognized for ... unused tax losses and income tax reductions. The amount recognized should be limited to the amount that is more likely than not to be realized." That Section also provides criteria for assessing the probability of future taxable income against which the unused tax losses and reductions can be utilized. Those criteria are applied at the end of each interim period to tax losses and income tax reductions arising in prior fiscal years. To the extent that the criteria are met at the end of an interim period and the benefit of the income tax losses and reductions carried forward has not been recognized previously, the benefit is recognized as follows:

(a)   When the tax benefit is expected to be realized in the current fiscal year, it is generally reflected in the computation of the estimated average annual effective income tax rate and, accordingly, recognized over the current and future interim periods of the current fiscal year. However, when a tax loss carryforward is applicable against a specific category of income that is presented separately, such as a capital gain classified as an extraordinary item, the tax benefit of the loss is recognized separately in the interim period in which the specific category of income is recognized.

(b)   When the tax benefit is expected to be realized in future fiscal years, it is recognized fully in the interim period.

16-150.   When an enterprise reassesses its ability to realize a previously recognized tax asset and determines that it is no longer more likely than not to realize the benefit, it recognizes the reduction in the carrying amount of the tax asset in the interim period in which it makes such a determination.

16-151.   To illustrate, an enterprise that reports quarterly has a non-capital loss carryforward of $11,250 for income tax purposes at the start of the current fiscal year. A future tax asset has not been recognized because the enterprise did not expect to realize sufficient taxable income to utilize the loss carryforward. The enterprise realized losses of $5,000 in the first quarter and $7,000 in the second quarter. As of the end of each of those quarters, it expected to make only enough income over the remainder of the fiscal year to realize the benefit of those losses. Accordingly, for the current fiscal year, the estimated average annual effective tax rate applied in the first and second quarters did not reflect the utilization of any of the loss carryforward. However, the enterprise earns $30,000 in the third quarter and concludes at the end of that quarter that it is likely to earn income of $20,000 in the fourth quarter. Accordingly, at the end of the third quarter, the enterprise recognizes the benefit of the loss carryforward of prior years. Excluding the effect of the non-capital loss carryforward, the estimated average annual income tax rate is expected to be 40 percent. Tax expense (benefit) is as follows:

	1st Quarter	2nd Quarter	3rd Quarter	4th Quarter	Annual
Income (loss) before taxes for the period	$(5,000)	$(7,000)	$30,000	$20,000	$38,000
Tax rate (See Note)	40%	40%	31%	31%	28.16%
Tax expense (benefit)	$(2,000)	$(2,800)	$ 9,300	$ 6,200	$10,700

Note   The effective tax rate for the 1st and 2nd quarters is 40 percent, the expected average rate for the year (this would be the statutory rate as the expected income for the year is nil). For the 3rd and 4th quarters, the rate would be calculated as follows:

Estimated Annual Income (-$5,000 - $7,000 + $30,000 + $20,000)	$38,000
Loss Carryforward	(11,250)
Taxable Income	$26,750
Tax Rate	40%
Tax for the Year	$10,700

16-152. If this is the tax for the year, the tax for the 3rd and 4th quarters will total $15,500 ($10,700 + $2,000 + $2,800). Given that the expected income for the 3rd and 4th quarters will be $50,000 ($30,000 + $20,000), the tax rate applicable to these quarters will be 31.00 percent ($15,500 ÷ $50,000). For the year, the rate will be 28.16 percent ($10,700 ÷ $38,000).

16-153. The tax benefits of losses that arise in the early portion of a fiscal year are recognized only when those benefits are expected to be realized through:

(a) application of the losses against income of interim periods later in the same fiscal year;

(b) application of the losses against income of a prior fiscal year, as a tax loss carryback; or

(c) recognition as a future tax asset at the end of the year in accordance with the requirements of INCOME TAXES, Section 3465.

16-154. When the tax benefits of losses that arise in early interim periods of a fiscal year meet the criteria for recognition, those tax benefits are recognized at the estimated average annual effective tax rate (see Paragraphs 16-80 and 16-88). However, losses that arise in early interim periods of a fiscal year may exceed the expected income of subsequent interim periods of that year and the tax benefit of the resulting loss for the fiscal year cannot be realized through application against income of prior years. In such circumstances, an enterprise assesses the extent to which the tax loss carryforward expected to arise at the end of the year will be realizable and, consequently, recognized as a future tax asset at that time. Losses of an interim period that are not expected to qualify for recognition as a future tax asset at the end of the fiscal year are not included in the tax benefit for that interim period.

16-155. In determining the balance of current and future income tax assets and liabilities at each interim period end, an enterprise makes its best estimates of the extent to which:

(a) transactions in the current fiscal year to date give rise to temporary differences;

(b) temporary differences existing at the beginning of the current fiscal year have reversed;

(c) the tax benefit of unused tax losses and tax reductions, other than investment tax credits, carried forward from prior fiscal years has been realized, or will be realizable in the future and meets the criteria for recognition as a future tax asset; and

(d) the tax benefit of losses and tax reductions, other than investment tax credits, arising in the current fiscal year to date has been realized, or will be realizable in the future and meets the criteria for recognition as a future tax asset.

Contractual or anticipated purchase price changes

16-156. The buying or selling prices of raw materials, labour, or other goods and services may be affected by volume rebates, discounts or other contractual changes. Such price changes are accrued in interim periods, by both the buyer and the seller, when they have been earned or will take effect. In such circumstances, the rebate or discount satisfies the definitions in "Financial Statement Concepts", Section 1000, as an asset of the recipient and a liability of the payer, and also the criteria for recognition in their Balance Sheets. However, a discretionary rebate or discount does not satisfy the recognition criteria and is not accrued. For example, a rebate arrangement may provide for payments based on a purchaser making a certain level of annual purchases. As of the end of a particular interim period, the required annual level of purchases has not been achieved but it is expected that the required level will be achieved before the end of the current fiscal year. Accordingly, as of the end of the interim period, the seller has a contingent obligation, because it has no realistic alternative but to make the future rebate payment. The purchaser has a corresponding contingent right. In such circumstances, the seller accrues a liability and expense. The purchaser accrues an asset and a cost reduction only when it has purchased the amount required to obtain a rebate, i.e., when the contingency has been resolved. The cost reduction may have been reflected previously through standard costing of inventories, in which case the accrual of the rebate receivable is reflected as an adjustment to inventory variances.

Amortization

16-157.   Amortization for an interim period is based only on assets owned during that interim period. It does not take into account asset acquisitions or dispositions planned for later in the fiscal year. However, under a unit of production method of amortization, the rate of amortization of assets owned may take into account future costs expected to be expended on those assets (for example, estimated future costs to be incurred in developing proved reserves in the case of an enterprise that has adopted the full cost method of accounting for oil and gas properties).

Inventories

16-158.   Inventories are measured at the end of an interim period by the same principles as at the end of a fiscal year, subject only to the special accounting methods discussed in Paragraph 16-46 through 16-48. "Inventories", Section 3030, provides guidance for recognizing and measuring inventories. Inventories pose particular problems at the end of any period because of the need to determine inventory quantities, costs, and net realizable values. Nonetheless, the same measurement principles are applied for inventories at the end of each period. To save cost and time, enterprises often use estimates to measure inventories at the end of interim periods to a greater extent than at the end of fiscal years.

16-159.   The net realizable value of inventories is determined by reference to selling prices and related costs to complete and dispose at the end of an interim period. An enterprise will reverse a write-down to net realizable value in a subsequent interim period only when it would be appropriate to do so at the end of a fiscal year.

Foreign currency translation gains and losses

16-160.   Foreign currency translation gains and losses for an interim period are determined in accordance with the same principles as at the end of a fiscal year.

16-161.   "Foreign Currency Translation", Section 1650, specifies how to translate the financial statements of foreign operations into the reporting currency, including guidelines for using historical, average, or closing foreign exchange rates and guidelines for including the resulting adjustments in income or in equity. Consistent with that Section, the actual average and closing rates for the interim period are used. It is not appropriate to estimate future changes in foreign exchange rates in the remainder of the current fiscal year in translating foreign operations at the end of an interim period.

16-162.   When "Foreign Currency Translation", Section 1650, requires that translation adjustments be recognized as income or as expenses in the period in which they arise, that principle is applied during each interim period. Enterprises do not defer a foreign currency translation adjustment at the end of an interim period on the basis that the adjustment is expected to reverse before the end of the fiscal year.

Impairment Of Assets

16-163.   Various other Sections contain requirements for recognizing and measuring the impairment of different types of assets, including:

  (a) "Temporary Investments", Section 3010;
  (b) "Accounts and Notes Receivable", Section 3020;
  (c) "Impaired Loans", Section 3025;
  (d) "Long-Term Investments", Section 3050;
  (e) "Property, Plant and Equipment, Section 3061;
  (f) "Goodwill and Other Intangible Assets, Section 3062;
  (g) "Research and Development Costs", Section 3450;
  (h) "Employee Future Benefits", Section 3461; and
  (i) "Income Taxes", Section 3465.

16-164.   This Section requires an enterprise to apply the same impairment testing, recognition, and reversal criteria at the end of an interim period as it does at the end of its fiscal year. That does not necessarily mean, however, that an enterprise must make a detailed impairment calculation at the end of each interim period.   Rather, an enterprise will review the carrying amount of its assets relative to their recoverable amount for indications of impairment since the end of the most recently completed fiscal year to determine whether such a calculation is needed.   The Sections listed the preceding Paragraphs provide guidance on when to undertake an impairment review, how to determine the recoverable amount of an asset, and how to reflect any impairment in an enterprise's financial statements.   A write-down for impairment in an interim period will be reflected in the financial statements for the fiscal year unless the write-down is reversed in a subsequent interim period. Reversals of asset write-downs are not permitted for certain asset types. For those assets, such as loans, for which a write-down may be reversed, any reversal must be justified by a change during a subsequent period in the circumstances originally giving rise to the write-down.

Earnings Per Share

16-165.   Basic and diluted earnings per share amounts for an interim period are determined on the basis of the earnings (income before discontinued operations and extraordinary items and net income) and the weighted average number of common shares outstanding for that period, both as adjusted in accordance with "Earnings Per Share", Section 3500. The calculations for the current interim period and cumulatively for the current fiscal year to date are done separately. Each amount is calculated as though the period were a fiscal year.

16-166.   Earnings per share amounts in annual financial statements and for the year to date in interim financial statements (other than in the first interim period in a fiscal year) may differ from the sum of the earnings per share amounts for each of the interim periods within that fiscal year. When a difference arises, an enterprise should consider the need to explain the reasons for it.

Assignment Problems

(The solutions for these problems are only available in
the solutions manual that has been provided to your instructor.)

Assignment Problem Sixteen - 1

In each of the following independent cases, information on the various operating segments of
a particular enterprise is provided. Operating segments have been identified using the guidance provided by Section 1701 of the *CICA Handbook*.

Case A Quantitative information with respect to identified operating segments for the Allen
Company is as follows:

Segment	Profit (Loss)	Assets	Revenues External	Intersegment
1	$125,000	$273,000	$206,000	Nil
2	91,000	342,000	172,000	$ 4,000
3	56,000	147,000	112,000	46,000
4	(104,000)	406,000	73,000	Nil
5	(26,000)	204,000	104,000	116,000
6	(427,000)	526,000	346,000	26,000
7	485,000	407,000	382,000	56,000
8	236,000	268,000	246,000	24,000
Totals	$436,000	$2,573,000	$1,641,000	$272,000

The total revenue reported by the enterprise is equal to the $1,641,000 total shown for the
eight identified operating segments.

Case B Quantitative information with respect to identified operating segments for the
Bakin Company is as follows:

Segment	Profit (Loss)	Assets	Revenues External	Intersegment
1	$126,000	$ 310,000	$ 323,000	$250,000
2	82,000	170,000	120,000	Nil
3	94,000	165,000	115,000	Nil
4	573,000	895,000	562,000	375,000
5	55,000	155,000	96,000	Nil
6	23,000	105,000	84,000	Nil
Totals	$953,000	$1,800,000	$1,300,000	$625,000

The total revenue reported by the enterprise is equal to the $1,300,000 total shown for the six
identified operating segments.

Case C Quantitative information with respect to identified operating segments for the Cello
Company is as follows:

Segment	Profit (Loss)	Assets	Revenues External	Intersegment
1	($172,000)	$ 273,000	$ 319,000	$ 26,000
2	46,000	252,000	119,000	Nil
3	32,000	173,000	191,000	34,000
4	(478,000)	561,000	362,000	171,000
5	72,000	219,000	123,000	4,000
6	(342,000)	402,000	247,000	Nil
7	132,000	148,000	429,000	Nil
8	(104,000)	289,000	113,000	Nil
9	28,000	83,000	47,000	8,000
Totals	($786,000)	$2,400,000	$1,950,000	$243,000

The total revenue reported by the enterprise is equal to the $1,950,000 total shown for the nine identified operating segments.

Required: Using the quantitative information provided, indicate which of the operating segments listed in each Case should be considered reportable operating segments. Briefly explain your conclusions.

Assignment Problem Sixteen - 2

Company Background
Integrated Inc.'s major business involves the manufacture, wholesale distribution, and retail sales of two unique groups of products. The first group of products is designed to help with home organization. These are marketed under the brand name Home Assistant (HA). The second group of products is directed towards assisting with the management of commercial offices. These are marketed under the brand name Office Assistant (OA).

Retail sales are handled exclusively through the Company's own outlets, with each outlet handling both the Home Assistant line and the Office Assistant line. While the head office of the Company is in Canada, it operates wholly owned subsidiaries in Mexico, France, and Japan.

All of the Company's manufacturing operations are in Mexico. While there are some external sales of manufactured product in Mexico, the majority of the production is shipped to the Company's operations in Canada, France, and Japan. There is no wholesale or retail activity in Mexico. In Canada, France, and Japan, the Company has wholesale and retail operations for both Home Assistant products and Office Assistant products.

When goods are moved from manufacturing to wholesale operations, or from wholesale operations to retail operations, they are transferred at prices which are the same as those used for sales to enterprises outside Integrated's consolidated group.

After trying alternative approaches, management of the Company has concluded that control of enterprise activities should be based on business functions, as opposed to geographic areas or product lines. As a consequence, the chief operating decision maker receives reports on the basis of manufacturing activities, wholesale activities, and retail operations.

At the retail level, interest is charged on overdue receivables. Interest expense is not allocated to operating segments.

Parent And Subsidiary Data
Separate records are kept for Integrated Inc. and each of its subsidiaries. The following information is taken from these records and reflects activities for the current year. This information is used to prepare the reports required by the chief operating decision maker.

Canadian Operations

	Wholesale Operations		Retail Operations	
	HA Products	OA Products	HA Products	OA Products
Profit (Loss)*	$ 47,000	$ 38,000	($ 64,000)	$ 28,000
Total Capital Assets	250,000	164,000	273,000	184,000
External Revenue	32,000	14,000	672,000	239,000
Intersegment Revenue	294,000	156,000	Nil	Nil
Amortization Expense	22,000	13,400	14,600	9,800
Income Tax Expense (Benefit)	23,400	19,500	(31,200)	13,200
Capital Expenditures	16,200	8,600	34,000	26,000
Interest Revenue	Nil	Nil	3,500	4,200

Because of an expropriation of Land by a local government unit, the retail operations of Canadian OA products experienced an Extraordinary Gain (Net Of Tax) of $5,400.

Mexican Subsidiary

	Manufacturing Operations	
	HA Products	OA Products
Profit (Loss)*	$ 233,000	$ 32,000
Total Capital Assets	1,456,000	824,600
External Revenue	123,200	78,300
Intersegment Revenue	326,400	142,600
Amortization Expense	123,200	75,400
Income Tax Expense (Benefit)	106,500	11,300
Capital Expenditures	223,400	87,500
Interest Revenue	Nil	Nil

French Subsidiary

	Wholesale Operations		Retail Operations	
	HA Products	OA Products	HA Products	OA Products
Profit (Loss)*	$ 23,000	$ 19,000	$ 32,000	$ 14,000
Total Capital Assets	126,000	87,000	134,000	98,000
External Revenue	Nil	7,200	356,000	114,000
Intersegment Revenue	142,000	72,000	Nil	Nil
Amortization Expense	14,000	6,200	7,800	5,500
Income Tax Expense (Benefit)	14,100	11,300	18,400	8,100
Capital Expenditures	7,500	4,500	16,000	Nil
Interest Revenue	Nil	Nil	3,200	4,100

Japanese Subsidiary

	Wholesale Operations		Retail Operations	
	HA Products	OA Products	HA Products	OA Products
Profit (Loss)*	$ 12,000	$ 8,500	$ 22,000	$ 24,000
Total Capital Assets	63,100	41,200	82,400	73,500
External Revenue	21,200	7,300	192,000	94,000
Intersegment Revenue	74,500	41,400	Nil	Nil
Amortization Expense	12,100	4,300	3,900	2,600
Income Tax Expense (Benefit)	4,300	2,900	7,400	8,200
Capital Expenditures	3,500	2,300	8,400	Nil
Interest Revenue	Nil	Nil	1,200	1,600

*Segment profit or loss is determined on the basis of total external and intersegment revenues for the segment, reduced by expenses other than taxes that can be directly allocated to the segment.

Consolidated Information

The following information will be included in the consolidated financial statements of Integrated Inc. and its subsidiaries:

Total Revenues*	$2,347,000
Income Before Taxes And Extraordinary Items	536,700
Total Capital Assets	4,723,200
Amortization Expense	346,400
Income Tax Expense	231,800
Capital Expenditures	482,300

*No single customer accounts for more than 10 percent of this total.

Required: Provide all of the disclosure that would be required by Section 1701 of the *CICA Handbook* for the current year's annual report of Integrated Inc.

Assignment Problem Sixteen - 3

The Interval Company anticipates that its total annual sales will amount to 3,000,000 units at a price of $10 per unit. The Company provides interim reports for each quarter of the calendar year and its sales follow a seasonal pattern. Over the past 8 years the pattern has been 20 percent of sales in the first quarter, 10 percent in the second quarter, 50 percent in the third quarter and 20 percent in the last quarter of the year. With respect to variable costs, the annual budget calls for $4 per unit in variable manufacturing costs and $1.50 per unit in variable selling and administrative expenses. The annual fixed manufacturing costs are estimated at $6,000,000 and the annual fixed selling and administrative costs are anticipated to be $4,500,000.

The budget presented in the preceding paragraph, can be summarized as follows:

Total Estimated Sales		$30,000,000
Variable Costs:		
Manufacturing	$12,000,000	
Selling And Administrative	4,500,000	$16,500,000
Fixed Costs:		
Manufacturing	$6,000,000	
Selling And Administrative	4,500,000	10,500,000
Total Estimated Costs		$27,000,000
Budgeted Annual Profit		$ 3,000,000

The actual sales for the year did not equal the budgeted sales. The actual sales figures for the four quarters are as follows:

Quarter	Units Sold	Price Per Unit	Sales
First	550,000	$ 10	$ 5,500,000
Second	200,000	10	2,000,000
Third	1,200,000	10	12,000,000
Fourth	500,000	10	5,000,000
Total	2,450,000		$24,500,000

The actual costs that were incurred in each of the four quarters were as follows:

| | Variable Costs | | Fixed Costs | |
| | Manufacturing | Selling | Manu. | Selling |
Quarter				
First	$ 2,200,000	$ 825,000	$1,500,000	$1,125,000
Second	800,000	300,000	1,500,000	1,125,000
Third	5,000,000	1,900,000	1,500,000	1,200,000
Fourth	2,300,000	900,000	1,700,000	1,400,000
Total	$10,300,000	$3,925,000	$6,200,000	$4,850,000

The number of units produced was equal to the number of units sold in each of the four quarters and there were no inventories on hand at the beginning of the year.

Required:

A. Prepare Income Statements for the Interval Company for each of the four quarters using the discrete approach to the measurement of interim earnings.

B. Prepare Income Statements for the Interval Company for each of the four quarters using the integral approach to the measurement of interim earnings. All of the variances of the fixed costs from the budgeted figures should be charged to income in the results of the fourth quarter.

Assignment Problem Sixteen - 4

The Pert Company estimates that its total sales for the year will be 600,000 units at a price of $40 per unit. The Company provides interim reports for each quarter of the calendar year and its sales follow an extremely seasonal pattern. The pattern in past years has been 10 percent of sales in the first quarter, 40 percent in the second quarter, 30 percent in the July to September quarter and 20 percent in the last quarter of the year. With respect to variable costs, the annual budget calls for $15 per unit in variable manufacturing costs and $10 per unit in variable selling and administrative expenses. The annual fixed manufacturing costs are estimated at $2,400,000 and the annual fixed selling and administrative costs are anticipated to be $1,800,000.

This budget, presented in narrative form in the preceding paragraph, can be summarized in the table which follows:

Total Sales		$24,000,000
Variable Costs:		
Manufacturing	$9,000,000	
Selling And Administrative	6,000,000	$15,000,000
Fixed Costs:		
Manufacturing	$2,400,000	
Selling And Administrative	1,800,000	4,200,000
Total Estimated Costs		$19,200,000
Budgeted Annual Profit		$ 4,800,000

The actual sales for the year were somewhat different than anticipated. The actual sales for the four quarters of the year were as follows:

Quarter	Units Sold	Price Per Unit	Sales
First	50,000	$ 40	$ 2,000,000
Second	200,000	40	8,000,000
Third	150,000	40	6,000,000
Fourth	100,000	40	4,000,000
Total	500,000	$ 40	$20,000,000

The actual costs that were incurred in each of the four quarters were as follows:

	Variable Costs		Fixed Costs	
	Manufacturing	Selling	Manu.	Selling
First Quarter	$ 750,000	$ 500,000	$ 600,000	$ 450,000
Second Quarter	3,200,000	1,900,000	600,000	450,000
Third Quarter	2,100,000	1,700,000	650,000	475,000
Fourth Quarter	1,500,000	1,000,000	700,000	500,000
Total	$7,550,000	$5,100,000	$2,550,000	$1,875,000

The number of units produced equals the number of units sold in each of the four quarters and there were no inventories on hand at the beginning of the year.

Required:

A. Prepare Income Statements for each of the four quarters of the year using the integral approach to the measurement of interim earnings. All of the variances of the fixed costs from the budgeted figures should be charged to income in the results of the fourth quarter.

B. Prepare Income Statements for each of the four quarters of the year using the discrete approach to the measurement of interim earnings.

Assignment Problem Sixteen - 5

In today's rapidly changing financial markets, financial statement users are demanding more information, released more promptly than in the past. You have been asked your opinion on this issue by colleagues at a symposium on financial reporting who are engaged in a lively discussion. One is a CA and controller of an international public company, while the other is a senior financial analyst in a securities firm.

Financial Analyst: My review of the *CICA Handbook* leads me to conclude that the objectives of interim reporting should be the same as those of annual reporting.

Controller: I disagree. Interim reports are aimed at different users, serve different purposes, and must be published more quickly than annual reports. It follows that the underlying objectives should also differ.

Financial Analyst: Regardless of the content of interim reports, the interim operating results should be measured on the same basis as the annual results because the interim period is an integral part of the annual period.

Controller: I agree that there is a measurement problem for interim reporting, but I don't see a simple solution. For example, I find it difficult to make interim estimates for various expenses given the cyclical nature of our business. After all, the interim period is only a portion of the annual period.

Required: Prepare a memo discussing the main issues raised in the preceding conversation.

(CICA Adapted)

Appendix

Solutions To Exercises and

Self Study Problems

The following pages contain detailed solutions to the exercises and self study problems found at the end of Chapters 2 through 16.

Solution to Chapter Two Exercises

Exercise Two - 1 Solution

Morton has direct control over Salt and would classify this investment as a subsidiary. Morton would account for this investment using the full consolidation method.

Morton has direct ownership of 40 percent of the Backy shares and, in addition, has indirect control of a further 15 percent through its control of Salt. Given this, Morton has control of Backy and would classify the investment as a subsidiary. Based on this classification, Morton would account for its investment in Backy using the full consolidation method.

Exercise Two - 2 Solution

As Placor does not have significant influence over Placee, the cost method will be used. Given this, the required journal entries are as follows:

Year Ending December 31, 2002

Cash [(20%)($100,000)]	$20,000	
Investment Income		$20,000

Year Ending December 31, 2003

Cash [(20%)($50,000)]	$10,000	
Investment in Placee [(20%)($40,000)]		$8,000
Investment Income [(20%)($50,000 - $40,000)]		2,000

[This dividend was paid out of Retained Earnings at acquisition. After this payment, the cumulative Retained Earnings since acquisition balance is a negative $40,000 ($150,000 - $100,000 - $40,000 - $50,000).]

Year Ending December 31, 2004

Cash [(20%)($80,000)]	$16,000	
Investment Income		$16,000

[At this point, there is still a negative balance in Retained Earnings since acquisition of $30,000 (-$40,000 + $90,000 - $80,000). However, the investment was written down for this last year and, as a consequence, all of the dividends can be credited to Investment Income.]

Exercise Two - 3 Solution

As Placor does have significant influence over Placee, the equity method will be used. Given this, the required journal entries are as follows:

Year Ending December 31, 2002

Cash [(20%)($100,000)]	$20,000	
Investment in Placee [(20%)($150,000 - $100,000)]	10,000	
Investment Income [(20%)($150,000)]		$30,000

Year Ending December 31, 2003

Cash [(20%)($50,000)]	$10,000	
Investment Loss [(20%)($40,000)]	8,000	
Investment in Placee [(20%)(-$40,000 - $50,000)]		$18,000

Year Ending December 31, 2004

Cash [(20%)($80,000)]	$16,000	
Investment in Placee [(20%)($90,000 - $80,000)]	2,000	
Investment Income [(20%)($90,000)]		$18,000

Exercise Two - 4 Solution

Part A The required journal entry would be as follows:

Cash [(15%)($103,000)]	$15,450	
Investment In Muddle [(15%)($103,000 - $20,000 - $46,000)]		$5,550
Investment Income		9,900

Part B   The required journal entry would be as follows:

Cash [(15%)($103,000)]	$15,450	
Loss From Discontinued Operations [(15%)($300,000)]	45,000	
Investment Income [(15%)($346,000)]		$51,900
Investment In Muddle [(15%)($103,000 - $46,000)]		8,550

Exercise Two - 5 Solution

Aussor's share of the Aussee Net Loss would be $600,000 [(40%)($1,500,000)], an amount that exceeds the carrying value of the Investment in Aussee. This means that, if the usual Investment Income entry was used, the Investment in Aussee would become a credit balance that would have to be disclosed as a liability. In the absence of a commitment on the part of Ausser to provide financial support, recording a liability would be inappropriate and, as a consequence, the following entry would be made for the year ending December 31, 2002 to reduce the carrying value to nil:

| Investment Loss | $400,000 | |
| Investment In Aussee | | $400,000 |

Before Investment Income can be recorded in the year ending December 31, 2003, the deficit in the Investment in Aussee account must be recovered. This would require the first $500,000 of Ausser's 2003 Net Income, leaving only $300,000 as a basis for recording Investment Income. Given this, the required entry would be as follows:

| Investment In Aussee [(40%)($800,000 - $500,000)] | $120,000 | |
| Investment Income | | $120,000 |

Exercise Two - 6 Solution

The annual discount amortization is $20,000 [($3,000,000 - $2,840,000) ÷ 8]. The carrying value of the bonds on January 1, 2005 would be $2,900,000 ($2,840,000 + 3 years @ $20,000). Based on this, the required journal entry would be as follows:

Cash	$3,050,000	
Gain on Bond Disposition		$ 150,000
Bond Investment		2,900,000

Exercise Two - 7 Solution

The total cost and total number of shares for Salson's holding of Tofal shares would be calculated as follows:

	Number Of Shares	Cost
1st Purchase	2,400	$ 27,600
2nd Purchase	3,450	42,600
3rd Purchase	1,740	22,450
4th Purchase	4,360	72,400
Totals	11,950	$165,050

Given the preceding totals, the average cost of the shares would be $13.81 and the gain on the sale of 5,250 shares would be calculated as follows:

Proceeds Of Disposition [(5,250)($28)]	$147,000
Adjusted Cost Base [(5,250)($13.81)]	(72,503)
Gain On Sale Of Shares	$ 74,497

Solution to Self Study Problem Two - 1

The appropriate accounting treatment for these investments would be as follows:

Best Parts Inc.   While Carson does not own the majority of the voting shares of Best Parts Inc., it would appear to have control. Carson owns 45 percent of the voting shares, owns a majority of the preferred shares, and is the purchaser for 90 percent of Best's sales. Unless the other 55 percent of the voting shares of Best are held by a single investor or related group of investors, these factors should give Carson control over Best. Given this, Best would be classified as a subsidiary of Carson and consolidation procedures would be applied.

With respect to Carson's investment in the Best preferred shares, if Best accounts were consolidated with those of Carson, this intercompany holding would be eliminated.

Research Tech Ltd.   As there appears to be a management agreement under which Carson has joint control over the affairs of this investee, it would appear that Research Tech is a joint venture. Given this, Section 3055 would require the use of proportionate consolidation.

Entell Ltd.   With Carson's share ownership at the 46 percent level, this investment would be classified as a significantly influenced company and the equity method would be used. With respect to Entell's investment in Chelsea, it would appear to be a portfolio investment to be carried by the cost method. The fact that Chelsea may not be a going concern suggests that a write down to reflect a non temporary decline in value might be appropriate.

Chelsea Distributors Inc.   As Carson does not control Entell Ltd. (see preceding paragraph), it does not control Entell's 18 percent shareholding in Chelsea Distributors Inc. Carson's 37 percent shareholding means that Chelsea is not a subsidiary but, rather, a significantly influenced company for which the equity method would be appropriate. Note that Carson may also consider writing down this investment to reflect Chelsea's going concern problems.

With respect to Chelsea's investment in Carson, this is a reciprocal shareholding that would be classified by Chelsea as a portfolio investment. This would require the use of the cost method by Chelsea. (As covered in Chapter 8, this investment would also be disclosed on the books of Carson as a reduction in total shareholders' equity.)

Solution to Self Study Problem Two - 2

Part A   As we are assuming here that a 25 percent investment does not give the Miser Company significant influence over the Mercy Company, the use of the cost method would be appropriate. The required journal entries under this method would be as follows:

2002 Journal Entries

Investment In Mercy	$4,000,000	
Cash		$4,000,000

Cash [(50%)(25%)($600,000)]	$ 75,000	
Investment Income		$ 75,000

(To record the investment transaction and Miser's 25 percent share of Mercy's dividends since acquisition. At this point, Retained Earnings since acquisition are nil.)

2003 Journal Entry

Cash $ 100,000
    Investment In Mercy $ 100,000
(To record Miser's 25 percent share of the dividends which Mercy has paid out of earnings retained prior to Miser's investment. At this point, Retained Earnings since acquisition are a negative amount of $2,400,000 and the dividend is a return of capital.)

2004 Journal Entry

Cash $ 125,000
    Investment In Mercy $ 125,000
(To record Miser's 25 percent share of the dividends which Mercy has paid out of earnings retained prior to Miser's investment. At this point, Retained Earnings since acquisition are a negative amount of $1,400,000, the opening amount of negative $2,400,000, reduced by the $1,500,000 in Net Income, but increased by the $500,000 in Dividends Declared.)

2005 Journal Entry

Cash $ 250,000
    Investment Income $ 250,000

Or

Cash $ 250,000
Investment In Mercy 225,000
    Investment Income $ 475,000
(To record Miser's 25 percent share of Mercy's dividends which have been paid out of earnings retained subsequent to acquisition.)

With respect to the entry for 2005, the *CICA Handbook* is not clear as to the appropriate treatment. The Investment In Mercy was written down in both 2003 and 2004 to reflect the fact that dividends were being paid out of Retained Earnings that were present at the time of the Miser Company's acquisition of the Mercy Company shares. By the end of 2005, earnings have been sufficient to more than replace the Retained Earnings balance that was present on July 1, 2002. The first of the preceding entries treats this situation prospectively and is probably more consistent with other *CICA Handbook* recommendations. The second entry reflects a retroactive treatment of this situation and has the advantage of maintaining the integrity of the cost method definitions.

Part B   Given the assumption that the Miser Company has significant influence over the Mercy Company, the use of the equity method would be required. The entries under this method would be as follows:

2002 Journal Entries

Investment In Mercy $4,000,000
    Cash $4,000,000

Cash $ 75,000
    Investment Income $ 75,000
(To record the investment transaction and Miser's 25 percent share of Mercy's income since acquisition which also equals dividends paid.)

2003 Journal Entry

Cash $ 100,000
Investment Loss 500,000
    Investment In Mercy $ 600,000
(To record Miser's 25 percent share of Mercy's loss and dividends.)

2004 Journal Entry

Cash	$ 125,000	
Investment In Mercy	250,000	
Investment Income		$ 375,000

(To record Miser's 25 percent share of Mercy's income and dividends.)

2005 Journal Entry

Cash	$ 250,000	
Investment In Mercy	500,000	
Extraordinary Loss	200,000	
Investment Income		$ 950,000
[(25%)($3,000,000 + $800,000)		

(To record Miser's 25 percent share of Mercy's ordinary income, extraordinary loss and dividends.)

Solution to Self Study Problem Two - 3

Part A - Income Statement Under Equity Method - If the Buy Company used the equity method to account for its investment in Sell Company, its Income Statement for the year ending December 31, 2005 would be as follows:

Buy Company
Income Statement (Equity Method)
For the Year Ending December 31, 2005

Sales	$5,000,000
Cost of Goods Sold	$3,000,000
Other Expenses	800,000
Investment Loss - Ordinary [(25%)($200,000)]	50,000
Total Expenses and Losses	$3,850,000
Income Before Extraordinary Items	$1,150,000
Extraordinary Investment Income (Net of Taxes of $100,000)	150,000
Net Income	$1,300,000

Part A - Statement Of Retained Earnings Under Equity Method - The Buy Company's Statement of Retained Earnings for the year ending December 31, 2005, if its Investment in Sell was accounted for by the equity method would be as follows:

Buy Company
Statement of Retained Earnings (Equity Method)
For the Year Ending December 31, 2005

Opening Balance - As Previously Stated	$15,000,000
Prior Period Error (Net of Taxes of $5,000)	(12,500)
Opening Balance - As Restated	$14,987,500
Net Income	1,300,000
Balance Available	$16,287,500
Dividends	(500,000)
Closing Balance	$15,787,500

Part B - Income Statement Under Cost Method - The Buy Company's Income Statement for the year ending December 31, 2005, if its Investment in Sell was accounted for by the cost method, would be as follows:

Buy Company
Income Statement (Cost Method)
Year Ending December 31, 2005

Sales	$5,000,000
Investment Income [(25%)($150,000)]	37,500
Total Revenues	$5,037,500
Cost of Goods Sold	$3,000,000
Other Expenses	800,000
Total Expenses	$3,800,000
Net Income	$1,237,500

Part B - Statement Of Retained Earnings Under Cost Method - If the Buy Company had used the cost method to account for its Investment in Sell since its acquisition, the January 1, 2005 Retained Earnings balance of the Buy Company would not have been the $15,000,000 stated in the problem. The difference arises from the fact that the equity method includes in that $15,000,000, Buy Company's share of the Sell Company's Net Income between January 1, 2002 and December 31, 2004, while the cost method would have included instead the Buy Company's share of the dividends declared by Sell Company. This means that the January 1, 2005 Retained Earnings of the Buy Company would have been equal to $14,750,000 [$15,000,000 - (25%)($3,000,000) + (25%)($2,000,000)], if its Investment in Sell had been carried using the cost method since its acquisition. The Statement of Retained Earnings under this assumption would be as follows:

Buy Company
Statement of Retained Earnings (Cost Method)
Year Ending December 31, 2005

Opening Balance	$14,750,000
Net Income	1,237,500
Balance Available	$15,987,500
Dividends	(500,000)
Closing Balance	$15,487,500

Part C - Investment Account Balance Under Equity Method - The December 31, 2005 balance in the Investment in Sell account would be $1,800,000 if the equity method of accounting was used. This amount can be calculated as follows:

Investment Cost	$1,500,000
Equity Pickup to December 31, 2004	
[(25%)($3,000,000 - $2,000,000)]	250,000
Ordinary Investment Loss	(50,000)
Dividends Received	(37,500)
Extraordinary Investment Income	150,000
Prior Period Error	(12,500)
Balance in Investment in Sell Account	$1,800,000

An alternate calculation, using end of period figures, is as follows:

Investment Cost	$1,500,000
Equity Pickup to December 31, 2005	
([25%][$3,400,000 - $2,150,000])	312,500
Prior Period Error	(12,500)
Balance in Investment in Sell Account	$1,800,000

Solution to Chapter Three Exercises

Exercise Three - 1 Solution
Part A   Acquisition of Assets For Cash and Debt Securities

Blocker Company
Balance Sheet As At December 31, 2002

Current Assets ($1,406,000 - $795,000 + $987,000)	$1,598,000
Non-Current Assets ($2,476,000 + $1,762,000)	4,238,000
Total Assets	$5,836,000
Liabilities ($822,000 + $454,000 + $1,500,000)	$2,776,000
Common Stock (Blocker's Only)	1,800,000
Retained Earnings (Blocker's Only)	1,260,000
Total Equities	$5,836,000

Part B   Acquisition of Shares Through Issuance of Shares
The issued shares have a value of $2,295,000 [(135,000)($17)], an amount that is equal to the market and carrying value of the Blockee shares. Given this, the consolidated Balance Sheet would be as follows:

Blocker Company and Subsidiary
Consolidated Balance Sheet
As At December 31, 2002

Current Assets ($1,406,000 + $987,000)	$2,393,000
Non-Current Assets ($2,476,000 + $1,762,000)	4,238,000
Total Assets	$6,631,000
Liabilities ($822,000 + $454,000)	$1,276,000
Common Stock ($1,800,000 + $2,295,000)	4,095,000
Retained Earnings (Blocker's Only)	1,260,000
Total Equities	$6,631,000

Part C   Acquisition of Shares by New Corporation

Blockbuster Inc.
Balance Sheet As At December 31, 2002

Current Assets ($1,406,000 + $987,000)	$2,393,000
Non-Current Assets ($2,476,000 + $1,762,000)	4,238,000
Total Assets	$6,631,000
Liabilities ($822,000 + $454,000)	$1,276,000
Common Stock [(204,000 + 153,000)($15)]	5,355,000
Total Equities	$6,631,000

As Blockbuster Inc. is a new company, it would not have a balance in its Retained Earnings account.

Exercise Three - 2 Solution

Part A   As the former shareholders of Epsilon now hold the majority of shares in the combined company, Epsilon would be identified as the acquirer. This is, of course, a reverse takeover.

Part B   While Delta does not have a majority of voting shares in Epsilon, the fact that no other shareholder has a large block of shares would suggest that they have acquired control of this Company. Given this, Delta would be identified as the acquirer.

Part C   None of the four combining companies has a large enough interest in Alphamega to have full legal control over the new Company. In this type of situation, the *Handbook* suggests that the relative size of the companies may be the determining factor. Given this, Gamma would be identified as the acquirer.

Part D   While the original Delta shareholders do not have a majority interest in the combined company, their management team is scheduled to continue in place. This would suggest that Delta should be identified as the acquirer.

Exercise Three - 3 Solution

The entry to record the issuance on June 30, 2002, would be as follows:

Investment in Lee [(1,250,000)($11)]	$13,750,000	
No Par Common Stock		$13,750,000

The required entry on March 1, 2003, would be as follows:

Investment in Lee [(250,000)($11.50)]	$2,875,000	
No Par Common Stock		$2,875,000

Exercise Three - 4 Solution

As Lor is arguing that the shares are actually worth $12.50 per share, the initial issuance would be recorded at that value:

Investment in Lee [(1,250,000)($12.50)]	$15,625,000	
No Par Common Stock		$15,625,000

When the additional shares are issued, it would not be an addition to the Investment in Lee. Rather, it would reflect the fact that the shares that were originally issued were not worth $12.50. As a consequence, no entry would be required to record the issuance of additional shares. The value for the No Par Common Stock would remain at $15,625,000, with only the number of issued shares changed from 1,250,000 to 1,500,000.

Exercise Three - 5 Solution

Part A   If Gor acquires the shares of Gee, the tax basis (UCC) of the assets will remain unchanged at $842,000. As the consolidated statements will include the $1,863,000 fair value of these assets, the temporary difference will be $1,021,000. Given this, the Future Income Tax Liability will be $357,350 [(35%)($1,021,000)].

Part B   If Gor acquires the assets of Gee, both their tax basis and their carrying value will be the fair value of $1,863,000. As the tax basis of the assets is equal to their carrying value, no temporary difference is present and no Future Income Tax Liability will be recorded in the financial statements of Gor.

Exercise Three - 6 Solution

Given the purchase price of $1,850,000, there is negative goodwill of $525,000 ($2,375,000 - $1,850,000). Applying Paragraph 1581.50 will result in this amount being deducted from the non-financial assets of Manee Ltd. on a pro rata basis. The total value of these assets is $2,195,000 ($855,000 + $1,340,000). Based on this value, the pro rata percentages are as follows:

Inventories ($855,000 ÷ $2,195,000)	39.0%
Property, Plant, and Equipment ($1,340,000 ÷ $2,195,000)	61.0
Total	100.0%

Using these calculations, the required asset and liability values would be as follows:

Cash (Unchanged)	$ 265,000
Accounts Receivable (Unchanged)	340,000
Inventories [$855,000 - (39%)($525,000]	650,250
Property, Plant, and Equipment [$1,340,000 - (61%)($525,000)]	1,019,750
Liabilities (Unchanged)	(425,000)
Total (Equals Investment Cost)	$1,850,000

Exercise Three - 7 Solution

As Saller had 423,000 shares outstanding prior to the business combination and only 135,000 additional shares were issued to Sallee, Saller would be identified as the acquirer. With the market value of Saller's shares at $52 per share, the purchase price would be $7,020,000. Based on this value, the investment analysis would be as follows:

Investment Cost	$7,020,000
Book Value - Sallee's Net Assets ($8,953,000 - $2,237,000)	(6,716,000)
Differential	$ 304,000
Fair Value Changes:	
Inventories ($2,732,000 - $2,485,000)	(247,000)
Property, Plant, and Equipment ($4,672,000 - $4,512,000)	160,000
Liabilities ($2,237,000 - $2,115,000)	(122,000)
Goodwill	$ 95,000

Based on this analysis, the combined Balance Sheet would be prepared as follows:

Saller Company
Balance Sheet
As At December 31, 2002

Cash ($1,876,000 + $564,000)	$ 2,440,000
Accounts Receivable ($3,432,000 + $1,232,000)	4,664,000
Inventories ($5,262,000 + $2,732,000)	7,994,000
Property, Plant, and Equipment (Net) ($6,485,000 + $4,512,000)	10,997,000
Goodwill (From Investment Analysis Schedule)	95,000
Total Assets	$26,190,000

Liabilities ($4,843,000 + $2,115,000)	$ 6,958,000
Common Shares ($9,306,000 + $7,020,000)	16,326,000
Retained Earnings (Saller's Only)	2,906,000
Total Equities	$26,190,000

As the business combination took place on December 31, none of Sallee's income would be included in Net Income for the year ending December 31, 2002. This means that the figure that would be reported would be $1,465,000. While there are actually 558,000 (423,000 + 135,000) shares outstanding on December 31, 2002, the weight attached to the new shares would be nil. This means that Earnings Per Share for the year ending December 31, 2002 would be $3.46 ($1,465,000 ÷ 423,000).

Solution to Self Study Problem Three - 1

While both shareholder groups wind up with an equal number of shares, the fact that the management of Graber will direct the operations of the combined company suggests that Graber should be identified as the acquirer. Based on this, the following investment analysis is required:

Investment Cost [(40,000) ($35) + $10,000]	$1,410,000
Book Value	(1,200,000)
Differential	$ 210,000
Fair Value Increase On Plant	(200,000)
Fair Value Decrease On Land	100,000
Fair Value Increase On Long Term Liabilities	50,000
Fair Value Decrease On Future Income Tax Liabilities	(100,000)
Fair Value Decrease On Grabee's Goodwill	50,000
Goodwill	$ 110,000

Note One   Paragraph 1581.45 clearly notes that acquiree goodwill should not be carried forward to the books of the combined company. Given this, it will be assigned a fair value of nil, resulting in a fair value change equal to its carrying value.

Note Two   When the legal form of the business combination involves an acquisition of assets and no rollover provision is used, there is no carry over of any of the acquiree's tax factors to the acquiring business. All of the acquired assets would have a new tax basis equal to their new accounting values. As there would be no temporary differences, it would not be appropriate to record any future income tax liability.

Based on this analysis, the required Balance Sheet would be as follows:

Graber Company
Balance Sheet
As At December 31, 2002

Cash ($50,000 + $70,000 - $10,000)	$ 110,000
Accounts Receivable ($250,000 + $330,000)	580,000
Inventories ($400,000 + $300,000)	700,000
Plant and Equipment (Net) ($1,200,000 + $800,000)	2,000,000
Land ($800,000 + $300,000)	1,100,000
Goodwill (See note which follows)	260,000
Total Assets	$4,750,000

Current Liabilities ($75,000 + $50,000)	$ 125,000
Long Term Liabilities ($800,000 + $450,000)	1,250,000
Future Income Tax Liabilities (Graber's Only)	200,000
Common Stock - Par $20	1,600,000
Contributed Surplus ($400,000 + $600,000)	1,000,000
Retained Earnings (Graber's Only)	575,000
Total Equities	$4,750,000

Notes   As Graber acquired the assets of Grabee, their accounting value and their tax base will be the same. Therefore, no future income tax asset or liability of Grabee's is included in the combined Balance Sheet. The $260,000 Goodwill consists of the $150,000 that was initially on the books of the Graber Company plus an additional $110,000 resulting from the business combination transaction(see investment analysis schedule).

Net Income And Earnings Per Share   Under the purchase method, the Net Income of the combined company for the year ending December 31, 2002 is equal to the Graber Company's Net Income of $125,000. While there are actually 80,000 shares outstanding at the end of the year, the weight that would be attached to the shares issued in the business combination transaction would be nil. This means that Earnings Per Share for the year amount to $3.13 per share ($125,000 ÷ 40,000).

Since the intercompany sales occurred before the business combination transaction, it is not necessary to eliminate any of the unrealized intercompany profits. As a result, no adjustment is required for the $20,000 gain on the land sale or the $50,000 gain on merchandise sales.

Solution to Self Study Problem Three - 2

Case A   As the shareholders of the Ero Company remain the majority shareholder group in the combined company, this Company will be deemed the acquirer. The resulting solution would be prepared as follows:

Investment Analysis

Investment Cost [(100,000)($40)]	$4,000,000
Book Value	(4,200,000)
Differential	($ 200,000)
Fair Value Decrease on Non-Monetary Assets	600,000
Goodwill	$ 400,000

Depreciation   The depreciation decrease resulting from the fair value change on Tick's Non-Monetary Assets would be $150,000 per year ($600,000 ÷ 4). As per *CICA Handbook* Section 3062, the goodwill is not amortized.

Ero Company
Balance Sheet
As At December 31, 2002

Monetary Assets ($200,000 + $1,000,000)	$1,200,000
Non-Monetary Assets ($3,800,000 + $4,000,000 - $600,000)	7,200,000
Goodwill (As per the investment analysis)	400,000
Total Assets	$8,800,000
Monetary Liabilities ($100,000 + $800,000)	$ 900,000
Common Stock ($2,500,000 + $4,000,000)	6,500,000
Retained Earnings (Ero's Balance)	1,400,000
Total Equities	$8,800,000

Net Income and Earnings Per Share   As the combination took place on December 31, 2002, none of Tick's earnings would be included in the combined Net Income, giving a figure for the year ending December 31, 2002 of $400,000. While there are actually 300,000 shares outstanding on December 31, 2002, the weight attached to the shares issued on that date would be nil. This gives an Earnings Per Share figure of $2.00 per share ($400,000 ÷ 200,000).

For the year ending December 31, 2003, the Net Income would be $1,650,000. This is made up of Ero's $700,000, Tick's $800,000, plus $150,000 ($600,000 ÷ 4) amortization of the fair value decrease on the non-monetary assets. Earnings Per Share would be $5.50 ($1,650,000 ÷ 300,000).

Case B   Since the shareholders of the Tick Company received a majority of the shares in the newly formed Erotick Company, this Company would be deemed the acquirer. In order to determined the consideration given for Ero, it is necessary to place a value on the shares of the new Erotick Company. The total fair market value of the acquiring company Tick was $7,200,000 [($72)(100,000)]. As the shareholders of Tick received 180,000 of the Erotick shares, this implies a value for these shares of $40 per share. Using this value for the 120,000 shares given to the Ero shareholders indicates an investment cost of $4,800,000 [($40)(120,000)]. Based on this figure, the required investment analysis is as follows:

Investment Analysis

Investment Cost	$4,800,000
Book Value	(3,900,000)
Differential	$ 900,000
Fair Value Increase on Non-Monetary Assets	(400,000)
Goodwill	$ 500,000

Depreciation   The increased depreciation due to the fair value change on Ero's Non-Monetary Assets would be $100,000 per year ($400,000 ÷ 4). As per *CICA Handbook* Section 3062, the goodwill is not amortized.

Erotick Company
Balance Sheet
As At December 31, 2002

Monetary Assets ($200,000 + $1,000,000)	$1,200,000
Non-Monetary Assets ($3,800,000 + $400,000 + $4,000,000)	8,200,000
Goodwill (As per investment analysis)	500,000
Total Assets	$9,900,000
Monetary Liabilities ($100,000 + $800,000)	$ 900,000
Common Stock ($3,000,000 + $4,800,000)	7,800,000
Retained Earnings (Tick's Balance)	1,200,000
Total Equities	$9,900,000

Net Income And Earnings Per Share   Since the date of formation of the Erotick Company is December 31, 2002, there is no income earned by the Company for the year ending December 31, 2002 and no Earnings Per Share. For the year ending December 31, 2003 the Net Income is $1,400,000 ($700,000 + $800,000 - $100,000) and the Earnings Per Share is $4.67 ($1,400,000 ÷ $300,000) per share.

Solution to Self Study Problem Three - 3

Case A   As the shareholders of the Medal Company become the majority shareholder group in the combined company, this Company will be deemed the acquirer. The resulting solution would be prepared as follows:

Investment Analysis

Investment Cost [(90,000)($65)]	$5,850,000
Book Value	(5,700,000)
Differential	$ 150,000
Fair Value Increase on Non-Monetary Assets	(500,000)
Goodwill (Negative)	($ 350,000)

Depreciation and Amortization   Since the negative goodwill will have to be deducted from the fair value increase on the Non-Monetary Assets, the depreciation increase resulting from the fair value change on Gold's Non-Monetary Assets would be $30,000 per year ($150,000 ÷ 5).

Medal Company
Balance Sheet
At December 31, 2002

Monetary Assets ($500,000 + $300,000)	$ 800,000
Non-Monetary Assets ($6,000,000 + $3,200,000 - $350,000)	8,850,000
Total Assets	$9,650,000
Monetary Liabilities ($300,000 + $100,000)	$ 400,000
Common Stock Par $ ($2,000,000 + $5,850,000)	7,850,000
Retained Earnings (Medal's Balance)	1,400,000
Total Equities	$9,650,000

Net Income and Earnings Per Share   For the year ending December 31, 2002, the Net Income would be $200,000 (Medal's only). While there are actually 190,000 shares outstanding on December 31, 2002, the weight applicable to the additional 90,000 would be nil. This gives an Earnings Per Share of $2.00 ($200,000 ÷ 100,000). For the year ending December 31, 2003, the Net Income would be $1,970,000 ($1,500,000 + $500,000 - $30,000) and the Earnings Per Share would be $10.37 ($1,970,000 ÷ 190,000).

Case B   As the shareholders of the Gold Company remain the majority shareholder group in the combined company, this Company will be deemed the acquirer. The resulting solution would be prepared as follows:

Investment Analysis

Investment Cost [(80,000)($50)]	$4,000,000
Book Value	(3,400,000)
Differential	$ 600,000
Fair Value Decrease on Non-Monetary Assets	200,000
Goodwill	$ 800,000

Depreciation and Amortization: The depreciation decrease resulting from the fair value change on Medal's Non-Monetary Assets would be $40,000 per year ($200,000 ÷ 5).

Gold Company
Balance Sheet
At December 31, 2002

Monetary Assets ($500,000 + $300,000)	$ 800,000
Non-Monetary Assets ($5,500,000 + $3,000,000)	8,500,000
Goodwill (As per the investment analysis)	800,000
Total Assets	$10,100,000
Monetary Liabilities ($300,000 + $100,000)	$ 400,000
Common Stock ($4,200,000 + $4,000,000)	8,200,000
Retained Earnings (Gold's Balance)	1,500,000
Total Equities	$10,100,000

Net Income and Earnings Per Share   For the year ending December 31, 2002, the Net Income would be $1,000,000 (Gold's only). While there are 180,000 Gold shares outstanding on December 31, 2002, the weight for the newly issued 80,000 would be nil. This gives an Earnings Per Share of $10.00 ($1,000,000 ÷ 100,000). For the year ending December 31, 2003, the Net Income would be $2,040,000 ($1,500,000 + $500,000 + $40,000) and the Earnings Per Share would be $11.33 ($2,040,000 ÷ 180,000).

Case C   Since the shareholders of the Gold Company received a majority of the shares in the newly formed Goldmedal Company, this Company would be deemed the acquirer. Establishing the investment cost will require putting a value on the shares of the new Goldmedal Company.   The total market value of Gold, the acquiring company, was $7,500,000 [(100,000)($75)]. Given this value, along with the fact that the Gold shareholders received 50,000 of the new Goldmedal shares, the value of the Goldmedal shares would be $150 per share ($7,500,000 ÷ 50,000). Based on this, the investment cost for Medal would be $4,500,000 [(30,000)($150)]. This information is used in the following investment analysis.

Investment Analysis

Investment Cost	$4,500,000
Book Value	(3,400,000)
Differential	$1,100,000
Fair Value Decrease on Non-Monetary Assets	200,000
Goodwill	$1,300,000

Depreciation and Amortization   The decreased depreciation due to the fair value change on Medal's Non-monetary Assets would be $40,000 per year ($200,000 ÷ 5).

Balance Sheet

Monetary Assets ($500,000 + $300,000)	$ 800,000
Non-Monetary Assets ($5,500,000 + $3,000,000)	8,500,000
Goodwill (As per the investment analysis)	1,300,000
Total Assets	$10,600,000
Monetary Liabilities ($300,000 + $100,000)	$ 400,000
Common Stock ($4,200,000 + $4,500,000)	8,700,000
Retained Earnings (Gold's Balance)	1,500,000
Total Equities	$10,600,000

Net Income And Earnings Per Share: Since the date of formation of the Goldmedal Company is December 31, 2002, there is no income earned by the Company for the year ending December 31, 2002. For the year ending December 31, 2003, the Net Income is $2,040,500 ($1,500,000 + $500,000 + $40,000) and the Earnings Per Share is $25.50 per share ($2,040,500 ÷ 80,000).

Solution to Chapter Four Exercises

Exercise Four-1 Solution

Part A   Under the entity approach, the consolidated Plant and Equipment (Net) would be as follows::

Consolidated Plant and Equipment At Cost	
Placard's Carrying Value	$1,500,000
Sign's Fair Value	520,000
Consolidated Amount	$2,020,000

Part B   Under the proprietary approach, the consolidated Plant and Equipment (Net) would be as follows::

Consolidated Plant and Equipment At Cost	
Placard's Carrying Value	$1,500,000
Placard's Share of Sign's Fair Value [(75%)($520,000)]	390,000
Consolidated Amount	$1,890,000

Part C   Under the parent company approach, the consolidated Plant and Equipment (Net) wold be as follows::

Consolidated Plant and Equipment At Cost	
Placard's Carrying Value	$1,500,000
Sign's Carrying Value	400,000
Placard's Share of the Fair Value Change [(75%)($520,000 - $400,000)]	90,000
Consolidated Amount	$1,990,000

or

Consolidated Plant and Equipment At Cost	
Placard's Carrying Value	$1,500,000
Sign:	
75 Percent of Fair Value [(75%)($520,000)]	390,000
25 Percent of Carrying Value [(25%)($400,000)]	100,000
Consolidated Amount	$1,990,000

Exercise Four-2 Solution

The journal entry required to eliminate the Investment in San and San's shareholders' equity accounts would be as follows:

No Par Common Stock	$1,250,000	
Retained Earnings	1,380,000	
Investment in San		$2,630,000

Given this entry, the required consolidated Balance Sheet would be prepared as follows:

Pan Inc. and Subsidiary
Consolidated Balance Sheet
As At December 31, 2002

Cash ($426,000 + $345,000)	$ 771,000
Accounts Receivable ($727,000 + $623,000)	1,350,000
Inventories ($1,753,000 + $1,265,000)	3,018,000
Investment In San ($2,630,000 - $2,630,000)	Nil
Plant And Equipment (Net) ($3,259,000 + $2,234,000)	5,493,000
Total Assets	$10,632,000
Current Liabilities ($398,000 + $362,000)	$ 760,000
Long-Term Liabilities ($1,272,000 + $1,475,000)	2,747,000
No Par Common Stock	4,450,000
Retained Earnings	2,675,000
Total Equities	$10,632,000

Exercise Four-3 Solution

The required investment analysis would be as follows:

Investment Cost	$2,508,000
Book Value ($830,000 + $1,687,000)	(2,517,000)
Differential	($ 9,000)
Fair Value Decrease on Inventories	35,000
Fair Value Increase on Liabilities	57,000
Goodwill	$ 83,000

Based on this schedule, the required journal entry would be as follows:

No Par Common Stock (Sum's)	$ 830,000	
Retained Earnings (Sum's)	1,687,000	
Goodwill	83,000	
Inventories		$ 35,000
Long-Term Liabilities		57,000
Investment in Sum		2,508,000

Given this entry, the required consolidated Balance Sheet would be prepared as follows:

Partial Ltd. and Subsidiary
Consolidated Balance Sheet
As At December 31, 2002

Cash ($612,000 + $256,000)	$ 868,000
Accounts Receivable ($1,346,000 + $632,000)	1,978,000
Inventories ($2,111,000 + $943,000 - $35,000)	3,019,000
Investment In Sack ($2,508,000 - $2,508,000)	Nil
Plant And Equipment (Net) ($3,562,000 + $1,866,000)	5,428,000
Goodwill	83,000
Total Assets	$11,376,000

Current Liabilities ($726,000 + $396,000)	$ 1,122,000
Long-Term Liabilities ($2,212,000 + $784,000 + $57,000)	3,053,000
No Par Common Stock (Partial's Only)	3,970,000
Retained Earnings (Partial's Only)	3,231,000
Total Equities	11,376,000

Exercise Four-4 Solution

As the investment cost of $2,440,000 is equal to 80 percent of book value [(80%)($1,215,000 + $1,835,000)] and there are no fair value changes on the identifiable net assets of Sock, no investment analysis is required. The required journal entry would be as follows:

No Par Common Stock (Sock's)	$1,215,000	
Retained Earnings (Sock's)	1,835,000	
Investment In Sock		$2,440,000
Non-Controlling Interest [(20%)($1,215,000 + $1,835,000)]		610,000

Pock Inc. and Subsidiary
Consolidated Balance Sheet
As At December 31, 2002

Cash ($943,000 + $347,000)	$ 1,290,000
Accounts Receivable ($1,712,000 + $963,000)	2,675,000
Inventories ($3,463,000 + $1,876,000)	5,339,000
Investment In Sock($2,440,000 - $2,440,000)	Nil
Plant And Equipment (Net) ($4,692,000 + $1,921,000)	6,613,000
Total Assets	$15,917,000
Current Liabilities ($987,000 + $784,000)	1,771,000
Long-Term Liabilities ($3,462,000 + $1,273,000)	4,735,000
Total Liabilities	$ 6,506,000
Non-Controlling Interest	610,000
Shareholders' Equity:	
No Par Common Stock (Pock's Only)	5,460,000
Retained Earnings (Pock's Only)	3,341,000
Total Equities	$15,917,000

Exercise Four-5 Solution

The required investment analysis would be as follows:

	90 Percent	100 Percent
Investment Cost	$1,480,000	$1,644,444
Book Value	(1,350,000)	(1,500,000)
Differential	$ 130,000	$ 144,444
Fair Value Decrease on Plant	144,000	160,000
Fair Value of Unrecorded Intangibles	(207,000)	(230,000)
Goodwill	$ 67,000	$ 74,444

The required journal entry would be as follows:

No Par Common Stock	$ 490,000	
Retained Earnings	1,010,000	
Intangibles Other Than Goodwill	207,000	
Goodwill	67,000	
Plant and Equipment (Net)		$ 144,000
Investment In Sickle		1,480,000
Non-Controlling Interest [(10%)($1,500,000)]		150,000

Based on this entry, the required Balance Sheet would be prepared as follows:

Pickle Company and Subsidiary
Consolidated Balance Sheet
As At December 31, 2002

Cash ($1,365,000 + $264,000)	$ 1,629,000
Accounts Receivable ($2,789,000 + $657,000)	3,446,000
Inventories ($2,126,000 + $1,206,000)	3,332,000
Investment In Sickle ($1,480,000 - $1,480,000)	Nil
Plant And Equipment (Net) ($3,972,000 + $1,249,000 - $144,000)	5,077,000
Intangibles Other Than Goodwill	207,000
Goodwill	67,000
Total Assets	$13,758,000
Current Liabilities ($1,349,000 + $764,000)	$ 2,113,000
Long-Term Liabilities ($2,718,000 + $1,112,000)	3,830,000
Total Liabilities	$5,943,000
Non-Controlling Interest	150,000
Shareholders' Equity:	
No Par Common Stock (Pickle's Only)	5,420,000
Retained Earnings (Pickle's Only)	2,245,000
Total Equities	$13,758,000

Exercise Four-6 Solution

Using the investment analysis from Exercise Four-5, the journal entry on the books of Sickle to record the push-down values would be as follows:

Retained Earnings [(90%)($1,010,000)]	$909,000	
Intangibles Other Than Goodwill	207,000	
Goodwill	67,000	
Capital Arising on Comprehensive		
Revaluation of Assets*		$130,000
Plant and Equipment (Net)		144,000
Contributed Surplus [(90%)($1,010,000)]		909,000

*The Capital Arising on Comprehensive Revaluation of Assets is the difference between the investment's cost and Pickle Company's share of the book value. This is the Differential in the investment analysis schedule in Exercise Four-5.

Subsequent to this entry, the push-down accounting Balance Sheet of Sickle would be prepared as follows:

Sickle Company
Push-Down Accounting Balance Sheet
As At December 31, 2002

Cash	$ 264,000
Accounts Receivable	657,000
Inventories	1,206,000
Plant And Equipment (Net) ($1,249,000 - $144,000)	1,105,000
Intangibles Other Than Goodwill	207,000
Goodwill	67,000
Total Assets	$3,506,000

Current Liabilities	$ 764,000
Long-Term Liabilities	1,112,000
No Par Common Stock	490,000
Contributed Surplus [(90%)($1,010,000)]	909,000
Capital Arising on Comprehensive Revaluation of Assets	130,000
Retained Earnings [(10%)($1,010,000)]	101,000
Total Equities	$3,506,000

Based on this Balance Sheet, the entry required for the preparation of the consolidated Balance Sheet would be as follows:

No Par Common Stock	$ 490,000	
Contributed Surplus	909,000	
Capital Arising on Comprehensive Revaluation of Assets	130,000	
Retained Earnings	101,000	
Investment in Sickle		$1,480,000
Non-Controlling Interest [(10%)($490,000 + $1,010,000)]		150,000

The resulting consolidated Balance Sheet would be as follows. Note that this Balance Sheet is identical to the one in Exercise Four-5 when push-down accounting was not used.

Pickle Company and Subsidiary
Consolidated Balance Sheet
As At December 31, 2002

Cash ($1,365,000 + $264,000)	$ 1,629,000
Accounts Receivable ($2,789,000 + $657,000)	3,446,000
Inventories ($2,126,000 + $1,206,000)	3,332,000
Investment In Sickle ($1,480,000 - $1,480,000)	Nil
Plant And Equipment (Net) ($3,972,000 + $1,249,000 - $144,000)	5,077,000
Intangibles Other Than Goodwill	207,000
Goodwill	67,000
Total Assets	$13,758,000

Current Liabilities ($1,349,000 + $764,000)	$ 2,113,000
Long-Term Liabilities ($2,718,000 + $1,112,000)	3,830,000
Total Liabilities	$5,943,000
Non-Controlling Interest	150,000
Shareholders' Equity:	
No Par Common Stock (Pickle's Only)	5,420,000
Retained Earnings (Pickle's Only)	2,245,000
Total Equities	$13,758,000

Exercise Four-7 Solution

Subsequent to the business combination, the former Marco shareholders now own 57.5 percent [115,000 ÷ (85,000 + 115,000)] of the outstanding Revco shares. This means that Marco, despite the fact that it is the subsidiary of Revco, would be deemed the acquiring company. As a consequence, the reverse takeover procedures discussed in EIC Abstract No. 10 are applicable.

Had this combination been carried out through an issue of Marco shares, Marco would have had to issue 18,478 new shares in order to give the Revco shareholders the same 42.5 percent interest [18,478 ÷ (18,478 + 25,000)] in the combined company that resulted from the legal form that was used. Using the $160 per share value for the Marco shares, we arrive at an investment cost of $2,956,480 [($160)(18,478)]. Given this, the investment analysis is as follows:

Purchase Price	$2,956,480
Book Value	(2,465,000)
Goodwill	$491,480

Based on these calculations, the resulting consolidated Balance Sheet would be as follows:

Revco Inc. and Subsidiary
Consolidated Balance Sheet
At December 31, 2002

Net Identifiable Assets ($2,465,000 + $3,898,000)	$6,363,000
Goodwill	491,480
Total Assets	$6,854,480
Common Shares ($2,625,000 + $2,956,480)	$5,581,480
Retained Earnings (Marco's Only)	1,273,000
Shareholders' Equity	$6,854,480

As the business combination took place on December 31, 2002, the year end for both companies, none of Revco's earnings would be included in the consolidated Net Income for 2002. The result is a consolidated Net Income figure of $378,000. Despite the fact that this is based on Marco's Net Income for the year, the Earnings Per Share would have to be calculated using the Revco shares issued to acquire Marco. This would be 115,000 shares, resulting in an Earnings Per Share figure of $3.29 ($378,000 ÷ 115,000).

Solution to Self Study Problem Four - 1

Investment Analysis - The analysis of Shark's investment in the Peril Company is as follows:

	70 Percent	100 Percent
Investment Cost	$ 910,000	$1,300,000
Book Value	(1,120,000)	(1,600,000)
Differential	($ 210,000)	($ 300,000)
Fair Value Changes:		
Decrease On Accounts Receivable	35,000	50,000
Increase On Inventories	(35,000)	(50,000)
Decrease On Plant And Equipment (Net)	210,000	300,000
Increase On Liabilities	70,000	100,000
Goodwill	$ 70,000	$ 100,000

Consolidated Balance Sheet - Based on the preceding analysis, the required Balance Sheet is as follows:

Shark Company and Subsidiary
Consolidated Balance Sheet
At December 31, 2002

Cash	$ 790,000
Accounts Receivable	2,265,000
Inventories	3,035,000
Plant And Equipment (Net)	4,790,000
Goodwill	70,000
Total Assets	**$10,950,000**
Liabilities	$ 2,470,000
Non Controlling Interest	480,000
Common Stock (No Par)	4,000,000
Retained Earnings	4,000,000
Total Equities	**$10,950,000**

Solution to Self Study Problem Four - 2

Investment Analysis   The analysis of Potvin Company's investment in the Shroder Company is as follows:

	60 Percent	100 Percent
Investment Cost	$1,200,000	$2,000,000
Book Value	(600,000)	(1,000,000)
Differential	$ 600,000	$1,000,000
Fair Value Changes:		
Increase On Inventories	(30,000)	(50,000)
Decrease On Plant And Equipment (Net)	150,000	250,000
Increase On Long-Term Liabilities	60,000	100,000
Recognition Of Copyright	(120,000)	(200,000)
Goodwill	$ 660,000	$1,100,000

Since, Potvin Company does not carry forward the accumulated depreciation of the acquired enterprise, the fair value change is calculated using the $800,000 ($1,300,000 - $500,000) net book value of Shroder's Plant and Equipment.

Consolidated Balance Sheet   Based on the preceding analysis, the required Balance Sheet is as follows:

Potvin Distributing Company and Subsidiary
Consolidated Balance Sheet
As At December 31, 2002

Cash	$ 400,000
Accounts Receivable	2,190,000
Inventories	3,430,000
Plant And Equipment	6,650,000
Accumulated Depreciation (Potvin's Only)	(2,000,000)
Copyright	120,000
Goodwill	660,000
Total Assets	$11,450,000

Accounts Payable	$ 1,690,000
Long-Term Liabilities	2,360,000
Non-Controlling Interest	400,000
Common Stock (No Par) (Potvin's Only)	3,000,000
Retained Earnings (Potvin's Only)	4,000,000
Total Equities	$11,450,000

Solution to Self Study Problem Four - 3

Investment Analysis　　The analysis of the Pentogram Company's investment in the Square Company is as follows:

	70 Percent	100 Percent
Cost	$875,000	$1,250,000
Book Value	(980,000)	(1,400,000)
Differential	($105,000)	($ 150,000)
Fair Value Changes:		
Decrease On Plant And Equipment	210,000	300,000
Increase On Inventories	(70,000)	(100,000)
Increase On Long-Term Liabilities	35,000	50,000
Goodwill	$ 70,000	$ 100,000

Consolidated Balance Sheet　　The required Consolidated Balance Sheet is as follows:

Pentogram Company and Subsidiary
Consolidated Balance Sheet
As At December 31, 2003

Cash ($1,200,000 + $50,000 - $875,000)	$ 375,000
Accounts Receivable ($400,000 + $250,000)	650,000
Inventories ($2,000,000 + $500,000 + $70,000)	2,570,000
Plant And Equipment ($4,000,000 + $1,100,000 - $210,000)	4,890,000
Accumulated Depreciation (Pentogram's Only)	(1,000,000)
Goodwill (as per investment analysis)	70,000
Total Assets	$7,555,000

Current Liabilities ($200,000 + $150,000)	$ 350,000
Long-Term Liabilities ($1,000,000 + $350,000 + $35,000)	1,385,000
Non-Controlling Interest [(30%)($1,400,000)]	420,000
No Par Common Stock (Pentogram's Only)	2,000,000
Retained Earnings (Pentogram's Only)	3,400,000
Total Equities	$7,555,000

Solution to Self Study Problem Four - 4

While Taken is legally the parent of Revok, the former shareholders of Revok now hold 60 percent (300,000 ÷ 500,000) of the outstanding shares of Taken. This means that Revok is the acquirer in this business combination and, since Revok is the legal subsidiary, we have a reverse takeover situation.

Using the provisions of EIC Abstract No. 10, the purchase price will be based on the value of the Revok shares. If the business combination had been carried out using Revok shares, Revok would have had to issue 100,000 new shares to Taken in order to give them the same 40 percent (100,000 ÷ 250,000) interest that they have in the combined company that resulted from the issue of Taken shares. This provides a purchase price of $900,000 [($9)(100,000)].

Part A   The required amount of goodwill to be included in the consolidated Balance Sheet would be calculated as follows:

Purchase Price	$900,000
Book Value	(840,000)
Differential	$ 60,000
Fair Value Increase On Taken's Land	(12,000)
Goodwill	$ 48,000

Part B   The Shareholders' Equity section would be prepared as follows:

Contributed Capital:	
Preferred Shares	$ 100,000
Common Shares (Note)	1,350,000
Retained Earnings (Revok's)	375,000
Total	$1,825,000

Note   The Common Shares would be equal to Revok's original value of $450,000, plus the purchase price of $900,000.

Part C   The consolidated Net Income for the year ending December 31, 2002 would be Revok's $56,000 (Revok is the acquirer).

Part D   The Earnings Per Share figure would be calculated using the 300,000 shares issued to acquire Revok. This would give a figure of $0.187 per share ($56,000 ÷ 300,000).

Solution to Chapter Five Exercises

Exercise Five - 1 Solution

The required consolidated Income Statement would be prepared as follows:

Part Company and Subsidiary
Consolidated Income Statement
Year Ending December 31, 2002

Revenues ($982,000 + $463,000)	$1,445,000
Expenses:	
Cost of Goods Sold ($448,000 + $219,000)	$ 667,000
Other Expenses ($374,000 + $115,000)	489,000
Non-Controlling Interest [(35%)($129,000)]	45,150
Total Expenses	$1,201,150
Income Before Results Of Discontinued Operations	$ 243,850
Loss From Discontinued Operations [(65%)($63,000)]	(40,950)
Net Income	$ 202,900

The final Net Income figure can be verified by noting that it is equal to Part's $160,000, plus $42,800 [(65%)($66,000)]

Exercise Five - 2 Solution

Step A Procedures   The required investment analysis would be as follows:

	65 Percent	100 Percent
Investment Cost	$1,350,000	$2,076,923
Book Value At Acquisition	(1,105,000)	(1,700,000)
Differential	$ 245,000	$ 376,923
Fair Value Increase On Non-Monetary Assets	(97,500)	(150,000)
Goodwill	$ 147,500	$ 226,923

The fair value change on the Non-Monetary Assets would be amortized at the rate of $6,500 per year ($97,500 ÷ 15).

Based on this schedule, the investment elimination entry would be as follows:

No Par Common Stock	$ 700,000	
Retained Earnings (At Acquisition Balance)	1,000,000	
Non-Monetary Assets	97,500	
Goodwill	147,500	
Investment In Schaffer		$1,350,000
Non-Controlling Interest [(35%)($1,700,000)]		595,000

Step B Procedures

The entry to eliminate the intercompany receivables would be as follows:

Liabilities	$15,000	
Monetary Assets		$15,000

The entry to record the fair value write-off of non-monetary assets would be as follows:

Retained Earnings [(4)($6,500)]	$26,000	
Total Expenses (Amortization)	6,500	
Non-Monetary Assets		$32,500

The entry to record the 2004 and current goodwill impairment would be as follows:

Retained Earnings	$35,000	
Goodwill Impairment Loss	25,000	
Goodwill		$60,000

The entry to eliminate the intercompany sales would be as follows:

Sales	$85,000	
Total Expenses (Cost Of Goods Sold)		$85,000

The entry to eliminate the subsidiary Dividends Declared would be as follows:

Dividend Revenue	$32,500	
Non-Controlling Interest (Balance Sheet)	17,500	
Dividends Declared		$50,000

Step C - Distribution Of Subsidiary Retained Earnings

Balance As Per The Trial Balance	$1,550,000
Balance At Acquisition	(1,000,000)
Balance Since Acquisition	$ 550,000
Non-Controlling Interest [(35%)($550,000)]	(192,500)
Available To The Controlling Interest	$ 357,500
Step B Adjustments:	
Plant And Equipment (4 Years At $6,500)	(26,000)
Goodwill Impairment (From 2004)	(35,000)
To Consolidated Retained Earnings	$ 296,500

Based on this Schedule, the Retained Earnings distribution entry would be as follows:

Retained Earnings	$489,000	
Non-Controlling Interest (Balance Sheet)		$192,500
Consolidated Retained Earnings		296,500

Consolidated Income Statement   The required consolidated Income Statement would be prepared as follows:

Parker Company And Subsidiary
Consolidated Income Statement
Year Ending December 31, 2006

Sales ($3,225,000 + $675,000 - $85,000)	$3,815,000
Dividend Revenue ($32,500 - $32,500)	Nil
Total Revenues	$3,815,000
Expenses And Losses:	
Total Expenses ($2,940,000 +	
$530,000 - $85,000 + $6,500)	$3,391,500
Non-Controlling Interest [(35%)($145,000)]	50,750
Goodwill Impairment Loss	25,000
Total Expenses And Losses	$3,467,250
Net Income	$ 347,750

Consolidated Statement Of Retained Earnings   The required consolidated Statement Of Retained Earnings would be prepared as follows:

Parker Company And Subsidiary
Consolidated Statement Of Retained Earnings
Year Ending December 31, 2006

Opening Balance ($5,895,000 + $296,500)	$6,191,500
Consolidated Net Income	347,750
Available For Distribution	$6,539,250
Dividends (Parker's Only)	(250,000)
Closing Balance	$6,289,250

Consolidated Balance Sheet   The required consolidated Balance Sheet would be prepared as follows:

Parker Company And Subsidiary
Consolidated Balance Sheet
At December 31, 2006

Monetary Assets ($2,850,000 + $725,000 - $15,000)	$ 3,560,000
Investment In Schaffer ($1,350,000 - $1,350,000)	Nil
Non-Monetary Assets ($6,475,000	
+ $2,045,000 + $97,500 - $32,500))	8,585,000
Goodwill ($147,500 - $35,000 - $25,000)	87,500
Total Assets	$12,232,500
Liabilities ($1,712,500 + $425,000 - $15,000)	$ 2,122,500
Non-Controlling Interest [(35%)($700,000 + $1,645,000)]	820,750
No Par Common Stock (Parker's Only)	3,000,000
Retained Earnings (See Statement)	6,289,250
Total Equities	$12,232,500

Exercise Five - 3 Solution
The following investment analysis and investment elimination entry are identical to those used in Exercise Five-2.

Step A Procedures   The required investment analysis would be as follows:

	65 Percent	100 Percent
Investment Cost	$1,350,000	$2,076,923
Book Value At Acquisition	(1,105,000)	(1,700,000)
Differential	$ 245,000	$ 376,923
Fair Value Increase On Non-Monetary Assets	(97,500)	(150,000)
Goodwill	$ 147,500	$ 226,923

The fair value change on the Non-Monetary Assets would be amortized at the rate of $6,500 per year ($97,500 ÷ 15).

Based on this schedule, the investment elimination entry would be as follows:

No Par Common Stock	$ 700,000	
Retained Earnings (At Acquisition Balance)	1,000,000	
Non-Monetary Assets	97,500	
Goodwill	147,500	
Investment In Schaffer		$1,350,000
Non-Controlling Interest [(35%)($1,700,000)]		595,000

Step B Procedures

The entry to eliminate the intercompany receivables would be as follows:

Liabilities	$15,000	
Monetary Assets		$15,000

The entry to record the fair value write-off of non-monetary assets would be as follows:

Retained Earnings [(5)($6,500)]	$32,500	
Non-Monetary Assets		$32,500

The entry to record the 2004 and current goodwill impairment would be as follows:

Retained Earnings	$60,000	
Goodwill		$60,000

Entries to eliminate the intercompany sales and subsidiary dividends would not be required in this closed trial balance problem.

Step C - Distribution Of Subsidiary Retained Earnings

Balance As Per The Trial Balance	$1,645,000
Balance At Acquisition	(1,000,000)
Balance Since Acquisition	$ 645,000
Non-Controlling Interest [(35%)($645,000)]	(225,750)
Available To The Controlling Interest	$ 419,250
Step B Adjustments:	
Plant And Equipment (5 Years At $6,500)	(32,500)
Goodwill Impairment ($35,000 + $25,000)	(60,000)
To Consolidated Retained Earnings	$ 326,750

Based on this Schedule, the Retained Earnings distribution entry would be as follows:

Retained Earnings	$552,500	
Non-Controlling Interest (Balance Sheet)		$225,750
Consolidated Retained Earnings		326,750

Consolidated Balance Sheet   The required consolidated Balance Sheet, which is identical to the Balance Sheet in Exercise Five-2, would be prepared as follows:

Parker Company And Subsidiary
Consolidated Balance Sheet
At December 31, 2006

Monetary Assets ($2,850,000 + $725,000 - $15,000)	$ 3,560,000
Investment In Schaffer ($1,350,000 - $1,350,000)	Nil
Non-Monetary Assets ($6,475,000	
+ $2,045,000 + $97,500 - $32,500))	8,585,000
Goodwill ($147,500 - $35,000 - $25,000)	87,500
Total Assets	$12,232,500
Liabilities ($1,712,500 + $425,000 - $15,000)	$ 2,122,500
Non-Controlling Interest [(35%)($700,000 + $1,645,000)]	820,750
No Par Common Stock (Parker's Only)	3,000,000
Retained Earnings ($5,962,5000 + $326,750)	6,289,250
Total Equities	$12,232,500

Exercise Five - 4 Solution

The following investment analysis is identical to the one used in Exercises Five-2 and Five-3.

	65 Percent	100 Percent
Investment Cost	$1,350,000	$2,076,923
Book Value At Acquisition	(1,105,000)	(1,700,000)
Differential	$ 245,000	$ 376,923
Fair Value Increase On Non-Monetary Assets	(97,500)	(150,000)
Goodwill	$ 147,500	$ 226,923

Using this analysis, along with the other information, Investment Income under the equity method would be calculated as follows:

Parker's Interest In Schaffer's Net Income [(65%)($145,000)]	$94,250
Fair Value Amortization ($97,500 ÷ 15)	(6,500)
Loss On Goodwill Impairment (Given)	(25,000)
Equity Method Investment Income	$62,750

Given this calculation, the required Income Statement would be as follows:

Parker Company
Income Statement
Years Ended December 31, 2006

Sales	$3,225,000
Investment Income	62,750
Dividend Revenue	Nil
Total Revenues	$3,287,750
Total Expenses	(2,940,000)
Net Income	$ 347,750

Note that this is the same Net Income that was disclosed in Exercise Five-2 when we prepared consolidated financial statements. The $32,500 Dividend Revenue under the cost method would be nil if the investment was accounted for using the equity method.

With respect to the Investment In Schaffer amount that would be included in Parker's single entity Balance Sheet under the equity method, it would be calculated as follows:

Investment In Schaffer At Cost		$1,350,000
Equity Pickup:		
Schaffer's December 31 Retained Earnings	$1,645,000	
Balance At Acquisition	(1,000,000)	
Balance Since Acquisition	$ 645,000	
Parker's Share	65%	419,250
Adjustments:		
Fair Value Amortization [(5)($6,500)]		(32,500)
Goodwill Impairment Loss ($35,000 + $25,000)		(60,000)
Investment In Schaffer At Equity		$1,676,750

This will result in an increase in Parker's assets of $326,750 ($1,676,750 - $1,350,000). To complete Parker's single entity Balance Sheet, the same amount will have to be added to the Retained Earnings of Parker, resulting in a total of $6,289,250. Using these figures, the required Balance Sheet would be as follows:

Parker Company
Balance Sheet
As At December 31, 2006

Monetary Asssets	$ 2,850,000
Investment In Schaffer (At Equity)	1,676,750
Non-Monetary Assets	6,475,000
Total Assets	$11,001,750
Liabilities	$ 1,712,500
No Par Common Stock	3,000,000
Retained Earnings	6,289,250
Total Equities	$11,001,750

Note that this is the same Retained Earnings figure that was disclosed in Exercises Five - 2 and Five - 3 when consolidated financial statements were prepared.

Exercise Five - 5 Solution

Step A Investment Analysis   The analysis of the Investment in Subco is as follows:

	80 Percent	100 Percent
Cost	$1,000,000	$1,250,000
Book Value	(960,000)	(1,200,000)
Differential	$ 40,000	$ 50,000
Fair Value Decrease On Inventories	320,000	400,000
Fair Value Increase On Plant And Equipment	(240,000)	(300,000)
Goodwill	$ 120,000	$ 150,000

The fair value change on equipment will be amortized over 10 years at the rate of $24,000 per year.

Part A - Consolidated Net Income   Consolidated Net Income would be calculated as follows:

Parco's Net Loss	($300,000)
Intercompany Dividends [(80%)($400,000)]	(320,000)
Parco's Adjusted Net Loss	($620,000)
Equity Pickup [(80%)($500,000)]	400,000
Combined Income Before Adjustments	($220,000)
Fair Value Amortization on Equipment ($240,000 ÷ 10)	(24,000)
Consolidated Net Income (Loss)	($244,000)

Part B   In order to prepare the required Cash Flow Statement, several calculations are required. The first is consolidated Amortization Expense.

Combined Plant On December 31, 2006 ($6,400,000 + $800,000)	$7,200,000
Write-Down By Parco During The Year	(800,000)
Total	$6,400,000
Combined Plant On December 31, 2007 ($4,800,000 + $600,000)	(5,400,000)
Total Single Entity Amortization Expense for 2007	$1,000,000
Fair Value Increase Amortization	24,000
Consolidated Amortization Expense for 2007	$1,024,000

The cash from operating activities, on a consolidated basis can be calculated as follows:

Consolidated Net Income (Loss)	($ 244,000)
Consolidated Amortization Expense	1,024,000
Plant Write-Down (Parco)	800,000
Amortization Of Bond Premium (Subco)	(5,000)
Non-Controlling Interest In Subco's Income [(20%)($500,000)]	100,000
Cash Increase Before Current Asset Changes	$1,675,000
Cash From Decrease in Accounts Receivable	
($1,500,000 + $900,000 - $1,800,000 - $650,000)	50,000
Cash From Decrease in Inventories	
($2,000,000 + $800,000 - $2,600,000 - $500,000)	300,000
Cash Used For Decrease in Accounts Payable	
($400,000 + $700,000 - $1,000,000 - $750,000)	(650,000)
Cash From Operating Activities	$1,375,000

The increase in cash for the year is $495,000 ($800,000 + $365,000 - $400,000 - $270,000).

Given the preceding calculations, the required consolidated Cash Flow Statement is prepared as follows:

**Parco Company And Subsidiary
Consolidated Cash Flow Statement
For The Year Ending December 31, 2007**

Cash Flows From (Used In):

Operating Activities

Cash From Operating Activities		$1,375,000

Financing Activities

Retirement of Long Term Debt	($1,000,000)	
Dividends Paid To Non-Controlling Interest		
[(20%)($400,000)]	(80,000)	(1,080,000)

Investing Activities

Parco's Acquisition Of Land	($200,000)	
Subco's Sale Of Land	400,000	200,000
Increase in Cash		$ 495,000

Exercise Five - 6 Solution

The analysis of the investments would be as follows:

	40 Percent	100 Percent
Investment Cost	$1,875,000	$4,687,500
Book Value - Net Assets	(1,300,000)	(3,250,000)
Differential	$ 575,000	$1,437,500
Fair Value Increase On Plant And Equipment	(290,000)	(725,000)
Goodwill	$ 285,000	$ 712,500

	15 Percent	100 Percent
Investment Cost	$820,000	$5,466,667
Book Value - Net Assets	(637,500)	(4,250,000)
Differential	$182,500	$1,216,667
Fair Value Increase On Plant And Equipment	(105,000)	(700,000)
Goodwill	$ 77,500	$ 516,667

Part A   The Plant And Equipment balance would be calculated as follows:

Best's Balance		$3,520,000
Worst's Balance		1,600,000
Fair Value Increase - 1st Purchase	$290,000	
Amortization [($290,000 ÷ 4)(2)]	(145,000)	145,000
Fair Value Increase - 2nd Purchase	$105,000	
Amortization [($105,000 ÷ 3)(1)]	(35,000)	70,000
Consolidated Plant And Equipment		$5,335,000

Part B   Consolidated Goodwill would be $362,500 ($285,000 + $77,500).

Part C   The consolidated Retained Earnings would be calculated as follows:

Best's Balance	$4,275,000
Equity Pickup - 1st Purchase [(40%)($2,450,000 - $1,250,000)]	480,000
Equity Pickup - 2nd Purchase [(15%)($2,450,000 - $2,250,000)]	30,000
Amortization Of Fair Value Increase ($145,000 + $35,000)	(180,000)
Consolidated Retained Earnings	$4,605,000

Solution to Self Study Problem Five - 1

Investment Analysis   The analysis of the Pastel Company's Investment In Shade as at the acquisition date is as follows:

	90 Percent	100 Percent
Purchase Price	$5,175,000	$5,750,000
Book Value	(5,400,000)	(6,000,000)
Differential	($ 225,000)	($ 250,000)
Fair Value Decrease On Equipment	900,000	1,000,000
Fair Value Increase On Land	(90,000)	(100,000)
Fair Value Decrease On Receivables	45,000	50,000
Fair Value Decrease On Long-Term Liabilities	(180,000)	(200,000)
Goodwill	$ 450,000	$ 500,000

Step A - Investment Elimination   The journal entry that would be required to eliminate the Pastel Company's Investment In Shade would be as follows:

Common Stock - No Par	$2,000,000	
Retained Earnings	4,000,000	
Land	90,000	
Long-Term Liabilities	180,000	
Goodwill	450,000	
Investment In Shade		$5,175,000
Equipment (Net)		900,000
Accounts Receivable		45,000
Non-Controlling Interest		600,000

Step B - Depreciation Of The Fair Value Change On Equipment   The entry to record the reduction in Depreciation Expense related to the fair value change on the equipment would be as follows:

Equipment (Net)	$450,000	
Depreciation Expense		$ 90,000
Retained Earnings		360,000

(Annual Adjustment = $900,000/10 = $90,000)

Step B - Fair Value Change On Land   No adjustment is required.

Step B - Realization Of The Fair Value Change On Accounts Receivable   The entry to record the realization of the fair value change on Accounts Receivable is as follows:

Accounts Receivable	$45,000	
Retained Earnings		$45,000

Step B - Amortization Of The Fair Value Change On The Liabilities   The entry to record the increase in Other Expenses (interest expense) related to the fair value change on liabilities is as follows:

Other Expenses	$ 36,000	
Retained Earnings	144,000	
Long-Term Liabilities		$180,000

(Annual Adjustment = $180,000/5 = $36,000)

Step B - Goodwill Impairment Loss   The entry to record the Goodwill Impairment Loss is as follows:

Goodwill Impairment Loss	$15,000	
Goodwill		$15,000

Step B - Intercompany Management Fees   Two entries are required here. The first is to eliminate the $100,000 in intercompany revenue and expense while the second is required to eliminate the intercompany asset and liability. The entries are as follows:

Other Revenues	$100,000	
Other Expenses		$100,000

Current Liabilities	$100,000	
Current Receivables		$100,000

Step B - Intercompany Merchandise Sales   Two entries are also required here. The first will eliminate the total intercompany merchandise sales of $650,000 ($500,000 downstream + $150,000 upstream) while the second will eliminate the intercompany asset and liability of $225,000 ($75,000 downstream + $150,000 upstream). The entries are as follows:

Sales	$650,000	
Cost Of Goods Sold		$650,000

Current Liabilities	$225,000	
Current Receivables		$225,000

Step B - Intercompany Dividends   Two entries are also required here. The first will eliminate the intercompany Dividends Declared against the Other Revenues and Non-Controlling Interest while the second will be required to eliminate the unpaid balance from the consolidated assets and liabilities. The entries are as follows:

Other Revenues	$90,000	
Non-Controlling Interest (Balance Sheet)	10,000	
Dividends Declared		$100,000

Dividends Payable	$90,000	
Current Receivables		$ 90,000

Step C - Distribution Of Retained Earnings   The analysis of the opening balance of the Shade Company's Retained Earnings is as follows:

Retained Earnings - Opening Balance	$5,500,000
Balance At Acquisition	(4,000,000)
Balance Since Acquisition	$1,500,000
Non-Controlling Interest [(10%)($1,500,000)]	(150,000)
Available To The Controlling Interest	$1,350,000
Fair Value Depreciation On Equipment	360,000
Fair Value Realization On Accounts Receivable	45,000
Fair Value Amortization On Long-Term Liabilities	(144,000)
To Consolidated Retained Earnings	$1,611,000

Based on the preceding analysis, the journal entry required to distribute the opening Retained Earnings balance of the Shade Company is as follows:

Retained Earnings - Shade	$1,761,000	
Consolidated Retained Earnings		$1,611,000
Non-Controlling Interest		150,000

Part A - Consolidated Income Statement   The consolidated Income Statement for the Pastel Company and its subsidiary, the Shade Company, is as follows:

Pastel Company and Subsidiary
Consolidated Income Statement
For The Year Ending December 31, 2007

Sales ($8,000,000 + $2,000,000 - $650,000)	$ 9,350,000
Gain on Sale of Land	500,000
Other Revenues ($800,000 + $100,000 - $100,000 - $90,000)	710,000
Total Revenues	$10,560,000
Cost Of Goods Sold ($3,800,000 + $800,000 - $650,000)	$ 3,950,000
Depreciation Expense ($1,400,000 + $300,000 - $90,000)	1,610,000
Other Expenses ($2,000,000 + $400,000 + $36,000 - $100,000)	2,336,000
Goodwill Impairment Loss	15,000
Non-Controlling Interest [(10%)($600,000)]	60,000
Total Expenses	$ 7,971,000
Consolidated Net Income	$ 2,589,000

Part B - Consolidated Statement Of Retained Earnings   The opening balance of consolidated Retained Earnings consists of the Pastel Company's opening balance in the amount of $18,100,000 plus the allocation that was established in Step C in the amount of $1,611,000. Beginning with this total of $19,711,000, the consolidated Statement Of Retained Earnings for the Pastel Company and its subsidiary, the Shade Company, is as follows:

Pastel Company and Subsidiary
Consolidated Statement Of Retained Earnings
For The Year Ending December 31, 2007

Opening Consolidated Retained Earnings	$19,711,000
Net Income (From Part A)	2,589,000
Balance Available	$22,300,000
Less Dividends Declared (Pastel's Only)	200,000
Closing Consolidated Retained Earnings	$22,100,000

Verification Of The Closing Balance   The closing balance in the consolidated Retained Earnings can be verified as follows:

Pastel's Closing Retained Earnings	$20,000,000
Equity Pickup ([90%][$6,000,000 - $4,000,000])	1,800,000
Fair Value Depreciation On Equipment	450,000
Fair Value Realization On Accounts Receivable	45,000
Fair Value Amortization On Long-Term Liabilities	(180,000)
Goodwill Impairment Loss	(15,000)
Closing Consolidated Retained Earnings	$22,100,000

Part C - Consolidated Balance Sheet The consolidated Balance Sheet for the Pastel Company and its subsidiary, the Shade Company, is as follows:

Pastel Company and Subsidiary
Consolidated Balance Sheet
As At December 31, 2007

Cash And Current Receivables ($2,625,000 + $800,000	
- $45,000 + $45,000 - $100,000 - $225,000 - $90,000)	$ 3,010,000
Inventories ($8,000,000 + $2,000,000)	10,000,000
Equipment (Net)($24,000,000 + $4,000,000 - $900,000 + $450,000)	27,550,000
Buildings (Net)($10,000,000 + $2,000,000)	12,000,000
Investment In Shade ($5,175,000 - $5,175,000)	-0-
Land ($2,000,000 + $1,200,000 + $90,000)	3,290,000
Goodwill ($450,000 - $15,000)	435,000
Total Assets	$56,285,000
Dividends Payable ($100,000 - $90,000)	$ 10,000
Current Liabilities ($1,800,000 + $900,000 - $100,000 - $225,000)	2,375,000
Long-Term Liabilities ($10,000,000 + $1,000,000	
- $180,000 + $180,000)	11,000,000
Non-Controlling Interest [(10%)($8,000,000)]	800,000
Common Stock - No Par (Pastel's Only)	20,000,000
Retained Earnings (See Part B)	22,100,000
Total Equities	$56,285,000

Note that, as you would expect in the absence of unrealized intercompany profits, the Non-Controlling Interest is simply 10 percent of the book value of the Shade Company's net assets.

Solution to Self Study Problem Five - 2

Investment Analysis The analysis of the Prude Company's Investment in Sybarite as at the acquisition date is as follows:

	60 Percent	100 Percent
Investment Cost	$750,000	$1,250,000
Book Value at Acquisition	(780,000)	(1,300,000)
Differential	($ 30,000)	($ 50,000)
Fair Value Decrease on Receivables	30,000	50,000
Fair Value Decrease on Inventories	270,000	450,000
Fair Value Increase on Plant	(210,000)	(350,000)
Fair Value Increase on Long-Term Liabilities	60,000	100,000
Goodwill	$120,000	$ 200,000

Step A - Investment Elimination   The journal entry that would be required to eliminate the Prude Company's Investment in Sybarite would be as follows:

Common Stock - No Par	$1,000,000	
Retained Earnings	300,000	
Accumulated Depreciation	300,000	
Goodwill	120,000	
Plant and Equipment		$ 90,000
Investment in Sybarite		750,000
Non-Controlling Interest		520,000
Current Receivables		30,000
Inventories		270,000
Long-Term Liabilities		60,000

While there is a net increase in Plant and Equipment of $210,000, it is accomplished by removing all of the Accumulated Depreciation of Sybarite on the acquisition date. This reflects the fact that, from the point of view of the newly combined company, these assets are newly acquired and it would not be appropriate for Accumulated Depreciation to be recorded.

Step B - Realization Of The Fair Value Change On Accounts Receivable   The entry to record the realization of the fair value change on Accounts Receivable is as follows:

Current Receivables	$30,000	
Retained Earnings		$30,000

Step B - Fair Value Change On Inventories   The entry to record the fair value change on the Inventories is as follows:

Inventories	$270,000	
Retained Earnings		$270,000

Step B - Depreciation Of The Fair Value Change On The Plant   The entry to record the increased Accumulated Depreciation related to the fair value change on the Plant would be as follows:

Retained Earnings	$105,000	
Accumulated Depreciation		$105,000
(Annual Adjustment = $210,000/14 = $15,000/year)		

Step B - Amortization Of The Fair Value Change On The Liabilities   The entry to record the amortization of the fair value change on the Long-Term Liabilities is as follows (this adjustment is required even though the Long-Term Liabilities have matured):

Long-Term Liabilities	$60,000	
Retained Earnings		$60,000
(Annual Adjustment = $60,000/5 = $12,000/year)		

Step B - Goodwill Impairment Loss   The entry to record the 2005 Goodwill Impairment Loss is as follows:

Retained Earnings	$42,000	
Goodwill		$42,000

Step B - Intercompany Merchandise Sales   Since no Income Statement is required, no entry is necessary to eliminate the intercompany sales of $50,000. An entry is required to eliminate the intercompany asset and liability arising from the outstanding merchandise payable of $50,000 and the accrued interest of $5,000 which is also outstanding. This entry is as follows:

Current Liabilities	$55,000	
Current Receivables		$55,000

Step C - Distribution Of Retained Earnings   The analysis of the closing balance of the Sybarite Company's Retained Earnings is as follows:

Sybarite's Balance At December 31, 2008	$1,400,000
Balance At Acquisition	(300,000)
Balance Since Acquisition	$1,100,000
Non-Controlling Interest [(40%)($1,100,000)]	(440,000)
Balance Available to the Controlling Interest	$ 660,000
Fair Value Realization on Current Receivables	30,000
Fair Value Realization on Inventories	270,000
Fair Value Depreciation on Plant (7 years @ $15,000)	(105,000)
Fair Value Amortization on Long-Term Liabilities (5 years @ $12,000)	60,000
Goodwill Impairment Loss	(42,000)
To Consolidated Retained Earnings	$ 873,000

Based on the preceding analysis, the journal entry required to distribute the closing Retained Earnings balance of the Sybarite Company is as follows:

Retained Earnings - Sybarite	$1,313,000	
Non-Controlling Interest		$440,000
Consolidated Retained Earnings		873,000

This results in a December 31, 2008 balance in consolidated Retained Earnings of $3,373,000 ($2,500,000 + $873,000).

Non-Controlling Interest   Using the steps in the general procedures, the Non-Controlling Interest would be calculated as follows:

Step A Allocation at Acquisition	$520,000
Step C Allocation Since Acquisition	440,000
Non-Controlling Interest, December 31, 2008	$960,000

This same balance can be calculated more directly by noting that on December 31, 2008, the Sybarite Company has No Par Common Stock of $1,000,000 and Retained Earnings of $1,400,000. If we multiply this total net worth of $2,400,000 by the non-controlling ownership percentage of 40 percent, we arrive at the same $960,000.

Consolidated Balance Sheet   Given the preceding calculations, the consolidated Balance Sheet for the Prude Company and its subsidiary, the Sybarite Company, would be as follows:

Prude Company And Subsidiary
Consolidated Balance Sheet
As At December 31, 2008

Cash ($50,000 + $300,000)	$ 350,000
Current Receivables ($300,000 + $400,000	
- $30,000 + $30,000 - $55,000)	645,000
Inventories ($700,000 + $1,750,000 - $270,000 + $270,000)	2,450,000
Investment in Sybarite ($750,000 - $750,000)	-0-
Plant and Equipment ($9,000,000 + $1,000,000 - $90,000)	9,910,000
Accumulated Depreciation ($3,000,000 + $650,000	
- $300,000 + $105,000)	(3,455,000)
Goodwill ($120,000 - $42,000)	78,000
Total Assets	$9,978,000
Current Liabilities ($300,000 + $100,000 - $55,000)	$ 345,000
Long-Term Liabilities ($1,000,000 + $300,000+ $60,000 - $60,000)	1,300,000
Non-Controlling Interest	960,000
No Par Common Stock (Prude's Only)	4,000,000
Retained Earnings	3,373,000
Total Equities	$9,978,000

Solution to Self Study Problem Five - 3

Investment Analysis For First Purchase   The investment analysis for the first purchase would be as follows:

	30 Percent	100 Percent
Cost	$3,000,000	$10,000,000
Book Value	(2,100,000)	(7,000,000)
Differential	$ 900,000	$ 3,000,000
Fair Value Increase on Plant	(600,000)	(2,000,000)
Goodwill	$ 300,000	$ 1,000,000

Write-Off Of Fair Value Change   The depreciation of the fair value change on the Plant and Equipment would increase expenses by $60,000 per year ($600,000/10).

Investment Analysis For Second Purchase   The investment analysis for the second purchase would be as follows:

	30 Percent	100 Percent
Cost	$3,600,000	$12,000,000
Book Value	(2,400,000)	(8,000,000)
Differential	$1,200,000	$ 4,000,000
Fair Value Increase on Plant	(900,000)	(3,000,000)
Goodwill	$ 300,000	$ 1,000,000

Write-Off Of Fair Value Change   The depreciation of the fair value change on the Plant and Equipment would increase expenses by $100,000 per year ($900,000/9).

Plant And Equipment   The consolidated value for Net Plant and Equipment is independently calculated in the schedule which follows:

Port's Book Value		$10,000,000
Ship's Book Value		4,000,000
Fair Value Changes:		
First Purchase	$600,000	
Two Years Depreciation @ $60,000/year	(120,000)	480,000
Second Purchase	$900,000	
One Year of Depreciation	(100,000)	800,000
Consolidated Net Plant and Equipment		$15,280,000

Consolidated Retained Earnings   The December 31, 2004 balance for this account would be as follows:

Port's Balance	$10,000,000
Equity Pickup from First Purchase	
[(30%)($4,500,000 - $3,000,000)]	450,000
Equity Pickup from Second Purchase	
[(30%)($4,500,000 - $4,000,000)]	150,000
Fair Value Depreciation ($120,000 + $100,000)	(220,000)
Consolidated Retained Earnings	$10,380,000

Consolidated Balance Sheet   Given the preceding computations, the consolidated Balance Sheet would be prepared as follows:

Port Company And Subsidiary
Consolidated Balance Sheet
As At December 31, 2004

Net Monetary Assets	$ 7,900,000
Plant and Equipment (Net)	15,280,000
Goodwill	600,000
Total Assets	$23,780,000
Non-Controlling Interest [(40%)($8,500,000)]	$ 3,400,000
Common Stock - No Par	10,000,000
Retained Earnings	10,380,000
Total Equities	$23,780,000

Solution to Self Study Problem Five - 4

Investment Analysis   The analysis of the Puberty Company's Investment in Senile Company as at the acquisition date is as follows:

	80 Percent	100 Percent
Purchase Price	$4,000,000	$5,000,000
Book Value	(2,400,000)	(3,000,000)
Differential	$1,600,000	$2,000,000
Fair Value Increase on Building	(3,200,000)	(4,000,000)
Fair Value Increase on Liabilities	1,600,000	2,000,000
Senile's Goodwill	800,000	1,000,000
Consolidated Goodwill	$ 800,000	$1,000,000

Paragraph 1581.40 indicates that none of the cost of the purchase should be allocated to goodwill of the acquiree that is present at acquisition. However, Paragraph 1600.15 requires the non-controlling interest in subsidiary assets to be based on the carrying values that are recorded in that company's records. This Recommendation means that the non-controlling interest's share of the subsidiary's recorded goodwill must remain in the consolidated financial statements. The combined effect of these two Recommendations is to require that the parent's share of the subsidiary's recorded goodwill be eliminated against the cost of the investment, while the non-controlling interest's share of this balance be included in the consolidated Balance Sheet.

Step A - Investment Elimination   The journal entry that would be required to eliminate the Puberty Company's Investment In Senile would be as follows:

Common Stock - No Par Value	$1,000,000	
Retained Earnings	2,000,000	
Plant and Equipment (Net)	3,200,000	
Consolidated Goodwill	800,000	
Investment In Senile		$4,000,000
Long-Term Liabilities		1,600,000
Senile's Goodwill		800,000
Non-Controlling Interest		600,000

Step B - Senile's Goodwill   Since there has been no impairment of Senile's Goodwill since the acquisition date, there is no adjustment necessary to this account.

Step B - Fair Value Change On Building   The entry to record the increase in Depreciation Expense related to the fair value change on the building would be as follows:

Retained Earnings	$ 768,000	
Other Expenses	128,000	
Plant and Equipment (Net)		$ 896,000

(Annual Adjustment = $3,200,000/25 = $128,000/Year)

Step B - Fair Value Change On Liabilities   The entry to record the decrease in Other Expenses (interest expense) related to the fair value change on liabilities is as follows:

Long-Term Liabilities	$ 700,000	
Retained Earnings		$ 600,000
Other Expenses		100,000

(Annual Adjustment = $1,600,000/16 = $100,000/Year)

Step B - Goodwill Impairment Loss   The entry to record the Goodwill Impairment Loss is as follows:

Goodwill Impairment Loss	$140,000	
Consolidated Goodwill		$ 140,000

Step B - Intercompany Merchandise Sales   The entry to eliminate intercompany merchandise sales is as follows:

Sales	$1,000,000	
Cost of Goods Sold		$1,000,000

Step B - Intercompany Note And Interest   Three entries are required here. The first is to eliminate the intercompany note payable and receivable, the second is required to eliminate the related interest expense and revenue and the third is to eliminate the interest payable and receivable at the year end. The entries are as follows:

Notes Payable	$500,000	
Long-Term Receivables		$500,000

Other Revenues	$ 30,000	
Other Expenses		$ 30,000
[($500,000)(12%)(1/2 year)]		

Current Liabilities	$ 15,000	
Cash and Current Receivables		$ 15,000
[($500,000)(12%)(1/4 year)]		

Step B - Intercompany Dividends   The entry to eliminate the intercompany dividends declared is as follows:

Other Revenues	$ 240,000	
Non-Controlling Interest	60,000	
Dividends Declared		$ 300,000

Step B - Intercompany Management Fees   Two entries are required. The first entry is to eliminate the intercompany revenue and expense while the second is required to eliminate the intercompany asset and liability. The entries are as follows:

Other Revenues	$100,000	
Other Expenses		$100,000

Current Liabilities	$100,000	
Cash and Current Receivables		$100,000

Step C - Distribution Of Retained Earnings   The analysis of the opening balance of the Senile Company's Retained Earnings is as follows:

Retained Earnings - Opening Balance	$3,200,000
Balance At Acquisition	(2,000,000)
Balance Since Acquisition	$1,200,000
Non-Controlling Interest [(20%)($1,200,000)]	(240,000)
Balance Available to the Controlling Interest	$ 960,000
Fair Value Depreciation on Plant	(768,000)
Fair Value Amortization On Long-Term Liabilities	600,000
To Consolidated Retained Earnings	$ 792,000

Based on the preceding analysis, the journal entry required to distribute the opening Retained Earnings balance of the Senile Company is as follows:

Retained Earnings - Senile	$1,032,000	
Consolidated Retained Earnings		$792,000
Non-Controlling Interest		240,000

Part A - Consolidated Income Statement   The consolidated Income Statement for the Puberty Company and its subsidiary, the Senile Company is as follows:

Puberty Company and Subsidiary
Consolidated Income Statement
For The Year Ending December 31, 2008

Sales ($9,000,000 + $2,500,000 - $1,000,000)	$10,500,000
Other Revenues ($1,000,000 + $300,000 - $30,000 - $240,000 - $100,000)	930,000
Total Revenues	$11,430,000
Cost of Goods Sold ($5,000,000 + $1,500,000 -$1,000,000)	$ 5,500,000
Other Expenses ($3,000,000 + $1,800,000 + $128,000 - $100,000 - $30,000 - $100,000)	4,698,000
Goodwill Impairment Loss	140,000
Total Expenses	$10,338,000
Combined Income	$ 1,092,000
Non-Controlling Interest [(20%)($500,000)]*	100,000
Consolidated Net Income	$ 1,192,000

*Note that due to the loss of Senile, the Non-Controlling Interest is an addition to consolidated Net Income rather than the usual reduction.

Part B - Consolidated Statement Of Retained Earnings   The opening balance of consolidated Retained Earnings consists of the Puberty Company's opening balance of $8,000,000 plus the allocation of $792,000 that was established in Step C. Beginning with this total of $8,792,000, the consolidated Statement of Retained Earnings for the Puberty Company and its subsidiary, the Senile Company is as follows:

Puberty Company and Subsidiary
Consolidated Statement Of Retained Earnings
For The Year Ending December 31, 2008

Opening Consolidated Retained Earnings	$8,792,000
Consolidated Net Income (From Part A)	1,192,000
Balance Available	$9,984,000
Dividends (Puberty's Only)	400,000
Closing Consolidated Retained Earnings	$9,584,000

The closing balance of consolidated Retained Earnings can be verified as follows:

Puberty's Closing Retained Earnings	$9,600,000
Equity Pickup ([80%][$2,400,000 - $2,000,000])	320,000
Fair Value Depreciation On Plant	(896,000)
Fair Value Amortization On Long-Term Liabilities	700,000
Goodwill Impairment Loss	(140,000)
Closing Consolidated Retained Earnings	$9,584,000

Part C - Consolidated Balance Sheet   The consolidated Balance Sheet for the Puberty Company and its subsidiary, the Senile Company is as follows:

Puberty Company and Subsidiary
Consolidated Balance Sheet
As At December 31, 2008

Cash and Current Receivables ($1,100,000 + $400,000 - $15,000 - $100,000)	$ 1,385,000
Long-Term Receivables ($1,000,000 + $200,000 -$500,000)	700,000
Inventories ($4,000,000 + $1,300,000)	5,300,000
Plant and Equipment (Net) ($6,000,000 + $4,000,000 + $3,200,000 - $896,000)	12,304,000
Investment in Senile ($4,000,000 - $4,000,000)	-0-
Goodwill ($1,000,000 - $800,00 + $800,000 - $140,000)	860,000
Total Assets	$20,549,000

Current Liabilities ($300,000 + $400,000 - $15,000 - $100,000)	$ 585,000
Notes Payable ($200,000 + $600,000 - $500,000)	300,000
Long-Term Liabilities ($2,000,000 + $2,500,000 + $1,600,000 - $700,000)	5,400,000
Non-Controlling Interest [(20%)($3,400,000)]	680,000
Common Stock - No Par Value (Puberty's Only)	4,000,000
Retained Earnings	9,584,000
Total Equities	$20,549,000

Solution to Self Study Problem Five - 5

Part A Solution - Consolidated Net Income   Since the book value of Savage at acquisition was $1,000,000 and there were no fair value changes, the purchase of 80 percent of the shares for $800,000 in cash means that there was no Goodwill in this business combination.

As the Saber T. Company shares were purchased on December 31, 2007, the equity pickup includes only the income of Savage. The 2007 consolidated Net Income is as follows:

Primate's Net Income	$400,000
Intercompany Dividends [(80%)($100,000)]	(80,000)
Equity Pickup [(80%)($200,000)]	160,000
Consolidated Net Income	$480,000

Part A Solution - Consolidated Statement Of Retained Earnings   The opening balance that is required for this Statement is calculated as follows:

Primate's Opening Balance	$3,000,000
Equity Pickup In Savage [(80%)($1,000,000 - $500,000)]	400,000
Opening Balance	$3,400,000

Using this opening balance, the required consolidated Statement Of Retained Earnings would be prepared as follows:

Opening Balance	$3,400,000
Consolidated Net Income	480,000
Balance Available	$3,880,000
Dividends Declared (Primate's Only)	(200,000)
Closing Balance	$3,680,000

The closing balance of consolidated Retained Earnings can be verified as follows:

Primate's Closing Balance	$3,200,000
Equity Pickup [(80%)($1,100,000 - $500,000)]	480,000
Closing Balance	$3,680,000

Part B - Consolidated Cash Flow Statement - A number of items must be calculated before this statement can be prepared. The first is the combined Depreciation Expense:

Combined Plant and Equipment	
December 31, 2006 ($1,490,000 + $700,000)	$2,190,000
Purchase By Savage (For Long-Term Bonds)	100,000
Purchase by Primate	400,000
Cost of Plant and Equipment Sold by Primate	(300,000)
Accumulated Depreciation on Plant Sold	200,000
Total	$2,590,000
Combined Plant and Equipment	
December 31, 2007 ($1,590,000 + $750,000)	(2,340,000)
Depreciation Expense	$ 250,000

In order to determine cash from operations, it is necessary to have the change in non-cash working capital items for the year. This calculation is as follows (the 2007 figures include the balances of Saber T. Company):

| | December 31 | | Change |
	2007	2006	
Accounts Receivable	$1,150,000	$ 700,000	$450,000
Inventories	1,800,000	1,400,000	400,000
Current Liabilities	(2,000,000)	(1,500,000)	(500,000)
Totals	$ 950,000	$ 600,000	$350,000

The acquisition of Saber T. Company resulted in an increase of $500,000 in non-cash working capital items ($200,000 in Accounts Receivable, $400,000 in Inventories, less the $100,000 in Current Liabilities). This means that, since the overall change calculated in the preceding schedule was only $350,000, consolidated operations must have resulted in a decrease of $150,000 ($350,000 - $500,000) in non-cash working capital items.

Using the preceding calculations, we can now provide the required schedule which reconciles consolidated Net Income with cash from operating activities. The calculation is as follows:

Consolidated Net Income	$480,000
Depreciation Expense	250,000
Non-Controlling Interest in Savage [(20%)($200,000)]	40,000
Equity Pickup In Mastodon [(30%)($100,000 - $50,000)]	(15,000)
Gain On Sale Of Plant by Primate	(100,000)
Total Working Capital From Operations	$655,000
Decrease In Non-Cash Working Capital Items	150,000
Cash From Operating Activities	$805,000

A further calculation is required to determine the dividend figure to be include in the consolidated Cash Flow Statement. While only the parent company's dividends are deducted in the consolidated Statement of Retained Earnings, all dividends involving cash outflows must be included in the Statement Of Changes In Financial Position. This would include dividends paid to any non-controlling interests. In this problem the calculation is as follows:

Primate Company's Dividends	$200,000
Non-Controlling Interest's Share of Savage's Dividends [(20%)($100,000)]	20,000
Total Dividends Affecting Cash	$220,000

Using the preceding calculations, the consolidated Cash Flow Statement can be prepared. The following statement would comply with the Recommendations of Section 1540 of the *CICA Handbook*, including those relating to the disclosure of business combination transactions:

Primate Company And Subsidiaries
Consolidated Cash Flow Statement
For The Year Ending December 31, 2007

Cash Flows From (Used In):

Operating Activities
  Cash From Operating Activities $805,000

Financing Activities:
  Dividends Paid (Note One):
    To Primate Shareholders   ($200,000)
    To Non Controlling Interest   (20,000)   (220,000)

Investing Activities:
  Proceeds From The Sale Of Plant by Primate $200,000
  Proceeds From Sale of Land By Savage   100,000
  Land Acquired By Primate For Cash   (125,000)
  Plant Acquisitions Requiring Cash   (400,000)
  Acquisition of Saber T. Company:
    Net Cash Outflow (Note Two)   (300,000)   (525,000)

Increase in Cash (Note Three) $ 60,000

Note One   Paragraph 1540.35 indicates that dividends not included in the determination of Net Income should be classified according to their nature. This Paragraph requires that dividends charged to Retained Earnings should be classified as a financing activity. It also requires that dividends paid to a non-controlling interest be given separate disclosure as a financing activity.

Note Two   On December 31, 2007, Primate acquired 100 percent of the outstanding voting shares of Saber T. Company. The acquisition included Goodwill of $100,000 ($500,000 + $1,000,000 - $500,000 - $700,000 - $200,000). Details of the transaction are as follows:

Cash Acquired $ 200,000
Other Assets Acquired (Includes Fair Value
    Change On Plant And Goodwill)   1,400,000

Total Assets Acquired $1,600,000
Liabilities Assumed   (100,000)

Total Purchase Price $1,500,000
Shares Issued   (1,000,000)

Cash Paid $ 500,000
Cash Acquired From Saber T. Company   (200,000)

Net Cash Outflow $ 300,000

Note Three   The increase in cash calculated from the Balance Sheets totals $60,000 ($1,060,000 + $200,000 - $1,200,000) which reconciles with the Cash Flow Statement. This reconciliation is required by Paragraph 1540.48.

Note Four - Other Matters   The issuance of long-term bonds in return for $100,000 of Plant And Equipment would not be included in the Cash Flow Statement. It would, however, have to be disclosed somewhere in the financial statements or the accompanying notes.

The disclosure of the nature of cash and cash equivalents is required. As the Cash Flow Statement is based only on cash, additional disclosure is not required.

Section 1540 requires separate disclosure of the cash paid for interest and income taxes that was included in the determination of Net Income for the period. Given that the problem does not provide Income Statement details, it is not possible to provide this information.

Solution to Chapter Six Exercises

Exercise Six-1 Solution
The required consolidated Income Statement would be prepared as follows:

Part Company and Subsidiary
Consolidated Income Statement
Year Ending December 31, 2002

Revenues ($982,000 + $463,000 - $75,000 - $82,000)	$1,288,000
Expenses:	
Cost of Goods Sold ($448,000 + $219,000 - $82,000)	$ 585,000
Other Expenses ($374,000 + $115,000)	489,000
Non-Controlling Interest [(35%)($129,000 - $75,000)]	18,900
Total Expenses	$1,092,900
Income Before Results Of Discontinued Operations	$ 195,100
Loss From Discontinued Operations [(65%)($63,000)]	(40,950)
Net Income	$ 154,150

The Revenues are reduced by the $75,000 sale of land. The Revenues and Cost Of Goods Sold are both reduced by the $82,000 in intercompany sales. The final Net Income figure can be verified by noting that it is equal to Part's $160,000, less the (negative) equity pickup of $5,850 [(65%)($66,000 - $75,000)].

Exercise Six-2 Solution
The following investment analysis and investment elimination entry are identical to those used in Exercise Five-2.

Step A Procedures   The required investment analysis would be as follows:

	65 Percent	100 Percent
Investment Cost	$1,350,000	$2,076,923
Book Value At Acquisition	(1,105,000)	(1,700,000)
Differential	$ 245,000	$ 376,923
Fair Value Increase On Non-Monetary Assets	(97,500)	(150,000)
Goodwill	$ 147,500	$ 226,923

The fair value change on the Non-Monetary Assets would be amortized at the rate of $6,500 per year ($97,500 ÷ 15).

Based on this schedule, the investment elimination entry would be as follows:

No Par Common Stock	$ 700,000	
Retained Earnings (At Acquisition Balance)	1,000,000	
Non-Monetary Assets	97,500	
Goodwill	147,500	
Investment In Schaffer		$1,350,000
Non-Controlling Interest [(35%)($1,700,000)]		595,000

Step B Procedures

The entry to eliminate the intercompany receivables would be as follows:

Liabilities	$15,000	
Monetary Assets		$15,000

The entry to record the fair value write-off of non-monetary assets would be as follows:

Retained Earnings [(4)($6,500)]	$26,000	
Total Expenses (Amortization)	6,500	
Non-Monetary Assets		$32,500

The entry to record the 2004 and current goodwill impairment would be as follows:

Retained Earnings	$35,000	
Loss On Goodwill Impairment	25,000	
Goodwill		$60,000

The entry to eliminate the intercompany sales would be as follows:

Sales	$85,000	
Total Expenses (Cost Of Goods Sold)		$85,000

The entry to eliminate the intercompany profit in the closing inventories of Parker would be as follows:

Total Expenses (Cost Of Goods Sold)	$12,750	
Inventories		$12,750
[($85,000)(1/2)(30%)]		

The gain on the intercompany equipment sale is $20,000 ($120,000 - $100,000). This amount would be recognized at the rate of $5,000 per year over the four year remaining life of the asset. The required entry would be as follows:

Retained Earnings ($20,000 - $5,000)	$15,000	
Total Expenses (Amortization)		
[($120,000 - $100,000) ÷ 4]		$ 5,000
Non-Monetary Assets [$20,000 - (2)($5,000)]		10,000

The entry to eliminate the subsidiary Dividends Declared would be as follows:

Dividend Revenue	$32,500	
Non-Controlling Interest (Balance Sheet)	17,500	
Dividends Declared		$50,000

Step C - Distribution Of Subsidiary Retained Earnings

Balance As Per The Trial Balance	$1,550,000
Balance At Acquisition	(1,000,000)
Balance Since Acquisition	$ 550,000
Unrealized Upstream Gain On Equipment	(15,000)
Adjusted Balance Since Acquisition	$ 535,000
Non-Controlling Interest [(35%)($535,000)]	(187,250)
Available To The Controlling Interest	$ 347,750
Step B Adjustments:	
Plant And Equipment (4 Years At $6,500)	(26,000)
Goodwill Impairment (From 2004)	(35,000)
To Consolidated Retained Earnings	$ 286,750

Based on this Schedule, the Retained Earnings distribution entry would be as follows:

Retained Earnings	$474,000	
Non-Controlling Interest (Balance Sheet)		$187,250
Consolidated Retained Earnings		286,750

Consolidated Income Statement   The required consolidated Income Statement would be prepared as follows:

Parker Company And Subsidiary
Consolidated Income Statement
Year Ending December 31, 2006

Sales ($3,225,000 + $675,000 - $85,000)	$3,815,000
Dividend Revenue ($32,500 - $32,500)	Nil
Total Revenues	$3,815,000
Expenses And Losses:	
Total Expenses ($2,940,000 + $530,000	
- $85,000 + $6,500 + $12,750 - $5,000)	$3,399,250
Non-Controlling Interest	
[(35%)($145,000 - $12,750 + $5,000)]	48,038
Goodwill Impairment Loss	25,000
Total Expenses And Losses	$3,472,288
Net Income	$ 342,712

Consolidated Statement Of Retained Earnings   The required consolidated Statement Of Retained Earnings would be prepared as follows:

Parker Company And Subsidiary
Consolidated Statement Of Retained Earnings
Year Ending December 31, 2006

Opening Balance ($5,895,000 + $286,750)	$6,181,750
Consolidated Net Income	342,712
Available For Distribution	$6,524,462
Dividends (Parker's Only)	(250,000)
Closing Balance	$6,274,462

Consolidated Balance Sheet   The required consolidated Balance Sheet would be prepared as follows:

Parker Company And Subsidiary
Consolidated Balance Sheet
At December 31, 2006

Monetary Assets ($2,850,000 + $725,000 - $15,000)	$ 3,560,000
Investment In Schaffer ($1,350,000 - $1,350,000)	Nil
Non-Monetary Assets ($6,475,000 + $2,045,000	
+ $97,500 - $32,500 - $12,750 - $10,000)	8,562,250
Goodwill ($147,500 - $35,000 - $25,000)	87,500
Total Assets	$12,209,750
Liabilities ($1,712,500 + $425,000 - $15,000)	$ 2,122,500
Non-Controlling Interest [(35%)($700,000	
+ $1,645,000 - $12,750 - $10,000)]	812,788
No Par Common Stock (Parker's Only)	3,000,000
Retained Earnings (See Statement)	6,274,462
Total Equities	$12,209,750

Exercise Six-3 Solution

The following investment analysis and investment elimination entry are identical to those used in Exercise Six-2 (and Five-2 and Five-3).

Step A Procedures   The required investment analysis would be as follows:

	65 Percent	100 Percent
Investment Cost	$1,350,000	$2,076,923
Book Value At Acquisition	(1,105,000)	(1,700,000)
Differential	$ 245,000	$ 376,923
Fair Value Increase On Non-Monetary Assets	(97,500)	(150,000)
Goodwill	$ 147,500	$ 226,923

The fair value change on the Non-Monetary Assets would be amortized at the rate of $6,500 per year ($97,500 ÷ 15).

Based on this schedule, the investment elimination entry would be as follows:

No Par Common Stock	$ 700,000	
Retained Earnings (At Acquisition Balance)	1,000,000	
Non-Monetary Assets	97,500	
Goodwill	147,500	
Investment In Schaffer		$1,350,000
Non-Controlling Interest [(35%)($1,700,000)]		595,000

Step B Procedures

The entry to eliminate the intercompany receivables would be as follows:

Liabilities	$15,000	
Monetary Assets		$15,000

The entry to record the fair value write-off of non-monetary assets would be as follows:

Retained Earnings [(5)($6,500)] $32,500
    Non-Monetary Assets $32,500

The entry to record the 2004 and current goodwill impairment would be as follows:

Retained Earnings $60,000
    Goodwill $60,000

The entry to record the intercompany profit in the inventories would be as follows:

Retained Earnings [($85,000)(1/2)(30%)] $12,750
    Inventories $12,750

The entry to record the remaining unrealized intercompany profit on the sale of equipment would be as follows:

Retained Earnings [$20,000 - (2)($5,000)] $10,000
    Non-Monetary Assets $10,000

Entries to eliminate the intercompany sales and subsidiary dividends would not be required in this closed trial balance problem.

Step C - Distribution Of Subsidiary Retained Earnings

Balance As Per The Trial Balance		$1,645,000
Balance At Acquisition		(1,000,000)
Balance Since Acquisition		$ 645,000
Unrealized Profit In Inventories	($12,750)	
Unrealized Profit In Non-Monetary Assets	(10,000)	(22,750)
Adjusted Balance Since Acquisition		$ 622,250
Non-Controlling Interest [(35%)($622,250)]		(217,788)
Available To The Controlling Interest		$ 404,462
Step B Adjustments:		
Plant And Equipment (5 Years At $6,500)		(32,500)
Goodwill Impairment ($35,000 + $25,000)		(60,000)
To Consolidated Retained Earnings		$ 311,962

Based on this Schedule, the Retained Earnings distribution entry would be as follows:

Retained Earnings $529,750
    Non-Controlling Interest (Balance Sheet) $217,788
    Consolidated Retained Earnings   311,962

Consolidated Balance Sheet   The required consolidated Balance Sheet would be prepared as follows:

Parker Company And Subsidiary
Consolidated Balance Sheet
At December 31, 2006

Monetary Assets ($2,850,000 + $725,000 - $15,000)	$ 3,560,000
Investment In Schaffer ($1,350,000 - $1,350,000)	Nil
Non-Monetary Assets ($6,475,000 + $2,045,000	
+ $97,500 - $32,500 -12,750 - 10,000)	8,562,250
Goodwill ($147,500 - $35,000 - $25,000)	87,500
Total Assets	$12,209,750

Liabilities ($1,712,500 + $425,000 - $15,000)	$ 2,122,500
Non-Controlling Interest [(35%)($700,000	
+ $1,645,000 - $12,750 - $10,000)]	812,788
No Par Common Stock (Parker's Only)	3,000,000
Retained Earnings ($5,962,500 + $311,962)	6,274,462
Total Equities	$12,209,750

Exercise Six-4 Solution

The following investment analysis is identical to the one used in Exercise Six-2 (and Five-4).

	65 Percent	100 Percent
Investment Cost	$1,350,000	$2,076,923
Book Value At Acquisition	(1,105,000)	(1,700,000)
Differential	$ 245,000	$ 376,923
Fair Value Increase On Non-Monetary Assets	(97,500)	(150,000)
Goodwill	$ 147,500	$ 226,923

The fair value change on the Non-Monetary Assets would be amortized at the rate of $6,500 per year ($97,500 ÷ 15).

Using this analysis, along with the other information, Investment Income under the equity method would be calculated as follows:

Parker's Net Income		$145,000
Unrealized Upstream Profits:		
Inventories	($12,750)	
Equipment	5,000	(7,750)
Parker's Adjusted Net Income		$137,250
Ownership Percentage		65%
Equity Pickup		$ 89,212
Fair Value Amortization ($97,500 ÷ 15)		(6,500)
Goodwill Impairment Loss (Given)		(25,000)
Equity Method Investment Income		$57,712

Given this calculation, the required Income Statement would be as follows:

Parker Company
Income Statement
Years Ended December 31, 2006

Sales	$3,225,000
Investment Income	57,712
Dividend Revenue	Nil
Total Revenues	$3,282,712
Total Expenses	(2,940,000)
Net Income	$ 342,712

Note that this is the same Net Income that was disclosed in Exercise Six-2 when we prepared consolidated financial statements.

With respect to the Investment In Schaffer amount that would be included in Parker's single entity Balance Sheet under the equity method, it would be calculated as follows:

Investment In Schaffer At Cost		$1,350,000
Equity Pickup:		
Schaffer's December 31 Retained Earnings	$1,645,000	
Balance At Acquisition	(1,000,000)	
Balance Since Acquisition	$ 645,000	
Unrealized Inventory Profit	(12,750)	
Unrealized Gain On Non-Monetary Assets	(10,000)	
Adjusted Balance Since Acquisition	$ 622,250	
Parker's Share	65%	404,462
Adjustments:		
Fair Value Amortization [(5)($6,500)]		(32,500)
Loss On Goodwill Impairment ($35,000 + $25,000)		(60,000)
Investment In Schaffer At Equity		$1,661,962

This will result in an increase in Parker's assets of $311,962 ($1,661,962 - $1,350,000). Note that this increase is equal to the addition to consolidated Retained Earnings calculated in Step C in Exercise Six-3. To complete Parker's single entity Balance Sheet, the same amount will have to be added to the $5,962,500 Retained Earnings of Parker, resulting in a total of $6,274,462. Using these figures, the required Balance Sheet would be as follows:

Parker Company
Balance Sheet
As At December 31, 2006

Monetary Assets	$ 2,850,000
Investment In Schaffer	1,661,962
Non-Monetary Assets	6,475,000
Total Assets	$10,986,962
Liabilities	$ 1,712,500
No Par Common Stock	3,000,000
Retained Earnings	6,274,462
Total Equities	$10,986,962

Note that this is the same Retained Earnings figure that was disclosed in Exercises Six-2 and Six-3 when consolidated financial statements were prepared.

Exercise Six-5 Solution
Step A Investment Analysis   The analysis of the Investment in Subco is as follows:

	80 Percent	100 Percent
Cost	$1,000,000	$1,250,000
Book Value	(960,000)	(1,200,000)
Differential	$ 40,000	$ 50,000
Fair Value Decrease On Inventories	320,000	400,000
Fair Value Increase On Plant And Equipment	(240,000)	(300,000)
Goodwill	$ 120,000	$ 150,000

The fair value change on equipment will be amortized over 10 years at the rate of $24,000 per year.

Part A - Consolidated Net Income   The required calculation of consolidated Net Income would be as follows:

Parco's Net Income (Loss)		($300,000)
Less: Intercompany Dividends [(80%)($400,000)]		(320,000)
Equity Pickup:		
Subco's Net Income	$500,000	
Upstream Unrealized Profits (Losses)		
Unrealized Loss On Sale Of Land	200,000	
Unrealized Closing Inventory Profits	(40,000)	
Adjusted Subco Net Income	$660,000	
Controlling Interest's Share	80%	528,000
Fair Value Depreciation on Equipment ($240,000/10)		(24,000)
Consolidated Net Income (Loss)		($116,000)

Part B   In order to prepared a consolidated Cash Flow Statement, several calculations are required. The first is consolidated Amortization Expense.

Combined Plant On December 31, 2006 ($6,400,000 + $800,000)	$7,200,000
Write-Down By Parco During The Year	(800,000)
Total	$6,400,000
Combined Plant On December 31, 2007 ($4,800,000 + $600,000)	(5,400,000)
Total Single Entity Amortization Expense for 2007	$1,000,000
Fair Value Increase Amortization	24,000
Consolidated Amortization Expense for 2007	$1,024,000

Consolidated cash from operating activities would be calculated as follows:

Consolidated Net Income (Loss)	($ 116,000)
Consolidated Amortization Expense	1,024,000
Plant Write-Down (Parco)	800,000
Amortization Of Bond Premium (Subco)	(5,000)
Non-Controlling Interest In Subco's Income	
[(20%)($500,000 + $200,000 - $40,000)]	132,000
Cash Increase Before Current Asset Changes	$1,835,000
Cash From Decrease in Accounts Receivable	
($1,500,000 + $900,000 - $1,800,000 - $650,000 - $100,000)	150,000
Cash From Decrease in Inventories	
($2,000,000 + $800,000 - $2,600,000 - $500,000 - $40,000)	340,000
Cash Used For Decrease in Accounts Payable	
($400,000 + $700,000 - $1,000,000 - $750,000 - $100,000)	(750,000)
Cash From Operating Activities	$1,575,000

The increase in cash for the year is $495,000 ($800,000 + $365,000 - $400,000 - $270,000).

Given the preceding calculations, the required consolidated Cash Flow Statement is prepared as follows:

Parco Company And Subsidiary
Consolidated Cash Flow Statement
For The Year Ending December 31, 2007

Cash Flows From (Used In):

Operating Activities		
Cash From Operating Activities		$1,575,000
Financing Activities		
Retirement of Long Term Debt	($1,000,000)	
Dividends Paid To Non-Controlling Interest		
[(20%)($400,000)]	(80,000)	(1,080,000)
Investing Activities*		Nil
Increase in Cash		$ 495,000

*While Parco acquired $200,000 in Land and Subco sold Land with a carrying value of $400,000, it was an intercompany transaction and would be eliminated in the consolidation process.

Exercise Six - 6 Solution
The analysis of the investments would be as follows:

	40 Percent	100 Percent
Investment Cost	$1,875,000	$4,687,500
Book Value - Net Assets	(1,300,000)	(3,250,000)
Differential	$ 575,000	$1,437,500
Fair Value Increase On Plant And Equipment	(290,000)	(725,000)
Goodwill	$ 285,000	$ 712,500

	15 Percent	100 Percent
Investment Cost	$820,000	$5,466,667
Book Value - Net Assets	(637,500)	(4,250,000)
Differential	$182,500	$1,216,667
Fair Value Increase On Plant And Equipment	(105,000)	(700,000)
Goodwill	$ 77,500	$ 516,667

Part A   The Plant And Equipment balance would be calculated as follows:

Best's Balance		$3,520,000
Worst's Balance		1,600,000
Fair Value Increase - 1st Purchase	$290,000	
Amortization [($290,000 ÷ 4)(2)]	(145,000)	145,000
Fair Value Increase - 2nd Purchase	$105,000	
Amortization [($105,000 ÷ 3)(1)]	(35,000)	70,000
Consolidated Plant And Equipment		$5,335,000

Part B   Consolidated Goodwill would be $362,500 ($285,000 + $77,500).

Part C   The consolidated Retained Earnings would be calculated as follows:

In this calculation, we would have to recognize that there was an unrealized upstream profit on the 2003 Land sale of $50,000 ($250,000 - $200,000), as well as an unrealized upstream profit on the 2004 sale of merchandise of $37,500 [($450,000)(1/3)(25%)]. The unrealized land profit affects the equity pickup of only the first purchase as it occurred before the second purchase. Using this information, the calculation would be as follows:

Best's Balance		$4,275,000
Equity Pickup:		
1st Purchase [(40%)($2,450,000 - $1,250,000 - $50,000 - $37,500)]	$445,000	
2nd Purchase [(15%)($2,450,000 - $2,250,000 - $37,500)]	24,375	469,375
Amortization Of Fair Value Increase ($145,000 + $35,000)		(180,000)
Consolidated Retained Earnings		$4,564,375

The equity pickup could also be calculated as $380,000 [(40%)($2,250,000 - $1,250,000 - $50,000)] plus $89,375 [(55%)($2,450,000 - $2,250,000 - $37,500)], an approach which gives the same $469,375 total as the calculation in the table.

Solution to Self Study Problem Six - 1

Investment Analysis   The analysis of the Pastel Company's Investment In Shade as at the acquisition date is as follows:

	90 Percent	100 Percent
Purchase Price	$5,175,000	$5,750,000
Book Value	(5,400,000)	(6,000,000)
Differential	($ 225,000)	($ 250,000)
Fair Value Decrease On Equipment	900,000	1,000,000
Fair Value Increase On Land	(90,000)	(100,000)
Fair Value Decrease On Receivables	45,000	50,000
Fair Value Decrease On Long-Term Liabilities	(180,000)	(200,000)
Goodwill	$ 450,000	$ 500,000

Step A - Investment Elimination   The journal entry that would be required to eliminate the Pastel Company's Investment In Shade would be as follows:

Common Stock - No Par	$2,000,000	
Retained Earnings	4,000,000	
Land	90,000	
Long-Term Liabilities	180,000	
Goodwill	450,000	
Investment In Shade		$5,175,000
Equipment (Net)		900,000
Accounts Receivable		45,000
Non-Controlling Interest		600,000

Step B - Depreciation Of The Fair Value Change On Equipment   The entry to record the reduction in Depreciation Expense related to the fair value change on the Equipment would be as follows:

Equipment (Net)	$450,000	
Depreciation Expense		$ 90,000
Retained Earnings		360,000

(Annual Adjustment = $900,000/10 = $90,000)

Step B - Fair Value Change On Land   No adjustment is required.

Step B - Realization Of The Fair Value Change On Accounts Receivable   The entry to record the realization of the fair value change on Accounts Receivable is as follows:

Accounts Receivable	$45,000	
Retained Earnings		$45,000

Step B - Amortization Of The Fair Value Change On The Liabilities   The entry to record the increase in Other Expenses (interest expense) related to the fair value change on Liabilities is as follows:

Other Expenses	$ 36,000	
Retained Earnings	144,000	
Long-Term Liabilities		$180,000

(Annual Adjustment = $180,000/5 = $36,000)

Step B - Goodwill Impairment Loss   The entry to record the Goodwill Impairment Loss is as follows:

Goodwill Impairment Loss	$15,000	
Goodwill		$15,000

Step B - Intercompany Management Fees   Two entries are required here. The first is to eliminate the $100,000 in intercompany revenue and expense while the second is required to eliminate the intercompany asset and liability. The entries are as follows:

Other Revenues	$100,000	
Other Expenses		$100,000
Current Liabilities	$100,000	
Current Receivables		$100,000

Step B - Intercompany Merchandise Sales   Two entries are also required here. The first will eliminate the total intercompany merchandise sales of $650,000 ($500,000 upstream + $150,000 downstream) while the second will eliminate the intercompany asset and liability of $225,000 ($75,000 upstream + $150,000 downstream). The entries are as follows:

Sales	$650,000	
Cost Of Goods Sold		$650,000
Current Liabilities	$225,000	
Current Receivables		$225,000

Step B - Unrealized Intercompany Inventory Profits   Two entries are required to eliminate the unrealized intercompany profits in both the opening inventories and the closing inventories. The unrealized opening inventory profits equal $240,000 [(60%)($300,000) + $60,000] while the unrealized inventory profits in the closing inventories equal $165,000 [(60%)($125,000] + $90,000]. The entries are as follows:

Retained Earnings	$240,000	
Cost of Goods Sold		$240,000
Cost of Goods Sold	$165,000	
Inventories		$165,000

Step B - Realization Of Equipment Sale Loss   The piece of equipment was sold at a loss of $30,000 ($120,000 - $150,000) on January 1, 2004. This upstream loss will be realized through an increase of Depreciation Expense of $2,000 per year ($30,000/15). The entry to record this adjustment is as follows:

Depreciation Expense	$ 2,000	
Equipment (Net)	22,000	
Retained Earnings		$24,000

Step B - Elimination Of Gain On Land And Building Sale   The total gain of $500,000 must be eliminated against the Building and Land accounts by the amounts that they have been increased over their carrying values on Pastel's books. The entry to record this adjustment is as follows:

Gain on Sale of Land	$500,000	
Building (Net)		$300,000
Land		200,000

Step B - Intercompany Dividends   Two entries are required here. The first will eliminate the intercompany Dividends Declared against the Other Revenues and Non-Controlling Interest, while the second will be required to eliminate the unpaid balance from the consolidated assets and liabilities. The entries are as follows:

Other Revenues	$90,000	
Non-Controlling Interest (Balance Sheet)	10,000	
Dividends Declared		$100,000

Dividends Payable	$90,000	
Current Receivables		$ 90,000

Step C - Distribution Of Retained Earnings   The analysis of the opening balance of the Shade Company's Retained Earnings is as follows:

Retained Earnings - Opening Balance	$5,500,000
Balance At Acquisition	(4,000,000)
Balance Since Acquisition	$1,500,000
Unrealized Upstream Opening (Profits) Losses:	
Inventories	(180,000)
Sale of Equipment	24,000
Realized Profits Since Acquisition	$1,344,000
Non-Controlling Interest [(10%)($1,344,000)]	(134,400)
Available To The Controlling Interest	$1,209,600
Fair Value Depreciation On Equipment	360,000
Fair Value Realization On Accounts Receivable	45,000
Fair Value Amortization On Long-Term Liabilities	(144,000)
To Consolidated Retained Earnings	$1,490,600

Based on the preceding analysis, the journal entry required to distribute the opening Retained Earnings balance of the Shade Company is as follows:

Retained Earnings - Shade	$1,605,000	
Consolidated Retained Earnings		$1,470,600
Non-Controlling Interest		134,400

Part A - Consolidated Income Statement   The consolidated Income Statement for the Pastel Company and its subsidiary, the Shade Company, is as follows:

Pastel Company and Subsidiary
Consolidated Income Statement
For The Year Ending December 31, 2007

Sales ($8,000,000 + $2,000,000 - $650,000)	$ 9,350,000
Gain on Sale of Land ($500,000 - $500,000)	- 0 -
Other Revenues ($800,000 + $100,000 - $100,000 - $90,000)	710,000
Total Revenues	$10,060,000
Cost Of Goods Sold ($3,800,000 + $800,000	
- $650,000 - $240,000 + $165,000)	$ 3,875,000
Depreciation Expense ($1,400,000 + $300,000	
- $90,000 + $2,000)	1,612,000
Other Expenses ($2,000,000 + $400,000 + $36,000 - $100,000)	2,336,000
Goodwill Impairment Loss	15,000
Non-Controlling Interest [(10%)($600,000 + $180,000	
- $75,000 - $2,000)]	70,300
Total Expenses	$ 7,908,300
Consolidated Net Income	$ 2,151,700

Part B - Consolidated Statement Of Retained Earnings   The opening balance of consoli-dated Retained Earnings consists of the Pastel Company's opening balance in the amount of $18,100,000 plus the $1,470,600 allocation that was established in Step C less the down-stream unrealized opening inventory profits of $60,000.   Beginning with this total of $19,510,600, the consolidated Statement Of Retained Earnings for the Pastel Company and its subsidiary, the Shade Company, is as follows:

Pastel Company and Subsidiary
Consolidated Statement Of Retained Earnings
For The Year Ending December 31, 2007

Opening Consolidated Retained Earnings	$19,510,600
Net Income (From Part A)	2,151,700
Balance Available	$21,662,300
Less Dividends Declared (Pastel's Only)	200,000
Closing Consolidated Retained Earnings	$21,462,300

Verification Of The Closing Balance   The closing balance in the consolidated Retained Earnings can be verified as follows:

Pastel's Closing Retained Earnings	$20,000,000
Equity Pickup [(90%)($6,000,000 - $4,000,000	
- $75,000 + $22,000)]	1,752,300
Fair Value Depreciation On Equipment	450,000
Fair Value Realization On Accounts Receivable	45,000
Fair Value Amortization On Long-Term Liabilities	(180,000)
Goodwill Impairment Loss	(15,000)
Downstream Unrealized Closing Intercompany Profits:	
On Inventories	(90,000)
On Building and Land Sale	(500,000)
Closing Consolidated Retained Earnings	$21,462,300

Part C - Consolidated Balance Sheet   The consolidated Balance Sheet for the Pastel Company and its subsidiary, the Shade Company, is as follows:

Pastel Company and Subsidiary
Consolidated Balance Sheet
As At December 31, 2007

Cash And Current Receivables ($2,625,000 + $800,000	
- $45,000 + $45,000 - $100,000 - $225,000 - $90,000)	$ 3,010,000
Inventories ($8,000,000 + $2,000,000 - $165,000)	9,835,000
Equipment (Net)($24,000,000 + $4,000,000	
- $900,000 + $450,000 + $22,000)	27,572,000
Buildings (Net)($10,000,000 + $2,000,000 - $300,000)	11,700,000
Investment In Shade ($5,175,000 - $5,175,000)	-0-
Land ($2,000,000 + $1,200,000 + $90,000 - $200,000)	3,090,000
Goodwill ($450,000 - $15,000)	435,000
Total Assets	$55,642,000
Dividends Payable ($100,000 - $90,000)	$ 10,000
Current Liabilities ($1,800,000 + $900,000 - $100,000 - $225,000)	2,375,000
Long-Term Liabilities ($10,000,000 + $1,000,000	
- $180,000 + $180,000)	11,000,000
Non-Controlling Interest [(10%)($8,000,000	
- $75,000 + $22,000)]	794,700
Common Stock (Pastel's Only)	20,000,000
Retained Earnings (See Part B)	21,462,300
Total Equities	$55,642,000

Solution to Self Study Problem Six - 2

Step A - Investment Analysis   The analysis of the Investment in Stone is as follows:

	80 Percent	100 Percent
Cost	$7,800,000	$9,750,000
Book Value	(5,600,000)	(7,000,000)
Differential	$2,200,000	$2,750,000
Fair Value Increase On Inventories	(800,000)	(1,000,000)
Fair Value Decrease On Land	400,000	500,000
Fair Value Increase On Plant And Equipment (Net)	(1,600,000)	(2,000,000)
Fair Value Increase On Software	(400,000)	(500,000)
Fair Value Increase On Long-Term Liabilities	1,200,000	1,500,000
Goodwill	$1,000,000	$1,250,000

Step A - Elimination Entry   The Step A journal entry that would be required to eliminate the Investment would be as follows:

Common Stock - No Par	$3,000,000	
Retained Earnings	3,000,000	
Reserve For Contingencies	1,000,000	
Inventories	800,000	
Software	400,000	
Goodwill	1,000,000	
Plant and Equipment	1,600,000	
Accumulated Depreciation (Note)	3,000,000	
Plant And Equipment (Note)		$3,000,000
Land		400,000
Long-Term Liabilities		1,200,000
Investment In Stone		7,800,000
Non-Controlling Interest [(20%)($7,000,000)]		1,400,000

Note   The debit to Accumulated Depreciation and the credit to Plant and Equipment for $3 million is necessary since the accumulated depreciation of the acquired company cannot be brought forward to the consolidated books.

Step B - Adjustment   The entry to adjust the fair value increase on the acquisition date Inventories is as follows:

Retained Earnings	$800,000	
Inventories		$800,000

Step B - Adjustment   The entry to adjust the Plant And Equipment for the depreciation on the fair value change is as follows:

Retained Earnings	$320,000	
Other Expenses	80,000	
Accumulated Depreciation		$400,000
(Annual Adjustment = $1,600,000/20 = $80,000)		

Step B - Adjustment   The entry to adjust for the realization of the fair value change on the obsolete Software is as follows:

Retained Earnings	$400,000	
Software		$400,000

Step B - Adjustment   The entry to adjust the interest for the fair value change on the Long-Term Liabilities is as follows:

Long-Term Liabilities	$600,000	
Other Expenses ($1,200,000/10)		$120,000
Retained Earnings		480,000

Step B - Elimination   The entry to eliminate the intercompany dividend payment is as follows:

Total Revenues	$800,000	
Non-Controlling Interest (Balance Sheet)	200,000	
Dividends Declared		$1,000,000

Step B - Elimination   The entry to eliminate the unrealized profit on the intercompany sale of the Patent is as follows:

Retained Earnings	$800,000	
Other Expenses ($1,000,000/10)		$100,000
Patents		700,000

Step B - Elimination   The entry to eliminate the unrealized profit on the intercompany sale of Land is as follows:

Total Revenues	$500,000	
Land		$500,000

Step B - Elimination   The entry to eliminate intercompany sales of merchandise is as follows:

Total Revenues	$2,000,000	
Cost Of Goods Sold		$2,000,000

Step B - Elimination   The entry to eliminate unrealized intercompany profits in the closing inventories is as follows:

Cost Of Goods Sold [(30%)($500,000)]	$150,000	
Inventories		$150,000

Step B - Elimination   The entry to eliminate the unrealized intercompany profits in the opening inventories is as follows:

Retained Earnings [(30%)($800,000)]	$240,000	
Cost Of Goods Sold		$240,000

Step C - Distribution Schedule   The allocation of the balance in the Retained Earnings account of the Stone Company would be as follows:

Opening Balance		$6,700,000
Retained Earnings At Acquisition		(4,000,000)
Balance Since Acquisition		$2,700,000
Upstream Unrealized Profits:		
On Patent Sale	($800,000)	
Opening Inventories	(240,000)	(1,040,000)
Adjusted Balance Since Acquisition		$1,660,000
Non-Controlling Interest [(20%)($1,660,000)]		(332,000)
Available To Controlling Interest		$1,328,000
Fair Value Change On Inventory Realization		(800,000)
Fair Value Depreciation On Plant And Equipment		(320,000)
Fair Value Change On Software		(400,000)
Fair Value Amortization On Long-Term Liability		480,000
To Consolidated Retained Earnings		$ 288,000

Step C - Distribution Entry The entry to distribute the Stone Company's Retained Earnings as per the allocation in the preceding schedule is as follows:

Retained Earnings	$620,000	
Consolidated Retained Earnings		$288,000
Non-Controlling Interest		332,000

The opening consolidated Retained Earnings is $11,288,000, the total of Plate's opening Retained Earnings of $11,000,000 and the preceding $288,000 allocation to consolidated Retained Earnings.

Part A - Income Statement The required consolidated Income Statement would be prepared as follows:

The Plate Company And Subsidiary
Consolidated Income Statement
For The Year Ending December 31, 2007

Total Revenues ($16,500,000 + $7,000,000 - $800,000 - $500,000 - $2,000,000)	$20,200,000
Cost Of Goods Sold ($6,400,000 + $3,400,000 - $2,000,000 + $150,000 - $240,000)	$ 7,710,000
Other Expenses ($3,800,000 + $1,600,000 + $80,000 - $120,000 - $100,000)	5,260,000
Non-Controlling Interest [(20%)($2,000,000 + $100,000 - $150,000 + $240,000)]	438,000
Total Expenses	$13,408,000
Consolidated Net Income	$ 6,792,000

Part B - Statement Of Retained Earnings The required consolidated Statement Of Retained Earnings would be prepared as follows:

The Plate Company And Subsidiary
Consolidated Statement Of Retained Earnings
For The Year Ending December 31, 2007

Opening Balance	$11,288,000
Consolidated Net Income	6,792,000
Balance Available	$18,080,000
Dividends Declared (Plate Company's Only)	2,000,000
Closing Balance	$16,080,000

Part C - Balance Sheet   The required consolidated Balance Sheet would be prepared as follows:

The Plate Company And Subsidiary
Consolidated Balance Sheet
As At December 31, 2007

Cash ($3,000,000 + $700,000)	$ 3,700,000
Accounts Receivable ($7,500,000 + $2,100,000)	9,600,000
Inventories ($14,300,000 + $5,600,000	
+ $800,000 - $800,000 - $150,000)	19,750,000
Land ($9,000,000 + $2,500,000 - $400,000 - $500,000)	10,600,000
Plant And Equipment	
($26,400,000 + $12,000,000 - $1,400,000)	37,000,000
Accumulated Depreciation	
($10,600,000 + $6,500,000 - $3,000,000 + $400,000)	(14,500,000)
Patents ($1,400,000 - $700,000)	700,000
Goodwill (Note)	1,000,000
Total Assets	$67,850,000
Current Liabilities ($8,500,000 + $1,200,000)	$ 9,700,000
Long-Term Liabilities	
($15,000,000 + $4,500,000 + $1,200,000 - $600,000)	20,100,000
Non-Controlling Interest	
[(20%)($10,700,000 - $700,000 - $150,000)]	1,970,000
Common Stock (Plate Company's Only)	20,000,000
Retained Earnings (See Part B Solution)	16,080,000
Total Equities	$67,850,000

Note   As there has been no goodwill impairment loss in any year since the acquisition of Stone, the original value of $1,000,000 remains unchanged.

Solution to Self Study Problem Six - 3

Step A - Investment Analysis   The analysis of the Prime Company's investment in the Sublime Company would be as follows:

	60 Percent	100 Percent
Investment Cost	$3,000,000	$5,000,000
Book Value	(3,000,000)	(5,000,000)
Differential	$ -0-	$ -0-
Fair Value Decrease On Accounts Receivable	60,000	100,000
Fair Value Decrease On Plant And Equipment (Net)	240,000	400,000
Goodwill	$ 300,000	$ 500,000

Step A - Investment Elimination Entry   The entry to eliminate the Investment In Sublime would be as follows:

No Par Common Stock	$3,000,000	
Retained Earnings	2,000,000	
Goodwill	300,000	
Investment In Sublime		$3,000,000
Non-Controlling Interest		2,000,000
Current Receivables		60,000
Plant And Equipment (Net)		240,000

Step B - Adjustment   The entry to adjust the fair value change on the Accounts Receivable is as follows:

Current Receivables	$60,000	
Retained Earnings		$60,000

Step B - Adjustment   The entry to adjust the fair value change on Plant And Equipment would be as follows:

Plant And Equipment (Net)	$160,000	
Retained Earnings		$160,000

(Annual Adjustment = $240,000/3 = $80,000 Per Year)

Step B - Elimination   No elimination is required in the preparation of an end of the year Balance Sheet for the upstream profits that were unrealized at the beginning of the year. Sublime's cost for the merchandise that remains in Prime's Inventories is $160,000 ($200,000/1.25) resulting in an unrealized profit of $40,000. The entry to eliminate the unrealized profits of Sublime that are in the ending inventories of Prime is as follows:

Retained Earnings	$40,000	
Inventories		$40,000

Step B - Elimination   The entries to eliminate the unrealized loss on the intercompany sale of Plant And Equipment and the related asset/liability balance are as follows:

Plant And Equipment (Net)	$45,000	
Retained Earnings		$45,000

(Annual Adjustment = $50,000/5 = $10,000 Per Year. The remaining life on December 31, 2003 is 4.5 years.)

Current Liabilities [(80%)($150,000)]	$120,000	
Current Receivables		$120,000

Step B - Elimination   The entries to eliminate the intercompany profit on the sale of Land and the related asset/liability balance are as follows:

Retained Earnings	$1,000,000	
Land		$1,000,000
Current Liabilities (January 1, 2004)	$ 400,000	
Current Receivables		$ 400,000
Long-Term Liabilities	$1,200,000	
Long-Term Receivables		$1,200,000

Step C - Distribution Schedule   The schedule for the allocation of the balance in the Retained Earnings account of Sublime is as follows:

Sublime's Closing Balance		$5,000,000
Balance At Acquisition		(2,000,000)
Balance Since Acquisition		$3,000,000
Upstream Unrealized Profits:		
Closing Inventories	($40,000)	
Loss On Equipment	45,000	5,000
Adjusted Balance Since Acquisition		$3,005,000
Non-Controlling Interest [(40%)($3,005,000)]		(1,202,000)
Available To Controlling Interest		$1,803,000
Fair Value Decrease On Accounts Receivable		60,000
Fair Value Depreciation On Plant And Equipment		160,000
To Consolidated Retained Earnings		$2,023,000

Step C - Distribution Entry   The entry to allocate the remaining balance of Sublime's Retained Earnings would be as follows:

Retained Earnings	$3,225,000	
Non-Controlling Interest		$1,202,000
Consolidated Retained Earnings		2,023,000

The December 31, 2003 consolidated Retained Earnings would be made up of Prime's $12,000,000, the above allocation of $2,023,000, less the downstream unrealized profit on land of $1,000,000. This gives a total of $13,023,000.

Non-Controlling Interest   The Non-Controlling Interest shown on the consolidated Balance Sheet consists of the Non-Controlling Interest at acquisition of $2,000,000 from the Step A elimination entry and the Non-Controlling Interest since acquisition of $1,202,000 that was calculated in the Step C Retained Earnings distribution schedule.

Solution   The required consolidated Balance Sheet is as follows:

The Prime Company And Subsidiary
Consolidated Balance Sheet
As At December 31, 2003

Cash And Current Receivables ($1,600,000 + $1,000,000	
- $60,000 + $60,000 - $120,000 - $400,000)	$ 2,080,000
Inventories ($2,400,000 + $1,500,000 - $40,000)	3,860,000
Investment In Sublime ($3,000,000 - $3,000,000)	-0-
Long-Term Receivables ($1,500,000 - $1,200,000)	300,000
Plant And Equipment ($14,000,000 + $8,500,000	
- $240,000 + $160,000 + $45,000)	22,465,000
Land ($5,000,000 + $2,000,000 - $1,000,000)	6,000,000
Goodwill (Note)	300,000
Total Assets	$35,005,000
Current Liabilities ($4,500,000 + $2,000,000	
- $120,000 - $400,000)	$ 5,980,000
Long-Term Liabilities ($5,000,000 + $3,000,000 - $1,200,000)	6,800,000
Non-Controlling Interest ($2,000,000 + $1,202,000)	3,202,000
No Par Common Stock (Prime's Only)	6,000,000
Retained Earnings (See Step C)	13,023,000
Total Equities	$35,005,000

Note   As there has been no goodwill impairment loss in any year since the acquisition of Sublime, the original value of $300,000 remains unchanged.

Solution to Self Study Problem Six - 4

Step A - Investment Analysis   The analysis of the Pork Company's investment in Salt is as follows:

	80 Percent	100 Percent
Investment Cost	$1,000,000	$1,250,000
Book Value	(800,000)	(1,000,000)
Differential	$ 200,000	$ 250,000
Fair Value Decrease On Bonds Payable	(80,000)	(100,000)
Goodwill	$ 120,000	$ 150,000

Step B - Bonds Payable Adjustment   The amortization of the fair value change on the Bonds Payable will be charged to income at the rate of $8,000 per year ($80,000/10).

Step B - Realization Of The Gain On Building Sale   The total unrealized gain on the intercompany sale of the building was $375,000 ($4,500,000 - $4,125,000). This will be realized as a reduction in Other Expenses at the rate of $25,000 per year ($375,000/15).

Part A   The consolidated Income Statement is as follows:

The Pork Company And Subsidiary
Consolidated Income Statement
For The Year Ending December 31, 2005

Sales ($600,000 + $400,000)	$1,000,000
Cost Of Goods Sold ($250,000 + $300,000)	$ 550,000
Other Expenses ($300,000 + $150,000 + $8,000 - $25,000)	433,000
Goodwill Impairment Loss	40,000
Non Controlling Interest [(20%)(- $50,000 + $25,000)]	(5,000)
Total Expenses	$1,018,000
Income (Loss) Before Extraordinary Items	($ 18,000)
Extraordinary Gain (Pork's)	100,000
Extraordinary Loss [(80%)($200,000)]	(160,000)
Consolidated Net Income (Loss)	($ 78,000)

Part B   If we assume that the Pork Company uses the equity method to account for its investment in Salt, there are two alternate ways to adjust for the effects of the realization of the intercompany gain in its Income Statement. Paragraph 3050.15 of the *CICA Handbook* describes these alternatives as follows:

The elimination of an unrealized intercompany gain or loss has the same effect on net income whether the consolidation or equity method is used. However, in consolidated financial statements, the elimination of a gain or a loss may affect sales and cost of sales otherwise to be reported. In the application of the equity method, the gain or loss is eliminated by adjustment of investment income from the investee or by separate provision in the investor's financial statements, as is appropriate in the circumstances.

The solution which follows is based on an adjustment of Investment Income rather than disclosure through a separate provision. The Income Statement of the Pork Company would be as follows:

Pork Company
Income Statement
For The Year Ending December 31, 2005

Sales	$600,000
Cost Of Goods Sold	$250,000
Other Expenses	300,000
Investment Loss - Ordinary (Note One)	68,000
Total Expenses	$618,000
Income (Loss) Before Extraordinary Items	($ 18,000)
Extraordinary Gain	100,000
Investment Loss - Extraordinary [(80%)($200,000)]	(160,000)
Net Income (Loss)	($ 78,000)

Note One   The Ordinary Investment Loss would be calculated as follows:

Salt's Ordinary Income (Loss)	($50,000)
Realization Of Intercompany Gain	25,000
Adjusted Loss	($25,000)
Pork's Ownership Percent	80%
Pork's Share Of The Loss	($20,000)
Bonds Payable Amortization	(8,000)
Goodwill Impairment Loss	(40,000)
Ordinary Investment Loss	($78,000)

Pork's Net Loss of $78,000 when the equity method is used is equal to the previously calculated consolidated Net Loss. This result is a reflection of a requirement stated in Paragraph 3050.08 of the *CICA Handbook* as follows:

> *Investment income as calculated by the equity method should be that amount necessary to increase or decrease the investor's income to that which would have been recognized if the results of the investee's operations had been consolidated with those of the investor.*

The goodwill impairment loss for an investment under the equity method is accounted for as part of investment income, not as a goodwill impairment loss. This is stated in Paragraph 3050.12 of the *CICA Handbook*:

> ... The portion of the difference between the investor's cost and the amount of its underlying equity in the net assets of the investee that is similar to goodwill (equity method goodwill) is not amortized. No part of an impairment write-down of an investment accounted for by the equity method is presented in the income statement as a goodwill impairment loss (see GOODWILL AND OTHER INTANGIBLE ASSETS, Section 3062).

Solution to Self Study Problem Six - 5

Investment Analysis For First Purchase   The investment analysis for the first purchase would be as follows:

	20 Percent	100 Percent
Purchase Price	$600,000	$3,000,000
Book Value	(500,000)	(2,500,000)
Differential	$100,000	$ 500,000
Fair Value Decrease on Inventories	40,000	200,000
Fair Value Increase on Plant	(80,000)	(400,000)
Goodwill	$ 60,000	$ 300,000

Investment Analysis For Second Purchase   The investment analysis for the second purchase would be as follows:

	55 Percent	100 Percent
Purchase Price	$1,705,000	$3,100,000
Book Value	(1,540,000)	(2,800,000)
Differential	$ 165,000	$ 300,000
Fair Value Increase on Land	(27,500)	(50,000)
Fair Value Increase on Plant	(110,000)	(200,000)
Fair Value Increase on Long-Term Liabilities	55,000	100,000
Goodwill	$ 82,500	$ 150,000

While the fact that a subsidiary acquisition occurs in more than one step does not change the general principles involved in the preparation of consolidated financial statements, it does make their application more complex. This is largely related to two factors. First, there will be an allocation of fair values and a goodwill calculation for each step in the acquisition. This will subsequently be reflected in the need to amortize and depreciate all of the various balances arising in the two or more steps required by the acquisition. In addition, the Step A Elimination Entry necessary for each acquisition ignores the fact that there is more than one acquisition. As a result, the combination of the two elimination entries has meaningless results for some accounts, such as Ginko's Common Stock and Retained Earnings and the Non-Controlling Interest.

The second complicating factor relates to the calculation of consolidated Retained Earnings. Because the acquisition takes place over a period of time, there is no single figure that can be designated as Retained Earnings since acquisition. This results in the need to calculate the parent's share of post-acquisition Retained Earnings for each step in the purchase.

Step B - Adjustment   The entry to adjust the fair value decrease on the inventories at the first acquisition date is as follows:

Inventories	$40,000	
Retained Earnings		$40,000

Step B - Adjustment   The entry to adjust the Plant And Equipment for the depreciation on the fair value changes at both acquisition dates is as follows:

Retained Earnings (7 years) $56,000
Retained Earnings (4 years)   62,856
Other Expenses   23,714
    Plant and Equipment (Net) $142,570
(Annual Adjustment - First Purchase = $80,000/10 = $8,000)
(Annual Adjustment - Second Purchase = $110,000/7 = $15,714)

Step B - Fair Value Change On Land   No adjustment is required.

Step B - Adjustment   The entry to adjust the interest for the fair value change on the Long-Term Liabilities is as follows:

Long-Term Liabilities $13,750
    Other Expenses $ 2,750
    Retained Earnings (4 years)   11,000
(Annual Adjustment = $55,000/20 = $2,750)

Step B - Elimination   The entry to eliminate the unrealized loss on the intercompany sale of the machine of $100,000 [$300,000 - (2)($300,000/6) - $100,000] is as follows:

Plant and Equipment (Net) $25,000
Other Expenses and Losses   25,000
    Retained Earnings $50,000
(Annual Adjustment = $100,000/4 = $25,000)

Step B - Elimination   The entry to eliminate the unrealized upstream loss and receivable and payable resulting from the intercompany sale of land is as follows:

Land $43,000
    Other Expenses and Losses $43,000

Current Liabilities $37,500
    Current Receivables $37,500

Step B - Elimination   The entry to eliminate the intercompany dividend payment is as follows:

Other Revenues $75,000
Non-Controlling Interest (Balance Sheet)   25,000
    Dividends Declared $100,000

Step B - Elimination   The entry to eliminate intercompany sales of merchandise is as follows:

Sales of Merchandise - Downstream $550,000
Sales of Merchandise - Upstream   190,000
    Cost Of Goods Sold $740,000

Step B - Elimination   The entry to eliminate unrealized intercompany profits in the closing inventories and the receivable and payable resulting from the merchandise purchases is as follows:

Cost Of Goods Sold - Downstream [(50%)($220,000)]	$110,000	
Cost Of Goods Sold - Upstream [(60%)($45,000)]	27,000	
Inventories		$137,000
Current Liabilities	$175,000	
Current Receivables		$175,000

Step B - Elimination The entry to eliminate the unrealized intercompany profits in the opening inventories is as follows:

Retained Earnings - Downstream [(50%)($150,000)]	$75,000	
Retained Earnings - Upstream [(60%)($20,000)]	12,000	
Cost Of Goods Sold		$87,000

Step C - Distribution Schedule The allocation of the opening balance in the Retained Earnings account of the Ginko Company would be as follows:

Balance at December 31, 2005		$1,800,000
Balance at December 31, 2002		(1,500,000)
Retained Earnings Realized Before Second Purchase		$ 300,000
Percentage Ownership		20%
To Consolidated Retained Earnings		$ 60,000
Balance at January 1, 2010		$2,200,000
Balance at Second Purchase		(1,800,000)
Balance Since Second Acquisition		$ 400,000
Upstream Unrealized (Profits) Losses:		
On Machine Sale	$ 50,000	
Opening Inventories	(12,000)	38,000
Adjusted Balance Since Acquisition		$ 438,000
Non-Controlling Interest [(25%)($438,000)]		(109,500)
Available To Controlling Interest		$ 328,500
Inventory Realization		40,000
Plant And Equipment Depreciation:		
First Purchase (7 years @ $8,000)		(56,000)
Second Purchase (4 years @ $15,714)		(62,856)
Long-Term Liability Amortization (4 years @ $2,750)		11,000
To Consolidated Retained Earnings		$ 260,644

Step C - Distribution Entry The entry to distribute the Ginko Company's Retained Earnings based on the allocation in the preceding schedule is as follows:

Retained Earnings	$430,144	
Consolidated Retained Earnings		$ 60,000
Consolidated Retained Earnings		260,644
Non-Controlling Interest		109,500

The required consolidated Income Statement would be prepared as follows:

The Rosebud Company And Subsidiary
Consolidated Income Statement
For The Year Ending December 31, 2010

Sales Of Merchandise ($5,000,000 + $2,000,000 - $550,000 - $190,000)	$6,260,000
Other Revenues ($200,000 + $100,000 - $75,000)	225,000
Total Revenues	$6,485,000
Cost Of Goods Sold ($2,500,000 + $800,000 - $550,000 - $190,000 + $137,000 - $87,000)	$2,610,000
Other Expenses and Losses ($1,000,000 + $900,000 + $8,000 + $15,714 - $2,750 + $25,000 - $43,000)	1,902,964
Non-Controlling Interest [(25%)($400,000 - $25,000 + $12,000 - $27,000)]	90,000
Total Expenses	$4,602,964
Consolidated Net Income	$1,882,036

The required consolidated Statement Of Retained Earnings would be prepared as follows:

The Rosebud Company And Subsidiary
Consolidated Statement Of Retained Earnings
For The Year Ending December 31, 2010

Opening Balance	$2,745,644
Consolidated Net Income	1,882,036
Balance Available	$4,627,680
Dividends Declared (Rosebud Company's Only)	600,000
Closing Balance	$4,027,680

The Opening Consolidated Retained Earnings balance consists of the opening balance for the Rosebud Company of $2,500,000 plus the $60,000 and the $260,644 from the Ginko Company less the opening downstream unrealized inventory profits of $75,000.

The required consolidated Balance Sheet would be prepared as follows:

The Rosebud Company And Subsidiary
Consolidated Balance Sheet
As At December 31, 2010

Cash and Current Receivables ($500,000 + $600,000 - $37,500 - $175,000)	$ 887,500
Inventories ($600,000 + $1,200,000 - $40,000 + $40,000 - $137,000)	1,663,000
Investment in Ginko ($2,305,000 - $600,000 - $1,705,000)	-0-
Land ($795,000 + $500,000 + $27,500 + $43,000)	1,365,500
Plant And Equipment ($2,900,000 + $2,200,000 + $80,000 + $110,000 + $25,000 - $142,570)	5,172,430
Goodwill ($60,000 + $82,500)	142,500
Total Assets	$9,230,930

Current Liabilities ($500,000 + $400,000 - $37,500 - $175,000)	$ 687,500
Long-Term Liabilities ($1,000,000 + $600,000 + $55,000 - $13,750)	1,641,250
Non-Controlling Interest (See Following)	874,500
Common Stock - No Par	2,000,000
Retained Earnings (See Statement)	4,027,680
Total Equities	$9,230,930

Non-Controlling Interest   The Non-Controlling Interest can be calculated as follows:

Book Value of Ginko - December 31, 2010	$3,500,000
Unrealized Upstream Loss on Machine	25,000
Unrealized Upstream Profits in Closing Inventories	(27,000)
Total	$3,498,000
Non-Controlling Interest Percent	25%
Non-Controlling Interest	$ 874,500

An alternate calculation is as follows:

Non-Controlling Interest - December 31, 2005 [(25%)($2,800,000)]	$700,000
Non-Controlling Interest Subsequent to Second Acquisition	109,500
Non-Controlling Interest in Consolidated Net Income	90,000
Non-Controlling Interest in Ginko's Dividends Declared	(25,000)
Non-Controlling Interest	$874,500

Solution to Self Study Problem Six - 6

Investment Analysis   The analysis of Patco's investment in Stand is as follows:

	80 Percent	100 Percent
Investment Cost	$720,000	$900,000
Book Value	(600,000)	(750,000)
Differential	$120,000	$150,000
Fair Value Decrease On Fixed Assets	96,000	120,000
Fair Value Increase On Copyright	(24,000)	(30,000)
Goodwill	$ 192,000	$ 240,000

The fair value change on fixed assets would be depreciated over four years at a rate of $24,000 per year. Note, however, that only one-half year's depreciation or $12,000 would be taken for 2002. The fair value change on Stand's copyright will be amortized at ten percent for the half year, the same rate that Stand appears to be using on its books ($6,000/$60,000 for July 1 to December 31).

Part A   The calculation of consolidated Net Income for the year ending December 31, 2002 would be as follows:

Patco's Net Income		$300,000
Equity Pickup:		
Stand's Net Income	$69,000	
Inventory Profits ($85,000 - [$85,000/125%])	(17,000)	
Loss On Equipment ($112,000 - $98,000)	14,000	
Loss Realization - 3 Months [($14,000/10)(3/12)]	(350)	
Realized Income Of Stand	$65,650	
Percentage Ownership	80%	52,520
Amortization - Fair Value Increase On Copyright		(2,400)
Depreciation - Fair Value Decrease On Fixed Assets		12,000
Consolidated Net Income		$362,120

Part B(1)   The consolidated Intangible Assets would be calculated as follows:

Patco's Balance	$525,000
Stand's Balance	54,000
Fair Value Increase On Copyright	24,000
Amortization Of The Fair Value Increase On Copyright	(2,400)
Consolidated Goodwill	192,000
Intangible Assets	$792,600

Part B(2)   The Non-Controlling Interest would be calculated as follows:

Stand's December 31, 2002 Book Value	$819,000
Inventory Profits ($85,000 - [$85,000/125%])	(17,000)
Loss On Equipment ($112,000 - $98,000)	14,000
Loss Realization - 3 Months [($14,000/10) (3/12)]	(350)
Adjusted Book Value	$815,650
Non-Controlling Percent	20%
Non-Controlling Interest	$163,130

Part B(3)   The consolidated Retained Earnings would be as follows:

Patco's Balance	$ 975,000
Equity In Stand's Earnings Since Acquisition [(80%)($69,000 - $17,000+ $14,000 - $350)]	52,520
Amortization - Fair Value Increase On Copyright	(2,400)
Depreciation - Fair Value Decrease On Fixed Assets	12,000
Retained Earnings	$1,037,120

This figure can be verified by taking the opening consolidated Retained Earnings which is Patco's January 1 balance plus the consolidated Net Income from Part A which equals $1,037,120 ($675,000 + $362,120).

Part C   Cash From Operating Activities can be calculated as follows:

Consolidated Net Income	$ 362,120
Depreciation ($525,000 + $120,000 - $12,000)	633,000
Amortization Of Intangibles ($175,000 + $6,000 + $2,400)	183,400
Non-Controlling Interest	
[(20%)($69,000 - $17,000 + $14,000 - $350)]	13,130
Funds from Operations	$1,191,650
Decrease in Non-Cash Current Assets From Operations	
($1,000,000 + $140,000 - [$663,000 +	
$84,000 -$17,000])	410,000
Increase in Current Liabilities ($450,000 + $60,000	
- [$450,000 + $75,000])	15,000
Cash From Operating Activities	$1,616,650

The acquisitions of Fixed Assets for cash can be calculated as follows:

December 31 Balance ($1,680,000		
+ $1,050,000 + $14,000 - $350)		$2,743,650
January 1 Balance (Patco Only)	$1,500,000	
Depreciation Expense ($525,000 + $120,000)	645,000	
December 31 Balance Before Acquisitions		(855,000)
Total Acquisitions		$1,888,650
Stand's Fixed Assets At Acquisition		(900,000)
Other Acquisitions		$ 988,650
Mortgage		(75,000)
Other Acquisitions For Cash		$ 913,650

The consolidated Cash Flow Statement would be prepared as follows:

Patco Company And Subsidiary
Consolidated Cash Flow Statement
Year Ending December 31, 2002

Cash Flows From (Used In):

Operating Activities

Cash From Operating Activities		$1,616,650
Financing Activities		Nil
Investing Activities		
Acquisition Of Subsidiary (Note One)	($710,000)	
Acquisition Of Fixed Assets For Cash	(913,650)	(1,623,650)
Decrease in Cash (Note Two)		($ 7,000)

Note One   On July 31, 2002, Patco acquired 80 percent of the outstanding voting shares of Stand. Details of the transaction are as follows:

Cash Acquired From Stand	$ 10,000
Assets Acquired Other Than Cash* ($140,000 + 900,000 + 60,000 - $96,000 + $24,000 + $192,000)	1,220,000
Total Assets Acquired	$1,230,000
Liabilities Assumed ($60,000 + $300,000)	(360,000)
Non-Controlling Interest In Net Assets [(20%)($750,000)]	(150,000)
Total Purchase Price (Cash Paid)	$ 720,000
Cash Acquired From Stand	(10,000)
Net Cash Outflow	$ 710,000

*(Includes Fair Value Changes And Goodwill)

Note Two   This agrees with the decrease in cash for the year of $7,000 ($12,000 + $6,000 - $25,000).

Note Three   The intercompany sale of the equipment for $98,000 is not disclosed in the consolidated Cash Flow Statement. The unrealized loss was eliminated in the consolidated Net Income calculation. Since the sale was not arms-length, neither the proceeds nor the purchase of the machine affect consolidated cash.

Note Four - Other Matters   The mortgage for $75,000 of the Building purchase would not be included in the Cash Flow Statement. It would, however, have to be disclosed somewhere in the financial statements or the accompanying notes.

The disclosure of the nature of cash and cash equivalents is required. As the Cash Flow Statement is based only on cash, additional disclosure is not required.

Section 1540 requires separate disclosure of the cash paid for interest and income taxes that was included in the determination of Net Income for the period. Given that the problem does not provide provide this information, this requirement cannot be complied with.

Solution to Chapter Seven Exercises

Exercise Seven - 1 Solution
The required information for the four companies would be as follows:

Company 1 would classify the investment as a portfolio investment and account for it using the cost method.

Company 2 would classify the investment as a joint venture and account for it using the proportionate consolidation method.

Company 3 would classify the investment as a joint venture and account for it using the proportionate consolidation method.

Company 4 would classify the investment as a portfolio investment and account for it using the cost method.

Exercise Seven - 2 Solution

As this is an exchange of non-monetary assets that is not the culmination of an earnings process, the transaction will have to be recorded at the carrying value of the capital assets given up. The entry would be as follows:

Investment In Joint Venture	$600,000	
Property, Plant, and Equipment		$600,000

Exercise Seven - 3 Solution

Under Paragraph 3055.26, the required entry would be as follows:

Investment In Joint Venture	$190,000	
Loss [(75%)($480,000 - $840,000)]	270,000	
Cash	380,000	
Capital Assets		$840,000

The preceding entry only recognizes 75 percent of the loss. If the transaction provides evidence of a non-temporary decline in the value of the asset, 100 percent of the loss would be recognized and the following entry would be required instead:

Investment In Joint Venture	$100,000	
Loss [(100%)($480,000 - $840,000)]	360,000	
Cash	380,000	
Capital Assets		$840,000

Exercise Seven - 4 Solution

Since only an equity interest was received, none of the recognized gain can be included in income. The required entry would be as follows:

Investment In Joint Venture*	$309,750	
Deferred Gain [(75%)($325,000 - $264,000)]		$ 45,750
Capital Assets		264,000

*[$264,000 + (75%)($325,000 - $264,000)]

Exercise Seven - 5 Solution

The total gain to be recognized would be $92,800 [(80%)($426,000 - $310,000)]. The amount to be included in income would be calculated as follows:

Proceeds of Disposition (All Unencumbered)	$176,000
Cost Of Assets Considered To Be Sold	
[($176,000 ÷ $426,000)($310,000)]	(128,075)
Gain To Be Included In Income At Time Of Transfer	$ 47,925

The Deferred Gain would be $44,875, the difference between the total gain to be recognized of $92,800 and the $47,925 that is included in income.

The investment amount of $266,800 is the $310,000 carrying value of the capital assets, less the $176,000 in cash received, plus the $92,800 gain to be recognized.

The required entry would be as follows:

Investment In Joint Venture	$226,800	
Cash	176,000	
Deferred Gain ($92,800 - $47,925)		$ 44,875
Income Gain		47,925
Capital Assets		310,000

Exercise Seven - 6 Solution

The total gain to be recognized is $157,333 [(2/3)($723,000 - $487,000)]. The amount to be included in income would be calculated as follows:

Gross Proceeds	$123,000
Share Of Cash Borrowed [(1/3)($123,000 - $100,000)]	(7,667)
Net Proceeds	$115,333
Cost Of Assets Considered To Be Sold	
[($115,333 ÷ $723,000)($487,000)]	(77,686)
Gain To Be Included In Income At Time Of Transfer	$ 37,647

The Deferred Gain is $119,686, the difference between the total gain to be recognized of $157,333 and the $37,647 that is included in income.

The investment amount of $521,333 is the $487,000 carrying value of the capital assets, plus the $157,333 total gain that can be recognized, less the $123,000 in cash received.

The required entry would be as follows:

Investment In Joint Venture	$521,333	
Cash	123,000	
Deferred Gain ($157,333 - $37,647)		$119,686
Income Gain		37,647
Capital Assets		487,000

Exercise Seven - 7 Solution

The first step would be to eliminate the Investment in Combo account, CI's Common Stock, and the 75 percent interest of the other joint venturers in CI's assets. The entry would be as follows:

Common Stock (CI)	$465,000	
Cash [(75%)($381,000)]		$285,750
Inventory [(75%)($84,000)]		63,000
Investment In Combo		116,250

The only other elimination entry is the one required to deal with the downstream sale. As BL can recognize this transaction to the extent of the interests of the other joint venturers, only BL's share of the Sales, Cost Of Sales, and unrealized profit will have to be eliminated. The required entry is as follows:

Sales [(25%)($84,000)]	$21,000	
Inventory [(25%)($84,000 - $56,000)]		$ 7,000
Cost Of Sales [(25%)($56,000)]		14,000

Given the preceding eliminations, the proportionate consolidation Balance Sheet and Income Statement can be prepared as follows:

Bonder Ltd.
Proportionate Consolidation Balance Sheet (Downstream Profits)
As At December 31, 2002

Cash ($84,000 + $381,000 - $285,750)	$179,250
Inventory (Nil + $84,000 - $63,000 - $7,000)	14,000
Investment In Combo ($300 - $300)	Nil
Total Assets	$193,250
Accounts Payable	$ 56,000
Common Stock	116,250
Retained Earnings ($28,000 - $7,000)	21,000
Total Equities	$193,250

Bonder Ltd.
Proportionate Consolidation Income Statement (Downstream Profits)
Year Ending December 31, 2002

Sales ($84,000 - $21,000)	$63,000
Cost Of Sales ($56,000 - $14,000)	42,000
Net Income	$21,000

Exercise Seven - 8 Solution

A first entry is required to eliminate BL's Investment in Combo, CI's Common Stock , and the other venturers' interest in the assets, liabilities, expenses, and revenues of CI:

Common Stock (CI)	$465,000	
Sales [(75%)($48,000)]	36,000	
Cost Of Sales [(75%)($32,000)]		$ 24,000
Cash [(75%)($433,000)]		324,750
Accounts Receivable [(75%)($48,000)]		36,000
Investment In Combo		116,250

A second entry is required to eliminate the remaining 25 percent of CI's receivable as it is due to Bonder:

Account Payable [(25%)($48,000)]	$12,000	
Accounts Receivable		$12,000

A final entry is required to eliminate BL's share of the intercompany Sales, Cost Of Sales, and the unrealized profit in the ending Inventory:

Sales [(25%)($48,000)]	$12,000	
Inventory [(25%)($48,000 - $32,000)]		$4,000
Cost Of Sales [(25%)($32,000)]		8,000

Using the preceding journal entries, the proportionate consolidation Balance Sheet and Income Statement can be prepared as follows:

Bonder Ltd.
Proportionate Consolidation Balance Sheet (Upstream Profits)
As At December 31, 2002

Cash (Nil + $433,000 - $324,750)	$108,250
Accounts Receivable (Nil + $48,000 - $36,000 - $12,000)	Nil
Inventory ($48,000 + Nil - $4,000)	44,000
Investment In Combo ($116,250 - $116,250)	Nil
Total Assets	$152,250

Accounts Payable ($48,000 - $12,000)*	$ 36,000
Common Stock	116,250
Retained Earnings	Nil
Total Equities	$152,250

*Note that 75 percent of the payable remains in the consolidated Balance Sheet. This is inherent in proportionate consolidation which views the other venturers as arm's length parties outside of the consolidated entity.

Bonder Ltd.
Proportionate Consolidation Income Statement (Upstream Profits)
Year Ending December 31, 2002

Sales ($48,000 - $36,000 - $12,000)	Nil
Cost Of Sales ($32,000 - $24,000 - $8,000)	Nil
Net Income	Nil

Solution to Self Study Problem Seven - 1

Case One   The potential loss on the transfer of non-monetary assets to CVL by AL is $250,000, calculated as follows:

Fair Value At Transfer	$ 750,000
Carrying Value At Transfer	(1,000,000)
Potential Loss	($ 250,000)

Paragraph 3055.26 requires that such losses be recognized to the extent of the interests of the other non-related venturers. This means that a loss of $187,500 ([75%][$250,000]) would have to be recognized at the time of the asset contribution. In addition, this transfer to CVL would probably provide sufficient evidence of a non-temporary decline in the value of the assets, that Paragraph 3061.38 of the *CICA Handbook*, "Property, Plant and Equipment", would require a write down of the 25 percent of the assets retained by AL through its interest in CVL. This would result in the recognition of the remaining $62,500 ($250,000 - $187,500) of the loss.

Case Two   In this Case, the recognizable gain is calculated as follows:

Fair Value At Transfer	$1,100,000
Carrying Value At Transfer	(600,000)
Total Gain	$ 500,000
AL's Share (25 Percent)	(125,000)
Gain To Be Recognized	$ 375,000

Paragraph 3055.27 limits the amount of the gain that can be recognized to the interests of the other non-related joint venturers. As calculated above, this amount would be $375,000 ([75%][$500,000]). In addition, inclusion of the gain in income at the time of transfer is limited by Paragraph 3055.28 to the portion of the total value of the asset that is received in the form of cash or other assets. The required calculation here is:

Cash Received At Transfer	$350,000
Cost Of Assets Considered To Be Sold*	(190,909)
Gain To Be Included In Income At Time Of Transfer	$159,091

*The Cost Of Assets Considered To Be Sold is based on the ratio of cash received over the fair value of non-cash assets contributed, multiplied by the carrying value of the assets contributed. In this Case, the calculation is as follows:

$$[(\$350,000 \div \$1,100,000)(\$600,000)] = \$190,909$$

Note that, under Paragraph 3055.29, the $215,909 ($375,000 - $159,091) unrecognized portion of the other venturers' share of the gain will be taken into income over the remaining life of the assets contributed. AL's $125,000 [(25%)($500,000)] share of the gain would not be recognized.

Case Three   The potential gain and maximum recognizable gain on the transfer of non-monetary assets to CVL by AL is calculated as follows:

Fair Value At Transfer	$400,000
Carrying Value At Transfer	(250,000)
Total Gain	$150,000
AL's Share (25 Percent)	(37,500)
Gain To Be Recognized	$112,500

The maximum amount of this gain that could be recognized under Paragraph 3055.27 is $112,500, the 75 percent share of the other non-affiliated venturers. However, since AL receives only an equity interest in return for its contributions, none of the gain can be included in income at the time of transfer. As per the Recommendation in Paragraph 3055.29, the $112,500 gain would be amortized to income over the remaining life of the assets.

Case Four   The potential gain and maximum recognizable gain on the transfer of non-monetary assets to CVL by AL is calculated as follows:

Fair Value At Transfer	$1,400,000
Carrying Value At Transfer	(1,100,000)
Total Gain	$ 300,000
AL's Share (25 Percent)	(75,000)
Gain To Be Recognized	$ 225,000

Under Paragraph 3055.27, recognition of the gain would be limited to $225,000, the 75 percent share of the other non-affiliated venturers. The amount of the gain to be included in income would be further limited by the amount of cash received, reduced by the portion of that cash which represents borrowings by the joint venture. In this Case, the $1,000,000 ($600,000 + $400,000) in cash contributed by the other joint venturers is more than sufficient to cover the $650,000 payment to AL. This means that the gain to be included in income at time of transfer can be calculated as follows:

Gross Proceeds	$650,000
Cost Of Assets Considered To Be Sold*	(510,714)
Gain To Be Taken Into Income At Time Of Transfer	$139,286

*The Cost Of Assets Considered To Be Sold is based on the ratio of cash received over the fair value of non-cash assets contributed, multiplied by the carrying value of the assets contributed. In this Case, the calculation is as follows:

$$[(\$650,000 \div \$1,400,000)(\$1,100,000)] = \$510,714$$

As per the Recommendation in Paragraph 3055.29, the $85,714 ($225,000 - $139,286) remaining portion of the other venturers' share of the gain will be taken into income over the remaining life of the assets contributed.

Case Five   The recognizable gain on the transfer of non-monetary assets to CVL by AL is calculated as follows:

Fair Value At Transfer	$2,500,000
Carrying Value At Transfer	(2,000,000)
Total Gain	$ 500,000
AL's Share (25 Percent)	(125,000)
Maximum Recognizable Gain	$ 375,000

Under Paragraph 3055.27, recognition of the gain would be limited to $375,000, the 75 percent share of the other non-affiliated venturers.

In this Case, the $1,000,000 in cash contributed by BL and CL is not sufficient to provide for the $1,750,000 in cash paid to AL. As a consequence, the gain to be included in income at time of transfer must be based on the cash received, reduced by AL's proportionate share of the borrowings used to finance the $750,000 additional payment to AL. Given this, the calculation would be as follows:

Gross Proceeds	$1,750,000
AL's Share Of Cash Borrowed [(25%)($1,750,000 - $1,000,000)]	(187,500)
Net Proceeds	$1,562,500
Cost Of Assets Considered To Be Sold*	(1,250,000)
Gain To Be Included In Income At Time Of Transfer	$ 312,500

*The Cost Of Assets Considered To Be Sold would be calculated as follows:

$$[(\$1,562,500 \div \$2,500,000)(\$2,000,000)] = \$1,250,000$$

As per the Recommendation in Paragraph 3055.29, the $62,500 ($375,000 - $312,500) remaining portion of the other venturers' share of the gain will be taken into income over the remaining life of the assets contributed.

Solution to Self Study Problem Seven - 2

Part A - Investment Analysis   The fair value of the net assets of Numa Inc. is $1,000,000 ($100,000 + $900,000). As both investor companies have paid a purchase price equal to their proportionate share of Numa Inc.'s fair value, there is no goodwill arising from this acquisition. In addition, since the difference between the fair value and carrying value of the Non-Current Assets arises from Land, there is no amortization of this fair value increase.

Part A - Proportionate Consolidation Balance Sheet   Under the Recommendations of Section 3055 of the *CICA Handbook*, Sentinel Resources Ltd. would have to use proportionate consolidation to account for its investment in Numa. Given this requirement, the consolidated Balance Sheet of Sentinel Resources and its investee Numa Inc., is as follows:

Sentinel Resources Ltd. And Investee
Consolidated Balance Sheet (Proportionate Consolidation Basis)
As At April 1, 2002

Net Current Assets [$1,050,000 + $100,000 - (55%)($100,000)]	$1,095,000
Investment in Numa ($450,000 - $450,000)	-0-
Other Non-Current Assets [$5,300,000 + $900,000 - (55%)($900,000)]	5,705,000
Total Assets	$6,800,000
Common Stock - No Par (Sentinel's Only)	$4,000,000
Retained Earnings (Sentinel's Only)	2,800,000
Total Equities	$6,800,000

Part B - Proportionate Consolidation Income Statement   Under the Recommendations of Section 3055, intercompany gains and losses can only be recognized to the extent of the interests of the other non-affiliated venturers. Given this general provision, Sentinel would have to remove its $36,000 [(45%)($175,000 - $95,000)] share of the $80,000 loss resulting from Numa's sale of Equipment to Sentinel. With respect to the remaining $44,000 or 55 percent of the loss, it would be removed from the consolidated Income Statement as a result of applying proportionate consolidation procedures (these procedures remove the interests of other non-affiliated venturers from all of the joint venture's accounts). Taken together, these procedures remove 100 percent of the upstream loss from the proportionate consolidation Income Statement. Note, however, only 45 percent of the loss would be removed from the equipment balance in the proportionate consolidation Balance Sheet. This difference reflects the fact that the equipment is on the books of the venturer and would not be reduced by proportionate consolidation procedures.

Given this analysis, the proportionate consolidation Income Statement of Sentinel Resources and its investee Numa Inc., is as follows:

Sentinel Resources Ltd. And Investee
Consolidated Income Statement (Proportionate Consolidation Basis)
As At March 31, 2003

Revenues [$7,800,000 + $660,000 - (55%)($660,000)]	$8,097,000
Expenses and Losses	
[$6,400,000 + $480,000 - (55%)($480,000) - (45%)(80,000)]	6,580,000
Consolidated Net Income	$1,517,000

When the intercompany transaction results in a loss, Section 3055 indicates that this may serve as evidence of a reduction in the net realizable value of the asset. In these circumstances, the venturer should recognize the full amount of the loss. If this approach is taken here, the Expenses And Losses would be $6,616,000 [$6,400,000 + $480,000 - (55%)($480,000)] and consolidated Net Income would be $1,481,000 ($8,097,000 - $6,616,000).

Part C - Proportionate Consolidation Income Statement   In this case we have an upstream profit of $76,000 ($390,000 - $314,000). The Recommendations of Section 3055 will require that Molar's 55 percent share of this intercompany transaction be removed from consolidated revenues and expenses. In addition, proportionate consolidation procedures will require the removal of the remaining 45 percent that reflects the interest of the other non-affiliated venturers. The resulting proportionate consolidation Income Statement would be as follows:

Molar Oil Company And Investee
Consolidated Income Statement (Proportionate Consolidation Basis)
As At March 31, 2003

Revenues [$9,600,000 + $660,000 - (45%)($660,000) - (55%)($390,000)]	$9,748,500
Expenses And Losses [$8,500,000 + $480,000 - (45%)($480,000) - (55%)($314,000)]	8,591,300
Consolidated Net Income	$1,157,200

Note again that, in upstream transactions such as this, only 55 percent of the gain would be removed from the inventory balance on the books of Molar.

Solution to Self Study Problem Seven - 3

Part A - Investment Analysis   The analysis of the Joffry Company's investment in DEL Ltd. is as follows:

	80 Percent	100 Percent
Investment Cost (From Balance Sheet)	$720,000	$900,000
Book Value	(640,000)	(800,000)
Differential	$ 80,000	$100,000
Fair Value Changes:		
Increase On Current Assets	(16,000)	(20,000)
Decrease On Non-Current Assets	40,000	50,000
Decrease On Liabilities	(32,000)	(40,000)
Goodwill	$ 72,000	$ 90,000

Part A - Balance Sheet   The required proportionate consolidation Balance Sheet is as follows:

Joffry Company And Investee
Consolidated Balance Sheet (Proportionate Consolidation Basis)
As At December 31, 2002

Current Assets ($780,000 + $300,000 - $60,000 + $16,000)	$1,036,000
Non-Current Assets ($1,500,000 + $700,000 - $140,000 - $40,000)	2,020,000
Goodwill (Preceding Schedule)	72,000
Total Assets	$3,128,000
Liabilities ($500,000 + $200,000 - $40,000 - $32,000)	$ 628,000
Non-Controlling Interest	-0-
Common Stock (No Par)	1,000,000
Retained Earnings	1,500,000
Total Equities	$3,128,000

Part B - Balance Sheet   The required consolidated Balance Sheet is as follows:

Joffry Company And Subsidiary
Consolidated Balance Sheet
As At December 31, 2002

Current Assets ($780,000 + $300,000 + $16,000)	$1,096,000
Non-Current Assets ($1,500,000 + $700,000 - $40,000)	2,160,000
Goodwill (See Part A)	72,000
Total Assets	$3,328,000
Liabilities ($500,000 + $200,000 - $32,000)	$ 668,000
Non-Controlling Interest	160,000
Common Stock (No Par)	1,000,000
Retained Earnings	1,500,000
Total Equities	$3,328,000

Part C - Investment Income - Etna Company   The agreement described in the problem establishes that DEL Ltd. is an incorporated joint venture. The Investment Income of the Etna Company would be calculated as follows:

Reported Income Of DEL Ltd.	$475,000
Less: Intercompany Gain on Patent Sale	(83,000)
Adjusted Income Of DEL Ltd.	$392,000
Etna Company's Percentage Of Ownership	40%
Investment Income	$156,800

The loss on the chemicals has already been deducted from the Income of DEL Ltd. The journal entry to record the Etna Company's income and dividends from its Investment in DEL Ltd. is as follows:

Cash	$ 30,000	
Investment In DEL Ltd.	120,800	
Investment Income		$156,800

(To record Etna's 40 percent share of DEL Ltd.'s income and dividends)

Solution to Self Study Problem Seven - 4

Analysis Of Gain   In transferring the Building to NVI, BL recognized a gain of $800,000 ($1,200,000 - $400,000). Under the provisions of Section 3055, this gain can only be recognized to the extent of the interest of the other non-affiliated venturer. This provides the following analysis:

Total Gain	$800,000
BL's Share (45 Percent)	(360,000)
Gain To Be Recognized	$440,000

To the extent that BL received cash or assets other than an equity interest in NVI, this gain can be taken into income at the time of transfer. The calculation of the amount to be taken into income at the time of transfer is as follows:

Cash Received At Transfer	$300,000
Cost Of Asset Considered To Be Sold:	
[($300,000 ÷ $1,200,000)($400,000)]	(100,000)
Gain To Be Taken Into Income At Transfer	$200,000

The remaining $240,000 ($440,000 - $200,000) of the gain that can be recognized, will be taken into income over the 10 year life of the Building. This will be at a rate of $24,000 per year.

As the $360,000 unrecognized gain will have to be removed from the consolidated carrying value of the Building, the consolidated Depreciation Expense will have to be decreased annually by $36,000 ($360,000 ÷ 10 Years).

Journal Entries   Journal entries can be used to assist in the preparation of the required consolidated financial statements. The first of these entries would eliminate the Investment In NVI, NVI's Common Stock - No Par, NVI's Retained Earnings at Acquisition, and SI's share of the individual assets, liabilities, expenses, and revenues of NVI:

Common Stock - No Par (NVI's)	$2,000,000	
Retained Earnings At Acquisition	Nil	
Accumulated Depreciation (55%)	66,000	
Liabilities (55%)	66,000	
Sales (55%)	1,265,000	
Cash And Receivables (55%)		$231,000
Inventories (55%)		638,000
Building (55%)		660,000
Cost Of Goods Sold (55%)		819,500
Depreciation Expense (55%)		66,000
Other Expenses (55%)		82,500
Investment In NVI		900,000

Note that, at this point, we are left with 45 percent of the carrying values of NVI's assets, liabilities, expenses, and revenues. Because we are using proportionate consolidation, there is no account balance to reflect SI's interest in the assets, liabilities, expenses, and revenues of NVI.

A second entry is required to deal with the gain recognized by BL on the transfer of the building.

The entry will leave the $200,000 of the gain that can be recognized at transfer in the Gain On Sale Of Building account. The $360,000 of the gain that cannot be recognized will be removed from the Building account, while the $240,000 portion of the gain that can be recognized over the life of the Building will be allocated to a Deferred Gain account. The required entry is as follows:

Gain On Sale Of Building ($800,000 - $200,000)	$600,000	
Building (Unrecognized Portion)		$360,000
Deferred Gain		240,000

This entry, when combined with the earlier elimination of SI's 55 percent share of the Building, leaves a balance of $180,000 ($1,200,000 - $660,000 - $360,000). As would be expected, this is equal to BL's 45 percent share of the original $400,000 carrying value for the Building.

As one year has passed since the Building was transferred to NVI, one-tenth of the Deferred Gain has been realized and can be taken into income. The appropriate entry is as follows:

Deferred Gain	$24,000	
Gain On Sale Of Building		$24,000

As NVI has recorded depreciation on the $1,200,000 fair value of the Building, this must be adjusted to reflect the removal of the $360,000 unrecognized gain from this asset. This will require an annual adjustment of $36,000 ($360,00 ÷ 10 Years) as follows:

Accumulated Depreciation	$36,000	
Depreciation Expense		$36,000

This entry, when combined with the earlier elimination in our first journal entry of SI's 55 percent share of these accounts, leaves Accumulated Depreciation and Depreciation Expense at $18,000. As was the case with the Building account, this is equal to depreciation at 10 percent on BL's $180,000 share of the original carrying value of the building.

There are intercompany expenses and revenues arising from both upstream ($250,000) and downstream ($940,000) sales of merchandise. In the case of joint ventures, intercompany sales and any related intercompany profit can be recognized to the extent of the share of the other non affiliated venturers (Paragraphs 3055.36 and 3055.37). In the case of downstream transactions, this means that we must eliminate the selling venturer's share of the sale and any unrealized profit resulting from the transaction. The remainder of the downstream sale and the related profit will remain in the proportionate consolidation results. When an upstream transaction is involved, all of the sale and unrealized profit must be eliminated. While we can recognize the other non-related venturer's share of the profit in the consolidated Balance Sheet (it is an asset of the venturer), the sale and profit belong to the other non related venturer and will be removed by the proportionate consolidation procedures.

With respect to the entry to eliminate the intercompany sales, SI's 55 percent share of the upstream sale was eliminated in our first journal entry. This means that we will only need to eliminate $535,500 ([45%][$250,000 + $940,000]) of these sales. The required entry is as follows:

Sales	$535,500	
Cost Of Goods Sold		$535,500

As some of the merchandise has not been resold, there are also unrealized intercompany profits to be eliminated. The upstream amount is $50,000 ([100%][$250,000 - $200,000]) and the downstream amount is $40,000 ([50%][$940,000 - $860,000]). As was the case with upstream intercompany sales, we have already eliminated SI's 55 percent share of all NVI's profits and, as a consequence, we only need to eliminate $22,500 ([45%][$50,000]) of the unrealized upstream profit of $50,000. With respect to the downstream profit, we will need to eliminate 45 percent of this total, an amount of $18,000 ([45%][$40,000]). The entry to eliminate this total of $40,500 ($22,500 + $18,000) is as follows:

Cost Of Goods Sold - Upstream	$22,500
Cost Of Goods Sold - Downstream	18,000
Inventories	$40,500

Given these entries, the required consolidated Balance Sheet can be prepared as follows:

BL And Investee NVI
Consolidated Balance Sheet (Proportionate Basis)
As At December 31, 2002

Cash And Receivables ($1,600,000 + $420,000 - $231,000)	$1,789,000
Inventories ($3,420,000 + $1,160,000 - $638,000 - $40,500)	3,901,500
Investment In NVI ($900,000 - $900,000)	-0-
Land	620,000
Building ($2,120,000 + $1,200,000 - $660,000 - $360,000)	2,300,000
Accumulated Depreciation ($630,000 + $120,000 - $66,000 - $36,000)	(648,000)
Total Assets	**$7,962,500**
Liabilities ($470,000 + $120,000 - $66,000)	$ 524,000
Deferred Gain ($240,000 - $24,000)	216,000
Common Stock - No Par (BL's Only)	4,800,000
Retained Earnings (See Note)	2,422,500
Total Equities	**$7,962,500**

Note   The balance in consolidated Retained Earnings can be verified with the following calculation:

BL's Balance - December 31, 2002		$2,760,000
Unrecognized Gain On Building Transfer	($360,000)	
Depreciation Adjustment	36,000	(324,000)
Deferred Gain On Building Transfer	($240,000)	
Gain Realized During 2002	24,000	(216,000)
Downstream Inventory Profit [(45%)($40,000)]		(18,000)
BL's Adjusted Balance		$2,202,000
Equity Pickup [(45%)($540,000 - $50,000)]		220,500
Consolidated Retained Earnings		**$2,422,500**

The required consolidated Income Statement would be prepared as follows:

BL And Investee NVI
Consolidated Income Statement (Proportionate Basis)
Year Ending December 31, 2002

Sales ($3,500,000 + $2,300,000 - $1,265,000 - $535,500)	$3,999,500
Gain On Sale Of Building ($800,000 - $600,000 + $24,000)	224,000
Total Revenues	$4,223,500
Cost Of Goods Sold ($2,200,000 + $1,490,000 - $819,500 - $535,500 + $22,500 + $18,000)	$2,375,500
Depreciation Expense ($220,000 + $120,000 - $66,000 - $36,000)	238,000
Other Expenses ($340,000 + $150,000 - $82,500)	407,500
Total Expenses	$3,021,000
Consolidated Net Income	$1,202,500

The consolidated Net Income figure can be verified with the following calculation:

BL's 2002 Net Income		$1,540,000
Unrecognized Gain On Building Transfer	($360,000)	
Depreciation Adjustment	36,000	(324,000)
Deferred Gain On Building Transfer	($240,000)	
Gain Realized During 2002	24,000	(216,000)
Downstream Inventory Profit [(45%)($40,000)]		(18,000)
BL's Adjusted Net Income		$ 982,000
Equity Pickup [(45%)($540,000 - $50,000)]		220,500
Consolidated Net Income		$1,202,500

Note that the preceding adjustments to BL's Net Income are the same as the adjustments in the verification of consolidated Retained Earnings. This is because it is the first year of operations of NVI.

Note　An additional verification of consolidated Retained Earnings is as follows:

BL's December 31, 2002 Retained Earnings	$2,760,000
BL's December 31, 2002 Net Income	(1,540,000)
Consolidated Net Income	1,202,500
Consolidated Retained Earnings	$2,422,500

Chapter Eight Problems

Chapter 8, Advanced Topics In Consolidations, is available only on the CD-ROM. There are no Exercises or Self Study problems related to this Chapter.

Solution to Chapter Nine Exercises

Exercise Nine - 1 Solution

1. Current Rate
2. Historic Rate
3. Current Rate
4. Historic (prepaid rent is a non-monetary asset)
5. Current Rate
6. Historic Rate
7. Historic Rate
8. Current Rate
9. Historic Rate (the estimated liability for warranties is a non-monetary item)
10. Current Rate
11. Current Rate
12. This could be either. If the shares are classified as equity, they would be translated at the historic rate. If they are classified as debt, they would be translated at the current rate.

Exercise Nine - 2 Solution

One Transaction Perspective Results

	2003	2004	Cumulative
Sales			
[(50,000)(€8)($1.38)]	$552,000	N/A	$552,000
[(75,000)(€8)($1.42)]	N/A	$852,000	852,000
[(50,000)(€8)($1.42 - $1.38)	N/A	16,000	16,000
Cost Of Goods Sold	(250,000)	(450,000)	(700,000)
Net Income	$302,000	$418,000	$720,000

Two Transaction Perspective Results

	2003	2004	Cumulative
Sales			
[(50,000)(€8)($1.38)]	$552,000	N/A	$552,000
[(75,000)(€8)($1.42)]		$852,000	852,000
Cost Of Goods Sold	(250,000)	(450,000)	(700,000)
Operating Income	$302,000	$402,000	$704,000
Exchange Gain			
[(50,000)(€8)($1.42 - $1.38)]	N/A	16,000	16,000
Net Income	$302,000	$418,000	$720,000

Note that, in this example, Net Income is the same in both years, without regard to the perspective adopted. This reflects the fact that, while the $16,000 adjustment of sales relates to 2003 sales (the 2003 receivable was not collected until 2004 and the value of the Canadian dollar had increased), there is no mechanism under current GAAP for adjusting the sales of a previous year.

Exercise Nine - 3 Solution
The required journal entries are as follows:

January 1, 2002

Cash [(€585,000)($1.40)]	$819,000	
Loan Payable		$819,000

December 31, 2002

Interest Expense [(7%)(€585,000)($1.40)]	$57,330	
Cash		$57,330

December 31, 2003

Interest Expense {[(7%)(€585,000)][($1.40 + $1.45) ÷ 2]}	$58,354	
Cash		$58,354

Exchange Loss [(€585,000)($1.45 - $1.40)]	$29,250	
Loan Payable		$29,250

The Interest Expense is translated at the average rate for the year as the exchange rate changed evenly throughout the year.

December 31, 2004

Interest Expense [(7%)(€585,000)($1.45)]	$59,378	
Cash		$59,378

Loan Payable [(€585,000)($1.45 - $1.42)]	$17,550	
Exchange Gain		$17,550

Loan Payable [(€585,000)($1.42)]	$830,700	
Cash		$830,700

Since the exchange rate did not change until the last day of the year, the Interest Expense is translated at the rate for the year prior to the change.

Exercise Nine - 4 Solution
Part A   The required journal entries would be as follows:

June 30, 2002

Merchandise [(US$275,000)(C$1.55)]	$426,250	
Accounts Payable		$426,250

Investments [(US$300,000)(C$1.55)]	$465,000	
Cash		$465,000

December 31, 2002

Accounts Payable [(US$275,000)(C$1.55)]	$426,250	
Exchange Loss [(US$275,000)(C$1.60 - C$1.55)]	13,750	
Cash [(US$275,000)(C$1.60)]		$440,000

Cash [(US$300,000)(C$1.60)]	$480,000	
Exchange Gain		$ 15,000
Investments [(US$300,000)(C$1.55)]		465,000

Part B   The only difference in this case, with the certificate of deposit designated a hedging item, is that the income components of the December 31, 2002 entries would be netted. One entry could be used for this purpose:

Accounts Payable [(US$275,000)(C$1.55)]	$426,250	
Cash [(US$300,000 - US$275,000)(C$1.60)]	40,000	
Exchange Gain		$ 1,250
Investments [(US$300,000)(C$1.55)]		465,000

Exercise Nine - 5 Solution
Part A   The required journal entries would be as follows:

September 30,2002

Temporary Investments [(£375,000)($2.30)]	$862,500	
Cash		$862,500

December 1, 2002

Cash [($385,000)($2.27)]	$873,950	
Exchange Loss [(£375,000)($2.30 - $2.27)]	11,250	
Gain On Sale Of Investments		
[(£385,000 - £375,000)($2.27)]		$ 22,700
Temporary Investments		862,500

Part B   The required journal entries would be as follows:

September 30,2002

Temporary Investments [(£375,000)($2.30)]	$862,500	
Cash		$862,500

December 1, 2002

Deferred Exchange Loss [(£375,000)($2.30 - $2.27)]	$11,250	
Temporary Investments		$11,250
Cash [(£385,000)($2.27)]	$873,950	
Gain On Sale Of Investments		
[(£385,000 - £375,000)($2.27)]		$ 22,700
Temporary Investments ($862,500 - $11,250)		851,250

December 31, 2002

Equipment [(£375,000)($2.27)]	$851,250	
Deferred Exchange Loss		$ 11,250
Cash [(£375,000)($2.25)]		840,000

Exercise Nine - 6 Solution
The required journal entries would be as follows:

October 15, 2002

Merchandise [(€425,000)($1.38)]	$586,500	
Accounts Payable		$586,500
Temporary Investments [(€425,000)($1.38)]	$586,500	
Cash		$586,500

December 31, 2002

Deferred Exchange Loss [(€425,000)($1.40 - $1.38)]	$8,500	
Accounts Payable		$8,500

March 1, 2003

Deferred Exchange Loss [(€425,000)($1.43 - $1.40)]	$12,750	
Accounts Payable		$12,750

Accounts Payable [(€425,000)($1.43)]	$607,750	
Loss On Temporary Investments		
[(€425,000 - €410,000)($1.43)]	21,450	
Deferred Exchange Loss ($8,500 + $12,750)		$ 21,250
Cash [(€425,000 - €410,000)($1.43)]		21,450
Temporary Investments [(€425,000)($1.38)]		586,500

Exercise Nine - 7 Solution

The required journal entries would be as follows:

September 30, 2002

Temporary Investments [(P260,000)($0.50)]	$130,000	
Cash		$130,000

December 31, 2002

Deferred Exchange Loss [(P260,000)($0.50 - $0.48)]	$5,200	
Temporary Investments		$5,200

January 4, 2003

Exchange Loss	$7,800	
Deferred Exchange Loss		$5,200
Temporary Investments [(P260,000)($0.48 - $0.47)]		2,600

Cash [(P270,000)($0.47)]	$126,900	
Gain On Temporary Investments [(P10,000)($0.47)]		$ 4,700
Temporary Investments [(P260,000)($0.47)]		122,200

Exercise Nine - 8 Solution

The required journal entries would be as follows:

November 15, 2002

No entry required.

December 31, 2002

No entry required.

February 15, 2003

Cash [(A$625,000)(C$0.88)]	C$550,000	
Sales		C$550,000

Exercise Nine - 9 Solution
The required journal entries would be as follows:

November 15, 2002

Accounts Receivable[(A$625,000)(C$0.87)]	C$543,750	
Sales		C$543,750

December 31, 2002

Accounts Receivable [(A$625,000)(C$0.91 - C$0.87)]	C$25,000	
Forward Exchange Contract		C$25,000
(The Forward Exchange Contract would be disclosed as a liability.)		
Premium Receivable [(1.5/3)(A$625,000)(C$0.88 - C$0.87)]	C$3,125	
Discount Revenue		C$3,125

February 15, 2003

Accounts Receivable [(A$625,000)(C$0.93 - C$0.91)]	C$12,500	
Forward Exchange Contract		C$12,500
Premium Receivable [(1.5/3)(A$625,000)(C$0.88 - C$0.87)]	C$3,125	
Discount Revenue		C$3,125
Cash [(A$625,000)(C$0.88)]	C$550,000	
Forward Exchange Contract (C$25,000 + C$12,500)	37,500	
Premium Receivable (C$3,125 + C$3,125)		C$ 6,250
Accounts Receivable		
(C$543,750 + C$25,000 + C$12,500)		581,250

Exercise Nine - 10 Solution
The required entries would be as follows:

November 15, 2002

No entry required.

December 31, 2002

Exchange Loss [(A$625,000)(C$0.94 - C$0.88)]	C$37,500	
Forward Exchange Contract		C$37,500

February 15, 2003

Forward Exchange Contract	C$37,500	
Exchange Gain [(A$625,000)(C$0.94 - C$0.93)]		C$ 6,250
Cash [(A$625,000)(C$0.93 - C$0.88)]		31,250

Solution to Self Study Problem Nine - 1

The journal entries that would be required to account for the loan on December 31 of the years 2002 through 2006 would be as follows:

December 31, 2002

Cash [(D5,000,000)($1.80)]	$9,000,000	
Long-Term Liability		$9,000,000

December 31, 2003

Exchange Loss		
[(D5,000,000)($2.10 - $1.80)]	$1,500,000	
Long-Term Liability		$1,500,000

December 31, 2004

Long-Term Liability		
[(D5,000,000)($2.00 - $2.10)]	$500,000	
Exchange Gain		$500,000

December 31, 2005

No Entry

December 31, 2006

Long-Term Liability		
[(D5,000,000)($2.00 - $1.70)]	$1,500,000	
Exchange Gain		$1,500,000
Long-Term Liability [(D5,000,000)($1.70)]	$8,500,000	
Cash		$8,500,000

Solution to Self Study Problem Nine - 2

Part A   In this Case, the forward exchange contract would be classified as the hedge of a commitment to purchase goods. Given this classification, the journal entries would be as follows:

December 1, 2002

No Entry Required

December 31, 2002

It would be possible to set up the forward exchange contract as an asset and credit a deferred gain for a total of $40,000 [(SF2,000,000)($.98 - $.96)]. However, it is clear that any gain that is recorded will never be taken into income and that the forward contract has no value beyond its ability to establish the price to be paid for the inventories that will be acquired on March 31. As a result, we would not make any entry at this point.

March 31, 2003

Inventories	$2,000,000	
Cash		$2,000,000
[(SF2,000,000)($1.00)]		

Part B   In this Case, the forward exchange contract would be classified as the hedge of a monetary liability position. Given this classification, the journal entries would be as follows:

December 1, 2002

Inventories	$1,920,000	
Accounts Payable		$1,920,000
[(SF2,000,000)($.96)]		

December 31, 2002

Forward Exchange Contract	$40,000	
Accounts Payable		$40,000
[(SF2,000,000)($.98 - $.96)]		
Hedge Expense	$20,000	
Premium Liability		$20,000
[(1/4)(SF2,000,000)($1.00 - $.96)]		

March 31, 2003

Forward Exchange Contract	$ 100,000	
Accounts Payable		$ 100,000
[(SF2,000,000)($1.03 - $.98)]		
Hedge Expense	$ 60,000	
Premium Liability		$ 60,000
[(3/4)(SF2,000,000)($1.00 - $.96)]		
Accounts Payable	$2,060,000	
Premium Liability	80,000	
Forward Exchange Contract		$ 140,000
Cash		2,000,000

Part C   In this Case, the forward contract is not serving as a hedge but, rather, is being used for purely speculative purposes. Given this, the required journal entries would be as follows:

December 1, 2002

No Entry Required

December 31, 2002

Forward Exchange Contract	$100,000	
Exchange Gain		$100,000
[(SF2,000,000)($1.05 - $1.00)]		

March 31, 2003

Cash [(SF2,000,000)($1.03 - $1.00)]	$60,000	
Exchange Loss [(SF2,000,000)($1.03 - $1.05)]	40,000	
Forward Exchange Contract		$100,000

Solution to Self Study Problem Nine - 3

Note that in this solution, $ without the prefix NZ denotes the Canadian dollar.

November 1, 2002   The journal entry required on this date would be as follows:

Accounts Receivable [(NZ$5,000,000)($.70)]	$3,500,000	
Sales		$3,500,000

No entries would be required to record the forward exchange contracts.

December 31, 2002   The following journal entries would be required on this date for the receivable and its related hedge contract:

Accounts Receivable [(NZ$5,000,000)($.73 - $.70)]	$150,000	
Forward Exchange Contract		$150,000
Hedge Expense [(2/3)(NZ$5,000,000)($.70 - $.69)]	$ 33,333	
Premium Liability		$ 33,333

December 31, 2002   With respect to the contract which was entered in order to hedge the purchase commitment, it would be possible to make an entry setting up the forward exchange contract as an asset and crediting a deferred gain for $600,000 [(NZ$20,000,000)($.73 - $.70)]. However, it is clear that any gain that is recorded will never be taken into income and that the forward contract has no value beyond its ability to establish the price to be paid for the equipment that will be acquired on March 1, 2003. As a result, we would make no entry at this point.

December 31, 2002   With respect to the speculative contract, the following entry would be required:

Exchange Loss [(NZ$10,000,000)($.81 - $.80)]	$100,000	
Forward Exchange Contract		$100,000

February 1, 2003   The following journal entries would be required for the receivable and its related hedge contract:

Accounts Receivable [(NZ$5,000,000)($.74 - $.73)]	$50,000	
Forward Exchange Contract		$50,000
Hedge Expense [(1/3)(NZ$5,000,000)($.70 - $.69)]	$16,667	
Premium Liability		$16,667
Cash	$3,450,000	
Forward Exchange Contract	200,000	
Premium Liability	50,000	
Accounts Receivable		$3,700,000

March 1, 2003   The following journal entry would be required to record the use of the contract to implement the purchase commitment.

Equipment [(NZ$20,000,000)($.75)]	$15,000,000	
Cash		$15,000,000

June 1, 2003   The following journal entry would be required to record the fulfillment of the speculative contract:

Exchange Loss [(NZ$10,000,000)($.82 - $.81)]	$100,000	
Forward Exchange Contract	100,000	
Cash [(NZ$10,000,000)($.82 - $.80)]		$200,000

Solution to Chapter Ten Exercises

Exercise Ten - 1 Solution
As Canadian accounting principles would be required, the revenues would have to be converted to an accrual basis prior to translation:

Cash Basis Revenue	FC926,000
Opening Accounts Receivable	(48,000)
Closing Unearned Revenue	22,000
Accrual Basis Revenue	FC900,000

This would translate into a Canadian dollar revenue figure of $360,000 [(FC900,000)($0.40)].

Exercise Ten - 2 Solution
- The German subsidiary appears to be a self-sustaining operation.
- The Brazilian subsidiary is clearly an integrated foreign operation.
- The Swiss subsidiary appears to be a self-sustaining operation with respect to the Canadian parent. The issue, however, is complicated by the difference between the currency of record and currency of operations or functional currency. It is likely that a dual transaction process would be used here (Swiss francs to Euros, followed by a translation of Euros to Canadian dollars). This topic is discussed later in the Chapter under the section, "U.S. Functional Currency Approach".
- The U.S. subsidiary appears to be a self-sustaining operation with respect to the Canadian parent. Here again, however a multiple currency translation process might be used (conversion of all of the other currency values to U.S. dollars, followed by conversion of U.S. dollars to Canadian dollars).

Exercise Ten - 3 Solution
The required Income Statement would be as follows:

Temp Company
Income Statement
Current Year

Sales [(€920,000)($1.40)]		$1,288,000
Gain On Sale Of Land:		
Proceeds [(€130,000)($1.40)]	$182,000	
Cost [(€80,000)($1.35)]	(108,000)	74,000
Total Revenues		$1,362,000
Expenses:		
Cost Of Sales		
Opening Inventory [(€50,000)($1.37)]	$ 68,500	
Purchases [(€490,000)($1.40)]	686,000	
Closing Inventory [(€70,000)($1.39)]	(97,300)	$ 657,200
Amortization Expense [(€132,000)($1.35)]		178,200
Other Expenses [(€220,000)($1.40)]		308,000
Total Expenses		$1,143,400
Net Income		$ 218,600

Exercise Ten - 4 Solution
The required Income Statement would be as follows:

Temp Company
Income Statement
Current Year

Sales [(€920,000)($1.40)]	$1,288,000
Gain On Sale Of Land [(€50,000)($1.40)]	70,000
Total Revenues	$1,358,000
Expenses:	
Cost Of Sales [(€470,000)($1.40)]	$ 658,000
Amortization Expense [(€132,000)($1.40)]	184,800
Other Expenses [(€220,000)($1.40)]	308,000
Total Expenses	$1,150,800
Net Income	$ 207,200

Solution to Self Study Problem Ten - 1

Account	Temporal	Current Rate
Cash	$125,000	$ 125,000
Long-Term Receivables	375,000	375,000
Inventories	500,000	500,000
Plant And Equipment	500,000	1,250,000
Accounts Payable	(175,000)	(175,000)
Long-Term Liabilities	(300,000)	(300,000)
Accumulated Depreciation on Plant and Equipment	(250,000)	(625,000)
Net Asset Balance	$775,000	$1,150,000

Solution to Self Study Problem Ten - 2

Part A - Integrated Foreign Operation

Income Statement
For The Year Ended December 31, 2002

	Barbados$	Rate	Canadian$
Revenue	1,000,000	.80	$ 800,000
Expenses:			
Interest Expense	990,000	.80	$ 792,000
Other Expenses	10,000	.80	8,000
Exchange Loss	- 0 -	Note 1	900,000
Total Expenses	1,000,000		$1,700,000
Income (Loss)	- 0 -		($ 900,000)

Note 1 Loss On Long-Term Debt

	Barbados$	Rate	Canadian$
Closing	9,000,000	.85	$7,650,000
Opening	9,000,000	.75	(6,750,000)
Exchange Loss			$ 900,000

Balance Sheet
As At December 31, 2002

	Barbados$	Rate	Canadian$
Cash	- 0 -		$ -0-
Land	12,000,000	.75	9,000,000
Total Assets	12,000,000		$9,000,000
Bond	9,000,000	.85	$7,650,000
Common Stock	3,000,000	.75	2,250,000
Retained Earnings (Deficit)	- 0 -		(900,000)
Total Equities	12,000,000		$9,000,000

Part A - Self-Sustaining Foreign Operation

Income Statement
For The Year Ended December 31, 2002

	Barbados$	Rate	Canadian$
Revenue	1,000,000	.80	$800,000
Expenses:			
Interest Expense	990,000	.80	$792,000
Other Expenses	10,000	.80	8,000
Total Expenses	1,000,000		$800,000
Income	- 0 -		$ - 0 -

Balance Sheet
As At December 31, 2002

	Barbados$	Rate	Canadian$
Cash	- 0 -		$ - 0 -
Land	12,000,000	.85	10,200,000
Total Assets	12,000,000		$10,200,000
Bond	9,000,000	.85	$ 7,650,000
Common Stock	3,000,000	.75	2,250,000
Cumulative Translation Adjustment	- 0 -	Note 2	300,000
Total Equities	12,000,000		$10,200,000

Note 2   Translation Adjustment On Net Assets

	Barbados$	Rate	Canadian$
Net Assets, Opening	3,000,000	.75	$2,250,000
Net Assets, Closing	3,000,000	.85	2,550,000
Cumulative Translation Adjustment			$ 300,000

Part B   Economic exposure is the impact of changes in the relative values of the currencies on the earnings ability of the foreign subsidiary. The foreign debt is hedged by the foreign non-monetary land investment if B$ proceeds from the sale of the land in five years are adequate to pay off the B$ debt. Therefore, reflecting an exchange loss on the bond (temporal method) does not reflect economic exposure.

The current rate method better reflects economic exposure. Investco Ltd. is exposed to the extent of this net asset investment (B$3,000,000 at historic values) and in fact enjoyed favorable unrealized exchange gains on this investment during the year since the Canadian dollar was depreciating relative to the Barbadian dollar.

Part C   According to the criteria of Section 1650, the Barbadian subsidiary is a self-sustaining foreign operation because:

1. There is no interrelationship between the day-to-day activities of the Barbadian subsidiary and the Canadian parent.

2. The activities of the Barbadian subsidiary are financed by B$ debt and B$ rental inflows.

3. The B$ debt will be repaid out of B$ proceeds from the sale of the land in five years.

In effect, there is no exposure of the Canadian parent to short-term fluctuations in the B$ exchange rate and it would be inappropriate to include unrealized foreign exchange gains or losses in the Canadian parent's income for each of the five years. Therefore, the current rate method would be required.

Part D   If the bond is translated at the current exchange rate and the exchange loss is expensed, then the company will recognize a loss on the bond without recognizing any change in the value of the land. In effect, the foreign currency debt is hedged by a non-monetary item (land)   accordingly, any loss on the bond is deferred entirely until the maturity date in four years, in accordance with Section 1650.54 of the *CICA Handbook*. If B$ proceeds from the sale of land are sufficient to repay the B$ debt (which they are expected to be), then there is no exposure to B$ exchange rate fluctuations. In other words, Canadian dollars are not expected to be required to repay the B$ debt when it comes due. According to Section 1650.48, deferral is acceptable if the land is identified as a hedge and there is reasonable assurance that the land will be effective as a hedge.

The CICA Accounting Guideline, No. 13 "Hedging Relationships" provides additional guidance on hedge accounting. It requires periodic assessment of the effectiveness of hedging relationships. Hedge accounting can only be used if the hedging relationship is judged effective.

Solution to Self Study Problem Ten - 3

Part A   The temporal method of translation should be adopted because Cellular is dependent on its parent and therefore is not a self-sustaining foreign operation. Factors that lead to this conclusion are:

1. All management have been appointed by Sentex.
2. Top management of Cellular are paid directly by Sentex.
3. Seventy-five percent of Cellular's sales are to Sentex.
4. The majority of the profits will be distributed to the parent after the two-year freeze on profit distributions.
5. Eighty percent of initial financing was provided by Sentex.

Part B   The exchange gain would be calculated as follows:

	Cuzos	Rate	Dollars
Opening Net Monetary Liabilities	(150,000)	2.00	(300,000)
Sales	600,000	1.82	1,092,000
Purchases Of Raw Materials And Labour	(370,000)	1.82	(673,400)
Selling And Administrative Expenses	(70,000)	1.82	(127,400)
Interest	(20,000)	1.82	(36,400)
Income Taxes	(4,500)	1.82	(8,190)
Land Held For Future Development	(10,000)	1.65	(16,500)
Calculated Closing Net Monetary Liabilities			(69,890)
Actual Closing Net Monetary Liabilities	(24,500)	1.65	(40,425)
Exchange Gain			29,465

Part C   The translated Income Statement and Balance Sheet of Cellular Company Inc., would be as follows:

Cellular Company Inc.
Income Statement
For the year ending December 31, 2002

	Cuzos	Rate	Dollars
Sales	600,000	1.82	1,092,000
Depreciation Included In Cost Of Sales	(98,000)	2.00	(196,000)
Raw Materials And Labour Included In Cost Of Sales ($400,000 - $98,000)	(302,000)	1.82	(549,640)
Selling And Administrative Expenses	(70,000)	1.82	(127,400)
Interest Expense	(20,000)	1.82	(36,400)
Income Taxes	(4,500)	1.82	(8,190)
Net Income Before Foreign Exchange Gain	105,500		174,370
Foreign Exchange Gain	N/A		29,465
Closing Retained Earnings	105,500		203,835

Cellular Company Inc.
Balance Sheet
As At December 31, 2002

	Cuzos	Rate	Dollars
Cash	25,000	1.65	41,250
Note Receivable	100,000	1.65	165,000
Accounts Receivable	65,000	1.65	107,250
Inventory	22,000	2.00	44,000
	68,000	1.82	123,760
Fixed Assets - Net	230,000	2.00	460,000
Land For Future Development	10,000	1.65	16,500
Total Assets	520,000		957,760
Accounts Payable	30,000	1.65	49,500
Taxes Payable	4,500	1.65	7,425
Long-Term Debt	180,000	1.65	297,000
Common Stock	200,000	2.00	400,000
Retained Earnings (see Income Statement)	105,500		203,835
Total Equities	520,000		957,760

Solution to Self Study Problem Ten - 4

Part A - Balance Sheets   Using the translation procedures required for integrated foreign operations, the Brazal Company's Balance Sheets are as follows:

Brazal Company (Integrated Foreign Operation)
Balance Sheet
As At December 31, 2001

Cash And Current Receivables (NC6,500,000 @ $.040)	$ 260,000
Long-Term Receivable (NC5,000,000 @ $.040)	200,000
Inventories (NC9,500,000 @ $.045)	427,500
Plant And Equipment (NC17,000,000 @ $.100)	1,700,000
Accumulated Depreciation (NC4,000,000 @ $.100)	(400,000)
Land (NC3,000,000 @ $.060)	180,000
Total Assets	$2,367,500
Current Liabilities (NC5,000,000 @ $.040)	$ 200,000
Long Term Liabilities	-0-
No Par Common Stock (NC18,000,000 @ $.100)	1,800,000
Retained Earnings (Balancing Figure)	367,500
Total Equities	$2,367,500

Brazal Company (Integrated Foreign Operation)
Balance Sheet
As At December 31, 2002

Cash And Current Receivables (NC11,000,000 @ $.030)	$ 330,000
Long-Term Receivable (NC5,000,000 @ $.030)	150,000
Inventories (NC8,000,000 @ $.032)	256,000
Plant And Equipment (NC13,000,000 @ $.100	
+ NC10,000,000 @ $.038)	1,680,000
Accumulated Depreciation (NC4,250,000 @ $.100	
+ NC750,000 @ $.038)	(453,500)
Land (NC3,000,000 @ $.060 + NC3,000,000 @ $.035)	285,000
Total Assets	$2,247,500
Current Liabilities (NC3,000,000 @ $.030)	$ 90,000
Long-Term Liabilities (NC10,000,000 @ $.030)	300,000
No Par Common Stock (NC18,000,000 @ $.100	
+ NC2,000,000 @ $.038)	1,876,000
Retained Earnings (Deficit) ($367,500 - $386,000)	(18,500)
Total Equities	$2,247,500

Part A - Statement Of Income And Change In Retained Earnings   Using the translation procedures required for integrated foreign operations, the Brazal Company's Statement of Income and Change in Retained Earnings would be as follows:

Brazal Company (Integrated Foreign Operation)
Statement of Income and Change in Retained Earnings
Year Ending December 31, 2002

Sales (NC50,000,000 @ $.035)	$1,750,000
Interest Revenue (NC1,000,000 @ $.035)	35,000
Total Revenues	$1,785,000
Opening Inventories (NC9,500,000 @ $.045)	$ 427,500
Purchases (NC28,500,000 @ $.035)	997,500
Closing Inventories (NC8,000,000 @ $.032)	(256,000)
Taxes (NC10,000,000 @ $.035)	350,000
Depreciation Expense (NC1,250,000 @ $.100	
+ NC750,000 @ $.038)	153,500
Other Expenses (NC5,000,000 @ $.035)	175,000
Exchange Loss (See Note One)	31,500
Total Expenses	$1,879,000
Income (Loss) Before Extraordinary Items	($ 94,000)
Extraordinary Loss (See Note Two)	(260,000)
Net Income (Loss)	($ 354,000)
Dividends (NC1,000,000 @ $.032)	(32,000)
Increase (Decrease) in Retained Earnings	($ 386,000)

Note One   The exchange loss is as follows:

Opening Net Monetary Assets (NC6,500,000 @ $.040)	$ 260,000
Sales (NC50,000,000 @ $.035)	1,750,000
Interest Revenue (NC1,000,000 @ $.035)	35,000
Proceeds From Equipment	
Expropriation (NC1,000,000 @ $.040)	40,000
Sale Of Common Stock (NC2,000,000 @ $.038)	76,000
Purchases (NC28,500,000 @ $.035)	(997,500)
Taxes (NC10,000,000 @ $.035)	(350,000)
Other Expenses (NC5,000,000 @ $.035)	(175,000)
Land Purchase (NC3,000,000 @ $.035)	(105,000)
Dividends (NC1,000,000 @ $.032)	(32,000)
Equipment Purchased (NC10,000,000 @ $.038)	(380,000)
Computed Closing Net Monetary Assets	$ 121,500
Actual Closing Net Monetary Assets (NC3,000,000 @ $.030)	(90,000)
Exchange Loss	$ 31,500

Note Two   The amount of the translated Extraordinary Loss is calculated as follows:

Proceeds From Expropriation (NC1,000,000 @ $.040)	$ 40,000
Net Book Value (NC3,000,000 @ $.100)	(300,000)
Extraordinary Loss	($260,000)

Part B - Balance Sheets   Using the translation procedures required for self-sustaining foreign operations, the Brazal Company's Balance Sheets are as follows:

Brazal Company (Self Sustaining Foreign Operation)
Balance Sheet
As At December 31, 2001

Cash And Current Receivables (NC6,500,000 @ $.040)	$ 260,000
Long-Term Receivable (NC5,000,000 @ $.040)	200,000
Inventories (NC9,500,000 @ $.040)	380,000
Plant And Equipment (NC17,000,000 @ $.040)	680,000
Accumulated Depreciation (NC4,000,000 @ $.040)	(160,000)
Land (NC3,000,000 @ $.040)	120,000
Total Assets	$1,480,000

Current Liabilities (NC5,000,000 @ $.040)	$ 200,000
No Par Common Stock (NC18,000,000 @ $.100)	1,800,000
Cumulative Translation Adjustment (Note Three)	(887,500)
Retained Earnings (Part A Solution)	367,500
Total Equities	$1,480,000

Note Three   The calculation for determining the balance in this account at the end of the year preceding the first application of the requirements for a self sustaining foreign operation is as follows:

Net Assets As Per Current Rate Method On December 31, 2001	
(NC32,000,000 @ $.040)	$1,280,000
Net Assets As Per Temporal Method On December 31, 2001	
(See Part A Solution)	(2,167,500)
Beginning Cumulative Translation Adjustment	($ 887,500)

Brazal Company (Self Sustaining Foreign Operation)
Balance Sheet
As At December 31, 2002

Cash And Current Receivables (NC11,000,000 @ $.030)	$ 330,000
Long Term Receivable (NC5,000,000 @ $.030)	150,000
Inventories (NC8,000,000 @ $.030)	240,000
Plant And Equipment (NC13,000,000 @ $.030 + NC10,000,000 @ $.030)	690,000
Accumulated Depreciation (NC4,250,000 @ $.030 + NC750,000 @ $.030)	(150,000)
Land (NC3,000,000 @ $.030 + NC3,000,000 @ $.030)	180,000
Total Assets	$1,440,000
Current Liabilities (NC3,000,000 @ $.030)	$ 90,000
Long-Term Liabilities (NC10,000,000 @ $.030)	300,000
No Par Common Stock (NC18,000,000 @ $.100 + NC2,000,000 @ $.038)	1,876,000
Cumulative Translation Adjustment (Note Five)	(1,221,500)
Retained Earnings (Note Four)	395,500
Total Equities	$1,440,000

Note Four   The Retained Earnings balance in the Brazal Company's December 31, 2002 Balance Sheet can be calculated as follows:

Balance - December 31, 2001	$367,500
Increase in Retained Earnings for 2002	28,000
Balance - December 31, 2002	$395,500

Note Five   On December 31, 2001, the balance in the Cumulative Translation Adjustment account was a debit of $887,500. The closing balance on December 31, 2002 is a debit of $1,221,500 and this represents an increase of $334,000. This increase is calculated as follows:

Opening Net Assets (NC32,000,000 @ $.040)	$1,280,000
Sales (NC50,000,000 @ $.035)	1,750,000
Interest Revenue (NC1,000,000 @ $.035)	35,000
Proceeds From The Sale Of Common Stock (NC2,000,000 @ $.038)	76,000
Cost Of Goods Sold (NC30,000,000 @ $.035)	(1,050,000)
Taxes (NC10,000,000 @ $.035)	(350,000)
Depreciation Expense (NC2,000,000 @ $.035)	(70,000)
Other Expenses (NC5,000,000 @ $.035)	(175,000)
Extraordinary Loss (See Income Statement)	(80,000)
Dividends (NC1,000,000 @ $.032)	(32,000)
Computed Closing Net Assets	$1,384,000
Actual Closing Net Assets (NC35,000,000 @ $.030)	1,050,000
Change In Cumulative Translation Adjustment	$ 334,000

Part B - Statement Of Income And Change In Retained Earnings   Using the translation procedures required for self-sustaining foreign operations, the Brazal Company's Statement of Income and Change in Retained Earnings would be as follows:

Brazal Company (Self Sustaining Foreign Operation)
Statement of Income and Change in Retained Earnings
Year Ending December 31, 2002

Sales (NC50,000,000 @ $.035)	$1,750,000
Interest Revenue (NC1,000,000 @ $.035)	35,000
Total Revenues	**$1,785,000**
Cost Of Goods Sold (NC30,000,000 @ $.035)	$1,050,000
Taxes (NC10,000,000 @ $.035)	350,000
Depreciation Expense (NC2,000,000 @ $.035)	70,000
Other Expenses (NC5,000,000 @ $.035)	175,000
Total Expenses	**$1,645,000**
Income Before Extraordinary Items	$ 140,000
Extraordinary Loss (See Note Six)	(80,000)
Net Income (Loss)	$ 60,000
Dividends (NC1,000,000 @ $.032)	(32,000)
Increase (Decrease) in Retained Earnings	**$ 28,000**

Note Six   The amount of the translated Extraordinary Loss is calculated as follows:

Proceeds (NC1,000,000 @ $.040)	$ 40,000
Net Book Value (NC3,000,000 @ $.040)	(120,000)
Extraordinary Loss	**($ 80,000)**

Solution to Chapter Eleven Exercises

Exercise Eleven - 1 Solution
Part A: Taxes Payable Solution

	Year 2002	Year 2003	Year 2004
Revenues	$155,000	$155,000	$155,000
Depreciation Expense	(80,000)	(80,000)	(80,000)
Tax Expense			
[(60%)($155,000 - $120,000)]	(21,000)	(21,000)	N/A
[(40%)($155,000 - Nil)]			(62,000)
Net Income	**$ 54,000**	**$ 54,000**	**$ 13,000**

	December 31 2002	December 31 2003	December 31 2004
Cash	$134,000	$268,000	$361,000
Capital Asset (Net)	160,000	80,000	Nil
Total Assets	**$294,000**	**$348,000**	**$361,000**
Common Stock	$240,000	$240,000	$240,000
Retained Earnings	54,000	108,000	121,000
Total Equities	**$294,000**	**$348,000**	**$361,000**

Part B: FITAL Solution

	Year 2002	Year 2003	Year 2004
Revenues	$155,000	$155,000	$155,000
Depreciation Expense	(80,000)	(80,000)	(80,000)
Tax Expense			
Current (See Part A)	(21,000)	(21,000)	(62,000)
Future*	(48,000)	(48,000)	96,000
Net Income	$ 6,000	$ 6,000	$109,000

	December 31 2002	December 31 2003	December 31 2004
Cash	$134,000	$268,000	$361,000
Capital Asset (Net)	160,000	80,000	Nil
Total Assets	$294,000	$348,000	$361,000
Future Income Tax Liability*	$ 48,000	$ 96,000	Nil
Common Stock	240,000	240,000	$240,000
Retained Earnings	6,000	12,000	121,000
Total Equities	$294,000	$348,000	$361,000

*For 2002 and 2003, the addition to this account would be $48,000 [(60%)($120,000 - $80,000)], leaving a cumulative amount of $96,000 at the end of 2003. At the end of 2004, the asset has been completely written off for both tax and accounting purposes. therefore there is no temporary difference and no Future Income Tax Liability.

Exercise Eleven - 2 Solution

A. Assuming that a reserve equal to $18,000 has been taken for tax purposes, the tax basis of the Accounts Receivable would be $244,000 ($262,000 - $18,000), an amount equal to the net carrying value of the Accounts Receivable.

B. As LIFO is not acceptable for tax purposes, the tax basis of the Inventories would be $171,500 ($164,000 + $7,500).

C. The tax basis of the Temporary Investments is $45,250, their cost of $46,000, less the non-deductible one-half of the $1,500 capital loss that would result from the recovery of their carrying value.

D. The tax basis of the Land would be its cost of $50,000.

E. The tax basis of the Long-Term Investments would be $220,000, their cost of $210,000 plus the non-taxable one-half of the capital gain that would arise if the carrying value were recovered through their sale.

F. The tax basis of the Class 8 assets would be their UCC of $132,000.

G. As the special rules applicable to luxury passenger vehicles do not permit recognition of recapture or terminal losses on their disposition, the tax basis of this vehicle is equal to its carrying value of $72,000.

H. The tax basis of this Patent is $11,000, the UCC balance in Class 44.

I. As all of these development costs have been deducted for tax purposes, the tax basis of the capitalized value is nil.

J. Three-quarters of the cost of the goodwill will be added to the Cumulative Eligible Capital (CEC) balance of the enterprise. The tax basis of the goodwill will be the CEC balance of $107,250, plus the non-taxable one-quarter of the $143,000 in proceeds that would result from the recovery of the carrying value of the goodwill, a total of $143,000.

Exercise Eleven - 3 Solution

A. The tax basis of the outstanding bank loan is the carrying value of $326,000. No amount would be deductible when the liability is settled.

B. The tax basis of the Accounts Payable is $54,000, the carrying value of the liability. No amount is deductible when the liability is settled.

C. The tax basis of the liability for membership fees is $18,000, the carrying value of the liability. No amount is deductible when the liability is settled.

D. If the enterprise has deducted a reserve for undelivered goods [ITA 20(1)(m)] with respect to the $31,000 advance, the tax basis of the liability is equal to the $31,000 carrying value of the liability. The full amount of the advance will be taxable when the liability is settled. If no reserve was deducted, the tax basis of the liability is nil, reflecting the fact that none of the $31,000 would be taxable when the goods are delivered.

E. The tax basis of the Liability For Estimated Warranty Costs is nil, the carrying value, less the $11,000 that will be deductible when the warranty costs are incurred.

F. The tax basis of the Wages Payable is $15,000, the carrying value of the liability. As the wages were almost certainly deducted when they were accrued, no amount is deductible when this liability is settled.

G. The tax basis of the long term bonds is $1,250,000, their carrying value of $1,240,000, plus the $10,000 ($1,250,000 - $1,240,000) that would be taxable if the bonds were settled at their carrying value of $1,240,000. This conclusion reflects the fact that bond premium is not amortized for tax purposes and retirement of the bonds at their amortized value of $1,240,000 would result in a $10,000 gain.

H. The tax basis of these liabilities is their $860,000 carrying value. No amount would be deductible if they were settled (redeemed) at their carrying value of $860,000.

Exercise Eleven - 4 Solution

A. There would be a deductible temporary difference of $9,000, the excess of the $133,000 tax basis of the Inventories over their $124,000 carrying value.

B. As no amount will be deductible on settlement of this liability, its tax basis is equal to its carrying value of $72,000. There is no temporary difference on this liability.

C. As $1,650,000 has been funded and only $200,000 has been charged to expense, the enterprise would have Prepaid Pension Costs with a carrying value of $1,450,000. As the full $1,650,000 would have been deducted for tax purposes when it was funded, the tax basis of the Prepaid Pension Costs is nil. This means that there is a taxable temporary difference of $1,450,000.

D. The tax basis of the long term bonds is $3,200,000, their carrying value of $3,110,000, plus the $90,000 taxable gain that would arise if they were settled at their carrying value of $3,110,000. This means that there is a taxable temporary difference of $90,000.

E. The tax basis of both the leased asset and the lease liability are nil. This means that there is a taxable temporary difference on the asset of $252,000 and a deductible temporary difference on the liability of $276,000. Considered together, there is a net deductible temporary difference of $24,000.

F. The tax basis of the specialized capital assets is nil, resulting in a taxable temporary difference of $912,000.

G. The tax basis of the depreciable assets is the UCC of $1,000,000, resulting in a taxable temporary difference of $1,150,000 ($2,150,000 - $1,000,000).

H. The tax basis of the Temporary Investments is $54,500, the original cost of $56,000 less $1,500, the non-deductible one-half of the $3,000 capital loss that would result from the recovery of the carrying value of the assets. This results in a deductible temporary difference of $1,500 ($54,500 - $53,000).

Exercise Eleven - 5 Solution

- Part IV tax on dividends received by a private corporation. This is a refundable tax and, as such, is within the scope of Section 3465.

- Capital taxes are a form of minimum tax. Such taxes are only within the scope of Section 3465 if they may be used to reduce income taxes in another period. This is not the case with the tax as described and, as a consequence, it would not fall within the scope of Section 3465.

- Goods and services taxes are covered in EIC Abstract No. 18 and do not fall within the scope of Section 3465.

- The harmonized sales tax in these Provinces is a combined federal and provincial goods and services tax. Such taxes are not within the scope of Section 3465. Rather the appropriate procedures for dealing with such taxes are found in EIC Abstract No. 18.

- Provided that future income taxes are expected to be included in the approved rate charged to customers in the future and are expected to be recovered from future customers, enterprises in regulated industries are not required to record future income tax assets and future income tax liabilities.

- As payment of this tax can be reduced by the federal surtax on corporate income, it would fall within the scope of Section 3465.

Exercise Eleven - 6

The required journal entry would be as follows:

Taxes Receivable [(23%)($85,000)]	$19,550	
Tax Benefit [(23%)($85,000)]		$19,550

The Taxes Receivable reflect the amount that will be recovered through the $85,000 loss carry back. It will be disclosed as a current asset on the Balance Sheet.

Exercise Eleven - 7

The company's overall tax rate will depend on whether the income is eligible for the small business deduction (first $200,000 of active business income) and the applicable provincial rates. The various overall rates, ignoring the general and accelerated rate reductions, are as follows:

	Eligible For The SBD		Not Eligible For The SBD	
	Alberta	Sask.	Alberta	Sask.
	%	%	%	%
Basic Federal Rate	38.0	38.0	38.0	38.0
Abatement	(10.0)	(10.0)	(10.0)	(10.0)
Pre Surtax	28.0	28.0	28.0	28.0
Surtax [(4%)(28%)]	1.1	1.1	1.1	1.1
	29.1	29.1	29.1	29.1
Small Business Deduction	(16.0)	(16.0)	N/A	N/A
Provincial Rate	6.0	8.0	15.5	17.0
Combined Rates	19.1	21.1	44.6	46.1

Applying these four combined rates to the applicable shares of Taxable Income produces a weighted average rate of 28.7%, calculated as follows:

Alberta Small Business [(40%)($200,000/$300,000)(19.1%)]	5.09%
Saskatchewan Small Business [(60%)($200,000/$300,000)(21.1%)]	8.44
Alberta Regular [(40%)($100,000/$300,000)(44.6%)]	5.95
Saskatchewan Regular [(60%)($100,000/$300,000)(46.1%)]	9.22
Weighted Average Rate	28.70%

Exercise Eleven - 8 Solution

The analysis schedule would be as follows:

	Accounting Income	Taxable Income	Change In Temporary Differences
Income Before Taxes	$325,000	$325,000	
One-Half Capital Gain	(25,000)	(25,000)	
Depreciation		92,000	($92,000)
Capital Cost Allowance		(71,000)	71,000
Balances	$300,000	$321,000	($21,000)
Tax Rate	37%	37%	37%
Current Tax Balances	$111,000	$118,770	($ 7,770)
Effect Of Change In Tax Rate [(41% - 37%)($560,000)]	(22,400)	N/A	(22,400)
Total Tax Balances	$ 88,600	$118,770	($30,170)

Based on this schedule, the appropriate journal entry is as follows:

Tax Expense	$88,600	
Future Income Tax Liability	30,170	
Taxes Payable		$118,770

The Income Statement for 2002, including disclosure of the split between current and future Tax Expense, would be as follows:

Saxon Ltd.
Condensed Income Statement
Year Ending December 31, 2002

Income Before Taxes		$325,000
Tax Expense:		
Current	$118,770	
Future	(30,170)	88,600
Net Income		$236,400

As the reported tax expense does not reflect the current tax rate of 37 percent, additional disclosure is required under Paragraph 3465.92(c) to reconcile these amounts. Appropriate disclosure would be as follows:

Taxes At Statutory Rate [(37%)($325,000)]	$120,250
Tax Savings From Non-Taxable Portion Of	
Capital Gain [(37%)($25,000)]	(9,250)
Adjustment of Future Income Tax Liability [(41% - 37%)($560,000)]	(22,400)
Income Tax Expense Reported	$ 88,600

Exercise Eleven - 9 Solution

The analysis of Ondine Inc.'s tax balances for 2002 would be as follows:

	Accounting Income	Taxable Income	Change In Temporary Differences
Income Before Taxes And Extraordinary Items	$423,000	$423,000	
Depreciation		93,000	($ 93,000)
Capital Cost Allowance		(134,000)	134,000
Ordinary Balance	$423,000	$382,000	$ 41,000
Tax Rate	42%	42%	42%
Tax Balances Before Rate Change	$177,660	$160,440	$ 17,220
Rate Change [($670,000)(42% - 20%)]	147,400	N/A	147,400
Tax Balances - Ordinary Income	$325,060	$160,440	$164,620
Extraordinary Loss	($ 92,000)	N/A	($ 92,000)
Non-Deductible One-Half	46,000		46,000
Extraordinary Balance	($ 46,000)		($ 46,000)
Tax Rate	42%		42%
Tax Balances - Extraordinary Item	($ 19,320)	Nil	($ 19,320)
Prior Period Adjustment	($ 73,000)	N/A	($ 73,000)
Tax Rate	42%		42%
Tax Balances - Prior Period Adjustment	($ 30,660)	Nil	($ 30,660)

Part A   The required journal entry would be as follows:

Income Tax Expense - Ordinary	$325,060	
Future Income Tax Asset - Non-Current		
($19,320 + $30,660)	49,980	
Taxes Payable		$160,440
Future Income Tax Liability - Non-Current		164,620
Income Tax Benefit - Extraordinary		19,320
Income Tax Benefit - Prior Period Adjustment		30,660

The $30,660 that relates to the prior period adjustment is credited directly to Retained Earnings.

Part B   The required Income Statement would be as follows:

Ondine Inc.
Condensed Income Statement
Year Ending December 31, 2002

Income Before Taxes And Extraordinary Item		$ 423,000
Tax Expense:		
Current	($160,440)	
Future	(164,620)	(325,060)
Income Before Extraordinary Item		$ 97,940
Extraordinary Loss	($ 92,000)	
Tax Benefit (All Future)	19,320	(72,680)
Net Income		$ 25,260
Opening Retained Earnings		
As Previously Reported	$2,896,000	
Prior Period Adjustment	($73,000)	
Tax Benefit (All Future)	30,660	(42,340)	2,853,660
Closing Retained Earnings		$2,878,920

Exercise Eleven - 10 Solution
Part A   The required journal entry for 2002 would be as follows:

Future Income Tax Asset [(43%)($375,000)]	$161,250	
Income Tax Benefit		$161,250

Based on this entry, the condensed Income Statement for Finder Inc. for the year ending December 31, 2002 would be as follows:

Finder Inc.
Condensed Income Statement
Year Ending December 31, 2002

Loss Before Income Taxes	($375,000)
Income Tax Benefit (All Future)	161,250
Net Loss	($213,750)

The journal entry for the year ending December 31, 2003 would be as follows:

Income Tax Expense	$179,700	
Future Income Tax Asset (Balance)		$161,250
Taxes Payable [(41%)($420,000 - $375,000)]		18,450

Based on this entry, the condensed Income Statement for Finder Inc. for the year ending December 31, 2003 would be as follows:

Finder Inc.
Condensed Income Statement
Year Ending December 31, 2003

Income Before Income Taxes		$420,000
Income Tax Expense:		
Current	($ 18,450)	
Future	(161,250)	(179,700)
Net Income		$240,300

Additional disclosure would be required to explain why the Income Tax Expense does not reflect the current rate of 41 percent.

Part B   The required journal entry for 2002 would be as follows:

Future Income Tax Asset [(43%)($375,000)]	$161,250	
Income Tax Benefit [(43%)($200,000)]		$86,000
Valuation Allowance [(43%)($375,000 - $200,000)]		75,250

Based on this entry, the condensed Income Statement for Finder Inc. for the year ending December 31, 2002 would be as follows:

Finder Inc.
Condensed Income Statement
Year Ending December 31, 2002

Loss Before Income Taxes	($375,000)
Income Tax Benefit (All Future)	86,000
Net Loss	($289,000)

The journal entry for the year ending December 31, 2003 would be as follows:

Valuation Allowance (Balance)	$ 75,250	
Income Tax Expense	104,450	
Future Income Tax Asset (Balance)		$161,250
Taxes Payable [(41%)($420,000 - $375,000)]		18,450

Based on this entry, the condensed Income Statement for Finder Inc. for the year ending December 31, 2003 would be as follows:

Finder Inc.
Condensed Income Statement
Year Ending December 31, 2003

Income Before Income Taxes		$420,000
Income Tax Expense:		
Current	($18,450)	
Future	(86,000)	(104,450)
Net Income		$315,550

Additional disclosure would be required to explain why the Income Tax Expense does not reflect the current rate of 41 percent.

Part C   The required journal entry for 2002 as the same as the one in Part A as follows:

Future Income Tax Asset [(43%)($375,000)]	$161,250	
Income Tax Benefit		$161,250

Based on this entry, the condensed Income Statement for Finder Inc. for the year ending December 31, 2002 would be as follows:

Finder Inc.
Condensed Income Statement
Year Ending December 31, 2002

Loss Before Income Taxes	($375,000)
Income Tax Benefit (All Future)	161,250
Net Loss	($213,750)

The journal entry for the year ending December 31, 2003 would be as follows:

Income Tax Expense	$161,250	
Future Income Tax Asset (Balance)		$161,250
Taxes Payable		Nil

Based on this entry, the condensed Income Statement for Finder Inc. for the year ending December 31, 2003 would be as follows:

Finder Inc.
Condensed Income Statement
Year Ending December 31, 2003

Income Before Income Taxes		$ 10,000
Income Tax Expense:		
Current	$ Nil	
Future	(161,250)	(161,250)
Net Income (Loss)		($151,250)

Additional disclosure would be required to explain why the Income Tax Expense does not reflect the current rate of 41 percent.

Exercise Eleven - 11 Solution

Part A   Letting X stand for the value to be recorded for the asset, the appropriate amount would be calculated as follows:

X = $230,000 +[(35%)(X - $95,000)]
X = $302,692

Asset	$302,692	
Future Income Tax Liability		$ 72,692
Cash		95,000
No Par Value Common Stock		135,000

This result can be verified by noting that, if the asset were sold for $302,692, the resulting tax liability would be $72,692 [(35%)($302,692 - $95,000)].

Part B   Letting X stand for the value to be recorded for the asset, the appropriate amount would be calculated as follows:

X = $285,000 +[(40%)(X - $427,500)]
X = $190,000

Asset	$190,000	
Future Income Tax Asset	95,000	
Cash		$285,000

This result can be verified by noting that, if the asset were sold for $190,000, the resulting tax deduction would be $95,000 [(40%)($190,000 - $427,500)].

Solution to Self Study Problem Eleven - 1

The analysis of BLM's income taxes for the year ending December 31, 2002 is as follows:

	Accounting Income	Taxable Income	Changes In Temporary Differences
Accounting Income	$ 78,000	$ 78,000	
Deferred Development Costs		(20,000)	$20,000
Depreciation Expense		16,000	(16,000)
CCA		(28,000)	28,000
Warranty Costs		6,000	(6,000)
Non-Deductible Fine	45,000	45,000	
Post Retirement Benefits		8,000	(8,000)
Totals	$123,000	$105,000	$18,000
Tax Rates	40%	40%	40%
Tax Balances	$ 49,200	$ 42,000	$ 7,200

Based on this analysis, the required entry to record income taxes for the year would be as follows:

Income Tax Expense	$49,200	
Income Tax Payable		$42,000
Future Income Tax Liability		7,200

Income Statement   Given this entry, the condensed Income Statement would be as follows:

BLM Inc.
Condensed Income Statement
Year Ending December 31, 2002

Income Before Taxes		$ 78,000
Income Tax Expense:		
Current	($42,000)	
Future	(7,200)	(49,200)
Net Income		$ 28,800

Balance Sheet   The required Balance Sheet is as follows:

BLM Inc.
Balance Sheet
As At December 31, 2002

Cash And Receivables	$ 96,000
Inventory	323,000
Deferred Development Costs	20,000
Investments	35,000
Land	25,000
Depreciable Capital Assets (Net)	279,000
Total Assets	$778,000

Current Income Tax Payable	$ 42,000
Accounts Payable	36,000
Provision For Warranties	6,000
Fine Payable	45,000
Accrued Post Retirement Benefits	8,000
Long-Term Debt	255,000
Future Income Tax Liability	7,200
Common Stock	350,000
Retained Earnings	28,800
Total Equities	$778,000

As BLM Inc. is a public company, additional disclosure is required as follows:

Paragraph 3465.92(a)   The Future Income Tax Liability reflects the net amount related to taxable temporary differences on depreciable assets and development costs, and deductible temporary differences on warranty liabilities and accrued post retirement benefits.

Paragraph 3465.92(b)   The components of Income Tax Expense are current income taxes of $42,000 and future income taxes of $7,200.

Paragraph 3465.92(c)   The Company's actual Income Tax Expense of $49,200, can be reconciled with the amount calculated using the 40 percent rate applicable to the company as follows:

Taxes At 40 Percent [(40%)($78,000)]	$31,200
Non-Deductible Fine [(40%)($45,000)]	18,000
Actual Income Tax Expense	$49,200

Solution to Self Study Problem Eleven - 2

Analysis   The analysis of Curton Inc.'s tax position is as follows:

	Accounting Income (Loss)	Taxable Income (Loss)	Temporary Differences
Income Before Results Of			
Discontinued Operations	$200,000	$200,000	N/A
Depreciation		350,000	($350,000)
CCA		(425,000)	425,000
Gain On Asset Sale*		(10,000)	10,000
One-Half Capital Gain	(7,500)	(7,500)	N/A
Warranty Reserve		15,000	(15,000)
Balances	$192,500	$122,500	$ 70,000
Tax Rate	40%	40%	40%
Balances	$ 77,000	$ 49,000	$ 28,000
Effect Of Rate Change			
[(40% - 35%)($50,000)]	2,500	N/A	2,500
Tax Balances	$ 79,500	$ 49,000	$ 30,500
Discontinued Operations Loss	($800,000)	($800,000)	N/A
Tax Rate	40%	40%	40%
Discontinued Operations			
Tax Balances	($320,000)	($320,000)	N/A

* The portion of the gain that represents the capital cost of $90,000 less the NBV of $80,000.

The total taxable loss for the year amounts to $677,500 ($800,000 - $122,500). Of this total, $200,000 can be applied to the previous year's taxable income in order to claim a refund of $70,000. The balance of $477,500 will become a loss carry forward. As management cannot claim that it is more likely than not that the $191,000 [(40%)($477,500)] benefit of this carry forward will be realized, no Future Income Tax Asset can be recognized.

Also of note in the journal entry to record the results of the preceding analysis is the fact that the deductible temporary difference related to the warranty provision will be reversed within one year. As a consequence, the related Future Income Tax Asset should be classified as current.

Journal Entry   The required journal entry is as follows:

Taxes Receivable [(35%)($200,000)]	$ 70,000	
Tax Expense - Income Before Results Of		
Discontinued Operations	79,500	
Future Income Tax Asset - Current	6,000	
Income Tax Benefit - Discontinued Operations Loss*		$119,000
Future Income Tax Liability - Non Current		36,500

*[($200,000)(35%) + ($122,500)(40%)]

The net taxable temporary differences at the end of 2002 total $120,000 ($50,000 + $70,000). This would create a net future income tax liability of $48,000 [($120,000)(40%)]. This can be verified by totalling the FITAL balances for the preceding and current years ($17,500 - $6,000 + $36,500).

Income Statement   Based on the preceding journal entry, the required Income Statement is as follows:

Curton Inc.
Income Statement
Year Ending December 31, 2002

Sales And Other Revenues		$2,600,000
Cost Of Goods Sold		($1,400,000)
Depreciation Expense		(350,000)
Other Expenses Except Taxes		(650,000)
Total Expenses Except Taxes		($2,400,000)
Income Before Tax Expenses And Discontinued Operations		$ 200,000
Income Tax Expense:		
Current	($ 49,000)	
Future	(30,500)	(79,500)
Income Before Results Of Discontinued Operations		$ 120,500
Discontinued Operations Loss	($800,000)	
Tax Benefit (All Current)	119,000	(681,000)
Net Income (Loss)		($ 560,500)

While no taxes are, in fact, currently payable, $49,000 would have been paid on income in the absence of the discontinued operations loss. This means that the discontinued operations loss, in addition to creating a current receivable of $70,000 on the loss carry back, has saved an additional $49,000 on the income before discontinued operations loss component of this year's taxes payable.

Other Disclosure   It is necessary to disclosure that there is an unrecognized benefit associated with a loss carry forward of $477,500 ($800,000 - $200,000 - $122,500). The disclosure would also indicate that the carry forward would expire in 2009.

In addition, a note is required to reconcile the $79,500 Tax Expense Before Discontinued Operations Loss with the $200,000 in Income Before Taxes. This reconciliation is as follows:

Tax Expense At Statutory Rate On Income Before Taxes	
And Discontinued Operations [(40%)($200,000)]	$80,000
One-Half Of Capital Gain [(40%)($7,500)]	(3,000)
Rate Change [(40% - 35%)($50,000)]	2,500
Tax Expense Before Discontinued Operations Loss	$79,500

A further note is required to reconcile the $119,000 tax benefit on discontinued operations with the statutory rate of 40 percent.

Tax Expense At Statutory Rate On Discontinued	
Operations Loss [(40%)($800,000)]	($320,000)
Unrecognized Loss Carry Forward	
[($800,000 - $322,500)(40%)]	191,000
Carry Back At 35 Percent [($200,000)(40% - 35%)]	10,000
Income Tax Expense (Benefit) Reported	($119,000)

Solution to Self Study Problem Eleven - 3

Analysis Of Tax Position

	Accounting Income	Taxable Income	Temporary Differences
Ordinary Income	$546,000	$546,000	
Depreciation		87,000	($ 87,000)
Capital Cost Allowance		(111,000)	111,000
One-Half Business Meals	19,000	19,000	
Warranty Costs		31,000	(31,000)
Balance	$565,000	$572,000	($ 7,000)
Rate	44%	44%	44%
Tax Balances Before Rate Change	$248,600	$251,680	($ 3,080)
Effect Of Rate Change			
[($2,200,000)(44% - 42%)]	44,000	N/A	44,000
Tax Balances	$292,600	$251,680	$ 40,920

Loss On Discontinued Operation	($1,200,000)	($1,200,000)
Non-Deductible One-Half Capital Loss	75,000	75,000
Balance	($1,125,000)	($1,125,000)
Tax Rate	44%	44%
Tax Benefit - Discontinued Operation	($ 495,000)	($ 495,000)

The total Taxable Loss is $553,000 ($1,125,000 - $572,000). This includes all of the $75,000 allowable capital loss as none of this amount could be applied against ordinary income. Of this amount, $123,000 can be carried back to claim a refund of $51,660 [(42%)($123,000)]. The fact that the benefit is $2,460 [(44% - 42%)($123,000)] less than it would be at current rates will result in it being deducted from the tax benefit associated with the discontinued operation.

The remaining $430,000, made up of a $75,000 allowable capital loss and a $355,000 non-capital loss, can be carried forward. A Future Income Tax Asset of $94,600 [($430,000)(1/2)(44%)] can be recognized. The unrecognized benefit of $94,600 will also be deducted from the tax benefit on the discontinued operation. This results in a net benefit of $397,940 ($495,000 - $2,460 - $94,600).

Required Journal Entry

Tax Expense - Ordinary	$292,600	
Current Income Tax Asset	51,660	
Future Income Tax Asset	94,600	
Tax Benefit - Discontinued Operation		$397,940
Future Income Tax Liability		40,920

Required Income Statement

Quern Inc.
Condensed Income Statement
Year Ending December 31, 2002

Income Before Taxes And Results Of Discontinued Operations		$546,000
Tax Expense:		
Current	($251,680)	
Future	(40,920)	(292,600)
Income Before The Results Of Discontinued Operations		$253,400
Loss From Discontinued Operations	($1,200,000)	
Tax Benefit	397,940	(802,060)
Net Income (Loss)		($548,660)

Required Disclosure

Ordinary Tax Expense   The Income Tax Expense included in the determination of Income Before The Results Of Discontinued Operations reflects an income tax rate that differs from the Company's statutory tax rate for the following reasons:

Taxes at Statutory Rate [(44%)($546,000)]	$240,240
Cost Of Non-Deductible Meals [(44%)($19,000)]	8,360
Adjustment Of Opening Future Income Tax Liability [(44% - 42%)($2,200,000)]	44,000
Income Tax Expense Reported	$292,600

Discontinued Operations Tax Benefit   The Tax Benefit used to reduce the Loss From Discontinued Operations reflects an income tax rate that differs from the Company's statutory tax rate for the following reasons:

Tax Benefit At Statutory Rate [(44%)($1,200,000)]	$528,000
Non-Deductible One-Half Of Capital Loss [(44%)($75,000)]	(33,000)
Loss Carry Back At 42 Percent Rate [(44% - 42%)($123,000)]	(2,460)
Loss Carry Forward With Unrecognized Benefit [(44%)($215,000)]	(94,600)
Tax Benefit Reported	$397,940

Additional disclosure would be required to indicate that the Company has a loss carry forward of $215,000 for which the benefit has not been recognized. Of this amount, $37,500 [(1/2)($75,000)] is an allowable capital loss that can be carried forward indefinitely. The remaining $177,500 [(1/2)($355,000)] will expire in 2010.

Solution to Self Study Problem Eleven - 4

Case A   The analysis of the Martin Company's 2002 tax situation in this case would be as follows:

	Accounting Income (Loss)	Taxable Income (Loss)	Temporary Differences
Loss Before Taxes	($2,000,000)	($2,000,000)	
Depreciation		1,500,000	($1,500,000)
Capital Cost Allowance		(800,000)	800,000
Balances	($2,000,000)	($1,300,000)	($ 700,000)
Rate	40%	40%	40%
Tax Balances	($ 800,000)	($ 520,000)	($ 280,000)

Based on this analysis, the required journal entry would be as follows:

Future Income Tax Asset	$520,000	
Future Income Tax Liability	280,000	
Income Tax Benefit		$800,000

The preceding journal entry would be incorporated into the following condensed Income Statement:

Martin Company
Condensed Income Statement
Year Ending December 31, 2002

Loss Before Taxes	($2,000,000)
Income Tax Benefit (All Future)	800,000
Net Loss	($1,200,000)

As the Income Tax Benefit reflects the current statutory rate of 40 percent, no additional disclosure would be required in this Case.

For 2003, no analysis of Martin's tax position is required because taxable income is equal to accounting income. The only feature to be noted in this year is that the 2002 loss carry forward of $1,300,000 would be used to reduce Taxes Payable from $2,000,000 (40 percent of $5,000,000) to $1,480,000 (40 percent of $3,700,000). The required journal entry would be as follows:

Tax Expense [(40%)($5,000,000)]	$2,000,000	
Future Income Tax Asset		$ 520,000
Taxes Payable [(40%)($5,000,000 - $1,300,000)]		1,480,000

This journal entry would be incorporated into the following condensed Income Statement:

Martin Company
Condensed Income Statement
Year Ending December 31, 2003

Income Before Taxes		$5,000,000
Tax Expense:		
Current	($1,480,000)	
Future	(520,000)	(2,000,000)
Net Income		$3,000,000

No additional disclosure would be required for 2003.

Case B   The 2002 analysis of the Martin Company's tax situation in this Case would be identical to that in Case A. However, as the Company cannot claim that it is more likely than not that the loss carry forward benefit will be realized, no Future Income Tax Asset can be recorded. The required entry is as follows (we have not used the valuation allowance approach for the Future Income Tax Asset).

Future Income Tax Liability	$280,000	
Income Tax Benefit		$280,000

The required condensed Income Statement would be as follows:

Martin Company
Condensed Income Statement
Year Ending December 31, 2002

Loss Before Taxes	($2,000,000)
Income Tax Benefit (All Future)	280,000
Net Loss	($1,720,000)

Disclosure would include the fact that there is a $1,300,000 loss carry forward for which no benefit has been recognized. The carry forward expires in 2009. In addition, the actual Income Tax Benefit would have to be reconciled with the amount that would have been recorded at the applicable statutory rate:

Tax Benefit At Statutory Rate [(40%)($2,000,000)]	$800,000
Unrecognized Loss Carry Forward Benefit [(40%)($1,300,000)]	(520,000)
Actual Tax Benefit	$280,000

The journal entry for 2003 would be as follows:

Tax Expense [(40%)($5,000,000 - $1,300,000)]	$1,480,000	
Taxes Payable		$1,480,000

The 2003 condensed Income Statement would be as follows:

Martin Company
Condensed Income Statement
Year Ending December 31, 2003

Income Before Taxes	$5,000,000
Tax Expense (All Current)	(1,480,000)
Net Income	$3,520,000

A reconciliation of the actual Tax Expense with the amount that would have been recorded at the applicable statutory rate is required:

Tax Expense At Statutory Rate [(40%)($5,000,000)]	$2,000,000
Realization Of Unrecognized Loss Carry Forward Benefit [(40%)($1,300,000)]	(520,000)
Actual Tax Expense	$1,480,000

Case C   The analysis of the Martin Company's 2002 tax situation in this case would be as follows:

	Accounting Income (Loss)	Taxable Income (Loss)	Temporary Differences
Loss Before Taxes	($2,000,000)	($2,000,000)	
Depreciation		1,500,000	($1,500,000)
Balances	($2,000,000)	($ 500,000)	($1,500,000)
Rate	40%	40%	40%
Tax Balances	($ 800,000)	($ 200,000)	($ 600,000)

Based on this analysis, the required journal entry would be as follows:

Future Income Tax Asset [(1/2)($200,000)]	$100,000	
Future Income Tax Liability	600,000	
Income Tax Benefit		$700,000

The required Income Statement would be as follows:

Martin Company
Condensed Income Statement
Year Ending December 31, 2002

Loss Before Taxes	($2,000,000)
Income Tax Benefit (All Future)	700,000
Net Loss	($1,300,000)

Disclosure would include the fact that there is a $250,000 loss carry forward for which no benefit has been recognized. The carry forward expires in 2009. In addition, the actual Income Tax Benefit must be reconciled with the amount that would have been recorded at the applicable statutory rate:

Tax Benefit At Statutory Rate [(40%)($2,000,000)]	$800,000
Unrecognized Loss Carry Forward Benefit [(40%)($250,000)]	(100,000)
Actual Tax Benefit	$700,000

The journal entry for 2003 would be as follows:

Tax Expense	$1,900,000	
Future Income Tax Asset		$ 100,000
Taxes Payable [(40%)($5,000,000 - $500,000)]		1,800,000

The 2003 condensed Income Statement would be as follows:

Martin Company
Condensed Income Statement
Year Ending December 31, 2003

Income Before Taxes		$5,000,000
Tax Expense:		
Current	($1,800,000)	
Future	(100,000)	(1,900,000)
Net Income		$3,100,000

A reconciliation of the actual Tax Expense with the amount that would have been recorded at the applicable statutory rate is required:

Tax Expense At Statutory Rate [(40%)($5,000,000)]	$2,000,000
Realization Of Unrecognized Loss Carry Forward Benefit	
[(40%)($250,000)]	(100,000)
Actual Tax Expense	$1,900,000

Note the total of the two years' income for all three cases is $1,800,000.

Solution to Self Study Problem Eleven - 5

2000 Solution The solution for this year would begin with the following analysis of the Loser Company's tax position:

	Accounting Income (Loss)	Taxable Income	Temporary Differences
Accounting Loss	($75,000)	($ 75,000)	
Club Dues	15,000	15,000	
Depreciation		100,000	($100,000)
Capital Cost Allowance		(100,000)	100,000
Balances	($60,000)	($ 60,000)	$ -0-

2000 Journal Entry Based on the preceding analysis, the required journal entry to record the taxes would be as follows:

Taxes Receivable	$20,000	
Future Income Tax Asset	4,000	
Income Tax Benefit		$24,000

Of the total loss of $60,000, $50,000 can be carried back to apply against 1999 taxable income and to claim a refund of $20,000. The remaining amount of $10,000 is a loss carry forward and its benefit can be recognized as an asset if management indicates that it is more likely than not to be realized. The problem indicates that this can be done to the extent of temporary differences that can be reversed.

2000 Income Statement The Income Statement resulting from the preceding analysis and entry would be as follows:

Loser Company
Condensed Income Statement
Year Ending December 31, 2000

Income (Loss) Before Taxes		($75,000)
Income Tax Benefit:		
Current	$20,000	
Future	4,000	24,000
Net Income (Loss)		($51,000)

A note is required which discloses the components of the variation from the statutory income tax rate. For this year, the note would be as follows:

The income tax benefit reflects an income tax rate that differs from the Company's statutory tax rate for the following reasons:

Income Tax Benefit At Statutory Rate [(40%)($75,000)]	$30,000
Reduction From Non-Deductible Club Dues [(40%)($15,000)]	(6,000)
Income Tax Benefit Reported	$24,000

2001 Solution   The solution for 2001 would begin with the following analysis of the Loser Company's tax position:

	Accounting Income (Loss)	Taxable Income	Temporary Differences
Accounting Loss	($1,000,000)	($1,000,000)	
Club Dues	15,000	15,000	
Depreciation		100,000	($100,000)
Balances	($ 985,000)	($ 885,000)	($100,000)

2001 Journal Entry   At this point, we have a total tax loss carry forward of $895,000 ($885,000 plus $10,000 from 2000). As we have indicated, this can be recognized to the extent that temporary differences are available to be reversed. At the end of 1999, there were $700,000 in temporary differences, a balance that remained unchanged during 2000. However, we recognized a $4,000 Future Income Tax Asset in 2000 based on $10,000 of these differences. After recognition of the $100,000 reduction of these differences during 2001, this means that there are $590,000 left for recognition of further loss carry forward benefits. This can implemented with the following journal entry:

Future Income Tax Liability [(40%)($100,000)]	$ 40,000	
Future Income Tax Asset [(40%)($690,000 - $100,000)]	236,000	
Income Tax Benefit		$276,000

2001 Income Statement   The Income Statement resulting from the preceding analysis and entry would be as follows:

Loser Company
Condensed Income Statement
Year Ending December 31, 2001

Income (Loss) Before Taxes		($1,000,000)
Income Tax Benefit:		
Current	$ - 0 -	
Future	276,000	276,000
Net Income (Loss)		($ 724,000)

The total loss carry forward for tax purposes is $895,000, with a potential benefit of $358,000 [(40%)($895,000)]. We have recognized the benefit associated with $600,000 of this amount. The benefit associated with the remaining $295,000 is unrecognized. Paragraph 3465.91(f) would require the disclosure of this unrecognized loss carry forward as well as the fact that it expires at the end of 2008.

In addition, a note such as the following is required which would illustrate the components that cause the tax rate in the Income Statement to differ from the statutory tax rate.

Note   The income tax benefit reflects an income tax rate that differs from the Company's statutory tax rate for the following reasons:

Income Tax Benefit At Statutory Rate [(40%)($1,000,000)]	$400,000
Reduction From Non-Deductible Club Dues [(40%)($15,000)]	(6,000)
Reduction From Unrecognized Loss Carry Forward [(40%)($295,000)]	(118,000)
Income Tax Benefit Reported	$276,000

2002 Solution   The solution for 2002 would begin with the following analysis of the Loser Company's tax position:

	Accounting Income (Loss)	Taxable Income	Temporary Differences
Accounting Income	$250,000	$250,000	
Dividends	(35,000)	(35,000)	
One-Half Capital Gain	(5,000)	(5,000)	
Depreciation		100,000	($100,000)
Balances	$210,000	$310,000	($100,000)
Tax Rate	50%	50%	50%
Tax Balances Before Rate Change	$105,000	$155,000	($ 50,000)
Effect Of Rate Change*	Nil	Nil	Nil
Tax Balances	$105,000	$155,000	($ 50,000)

*Both the Future Income Tax Asset and the Future Income Tax Liability accounts would have to be written up to reflect the new 50 percent tax rate. However, as both of these accounts are based on the total temporary differences of $600,000, the two adjustments would offset each other in this schedule.

2002 Journal Entries   A first entry would be required to recognize the effect of the tax rate change on the Future Income Tax Asset and the Future Income Tax Liability balances:

Future Income Tax Asset [(50% - 40%)($600,000)]$60,000		
Future Income Tax Liability		$60,000

The next entry would recognize the Tax Expense without consideration of the loss carry forward:

Tax Expense	$105,000	
Future Income Tax Liability	50,000	
Taxes Payable		$155,000

An additional entry would be required to recognize the use of the loss carry forward to eliminate Taxes Payable:

Taxes Payable	$155,000	
Tax Expense		$105,000
Future Income Tax Asset		50,000

The credit to Tax Expense reflects the fact that we have realized the benefit associated with another $210,000 of the loss carry forward. The total remaining loss carry forward is $585,000 ($895,000 - $310,000) and the remaining unrecognized portion is $85,000 ($295,000 - $210,000). The $500,000 difference between these two figures is reflected in the $250,000 ($300,000 - $50,000) balance remaining in the Future Income Tax Asset account.

2002 Income Statement   The Income Statement resulting from the preceding analysis and entries would be as follows:

Loser Company
Condensed Income Statement
Year Ending December 31, 2002

Income Before Taxes	$250,000
Tax Expense ($105,000 - $105,000)	Nil
Net Income	$250,000

A note would be required indicating that there is an $85,000 loss carry forward for which no benefit has been recognized, and that it expires in 2008. A further note would be required to illustrate the components that cause the tax rate in the Income Statement to differ from the statutory tax rate:

Tax Expense At Statutory Rate [(50%)($250,000)]	($125,000)
Tax Savings From Non-Taxable Dividends [(50%)($35,000)]	17,500
Reduction From Non-Taxable One-Half Of	
Capital Gain [(50%)($5,000)]	2,500
Realization Of Previously Unrecognized Loss	
Carry Forward Benefit [(50%)($210,000)]	105,000
Tax Expense Reported	$ Nil

2003 Solution   The solution for 2003 would begin with the following analysis of the Loser Company's tax position:

	Accounting Income	Taxable Income	Temporary Differences
Accounting Income	$1,800,000	$1,800,000	
Dividends	(35,000)	(35,000)	
Depreciation		100,000	($100,000)
Capital Cost Allowance		(250,000)	250,000
Balances	$1,765,000	$1,615,000	$ 150,000
Tax Rates	50%	50%	50%
Tax Balances	$ 882,500	$ 807,500	$ 75,000

2003 Journal Entries   Based on the preceding analysis, the required journal entries to record the 2000 taxes would be as follows:

Tax Expense	$882,500	
Future Income Tax Liability		$ 75,000
Taxes Payable		807,500
Taxes Payable [(50%)($585,000)]	$292,500	
Future Income Tax Asset		$250,000
Tax Expense [(50%)($85,000)]		42,500

The first entry uses the balances calculated in the schedule which ignores the tax loss carry forward. The second entry accounts for the realization of the tax loss benefit. The debit to Taxes Payable is the decrease due to the tax loss carry forward of $585,000. The credit to Future Income Tax Asset eliminates the balance in that account, reflecting the fact that all of the benefit of the loss carry forward has now been realized. The $42,500 reduction of the Tax Expense is for the recognition of the benefit associated with the $85,000 loss carry forward for which no benefit has previously been recognized.

2003 Income Statement   The Income Statement resulting from the preceding analysis and entry would be as follows:

Loser Company
Condensed Income Statement
Year Ending December 31, 2003

Income Before Taxes		$1,800,000
Tax Expense:		
Current ($807,500 - $292,500)	($515,000)	
Future ($75,000 + $250,000)	(325,000)	(840,000)
Net Income		$ 960,000

A note is required which would illustrate the components that cause the tax rate in the Income Statement to differ from the statutory tax rate as follows:

Tax Expense At Statutory Rate [(50%)($1,800,000)]	($900,000)
Tax Savings From Non-Taxable Dividends [(50%)($35,000)]	17,500
Realization of Previously Unrecognized Loss Carry Forward Benefit [(50%)($85,000)]	42,500
Tax Expense Reported	($840,000)

Chapter Twelve Problems

There are no Exercises or Self Study problems related to this Chapter.

Solution to Self Study Problem Thirteen - 1

Part A   The capital balances of the two partners on February 28 of the current year are as follows:

	George Brown	Terry Green
Assets Contributed	$50,000	$ 170,000
Liabilities Assumed	-0-	30,000
Net Capital Balances	$50,000	$ 140,000

Part B   The total capital balance would be $190,000 ($50,000 + $140,000) and, if the agreement called for this amount to be split equally, George Brown and Terry Green would each be allocated $95,000 ($190,000/2).

Part C   Given the large difference in tangible assets contributed by the two partners, it would appear that George Brown is bringing goodwill into the Partnership. The amount would be calculated as follows:

Identifiable Assets From Green	$140,000
Identifiable Assets From Brown	(50,000)
Implied Goodwill	$ 90,000

George Brown and Terry Green would each be allocated $140,000 in capital.

Solution to Self Study Problem Thirteen - 2

Part A   Under the profit sharing agreement described in Part A, we would first have to calculate the average capital balances for the two partners. This would be done as follows:

Jim Bond Average Capital

[($20,000)(1)]	$20,000
[($5,000)(3/4)]	3,750
[($5,000)(1/4)]	1,250
Total	$25,000

Bob Ray Average Capital

[($40,000)(1)]	$40,000
[($10,000)(5/6)]	(8,333)
[($10,000)(1/3)]	(3,333)
[($10,000)(1/6)]	1,666
Total	$30,000

We can now calculate the amounts to be distributed to each of the partners under the terms of the agreement:

	Jim Bond	Bob Ray	Total
Interest At 4 Percent	$1,000	$ 1,200	$ 2,200
Balance Equally	8,900	8,900	17,800
Total Distribution	$9,900	$10,100	$20,000

Part B   The distribution to be made under the profit sharing agreement in Part B is calculated as follows:

	Jim Bond	Bob Ray	Total
Salary	$ -0-	$ 9,000	$ 9,000
Interest At 4 Percent	1,200	1,200	2,400
Balance 60:40	5,160	3,440	8,600
Total Distribution	$6,360	$13,640	$20,000

Part C   The distribution to be made under the profit sharing agreement in Part C is calculated as follows:

	Jim Bond	Bob Ray	Total
Salaries	$8,300	$ 9,500	$17,800
Balance 25:30	1,000	1,200	2,200
Total Distribution	$9,300	$10,700	$20,000

Part D   Prior to calculating the complete profit sharing distribution, a calculation of the bonus is required. This calculation would be as follows:

$$\text{Bonus} = [(.20)(\$20,000 - \$5,000 - \text{Bonus})]$$
$$[(1.2)(\text{Bonus})] = \$3,000$$
$$\text{Bonus} = \$2,500$$

Given the preceding calculation, the profit sharing distribution would be as follows:

	Jim Bond	Bob Ray	Total
Bonus	$2,500	$ -0-	$ 2,500
Salary	-0-	5,000	5,000
Balance Equally	6,250	6,250	12,500
Total Distribution	$8,750	$11,250	$20,000

Solution to Self Study Problem Thirteen - 3

Part A   There are three alternative methods that could be used to record the admission of Douglas to the Partnership. The recorded value of the partnership is $400,000 and if we assume that these values are appropriate for 80 percent of the business after the admission of Douglas, the implied total value is $500,000. This would indicate that Douglas is bringing Goodwill of $20,000 into the Partnership and the admission would be recorded as follows:

Goodwill	$ 20,000
Cash	80,000
Douglas, Capital	$100,000

Alternatively, if we assume that the amount paid by Douglas is an appropriate measure of the value of the business, the total value after his admission would be $400,000. This means that the business prior to his payment of $80,000 would only be worth $320,000 and assets would have to be revalued as follows:

Allison, Capital (60 Percent)	$48,000	
Brook, Capital (30 Percent)	24,000	
Carey, Capital (10 Percent)	8,000	
Assets		$80,000

After this adjustment, the entry to record the admission of Douglas would be as follows:

Cash	$80,000	
Douglas, Capital		$80,000

A final alternative would involve no adjustment of asset values or recognition of Goodwill. Under this alternative we would assume that the existing partners are paying a bonus to Douglas and the admission would be recorded as follows:

Cash	$80,000	
Allison, Capital (60 Percent)	9,600	
Brook, Capital (30 Percent)	4,800	
Carey, Capital (10 Percent)	1,600	
Douglas, Capital (20 Percent Of $480,000)		$96,000

Part B   Here the question is whether or not to recognize the Goodwill implied in the price paid by Douglas. His price of $84,000 for 20 percent of the Partnership implies a total value of $420,000, an amount $20,000 in excess of the current book values. This could be recorded as follows:

Goodwill	$20,000	
Allison, Capital (60 Percent)		$12,000
Brook, Capital (30 Percent)		6,000
Carey, Capital (10 Percent)		2,000

With this adjustment recorded, the entry to admit Douglas would be as follows:

Allison, Capital [(20%)($206,000)]	$41,200	
Brook, Capital [(20%)($136,000)]	27,200	
Carey, Capital [(20%)($78,000)]	15,600	
Douglas, Capital [(20%)($420,000)]		$84,000

An alternative solution involving no recognition of Goodwill would be as follows:

Allison, Capital [(20%)($194,000)]	$38,800	
Brook, Capital [(20%)($130,000)]	26,000	
Carey, Capital [(20%)($76,000)]	15,200	
Douglas, Capital		$80,000

Solution to Self Study Problem Thirteen - 4

Part A   The entry to record the transfer of interest of Tom Jones to his sister Shirley would be as follows:

Tom Jones, Capital	$26,000	
Shirley Jones, Capital		$26,000

As the transfer took place directly between the two individuals, no further explanation of this entry is required.

Part B   Under the new entity approach, assets would be revalued on the basis of the price paid by Shirley. The fact that she paid $40,000 for a 20 percent interest in the Partnership would indicate that the equity interest will be worth $200,000 ($40,000/.20) after her admission. This means that the present ownership interests would have a current value of $160,000 ($200,000 - $40,000) and that the total assets would be valued at $205,000 ($160,000, plus the Liabilities of $45,000). As the fair value given for the Partnership's Identifiable Assets is only $189,000, Goodwill in the amount of $16,000 appears to be present. The entries to record the fair value change on the Identifiable Assets and to admit Shirley to the Partnership are as follows:

Identifiable Assets ($189,000 - $164,000)	$25,000	
Goodwill	16,000	
Tom Jones, Capital (20%)		$ 8,200
Dick Jones, Capital (30%)		12,300
Harry Jones, Capital (50%)		20,500
Cash	$40,000	
Shirley Jones, Capital		$40,000

Part C   As the Partnership assets will not be revalued in this Case, the excess of the retirement price over the book value of Dick Jones' equity interest must be allocated to the other partners on the basis of their profit and loss sharing ratios. The required entry would be as follows:

Dick Jones, Capital	$41,000	
Tom Jones, Capital ([2/7][$13,000])	3,714	
Harry Jones, Capital ([5/7][$13,000])	9,286	
Cash		$54,000

Part D   If the assets were sold for $189,000, the transaction would result in a gain of $25,000 ($189,000 - $164,000). This would be allocated to the three partners on the basis of their profit sharing ratios. This means the sale of the assets would be recorded as follows:

Cash	$189,000	
Tom Jones, Capital (20%)		$ 5,000
Dick Jones, Capital (30%)		7,500
Harry Jones, Capital (50%)		12,500
Identifiable Assets		164,000

Given the preceding entry, the entry to record the distribution of the final cash balance to the partners would be as follows:

Liabilities	$ 45,000	
Tom Jones, Capital ($26,000 + $5,000)	31,000	
Dick Jones, Capital ($41,000 + $7,500)	48,500	
Harry Jones, Capital ($52,000 + $12,500)	64,500	
Cash		$189,000

Solution to Self Study Problem Thirteen - 5

Case 1 The price paid by Breem for a one-third interest implies a total value for the partnership of $1,620,000 [(3)($540,000)] and a value for the partnership prior to this admission of $1,080,000 ($1,620,000 - $540,000). Given the book value for the Partners' capital of $1,000,000, this would imply Goodwill of $80,000. The entries to record this Goodwill and the admission of Breem would be as follows:

Goodwill	$ 80,000	
Jones, Capital (30 Percent)		$ 24,000
Smith, Capital (45 Percent)		36,000
Doe, Capital (25 Percent)		20,000
Cash	$540,000	
Breem, Capital		$540,000

Case 2 Doe is giving up his interest in the Partnership for an amount that is $20,000 less than its book value. If assets are not to be revalued, this deficiency will have to be viewed as a bonus to the other Partners. The entry which reflects this interpretation of the retirement of Doe is as follows:

Doe, Capital	$191,000	
Jones, Capital [(30/75)($20,000)]		$ 8,000
Smith, Capital [(45/75)($20,000)]		12,000
Cash		171,000

Case 3 On December 31 of the current year, the total capital of the Partners is $1,000,000 and, if we assume that the $100,000 is the only payment that will be received by the Partners, the loss would be $900,000. Based on this assumption, the distribution to the Partners can be calculated as follows:

	Jones	Smith	Doe
Capital Before Installment	$327,000	$482,000	$191,000
Share Of Liquidation Loss	(270,000)	(405,000)	(225,000)
Adjusted Capital	$ 57,000	$ 77,000	($ 34,000)
Distribution Of Doe's			
Capital Deficiency	(13,600)	(20,400)	34,000
Cash Distribution	$ 43,400	$ 56,600	$ -0-

Based on the preceding analysis, the journal entry to reflect the distribution of the first $100,000 would be as follows:

Jones, Capital	$ 43,400	
Smith, Capital	56,600	
Cash		$100,000

Solution to Self Study Problem Thirteen - 6

The development of a distribution schedule must take into account the amount of loss that can be absorbed by each partner's capital account. If we assume that in liquidation Portly's loan will be added to his capital account, the loss bearing capability of each partner can be calculated as follows:

Portly = $160,000/.10 = $1,600,000
Brawn = $320,000/.40 = $ 800,000
Large = $480,000/.50 = $ 960,000

Portly's loss bearing capability exceeds that of Large by $640,000 and, as a consequence, he would receive the first $64,000 to be distributed to the partners (10 percent of $640,000). This would leave the partners with the following loss bearing capabilities:

Portly = $ 96,000/.10 = $960,000
Brawn = $320,000/.40 = $800,000
Large = $480,000/.50 = $960,000

In order to reduce the loss bearing capabilities of Portly and Large they would receive the next $96,000 with $16,000 going to Portly (10 percent of $160,000) and $80,000 going to Large (50 percent of $160,000). At this point each partner would have a loss sharing capability of $800,000. Alternatively, it can be seen that the partners' remaining capital balances ($80,000, $320,000 and $400,000) are in the same ratio as their profit sharing ratios. Subsequent distributions would be made on the basis of their profit and loss sharing ratios.

The schedule of distributions would be as follows:

	Creditors	Portly	Brawn	Large
First $72,000	$72,000			
Next $64,000		$64,000		
Next $96,000		$16,000		$80,000
Any Balance		10%	40%	50%

Chapter Fourteen Problems

There are no Exercises or Self Study problems related to this Chapter.

Solution to Chapter Fifteen Exercises

Exercise Fifteen - 1 Solution
1. Cash and cash equivalents: Financial asset type (i)
2. Accounts receivable: Financial asset type (ii)
3. Inventories: Not a financial instrument
4. Shares in portfolio investments: Financial asset type (iv)
5. Property, plant and equipment: Not a financial instrument
6. Bank loans outstanding: Financial liability type (i)
7. Accounts payable and accrued liabilities: Financial liability type (i)
8. Current portion of long-term debt: Financial liability type (i)
9. Long-term debt: Financial liability type (i)
10. Future income taxes: Not a financial instrument
11. Shares and warrants: Equity instrument
12. Retained earnings: Not a financial instrument

Exercise Fifteen - 2 Solution
Part A   In this case, the Preferred Stock would be accounted for on the basis of its legal form. The required Income Statement would be as follows:

Classify Inc.
Income Statement
Year Ending December 31, 2002

Operating Revenues	$660,000
Operating Expenses	(440,000)
Net Income	$220,000

The $270,000 [(6%)($4,500,000)] dividends on the Preferred Stock would be disclosed in the Statement Of Retained Earnings as a distribution of Net Income.

The required journal entry on January 1, 2003 would be as follows:

Preferred Stock - Stated Value	$4,500,000	
Cash		$4,200,000
Contributed Capital		300,000

Part B   In this case, the Preferred Stock would be accounted for as a liability, resulting in the following Income Statement:

Classify Inc.
Income Statement
Year Ending December 31, 2002

Operating Revenues	$660,000
Operating Expenses	(440,000)
Operating Income	$220,000
Interest Expense [(6%)($4,500,000)]	(270,000)
Net Income (Loss)	($ 50,000)

The required journal entry on January 1, 2003 would be as follows:

Preferred Stock - Stated Value	$4,500,000	
Cash		$4,200,000
Gain On Bond Retirement		300,000

Exercise Fifteen - 3 Solution

As we have no values for using an option pricing model for the conversion option, it will have to be valued as a residual amount. Given this, the journal entry to record the issuance of the convertible bonds on January 1, 2002 would be as follows:

Cash	$4,575,360	
Bonds Payable - Face Value		$4,500,000
Common Stock - Conversion Option		75,360

The entry required to record the conversion on January 1, 2006 would be as follows:

Bonds Payable - Face Value	$4,500,000	
Common Stock - Conversion Option	75,360	
Common Stock		$4,575,360

Solution to Self Study Problem Fifteen - 1

1. True
2. False. For example, investments in equity securities are financial assets, but they are not monetary in nature.
3. False
4. False   *CICA Handbook* Section 3860, "Financial Instruments – Disclosure and Presentation" was published in 1995. A number of other sections deal with specific financial instruments such as receivables and investments in equity securities.
5. False. It deals with disclosure and presentation issues only.
6. True
7. False
8. False
9. False
10. False

Solution to Self Study Problem Fifteen - 2

1. No
2. No. Since most warranty obligations are honoured by providing repair services instead of giving cash refunds, warranty obligations are normally not considered financial instruments
3. No
4. Yes
5. No
6. No
7. No, since the lessee is expected to receive the benefit of this deposit by using the premises for the last month. More generally, since most prepaids are honoured by receiving services rather than cash refunds, they are normally not considered financial instruments.
8. Yes
9. Yes
10. No
11. No
12. Yes
13. No
14. Yes
15. Yes
16. No
17. Yes
18. Yes

19. No. Although this obligation will be extinguished by paying cash, the profession has taken the position that this payment is imposed by statutory authority and is not the result of a contract per se. Therefore it is not considered to be a financial instrument.
20. No. Since the company will provide goods or services, not cash or other financial assets, to extinguish this obligation, it is not a financial instrument.
21. Yes
22. No
23. No. See the discussion for taxes payable in #19 above.
24. Yes

Solution to Self Study Problem Fifteen - 3

1. Cash and cash equivalents: Face (maturity or future) value

2. Accounts receivable   Net realizable value

3. Inventories: Lower of cost and market

4. Shares in portfolio investments: Historical transaction amount

5. Property, plant and equipment, net: Historical cost, net of amortization to date

6. Bank loans: Face (maturity or future) value

7. Accounts payable and accrued liabilities: Face (maturity or future) value

8. Current portion of long-term debt: Present value, calculated by using yield rate at issue date

9. Long-term debt: Present value, calculated by using yield rate at issue date

10. Future income taxes: Face (maturity or future) value

11. Shares and warrants: Historical transaction amount

12. Retained earnings: Cumulative balance over time, no fixed valuation method

Solution to Self Study Problem Fifteen - 4

January 1, 2002

Cash	$10,000,000	
Bonds payable		$10,000,000

December 31, 2002

Interest expense	$800,000	
Cash (paid to bondholders)		$800,000
[($10,000,000)(8%)]		
Cash (receive fixed)	$800,000	
Interest expense		$800,000
Interest expense	$680,000	
Cash (pay variable)		$680,000
[($10,000,000)(6.8%)]		
Swap contract	$400,000	
Gain in value of swap contract		$400,000
Loss in value of bonds	$400,000	
Bonds payable		$400,000

Solution to Self Study Problem Fifteen - 5

Part A   The issue price of bonds without conversion rights would be calculated as follows:

PV Of Principal [($10,000,000)(.12403)]	$1,240,300
PV On Interest [($800,000)(7.96333)]	6,370,664
Total	$7,610,964

The required journal entries would be as follows:

March 31, 2002

Cash	$8,500,000	
Discount on bonds [$10,000,000 - $7,610,964]	2,389,036	
Bonds payable		$10,000,000
Common stock conversion rights		889,036

December 31, 2002

Interest expense [(11%)($7,610,964)(9/12)]	$627,905	
Discount on bonds		$ 27,905
Interest payable [($10,000,000)(8%)(9/12)]		600,000

March 31, 2003

Interest expense [(11%)($7,610,964)(3/12)]	$209,302	
Interest payable	600,000	
Discount on bonds		$ 9,302
Cash [($10,000,000)(8%)]		800,000

December 31, 2003

Interest expense [(11%)($7,610,964 + $27,905 + $9,302)(9/12)]	$630,974	
Discount on bonds		$ 30,974
Interest payable [($10,000,000)(8%)(9/12)]		600,000

Part B   Using this approach would require that the $8,500,000 proceeds be allocated to the bonds and the conversion rights using the following pro rata calculation:

Fair Value Of Bonds [($7,610,964 ÷ $8,610,964)($8,500,000)]	$7,512,886
Fair Value Of Rights [($1,000,000 ÷ $8,610,964)($8,500,000)]	987,114
Total Proceeds	$8,500,000

March 31, 2002

Cash	$8,500,000	
Discount on bonds [$10,000,000 - $7,512,886]	2,487,114	
Bonds payable		$10,000,000
Common stock conversion rights		987,114

December 31, 2002

Interest expense [(11%)($7,512,886)(9/12)]	$619,813	
Discount on bonds		$ 19,813
Interest payable [($10,000,000)(8%)(9/12)]		600,000

March 31, 2003

Interest expense [(11%)($7,512,886)(3/12)]	$206,604	
Interest payable	600,000	
Discount on bonds		$ 6,604
Cash		800,000

December 31, 2003

Interest expense		
[(11%)($7,512,886 + $19,813 + $6,604)(9/12)]	$621,992	
Discount on bonds		$ 21,992
Interest payable [($10,000,000)(8%)(9/12)]		600,000

Part C The required entry on April 1, 2012 would be as follows:

April 1, 2012

Common stock conversion rights [(10%)($987,114)]	$ 98,711	
Bonds payable [(10%)($10,000,000)]	1,000,000	
Discount on bonds [($2,487,114)(10/20)(10%)]		$124,356
Common shares		974,335

Some accountants argue that the market value [20,000 x $45] should be used to record the shares when debt is converted, which in this case would trigger a $74,355 gain on conversion. There is currently no pronouncement on this issue in Canada. This entry uses the book value method, which is the most common method used in practice.

Solution to Self Study Problem Fifteen - 6

Since the "loan" does not bear interest, has no maturity date and the company has no intention of repaying it in the foreseeable future, it appears to be more like equity than debt. According to *Handbook* Section 3860, these advances should be classified as equity, with full note disclosure. This treatment will also give Tripp some breathing room, since the debt to equity ratio is currently at the contractual limit of 1.5:1. A small change in their numbers could trigger a violation of their loan agreement with the bank, and the bank may have the right to call in Tripp's loan if this occurs.

Solution to Self Study Problem Fifteen - 7

The required journal entries would be as follows:

January 1, 2002

Cash	$104,213	
Bonds Payable		$100,000
Bond Premium		4,213

December 31, 2002

Interest Expense [($104,213)(6%)]	$6,253	
Bond Premium	747	
Cash [($100,000)(7%)]		$7,000

In order to deal with the remaining entries, we need to know the fair value of the bonds on December 31, 2002. This value, along with the required fair value adjustment, would be calculated as follows:

PV Of Principal [($100,000)(.73503)]	$ 73,503
PV Of Interest [($7,000)(3.31213)]	23,185
Fair Value	$ 96,688
Carrying Value ($104,213 - $747)	103,466
Fair Value Adjustment - Gain	$ 6,778

Based on this calculation, the required journal entry would be as follows:

December 31, 2002

Bond Premium (Balance)	$3,466	
Bond Discount ($100,000 - $96,688)	3,312	
Gain On Market Value Of Bonds		$6,778

December 31, 2003

Interest Expense [($96,688)(8%)]	$7,735	
Bond Discount		$ 735
Cash [($100,000)(7%)]		7,000

Solution to Self Study Problem Fifteen - 8

The required journal entries would be as follows:

January 2, 2002

Compensation Expense	$8,000	
Stock Options		$8,000
[(4,000)($4) ÷ 2 Years]		

December 31, 2003

Compensation Expense	$8,000	
Stock Options		$8,000

January 2, 2004

Cash [(2,000)($50)]	$100,000	
Stock Options [((1/2)($16,000)]	8,000	
Common Shares (2,000 Shares)		108,000

Note that the shares are recorded at the value of the consideration received for them ($100,000 plus Ms. Patrick's effort), not their market value of $124,000 at issue date.

Chapter Sixteen Problems

There are no Exercises or Self Study problems related to this Chapter.

Index

J

ADVANCED FINANCIAL ACCOUNTING COMPANION CD-ROM
INSTALLATION INSTRUCTIONS

Canadian Institute of Chartered Accountants has created this Companion CD-ROM, which includes Folio infobases for *to Canadian Financial Reporting* and *Financial Reporting in Canada*, 26th edition, and also a PDF file for *Advanced s in Consolidations*.

: There are a significant number of hypertext links in the infobases to the *CICA Handbook*. In order to make these links properly, you should install these infobases in the same folder as the *CICA Handbook* infobase (e.g., C:\Program CICA\CICA Handbook) at Step 5, below.

lling the Infobases

sert the CD-ROM in your CD drive. From your START button, select Run.

 the Run dialogue box, key in your CD-drive letter followed by **:\SETUP.EXE** and press OK.

ollow the on-screen instructions until you reach the Setup Type screen.

t the Setup Type screen, select the type of installation you want to perform and press Next:

Hard Drive Install (typical)
Install to run from the CD
Network (Administrator)—*for network installations*

t the Choose Destination Location screen, accept the default location and press Next, or Browse to select another location e sure to create a directory); if choosing another location, we recommend **:\CICA.**). Press OK and then press Next to ntinue.

t the Setup Complete screen, press Finish. If doing a network installation, proceed to Step 7, otherwise you may now en your infobases from your desktop.

t each workstation, run the **SETUP.EXE** file created in the **:\CICA** directory on your network. Follow the on-screen structions to proceed with the workstation installation. At the Setup Complete screen, press Finish and you will now be le to open your infobases from your desktop.

ter 7

stall process will also add an icon to your desktop for Chapter 7, "Advanced Topics in Consolidations." This is a PDF file u will need Adobe Acrobat 4.0 or higher to open this file. If you do not already have Acrobat Reader on your computer, go to http://www.adobe.com to download your free update.

see the proceding page for the Pearson Education Canada License Agreement. Do not open the CD-ROM package until ve read this license.

NOTE: Please see the preceding page for the Installation Instructions for the Advanced Financial Accounting Companion CD-ROM.

"AS IS" LICENSE AGREEMENT AND LIMITED WARRANTY

READ THIS LICENSE CAREFULLY BEFORE OPENING THIS PACKAGE. BY OPENING THIS PACKAGE, YOU ARE AGREEING TO THE TERMS AND CONDITIONS OF THIS LICENSE. IF YOU DO NOT AGREE, DO NOT OPEN THE PACKAGE. PROMPTLY RETURN THE UNOPENED PACKAGE AND ALL ACCOMPANYING ITEMS TO THE PLACE YOU OBTAINED THEM. *THESE TERMS APPLY TO ALL LICENSED SOFTWARE ON THE DISK EXCEPT THAT THE TERMS FOR USE OF ANY SHAREWARE OR FREEWARE ON THE DISKETTES ARE AS SET FORTH IN THE ELECTRONIC LICENSE LOCATED ON THE DISK:*

1. GRANT OF LICENSE and OWNERSHIP: The enclosed computer programs <<and any data>> ("Software") are licensed not sold, to you by Pearson Education Canada Inc. ("We" or the "Company") in consideration of your adoption of the accompanying Company textbooks and/or other materials, and your agreement to these terms. You own only the disk(s) but we and/or our licensors own the Software itself. This license allows instructors and students enrolled in the course using the Company textbook that accompanies this Software (the "Course") to use and display the enclosed copy of the Software for academic use only, so long as you comply with the terms of this Agreement. You may make one copy for back up only. We reserve any rights not granted to you.

2. USE RESTRICTIONS: You may <u>not</u> sell or license copies of the Software or the Documentation to others. You may <u>not</u> transfer, distribute or make available the Software or the Documentation, except to instructors and students in your school who are users of the adopted Company textbook that accompanies this Software in connection with the course for which the textbook was adopted. You may <u>not</u> reverse engineer, disassemble, decompile, modify, adapt, translate or create derivative works based on the Software or the Documentation. You may be held legally responsible for any copying or copyright infringement which is caused by your failure to abide by the terms of these restrictions.

3. TERMINATION: This license is effective until terminated. This license will terminate automatically without notice from the Company if you fail to comply with any provisions or limitations of this license. Upon termination, you shall destroy the Documentation and all copies of the Software. All provisions of this Agreement as to limitation and disclaimer of warranties, limitation of liability, remedies or damages, and our ownership rights shall survive termination.

4. DISCLAIMER OF WARRANTY: THE COMPANY AND ITS LICENSORS MAKE <u>NO</u> WARRANTIES ABOUT THE SOFTWARE, WHICH IS PROVIDED "<u>AS-IS</u>." IF THE DISK IS DEFECTIVE IN MATERIALS OR WORKMANSHIP, YOUR ONLY REMEDY IS TO RETURN IT TO THE COMPANY WITHIN 30 DAYS FOR REPLACEMENT UNLESS THE COMPANY DETERMINES IN GOOD FAITH THAT THE DISK HAS BEEN MISUSED OR IMPROPERLY INSTALLED, REPAIRED, ALTERED OR DAMAGED. THE COMPANY DISCLAIMS ALL WARRANTIES, EXPRESS OR IMPLIED, INCLUDING WITHOUT LIMITATION, THE IMPLIED WARRANTIES OF MERCHANTABILITY AND FITNESS FOR A PARTICULAR PURPOSE. THE COMPANY DOES NOT WARRANT, GUARANTEE OR MAKE ANY REPRESENTATION REGARDING THE ACCURACY, RELIABILITY, CURRENTNESS, USE, OR RESULTS OF USE, OF THE SOFTWARE.

5. LIMITATION OF REMEDIES AND DAMAGES: IN NO EVENT, SHALL THE COMPANY OR ITS EMPLOYEES, AGENTS, LICENSORS OR CONTRACTORS BE LIABLE FOR ANY INCIDENTAL, INDIRECT, SPECIAL OR CONSEQUENTIAL DAMAGES ARISING OUT OF OR IN CONNECTION WITH THIS LICENSE OR THE SOFTWARE, INCLUDING, WITHOUT LIMITATION, LOSS OF USE, LOSS OF DATA, LOSS OF INCOME OR PROFIT, OR OTHER LOSSES SUSTAINED AS A RESULT OF INJURY TO ANY PERSON, OR LOSS OF OR DAMAGE TO PROPERTY, OR CLAIMS OF THIRD PARTIES, EVEN IF THE COMPANY OR AN AUTHORIZED REPRESENTATIVE OF THE COMPANY HAS BEEN ADVISED OF THE POSSIBILITY OF SUCH DAMAGES. SOME JURISDICTIONS DO NOT ALLOW THE LIMITATION OF DAMAGES IN CERTAIN CIRCUMSTANCES, SO THE ABOVE LIMITATIONS MAY NOT ALWAYS APPLY.

6. GENERAL: THIS AGREEMENT SHALL BE CONSTRUED AND INTERPRETED ACCORDING TO THE LAWS OF THE PROVINCE OF ONTARIO. This Agreement is the complete and exclusive statement of the agreement between you and the Company and supersedes all proposals, prior agreements, oral or written, and any other communications between you and the company or any of its representatives relating to the subject matter.

Should you have any questions concerning this agreement or if you wish to contact the Company for any reason, please contact in writing: Editorial Manager, Pearson Education Canada, 26 Prince Andrew Place, Don Mills, Ontario, M3C 2T